The Cambridge Old English Reader

Old English was the language spoken by the An_ ... ..e Norman Conquest. This is the first major new reader of Old ... ...e and verse to be published for thirty years. Designed for beginning stu ...nts, it breaks new ground in two ways, first in its range of texts, and second in the degree of annotation it offers.

The fifty-six individual texts include the established favourites such as *The Battle of Maldon* and King Alfred's *Preface*, but also others which have not before been readily available, such as a complete Easter homily, Ælfric's life of Saint Æthelthryth and all forty-six Durham proverbs.

Modern English glosses for every prose-passage or poem are provided on the same page as the text, along with extensive notes. At the back, a succinct reference grammar is included, along with a guide to grammatical terminology. A comprehensive glossary lists and analyses all the Old English words that occur in the book. Headnotes to each of the six sections, and to every text, establish their literary and historical contexts, and illustrate the rich cultural variety of Anglo-Saxon England.

Richard Marsden is Senior Lecturer in English at the University of Nottingham, where he teaches Old English, Anglo-Saxon studies and the history of the English language. In addition to numerous articles on Old English Literature and language, he has published *The Text of the Old Testament in Anglo-Saxon England* (Cambridge University Press, 1995).

The Cambridge Old English Reader

RICHARD MARSDEN

School of English Studies
University of Nottingham

PUBLISHED BY THE PRESS SYNDICATE OF THE UNIVERSITY OF CAMBRIDGE
The Pitt Building, Trumpington Street, Cambridge, United Kingdom

CAMBRIDGE UNIVERSITY PRESS
The Edinburgh Building, Cambridge, CB2 2RU, UK
40 West 20th Street, New York, NY 10011-4211, USA
477 Williamstown Road, Port Melbourne, VIC 3207, Australia
Ruiz de Alarcón 13, 28014 Madrid, Spain
Dock House, The Waterfront, Cape Town 8001, South Africa

http://www.cambridge.org

First published 2004
Reprinted 2005

Printed in the United Kingdom at the University Press, Cambridge

Typeface Times 10/13 pt   *System* LATEX 2$_\varepsilon$ [TB]

A catalogue record for this book is available from the British Library

Library of Congress Cataloguing in Publication data

Marsden, Richard.
The Cambridge Old English reader / Richard Marsden.
     p.   cm.
Includes bibliographical references and index.
ISBN 0 521 45426 3 (hardback) – ISBN 0 521 45612 6 (paperback)
1. English language – Old English, ca. 450–1100 – Readers.   2. Anglo-Saxons –
Literary collections.   3. Anglo-Saxons – Sources.   I. Title.
PE137.M46   2003
429′.86421–dc21   2003043579

ISBN 0 521 45426 3 hardback
ISBN 0 521 45612 6 paperback

Contents

Preface

This book was planned nearly ten years ago to meet the need for a reader in Old English which would offer teachers and students two things: first, a range of texts far wider than the narrow canon available in the primers and readers in print; second, texts edited to modern standards of 'userfriendliness', in the way of presentation, glossing and annotation. The established canon is still properly represented in this volume but the addition of many new texts will I hope open up areas of Anglo-Saxon literary life which are usually ignored by all but the specialist, and will enable teachers at all levels to plan more adventurous courses. The innovations in presentation recognise the problems of today's readers, especially students in the many universities where modularisation has resulted in the compression of courses and the consequent demand that students do more in a shorter time (and with less supervision). They recognise also that few new readers of Old English today will have had the sort of rigorous linguistic training whose lack some of us spend so much time lamenting. The decision to supply every text with same-page glosses, in addition to explanatory notes that are fuller than in most previous works of this kind, was not taken lightly – not least because of the inevitable technical complications involved. The great Victorian scholar Henry Sweet averred grumpily (in the preface to his edition of Alfred's translation of Gregory's *Regula pastoralis*, p. ix) that a student tackling an Old English text ought simply to sit down with a grammar and a dictionary and get on with it; but that time has long gone, as though it had never been. The aim of this Reader is both to enable students to read Old English texts and positively to encourage them to do so. There is no virtue, as far as I can see, in withholding anything that might help them.

At the start of this project, I was lucky to secure my then Cambridge colleague, Andy Orchard, as a collaborator, and the initial work was done by us in tandem. Eventually, however, it became clear that his many other commitments would delay indefinitely the completion of his portion of the work, and so I decided to go it alone. Nevertheless, his involvement at the planning stage was crucial. Much that may find favour with users of this volume is owed to him, and some of the material for Texts 27 and 29 is based on his original drafts. I thank him warmly for his contribution and hope that the result will not disappoint him too much.

Many other debts have been incurred during the final two years of preparation. First, I heartily thank Sarah Stanton of Cambridge University Press for her great patience. The Press's official readers, including Katherine O'Brien O'Keeffe, offered immensely pertinent comments just when they were needed. Advice in connection with specific texts was freely given by many other scholars, including Elizabeth Baldwin, Debbie Banham, Carole Hough, Roy Liuzza, Lisi Oliver, Jane Page and Mary P. Richards. Simon Keynes kindly supplied me with *The Fonthill Letter* on disk. Jayne Carroll, Stuart Lee and Susan Rosser read and commented on specific sections. My colleagues at Nottingham have been using some of the texts in their teaching for several years and their input has been invaluable; Paul Cullen and David Parsons advised on place-names, Christina Lee answered a succession of queries, and Paul Cavill read all the headnotes, to their great improvement. Students in Cambridge, Leeds and Seattle, as well as Nottingham, have tried out many of the texts, and their comments have been an enormous help. The making of the combined Glossary was undertaken during a long summer by Robbie Dewa; Martin Blake, Gemma Hobbs and Tim Knebel worked assiduously to get the line references right. The University of Nottingham and the School of English Studies generously funded some of the production costs.

Last but not least, my friend and colleague Paul Remley of the University of Washington became a mentor during the final years of preparation, reading all the material, recommending and facilitating modifications, and tackling with patience and enthusiasm a succession of questions and problems relating to all aspects of the project. Without his wisdom, scholarship and sharp-sightedness, this book would be much the poorer; without his encouragement, it is unlikely that it would yet be finished.

Despite the best efforts of all the above named, some of my errors and infelicities will no doubt remain, and I trust that readers will let me know of them.

Nottingham, St Brice's Day, 2002

Abbreviations

(used in headnotes, text-notes, and Reference Grammar)

acc.	accusative (case)
adj.	adjective, adjectival
adv.	adverb, adverbial
antec.	antecedent (as noun or adjective)
art.	article
auxil.	auxiliary (verb)
BritE	British English
c.	approximately (Lat. *circa*)
cent.	century
cf.	compare (Lat. *confer*)
conj.	conjunction, conjunctive
correl.	correlative
dat.	dative (case)
def.	definite (article)
demons.	demonstrative (pronoun)
dir.	direct (object, statement)
fol(s).	folio(s) (referring to a manuscript leaf)
fut.	future (tense)
gen.	genitive (case)
imper.	imperative
imperf.	imperfect (tense)
impers.	impersonal
indecl.	indeclinable
indef.	indefinite (article, phrase)
indic.	indicative (mood of verb)
indir.	indirect (object, statement)
inf.	infinitive
infl.	inflected
instr.	instrumental (case)
interj.	interjection
intrans.	intransitive (verb)

Lat.	Latin
lit.	literal, literally
ME	Middle English (*c.* 1200–1500)
ModE	Modern English (*c.* 1500–)
n	note (as in 12/34n: 'see note to Text 12, line 34')
neg.	negative
nom.	nominative (case)
NT	New Testament
num.	numeral, numerical
obj.	object
OE	Old English
om.	omits, omitted
OT	Old Testament
part.	participle; particle
perf.	perfect (tense)
pers.	person (of verb); personal (pronoun)
phr(s).	phrase(s)
pl.	plural
pluperf.	pluperfect (tense)
poss.	possessive
prep.	preposition, prepositional
pres.	present (tense, participle)
pret.	preterite (tense)
pron.	pronoun, pronominal
r	recto (front of a manuscript leaf)
rel.	relative (particle, pronoun, clause)
rflx.	reflex, reflexive
sbj.	subjunctive (mood of verb)
sg.	singular
subj.	subject
subord.	subordinate (clause)
trans.	transitive (verb); translate(d), translation
v	verso (back of a manuscript leaf)
var.	variant
vb.	verb, verbal
WS	West Saxon (OE as written in Wessex)
<	is derived from
>	gives rise to
§	see numbered section in Reference Grammar

Additional abbreviations are used in the Glossary and in the same-page glosses which accompany the texts: see p. 000.

Abbreviations used in bibliographies

JOURNALS AND SERIES

ASE	*Anglo-Saxon England*
ASPR	Anglo-Saxon Poetic Records
CSASE	Cambridge Studies in Anglo-Saxon England
EEMF	Early English Manuscripts in Facsimile
EETS	Early English Text Society (original series)
ELN	*English Language Notes*
ES	*English Studies*
JEGP	*Journal of English and Germanic Philology*
LSE	*Leeds Studies in English*
MÆ	*Medium Ævum*
MLN	*Modern Language Notes*
MLQ	*Modern Language Quarterly*
MS	*Medieval Studies*
Neophil.	*Neophilologus*
NM	*Neuphilologische Mitteilungen*
n.s.	new series
PMLA	The journal of the Modern Language Association
Settimane	*Settimane di studio del Centro italiano di Studi sull'alto medioevo* (Spoleto)
SN	*Studia Neophilologica*
SP	*Studies in Philology*
s.s.	supplementary series

BOOK TITLES

Cambridge Companion	*The Cambridge Companion to Old English Literature*, ed. M. R. Godden and M. Lapidge (Cambridge, 1991)
OE Elegies, ed. Klinck	*The Old English Elegies: a Critical Edition and Genre Study*, ed. A. L. Klinck (Montreal, 1992; 2nd edn 2001)
OE Literature, ed. Liuzza	*Old English Literature: Critical Essays*, ed. R. M. Liuzza (New Haven and London, 2002)

Biblical reference

The names of books of the Bible referred to in headnotes and text-notes are abbreviated as indicated by the brackets:

OLD TESTAMENT	NEW TESTAMENT
Gen(esis)	M(a)t(thew)
Ex(odus)	M(ar)k
Deut(eronomy)	L(u)k(e)
Lev(iticus)	J(oh)n
J(u)dg(es)	Rom(ans)
2 K(in)gs	2 Cor(inthians)
2 Sam(uel)	Gal(atians)
1 and 3 Esd(ras)	Eph(esians)
J(u)d(i)th	2 Thes(salonians)
Ps(alm)s	Heb(rews)
Eccl(esiastic)us	1 and 2 J(oh)n
Isa(iah)	Rev(elation)

The Bible known to the Anglo-Saxons was the Latin Vulgate and all modern English quotations are based on the 'Douay-Rheims' translation of this work. The numbering of the psalms follows Vulgate usage, which differs slightly from the system familiar to users of Protestant Bibles in English.

Introduction

The period of English history which we now call 'Anglo-Saxon' lasted from the mid-fifth century until about the end of the eleventh, after the Norman Conquest. Most surviving Anglo-Saxon manuscripts date from the latter part of that period and the majority of them are in Latin, but England was unique in early medieval Europe in having a thriving vernacular literature also – written in the language that we now call 'Old English', to distinguish it from the 'Middle English' stage of the evolving language, which culminated in the works of Chaucer and Malory.

THE TEXTS

The fifty-six vernacular reading texts selected for this book have been organised under forty headings and in six thematic sections, in a way which it is hoped will provide a coherent view of the range and variety of the preserved OE corpus. Section introductions give a brief overview of those themes and their significance in the history and the literature of the Anglo-Saxons. However, the sections are not mutually exclusive, and many of the texts could certainly claim a place in more than one. Each text within the sections has its own headnote, which sets it in its historical and literary context and alludes to any major critical problems involved in the editing or reading of it. In a few cases, where the narrative is particularly complex, a brief summary or paraphrase is given. Some points of linguistic and orthographical interest are noted also (see below), but these are inevitably brief, and readers with an interest in such matters should always turn to the standard editions for fuller details. The items of 'Further reading', given after each headnote, begin with available printed facsimiles and recommended editions, followed (in chronological order of publication) by useful critical works. The lists are necessarily short, but the works cited will themselves suggest avenues for further study. To help readers to trace themes, persons and topics treated in the headnotes, texts and text-notes, an index is provided on pp. 526–32.

Inevitably, the texts vary greatly in terms of the difficulties they present for the modern reader, according to complexity of syntax above all but also to matters of vocabulary and spelling. In editing the texts, I have been conscious that some of them will obviously be more suitable for tackling by new students of OE than others, and consequently these have been rather more generously glossed and annotated; so too have the great 'canonical' texts, such as *The Battle of Maldon* and Alfred's preface to his translation of Gregory's *Cura pastoralis*, which are often a staple of courses in Anglo-Saxon studies. In my view, the most accessible first text for beginners will be no. 13 (After the Flood), closely followed by nos. 1 (In the Schoolroom) and 2 (A Personal Miscellany); and nos. 27 (Falling in Love) and 8 (England under Attack) present relatively few difficulties. Among the poems, nos. 33 (Truth is Trickiest), 35e (the 'Bookworm' riddle) and sections of 30 (*The Battle of Maldon*) may be good places to start. At the other end of the scale, nos. 18 (The Drowning of Pharaoh's Army), 31a and 31b (extracts from *Beowulf*) and 32 (*The Fight at Finnsburh*) will prove the most challenging.

SAME-PAGE GLOSSES AND NOTES

Each text is provided with same-page glosses, the glossed words being marked with a superscript circle (°) in the text. For poems, the glosses appear on the same line on the far right of the page; for prose pieces, such an arrangement was not feasible, and the glosses are in a separate register immediately beneath the texts, where the relevant line-numbers are highlighted in bold type. The glosses are a guide to interpretation only. In general, space allows for only a single modern equivalent for an Old English word and readers should not feel constrained to adopt this mechanically in a translation; other possibilities will be found in the integrated Glossary at the back of the book. In the case of compound words, including the riddle-like 'kennings', such as *wīgsmiþas*, which characterise OE poetic diction, the same-page gloss will sometimes consist of a literal translation within quotation marks ('war-smiths'); a modern interpretation may be given in parenthesis ('warriors'), but where it is not, readers can easily supply their own version – or keep the literal rendering, if this seems acceptable (and it often does). Where the glossed word has an unusual form, the more familiar form may be given after the translation, in italics and within square brackets. Some glosses are accompanied by brief grammatical information, in italics, using the abbreviating conventions of the main Glossary, but only in cases where the function of the word is crucial and/or may not be obvious. It should be noted that where words are repeated in a text, even if in a different grammatical form, they are *not* normally glossed again.

Words or phrases in the texts on which notes are given, at the bottom of the page, are enclosed between superscript angle-brackets. The relevant note is keyed by line-number, with the word or words under review (sometimes shortened by ellipsis) given in bold type. The notes are as full as space has allowed and cover historical context, as well as matters of grammar, syntax and vocabulary. In the elucidation of problematical words or phrases, I have tried hard to avoid prescription, preferring to offer two (and occasionally more) alternative interpretations in those cases where certainty is impossible. My primary aim throughout has been to guide students towards an understanding of what the OE writers appear to *say*, not to insist on what they 'mean', nor merely to facilitate the production of a honed modern version which smoothes out all the wrinkles. Those wrinkles may be important, especially in poetry. It is curious that we applaud allusiveness, enigma, paradox and ambiguity when they are used by poets of later periods, yet when such features appear in OE poetry we see them all too often as problems in need of a solution. It cannot be stressed too much that there is no such thing as the 'perfect' translation, from OE or any other language. In this Reader, the modern renderings given in notes, glosses or Glossary should be taken as informed suggestions only and the user should not hesitate to reject the idiolect of this particular (British) editor, if it seems appropriate to do so.

Students should be especially aware of the problem of the 'etymological fallacy', whereby we assume that apparently familiar Old English words have the same meanings as their modern equivalents. That may indeed be the case, but there are many exceptions. The most notorious is Old English *mann*, which signifies a 'person', man *or* woman, not simply a male. Adjectives need particular care; *brūn*, which we recognise as modern 'brown', has a basic meaning of 'bright' or 'gleaming' and the sense of darkness or brownness is only secondary.

THE GLOSSARY

In the integrated Glossary on pp. 396–516, I have endeavoured to list every different word used in the texts, and every inflected or variant form of those words. These are sourced with text-number and, separated by a slash, line-number: thus 10/23 refers to line 23 in Text 10. I have not, however, included every single occurrence of those words and forms; to have done so would have increased the length of the Glossary greatly but offered little extra benefit to the user. Coverage of the less frequently occurring words is comprehensive, but in the case of much-used words (or the most used forms of them), a limited number of occurrences is listed; curtailment of entries is signalled by '*etc.*' at the end of a string of citations and by this the user will be warned that some texts may have been omitted altogether from the citations and that, even from the cited texts, some occurrences may have been omitted. Entries for the most frequently occurring words and their variations have been treated rather differently. In these cases, a representative sample of occurrences only is given. Such entries are identifiable by the '*etc.*' which appears within square brackets at the end of the whole entry. The words thus treated include most of the demonstrative and personal pronouns, the 'pronoun-adjectives' (such as *manig* and *ōþer*), conjunctions, the more common adverbs, particles and prepositions, and most of the anomalous, modal and preterite-present verbs (such as *bēon-wesan*, *habban*, *weorþan*, *magan*, *sculan* and *willan*), along with a few others. The head-words are described, and their varying forms parsed, by means of the system of abbreviation explained at the start of the Glossary. For nouns, gender definition is accompanied by an indication of the pattern of declension which the noun follows, using a code keyed to the analysis of nouns in section B of the Reference Grammar. It is hoped that such information will help the serious student of language to analyse the texts successfully. In the Glossary, no attempt has been made to 'standardise' the spelling of OE words (on which see further below). Choices about which forms to prioritise (whether, say, the head-word should be *riht* or *ryht*) have been made on a pragmatic, word by word, basis – usually according to which form occurs most frequently in this collection of texts.

THE REFERENCE GRAMMAR

Unlike ModE (but like German and many other living languages), OE is a highly inflected language, in which the grammatical function of a word within a sentence is as often as not indicated by a variant ending (or inflection) on the word, and sometimes by a change in the stem-form of the word. One consequence of this system is that word order in an OE sentence can be more flexible than in ModE, in which the order of subject, verb and object rigidly dictates meaning (so that the victim in the statement 'the dog bit the man' is unambiguous). Furthermore, OE uses far fewer prepositions and other 'marker' words than does ModE, relying instead on the inflections. Thus 'the dog' is *se hund*, and to say '*to* the dog' we inflect both the word for 'the' and the word for 'dog', i.e. *þām hunde*; we do not need the preposition *tō* (though, confusingly, OE *can* use it also: *tō þām hunde*). It is not unusual today for students in universities to be required to learn OE simply by reading it, with little or no formal training in the grammar of the language, and this is possible; but it will be neither a simple nor a completely successful process unless some effort is made to understand the grammatical forms being used. The Reference Grammar is intended to provide a summary of the necessary information. A key to the grammatical terminology used in it (and throughout the Reader) is given on pp. 517–25. The recurrent problem of how to present the classification of noun inflections in all their variety has been tackled here by using a system based largely on gender. To classify in the traditional way, on historical linguistic principles, would be to encroach on a subject better treated at length in books devoted to OE and Germanic philology (on which, see the section on 'Further study', below). The traditional categorisation of the declensions is nevertheless alluded to in the Reference Grammar; students will encounter it in the glossaries of many of the older, and a few of the more recent, editions of OE texts. Though the Reference Grammar has been designed to answer specific questions raised by the texts in this Reader, it is hoped that it may prove useful for students tackling other texts also.

THE EDITING OF THE TEXTS

The texts have been edited from the original manuscripts, from microfilms or from facsimiles. Published editions have been consulted constantly. In the transcription of the texts, the following minimal modifications have been made. Contractions (mainly þ for *þæt* and *ū* for *-um*, with a few others) have been expanded silently; so too has 7, the 'Tironian' symbol for *and* or *ond* (the choice of vowel in the expansion depending on the conventions followed elsewhere in the particular manuscript). Proper names and the two principal names for the deity (*God* and *Drihten*) have been given initial capital letters, as have first words in sentences. Manuscript word-separation in general has been retained (so that, for instance, both *oþ þæt* and *oþþæt* may be found), but in cases where this might cause confusion (as in the apparently arbitrary separation of place-name elements in parts of the *Anglo-Saxon Chronicle*), compounding has been effected. Dates and hands of corrections to manuscripts, whether written over an erasure or inserted above the line or in the margin, are usually very hard to identify; those which appear to be by the copyist himself (probably checking his copy against the exemplar), or at least were made while the manuscript was being used during the Anglo-Saxon period, have been accepted silently. On emendation, see below.

Punctuation always presents problems for editors of OE texts, for little is used in the manuscripts and, when it does occur, it is not always helpful to the modern reader. Many editors justifiably fear that the imposition of modern conventions may interfere with the syntactical dynamics of the original, especially in poetry, but recent attempts to produce editions of poems with minimal punctuation have not seemed particularly helpful, especially for new readers. The decisions on punctuation made by this editor have been pragmatic ones, suited to the individual texts and the perceived needs of the reader. In general, more guidance in the way of commas is given in the 'beginners' texts' listed above than in the more advanced ones. In those cases in which the interpretation of a passage may vary significantly according to where we place a notional comma or full-stop, this is pointed out in the explanatory notes.

THE LANGUAGE OF THE TEXTS: SPELLING VARIATION

Varied and sometimes eccentric spelling is a fundamental characteristic of OE writings, and no attempt has been made in this book to present texts in 'standard' OE – that is, to convert word-forms to those of the dialect of Wessex (i.e. West Saxon) in the later OE period. This is indeed the dialect (or, more likely, range of dialects) in which most of our surviving texts are written, but it was itself subject to much variation. A complex and interrelated set of factors produced variety in the spelling of OE, primary among them being developments in pronunciation through time, with regional dialectal differences continuously making their major contribution also. The results may be seen in many of the texts. Within the space of a few lines in the extract from the OE *Apollonius of Tyre* used for Text 27, for instance, we find *cyning* for 'king' alternating with both *cyningc* (showing 'intrusive c' after *g*, a common feature of late OE) and the increasingly used 'syncopated' (i.e. contracted) form, *cyng*; and a check in the Glossary will show that the forms *cing*, *cincg* and even *kyning* occur in other texts. The scribe whose manuscript of *The Letter of Alexander* supplies our Text 28 wrote both *trēowum* and *trīowum* for 'trees' (here in the dative plural). This example nicely illustrates one of an important set of sound-changes – occurring initially in the spoken language, and eventually showing up in writing also – which took place in the WS dialect between the earlier King Alfred's time (late ninth century) and that of Abbot Ælfric (late tenth century), namely, the shift of the diphthong *io/īo* to *eo/ēo*. It is a fair bet that the early eleventh-century scribe of *The Letter of Alexander* (or possibly a predecessor), though copying from an exemplar which preserved the older spelling of the word for 'tree', with *īo*, was influenced by his own familiarity with the contemporary version using *ēo* to make modifications (perhaps unconsciously, certainly with no zeal for consistency). It is quite possible to draw up lists of word-forms by which to distinguish 'Alfredian' texts (those, at least, preserved in 'unmodernised' copies) from later ones. In the former (our Texts 5 and 6, for example), we expect to see *biþ*, *hwelc*, *mon*, *sīo* and *þǣm*; in the latter (such as Texts 4, 21a and 22), we will not be surprised to find *byþ*, *hwilc* (or *hwylc*), *man*, *sēo* and *þām*. We might want to add the syncopated form of the word for 'king', *cyng*, to our list; but the relationship alluded to above between variation through time (diachronism) and variation across geographical boundaries at a single time (synchronism) is a complex one. The form *cyng* is indeed increasingly common in the WS dialect after 1000, but not exclusively so, for it is a form found also in Mercian writings of the tenth century.

Another factor contributing importantly to variation in OE during the later years of the Anglo-Saxon period was the decay of the inflection system. The end-product of this process would be, by the time of Chaucer and Malory, a language in which inflections had all but disappeared, though echoes of them long persisted in spelling (and sporadically in pronunciation also). A 'levelling' process was already under way long before the Norman Conquest, whereby, for instance, the dative ending *-um* came to be written *-an* or *-on*; the distinction between the verb-endings *-an*, *-on* and *-en* (markers of the infinitive, the past plural indicative and the plural subjunctive, respectively) became more and more blurred as well, so that all these inflections 'fell together'. Similarly, the distinction between the present-tense endings *-eþ* and *-aþ* (notionally singular and plural, respectively, in many classes of verb) became lost. Such changes, beginning in the spoken language and then reflected graphemically, were accelerated by the fact that stress was on the initial main syllable of an OE word (as still in ModE), with a consequent tendency for final syllables to be pronounced indistinctly. With word order increasingly regularised as we know it today (subject–verb–object), and with prepositions more and more used to express grammatical relationships previously signalled by a special inflection on the relevant noun, endings ceased to matter very much.

In the headnote to each text, major linguistic peculiarities (mainly related to spelling) are pointed out, but no attempt is made to present an exhaustive analysis. Readers will soon come to take 'irregularities' in their stride and to see them, not as an obstacle to the understanding of Old English, but as an integral part of the language.

EMENDATION

In the light of the foregoing remarks, it will be clear that wholesale emendation of texts to produce some sort of consistency cannot be justified. In this book, it has been kept to a minimum (with the exception of Text 1, where the fact that the OE material is based on a word-for-word gloss of a Latin text has made a certain amount of rearrangement of words desirable). Whenever a reasonable case can be made for an unusual or unexpected word-form having been the deliberate choice of a copyist, and assuming that it can be shown (albeit sometimes with difficulty) to 'make sense', it is retained. In some cases, however, emendation does seem desirable or is simply unavoidable. We can rarely be confident that we are restoring an 'original' reading. If another manuscript copy of the text in question happens to have been preserved (almost unheard of for the verse texts), that may be a good guide to the form which the emendation should take; otherwise it depends on personal editorial judgement. All emendations made in the texts are listed, along with manuscript details, on pp. 345–54.

READING ALOUD

The reading aloud of texts is highly recommended as a way of mastering the rhythms and idioms of the OE language – and the process may be undertaken with a minimum of initial preparation. Despite the orthographical instability described above, the Anglo-Saxons were innocent of the major dislocations between sound and spelling which were to become established during the fourteenth and fifteenth centuries and would produce the baffling inconsistencies which we know today. Broadly speaking, they spelled words as they spoke them. The notes on pp. xxix–xxxiv offer a rough guide to the probable sounds of OE in Wessex at the time when most of the preserved manuscripts were copied.

OLD ENGLISH POETRY

The poems included in this book are printed in a familiar way, line after line, but it is one of the curiosities of OE verse as written out in the manuscripts that, almost without exception, it is presented continuously, without line-breaks and with a minimum of punctuation (though recent work suggests that, in some cases, the varying amounts of space left between words may give a clue as to how a given line ought to be read). Yet editors rarely have much difficulty deciding how the poems should be presented on the printed page. This is because of the distinctive metrical structure of OE verse, which is based on a system of half-lines with alternating stressed syllables. A poetic line consists of two of these half-lines (often referred to as the *a* and *b* verses), which are separated by a 'caesura' (a notional pause, which we show distinctly in printing the poems) but at the same time are linked by alliteration – the repetition of initial sounds, as defined more precisely below. The system was part of a common Germanic legacy, deriving from the prominent phonetic characteristic of the Germanic languages to place stress on the initial syllable of a word; and because the speech rhythms on which OE metre is based are basically unchanged in the modern language, it will be found easy to grasp intuitively. Usually, each of the two half-lines, *a* and *b*, more or less equal in length, contains two strongly stressed syllables ('lifts') and a variable number, from two upwards, of lightly stressed ones (constituting a 'fall'). Alliteration links at least one stress, and more often both, in the *a*-verse with the first stress in the *b*-verse, making two or three alliterating stresses in all; the second stress in *b* does *not* alliterate. The alliterating syllable of the second half-line is called the 'head stave' and sets off the most emphatic word in that half-line. The alliteration may involve single initial consonants, identical double consonants (such as *sc*, *sp* or *cn*) or any pattern of initial vowels or diphthongs. These points are illustrated in the first three complete lines of *The Battle of Maldon* (Text 30, lines 2–4), with the stressed syllables given here in bold type:

> **Hēt** þā **hyss**a hwæne   **hors** forl**æt**an
> **feor** āf**ȳ**san   and **forð gang**an,
> **hic**gan tō **hand**um   and tō **hige gōd**um.
>
> '(He) ordered then each warrior to let go his horse/ send it far off and march forth/ to think about their hands and good courage.'

In each full line there are four main stresses, and in each case the consonants of the first three stressed syllables alliterate – *h* in the first line, *f* in the second and *h* again in the third (this repetition of *h* being coincidental); in each line, the fourth stressed syllable breaks from the alliterative pattern. It will be noted that prefixes do not count in the scheme: the *ā* of *āfȳsan* is ignored, for alliteration is always on a word that bears a primary stress and prefixes (including the most common one, *ge*) do not carry such stress. The next line in the poem is as follows:

> Þā þæt **Off**an **mæg**   **æ**rest on**fund**e
>
> 'When the kinsman of Offa first realised . . .'

The 'regular' pattern of two main stresses on each side of the caesura is maintained, but only one of each pair alliterates, namely the vowels in the first syllables of *Offan* and *ærest*.

It is unlikely that the Anglo-Saxon poets had rules as to how many *un*stressed elements in a line there ought to be; there are usually between two and four. A nineteenth-century German scholar, Eduard Sievers, categorised regular OE poetic half-lines in just five main 'types' (with slightly varying alternatives within one of them), according to their stress patterns. Here Sievers's types are illustrated from *The Battle of Maldon*; in the schematic analysis, / represents a 'lift' (i.e. main stress) and x a 'fall', and a secondary stress is shown by \x:

Type A	**hors** forl**æt**an (2)	/ x / x
Type B	and **ealde swurd** (47)	x / x /
Type C	and **forð gang**an (3)	x / / x
Type D	**grim gūð**plega (61)	/ / \x x
	bord ord onfēng (110)	/ / x \x
Type E	**æt**trene **ord** (47)	/ x x /

Sometimes, however (and apparently for special effect), poets extend their lines beyond normal metrical limits, by accommodating three main stresses in each half-line, and a number of extra unstressed syllables; the lines are then said to be 'hypermetric'. *The Dream of the Rood* is a good poem in which to see such lines in action (Text 23 and headnote). Moreover, an initial sequence of unstressed syllables may be disregarded altogether in the metrical scheme; such a sequence is termed an 'anacrusis'. In general, rhyme as we know it today (that is, end-rhyme) is absent from OE verse, but sporadic exceptions occur in *The Battle of Maldon* itself (see 30/271n) and in other poems (see 37/headnote), and there is one poem – known today appropriately enough as *The Rhyming Poem* – which rhymes throughout.

A poet composing alliterative lines needs an abundant word-hoard of synonyms in order to be able to provide the right one in the right place, and the OE poetical vocabulary is consequently very large, containing many words which are never found in prose and which seem to have been inherited from ancient Germanic tradition perpetuated. Examples are a much-used poetic word for 'sword', *mēce* (with *sweord* the usual word in prose), and one for 'battle', *gūð* (with *gefeoht* a frequent prose alternative). The poets used many words metaphorically, and often 'metonymically' – that is, using one aspect or attribute of something for the whole: thus *ceol* 'keel' is used for 'ship' and *lind* 'linden-wood' for 'shield' (for that was one of materials used for making shields). A substantial part of the poetic vocabulary is made up of compound words or two-word phrases composed from basic nouns and known as 'kennings'. Examples are *eardstapa*, literally 'earth-stepper', one who wanders across the earth, *bānhūs*, 'bone-house', 'a body', and *hronrād*, 'whale-road', the 'ocean'. In context, the effect of kennings is often far greater than the sum of their parts, because of the expanding associations they spark off in the mind of the reader or listener.

Old English poetry has traditionally been characterised as 'formulaic', in the sense that it exhibits a high amount of verbal and thematic repetition. Examples of the sharing of phrases or half-lines between different poems are noted in the Reader: see, for example, 30/163n and 37/34n. This fact in turn has led critics to link OE poetry to the sort of oral tradition (well known in other cultures) in which unlettered poets extemporise poems by building on and varying well-known basic patterns and structures. There is certainly no doubt that the poetry of the Anglo-Saxons derived both its language and its themes from a preliterate Germanic age, but the reworking of old material and the reuse of remembered lines are time-honoured aspects of written *literary* production, too, and the context in which the poetry preserved from Anglo-Saxon England seems to have been composed and recorded is indubitably that of a literate age.

As for the distinctive style of OE poetry, two techniques may be singled out here – understatement and variation. Understatement is used to great ironical effect by many poets; when it involves expressing negation by using an apparently affirmative phrase, it may be termed 'litotes'. In *The Wife's Lament*, for instance, the wife tells us she has *lēofra lȳt*, 'few loved ones' (40/16): she appears to mean none at all. Other examples may be seen in 18/9 and 49, and 38/31 and 54–5. Variation, in its simplest form, is the multiple statement (twice or more) of the same idea within a few lines; each variation augments the original idea or image with extra qualities or attributes. In this example from *The Battle of Maldon*, the 'varied' words are italicised:

> Lēofsunu gemǣlde   and his *linde* āhōf
> *bord tō gebeorge* (244–5)
>
> 'Leofsunu spoke and raised up his linden-wood, board as protection'

First Leofsunu's shield is called a 'linden-wood' – it is made from the wood of a lime tree; then the idea of the shield is varied, with a phrase which describes its function, and a synonym is used for the thing itself: it is 'a board for protection'. In this second example, there are two sets of variation – of verb (shown here in italics) and of subject (in boldface) – interwoven:

> Swā hī *bylde forð*   **bearn Ælfrices,**
> **wiga wintrum geong,**   *wordum mǣlde,*
> **Ælfwine** þā *cwæð,*   hē *on ellen sprǣc* (209–11)
>
> 'thus he *urged* them onwards, the **son of Ælfric, warrior young in winters**, he *declared in words,* **Ælfwine** then *pronounced,* he *spoke with courage*'.

The variation on Ælfwine's speaking is fourfold: he (verbally) urges forth, declares in words, pronounces and speaks with courage; and he himself is described in three ways: as the son of Ælfric (for the announcement of lineage is a characteristic priority among heroic men), as a warrior young in years and, lastly, by name. There has only been one subject in these three lines, and one action, but variation has given us a multiple view. Such a technique makes great demands, of course, on the poet and his word-hoard – and on the modern translator, too.

FURTHER STUDY

A great variety of published materials is available for the would-be scholar of OE language and literature. The following works will provide a solid core on which to build.

Dictionaries

An excellent dictionary for general purposes is J. R. C. Hall, *A Concise Anglo-Saxon Dictionary*, 4th edn with suppl. by H. D. Meritt (Cambridge, 1969). The monumental J. Bosworth and T. N. Toller, *An Anglo-Saxon Dictionary* (Oxford, 1882–98; with *Supplement*, 1908–21, and *Enlarged Addenda and Corrigenda to the Supplement*, ed. A. Campbell, 1972), is still a mine of essential information but is unwieldy. It is being replaced, on microfiche initially and now CD, by the *Dictionary of Old English*, ed. A. Cameron *et al.* (Toronto, 1986–); the CD of letters

A–F is now available (2003). The address of the *Dictionary* is www.doe.vtoronto. ca. A survey of lexical scholarship will be found in A. Cameron, A. Kingsmill and A. C. Amos, *Old English Word Studies* (Toronto, 1983). For semantic study, *A Thesaurus of Old English in Two Volumes*, ed. J. Roberts and C. Kay with L. Grundy (London, 1995) is recommended.

Language

On grammar, essential reference works are A. Campbell, *Old English Grammar* (Oxford, 1959), and R. Hogg, *A Grammar of Old English* (Cambridge, 1992). Both are advanced works, based on historical principles; R. Lass, *Old English: a Historical Linguistic Companion* (Cambridge, 1994) offers a gentler ride. Accessible short grammatical surveys include R. Quirk and C. L. Wrenn, *An Old English Grammar*, 2nd edn (London, 1957); H. Sweet, *Anglo-Saxon Primer*, rev. N. Davis, 9th edn (Oxford, 1953); and S. Moore and T. A. Knott, *The Elements of Old English*, 9th edn (Ann Arbor, MI, 1942). On all syntactical matters, B. Mitchell, *Old English Syntax*, 2 vols. (Oxford, 1985), is indispensable. It is supplemented by B. Mitchell, *A Critical Bibliography of Old English Syntax to the end of 1984*, including Addenda and Corrigenda to 'Old English Syntax' (Oxford, 1990), and B. Mitchell and S. Irvine, 'A Critical Bibliography of Old English Syntax: Supplement', *Neuphilologische Mitteilungen*, 93 (1992), 1–56, and 97 (1996), 1–28, 121–61 and 255–78.

For readers interested in the history of the OE language and its subsequent development, recommended introductions are A. C. Baugh and T. Cable, *A History of the English Language*, 5th edn (London, 2002); C. Barber, *The English Language: a Historical Introduction* (Cambridge, 1993); and T. Pyles and J. Algeo, *The Origins and Development of the English Language*, 4th edn (Fort Worth, TX, 1992). Specialist studies will be found in *The Cambridge History of the English Language*, Vol. I: *The Beginnings to 1066*, ed. R. M. Hogg (Cambridge, 1992), and in subsequent volumes of this series. Of great interest for anyone with an interest in other contemporary Germanic languages, including Old Norse, is O. W. Robinson, *Old English and its Closest Relatives: a Survey of the Earliest Germanic Languages* (London, 1992).

Manuscripts and texts

For information on surviving manuscripts and the OE texts which they contain, collectively indispensable are N. R. Ker, *Catalogue of Manuscripts Containing Anglo-Saxon* (Oxford, 1957; repr. with suppl. 1990); H. Gneuss, *Handlist of Anglo-Saxon Manuscripts* (Tempe, AZ, 2001); A. Cameron, 'A List of Old English Texts', in *A Plan for the Dictionary of Old English*, ed. R. Frank and A. Cameron (Toronto, 1973), pp. 25–306; and A. diP. Healey and R. L. Venezky, *A Microfiche Concordance to Old English*, with *The List of Texts and Index of Editions* (Toronto, 1980). Instructive background studies will be found in M. P. Richards, ed., *Anglo-Saxon Manuscripts: Basic Readings* (New York and London, 2001), and in P. Pulsiano and E. M. Treharne, eds., *Anglo-Saxon Manuscripts and their Heritage* (Aldershot, 1998).

Published editions of the texts are listed in Cameron (1973) and Healey and Venezky (1980), above, and in S. B. Greenfield and F. C. Robinson, *A Bibliography of Publications on Old English Literature* (Toronto, 1980), which offers also a classified list of the critical literature on the texts. The latter work, however, covers only the period until 1972, at which point the annual volumes of the periodical *Anglo-Saxon England* (1972–) become essential (for all the subjects covered in this survey), along with *Old English Newsletter* (1967–).

The literature and its background

For an overview of the literary corpus, a starting point is S. B. Greenfield and D. G. Calder, *A New Critical History of Old English Literature*, with a survey of the Anglo-Latin background by M. Lapidge (New York, 1986), and, for excellent introductory essays on a variety of literary and linguistic themes, *The Cambridge Companion to Old English Literature*, ed. M. R. Godden and M. Lapidge (Cambridge, 1991) and *Reading Old English Texts*, ed. K. O'B. O'Keeffe (Cambridge, 1997). A good collection of essays both on general literary topics and on specific texts is *Old English Literature: Critical Essays*, ed. R. M. Liuzza (New Haven and London, 2002). A range of survey essays will be found in *A Companion to Anglo-Saxon Literature*, ed. P. Pulsiano and E. Treharne (Oxford, 2001). For the cultural and historical background, *The Blackwell Encylopaedia of Anglo-Saxon England*, ed. M. Lapidge *et al.* (Oxford, 1999) and D. Hill, *An Atlas of Anglo-Saxon England* (Oxford, 1981) are invaluable reference works. The individual texts in the Reader have their own bibliographies, but one work warrants mentioning here in connection with poetry: *The Anglo-Saxon Poetic Records: a Collective Edition*, edited in six volumes by G. P. Krapp and E. V. K. Dobbie (New York, 1931–42), contains editions and valuable commentary on all the surviving OE poems.

Translations

Much OE literature is available in translation. Prose renderings of almost all the poetry are given in S. A. J. Bradley, *Anglo-Saxon Poetry*, 2nd edn (London, 1995). Many translators have attempted renderings in verse, but students looking for 'cribs' to help with their study of the poems in this Reader should beware of these. They may be enjoyable enough to read, and in some cases they are highly accomplished, but they stray regularly from literal meaning and all too often from the original poet's intentions. As for the vast prose literature in OE, all the earlier (and some of the more recent) editions from the Early English Text Society give parallel modern translations. A useful range of important prose texts is translated in M. Swanton, *Anglo-Saxon Prose*, 2nd edn (London and Rutland, VT, 1993), and a good selection of both prose and verse is available in K. Crossley-Holland, *The Anglo-Saxon World: an Anthology* (Oxford, 1999).

On-line resources

On-line resources for students of OE literature multiply at a confusing rate, but one of the best gateways to them is through the Georgetown-based *Labyrinth Library: Old English Literature*; the address is: http://www.georgetown.edu/labyrinth/library/oe/oe.html. At the same university, Cathy Bell's *Old English Pages* comprise another valuable resource: http://www.georgetown.edu/cbell/oe/old_english.html.

The writing and pronunciation of Old English

WRITING

The Latin alphabet was introduced for the writing of OE by Christian monks soon after AD 600. It had twenty-three letters, lacking *v* (whose function was shared with *u*), *j* (which was not distinguished from *i*), and *w*. The letters *q*, *x* and *z* were used rarely in OE (though *x* and *z* do appear in some words taken from Greek), and *k* was little used until towards the end of the Anglo-Saxon period (*c* being written instead). The letter-shapes in the manuscripts are mostly those we recognise today, though the handwriting used by Anglo-Saxons was continuously evolving over the centuries, a fact which often enables palaeographers to date manuscripts with a fair degree of precision. The shapes of *e*, *f*, *g*, *r* and *s* can cause particular difficulties for those reading the manuscripts, especially when in ligature, i.e. joined to other letters. For instance, *r*, with a descending tail, may resemble a *p*, and *s* is often written in a long form. The letter *g* was usually shaped ᴣ, a symbol we call 'yogh'; most editors of OE texts today (including this one) simply print *g*.

The letters of Latin were augmented by four further characters – either invented, or borrowed from the runic alphabet, which had long been in use among the Germanic peoples, mainly for inscriptions. They are (with 'capital' forms in brackets):

þ (Þ) for 'th', a runic character with the name *þorn* ('thorn');

ð (Ð) also for 'th', formed by adding a cross-stroke to a *d* written in the Irish way, with a round back, and known by the Anglo-Saxons as *ðæt*, but today as 'eth'. Thorn and eth were used without distinction: a word such as *siþþan* might also be written *siððan* or even *siþðan* or *siðþan*.

æ (Æ) for a 'fronted' a-sound (see below); known by the Anglo-Saxons as *æsc* ('ash').

ƿ (Ƿ) for 'w', a runic character with the name *wynn* ('joy'). In most modern printing of OE, as in this book, wynn is replaced by *w*.

These new characters were not in full use among the Anglo-Saxons until the end of the seventh century. Until then, *th* or *d* may be found instead of *ð* or *þ* (the latter taking longer to become established than *ð*), *ae* or *e* for *æ*, and *uu* or *u* for *w*. For examples, see Text 20a. In manuscripts written at the close of the Anglo-Saxon period, too, under Norman French influence, the digraph *th* is increasingly found again.

PRONUNCIATION

The relationship between sound and symbol is consistent in OE, which thus differs from the notorious modern language. *All* letters should be pronounced, including each character in pairs of doubled consonants, such as *dd* or *ll*, and each consonant in pairs such as *cn, gn, hn, hl, wl, hr* and *wr*. Final *-e* is always sounded (and pronounced like the *e* in ModE *met*). Most **consonants** may be pronounced as in ModE, and as in the modern language, so in OE *f*, *s* and *þ/ð* (i.e. 'th') may be pronounced 'voiced' (with the vocal cords vibrating) or 'unvoiced'; see below. The consonants *c* and *g* give some trouble, because they may be pronounced 'hard' (velar or guttural) or 'soft' (palatalised); guidance is given below. In the Reference Grammar and Glossary only, the distinction is marked by the use of a small dot over the 'soft' versions – *ċ* and *ġ*. The main thing to remember about **vowels** is that they are 'pure', which poses a problem for speakers of British and some other varieties of English, who tend to slur them. Vowels may be 'short' or 'long' – and the difference can make a difference to meaning (as between the verb *mæg* and the noun *mæġ*); for the convenience of learners, in this book all long vowels are marked with a macron, as in *ē*. It should be noted, however, that this is *not* an OE symbol and does not appear in the manuscripts; nor is it used in most printed editions of OE texts, and students quoting OE in written work should not normally reproduce it (or the 'dot' described above). The **diphthongs** (two vowels combined) can be produced simply by saying the constituent vowels in quick succession, as a continuous and shifting (but not distinctly double) sound.

Consonants

b d k l m n t w	These may be pronounced as in ModE.
c, ċ	1. 'Hard' (velar) as *c* in ModE 'come': before and, when final, after *a*, *o*, *u* or *y*, and finally after short *æ* and *e*, and before consonants: *bōc* 'book', *bæc* 'back', *cuman* 'come', *cniht* 'boy'. 2. 'Soft' (palatalised) as *ch* in ModE 'church': before or between *e* or *i* (short and long) and finally after *i* (short and long), *ē* and *ǣ*: *ic* 'I', *ċiriċe* 'church', *ċild* 'child', *tǣċan* 'teach'. 3. There are exceptions; a good guide *may* be the pronunciation of the ModE equivalent; thus OE *cēne* has the 'hard' *c*, as in 'keen', *hwilċ* has 'ch', as in 'which'. But see note below.
cg	As ModE *dg*, so that OE *ecg* sounds very like ModE 'edge'.
f	1. ModE 'voiceless' *f*, as in 'father': when initial or final: *fæder* 'father', *hlāf* 'loaf', *wīf* 'woman', 'wife'. 2. ModE 'voiced' *v*, as in 'weave': when between vowels or other 'voiced' sounds: *hlāfas* 'loaves', *hæfde* 'had'.
g, ġ	1. 'Hard' (velar) as in ModE 'god': before *a*, *o* and *u*, and initially before consonants: *god* 'a god', *lagu* 'law', *gnornian* 'mourn'. 2. 'Soft' (palatalised) as *y* in ModE 'yet': initially before or after *e* or *i* (short or long), and finally after *e*, *i* and *æ*: *ġēar* 'year', *ġif* 'if', *þeġn* 'thegn', *dæġ* 'day', *hiġ* (late form of *hī*) 'they'. 3. Something like the *ch* of ModE 'loch' pronounced abruptly without 'voicing' (*g* in dialectal *sagen* is a guide for German-speakers): after or between *a*, *o* and *u*: *magan* 'can', *bōga* 'bow', *burg* 'stronghold'. A sort of 'swallowed' hard *g* will do here; the sound often modified into *w* in later English.
h	1. As in ModE 'he': initially: *hūs* 'house', *hwǣr* 'where'. 2. A sound like *ch* in German *ich* or *nicht*: after *e* or *i*: *fēhþ* 'seizes', *riht* 'right'. 3. Elsewhere *h* sounds something like *ch* in ModE 'loch' or German *nach*: *hēah* 'high', *þūhte* 'thought'.
r	1. Probably trilled when initial. 2. Probably sounded with the tip of the tongue curled back, as often in American English, when final, or following a consonant.
s	1. *z* as in ModE 'zoo': between vowels or next to voiced consonants: *rīsan* 'rise', *wīsdom* 'wisdom'. 2. *s* as in ModE in 'sit': elsewhere: *sittan* 'sit', *eorlas* 'earls'.
sc	As ModE *sh* in 'ship': *scip* 'ship', *scūr* 'shower', *disc* 'dish'. There are a few exceptions, such as *āscian* 'ask' and *Scottas* 'Scots', in which *sc* is pronounced *sk*.
ð, þ	1. 'Voiced' as in ModE 'this' or 'father': at the start of a word or medially: *þis* 'this', *hwæþer* 'whether'. 2. 'Voiceless' as in ModE 'path': at the end of a word: *pæþ* 'path'.

Vowels

a	As *a* in ModE 'man': *mann* 'person'
ā	As *a* in BritE 'father' or 'ah!': *fāh* 'hostile', *bān* 'bone'
æ	As *a* in BritE 'that' or 'mat', a brisk 'fronted' sound: *þæt* 'that', *fæt* 'vessel'
ǣ	A longer verson of *æ*: the vowel in ModE 'mad' is usually pronounced long, far longer than in 'mat': *þǣr* 'there'. Many readers of OE use a lengthened *e*, so that *þǣr* sounds rather like ModE 'there'.
e	As in ModE 'met': *bet* 'better', *wendeþ* 'turns'; it should be sounded finally also: *reste* 'at rest'
ē	As *a* in southern BritE 'hate' (but a single unbroken sound): *mē* 'to me', *wēste* 'deserted'
i	As in ModE 'bit': *siþþan* 'then'
ī	As in ModE 'beet': *sīþ* 'journey'
o	As in BritE 'not': *God* 'God'
ō	As in ModE 'note': *gōd* 'good', *mōder* 'mother'
u	As in ModE 'put' (*not* 'putt'): *up* 'up', *sunu* 'son'
ū	As *oo* in southern BritE 'boot' (with lips rounded: a single unbroken sound): *þū* 'you'
y	As *u* in French *tu* or *ü* in German *müde*; made by trying to pronounce *i* with the lips pursed: *byrġen* 'burying place'
ȳ	A long version of *y*, made by trying to pronounce ModE *ee* with the lips pursed: *sȳ* 'be', *fȳr* 'fire'

Diphthongs

ea	æ + a
ēa	ǣ + a
eo	e + o
ēo	ē + o
ie	i + e
īe	ī + e
io	i + o
īo	ī + o

The emphasis in diphthongs is usually given to the first vowel, and this should be pronounced long, if it is so marked. They should thus *not* be pronounced as *ao* in ModE *chaos*, where there are two separate sounds. In the case of *ea*/*ēa*, it should be noted that the first element was probably nearer to *æ/ǣ* than *e/ē*. The pronunciation of *ie/īe* seems to have undergone 'smoothing' from an early period, to judge from the frequent spellings with simply *i/ī* or *y/ȳ*. Conversely, the accusative masculine pronoun *hine* is often spelled *hiene* in late manuscripts, but it is highly unlikely that a diphthong was used in articulating such an unstressed word. The diphthongs *io* and *īo* occur in early WS and some other dialects.

Stress

Stress is nearly always on the first *main* syllable of a word, as in ModE. Prefixes are ignored in this rule, so that the ubiquitous *ge-* and the many verbal and other prefixes such as *a-*, *æt-*, *be-*, *for-* and *on-* do not count. Thus *cúman*, *léofodon*, *ándswaru*, but *ġebrécan*, *onstéllan*, *forstándan*.

Note on c, g and long vowels

The question of the circumstances in which *c* and *g*, both historically 'hard' (velar or guttural) sounds, were 'softened' (palatalised) in OE is a complex one. Although modern pronunciation is often a good guide, there are many exceptions. For instance, OE *gest* (also spelled *gist* and *gyst*), 'guest', was pronounced with a 'soft' *g* (*ġest*); but during the ME period the word was 'reborrowed' from Old Norse *gestr*, with a 'hard' *g*, and this is the pronunciation which was preserved. OE *cald*, 'cold', with hard *g* in the Northumbrian and Mercian dialects, seems to have developed a soft *ċ* in Wessex, which explains the alternative spelling *ċeald* in many manuscripts. As the language developed after the Norman Conquest, however, the midland and northern pronunciation, with hard *c*, became the standard one.

The lengthening of vowels is another problem area, especially in relation to personal pronouns and to the endings of adjectives and adverbs. In general, the vowels of stressed words or syllables are given more emphasis, and consequently length, in pronunciation than those that are unstressed. In this book, therefore, on the assumption that the personal pronouns *hē*, *mē*, *þē*, *wē* and *gē* usually have an emphatic role in a clause or sentence, their vowels are always marked long. In the case of the demonstrative *se*, when it is fulfilling its function as the definite article ('the') or the relative pronoun ('who', 'which' or 'that'), it carries little stress and so will have been pronounced with a short vowel: *se tōþ se bistandeþ*, 'the tooth *which* stands next'; but when used as a pronoun (for 'he'), it becomes more emphatic and so the convention of marking the vowel long in such cases is followed in this book: *sē wæs eald*, '*he* was old'. Similarly, a difference in stress between the adjectival ending *-lic* and adverbial ending *-līce* justifies varied vowel-marking. In adjectives, the ending *-lic* and its inflected forms carry little stress and are therefore left unmarked. In adverbs, however, -*līce* and its inflected forms carry much more stress, albeit still secondary in relation to the whole word, and so their vowels are marked long.

Among editors of OE texts there is inevitably much variation (and not a little inconsistency) in the tackling of matters such as these – which are, in any case, of minor importance. We can be confident that there was as much variety in the speaking of OE in the kingdom(s) of Anglo-Saxon England, according to time and place – and even, perhaps, social situation, though we have no evidence of this – as there is in the speaking of the modern language.

I

TEACHING AND LEARNING

Centuries before their continental neighbours, for whom Latin long remained the major language of writing, the Anglo-Saxons had an extensive literature in their own vernacular – Old English. The opportunity for widespread literacy had come to them with their conversion to Christianity, which began with St Augustine's mission to Canterbury in 597. Within only a few years, the lawcode of the kingdom of Kent had been put into English, the first vernacular document that we know of (see Section II), and by the time of the Norman Conquest in 1066 there was no area of written discourse not represented by works in OE, whether as translations or original compositions. Nevertheless, it was Latin which remained the official language of the church throughout the Anglo-Saxon period, and far beyond it. Key theological texts and the Bible were all in Latin, and so were divine services, and therefore would-be monks and priests among the native population (whose mother tongue was OE in its various dialectal varieties) had to learn it. A priority for the missionaries at Canterbury, and their successors throughout the group of Anglo-Saxon kingdoms which would eventually become England, was thus the setting up of schools. All monasteries and cathedrals of any size needed one, and naturally the medium of instruction, to begin with at least, would have to be the vernacular. OE 'glosses' to Latin school-texts from Canterbury have been preserved, and Bede tells us (in his *Historia ecclesiastica gentis Anglorum*: see p. 69) how he used English in order to teach novice monks the Creed and other essential elements of the Christian faith.

This bilingual process of teaching and learning persisted throughout the Anglo-Saxon period, as surviving teaching materials show. Some of these are the work of the monk and scholar Ælfric, who was in charge of the monastic school at Cerne Abbas in Dorset during the closing years of the tenth century. He was the product of a great revival in learning that had taken place in the wake of the important mid-century reform and expansion of the Benedictine monastic system in England. He devised his own teaching materials for the novice monks, including very young boys, in his charge. These materials included a 'colloquy', a sort of staged dialogue which Ælfric will have used to develop his pupils' skills in the Latin language; but someone later added an OE translation above the Latin text and today, one thousand years on, this performs a function for students of OE similar to that of the original Latin (Text 1). The schoolboys needed a good Latin primer, too, and Ælfric wrote one for them, the first ever in Europe in a vernacular language; extracts from it are given here, including the preface in which Ælfric expresses the motivation of his life's work with precision: 'through learning is faith maintained' (Text 4).

The relative importance of the vernacular in relation to Latin had changed dramatically during the reign of Alfred (871–99) in Wessex, the last Anglo-Saxon kingdom to remain independent of the encroaching Danes (see p. 37). Alfred realised that Latin learning had been all but wiped out in England (though we know that in parts of Mercia, at least, some sort of pedagogical tradition had in fact survived), and he instigated a programme to establish widespread education in English. This involved initially the translation from Latin of a series of essential books of Christian instruction and their distribution round the country. Remarkably, we can read about Alfred's aims in his own words, in a letter which he sent out from his base at Winchester, attached to copies of a book newly translated from Latin (Text 5). His programme laid firm foundations for Anglo-Saxon vernacular learning and pushed OE prose beyond its limited role as the vehicle for legal texts, the narratives of saints' lives and minor devotional works into a medium for the transmission of all the basic tools of Christian scholarship. One of Alfred's own contributions was his translation of a popular medieval philosophical treatise, the *De consolatione Philosophiae* ('On the Consolation of Philosophy') by Boethius, a dialogue text teaching wisdom in adversity. In his version, Alfred emphasised the Christian interpretation of fate and fortune as God's will, and showed his own gifts as a teacher by using everyday similes to explain the relationship between God and humankind – as in the example of 'The Wagonwheel of Fate' (Text 6).

The bilingual character of an educated monk's life in the later Anglo-Saxon period is nicely illustrated by a little book that was once the personal property of a Winchester monk called Ælfwine. It is known as *Ælfwine's Prayerbook* and has the flavour of a personal commonplace book, packed as it is with both devotional and practical texts and also some more curious items, such as rules for 'prognostication' (the foretelling of future events). The texts are mostly in Latin but several are in OE, including the three given below (Text 2). The use of the vernacular for practical purposes is further illustrated by the extensive medical literature of the Anglo-Saxons. Among the preserved works is a compilation known as *Bald's Leechbook*, and three helpful medical recipes from it, based on plants, are given here (Text 3).

Further reading

D. Bullough, 'The Educational Tradition in England from Alfred to Ælfric: Teaching *utriusque linguae*', *Settimane* 19 (1972), 453–94

J. M. Bately, 'Old English Prose Before and During the Reign of Alfred', *ASE* 17 (1988), 93–138

P. Lendinara, 'The World of Anglo-Saxon Learning', in *Cambridge Companion*, pp. 264–81

S. Foot, 'The Making of *Angelcynn*: English Identity Before the Norman Conquest', *Transactions of the Royal Historical Society*, 6th ser. 6 (1996), 25–49; repr. in *OE Poetry*, ed. Liuzza, pp. 51–78

D. Scragg, 'Secular Prose', in *A Companion to Anglo-Saxon Literature*, ed. P. Pulsiano and E. Treharne (Oxford, 2001), pp. 268–80

1

In the Schoolroom
(from Ælfric's *Colloquy*)

A 'colloquy' is a sort of formal dialogue between a master and his pupil and was a format much used as an educational tool in the Middle Ages, both for imparting essential knowledge and in the learning of languages, especially Latin. The text known today as 'Ælfric's *Colloquy*' is ascribed to Ælfric on the strength of a note written in one of the manuscripts by someone who may have been a pupil at Cerne Abbas in Dorset, where Ælfric spent some twenty years teaching in the monastic school. Ælfric was the most prolific and influential of the writers who made the later tenth century, following the reform and expansion of the monasteries, the most productive in Anglo-Saxon letters. Little is known about the man himself, but he was probably born about *c.* 950 somewhere in Wessex and entered the Old Minster at Winchester as a boy, attending the monastic school run by Æthelwold. Probably in 987, he moved to the monastery at Cerne Abbas, newly founded by Æthelmær, son of the wealthy Æthelweard, who was a kinsman of King Æthelred and ealdorman (i.e. ruler under the king) of the West Country. Æthelmær and Æthelweard were great patrons of the church, and thus of learning, and Ælfric dedicated a number of his works to them, including his two great series of *Catholic Homilies* (see p. 181) and his *Lives of Saints* (see p. 170). Ælfric did most of his writing at Cerne Abbas, but in 1004 or 1005 he moved to Eynsham, near Oxford, to become abbot of another foundation endowed by Æthelmær, and there he died *c.* 1010.

Thus the *Colloquy* fits well with Ælfric's role as an educator, and it would have been an obvious companion for two other teaching aids which he prepared – a beginner's grammar of Latin (the *Excerptiones*: see Text 4) and a Latin–English *Glossary*, which appears with the grammar in some manuscripts. The OE version of the *Colloquy* given here was not, however, the work of Ælfric (who would scarcely have needed it and would not have made the errors of translation which characterise it) but was added later above a copy of his Latin text. Although four manuscripts of this are preserved, only one of them (British Library, Cotton Tiberius A. iii, fols. 60v–64v) has the complete OE gloss; text and gloss were probably copied together in the second quarter of the eleventh century from an older manuscript, perhaps at Canterbury, for the manuscript belonged to the library of Christ Church. The OE gloss was perhaps made by a pupil, or even by a teacher who was less accomplished than Ælfric and in need of a crib for himself. Such glosses usually

follow strictly the order of the glossed language (here Latin) and therefore d
read idiomatically as a continuous text. Nevertheless, the glossator of the *Colloquy*
has usually preferred natural OE word order in short phrases: thus he writes *ic eom
bysgod*, 'I am occupied', above the Latin *occupatus sum*, not a literal rendering,
'occupied am'. In the edited extracts given below, a few alterations have been
made, mainly in the word order, and in a few cases frequently used phrases which
the glossator did not bother to repeat have been supplied.

Apart from its proven usefulness as a learning text, one of the most fascinating
aspects of the *Colloquy* is the light it throws on the everyday life of members
of feudal Anglo-Saxon society who are otherwise hardly known to us, such as
ploughmen and shepherds. The extracts given here are from the opening section,
where we meet some impressively virtuous pupils, and the closing section, where
a youngster who might be from the classroom itself is quizzed about his day in
the monastery. It is a wearying day (and night). Monks were required to attend
a series of eight church services (the canonical 'hours' or 'offices', specified in
the Benedictine Rule), each of which consisted of its own arrangement of psalms,
hymns, readings and prayers. They began around 2 a.m. or 3 a.m. with the longest
and most elaborate, the 'Night Office' (also known as 'Nocturns' or 'Matins'),
and ended in the late evening with 'Compline'. But, as will be seen below, the
simple series became elaborated considerably by additions; many of these were
made in the tenth century by the industrious continental reformer Benedict of
Aniane. In its original form, the Latin component of the dialogue was obviously
contrived to give schoolboys practice in the use of the correct terms for all these
devotions.

Bede

The language shows many of the characteristics of WS written in the first half
of the eleventh century, but with much inconsistency. Late variations in unstressed
word-endings (the result of 'levelling': see p. xxi) include *-on* for *-um* in *mīnon*
(37; but cf. *hundum* in 34) and *-on* for *-an* in *oxon* (20, but cf. *oxan* in 25). In
scēphyrdas (15) there is typical late WS 'smoothing' of the diphthong of *scēap-*,
but cf. *scēap* (33). The writing of *k* for *c* is common in late OE texts, as in *geiukodan*
(21), *melke* (35) and *weorkes* (10), but cf. *weorc* (18); *t* for *d* is written in *mit* (22)
and *synt* (15), but cf. *mid* (11, 25, etc) and *synd* (45); and intrusive *c* is written
after final *g* in *yrþlingc* (18) and *þingc* (56), but cf. *þing* (39). Other orthographical
variation includes the frequent use of *y* for the short vowel *i*: thus *byþ, syndon, ys,
sprycst, syngan*, etc; but both *hit* and *hyt* occur (4 and 30), *þisum* and *þysum* (43
and 42), and so on. For the second-person present tense of *etan*, 'eat', both *etst*
(58) and *ytst* (53, 55) are used. The glossator of the *Colloquy* committed many
clear errors (that is, spellings which it is hard or impossible to accept as variant
forms or mere inconsistencies); these have been corrected in the text below (and
are listed on p. 345).

Jarrow

monastic education
Latin

Further reading

G. N. Garmonsway, ed., *Ælfric's Colloquy*, rev. edn. (Exeter, 1978)

G. N. Garmonsway, 'The Development of the Colloquy', in *The Anglo-Saxons: Studies in some Aspects of their History and Culture presented to Bruce Dickins*, ed. P. A. M. Clemoes (London, 1959), pp. 212–47

E. R. Anderson, 'Social Idealism in Ælfric's Colloquy', *ASE* 3 (1974), 153–62; repr. in *OE Poetry*, ed. Liuzza, pp. 204–14

J. Ruffing, 'The Labor Structure of Ælfric's Colloquy', *The Work of Servitude, Slavery and Labor in Medieval England*, ed. A. J. Frantzen and D. Moffatt (Glasgow, 1994), pp. 55–70.

D. W. Porter, 'Ælfric's *Colloquy* and Ælfric Bata', *Neophil.* 80 (1996), 639–60

'Wē cildra° biddaþ° þē°, ēalā° lārēow°, þæt þū° tǣce° ūs sprecan°, forþām° ungelǣrede° wē syndon° and gewæmmodlīce° wē sprecaþ°.'

'Hwæt ⌐wille gē⌐ sprecan?'

⌐Hwæt rēce wē⌐ hwæt wē sprecan, būton° hit riht° sprǣc° sȳ° and behēfe°, næs° īdel° oþþe° fracod°?' *what do we care as long as its proper not frivolous or base?*

'Wille gē bēon° beswungen° on° leornunge?' *do you want to be beaten while learning*

⌐Lēofre ys ūs bēon⌐ beswungen for° lāre° þænne° ⌐hit⌐ ne° cunnan°. Ac° wē witun° þē bilewitne° wesan° and ⌐nellan onbelǣden ūs swincgla⌐, būton° þū bī° tōgenȳdd° fram° ūs.'

10   'Ic āxie° þē, hwæt sprycst þū? Hwæt hæfst° þū ⌐weorkes⌐?'

---

1 children beg you O master you teach *sbj* to speak because **2** ignorant are badly (*i.e.* ungrammatically) speak **4** as long as correct speech is *sbj* proper **5** not frivolous or base **6** be beaten during **7** for (the sake of) learning than not to know But **8** know [*witon*] kind to be unless be *sbj* [*bēo*] **9** compelled by **10** ask have

---

3 **wille gē** 'want you', i.e. 'do you want'. The pl. inflection on the vb. is reduced (*wille*, not *willaþ*) because it precedes its pron. [§G6f].

4 **Hwæt rēce wē** 'What care we?', i.e. 'What do we care?'; again, -*e* for -*aþ*. The Benedictine Rule stressed the importance of the correct articulation of Latin, both in reading aloud and in chanting. Boys were punished for errors; see also 48n.

7 **Lēofre ys ūs bēon** 'It is dearer to us to be', i.e. 'We would rather be'. **hit** The antec. is *lāre*, a fem. noun, so the obj. pron. 'ought' to be *hēo*, 'her' (not 'it') in OE, but here 'natural' gender is being used [§B/overview].

8 **nellan onbelǣden ūs swincgla** The infin. vb. *nellan* (a conflation of *ne* and *willan*) is, like *wesan* in the same line, governed by *wē witun*: '(we know you) to be unwilling to inflict strokes on us'; infin. *onbelǣden* would more regularly end with -*an*.

10 **weorkes** gen. of respect: 'by way of work'; *k* for *c* is a late spelling.

'Ic eom geanwyrde° monuc and ic sincge° ælce° dæg seofon tīda° mid°
gebrōþrum°, and ic eom bysgod° on° sange° ac þēahhwæþere° ic wolde°
betwēnan° leornian sprecan on lēden° gereorde°.'

ꞌHwæt cunnon þās þīne gefēranꞋ?'

15   'Sume synt° yrþlincgas°, sume scēphyrdas, sume oxanhyrdas, sume Ꞌēac
swylceꞋ huntan°, sume fisceras, sume fugeleras°, sume cȳpmenn°, sume
scēwyrhtan°, ꞋsealterasꞋ, bæceras°.'

'Hwæt sægest þū, yrþlingc? Hū° begæst° þū þīn weorc?'

'Ēalā Ꞌlēof hlāfordꞋ, þearle° ic deorfe°. Ic gā° ūt on° dægrǣd°, þȳwende°
20   oxon tō felda°, and iugie° hig° tō syl°. ꞋNys hit swā stearc winter þætꞋ ic durre°
lūtian° æt hām° for ege° hlāfordes mīnes; ac, Ꞌgeiukodan oxan and gefæstnodon
sceare and cultre mit þǣre sylꞋ, ælce dæg ic sceal° erian° fulne° æcer° oþþe
māre°.'

'Hæfst° þū ænigne gefēran?'

25   'Ic hæbbe sumne° cnapan° þȳwende oxan mid gādīsene°, þe° ēac swilce nū
hās° ys for° cylde° and hrēame°.'

'Hwæt māre dēst° þū on° dæg?'

'Gewyslīce° þænne° māre ic dō. Ic sceal fyllan oxena° binnan° mid hīge°
and wæterian hig, and heora° scearn° beran° ūt.'

11 professed each times with **12** (my) brothers (*i.e.* fellow-monks) occupied with
singing nevertheless would like **13** in the meantime Latin language **15** are
ploughmen **16** hunters fowlers merchants **17** shoe-makers bakers **18** How carry
out **19** very hard labour go at daybreak driving **20** (the) field yoke them (the)
plough dare **21** hide home fear (of +*g*) **22** must plough full (*i.e.* complete) field (*or*
acre) **23** more **24** Have **25** a (certain) boy 'goad-iron' (*i.e.* cattle-prod) who
26 hoarse because of cold shouting **27** do during **28** Certainly still of (the) oxen
bins *ap* hay **29** their muck *as* carry

14 **Hwæt cunnon þās þīne gefēran** The vb. is used in its sense of 'know how to' or 'be
able to (do something)': 'What can these friends of yours [lit. "these your friends"] do?'

15–16 **ēac swylce** 'also likewise', or simply 'again'; see 25 also.

17 **sealteras** 'salters'. The salting of meat to preserve it was a crucial aspect of food
production.

19 **lēof hlāford** *lēof* is the adj. 'dear', so the phr. is lit. 'dear lord', but *lēof* can also
mean 'sir', as in 31 and 33; the phr. here may best be translated simply as 'master'.

20 **Nys hit swā stearc winter þæt** lit. 'It isn't so stark a winter that...', i.e. 'There is
no winter so severe that...'; *nys* is a contraction of *ne ys*.

21–2 **geiukodan ... mit þǣre syl** '(with the) oxen yoked and the share and coulter
fastened to [*mit* for *mid*, lit. "with"] the plough...' The OE imitates a Latin construction
known as the 'ablative absolute'. The share and the coulter are iron blades which perform
the cutting action of the plough.

30   '⌐Hig! Hig!⌐ Micel° gedeorf° ys hyt.'
      'Gēa° lēof°, micel gedeorf hit ys, forþām ⌐ic neom° frēoh°⌐.'

      'Hwæt sægest þū, scēaphyrde, hæfst þū ænig gedeorf?'
      'Gēa lēof, ic hæbbe. On forewerdne° morgen ic drīfe mīne scēap tō heora
      læse° and stande ofer hig on hǣte° and on cyle° mid hundum°, ⌐þē lǣs⌐ wulfas
35   forswelgen° hig; and ic āgēnlǣde° hig on heora loca° and melke° hig tweowa°
      on dæg, and heora loca ic ⌐hæbbe⌐; and cȳse° and buteran ic dō° þærtō°. And ic
      eom getrȳwe° hlāforde mīnon.'

      'Þū, cnapa, hwæt dydest tōdæg?'
      'Manega° þing ic dyde. ⌐On þisse niht, þā þā⌐ cnyll° ic gehȳrde°, ic ārās°
40   on° mīnon bedde and ēode° tō cyrcean° and sang ⌐ūhtsang⌐ mid gebrōþrum.
      Æfter þām, wē sungon be° eallum hālgum° and ⌐dægrēdlīce lofsanges⌐; æfter
      þysum, ⌐prīm⌐ and seofon seolmas° mid letanīan° and capitolmæssan°; syþþan°

30 Great labour **31** Yes sir am not [*ne eom*] free **33** early **34** pasture heat cold
dogs **35** devour *sbj* lead back folds *ap* milk twice **36** cheese make as well
37 loyal (to +*d*) **39** Many 'knell' (*i.e.* sounding of the bell) heard got up **40** from
went church **41** about saints **42** psalms the litany first mass then

30 **Hig! Hig!** Here *hig* represents an exclamation, 'O!' or 'Ho!' In 20, 29, etc, the same
spelling is used for the pl. pron. (nom. or acc.) *hī* (or *hīe*) and in 28 it is the word for 'hay'
(with long vowel, and given the dat. ending -*e*).
      31 **ic neom frēoh** Ploughmen in Anglo-Saxon England generally were slaves (see
7/headnote).
      34 **þē lǣs** lit. 'the less', i.e. 'lest' or 'in case' (*þē* is instr.).
      36 **hæbbe** 'hold', in the sense of 'look after'. In fact, the glossator has misunderstood
Lat. *moueo*, 'I move'.
      39 **On þisse niht** The Anglo-Saxons associated the night-time with the day following;
thus 'this night' (lit. 'in this night', acc.) would for us be 'last night'. **þā þā** lit. 'then when',
but simply 'when' in trans. The noun *cnyll* is without a def. art., which would be *þone*, acc.
sing. masc.
      40 **ūhtsang** lit. 'dawn-song', i.e. 'Matins' or 'Nocturns', the name given to the first of
the series of fixed 'offices' or services; it might be held at 2 a.m. or 3 a.m., depending on
the time of year, and could last as long as two hours.
      41 **dægrēdlīce lofsanges** 'morning hymns [lit. "songs of praise"]'. This refers to the
second fixed office, that of 'Lauds', sung at first light – and here apparently elaborated to
include hymns to 'all saints'. *Lofsanges* is a late (or simply erroneous) spelling of acc. pl.
lofsangas.
      42 **prīm** 'Prime'. The first of several shorter fixed offices for the day. It was held at
6 a.m., the time considered to be the start of the day and thus called in Latin *prima hora*, the
'first hour'. Prime for our schoolboy is followed by yet more 'extras': recitation of the seven
so-called 'penitential' psalms (pss 6, 32, 38, 51, 102, 130 and 143), a litany (an invocation
for mercy addressed to God through a series of named saints as intercessors), and a 'first
mass'.

⌐undertīde⌐, and dydon° ⌐mæssan be dæge⌐. Æfter þisum wē sungon ⌐middæg⌐,
and æton° and druncon and slēpon°, and eft° wē ārison and sungon ⌐nōn⌐. And
45   nū⌐ wē synd° hēr ætforan° þē, gearuwe° gehȳran hwæt þū ūs secge°.'
      'Hwænne wylle gē syngan ⌐æfen oþþe nihtsangc⌐?'
      'Þonne° hyt tīma ⌐byþ⌐.'
      'Wære þū tōdæg ⌐beswuncgen⌐?'
      'Ic næs°, forþām wærlīce° ⌐ic mē hēold⌐.'
50   'And ⌐hū þīne gefēran⌐?'
      'Hwæt° mē āhsast° be° þām°? Ic ne dear° yppan° þē digla° ūre°.' ⌐Ānra
gehwylc⌐ wāt° gif hē beswuncgen wæs oþþe nā°.'
      'Hwæt ytst° þū on dæg?'
      '⌐Gȳt flæscmettum ic brūce⌐, forðām cild ic eom under gyrda° drohtniende°.'
55   'Hwæt māre ytst þū?'
      'Wyrta° and æigra°, fisc and cȳse, buteran and bēana and ⌐ealle clǣne þingc⌐
ic ete mid micelre þancunge°.'
      'Swȳþe° waxgeorn° eart þū þonne° þū ealle þingc etst þe° þē tōforan° synd.'

---

43 (we) attended   **44** ate slept next   **45** are before ready may say *sbj*   **47** When
49 was not [*ne wæs*] carefully   **51** Why (you) ask about that dare betray (to +*d*)
secrets our   **52** knows not   **53** eat   **54** rod living   **56** Vegetables eggs
57 thankfulness   **58** Very greedy when that before

---

43 **undertīde** This is 'Terce', the next fixed office, which took place at 9 a.m. (at the 'third hour', Lat. *tertia hora*). The OE word, properly *underntīd*, means 'morning-time', *undern* referring to the period between 9 a.m. and noon.   **mæssan be dæge** 'the mass for the day'; another extra act of devotion.   **middæg** The next fixed office, 'Sext', so called because held at the 'sixth hour' (Lat. *sexta hora*) or 'midday', as the OE has it. Only after this office do the monks have their first meal of the day, followed by a little sleep.

44–5 **nōn** 'None'; the fixed office held at 3 p.m. (the 'ninth hour', Lat. *nona hora*).   **And nū** Finally, in the late afternoon, the boys reach the classroom.

46 **æfen ... nihtsangc** These are the last two of the eight fixed offices: evening 'Vespers' (lit. 'even(song)') and finally the Night Office, 'Compline' (lit. 'night song').

47 **byþ** 'is' or 'will be'. On the use of *byþ*, see §G1a.iv.

48 **beswuncgen** Beating students for poor performance in chanting the psalms and for falling asleep, among other transgressions, seems to have been a common practice. See also the references in 54 and 72–3.

49 **ic mē hēold** 'I kept myself', i.e. 'I conducted myself'.

50 **hū þīne gefēran** 'how (about) your companions?' Along with beatings, reporting others' transgressions appears to have been a central element of monastic discipline.

51–2 **Ānra gehwylc** 'Everyone'; lit. 'each of ones' (partitive gen.).

54 **Gȳt flæscmettum ic brūce** 'I still partake of meat'. The Benedictine Rule (chs. 39–40) forbids monks to eat red meat but there is latitude for youngsters who are as yet novices. The vb. *brūcan* here (and in 62) takes a dat. obj. (though more usually it takes a gen. in OE).

56 **ealle clǣne þingc** 'every clean thing'. There were strict rules about what could be eaten by monks; taboo foods included especially those contaminated by blood (see previous note).

'Ic neom swā micel swelgere° þæt ic ealle cynn° metta° on ānre gereordinge°
60　etan mæge°.'

ᴦAc hū?ᴾ

'Ic brūce hwīlon° þisum mettum, hwīlon ōþrum, mid sȳfernysse°, ᴦswā swāᴾ
dafnað° munuce, næs° mid oferhropse°, forþām ic eom nān° ᴦglutoᴾ.'

'And hwæt drincst þū?'
65　'Ealu°, gif ic hæbbe, oþþe wæter gif ic næbbe° ealu.'

'Ne drincst þū ᴦwīnᴾ?'

'Ic neom swā spēdig° þæt ic mæge bicgean° mē wīn. And wīn nys drenc°
cilda° ne dysgra° ac ealdra° and wīsra°.'

'Hwǣr slǣpst þū?'
70　'On slǣpern° mid gebrōþrum.'

'Hwā° āwecþ° þē tō° ūhtsancge?'

'Hwīlon ic gehȳre cnyll and ic ārīse, hwīlon lārēow mīn āwecþ mē stīþlīce°
mid gyrde.'

---

59 glutton　kinds　of food(s)　meal　**60** could *sbj*　**62** sometimes　moderation　**63** (it) is
fitting for (+*d*)　not　voracity　no　**65** Ale　don't have [*ne hæbbe*]　**67** wealthy　buy
drink　**68** of children　of foolish (men)　of old (men)　of wise (men)　**70** dormitory
71 Who　wakes　for　**72** sternly

61　**Ac hū?** lit. trans. of Lat. *sed quomodo*: 'but in what way?'; perhaps, 'But how
is that?'

62　**swā swā** Double conj. (lit. 'so so' or 'as as'): 'just as'.

63　**gluto** The Latin word is used to gloss itself, though *swelgere* was used earlier (59).
Later English adopted the word, initially as 'glutun', then 'glutton'.

66　**wīn** The Benedictine Rule in fact allowed novices a little wine in the morning; but
in England all wine was imported, and thus expensive.

2

A Personal Miscellany
(from *Ælfwine's Prayerbook*)

Between about 1023 and 1031, a small book of some eighty pages was compiled at the New Minster, Winchester, for Ælfwine, later abbot of the Minster (from about 1035) but at the time a dean, an important administrative official under the abbot. One of the two scribes involved was probably Ælfwine himself. We can be confident that the book (now divided into two volumes, London, British Library, Cotton Titus D. xxvi–xxvii) was indeed Ælfwine's private prayerbook from the number of references to him throughout, including a prayer with his name as the supplicant. More than half of the seventy-eight items are devotional texts, mostly prayers. There are also scriptural passages and a litany (a formal list of saints to be invoked as intercessors), and three full-page line drawings, including one of the Crucifixion. The book opens with an ecclesiastical calendar and tables, enabling Ælfwine to find the dates of the 'moveable' feasts of the church year, above all Easter, which are not fixed but depend on the phases of the moon. This would have been a vital resource if, as is likely, his job as dean necessitated frequent journeys away from the monastery. But there are also secular texts, several of them revealing a characteristic medieval curiosity about numerology and natural phenomena, and these include 'prognostications', which give, for example, days considered lucky or unlucky for the performance of certain activities, such as blood-letting. Although the book is written predominantly in Latin, ten of the items are in OE, and another has an OE rubric. The longest is a vernacular version of Ælfric's *De temporibus anni* ('On the seasons of the year') but they include also a medical remedy for boils (which occurs also in *Bald's Leechbook*: see Text 3), and the three items presented below.

Given here in sequence, they are among five short texts to be found on fols. 54v to 56v, between the work by Ælfric and an account of the passion of Christ according to St John. The 'Alphabet and Sentences' is a curiosity, deriving it seems from the 'prognostic' tradition, in which alphabet texts were used for dream interpretation. Several survive in Latin and in Middle High German, most of them written between the twelfth and the fifteenth centuries, but although there are analogies between these and Ælfwine's version, no direct connection is apparent. To learn the meaning of a dream, you would, on waking, open a book at random and (according to one of several possible procedures) note the first letter on the left-hand page. You would then turn to your alphabetical list of prognostications or precepts and read off the meaning of the letter – and thus of the dream. No doubt for Ælfwine the book to be used would be the Bible. His version of the alphabet text has in fact been thoroughly Christianised and many of the sentences are commands or advice about proper conduct for a Christian, some explicitly so (six mention God), others implicitly (such as those which talk of how to achieve 'bliss'). Thus, if D is the letter that comes up, the interpretation of your dream (whatever its details may have been) is that you will not have things all your own way. In three cases, for the letters C, F and Y, the interpretative formula survives with the use of a word meaning 'signifies' – *blycnað* or (*ge*)*tacnað*; thus the letter C 'signifies happiness', though not apparently in this life. The sentence for the letter Z, in verse, is simply a version of the *Gloria patri* ('Glory be to the Father . . .'), the formulaic utterance of devotion to the Trinity much used in Christian worship. There is no J or U in the alphabet, because no distinction was yet made in the writing of English between *i* and *j* or *u* and *v* (see p. xxix). The elliptical style of many of the sentences is very reminiscent of that used in the sorts of sayings collected in the *Durham Proverbs* (Text 34). A two-part structure is apparent in most of the sentences, two syntactically discrete clauses being joined by a notional conjunction, which may be 'and' or 'but'. Often a neuter pronoun 'it' or 'that' features as the subject or object of a clause; this presumably refers to something dreamt about.

The second item from *Ælfwine's Prayerbook* is a memorandum on the varying heights of the tides of the sea, which change continually in direct relation to the behaviour of the moon. The note reminds Ælfwine how there are in effect four different phases within every period of about thirty days. It will be seen that the highest tides correspond – but not exactly – with full and new moons. A curiosity of this short and informal piece is the amount of linguistic variation in it: three different prepositions are used to convey ModE 'from' – *on* (first with acc., then with dat.), *of* and *fram* – and a four-times repeated 'until' clause is expressed in two different ways (see 2, 3, 4 and 5).

The third item reflects a recurring medieval preoccupation with the ages of Christ and of his mother, the Virgin Mary. Nothing direct is said on the issue of Christ's age in the gospels, and figures between thirty years and thirty-three years and three months were arrived at by various ingenious means. Thirty-three seems always to have been chosen for the calculations of the Virgin's age. She is said to have given birth to her son at the age of fourteen (though some sources say this is her age at the Annunciation, when she was told she would give birth, after which nine months must be added for her pregnancy). If Christ then lived thirty-three years and Mary, after his Ascension, for another sixteen (though many sources say fifteen), then a total of sixty-four years is reached.

The language of the OE texts in *Ælfwine's Prayerbook* is characteristic of late WS of the early eleventh century, with the exception of *hīo*, not *hēo* ('she'), consistently used in the third item (lines 1, 2, etc; cf. *sēo*, *þrēo*, etc, in the other items); this is associated with much earlier WS (as well as Kentish) texts. For the full OE equivalents for the Roman numerals in Texts 2b and 2c, see §E1.

Further reading

B. Günzel, ed., *Ælfwine's Prayerbook (London, British Library, Cotton Titus D. xxvi + xxvii)*, Henry Bradshaw Society 108 (London, 1993)

T. N. Hall, 'The Ages of Christ and Mary in the Hyde Register and in Old English Literature', *Notes and Queries* n.s. 35 (1988), 4–11

M. Clayton, *The Cult of the Virgin Mary in Anglo-Saxon England*, CSASE 2 (Cambridge, 1990)

V. Flint, *The Rise of Magic in Early Medieval Europe* (Princeton, 1991), pp. 273–87

R. M. Liuzza, 'Anglo-Saxon Prognostics in Context: a Survey and Handlist of Manuscripts', *ASE* 30 (2001), 181–230

2a
A Divinatory Alphabet

A ⌐Hē gangeð⌐ ond biþ° his sīðfæt° gesund°.
B ⌐Gōd⌐ þū° fintst° gyf ðū ⌐hit⌐ onginst° ond þē° bið wel.
C Blīðnysse° getācnaþ°: ⌐nis hit on þissum lēohte⌐.
D Ne° gewealdest° þū ⌐þæs⌐ ðū wilt°, ne° þū hit æfre° fintst.

1 will be   journey   safe   **2** you   (will) find   begin   with you   **3** Happiness *as*   (it) signifies   **4** Not   (will) possess   wish   nor   ever

1 **Hē gangeð** By definition, prognostications look forward, so the pres. vbs. all have a future meaning; this one has a sense of marching or going forward: 'He (*or* one) will go forth'.

2 **Gōd** Probably this is the noun 'goodness' or 'benefit' (here the acc. obj. of the vb.); a case could be made, however, for interpreting it as 'God' (in which case the OE word would be pronounced with a short vowel).   **hit** Presumably some project, perhaps the *sīðfæt* of *A*.

3 **nis hit** The sense seems to be '*but* it is not' or 'will not be . . .'; *nis* is a contraction of *ne is*.   **on þissum lēohte** 'in this world'. This noun (lit. 'light') is often used in such a sense in devotional writings.

4 **þæs** The vb. *gewealdan* takes a gen. obj.: 'what'.

5　　*E*　⌐Becume blisse ðē⌐ ond þū bist° symble °gesund°.

　　　F　Tācnað° ⌐dēaþ fram dēaþe⌐: on þyssum gēare° ⌐bīde gōd Godes⌐.

　　　G　Þū scealt° gedēon° be° þisse geþōhtnunge°.

　　　H　Ðæt ðē° ne biþ geseald°: ⌐þenc þū on ōðer⌐.

　　　I　Ongin° þæt° þū wille°: ⌐þæt þē bið geendod⌐.

10　　*K*　Beorh° þē° þæt þū ne gange on° frēcnysse°.

　　　L　Hera° ðū God on ealle tīd° þīnes līfes.

　　　M　God þē gemiclað° ⌐þæt ðē forþ gespēwð þæt þū dōn wilt⌐.

　　　N　⌐Hylt þū ðæt tō dōnne: ne bið seald þīnum dǣdum⌐.

　　　O　Ealle° friðsumaþ° God on° eallum his mihtum°.

15　　*P*　Gyf þū riht° nimst°, ⌐nelt þū wīfes wesan⌐.

　　　Q　⌐For þām⌐ micel° God is ond ⌐nergendlic swȳðe⌐, ond þū fintst blisse.

---

5 will be always healthy　**6** (It) signifies year　**7** shall (*or* ought to) prosper through counsel　**8** to you given　**9** Begin what will *sbj*　**10** Guard yourself into danger　**11** Praise time　**12** (will) magnify　**14** All (things *or* people) *ap* reconciles with powers　**15** (what is) right accept　**16** great

---

　　5 Becume blisse ðē The inflection on the pl. vb., coming before its subject, is reduced to -*e* [§G6f]. The full form is probably sbj. (*becumen*), with an optative sense: 'Let joys come to you', but the positive 'will come' (*becumaþ*) is a possible interpretation also.

　　6 dēaþ fram dēaþe 'death from death'. There are many references in the NT to the idea that Christ destroyed death's dominion over humankind: see, for instance, Rom. 6.9, I Cor. 15.26 and 54–5, and Rev. 1.18 and 20.14.　**bīde gōd Godes** 'expect goodness of [i.e. from] God'. Presumably this is an intimation of death – theoretically a welcome event for the Christian. It is conceivable that we should read *God gōdes*, with *bide* then the imp. form of *biddan*, 'pray', which takes acc. of person prayed to and gen. of thing prayed for: 'pray God for (his) goodness'.

　　8 þenc þū on ōðer Presumably, 'think about another thing', i.e. 'about something else', in place of whatever it is that you are not going to get.

　　9 þæt þē bið geendod 'it will be finished for you'. The sense may be that with God's help you can finish whatever you start.

　　12 þæt ðē . . . dōn wilt 'so that what (*þæt*) you wish to do will henceforth prosper (*gespēwð*) for you'.

　　13 Hylt þū ðæt tō dōnne 'restrain yourself [lit. "hold you"] from doing that'; *tō dōnne* is infl. inf., lit. 'to do that'.　**ne bið seald þīnum dǣdum** Perhaps, '(it) will not be given by your deeds', meaning 'it' will not be achieved by your efforts.

　　15 nelt þū wīfes wesan 'you will not wish to be with a woman' (*nelt* for *ne wilt*). The idiom (with the noun in the gen. of respect or location) is unusual, but Latin analogues confirm that this is the likely interpretation.

　　16 For þām lit. 'on account of that'. Presumably, this means that, as a result of reading this particular letter, you can be sure that the following is the case. This sentence could be linked with the previous one, with *for þām* being interpreted as 'because', but its discrete function would then be lost.　**nergendlic swȳðe** *nergendlic* seems to be an adj. meaning 'saving', so lit. 'very saving'; a paraphrase seems necessary: perhaps, 'a great saviour'.

R   Forlǣt° al° ðā ⌜syn⌝.
S   Þū bist hāl° gyf þū tō Gode gehwyrfst°: ⌜sē sit⌝ hāl ond mihtig.
T   ⌜Ne fyrhteð⌝ þā° þe° on° synnum lyfiað° ond yfel þencað°.
20 V   ⌜Blisse⌝ ðē biþ geseald ond ⌜weg on geweald⌝.
X   Blisse ond weg ond ēce° līf.
Y   Bȳcnaþ° sibbe° ond gesynta°.
Z   Wuldor° sȳ° ðē ond wurðmynt°,   wereda° Drihten°,
      fæder on foldan°,   ⌜fægere gemǣne⌝
25 mid sylfan° sunu°   ond sōðum° gāste°.
    Āmen.

17 Abandon all [*eal*]   **18** safe turn   **19** those   who   in   live   intend   **21** eternal
22 (It) signifies   love   salvation   **23** Glory   be *sbj*   honour   of hosts   Lord   **24** earth
25 (your) own   son *ds*   righteous   spirit *ds*

17 **syn** The form *synne* (acc. sg. fem.) would be expected.

18 **sē sit** 'he dwells' or 'remains', using an extended sense of the vb. *sittan*, 'sit'. It is assumed here that *sē* is the pers. pron. (for *hē*), but it could be the rel. pron. *se*, 'who' (with short vowel), in which case we would punctuate with a comma, not a colon.

19 **Ne fyrhteð** The form is indic., 'one will not fear', but the sense seems more likely to be optative: 'let him not fear'.

20 **Blisse** Presumably nom., and therefore pl., 'joys', despite the sg. vb., *biþ*. **weg on geweald** It seems that *weg* must mean 'way' in the sense of 'the course of life', or simply 'life', which is to be given 'into (your) power'. The two gifts are repeated succinctly under *X*, with the addition of a third.

24 **fægere gemǣne** A second part of the subj., parallel with *wuldor*: '(and) beautiful fellowship'.

2b
The Moon and Tide

Hēr is sēo endebyrdnes° ⌜mōnan gonges ond sǣflōdes⌝. ⌜On þrēora nihta ealdne

1 sequence

1 **mōnan gonges ond sǣflōdes** A double gen. construction: 'of the moon's motion (*or* course) and the tide's [lit. "sea-flood's"]', i.e. 'of the motion of the moon and the tide'. OE tends to split so-called 'heavy groups', i.e. pairs of nouns dependent on another noun, putting one later, as here. *Mōnan* is the gen. form of the weak masc. noun *mōna* [§B5a].

mōnan⌐, wanað° se sǣflōd oþþæt° se mōna bið XI nihta eald oþþe° XII. Of° XI
nihta ealdum mōnan, weaxeð° se sǣflōd oþ° XVIII nihta ealdum mōnan. Fram
XVIII nihta ealdum mōnan, wanaþ se sǣflōd oþ XXVI nihta ealdum mōnan. Of
5   XXVI nihta ealdum mōnan, weaxeð se sǣflōd oþþæt se mōna bið eft° ðrēora
nihta eald

2 diminishes (*or* wanes) until or From **3** grows until **5** again

1–2 **On þrēora nihta ealdne mōnan** lit. 'From the old-by-three-nights moon' (with
þrēora nihta in the gen. of respect), i.e. 'From when the moon is three nights old'. *On* is
here followed by the acc. form of the adj. and its noun (*ealdne mōnan*), but subsequently
of or *fram* are used (both meaning 'from'), with the dat. (*ealdum mōnan*).

2c
The Age of the Virgin

⌐Sancta⌐ Māria wæs ⌐on þrēo ond syxti wintra⌐ þā° hīo° of° middanearde°
fērde°. Ond hīo wæs fēowortȳne° gēara eald þā hīo Crīst ācende° ond hīo wæs
mid° him XXXIII gēara on middanearde. Ond hīo wæs ⌐XVI gēar⌐ æfter him
on° worulde.

1 when she from earth ('middle-earth') **2** departed fourteen gave birth to +*a* **3** with
4 in

1 **Sancta** Mary's Latin title (fem.): 'Saint' or 'Holy'.   **on þrēo ond syxti wintra** 'sixty-
three winters old' (lit. 'at three-and-sixty of winters'); the number is followed by the partitive
gen., as are 'fourteen' and 'thirty-three' in 2 and 3. The Anglo-Saxons often counted in
winters but, as the next line shows, used years also.
3 **XVI gēar** acc. of time, rather than the gen. construction used three times already.

3
Medicinal Remedies
(from *Bald's Leechbook*)

Uniquely in western Europe before 1100, Anglo-Saxon England had its own medical literature in the vernacular, and four major medical treatises in OE have survived. Much of the material in them was translated directly from Latin works and
thus continued the Graeco-Roman tradition associated especially with Hippocrates
and Galen (who themselves drew on traditions going back four thousand years in
the Near East). It is probable that the Anglo-Saxon compilers were influenced
by a 'native' northern European tradition as well. This may originally have been
transmitted orally.

Bald's Leechbook (now London, British Library, Royal 12 D. xvii) is one of
the four treatises. It is so called because a Latin colophon (concluding statement)
written by the scribe declares: 'Bald is owner of this book, which he ordered Cild
to write'. Nothing is known about Bald (or indeed about Cild himself), but this
'leechbook' – *lǣcebōc* was the Anglo-Saxons' own term for such a book – was
clearly intended for use by a professional 'leech' (*lǣce*, 'physician'). It is a com-
pendium of medical knowledge in two parts. The first has eighty-eight numbered
chapters giving remedies for specific disorders, starting with those affecting the
head and working systematically down the body (the method of the Greek physicians); the second is a more discursive and learned account of mainly internal
disorders, with sixty-seven chapters. Extract (a) below is from item 2 in part one;
extracts (b) and (c) are from items 12 and 65, respectively, in part two. A third
part (known as *Leechbook III*), with seventy-six chapters, was added to the British
Library manuscript but is from a separate source. All the material was probably
put together in King Alfred's time (the end of the ninth century), though our copy
of it was made around the middle of the tenth century, probably at Winchester.

Much can be deduced about the health and habits of the Anglo-Saxons from
their medical literature. The number of entries concerned with what is termed
'dimness (or mistiness) of the eyes', for example, as in (a), suggests that eye ail-
ments were especially common. Although a condition such as astigmatism may
have been involved in some cases, the problem was no doubt more usually the
result of infection or injury. Inflammation and irritation would be exacerbated by
the smoky atmosphere inside buildings without chimneys, and unsanitary con-
ditions would encourage the spread of a wide range of diseases. Many of the
Anglo-Saxon medical remedies contain incantations (often Christian in origin)

and evidently magical, or at the very least superstitious and apparently unscientific, elements. Earlier commentators were tempted to dismiss the remedies as worthless, and yet such elements invariably apply to the presentation of the cure, not to its basic component – a point well illustrated in remedy (c). Research has shown conclusively that most Anglo-Saxon medical remedies make good sense on strictly pharmacological grounds and there are sound scientific reasons for many of the ostensibly irrational instructions in the recipes. The rather bizarre terms in which these may be given perhaps supply the additional element of psychological reassurance, a dimension of cure no less valued today than a thousand years ago. The common names of plants are notoriously variable and specific Latin names are indicated in the notes below, where these can be established with some degree of certainty.

The text shows clear evidence of 'Alfredian', i.e. early WS, forms, such as *hiora* (3a/6), *monige* (3a/6), *mon* (3a/11), and the inflection -*un* for dat. pl. -*um* in *sīþun* (3c/3), but there are signs also that the scribe was influenced by later developments, as in *sȳn* (3a/10), alongside *sīen* (3c/1).

Further reading

C. E. Wright, ed., *Bald's Leechbook (British Museum Royal Manuscript 12. D. xvii)*, EEMF 5 (Copenhagen, 1955)

O. Cockayne, ed. and trans., *Leechdoms, Wortcunning, and Starcraft of Early England*, 3 vols. (London, 1864–6; repr. New York, 1965)

S. Rubin, *Medieval English Medicine* (London, 1974)

A. L. Meaney, 'Variant Versions of the Old English Medical Remedies and the Compilation of Bald's *Leechbook*', *ASE* 13 (1984), 235–68

M. L. Cameron, 'Anglo-Saxon Medicine and Magic', *ASE* 17 (1988), 191–215

'Bald's *Leechbook* and Cultural Interactions in Anglo-Saxon England', *ASE* 19 (1990), 5–12

Anglo-Saxon Medicine, CSASE 7 (Cambridge, 1993)

S. Pollington, *Leechcraft. Early English Charms, Plantlore and Healing* (Hockwold-cum-Witon, Norfolk, 2000)

3a
For Dimness of the Eyes

Lǣcedōmas° wiþ° ēagna° miste°: Genim° ⌐celþenian⌐ sēaw° oþþe blōstman°;
gemeng° wið° ⌐dorena hunig⌐; gedō° ⌐on ǣrenfæt⌐, wlece° listum° ⌐on wearmum
glēdum⌐ oþþæt° hit gesoden° sīe°. Þis bið gōd lǣcedom wiþ ēagna dimnesse.
⌐Wiþ þon ilcan⌐ eft°, ⌐wildre rūdan⌐ gedēawre° ond getrifuladre° sēaw; gemeng
5   wið āsēownes° huniges ⌐em micel⌐: smyre° mid° þā ēagan. Wiþ ēagna miste,
monige° men, ⌐þȳ lǣs⌐ hiora ēagan þā ādle° þrōwian°, lōciað° on° ceald wæter
ond þonne magon° fyr° gesēon°; ⌐ne wyrt þæt þā sēon⌐ ac micel wīngedrinc ond
ōþre geswette° drincan ond mettas°, ond ⌐þā swīþost⌐ þā ðe⌐ on ðǣre uferan°
wambe° gewuniað° ond ne magon meltan° ac þǣr yfele wǣtan° wyrceað° ond
10   ⌐þicce⌐; por° ond cawel° ond eal þā þe sȳn° swā° āfer° ⌐sind tō flēoganne⌐, ond
þæt þe⌐ mon on bedde dæges° ūpweard° ne licge°. Ond cyle° ond wind ond rēc°
ond dūst – þās° þing ond ⌐þisum gelīc⌐ ǣlce° dæge sceþþað° þām ēagum. Wiþ

1 Remedies for of (the) eyes dimness Take juice *as* flower *as*   **2** mix with put warm
carefully   **3** until cooked is *sbj*   **4** again moist crushed   **5** strained smear with (it)
6 many disease suffer *sbj* look into   **7** are able further see   **8** sweetened foods most
of all upper   **9** stomach remain dissolve (*i.e.* be digested) humours cause   **10** leek
cabbage are *sbj* likewise bitter   **11** by day (facing) upwards lies cold smoke
12 these to these like every harm +*d*

1 **celþenian** 'of celandine' (gen. sg.). The medicinal properties of the greater celandine
(*Chelidonium majus*) are well established.
2 **dorena hunig** 'the honey of bumble-bees'. Honey is a bactericide.   **on ǣrenfæt** 'in
a brass vessel'; this produces copper salts, which can destroy bacteria.
2–3 **on wearmum glēdum** 'on warm embers'. Both celandine juice and honey are thick
liquids, easily burned when heated, so care is needed; glowing coals provide a suitably gentle
heat.
4 **Wiþ þon ilcan** 'For the same' (*wiþ* with instr.).   **wildre rūdan** 'of wild rue'. Perhaps
the species *Ruta sylvestris*; the two following adjs., also gen. sg., describe it.
5 **em micel** 'equally much', i.e. 'an equal quantity of' (with gen.).
6 **þȳ lǣs** 'the less', i.e. 'in case' (*þȳ* is instr.), followed by sbj. vb. (*þrōwian* for *þrōwien*).
7 **ne wyrt þæt þā sēon** The emphasis is on the subj. pron.: '*that* [i.e. looking into cold
water, presumably *under* water] does not harm (*wyrt*) the sight' – but (*ac*) the activities now
listed do. The fem. *n*-noun *sēo* (here acc.) is usually glossed specifically as 'pupil (of the
eye)', but the more general trans. is appropriate here.
8 **þā ... þā ðe** 'those [i.e. those foods] that ...'; the second *þā* simply echoes the first.
10 **þicce** adj. parallel with *yfele*, describing *wǣtan*: 'thick'.
10–11 **sind tō flēoganne** infl. inf. with passive sense [§G6d.ii.1]: 'are to be avoided';
flēogan is normally a trans. vb.   **ond þæt þe** 'and (care should also be taken) that ...'.
12 **þisum gelīc** 'like to this (*or* these)', i.e. 'things like this'.

ēagna miste, genim grēnne° ⌐finul⌐, gedō on wæter XXX nihta on ǣnne croccan°,
þone° þe sīe gepīcod° ūtan°; gefylle þonne mid rēnwætere. Æfter þon° āweorpe°
15   of° þone finul ond mid þȳ° wætere ælce dæge þwēah° þā ēagan ond ontȳne°.

13 green (*i.e.* young) pot **14** one 'pitched' (*i.e.* covered with pitch) on the outside that
isn throw **15** off that *isn* wash open (them)

13 **finul** 'fennel' (*Foeniculum vulgare*); recommended in the old herbals against wind
and poisoning, and for cleansing the stomach. It is used in the next remedy also.

3b
For Vomiting

Wið spiwþan° ond ⌐wið þon þe him mete⌐ under° ne gewunige°, genim
⌐sinfullan⌐, gegnīd° on° scearp° wīn: sele° bollan° fulne° tō gedrincanne æfter
ǣfengeweorce°. Genim wiþ þon ilcan finoles sēawes twēgen° dǣlas°, huniges
ǣnne°; sēoþ oþþæt þæt° hæbbe huniges þicnesse: sele þonne, ⌐neahtnestigum⌐,
5   cuclermǣl° full; þæt wlættan° gestīreð°, þæt lungenne° bēt°, þæt lifre° hǣlð°.
Wið miclan spiweþan ⌐ond hē ne mæge nānne mete gehabban⌐, genim diles°
sǣdes° āne yntsan°, pipores° fēower, cymenes° þrēo. Gegnīd swīþe smale, dō°
þonne on wæter ⌐þe wǣre minte on gesoden ond⌐ sūre° æppla oððe ⌐wīngeardes
twigu ufeweard merwe⌐. Gif se mon ne sīe on fefre°, ȳce° mid wīne ond sele

1 'spewing' *ds* down stays **2** crumble (it) into bitter give bowl full **3** evening
work two parts (of +*g*) **4** one boil it **5** spoonful nausea controls lungs
improves liver heals **6** of dill **7** of the seed ounce of pepper of cumin put **8** sour
9 fever augment

1 **wið þon þe** 'in the case that' (*wið* with instr.). **him mete** poss. dat. [§D4b]: 'his [i.e.
the sick person's] food'.
2 **sinfullan** 'house-leek' (*Sempervivum tectorum*), well known in the old herbals.
4 **neahtnestigum** The main elements of the adj. *neahtnestig* are *neaht* (= *niht*, 'night')
and *nest*, a contraction of *ne wist* ('does not eat', from *wistian*, 'feast'); the dat. pl. ending
turns it into an adv. of manner. An effective rendering is 'after a night's fasting'.
6 **ond hē . . . gehabban** 'and (when) he [i.e. the sick person] is not able to hold (down)
any food'.
8 **þe wǣre minte on gesoden** 'which mint has been boiled in'. **ond** i.e. along with.
8–9 **wīngeardes twigu ufeweard merwe** *uferweard* is an adj meaning 'top' or 'top part
of'; perhaps, 'the tender upper parts of the twigs of a vine [lit. "vineyard"]'.

10   drincan þonne hē tō reste gān° wille, ond le° ūtan on þone magan° gesodene
⌜wuduæpla⌝ ond hlāfes° cruman° ond swilce° onlegena°.

10 go   apply   stomach   **11** of bread   crumbs   similar   applications

11 **wuduæpla** 'crab-apples' (acc. pl.); probably the species *Malus sylvestris*.

3c
For Dysentery

Wiþ ūtwærce°, ⌜brēmbel þe sīen bēgen endas on eorþan⌝. Genim þone nēowran°
wyrttruman°, delf° ūp, þwīt° nigon° spōnas° on þā wynstran° hand ond sing
þriwa° ⌜*miserere mei Deus*⌝ ond ⌜nigon sīþun *Pater Noster*⌝. Genim þonne
⌜mucgwyrt⌝ ond ⌜efelāstan⌝. Wyl° ⌜þās þrēo on meolcum⌝ oþþæt hȳ rēadian°.
5   Sūpe° þonne ⌜on neaht nestig⌝ gōde blede° fulle, hwīle° ær hē ōþerne mete
þicge°. Reste° hine sōfte° ond wrēo° hine wearme. Gif mā° þearf° sīe, dō eft°
swā; gif þū þonne gīt° þurfe°, dō þriddan° sīþe. Ne þearft þū oftor°.

1 dysentery newer **2** root dig cut off nine shavings left **3** three (times) **4** Boil
become red *sbj* **5** Let (him) sip bowl a while **6** consumes Let (him) rest quietly
wrap up more need again **7** still need (to) *sbj* third more often

1 **brēmbel** 'bramble' (*Rubus fructicosus*). The root contains tannin, a known remedy
for diarrhoea. **þe sīen begen endas on eorþan** '(of) which both ends are in the ground'.
Bramble stems have the habit of looping over and re-rooting in the ground, this end thus
being the 'newer' root.

3 *miserere mei Deus* Lat. 'God have pity on me'; a frequent refrain in penitential
prayers. **nigon sīþun** dat. of time: 'nine times' (*sīþun* for *sīþum*). **Pater Noster** Lat.
'Our Father'; i.e. the Lord's Prayer.

4 **mucgwyrt** 'mugwort' (*Artemisia vulgaris*). Apart from such empirical uses, this
plant was renowned in the Anglo-Saxon period for warding off evil spirits. **efelāstan**
'everlasting'. This appears consistently in medieval herbals as a remedy for loose bowels;
it is not clear which specific plant is meant (though *Mercurialis perennis*, dog's mercury, or
Mercurialis annua have been suggested). **þās þrēo** i.e. bramble, mugwort and everlasting.
on meolcum 'in milk'; pl. with sg. sense [§B4b.iii].

5 **on neaht nestig** 'fasting at night'; presumably, 'after a night's fast' (see 3b/4n).

4

Learning Latin
(from Ælfric's *Excerptiones de arte grammatica anglice*)

One of the works which Ælfric probably composed in the first instance to meet his own needs as a teacher in the monastic school at Cerne Abbas (see p. 4) is the *Excerptiones de arte grammatica anglice* ('Extracts on Grammar in English'). It is a schoolboys' Latin grammar-book, written at a fairly elementary level and intended, as Ælfric explains in the preface (given below), to make Latin accessible to boys at an early stage in their monastic careers. These boys, known as 'oblates' or 'novices' (who in many cases, like Ælfric himself, would have been placed in a monastery at the age of about seven), had to learn not only to read and write but also to speak Latin. From the start, they had to participate in the Divine Office, the series of services performed daily in Latin in the monastic church according to a strict timetable set out in the Benedictine Rule (see 1/headnote). They were expected to learn by heart the psalter (with its one hundred and fifty psalms) and hymnal (dozens of hymns and chants regularly used in the liturgy), and in the classroom they would have to progress eventually to the texts which constituted the standard medieval curriculum, covering subjects such as rhetoric and dialectic, and grammar itself.

Well-known grammars such as the *Ars minor* of Donatus had long been adapted for the use of English-speaking learners, but they were still written in Latin. Ælfric's *Excerptiones* – based primarily on an abridgement of the work of another sixth-century Latin grammarian, Priscian – was the first to be written in English (or indeed in any other European vernacular). The widespread and continuing use of the work is confirmed by the preservation of copies of it in thirteen manuscripts, the last made as late as the thirteenth century. Appended to seven copies is a *Glossary*, a list of Latin words with OE equivalents which we assume was also compiled by Ælfric; it contains several hundred words, arranged not alphabetically but according to topic. For his *Excerptiones*, Ælfric needed a set of English grammatical terms to represent the latinate ones. Most were created (by Ælfric himself or predecessors) by literal translation. Thus, *infinitiuus* (Latin for the 'infinitive' form of the verb) became *ungeendigendlic* ('unending') and *accusatiuus* (the accusative or object case) was *wregendlic* (from *wregan* 'to accuse' or 'impeach'). Some terms, such as *wordes gefēra* ('a word's companion') for 'adverb', have great charm, though others are more than a little cumbersome. They did not survive into the modern era, so that today of course we use the latinate terms themselves, semantically opaque though they may be to the student untutored in Latin. Ælfric's use of some very common OE words in technical ways can be confusing. Thus *cyn(n)* and *gecynd* are both sometimes used in the sense of 'gender', but may also have their more familiar meanings of 'kind' or 'sort' and 'nature' or 'character', respectively; and *dæl* ('part' or 'portion') is used for both 'letter' and 'word'. Verb 'tense' is signified by *tīd* ('time').

The manuscript from which the following extracts are taken is probably the oldest to survive, Oxford, St John's College 154, fols. 1–160, copied at the beginning of the eleventh century. The language is good late WS, written with great consistency. There is some evidence of late levelling of unstressed endings, as in *ōðron* for *ōðrum* (91) and the consistent use of *-on* for the plural subjunctive ending *-en* (*becumon*, 5, *leornion*, 10, *sceolon*, 14, etc). The variation *cwest* (56) for *cwyst* (55, 81 and 83) will also be noted, and *d* for *ð* is written in *erad* (93). In line 37, *þar* is presumably for dative *þām*, not an instrumental pronoun (cf. *forþan* throughout). The headings to the extracts below are those given in the manuscript. Only Latin words and phrases which Ælfric himself does not put directly into English are translated in the notes.

Further reading

J. Zupitza, ed., *Ælfrics Grammatik und Glossar. Erste Abteilung: Text und Varianten*, Sammlung englischer Denkmäler 1 (Berlin, 1880; repr. with new introd. by H. Gneuss, 1966)

E. R. Williams, 'Ælfric's Grammatical Terminology', *PMLA* 73 (1958), 453–62

M. Lapidge, 'Schools, Learning and Literature in Tenth-Century England', in his *Anglo-Latin Literature 900–1066* (London, 1993), pp. 1–48

V. Law, *Grammar and Grammarians in the Early Middle Ages* (London, 1997), ch. 10

M. J. Menzer, 'Ælfric's *Grammar*: Solving the Problem of the English-Language Text', *Neophil.* 83 (1999), 637–52

Ic, Ælfric, wolde þās lȳtlan bōc āwendan° tō Engliscum gereorde° of° ðām stæfcræfte° þe is gehāten° *grammatica* syððan° ic ˹ðā twā bēc˺ āwende on

1 translate   language   about   **2** grammar   called   after

2 ðā twā bēc Ælfric refers to his two series of *Catholic Homilies*, each with forty items (see p. 181).

hundeahtatigum° spellum°, ⌜forðan ðe⌝ stæfcræft is sēo cæg° ðe ðæra bōca
andgit° unlīcð°. And ic þōhte þæt ðēos bōc mihte fremian° iungum cildum
5 ⌜tō anginne þæs cræftes⌝ oððæt° hī tō māran° andgyte° becumon°. Ælcum men
gebyrað°, þe ænigne gōdne° cræft hæfð, ⌜þæt hē ðone dō nytne ōðrum mannum⌝
and ⌜befæste þæt pund þe him God befæste⌝ sumum ōðrum men°, þæt Godes
fēoh° ne ætlicge° and ⌜hē⌝ bēo° lȳðre° þēowa° gehāten and bēo gebunden° and
geworpen° intō ðēostrum°, swāswā° þæt hālige godspel segð. Iungum mannum
10 gedafenað° þæt hī leornion sumne wīsdōm and ðām ealdum gedafenað þæt
hī tæcon sum gerād° heora iunglingum°, forðan ðe ðurh lāre° byð se gelēafa°
gehealden°. And ælc man ðe wīsdōm lufað byð gesælig° and sē ðe nāðor° nele°
ne leornian ne tæcan gif hē mæg, þonne ācōlað° his andgyt fram ðære hālgan lāre
and hē gewīt° swā° ⌜lȳtlum and lȳtlum⌝ fram Gode. Hwanon° sceolon° cuman
15 wīse lārēowas° on° Godes folce būton° hī on iugoðe° leornion? And hū mæg se
gelēafa bēon forðgenge° gif sēo lār and ðā lārēowas ātēoriað°?

 ⌜Is nū for ðī Godes þēowum and mynstermannum georne tō warnigenne⌝
þæt sēo hālige lār on ūrum dagum ne ācōlige oððe ātēorige, swāswā hit wæs

---

3 eighty homilies key **4** meaning unlocks benefit *+d* **5** until greater understanding
reach *sbj* **6** (it) is desirable for *+d* worthy **7** man *ds* **8** wealth lie idle *sbj* be *sbj*
wicked servant bound **9** thrown darkness *dp* just as **10** it befits *+d* **11** understanding
young men *dp* teaching faith **12** maintained blessed neither will not [*ne wille*]
13 wanes **14** goes away thus From where are to **15** teachers among unless youth
16 advanced fall away

 3 **forðan ðe** conj. phr.: 'because' (also 11, 25, etc.).

 5 **tō anginne þæs cræftes** 'at the start of this subject'. The children described are boys
in the monastic school.

 6 **þæt hē ðone . . . mannum** The antec. of *ðone* ('it', acc. sg. masc.) is *cræft*: ('skill'),
and *dō* is sbj.: 'that he make it useful to other people', or 'that he put it to the use of other
people'.

 7 **befæste . . . befæste** 'entrust . . . entrusted'. Simplification of the pret. form [§G4.iii]
makes it identical with that of the pres. sbj.; the vb. takes a dat. indir. obj. ('to . . .'). The
reference is to the parable of the 'talents' (the term 'pound' is used here), told in Mt 25.14–
30 and Lk 19.12–28 (hence the reference to 'the holy gospel' in 9). The wicked servant
who fails to 'invest' his God-given portion will go to hell.

 8 **hē** i.e. the 'any man' who has a God-given skill.

 14 **lȳtlum and lȳtlum** adv. dat.: 'by little and by little', i.e. 'little by little'.

 17 **Is nū . . . tō warnigenne** The infl. inf. construction is passive in sense; the vb. takes
the dat.: 'Now therefore [*for ðī*, instr.: also 22, 39] God's servants and monks are earnestly
to be cautioned'.

gedōn° on Angelcynne ⌐nū for ānum fēawum gēarum⌐, swā þæt nān Englisc
20 prēost ne cūðe° dihtan° oððe āsmēagean° ānne pistol° on Lēden° oðþæt Dūnstān
arcebisceop and Aðelwold bisceop eft° þā lāre on munuclīfum° ārǣrdon°. Ne
cweðe ic nā° for ðī þæt ðēos bōc mæge ⌐micclum tō lāre fremian⌐, ac hēo byð
⌐swā ðēah⌐ sum angyn° ⌐tō ǣgðrum gereorde, gif hēo hwām līcað⌐. Ic bidde
nū on Godes naman, gyf hwā° ðās bōc ⌐āwritan⌐ wylle, þæt hē hī gerihte° wel
25 be° ðǣre bysne°, forðan ðe ic nāh° geweald° ⌐þēah hī hwā tō wōge gebringe⌐
þurh lēase° wrīteras° and hit bið ðonne his plēoh°, nā mīn. Micel yfel dēð° se
unwrītere°, gyf hē nele his wōh gerihtan.

DE LITTERA°

Littera is 'stæf°' on Englisc and is ⌐se lǣsta dǣl on bōcum⌐ and untōdǣledlic°.
30 Wē tōdǣlað° þā bōc tō cwydum° and syððan° ðā cwydas tō dǣlum°, eft ðā dǣlas
tō stæfgefēgum° and syððan þā stæfgefēgu tō stafum. Þonne bēoð ðā stafas
untōdǣledlīce, forðan ðe ⌐nān stæf ne byð nāht⌐, gif hē ⌐gǣð on twā⌐. Ǣlc° stæf
hæfð þrēo ðing°: NOMEN, FIGURA, POTESTAS, þæt is 'nama' and ⌐hīw⌐ and

19 done (*or* happened) **20** could compose explicate letter Latin **21** again monastic
life established **22** not at all **23** start **24** anyone correct *sbj* **25** from exemplar do
not have [*ne āh*] control **26** unreliable scribes responsibility does **27** bad copyist
28 *Concerning letters* **29** letter indivisible **30** divide sentences then words
31 syllables **32** Each **33** properties

19 **nū for ānum fēawum gēarum** 'a few years ago now'. Ælfric refers to the years
before the great monastic reforms of the mid-tenth century and echoes King Alfred's
assessment of the state of learning in England in the ninth century (Text 5). Dunstan,
Archbishop of Canterbury (959–88), and Æthelwold, Bishop of Winchester (963–84), who
taught Ælfric, were prominent monastic reformers. Ælfric's following comment on priests
may be compared with his words in 16/23–38.
22 **micclum tō lāre fremian** *micclum* is a pron., dat. obj. of the vb.: 'help many towards
learning'.
23 **swā ðēah** 'nevertheless' (also in 92). **tō ǣgðrum gereorde** 'to each language',
i.e. English and Latin. **gif hēo hwām līcað** impers.: 'if it [i.e. *bōc*, fem.] is pleasing to
anyone'.
24 **āwritan** 'copy out'; but perhaps 'have a copy made' is more accurate here, in view
of the fact that more than one scribe is indicated below (*wrīteras*).
25 **þēah hī hwā tō wōge gebringe** 'even though someone may bring it [*hī*, acc. sg. fem.]
into error'; we would say today, 'introduce error into it'. Cf. the same remark in 16/107–8.
29 **se lǣsta dǣl on bōcum** 'the smallest unit [lit. "least part"] in books'. Confusingly,
Ælfric in the next sentence uses *dǣl* as the unit or part of a sentence, i.e. 'word'.
32 **nān stæf ne byð nāht** A triple neg. statement: 'a letter is nothing', or 'no letter is
anything'. **gǣð on twā** 'goes into two', i.e. 'is divided into two'.
33 **hīw** Here *hīw* (rendering Lat. *figura*) clearly indicates the 'shape' or 'form' of the
letter. Cf. 69n, below.

'miht'°. Nama: hū hē gehāten byð (*a, b, c*); hīw: hū hē gesceapen° byð; miht:
35   ⌜hwæt hē mæge⌝ betwux° ōðrum stafum.

Sōðlīce on Lēdensprǣce synd þrēo and twēntig stafa: *a, b, c, d, e, f, g, h, i, k,*
l, m, n, o, p, q, r, s, t, u, x, y, z. Of ðan syndon fīf VOCALES, ⌜þæt synd 'clypiendlice'⌝: *a, e, i, o, u.* Ðās fīf stafas ætēowiað° heora naman þurh hī sylfe and
būtan° ðām stafum ne mæg nān word bēon āwriten and ⌜for ðī⌝ hī synd *quinque*
40   *uocales* gehātene. Tō ðisum is genumen° se grēcisca *y* ⌜for intingan grēciscra
namena⌝ and se ylca° is on Engliscum gereorde swīðe gewunelic°. Ealle ðā ōðre
stafas syndon gehātene CONSONANTES, þæt is ⌜'samod swēgende'⌝, forðan
ðe hī swēgaþ° mid ðām fīf clypiendlicum. Ðonne bēoð gȳt° of þām samod
swēgendum sume SEMIVOCALES, þæt synd ⌜'healfclypiende'⌝; sume syndon
45   *mutae*, þæt synd 'dumbe°'. *Semiuocales* syndon seofan: *f, l, m, n, r, s, x.* Þās
syndon 'healfclypiende' gecīgede°, forðan ðe hī nabbað fulle clypunge° swāswā
ðā *quinque*° *uocales.* And þā syx ongynnað of° ðām stæfe *e* and ⌜geendiað on
him sylfum⌝; *x* āna° ongynð of þām stæfe *i,* æfter° ūðwitena° tæcinge. Þā ōðre
nigon *consonantes* synd gecwedene° *mutae,* þæt synd 'dumbe'. Hī ne synd nā
50   ⌜mid ealle⌝ dumbe ac hī habbað lȳtle clypunge. Þā synd: *b, c, d, g, h, k, p, q,*
t. Þās ongynnað on him sylfum and geendiað of ðām clypiendlicum stafum:

34 function shaped **35** among **38** reveal **39** without **40** added **41** same
common **43** sound further **45** silent **46** called sounding **47** *five* with **48** alone
according to of scholars **49** said to be

35 **hwæt hē mæge** 'what it has the power (to do)'.
37–8 **þæt synd** 'that is', but Ælfric uses the pl. vb. because the referent is pl.; see also
44 and 45, but cf. 42. **clypiendlice** 'calling', i.e. 'vocalic (letters)' or 'vowels', which are
sounds made by the voice without audible friction. Ælfric characteristically gives a lit. trans.
of Lat. *uocales,* which, like its OE equivalent, can be used as a noun as well as adj. Vowels
can themselves form syllables and hence, as Ælfric points out, the five vowels (*quinque*
uocales) make their own names.
39 **for ðī** 'therefore' (instr.); i.e. because they 'call out' their own names.
40–1 **for intingan grēciscra namena** 'for the matter of Greek names', i.e. 'for dealing
with Greek names'.
42 **samod swēgende** 'sounding with', a lit. interpretation of Lat. *con* + *sonantes.* 'Consonants' are letters which sound along with the vowels. They are produced with at least
partial obstruction of the breath and can only make syllables when combined with a vowel.
44 **healfclypiende** The 'half-sounding' consonants, i.e. 'semi-vowels'. As we see,
Ælfric means those whose names begin with a vowel (not what we understand today by
'semi-vowels').
47–8 **geendiað on him sylfum** Thus the names of the letters are 'ef', 'el', 'em', 'en',
'er', and 'es', and 'ix'. In ModE we say 'ex' for *x* and 'ar' for *r.*
50 **mid ealle** 'completely'.

b, c, d, g, p, t geendiað on *e*; *h* and *k* geendiað on *a* ⌐æfter rihte¬; *q* geendað
on *u*. Z ēac, se grēcisca stæf, geendað on *a*; se stæf is genumen of Grēcum tō

⁵⁵ Ledensprǣce for grēciscum wordum. ⌐*I* and *u*¬ bēoð āwende tō *consonantes*
gif hi bēoð tōgædere gesette° oððe mid ōðrum swēgendlicum. Gyf ðū cwyst nū
iudex°, þonne byð se *i consonans*. Gif ðū cwest *uir*°, þonne bið se *u consonans*.
Ianua°: hēr is se *i consonans*; *uatis*°: hēr is se *u consonans*. Ðās twēgen stafas
habbað māran mihte° þonne wē hēr secgan wyllað. Ēac wē mihton be eallum
þām ōðrum stafum menigfealdlīce° sprecan, gif hit on Englisc gedafenlic°

⁶⁰ wǣre.

⌐INCIPIT DE VERBO¬

⌐*Verbum est pars orationis*¬ *cum tempore et persona sine casu aut
agere aliquit aut pati aut neutrum significans*: 'VERBUM ys ⌐word ān dǣl¬
Lēdensprǣce mid tīde° and hāde° būtan cāse°, getācniende° oððe° ⌐sum ðing tō

⁶⁵ dōnne oððe sum ðing tō þrōwigenne oððe nāðor¬'. *Verbum habet*

---

55 placed **56** *judge* *man* **57** *door* *oracle* [standard Lat. *uates*] **58** functions **59** in
various ways appropriate **64** tense person case signifying either

---

52 **æfter rihte** 'according to right', i.e. 'properly speaking'; this suggests that some
people say the names of 'h' and 'k' differently (as we do, of course, in ModE). The name
of 'z' is presumably a form of the Greek *z(et)a*.

54 *I* **and** *u* Although the consonant represented by *v* was considered by ancient grammarians as separate from the vowel *u*, the same letter (*u*) was used by early medieval scribes
to represent both; moreover, because the pronunciation of *v* was something like our modern
w, the former often passed into the latter. A similar process occurred with *j*, which was
represented by the same character as for the vowel *i* and which was pronounced something
like *y* in ModE 'yet'.

61 *Incipit de uerbo* '(Here) begins (the section) concerning the verb'. There are eighteen
sub-sections, the first two of which are given here.

62 *Verbum est pars orationis* 'The verb is a part of speech...'. In his following
trans., Ælfric specifies 'a part of *the Latin language*', but the rest of the rendering is
close.

63 **word ān dǣl** 'a word (which is) a part (of...)'.

64–5 **sum ðing...tō þrōwigenne** The infl. infin. may express purpose: 'a certain thing
to be done or a certain thing to be suffered', or 'the doing of something or the enduring
of something'. The distinction is between active vbs. (specifically trans., i.e. taking a dir.
obj.) and passive vbs. **oððe nāðor** 'or neither'. The third possibility is the intrans. category of active vbs., which Ælfric discusses below, citing 'live' and 'breathe' among his
examples.

septem accidentia: ⌐"word⌐ hæfð seofon ⌐gelimplice ðing"⌐. ⌐Him gelimpð
SIGNIFICATIO⌐, þæt ys 'getācnung°', hwæt þæt word getācnige: dæde°
oðða þrōwunge° oðða nāðor; TEMPUS 'tīd', MODUS 'gemet°', ⌐SPECIES⌐
'hīw', ⌐FIGURA⌐ 'gefēgednyss', CONIUGATIO 'geþēodnyss°', PERSONA 'hād',
70   NUMERUS 'getel°'. Wē wyllað nū secgan endebyrdlīce° and gewīslīce° be°
eallum þisum.

Significatio ys getācnung, hwæt þæt word getācnige. Ælc fulfremed° word
geendað on *o* oðða on *or*. On *o* geendiað *actiua uerba*, þæt synd 'dædlice° word',
þā° ðe geswuteliað° hwæt men dōð: *amo* 'ic lufige' geswutelað mīn weorc°;
75   ealswā° *doceo* 'ic tæce°', *lego* 'ic ræde°', *audio* 'ic gehȳre°'. On eallum þisum
wordum ys mīn weorc geswutelod. Þās and ðyllīce° synd *actiua* gehātene, þæt
synd 'dædlice', forðan ðe hī geswuteliað dæda. Dō° ænne *r* tō ðisum wordum,
þonne bēoð hī *passiua*, þæt synd 'ðrōwiendlīce°', ⌐nā swylce⌐ hī æfre pīnunge°
getācnion° ac þonne° ōðres mannes dæd befylð° on mē oðða on ðē; þonne byþ
80   þæt on Lēdensprǣce *passiuum uerbum*. Ic cweðe nū *amo* 'ic lufige', þonne
cwyst ðū *quem amas?* 'hwæne° lufast ðū'? Ic cwepe *te amo* 'þē ic lufige' þonne
befylð mīn lufu on ðē, and ðū miht cwedan *amor a te* 'ic eom gelufod fram°
ðē'; *doceo te* 'ic tæce ðē', and ðū cwyst: *doceo a te* 'ic eom gelæred° fram ðē',
et cetera.

85   Nū synd þā word gehātene *actiua*, þæt synd 'dædlice', þā ðe geendiað on *o*
and maciað of him sylfum *passiua uerba*, þæt synd 'þrōwiendlīce word', gif se
r byþ þærtō genumen, swāswā wē nū° sǣdon. Þā word þe geendiað on *o* and ne

---

67 meaning action 68 enduring (an action) mood 69 conjugation 70 number in order
carefully about 72 complete 73 active 74 those show action 75 likewise teach
read hear 76 the like 77 Add 78 passive suffering 79 denote *sbj* rather that falls
81 whom 82 by 83 taught 87 (just) now

---

66 **word** Here, and in much of what follows, Ælfric uses OE *word* (like Lat. *uerbum*) in
the restricted sense of 'a verb'. **gelimplice ðing** 'things belonging (to it)', i.e. 'properties'
(Lat. *accidentia*).

66–7 **Him gelimpð** 'belongs to it' or 'it possesses'. **SIGNIFICATIO** Today we give the
name 'voice' to this particular area of 'signification', with its two categories, active and
passive; after completing his brief overview of the vb. system, Ælfric begins a detailed
description of these.

68 **SPECIES** Ælfric translates this as *hiw* 'form', and in a later section of the *Excerptiones*
under this heading he discusses the function of the various vb. forms ('simple', 'derived',
and so on). Cf. 33n. above.

69 **FIGURA** This category, which Ælfric translates here as *gefegednys*, 'structure' or
'form', relates to the basic formation or derivation of a vb.; in a later section he describes,
for instance, how vbs. may be derived from other parts of speech, such as adjs.

78 **nā swylce** 'not such that', or 'not in the sense that'.

magon æfter° andgyte° bēon *passiua*, þā synd *neutra* gehātene, þæt is 'nāðres
cynnes°': *uiuo* 'ic lybbe', *spiro* 'ic orðige°', *sto* 'ic stande', *ambulo* 'ic gange°',
90   *sedeo* 'ic sitte'. Ne mæg hēr bēon nān *passiuum* on ðisum wordum, forðan ðe
heora getācnung ne befylð on nānum ōðron menn būton° on ðām ðe hit cwyð.
Swā ðēah ⌐sume of ðisum *neutrum* maciað *passiuum*¬ on ðām ðriddan° hāde, nā
tō° mannum ac tō ōðrum ðingum: *aro* 'ic erige°', *aras* 'þu erast', *arat* 'hē e1rað'.
Ne cweð nān mann 'ic eom geerod°' ac on ðām ðriddan hāde ys gecweden:
95   *aratur terra* 'þæt land ys geerod'; *bibo* 'ic drince', *bibitur uinum* 'þæt wīn ys
gedruncen'; *manduco* 'ic ete', *manducatur panis* 'se hlāf is geeten'; *laboro* 'ic
swince°', *laboratur uestis* 'þæt hrægl° is beswuncen°', *et cetera*.

88 according to meaning   **89** kind   breathe   walk   **91** but   **92** third   **93** (in relation) to
plough   **94** ploughed   **97** toil   clothing   worn out

92 **sume . . . maciað** *passiuum* 'some of these neutral (verbs) form the passive'.

5

A New Beginning
(Alfred's preface to his translation
of Gregory's *Cura pastoralis*)

As part of his efforts to revive education in England (see p. 2), King Alfred (877–99) distributed copies of a translation of Gregory the Great's *Cura pastoralis*, a handbook for priests, to churches throughout his kingdom (which now extended beyond Wessex to include Mercia). The letter which he wrote to accompany these manuscripts has become a keystone in our study of the intellectual history of England in the late ninth century. It acts as a preface, presenting first the king's stark – some would say overstated and ideologically driven – view of the dire state of ecclesiastical (i.e. Latin) learning at this time. He notes that in days gone by learning and piety went hand in hand and books were even exported abroad (a clear reference to the time of Bede in Northumbria during the first decades of the eighth century). Now, however, few people can read English, let alone Latin. Alfred implicitly links this decline to a neglect of Christian duty by the English and consequent divine punishment in the form devastation by Viking attacks. Before the knowledge of Latin had declined, no one had thought of making vernacular translations, but now Alfred has embarked on a remedial programme of translation which will make available to the people of England a selection of texts essential for a Christian education. He has assembled a team of learned men from other parts of Britain and the Continent to help with the task. Now it is up to local bishops to organise the learning process using the materials provided. In justifying his ground-breaking experiment – promoting Christian learning by means of vernacular texts – Alfred analyses the history of translation from the sacred languages and shows it to have been a logical and justifiable process. For him, pedagogy is a sacred duty; wisdom is equated with piety, and piety with spiritual wealth.

Four copies of Alfred's letter are preserved. The text below is based on that in Oxford, Bodleian Library, Hatton 20, the version sent with a copy of the *Cura pastoralis* to Wærferth, bishop of Worcester (873–915), one of the team of helpers whom Alfred gathered round him and who, at Alfred's request, translated into English another work by Gregory, the *Dialogi* ('Dialogues'). The manuscript remained in Worcester until the mid-seventeenth century.

Alfred's letter is not consistently easy to read. He wrote at a period when the clear and confident native prose style we associate above all with Ælfric one hundred years later was not yet fully developed, and his style is still heavily influenced by Latin syntax. This often results in cumbersome sentences, consisting of a succession of dependent clauses whose connections are tricky to unravel. Help with these is given in the notes below. Alfred's language, as we would expect, shows many early WS forms. Most notable is the use of *io* to represent both the short vowel *i* and the diphthong *eo*; thus *hiora* (7, etc), *hiene* (21, etc) and *wiotan* (4), and *īow* (48), *sīo* (40, etc), *giond* (5, etc), *liornunga* (10, 53) and *gehīoldon* (8). Before *n*, the characteristic vowel is *o*, rather than *a*, as in *monige* (16 and 58), *monnum* (23 and 49) and *mon* (32, 55, etc). The stem-vowel of *hwelce* (4) and *swelce* (31) has not yet given way to *i* or *y*; *swǣ* is still used, rather than *swā* (13, 45, etc), and *meahte* (65) rather than *mihte*. The adjectival ending -*ǣ* is used rather than -*e* (as in *gefyldǣ*, 28, *oðrǣ*, 47, etc), and *ðǣtte* (a contraction of *ðǣt ðe*) is used more often than not for the relative pronoun *ðǣt* (16, 18, etc). Use of *k* for non-palatalised ('hard') *c* is also characteristic (*kyning(as)*, 2 and 6, and *kynerīces*, 59).

Further reading

N. R. Ker, ed., *The Pastoral Care*, EEMF 6 (Copenhagen, 1956)

H. Sweet, ed., *King Alfred's West-Saxon Version of Gregory's Pastoral Care*, 2 vols., EETS 45 and 50 (London, 1871)

B. F. Huppé, 'Alfred and Ælfric: a Study of Two Prefaces', in *The Old English Homily and its Backgrounds*, ed. P. E. Szarmach and B. F. Huppé (Albany, NY, 1978), pp. 119–37

P. E. Szarmach, 'The Meaning of Alfred's *Preface* to the *Pastoral Care*', *Mediaevalia* 6 (1982 for 1980), 57–86

S. Keynes and M. Lapidge, eds. and trans., *Alfred the Great* (Harmondsworth, 1983)

A. J. Frantzen, *King Alfred* (Boston, MA, 1986)

M. Lapidge, 'Latin Learning in Ninth-Century England', in his *Anglo-Latin Literature 600–899* (London and Rio Grande, 1996), pp. 409–54

S. C. Hagedorn, 'Received Wisdom: the Reception History of Alfred's Preface to the *Pastoral Care*', in *Anglo-Saxonism and the Construction of Social Identity*, ed. A. J. Frantzen and J. D. Niles (Gainesville, FL, 1997), pp. 86–107

N. G. Discenza, 'Wealth and Wisdom: Symbolic Capital and the Ruler in the Translation Program of Alfred the Great', *Exemplaria* 13 (2001), 433–67

✠ ⌐ÐĒOS BŌC SCEAL TŌ WIOGORACEASTRE⌐.

Ælfred kyning ⌐hāteð grētan Wǣrferð biscep his wordum⌐ luflīce° ond
frēondlīce° ond ⌐ðē cȳðan hāte⌐ ðæt mē° cōm° swīðe° oft on gemynd°
hwelce° wiotan° iū° wǣron giond° Angelcynn°, ⌐ǣgðer ge godcundra hāda ge
5   woruldcundra⌐, ond hū gesǣliglica° tīda° ðā wǣron giond Angelcynn ond hū
ðā kyningas ðe ðone onwald° hæfdon ðæs folces Gode ond his ǣrendwrecum°
hīersumedon°; ond hīe ǣgðer ge hiora sibbe° ge hiora siodo° ge hiora onweald
innanbordes° wel gehīoldon° ond ēac ūt° hiora ēðel° gerȳmdon°; ond hū ⌐him
ðā spēow⌐ ǣgðer ge mid wīge° ge mid wīsdōme; ond ēac ðā godcundan hādas
10   hū giorne° hīe wǣron ǣgðer ge ymb° lāre° ge ymb liornunga ge ymb ealle ðā
ðīowotdōmas° ðe hīe Gode dōn° scoldon; ond hū man ⌐ūtanbordes⌐ wīsdōm ond
lāre hieder° on lond° sōhte° ond hū wē ⌐hīe⌐ nū sceoldon° ūte begietan° gif wē
hīe habban sceoldon. Swǣ° clǣne° ⌐hīo⌐ wæs oðfeallenu° on Angelcynne ðæt
swīðe fēawa° wǣron behionan° Humbre° ðe hiora ðēninga° cūðen° understondan
15   on Englisc oððe furðum° ān ǣrendgewrit° of Lǣdene° on Englisc āreccean°, ond
ic wēne° ðætte nōht° monige° ⌐begiondan Humbre⌐ nǣren°. Swǣ fēawa hiora

2 warmly   3 affectionately to me   has come   very   mind   4 what   wise men   formerly
throughout   English nation   5 happy   times   6 rule (over +*g*)   ministers   7 obeyed +*d*
peace   morality   8 at home   maintained   abroad   territory *as*   extended   9 warfare
10 zealous   in (*or* as regards)   teaching   11 services   perform (for +*d*)   12 here   (this) land
came seeking   would have to *sbj*   obtain   13 So [*swā*]   completely   fallen away   14 few
on this side of +*d*   the (river) Humber   services   could   15 moreover   letter   Latin
translate   16 imagine   not   many   were not *sbj*

1 **DĒOS ... WIOGORACEASTRE** 'This book is meant (to go) to Worcester', with
om. of the vb. of motion [§G2d]. The direction was written in large capitals at the top of
the page in Hatton 20 after the volume of Gregory had been put together. The diocese of
Worcester, in Mercia, had been founded by 680. Remote from the main areas of Danish
depredation, it seems to have retained a good level of learning until Alfred's time.

2 **hāteð grētan ... wordum** The infin. after *hāteð* may be trans. with a passive
[§G6d.i.2]: 'commands bishop Wǣrferth to be greeted with his words'. It is a way of
saying 'sends greetings to bishop Wǣrferth'.

3 **ðē cȳðan hāte** After the formal greeting, Alfred switches to the 1st pers.: '(I) command
you to be informed'.

4–5 **ǣgðer ge ... woruldcundra** gen. of respect: 'both in sacred orders and in secular
(ones)'.

8–9 **him ðā spēow** impers. vb. with dat.: 'it prospered for them', i.e. 'they prospered'.

11 **ūtanbordes** 'from abroad'. In the age of Bede, Northumbria had been a leading
centre of Christian learning and many manuscripts were copied at Wearmouth–Jarrow to
meet demand from the Continent.

12 **hīe** acc. sg. fem.; the antec. is *lār*.

13 **hīo** for *hīe*, nom. sg. fem.

16 **begiondan Humbre** i.e. in Northumbria; even here, learning had decayed.

wǣron ðæt ic furðum ānne ānlēpne° ne mæg geðencean° ᴦbe sūðan Temese, ðā
ðāᴸ ic tō rīce fēng°. Gode ælmihtegum sīe° ðonc° ðætte wē nū ænigne onstal°
habbað lārēowa°. ᴦOnd forðon° ic ðē bebīode° ðæt ðū dō swǣ ic gelīefe° ðæt
20 ðū wille°, ðæt ðū ðē ðissa woruldðinga tō ðǣm geǣmetige, swǣ ðū oftost°
mǣge, ðæt ðū ðone wīsdōm ðe ðē God sealde°, ðǣr ðǣr ðū hiene befæstan°
mǣge, befæsteᴸ. Geðenc° hwelc wītu° ūs° ðā becōmon° for° ðisse worulde, ðā
ðā wē ᴦhitᴸ nōhwæðer° ne selfe° ne lufodon ne ēac ōðrum monnum ne lēfdon°:
ᴦðone naman ǣnne wē lufodon ðætte wē Crīstne wǣrenᴸ ond ᴦswīðe fēawe ðā
25 ðēawasᴸ.

Ðā ic ðā ðis eall gemunde°, ðā gemunde ic ēac hū ic geseah°, ᴦǣr ðǣm ðeᴸ
hit eall forhergod° wǣre ond forbærned°, hū ðā ciricean° giond eall Angelcynn
stōdon māðma° ond bōca gefyldæ° ᴦond ēacᴸ micel mengeo° Godes ðīowa°, ond
ðāᴸ swīðe lȳtle fiorme° ðāra bōca wiston°, ᴦfor ðǣm ðeᴸ hīe hiora° nānwuht°
30 ongiotan° ne meahton, for ðǣm ðe hīe nǣron on hiora āgen° geðīode° āwritene.

17 single   think of   **18** succeeded   be   thanks (to +*d*)   supply   **19** teachers *gp*   therefore
command   believe   **20** wish   most often   **21** gave   apply   **22** Think   punishments   upon
us   came   because of (*or* in respect to) +*d*   **23** neither   (our)selves   allowed (to +*d*)
26 remembered   saw   **27** plundered   burnt   churches   **28** treasures   filled (with +*g*)
multitude   servants   **29** they   benefit *as*   knew   of them   nothing   **30** understand   own
language

17–18   **be sūðan Temese** 'to the south of the Thames'. **ðā ðā** double conj.: 'when' (lit.
'then when'); also 22–3.

19–22   **Ond forðon ... befæste** A cumbersome sentence. The main statement is: *ic ðē
bebīode ... ðæt ðū ðē ðissa woruldðinga tō ðǣm geǣmetige ... ðæt ðū ðone wīsdōm ...
befæste*. In the long rel. clause, *tō ðǣm* ('to that extent' or 'end') and *ðæt* may be taken as
correl. and be trans. together: 'that you should empty yourself of (*or* detach yourself from)
the affairs of this world, to the end that you may acquire wisdom'; alternatively, *tō ðǣm*
may be interpreted absolutely: '... for these (things), namely that you ...' The clause *ðǣr
ðǣr ... mǣge* then follows: 'there where (*or* wherever) you may acquire it (*hine*)'.

23   **hit** The antec. is *wīsdōm*, though this is a masc. noun, and so the masc. pron. *hē*
might be expected; an example of the use of 'natural' gender [§B/overview].

24   **ðone naman ... wǣren** 'we loved only the name that we were Christians', i.e.
'we loved only to be called Christians'. It has been argued, on the basis of a well-known
passage from St Augustine, that Alfred did not here write *lufodon* but *hæfdon*, 'had', and
this is indeed the reading in two of the manuscripts. A copyist may have repeated *lufodon*
inadvertently from the previous line.

24–5   **swīðe fēawe ðā ðēawas** *fēawe* may be an adj. describing *ðēawas* (acc. pl. masc.):
'(we loved) very few (of the) practices'; or a noun/pron. (nom. pl. masc.): 'very few [*i.e.*
of us] (loved) the practices'. In 14 and 16 the indecl. form *fēawa*, made on the analogy of
fela, 'many', has been used in this latter sense.

26   **ǣr ðǣm ðe** compound conj.: 'before'.

28   **ond ēac** 'and (how there was) also'.

29   **for ðǣm ðe** conj. phr.: 'because'.

Swelce° hīe cwǣden°: 'Ūre ieldran°, ðā° ðe ðās stōwa° ǣr hīoldon°, hīe lufodon wīsdōm ond ðurh ðone° hīe begēaton° welan° ond ūs lǣfdon°. Hēr mon mæg gīet° gesīon° hiora ⌐swæð°¬ ac wē ⌐him ne cunnon¬ æfter¬ spyrigean°. Ond ⌐for ðǣm¬ wē habbað nū ǣgðer forlǣten° ge ðone welan ge ðone wīsdōm, for ðǣm
35 ðe wē noldon° tō ðǣm spore° mid ūre mōde° onlūtan°.'

Ðā ic ðā ðis eall gemunde, ðā wundrade° ic ⌐swīðe swīðe ðāra gōdena wiotona¬ ðe giū° wǣron giond Angelcynn ond ðā bēc° ⌐eallæ be fullan¬ geliornod° hæfdon, ðæt hīe ⌐hiora ðā nǣnne dǣl¬ noldon on hiora āgen geðīode wendan°. Ac ic ðā sōna° eft° mē selfum andwyrde° ond cwæð: 'Hīe ne
40 wēndon° ðætte ǣfre menn sceolden swǣ reccelēase° weorðan° ond sīo lār ⌐swǣ oðfeallan¬. ⌐For ðǣre wilnunga¬ hīe hit forlēton° ond woldon° ðæt hēr ⌐ðӯ māra wīsdōm on londe wǣre ðӯ wē mā¬ geðēoda° cūðon°.'

Ðā gemunde ic hū ⌐sīo ǣ¬ wæs ǣrest on Ebreiscgeðīode° funden° ond eft, ðā hīe Crēacas° geliornodon, ðā wendon hīe ⌐hīe on° hiora āgen geðīode ealle¬

---

31 (It was) as though said *sbj* forefathers those places occupied **32** it acquired wealth left (it) **33** still see track cannot follow **34** lost **35** would not track mind bend **36** marvelled (about +*g*) **37** long ago books **38** studied **39** translate immediately after answered +*d* **40** imagined careless become **41** left wanted (*i.e.* hoped) **42** languages knew **43** the Hebrew language found **44** the Greeks in

---

33 **swæð** Along with *spyrigean* (33) and *spore* (35), this constitutes a hunting metaphor.
him ... æfter 'after them'.

33–4 **for ðǣm** adv. phr. correl. with conj. *for ðǣm* later in the sentence: 'therefore ... (because ...)'.

36–7 **swīðe swīðe** 'very much'. **ðāra gōdena wiotona** 'about [lit. "of"] those good wise men'.

37 **eallæ** pron. (for *ealle*) in apposition with *ðā bēc*: 'all the books'. **be fullan** 'fully'.

38 **hiora ... nǣnne dǣl** 'not any part of them [i.e. the books]'.

40–1 **swǣ oðfeallan** A notional *sceolde* may be supplied before this phr.: 'should so decay'. Alternatively, *oðfeallan* could be taken as a past part. (for *oðfeallen*), parallel with the adj. *reccelēase*: '(become) so decayed'.

41 **For ðǣre wilnunga** Apparently, 'by desire', i.e. 'deliberately'.

41–2 **ðӯ māra ... ðӯ wē mā ...** 'the more ... the more we ...'; *māra* is an adj. describing *wīsdōm*, *mā* is a noun governing *geðēoda* in the partitive gen., and *wē* belongs with *cūðon*. Learning would increase as an inevitable consequence of the study of languages, and translation would be unnecessary.

43 **sīo ǣ** 'the Law' here means the Pentateuch, the first five books of the OT, the so-called 'books of Moses'. Alfred shows a sound understanding of the history of Bible translation. Originally composed mostly in Hebrew, the books of the OT were later put into Greek for the Jews of north Africa, then into Latin for the Christians of the Roman Empire. Alfred uses this to justify his own programme of vernacular translation of Christian works. He himself put fifty psalms into English (see Text 15).

44 **hīe ... ealle** acc. sg. fem. pron., with antec. *ǣ*: 'it all'.

45 ond ēac ⌐ealle ōðre bēc⌐. Ond eft Lǣdenware° ⌐swǣ same⌐, siððan° hīe ⌐hīe⌐ geliornodon, hīe hīe wendon ealla ðurh wīse° wealhstodas° on hiora āgen geðīode.
Ond ēac ealla ōðræ Crīstnæ ðīoda° ⌐sumne dǣl hiora⌐ on hiora āgen geðīode
wendon. ⌐Forðȳ°⌐ mē ðyncð° betre, ⌐gif īow swǣ ðyncð⌐, ðæt wē ēac sumæ°
bēc, ðā ðe nīedbeðearfosta° sīen° ⌐eallum monnum⌐ tō wiotonne°, ⌐ðæt wē ðā⌐
50 on ðæt geðīode wenden ðe wē ealle gecnāwan° mægen, ond gedōn° swǣ wē
swīðe ēaðe° magon mid Godes fultume°, gif wē ðā stilnesse° habbað, ðætte eall
sīo gioguð° ðe nū is on Angelcynne ⌐frīora monna⌐, ðāra ðe ðā spēda° hæbben
ðæt hīe ðǣm befēolan° mægen, sīen tō liornunga oðfæste°, ⌐ðā hwīle ðe hīe tō
nānre ōðerre note ne mægen⌐, oð ðone first° ðe hīe wel cunnen° Englisc gewrit°
55 ārǣdan°. Lǣre° mon siððan furður on Lǣdengeðīode ðā° ðe mon furðor lǣran
wille ond ⌐tō hīeran hāde⌐ dōn° wille.

　　　Ðā ic ðā gemunde hū sīo lār Lǣdengeðīodes ǣr ðissum āfeallen° wæs giond
Angelcynn, ond ðēah° monige cūðon Englisc gewrit ārǣdan, ðā ongan° ic
ongemang° ōðrum mislicum° ond manigfealdum° bisgum° ðisses kynerīces°
60 ðā bōc wendan on Englisc ðe is genemned on Lǣden ⌐Pastoralis⌐, ond on

45 the Romans when **46** learned interpreters **47** peoples **48** Therefore (it) seems
certain **49** most necessary are *sbj* know **50** understand do **51** easily support
peace **52** youth means **53** apply (themselves) set **54** time can writing **55** read
Teach *sbj* those **56** promote **57** decayed **58** yet began **59** amidst various
numerous cares kingdom

　　　45 **ealle ōðre bēc** i.e. the other books of the OT. **swǣ same** 'in the same way'.
hīe acc. pl. pron., 'them', with antec. *bēc*; similarly *hīe* (before *wendon*) in the next line.
　　　47 **sumne dǣl hiora** 'some part of them [i.e. the biblical books]'.
　　　48 **Forðȳ . . .** Another complex sentence begins (ending at *ārǣdan*, 55). It is best tackled
by first extracting the essential thought expressed: *mē ðyncð betre . . . ðæt wē ēac sumæ
bēc . . . on ðæt geðīode wenden ðe wē ealle gecnāwan mægen, ond gedōn . . . ðætte eall sīo
gioguð . . . on Angelcynne . . . sīen tō liornunga oðfæste*. All the qualifying clauses may now
be added, one by one.
　　　48 **gif īow swǣ ðyncð**, 'if it seems so to you' (*īow* for *ēow*). Alfred now addresses
all the bishops who are to receive copies of the translation of *Cura pastoralis*, not just
Wǣrferth.
　　　49 **eallum monnum** 'for all people'. **ðæt wē** This simply repeats the words in the
previous line, taking up the thread again. **ðā** Probably the acc. pl. pron., 'them', referring
to *sumæ bēc*, but possibly the adv. 'then'.
　　　52 **frīora monna** gen. of definition: '(who are) free men'.
　　　53–4 **ðā hwīle ðe . . . ne mægen** 'as long as they are not competent (*or* able) for any
other employment'.
　　　56 **tō hīeran hāde** 'to higher office'; i.e. to a position in the church.
　　　60 *Pastoralis* The usual medieval title of Gregory's book was *Liber pastoralis*, 'the
pastoral book'.

Englisc 'Hierdebōc', ⌐hwīlum word be° worde hwīlum andgit° of° andgiete,
swǣ swǣ⌐ ic hīe geliornode æt° ⌐Plegmunde mīnum ærcebiscepe ond æt Assere
mīnum biscepe ond æt Grimbolde mīnum mæsseprīoste ond æt Iōhanne⌐ mīnum
mæsseprēoste. Siððan ic hīe ðā geliornod hæfde, swǣ swǣ ic hīe forstōd° ond
65   swǣ ic hīe andgitfullīcost° āreccean° meahte, ic hīe on Englisc āwende: ond
tō ælcum biscepstōle° on mīnum rīce wille āne onsendan ond on ælcre bið ān
⌐æstel⌐ se° bið ⌐on fīftegum mancessa⌐. Ond ic bebīode on Godes naman ðæt nān
mon ðone æstel from ðǣre bēc ne dō°, ne ðā bōc from ðǣm mynstre. Uncūð° hū
longe ðǣr swǣ° gelǣrede° biscepas sīen° swǣ swǣ nū, Gode ðonc, welhwǣr°
70   siendon. Forðȳ ic wolde ðætte ⌐hīe⌐ ealneg° æt ⌐ðǣre stōwe⌐ wǣren, būton° se
biscep hīe mid him habban wille oððe hīo hwǣr° tō° lǣne° sīe oððe ⌐hwā ōðre
bī wrīte⌐.

61 for sense for **62** from **64** understood **65** most intelligibly render **66** bishopric
67 which **68** take (It is) unknown **69** such learned may be almost everywhere
70 always unless **71** somewhere on loan

61–2 hwīlum word ... of andgiete Alfred highlights the two basic methods of translating: literally, word for word, or more freely according to sense. The choice of method for
sacred texts was much debated in the medieval period; cf. Ælfric's comments in 16/85–93.
swǣ swǣ conj. phr.: 'just as'.
62–3 Plegmunde ... Assere ... Grimbolde ... Iōhanne The men from outside Wessex
whom Alfred seconded for his programme of translation and teaching. Plegmund (Archbishop of Canterbury, 890–914) was Mercian; Asser (who became bishop of Sherborne
and wrote a biography of the king) was Welsh; Grimbald (a priest) was a Frank from
Flanders; and John (whom Alfred made abbot of a new monastery at Athelney, Dorset) was
a continental Saxon. On the 'mass-priest', see 16/12n.
67 æstel A rare word thought to denote an elaborate marker or pointer for use by the
reader of a book, made of precious metals and perhaps having a jewelled handle. **on
fīftegum mancessa** 'at fifty mancuses' (with noun in the partitive gen.); either made with,
or simply worth, that amount of gold. The mancus was a gold coin equivalent to the weight
of thirty silver pence.
70 hīe i.e. book and æstel. **ðǣre stōwe** 'that place' is the church.
71–2 hwā ōðre bī wrīte 'someone should be copying another', i.e. is making another
copy. This interpretation takes *ōðre* as the acc. sg. fem. pron. and *bīwrītan* (with *bī* a form
of the prep. *be* and *wrīte* here pres. sbj.) as an idiom meaning 'to copy'.

6

The Wagonwheel of Fate
(from Alfred's translation of Boethius's
De consolatione Philosophiae)

Boethius's *De consolatione Philosophiae* ('On the Consolation of Philosophy') was one of the most widely read and influential books of the Middle Ages, as its survival in more than four hundred manuscripts attests. Written in Latin, the work inspired many translations, including one by Chaucer. Boethius, born about AD 480, was a patrician Roman with a passion for philosophy and education. He was appointed to high political office in the Roman Empire under the Ostrogoth king, Theodoric (493–526), but during a period of political unrest was suspected by the king of plotting against him and was imprisoned, before being executed without trial *c.* 526. His *De consolatione*, written in prison, was Boethius's way of coming to terms with his unexpected fate. It purports to be a dialogue between himself and a figure called *Philosophia* (often rendered as 'Lady Philosophy'), who visits him in his cell. As he rails against the injustice of fortune, she counters with careful comments and elucidations which point insistently to the existence of a divine scheme of things. From this Boethius obtains some peace of mind in his trouble.

It is not surprising that Alfred felt a special sympathy for the work. He, too, had experienced the lowest ebb of misfortune, in his case when the Danes had overrun Wessex and forced him into hiding. Even after the surprise victory at Edington in 878, which enabled him to come back and build the basis of a stable English kingdom, the Danish threat continued, and he was afflicted by illness. His name for the *De consolatione* was *frōforbōc*, 'comfort book', and he made many changes which reflect his personal identification with the subject. Although Boethius had been a Christian, this is not immediately apparent in the original work, and one of Alfred's aims in his reworking of it was to present explicit Christian teaching on Providence and the divine order. He eliminated the autobiographical references to Boethius and presented the dialogue as that between the inquirer's mind and the (male) personification of Wisdom, rather than *Philosophia*.

The extract here is from the fourth book, Alfred's ch. 39. The inquirer has asked Wisdom to explain the fact that often good people suffer while evil people find happiness, according, it seems, to pure chance. Wisdom acknowledges that this is the trickiest of questions, involving as it does the issues of free will and predestination, and of Providence and fate. He explains first that Providence is divine reason, which is eternal and in which events unfold as though in God's forethought, just as a craftsman plans in advance what he will make; what we call 'fate' is the unfolding of those events through time. In an expansion of his source by Alfred, Wisdom then explains the stability at the heart of Providence in terms of the fixed axle at the centre of a revolving wagonwheel (thus replacing Boethius's original abstract image of concentric circles with a concrete metaphor). The movements of fate, says Wisdom, are the movements of the various parts of the wheel, which move faster the more remote they are from the centre. This centre is the hub, into which fit the spokes, while at their other end the spokes fit into segments now known as 'felloes' or 'fellies', making up the outer rim of the wheel which actually rolls over the ground as the wagon moves. People, according to their relative closeness to God, are seen as being at appropriate points between the outer and inner ends of the spokes; and the relationship of the temporal to the eternal world is like that of the wheel to the axle, which governs the whole wagon.

Two complete copies of Alfred's Boethius survive. The elder, in a manuscript produced in the mid-tenth century (London, British Library, Cotton Otho A. vi), was badly damaged by fire in the eighteenth century but a transcription of it had been made earlier; a second copy, from the first half of the twelfth century (Oxford, Bodleian Library, Bodley 180), is intact. The relationship between the two surviving texts is complex. Neither seems to represent the work in its final form but, rather, different stages in its composition. The text below is based on the Cotton manuscript, with emendations and restorations made mostly from Bodley 180 (see p. 346). The language of the Cotton text shows many of the early WS spellings characteristic of 'Alfredian' texts (see 5/headnote). They include words with the diphthong *io*, which in later WS fell together with *eo*, such as *fiorran* (1), *sīo* (14, etc), *gesīoð* (17) and *hiora* (19). Other spellings of note are *ānfaldnesse* and *manigfaldlic* (7 and 26; cf. later WS *-feald-*), *weorulde* (34 and 59; cf. *worulde*) and *wunigan* (59; cf. *wunian*). Old spellings (before a change of *e* to *i*) are represented also in *manega* (8), *misleca* (8), *ælmehtigan* (21) and *cræftega* (23). Long *o* is represented by *oo* in *good(e)* (26 and 27), but cf. *gōd* in 45.

Further reading

W. J. Sedgefield, ed., *King Alfred's Old English Version of Boethius, 'De consolatione Philosophiae'* (Oxford, 1899; repr. Darmstadt, 1968)

W. J. Sedgefield, trans., *King Alfred's Version of the 'Consolations' of Boethius* (Oxford, 1900)

D. Whitelock, 'The Prose of Alfred's Reign', in *Continuations and Beginnings: Studies in Old English Literature*, ed. E. G. Stanley (London, 1966), pp. 67–103

F. A. Payne, *King Alfred and Boethius: an Analysis of the Old English Version of the 'Consolation of Philosophy'* (Madison, Milwaukee and London, 1968)

D. K. Bolton, 'The Study of the *Consolation of Philosophy* in Anglo-Saxon England', *Archives d'histoire doctrinale et littéraire du Moyen Age* 44 (1977), 33–78

J. S. Wittig, 'King Alfred's *Boethius* and its Latin Sources: a Reconsideration', *ASE* 11 (1982), 157–98

A. J. Frantzen, *King Alfred* (Boston, 1986), ch. 4

Þā ongan° hē° sprecan ⌜swīðe fiorran ymbūtan⌝ swelce° hē nā° þā sprǣce° ne mǣnde° ond tiohhode° hit ðēah° þiderweardes° ond cwæð: 'Ealla gesceafta°, gesewenlica° ond ungesewenlica, stillu° ond unstillu, ⌜onfōð⌝ æt° þǣm stillan ond æt þǣm gestæððegan° ond æt þǣm ānfealdan° Gode endeberdnesse° ond
5 andwlitan° ond gemetgunge°. Ond ⌜forþǣm hit swā gesceapen° wæs, forðǣm⌝ hē wāt° hwȳ° hē gescēop eall þæt hē gescēop. Nis° him nānwiht° unnyt° ⌜þæs þe⌝ hē gescēop. Se God wunað° symle° on þǣre hēan° ceastre° his ānfaldnesse° ond bilewitnesse°. Þonan° hē dǣlð° manega ond misleca° gemetgunga° eallum his gesceaftum, ond þonan hē welt° eallra. Ac ⌜ðæt ðætte⌝ wē hātað° Godes
10 foreþonc° ond his forescēawung°, ⌜þæt bið þā hwīle þe⌝ hit ðǣr mid him bið on his mōde° ⌜ǣr ðǣm þe⌝ hit gefremed° weorðe°, þā hwīle ðe hit geþōht° bið. Ac siððan° hit fullfremed° bið, þonne hātað wē hit "wyrd".

1 began   he (*i.e.* Wisdom)   as though   not   subject   2 had in mind   directed   nevertheless   that way   created things   3 visible   unmoving   from   4 unchanging   single   (their) order   *as*   5 form   measure   created   6 knows   why   Is not   nothing   useless   7 dwells   always   sublime   city   oneness *gs*   8 mercy *gs*   From there   dispenses   various   ordinances   9 controls   +*g*   call   10 providence   foresight   11 mind   brought about   becomes (*i.e.* is)   thought about   12 when   accomplished

1 **swīðe fiorran ymbūtan** lit. 'very far-off around', i.e. 'in a very round-about way'. Wisdom does not appear at first to be alluding to the subject in hand (i.e. Fate) at all (*swelce ... ne mǣnde*).

3 **onfōð** The obj. of the vb. is the trio *endeberdnesse*, *andwlitan* and *gemetgunge* in 4–5; the intervening description of the source of what is received (i.e. God), using three adjs. in prep. phrs. (*æt ... Gode*), gives the sentence strength.

5 **forþǣm ... forðǣm** correl. adv. and conj.: 'for this reason (*or* thus) ... because ...'.

6–7 **þæs þe** '(in respect) of that which', or simply 'of what'. See also 17.

9 **ðæt ðætte** 'that which' (lit. 'that, that which'; *ðætte = ðæt ðe*); the next *þæt* is correl. and may be om. in trans.

10 **þæt bið þā hwīle þe** '(that) exists as long as'. Wisdom explains a crucial point: everything that happens in the world pre-exists in God's mind as 'providence' or 'fore-thought'; only when it has happened do we become aware of it and, retrospectively, call it 'fate'.

11 **ǣr ðǣm þe** conj. phr.: 'before'.

'Be° þȳ° mæg ælc mon witan° þæt ⌜hī sint ægþer ge twēgen° naman ge⌝ twā°
þincg, foreþonc ond wyrd. Se foreþonc is sīo godcunde° gesceadwīsnes°. Sīo is

15 fæst° on þǣm hēan° sceppende° þe ⌜eall fore° wāt hū hit geweorðan sceall ǣr,
ǣr⌝ hit geweorðe. Ac þæt þæt wē 'wyrd' hātað, þæt bið Godes weorc° þæt ħe
ælce dæg wyrcð°, ægþer ge þæs ðe wē gesīoð° ge þæs þe ūs ungesewenlic bið.
Ac se godcunda foreþonc heaðerað° ealle gesceafta, þæt hī ne mōton° tōslūpan°
of hiora endebyrdnesse. ⌜Sīo wyrd þonne⌝ dǣlð eallum gesceaftum anwlitan ond

20 stōwa° ond tīda° ond gemetgunga°; ac sīo wyrd cymð of ðǣm gewitte° ond of
ðǣm foreþonce þæs ælmehtigan Godes, se° wyrcð æfter° his unāsecgendlicum°
foreþonce þonne° ⌜swā hwæt swā⌝ hē wile.

⌜Swā swā⌝ ælc cræftega° ðencð° ond mearcað° his weorc on his mōde ǣr, ǣr
hē hit wyrce, ond wyrcð siððan eall, þīos wandriende° wyrd þe wē wyrd hātað

25 fǣrð° æfter his forþonce ond æfter his geþeahte°, swā swā hē tiohhað° þæt
hit sīe°. Þēah hit ūs manigfaldlic° ðince°, sum good, sum ȳfel, hit is ðēah him
anfeald° good, forðæm hē hit eall tō gōdum ende brengð ond for goode dēð° eall
þæt þæt hē dēð. ⌜Siððan wē hit hātað wyrd, siððan⌝ hit geworht bið; ǣr hit wæs
Godes foreþanc ond his foretiohhung°. ⌜Ðā wyrd⌝ hē þonne wyrcð oððe° þurh

30 ðā goodan englas oððe þurh monna sāwla° oððe þurh ōðerra gesceafta līf oððe
þurh heofones tungl° oððe ðurh þāra scuccena° mislice° lotwrencas°; hwīlum°
þurh ān ðāra°, hwīlum þurh eall ðā. Ac þæt is openlīce° cūð° þæt sīo godcunde
foretiohhung is ānfeald ond unandwendlic° ond welt ælces þinges endebyrdlīce°
ond eall þing gehīwað°. Sumu þing þonne on þisse weorulde sint underðīed°

35 þǣre wyrde, sume hire° nānwuht° underðīed ne sint. Ac sīo wyrd, ond eall ðā
þing þe hire underðīed sint, sint underðīed ðǣm godcundan foreþonce. Be ðǣm

---

13 From this *isn* understand two *npm* two *npn* **14** divine reason **15** constant
sublime creator beforehand **16** action **17** carries out see **18** controls may fall
away **20** places seasons proportions mind **21** who according to ineffable **22** then
(*i.e.* henceforth) **23** craftsman thinks out designs **24** changing **25** proceeds purpose
intends **26** should be *sbj* complex seems **27** uniform does **29** preordaining
either **30** souls *ap* **31** stars evil spirits *gp* various tricks *ap* sometimes **32** of those
plainly known **33** unchanging in an orderly way **34** gives shape to subject to +*d*
35 to it not at all

---

13 **hī sint** '(they) are'; the anticipated subjs. of the vb. are *foreþonc* and *wyrd*, which are
two names, as Wisdom explains, for two (different) things.   **ægþer ge . . . ge** 'both . . . and'.
15–16 **eall . . . hū hit geweorðan sceall** 'how everything must (*or* shall) happen (*or* turn
out)'. **ǣr, ǣr** adv. plus conj.: 'first [repeating the sense of *fore*], before . . .'; so also in 23.
19 **Sīo wyrd þonne** Again, fate is the practical manifestation of providence.
22 **swā hwæt swā** 'what(so)ever'.
23 **Swā swā** conj. phr. correl. with adv. *swā swā* in 25: 'Just as . . . (so . . .)'.
28 **Siððan . . . siððan** correl. conj. and adv.: 'Then . . . , when . . .'; but it may be better
to transpose the clauses: 'When it is done, (then) we call it fate'.
29 **Ðā wyrd** acc. obj. of *wyrcð*.

ic ðē mæg ˹sum bīspell˺ secgan þæt þū meaht þȳ° sweotolor° ongitan° hwilce men bīoð underðīed þǣre wyrde, hwylce ne bīoð.

'Eall ðios unstille gesceaft° ond þios ˹hwearfiende˺ hwearfað° on° ðǣm

40 stillan Gode ond on ðǣm gestæððegan ond on ðǣm ānfealdan, ond hē welt eallra gesceafta swā swā hē æt fruman° getiohhod° hæfde ond ˹gēt hæfð˺, swā swā on wǣnes° eaxe° hwearfiað þā hwēol ond sīo eax stint° stille ond byrð° þēah ealne þone wǣn ond welt ealles þæs fǣreltes°. Þæt hwēol hwerfð ymbūtan° ond sīo nafu° nēxt þǣre eaxe ˹sīo˺ færð micle° fæstlīcor° ond orsorglīcor° þonne ˹ðā

45 felgan˺ dōn. Swelce° sīo eax sīe þæt hēhste° gōd þe wē nemnað° God ond þā sēlestan° men faren nēhste Gode, swā swā sīo nafu færð nēahst þǣre eaxe; ond ˹þā midmestan swā swā˺ ðā spācan°, forðǣm þe ˹ǣlces spācan bið ōðer ende˺ fæst° on ðǣre nafe, ōðer on þǣre felge. Swā bið þǣm midlestan monnum: ōðre hwīle hē smēað° on his mōde ymb° þis eorðlice līf, ōðre hwīle ymb ðæt

50 godcundlice°, swilce° hē lōcie° mid ōðre ēagan° tō heofonum, mid ōðre tō eorþan. Swā swā þā spācan sticiað° ōðer ende on þǣre felge, ōþer on þǣre nafe, middeweard° se spāca bið ǣgðrum° emnnēah°, ðēah ōðer ende bīo fæst on þǣre nafe, ōðer on þǣre felge; swā bīoð þā midmestan men onmiddan þām spācan ond þā betran° nēar° þǣre nafe ond þā mǣtran° nēar ðǣm felgum: ˹bīoð þēah

55 fæste˺ on ðǣre nafe ond se ˹nafa˺ on ðǣre eaxe.

'Hwæt°, þā felga ˹þēah hongiað° on þǣm spācan, þēah˺ hī eallunga° wealowigen° on þǣre eorðan. Swā dōð þā mǣtestan men on þǣm midmestum

---

37 the [*adv*] more clearly understand 39 creation revolves round 41 beginning intended 42 cart's axle remains bears 43 movement around 44 nave much faster more safely 45 Likewise highest call 46 best 47 spokes 48 fixed 49 meditates about 50 heavenly as though looks *sbj* eye 51 fix 52 (and) in the middle to both equally near 54 better nearer baser 56 Now depend entirely 57 roll

---

37 **sum bīspell** Wisdom will now attempt with 'a parable' to explain why fate appears to act indiscriminately.

39 **hwearfiende** 'changing'; adj., parallel with *unstille* and qualifying *gesceaft*. Similarly, there follow three adjs. describing God, two coming after the noun.

41 **gēt hæfð** 'still has', i.e. still intends.

44 **sīo** This simply repeats the subj. and is unnecessary in trans.

44–5 **ðā felgan** 'the felloes'. A 'felloe' or 'felly' is one of the curved segments which together make up the rim of the wheel.

47 **þā midmesten swā swā** 'the middle sort (of people) (are) as . . .'. **ǣlces spācan . . . ōðer ende** 'the one end of each spoke'; the next *ōðer* (48) should be trans. 'the other'.

54–5 **bīoð þēah fæste** 'nevertheless (they) are fixed'. The antec. of 'they' is probably just the 'baser' sort of people, though of course all three degrees are joined to the nave and thus also the axle.

55 **nafa** The masc. *n*-stem form of the word [§B5a]; elsewhere, 'strong' fem. *nafu* is used [§B3a].

56 **þēah . . . þēah** The first of this correl. pair is better not trans.

ond þā midmestan on þǣm betstan ond þā betstan on Gode. Þēah þā mǣtestan
ealle hiora lufe wenden° tō ðisse weorulde, hī ne magon þǣron° wunigan°, ˊne
60 tō nāuhte ne weorðað˺ gif hī ˊbe nānum dǣle˺ ne bēoð gefæstnode tō Gode,
ˊþon mā þe˺ þæs hwēoles felga magon bīon on ðǣm fǣrelte gif hī ne bīoð
fæste on þǣm spācum ond þā spācan on þǣre eaxe. Þā felgea bīoð fyrrest° ðǣre
eaxe, forðǣm° hī farað ungerēdelīcost°. Sīo nafu færð nēaxst þǣre eaxe, forðȳ°
hīo færð gesundlīcost°. Swā dōð ðā sēlestan men; swā hī hiora lufe nēar Gode
65 lǣtað° ond swīðor° þās eorðlicon þing forsīoð°, swā hī bēoð orsorgran° ond lǣs
reccað° hū sīo wyrd wandrige° oððe hwæt hīo brenge. ˊSwā swā sīo nafu bið
symle swā gesund, hnæppen þā felga on þæt ðe hī hnæppen˺, ond þēah bið
sīo nafu hwæthwugu° tōdǣled° from þǣre eaxe. Be þȳ þū meaht ongitan þæt
se wǣn bið micle leng° gesund þē lǣs bið° tōdǣled from þǣre eaxe; swā bīoð
70 ˊþā men eallra orsorgestæ˺ ǣgðer ge þisses andweardan° līfes earfoða° ge þæs
tōweardan°, þā° þe fæste bīoð on° Gode. Ac ˊswā hī swīður bīoð āsyndrede°
from Gode, swā hī swīður˺ bīoð gedrēfde° ond geswencte° ǣgþer ge on mōde°
ge on līchoman°.

ˊSwylc is þæt þæt we "wyrd" hātað, be þǣm godcundan foreþonce, swylce˺
75 sīo smēaung° ond sīo gesceadwīsnes is, ˊtō metanne wið þone gearowitan˺ ond
swylce þās lǣnan° þing bīoð, tō metanne wið ðā ēcan°, ond swilce þæt hwēol
bið, tō metanne wið ðā eaxe, forðǣm sīo eax welt ealles þæs wǣnes. Swā dēð
se godcunda foreðonc.'

59 direct in it stay **62** farthest (from +*d*) **63** (and) therefore most roughly (and)
therefore **64** most soundly **65** set more firmly renounce more secure **66** care may
change **68** somewhat separated **69** longer (it) is **70** present troubles **71** future
those to separated **72** afflicted oppressed spirit **73** body **75** reflection **76** transitory
eternal

59–60 **ne tō nauhte ne weorðað** 'nor come [lit. "become" or "turn out"] to anything'.
60 **be nānum dǣle** lit. 'in no portion', i.e. 'to any extent'.
61 **þon mā þe** instr. phr.: 'any more than'.
66–7 **Swā swā ... hī hnæppen** The repeated vb. is pres. sbj.: 'Thus also the nave is
always sound, let the felloe strike whatever it may strike'.
70 **þā men eallra orsorgestæ** 'the people who are most unconcerned of all [*eallra*, gen.
pl. neut. pron.]'. The adj. has the gen. pl. complement *earfoða*, 'about troubles'.
71–2 **swā hī swīður ... swā hī swīður** 'the further they ... the more heavily they ...'.
74 **Swylc is ... swylce** 'What we call fate, alongside divine foresight, is such as ...'.
75 **tō metanne wið** The infl. infin. forms an adv. phr.: 'when measured against'. **þone
gearowitan** 'understanding'; what is meant is *complete* understanding.

II

KEEPING A RECORD

Writing about King Æthelberht of Kent, the first Anglo-Saxon king to convert to Christianity, Bede (*d.* 735) records that 'among the many benefits that his wisdom conferred on the nation, he introduced . . . a code of law after the example of the Romans which was written in English and remains in force to this day'. This noteworthy event took place within a few years of arrival in Kent of the Christian mission headed by Augustine in 597, and Æthelberht's lawcode – though it is preserved only in a copy made five hundred years later – is the earliest-known example of English used as a language of written record. This section begins with extracts from it (Text 7). The writing of Germanic languages across Europe had previously been restricted to inscriptions made laboriously on wood or stone in versions of the 'runic' alphabet, but Christianity had brought Latin letters to the Anglo-Saxons and the opportunity for literacy. Bede's remark about 'the example of the Romans' seems to stress just that: the Anglo-Saxons, too, had now written their laws down, and no longer relied simply on oral tradition.

The lawcodes of successive Anglo-Saxon kings, right up to the time of Cnut (1016–35), would now be cast in OE – centuries before vernaculars were used in such a way by England's continental neighbours – but the widespread use of the vernacular for general purposes took a little longer to become established. The language of the church and of learning remained Latin, and this is the language in which Bede naturally wrote his great *Historia ecclesiastica gentis Anglorum* ('The Ecclesiastical History of the English People'). It is a record of the history of the nation of 'the English', as Bede (echoing a description by Pope Gregory in the sixth century) was now calling them, set firmly in the context of Christian history. But the relative importance of the vernacular changed dramatically during the reign of Alfred (877–99) in Wessex (see Section I/headnote), when the king instigated the translation of essential books of Christian instruction from Latin. Now Bede's *Historia ecclesiastica* was itself put into English. Literate Anglo-Saxons could for the first time read in their own language about the arrival of their ancestors in Britain in the fifth century (Text 9a) and could enjoy the many anecdotes told by Bede to illustrate the moulding of the nation, including one about the miraculous 'invention' of OE Christian poetry by a cowherd of Whitby called Cædmon (Text 9b).

It was also during Alfred's reign that the systematic recording of historical annals was begun in earnest. Versions of what we now know as the *Anglo-Saxon Chronicle* would continue to be made for three centuries, maintaining a record of selected events on a yearly basis and thereby giving shape to an evolving concept of English national identity. It is from the Chronicle in its later years that we get a clear sense of the political chaos which increasingly threatened the English during the reign of Æthelred (978–1016), when the Danes were attacking with impunity and the king and his advisers felt obliged to hand over huge sums of money to buy them off; it had little effect, as the extracts from the 'Peterborough' version of the Chronicle reveal (Text 8). But there had been victories, too, in the history of the English. In 937 King Athelstan resoundingly defeated an army of the Vikings and their allies at a place called Brunanburh, and in some copies of the Chronicle the bare annalistic record of that battle was replaced by a celebratory poem (Text 10).

From the end of the ninth century, legal documents such as wills were increasingly written, in whole or in part, in the vernacular. One of about sixty which survive is that of an aristocratic woman called Ælfgifu, who leaves her property and lands to various churches and monasteries in southern England (Text 11). The extent to which Anglo-Saxon kings may have been involved in the everyday administration of the law in relation to property matters is revealed in a document known as *The Fonthill Letter*, which records the settlement of a complex land dispute during the reigns of King Alfred and his son and successor Edward (Text 12).

Further reading

F. E. Harmer, ed. and trans., *Select English Historical Documents of the Ninth and Tenth Centuries* (Cambridge, 1914)

K. Harrison, *The Framework of Anglo-Saxon History to A.D. 900* (Cambridge, 1976)

D. Whitelock, ed. and trans., *English Historical Documents, I: c. 500–1042*, 2nd edn. (London, 1979)

D. Whitelock, M. Brett and C. N. L. Brooke, eds. and trans., *Councils and Synods, with Other Documents Relating to the English Church, I, 871–1204: Part 1, 871–1066* (Oxford, 1981)

S. Kelly, 'Anglo-Saxon Lay Society and the Written Word', in *The Uses of Literacy in Early Mediaeval Europe*, ed. R. McKitterick (Cambridge, 1990), pp. 36–62; repr. in *OE Poetry*, ed. Liuzza, pp. 23–50

A. J. Frantzen and J. D. Niles, eds., *Anglo-Saxonism and the Construction of Social Identity* (Gainesville, FL, 1997)

J. Hines, *The Anglo-Saxons from the Migration Period to the Eighth Century: an Ethnographic Perspective* (Woodbridge, 1997)

7

Laws of the Anglo-Saxon Kings

Within a few years of Augustine's arrival in Kent in 597 – on a mission which, combined with that of Aidan a few years later in the north, would lead to the Christianisation of most of England by the mid-seventh century – the lawcode of the Kentish king, Æthelberht (*d.* 616), had been written down in English. One of the priorities of the law-makers (and Augustine himself was presumably involved) was to integrate the needs of the new church within the established legal system, whose origins lay in the Germanic traditions of the Continent. Bede notes with obvious approval, in his *Historia ecclesiastica*, that the Kentish lawcode opens with an article for the protection of the new religion, especially the property of the church and its officials; thus he corroborates the content of the received text, without citing it directly. From now on this would be a distinctive feature of all the English lawcodes.

Another primary object of Anglo-Saxon law was to formalise and contain the more destructive aspects of the Germanic feud system, whose structure of reciprocal loyalties demanded the exacting of revenge for wrongs done to kin or to associates. Æthelberht's laws, and those of his successors, sought to limit the circumstances under which private revenge might be taken and to set out a sliding scale of compensatory payments, dependent on the status of both the victim and the perpetrator of crime and the circumstances under which it was committed.

Two essential concepts dominate the lawcodes. First, *mundbyrd*, or simply *mund*, 'protection', which is the right of individuals to peace and security when under the protection of the king, the church, a lord, or even (if you were his employee) a simple freeman; and second, *wergeld*, literally 'man-money' (but, in the absence of a modern equivalent, we use the untranslated OE term today), which is the money, or goods in kind, due to a dead person's kin to compensate for his or her death (see also 7a/22n).

An important development in the formulation of law between the reign of Æthelberht of Kent and that of Alfred of Wessex (871–99) was the association of social order with loyalty to the monarch. It was barely present in Æthelberht's code, but Alfred makes it explicit. Law-making had by now become a public display of royal power and prerogative, and it was an opportunity also to set out ideological aspirations. Characteristically, Alfred headed his laws with an English translation of a passage of Mosaic law from the Old Testament. This was an assertion of the continuity of English history within the greater scheme of Christian history, with the clear implication that the English were destined to be the new chosen people of God – a theme at the heart of Bede's historical writings also.

In the extract given here from one of several lawcodes issued in the name of King Æthelred, more than a hundred years later, the central involvement of the church in the promulgation and operation of law is now clear. Enshrined in the laws themselves is the symbiotic relationship between monarchy and church, which had been deliberately nurtured by the monastic reformers of the second half of the tenth century and which would last in England until the Reformation (and, symbolically at least, into more modern times). There was benefit to both monarchy and church but above all to the latter, which gained vital political and financial support. The function of the king as *vicarius Dei*, 'vicar (i.e. deputy) of God', is explicitly spelled out in 'Æthelred VIII' (see lines 12–13). It will be noted from these texts that slavery existed in Anglo-Saxon England. The slaves came from Celtic areas of Britain, from overseas, or even from rival Anglo-Saxon kingdoms. Relatively benign laws gave them certain rights, though at least until Alfred's time an owner was allowed to kill a slave.

The prose used in the lawcodes, especially the earlier ones, is concise and un-adorned and reflects their oral and formulaic origins in Germanic law-making; they were memoranda of established custom, couched in familiar and easily re-membered form. Often, indeed, the language may seem economic to the point of obscurity for those unused to the specialised phrasing and the context.

Further reading

P. Sawyer, ed., *Textus Roffensis: Rochester Cathedral Library Manuscript A. 3. 5. Part 1*, EEMF 7 (Copenhagen, 1957) [includes a facsimile of Æthelberht's laws]

R. Flower and H. Smith, *The Parker Chronicle and Laws (Corpus Christi College, Cambridge, MS. 173)*, EETS 208 (London, 1941) [facsimile of Alfred's laws]

F. Liebermann, ed., *Die Gesetze der Angelsachsen*, 3 vols. (Halle, 1903–16) [still the stan-dard edition]

F. L. Attenborough, trans., *The Laws of the Earliest English Kings* (Cambridge, 1922)

H. G. Richardson and G. O. Sayles, *Law and Legislation from Æthelberht to Magna Carta* (Edinburgh, 1966)

P. Wormald, 'Æthelred the Lawmaker', in *Ethelred the Unready: Papers for the Millenary Conference*, ed. D. Hill (Oxford, 1978), pp. 47–80

M. P. Richards and B. J. Stanfield, 'Concepts of Anglo-Saxon Women in the Laws', in *New Readings on Women in Old English Literature*, ed. H. Damico and A. H. Olsen (Bloomington, IN, 1990), pp. 89–99

M. P. Richards, 'Anglo-Saxonism in the Old English Laws', in *Anglo-Saxonism and the*

Construction of Social Identity, ed. A. J. Frantzen and J. D. Niles (Gainesville, FL, 1997), pp. 40–59

P. Wormald, *The Making of English Law: King Alfred to the Twelfth Century*, 2 vols. (Oxford, 1999)

C. Hough, 'Legal and Documentary Writings', in *A Companion to Anglo-Saxon Literature*, ed. P. Pulsiano and E. Treharne (Oxford, 2001), pp. 170–87

C. Hough, 'Two Kentish Laws Concerning Women: a New Reading of Æthelberht 73 and 74', *Anglia* 119 (2001), 554–78

7a
Laws of Æthelberht of Kent (*c.* 614)

The first part of a manuscript known as the *Textus Roffensis* ('Rochester Book'), copied at Rochester, Kent, in the early twelfth century (now Rochester, Cathedral Library, A. 3. 5, fols. 1–118), is a collection of legal texts relating to Anglo-Saxon and later medieval England. The first item (fols. 1–3) is the lawcode of King Æthelberht of Kent, the start of whose reign has not yet been dated more accurately than between 560 and 585 but who died in 616; dates of *c.* 600 (or earlier) to *c.* 615 have been assigned to the laws, all of them tentatively. There is no reason to think that our version of Æthelberht's code has not survived essentially in its original form, but linguistically it shows evidence of its much later copying, with predominantly WS forms, though the spelling of the third-person singular present tense of the verb *slēan* 'strike' in the compound verbs *ofslēan, ofāslēan* and *forslēan* betrays the influence of earlier forms. In lines 11, 12 and 20, the variations *ofslēahþ, ofslēhð and ofslǣhþ* occur; the latter is not a WS form, and could indeed be Kentish, and is the form used consistently in the injury tariff (33–8). Subjunctive *sīo* (18) for *sīe* could also be a Kentish relic. The forms *heom* (5, for *him*) and *drincæþ* (7, for *drinceþ*) are early (or non-) WS. The text is written continuously (though with a bold capital to start the first word of each new law), but there are five notional sections, covering (1) the extension of legal rights to the property of the new church and its bishops and clergy; (2) offences against the king, noblemen and free men (in that order); (3) miscellaneous criminal offences; (4) compensations for personal injury; and (5) offences against women, servants and slaves. Sections 1, 2, and parts of 4 and 5 are given here; according to the consecutive numbering system used by modern editors, they are laws 1–16, 50–54 and 73–85. The personal injury tariff is characteristic of early Germanic law-making and reached Alfred's lawcode in a very similar form.

Ðās° syndon° þā dōmas° þe° Æðelbirht cyning āsette° ⌐on Agustinus dæge⌐.

Godes feoh° ond ciricean° ⌐XII.gylde⌐. Biscopes feoh XI.gylde°. Prēostes feoh IX.gylde°. ⌐Dīacones feoh VI.gylde°. Cleroces⌐ feoh III.gylde°. ⌐Ciricfriþ⌐ II.gylde°. Mæthlfriþ° II.gylde.

5   Gif cyning his lēode° tō him gehāteþ° ond heom° mon° þær yfel° ⌐gedō⌐, ⌐II.bōte⌐ ond cyninge° ⌐L scillinga⌐.

Gif cyning æt mannes hām° drincæþ° ond ðær man ⌐lyswæs hwæt⌐ gedō, twibōte ⌐gebēte⌐.

Gif ⌐frīgman⌐ cyninge stele°, IX.gylde forgylde°.

---

1 These are decrees which set down   **2** property the church's elevenfold [*endlyfengylde*]   **3** ninefold [*nigongylde*]   sixfold [*sixgylde*]   threefold [*þrigylde*] **4** twofold [*twigylde*]   Peace at a meeting   **5** people   summons   to them   someone   injury **6** to the king   **7** dwelling   is drinking [*drinceþ*]   **9** steals *sbj* (from +*d*)   let   him repay *sbj*

---

1 **on Agustinus dæge** 'in Augustine's day'; the nom. form of the name in Latin approximates to a gen. form in OE.

2 **XII.gylde** [*twelfgylde*] 'twelvefold'. In the elliptic style of the laws, this is shorthand for 'is to be paid for with a twelvefold compensation'. Thus, if you steal God's or the church's property, your punishment is to pay a sum twelve times the value of that property. Free-standing numbers are invariably given in Roman numerals in the laws; often, as here, numbers forming the first element of adverbs or adjectives are also given thus.

3 **Dīacones . . . Cleroces** In the church hierarchy, *diacones* ('deacons') came after bishops and priests in the so-called 'major orders'; the *cleroces* ('clerks') referred to here are probably clergy of the 'minor orders', who would include officials such as cantors, sub-deacons and vergers.   **Ciricfriþ** 'the church-peace'; here shorthand for '*breaking* the peace in church'. The next law is similarly abbreviated.

5 **gedō** 'does' or 'should do'. The sbj. mood is commonly used for vbs. in the laws (see also 8n), but the indic. is used too: thus *ofslē(a)hþ* in 11 and 12 (but sbj. *ofslēa* in 10), *stelþ* in 15 and *geligeþ* in 17. We may still use sbj. forms in ModE ('if anyone do harm', 'if the king drink'), though the indic. is preferred ('if anyone does harm', 'if the king drinks').

6 **II.bōte** [*twibōte*] '(let him be) subject to double compensation'.   **L scillinga** 'fifty shillings'. In the manuscript, the abbreviation *scill* is most often used; as numbers above two are commonly followed by the partitive gen. in OE [§E3d], that is the expansion which has been made silently throughout, as here. However, where the word is written in full by the scribe, other forms are sometimes used; thus nom. pl. in 22 and dat pl. in 23 (see note). The shilling was a gold coin.

7 **lyswæs hwæt** 'something of evil' (partitive gen.) or 'an evil deed'. The phr. probably refers to acts of violence committed while the king is being entertained on someone's estate, thus complementing the previous law about violence when the king invites people to him.

8 **gebēte** sbj. vb. with optative meaning: 'let him [the criminal] make good', i.e. 'he [the victim] is to compensated'.

9 **frīgman** 'a free [i.e. freeborn] man'; not a slave, probably a smallholder. A person of either gender may be meant; but in 11, the expression using *manna* (see next note) might refer specifically to a male. See also 40, where a free woman is explicitly designated.

10   Gif in cyninges tūne° ⌐man mannan⌐ ofslēa°, L scillinga gebēte.

Gif man frīgne° mannan ofslēahþ, cyninge L scillinga tō° ⌐drihtinbēage⌐.

Gif cyninges ⌐ambihtsmið⌐ oþþe° ⌐laadrincmannan⌐ ofslēhð, ⌐meduman lēodgelde forgelde⌐.

⌐Cyninges mundbyrd⌐: L scillinga.

15   Gif frīgman ⌐frēum⌐ stelþ, III° gebēte, ond cyning āge° þæt wīte° ond ealle þā æhtan°.

Gif man wið cyninges mægdenman° geligeþ°, L scillinga gebēte. Gif hīo° ⌐grindende þēowa⌐ sīo°, XXV scillinga gebēte. ⌐Sīo þridde⌐, XII scillingas.

Cyninges ⌐fēdesl⌐, XX scillinga forgelde.

20   Gif on eorles° tūne man mannan ofslæhþ, XII scillinga gebēte. Gif wið eorles birele° man geligeþ, XII scillinga gebēte.

---

10 manor kills *sbj* **11** free as **12** or **15** three(fold) (is to) have fine **16** possessions **17** a maiden lies she **18** is *sbj* **20** nobleman's **21** serving-woman

10 man mannan *man* is the impers. pron. 'one' or 'someone'; *mannan* is acc. sg. of the *n*-noun *manna*, 'man' [§B5a].

11 **drihtinbēage** lit. 'lord-ring'. This seems to be an ancient term for the fine to be paid to one's lord for killing a freeman, dating from a time when the fine might be paid with rings rather than in coin.

12 **ambihtsmið** Perhaps 'official smith'; i.e. metalworker. **laadrincmannan** The word occurs uniquely here; lit. 'escort-man', probably a 'herald' or 'messenger'. Both occupations specified in this law seem to have a relatively high status.

12–13 **meduman lēodgelde forgelde** 'pay with the ordinary [*meduman*, "middling"] wergeld'. On 'wergeld' (for which *lēodgeld* is a synonym), see main headnote. The point of this law appears to be that servants of the king, though not themselves free, have sufficient status to be entitled to the compensation normally due to freemen. *Forgieldan* takes a dat. obj.: you pay back 'with' or 'by means of' something; *forgelde* is a variant form of *forgylde* in 9.

14 **Cyninges mundbyrd** '(breach of) the king's protection', which includes offences of disrespect to the king and crimes against anyone under his protection.

15 **frēum** adj. as noun, dat. sg.: 'from a free (man)'.

18 **grindende þēowa** 'grinding slave'; presumably one who grinds the corn to make the king's bread. **Sīo þridde** '(if she) is (of) the third (class)'. Thus there appears to be a hierarchy of female slaves serving the king – first maidservant (17), then grinding slave, then others. The pattern is echoed in connection with the female servants of a *ceorl*: see 22–4.

19 **fēdesl** The noun is related to the vb. *fēdan* ('feed') and has traditionally been interpreted as 'boarder'. However, it has also been suggested that, when coupled with *cyning*, *fēdesl* may instead refer to a class of nobleman above that of *eorl*. The context would thus be a series of laws referring to offences against persons under the protection of king and arranged hierarchically: *fēdesl*, then (see below) *eorl* followed by *ceorl*.

⌜Ceorles mundbyrd⌝: VI scillingas. Gif wið ceorles ⌜birelan⌝ man geligeþ, ⌜VI scillingum⌝ gebēte. ⌜Æt þǣre ōþere ðēowan L scætta⌝. Æt þāre þriddan XXX scætta.

25   Sē° þe° cinbān° forslǣhð°, mid XX scillingum forgelde.

Æt° þām fēower° tōðum° fyrestum°, æt gehwylcum° VI scillingas. Se tōþ se° þanne° bīstandeþ°, IIII scillinga. Sē þe ðonne bi° ðām° standeþ, III scillinga. Ond þonne siþþan° gehwylc, scilling.

Gif sprǣc° āwyrd° ⌜weorþ⌝, XII scillingas.

30   Gif widobāne° gebroced° weorðeþ, VI scillinga gebēte.

Sē þe earm° þurhstinð°, VI scillingum gebēte. Gif earm forbrocen° weorð, VI scillinga gebēte.

Gif þuman° ⌜ofāslǣhð⌝, XX scillinga. Gif ⌜ðuman nægl⌝ of weorðeþ, III scillinga gebēte.

35   Gif man scytefinger° ofāslǣhð, VIIII scillinga gebēte.

Gif man middelfinger ofāslǣhð IIII scillinga gebēte.

Gif man goldfinger° ofāslǣhð, VI scillinga gebēte.

Gif man þone lȳtlan finger ofāslǣhð, XI scillinga gebēte . . .

---

25 He who jaw-bone breaks **26** For four teeth 'foremost' (*i.e.* front) each which **27** then [*þonne*] stands next next to +*d* that **28** after that **29** (power of) speech impaired **30** collar-bone broken **31** arm *as* punctures broken **33** thumb **35** shooting finger (*i.e.* forefinger) **37** gold finger (*i.e.* ring finger)

22 **Ceorles mundbyrd** A *ceorl*, perhaps 'commoner' (or 'yeoman'), is one of the mass of free men who own a small amount of land in their own right but are very low in the social hierarchy. On *ceorl* as 'man' or 'husband', see 34/10n; on the later derogatory sense of the term ('churl'), see 8/71–2n. **birelan** *birele* is here being treated as an *n*-noun [§B5c], even though in 21 it was 'strong' [§B3c]; the form is dat. sg. in both cases.

23 **VI scillingum** Here the numeral is treated as an adj. with dat. pl. noun: 'with six shillings'. **Æt þǣre ōþere ðēowan** 'with a slave-woman of the second (class)'; see 18n. **L scætta** A *sceat* was a small gold coin equal in weight to a grain of barley, and there were twenty to a shilling in Kent. It was later replaced by the penny.

29 **weorþ** 'becomes' or 'is'. This is the 'syncopated' form of the vb.; the full form, *weorðeþ*, is used in 30 and 33.

33 **ofāslǣhð** '(he) cuts off', with subj. understood as 'he who' in 31. **ðuman nægl** Here *ðuman*, an *n*-noun, is gen. sg.: lit. 'a thumb's nail'.

Gif ⌐frīwīf locbore lēswæs hwæt⌐ gedēþ°, XXX scillinga gebēte.

40   ⌐Mægþbōt sȳ swā frīges mannes⌐.

⌐Mund þāre betstan widuwan eorlcundre⌐ L scillinga gebēte. ⌐Ðāre ōþre⌐ XX scillinga, ðāre þriddan XII scillinga, þāre fēorðan VI scillinga.

Gif man widuwan ⌐unāgne⌐ genimeþ°, II.gelde° sēo mund sȳ.

Gif mon mǣgþ° gebigeð°, ⌐cēapi gecēapod sȳ⌐ gif hit unfācne° is. Gif hit

45   þonne° fācne° is, eft° þǣr ⌐æt hām gebrenge⌐ ond ⌐him⌐ man his scæt° āgefe°.

Gif hīo cwic° bearn° gebyreþ°, ⌐healfne scæt āge⌐ gif ceorl° ǣr° swylteþ°.

---

39 commits *sbj*   **43** carries off   twofold   **44** virgin   buys   without deceit   **45** however deceitful   back   money   (may) return   **46** live   child   gives birth to   husband   first   dies

---

39 **frīwīf** 'a free(born) woman'; see 9n.   **locbore** The word occurs uniquely here. The traditional interpretation has been as a noun (or adj.) meaning '(One) wearing long hair' (taking *loc(c)* to be 'lock of hair'), with the assumption (for which there is in fact no supporting evidence) that wearing the hair long was the symbol either of a freeborn woman or of a virgin in Anglo-Saxon England. A more likely interpretation is '(one) carrying responsibility for the locks' (*loc*, 'lock' or 'bolt'), and thus a woman of responsibility in general. A recent interpretation has a similar result but is based on *loc* in a further sense, 'a close' or 'settlement', taking the compound to describe an adult woman (presumably married) competent to enter into a legal contract, and therefore 'in a position of responsibility'. **lēswæs hwæt** As in 7, this phr., 'something of evil', probably refers to 'violence', rather than (as in the traditional interpretation of the present context) some sexual misdemeanour.

40 **Mægþbōt sȳ swā frīges mannes** 'Perhaps, 'Let the remedy due from a maiden (*or* unmarried woman) be as (that) of a freeborn woman' – i.e. as defined in the previous law. This is a recent reinterpretation. Traditionally, *mægþbōt* has been assumed to mean the remedy due *to* an injured *mægþ*, but the law then seems to be out of place here, belonging better with the earlier injury tariff, and it is hard to identify which 'freeborn person' is being referred to. But taking *frīges mannes* simply to refer back to the 'freeborn woman' of the previous law (and *mann* can refer to male or female) makes good sense; this law is then complementary, defining a second type of female miscreant.

41 **Mund þāre betstan widuwan eorlcundre** '(Breach of) the protection of (*or* due to) a widow of the best class [lit. "the best widow"], a noble (woman)'. *þāre* (here and in its next three occurrences), along with the three words complementing it, is probably gen., but could be interpreted as dat. **Ðāre ōþre** 'Of the second (class)'. Again, a graded system of penalties matches the social hierarchy. The precise details of this are unclear but the similar range of penalties listed earlier in the code for sexual misdemeanours (see 17–24) may be compared.

43 **unāgne** 'not (his) own'; i.e. not his by right of ownership or familial relation.

44 **cēapi gecēapod sȳ** The *-i* on *cēapi* may be an archaic instr. inflection [§D5], or a dat., and the phr. seems to be impers.; perhaps 'let (it) be bought at the price (bargained for)'. The meaning thus seems to be, 'let the bargain stand'. Interpretations of the phr. with *cēap* in the sense of 'cattle' are less convincing.

45 **æt hām gebrenge** 'let (her) be brought back to (her) home'. **him** 'to him'; i.e. to the man who tried to buy the widow.

46 **healfne scæt āge** 'let (her) have half the property', i.e. the property left by her dead husband.

Gif mid bearnum būgan° wille°, healfne scæt āge.

Gif ceorl āgan° wile, ⌐swā ān bearn⌐.

Gif hīo bearn ne gebyreþ, fæderingmāgas° fīoh āgan° ond ⌐morgengyfe⌐.

50   Gif man mǣgþmon° nēde° genimeþ, ðām āgende° L scillinga, ond eft æt° þām āgende ⌐sīnne willan ætgebicge⌐.

Gif hīo ōþrum mæn° ⌐in sceat⌐ bewyddod° sȳ, XX scillinga gebēte.

Gif ⌐gǣngang geweorðeþ⌐, XXXV scillinga ond cyninge XV scillingas.

Gif man mid esnes° cwynan° geligeþ, ⌐be cwicum ceorle⌐, II gebēte ...

47 depart (she) wishes *sbj*   **48** to have (the child)   **49** paternal kin   may have *sbj* [*āgen*]
50 unmarried woman   by force   owner   from   **52** man *ds* [*men*]   betrothed (to +*d*)   **54** of
a servant   wife *ds*

48 **swā ān bearn** lit. 'as for one child', i.e. he is to have a share of the property equal to one child's.

49 **morgengyfe** 'morning-gift'. This was a gift to the woman from her husband on the morning after their wedding. She was entitled to keep it, unless she married again within a year of her husband's death.

51 **sīnne willan ætgebicge** 'let him buy his [the owner's] consent'. On *sīnne*, see §A4i.

52 **in sceat** 'for a sum of money'.

53 **gǣngang geweorðeþ** *gǣngang* occurs uniquely here. A plausible interpretation is to read a noun *gēan-gang*, 'again-going' or 'returning', so that the phr. might mean lit. 'becomes returning', i.e. 'returns', or perhaps 'is returned'.

54 **be cwicum ceorle** 'with the husband living', i.e. while the servant is alive.

7b
Laws of Alfred of Wessex (*c.* 890)

In prefatory remarks to his laws (lines 1–11, below), Alfred (871–99) stresses that they are based on precedent, and among those whom he acknowledges as predecessors are Æthelberht of Kent, Offa of Mercia (757–96) and an earlier king of Wessex, Ine (688–726), whose laws Alfred thought important enough to append to his own in full. Offa may not in fact have issued his own code, but Alfred by now presided over a kingdom which effectively included Mercia, so he had good political reason to mention Offa. As noted above, Alfred makes an explicit association between social order and loyalty to the monarch, which is to take precedence even over ties of kinship (see lines 40–7). The manuscript from which the extracts below are taken, Cambridge, Corpus Christi College 173, was copied in the mid-tenth century, and many early WS forms are evident. Most obvious are words with *io* for later *eo*, such as *trīowan* (22), *fiorh* (24, but cf. *feorh*, 20) and *getrīowe* (25), and the pronouns *hīo* (28, 29) and *hiora* (31). Other early forms include *monege* (1), *ǣghwelc* (12), *hwelcere* (34) and *genēde* (39, but cf. *genīed*, 13). The text in the Corpus manuscript is divided into one hundred and twenty sections, identified by Roman numerals; sections I–XLIV contain Alfred's laws, the rest those of Ine. This numbering is retained here, though modern translators and commentators impose a more complex, analytical, system of division.

I ... ⌈Ic ðā⌉ Ælfred cyning ⌈þās⌉ tōgædere gegaderode° ond ⌈āwrītan hēt monege þāra þe⌉ ūre° foregengan° heoldon°, ⌈ðā ðe mē līcodon⌉; ond manege þāra þe mē ne līcodon ic āwearp° mid° mīnra witena° geðeahte° ond ⌈on ōðre wīsan bebēad tō healdanne⌉. ⌈Forðām⌉ ic ne dorste° geðrīstlæcan° ⌈þāra mīnra āwuht
5 fela⌉ on° gewrit° settan°, forðām mē wæs uncūð° ⌈hwæt þæs ðām līcian wolde ðe æfter ūs wæren⌉. Ac ðā ðe ic gemētte° ⌈āwðer oððe on Ines dæge, mīnes mæges, oððe⌉ on Offan Mercna° cyninges oððe on Æþelbryhtes°, þe ⌈ærest° fulluhte° onfēng° on° Angelcynne°⌉, ⌈þā ðe⌉ mē° ryhtoste° ðūhton° ic þā hēron° gegaderode ond þā ōðre forlēt°. Ic ðā Ælfred Westseaxna cyning eallum mīnnum

1 gathered **2** our predecessors observed **3** rejected with councillors' advice
4 dared to presume **5** into writing put unknown **6** found **7** of the Mercians
Æthelberht's first **8** baptism received among the English to me most just seemed
herein **9** omitted

1 **Ic ðā** i.e. *Ðā ic* ... **þās** 'these', referring to the laws (*dōmas*) of his royal predecessors which Alfred has been discussing earlier in this preamble.

1–2 **āwrītan hēt** 'commanded (someone) to write down', or, better, 'commanded to be written down'. **monege þāra þe** 'many of those which ...'.

2 **ðā ðe mē līcodon** 'those which I liked'; impers. vb. with dat. obj. [§G5], as also in 5 and 10.

3–4 **on ōðre wīsan bebēad tō healdanne** 'ordered to be held [lit. 'to hold', infl. inf.] in another way'. Such laws were presumably modified. **Forðām** The adv. is correl. with conj. *forðām* in 5: 'For this reason ..., (namely) because ...', but it is better om. in trans.

4–5 **þāra mīnra āwuht fela** The adv. *āwuht* invades the gen. clause: 'by any means many of my own (laws)'. Alfred explains that, as far as possible, he has chosen to use existing laws rather than to introduce new ones of his own.

5–6 **hwæt þæs ðām līcian wolde** *þæs* is here best treated as an adv.: 'regarding this' or 'in this respect'; for *līcian*, see 2n: 'what in this respect would please those (*ðām*) ...' **ðe æfter ūs wæren** 'who would be [sbj.] after us', i.e. 'come after us'.

6–7 **āwðer oððe ... oððe** 'either in Ine my kinsman's day, or ...' (with the first *oððe* redundant in trans). In the next two clauses, *dæge* is understood after *cyninges* and *Æþelbryhtes*.

7–8 **ærest ... on Angelcynne** Bede reports that Æthelberht of Kent was the first English king to die a Christian, in 616. Although his Frankish queen, a Christian, had established a chapel on royal land even before Augustine's arrival, it is not clear exactly when he was converted. **þā ðe** 'those that'; correl. with the same phr. in 6 and best not trans.

10   witum þā° geēowde° ond hīe ðā cwǣdon þæt ⌜him þæt līcode eallum⌝ tō
      healdanne°.

      II Æt ǣrestan° wē lǣrað° þæt° mǣst° ðearf° is, þæt ǣghwelc° mon his āð°
      ond his wed° wǣrlīce° healde. Gif hwā° ⌜tō hwæðrum þissa⌝ genīed° sīe° ⌜on
      wōh⌝, oððe tō hlāfordsearwe° oððe tō ǣngum unryhtum° fultume°, ⌜þæt is þonne
15   ryhtre tō ālēoganne⌝ þonne° tō gelǣstanne°. ⌜Gif hē þonne ðæs weddie þe hym°
      riht sȳ° tō gelǣstanne⌝, ond þæt ālēoge°, selle° mid ēaðmēdum° his wǣpn ond
      his ǣhta° his frēondum tō gehealdanne° ond bēo° fēowertig nihta on carcerne°
      on cyninges tūne°; ðrowige° ðǣr ⌜swā biscep him scrīfe⌝ ond his mǣgas° hine
      fēden° gif hē self mete° næbbe°.

20   V Gif hwā ymb° cyninges feorh° sierwe°, ⌜ðurh hine⌝ oððe ðurh wreccena°
      feormunge° oððe ⌜his manna⌝, sīe hē ⌜his fēores scyldig⌝ ond ealles þæs ðe hē
      āge°. Gif hē hine selfne trīowan° wille, ⌜dō þæt be cyninges wergelde⌝. Swā° wē

10 those *ap* showed (to +*d*)   **11** observe (them)   **12** first direct what (the) greatest
need each oath   **13** pledge carefully anyone compelled is   **14** treachery against (his)
lord illegal aid   **15** than perform for him   **16** is leaves unfulfilled let him give
humility *dp*   **17** possessions keep be prison   **18** estate let him endure kinsmen
19 feed food does not have [*ne hæbbe*]   **20** against life plots of exiles   **21** harbouring
22 owns clear Thus

10 **him . . . eallum** 'them all'.

13–14 **tō hwæðrum þissa** 'to either of these'; i.e. to either of the two eventualities
following (*oððe . . . oððe . . .*, 'either . . . or . . .'). **on wōh** 'in error', i.e. 'wrongfully'.

14–15 **þæt is þonne ryhtre tō ālēoganne** 'that [i.e. the promise of treachery or of illegal
aid] is then more proper (*ryhtre*) to be left unfulfilled [lit. "denied"]'. Thus the requirement
of the previous law, about keeping an oath, is removed if it has been forced out of someone
and if its fulfilment would involve a greater crime.

15–16 **Gif hē . . . gelǣstanne** This clause, missing from the manuscript, has been supplied from the *Textus Roffensis* (see headnote). **ðæs weddie þe** 'pledges that (*ðæs*) which';
the vb. takes a gen. obj.

18 **swā biscep him scrīfe** 'as the bishop prescribes for him'; i.e. he is to endure whatever
penance the bishop decides.

20 **ðurh hine** 'by himself'; i.e. directly.

21 **his manna** The reference is presumably to any of the king's people who may be
disloyal to him. **his fēores scyldig** gen. of respect: 'liable for his life'; i.e. liable to forfeit
his life.

22 **dō þæt be cyninges wergelde** 'let him do it by (an oath equivalent to) the
king's wergeld'; i.e. he must make a pledge to pay this sum. Wergeld (see main headnote) was compensation for a death; the killer and his kin, and in some cases his companions, are responsible collectively for payment. As with all compensation, the actual amount varied according to the rank and status of the victim. A king's wergeld
in late ninth-century Wessex has been estimated to be at least 30,000 pence or 6,000
shillings.

ēac settað° be° eallum hādum°, ⌜ge ceorle ge eorle⌝: sē° ðe ymb his hlāfordes
fiorh sierwe, sīe hē wið° ðone° his fēores scyldig ond ealles ðæs ðe hē āge, oððe
25 ⌜be his hlāfordes were⌝ hine getrīowe°.

VIIII Gif hwā nunnan° of° mynstere° ūt ālæde° būtan° kyninges lēfnesse°
oððe biscepes, geselle hundtwelftig° scillinga, healf cyninge, healf biscepe ond
þǣre cirican° hlāforde ⌜ðe ðone munuc āge⌝. Gif hīo leng° libbe° ðonne sē ðe
hīe° ūtlǣdde, ⌜nāge° hīo his ierfes° ōwiht°. Gif hīo bearn gestrīene°, næbbe⌝
30 ðæt° ðæs ierfes ⌜ðon māre ðe⌝ sēo mōdor. Gif hire bearn mon° ofslēa°, ⌜gielde°
cyninge þāra mēdrenmǣga dǣl; fædrenmǣgum° hiora° dǣl mon āgife⌝.

XXI Gif hund° mon° tōslīte° oððe ābīte°, æt forman° misdǣde° ⌜geselle⌝ VI
scillinga, gif hē him mete° selle, æt æfteran° cerre° XII scillinga, æt ðriddan°
XXX scillinga. Gif æt ðissa misdǣda hwelcere° se hund ⌜losige⌝, ⌜gā ðēos bōt
35 hwæðre forð⌝. Gif se hund mā° misdǣda gewyrce° ond ⌜hē⌝ hine hæbbe°, bēte°
be° fullan were ⌜swā dolgbōte swā hē wyrce⌝.

23 set out (*or* determine) concerning ranks he **24** 'against' (*i.e.* on account of) that
25 clear **26** a nun from nunnery brings without permission **27** one hundred and
twenty **28** church *gs* longer lives **29** her is not to have [*ne āge*] inheritance *gs*
anything bears **30** it (the child) someone *ns* kills give (to +*d*) **31** (to) the father's kin
their **32** dog someone *as* tears apart bites first offence **33** food second occasion
third **34** any (of +*gp*) **35** more commits retains (let him) compensate **36** with

23 ge ceorle ge eorle 'both commoner and nobleman'. This rhyming formula, epit-
omising the social polarities of Alfred's England, reminds us of the mnemonic character of Germanic law. The use of *eorl* for 'nobleman' was already becoming obsolete in
Alfred's time, being replaced by *þegn* (see 8/12n and 33/16n); what is meant is a substantial
landowner. On *ceorl*, see 7a/22n.
25 be his hlāfordes were 'at his lord's wergeld' (*wer*, 'man', short for *wergild*); i.e. he
may exculpate himself by taking an oath on a sum equivalent to his lord's 'man-price'.
28 ðe ðone munuc āge 'which possesses the nun'. The antec. of *ðe* is *cirican*; *munuc*
was used to refer to both male and female religious. The second half of the fine is to be
divided between the bishop and the patron of the church.
29 nāge . . . næbbe . . . These harsh laws, designed to discourage the marriage of nuns,
deny legal status to both the nun and her child.
30 ðon māre ðe instr. phr.: 'the more than', i.e. 'any more than'.
30–1 gielde . . . āgife The nun's kin, too, are prohibited from gaining, though not the
kin of her 'husband', the child's father.   **þāra mēdrenmǣga dǣl** 'the portion of [i.e. due
to] the mother's kin'.
32 geselle 'let (the owner) pay'. Presumably ownership is confirmed by the action of
giving the dog food (see 33).
34 losige 'be lost', probably in the sense of 'perish' or 'be destroyed', but perhaps
simply 'escape'.
34–5 gā ðēos bōt hwæðre forð 'let this compensation nevertheless go forward [i.e.
continue]'; it is still to be paid.   **hē** i.e. the dog's owner.
36 swā dolgbōte swā hē wyrce 'such wound-compensation as it (*hē*) inflicts', i.e.
'compensation for such wounds as it inflicts'.

XXIII Gif mon ceorles mennen° ⌐tō nēdhǣmde geðrēataðᒣ, mid V scillingum gebēte þām ceorle ond LX scillinga tō wīte°. Gif ðēowmon° þēowne° tō nēdhǣmde genēde°, ⌐bēte mid his ēowendeᒣ.

40   **XXXVIII** ...Ēac° wē cweðað þæt mon mōte mid° his hlāforde feohtan ⌐orwīgeᒣ, gif mon on° ðone hlāford fiohte; swā° mōt° se hlāford ⌐mid þȳ menᒣ feohtan. Æfter þǣre ilcan wīsan° mon mōt feohtan mid his geborene° mǣge, gif hine mon on wōh onfeohteð°, ⌐būton wið his hlāfordeᒣ: þæt wē ne līefað°. Ond mon mōt feohtan orwīge, gif hē gemēteð ōþerne° æt° his ǣwum° wīfe
45   ⌐betȳnedum durumᒣ oððe under ānre° rēon°, oððe æt his dehter° ⌐ǣwum borenreᒣ oððe æt his swistær ǣwum borenre oððe æt his mēdder° ðe wǣre tō ǣwum wīfe forgifen° his fǣder.

    XXXVIIII Eallum frīoum monnum ⌐ðās dagasᒣ sīen° forgifene, būtan þēowum° monnum ond ⌐esnewyrhtanᒣ: XII dagas on ⌐Gēhholᒣ ond ⌐ðone dægᒣ
50   þe° Crīst ðone dēofol oferswīðde°ᒣ ond ⌐Sanctus Gregorius gemynddægᒣ ond

---

37 slave-woman **38** penalty   male slave   woman slave *as*   **39** forces   **40** Further on behalf of   **41** against   likewise   may   **42** way   born   **43** attacks   allow   **44** another (man)   with   lawful   **45** one   blanket   daughter *ds*   **46** mother *ds*   **47** given **48** are to be *sbj*   **49** enslaved   **50** (on) which   overcame

---

37 **tō nēdhǣmde geðrēatað** 'forces to rape', i.e. 'rapes'.

39 **bēte mid his ēowende** 'he is to pay compensation with his genitals'; i.e. he is to be castrated.

41 **orwīge** 'without battle'; i.e. without the process of revenge, which is regulated by its own complex laws. Homicide committed in support of a lord does not attract the usual legal consequences.   **mid þȳ men** 'on behalf of the [i.e. his] man'. Unusually, *mid* is here followed by the instr.; *men* is both dat. and instr. sg. of *mann*.

43 **būton wið his hlāforde** On the theme that loyalty to one's lord transcends kinship obligations, see Text 29.

45 **betȳnedum durum** dat. of place: 'within closed doors'.   **ǣwum borenre** 'legally born'; i.e. legitimate. The phr. is elided to just *borenre* in the next line.

48 **ðās dagas** In passive sentences, the obj. of a vb. becomes its subj. ('these days are to be given'), so *dagas* here may be assumed to be nom. However, in the list of days which follows, in those cases where acc. and nom. forms would be different, the writer has clearly used the acc. (*ðone dæg*, 49, *ðā fullan wican*, 52, *ānne dæg*, 53), except for nom. *ān dæg* in 51.

49 **esnewyrhtan** 'unfree labourers' (dat. pl.). The distinction between these and slaves just mentioned is not clear (and the word *esne* is itself used often to mean 'slave'), but it cannot have been great. Both categories of worker are presumably included in the 'slaves' who are allocated four days off per year in the next law.   **Gēhhol** Our archaic word for Christmas, 'Yule', derives from this OE word, which is more commonly spelled *gēol*. There is an Old Norse cognate, *jól*, but the word's origin is obscure.

49–50 **ðone dæg þe ... oferswīðde** 15 Feb., the day commemorating Christ's temptation in the wilderness (Mt 4.1–11).

VII dagas tō° Ēastron° ond VII ofer° ond ān dæg æt Sancte ⌜Pētres tīde° ond
Sancte Paules, ond on hærfeste° ðā fullan wican° ær Sancta Mārian mæssan°,
ond æt Eallra Hāligra⌝ weorðunge° ānne dæg. Ond IIII Wōdnesdagas° ⌜on IIII
Ymbrenwicum⌝ ðēowum monnum eallum sīen forgifen, ⌜þām þe him lēofost
55   sīe tō sellanne⌝ æghwæt° ðæs° ðe him ænig mon for° Godes noman geselle oððe
hīe on ænegum hiora hwīlsticcum° geearnian° mægen.

51 before Easter after feast-day   **52** harvest-time week mass(-day) (*i.e.* feast-day)
53 celebration (of +*g*) (the four) Wednesdays   **55** anything of what in   **56** spare
moments earn

50 **Sanctus Gregorius gemynddæg** 'the feast-day [lit. "remembrance day"] of Saint
Gregory'; celebrated on 12 Mar. Gregory the Great instigated St Augustine's mission to
convert the English in 597, and his feast was ranked high in Anglo-Saxon times. The Latin
nom. forms *sanctus* and *Gregorius* are used, though they function as gen.; in 51, *sancte*
is derived from the Latin gen. sg. masc. *sancti*, but in 52 *sancta* is the Latin fem. form.
Although *sanctus* was borrowed into OE as *sanct* (masc. or fem.), Latin forms, as here, are
usually retained before names. The names themselves in 51–3 are given OE inflections.
   51–3 **Pētres . . . Paules . . . Mārian . . . Eallra Hāligra** The feast of SS Peter and Paul
was on 29 Jun.; that of St Mary (the Virgin Mary) on either 15 Aug. (commemorating her
Assumption) or 8 Sept. (her Nativity); and that of All Saints on 1 Nov.
   53–4 **on IIII Ymbrenwicum** 'in the four Ember weeks'. Each of these weeks, three
months apart, had three 'Ember' days set aside for fasting and abstinence: they were the
Wednesdays, Fridays and Saturdays following the first Sunday in Lent, Whit Sunday, Holy
Cross Day (14 Sept.) and St Lucy's Day (13 Dec.). They were known as the 'fasts of the
four seasons' in the early church, and OE *ymbryne* (lit. 'around-course') means 'circuit' or
'period of time', and thus 'season'.
   54–5 **þām þe him lēofost sīe tō sellanne** 'in order to sell to whomever (*þām*) it be most
agreeable to them (*him*)'; i.e. to whomever they choose. *Sellan* (normally 'give') here has
its ModE meaning. This is a chance, it seems, for slaves to make some money from anything
they have acquired through charity or hard work.

7c
Laws of Æthelred of England (1014)

A number of lawcodes were drawn up during the long reign of Æthelred (978–
1016). The one whose opening articles are given below, known as 'Æthelred VIII',
was composed in 1014 and is one of several with a style unmistakably that of
Archbishop Wulfstan (see p. 204). The only manuscript in which it survives in full
(Cambridge, Corpus Christi College 201) is associated with him. It was copied in

the mid-eleventh century, and the language is late WS, with characteristic forms such as *gesille* (10; cf. earlier *geselle*) and *silfne* (11; cf. *selfne*), and *ðāre* (15, 21; cf. *ðǣre*) and *þārtō* (16; cf. *þērtō*). For the subjunctive verb 'be', both *sī* and *sȳ* (the later form) are used (19, 20, etc). Inconsistency in the forms of *cyning* will be noted; it occurs both with syncopation and without, with intrusive *c* and without (see 2, 12, 14, etc). Æthelred VIII is taken up entirely with matters of church and monastery and with the conduct of the clergy and monks. The opening decrees of the code are concerned with the church's jealously guarded rights of 'sanctuary', or asylum, whereby a criminal who had taken refuge in a church could not be removed but was allowed to take a special oath before a law officer. The latter would then specify a port from which the criminal could leave the country unhindered, as long as he did this within a specified period. It will be noted how in its hierarchy of buildings (from humble country church to great cathedral) and of officials (from lowly deacons to lordly bishops), the institutionalised church shadows closely the social hierarchy.

⌐*Anno MXIIII ab incarnatione Domini nostri Iesu Christi*⌐.

Þis is ān ðāra gerǣdnessa° þe Engla° cyningc gedihte° mid his witena° geþeahte°.

Þæt is ǣrest þæt hē wile° þæt ealle Godes circan bēon ⌐fulles grides wurðe⌐.

5   Ond gif ǣfre° ǣnig man heonan° forð ⌐Godes ciricgrið⌐ swā ābrece° þæt hē binnon° ciricwāgum° manslēaga° wurðe°, þonne sȳ° þæt bōtlēas° ond ⌐ēhte his⌐ ǣlc þāra þe Godes frēond sȳ, būton° þæt gewurðe° þæt hē þanon° ætberste° ond ⌐swā dēope friðsōcne⌐ gesēce° þæt se cyningc him þurh° þæt fēores° geunne° wið° fulre bōte° ge° wið° God ge° wið men.

2 decrees of the English composed counsellors'   **3** advice   **4** wills   **5** ever hence violates   **6** within church walls murderer becomes is *sbj* beyond compensation **7** unless happens from there escapes   **8** reaches on account of life grants +*g* **9** in return for compensation both to and

1 *Anno . . . Christi* Lat. 'In the 1014th year from the incarnation of our Lord Jesus Christ'.

4 **fulles griðes wurðe** 'entitled to full (right of) sanctuary'. The adj. *wurðe* governs the gen.; it is spelled *wirðe* in 22. On the ecclesiastical right of sanctuary, see headnote.

5 **Godes ciricgrið** 'God's church-sanctuary', i.e. 'the sanctuary of God's church'.

6 **ēhte his** 'let (each . . .) persecute (*or* pursue) him'; *ēhtan* (here in the sbj., with optative meaning) takes a gen. obj.

8 **swā dēope friðsōcne** 'such solemn sanctuary'. As later decrees in this code make clear (see 22–3), the status of individual churches (and thus the security of the sanctuary they offer) varies considerably.

10   Ond þæt is þonne ærest þæt hē his āgenne° wer° gesille° þām cyninge ond
       ⌈Chrīste⌉ ond ⌈mid þām hine silfne inlagige tō bōte⌉.
       Forðām° crīsten cyning is Crīstes gespelia° on° crīstenre þēode° ond hē sceal°
       Crīstes ābilgðe° wrecan° swīðe georne°.
       Ond gif hit þonne tō bōte gegā°, ond se cyngc þæt geþafige°, þonne ⌈bēte
15   man þæt ciricgrið intō ðāre circan be þæs cyninges fullan mundbryce⌉, ond þā
       ⌈mynsterclǣnsunge⌉ begite° swā þārtō° gebirige°, ond wið God hūru° ⌈þingian⌉
       georne.
       Ond gif ⌈be cwicum mannum⌉ ciricgrið ābrocen bēo, bētan man georne ⌈be
       þām þe sēo dǣd sȳ⌉, ⌈sȳ hit⌉ þurh feohtlāc°, sī hit þurh rēaflāc°, sī hit þurh
20   unriht° hǣmed°; ⌈sī þurh þæt þæt hit sȳ⌉, bēte man ǣfre° ǣrest þone griðbryce°
       intō ðāre circan be þām þe sēo dǣd sȳ ond be þām þe þāre circan mǣð° sȳ.
       Ne sȳn ealle cyrcan nā° ⌈gelīcre mǣðe worldlīce° wirðe⌉, þēah hī god-
       cundlīce° ⌈habban hālgunge gelīce⌉.
       Hēafodmynstres° griðbryce, ⌈æt bōtwurðan þingan⌉, bēte man ⌈be cyninges
25   munde⌉, þæt is mid V pundum on Engla lage°; ond medemran° mynstres mid

10 own wergeld give **12** Because deputy among people must **13** offences
(against +g) avenge zealously **14** comes permits **16** be obtained *sbj* for that is
appropriate indeed **19** fighting robbery **20** unlawful sexual intercourse always
breach of sanctuary **21** status **22** not in temporal matters **23** in divine matters
24 Chief minister *gs* **25** law 'more middling' (*i.e.* rather smaller)

11 **Chrīste** 'to Christ'; i.e. to the church. **mid þām...tō bōte** The vb. *inlagian* means
to reverse a legally imposed sentence (*lagian*, without the neg. prefix, 'ordain') and so the
sense is: 'free himself with that [i.e. payment of his wergeld] in compensation'. The wergeld
is only the first payment, and more will be required (see 14–17).
      14–15 **bēte man...mundbryce** 'let (the violation of) the sanctuary be compen-
sated for to the church by (the amount of) the full (fine for) breach of the king's
protection'.
      16 **mynsterclǣnsunge** 'purification of the church'; a further procedure required fol-
lowing the violation. **þingian** Instead of the usual sbj. vb. with optative meaning ('let
him...' or 'he is to...'), here (and in 18, *bētan*) the infin. is used, as though a modal vb.
is implied: *sceal þingian*, 'must supplicate'.
      18 **be cwicum mannum** 'with living people', i.e. 'without anyone being killed'.
      18–19 **be þām þe sēo dǣd sȳ** 'according to what the deed may be', i.e. 'in proportion
to the deed'. **sȳ hit** 'whether it be...'.
      20 **sī þurh þæt þæt hit sȳ** 'whatever it may be a result of' (lit. 'be it through that that
it may be').
      22 **gelīcre mǣðe...wirðe** 'entitled to the like [i.e. same] status'.
      23 **habban hālgunge gelīce** 'have [i.e. are subject to] the same consecration'.
      24 **æt bōtwurðan þingan** 'for [i.e. in the case of] matters [i.e. crimes] that can be
atoned for'; *þingan* is for *þingum*.
      24–5 **be cyninges munde** 'at (the rate of the breach of) the king's protection'; see main
headnote.

hundtwelftigan° scillingum, þæt is be° cyninges wīte°; ond þonne gīt° læssan°
mid sixtigan scillingum; ond ⌜æt feldcircan⌝ mid XXX scillingum.

Ā° sceal° mid° rihte dōm° æfter° dæde, ond medmung° be° mæþe.

26 one hundred and twenty according to penalty yet (a) smaller **28** Ever (it) must
(be) by judgement according to the amount (of a fine) according to

27 **æt feldcircan** 'in a field-church'; i.e. a country church (Lat. *campestris ecclesia*).

8

England under Attack
(from the *Anglo-Saxon Chronicle*:
annals for 981–93, 995–8 and 1002–3)

The collection of annals we now call the *Anglo-Saxon Chronicle* was first compiled systematically during the reign of King Alfred (871–99). There is no conclusive evidence of his personal involvement, but the ambitious scheme to present a chronological record of the history of the English kingdoms in the vernacular fits well with Alfred's programme of educational revival (see p. 2), promoted in the context of an increasing sense of English nationalism. The *Chronicle* in fact records, in its characteristically terse and formulaic way, events from the invasion of Britain by Julius Caesar in AD 43 up to the Alfredian period itself. Subsequently it was continued up to the Norman Conquest and beyond, stopping only in the year 1154, when King Stephen died.

The history of the *Chronicle* is complex. Seven main versions are preserved, each differing in some way from the others, often radically, though they can be divided into four distinct groups. A prototype was probably produced somewhere in Wessex around 891 by at least two compilers, presumably working in a monastic setting, where annalistic writing would have been practised. For the entries covering the previous 850 years, the compilers relied on Bede's *Historia ecclesiastica* (see p. 69), along with genealogies, classical sources and probably some pre-existing annals in Latin; thereafter, events were recorded soon after their occurrence. It seems that copies of the prototype *Chronicle* were distributed through the kingdom and that later bulletins were then sent out to be added to these. It was common, however, for additions of purely local significance to be made, such as the references to the abbots of Peterborough in the extracts below. The chronology of events as presented in the *Chronicle* is often suspect, and some obvious facts are missing, but it remains a fruitful source for historians.

Chronicle entries start characteristically with *hēr*, or sometimes the fuller *hēr on þissum gēare* ('here, in this year'), referring, originally at least, to the space already allotted in the annal for the particular year. The prose style of entries for the years up to 891 tends to be blunt, factual and formulaic, though this does not preclude some variety. Occasionally expansive narrative episodes are interpolated, such as that for the year 755, relating a struggle between Cynewulf and Cyneheard for the throne of Wessex (see Text 29). After 891, expansion is more frequent and there is a greater tendency to weave interpretation or political comment into the factual account, as in the entry for 1003, below. Verse narratives are sometimes included, too – such as that for 937, about an English victory against the Vikings (see Text 10).

The extracts below cover parts of the period 981–1003 and are taken from the so-called 'Peterborough Chronicle' (Oxford, Bodleian Library, Laud 636), which gives the fullest account of these years. Even though it is an important witness to OE, it was produced in the early Middle English period and provides valuable evidence for the transition from OE to Middle English. We may deduce that it was written at Peterborough, in eastern England, soon after 1121, for all the annals up to that year have been copied out by one main scribe, apparently from a Kentish source, and probably because the Peterborough monastery's previous copy of the *Chronicle* had been destroyed in a fire; thereafter entries were added in stages up to 1154. The annals given here report on the earlier part of the ultimately disastrous reign of Æthelred (978–1016), who is known now as 'the Unready'. This is in fact a misinterpretation of the OE epithet *unrǣd*, which means 'bad counsel' or 'without counsel', and is a pun on the king's name, *æþelrǣd*, 'noble counsel'. Æthelred came to the throne after the mysterious murder of the previous king, his half-brother Edward. In the early stages, his rule was probably not quite as bad as most accounts suggest, but subsequent events would colour perceptions of his whole reign. From 981 onwards (with an apparent respite only in 995–6), the Danes relentlessly attacked an England which was weakened internally by indecision, treachery and cowardice. Among the outside aggressors was the Danish king, Svein Forkbeard, who would seize the English throne in 1013, after Æthelred's flight to Normandy. Only Svein's death in the following year allowed Æthelred to return and reign until his death in 1016, when Svein's son Cnut (or Canute) overwhelmed the forces of Edmund, Æthelred's son, and initiated twenty-five years of Danish rule.

As we would expect in OE material copied in the early years of the twelfth century, the language shows many late forms, though they are not consistently used. Variant spellings to look out for are *muhton* for *mihton* (30), *þæne* for *þone* (24), *þet* for *þæt* (9 and 62), *wes* for *wæs* (11) and *dæi* for *dæg* (32). The preposition *būtan* (or *būton*) is used with following accusative, rather than the more usual dative (15 and 33). The use of the preposition *of* in the phrase *abbod of Burch* (37) anticipates its function in later English, indicating 'belonging to', rather than simply 'from'. The scribe of the Peterborough Chronicle uses abbreviation extensively, with an overhead bar (known as a 'suspension mark') signalling the fact. In the manuscript of the passages given below, *arcebiscop* is written *arcēb* or *arcb̄* and *biscop* simply *b̄*; *abbod* is invariably *ab̄b̄*; *e* is often suspended, as also is *m*, in words other than those ending in *um* (for which abbreviation to *ū* is very frequent in manuscripts of OE): thus *ponñ* for *þonne* and *cō* for *com*; and *Xr̄es* is written for *Christes*.

Below, all these abbreviations are silently expanded, with inflections supplied as appropriate.

Further reading

D. Whitelock, ed., *The Peterborough Chronicle (the Bodleian Manuscript Laud Misc. 636)*, EEMF 4 (Copenhagen, 1954)

J. Earle and C. Plummer, ed., *Two of the Saxon Chronicles Parallel with Supplementary Extracts from the Others*, 2 vols. (Oxford, 1892–9; repr. 1952)

J. Bately, *et al.*, eds., *The Anglo-Saxon Chronicle: a Collaborative Edition* (Cambridge, 1982–)

D. Whitelock, ed., *The Anglo-Saxon Chronicle*, rev. edn. (London, 1961)

M. Swanton, trans., *The Anglo-Saxon Chronicle* (London, 1996)

J. Bately, *The Anglo-Saxon Chronicle: Texts and Textual Relationships*, Reading Medieval Studies, Monograph 3 (Reading, 1991)

C. Clark, 'The Narrative Mode of The Anglo-Saxon Chronicle', in *England before the Conquest: Studies in Primary Sources presented to Dorothy Whitelock*, ed. P. A. M. Clemoes and K. Hughes (Cambridge, 1971), pp. 215–35

R. P. Horvath, 'History, Narrative and the Ideological Mode of *The Peterborough Chronicle*', *Mediaevalia* 17 (1994 for 1991), 123–48

⌐*Anno dcccc lxxxi*⌐. Hēr cōmon° ǣrest° þā° VII scipu and gehergoden° Hamtūn°.

⌐*Anno dcccc lxxxii*⌐.

Anno dcccc lxxxiii. Hēr forðfērde° Ælfere ealdorman and fēng° Ælfrīc ⌐tō

5 þām ilcan ealdordōme⌐.

1 came first then ravaged   2 Southampton   4 went forth (died) succeeded

1 *Anno dcccc lxxxi* Lat. 'in the year 981'. The Roman numerals are divided, as here, in the manuscript.

3 *Anno dcccc lxxxii* The year is recorded but the chronicler has found nothing of note to enter; the same happens in 990, below.

4–5 **tō þām ilcan ealdordōme** 'to that same caldormanry [office of ealdorman]', i.e. that of Mercia. Ælfric was a very common name and this one has no connection with the famous teacher of Cerne Abbas (see p. 4); nor should he be confused with another ealdorman Ælfric, of Hampshire, whose treachery in 992 is chronicled below. In the tenth century, 'ealdorman' came to signify a local ruler acting in the king's name, a wealthy nobleman often with responsibility for areas equivalent to the former separate Anglo-Saxon kingdoms (such as Mercia). Earlier, the term could also be used more generally for a leader or superior (see, for example, 9b/43).

Anno dcccc lxxxiiii. Hēr forðfērde se hālga° biscop Aðelwold ⌐muneca fæder⌐ and hēr wæs Ēadwine tō° abbod gehālgod° tō° Abbandūne°.

Anno dcccc lxxxv. Hēr Ælfrīc ealdorman wæs ūt ādrǣfed°.

Anno dcccc lxxxvi. Hēr se cyning fordyde° þet biscoprīce°æt Hrōfeceastre°.

10 ⌐And hēr cōm ǣrest se myccla° yrfcwalm° on° Angelcyn°⌐.

Anno dcccc lxxxvii. Hēr ⌐Wecedport⌐ wes gehergod.

Anno dcccc lxxxviii. Hēr wæs Goda ⌐se Dæfenisca þægn⌐ ofslagen and ⌐mycel wæl⌐ mid him. And hēr ⌐Dūnstān⌐ se hālga arcebiscop forlēt° þis līf and gefērde° þæt heofonlīce°. And Æðelgār biscop fēng æfter him tō arce-

15 biscopstōle° and hē ⌐lītle hwīle⌐ æfter þām° leofode°, būtan° ān gēar and III mōnðas.

⌐*Anno dcccc lxxxix*⌐. Hēr Ǣdwine abbod forðfērde and ⌐fēng Wulfgār tō⌐, and hēr Sirīc wæs gehādod° tō arcebiscope.

Anno dcccc xc.

---

6 holy   **7** as consecrated at Abingdon   **8** driven   **9** laid waste   diocese   Rochester
10 great   cattle-plague   to   England   **13** left   **14** attained   (the) heavenly (life)
15 archiepiscopal see   that   lived   only   **18** consecrated

---

6–7 **muneca fæder** A conventional epithet, but the chronicler is perhaps also acknowl-edging Æthelwold as a key figure in the monastic reform movement and promulgator of a trans. of the Benedictine Rule. One of the monasteries Æthelwold was responsible for reviving, after he became bishop of Winchester in 963, was Peterborough, where this ver-sion of the *Chronicle* was made. His first reforming efforts had been carried out as abbot of Abingdon, to which position Eadwine now succeeds. The 'Parker' version of the *Chronicle* (see p. 87) simply calls Æthelwold *wellwillenda* ('benevolent').

10 **And hēr . . . on Angelcyn** The juxtaposition by the chronicler of this and the previous event is deliberate, suggesting cause and effect. At Rochester, it seems that the king was retaliating against some sort of civil dissension and there is a tradition that Archbishop Dunstan (see 13n) had to pay him off with a hundred pounds of silver to stop his depredations against church property, and at the same time pronounced a prophesy of coming ills against him. Æthelred is reported to have said later that he had acted out of ignorance, not malice.

11 **Wecedport** 'Watchet', on the Somerset coast, the site of a royal mint and a former royal estate.

12 **se Dæfenisca þægn** 'the Devonshire thegn'. A thegn (or thane) was a nobleman, a member of the landed aristocracy, though lower-ranking than an ealdorman, to whom he would owe a duty as a retainer; the word means lit. 'one who serves' (cf. the vb. *þegnian*).

13 **mycel wæl** 'much slaughter'; i.e. along with Goda, many others were slain. **Dūnstān** He was one of the leaders, with Æthelwold and Oswald, of the monastic reform movement.

15 **lītle hwīle** acc. of duration of time: 'for a little while'.

17 **Anno dcccc lxxxix.** An emended reading; the chronicler or copyist got a bit ahead of himself here, writing *millesimo dccc lxxxix*, 'in the millennium (plus) 89', i.e. 1089.   **fēng Wulfgār tō** 'Wulfgar succeeded'.

20   ***Anno dcccc xci.*** Hēr wæs Gypeswīc° gehergod and æfter þām swȳðe° raðe°
⌐wæs Brihtnōð ealdorman ofslægen æt Mældūne⌐. And on° þām gēare man
gerædde° þæt man geald° ǣrest gafol° Deniscan mannum for° þām mycclan
brōgan° þe hī worhtan° be° þām sǣriman°. Þæt wæs ǣrest X þūsend punda;
þæne° rǣd° gerædde Sirīc arcebiscop.

25   ***Anno dcccc xcii.*** Hēr Ōswald se ēadiga arcebiscop forlēt þis līf and gefērde
þæt heofonlice and ⌐Æðelwine⌐ ealdorman gefōr° on þām ilcan gēare. Ðā
gerædde se cyng and ealle his witan þæt man gegaderode° þā scipu þe ⌐āhtes⌐
wǣron tō° Lundenbyrig°. And se cyng þā ⌐betǣhte þā fyrde tō lǣdene Ealfrīce
ealdorman⌐ and ⌐Þorode eorl and Ælfstāne biscop and Æscwīge biscop⌐, and
30   ⌐sceoldan cunnian⌐ gif hī muhton° þone here° ⌐āhwǣr ūtene⌐ betræppen°. Ðā
sende se ealdorman Ælfrīc and ⌐hēt warnian þone here⌐. And þā ⌐on þēre nihte ðe
hī on ðone dæi tōgædere cumon sceoldon⌐, ðā scēoc° hē on niht fram þǣre fyrde

20 Ipswich very quickly   **21** in   **22** decided (*or* advised)   should give *sbj* (to +*d*)
tribute because of   **23** terror caused along sea-coast   **24** that [*þone*] course of action
26 died   **27** should collect *sbj*   **28** at London   **30** might be able to   army (*i.e.* Vikings)
entrap   **32** fled

21 **wæs Brihtnōð... æt Mældūne** A reference to the episode commemorated in *The
Battle of Maldon* (Text 30). The 'Parker' version (under 993) says a little more: ... *and
swā tō Mældūne and him þēr cōm tōgēannes Byrhtnoð ealdorman mid his fyrde and him
wið gefeaht and hȳ þone ealdorman þēr ofslogon and wælstōwe geweald āhtan* ('and so
to Maldon, and there Ealdorman Byrhtnoth came against them with his army and fought
against them, and they slew the ealdorman there and held the battlefield').
26 **Æðelwine** He was ealdorman of East Anglia and a close friend of Oswald (see 13n).
27 **āhtes** gen. of definition: 'of aught', i.e. 'of any value'.
28–9 **betǣhte þā fyrde tō lǣdene** 'entrusted for leading [infl. inf.] the army', i.e.
'entrusted leadership of the army'. *Fyrde*, 'army', is commonly used, as here, for the English
militias gathered to combat the Vikings.   **Ealfrīce ealdorman** 'to ealdorman Ælfric'. Here,
and in the references to the other three leaders that follow, the name is correctly in the dat.
case, but the title remains uninflected. *Ealfrīc* is a variant spelling of *Ælfrīc*; this one is
the treacherous ealdorman of Hampshire, not the Mercian ealdorman mentioned above
(see 4–5n).
29 **Þorode** A resident of Northumbria.   **Ælfstāne** There were bishops of this name at
both London and Rochester at this time.   **Æscwīge** Bishop of Dorchester.
30 **sceoldan cunnian** 'they were to try'; i.e. the king had instructed them to try.
āhwǣr ūtene 'somewhere outside'; i.e. somewhere away from land, in the estuary or out
at sea.
31 **hēt warnian þone here** 'commanded to warn the army' [§G6d.i.2], i.e. 'commanded
the army to be warned' or 'had the army warned'.
31–2 **on þēre nihte ðe hī on ðone dæi** 'on the night before the day when' (*þēre* for
þǣre, *dæi* for *dæg*). The Anglo-Saxons regarded the day as going with the previous night.
tōgædere cumon sceoldon 'ought to have come together' (i.e. joined battle); see also 42–3.

⌐him sylfum tō mycclum bismore⌐. And se here þā ætbærst°, būton ān scip ⌐þǣr man ofslōh⌐. And þā gemǣtte° se here ðā scipu of° Ēastenglum and of Lunden
35   and ⌐hī⌐ ðǣr ofslōgon mycel wæl and þæt scip genāmon° eall gewǣpnod° and gewǣdod° þe se ealdorman on wæs. And ðā, æfter Ōswaldes arcebiscopes forðsīðe°, fēng Ealdulf abbod of Burch° tō Eoferwīcstōle° and tō Wigeraceastre° and Kenulf tō þām abbotrīce° æt Burch.

   Anno dcccc xciii. Hēr on ðissum gēare wæs Bæbbanburh° tōbrocon° and
40   mycel herehuðe° þǣr genumen° and æfter þām cōm tō Humbran° ⌐mūðe⌐ se here and þǣr mycel yfel° gewrohtan° ⌐ǣgðer ge on° Lindesīge° ge⌐ on Norðhymbran°. Þā gegaderode man swīðe mycele fyrde and þā hī tōgædere gān° sceoldan, þā onstealdon° þā heretogan° ǣrest þone flēam°. Þæt wæs Frǣna and Godwine and Friðegist. On þysum ilcan gēare hēt se cyng āblendan° ⌐Ælfgār⌐, Ælfrīces sunu
45   ealdormannes...

   Anno dcccc xcv. Hēr on þissum gēare æteowde° ⌐cometa se steorra⌐. And Sirīc arcebiscop forðfērde.

   Anno dcccc xcvi. Hēr on þissum gēare wæs Ælfrīc gehālgod tō arcebiscope ⌐tō Crīstes cyrcean⌐.
50   ***Anno dcccc xcvii***. Hēr on þissum gēare fērde° se here ābūtan° Defnanscīre intō Sǣfern° mūðon and þǣr gehergodon ǣgðer on Cornwealum° ge on

33 escaped   **34** encountered   from   **35** captured   armed   **36** 'dressed' (*i.e.* in sail)
37 death   Peterborough   (see) of York   (see of) Worcester   **38** abbacy   **39** Bamburgh
destroyed   **40** plunder   taken   of the Humber   **41** harm   inflicted   in   Lindsey
Northumbria   **42** come   **43** 'set up' (*i.e.* set the example of)   leaders   flight   **44** be blinded
46 appeared   **50** went   around   **51** of the Severn   the Cornish (*or* Cornwall)

33 **him sylfum tō mycclum bismore** 'as a great disgrace to himself', or 'to his own great disgrace'.

33–4 **þǣr man ofslōh** 'where one slaughtered', i.e. 'on which (the crew) was slaughtered'.

35 **hī** 'they'; the antec. is *se here*. In 41, the army is similarly treated as a collective noun with pl. vb. (*gewrohtan*).

40 **mūðe** 'mouth' or 'estuary', dat. sg. masc. In 51 and 54, the *n*-form of the noun, *mūða* (dat. sg. *mūðon/-an*), is used [§B5a].

41 **ǣgðer ge ... ge** 'both ... and ...'.

44 **Ælfgār** As the son of ealdorman Ælfric of Hampshire, Ælfgar was presumably given this cruel (but not unusual) punishment in retribution for his father's treachery and cowardice.

46 **cometa se steorra** 'the star (called) a "comet" '. In his *Enchiridion*, Byrhtferth of Ramsey (pt. 2, ch. 3) explains that a comet is a star whose appearance foreshadows catastrophes such as famine, pestilence and war. Bede, too, in his *Historia ecclesiastica* (bk. 4, ch. 12), reports the appearance of a comet (in 678).

49 **tō Crīstes cyrcean** 'at Christ Church', Canterbury. The archbishop (995–1005) is yet another Ælfric; he has often been confused with his contemporary, Ælfric of Cerne Abbas.

Norðwālum° and on Defenan and ⌜ēodon him þā ūp⌝ æt Wecedport and þær
mycel yfel wrohtan on° bærnette° and on manslihtum° and æfter þām wendon°
eft° ābūtan Penwihtsteort° on° ðā sūðhealfe° and wendon þā in tō Tamer° mūðan
55   and ēodon þā ūp oð° þæt hī cōmon tō Hlidaforda° and ælc° þing bærndon and
slōgon° þæt hī gemētton°, and Ordulfes mynster ⌜æt Tefingstoce⌝ forbærndon°
and unāsecgendlice° herehuðe mid him to scipa brohtan° . . .
      Millesimo ii. Hēr on þissum gēare se cyng gerǣdde and his witan þæt man
sceolde gafol gyldon° þām flotan° and frið° wið° hī geniman° ⌜wið þon þe⌝
60   hī heora yfeles geswīcan° sceoldan. Ðā sende se cyng tō þām flotan ⌜Lēofsīg⌝
ealdorman and hē þā, ⌜þæs cynges worde and his witena⌝, grið° wið hī gesætte°
⌜and þet hī tō metsunge fēngon and tō gafle⌝. And hī þā þæt underfēngon°
and him man þā geald XXIIII þūsend punda. Ðā ⌜on gemang þysum⌝ ofslōh
Lēofsīg ealdorman Æfic þæs cynges hēahgerēfan° and se cyng hine ðā geūtode°
65   of earde°. And þā on þām ilcan lengtene° cōm ⌜sēo hlǣfdige⌝ Ricardes dohtor
hider° tō lande. On ðām ilcan sumera Ealdulf arcebiscop forðfērde. And on
ðām gēare se cyng hēt ofslēan ealle ðā Deniscan men þe on Angelcynne wǣron
⌜on Bricius messedæg⌝, forþon° þām cynge wæs° gecydd° þæt hī woldon ⌜hine

---

52 the Welsh (*or* Wales)   **53** by way of burning manslaughter(s) turned   **54** next
Land's End to south side of the Tamar   **55** until Lydford every   **56** destroyed came
across burned down   **57** indescribable brought   **59** give fleet (*i.e.* Vikings) peace   from
accept   **60** cease (from +*g*)   **61** truce arranged   **62** accepted   **64** high-sheriff *as* banished
65 the land   Lent (*or* spring)   **66** here   **68** because (it) had been   made known (to +*d*)

---

52 **ēodon him þā ūp** 'went then ashore'; the dat. pron. is rflx. [§D4c].

56 **æt Tefingstoce** The founding of the monastery at Tavistock, *c*. 974, had been super-
vised by Ordwuld, King Edgar's brother-in-law.

59 **wið þon þe** instr. phr.: 'on condition that'.

60 **Lēofsīg** He succeeded Byrhtnoth as ealdorman of Essex in 991.

61 **þæs cynges worde and his witena** 'by command of the king and his counsellors';
see 29/1n.

62 **and þet hī tō metsunge fēngon and tō gafle** This clause is still governed by *gesætte*:
'and (arranged) that they received provisions and tribute . . .'. The idiom *fōn tō*, here 'receive',
also means 'succeed', as in 4–5, above.

63 **on gemang þysum** 'in the midst of this (*or* these events)'.

65 **sēo hlǣfdige** 'the lady', here used as a title. This was Emma, daughter of Richard I,
duke of Normandy, and sister of his successor, Richard II. In this same year, Emma married
Æthelred, a crucial event in the lead-up to the Norman Conquest of 1066.

68 **on Bricius messedæg** 'on St Brice's feast-day' (13 Nov.; Brice was an early Gaul-
ish bishop, *d.* 444). It is not clear how many Danes were slaughtered in the St Brice's
day massacre, which Æthelred later claimed he had ordered with the advice of his leading
counsellors. The victims are more likely to have been dispersed Danish settlers than members of dominant communities such as those at York and Lincoln. The dire event was long
remembered, and if the tradition which suggests that the sister of King Svein of Denmark
was among the victims is true, his invasion in the following year (see 1003) may have been
spurred by a desire for revenge.

besyrewian æt his līfe⌐ and syððan° ⌐ealle his witan⌐ and habban syþðan his
70   rīce°.

Millesimo iii. Hēr wæs Eaxeceaster° ābrocen° þurh ⌐þone Frenciscan ceorl
Hugon⌐ þe sēo hlēfdige ⌐heafde hire gesett tō gerēfan⌐, and se here ⌐þā burh⌐
mid ealle fordyde and mycle herehuðe þǣr genāmen. Ðā gegaderode man swīðe
mycele fyrde of Wiltūnscīre° and of Hamtūnscīre° and ⌐swīðe ānrǣdlīce wið
75   þæs heres weard wǣron⌐. Ðā sceolde se ealdorman Ælfrīc lǣdan þā fyrde ac°
⌐hē tēah forð⌐ þā his ealdan wrenceas°. ⌐Sōna swā⌐ hī wǣron swā gehende°
þet ǣgðer° heora on ōðer hāwede°, þā ⌐gebrǣd hē hine sēocne⌐ and ongan
⌐hine brecan⌐ tō spīwenne° and cweð þet hē gesīclod° wǣre and swā þæt folc
beswāc° þæt hē lǣdan sceolde. Swā hit gecweðen° is, '⌐ðonne se heretoga
80   wācað° þonne⌐ bið eall se here swīðe gehindred°'. Ðā Swegen° geseah° þæt hī
ānrǣde° nǣron° and ealle tōhwurfon°, þā lǣdde hē his here intō Wiltūne°. And
hī ðā burh gehergodon and forbærndon and ēodon þā tō Searbyrig° and þanon°
eft tō sǣ. Fērde þǣr he ⌐wiste⌐ his ȳðhengestas°.

69 after that   **70** kingdom   **71** Exeter   destroyed   **74** Wiltshire   Hampshire   **75** but
76 tricks   close   **77** both (of)   looked   **78** vomit   ill   **79** betrayed   said   **80** weakens
impeded   Svein   saw   **81** resolute   were not [*ne wǣron*]   were dispersing   Wilton
82 Salisbury   from there   **83** 'wave-stallions' (ships)

68–9 **hine besyrewian æt his līfe** 'trick him from his life', i.e. 'treacherously deprive
him of his life'.   **ealle his witan** This is a further obj. of *besyrewian*.

71–2 **þone Frenciscan ceorl Hugon** Little is known about this 'French fellow', Hugh,
who was in fact a Norman count. We may be seeing here an early use of 'churl' in a derogatory
sense; on its more usual OE meaning, see 7a/22n.   **heafde hire gesett tō gerēfan** 'had for
herself appointed as reeve', i.e. 'had appointed as her reeve'.   **þā burh** 'the city', i.e. Exeter.

74–5 **swīðe ānrǣdlīce ... wǣron** 'were firmly resolved towards the [Danish] army',
i.e. 'were firmly resolved to march against the army'.

76 **hē tēah forð** 'he pulled out', i.e. 'got up to'.   **Sōna swā** 'As soon as'.

77 **gebrǣd hē hine sēocne** 'he feigned himself sick', 'i.e. 'pretended to be sick'.

78 **hine brecan** 'to force himself'.

79–80 **ðonne ... þonne ...** 'when ..., then ...' A similar proverbial statement constitutes one of the *Durham Proverbs* (34/31).

83 **wiste** A complement for the vb. is needed: 'knew ... to be'.

9

Bede's *Ecclesiastical History of the English People*

The Venerable Bede (*c.* 672–735) spent all his life from the age of seven at the monastery of Jarrow, part of the twinned institution of Wearmouth-Jarrow in Northumbria. This was at the time the most powerful of the independent Anglo-Saxon kingdoms, with kings willing and able to endow great centres of faith and learning. Wearmouth-Jarrow became one of the most important in the Christian West, largely owing to Bede. Ælfric of Eynsham, whose own works dominated a later period of Anglo-Saxon England (see p. 4), was to call Bede 'the wise teacher of the English people'. The range of his writings was immense: biblical exegesis, history, hagiography (writings about saints), grammar, poetry, natural science and computus (astronomical and chronological calculation). His works, which define for us the first great period of cultural development in Anglo-Saxon England, were in demand on the Continent also, both in Bede's own lifetime and throughout the Middle Ages. The thirteenth-century Italian poet Dante afforded him the rare privilege of a place among the blessed souls inhabiting 'the heaven of the sun' in his *Paradiso* (part of the *Divina Commedia*).

The *Historia ecclesiastica gentis Anglorum* ('Ecclesiastical History of the English People') was Bede's greatest achievement. In five books, it tells the story of his country from Julius Caesar's attempted invasion of Britain in 60 BC to the year in which Bede finished writing, AD 731. His aim was a fundamental Christian one: to record the growth of the English church and to reveal it, and England, as part of the divine scheme of history. To that end, the main narrative is filled out with letters, accounts of holy men and of miracles, and many anecdotes which became part of the literary heritage of England. Bede wrote in Latin, but when, at the end of the ninth century, King Alfred came to launch a revival of learning in Wessex (see p. 2), the *Historia ecclesiastica* was a natural choice for putting into OE, even though Alfred's direct involvement has not yet been proved. Like much early translation into OE, this one tends to stick close to the original Latin, sometimes at the expense of natural idiom, with awkward results; and there are occasional passages where the translator's misunderstanding of the Latin has caused problems (as indicated in the notes below). In many passages, however, a distinctive native style emerges, as in the use of doublets of OE verbs to render a single Latin verb; for example, *compian ond feohtan* in 9a/7 renders Latin *pugnare*, 'to fight'. Constructions using the present participle are much favoured, sometimes translating a Latin present participle but often (combined with the verb 'to be') a past participle or other verbal form; see, for example, 9a/48–50 and 9b/20–1 and 40. The reader of the OE Bede has to be especially careful in interpreting third-person pronouns, whose referent may change two or three times within a single sentence.

The OE translation is preserved in four main manuscripts and some fragments. Their texts derive from a common source which may have originated in Mercia, to judge from certain linguistic features (described in the individual headnotes, below). The most authoritative manuscript is considered to be the earliest, Oxford, Bodleian Library, Tanner 10, written late in the tenth century, and the text of the extract in 9b is edited from this. However, because Tanner 10 lacks most of bk. 1, chs. 1–15, the text of 9a (bk. 4, ch. 24) as far as line 47 (*forgefe*) is taken from a manuscript copied at Worcester in the second half of the eleventh century (Cambridge, University Library, Kk. 3. 18).

Further reading

T. Miller, ed. and trans., *The Old English Version of Bede's Ecclesiastical History*, 4 vols., EETS os 95, 96, 110 and 111 (London, 1890–8)

B. Colgrave and R. A. B. Mynors, eds. and trans., *Bede's Ecclesiastical History of the English People* (Oxford, 1969); rev. edn. of the trans. only, with additional notes, issued in the World Classics series (Oxford, 1994)

J. M. Wallace-Hadrill, *Bede's Ecclesiastical History of the English People: a Historical Commentary* (Oxford, 1988)

G. Bonner, ed., *Famulus Christi: Essays in Commemoration of the Thirteenth Centenary of the Birth of the Venerable Bede* (London, 1976)

D. H. Farmer, ed., and J. F. Webb, trans., *The Age of Bede*, rev. edn. (Harmondsworth, 1983)

G. H. Brown, *Bede the Venerable* (Boston, MA, 1987)

P. Hunter Blair, *The World of Bede*, reissued with corrections and additional bibliography (Cambridge, 1990)

9a
The Founding of England (Bk. 1, chs. 15–16)

Bede's account of the coming of the Germanic tribes to Britain is based on the work of the late fifth- or early sixth-century British monk, Gildas, whose idiosyncratic

De excidio Britanniae ('On the Ruin of Britain') was hugely influential on early historians. However, Bede adds many details of his own, including the division of the invaders into Angles, Saxons and Jutes (though it is to be noted that in the title of his history he subsumes them all under the term *gens Anglorum*, 'the English people'). Presumably, Bede got his information from oral traditions or other written records. Modern archaeology supports much of his account, including the distribution of the settling tribes, though Frisians and Franks should be added to the list. This distribution is reflected still today in county and regional names, such as Essex (East Saxons), Wessex (West Saxons) and East Anglia.

At the end of the chapter preceding the one given here, Bede has anticipated its content by stressing that it was God's will that the Britons (i.e. the native Celtish peoples, who had been more or less Christianised during the Roman occupation) should suffer invasion as punishment for their corruption and debauchery and their falling away from the worship of Christ. They have already been ravaged by plague; now renewed attacks by Picts from the north prompt one of their leaders to take the fateful step of seeking help from the Continent.

The fact that the first fifty lines of the extract below are taken from a late eleventh-century manuscript and the last dozen lines from one copied at the end of the tenth century (see main headnote) allows some characteristic differences between earlier and later WS to be observed. For example, in the 'late' section, the plural pronoun 'they'/'them' is consistently *hī*, but in the early part it is *hēo*. The levelling of unstressed endings in some preterite verbs is more notable in the later text, as in *sceoldan* (7) and *geslōgan* (9), but cf. *onhergedon* (8) and *sendon* (10). The earlier text's *gēr* for *gear* (60) might be of Mercian origin.

Further reading

Gildas, *The Ruin of Britain and Other Works*, trans. M. Winterbottom (London, 1978)

P. Sims-Williams, 'The Settlement of England in Bede and the *Chronicle*', *ASE* 12 (1983), 1–41

M. Lapidge and D. Dumville, eds., *Gildas: New Approaches* (Woodbridge, 1984)

J. N. L. Myres, *The English Settlements* (Oxford, 1986)

N. J. Higham, *The English Conquest: Gildas and Britain in the Fifth Century* (Manchester, 1994)

⌐Đā wæs ymb fēower hund wintra ond nigon ond fēowertig fram¬ ūres
Drihtnes° menniscnysse° þæt Martianus cāsere° rīce° onfēng° ond ⌐VII gēar
hæfde¬. Sē° wæs ⌐syxta ēac fēowertigum¬ fram ⌐Agusto¬ þām cāsere. Đā
⌐Angelþēod ond Seaxna¬ wæs gelaðod° fram° þām foresprecenan° ⌐cyninge¬
5   ond on Breotone cōm on þrim° ⌐myclum scypum¬, ond on ēastdæle° þyses
ēalondes eardungstōwe° onfēng þurh ðæs ylcan° cyninges bebod° þe° hī° hider
gelaðode þæt° hī sceoldan ⌐for heora ēðle compian ond feohtan¬. Ond hī sōna
compedon wið heora gewinnan° þe hī° oft ær° norðan° onhergedon° ond Seaxan
þā sige° geslōgan°. Þā sendan hī hām ærenddracan° ond hēton° secgan° þysses
10   landes wæstmbærnysse° ond Brytta° yrgþo°. Ond hī þā sōna hider sendon māran
sciphere° strengran° wighena° ⌐ond wæs unoferswīðendlic° weorud°¬, þā hī
tōgædere geþēodde° wæron. Ond him Bryttas sealdan° ond geafan eardung-

---

2 Lord's incarnation emperor power took **3** He **4** invited by aforementioned **5** three
dp eastern part **6** place of settlement same decree who them **7** (on condition) that
8 adversaries them (the British) previously from the north (had) harassed **9** victory
won messengers commanded (them) to tell about +*a* **10** fertility *as* of the Britons
cowardice *as* **11** ship-army stronger warriors *gp* invincible host **12** joined gave

---

1 **Đā wæs ymb … fram** In temporal expressions, *ymb* usually means 'after', but here
that sense is also given by *fram*, so it is best to trans. simply, '(It) was then 449 years
after …'. Bede is always careful to locate the history of the English precisely in the wider
scheme of (Christian) world history. Numerals from *fēower* upwards usually govern the
gen. [§E3d].
   2–3 **VII gēar hæfde** acc. of duration of time: 'held for seven years'; the obj. of the vb.
is again *rīce*. Marcian ruled the eastern Roman Empire, AD 450–7.
   3 **syxta ēac fēowertigum** 'the sixth-plus-fortieth', i.e. 'the forty-sixth (emperor)'; the
use of *eac* with dat. ('in addition to') in compound ordinal numbers is frequent in the trans.
of Bede. On the declension of ordinals see §E4.   **Augusto** The translator has taken over
the name *Augustus* complete with its Latin ablative case-ending to express the OE dat. after
fram. Augustus had been the first Roman emperor (27BC–AD14).
   4 **Angelþēod ond Seaxna** 'the Angle nation and (the nation) of Saxons', i.e. 'the
Anglo-Saxon people'. Compound subjs. ('heavy groups') are usually split thus in OE
(see 29/1n). **cyninge** The king has been named by Bede as Vortigern in the preceding chapter
(bk. 1, ch. 14).
   5 **myclum scypum** Bede's Latin describes them as 'long ships'.
   7 **for heora ēðle** The 'native land' in question is of course Britain, so that the poss. pron.
heora ('their') refers to the British, not to the invaders (*hī*); in the next sentence, however,
heora does indicate the latter.   **compian ond feohtan** 'strive and fight'. On the use of such
doublets, see the main headnote.
   11 **ond wæs unoferswīðendlic weorud** The awkward use of vbs. without their subj.
pron. (here a notional *þæt* must be inserted before *wæs*) results from Latin influence; see
also 21, 22, etc. The united force of the first and second waves of invaders would prove
irresistible.

stōwe betwih° him°, þæt hī for sibbe° ond hǣlo° heora ēðles campodon ond
wunnon° wið heora fēondum ond hī him andlyfne° ond āre° forgēafen° for
15   heora gewinne°.

Cōmon hī of° þrim folcum° ðām strangestan° Germānie°, þæt of Seaxum°
ond of ⌐Angle⌐ ond of Gēatum°. ⌐Of Gēata fruman syndon⌐ Cantware° ond
Wihtsǣtan°, þæt is sēo ðēod° þe Wiht þæt ēalond oneardað. Of Seaxum, þæt is
of ðām lande þe mon hāteð ⌐Ealdseaxan⌐, cōman Ēastseaxan ond Sūðseaxan ond
20   Westseaxan. Ond of Engle cōman Ēastengle ond Middelengle ond Myrce° ond
eall Norðhembra° cynn. ⌐Is þæt land ðe⌐ Angulus is nemned, betwyh Gēatum
ond Seaxum; ⌐is sǣd of þǣre tīde° þe hī ðanon° gewiton° oð tōdæge þæt⌐ hit
wēste° ⌐wunige⌐. Wǣron ðā ǣrest° heora lāttēowas° ond heretogan° twēgen
gebrōðra° ⌐Hengest ond Horsa⌐. Hī wǣron Wihtgylses suna, þæs° fæder wæs
25   Witta hāten, þæs fæder wæs Wihta hāten, ond þæs Wihta fæder wæs Wōden
nemned. Of ðæs strȳnde° monigra mǣgða° cyningcynn° ⌐fruman lǣdde⌐. Ne
wæs ðā ylding° ⌐tō þon þæt hī hēapmǣlum° cōman māran weorod⌐ of þām

13 among   them (the Britons)   peace   security   **14** contended   food   benefit   gave
15 labour   **16** from   tribes   most powerful   of the Germans   the Saxons   **17** the Jutes
inhabitants of Kent   **18** inhabitants of Wight   people   inhabit   **20** Mercians   **21** of the
Northumbrians   **22** time   from there   left   **23** desolate   at first   leaders   commanders
24 brothers *np*   whose   **26** stock   tribes *gp*   royal line *ns*   **27** delay   in droves

17 **Angle** dat. sg. of *Angel*, i.e. 'Angeln' (part of the province of Schleswig in modern
Denmark), from where the Angles came; the spelling *Engle* is used in 20. The pl. tribal
name, '(from) the Angles', may be used in trans., to match *Seaxum* and *Gēatum*.   **Of Gēata
fruman syndon** 'From the origin of the Jutes are . . .', i.e. 'Descended from the Jutes
are . . .'.

19 **Ealdseaxan** 'Old Saxony' was the name being given to the original continental
home of the Saxons by Bede's time, when Christian missionaries were active there. Literary
contacts would take place as a result, too (though they have not been specifically dated),
as is shown by the survival of parts of a poem on the biblical Genesis in the Old Saxon
language, which remained very close to OE; see 17/headnote.

21 **Is þæt land ðe** 'that is the land that . . .' The referent is *Engle* (or *Angle*) in the
previous line. The translator gives the Latin version of it, *Angulus*.

22 **is sǣd of þǣre tīde þe . . . þæt** Best trans. as *hit is sǣd þæt, of þǣre tīde þe . . .*

23 **wunige** 'remains', but the sense is past continuous: 'has remained'.

24 **Hengest ond Horsa** Earlier in the *Historia ecclesiastica* (bk. 1, ch. 15), Bede has
traced the genealogy of these legendary leaders back to the principal Germanic deity, Woden
(the Norse Óðinn); by such a tactic, the divinity of the 'god' is neatly neutralised: he was just
another human being (see 24/headnote). Similar origins were claimed in their genealogies
by most of the Anglo-Saxon royal families.

26 **fruman lǣdde** 'led' or 'took origin'; i.e. 'derived their origin'.

27 **tō þon** 'after that' (instr.).   **þæt hī . . . cōman māran weorod** The pron. 'they',
anticipating the subj., is superfluous: 'that more troops came'.

ðēodum þe wē ǣr gemynegodon°. Ond þæt folc ðe hider cōm ongan° weaxan° ond myclian° ⌜tō þan swīðe⌝ þæt hī wǣron ⌜on myclum ege⌝ þām sylfan
30 landbīgengan° ðe hī ǣr hider laðedon ond cȳgdon°.

Æfter þissum hī þā geweredon° tō° sumre° tīde wið° Pehtum°, þā° hī ǣr þurh gefeoht feor° ādrifan°. Ond þā wǣron Seaxan sēcende° intingan° ond tōwyrde° ⌜heora gedāles wið Bryttas⌝. Cȳðdon° him openlīce ond sǣdon, būtan° hī him māran andlyfne sealdon, þæt ⌜hī woldan him sylfe⌝ niman° ond hergian° þǣr
35 hī ⌜hit⌝ findan mihton. Ond sōna ðā bēotunge° dǣdum° gefyldon°: bærndon ond hergedon ond slōgan fram ēastsǣ oð westsǣ ond him nǣnig° wiðstōd. ⌜Ne wæs ungelīc wræcc þām ðe iū Chaldēas bærndon Hierusalēme weallas⌝ ond ðā cynelican° getimbro° mid fȳre fornāman° for ðæs Godes folces synnum. ⌜Swā þonne hēr⌝, fram° þēre ārlēasan° ðēode, ⌜hwæðere rihte Godes dōme⌝,
40 nēhceastra° gehwylce° ond land forheregeode° wǣron. Hruran° ond fēollan cynelico getimbro ond ānlīpie° ond gehwǣr° sācerdas° ond mæsseprēostas° betwih° wībedum° wǣron slægene ond cwylmde°. ⌜Biscopas mid folcum būton° ǣnigre āre° scēawunge° ætgædere⌝ mid īserne° ond līge° fornumene wǣron. Ond

---

28 mentioned   began   to grow   **29** to increase   **30** native inhabitants   summoned **31** made an alliance   at   a certain   with   the Picts   whom   **32** far   had driven away seeking   occasion   opportunity   **33** Proclaimed   unless   **34** seize   plunder   **35** threats *ap*   with deeds   fulfilled   **36** none   **38** public   buildings *ap*   destroyed   **39** on account of   impious   **40** neighbouring towns   each +*gp*   ravaged   Crumbled   **41** private everywhere   priests   mass-priests   **42** among   altars   murdered   without   **43** of respect show *ds*   iron (sword)   fire

---

29 **tō þan swīðe** instr. phr.: 'to such an extent'.   **on myclum ege** The phr. mimics the Latin dat. *terrori*: 'a cause of great terror' (lit. 'as a great terror').

33 **heora gedāles wið Bryttas** 'for their breaking from the Britons'.

34 **hī woldan him sylfe** Strictly speaking, *sylfe* is in concord with *hī*, 'they themselves', while *him* is the rflx. dat. pron., 'for them(selves)'; best simplified in trans.: 'they would... for themselves'.

35 **hit** i.e. a supply of food, although the antec. of the pron., *andleofen*, is fem., not neut.; an example of the use of 'natural' gender [§B/overview].

36–7 **Ne wæs ungelīc ... weallas** Possible trans.: 'It was a vengeance (*wræcc*) not unlike that of the Chaldeans who once (*iū*) burned the walls of Jerusalem', or 'not dissimilar to that in which the Chaldeans, when they ...'. Bede alludes here to the OT account (2 Kgs 25.8–10) of the destruction of Jerusalem and the Temple by invading Chaldeans, which preceded the Jewish exile. In drawing an explicit historical parallel, he implicitly interprets the disaster which overcame the Britons as another case of God's retribution against a disobedient people.

39 **Swā þonne hēr** 'Thus, therefore (*þonne*), at this time (*hēr*)'.   **hwæðere rihte Godes dōme** 'and indeed by God's just decree'.

42–3 **Biscopas mid folcum ... ætgædere** 'bishops and people together'.

⌐ne wæs ænig sē ðe⌐ bebyrignysse° sealde° þām° ðe swā hrēowlīce° ācwealde°
45　wǣron. Ond monige ðǣre earman° lāfe° on wēstenum° fanggene° wǣron ond
hēapmǣlum sticode°. Sume for hungre heora fēondum ⌐on hand ēodon⌐ ond
ēcne° þēowdōm° gehēton°, ⌐wið þon þe⌐ him mon andlifne forgefe°. Sume ofer
sǣ sārigende° gewiton°; sume forhtiende° in ēðle gebīdon° ond ⌐þearfende līf in
wuda ond in wēstenum ond in hēan cleofum° sorgiende mōde symle° dydon⌐.
50　　Ond þā ⌐æfter þon þe⌐ se here° ⌐wæs hām hweorfende⌐ ond ⌐hēo⌐ hæfdon
ūtamǣrede° þā bīgengan° þisses ēalondes, ðā ongunnon hēo sticcemǣlum° mōd°
ond mægen° ⌐monian⌐ ond forðēodon° of þǣm dēaglum° stōwum° þe hēo ǣr
in behȳdde° wǣron ond ⌐ealra ānmōdre geþafunge⌐ heofonrīces fultomes° him°
wǣron biddende° þæt hēo ⌐oð forwyrd ǣghwǣr fordīlgode ne wǣron⌐. Wæs in
55　ðā tīd heora heretoga ond lāttēow ⌐Ambrosius⌐ hāten, ⌐ōðre noman⌐ Aurelianus.
Wæs gōd mon ond gemetfæst°, Rōmanisces cynnes mon. In þisses monnes
tīd, mōd ond mægen Brettas onfēngon° ond hē hēo tō gefeohte forðgecegde°
ond him sige geheht°, ond hēo ēac° on þām gefeohte þurh Godes fultom
sige onfēngon. Ond þā of þǣre tīde hwīlum° Brettas hwīlum eft Seaxan sige

44 burial might give to those cruelly killed **45** wretched remnant wastelands
captured **46** butchered **47** perpetual servitude promised gave *sbj* **48** grieving went
in fear remained **49** crags continuously **50** army **51** driven out inhabitants
little by little heart **52** strength came out secret places **53** hidden help for themselves
54 praying **56** moderate **57** acquired called forth **58** promised moreover
59 sometimes

44 **ne wæs ænig sē ðe** 'there was none, he who...', i.e. 'there was no one who...'.

46 **on hand ēodon** 'went into the hand', i.e. 'yielded to' or 'surrendered to'.

47 **wið þon þe** conj. phr. (instr.): 'provided that'.

48–9 **þearfende līf...dydon** 'led a needy life (*or* a life of want)'.　**sorgiende mōde** dat of manner: 'with sorrowing heart'.

50 **æfter þon þe** conj. phr. (instr.): 'after'.　**wæs hām hweorfende** Past continuous construction ('was returning'), but the sense is pluperf.: 'had returned home(wards)'. Later events make it that the invaders did not return to the Continent, so 'home' must mean to the land within Britain which Vortigern had granted them.　**hēo** pron. 'they' (*hī* or *hīe* in later WS), referring plurally to the army (*here*), as also in 52 and 54.

52 **monian** 'to recover' or 'to revive', translating Lat. *resumere*. There is other evidence of this usage in Alfredian texts, but the OE vb. (with its variants *manian, manigian*) usually conveys a sense of reminding or inciting.

53 **ealra ānmōdre geþafunge** 'with the wholehearted assent of all'.

54 **oð forwyrd... ne wǣron** 'should not everywhere [i.e. completely] be destroyed to (the point of) annihilation'.

55 **Ambrosius** Gildas, Bede's source here, calls Ambrosius a Roman, not a Briton (see next line); the writer of a later Celtic source, the *Historia Brittonum*, implies that he may have been a relation of Vortigern's.　**ōðre noman** dat. of definition: '(and) by the other name'.

60   geslōgon° oð þæt gēr° ⌜ymbsetes þǣre Beadonescan dūne⌝, þā hēo micel wæl°
      on Ongolcynne geslōgon° ⌜ymb fēower ond fēowertig wintra Ongolcynnes
      cymes⌝ in Breotone.

60 won   year   slaughter   **61** inflicted

   60 **ymbsetes þǣre Beadonescan dūne** 'of the siege of Mount Badon'. This must have
taken place *c.* 500 somewhere in the west of England, but the site has not been identified.
   61–2 **ymb fēower ond fēowertig wintra...cymes** 'at forty-four years from [lit. 'of']
the arrival...', i.e. 'forty years after...'.

9b
The Miracle of Cædmon
(Bk. 4, ch. 24)

The miracle by which Cædmon, an unlettered cowherd attached to Whitby Abbey,
in Northumbria, was granted the divine gift of poetic composition is the subject
of one of the most celebrated of Bede's stories. Commanded in a vision to 'sing',
Cædmon does just that, and his gift of turning Christian history into song so
impresses Abbess Hild that she has him received into the monastery as a brother. He
lives out his days composing songs on biblical themes and eventually approaches
death with the devout self-possession of a saint. Whitby is comparatively close to
Jarrow and the alleged miracle will have happened during Bede's lifetime there,
perhaps about 670, though he would have been only a very small boy. Critics used
to ascribe the OE biblical poems *Genesis*, *Exodus* and *Daniel* (preserved in the
Junius manuscript: see p. 130) to Cædmon – and the books of Genesis and Exodus
are alluded to in Bede's narrative (lines 63–4) – but it is now generally accepted,
mainly for stylistic reasons, that these poems are not the work of a single author,
and no connection with Whitby can be proven.
    However fabulous Bede's account may be, the nine-line hymn of Creation which
it puts into the mouth of the inspired cowherd neatly illustrates a cultural synthesis
which was to shape much subsequent OE poetry – namely, the use of the traditional
'heroic' poetic idiom of the ancestors of the Anglo-Saxons to present and promote
the themes of Christianity. Words such as *dryhten* ('lord') are perhaps being used
in Cædmon's hymn for the first time in a Christian context ('Lord'). With its
alliteration and variation, the hymn is a good example of the type of composition
on secular themes which Cædmon would presumably have heard frequently at

those gatherings from which he used to leave early, as Bede tells it, because of his inability to join in. Bede himself gives only a Latin paraphrase of the hymn and apologises for its inadequacy. The manuscripts of the OE translation of the *Historia ecclesiastica* present the hymn in a WS form (as in the main text below), but the earliest surviving versions of it (there are some twenty of them) are in the Northumbrian dialect. They entered the Latin manuscript tradition, as marginal additions, long before the whole work was translated. One of the manuscripts dates from 737, only two years after Bede's death; its Northumbrian version is given below in the notes.

Structurally, the hymn is in two sections: the first four lines offer a general statement of why we should praise God, namely for his wonderful creation; the following five lines define the two principal aspects of that creation, heaven and earth. But the whole poem is tightly bound together by no fewer than seven epithets for God, with three different ones in the first part (*heofonrīces weard*, *meotod* and *wuldorfæder*) and three more in the second (*halig scyppend*, *monncynnes weard* and *frēa ælmihtig*), and one (*ēce Drihten*) used in both, a link reinforced by the use of a similar formula (but with differing focus) in lines 1b and 7b (*heofonrīces weard* and *monncynnes weard*). Thematically, the poem reminds us of the praise-motif which informs so many of the psalms of the OT; ps 135, for example, includes the lines, 'Praise the Lord, for he is good . . . Praise ye the Lord of lords . . . who alone does great wonders . . . who made the heavens in understanding . . . who established the earth above the waters . . .'.

The language of the extract of Bede given here (from a copy made in the late tenth century) shows many early WS features. They include forms such as *ðeosse* (1), *leomu* (22) and *wreoton* (62), in which *i* would later be written for *eo*, and the use of *ðætte* for the relative pronoun *ðæt* (3 and 98). The preterite singular ending *-ade*, as in *gewunade* (2) and *leornade* (11), suggests non-WS influence; 'standard' *-ode* occurs in *gedeofanode* (14), but here the diphthong *eo* for expected *a* might be Mercian. The alternative *-ede* in *ondswarede* (24) is an occasional variation in all dialects. The form *neahte* (21 and 82), later *nihte*, could be Mercian, and *ænde* for *ende* (76) is an early feature of several dialects. Vowel-doubling to indicate length, as in *booc* (64) and *wiites* (69), is frequent in Alfredian texts (and also in those of the very late WS period).

Further reading

A. H. Smith, ed., *Three Northumbrian Poems: Cædmon's Hymn, Bede's Death Song and the Leiden Riddle*, rev. edn. (Exeter, 1978)

P. R. Orton, 'Cædmon's Christian Poetry', *NM* 84 (1983), 163–70

K. S. Kiernan, 'Reading Cædmon's Hymn with Someone Else's Glosses', *Representations* 32 (1990), 157–74; repr. in *OE Literature*, ed. Liuzza, pp. 103–24

K. O'B. O'Keeffe, 'Orality and the Developing Text of *Cædmon's Hymn*', *Speculum* 62 (1987), 1–20; repr. in *OE Poetry*, ed. Liuzza, pp. 79–102, and *Anglo-Saxon Manuscripts: Basic Readings*, ed. M. P. Richards (New York and London, 1994), pp. 221–50

E. G. Stanley, 'New Formulas for Old: *Cædmon's Hymn*', in *Pagans and Christians: the Interplay between Christian Latin and Traditional Germanic Cultures in Early Medieval Europe*, ed. T. Hofstra *et al.* (Groningen, 1995), pp. 131–48

A. Orchard, 'Poetic Inspiration and Prosaic Translation: the Making of *Cædmon's Hymn*', in *Studies in English Language and Literature: 'Doubt Wisely': Papers in Honour of E. G. Stanley*, ed. M. J. Toswell and E. M. Tyler (London and New York, 1996), pp. 402–22

P. Cavill, 'Bede and Cædmon's *Hymn*', in *"Lastworda Betst": Essays in Memory of Christine E. Fell with her Unpublished Writings*, ed. C. Hough and K. A. Lowe (Donington, 2002), pp. 1–17

In ðeosse abbudissan° mynstre° wæs sum° brōðor syndriglīce° mid godcundre° gife° gemǣred° ond geweorðad°, forþon° hē gewunade° gerisenlice° lēoð° wyrcan°, ⌐þā ðe tō ǣfestnisse° ond tō ārfæstnisse° belumpen⌐, ⌐swā ðætte swā hwæt swā⌐ hē of godcundum stafum° þurh bōceras° geleornode, þæt hē æfter
5   medmiclum° fæce° in scopgereorde°, mid þā mǣstan swētnisse ond inbryrd-nisse° geglængde° ond in Englisc gereorde° wel geworht, forþbrōhte°. Ond for° his lēoþsongum° ⌐monigra monna mōd⌐ oft tō worulde° forhogdnisse° ond ⌐tō geþēodnisse þæs heofonlican līfes⌐ onbærnde° wǣron. Ond ēac° swelce° monige ōðre æfter him in Ongelþēode° ongunnon° æfeste° lēoð wyrcan. Ac

1 abbess's monastery a certain specially divine   **2** gift glorified honoured because used to fitting songs   **3** compose piety virtuous behaviour   **4** writings scholars **5** short time poetical language   **6** inspiration adorned speech produced   **7** on account of +*d* songs world *gs* contempt (for +*g*)   **8** inspired also likewise   **9** English language began pious

3 **þā ðe... belumpen** 'those which pertained'; *belumpen* is a sbj. form, but indic. *belumpon* (as in other manuscripts, and in 14) is more appropriate.

3–4 **swā ðætte swā hwæt swā** 'so that whatsoever'. Later in the line, *þæt* is correl. with *hwæt*; it may be rendered as 'it' or not trans.; its vb. (*forþbrōhte*) does not appear until after a long intervening subord. clause.

7 **monigra monna mōd** 'the hearts of many men'. The fact that *mōd* is pl. is only confirmed when we reach the vb. *wǣron*.

8 **tō geþēodnisse þæs heofonlican līfes** 'to association with [lit. "of"] the holy life'. Although this seems to make sense, the use of OE *geþēodnis* probably results from an error by the translator, for the meaning intended by Bede here was 'longing' (Lat. *appetitus*).

10 nænig° hwæðre° ⌐him þæt gelīce dōn meahte⌐, forþon hē ⌐nales from monnum
ne þurh mon⌐ gelǣred° wæs þæt hē þone lēoðcræft° leornade, ac hē wæs god-
cundlīce° gefultumed° ond þurh Godes gife þone songcræft onfēng°. Ond hē
forðon° nǣfre° ⌐nōht lēasunge ne īdles lēoþes⌐ wyrcan meahte, ac ⌐efne þā ān þā
ðe⌐ tō æfestnesse belumpon ond ⌐his þā æfestan tungan gedeofanode singan⌐.

15   Wæs ⌐hē se mon⌐ in weoruldhāde° geseted° oð þā tīde° þe hē wæs ⌐gelȳfdre
ylde⌐ ond nǣfre nænig lēoð geleornade. Ond hē forþon oft in° gebēorscipe°,
⌐þonne þǣr wæs blisse intinga gedēmed þæt hēo ealle scolden⌐ þurh° ende-
byrdnesse° be° hearpan singan, þonne hē geseah° þā hearpan him nēalēcan°,
þonne ārās hē for scome° from þǣm symble° ond hām ēode° tō his hūse. Þā hē

20 þæt þā ⌐sumre tīde⌐ dyde, þæt hē forlēt þæt hūs þæs gebēorscipes ond ūt ⌐wæs
gongende⌐ tō nēata° scipene°, þāra° heord° him wæs ⌐þǣre neahte⌐ beboden°,
þā hē ⌐ðā⌐ þǣr in gelimplice° tīde his leomu° on reste gesette° ond onslēpte°, þā
⌐stōd him sum mon æt⌐ þurh° swefn° ond hine hālette° ond grētte° ond hine be
his noman nemnde°: 'Cedmon, sing mē hwæthwugu°.' Þā ondswarede hē ond

10 no one however   **11** taught the art of song   **12** divinely helped received
13 therefore never   **15** secular life settled time   **16** at (a) feast   **17** in   **18** turn
with saw approach   **19** shame feast went   **21** of cattle shed of which the care
assigned   **22** appropriate limbs settled fell asleep   **23** in dream hailed greeted
24 called something

10 **him þæt gelīce dōn meahte** 'could do it (*þæt*) like him [dat.]'; *meahte* is sbj., for hypothesis.

10–11 **nales from monnum ne þurh mon** Bede emphasises the divine nature of Cædmon's gift with this echo of Gal 1.1: 'Paul, an apostle, *not by men, neither by man*, but by Jesus Christ and God the Father, who raised him from the dead'.

13–14 **nōht lēasunge ne īdles lēoþes** gen. of respect: 'nothing (by way) of frivolity or empty song'.   **efne þā ān þā ðe** lit. 'even those only, those which', i.e. 'those only which'.

14 **his þā æfstan ... singan** '(which it) befitted that pious tongue of his to sing' (*gedeofanade* for later WS *gedafenode*).

15–16 **hē se mon** Use of pron. as well as def. art. is redundant in ModE (as also in 73): 'the man'.   **gelȳfdre ylde** gen. of description: 'of advanced age'.

17 **þonne þǣr ... ealle scolden** lit. 'when a cause for merriment there had been decided, (namely) that they should all ...'. The awkward OE version again results from a translator's mistake with the Latin. Suggested rendering: 'when it had been decided that, for the sake of merriment, they should all ...'.

20 **sumre tīde** dat. of time: 'on a certain occasion'.

20–1 **wæs gongende** The form is continuous past but here renders a Latin pluperfect (*egressus esset*) and needs to be trans. as such: 'had gone'; but in 83, the same phr. has a fut. sense. Cf. also 97 and 105, where a simple past state is implied.   **þǣre neahte** dat. of time: 'that night'.

22 **ðā** A superfluous adv.

23 **stōd him ... æt** The prep. is separated from its (indir.) obj. pron.: 'stood next to him'.

25   cwæð: 'Ne con° ic nōht singan ond ic ⌐forþon of þeossum gebēorscipe ūt ēode
     ond hider gewāt°, forþon⌐ ic nāht singan ne cūðe°.' Eft° hē cwæð, sē ðe wið
     hine sprecende wæs: 'Hwæðre° þū meaht singan.' Þā cwæð hē: 'Hwæt sceal ic
     singan?' Cwæð hē: 'Sing mē ⌐frumsceaft⌐.' Þā hē ðā þās andsware onfēng, þā
     ongon° hē sōna° singan in herenesse° Godes scyppendes° þā fers° ond þā word
30   þe hē næfre gehȳrde°, ⌐þære endebyrdnes⌐ þis is:

> ⌐Nū⌐ sculon° herigean°   heofonrīces° weard°,
> meotodes° meahte°   ond his mōdgeþanc°,
> weorc° wuldorfæder°,   swā° hē ⌐wundra gehwæs,
> ēce° Drihten°,   or⌐ onstealde°.

25 know how **26** came could Again **27** Yet **29** began at once praise (of) the
creator verses **30** had heard **31** (we) must praise of the heavenly kingdom guardian
32 creator's power purpose of mind **33** action of the 'glory-father' how **34** eternal
Lord established

25–6 **forþon ... forþon** correl. conj. and adv.: 'For this reason ..., because ...'.
28 **frumsceaft** '(about) the beginning of creation'.
30 **þære endebyrdnes** 'the meaning of which'.
31 **Nū ...** The earliest known versions of this hymn, inserted into Latin copies of Bede's
work, are in a Northumbrian dialect. The following is preserved in Cambridge, University
Library, Kk. 5. 16, fol. 128v, a manuscript which can be dated precisely to 737, only two
years after Bede's death:

> Nū scylun hergan   hefaenrīcaes uard,
> metudæs maecti   end his mōdgidanc,
> uerc uuuldurfadur,   suē hē uundra gihuaes,
> ēci Dryctin,   or āstelidæ.
> Hē aērist scōp   aelda barnum
> heben til hrōfe   hāleg scepen;
> thā middungeard   monncynnæs uard,
> ēci Dryctin,   æfter tīadæ
> fīrum foldu,   frēa allmectig.

Several phonetic features of early Northumbrian are illustrated here, including the retention of 'unbroken' *a* before *r* + consonant (thus *barnum* not *bearnum*). Orthographical features include *ae*, with the letters not always joined as in later *æ*. There is only
one difference in vocabulary, in the fifth line, where *aelda barnum* 'for the children
of men' (which would closely correspond to a Lat. *filiis hominum*) is replaced in the
later, WS, version by *eorðan bearnum* 'for the children of the earth' (but see 35n,
below).
33–4 **wundra gehwæs ... or** 'the beginning (*or*) of all [lit. "each of"] marvels'; *or* is
given great emphasis at the head of 34b, alliterating with *ēce* in 34a.

35   Hē ǣrest° sceōp°   ⌐eorðan bearnum⌐

        heofon tō° hrōfe°,   hālig scyppend;

        þā° middangeard°   monncynnes° weard,

        ēce Drihten,   æfter tēode°

        ⌐fīrum foldan⌐,   frēa° ælmihtig.

40   Þā ārās hē from þǣm slǣpe ond ⌐eal þā þe⌐ hē slǣpende° song° fæste° in ge-

        mynde° hæfde, ond ⌐þǣm wordum⌐ sōna ⌐monig word in þæt ilce° gemet° Gode

        wyrðes songes⌐ tōgeþēodde°. Þā cōm hē on morgenne tō þǣm tūngerēfan°, þe his

        ealdormon° wæs; sægde° him hwylce° gife hē onfēng. Ond hē hine sōna tō þǣre

        abbudissan gelǣdde ond hire þā cȳðde° ond sægde. Þā heht° hēo gesomnian°

45   ealle þā gelǣredestan° men ond þā leorneras° ond ⌐him ondweardum⌐ hēt secgan

        þæt swefn ond þæt lēoð singan ⌐þæt ealra heora dōme gecoren wǣre, hwæt

        oððe hwonon þæt cumen wǣre⌐. Þā wæs him eallum gesegen°, ⌐swā swā hit

        wæs⌐, þæt him wǣre from Drihtne sylfum heofonlic gifu forgifen°. Þā rehton°

        hēo him ond sægdon sum hālig spell° ond godcundre lāre° word: bebudon° him

50   þā, gif hē meahte, þæt hē in swinsunge° lēoþsonges þæt gehwyrfde°. Þā hē ðā

        hæfde ⌐þā wīsan⌐ onfongne°, þā ēode hē hām tō his hūse ond cwōm° eft on

---

35 first created **36** as roof **37** then 'middle earth' (*i.e.* the world) *as* humankind's **38** made (*or* adorned) **39** lord **40** (while) sleeping had sung firmly **41** memory same manner **42** added estate steward **43** superior told what **44** explained commanded assemble **45** most learned scholars **47** seen (by +*d*) **48** given related **49** story teaching *gs* enjoined **50** melody should turn to *sbj* **51** accepted came

---

35 **eorðan bearnum** 'for the children of the earth' (i.e. humankind; for similar epithets, see 17/66, 19/24, etc). This interpretation, with *eorðan* as gen., is supported by the Latin version; *heofon* is then the single subj. of *scēop*. However, *eorðan* could be acc. and thus a first obj. of the vb., allowing a trans. of 35–6 as, 'He first created the earth for men, (and) heaven for a roof'.

39 **fīrum foldan** Either '(made/adorned) the earth for men', with *foldan* parallel with *middangeard* (37) as a second obj. of the vb., or '(made/adorned it [i.e. "middle-earth"]) for the men of the earth'.

40 **eal þā þe** 'all those (things) which'.

41–2 **þǣm wordum** 'to those words', governed by *tōgeþēodde* in 42. **monig word ...** **Gode wyrðes songes** To judge from the Latin, the intended meaning is: 'many words of song worthy of [lit. "to"] God'.

45 **him ondweardum** The translator mimics a Latin 'ablative absolute' construction, using the dat.: 'with them present'.

46–7 **þæt ealra ... cumen wǣre** 'so that by the judgement of all of them (it) could be decided what it [i.e. Cædmon's gift] was and (*oððe*) whence it had come'.

47–8 **swā swā hit wæs** 'just as it was'; i.e. as indeed was the case.

51 **þā wīsan** 'the matter' (*wīse* is a fem. *n*-noun, here acc. sing.), i.e. the task he had been set.

morgenne ond, ⌐þȳ betstan lēoðe¬ geglenged°, him° āsong° ond āgeaf° þæt him
beboden wæs.

55   Ðā ongan sēo abbudisse clyppan° ond lufigean° þā Godes gife in þǣm
men ond hēo hine þā monade° ond lǣrde° þæt hē woruldhād° ānforlēte° ond
munuchād° onfēnge, ond hē þæt wel° þafode°. Ond hēo hine in þæt mynster
onfēng⌐mid his gōdum¬ond hine geþēodde° tō gesomnunge° þāra Godes þēowa°
ond heht hine lǣran° þæt getæl° þæs hālgan° stǣres° ond spelles°. Ond hē
⌐eal þā¬ hē in gehȳrnesse° geleornian meahte ⌐mid hine gemyndgade¬ ond,

60   ⌐swā swā clǣne nēten eodorcende¬, in þæt swēteste lēoð gehwerfde°. Ond his
song ond his lēoð wǣron swā wynsumu° tō gehȳranne° þætte ⌐seolfan þā his
lārēowas¬ æt° his mūðe wreoton° ond leornodon. Song hē ǣrest be middangeardes gesceape° ond bī fruman° moncynnes ond eal þæt stǣr Genesis, þæt is
sēo ǣreste Moyses booc, ond eft° bī ūtgonge° Israhēla folces of Ægypta londe

65   ond bī ingonge° þæs gehātlandes° ond bī ōðrum monegum spellum ⌐þæs hālgan
gewrites canōnes bōca¬, ond bī Crīstes ⌐menniscnesse° ond bī his þrōwunge°
ond bī his ūpāstignesse°¬ in heofonas ond bī þæs Hālgan Gāstes° cyme° ond
þāra apostola lāre, ond eft bī þǣm dæge þæs tōweardan° dōmes° ond bī fyrhtu°
þæs tintreglican° wiites° ond bī swētnesse þæs heofonlecan rīces hē monig lēoð

70   geworhte. Ond swelce° ēac ōðer monig be þǣm godcundan fremsumnessum°
ond dōmum hē geworhte. In eallum þǣm hē geornlīce° gēmde° þæt hē men

52 adorned   to them   sang   gave back   **54** cherish   delight in   **55** urged   instructed   secular
life   abandon *sbj*   **56** monastic life   readily   consented to   **57** joined   community   servants
58 be taught   sequence   sacred   history   narrative   **59** listening   **60** turned   **61** delightful
hear   **62** from   wrote (down)   **63** creation   beginning   **64** then   exodus   **65** entry
promised land   **66** incarnation   passion   **67** ascension   Spirit's   coming   **68** future
judgement   terror   **69** infernal   torment   **70** likewise   blessings   **71** earnestly   took care

52 **þȳ betstan lēoðe** instr. phr.: 'with the best poetry'.

57 **mid his gōdum** 'with his possessions'; mistranslation of a Latin phr. meaning 'with
all her people'.

59 **eal þā** 'all those (things that)'.   **mid hine gemyndgade** 'remembered within
himself', or 'turned over in his mind'.

60 **swā swā... eodorcende** 'just like a clean beast chewing the cud'. According
to OT law, 'clean' animals are those such as cattle, sheep and goats which have cloven
(i.e. divided) hoofs, signifying discretion between good and evil, and which chew the cud
(i.e. food already partly digested), signifying meditation on God's law. See Lev 11.2–4 and
Deut 14.3–9.

61–2 **seolfan þā his lārēowas** 'those same teachers of his'.

65–6 **þæs hālgan gewrites canōnes bōca** A series of nouns in the gen.: 'of the books
of (*or* from) the canon of holy scripture'.

66–7 **menniscnesse... þrōwunge... ūpāstignesse** The original Latin has the resurrection inserted between the passion and the ascension in this list of the stages of Christ's
life, but it reached none of the OE manuscripts.

ātuge° ⌐from synna lufan ond māndǣda⌐ ond tō lufan ond tō geornfulnesse°
āwehte° gōdra dǣda. Forþon hē wæs se mon swīþe ǣfest ond ⌐regollecum
þēodscipum ēaðmōdlīce underþēoded⌐. Ond ⌐wið þǣm þā ðe⌐ in ōðre wīsan
75   dōn woldon, hē wæs mid welme° micelre° ellenwōdnisse° onbærned°. Ond hē
forðon ⌐fægre ænde⌐ his līf betȳnde° ond geendade°.

Forþon þā ⌐ðǣre tīde nēalǣcte⌐ his gewitenesse° ond forðfōre°, þā wæs hē
⌐fēowertȳnum dagum ǣr þæt hē wæs⌐ līchomlicre° untrymnesse° þrycced° ond
hefgad°, hwæðre ⌐tō þon gemetlīce þæt⌐ hē ealle þā tīd meahte ge° sprecan ge°
80   gongan°. Wæs þǣr in nēaweste° untrumra° monna hūs ⌐in þǣm⌐ heora þēaw°
wæs þæt hēo ⌐þā untrumran ond þā ðe æt° forðfōre° wǣron inlǣdon sceoldon⌐
ond him þǣr ætsomne° þegnian°. Þā bæd° hē his þegn° on ǣfenne þǣre neahte°
þe hē of worulde gongende wæs þæt hē in þǣm hūse him stōwe° gegearwode°
þæt hē gerestan meahte. Þā wundrode se þegn for hwon° hē ðæs° bæde, forþon
85   him þūhte° þæt his forðfōr swā nēah ne wǣre, dyde hwæðre swā swā hē cwæð
ond bibēad°. Ond ⌐mid þȳ⌐ hē ðā þǣr on reste ēode ond hē, ⌐gefēonde mōde⌐,
sumu þing ⌐mid him sprecende ætgædere° ond glēowiende° wæs þe þǣr ǣr inne
wǣron⌐, þā wæs ofer° middeneaht þæt hē frægn° hwæðer hēo° ǣnig ⌐hūsl⌐ inne

72 might draw *sbj* yearning for +*g*   **73** awoke   **75** fervour *ds* great   zeal *gs*   fired
76 concluded   ended   **77** departure   journey   forth (*i.e.* death)   **78** bodily *dsf* weakness
ds oppressed by   **79** burdened   both and   **80** walk   vicinity   infirm   custom   **81** near
death   **82** together   minister to   asked   attendant   night *gs*   **83** a place   should prepare
84 why   for that   **85** seemed   **86** commanded   **87** together   joking   **88** past   asked   they

72 **from synna lufan ond māndǣda** The double complement of *lufan* is broken up:
'from love of sin and wrongdoings'.

73–4 **regollecum þēodscipum ēaðmōdlīce underþēoded** 'humbly subject to the regular discipline(s)', i.e. 'to the monastic rule'. **wið þǣm þā ðe** 'against those, they who',
i.e. 'against those who'.

76 **fægre ænde** instr. phr.: 'with a beautiful end' (*ænde* for *ende*).

77 **ðǣre tīde nēalǣcte** impers. vb. with dat.: '(it) drew near to the time (of...)'.

78 **fēowertȳnum dagum ǣr** dat. of time, with the numeral declined as an adj. [§E3d]:
'fourteen days previously'. **þæt hē wæs** These superfluous words are best ignored in trans.

79 **tō þon gemetlīce þæt** 'to that extent [instr. phr.] mildly that', i.e. 'sufficiently mildly
that'.

80 **in þǣm** 'into which'.

81 **þā untrumran ... inlǣdon sceoldon** 'should bring the more infirm...'. The comp.
adj. *untrumran* is used as a noun; *inlǣdon* is inf. (for *inlǣdan*).

86 **mid þȳ** instr. phr.: 'when', correl. with *þā* in 88. **gefēonde mōde** instr. phr.: 'with
rejoicing heart'.

87–8 **mid him ... þe þǣr ǣr inne wǣron** 'with those who were already (*ǣr*) in there'.

88 **hūsl** 'eucharist (*or* housel)'. This is the consecrated bread and wine used in the
communion rite (itself called the eucharist), probably kept ready in the infirmary in case
they were suddenly needed by a dying monk.

hæfdon. Þā ondswarodon hēo ond cwǣdon: 'Hwylc þearf° is ðē° hūsles? Ne
90 þīnre forþfōre swā nēah is, nū° þū þus rōtlīce° ond þus glædlīce° tō ūs sprecende
eart.' Cwæð hē eft: 'Berað° mē hūsl tō.' Þā hē hit þā on honda hæfde, þā frægn
hē hwæþer hēo ealle ⌐smolt mōd ond būton eallum incan blīðe tō him hæfdon⌐.
Þā ondswaredon hȳ ealle ond cwǣdon þæt hēo nǣnigne° incan tō him wiston° ac
hēo ealle him swīðe blīðemōde° wǣron, ond hēo wrixendlīce° hine bǣdon þæt
95 hē him eallum blīðe wǣre. Þā ondswarade hē ond cwæð: 'Mīne brōðor, mīne
þā lēofan°, ic eom swīðe blīðemōd tō ēow ond tō eallum Godes monnum.' Ond
swā ⌐wæs hine getrymmende⌐ mid þȳ heofonlecan wegneste° ond him ⌐ōðres
līfes ingong⌐ gegearwode. Þā gȳt° hē frægn hū nēah þǣre tīde wǣre þætte þā
brōðor ārīsan scolden ond Godes lof° rǣran° ond heora ⌐ūhtsong⌐ singan. Þā
100 ondswaredon hēo: 'Nis hit feor tō þon°.' Cwæð hē: 'Teala!° Wuton° wē wel þǣre
tīde bīdan°.' Ond þā ⌐him gebæd⌐ ond hine° gesegnode° mid Crīstes rōdetācne°
ond his hēafod onhylde° tō þām bolstre° ond ⌐medmicel fæc⌐ onslēpte° ond
swā mid stilnesse° his līf geendade. Ond swā wæs geworden° ⌐þætte swā swā
hlūttre° mōde ond bilwitre° ond smyltre° wilsumnesse° Drihtne þēode°, þæt
105 hē ēac swylce swā⌐ smylte dēaðe middangeard ⌐wæs forlǣtende⌐ ond ⌐tō his
gesihðe⌐ becwōm°. ⌐Ond sēo tunge þe⌐ swā monig hālwende° word in þæs

89 need (of +*g*) for you **90** since cheerfully joyfully **91** Bring **93** no felt
94 kindly disposed (towards +*d*) in turn **96** beloved **97** 'journey-provisions' (*i.e.* the
eucharist) **98** further **99** praise lift up **100** that Good! Let us **101** await himself
signed sign of cross **102** lowered pillow fell asleep **103** peace (had) come about
104 pure innocent serene devotion had served **106** came salutary

92 **smolt mōd ... hæfdon** 'had a peaceful and cheerful (*blīðe*) spirit, without any rancour, towards him'.

97 **wæs hine getrymmende** '(he) was strengthened', with rflx. acc. pron. We would
expect the past part. *getrymmede*, rather than the pres. part. (though perhaps the sense is
'was being strengthened').

97–8 **ōðres līfes ingong** 'the entrance of [i.e. into] the next life'.

99 **ūhtsong** 'Matins', the office sung by the monks at about 2 or 3 a.m.; see
1/40n.

101 **him gebæd** 'prayed', with rflx. dat. pron.

102 **medmicel fæc** acc. of time: 'for a little while'.

103–5 **þætte swā swā ... þæt hē ēac swylce swā** The correl. *þæt* is redundant: 'that
just as ... so also he likewise ...'. A succession of dats. is used in the comparison ('with a
pure and innocent heart', etc).

105–6 **wæs forlǣtende** 'was leaving', i.e. 'left'. **tō his gesihðe** 'into his sight', i.e.
'into his presence', with *Drihtne* the acc. antec. of the pron.

106 **Ond sēo tunge þe** An apparent mistranslation of Lat. *illaque lingua* which, in the
context, ought to have been treated as an 'ablative' phr. ('and in the language'), not nom. It
is best to render it as though the OE were *ond mid þǣre tungan þe*: 'and, with the tongue
which ...'.

scyppendes lof gesette°, ⌜hē ðā swelce ēac þā ȳtmæstan° word in his herenisse°,
hine seolfne segniende° ond his gāst in his honda bebēodende°, betȳnde⌝. Ēac
swelce þæt is gesegen° þæt hē wǣre gewis° his seolfes forðfōre, ⌜of þǣm wē nū
110   secgan hȳrdon⌝.

107 (had) composed   last   praise   **108** crossing   commending   **109** seen   aware (of +g)

107–8 **hē ðā swelce ēac ... betȳnde** Not only does the vb. follow its subj. (*hē*) and obj.
(*þā ȳtmæstan word*), but it is also separated from them by a double subord. clause (*hine
seolfne ... bebēodende*): 'he then also likewise concluded ...'.
109–10 **of þǣm ... hȳrdon** 'from what we just now [i.e. in this narrative] have heard'.

10

The Battle of Brunanburh

Two of the seven extant versions of the *Anglo-Saxon Chronicle* (see p. 61) have the following brief entry for the year 937: 'In this year Athelstan and Edmund his brother led levies to Brunanburh and there fought with Olaf, and with the help of Christ they had the victory'. It was one episode out of many in an unceasing struggle between Wessex and its northern and western enemies during the tenth century and might have gone unremarked. But the other five versions of the *Chronicle* expand on the entry with an ardently nationalistic poem of seventy-three lines which celebrates the battle at Brunanburh as a decisive English triumph. There King Athelstan and his brother Edmund, leading the armies of Wessex and Mercia, overcame a combined force of Norsemen from Dublin led by Olaf (*Anláf* in the text), Scots under King Constantine III, and Britons from Strathclyde. Although the main events of the battle are corroborated in various later annals and histories, and in a much later Norse saga, the location of Brunanburh is not known for certain. It must have been quite near the English west coast, however, at some point between Chester and the Scottish border, and a plausible case has been made for Bromborough in the Wirral, Cheshire, in which case the 'Dingesmere' mentioned in the poem is likely to be the River Dee.

Some critics have suggested that the poet of *Brunanburh* was influenced by Latin or Norse panegyrics (laudatory verses about aristocrats or heroes), but the poem's emphasis is on English nationalism in an historical perspective, rather than on individual heroics, and nothing specific is said about Athelstan's feats (cf. the treatment of ealdorman Byrhtnoth in *The Battle of Maldon*, Text 30). *Brunanburh* concludes with an historical allusion which links the present victors to the conquering ancestral Anglo-Saxons of the fifth century. From this continuity the poet builds a sense of national destiny, using the style, diction and imagery of heroic poetry. Thus the king of Wessex is 'lord of men' (*eorla drihten*, 1), which is varied with 'ring-giver of warriors' (*beorna bēahgifa*, 2), and the original Anglo-Saxons themselves are 'proud war-smiths' (*wlance wigsmiþas*, 72) and 'glory-eager men' (*eorlas ārhwate*, 73). Several of the poet's stock phrases are shared with *Beowulf* (as noted below) and the 'beasts of battle' motif is used to full effect (60–5). We do not know whether the poem about Brunanburh was written specifically for inclusion in the *Chronicle*, or indeed how long after the battle it was written. It is interesting to compare the poet's perception of the fifth-century invasions as an Anglo-Saxon triumph with Bede's representation of them as a disaster for the native British, being retribution from God for their moral backsliding (Text 9a). Although there is a formulaic mention of the sun as 'God's candle' in the poem (15), the poet shows no interest in giving his poem a Christian perspective.

The text below is printed from the 'Parker' manuscript (Cambridge, Corpus Christi College 173), the oldest surviving version of the *Chronicle*, begun in the last years of the ninth century and continued at intervals, in Winchester, throughout the tenth; the annal for 937 was presumably written around mid-century. Various early WS spellings are preserved among later ones. Notably, the preterite plural verb-ending occurs as *-un* six times (10, 22, 27, 28, 47 and 48), but the ending is *-on* four times (4, 9, 24 and 58) and occurs eleven times in the later 'levelled' form, *-an* (5, 6, 12, etc); similarly, *o* occurs for *a* before nasal consonants three times (*condel*, 15, *ondlongne*, 21, and *hondplegan*, 25), but elsewhere the vowel is *a* (*land*, 9, 27 and 59, *campstede*, 29 and 49, etc). The dative ending *-um* is weakened four times, in *lāfan* (6), *mǣcan* and *gemānan* (40; see note) and *wundun* (43). The form *gīeta* (66) is early WS in its diphthong (cf. later *gȳt*); the final *-a* is characteristic of poetical use. Several corrections have been made in the edited text below, mostly with reference to an eleventh-century copy of the *Chronicle* in London, British Library, Cotton Tiberius B. i.

Further reading

R. Flower and H. Smith, eds., *The Parker Chronicle and Laws*, EETS 208 (London, 1941)

A. Campbell, ed., *The Battle of Brunanburh* (London, 1938)

B. J. Muir, *Leoð: Six Old English Poems: a Handbook* (New York, 1989)

J. McN. Dodgson, 'The Background of Brunanburh', *Saga Book of the Viking Society* 14 (1953/7), 303–16

A. S. Colman, 'The Rhetoric of *Brunanburh*', *PQ* 48 (1969), 166–77

J. McN. Dodgson, *The Place-Names of Cheshire* IV, English Place-Name Society 47 (Cambridge, 1972)

J. D. Niles, 'Skaldic Technique in *Brunanburh*', *Scandinavian Studies* 59 (1987), 356–66

P. Orton, 'On the Transmission and Phonology of *The Battle of Brunanburh*', *LSE* n.s. 24 (1994), 1–28

J. Thormann, 'The *Anglo-Saxon Chronicle* Poems and the Making of the English Nation', in *Anglo-Saxonism and the Construction of Social Identity*, ed. A. J. Frantzen and J. D. Niles (Gainesville, FL, 1997), pp. 60–85

N. J. Higham, 'The Context of Brunanburh', in *Names, Places and People: an Onomastic Miscellany in Memory of John McNeal Dodgson*, ed. A. R. Rumble and A. D. Mills (Stamford, 1997), pp. 144–56

⌐Hēr Æþelstān cyning¬ eorla° dryhten,   of men
beorna° bēahgifa° ond his brōþor ēac°,   warriors'   ring-giver   also
Ēadmund æþeling°, ealdorlangne° tīr°   prince life-long glory *as*
geslōgon° æt sæcce° ⌐sweorda ecgum¬   won   battle
5 ymbe° Brūnanburh. Bordweal° clufan°,   at (*or* near) Shield-wall *as* (they) split
hēowan° heaþolinde° ⌐hamora lāfan¬,   hacked   linden-shields *ap*
afaran° Ēadweardes, swā° him° geæþele° wæs   sons *np* as in them inborn
⌐from cnēomægum°¬ þæt hī æt campe° oft   (their) ancestors   combat
wiþ° lāþra° gehwæn° land ealgodon°,   against of foes each +*g* defended
10 hord° ond hāmas°. Hettend° crungun°,   treasure-hoard homes Enemies fell
⌐Sceotta lēoda ond scipflotan¬
fæge° fēollan, feld° ⌐dænede¬   fated   field
⌐secga swāte¬ ⌐siðþan sunne ūp
on morgentīd°, mære° tungol°,   morning glorious star
15 glād ofer grundas¬, Godes condel° beorht°,   candle bright
⌐ēces° Drihtnes¬, oð° sīo æþele° gesceaft°   eternal until noble creation
sāh° tō setle°. Þær læg° secg° mænig   sank rest lay (a) man
gārum° āgēted°, ⌐guma norþerna¬   by spears destroyed

1 **Hēr** 'Here', the characteristic introduction to entries in the *Chronicle* (see Text 8). It is metrically redundant and presumably was not part of the original poem. **Æþelstān** As the poet notes in 3, Athelstan (924–39) was brother to Edmund, who succeeded him as king (939–46) and was sixteen at the time of the battle. We learn in 7 that their father was Edward the Elder (899–924).

4 **sweorda ecgum** dat. of instrument: 'by the edges of swords'. The poet uses many dat. expressions: see next note and 13 (*swāte*), 18 (*gārum*), 24 (*mēcum*), 30 (*sweordum*), 43 (*wundun*), etc.

6 **hamora lāfan** 'with the legacies [dat. pl.] of hammers'; i.e. swords forged by the blacksmith's hammer. This was a popular figure among OE poets: see 35a/7 and *Beowulf* (2829).

8 **from cnēomægum** Their most illustrious forebear was their grandfather, Alfred (871–99).

11 **Sceotta lēoda ond scipflotan** 'People of the Scots and seamen (*i.e.* Vikings)'. These formed the two major elements of the attacking force. The poet does not mention the Strathclyde Britons, whom we know about from other sources.

12 **dænede** 'flowed'. A vb. *dennian*, 'flow' or 'stream', is conjectured here; in the manuscript a second *n* has been added above the line. Some editors emend to *dunnode*, pret. of *dunnian* 'darken'.

13 **secga swāte** dat. of manner: 'with the blood of men'. This is the most satisfactory emendation of the manuscript's *secgas hwate*.

13–15 **siðþan sunne ūp ... glād ofer grundas** 'from when ... the sun glided aloft (*ūp*) over the earth [lit. "grounds"]'. The battle lasted from sunrise to sunset.

16 **ēces Drihtnes** Parallel with *Godes* in 15.

18 **guma norþerna** To be construed with *mænig* in 17: 'many a north man (*i.e.* Norseman)'. The same must be done with *Scittisc* in 19.

ofer° scild scoten°, swilce° Scittisc° ēac,	above hit likewise Scots(man)
20 wērig, wīges° sæd°. ⌐Wesseaxe⌐ forð°	battle *gs* sated (with +*g*) onwards
⌐ondlongne dæg⌐ ēorodcistum°	in (their) troops
⌐on lāst legdun lāþum þēodum⌐,	
hēowan heref/ēman° hindan° þearle°	fugitives *ap* from behind violently
⌐mēcum mylenscearpan⌐. Myrce° ⌐ne wyrndon	Mercians
25 heardes hondplegan hæleþa nānum	
þæra þe⌐ mid ⌐Anlāfe⌐ ofer æra° gebland°	of waves turmoil
on lides° bōsme° land gesōhtun°,	ship's bosom invaded
fæge° tō gefeohte. Fīfe lægun°	fated (men) lay (dead)
on þām campstede° cyningas giunge°,	battlefield young
30 sweordum āswefede°, swilce seofene ēac	'put to sleep'
eorlas Anlāfes, unrīm° heriges°	(and) a countless number the army *gs*
⌐flotan⌐ ond Sceotta. Þær geflēmed° wearð°	put to flight was
Norðmanna bregu°, nēde° gebēded°,	chief by necessity forced
tō lides stefne° ⌐lītle weorode⌐;	prow *ds*
35 crēad° cnear° on flot°, cyning ūt gewāt°	hastened boat sea went
on fealene° flōd°, feorh° generede°.	grey tide life saved
Swilce þær ēac se frōda° mid° flēame° cōm°	wise (man) in flight went
on his cȳþþe° ⌐norð⌐, ⌐Costontīnus⌐;	native land
hār° hilderinc° hrēman° ne þorfte°	hoary warrior to exult had cause
40 ⌐mæcan gemānan⌐. Hē wæs his mæga° sceard°,	kinsmen *gp* bereft of

20 **Wesseaxe** Assimilated form of *Westseaxe*: 'the West Saxons'.

21 **ondlongne dæg** acc. of duration of time: 'for the entire day'.

22 **on lāst legdun lāþum þēodum** Unique idiom using *lecgan* ('lie') and poss. dat.: 'followed in the track (*or* pursued the trail) of the hostile peoples'.

24 **mēcum mylenscearpan** instr. dat.: 'with swords mill-sharp', i.e. 'sharpened by the grindstone'.

24–6 **ne wyrndon ... nānum þæra þe** The vb. takes a gen. obj.: 'did not withhold hard hand-to-hand combat from any [lit. "none"] of the warriors who...'. **Anlāfe** 'Olaf' was leader of the Vikings from Dublin.

32 **flotan** We would expect gen. pl., *flotena*, parallel with *Sceotta*: '(the army) of sailors (Vikings)'.

34 **lītle weorode** instr. of accompaniment: 'with little company'.

38 **norð** adv.: '(went) north'. **Costontīnus** Constantine III was king of the united Picts and Scots.

40 **mæcan gemānan** '(about) the shared swords', i.e. about the battle, taking -*an* as the dat. pl. inflection -*um* on both noun and adj. The vb. *hrēman* usually governs the gen., and two other manuscripts indeed have *mēc(e)a gemānan*, '(about) the meeting of swords' (treating *gemānan* as a noun).

⌐frēonda gefylled⌐ on folcstede°   battlefield
beslagen° æt sæcce ond his sunu° forlēt°   struck down sons left
on wælstōwe° wundun forgrunden°,   place of slaughter destroyed (by +*d*)
giungne° æt gūðe. Gelpan° ne þorfte   young (men) To boast (of +*g*)
45 beorn° blandenfeax° bilgeslehtes°,   warrior *ns* grey-haired sword-clash *gs*
eald inwidda°, ⌐ne Anlāf þȳ mā⌐.   malicious foe *ns*
Mid° heora herelāfum° hlehhan° ne   Among 'army-remnants' to rejoice
þorftun
þæt hēo° ⌐beaduweorca beteran wurdun⌐   they
on campstede cumbolgehnāstes°,   clash of standards
50 gārmittinge°, gumena gemōtes°,   meeting of spears encounter
wǣpengewrixles°, ⌐þæs⌐ hī on wælfelda° exchange of weapons field of slaughter
wiþ Ēadweardes afaran plegodan°.   contended
Gewitan° ⌐him⌐ þā Norþmen nægledcnearrum°, Departed in (their) nailed ships
drēorig° ⌐daraða lāf⌐, on ⌐Dinges-Mere⌐   sad
55 ofer dēop wæter Difelin° sēcan°   Dublin to make for
eft° Īraland, æwiscmōde°.   again humiliated
Swilce þā gebrōþer° bēgen° ætsamne°,   brothers both together
cyning ond æþeling, cȳþþe sōhton,
Wesseaxena land, wīges hrēmige°.   exulting (in +*g*)
60 Lētan° him behindan hrǣ° bryttian°   (They) left corpses *ap* to divide out
saluwigpādan°, þone sweartan° ⌐hræfn⌐,   dark-plumaged black
hyrnednebban°, ond þane hasewanpādan°   horny-beaked dusky-coated
⌐earn æftan hwīt⌐, ǣses° ⌐brūcan°⌐,   carrion to enjoy +*g*
grǣdigne° gūðhafoc° ond þæt grǣge° dēor°, greedy war-hawk grey beast

41 **frēonda gefylled** The noun is parallel with *mǣga* as a complement of *sceard*: '(bereft of kinsmen,) of friends felled . . .'.

46 **ne Anlāf þȳ mā** 'nor Olaf the more (instr. *þȳ*)', i.e. 'and no more did Olaf'.

48 **beaduweorca beteran wurdun** 'were (*or* had been) superior in battle-deeds'. The gen. of comparison is continued in the next three lines: *beteran . . . cumbolgehnastes, garmittinge*, etc.

51 **þæs** Best trans. as the conj. 'after' or 'because'.

53 **him** Reflx. dat. pron. with vb. of motion, best left untranslated.

54 **daraða lāf** 'the . . . remnant of spears'; i.e. those left untouched by the spears. **Dinges-Mere** Apparently the name of an estuary somewhere on the west coast of England, opposite Ireland; perhaps the River Dee (see headnote).

61 **hræfn** The 'raven' (the first of four 'beasts of battle' to be introduced) is the acc. obj. of *lētan* and has been left behind to divide up the corpses; *saluwigpādan, sweartan* and *hyrnednebban* all describe it.

63 **earn æftan hwīt** 'the eagle white from behind', i.e. with white tail. **brūcan** Like *bryttian* in 60, *brūcan* is governed by *lētan*.

65	wulf on° wealde°. ⌐Ne wearð wæl māre	from forest

65 wulf on° wealde°. ⌐Ne wearð wæl māre — from forest
    on þis ēiglande æfre gīeta° — yet
    folces gefylled⌐ beforan þissum
    sweordes ecgum, ⌐þæs þe⌐ ūs secgað bēc°, — books
    ealde ūðwitan°, ⌐siþþan⌐ ēastan hider — authorities
70 Engle ond Seaxe ūp° becōman° — ashore came
    ofer brād brimu° Brytene sōhtan°, — ocean sought out
    wlance° wīgsmiþas° Wēalas° ofercōman, — proud 'war-smiths' Welshmen
    eorlas ārhwate° eard begēatan°. — eager for glory acquired

65–7 **Ne wearð... folces gefylled** *folces* is best treated as dependent on *wæl*: 'Never yet ... had there been a greater slaughter of people killed ...'.

68 **þæs þe** 'according to what'.

69 **siþþan** 'since ...'. The poet refers back to the events of the fifth century, as recorded by the British historian Gildas – and noted by Bede (9a/*passim*) and Wulfstan (25/146–54), when the Angles, Saxons and other continental tribes began to settle at the expense of the native Britons.

11
The Will of Ælfgifu

There are some sixty vernacular documents of varying length which may loosely be described as Anglo-Saxon 'wills'. They were made by kings and ecclesiastics as well as laymen and laywomen. The beneficiaries may be family and friends when personal effects are involved, but in the case of land, it is the church or monastery which usually benefits. Because such institutions needed to maintain a record of dispositions, to guard against possible litigation over their property, many wills survive only as copies in 'cartularies' – volumes of charters kept by the churches. The 'Codex Wintoniensis' (now London, British Library, Additional 15350) is the cartulary of St Swithun's, Winchester, written in the first half of the twelfth century. Among the items there is the will of Ælfgifu. This woman has not been positively identified, but she was probably of royal descent and it has been conjectured that she was married to (but then divorced from) King Eadwig (957–9). Her will can be dated between 966 and 975 for two main reasons. First, she makes a bequest to Romsey Abbey in Hampshire, and this is likely to have been after the old foundation was re-established by King Edgar in 967. Second, the *Liber Eliensis* – 'Book of Ely', a twelfth-century compilation treating the history of Ely Abbey in Cambridgeshire – tells us that Edgar gave to Ely the estate at *Meassewyrthe*, which Ælfgifu, as she says (lines 13–15), left to him at her death; in other words, she must have died before Edgar.

Although Anglo-Saxon wills are the predecessors of the modern 'last will and testament', they are not documents which formally effect the transfer of bequests; they are more like written memoranda of the declared intention to make such transfer. Their oral character (attested by the use of *cwydes* in line 2) reflects their origin in Germanic legal practice.

The extant copy of Ælfgifu's will is full of unusual spellings, though it is not clear how many are original and how many due to the idiosyncrasies of its late copyist. The most prevalent is *æ* for *e*, whether medial or terminal, long or short (*Ælfgyfæ*, 1, *Godæs*, 2, *þǣ*, 3 and 26, *pæniga*, 28, and so on), and in fact, if this is ignored, the language is fairly conventional late WS. Other orthographical peculiarities include *ð* for *d* in *geþēowuð* (8), *cynehlāforð* (24, but cf. *cinehlāford*, 32), and *ig* for *ic* (26). Consonants intrude in *mandcussa* (8, but cf. *mancussa*, 10) and *ǣlchum* (28); the latter shows how the palatalised ('soft') *c* would in future be written, under the influence of Norman French practice. Loss of *n* from the possessive pronoun, as in *mīræ* (26, for *mīnre*), is frequent in late WS (and occurs also in 12/8). All the manuscript's spellings are retained here.

Establishing the uninflected forms of the place-names given in the will is not always possible, for several with apparent dat. pl. inflection here are unrecorded in any other form; thus *Hrisanbeorgan* (6), *Baþum* (13; see note) and *Weowungum* (13). As commonly happens in WS, most names with the second element *-hām*, and others, are endingless in the 'locatival' dative [§B6c]; thus *æt Wichām* (12), *æt Hæfæreshām* (14) and *æt Gyssīc* (15).

Further reading

D. Whitelock, ed. and trans., *Anglo-Saxon Wills* (Cambridge, 1930)

B. Danet and B. Bogoch, 'From Oral Ceremony to Written Document: the Transitional Language of Anglo-Saxon Wills', *Language and Communication* 12 (1992), 95–122

K. A. Lowe, 'The Nature and Effect of the Anglo-Saxon Vernacular Will', *Journal of Legal History* 19 (1998), 23–61

ÞIS ys Ælfgyfæ° gegurning° tō hiræ cinehlāfordæ°: þæt is þæt hēo hyne bitt° for Godæs lufun° and ⌐for cynescypæ⌐ þæt hēo mōte° bēon ⌐hyre cwydes wyrðæ⌐. Þonnæ cȳð° hēo þǣ° lēof°, bæ þīnre geþafiunga°, hwæt hēo for þǣ and for þȳræ° sāwlæ° tō Godæs ciricean dōn° wylæ. Þæt is ǣræst° þæt hēo ann° intō° ⌐Ealdan Mynstær⌐, þær hēo ⌐hiræ līcaman ræstan⌐ þæncþ°, þæs landæs æt Hrisanbeorgan° eallswā° hit stænt°, būton° þæt hēo wylæ bæ þīnre geþafunga

5

1 Ælfgifu's desire royal lord entreats **2** love *ds* [*lufan*] may **3** makes known to you lord consent **4** your [*þȳnre*] soul give first grants +*g* to **5** intends **6** Risborough just as stands except

2 for cynescypæ 'for (the sake of his) royal power'. **hyre cwydes wyrðæ** 'worthy of her will', i.e. that she may be entitled to make it. More common meanings of *cwyde* include 'saying' or 'speech'.

5 Ealdan Mynstær Winchester, in the heart of Wessex, was the site of a Roman city. The church known later as the 'Old Minster' was built in 648 and became a cathedral soon after. Two more foundations, the New Minster (see 9) and the Nunnaminster (see 10; later St Mary's Abbey), were built early in the tenth century, both of them planned by King Alfred (*d.* 899), whose capital the expanding city had become. There are gifts for these foundations also in Ælfgifu's will, below. **hiræ līcaman ræstan** 'to rest her body'; i.e. be buried.

þæt man frēoge° on ælcum tūnæ° ⌐ælne wītæþǣownæ mann⌐ þæ ⌐undær hiræ geþēowuð⌐ wæs, ⌐and twā hund mandcussa goldæs⌐ tō þām mynstær and ⌐hire scrīn⌐ mid hiræ hāligdōmæ°. And hēo an inntō Nīgean° Mynstær þæs landæs æt
10   Bleddanhlǣwe° and hund mancussa goldæs and ānnæ offringdisc° intō Nunna° Mynstær and þæs landæs æt Hwætædūnæ° ⌐intō Rummæsigæ Xrīste and Sanctan Mārian⌐, and æt° Cæstæleshammæ° ⌐intō Abbandūnæ⌐ and æt Wichām° ⌐intō Baþum⌐. And ic ann mīnæn cinæhlāfordæ þæs landæs æt Weowungum° and æt Hlincgeladæ° and æt Hæfæreshām° and æt Hæðfælda° and æt Mæssan-
15   wyrðæ° and æt Gyssīc°, and ⌐twēgea bǣagas⌐ (ǣigþær° ys ⌐on hundtwælftigum mancussum⌐) and ānræ ⌐sopcuppan⌐ and syx horsa and ⌐swā fala⌐ scylda and spæra. And ⌐þām æþelingæ⌐ þæs landæs æt Nīwanhām° and ānæs bēages on þrītægum° mancussum. And ⌐þæra hlǣfdigan⌐ ānæs swȳrbēages° on hundtweltifgum mancussum and ānæs bēages on þrītegum mancussum and

7 set free *sbj* estate   9 relics New   10 Bledlow   offering-dish (*or* paten)   Nuns'
11 Whaddon   12 (the land) at   Chesham   Wickham   13 Wing   14 Linslade   Haversham
Hatfield   15 Masworth   Gussage   'either' (*i.e.* both)   17 Newnham   18 thirty   necklace

7 **ælne wītæþǣownæ mann** 'each (*ealne*) penally enslaved man'; i.e. each man reduced to slavery as a punishment by law.

7–8 **undær hiræ geþēowuð** 'enslaved (*geþēowod*) under her', i.e. 'subject to her' (i.e. to Ælfgifu herself).   **and twā hund mandcussa goldæs** 'and (she grants) two hundred mancuses of gold'. The mancus was a gold coin equivalent to the weight of thirty silver pence.

8–9 **hire scrīn** 'her shrine' (acc. sg.): probably a box ornamented with gems and precious metals.

11–12 **intō Rummǣsigæ … Mārian** 'to (the nunnery of) Christ and St Mary at Romsey'. This was a Benedictine house, in Hampshire, re-established by King Edgar in 967. The inflexion on *Sanctan* is weak [§C2], presumably to match that of *Mārian* (dat. sg.); cf. 7b/50n.

12 **intō Abbandūnæ** The monastery at Abingdon (Berkshire) had been reformed by Æthelwold, one of the three key figures of the Benedictine Reform movement, who became bishop of Winchester in 963. He is mentioned again in 20.

13 **intō Baþum** King Edgar may have restored or reformed the monastery at Bath. See further 37/headnote. *Baþum* is a dat. pl. form, perhaps originally, '(place) with the baths'.

15 **twēgea bǣagas** 'two bracelets (*or* armlets)'. There is lack of concord here; the vb. *ann* governs the gen. and *twēgea*, used as an adj., has the gen. form but *bǣagas* is acc. pl. (cf. correct *ānræ sopcuppan*, 16, *ānæs bēages*, 17–18, etc).

15–16 **on hundtwælftigum mancussum** 'of (*or* worth) one hundred and twenty mancuses'. On the numeral see §E3b.

16 **sopcuppan** Apparently a special sort of cup in which a *sop*, a piece of bread soaked in wine or water, could be made.   **swā fala** 'as many (*fela*, with gen. pl.)', i.e. six.

17 **þām æþelingæ** 'to the prince'. Probably Edgar's son, Edward the Martyr (see p. 62).

18 **þæra hlǣfdigan** 'to the lady' (*þæra* for *þēre*, dat. sg. fem.); i.e. the atheling's wife.

20   ānre sopcuppan. And ic ann Aþelwoldæ bisceopæ þæs landæs æt ⌜Tæafersceat⌝
and bidde hinæ þæt hǣ symlie° þingiæ° for mīnæ mōdor an° for mē. And ic
ann bæ mīnæs hlāfordæs geþafiungæ þæs landæs æt Mundingwillæ° and æt
Beorhþanstædæ° Ælfwerdæ and Æþelwærdæ and Ælfwaræ ⌜him tō gemanan
hira dæg⌝ and ofær° hira dæg intō Ealdan Mynstær for mīnnæ cynehlāforð
25   and for mē. And ⌜syllan hī⌝ ælcæ gēare ⌜twā dægfæorman⌝ intō ⌜þām twām
mynstrum þā wīlæ þæ hī his brūcæn⌝. And ig° an Ælfwæræ mīræ swystær
eallæs þæs þæ ic hiræ ālēnæð° hæfdæ and Æþælflledæ mīnæs brōþur wīfæ þæs
bændes° þæ ic hire ālǣneð hæfdæ. And ælchum abbodæ° fīf pund° pæniga° tō
hira mynstres bōte°. And, lēof, be þīnre geþafiunga þæt° ic mōtæ bætæcen° þām
30   bisceope and þām abbodæ þonæ ofærēacan° tō þǣre stōwe° bōtæ and ⌜earmum
mannum for mē tō dǣlænne swā swā him þincæ þæt mǣ for Godæ þearflucustþ
sī⌝. And ic biddæ mīnnæ cinelāford for Godæs lufum þæt næ forlǣte° mīnæ
mænn ⌜þe hinæ gesǣcen⌝ and him wyrðæ° sȳn. And ic ann Ælfwerdæ ānræ
sopcuppan and Æþelwerdæ ānæs gerǣnodæs° drincæhornæs°.

---

21 always intercede and [*and*]   **22** Mongewell   **23** Berkhampstead   **24** after   **26** I [*ic*]
27 loaned   **28** headband (*or* chaplet) abbot pound-weight of pennies   **29** benefit
(I wish) that entrust (to +*d*)   **30** surplus place's (*i.e.* minster's)   **32** he (not) abandon
33 worthy of +*d*   **34** ornamented drinking-horn

20 **Tæafersceat** An unidentified place.

23–4 **him tō gemanan hira dæg** '(to them) in common for their lifetime'; *dæg* is acc.
of duration of time, or possibly an uninflected dat. [§B1c], as later in this line. We learn
in 26 that Ælfwaru is Ælfgifu's sister and it is probable that the two men named are their
brothers. One of them is alluded to again in 27.

25 **syllan hī** For *syllen*, sbj. pres. 3rd-pers. pl., with optative meaning: 'let them give'.
twā dægfæorman 'two days' provisions'; a *dægfeorm* (*feorm* 'food' or 'sustenance') is a
gift of food sufficient for a community for one day.

25–6 **þām twām mynstrum** i.e. the Old and New Minsters.   **þā wīlæ þæ** 'as long as'
(*þā hwīle þe*).   **hī his brūcæn** 'they possess it (*his*)'; *brūcan* takes a gen. obj. The referent
of 'it' is the land described in 22–3.

30–2 **earmum mannum ... þearflucustþ sī** '(for them) to distribute to poor men for
me, as may seem (*þincæ*) to them (*him*) to be most advantageous (*þearflucustþ*) for me
before God'.

33 **þe hinæ gesǣcen** 'who seek him out'; i.e. go to him for protection.

12

The Fonthill Letter

The 'Fonthill Letter' is a record of the evidence submitted to King Alfred's son and successor, Edward the Elder (899–924), by the prominent nobleman Ordlaf in connection with the disputed ownership of a piece of land at Fonthill, south of Warminster in the southern county of Wiltshire, part of Wessex. Ordlaf was ealdorman of Wiltshire from 897. We can deduce that the events related occurred between 897 and 901, and that the undated letter was probably written between about 920 and 924. It is preserved on a single sheet of parchment now in the library of Canterbury Cathedral (Dean and Chapter, Chart. Ant. C. 1282 [Red Book, no. 12]), which appears to be an original document. As such, it offers us a unique first-person account of the working of Anglo-Saxon law at the end of the ninth century and the beginning of the tenth, revealing the extent to which Alfred had been personally involved in its administration. All the places named in the letter are in Wiltshire.

The matter of the letter, following the opening address to King Edward, is complex, and may be summarised as follows.

3–30. Ordlaf wants to give the Fonthill estate to the bishop of Winchester in exchange for another piece of land, but his entitlement to Fonthill is being disputed by one Æthelhelm Higa, among others. To obtain King Edward's confirmation of the arrangement, therefore, Ordlaf must explain the complex way in which he himself acquired the land. It had belonged to his godson Helmstan, who appears to be something of a rogue. The letter explains that it was after Helmstan had stole a belt (clearly a valuable one) that Æthelhelm (presumably seeing this as an opportune moment) proceeded to press his own (unexplained) claim to the Fonthill estate. At this point Helmstan asked his godfather Ordlaf to intercede with King Alfred. This he did, and the king obliged by ordering an arbitration hearing, and various men, including Ordlaf himself, were appointed to hear the arguments of both sides.

31–44. At the hearing, at Wardour, Helmstan produced documentary evidence that he had acquired the Fonthill estate from Oswulf, who received it from a woman called Æthelthryth, who received it from her husband. This seems to the arbitrators to settle the question of ownership and they are ready to allow Helmstan to take an oath in the matter, but Æthelhelm is not happy and insists that the case be referred to the king himself. When the arbitrators, along with Æthelhelm, arrive at the king's chamber, he is washing, but when he has finished and has heard the arguments, he backs the arbitrators' decision and sets a day for Helmstan to take a formal oath about the matter. On the appointed day the oath is successfully taken (that is, sufficient numbers of people

willing to swear on Helmstan's behalf have come forward), but meanwhile Helmstan, in order
to ensure the full support of his influential godfather Ordlaf, has promised to give *him* the title to
the Fonthill estate. This he now does, but Ordlaf agrees that his godson can continue to use the
estate, so long as he stays out of trouble.

45–65. But that is not Helmstan's way. Within two years (during which time Alfred has died
and been succeeded by Edward), he steals some oxen and is caught, and the king's official,
Eanwulf, confiscates in the king's name property which Helmstan owns at Tisbury, adjacent to
Fonthill. Ordlaf now takes over the Fonthill estate – which could not itself be forfeited because,
of course, Helmstan had relinquished title to it – and the king outlaws Helmstan. But the latter is
not finished yet. In an obscure move which apparently involves making another oath at Alfred's
grave and obtaining a seal as proof, Helmstan persuades King Edward to remove the outlawry
and give him another estate, to which he retires. Now Ordlaf has in turn given the Fonthill estate
to the bishop of Winchester in exchange for land elsewhere, and he needs Edward to confirm his
right to do this. Clearly the king does so, for we hear, finally, in the endorsement that Æthelhelm
has withdrawn his claim.

The Fonthill Letter provides an excellent illustration of the impact which
Alfred's educational programme had on lay literacy. The orthography is remarkably consistent, and this may reflect a layman making a conscious effort of the
sort which would not be made by a professional scribe. Furthermore, the relative
informality of the letter, compared with most other legal documents, allows us a
glimpse of the register of contemporary colloquial speech. Several linguistic features seem to confirm an early (i.e. contemporary, *c.* 920) date for composition,
such as *o* before nasals, rather than the usual *a* of late WS (*lond*, 5, *mon*, 20). Other
features, such as the contracted form *cing*(*e*) (7, 18, etc), *specan* for *sprecan* (4),
gēt for *giet* (56), and the dative ending *-an*, *-un* or *-on* for *-um*, are usually associated
with late WS, but they do not preclude an earlier date of composition. In line 8,
mīre for *mīnre* is also a noted feature of late WS (see 11/26); in line 54, *gesāhte*
is written for *gesōhte*. A number of interlinear restorations of omitted letters or
words, and two corrections on erasures, seem to have been made by the original
scribe when checking his work; the only omission he appears to have missed is *re*
in *ærest* (17). It will be noted that the writer favours the instrumental case after
the preposition *on* (17, 42 and 62), as well as after *innan* (26). In line 33, the text
between square brackets (some twelve characters) has been lost at a crease in the
single sheet of parchment. Similar losses in lines 31 and 32 have been made good
with conjectured reconstructions (see p. 348).

Further reading

S. Keynes, 'The Fonthill Letter', in *Words, Texts and Manuscripts. Studies in Anglo-Saxon
    Culture Presented to Helmut Gneuss on the Occasion of his Sixty-Fifth Birthday,*

ed. M. Korhammer, with the assistance of K. Reichl and H. Sauer (Cambridge, 1992), pp. 53–97 [edition, with translation and commentary]

P. Wormald, 'A Handlist of Anglo-Saxon Lawsuits', *ASE* 17 (1988), 247–81

M. Gretsch, 'The Language of the "Fonthill Letter"', *ASE* 23 (1994), 57–102

M. Boynton and S. Reynolds, 'The Author of the Fonthill Letter', *ASE* 25 (1996), 91–5

✠ Lēof°, ic ðē cȳðe° hū hit wæs ymb° ðæt lond æt Funtial, ðā fīf ⌐hīda⌐ ðe Æðelm Higa ymb° spycð°.

Ðā Helmstān ðā undæde° gedyde°, ðæt hē Æðerēdes belt forstæl°, ðā ongon° Higa ⌐him specan sōna° on⌐, mid ōðran onspecendan°, ond wolde him° oðflītan° 5 ðæt lond. Ðā sōhte° hē mē ond bæd° mē ðæt ic him wære° forespeca°, forðon° ⌐ic his hæfde ær onfongen⌐ æt biscopes honda ær hē ðā undæde gedyde. Ðā spæc ic him fore° ond ðingade° him tō° Ælfrede cinge. Ðā, God forgelde° his sāule, ⌐ðā lyfde hē ðæt hē mōste bēon ryhtes wyrðe, for° mīre forspæce° ond ryhtrace°, wið⌐ Æðelm ymb ðæt lond. ⌐Ðā hēt hē hīe sēman⌐. Ðā wæs ic ðāra 10 monna sum° ðe ðærtō° genemned° wæran, ond Wihtbord ond Ælfrīc (wæs ðā hrælðēn°) ond Byrhthelm ond ⌐Wulfhun ðes blāca æt Sumortūne⌐ ond Strica ond Ubba ond mā° monna ðonne ic nū genemnan mæge.

1 Sir inform concerning **2** about speaks **3** crime committed stole began **4** at once claimants from him obtain by litigation **5** approached asked should be intercessor because **7** on behalf of (+*d*) interceded (for +*d*) with reward *sbj* **8** because of advocacy **9** true account **10** one (of +*gp*) for that named **11** 'clothing-thane' (master of the wardrobe) **12** more +*gp*

1 **hīda** A 'hide' was usually about twenty acres.

4 **him specan . . . on** 'to bring a charge against him' (lit. 'speak against').

6 **ic his hæfde ær onfongen** 'I had previously received him [lit. "of him"] from the bishop's hand'; i.e. the writer had 'stood sponsor' for Helmstan when he was confirmed in the church. Helmstan is thus Ordlaf's godson.

8–9 **ðā lyfde hē . . . ryhtes wyrðe . . . wið** 'he [the king] allowed that he [Helmstan] might be worthy of justice against', i.e. 'he allowed him to be entitled to prove his right against'; *ðā* is best om. in trans.

9 **Ðā hēt hē hīe sēman** 'Then he [the king] commanded them [Helmstan and Æthelhelm] to reconcile themselves' or 'be brought to an agreement'.

11 **Wulfhun ðes blāca æt Sumortūne** 'Wulfhun the Black of Somerton'. Nothing is known of this intriguing man.

Ðā reahte° heora ǣgðer° his spell°. Ðā ðūhte° ūs eallan ðæt Helmstān mōste
gān° forð mid ðon bōcon° ond geāgnigean° him° ðæt lond, ⌐ðæt hē hit hæfde⌐
15 swā° Æðeldrȳð hit ⌐Ōsulfe on æht⌐ gesealde° wið° gemēdan° fēo°, ond hēo
cwæð tō Ōsulfe ðæt ⌐hēo hit āhte him wel tō syllanne⌐, forðon hit wæs ⌐hire
morgengifu⌐ ðā° hēo ǣrest ⌐tō Aðulfe cōm⌐. Ond Helmstān ðis eal on° ðon
āðe° befēng°. Ond Ælfred cing ðā Ōsulfe his hondsetene° sealde°, ðā hē ðæt
lond æt° Æðeldrȳðe bōhte, ⌐ðæt hit swā stondan mōste⌐, ond Ēadweard ⌐his⌐
20 ond Æðelnāð his ond Deormōd his ⌐ond ǣlces ðāra monna ðe mon ðā habban
wolde⌐. Ðā wē hīe° ⌐æt Weardoran⌐ nū sēmdan°, ðā bǣr° mon ðā bōc° forð ond
rǣdde hīe. Ðā stōd ⌐sēo hondseten eal ðǣron⌐. Ðā ðūhte ūs eallan ðe æt ðǣre
sōme° wǣran ðæt Helmstān wǣre ⌐āðe ðæs ðē nēar⌐.

Ðā næs Æðelm nā fullīce° geðafa° ǣr wē ēodan° in ⌐tō cinge⌐ ond sǣdan eall
25 hū wē hit reahtan° ond ⌐be hwȳ⌐ wē hit reahtan, ond Æðelm stōd sylf ðǣrinne

13 related both story (it) seemed (to) **14** go charters *dp* prove his right to (+*a*) for
himself **15** just as had given for suitable price **17** when in **18** oath included
signature gave **19** from **21** them were settling brought charter **23** arbitration
24 fully in agreement went **25** had decided

14 ðæt hē hit hæfde '(namely) that he had possessed it...'. Thus begins the explanation of how Helmstan had acquired the disputed land in good faith. He received it from
Æthelthryth, just as she received it, at a fair price, from Oswulf.

15 Ōsulfe on æht 'to Oswulf into possession', i.e. 'into Oswulf's possession'.

16 hēo hit āhte him wel tō syllanne 'she possessed it fully (*wel*) for selling to him';
i.e. it was her property to sell as she pleased.

16–17 hire morgengifu 'her morning gift'; see 7a/49n.

17 tō ... cōm 'married'.

19 ðæt hit swā stondan mōste 'that it might remain thus'. Alfred with his seal had
endorsed Oswulf's purchase of the Fonthill land, and its validity was further confirmed by
the noblemen named as witnesses to the transaction. Edward is presumably Edward the
Elder, who succeeded his father Alfred as king.   **his** i.e. his signature (as in the next two
occurrences also).

20–1 ond ǣlces ... wolde 'and each of the men whom one then wished to have'; i.e.
those who at that time made suitably respectable witnesses.

21 æt Weardoran The attempted reconciliation between Helmstan and Æthelhelm took
place 'at Wardour', when the charter signed by Alfred and the others was duly brought out
as evidence.

22 sēo hondseten eal ðǣron 'the whole ratification on it'; i.e. all the signatures.

23 āðe ðæs ðē nēar 'the nearer to the oath on that account'; i.e. he has substantiated
his case to the extent that he might soon take the oath which would settle matters once and
for all. But Æthelhelm has other ideas.

24 tō cinge 'to *the* king' (as also in 26, 52 and 63).

25 be hwȳ 'for why [instr.]', i.e. 'why'.

mid°. Ond cing stōd – ⌐ðwōh° his honda – æt Weardoran innan ðon būre°⌐. Đā
hē ðæt gedōn hæfde, ðā āscade hē Æðelm hwȳ hit him ryht° ne ðūhte ⌐ðæt wē
him gereaht hæfdan⌐; cwæð ðæt hē nān° ryhtre° geðencan° ne meahte ðonne°
hē ðone āð agifan mōste° gif hē meahte. Đā cwæð ic ⌐ðæt hē wolde cunnigan⌐
30   ond bæd° ðone cing ðæt hē hit āndagade°, ond hē ðā swā dyde.

Ond hē gelǣdde° ðā tō° ðon āndagan° ðone āð be° fullan ond bæd mē ⌐ðæt
ic him fultemade°⌐ ond cwæð ðæt him wǣre lēofre° ðæt hē ðæt land mē sealde
ðonne se āð forburste° oððe hit æfr[.........g...]æde. Đā cwæð ic ðæt ic
him wolde fylstan° ⌐tō ryhte⌐, ond nǣfre tō nānan wō°, ⌐on ðā gerāda ðe⌐ hē
35   his° mē ūðe°; ond hē ⌐mē ðæt on wedde gesealde⌐. Ond wē rīdan° ðā tō ðon
āndagan: ic, ond Wihtbord rād mid mē, ond Byrhthelm rād ðider mid Æðelme.
Ond wē gehȳrdan ealle ðæt hē ðone āð be fulan āgeaf. Đā wē cwǣdan ealle
ðæt hit wǣre ⌐geendodu spǣc⌐, ðā se dōm° wæs gefylled°. Ond lēof, hwonne
bið engu° spǣc geendedu, gif mon ne mæg ⌐nōwðer ne mid fēo ne⌐ mid āða
40   geendigan°? Oððe gif mon ǣlcne dōm wile onwendan° ðe Ælfred cing gesette°,
⌐hwonne habbe wē ðonne gemōtad⌐? Ond hē mē ðā bōc ðā āgeaf swā hē mē
on ðon wedde ǣr geseald hæfde, sōna swā se āð āgifen was. Ond ic him gehēt°
ðæt hē mōste ðes londes brūcan° ðā hwīle ðe hē lifde, gif hē hine wolde būtan°
bysmore° gehealdan°.

26 with (us)   was washing   chamber   27 just   28 nothing   more just   think of   than that
29 should be allowed   30 asked   would fix a day for   31 performed   on   appointed day
in   32 should support *sbj*   preferable   33 should fail   34 help   wrong   35 it *gsn*   granted
sbj (+*g*)   rode   38 judgement   carried out   39 any [*ǣnigu*]   40 end (it)   change   made
42 promised   43 use   without   44 disgrace   keep

26 **ðwōh his honda . . . būre** Ordlaf clearly feels that these precise circumstantial details
will bolster his credibility.

27–8 **ðæt wē him gereaht hæfdan** 'what we had decided for him'.

29 **ðæt hē wolde cunnigan** 'that he wanted to attempt (it)', i.e. the oath (*cunnigan* for
cunnian).

31–2 **ðæt ic him fultemade** Helmstan clearly feels that he needs further support,
perhaps in the form of an additional oath from his respected godfather; he is prepared
to pay for it.

34 **tō ryhte** 'to (obtain) justice'.   **on ðā gerāda ðe** 'on condition that'. The neut. noun
gerād is sometimes treated as fem., as probably here (acc. sg.).

35 **mē ðæt on wedde gesealde** 'gave me that in a pledge', or 'gave me a pledge to that'.

38 **geendodu spǣc** 'a closed suit'. Everything seems to have been brought to a satisfactory conclusion.

39 **nōwðer ne . . . ne** 'neither . . . nor . . .'.

41 **hwonne habbe wē ðonne gemōtad** lit. 'when may we therefore have disputed?',
i.e. 'when shall we have done with disputing?'. The first of Ordlaf's rhetorical questions may indicate that a money settlement of the dispute with Æthelhelm had been tried
earlier.

45   Đā onufan° ðæt (ˈymban ōðer healf gēar nāt ic hweðer ðe ymb tūaˈ) ðā
forstæl hē ðā unlǣdan° oxan æt Funtial, ˈðe hē mid ealle fore forwearðˈ, ond
drāf° tō ˈCytlidˈ. Ond hine mon ðǣræt° āparade° ond his ˈsperemonˈ āhredde°
ðā ˈsporwreclasˈ. Đā hē flēah°, ðā tōrȳpte° hine ān brēber° ofer° ðæt nebb°; ðā hē
ætsacan° wolde, ðā ˈsǣde him mon ðæt tō tācneˈ. Đā ˈswāf Eanulf Penearding
50   onˈ (wæs gerēfa°), ðā genom° eal ðæt yrfe° ˈhim onˈ ðæt hē āhte tō° Tyssebyrig°.
Đā āscade ic hine hwȳ hē swā dyde, ðā cwæð hē ðæt hē° wǣre ðēof ond mon
gerehte° ðæt yrfe cinge forðon hē wæs cinges mon. Ond ˈOrdlāf fēng°ˈ tō his
londe; forðon° hit wæs ˈhis lǣnˈ ðæt hē ˈon sæt, hē ne meahte nā his forwyrcanˈ.
Ond ˈtū hine hēteˈ ðā flȳman°. ˈĐā gesāhte hē ðīnes fæder līcˈ ond brōhte insigle°
55   tō mē, ond ic wæs æt Cippanhomme° ˈmit tēˈ. Đā āgeaf ic ðæt insigle ðē ond
ðū him forgēafe° his eard° ond ˈðā āre° ðe hē gēt° on° gebogen° hæfðˈ.

45 on top of **46** untended **47** drove (them) there discovered rescued **48** fled
scratched bramble across face **49** deny (it) **50** reeve took property at Tisbury
51 he (*i.e.* Helmstan) **52** adjudged (to +*d*) succeeded **53** because **54** outlaw seal
55 Chippenham **56** gave land estate still to withdrawn

45 **ymban ... tūa** 'I don't know whether it was after a year and a half or after two'.
In OE, a certain number and a half is expressed by the ordinal of the next number above
plus *healf*: hence *ōðer healf*, lit. 'two half', might be interpreted '(one complete item and)
half-way to the second'. As ordinals are adjs., *ōðer healf* is, like *gēar*, in the acc., following
ymban.

46 **ðe hē mid ealle fore forwearð** 'because of which (*ðe ... fore*) he was ruined
completely'.

47 **Cytlid** 'Chicklade' is about three miles south of Fonthill. **speremon** 'track-man' or
'tracker'; i.e. the man who had traced him.

48 **sporwreclas** The otherwise unknown word must describe the cattle which had been
tracked down (with Helmstan): perhaps, 'traced cattle'.

49 **sǣde him mon ðæt tō tācne** 'that [i.e. the scratch] was declared as evidence against
him'.

49–50 **swāf ... on** 'intervened'.

50 **him on** 'from him [Helmstan]'.

52 **Ordlāf fēng** Ordlaf's sudden change from 1st pers. to 3rd may reflect the importance
of this passage in his argument, namely, the claim that land he held on lease cannot be
forfeited. He reverts to 1st pers. in 55.

53 **his lǣn** 'his [Ordlaf's] loan'. The land occupied by Helmstan was on lease from
Ordlaf. **on sæt** 'occupied'. **hē ne meahte nā his forwyrcan** 'he [Helmstan] could not
forfeit it' (*forwyrcan* takes the gen.).

54 **tū hine hēte** 'And you [the king] pronounced him [Helmstan]'. Ordlaf is of course
writing to Edward, Alfred's son and successor. The form *tū* for *þū* occurs through partial
assimilation of the *d* of preceding *and*. **Đā gesāhte ... līc** The significance of Helmstan
visiting King Alfred's 'body' (i.e. his grave) is not clear; *fæder* is gen. sg. [§B4c.i].

55 **mit tē** Double assimilation has modified *mid þē*.

56 **ðā āre ... hæfð** It appears that Helmstan has since remained in retirement on the
estate given him by King Edward.

Ond ic fēng tō mīnan londe ond sealde hit ðon biscope, ðā on ðīne gewitnesse ond ðīnra weotena°, ⌐ðā fīf hīda wið ðon londe æt Lidgeard wið fīf hīdan⌐. Ond biscop ond eal hīwan° forgēafan mē ðā fēower° ond ān was tēoðinglond°. Ðonne,

60   lēof, is mē micel° nēodðearf° ðæt hit mōte° stondan swā hit nū gedōn is ond gefyrn° wæs. Gif hit elleshwæt° bið, ðonne sceal ic, ond wylle, ⌐bēon gehealden on ðon ðe ðē tō ælmessan ryht ðincð⌐.

✠ And Æðelm Higa ēode° of ðām geflite°, ðā cing wæs æt Worgemynster°, on Ordlāfes gewitnesse ond on Ōsferðes ond on Oddan° ond on Wihtbordes

65   ond on Ælfstānes ðys° blerian° ond on Æðelnōðes.

---

58 counsellors *gp*   **59** community   four (hides)   tithe-land   **60** great   necessity   may
61 arranged   otherwise   **63** withdrew   suit   Warminster   **64** Odda's   **65** the [*þæs*]
bold *gs*

---

58 **ðā fīf hīda wið ðon londe ... wið fīf hīdan** 'the five hides (of the Fonthill estate) against [i.e. in exchange for] the land at Lydiard with (its) five hides'. In its first occurrence, *wið* has its usual OE sense; in the second, it corresponds to ModE usage.

61–2 **bēon gehealden on ... ryht ðincð** 'be satisfied with [lit."held to"] what seems to you right in charity'.

III

SPREADING THE WORD

'What page, what word in that divine authority, the Old and the New Testament, is not a most proper standard of human life?' So runs the rhetorical question asked in ch. 73 of the Benedictine Rule, the guide to daily life which was followed, allowing for regional variation, in most of the monasteries of late Anglo-Saxon England. But it was not just monks and nuns for whom the Bible provided a framework for everyday existence. It had a pervasive influence on all medieval life and thought, informing not only the spiritual dimension but the political and historical too. For the Christian, history was not the cyclical process conceived of in the classical and heroic worlds – involving the perpetual rise and fall of people and nations under the influence of blind fate or fickle gods – but a linear progression from a known beginning to a clearly anticipated end, the whole process operating within the all-embracing knowledge and will of a single, eternal God. The prelude to human history was Creation, whose paradisal promise was wrecked by Adam's and Eve's disobedience at the prompting of Satan (whose pride, in some accounts, had earlier lost him his position as God's brightest angel). It was their fall which brought pain and struggle into the world, and human history evolved under the burden of their 'original sin' until the moment when a merciful God presented humankind with the gift of his son, Christ. His sacrifice on the cross would offer the possibility of redemption and salvation. The end of history, in the Christian scheme of things, will be Doomsday (OE *dōmes dæg*, 'day of judgement'), when everyone will be assessed in relation to their conduct on earth, and only those found deserving will enjoy an eternity of bliss in heaven.

The two parts of the Bible are complementary. The OT (the scripture of the Jews) is in the first place a record of history, chronicling the Creation and Fall, and the subsequent covenants made by God with Noah, Abraham, and Moses to save his chosen people, Israel, and guide them into a promised land; but it is also a platform for God's prophets and sages, such as Isaiah, Jeremiah and Job, and the writers of the books of Psalms, Proverbs and Wisdom. The NT, in turn, gives meaning to the Old, by presenting the life and death of Christ as the fulfilment of its covenants and prophecies. The teaching of Christ is recorded in the gospels of Matthew, Mark, Luke and John, and the activities of his apostles are related in a further series of books, many of them 'epistles' written by Paul to members of the early Christian churches, elaborating on Christ's own preaching and establishing the structure of the evolving church, and of Christian worship within it. The NT looks forward, too, mapping out in its final book, Revelation (or Apocalypse), the events of the approaching last age.

It is in this Christian-historical context that all the scriptural, devotional, homiletic, hagiographical and regulatory prose and poetry of the Anglo-Saxon period must be read. Although there was never a complete Bible in OE, the four gospels, the psalms, and much from the early books of the OT had been translated by the end of the Anglo-Saxon period. Extracts from Genesis (Text 13) and the gospel of Matthew (Text 14) are given here, along with three of the fifty psalms translated by the devout King Alfred (Text 15). Biblical translation was not undertaken lightly in the medieval period, in view of the perceived dangers of heresy by the translator and likelihood of misinterpretation by the audience; such problems are discussed by Ælfric in a preface justifying his own translation of part of Genesis (Text 16). Anglo-Saxon poets, on the other hand, seem to have had no reservations about 'vernacularising' the Bible, whose stories and characters caught their imaginations. A series of four poems, for instance, was compiled early in the eleventh century to present in memorably dramatic form precisely the great narrative of Christian history outlined above; they are imaginative recreations of the scriptural events, in which character and incident are moulded into a distinctly Anglo-Saxon shape. Extracts from two of the poems are included here, featuring the anguished Satan from *Genesis B* (Text 17) and the doomed Egyptians from *Exodus* (Text 18). Another poet used the idiom of Germanic heroism to retell the story of the pious widow Judith, from the OT book of that name, who saved her nation from disaster by slaying the leader of their enemies (Text 19).

The originals of the biblical works used by the various translators and poets may be read in any ModE translation of the Bible (though see the comments on Judith in 19/headnote), but the 'Douay-Rheims' translation of the Vulgate (see p. xiv) brings us closer to the versions known by them.

Further reading

H. Mayr-Harting, *The Coming of Christianity to Anglo-Saxon England* (London, 1972)

G. Shepherd, 'English Versions of the Scriptures before Wyclif', in *The Cambridge History of the Bible*, II: *The West from the Fathers to the Reformation*, ed. G. W. H. Lampe (Cambridge, 1969), pp. 362–87

J. Gardner, *The Construction of Christian Poetry in Old English* (Carbondale and Edwardsville, IL, 1975)

G. H. Brown, 'Old English Verse as a Medium for Christian Theology', in *Modes of Interpretation in Old English Literature: Essays in Honour of Stanley B. Greenfield*, ed. P. R. Brown, G. R. Crampton and F. C. Robinson (Toronto, 1986), pp. 15–28

M. R. Godden, 'Biblical Literature: the Old Testament', in *Cambridge Companion*, pp. 206–26

B. C. Raw, 'Biblical Literature: the New Testament', in *Cambridge Companion*, pp. 227–42

J. Hill, 'Confronting *Germania Latina*: Changing Responses to Old English Biblical Verse', in *Latin Culture and Medieval Germanic Europe. Proceedings of the First Germania Latina Conference held at the University of Groningen, 26 May 1989*, Germania Latina 1, ed. R. North and T. Hofstra (Groningen, 1992), pp. 71–88

13

After the Flood
(The *Old English Hexateuch*:
Gen 8.6–18 and 9.8–13)

According to the story told in chs. 6–9 of the book of Genesis, God became so exasperated when he saw the corruption that had overcome the world he had created that he decided to destroy everything in it with a great flood. There was, however, one righteous man left – Noah. He was commanded by God to build an ark, into which he was to take his own family and representatives of all living animals. It rained for forty days and forty nights and the sinful world was drowned, but Noah and his companions survived in the ark. When God finally allowed the waters to recede, Noah began to send out birds. This was common practice among ancient navigators to see whether any dry land was near; if a bird did not return, it meant that it had found somewhere to land. After some delay, eventually Noah and his companions emerged from the ark and a new era for humankind began. God then made a covenant with them that he would never again destroy the earth, and he established a special sign as confirmation of this, a rainbow (a natural phenomenon which features in the mythologies of many religions). For Christian writers, the story of Noah's flood reveals key aspects of the relationship between God and the human race, especially the concepts of judgement (for humankind's sins) and salvation (for those, like Noah, who put their trust in God). The ark itself symbolised the Christian church, with its promise of hope for the faithful, who live according to God's will while on their 'pilgrimage' in this earthly world; they are the citizens of the 'City of God', described by Augustine in his great work, *De ciuitate Dei* ('On the City of God'; see bk. 15, ch. 26).

Genesis is the first of the crucial opening books of the OT which were translated, in large part, into OE. The translations are preserved in two main manuscripts, which bring together contributions from Ælfric (see 16/headnote) and from other, unnamed, translators. One manuscript (London, British Library, Cotton Claudius B. iv) is known as a 'Hexateuch', because it includes the first six books of the OT (Genesis to Judges), the other (Oxford, Bodleian Library, Laud. Misc. 509) as a 'Heptateuch', because it has the first seven (Genesis to Joshua). The former, from which the extract below is taken, was copied in the mid-eleventh century, and was in the possession of St Augustine's Abbey in Canterbury. It is lavishly illustrated with many fine colour drawings, including several showing the structure of Noah's ark.

Ælfric translated from the Latin Vulgate (not, like the authors of most modern translations, from the Hebrew) with meticulous accuracy, though striving always to produce idiomatic English, as he himself explained in his own account of the problems of translation (see Text 16). He abbreviated the narrative slightly in one or two places by the omission of repetitive material. The language of the copy used here is characteristic of the WS dialect as written in the later Anglo-Saxon period. Frequent minor variations in spelling will be noted, such as *hyre* (10, 'her') as well as *hire* (5), and *byð* (24, 'will be') as well as *bið* (21); the forms with *y* feature in later WS. Others are *wætera* (4, 'waters', nom. pl.) as well as *wæteru* (3), and *hrem* (2, 'raven') as well as *hremn* (2). There are two 'errors' in the text: *ðæra* is written for *ðære* (13, the dative singular demonstrative) and *ādȳdon* for *ādȳdan* (20, the infinitive form of the verb); but in both instances we are no doubt seeing evidence of just the sort of 'levelling' of unstressed word-endings characteristic of manuscripts written in the eleventh century (see p. xxi), so they have not been changed here. But an omission (*flæsc*, 20) has been made good from the other available manuscript. The following extract gives Gen 8.6–18 and 9.8–13. In the intervening passage (between lines 17 and 18), Noah and his sons, emerging from the ark, offer sacrifices, which are accepted by God.

Further reading

C. R. Dodwell and P. Clemoes, eds., *The Old English Illustrated Hexateuch. British Museum Cotton Claudius B.* IV, EEMF 18 (Copenhagen, 1974)

S. J. Crawford, ed., *The Old English Version of the Heptateuch, Ælfric's Treatise on the Old and New Testament and his Preface to Genesis*, EETS 160 (London, 1922; repr. 1969, with the text of two additional manuscripts transcribed by N. R. Ker)

M. McC. Gatch, 'Noah's Raven in *Genesis A* and the Illustrated *Old English Heptateuch*', *Gesta* 14.2 (1975), 3–15

R. Marsden, 'Ælfric as Translator: the Old English Prose Genesis', *Anglia* 109 (1991), 319–58

R. Barnhouse and B. Withers, eds., *The Old English Hexateuch: Aspects and Approaches* (Kalamazoo, MI, 2000)

Ðā° æfter feowertigum° dagum° undyde° Nōe his ēahðyrl°, ðe° hē on° ðām arce°
gemacode°, and āsende° ūt ænne° hremn°. Se hrem flēah° ðā ūt and ⌐nolde eft
ongēan cyrran⌐, ⌐ær ðan ðe⌐ ðā° wæteru° ādrūwodon° ofer eorðan. Hē āsende ðā
eft ūt āne culfran°, ðæt° hēo° scēawode° gyf° ðā wætera ðāgȳt° geswicon° ⌐ofer

5   ðǣre eorðan brādnysse⌐. Hēo ðā flēah ūt and ne° mihte° findan hwǣr° hēo hire°
fōt āsette°, ⌐for ðan ðe⌐ ðā wætera wǣron ofer ealle eorðan; and hēo gecyrde°
ongēan tō Nōe and hē genam° hī° intō ðām arce.

He ābād° ðāgȳt ōðre° seofan dagas and āsende ūt eft culfran. Hēo cōm° ðā
on ǣfnunge° eft tō Nōe, and brōhte° ān twig of° ānum elebēame° mid grēnum

10 lēafum on° hyre mūðe°. Ðā undergeat° Nōe ðæt ðā wætera wǣron° ādrūwode
ofer eorðan, and ābād ⌐swā ðēah⌐ seofan dagas and āsende ūt culfran. Swā° hēo
ne gecyrde ongēan tō him, ðā geopenode° Nōe ðæs arces hrōf°, and behēold°
ūt and geseah° ðæt ðǣra eorðan brādnis wæs ādrūwod.

God ðā spræc° tō Nōe, ðus cweðende°: 'Gang° ūt of ðām arce, ðū° and þīn°

15 wīf and ðīne suna° and heora° wīf°; and ⌐eal ðæt ðǣrinne is⌐ mid° ðē° lǣd° ūt
mid ðē ofer eorðan, and ⌐weaxe gē and bēoð gemænifylde⌐ ofer eorðan.' Nōe
ðā ūt ēode° of ðām arce, and ⌐hī ealle⌐, ofer eorðan.

God cwæð° eft° tō Nōe and tō his sunum: 'Efne° nū° ic sette° mīn wed° tō°
ēow° and tō ēowrum° ofspringe° and tō eallum libbendum° nȳtenum° ðe° of ðām

---

1 Then forty days undid (*or* opened) 'eye-hole' (window) which in ark **2** (had) made
sent a raven flew **3** the waters (had) dried up **4** dove (so) that she would see *sbj* if
yet (had) decreased **5** not could where her **6** might put down *sbj* returned **7** took
her **8** waited another came **9** (the) evening brought from olive-tree **10** in mouth
realised were **11** As **12** opened roof looked **13** saw **14** spoke saying Come you
your **15** sons their wives with you bring **17** came **18** said then Thus now
(shall) establish covenant with **19** you your descendant(s) living animals which

---

2–3 **nolde eft ongēan cyrran** 'would not (*ne wolde*) return back (*eft*) again'. According
to the original Hebrew version, the raven *did* return to the ark; the whole world, after all,
was still submerged. But the Vulgate, Ælfric's source, has the puzzling negative version.
What did the recalcitrant raven do to avoid returning until after dry land appeared? Some
church writers ingeniously suggested that it perched on a floating corpse. The dove, as we
see below, behaved better.   **ǣr ðan ðe** conj. phr.: 'before' or 'until'.

4–5 **ofer ðǣre eorðan brādnysse** 'across the breadth (*or* surface) of the earth'; *eorðan*
is the gen. sg. form of a fem. *n*-declension noun [§B5c].

6 **for ðan ðe** conj. phr.: 'because'.

11 **swā ðēah** adv. phr.: 'nevertheless'.

15 **eal ðæt ðǣrinne is** 'all that is there inside'; i.e. all the creatures.

16 **weaxe gē and bēoð gemænifylde** 'be fruitful [lit. "grow you"] and be multiplied'.
This was the command given by God to Adam and Eve in the Garden of Eden (Gen 1.28),
for it expressed the original purpose of creation.

17 **hī ealle** 'they all', i.e. 'all of them'.

1-40.

20   arce ēodon, ðæt ic nāteshwōn° nelle° heononforð° eal flǣsc° ādȳdon° mid flōdes°
     wæterum; ne° heononforð ⌐ne bið flōd tōsencende ðā eorðan⌐. Ðis bið ðæt tācn°
     mīnes weddes ðæt ic dō° betwux° mē and ēow and eallum libbendum nȳtenum
     ⌐on ēcum mǣgðum⌐ – ðæt is, ðæt ic sette mīnne rēnbogan° on wolcnum°, and hē
     byð tācn mīnes weddes betwux mē and ðǣre eorðan

20 never again   will not [*ne wille*]   henceforth   flesh (*i.e.* living creatures)   destroy   of (the)
flood   **21** nor   sign   **22** make   between   **23** rainbow   skies

   21 ne bið flōd tōsencende ðā eorðan lit. '(there) will not be a flood drowning the
earth'; perhaps, 'no flood will drown the earth'. *Bið* (a pres. 3rd-pers. sg. form of *bēon* 'be')
is often used for the fut. [§G1a.iv]; cf. *is*, used specifically for the pres. in 15 and 23.
   23 on ēcum mǣgðum 'for endless generations'. The covenant is not just with Noah
but with all future people.

14

The Crucifixion
(The *Old English Gospels*:
Mt 27.11–54)

The gospels of Matthew, Mark, Luke and John provide a narrative of the career of Christ, culminating in his crucifixion and resurrection. Our word 'gospel' derives from OE *gōdspel*, 'good news', a translation of Latin *euangelium*, which was itself a borrowing of the Greek *euangelion*; this meant originally a 'reward for good news' and then came to mean the 'good news' itself. The *Old English Gospels* (which are also known as the *West Saxon Gospels*) represent the earliest complete rendering of the gospels in English, made from the Latin Vulgate, probably in the second half of the tenth century. Six complete manuscript copies survive, along with fragments of two others. All were made in the eleventh or twelfth centuries. It is unlikely that the OE version was intended to give the common people access to scripture, as were the much later Middle English translations associated with the reformer Wyclif. The context of both its production and its use was probably the monastery. The addition of Latin annotations to some of the manuscripts may have been to allow cross-referencing with the Vulgate, which remained the official Bible of the church; and no doubt they would have been a help for monks learning Latin, too.

The extract given here covers the last hours of Christ's life as a man: his arrest by the Roman authorities, his 'trial' before Pilate and his execution, followed by his resurrection from the tomb. One of the central aims of the gospel-writers was to show Jesus to be the Messiah of the Jews, whose coming had been prophesied in the OT, and this idea of fulfilment is repeatedly emphasised by quotations from OT books. In the extract, for example (lines 40–42, translating Mt 27.35), we are told that the sharing out of Christ's clothes by his executioners fulfils the words of a prophet (see 41–2n).

The language of the preserved copies of the *Old English Gospels* is late WS. The eleventh-century manuscript used here (Cambridge, Corpus Christi College 140) was written by four different scribes with their own idiosyncrasies; the one who wrote the latter part of Matthew preferred the 'late' form *heom* to *him* for the dative plural third-person pronoun (17, 18, etc) but also wrote *hym* (25), another late form, and he preferred *hyne* to *hine* for the third-person accusative singular masculine pronoun. He almost invariably wrote late *hig* for the nominative and accusative third-person plural pronoun (but cf. *hī*, 21). For the verb 'answered', he wrote both *andwerde* (5) and *andwyrde* (16), and often *hǣlynd*, rather than *hǣlend*, and this has been identified as possibly a Kentish or south-eastern feature.

Further reading

R. M. Liuzza, ed., *The Old English Version of the Gospels*, 2 vols. (I, Text and Introduction, and II, Notes and Glossary), EETS 304 and 314 (Oxford, 1994–2000)

A. N. Doane and R. M. Liuzza, *Anglo-Saxon Manuscripts in Microfiche Facsimile, vol. 3* (Binghamton, NY, 1995)

R. M. Liuzza, 'Who Read the Gospels in Old English?', in *Words and Works: Essays for Fred C. Robinson*, ed. P. S. Baker and N. Howe (Toronto, 1998), pp. 3–24

Þā stōd se hǣlend° beforan þām ⌐dēman⌐ and se dēma hyne āxode°, þus cweðende°, 'Eart ðū Iūdēa° cyning?' Þā cwæð se hǣlend, '⌐Þæt ðū segst⌐. And ⌐mid þȳ ðe⌐ hyne wrēgdon° ⌐þǣra sācerda ealdras and þā hlāfordas⌐, nān þing hē ne andswarode. Ðā cwæð Pilātus tō him, 'Ne gehȳrst° þū hū fela° sagena°

5   hig° ongēn° þē secgeað?' And hē ne andwerde° mid° nānum worde, swā° þæt se dēma wundrode° swīþlīce°.

⌐Hig hæfdon heom tō gewunan⌐ tō° heora symbeldæge° þæt se dēma sceolde° forgyfan° þām folce ǣnne forwyrhtne° mann swylcne° hig habban woldon°. Hē hæfde þā ⌐sōðlīce⌐ ǣnne° strangne° þēofmann° gehæftne° se° wæs genemned°

1 Saviour asked   **2** saying of the Jews   **3** accused   **4** hear many +*gp* reports
5 they against answered with so   **6** marvelled greatly   **7** on feast-day should
8 release (to + *d*) condemned whichever one wanted   **9** a resolute (*i.e.* persistent)
thief 'shackled' (*i.e.* in custody) who named

    1 dēman 'judge', or, better here, 'governor'; i.e. Pontius Pilate, who was appointed procurator of the Roman province of Judaea in AD 26.

    2 þæt ðū segst 'You say it', or 'You say so'.

    3 mid þȳ ðe conj. phr.: 'when' (*þȳ* is instr.). **þǣra sācerda ealdras and þā hlāfordas** lit. 'the elders of the priests and the lords' (the subjs. of *wrēgdon*); traditionally rendered as 'the chief priests and elders'.

    7 Hig hæfdon heom tō gewunan 'They had for themselves as custom', i.e. 'It was their custom'. The practice of releasing a prisoner at festival times (here it is the Jewish feast of the Passover) was widespread in the ancient world.

    9 sōðlīce This adv., 'truly' (also in 12, 14, etc), and *witodlīce*, 'surely' or 'indeed' (in 18, 20, etc), are used interchangeably to render a number of the Latin advs. and conjs. which punctuate the scriptural narrative. 'Now', 'then' or 'but' may be the appropriate trans. in some contexts, or simple 'and (so)' may be sufficient.

10   Barrabbas. ⌐Þā þæt folc gesamnod° wæs, þā⌐ cwæð Pilātus: ⌐'Hwæþer wylle
      gē⌐ þæt ic ēow āgyfe°: þe Barrabban ðe þone hǣlynd ðe° is Crīst gehāten°?'
      Hē wiste° sōðlīce þæt hig hyne for° andan° him° sealdon°. ⌐Hē sæt þā Pilātus⌐
      on his dōmsetle°, þā sende° his wīf tō hym and cwæð: ⌐'Ne bēo þē nān þing
      gemǣne ongēn⌐ þisne rihtwīsan°. Sōðlīce fela° ic hæbbe geþolod° tōdæg þurh
15   gesyhðe° for° hym'. Ðā lǣrdon° þǣra sācerda ealdras and þā hlāfordas þæt folc
      þæt hig bǣdon° Barrabban and þone hǣlyn fordydon°. Ðā andwyrde se dēma
      and sǣde heom, 'Hwæþerne wylle gē þæt ic forgyfe ēow of þisum twām°?' Ðā
      cwǣdon hig: 'Barrabban'. Þā cwæð Pilātus tō heom: ⌐'Witodlīce⌐ hwæt dō ic
      be° þām hǣlende þe is Crīst genemned?' Ðā cwǣdon hig ealle: 'Sȳ° hē on rōde°
20   āhangen°'. Ðā cwæð se dēma tō heom: 'Witodlīce ⌐hwæt yfeles⌐ dyde þes°?'
      Hī ðā swīþor° clypodon°, þus cweðende: 'Sȳ hē āhangen'. Ðā geseah° Pilātus
      þæt ⌐hyt nāht ne fremode ac° gewurde māre gehlȳd⌐, þā genam° hē wæter and
      þwōh° hys handa beforan þām folce and cwæð: 'Unscyldig° ic eom fram° þyses
      rihtwīsan blōde, gē° gesēoð°'. Ðā andswarode eall þæt folc and cwæð: 'Sȳ hys
25   blōd ofer° ūs and ofer ūre bearn°'. Ðā forgeaf hē hym° Barrabban and þone
      hǣlynd hē ⌐lēt swingan⌐ and sealde heom° ⌐tō āhōnne⌐.
            Þā underfēngon° þæs dēman cempan° þone hǣlynd on° ðām dōmerne°

---

10 gathered   **11** give who called   **12** knew because of envy to him (*i.e.* Pilate)
(had) delivered   **13** judgement-seat sent   **14** righteous man much suffered
15 (a) dream on account of persuaded   **16** asked for did away with   **17** two   **19** with
Be *sbj* (*i.e.* let him be) cross   **20** hung (*i.e.* crucified) this (man)   **21** the more violently
called out saw   **22** but took   **23** washed guiltless of (+*d*)   **24** you see   **25** upon
children *ap* to them   **26** to them   **27** conducted soldiers *np* into judgement-hall

---

    10 **Þā . . . þā** 'When . . . , then . . .'; but the second *þā* (adv.) can be om. in trans. (see also
21–2).
    10–11 **Hwæþer** interrog. pron.: 'which of the two?'; this is complemented (in 11) with
the repeated particle *þe . . . þe*, 'either . . . or'. **wylle gē** Reduced inflection (*wylle*, not
wyllen) in a pl. vb. preceding its pron. [§G6f].
    12 **Hē . . . Pilātus** The use of both pron. and noun or name to define a subj. is common
in OE, though the name alone will usually be sufficient in trans. (see also *sume þā* in 58).
    13–14 **Ne bēo . . . ongēn** lit. 'Let there not be to you any shared thing towards', i.e. 'Do
not have anything to do with . . .'.
    18 **Witodlīce** 'Then'; see 9n.
    20 **hwæt yfeles** gen. of respect: 'what (by way) of evil', i.e. 'what evil' or 'what evil
thing'.
    22 **hyt nāht ne fremode** 'it availed nothing'; i.e. nothing he could do was of any use.
ac gewurde māre gehlȳd 'but there came about more uproar', i.e. 'the uproar became
greater'.
    26 **lēt swingan** part of an acc. and inf. construction [§G6d.i.3]: 'allowed to be scourged'.
tō āhōnne infl. inf. expressing purpose, with passive sense: 'to be crucified'. Crucifixion
was a Roman, not a Jewish, mode of execution and was usually preceded by flogging.

and ⌐gegaderodon° ealne° þone ðrēat° tō heom⌐ and unscrȳddon° hyne hys
āgenum° rēafe° and scrȳddon° hyne ⌐mid° weolcenrēadum° scyccelse° and
30 wundon° cynehelm° of þornum and āsetton° ofer hys hēafod and hrēod°⌐ on
hys swīðran° and bīgdon° heora cnēow° beforan him and bysmorudun° hyne,
þuss cweþende: ⌐Hāl wes þū⌐, Iūdēa cyning', and spǣtton on hyne and nāmon°
hrēod and bēotun° hys hēafod. And ⌐æfter þām þe⌐ hig hyne þus bysmerodon,
hig unscrȳddon hyne þām scyccelse and scrȳddon hyne mid hys āgenum rēafe
35 and lǣddon hyne tō āhōnne. Sōþlīce ðā hig ūtfērdon°, þā gemetton hig ǣnne
Cyrēniscne° mann cumende° heom tōgēnes° þæs° nama wæs Symon. Þone° hig
nȳddon° þæt hē bǣre° hys rōde. Ðā cōmon hig on° þā stōwe° þe is genemned
Golgotha, þæt is ⌐hēafodpannan stōw⌐. And hig sealdon hym wīn drincan wið
⌐eallan⌐ gemenged°. And þā hē hys° onbyrigde°, þā nolde hē hyt drincan.
40   Sōþlīce æfter þām þe hig hyne on rōde āhengon°, hig tōdǣldon° hys rēaf and
wurpon° hlot° þǣrofer°, ⌐þæt wǣre gefylled þæt ðe gecwēden wæs þurh ðone
wītegan, and þus cwæð⌐: 'Hig tōdǣldon heom° mīne rēaf and ofer mīne rēaf
hig wurpon hlot'. And ⌐hig behēoldon hyne sittende⌐. And hig āsetton ofer hys
hēafod hys gylt°, þuss āwritenne: 'Ðis ys se hǣlynd Iūdēa cyning'. Ðā wǣron
45 āhangen mid hym twēgen° sceaþan°, ān on þā swīðran healfe° and ōðer on þā
wynstran°. Witodlīce þā wegfērendan° hyne bysmeredon and cwehton° heora

28 gathered all troop stripped (of +*d*)   29 own clothing dressed with (*or* in) scarlet
cloak   30 wove crown placed (it) a reed   31 right (hand) bent knee *as* mocked
32 took   33 beat   35 went out   36 of Cyrene coming towards whose Him
37 compelled carry *sbj* to place   39 mixed it tasted +*g*   40 (had) crucified divided
41 cast lots for it   42 among themselves   44 crime   45 two criminals side   46 left
passers-by shook

28 **gegaderodon... tō heom** Pilate's guards bring in the rest of the soldiers in their
troop to deal with Christ.

29–30 **mid weolcenrēadum scyccelse... hrēod** A mock imperial robe (perhaps a soldier's scarlet cloak), a mock crown (of thorns) and a mock sceptre (the 'reed') are used to
humiliate Christ.

32 **Hāl wes þū** An Anglo-Saxon greeting: 'Be thou well!', or 'Hail!'

33 **æfter þām þe** conj. phr.: 'after'; see also 40.

38 **hēafodpannan stōw** 'the place of the skull', translating the Hebrew and Aramaic
name Golgotha. The place was so named either because it was held to be shaped like a skull
or because it abounded in the skulls of those killed there.

39 **eallan** 'gall'; a bitter fluid such as that produced by the gall-bladder.

41–2 **þæt wǣre... wītegan** 'so that was fulfilled which had been spoken by the
prophet'. The 'prophet' here is David, traditionally the author of the OT psalms, and the
quotation is from ps. 21.19. Executioners were allowed to keep the garments of their victims.
and þus cwæð 'and he spoke thus'.

43 **hig behēoldon hyne sittende** The pres. part. complements *hig*: 'they, sitting, watched
him', or 'they sat and watched him'.

hēafod and cwædon: ⌜Wā þæt ðes⌝ tōwyrpð° Godes templ and on þrīm° dagum°
hyt eft° getimbrað°! Gehǣl° nū þē sylfne! Gyf þū sȳ Godes sunu, gā° nyþer° of
þǣre rōde!' Ēac þǣra sācerda ealdras hyne bysmeredon mid þām bōcerum° and
50   mid þām ealdrum and cwǣdun: 'Ōþere° hē gehǣlde° and hyne sylfne gehǣlan
ne mæg°. Gyf hē Israhēla cyning sȳ, gā nū nyþer of þǣre rōde and wē gelȳfað°
hym. Hē gelȳfð° on God: ⌜ālȳse hē hyne⌝ nū gyf hē wylle. Witodlīce hē sǣde
"Godes sunu ic eom"'. Gelīce° þā sceaðan þe mid him āhangene wǣron hyne
hyspdun°.
55   Witodlīce ⌜fram þǣre sixtan tīde wǣron gewurden þȳstru° ofer ealle eorðan
oþ þā nigoþan tīd⌝. And ymbe° þā nygoðan tīd clypode se hǣlend ⌜mycelre
stefne⌝ and þuss cwæð: ⌜*Heli Heli lema zabdani*⌝?' Þæt ys on Englisc: 'Mīn
God, mīn God, ⌜tō hwī⌝ forlēte° þū mē?' Sōþlīce ⌜sume þā ðe þǣr stōdon⌝
and þis gehȳrdon° cwǣdon: 'Nū hē clypað Heliam°'. Ðā hrædlīce° arn° ān
60   heora and genam āne spongean° and fylde° hig mid ecede° and ⌜āsette ān
hrēod þǣron⌝ and sealde hym drincan. Witodlīce þā ōðre cwǣdon: 'Læt!° Utun°
gesēon hwæþer Helias cume° and wylle hyne ālȳsan°'. Þā clypode se hǣlynd
eft micelre stefne and āsende° hys gāst°. And þǣrrihte° ðæs temples wāhryft°
wearð° tōsliten° on twēgen dǣlas° fram ufeweardon° oð nyþeweard° and sēo
65   eorðe bīfode° and stānas tōburston°. And byrgena° wurdun geopenode and

47 destroys three days **48** again builds Heal come down **49** scholars **50** Others
ap healed **51** can will believe (in +*d*) **52** trusts **53** Likewise **54** scorned
55 darkness **56** at **58** have forsaken **59** heard Elijah quickly ran **60** sponge
filled vinegar **61** Let be! (*or* Leave off!) Let us **62** come *sbj* free **63** sent up spirit
at once veil **64** was torn parts top bottom **65** shook broke tombs

47 **Wā þæt ðes** The interj. *wā* expresses contempt, an ironical 'alas!' or 'so!'; perhaps,
'So! this is he who . . .' The passers-by are referring to the words said by Christ to the Jews
at the temple in Jerusalem, as reported in Jn 2.19 and Mt 26.61.

52 **ālȳse hē hyne** The vb. is sbj., with optative meaning: 'let him [God] release him
[Christ]'.

55–6 **fram þǣre sixtan tīde . . . oþ þā nigoþan tīd** 'from the sixth hour [i.e. midday]
until the ninth hour [i.e. three o'clock]'; on this time system, see 1/42n.

56–7 **mycelre stefne** dat. of manner: 'in a great voice'.

57 **Heli Heli lema zabdani** The words, supposed to have been spoken by Christ, are
from ps. 21.1 and are given in Aramaic (as copied from the Latin version of a Greek
transcription). *Heli* ('my God') is misheard by the onlookers as the name of the prophet
Elijah (Lat. *Helias*).

58 **tō hwī** 'why' (lit. 'for what', instr.).   **sume þā ðe þǣr stōdon** Probably *þā* is the
nom. pl. pron. 'they' or 'those', repeating the sense of *sume*: 'some of those who stood
there'.

60–1 **āsette ān hrēod þǣron** 'put a reed into it', i.e. 'put it on a reed'.

⌐manige hālige līchaman⌐ ðe ǣr° slēpon° āryson°. And þā hig ūt ēodon° of þām
byrgenum æfter hys° ǣryste°, hig cōmun ⌐on þā hāligan ceastre⌐ and ætēowdon°
hig° manegum°. Witodlīce ⌐þæs hundredes ealdor⌐ and ðā þe mid him wǣron
healdende° þone hǣlynd, þā hig gesāwon þā eorðbifunge° and þā ðing° ðe þǣr
gewurdon°, ⌐hig ondrēdon heom⌐ ðearle° ond cwǣdon: 'Sōðlīce Godes sunu
wæs þes'.

70

66 previously (had) slept arose came out   67 his (*i.e.* Christ's) resurrection showed
68 themselves to many   69 watching over earthquake things   70 happened sorely

66 **manige hālige līchaman** 'many holy (*or* saintly) bodies', i.e. 'the bodies of the
saints'.
67 **on þā hāligan ceastre** 'into the holy city'; i.e. Jerusalem.
68 **þæs hundredes ealdor** 'leader of the hundred', i.e. 'centurion', in charge of a
hundred men.
70 **hig ondrēdon heom** rflx. vb.: 'they were afraid'.

15

King Alfred's Psalms

The psalms of the Old Testament, which had been a part of Jewish worship since the eighth century BC, came to play a crucial role in the practice of Christianity, too, for they were interpreted as presenting prophecies which were later fulfilled in the life of Christ. Their poetic qualities – a 'psalm' is a song, originally in verse in the Hebrew – and their association (however tenuous) with the great but troubled king of Israel, David, made them a popular resource for personal devotion also. By the early Middle Ages, formal church worship (the 'divine office') was built around the psalms and they were circulated in self-contained books called psalters. In the monasteries, the whole of the psalter would be sung through every week, and monks were expected to know all the one hundred and fifty psalms by heart. Not surprisingly, therefore, the Latin psalter seems to have been the most widely copied book in Anglo-Saxon England. Eleven of the forty surviving examples have an OE translation (or 'gloss') written word by word between the lines of Latin, probably as a way to help monks to master that language.

Because it followed the Latin word-order slavishly, such a translation did not produce a coherent vernacular version of the psalter. A self-contained translation exists, however, in a bilingual psalter made in the mid-eleventh century and now in the Bibliothèque Nationale in Paris (lat. 8824). It is the most curiously shaped of Anglo-Saxon books, with pages three times as tall as wide (526 × 186 mm). All the psalms are there in Old English, the first fifty in prose and the rest (by a different translator) in verse, and they are accompanied by a Latin text in adjacent columns, though it differs somewhat from the one that must have been used by the translators. Scholars have established that the prose translations of the first fifty psalms are by King Alfred of Wessex (871–99) and were probably made near the end of his life. It is not known whether he ever intended to complete the whole psalter but the first group of fifty in itself is likely to have had a particular resonance for him, for it contains the lamentations of King David as he faces the hostility of his enemies. Alfred, as noted elsewhere (p. 37), suffered a long period of defeat and dejection before finally containing the Viking threat to Wessex and, like David, he had agonised about the workings of God's will and the demands of faith. In general, Alfred renders the Latin closely, but he frequently makes amplifications to clarify meaning or to render an abstract concept more concrete. Thus, for example, the Vulgate's *locus pascuae* ('place of pasture') becomes *swȳðe good feohland* ('very good land for cattle') in ps. 22 (15c/8–9). The lyrical voice of the Hebrew psalmist survives in these versions and is intensified by the voice of Alfred himself. They are a very personal work and give us an insight into the mind of a king whose piety was emphasised by Asser, his priest, who completed a sketch of the king's early years in 893. Alfred also supplied introductions to each psalm (though that for the first is missing from the Paris copy), which explains the historical circumstances of its writing and how it is to be interpreted in relation to future Jewish history, to the life of Christ and to the conduct of every Christian. These introductions appear to be original compositions by Alfred, though based on existing early medieval sources (and, for pss. 12 and 22, they are included below).

The Paris manuscript of the OE psalms is a late (mid-eleventh century) WS copy of an earlier WS text, and this is reflected in the language. Linguistic forms are consistently those of the later period: thus *byð* (15a/1, not *við*), *þām* (15a/1, not *þǣm*) and *swylce* (15a/7, not *swelce* or *swilce*). But there are clues to early composition in the use of words such as *smēagan* 'reflect' (15a/3), *seofian* 'lament' (15b/1) and *bēod* 'table' (15c/14), which are characteristic of Alfredian texts. The numbering of the psalms followed here is that of the Vulgate, which differs slightly from that of today's Protestant Bible, in which Vulgate pss. 1, 12 and 22 appear as pss. 1, 13 and 23, respectively. For convenience, conventional modern verse-division is indicated within each psalm, but it must be stressed that such divisions were unknown to the Anglo-Saxons and that the psalms will have been read as continuous narratives.

Further reading

B. Colgrave *et al.*, eds., *The Paris Psalter (Ms Bibliothèque Nationale fonds latin 8824)*, EEMF 8 (Copenhagen, 1958)

P. P. O'Neill, ed., *King Alfred's Old English Prose Translation of the First Fifty Psalms* (Cambridge, MA, 2001)

P. P. O'Neill, 'The Old English Introductions to the Prose Psalms of the Paris Psalter: Sources, Structure and Composition', in *Eight Anglo-Saxon Studies*, ed. J. Wittig (Chapel Hill, NC, 1981), pp. 20–38

J. M. Bately, 'Lexical Evidence for the Authorship of the Prose Psalms in the Paris Psalter', *ASE* 10 (1982), 69–95

A. J. Frantzen, *King Alfred* (Boston, MA, 1986), ch. 6

G. H. Brown, 'The Psalms as the Foundation of Anglo-Saxon Learning', in *The Place of the Psalms in the Intellectual Culture of the Middle Ages*, ed. N. van Deusen (Albany, NY, 1999), pp. 1–24

15a

Psalm 1

⌐Ēadig byð se wer⌐ þe ne gæð° ⌐on geþeaht unrihtwīsra⌐, ne ⌐on þām wege ne
stent synfulra⌐, ne on heora wōlbærendum° setle° ne sitt, ac his willa° byð on°
Godes æ° ond ymb° his æ hē byð smēagende° ⌐dæges ond nihtes⌐. ⌐Him byð swā
þām trēowe⌐ þe byð āplantod° ⌐nēah wætera rynum⌐, þæt sylð° his wæstmas°
5   tō° rihtre tīde°, ond his lēaf° ond his blæda° ne fealwiað° ⌐ne ne⌐ sēariað°. ⌐Swā
byð þām men⌐ þe wē ær ymbspræcon°: ⌐eall him cymð tō gōde þæt þæt hē
dēð⌐. Ac þā unrihtwīsan ne bēoð nā swylce°, ⌐ne him ēac swā ne limpð⌐, ac hī
bēoð dūste gelīcran° þonne° hit wind tōblæwð°. Þȳ° ne ārīsað þā unrihtwīsan on
dōmes° dæg, ne þā synfullan ne bēoð on geþeahte þæra rihtwīsena, ⌐for þām⌐
10 God wāt° hwylce° weg° þā rihtwīsan geearnedon° ac þā unrihtwīsan cumað tō
wītum°.

1 walks **2** pestilential seat desire for **3** law about thinking **4** planted gives fruits
5 at time leaves shoots wither dry up **6** spoke about **7** so **8** more like (to +*d*) when
blows Therefore **9** of judgement **10** knows what path (have) deserved **11** torments

    1 **Ēadig byð se wer** 'Blessed is the man', translating Lat. *beatus uir*, words which in
manuscript psalters are often enlarged and elaborately decorated. **on geþeaht unrihtwīsra**
To walk 'in the counsel of the unrighteous' means, in biblical idiom, to follow the teaching
or example of ungodly people.
    1–2 **on þām wege ne stent synfulra** 'does not stand in the way of the sinful'.
    3 **dæges ond nihtes** gen. of time: 'day and night'.
    3–4 **Him byð swā þām trēowe** 'for him it will be as (it is) for the tree', i.e. 'he will be
like a tree'. Most vbs. from this point on in the Latin version are fut. in form, and the OE
pres. tense may be rendered as such.
    4 **nēah wætera rynum** lit. 'near the flowings of waters', i.e. 'near running streams'.
    5 **ne ne** 'nor not', i.e. 'nor'.
    5–6 **Swā byð þām men** 'So it is with the man [dat. sg.]...'. This whole sen-
tence (referring to the blessed man of the opening) is an explanatory interpolation by
Alfred.
    6–7 **eall ... þæt hē dēð** 'all for him comes to good, that which he does', i.e. 'all that he
does prospers'.
    7 **ne him ēac swā ne limpð** impers. vb. with dat. pron.: 'nor also does it happen to him
thus'.
    9 **for þām** conj. phr.: 'because'.

15b
Psalm 12

Đā Dāfid þysne twelftan sealm sang, þā seofode° hē tō Drihtne on þām
sealme° be° his fēondum° ⌐ǣgþer ge gāstlicum° ge⌐ līchamlicum° ond swā dēð
ǣlc þǣra þe hine singð ond ⌐swā dyde Crīst be Iūdēum ond be dēoflum⌐ ond
swā dyde ⌐Ezēchias⌐ se cyng be Assīriam°, þā hī hine ymbseten° hæfdon on
5 þǣre byrig°:
    Hū lange wilt þū Drihten ⌐mīn⌐ forgitan, ⌐hwæðer þū oð mīnne ende wylle⌐?
Oððe hū lange wilt þū āhwyrfan° þīnne andwlitan° fram mē? Hū lange sceal°
ic settan° on° mīne sāwle þis sorhfulle geþeaht° ond þis sār° æt mīnre heortan,
⌐hwæþer ic ǣlce dæge scyle⌐? Hū lange sceal mīn fēond° bēon ūpp āhafen° ofer
10 mē? Besēoh° tō mē Drihten mīn God ond gehȳr° mē. Onlīht° mīne ēagan þæt
hī nǣfre° ne slāpan° ⌐on swylcum dēaðe, þȳ lǣs⌐ ǣfre° mīn fēond cweðe°, 'Ic
eom strengra° þonne hē'. Þā° þe mē swencað°, hȳ fægniað° gif ic onstyred°
bēo. Ac ic þēah° on þīne mildheortnesse° gelȳfe°. Mīn heorte blissað° on° þīnre
hǣlo° ond ic singe þām Gode þe mē eall gōd syleð° ond lofie° þīnne naman, þū
15 hēhsta° God.

1 lamented 2 psalm about enemies spiritual physical 4 the Assyrians besieged
5 city 7 turn away face must 8 put in thought pain 9 enemies raised 10 Have
regard hear Enlighten 11 never sleep ever should say *sbj* 12 stronger Those afflict
rejoice stirred up 13 nevertheless mercy believe (shall) rejoice in 14 salvation gives
praise 15 highest

2 **ǣþer ge ... ge** 'both ... and ...'.
3 **swā dyde ... be dēoflum** Perhaps an allusion to Lk 13.31–5.
4 **Ezēchias** In OT accounts, Hezekiah, king of Judah, was besieged by the forces of
Assyria, whose vassal he was, but refused to give up Jerusalem. The Assyrians withdrew,
apparently because of a divinely sent plague. See 2 Kgs 18–20 and Isa 36–9.
6 **mīn** 'me'; gen. after *forgitan* 'forget'. **hwæðer þū ... wylle** The conj. *hwæðer*
commonly expresses doubt or an element of special pleading on the part of a person asking
a direct question, and hence a sbj. vb. usually follows. Suggested trans.: 'or will you do so
until my end [i.e. death]?'
9 **hwæþer ic ... scyle** 'or must I ...?'
11 **on swylcum dēaðe** 'in such a death'; a rather abrupt paraphrase of the Latin, the
sense of which is 'lest I ever fall asleep in death', i.e. die. **þȳ lǣs** 'lest' or 'in case'; the
vb. that follows is sbj.

15c

Psalm 22

Dāuid sang þysne twā ond twēnteogeþan sealm þā hē wītegode° be Israēla
folces frēodōme, hū hȳ sceoldon bēon ālǣd° of° Babilōnia þēowdōme° ond
hū hī sceoldon ⸢Gode þancian þǣra āra⸣ þe hī ⸢be wege hæfdon hāmweardes⸣,
ond ēac be his āgenre° gehwyrftnesse° ⸢of his wræcsīðe°⸣. Ond ǣlc þǣra° ðe
5   hine singð, hē þancað Gode his ālȳsnesse° of his earfoðum° ond swā dydon þā
apostolas ond eall þæt Crīstene folc ⸢Crīstes ǣriste⸣, ond ēac þanciað Crīstene
men on þyson sealme hēora ālȳsnesse of hēora scyldum° æfter fulluhte°:
Drihten mē rǣt°, ⸢ne byð mē nānes gōdes wan⸣. Ond hē mē geset° on swȳðe
good feohland° ond fēdde mē be wætera° staðum° ond mīn mōd° gehwyrfde°
10   of unrōtnesse° on gefēan°. Hē mē gelǣdde ofer° þā wegas rihtwīsnesse° for° his
naman. Þēah ic nū gange° on midde° þā sceade° dēaðes ⸢ne ondrǣde ic mē⸣ nān
yfel, for þām þū byst mid mē Drihten. Þīn gyrd° ond þīn stæf° mē āfrēfredon°,
⸢þæt is⸣ þīn þrēaung° ond eft° þīn frēfrung°. Þū gegearwodest° beforan mē
⸢swīðe brādne bēod wið þāra willan þe mē hatedon⸣. Þū gesmyredest° ⸢mē⸣ mid

---

1 prophesied   **2** led   from   captivity   **4** own   return   exile   of those   **5** release
tribulations   **7** sins   baptism   **8** guides   (has) set down   **9** pasture   'of waters' (*i.e.* streams)
banks   soul   (has) turned   **10** sadness   joy   along   of righteousness   in   **11** walk
midst +*a*   shadow   **12** rod   staff   (have) comforted   **13** correction   also   consolation
(have) prepared   **14** (have) anointed

---

3   **Gode þancian þǣra āra** The vb. takes the dat. of person (*Gode*) and gen. of cause:
'thank God for the mercies'. See also 5 and 7.   **be wege... hāmweardes** 'on the way
home'.

4   **of his wræcsīðe** David went into exile when his son Absalom revolted against him,
and he was able to return only after Absalom's death. See II Sam 15–20.

6   **Crīstes ǣriste** Another gen. phr. dependent on *þancian*: 'for Christ's resurrection'.

8   **ne byð mē nānes gōdes wan** lit. 'to me is not lacking of any good (thing)', i.e. 'I
want for nothing good'.

11   **ne ondrǣde ic mē** 'I shall not fear'; rflx. *mē* need not be trans.

13   **þæt is** This explanation of the symbolic meaning of *gyrd* and *stæf* is Alfred's addition
to the biblical text. He or his advisers will have found the information in a patristic work,
such as St Augustine's *Enarrationes in psalmos* ('Commentaries on the Psalms').

14   **swīðe brādne bēod** 'a very ample table'. The Latin simply has *mensa* 'a table'
(OE *bēod*), but Alfred amplifies to emphasise the munificence of the feast which the Lord
prepares.   **wið þāra willan þe mē hatedon** Here *þāra* is the antec. of the rel. part. *þe*:
'against the desire (*or* wishes) of those who hated me'. The prep. *wið*, 'against', usually
takes the acc., and *willan*, as an *n*-noun, could be acc. sg. or pl. Implicit in this verse is an
ancient ideal of hospitality which includes protection against enemies.   **mē** obj. pron. not
needed in trans.

15   ele° mīn hēafod°. Drihten, hū mǣre° þīn folc nū is: ǣlce dæge hit symblað°. Ond
     ⌜folgie mē⌝ nū þīn mildheortnes° ealle dagas mīnes līfes, þæt ic mæge wunian°
     on þīnum hūse swīþe lange tiid° ⌜oð lange ylde⌝.

15 oil head illustrious feasts   **16** mercy dwell   **17** time

     16 **folgie mē** sbj. with optative sense: 'may . . . follow me'.
     17 **oð lange ylde** This phr., 'until a long old age', renders a Latin phr. meaning 'for the
length of my days'.

16

A Translator's Problems
(Ælfric's preface to his translation
of Genesis)

The Bible almost universally used in the medieval period was the Latin Vulgate, a name which denotes the version accepted by the *vulgus*, or common people. A recurring source of contention among many church writers and clergy was the question of whether one should or should not make its narratives directly available to the ordinary person – and to priests unable to read Latin – by putting them into vernacular languages. The problem would persist right up until the Reformation, when it was finally resolved in favour of the translators, though not before several of them or their supporters had suffered martyrdom in the cause of vernacular scripture. The Vulgate itself had originally been a 'vernacular' version, made for a Latin-speaking world, but soon its language was considered to be as sacred as the Hebrew and Greek in which the Old and New Testaments, respectively, had been written. Those dedicated to communicating the word of God had two main concerns: first, whether tampering with the 'original' language at all might be sacrilegious, given that the words and the very structure of the sentences (so it was believed) had been dictated by God; and, second, whether it might be dangerous anyway to allow direct access to the text of the Bible to people untrained in the complexities of scriptural history and interpretative disciplines such as 'typology' (the method by which events in the Old Testament are interpreted as prefiguring those in the New).

Both of these concerns are expressed by Ælfric in the preface he wrote to a translation of the first twenty-two chapters of Genesis (see Text 13). We learn that Ælfric's translation had been made at the request of his patron Æthelweard (*d. c.* 998), ealdorman of the western provinces (presumably Devon, Somerset and Dorset; see also p. 4). However, Ælfric declares that he will do no more such translation (though in fact he did); he fears that ignorant men will not realise the symbolic significance of Old Testament events but will take them as offering standards of behaviour for all ages. As for his method of working, although Ælfric claims that he dare not tamper with sacred scripture but will translate it literally, word for word, he crucially makes an exception for those cases where differences between Latin and English idiom do not allow meaningful literal translation – and thus (like translators before and after him) he permits himself in practice to adopt a more pragmatic approach, by translating sense for sense, not word for word.

The preface survives, attached to the translation of Genesis itself, in three manuscripts, though one version is incomplete and another is very badly reproduced. The text here is taken from Oxford, Bodleian Library, Laud misc. 509, a manuscript copied in the second half of the eleventh century. The late WS language shows some levelling of the dative *-um* inflection to *-on* (12, 17 and 65); late *hig* is written in the latter part of the preface (36, 37, etc) but *hī* in the former (23, 24, etc), and *sig* occurs for *sī* (67 and 105). The unstable stressed vowel in the word for 'Latin' will be noted (3, 88, 89, etc). Owing to damage to the edges of the first folio, some letters are now lost, but their restoration (effected silently below but noted in the list of emendations, p. 349) is straightforward.

Further reading

J. Wilcox, ed., *Ælfric's Prefaces*, Durham Medieval Texts 9 (Durham, 1994)

H. Hargreaves, 'From Bede to Wyclif: Medieval English Bible Translations', *Bulletin of the John Rylands Library* 48 (1965), 118–40

A. E. Nichols, 'Ælfric's Prefaces: Rhetoric and Genre', *ES* 49 (1968), 215–23

B. F. Huppé, 'Alfred and Ælfric: a Study of Two Prefaces', in *The Old English Homily and its Backgrounds*, ed. P. E. Szarmach and B. F. Huppé (Albany, NY, 1978), pp. 119–37

M. Griffith, 'How Much Latin Did Ælfric's *magister* Know?', *Notes and Queries* 244 (1999), 176–81

M. Griffith, 'Ælfric's Preface to Genesis: Genre, Rhetoric and the Origins of the *ars dictaminis*', *ASE* 29 (2000), 215–34

M. J. Menzer, 'The Preface as Admonition', in *The Old English Hexateuch: Aspects and Approaches*, ed. R. Barnhouse and B. Withers (Kalamazoo, MI, 2000), pp. 15–39

⌈*Incipit prefatio Genesis Anglice*⌉.

⌈Ælfrīc munuc° grēt° Æðelweard ealdormann ēadmōdlīce°⌉. Þū bæde° mē, lēof°, þæt ic sceolde ðē° āwendan° of Lȳdene° on Englisc þā bōc Genesis. Ðā ⌈þūhte mē⌉ hefigtīme° ⌈þē tō tīþīenne þæs⌉ and þū cwǣde° þā þæt ic ne þorfte°

2 (the) monk greets humbly asked 3 sir for you translate Latin 4 burdensome said had to

1 Lat. '(Here) begins the preface to Genesis in English'.

2 **Ælfrīc munuc...ēadmōdlīce** A formulaic beginning; see also the opening of Alfred's preface to his trans. of Gregory's *Cura pastoralis* (Text 5). On Ealdorman Æthelweard, see headnote.

4 **þūhte mē** impers. vb. with dat.: '(it) seemed to me' (compare ModE 'methought'). See also 6 and 41. **þē tō tīþīenne þæs** 'to grant [infl. inf.] that to you'; *tīþīan* takes a gen. obj.

5   nā° māre° āwendan þǣre bēc° būton° ⌐tō Īsaace⌐, Abrahāmes suna, ⌐for þām þe
sum ōðer man⌐ þe hæfde āwend fram Īsaace þā bōc oþ° ende. Nū þincð° mē, lēof,
þæt þæt weorc is swīðe plēolic° mē° oððe ænigum men tō underbeginnenne°,
for þan þe ic ondrǣde° gif° sum dysig° man þās bōc rǣt° oððe ⌐rǣdan gehȳrþ⌐,
þæt hē wille wēnan° þæt hē mōte° lybban° nū ⌐on þǣre nīwan ǣ° swā swā þā
10   ealdan fæderas° leofodon þā on þǣre tīde ǣr þan þe sēo ealde ǣ gesett° wǣre,
oþþe swā swā men leofodon under Moyses ǣ⌐.

Hwīlon° ic wiste° þæt sum ⌐mæsseprēost⌐, sē° þe mīn magister° wæs on
þām tīman, hæfde þā bōc Genesis and hē cūðe° ⌐be dæle⌐ Lȳden understandan.
⌐Þā cwæþ hē⌐ be° þām hēahfædere° Iācōbe þæt hē hæfde ⌐fēower wīf, twā
15   geswustra° and heora twā⌐ þīnena°. Ful sōð° hē sǣde ac hē nyste°, ⌐ne ic þā
gīt⌐, hū micel tōdāl° ys betweohx° þǣre ealdan ǣ and þǣre nīwan. On anginne°
þisere worulde nam° se brōþer hys swuster tō wīfe and hwīlon° ēac se fæder
tȳmde° be° his āgenre dehter and manega° hæfdon mā° wīfa tō° folces ēacan°
and man ne mihte þā æt fruman° wīfian° būton on° his siblingum°. Gyf hwā°
20   wyle nū swā lybban æfter Crīstes tōcyme° swā swā men leofodon ǣr Moises ǣ

5 no more (of +*g*) book *gs* except   **6** until (it) seems (to +*d*)   **7** dangerous for me
undertake   **8** fear lest foolish reads   **9** imagine may live law   **10** patriarchs
established   **12** At one time knew he master   **13** could   **14** about patriarch
15 sisters maidservants truth *as* did not know [*ne wyste*]   **16** distinction between
beginning   **17** took sometimes   **18** propagated with many more +*g* for increase
19 beginning take a wife among siblings anyone   **20** coming

5 **tō Īsaace** i.e. as far as Gen 22, the chapter in which, in a key test of faith, Abraham
obeys God's command to offer his only son Isaac as a sacrifice.

5–6 **for þām þe** conj. phr.: 'because'; also 43, etc, and the variation *for þan þe* in 8, 50,
etc.   **sum ōðer man** This 'certain other man' (or simply 'person') has not been identified,
but a trans. of the rest of Genesis is included in an early eleventh-century compilation of
substantial parts of the first six OT books in OE (see 13/headnote).

8 **rǣdan gehȳrþ** inf. of duration [§G6d.i.3]: 'hears read'.

9–11 **on þǣre nīwan ǣ...Moyses ǣ** The 'new law' is the NT and the 'old law'
is the OT, or more specifically the first five books of it (the Pentateuch), traditionally
said to have been written by Moses. The sexual licence alluded to was prevalent during the era of the earliest patriarchs, such as Abraham and Jacob, before the time of
Moses.   **ǣr þan þe** conj. phr.: 'before'.   **swā swā** double conj.: 'just as', or simply
'as'; also 20, etc.

12 **mæsseprēost** A 'mass-priest' was qualified to celebrate the eucharistic mass, in
which bread and water are consecrated as the body and blood of Christ.

13 **be dæle** 'in part' or 'to some extent'. It has been argued that this is understatement,
i.e. that the priest in fact understood Latin very well.

14 **Þā cwæþ hē** The priest talked of events related in Gen 29.16–30.13.

14–15 **fēower...twā...twā...** Both numerals are used as adjs., *twā* (from *twēgen*)
agreeing with the nouns *geswustra* and *þīnena* (acc. pl. fem.) [§E3d].

15–16 **ne ic þā gīt** 'nor I then yet', i.e. 'nor I up to then'.

oþþe under Moises ǣ, ⌐ne byð se man nā° Crīsten ne hē furþon° wyrðe° ne byð⌐ þæt ⌐him ǣnig Crīsten man mid ete⌐.

Ðā ungelǣredan° prēostas, gif hī ⌐hwæt lītles⌐ understandað of þām Lȳdenbōcum, þonne þingð him sōna° þæt hī magon° mǣre° lārēowas° bēon, ac

25 hī ne cunnon° ⌐swā þēah⌐ þæt gāstlice° andgit° þǣrtō° and hū sēo ealde ǣ wæs getācnung° tōweardra° þinga oþþe hū sēo nīwe gecȳþnis° æfter Crīstes menniscnisse° wæs gefillednys° ealra þǣra þinga þe sēo ealde gecȳðnis getācnode° tōwearde° be Crīste and be hys gecorenum°. ⌐Hī cweþaþ ēac oft be Pētre,⌐ hwī° hī ne mōton° habban wīf swā swā Pētrus se apostol hæfde, and hī nellað°

30 gehīran° ne witan° þæt se ēadiga° Pētrus leofede æfter° Moises ǣ oþ þæt Crīst, þe on þām tīman tō mannum cōm, began tō bodienne° his hālige godspel and gecēas° Pētrum ǣrest° him° tō° gefēran°. Þā forlēt° Pētrus þǣrrihte° his wīf and ealle þā twelf apostolas, þā þe wīf hæfdon, forlēton ⌐ǣgþer ge wīf ge⌐ ǣhta° and folgodon Crīstes lāre° tō þǣre nīwan ǣ and clǣnnisse° þe hē silf þā ārǣrde°.

35 Prēostas sindon gesette tō° lārēowum° þām lǣwedum° folce. Nū ⌐gedafnode him⌐ þæt hig cūþon þā ealdan ǣ gāstlīce° understandan and hwæt Crīst silf tǣhte° and his apostolas on þǣre nīwan gecȳðnisse, þæt hig mihton þām folce wel° wissian° tō Godes gelēafan° and wel bīsnian° tō° gōdum weorcum.

Wē secgað ēac ⌐foran tō⌐ þæt sēo bōc is swīþe dēop gāstlīce tō under-

40 standenne and wē ne wrītaþ nā māre būton þā nacedan° gerecednisse°. Þonne

21 not at all even worthy **23** ignorant **24** at once can great teachers **25** know spiritual meaning pertaining to it **26** prefiguration future testament **27** incarnation fulfilment signified **28** in advance 'chosen ones' (*i.e.* disciples) **29** why may will not **30** 'hear' (*i.e.* accept) understand blessed according to **31** preach **32** chose first for himself as companion abandoned at once **33** possessions **34** teaching purity established **35** as teachers lay **36** spiritually **37** taught **38** properly guide +*d* faith (in +*g*) set an example in **40** bare narrative

21 **ne byð... ne byð** A series of double negs.: 'that man is no Christian at all and is not even worthy'.
22 **him...mid ete** The syntax separates the prep. from its pron. obj.: 'should eat with him'.
23 **hwæt lītles** lit. 'something of a little (thing)', i.e. 'something' or 'a little'.
25 **swā þēah** adv. phr.: 'nevertheless' or 'however'.
28 **Hī cweþaþ ēac oft be Pētre** 'They speak also often about Peter...'. In the following two sentences, we hear how ignorant priests, wanting to be married, cite the example of the apostle Peter, but Ælfric points out that it was only until he received the word of Christ that Peter lived according to the 'old law' of Moses; afterwards he abandoned wife and home. The opening of the first sentence could be paraphrased, 'They often raise the subject of Peter, asking why they [the priests] may not have wives'. In the manuscript, *Pētre* had been erased and *Paul* written above, erroneously, in a modern hand.
33 **ǣþer ge... ge** 'both... and...'.
35–6 **gedafnode him** The impers. vb. is pret. sbj.: '(it) would befit them'.
39 **foran tō** 'beforehand', i.e. 'by way of introduction'.

þincþ° þām ungelǣredum þæt eall þæt andgit bēo belocen° on þǣre ānfealdan°
gerecednisse ac hit ys swīþe feor° þām°. Sēo bōc ys gehāten° Genesis, þæt ys
⸢gecyndbōc⸣, for þām þe hēo ys firmest° bōca and spricþ be ǣlcum gecinde°,
ac hēo ne spricð nā be ⸢þǣra engla gesceapenisse⸣. Hēo onginð þus: ⸢*In principio*
45   *creauit Deus celum and terram*⸣. Þæt ys on Englisc, 'On andginne gesceōp° God
heofenan and eorþan'. Hit wæs sōðlīce° swā gedōn þæt God ælmihtig geworhte
on anginne, ⸢þā þā⸣ hē wolde°, gesceafta°. Ac swā þēah æfter° gāstlicum andgite
þæt anginn ys Crist, swā swā hē sylf cwæþ tō þām Iūdēiscum°: ⸢'Ic eom angin⸣
þe tō ēow sprece'. Þurh þis angin worhte God fæder heofenan and eorþan,
50   for þan þe hē gesceōp ealle gesceafta þurh þone sunu, sē þe was ǣfre° of him
āccenned°, ⸢wīsdōm of þām wīsan fæder⸣.

Eft° stynt° on þǣre bēc on þām forman° ⸢ferse: *et spiritus Dei ferebatur super
aquas*⸣. Þæt is on Englisc, 'and Godes gāst wæs geferod° ofer wæteru'. Godes
gāst ys se hālga gāst, þurh þone° gelīffǣste° se fæder ealle þā gesceafta þe
55   hē gesceōp þurh þone sunu, and se hālga gāst færþ° geond° manna heortan
and silþ° ūs synna forgifnisse, ǣrest þurh wæter on þām fulluhte° and syþþan
þurh dǣtbōte°. And gif hwā° forsihð° þā forgifenisse þe se hālga gāst sylþ,
þonne biþ his synn ǣfre unmyltsiendlic° on ēcnysse°. Oft ys sēo hālige þrinnys°
geswutelod° on þisre bēc, ⸢swā swā ys⸣ on þām worde þe God cwæþ: ⸢'Uton°

41 (it) will seem (to +*d*) contained simple   **42** far from that called   **43** the first   species
45 created   **46** truly   **47** wanted   created beings   according to   **48** Jews   **50** eternally
51 begotten   **52** Then again   stands   first   **53** carried   **54** whom   brought to life
55 passes through   **56** gives baptism   **57** penance   anyone   rejects   **58** unforgivable
eternity   Trinity   **59** revealed   Let us

43 **gecyndbōc** Strictly speaking, Ælfric here translates Lat. *genus*, 'origin', 'kind' or
'species' ('book of origin'), not *genesis*, which signifies 'generation', 'birth' or 'creation'.

44 **þǣra engla gesceapenisse** 'the creation of the angels'. The problem of when and
how they were created greatly exercised medieval writers, but Ælfric avoids discussion here.

44–5 **In principio... terram** Lat. 'In the beginning, God created heaven and earth'
(Gen 1.1).

47 **þā þā** double conj., 'when'; lit. 'then when'.

48 **Ic eom angin** See Rev 1.8, 21.6 and 22.13. Understanding the theological puzzles and
paradoxes presented in the next dozen lines depends on an awareness of the Christian belief
that God, his son Christ and the Holy Spirit are unified in the Trinity (the 'three-in-one')
and that God exists eternally outside the framework of mere human time.

51 **wīsdōm of þām wīsan fæder** The Son (Christ) is seen as a manifestation of the
Father's (God's) wisdom.

52–3 **ferse** 'section' or 'paragraph' are better renderings than 'verse', for the biblical
verse-division used today was not known in Anglo-Saxon times. *et spiritus... aquas* Lat.:
'And the spirit of God was carried [i.e. moved] over the waters' (Gen 1.2).

59 **swā swā ys** subj. pron. unexpressed: 'just as (it) is'; similarly, *wæs beboden*, 81, *is
ēac to witenne*, 93, and *hine silfne gewyrð*, 99–100.

60 wircean° mannan tō° ūre ānlīcnisse°⌐. ⌐Mid þām þe⌐ hē cwæð 'uton wircean'
    ys sēo þrinnis gebīcnod°; mid þām þe hē cwæð 'tō ūre ānlīcnisse' ys sēo sōðe°
    ānnis° geswutelod. Hē ne cwæþ nā° menifealdlīce°, 'tō ūrum ānlīcnissum', ac
    ānfealdlīce°, 'tō ūre ānlīcnisse'. Eft cōmon ⌐þrī englas⌐ tō Abrahāme and hē
    spræc tō him eallon þrīm° swā swā tō ānum. Hū clipode° ⌐Abēles blōd⌐ tō
65 Gode būton° swā swā ælces mannes misdǣda° wrēgaþ° hine tō Gode būtan°
    wordum? Be þisum lītlum° man mæg understandan hū dēop sēo bōc ys on
    gāstlicum andgite, ⌐þēah þe⌐ hēo mid lēohtlicum° wordum āwriten sig°.
        Eft Iōsēp, þe wæs gesæld° tō Ēgipta lande, and hē āhredde° þæt folc wið°
    þone miclan hunger, hæfde Crīstes getācnunge þe° wæs geseald for ūs tō cwale°
70 and ūs āhredde ⌐fram þām ēcan hungre helle sūsle⌐. Ðæt micele ⌐geteld⌐ þe
    Moises worhte mid wunderlicum cræfte on þām wēstene°, swā swā him God
    sylf gedihte°, hæfde getācnunge Godes gelāþunge° þe hē silf āstealde° þurh
    his apostolas mid menigfældum frætewum° and fægerum° þēawum°. Tō þām
    geweorce° brōhte þæt folc gold and seolfor and dēorwirþe° gimstānas and
75 menigfælde mǣrþa°; sume ēac brōhton gātehǣr°, swā swā God bebēad°. Ðæt
    gold getācnode ūrne gelēafan and ūre gōde ingehīd° þe wē Gode offrian sceolon.
    Þæt seolfor getācnode Godes sprǣca° and þā hālgan lāra þe wē habban° sceolon
    ⌐tō Godes weorcum⌐. Ðā gimstānas getācnodon mislice° fægernissa° on Godes
    mannum. Ðæt gātehǣr getācnode þā stīþan° dǣdbōte þǣra manna þe heora
80 sinna behrēowsiað°. Man offrode ēac ⌐fela cinna orf⌐ Gode tō lāce° binnan°

60 make in likeness **61** signified true **62** unity not in the plural **63** in the singular
64 three *d* cried out **65** except sins accuse without **66** small (things) **67** lucid is *sbj*
68 sold saved from **69** who (*i.e.* Christ) death **71** desert **72** instructed church
established **73** adornments pleasing customs **74** construction precious **75** fine things
goat's hair commanded **76** intention **77** utterances keep **78** various excellent features
79 resolute **80** repent offering within

59–60 **Uton … ānlīcnisse** See Gen 1.26. **Mid þām þe** conj. phr.: 'When'.
63 **þrī englas** See Gen 18.1–5.
64 **Abēles blōd** Ælfric rather abruptly abandons his allusions to the Trinity in order to
add an unconnected further example of a biblical event with deep spiritual meaning. How
else, he asks, are we to interpret the incident when Abel's blood, shed by his killer (and
brother) Cain, 'cries out' to God (Gen 4.10) other than as a prefiguration of the way our
own sins silently condemn us before the all-knowing God?
67 **þēah þe** 'even though' (lit. 'though that').
70 **fram … helle sūsle** 'from the eternal hunger of hell's torment'. **geteld** 'tabernacle'
(or 'tent'); on its making, see Ex 35–9.
78 **tō Godes weorcum** 'for the works of God', i.e. 'in order to do God's works'.
80 **fela cinna orf** 'cattle of many kinds'. Here *fela* is an adj., describing gen. pl. *cinna*.
On the ritual sacrifice of animals, see Ex 29 and Lev 3, but Ælfric draws on patristic sources
as well.

þām getelde, ⌐be þām⌐ ys swīþe menigfeald getācnung. And wæs beboden° þæt
se tægel sceolde bēon gehāl° æfre on þām nȳtene° æt þǣre offrunge, for þǣre
getācnunge þæt God wile þæt wē simle° wel dōn oþ ende ūres līfes; ⌐þonne biþ
se tægel geoffrod on ūrum weorcum⌐.

85   Nū is sēo foresǣde° bōc on manegum stōwum° swīþe nærolīce° gesett° and
þēah° swīðe dēoplīce° on þām gāstlicum andgite, and hēo is swā geendebyrd°
swā swā God silf hig gedihte° þām wrītere Moise, and wē ne durron° nā māre
āwrītan on Englisc þonne þæt Līden hæfþ, ne þā endebirdnisse° āwendan°,
⌐būton þām ānum⌐ þæt þæt Lēden and þæt Englisc ⌐nabbað nā āne wīsan on
90 þǣre sprǣce fadunge⌐. Ǣfre sē þe āwent° oþþe sē þe tǣcþ° of° Lēdene on
Englisc, æfre hē sceal gefadian° hit swā þæt þæt Englisc hæbbe his āgene°
wīsan, elles° hit biþ swīþe gedwolsum° tō rǣdenne° þām° þe þæs Lēdenes
wīsan ne can°. ⌐Is ēac tō witanne⌐ þæt sume gedwolmen° wǣron þe woldon
āwurpan° þā ealdan ǣ and sume woldon habban þā ealdan and āwurpan þā
95 nīwan, swā swā þā Iūdēiscan dōð. Ac Crīst sylf and his apostolas ūs tǣhton°
ǣgþer° tō healdenne þā ealdan gāstlīce and þā nīwan sōþlīce mid weorcum°.
God gesceōp ūs twā ēagan and twā ēaran, twā nosþirlu° and twēgen weleras°,
twā handa and twēgen fēt, and hē wolde ēac habban twā gecȳðnissa on þissere
worulde geset°, þā ealdan and þā nīwan, for þan þe hē dēþ° swā swā hine silfne
100 gewyrð° and hē nænne° rǣdboran° næfð° ⌐ne nān man ne þearf him cweþan tō⌐,
'Hwī dēst þū swā?' Wē sceolon āwendan ūrne willan tō his gesetnissum° and
wē ne magon gebīgean° his gesetnissa tō ūrum lustum°.

    Ic cweþe nū þæt ic ne dearr° ne ic nelle° nāne bōc æfter þissere of Lēdene on
Englisc āwendan. And ic bidde þē, lēof ealdorman, þæt þū mē ⌐þæs⌐ nā leng°

81 commanded   82 whole beast   83 always   85 aforementioned places concisely
composed   86 yet profoundly set out   87 dictated dare   88 order change
90 translates interprets from   91 arrange own   92 or else confusing read
for him   93 know heretics   94 discard   95 taught   96 both deeds   97 nostrils
cheeks   99 composed does   100 pleases no adviser has not   101 laws   102 bend
desires   103 dare will not   104 longer

    81 **be þām** The pron. is rel.: 'concerning which'.
    83–4 **þonne biþ se tægel ... weorcum** 'then the tail will be offered among our works'.
The tail will signify the continuation of our good works for God.
    89 **būton þām ānum** 'except in the one (case)'.
    89–90 **nabbað nā ... fadunge** 'do not have a single way in the arrangement of the
language'; i.e. they do not have the same syntax. The 'Laud' manuscript (see headnote)
has *fandunge*, 'test' or 'testing', but *fadunge* is in the two other witnesses and is preferable,
especially in view of Ælfric's use of the related vb. *gefadian* in the next line.
    93 **Is ēac tō witanne** infl. inf. with pass. sense: '(It) is also to be understood'.
    100 **ne nān man ... tō** multiple neg.: 'nor need (*or* must) any person say to him'.
    104 **þæs** The gen. pron. is the obj. of *bidde*: 'for that'.

105   ne bidde, ⌐þī lǣs þe ic bēo þē ungehīrsum oþþe lēas gif ic dō⌐. God þē sig milde
⌐ā on ēcnisse⌐. Ic bidde nū on Godes naman, gif hwā þās bōc āwrītan° wylle,
þæt hē hig gerihte° wel be° þǣre bysne°, for þan þe ic nāh° geweald° ⌐þēah þe
hig hwā tō wōge bringe⌐ þurh lēase° wrīteras° and hit byð þonne his plēoh°, nā
mīn. Mycel yfel dēð se unwrītere° gif hē nele° hys wōh° gerihtan.

106 copy   **107** correct   from   exemplar   have not   control   **108** lax   scribes
responsibility   **109** bad scribe   will not   errors

105   **þī lǣs þe ... gif ic dō** Ælfric envisages himself in a double bind: 'lest I should be
(*bēo*, sbj.) disobedient to you (if I disobey your command to translate again) or false (to my
vow to do no more translating) if I do (translate again)'.

106   **ā on ēcnisse** 'ever in eternity', i.e. 'for ever more'.

107–8   **þēah þe ... bringe** 'even if someone (*hwā*) brings it (*hig*, acc. sg. fem. [i.e. the
book]) to error', i.e. 'even if someone corrupts it'. Cf. Ælfric's similar remarks in 4/23–8.

17

Satan's Challenge
(*Genesis B*, lines 338–441)

The 'Junius' manuscript (Oxford, Bodleian Library, Junius 11), named after the Dutch scholar who studied it and published its contents in the seventeenth century, contains three OE poems on Old Testament themes, *Genesis*, *Exodus* and *Daniel*, along with a fourth called *Christ and Satan*, which develops some of these themes from the perspective of the New Testament (but which may not have been part of the volume's earliest design). Together, these poems explore some of the major themes of Christian history. The manuscript was compiled in the second half of the tenth or the early eleventh century and the text is interspersed with line drawings, some embellished with coloured inks. *Genesis*, the longest of the poems with its 2936 surviving lines, presents an imaginative paraphrase of the first twenty-two chapters of Genesis. In fact, however, it is a hybrid work, for interpolated in it are over six hundred lines of a different origin from the rest, though they fit well into the narrative (lines 235–851, or thereabouts). The interpolated lines are known as *Genesis B* (formerly the *Later Genesis*) to distinguish them from the larger poem, *Genesis A*, into which they fit. *Genesis B* describes the fall from heaven of Lucifer and his followers, the temptation of Eve, the fall of her and Adam, and finally the expulsion of the pair from Eden. The poem is unique in the surviving literature, as far as we can tell, in being a close OE translation of an original work in Old Saxon. This was the language, nearly related to OE, spoken by the inhabitants of Saxony (part of present-day Germany), to whom the Anglo-Saxons sent Christian missionaries during the seventh and eighth centuries. Twenty-five lines of an Old Saxon version of the poem are preserved in a manuscript in the Vatican Library.

The story of the fall of the angels as a result of the subversive pride of Lucifer, God's brightest and most favoured angel (whose name means 'light-bearing one'), is not told in the Bible. For many church writers, however, it provides an explanation of the origin of sin and, according to some interpretations, gives a rationale for God's decision to create humankind – namely, to replace the expelled rebel angels. It also sets up the causal framework within which the temptation and subsequent fall are played out. Without the constraints of a canonical biblical version to curb his imaginative power, the poet of *Genesis B* has turned Lucifer's story into a human drama driven by psychological realism. Satan (the name given to Lucifer once he has fallen) is a vaunting warrior-chief in the heroic mould, who reminds his retainers of their obligations to him. Though shackled in the abyss, he is gripped by the self-delusive but magnificent rhetoric of defiance and revenge. It is not surprising that he has been compared with the Satan of *Paradise Lost* (1667) by the English poet John Milton, a contemporary of Junius. But the significance of the parallels may have been overstated, for this is an old and powerful story and Satan's character is a perfectly logical part of it. In the extract given below, Satan reviews his vain struggle with God, vents his anguish that Adam and Eve are now to share what was once 'his' kingdom, and promises a special reward to any of his followers who succeeds in persuading Adam and Eve to rebel against God's commands.

The language of *Genesis B*, like that of the other 'Junius' texts, is predominantly late WS in character, but a number of earlier forms have aroused speculation that the poem was translated from its Old Saxon original during the reign of Alfred, who brought over at least one scholar from Saxony to help him in his programme of educational renewal (see p. 36n). Examples of such forms are *nīobedd* (6; not *nēobed*) and *ǣnegum* (72; not *ǣnigum*, but cf. *ǣnige* in 54). There are also several words which either occur uniquely in *Genesis B* or never occur elsewhere with the meaning they have here. Some of these are modelled on Old Saxon words and include *rōmigan* (23; Old Saxon *rômon*) and *hearmscearu* (95; Old Saxon *harmskara*). But others have no known Old Saxon equivalent. These include the verb *rīdan* used in a special sense (35; see note), the noun *grindlas* (47), and the verbs *oðwendan* (66) and *āhwettan* (69). Particularly notable is the variety of verb-forms used by our scribe (though metrical needs dictate some of the variation): *syndon, synd* and *synt* (52, 83 and 84), *gȳman* and *gīeman* (9 and 12) and (for the present tense third-person singular of *weorþan*) *weorð, wurðeþ* and *wyrð* (68, 93 and 94). The lines of the extract are numbered here from 1, but their numbering in the *Genesis* poem as a whole is also indicated.

Further reading

B. J. Timmer, *The Later 'Genesis'*, rev. edn (Oxford, 1948)

A. N. Doane, *The Saxon 'Genesis': an Edition of the West Saxon 'Genesis B' and the Old Saxon Vatican 'Genesis'* (Madison, WI, 1991)

R. Woolf, 'The Devil in Old English Poetry', *Review of English Studies* n.s. 4 (1953), 1–12, repr. in her *Art and Doctrine: Essays on Medieval Literature*, ed. H. Donoghue (London, 1986), pp. 1–14

T. D. Hill, 'The Fall of Angels and Man in the Old English Genesis B', in *Anglo-Saxon Poetry: Essays in Appreciation for John C. McGalliard*, ed. L. E. Nicholson and D. W. Frese (Notre Dame, IN, 1975), pp. 279–90

Þā spræc se ofermōda° cyning   þe ǣr wæs° engla   proud   had been
  scȳnost°   brightest
hwītost° on heofne   ond his hearran° lēof°   most radiant   lord *ds*   dear (to +*d*)

[340]   drihtne dȳre°   oð° ⌐hīe⌐ tō dole° wurdon°   precious (to +*d*)   until   folly   turned
þæt° ⌐him for° gālscipe°   God sylfa wearð   so that   because of   wantonness

5   mihtig on mōde yrre⌐.   Wearp° ⌐hine⌐ on þæt morðer°   Threw   torment
  ⌐innan⌐,
niðer° on þæt nīobedd°,   ond scēop° him   down   'corpse-bed' (*i.e.* hell)   created
  naman siððan°:   thereafter
cwæð se hēhsta°   ⌐hātan sceolde⌐   'highest one' (*i.e.* God)
Sātan siððan,   hēt° hine þǣre sweartan° helle°   commanded   black   hell *gs*
grundes° gȳman°   nalles° wið God winnan°.   abyss *gs*   control +*g*   not   contend

10   ⌐Sātan maðelode°⌐,   sorgiende° spræc,   spoke out   sorrowing
sē° ðe helle forð°   healdan° sceolde   he   henceforth   possess
gīeman þæs grundes.   Wæs ǣr Godes engel,

[350]   hwīt on heofne,   oð hine his hyge° forspēon°   ambition (*or* pride)   seduced
ond his ofermētto°   ealra° swīðost°,   presumption   of all   most

15   þæt hē ne wolde   wereda° Drihtnes   of hosts
word wurðian°.   Wēoll° him oninnan°   respect   Welled   within +*d*
hyge ymb his heortan,   ⌐hāt wæs him ūtan°   outside
wrāðlic wīte⌐.   Hē þā ⌐worde cwæð⌐:
'Is þæs° ænga° styde°   ungelīc° swīðe   this   constricted   place   unlike +*d*

20   ⌐þām ōðrum⌐   þe wē ǣr cūdon°   knew
hēan° on heofonrīce°   þe mē mīn hearra   high   heavenly kingdom
  onlāg°,   granted (to +*d*)

---

3   **hīe** 'they'; i.e. the angels of 1.

4–5   **him ... on mōde yrre** The adj. *mihtig*, like *sylfa*, qualifies *God*, but is separated and given an emphatic position at the head of the next half-line; the dat. pron. is rflx.: 'mighty God himself became angry at heart'.

5   **hine** i.e. Satan.   **innan** adv., either repeating the sense of *on*, 'into', or meaning 'within', i.e. within hell, anticipating later lines.

7   **hātan sceolde** '(that he) must be called'. 'Satan' is from a Hebrew word meaning 'adversary'.

10   **Sātan maðelode** A formula much used in OE heroic poetry (e.g. *The Battle of Maldon*, 30/42 and 309); Satan does not in fact begin to speak until 19.

17–18   **hāt ... wrāðlic wīte** Both adjs. describe *wīte*: 'there was hot and cruel punishment'.   **worde cwæð** lit. 'spoke with (this) utterance'.

20   **þām ōðrum** 'the other (place)'. The half-line needs an extra syllable to be metrically complete, and in the Old Saxon poem from which the OE was apparently translated (see headnote), the equivalent of *þām ōðrum* does in fact have that extra syllable: *thesero oðrun*. Some editors add *hām*, 'home', to the OE version.

    þēah wē hine° for° þām alwaldan°   āgan° ne   it because of almighty possess
      mōston°,   could *sbj*

[360] rōmigan° ūres rīces. Næfð° hē þēah° riht gedōn   extend +*g* Has not however
    þæt hē ūs hæfð befælled°   ᚱfȳre tō botme   struck down
25 helle þǣre hātan˥, heofonrīce benumen°.   deprived (of +*d*)
    Hafað hit gemearcod° mid moncynne   designated
    tō gesettanne°. Þæt mē is sorga° mǣst   be settled *infl inf* of sorrows
    þæt Ādam sceal°, þe wæs of eorðan geworht°,   is to   made
    mīnne stronglican° stōl° behealdan°,   mighty throne occupy
30 ᚱwesan him on wynne˥ ond ᚱwē þis wīte þolien˥
    hearm° on þisse helle. Wālā°, ᚱāhte ic mīnra handa   affliction *as* Alas!
      geweald°   control
    ond mōste āne tīd˥ ūte° weorðan°,   outside (come) to be
[370] wesan° ᚱāne winterstunde˥, þonne ic ᚱmid þȳs werode°˥ –   be (outside) troop
    ac ᚱlicgað mē ymbe˥ īrenbenda°,   iron bonds
35 ᚱrīdeð racentan sāl˥. Ic eom rīces lēas°;   without +*g*
    habbað mē swā° hearde helle clommas°   such fetters *np*
    fæste° befangen°. Hēr is fȳr micel   tightly clasped
    ufan° ond neoðone°. Ic ā° ne geseah°   above below ever saw
    lāðran° landscipe°; līg° ne āswāmað°   more hateful region fire (will) cease
40 hāt ofer° helle. ᚱMē habbað hringa° gespong°   throughout of rings fastenings
    slīðhearda° sāl° sīðes āmyrred˥,   savagely cruel halter

24–5 **fȳre tō botme** double dat. construction: 'to the fire, to the bottom', i.e. 'to the bottom of the fire'. **helle þǣre hātan** dat. phr. parallel with 24b (the inflection of the adj. is weak dat. sg. fem.): 'to hell the hot', i.e. 'into hot hell'.

30 **wesan him on wynne** The rflx. dat. pron. is best not trans.: '(and is) to be in bliss'. **wē … þolien** The form of the vb. is sbj. but should probably be infin. (*þolian*), with the modal *sceal* (28) still understood: 'we (must) suffer'.

31–2 **āhte … mōste** Both pret. vbs. are sbj. in mood (though in both cases the pret. indic. forms would be the same): 'had I … could I …', i.e. 'if I had … if I were able to…'. **āne tīd** acc. of time: 'one time', or 'just once'.

33 **āne winterstunde** acc. of time: 'for (just) one winter's hour'; i.e. the briefest of periods. **mid þȳs werode** – *mid* here takes the instr. case. The poet has Satan break off his yearning for rhetorical effect.

34 **licgað mē ymbe** 'lie around me', i.e. 'encircle me' See also 45.

35 **rīdeð racentan sāl** The vb. suggests a ship 'riding' at anchor, but the action is being done to Satan and so an obj. pron. is needed; perhaps, 'a loop (*or* halter) of chain swings (me)', or, following a popular interpretation, 'chafes me'. The vb. is used to signify swinging on a gallows in *Beowulf* (2445).

40–1 **Mē habbað … sīðes āmyrred** The dat. pron. ('for me') is best seen as possessive: 'have hindered my movement' (*āmyrran* takes a gen. obj.). Similarly in 42 (though here 'from me' is also a possibility). The 'fastenings of rings' are presumably a chain.

āfyrred° mē° mīn fēðe°;   fēt synt   removed   from me   power of walking
   gebundene°,   fettered

[380]   handa gehæfte°.   Synt ⌐þissa heldora   shackled
   wegas⌐ forworhte°   ⌐swā ic mid wihte ne mæg   obstructed

45   of⌐ þissum lioðobendum°.   ⌐Licgað⌐ mē ymbe   'limb-bonds' (*i.e.* fetters)
   heardes īrenes   hāte° geslægene°   hotly   struck (*i.e.* forged)
   grindlas° grēate°.   ⌐Mid þȳ⌐ mē God hafað   bolts   huge
   gehæfted be þām healse°,   swā ic wāt° hē mīnne   neck   know
   hige cūðe°   knew
   ond ⌐þæt⌐ wiste° ēac,   weroda Drihten,   knew

50   þæt sceolde° ⌐unc Ādame⌐   yfele° gewurðan°   (it) must   evilly   turn out
   ymb° þæt heofonrīce,   ⌐þær⌐ ic āhte° mīnra handa geweald.   concerning   had
   Ac ðoliaþ° wē nū þrēa° on helle: þæt syndon   suffer   punishments
   þȳstro° ond hǣto°,   darkness   heat

[390]   ⌐grimme° grundlēase°⌐.   Hafað ūs God sylfa   fierce   boundless
   forswāpen° on þās sweartan mistas.   Swā° hē ūs°   swept away   Though   to us
   ne mæg ǣnige synne gestǣlan°,   impute

55   þæt wē him ⌐on þām lande⌐ lāð° gefremedon°,   hē hæfð   harm   did
   ūs þēah° þæs lēohtes bescyrede°,   yet   deprived (of +*g*)
   beworpen° ⌐on ealra wīta mǣste⌐.   Ne magon wē þæs°   cast (us)   for that
   wrace° gefremman,   vengeance
   gelēanian° him ⌐mid lāðes wihte⌐   þæt° hē ūs hafað   repay   because
   þæs lēohtes bescyrede?

43–4 **þissa heldora wegas** 'the ways of [*i.e.* through] these gates of hell'.

44–5 **swā ic mid wihte ne mæg of** A vb. of motion is om. after the modal vb.: 'so (that) I cannot escape at all from...'.

45 **Licgað** The subj. of the vb. is the phr. *grindlas grēate* ('huge bolts') in 47, as defined by the two half-lines in 46.

47 **Mid þȳ** conj. phr., correl. with *swā* in 48: 'Because..., (so...)'.

49 **þæt** correl. with *þæt* in 50 and best left untrans.

50 **unc Ādame** There are parallels in other OE poems for this awkwardly elliptical expression. Here *unc* is the dat. dual pron., 'for us two'. The 'me' of this pair is understood but the second party is defined by his name in apposition (i.e. parallel) and is so also in the dat. Thus, 'for us two, (me and) Adam', or simply 'for me and Adam'.

51 **þǣr** As the clause introduced here is the second part of a conditional statement set up by *sceolde*, *þǣr* (here the conj. 'where') is best trans. 'if': i.e. 'it must have turned out... if I had...'.

53 **grimme grundlēase** The adjs. may describe *þrēa, helle* or *þȳstro ond hǣto*, or indeed all of them.

55 **on þām lande** i.e. in heaven.

56 **on ealra wīta mǣste** 'into the greatest of all torments'.

57 **mid lāðes wihte** 'with anything of harm', i.e. 'with some harm'.

Hē hæfð nū gemearcod ānne middangeard°   þær hē hæfð mon   world
  geworhtne

⌐æfter his onlīcnesse°⌐;   mid° þām° hē wile eft°   image   through   him   again
  gesettan°   settle

60 heofona rīce mid hluttrum° sāulum°.   Wē þæs° sculon   pure   souls   about this
  hycgan° georne°:   think   earnestly

þæt wē on Ādame,   gif wē æfre mægen,

ond on his eafrum° ⌐swā some⌐,   andan°   descendants   (our) grudge
  gebētan°,   make good *sbj*

⌐onwendan him þær willan sīnes⌐   gif wē hit mægen wihte°   at all

[400] āþencan°.   contrive

Ne ⌐gelȳfe⌐ ic mē° nū þæs ⌐lēohtes⌐ furðor°   ⌐þæs þe⌐   for myself   any more
  hē him° penceð lange nīotan°,   for himself   enjoy +*g*

65 ⌐þæs ēades⌐, mid his engla cræfte°;   ne magon wē þæt ⌐on aldre⌐   strength
  gewinnan°   bring about

þæt wē mihtiges Godes mōd° onwæcen°.   Uton°   will   weaken *sbj*   Let us
  oðwendan° hit nū ⌐monna bearnum⌐,   take away

þæt heofonrīce, nū wē hit habban ne mōton,   ⌐gedōn þæt⌐
  hīe his hyldo° forlǣten°,   favour   loose *sbj*

þæt hīe þæt onwendon° þæt hē mid his worde bebēad°.   disregard *sbj*   ordered
  Þonne weorð° hē him° wrāð° on mōde,   will become   against them   angry

āhwet° hīe from his hyldo: þonne sculon hīe þās°   (he) will reject   this
  helle sēcan

70 ond þās grimman grundas°:   þonne mōton we hīe ⌐ūs tō⌐   depths
  giongrum⌐ habban,

⌐fīra bearn⌐ on þissum fæstum clomme°.   Onginnað°   grip   Let us begin
  nū ymb þā fyrde° þencean.   campaign

---

59 **æfter his onlīcnesse** See Gen 1.26.

62 **swā some** 'in the same way', or 'likewise'.

63 **onwendan him þær willan sīnes** 'upset for him in that respect (*þǣr*) his (God's) will', i.e. 'frustrate his will in this'.

64 **gelȳfe** The vb. is used in the sense of 'hope for' and governs the gen.   **lēohtes** The noun ('light' or 'splendour') is here a synecdoche for heaven.   **þæs þe** 'which', in concord with *leohtes*.

65 **þæs ēades** 'the blessedness'; a var. for *leohtes*, and hence in grammatical concord. **on aldre** 'in eternity', or 'ever'.

66 **monna bearnum** 'from the children of men (*or* people)'. This is a stock epithet for 'humans'; see also 71.

67 **gedōn þæt** Like *oðwendan* in 66, this infin. is governed by *uton*: '(and) let us act so that', or 'bring it about that'.

70 **ūs tō giongrum** 'to us as subordinates', i.e. 'as our subordinates'.

71 **fīra bearn** 'the children of men', parallel with *hīe* in 70 ('them'). Cf. 9b/35n.

⌐Gif ic⌐ ǣnegum° þegne°   þēodenmādmas°   to any follower princely treasures
[*410*] gēara° forgēafe°,   þenden° wē on þan gōdan rīce   once   gave   while
gesǣlige° sǣton°   ond hæfdon ūre setla° geweald,   happy   dwelt   thrones *gp*
75 þonne hē mē nā° on lēofran° tīd   ⌐lēanum⌐ ne meahte°   never   better   could *sbj*
mīne gife° gyldan° –   ⌐gif his gīen wolde   gift *as*   repay
mīnra þegna hwilc   geþafa wurðan⌐,
þæt° hē ūp heonon°   ūte mihte   (namely) that   from here
cuman° þurh þās clūstro°   ond hæfde cræft° mid°   go   barriers   strength   in
him
80 þæt hē mid feðerhoman°   flēogan meahte,   'feather-dress' (*i.e.* wings)
windan° on wolcne°   ⌐þær⌐ geworht° stondað   circle   sky   created
Ādam ond Ēue   on eorðrīce
mid welan° bewunden°,   ond wē synd   prosperity   surrounded
[*420*]   āworpene° hider   cast down
on þās dēopan dalo°.   Nū hīe Drihtne synt   valley
85 wurðran° micle°   ond mōton him°   more valued by +*d*   much   for themselves
þone welan āgan
þe wē on heofonrīce   habban sceoldon,
⌐rīce mid rihte⌐.   Is se rǣd° gescyred°   benefit   allotted (to +*d*)
monna cynne.   Þæt mē is on mīnum mōde swā sār°,   painful
on mīnum hyge hrēoweð°   þæt hīe heofonrīce   (it) grieves (me)
90 āgan tō aldre.   Gif hit ēower° ǣnig mǣge   of you
gewendan° mid wihte   þæt hīe word Godes,   bring about
lāre°, forlǣten°,   sōna° hīe ⌐him þē lāðran   (his) teaching   abandon *sbj*   at once
bēoð⌐.
[*430*] Gif hīe brēcað° his gebodscipe°,   þonne hē him°   breach   authority   with them
ābolgen° wurðeþ;   enraged

72 **Gif ic . . .** In the first part of this long sentence (which ends in 84), *Gif* is correl. with
þonne in 75: 'If . . . , then . . .', and the main statement finishes with *gyldan* in 76a. The rest of
the sentence – a series of subord. clauses instigated by another *gif* clause in 76b – is merely
an extension of that statement, describing in conditional tenses what action the followers
of Satan might take to repay him.

75 **lēanum** dat. of instrument: 'with returns'.

76–7 **gif his . . . geþafa wurðan** *his* is the gen. of *hit*, governed by *geþafa* in the next
line: 'if now (*gīen*) any of my thanes would turn out to be (*wurðan*, sbj.) consenting to it',
i.e. 'would consent to it'.

81 **þær** '(to where'. Some editors prefer to start a new sentence here, thus translating
'There . . .'.

87 **rīce mid rihte** '(our) kingdom by right'.

92 **him þē lāðran bēoð** 'will be the more loathsome to him' (*þē* is instr.).

	siððan bið him se wela onwended° ond wyrð him wīte	overturned
	gegarwod°,	prepared
95	sum heard hearmscearu°. ⌜Hycgað his⌝ ealle°	punishment all (of you)
	hū gē hī beswīcen°. Siððan ic mē sēfte° mæg	may deceive more easily
	restan on° þyssum racentum gif him° þæt rīce losað°.	in to them is lost
	Sē þe þæt gelæsteð°, him bið lēan° gearo°	achieves reward prepared
	æfter tō aldre ⌜þæs wē⌝ hērinne magon	
100	on þyssum fȳre forð fremena° gewinnan°.	(by way) of benefits gain
	⌜Sittan læte ic hine⌝ wið mē sylfne ⌜swā hwā swā	
	þæt⌝ secgan cymeð	
	on þās hātan helle, þæt ⌜hīe⌝ heofoncyninges	
[440]	unwurðlīce° wordum ond dædum	dishonourably
	⌜lāre ...⌝⌝	

95 **Hycgað his** The vb. takes the gen.: 'think about it', or 'give thought to it'.

99 **þæs wē** Construed with *lēan* (98): '(the reward) of what (*or* whatever) we ...'.

101 **Sittan læte ic hine** 'I shall allow him to sit'. **swā hwā swā** 'who(so)ever'. **þæt** correl. with *þæt* in 102 and best om. in trans.

102 **hīe** i.e. Adam and Eve.

104 **lāre** Construed with *heofoncyninges*. The sentence breaks off here at the bottom of a manuscript page and the text restarts on the next page at a later point in the narrative, owing probably to the loss of two leaves. Evidently the sentence would have been completed by a vb. conveying the sense of 'rejected' ('in word or deed'), with obj. *lāre* (see also 92).

18

The Drowning of Pharaoh's Army
(*Exodus*, lines 447–564)

The story told in *Exodus*, the second poem of the Junius manuscript (see p. 130), is at the heart of Jewish history, for it tells of the very survival of the race. The biblical version of the events covered in the poem is given very concisely in Ex 13.20–14.31. After a long captivity in Egypt, the Israelites have finally been allowed by Pharaoh to leave and are led away by Moses. But Pharaoh changes his mind and gives chase until he corners the fugitives at the Red Sea, whereupon Moses, at God's command, causes the waters to part so that the Israelites can pass safely across. When Pharaoh and his troops try to follow, the water returns and they are all drowned.

The extract given here comes from the dramatic climax of the poem. The terrified Egyptians have tried to follow the Israelites, only to find the sea overwhelming them. With impressive verbal virtuosity, the poet presents their destruction in a repetitive pattern of visual images of almost cinematographic intensity – using fourfold variation, for instance, to tell how the walls of water have come crashing down on the doomed army. There is an apocalyptic tone to all this, a clear allusion to the terrors of Judgement Day for the unrighteous. God's adversary, the poet declares, has found that God was greater than he was; the pride of the Egyptians has been smashed and such is the completeness of their annihilation that there is not even a messenger left to take the news of defeat back home. After the action, Moses spells out to the Israelites the nature of God's covenant with them (lines 108–18), but first there is a homiletic digression apparently by the poet himself, who is clearly well versed in biblical exegesis (lines 77–102). He exhorts his audience to be open to the lessons of scripture, to recognise the ephemeral nature of life on earth, and to prepare for Judgement Day. Deliverance from this exile on earth will be the reward of the righteous.

Syntactically, *Exodus* presents the modern reader with special challenges. It is not always clear, for instance, whether certain half-lines complement the previous half-line (or even the one before that) or anticipate the next, and the interpretations and punctuation given below are necessarily subjective. But there is no reason to doubt that much of the ambiguity of the poem was intended. As for vocabulary, the poet draws freely on his OE wordhoard to produce a bewildering number of more or less synonymous words for the sea, ocean, water and currents. Although the language of *Exodus* is predominantly WS in form, the sporadic appearance of forms generally considered to be non-WS (such as *genēop* not *genēap*, 30, and uncontracted *demeð*, 97, and *lædeð*, 98 and 109) has been sufficient to raise speculation about an earlier Anglian recension of the poem, and a possible origin in Northumbria, but the evidence is not conclusive. There is little doubt that the version of the poem that has come down to us is far removed from the poet's 'original'. It contains many apparent errors, the most obvious of which have been corrected in the extract below, but no attempt has been made to 'improve' the text simply on the grounds that difficulties of translation might be (though they cannot be proved to be) due to further corruptions or because the metrical scheme appears to be defective. The lines of the extract here are numbered from 1, but their numbering in the poem as a whole is also indicated.

Further reading

P. J. Lucas, ed., *Exodus* (London, 1977; rev. edn. Exeter, 1994)

E. B. Irving, ed., *The Old English Exodus*, Yale Studies in English 122 (repr. with suppl. bibliography, Yale, 1970)

E. B. Irving, 'New Notes on the Old English *Exodus*', *Anglia* 90 (1972), 289–324
  '*Exodus* Retraced', in *Old English Studies in Honor of John C. Pope*, ed. R. B. Burlin and E. B. Irving (Toronto, 1974), pp. 203–23

R. Frank, 'What Kind of Poetry Is *Exodus*?', in *Germania: Comparative Studies in the Old Germanic Languages and Literatures*, ed. D. G. Calder and T. C. Christy (Wolfeboro, NH, and Woodbridge, 1988), pp. 191–205

R. Marsden, 'The Death of the Messenger: the *spelboda* in the Old English *Exodus*', *Bulletin of the John Rylands Library* 77 (1995), 141–64

P. G. Remley, *Old English Biblical Verse*, CSASE 16 (Cambridge, 1996), ch. 3

Folc wæs āfǣred°, ⌐flōdegsa becwōm⌐		terrified
gāstas° gēomre°, geofon° ⌐dēaðe hwēop⌐.	spirits *ap* miserable	ocean *ns*
Wǣron ⌐beorhhliðu⌐ blōde bestēmed°,		bedewed (with +*d*)
[*450*] holm° ⌐heolfre spāw⌐. Hrēam° wæs on ȳðum°,	sea *ns* Shouting	(the) waves

1 **flōdegsa becwōm** The vb. is here used transitively, with obj. *gāstas gēomre*: 'flood-terror [*i.e.* (presumably) terror of the water] overcame ...'. In 10, *becwōm* has its more usual sense of 'came'. The element *cwōm* is an earlier, uncontracted form of *cōm*.

2 **dēaðe hwēop** 'threatened (them) with death' (dat. of instrument).

3 **beorhhliðu** The 'hill-slopes' or 'hillsides' are the walls of water drawn up on each side of the dry passage as ramparts or fortifications, allowing the Israelites to escape. See 18, 38 and 41 for variations.

4 **heolfre spāw** 'spewed (*or* spat) with gore (*or* blood)'. Water turning to blood is a sign of Judgement Day, as predicted in Ex 7.17 and described in Rev 8.8 and 16.3.

5	wæter wæpna ful°, ⌈wælmist⌉ āstāh°.		full (of) rose up
	Wæron Ēgypte° eft° oncyrde°,		the Egyptians again turned back
	flugon° forhtigende°, fær° ongēton°.	fled	'fearing' calamity *as* recognised
	Woldon herebleaðe° hāmas° findan,		battle-shy (men) homes *ap*
	⌈gylp weard gnornra; him ongēn genāp⌉		
10	⌈atol° ȳða gewealc°⌉. ⌈Ne ðær ænig becwōm		terrible churning *as*
	herges tō hāme ac behindan belēac		
	wyrd mid wæge⌉. Þær ær wēgas° lāgon°		paths had lain
	mere° mōdgode°, mægen° wæs ādrenced°,		sea raged army submerged
[*460*]	strēamas° ⌈stōdon⌉, storm° ūp gewāt°		currents turbulence went
15	hēah tō heofonum, ⌈herewōpa mæst⌉.		
	Lāðe° cyrmdon° lyft° ūp° geswearc°	Foes wailed sky above darkened
	⌈fægum stæfnum⌉, flōd° blōd gewōd°.		water *as* pervaded
	Randbyrig° wæron rofene°, ⌈rodor swipode		ramparts broken
	meredēaða mæst⌉. Mōdige° swulton°		Bold perished

5 **wælmist** 'slaughter-mist'; perhaps 'a pall of death'.

9 **gylp weard gnornra** Understatement: '(their) arrogance [*or* boasting] became more troubled'. **him ongēn genāp** 'darkened against them', with subj. *gewealc* in 10. The churning sea threatens the Egyptians with its dark waves (see *brūn yppinge* in 53), at the same time blocking out the light.

10 **atol ȳða gewealc** The same half-line appears in *The Seafarer* (26/6).

10–12 **Ne ðær ænig . . . herges** 'none of the army there'.   **ac behindan . . . wæge** The 'fate' (*wyrd*) alluded to here is clearly God's will, or Providence (cf. Text 6): 'but Providence shut (them) in from behind with water'.

14 **stōdon** The vb. *standan* has a wide semantic range in OE, encompassing both stasis and decisive movement; here perhaps, 'built up'.

15 **herewōpa mæst** lit. 'the greatest of army-wailings' (a theme continued in 16a). Either this is parallel with *storm* (i.e. the turbulence and the wailing rose up together) or the wailing *is* the turbulence.

17 **fægum stæfnum** dat. of manner: 'with doomed voices'. The phrase seems to complement *lāðe cyrmdon* (16), but in this passage of dislocated imagery the voices themselves may be darkening the sky.

18–19 **rodor swipode meredēaða mæst** The poet continues the apocalyptic conflation of celestial and terrestrial, concrete and abstract: hard to trans., but lit. 'the greatest quantity of sea-deaths scourged the sky'. *Meredēað* could also be interpreted as 'sea of death' or 'deadly sea', and these certainly might fit the context better when the compound is repeated in 67.

20	cyningas on° corðre°, ⸢cyre swiðrode	in (their) pomp
	sǣs æt ende⸣. Wīgbord° scinon°	Shields shone
	hēah ofer hæleðum°, holmweall° āstāh	warriors sea-wall
	merestrēam° mōdig. Mægen wæs on cwealme°	sea-current death
[470]	fæste gefeterod° forðganges° nēp°	bound of escape powerless
25	searwum° æsǣled°. ⸢Sand bāsnodon	war-gear encumbered (by +d)
	wītodre fyrde⸣ ⸢hwonne waðema° strēam,	of waves
	sincalda° sǣ sealtum ȳðum	ever-cold
	æflāstum gewuna° ēce staðulas°	accustomed to +d foundations
	nacud nȳdboda° nēosan° cōme,	herald of disaster to seek
30	fāh° fēðegāst°, sē ðe fēondum genēop°⸣.	hostile roving spirit engulfed +d
	Wæs sēo hæwene° lyft heolfre geblanden°.	blue mingled
	Brim° berstende° ⸢blōdegesan hwēop	Sea *ns* bursting
	sǣmanna sīð⸣ oðþæt sōð° metod°	true creator

20–1 **cyre swiðrode sǣs æt ende** *cyre* means 'choice' or 'free-will'; if, as assumed here, *swiðrode* is from *swiðrian* (or *sweðrian*), 'diminish' or 'abate', then *cyre* must be attributed to the 'kings', producing an effectively ironic litotes: '(their) free-will diminished at the edge (*ende*) of the sea'. If, however, the vb. is part of *swīðrian* (and thus *swīðrode*), 'become strong' or 'prevail', then *sǣs* must be construed with *cyre* and the words may be interpreted (appropriately enough): 'finally the will of the sea prevailed'. Emending *cyre* to *cyrm* ('noise' or 'tumult'), as suggested by some editors, is unnecessary.

25–6 **Sand bāsnodon wītodre fyrde** The problem is *wītodre*, which occurs uniquely here. Most editors have assumed, from the context and by analogy with similar OE words, that it has the sense of 'fated': 'Sand awaited the fated army' (i.e. the sand of the bottom of the sea). Conceivably, *wītodre* is an error for *wītrode*, 'battle-route' (a word used in 46). The meaning would then be, 'sands had awaited the battle-route of the army' – earlier in the poem, sand has represented the safety of the shore; *hwonne* (see next note) would now have to be trans. 'until'. *Bāsnodon* is itself an emendation, of *barenodon*.

26–30 **hwonne ... genēop** A complex passage. On the assumption that *æflāst* denotes deviance (i.e. *of* + *lāst*, 'off-track'), one interpretation could be: 'when the surge of waves, the ever-cold sea, with its salt waves accustomed to deviant paths – naked herald of disaster, hostile vagrant spirit [*feðegāst*: but this might be a form of *feðegest*, 'visitor on foot'] – came [*cōme*, sbj. vb. after the conj. *hwonne*, expressing anticipation] to seek out its eternal foundations (*i.e.* the sands of the sea-bed): that (sea) which engulfed (*or* overwhelmed) the enemies'. The sea is personified as a terrifying, anarchic force, and its return to its natural place emphasises the inevitability of the Egyptians' destruction.

32–3 **blōdegesan hwēop sǣmanna sīð** The poet inserts a restrospective comment: 'had threatened the seamen's journey with the terror of blood'. The 'seamen' are the Israelites (whose progress is described in terms of seafaring elsewhere in the poem). They too had been faced by death at the Red Sea, until God intervened.

[*480*]   þurh Moyses hand   ⸢mōd gerȳmde⸣.

35   Wīde wæðde°   wælfæðmum° swēop°,   roamed   with deadly embraces   swept

flōd fāmgode°   fǣge° crungon°,   foamed   (those) doomed to die   fell

lagu° land gefēol°   lyft wæs onhrēred°,   water   fell on +a   disturbed

wicon° weallfæsten°   wǣgas° burston,   gave way   ramparts *np*   waves *np*

multon° meretorras°   þā se mihtiga° slōh   dissolved   sea-towers *np*   almighty

40   mid hālige hand,   heofonrīces weard°,   guardian

wērbēamas°.   Wlance° ðēode°   protecting barriers *ap*   Proud   people

ne mihton forhabban°   ⸢helpendra pað⸣   hinder

merestrēames mōd°   ac ⸢hē⸣ manegum gescēod°   power *as*   destroyed +d

[*490*]   ⸢gyllende gryre⸣.   Gārsecg° wēdde°   Sea   became mad

45   ⸢ūp ātēah, on slēap⸣.   Egesan° stōdon°,   Terrors   arose

wēollon° wælbenna°   ⸢wītrod gefēol   seethed   mortal wounds *np*

hēah of heofonum⸣   handweorc° Godes   handiwork

fāmigbōsma°.   Flōdweard° geslōh°   foamy-bosomed   'Flood guardian'   struck

⸢unhlēowan wǣg   alde mēce⸣

50   þæt ⸢ðȳ dēaðdrepe⸣   drihte° swǣfon°,   troops   slept

synfullra° swēot°.   Sāwlum lunnon°,   of guilty ones   company   lost +d

fæste° befarene°,   ⸢flōdblāc here⸣   completely   surrounded

34 **mōd gerȳmde** The event referred to is the parting of the sea consequent on Moses's raising of his staff, but the phr. is ambiguous. If the *mōd* referred to is God's, the phrase means '(God) revealed his will (*or* power)'; if it is the ocean's, the meaning must be '(God) made space for (*i.e.* dissipated) its power'. The fact that *mōd* is attributed to the sea in 43, as a force which the heathen Egyptians cannot resist, makes the second alternative the more attractive.

42 **helpendra** These may be the *wērbeamas*, which have been 'helpers' or 'supports' to the Israelites, or alternatively the rushing waters, which are of course helping to save the Israelites.

43 **hē** The antec. noun is probably *mōd*, but *weard* (40) or *pað* (42) are other possibilities.

44 **gyllende gryre** instr.: 'with shrieking terror'.

45 **ūp ātēah, on slēap** A memorable half-line, in which the drama of the sea's rearing itself up and then inexorably sliding down is enacted through the parallel verbal phrases, with stressed and alliterating advs. and assonating vbs.: 'drew (itself) up, slid down onto (them)'.

46–7 **wītrod gefēol** The vb. is trans. with acc. obj. *wītrod*: 'attacked' or 'fell on the battle-route'; the subj. is God's 'handiwork', the *famigbosma* ('the foamy-bosomed one', i.e. the sea).   **hēah of heofonum** 'high from the heavens', i.e. 'from high in the heavens'.

49 **unhlēowan wǣg** 'the unprotective wave (*or* water)'; effective use of litotes: it is of course not simply 'unprotective' but unequivocally destructive.   **alde mēce** instr.: 'with ancient sword'.

50 **ðȳ dēaðdrepe** instr.: 'by that death-blow'.

52 **flōdblāc here** 'flood-pale army'. The subj. of *lunnon* (51). Either the Egyptians are white with the terror of drowning in the flood or that is their colour when drowned.

siððan° hīe ⌜onbugon   brūn yppinge⌝,   when
[*500*] mōdewǣga° mǣst.   Mægen eall gedrēas°   violent waves *gp*   perished
55 ⌜ðā þe gedrecte⌝,   dugoð° Ēgypta,   host
Faraon mid his folcum.   Hē onfond° hraðe°   discovered   quickly
siððan ⌜grund⌝ gestāh°   Godes andsaca°   reached   adversary
þæt wæs mihtigra°   mereflōdes° weard;   mightier   ocean-tide's
⌜wolde heorufæðmum   hilde gescēadan⌝
60 yrre ond egesfull°.   Ēgyptum wearð   awesome
⌜þæs dægweorces⌝   dēop° lēan° gescēod°   awful   reward   assigned (to +*d*)
forðām° þæs heriges°   hām eft ne cōm   because   army
⌜ealles ungrundes⌝   ǣnig tō° lāfe°   as   survivor
[*510*] þætte° sīð° heora   secgan mōste°,   so that   fate   might
65 bodigean° æfter° burgum   bealospella° mǣst,   proclaim   through   of ill tidings
⌜hordwearda hryre   hæleða cwēnum⌝
ac þā mægenþrēatas°   meredēað geswealh°,   mighty hosts *ap*   swallowed
⌜spelbodan ēac⌝.   Sē ðe spēd° āhte°   power   possessed
āgēat° gylp° wera°;   ⌜hīe wið God wunnon°⌝.   destroyed   boast   of men   vied
70 Þanon° Israhēlum   ⌜ēce rædas⌝   Thereupon
on merehwearfe°   Moyses sægde,   sea-shore

53 **onbugon brūn yppinge** The phr. after the vb. seems to be dat.: 'submitted [lit. "bowed"] to the dark mass (of water)', with the termination of the adj. (-*re*) elided before the following vowel; in the next half-line, however, *mǣst* is nom. *Onbugon* is an emendation of the manuscript's puzzling *on bogum*.

55 **ðā þe gedrecte** The pron. *ðā* is pl. but the form of the vb. is sg.: 'those who had caused affliction' (i.e. to the Israelites). Church writers interpreted the name of the Egyptians as 'those who cause affliction'.

57 **grund** 'bottom'. Not in the manuscript; a conjectural restoration.

59 **wolde ... gescēadan** The subj. is potentially ambiguous – either 'God's adversary' (Pharaoh) or 'the guardian of the ocean tide' (God himself); but the epithet which follows, *yrre ond egesfull* ('angry and awesome'), is clearly more appropriate for God (and is so used in the OE poem *Christ III*, 1528). Thus: 'he intended to decide the battle with deadly embraces', i.e. the embraces of the sea.

61 **þæs dægweorces** gen. of respect: 'for that day's work'.

63 **ealles ungrundes** The adj. phr. qualifies *þæs heriges* in 62: 'of all (that) vast (army)'.

66 **hordwearda ... cwēnum** '(and proclaim) to the wives of warriors the fall of (their) hoard-guardians', i.e. of their lords or princes.

68 **spelbodan ēac** 'the messenger(s) [*or* "tale-teller(s)"] too'. The manuscript has only *spelbodan* (which could be acc. sg. or pl.: §B5a) and clearly something is missing; *ēac* fits the context. Some editors put *ēac* plus def. art. (sg. *þone* or pl. *þā*) before *spelbodan*.

69 **hīe wið God wunnon** The actions of the damned are described thus in other OE poems, in reference to the biblical giants in *Beowulf* (113) and Satan in *Genesis B* (333).

70 **ēce rædas** 'eternal precepts'. This obj.-phr. (with its vars. *hālige sprēce*, 72, and *dēop ǣrende*, 73, and its distinct echo of *ēce staðulas*, 28) refers to the speech by Moses which starts at 108.

hēahþungen° wer, ⌐hālige sprǣce⌐,   illustrious

dēop° ǣrende°. ⌐Dægweorc ne mað°,   profound   message *as*   is (not) hidden

[520] swā gȳt° werðēode°   on gewritum° findað   still   nations   the scriptures

75 dōma° gehwilcne°⌐   ⌐þāra ðe him Drihten bebēad⌐   laws   each +*gp*

on þām sīðfate°   sōðum wordum.   journey

Gif onlūcan° wile   ⌐līfes wealhstōd   unlock

beorht° in brēostum,   bānhūses weard⌐,   radiant

⌐ginfæsten gōd   gāstes cǣgon⌐,

80 rūn° bið° gerecenod°,   rǣd° forð   mystery   will be   explained   wisdom

gǣð°.   will go

⌐Hafað⌐ wīslicu°   word on fæðme°,   wise *npn*   (its) embrace (*or* keeping)

wile meagollīce°   ⌐mōdum tǣcan⌐   earnestly

þæt wē gēsne° ne sȳn°   Godes þēodscipes°,   lacking +*g*   are *sbj*   law

[530] metodes miltsa°.   Hē ūs mā° onlȳhð°,   mercies *gp*   more   grants

85 nū ūs bōceras°   ⌐beteran secgað   scholars

lengran lyftwynna⌐. Þis is lǣne° drēam°,   temporary   happiness

wommum° āwyrged°   wreccum° ālȳfed°,   with sins   cursed   to exiles   granted

⌐earmra anbid⌐.   Ēðellēase°   Homeless

⌐þysne gystsele   gihðum⌐ healdeð°   (we) occupy

72 **hālige sprǣce** If the fem. noun and adj. are taken to be the acc. sg. obj. of the vb. *sægde*, the meaning is 'divine utterance'; but they could equally well be the acc. pl. obj. ('divine words'), or even a dat. sg. phr. complementing the vb. ('with divine utterance').

73–5 **Dægweorc ... dōma gehwilcne** The story of the escape through the Red Sea (the 'day's work') is not hidden (*ne mað* is an emendation of the manuscript's *nemnað*), for it is revealed in the scriptures (*on gewrītum*), just as are those laws which God enjoined on the Israelites during their journeyings (the *sīðfat* of 76). On the revelation of the Ten Commandments and other laws (*dōmas*) to Moses, see Ex 20–23.

75 **þāra ðe him Drihten bebēad** The gen. demons. adj. is in concord with *dōma* but need not be trans.: 'which the Lord enjoined on them'.

77–8 **līfes wealhstōd ... bānhūses weard** The 'interpreter of life' (*wealhstōd*) is the first subj. of the sentence. It is the intellectual faculty, which concerns itself with the well-being of the body; hence it is also expressed in a second kenning, *bānhūses weard*, 'guardian of the bone-house (*i.e.* body)'. **brēostum** The pl. is commonly used thus, with sg. meaning, in OE (§D4i).

79 **ginfæsten gōd** obj. of *onlūcan wile* (77): 'the wide benefits'. **gāstes cǣgon** adv. phr. modifying *onlūcan wile*: 'with the keys of the spirit' (*cǣgon* for *cǣgum*, dat. of instrument).

81 **Hafað** '(It) has'. The antec. subj. is *wealhstod*.

82 **mōdum tǣcan** 'teach (us) in (our) minds', or 'teach to our minds (*or* hearts)'.

85–6 **beteran secgað lengran lyftwynna** The two comp. adjs. are parallel: 'tell (us) of the better and longer(-lasting) joys of heaven'.

88 **earmra anbid** 'a period of waiting for [lit. "of"] wretched (people)'; the phr. is parallel with *lǣna drēam*.

89 **þysne gystsele** 'this lodging-house' (acc. sg.), a metaphor for the earthly life. **gihðum** dat. of manner: 'with anxieties'.

90 murnað° on mōde; ⌐mānhūs witon⌐	are anxious
fæst under foldan° þær bið fȳr ond wyrm,	earth
open ēce scræf° yfela gehwylces°,	pit of every
swā° nū regnþēofas° rīce° dǣlað:	in as far as arch-thieves dominion share
[540] yldo° oððe ǣrdēað°. ⌐Eftwyrd⌐ cymð,	age premature death
95 mægenþrymma° mǣst ofer middangeard,	of powerful forces
⌐dæg dǣdum fāh⌐. Drihten sylfa	
on þām meðelstede° manegum dēmeð°,	place of assembly will judge +d
⌐þonne⌐ hē sōðfæstra° sāwla° lǣdeð	of (those) steadfast in truth souls ap
ēadige° gāstas on° ūprodor°	blessed into high heaven
100 þær is lēoht ond līf ⌐ēac þon⌐ lissa° blǣd°.	of mercies blessing(s)
Dugoð° on drēame Drihten herigað°,	(The) company will praise
weroda° wuldorcyning° ⌐tō wīdan fēore⌐.	of hosts glorious king
Swā reordode°, rǣda gemyndig°,	spoke intent (on +g)
[550] manna mildost mihtum° swīðed°	in (his) powers fortified
105 ⌐hlūdan stefne⌐; here° stille° bād°	army silently awaited
⌐witodes willan⌐, wundor° ongēton°,	wondrous thing as (they) perceived
mōdiges° ⌐mūðhǣl⌐; hē tō mænegum° spræc:	of the spirited (man) multitudes
'Micel is þēos menigeo°, mægenwīsa° trum°,	company leader ns strong
fullesta° mǣst se° ðās fare° lǣdeð.	of supports who journey
110 ⌐Hafað ūs on Cananēa cyn° gelȳfed°	the people conceded
burh and bēagas°, brāde° rīce⌐.	treasures ap broad
Wile nū gelǣstan° þæt° hē lange gehēt°	fulfil what promised
mid āðsware°, engla Drihten,	'oath-swearing'
[560] in fyrndagum° fæderyncynne°	days of old to (our) forefathers

---

90 **mānhūs witon** '(we) know [*i.e.* are conscious of] the house of wickedness', i.e. hell.

94 **Eftwyrd** Possibly an adv., 'in (due) time', but usually interpreted as a noun. 'the after event', i.e. Judgement Day.

96 **dæg dǣdum fāh** The phr. varies *eftwyrd* in 94. Although *fāh* may mean 'hostile' (see 30) or 'guilty', it may also have the sense 'variegated', 'stained' or 'gleaming' (the latter used especially of decoration). The words here suggest 'a day marked by deeds' – a reference to the review of the past behaviour (gleaming with virtue or stained with sin) which will determine the future of each individual soul. For a similar instance of *fāh* used ambiguously, see 23/13.

98 **þonne** This may be treated as either the conj. 'when' or the adv. 'then'. There is similar syntactical ambiguity with *þēr* in 100.

100 **ēac þon** adv. phr. with instr. *þon*: 'in addition to that', or 'and also'.

102 **tō wīdan fēore** 'for ever more' (lit. 'to spacious life').

105 **hlūdan stefne** dat. of manner: 'in a loud voice'.

106 **witodes willan** 'the will of the appointed one', i.e. Moses, who finally speaks.

107 **mūðhǣl** 'wholesome speech', or 'speech of salvation' (acc. sg.).

110–11 **Hafað ūs ... rīce** See Ex 15.15 on the promised land of Canaan.

115 gif gē gehealdað° hālige lāre°:   keep teaching
 þæt gē fēonda gehwone° forð° ofergangað°, each +*gp* henceforth overrun
 gesittað° sigerīce° ⌜be sǣm twēonum⌝, occupy (a) victorious kingdom
 bēorselas° beorna°. Bið° ēower feast-halls *ap* of warriors (Shall) be
  blǣd° micel!'   glory

117 **be sǣm twēonum** 'between the seas'. A stock phr. in OE poetry (repeated in *Exodus*, 563, and used also in *Beowulf*, 858), perhaps emphasising the extent of the 'victorious kingdom', but more specifically echoing a description of the promised land in Ex 23.31, where we are told that it will stretch 'from the Red Sea to the Sea of Palestine', or a similar reference in Num 34.6–12. The form *twēonum* occurs only in this phr.; cf. *twēgen* 'two' and *twēon* 'hesitate'.

19
Judith

In a treatise on the books of the Old and New Testaments, written probably in the late 990s, at a time when Viking attacks on eastern and southern England were intensifying, abbot Ælfric exploited a reference to the Book of Judith to make a rare comment on events outside the monastery. He explained that he had put Judith's story into English (in a homiletic paraphrase) 'as an example to you people, so that you may defend your country with weapons against the threatening host'. Judith was a pious widow who saved the Israelites from destruction at the hands of the Assyrians by allowing herself to be taken into the bedroom of Holofernes, an enemy general laying siege to their city of Bethulia, and then chopping off his head. The courage and fortitude which Ælfric so admired caught the imagination of many later medieval writers and painters also. The Book of Judith is one of several books which, though immensely popular and influential, and still part of the Roman Catholic Bible, were excluded after the Reformation from the official 'canonical' books of the Protestant Bible. They may often be found there today, however, in a separate section of 'apocryphal' scripture.

There is no evidence that the version of Judith's story created by an anonymous OE poet was written with the specific purpose of encouraging the English in their own conflicts with invaders. It has come down to us in the early eleventh-century *Beowulf*-manuscript (London, British Library, Cotton Vitellius A. xv, fols. 202r–209v), written out by one of that poem's scribes and bound into the volume immediately after it. Skilfully paring down the biblical narrative to its essentials (by ignoring the events of the first half of the book and omitting all the characters but Judith, Holofernes and Judith's maid), the poet has produced a moral tale for all times, but it is distinctly coloured by the conventional diction and imagery of Germanic heroism and structured round the sort of polarisation of good and evil well known in saints' lives. For instance, the doughty widow of the biblical version dresses up and presents herself enticingly to Holofernes at a feast, but in the poem she is a young virgin whose role in the would-be seduction is entirely passive. Holofernes himself, presented simply as an inebriated boor in the Bible, becomes a raving, lecherous monster in the poem (the antithesis of a good heroic leader) – reason enough, some critics have thought, to explain the poem's inclusion in a codex with *Beowulf* and other texts about monstrous human beings. The parallel treatment of pagan and Christian worlds in the poem is nowhere better seen than in the use of traditional 'heroic' epithets to describe not only the earthly lord (Holofernes) but the heavenly one also (see the discussion of 'Cædmon's Hymn', pp. 76–7): the former, for instance, is called *sinces brytta*, 'distributor of treasure' (30), and, tellingly, *morðres brytta*[*n*], 'distributor of violent crimes' (90), while God is called *tīres brytta*, 'distributor of glory' (93). At the end of the poem, we are treated to a dramatic battle as the Israelites (called 'Hebrews' in the poem) rout the Assyrians, though in the biblical account the latter simply run away once Holofernes's death has been discovered. The poet's Israelites then distribute the treasures of the Assyrians in time-honoured Germanic fashion. The poem's message is clear: Faith will be rewarded and God will humble the proud. Judith is empowered through her righteousness and humility to take on the male role of executioner, and her strength comes as a direct result of her prayer to God, to whom she appeals with a formulaic invocation of the Trinity – Father, Son and Holy Spirit, though this is strictly speaking anachronistic in an OT story (lines 83–94).

As we have it, the poem is incomplete, lacking at least a beginning, but the coherent structure of what remains suggests that little is missing – perhaps just a page of manuscript which would have set the scene of the Assyrians' threat and Judith's determination to act. On stylistic grounds, the poem has been assigned to the tenth century. Our copy shows remarkable consistency in its use of 'standard' WS forms (with a few exceptions, such as earlier *monna*, 52 and 181, as well as *manna*, 235). There is some levelling of unstressed endings, as in *tōðon* (272, for *tōðum*) and *tōbrēdon* (247, for *tōbrēdan*). Arguments for derivation of the received text from an originally Anglian poem are not conclusive. The spelling of the two Latin-derived names 'Bethulia' and 'Judith' throughout with *th*, rather than *p/ð*, will be noted, but there is a scribal slip-up with *Iūdithðe* in 40. *Hōlofernus* is left in its nominative Latin form, whatever its case, except once, when an OE genitive is improvised (*Hōlofernes*, 336); the name alliterates throughout the poem with vowels.

Further reading

M. Griffiths, ed., *Judith* (Exeter, 1997)

A. Renoir, '*Judith* and the Limits of Poetry', *ES* 43 (1962), 145–55

J. J. Campbell, 'Schematic Technique in *Judith*', *English Literary History* 38 (1971), 155–72

D. Chamberlain, '*Judith*: a Fragmentary and Political Poem', in *Anglo-Saxon Poetry: Essays in Appreciation for John C. McGalliard*, ed. L. E. Nicholson and D. W. Frese (Notre Dame, IN, 1975), pp. 135–59

R. Woolf, 'The Lost Opening of *Judith*', in *Art and Doctrine: Essays on Medieval Literature*, ed. H. Donoghue (London and Ronceverte, 1986), pp. 119–24

M. Dockray-Miller, 'Female Community in the Old English *Judith*', *SN* 70 (1998), 165–72

... ⌐twēode

gifena in ðȳs⌐ ginnan° grunde°. Hēo ðǣr ðā gearwe°   wide earth readily
  funde°   found
⌐mundbyrd⌐ æt° ðām mǣran° þēodne°   þā hēo   from famous ruler
  āhte° mǣste° þearfe°,   had most need
hyldo° þæs hēhstan° dēman°,   þæt hē hīe°   support highest judge *gs* her
  wið° þæs hēhstan brōgan°   against danger
5 gefriðode°, ⌐frymða waldend⌐. ⌐Hyre ðæs fæder on   would protect
  roderum°   skies
torhtmōd tīðe gefremede⌐,   þe° hēo āhte trumne°   because firm
  gelēafan°   faith
ā° tō° ðām ælmihtigan. ⌐Gefrægen ic ðā Hōlofernus   always in
  wīnhātan° wyrcean⌐ georne°   ond ⌐eallum wundrum   invitations *ap* eagerly
  þrymlic
girwan ūp swǣsendo⌐. Tō ðām° hēt° se gumena°   it summoned of men
  baldor°   prince
10 ealle ðā yldestan° ðegnas;   hīe ðæt ⌐ofstum miclum⌐   most senior
  ræfndon°, rondwiggende°, ⌐cōmon tō ðām rīcan° did shield-warriors powerful
  þēodne
  fēran⌐, folces ræswan°. Þæt wæs ⌐þȳ fēorðan dōgore⌐   chief *ds*
  ⌐þæs ðe⌐ Iūdith hyne°, glēaw° on geðonce°   him wise purpose

---

1–2 **twēode gifena** 'doubted (*or* was suspicious of) gifts'; the vb. takes the gen. Judith is no doubt the subj. and the reference is to secular rewards.   **in ðȳs** Here *in* is followed by the instr.

3 **mundbyrd** 'protection'; a significant term in Anglo-Saxon lawcodes (see p. 45). It is varied with a parallel obj., *hyldo*, in 4.

5 **frymða waldend** An epithet for God: 'ruler of beginnings', the first of many.

5–6 **Hyre ðæs... tīðe gefremede** 'To her in respect of this [*ðæs*] he afforded favour [*tīðe*]', i.e. 'he granted her favour in this'.   **torhtmōd** This describes *fæder*: 'illustrious'.

7–8 **Gefrægen... wyrcean** *Gefrignan* is followed by acc. and infin. [§G5d.i.3]: 'I (have) heard (that) Holofernes [acc.] issued...'; the construction extends to infin. *girwan* in 9. See also 246.

8–9 **eallum wundrum... swǣsendo** The adj. *þrymlic* ('glorious') seems to modify *swǣsendo*: 'served up [*girwan*] a glorious feast with all wonderful things'.

10 **ofstum miclum** dat. (pl.) of manner: 'with great haste'; see also 35 and 70.

11–12 **cōmon... fēran** vb. of motion plus infin.: 'came preceding'; perhaps, 'made their way'.

12 **þȳ fēorðan dōgore** 'on the fourth day' (instr. *þȳ*). This is a detail from the biblical version (Jdth 12.10); the lost opening of the OE poem may have offered more explanation.

13 **þæs ðe** gen. phr. of specification: 'from that when', i.e. 'after'.

ides° ælfscīnu°,   ǣrest° gesōhte°.   woman of elfin beauty first visited
15 Hīe ðā tō ðām symle°   sittan ēodon°   feast went
wlance° tō wīngedrince°,   ealle his ⌜wēagesīðas⌝,   boastful wine-drinking
bealde° byrnwiggende°.   Þǣr wǣron bollan°   bold mailed warriors bowls
stēape°   deep
boren° æfter° bencum gelōme°,   swylce°   carried along frequently likewise
ēac° būnan° ond orcas°   also goblets pitchers
fulle° fletsittendum°.   ⌜Hīe þæt fǣge þēgon⌝,   full to hall-guests
20 rōfe° rondwiggende,   ⌜þēah° ðæs° se rīca ne   renowned though that
wēnde°⌝,   expect +g
egesful° eorla° dryhten.   Ðā ⌜wearð Hōlofernus,   terrible of warriors
goldwine° gumena,   on gytesālum⌝,   'gold-friend'
hlōh° ond hlȳdde°,   hlynede° ond dynede°, laughed shouted roared clamoured
þæt mihten° ⌜fīra bearn⌝   feorran° gehȳran   could *sbj* from afar
25 hū se stīðmōda°   styrmde° ond gylede°,   stern-hearted (man) bellowed yelled
mōdig° ond medugāl°,   manode° geneahhe°   proud mead-merry urged often
bencsittende°   þæt hī gebǣrdon° wel.   'bench-sitters' enjoyed (themselves)
Swā se inwidda°   ofer° ealne dæg   villain throughout
dryhtguman° sīne°   drencte° mid wīne,   retainers his 'drenched' (*i.e.* plied)
30 swīðmōd° sinces° brytta°,   oðþæt hīe ⌜on   arrogant of treasure dispenser
swīman⌝ lāgon,
⌜oferdrencte his duguðe ealle⌝,   swylce hīe wǣron ⌜dēaðe geslegene⌝,
⌜āgotene gōda gehwylces⌝.   Swā ⌜hēt se gumena baldor°   prince
fylgan fletsittendum⌝ oðþæt fīra bearnum

---

16 **wēagesīðas** 'companions in evil' or 'in misery' (or perhaps both).

19 **Hīe þæt fǣge þēgon** 'They consumed it (as) doomed (men)'.

20 **þēah...wēnde** i.e. he did not foresee that the men were fated to die.

21–2 **wearð...on gytesālum** The idiom (perhaps imperfectly copied) seems to mean 'became (merry) at the wine-pouring'.

24 **fīra bearn** 'the children of men'; a stock epithet for 'humans' or 'people'. See also 33 and 51, and 9b/35n.

30 **on swīman** 'in a stupor' or 'unconscious'; cf. an ironical repetition in 106.

31 **oferdrencte...ealle** *oferdrencte* may be a past part.: 'all of his retinue [gen. sg. after nom. pl. masc. pron. *ealle*] drenched (with drink)'; or possibly pret.: 'he [Holofernes] had drenched all his retinue [acc. sg., with adj. *ealle*]' or 'drenched his retinue completely [with adv. *ealle*]'. There is a nice antithesis between 'drenched' (or 'soaked') here and 'drained' on the next line. **dēaðe geslegene** dat. of instrument: 'conquered by death', i.e. 'struck dead'.

32 **āgotene gōda gehwylces** 'drained of every virtue (*or* faculty)'.

32–3 **hēt...fylgan fletsittendum** 'commanded that the hall-sitters [i.e. guests] be attended to [*fylgan*]'.

nēalæhte° niht sēo þ̄ystre°.   Hēt ðā ⌜nīða geblonden⌝   approached +d   dark

35 þā ēadigan° mægð°   ofstum fetigan°   blessed   maiden *as*   to be fetched

tō his bedreste°   bēagum° gehlæste°,   bed   with bracelets   decked

hringum gehrodene°.   Hīe hraðe° fremedon°,   adorned   quickly   did

anbyhtscealcas°,   swā him heora ealdor°   (his) servants   leader

   bebēad°,   ordered +d

byrnwigena° brego°:   bearhtme° stōpon°   mailed warriors'   leader   instantly   went

40 tō ðām gysterne°   þǣr hīe Iūdithðe   guest-hall

fundon° ferhðglēawe°   ond ðā fromlīce°   found   prudent   promptly

lindwiggende°   lǣdan° ongunnon°   shield-warriors *np*   to bring   preceded

þā torhtan° mægð   tō træfe° þām hēan°   radiant   tent   high

þǣr se rīca hyne°   reste° ⌜on symbel⌝   himself   rested

45 nihtes° inne°,   nergende° lāð°,   at night   within   to the saviour   loathsome

Hōlofernus.   Þǣr wæs eallgylden°   all-golden

flēohnet° fæger°   ond ymbe° þæs folctogan°   fly-net   fine   round   leader's

bed āhongen°,   þæt se bealofulla°   (it) hung   wicked (one)

mihte wlītan° þurh,   wigena° baldor,   look   warriors'

50 ⌜on æghwylcne   þe ðǣrinne cōm

hæleða bearna   ond on° hyne nǣnig⌝   at

monna cynnes°,   ⌜nymðe se mōdiga hwæne°   of the race

nīðe rōfra   him þē nēar hēte

rinca tō rūne gegangan⌝.   Hīe ðā on° reste° gebrōhton°   to   bed   brought

55 snūde° ðā snoteran° idese;   ēodon ðā stercedferhðe°   quickly   wise   determined

hæleð° heora hearran° cȳðan°   þæt wæs sēo hālige   men   lord *ds*   to inform +d

   mēowle°   woman

gebrōht on his būrgetelde°.   Þā wearð se brēma°   pavilion   famous (man)

   on mōde

blīðe°, burga° ealdor,   þōhte° ðā beorhtan°   joyful   of cities   intended   illustrious

   idese

mid wīdle° ond mid womme° besmītan°.   Ne wolde þæt   filth   sin   to defile

   wuldres° dēma   of glory

---

34 **nīða geblonden** '(the man) infected [lit. "mixed"] with evils [gen. pl.]'.

44 **on symbel** 'always'.

50–1 **on æghwylcne þe . . . hæleða bearna** 'at each of the sons of men who . . .'.   **ond on hyne nǣnig** i.e. none could see *him* in return.

52–4 **nymðe se mōdiga . . . gegangan** Not only is the subj. of this clause (*se mōdiga*) widely separated from its vb. (*hēte*, sbj. pret.) but also the obj. (*hwæne*, 'whom' or 'one') from its complement (*rinca*): 'unless the arrogant (man) should summon one of the warriors renowned for wickedness [*nīðe rōfra*] to go the nearer [instr. *þē* with comp. adv.] to him for council'.

60   geðafian°, þrymmes° hyrde°,   ac hē ⌐him þæs   *allow   of majesty   shepherd*
        ðinges gestȳrde⌐,
      Dryhten, dugeða° waldend.   Gewāt° ðā se   *of hosts   Went*
        dēofulcunda°   *devilish man*
      ⌐gālferhð° gumena ðrēate°⌐   *lustful   with a troop*
      bealofull° his beddes nēosan°,   ⌐þær hē sceolde⌐   *wicked   to seek +g*
      his blǣd° forlēosan°   *life   lose*
      ǣdre° binnan° ānre nihte.   Hæfde ðā his ende gebidenne°   *swiftly   in   endured*
65   on eorðan ⌐unswǣslicne°⌐,   ⌐swylcne hē ǣr æfter worhte⌐,   *unpleasant*
      þearlmōd° ðēoden gumena,   þenden° hē on ðysse worulde   *stern-hearted   while*
      wunode° under wolcna° hrōfe.   Gefēol° ðā, wīne°   *dwelt   skies'   Fell   wine d*
        swā druncen,
      se rīca ⌐on his reste middan⌐   ⌐swā hē nyste rǣda nānne
      on gewitlocan⌐.   Wiggend° stōpon   *The warriors*
70   ūt of ðām inne°   ofstum miclum,   *chamber*
      weras° wīnsade°   þe ðone wǣrlogan°,   *men np   wine-sated   liar as*
      lāðne lēodhatan°,   lǣddon tō bedde   *'people-hater' (i.e. tyrant)*
      ⌐nēhstan sīðe⌐.   Þā wæs nergendes
      þēowen° þrymful°,   þearle° gemyndig°   *handmaiden   glorious   keenly   intent on*
75   hū hēo þone atolan°   ēaðost° mihte   *monster   most easily*
      ealdre° benǣman°   ǣr se unsȳfra°   *life ds   deprive (of +d)   unclean (man)*
      womfull° onwōce°.   Genam° ðā ⌐wundenlocc⌐   *sinful   awoke   Seized*
      scyppendes mægð   scearpne mēce°   *sword as*
      ⌐scūrum heardne⌐   ond of sceaðe° ābrǣd°   *sheath   drew out*
80   ⌐swīðran folme⌐;   ongan° ðā swegles° weard°   *began   heaven's   guardian as*

60 **him þæs ðinges gestȳrde** 'prevented him [dat.] from that thing [gen.]', i.e. 'from that act'.

62 **gālferhð ... ðrēate** A half-line seems to be missing here, but the sense is not affected.

63 **þær hē sceolde** The poet looks forward: 'where he was to . . .'.

65 **unswǣslicne** This describes *ende* in 64.   **swylcne hē ǣr æfter worhte** 'such [i.e. such an end] as he had previously striven after (*or* towards)'.

68 **on ... middan** 'in the midst of' (with dat.).

68–9 **swā ... on gewitlocan** 'as if he didn't know any of the plans in his mind', or 'as if oblivious of . . .'.

73 **nēhstan sīðe** dat. of definition: 'for the last time'.

77 **wundenlocc** 'with wound locks' (describing *mægð* in 78), suggesting either 'curly-haired' or 'with braided hair'.

79 **scūrum heardne** dat. of instrument: 'hardened by showers'. Probably a reference to the manufacture of the sword, the hardening of which would involve quenching the red-hot iron in water; 'quench-hardened' has thus been suggested.

80 **swīðran folme** dat. of instrument: 'with (her) right hand'.

be naman nemnan°,   nergend ealra   call
woruldbūendra°,   ond ⌜þæt word⌝ ācwæð: 'world-dwellers' gp
'Ic ðē, frymða God   ond frōfre° gǣst°,   of comfort   spirit
bearn° alwaldan°,   biddan° wylle   son   of the almighty   entreat (for +g)
85   miltse° þīnre°   ⌜mē þearfendre⌝,   grace gs   your
⌜ðrȳnesse ðrym⌝.   Þearle ys mē nū ðā
heorte onhǣted°   ond hige° gēomor°,   inflamed   (my) mind   troubled
swȳðe mid sorgum° gedrēfed°.   Forgif° mē,   anxieties   afflicted   Give
    swegles ealdor,
sigor° ond sōðne gelēafan°   þæt ic mid þȳs sweorde   victory   faith
    mōte°   may
90   gehēawan° þysne morðres° bryttan.   ⌜Geunne mē   cut down   of violence
    mīnra gesynta⌝,
þearlmōd þēoden gumena.   ⌜Nāhte° ic þīnre nǣfre   Have not had
miltse þon māran° þearfe⌝.   Gewrec° nū mihtig Dryhten,   more   Avenge
torhtmōd tīres° brytta,   ⌜þæt mē ys þus torne on mōde,   of glory
hāte on hreðre mīnum⌝.'   Hī° ðā se hēhsta dēma   Her as
95   ǣdre mid elne° onbryrde°,   swā hē dēð ⌜ānra gehwylcne⌝   courage   inspired
hērbūendra°   ⌜þe hyne him tō helpe sēceð⌝   'here-dwellers' gp
mid rǣde° ond mid rihte gelēafan.   Þā ⌜wearð hyre rūme on mōde⌝   wisdom
⌜hāligre⌝ hyht° genīwod°;   genam ðā þone hǣðenan mannan   hope   renewed
fæste be feaxe° sīnum°,   tēah° hyne ⌜folmum wið hyre   hair   his   dragged
    weard⌝

---

82 **þæt word** 'the (following) utterance', or 'these words'.

85 **mē þearfendre** lit. 'for me needing', i.e. 'for myself in my need'.

86 **ðrȳnesse ðrym** 'majesty of the Trinity'. Judith addresses God with the collective name for his three persons – Father, Son and Holy Spirit – whom she has already invoked separately in 83a, 84a and 83b, respectively; on the anachronism, see headnote.

90 **Geunne mē mīnra gesynta** The vb. *geunnan* takes the dat. of pers. and gen. of thing: 'grant (to) me my safe deliverance[s]'.

91–2 **Nāhte ic … þearfe** i.e. *Nāhte ic nǣfre þon māran þearfe þīnre miltse*. Instr. *þon* is intensive 'the' before a comp. adj.

93–4 **þæt mē … on hreðre mīnum** Both *torne* and *hāte* are used adverbially; lit. '(avenge it) that to me it is thus grievously in my mind, hotly in my breast'; possible paraphrase: 'that my heart is thus grieving, my breast burning'.

95 **ānra gehwylcne** 'everyone of'; acc. obj. of *dēð*, 'does'.

96 **þe hyne him tō helpe sēceð** 'who seeks him [*hyne*, i.e. God] as a help for himself [*him*]'.

97 **wearð hyre rūme on mōde** lit. 'it became in her roomy in spirit', i.e. 'her spirit was enlarged'.

98 **hāligre** dat., parallel with *hyre* (97): 'in the holy (woman)'.

99 **folmum** dat. of instrument: 'with (her) hands'. **wið hyre weard** 'towards her'.

100	bysmerlīce° ond þone bealofullan°	ignominiously evil one *as*
	listum° ālēde°, lāðne mannan,	cunningly laid down
	swā° hēo ðæs unlædan° ēaðost° mihte	so that wretched (man) *gs* most easily
	wel° gewealdan°. Slōh ðā wundenlocc	effectively manage *+g*
	þone fēondsceaðan° ⌐fāgum mēce⌐	fiendish enemy
105	heteþoncolne° þæt hēo ⌐healfne forcearf°	savage (man) *as* cut through
	þone swēoran him⌐, þæt hē on swīman læg,	
	druncen ond dolhwund°. Næs° ðā dēad þā gȳt°,	wounded Was not yet
	ealles° orsāwle°. Slōh ðā eornoste°	completely lifeless resolutely
	ides ellenrōf° ōðre° sīðe°	daring (a) second time *ds*
110	þone hǣðenan hund°, þæt him þæt hēafod wand°	dog rolled
	forð on ðā flōre. Læg se fūla° lēap°	foul carcass
	gēsne° beæftan°, gæst ellor° hwearf°	'empty' (dead) behind elsewhere went
	under neowelne° næs° ond ðær genyðerad° wæs	deep ground prostrated
	sūsle° gesǣled° syððan° æfre,	in torment fettered afterwards
115	wyrmum bewunden° wītum° gebunden°,	coiled about by with tortures bound
	hearde° gehæfted° in hellebryne°	painfully imprisoned hell-fire
	æfter hinsīðe°. Ne ðearf° hē hopian°	(his) going-hence have occasion to hope
	nō°,	never
	þȳstrum° forðylmed°, þæt hē ⌐ðonan mōte⌐	darkness *dp* enveloped (by *+d*)
	of ðām wyrmsele° ac ðær wunian° sceal	hall of serpents dwell
120	⌐āwa tō aldre⌐ būtan° ende forð°	without henceforth
	in ðām heolstran° hām, hyhtwynna° lēas°.	dark joys of hope without *+g*
	Hæfde ðā gefohten° foremǣrne° blǣd°	won outstanding glory
	Iūdith æt gūðe° swā hyre God ūðe°,	battle granted *+d*
	swegles ealdor, þe hyre sigores onlēah°.	allotted *+g*
125	Þā sēo snotere mægð snūde gebrōhte	
	þæs herewǣðan° hēafod swā blōdig	warrior's
	on ðām fætelse° ⌐þe hyre foregenga,	bag
	blāchlēor° ides, hyra bēgea nest,	pale-cheeked
	ðēawum° geðungen°, þyder on lǣdde⌐,	in virtues excellent

104 **fāgum mēce** dat. of instrument: 'with decorated sword'. See also 194, 264 and 301.

105–6 **healfne . . . þone swēoran him** 'half his neck'; poss. dat. *him*, as also in 110.

118 **ðonan mōte** vb. of motion unexpressed after modal vb. [§G2d]: 'may (get away) from there'. For his statement of Holofernes's eternal doom, the poet has moved into the pres. (or fut.) tense.

120 **āwa tō aldre** 'always for ever', or 'in eternity'.

127–9 **þe hyre foregenga . . . on lǣdde** 'in which [*þe . . . on*] her attendant had brought there food [*nest*] for [lit. "of"] both of them'.

130 ond hit þā swā heolfrig° ⌈hyre on hond āgeaf,   bloody

higeþoncolre, hām tō berenne°,   carry

Iūdith gingran sīnre⌉. Ēodon ðā gegnum° þanonne°   directly from there

þā idesa bā° ellenþrīste°   both (of) boldly daring

oðþæt hīe becōmon°, collenferhðe°   came   elated

135 ēadhrēðige° mægð, ūt° of ðām herige°,   triumphant away army

þæt hīe sweotollīce° gesēon° mihten   clearly see

þǣre wlitegan° byrig° weallas° blīcan°,   beautiful city's walls ap shining inf

Bēthūliam. Hīe ðā bēahhrodene°   ring-adorned

⌈fēðelāste⌉ forð ōnettan°   hurried

140 oð hīe glædmōde° gegān° hæfdon   glad at heart reached

tō ðām wealgate°. Wiggend° sǣton,   wall-gate Warriors

weras wæccende° wearde° hēoldon°   watching guard as kept

in ðām fæstenne° swā° ðām folce ǣr   stronghold just as

geōmormōdum° Iūdith bebēad°,   sad-hearted (had) instructed +d

145 searoðoncol° mægð, þā hēo on sīð° gewāt°,   shrewd venture (had) set out

ides ellenrōf. Wæs ðā eft cumen

lēof° tō lēodum° ond ðā lungre° hēt   beloved (woman) people at once

glēawhȳdig° wīf gumena sumne°   prudent one (of) as

of ðǣre ginnan° byrig ⌈hyre tōgēanes gān⌉   broad

150 ond hī° ofostlīce° in forlǣton°   her speedily to let inf

þurh ðæs wealles geat, ond þæt word ācwæð

tō ðām sigefolce°: 'Ic ēow secgan mæg   'victory-people'

þoncwyrðe° þing, þæt gē ne þyrfen° leng°   'thanks-worthy' need sbj longer

murnan° on mode. Ēow ys metod° blīðe°,   grieve ordainer gracious

155 cyninga wuldor°. Þæt° gecȳðed° wearð°   glory It revealed has been

geond° woruld wīde þæt ēow ys wuldorblǣd°   through glorious success

torhtlic° tōweard° ond tīr° gifeðe°   splendid imminent fame granted

⌈þāra lǣðða⌉ þe gē lange drugon°.'   endured

Þā wurdon blīðe burhsittende°,   city-dwellers

160 syððan hī gehȳrdon hū sēo hālige sprǣc

ofer° hēanne° weall. Here° wæs ⌈on lustum⌉.   across high (The) army

Wið° þæs fæstengeates° folc ōnette,   Towards +g fortress-gate

weras wīf° somod° wornum° ond   (and) women together in swarms

hēapum°   in crowds

130–2 **hyre on hond ... gingran sīnre** lit. 'to her into the hand gave, to the discreet one, Judith to her servant', i.e. 'Judith put (it) into the hands of her discreet servant'.

139 **fēðelāste** dat. of place: 'on (their) way [lit. "foot-track"]'.

149 **hyre tōgēanes gān** 'to come to meet her' (lit. 'towards her [dat.]').

158 **þāra lǣðða** '(in respect) of those afflictions', or 'in return for...'.

161 **on lustum** 'in ecstasies', or 'joyful'.

ðrēatum ond ðrymmum°   þrungon° ond urnon°   — in bands thronged ran
165 ongēan° ðā ⌐þēoðnes⌐ mægð   þūsendmǣlum°,   — towards in thousands
ealde ge geonge. ⌐Ǣghwylcum wearð
men⌐ on ðǣre medobyrig°   mōd ārēted°   — 'mead-city' delighted
syððan hīe ongēaton   þæt wæs Iūdith cumen
eft tō ēðle°   ond ðā ofostlīce   — home
170 hīe° mid ēaðmēdum°   in forlēton.   — her humility *dp*
Þā sēo glēawe° hēt,   golde gefrætewod°,   — wise (woman) adorned
hyre ðīnenne°   þancolmōde°   — servant *as* attentive
þæs herewǣðan°   hēafod onwrīðan°   — warrior's to unwrap
ond hyt ⌐tō behðe   blōdig ætȳwan°   — to show (to +*d*)
175 þām burhlēodum°   hū hyre æt beaduwe° gespēow⌐.   — townspeople battle
Sprǣc ðā sēo æðele°   tō eallum þām folce: — noble woman
'Hēr gē magon sweotole°,   sigerōfe° hæleð°,   — openly victorious heroes
lēoda rǣswan°,   on ðæs lāðestan°   — leaders most loathsome
hǣðenes heaðorinces°   hēafod starian°,   — warrior's gaze
180 ⌐Hōlofernus unlyfigendes°⌐   — lifeless
⌐þe ūs monna mǣst   morðra gefremede⌐,
sārra° sorga°,   ond þæt swȳðor° gȳt   — painful miseries more greatly
ȳcan° wolde,   ac him ne ūðe God   — increase
lengran° līfes   þæt hē mid lǣððum ūs   — longer
185 eglan° mōste. Ic him° ealdor° oðþrong°   — plague from him life *as* forced
þurh Godes fultum°. Nū ic gumena gehwæne°   — help each +*gp*
þyssa burglēoda   biddan wylle,
randwiggendra,   þæt gē recene° ēow°   — instantly yourselves *ap*
fȳsan° tō gefeohte. Syððan frymða God,   — prepare
190 ārfæst° cyning,   ēastan° sende°   — gracious from the east sends *sbj*
lēohtne° lēoman°,   berað° linde° forð,   — radiant light *as* carry *imp* shields
bord° for° brēostum   ond byrnhomas°,   — shields before +*d* mail-coats
scīre° helmas   ⌐in sceaðena gemong⌐,   — shining

165 **þēoðnes** i.e. *þēodnes*; confusion of *d* and *ð* is frequent in late manuscripts.

166–7 **Ǣghwylcum... men** 'In every person'.

174–5 **tō behðe... hū hyre... gespēow** 'as proof of how... she had fared' (lit. 'how it had availed her [dat.]'); *blōdig* describes *hēafod* in 173.

180 **Hōlofernus unlyfigendes** The phr. is parallel with *þæs... heaðorinces* as gen. complement of *hēafod*.

181 **þe ūs... gefremede** *mǣst* should be construed with *morðra* (not *monna*) as the obj. of the vb.: 'who, of (all) men, perpetrated upon us the greatest number of violent crimes'. The gen. phr. *sārra sorga* in 182 is parallel with *morðra*.

193 **in sceaðena gemong** 'into the throng [*gemong*, acc. sg.] of enemies', or 'in the midst of...'; see also 225 and 303.

fyllan° folctogan° ⌐fāgum sweordum⌐,   to cut down   commanders *ap*

195   fǣge° frumgāras°. Fȳnd° syndon ēowere°   doomed leaders *ap* Enemies your

gedēmed° tō dēaðe   ond gē dōm° āgon°,   condemned honour (shall) have

tīr æt tohtan°,   swā ēow getācnod° hafað   battle   indicated

mihtig Dryhten   þurh mīne hand.'

Þā wearð snelra° werod°   snūde gegearewod°,   keen (men) *gp* troop prepared

200   cēnra° tō campe°. Stōpon cynerōfe°   bold (men) *gp* battle renowned

secgas° ond gesīðas°,   bǣron sigeþūfas°,   warriors   comrades   victory banners

fōron° tō gefeohte   forð ⌐on gerihte⌐   marched

hǣleð under helmum   of ðǣre hāligan byrig

⌐on ðæt dægred sylf⌐. Dynedan scildas°,   shields *np*

205   hlūde° hlummon°. Þæs° se ⌐hlanca⌐   loudly   resounded At that

    gefeah°   exulted

wulf in walde°   ond se wanna° hrefn°,   wood   black   raven

wælgīfre° fugel°. Wistan° bēgen°   carrion-greedy bird Knew both

þæt him° ⌐ðā þeodguman⌐ þōhton° tilian°   for them   intended   to provide

fylle° on° fǣgum°; ⌐ac him flēah°   (their) fill   among doomed (men) flew

on lāst⌐

210   earn° ætes° georn°,   ūrigfeðera°,   eagle   food   eager (for +*g*) dewy-feathered

⌐salowigpāda⌐ sang hildelēoð°,   dark-coated   war-song

hyrnednebba°⌐. Stōpon heaðorincas   horny-beaked

beornas tō beadowe,   bordum beðeahte°,   protected (by +*d*)

hwealfum° lindum,   þā° ðe hwīle° ǣr   curved   those   a while

215   elðēodigra° edwīt° þoledon°,   of foreigners abuse   suffered

hǣðenra hosp°. ⌐Him þæt hearde° wearð   scorn   harshly

æt ðām æscplegan° eallum⌐ forgolden°,   'spear-play'   repaid

Assȳrium,   syððan Ebrēas°   Hebrews

under gūðfanum° gegān hæfdon   battle-standards

---

194 **fāgum sweordum** dat. of instrument: 'with gleaming swords'.

202 **on gerihte** 'directly'.

204 **on ðæt dægred sylf** 'in the dawning itself', i.e. 'at the very dawning of the day'.

205 **hlanca** 'lank' or 'lean', defining *wulf* (206). Thus begins a formulaic 'beasts of battle' passage, a theme revisited in 295–6; see also 10/60–5, 30/106–7 and 32/5–6.

208 **ðā þeodguman** 'the men of that nation'; i.e. the Israelites.

209 **ac** The sense seems to be continuative, not adversative ('but'); perhaps 'moreover'. **him... on lāst** 'in their track (*or* wake)'.

211–12 **salowigpāda... hyrnednebba** The adjs. presumably continue to describe the eagle.

216–17 **Him... eallum** 'to them all'; *Assȳrium* in 218 is parallel.

220   tō ðām ⌜fyrdwīcum⌝.   Hīe ðā fromlīce°   promptly
      lēton forð flēogan   flāna° scūras,   of arrows
      hildenǣdran°,   of hornbogan°,   'battle-adders'   curved bows *dp*
      strǣlas° ⌜stedehearde⌝.   Styrmdon° hlūde   darts   Bellowed
      grame° gūðfrecan°,   gāras° sendon   fierce   fighting-men   spears
225   ⌜in heardra gemang⌝.   Hæleð wǣron yrre°,   angry
      landbūende°,   ⌜lāðum cynne⌝;   native people
      stōpon styrnmōde°,   stercedferhðe,   stern-minded
      wrehton° unsōfte°   ealdgenīðlan°   roused   roughly   ancient enemies *ap*
      medowērige°.   Mundum° brugdon°   mead-stupified   With hands   drew
230   scealcas° of sceaðum   scīrmǣled° swyrd   warriors   brightly decorated
      ⌜ecgum gecoste⌝,   slōgon eornoste
      Assīria°   ōretmæcgas°   of the Assyrians   warriors *ap*
      ⌜nīðhycgende⌝;   nānne° ne sparedon°   none *as*   spared
      þæs herefolces°,   hēanne° ne rīcne°,   army *gs*   lowly   mighty
235   ⌜cwicera manna⌝   þe hīe ofercuman mihton.
      Swā ðā magoþegnas°   on ðā morgentīd°   retainers   morning-hour
      ēhton° elðēoda°   ealle þrāge°   assailed +*g*   foreigners   time *as*
      oðþæt ongēaton   ⌜ðā ðe grame wǣron⌝,
      ðæs herefolces   ⌜hēafodweardas⌝,

220 **fyrdwīcum** This word usually occurs thus in the pl. (probably by analogy with the Latin equivalent *castra*), but with sg. meaning: 'army camp'.

223 **stedehearde** This is a unique word (and the form is not certain, owing to manuscript damage). *Stede* usually means 'place' and one interpretation is 'firmly fixed', with reference to the attachment of the shaft of an arrow to its iron point; another takes *stede* as cognate with Old Norse *steði* 'anvil' and gives 'anvil-hardened'.

225 **in heardra gemang** 'into the midst of the cruel ones', or 'in among (their) enemies'.

226 **lāðum cynne** 'towards the loathsome race'; i.e. the Assyrians, who have invaded the land of the Israelites.

231 **ecgum gecoste** dat. of respect: 'tried as to their edges', i.e. 'with proven edges'.

233 **nīðhycgende** It is not clear whether this is a pejorative variation for the Assyrian warriors, meaning 'evil schemers' (acc. pl.), or a more positive variation for the Israelite warriors who are the subj. of *slōgon*, meaning 'those intent on battle' or perhaps 'revenge' (nom. pl.).

235 **cwicera manna** This may be taken as a second complement of *nānne*: '(none) of the living men', or simply as a gen. phr. of specification: 'among the living men'; see also 323.

238 **ðā ðe grame wǣron** 'those who were hostile', i.e. 'those who were (their) enemies'; they are the subj. of *ongēaton*.

239 **hēafodweardas** Apparently 'chief watchmen' (of the army), echoing the Vulgate's *exploratores*, 'scouts'; the word is nom. pl., defining *ðā* in 238. These are the Assyrians, perceiving imminent defeat.

240 þæt ⌜him swyrdgeswing swīðlic ēowdon⌝	
weras Ebrisce. Hīe ⌜wordum⌝ þæt	
þām yldestan° ealdorþegnum°	most senior retainers *dp*
cȳðan ēodon, wrehton cumbolwigan°	warriors *ap*
ond ⌜him forhtlīce° fǣrspel° bodedon°,	fearfully dreadful news *as* announced
245 medowērigum, morgencollan°,	morning-slaughter *as*
atolne° ecgplegan°⌝. ⌜Þā ic ǣdre° gefrægn	terrible sword-play *as* quickly
slegefǣge° hæleð slǣpe tōbrēdon°⌝	death-doomed shake off *inf* (+d)
ond wið° þæs bealofullan būrgeteldes°	towards +g tent
weras wērigferhðe° hwearfum° þringan°,	demoralised in crowds throng
250 Hōlofernus. Hogedon° āninga°	(They) intended at once
hyra hlāforde hilde° bodian°,	battle *as* warn about +a
ǣrðon° ðe him se egesa° onufan° sǣte°,	before terror upon 'sat' (*i.e.* fell) *sbj*
⌜mægen° Ebrēa⌝. Mynton° ealle	force Supposed
þæt se beorna brego° ond sēo beorhte mægð	leader
255 in ðām wlitegan° træfe wæron ætsomne°,	splendid together
Iūdith sēo æðele ond se gālmōda°,	licentious man
egesfull° ond āfor°. Næs ðēah° eorla nān	fearsome ferocious however
þe ðone wiggend āweccan° dorste°	awaken dared
oððe gecunnian° ⌜hū ðone cumbolwigan	seek to know
260 wið ðā hālgan mægð hæfde geworden⌝,	
metodes mēowlan. Mægen nēalǣhte°,	approached
folc Ebrēa, fuhton° þearle	fought
⌜heardum heoruwǣpnum⌝, ⌜hæfte⌝ guldon°	repaid
hyra fyrngeflitu°, fāgum swyrdum,	former quarrels *ap*

240 **him swyrdgeswing swīðlic ēowdon** The pret. vb. (whose subj. is *weras*, 241) is best trans. as continuous past: lit. 'were displaying to them (many a) fierce sword-stroke'; something of an understatement.

241 **wordum** dat. of manner: 'with words', or perhaps, 'by word of mouth'.

244–6 **him ... ecgplegan** The vb. *bodedon* has three parallel objs.: *fǣrspel, morgencollan* and *atolne ecgplegan*; *medowērigum* ('mead-weary' or 'stupefied with mead') varies *him* ('to them'), indir. obj. of *bodedon*.

246–7 **Þā ic ... tōbrēdon** Best trans. as *Þā, ic gefrægn, slegefǣge hæleð ǣdre tōbrēdon* [an inf. form; see 7–8n] *slǣpe*. The main vb., *gefrægn*, seems to be construed with *þringan* in 249 also: 'I heard to throng', i.e. 'I heard that they thronged'.

253 **mægen Ebrēa** acc. phr. parallel with *hilde* in 251.

259–60 **hū ðone cumbolwigan ... geworden** vb. used impersonally, with acc. noun: 'how it had pleased the warrior with the holy maiden'.

263 **heardum heoruwǣpnum** dat. of instrument: 'with tough battle-weapons'. **hæfte** 'with hilt', i.e. 'with sword' or 'swords'.

265 ealde æfðoncan°. ⌜Assȳria wearð   grudges *ap*
    on ðām dægeweorce°   dōm⌝ geswiðrod°,   day's work   diminished
    bælc° forbīged°. Beornas stōdon   pride   brought low
    ymbe hyra þēodnes træf   þearle gebylde°,   agitated
    sweorcendferhðe°. Hī ðā somod ealle   gloomy-hearted
270 ongunnon cohhetan°,   cirman° hlūde   to clear (their) throats   to call
    ond ⌜grīstbitian,   gōde orfeorme,
    mid tōðon⌝, torn° þoligende°. Þā ⌜wæs hyra tīres æt ende⌝,   misery   suffering
    ēades° ond ellendǣda°. Hogedon þā   good fortune *gs*   brave deeds *gp*
       eorlas āweccan
    hyra winedryhten°; ⌜him wiht ne spēow⌝.   lord and friend
275 Þā ⌜wearð sīð° ond late°   sum tō ðām arod   tardily   at last
    þāra beadorinca⌝   þæt hē in þæt būrgeteld°   pavilion
    nīðheard° nēðde°,   swā hyne nȳd° fordrāf°. daringly   ventured   need   compelled
    Funde ðā on bedde   blācne° licgan   pale
    his goldgifan°   gǣstes gēsne°,   gold-giver   bereft (of +*g*)
280 līfes belidenne°. Hē þā lungre° gefēoll   deprived (of +*g*)   at once
    frēorig° tō foldan°,   ongan his feax° teran,   chilled (by fear)   ground   hair *as*
    hrēoh° on mōde,   ond his hrægl° somod°   distraught   clothing   as well
    ond þæt word ācwæð   tō ðām wiggendum,
    þe ðǣr unrōte°   ūte° wǣron: dejected   outside
285 'Hēr ys geswutelod°   ⌜ūre sylfra⌝ forwyrd°   made manifest   destruction
    tōweard getācnod,   ⌜þæt þǣre tīde ys
    mid nīðum nēah geðrungen⌝   ⌜þe° wē sculon losian°⌝,   when   perish
    somod æt sæcce° forweorðan°. Hēr līð° sweorde   conflict   be destroyed   lies
       gehēawen

265–6 **Assȳria ... dōm** 'the renown of the Assyrians'.

271–2 **grīstbitian ... mid tōðon** 'to grind' or 'gnash with their teeth'. **gōde orfeorme** 'destitute of [lit. "from"] benefit', i.e. 'without success' (though the first word could be *Gode*, giving 'alienated from God').

272 **wæs hyra tīres æt ende** impers. vb. and gen. of respect: '(it) was at an end as regards their glory', i.e. 'their glory was at an end'. Two more gen. nouns, parallel with *tīres*, follow in 273.

274 **him wiht ne spēow** 'to them it did not avail at all', i.e. 'they did not succeed at all'.

275–6 **wearð ... þāra beadorinca** Here *tō ðām* is adv. ('to that extent'): 'one of the warriors became so bold [*arod*]', or 'became bold enough'.

285 **ūre sylfra** 'of our selves', i.e. 'our own ...'.

286–7 **þæt þǣre tīde ... nēah geðrungen** lit. 'that to the time (it) is nearly pressed', i.e. 'it has nearly come to the time'. **þe ... losian** Many editors supply *nū* after *sculon* for metrical reasons.

	behēafdod° healdend° ūre.' Hī ðā hrēowigmōde°	decapitated lord dejected
290	wurpon° hyra wǣpen ofdūne°, ⌐gewitan him wērigferhðe	threw down
	on flēam° sceacan⌐. ⌐Him mon feaht on lāst⌐	flight
	mægenēacen° folc oð se mǣsta° dǣl	increased in strength greatest
	þæs heriges læg hilde gesǣged°	laid low (by +d)
	on ðām sigewonge°, sweordum gehēawen,	victory-field
295	wulfum tō° willan° ond ēac wælgīfrum	as enjoyment (for +d)
	fuglum tō frōfre°. ⌐Flugon ðā ðe lyfdon	joy (to +d)
	lāðra lindwīg⌐. Him on lāste° fōr°	track advanced
	swēot° Ebrēa sigore geweorðod°,	army ns honoured (with +d)
	dōme° gedȳrsod°: ⌐him fēng Dryhten God	decree exalted (by +d)
300	fægre° on fultum⌐, frēa° ælmihtig.	splendidly Lord
	Hī ðā fromlīce fāgum swyrdum	
	hæleð higerōfe° herpað° worhton	brave-hearted a way for the army as
	þurh lāðra gemong, linde hēowon°,	hacked
	scildburh° scǣron°. Scēotend°	shield-wall split 'Shooters' (*i.e.* spear-throwers)
	wǣron	
305	gūðe gegremede°, guman Ebrisce;	enraged (with +d)
	⌐þegnas on ðā tīd þearle gelyste	
	gārgewinnes⌐. Þǣr on grēot° gefēoll	dust
	se hȳhsta° dǣl hēafodgerīmes°	greatest 'head-count' (*i.e.* total number)
	Assīria ealdorduguðe°,	chief nobility gs
310	⌐lāðan cynnes°⌐. Lȳthwōn° becōm°	race Few +g came
	cwicera° tō cȳððe°. Cirdon° cynerōfe	of the living native land Turned
	wiggend on wiðertrod°, ⌐wælscel⌐ oninnan°,	return path amidst +a

290–1 **gewitan him... sceacan** 'they went hurrying away', with rflx. dat. pron. not trans.

291 **Him mon feaht on lāst** '(they) fought on the track of them', i.e. 'fought them in the rear'.

296–7 **Flugon... lindwīg** The noun *lindwīg* is a conjectured reconstruction of *lindw.* in the damaged manuscript and means either 'shield-army' or 'shield prowess'. It is likely to be the obj. of *flugon*, the pret. of the trans. vb. *flēon* 'to flee': 'Those who lived [i.e. the survivors] fled the shield prowess of their foes'. Alternatively *flugon* might be pret. of the intrans. vb. *flēogan* 'to flee': 'The survivors, the shield-army of foes, fled'.

299–300 **him fēng... on fultum** 'came [lit. "seized"] to their help'.

306–7 **þegnas... gelyste gārgewinnes** impers. vb. with acc. of person (*þegnas*) and gen. of thing: 'the thanes... desired spear-conflict'.

310 **lāðan cynnes** gen. phr. parallel with *hēafodgerīmes*.

312 **wælscel** The compound is otherwise unknown (though the first element is *wæl*, 'slaughter'); plausible guesses are 'carnage' or 'heaps of slain'.

rēocende° hrǽw°. ⌐Rūm wæs tō nimanne — reeking corpses *ap*
londbūendum⌐ on° ðām lāðestan°, — from most hateful ones *dp*
315 hyra ealdfēondum° unlyfigendum, — old enemies
heolfrig° hererēaf°, hyrsta° scȳne°, — bloodied war-booty trappings beautiful
bord ond brād swyrd, brūne° helmas, — burnished
dȳre° mādmas°. Hæfdon dōmlīce° — costly treasures gloriously
on ðām folcstede° fȳnd oferwunnen°, — battlefield conquered
320 ⌐ēðelweardas, ealdhettende⌐,
swyrdum āswefede°. ⌐Hīe on swaðe reston, — put to death
þā ðe⌐ him tō° līfe lāðost wǣron° — in had been
cwicera cynna. Þā sēo cnēoris° eall, — nation
mǣgða° mǣrost°, ānes mōnðes fyrst°, — of races most famous (for the) duration
325 wlanc, wundenlocc, wǣgon° ond lǣddon — carried
tō ðǣre beorhtan byrig Bēthūliam
helmas ond hupseax°, hāre° byrnan°, — hip-swords grey mail-coats
gūðsceorp° gumena golde gefrætewod – — war-apparel
⌐mǣrra mādma⌐ þonne ⌐mon ǣnig
330 āsecgan° mǣge searoþoncelra⌐. — tell
⌐Eal þæt⌐ ðā ðēodguman þrymme° geēodon° — by force (had) won
cēne° under cumblum° ond compwīge°, — bold banners (in the) fray
þurh ⌐Iūdithe⌐ glēawe° lāre°, — prudent advice *as*
mǣgð mōdigre. Hī tō° mēde° hyre° — as reward for her
335 of ðām sīðfate° sylfre° brōhton, — expedition (for) herself
eorlas æscrōfe°, Hōlofernes — 'spear-renowned'
sweord ond swātigne° helm, swylce ēac sīde° byrnan — bloody ample

313–14 **Rūm wæs tō nimanne londbūendum** 'It was an opportunity [*rūm*] for the land-dwellers to seize ...'. The dir. objs. of the vb. are *heolfrig hererēaf*, etc, in 316–18, all acc.

320 **ēðelweardas** 'guardians of the homeland'; i.e. the Israelites, the subj. of *hæfdon oferwunnen*. **ealdhettende** 'old antagonists', acc. obj. of the vb., parallel with *fȳnd*.

321–2 **Hīe on swaðe reston, þā ðe** 'They remained in their trail, those who...', i.e. 'Behind them remained those who...'.

329 **mǣrra mādma** Apparently, 'of more famous treasures', a descriptive gen. phr. complementing *gūðsceorp* in 328. Some editors emend to *māre*, which is then the subj. of an independent phr. parallel with *gūðsceorp*.

329–30 **mon ǣnig ... searoþoncelra** 'any man among [lit. "of"] discerning (men)'.

331 **Eal þæt** i.e. the booty.

333 **Iūdithe** gen.: 'Judith's'; in 334, the phr. *mǣgð mōdigre* is in concord.

gerēnode° rēadum° golde;   ond ⌐eal þæt se rinca   ornamented (with +d)   red
  baldor
swīðmōd° sinces⌐ āhte°   oððe sundoryrfes°,   arrogant   had   personal wealth
340 bēaga ond beorhtra māðma,   hī þæt þǣre beorhtan idese
āgēafon° gearoþoncolre°.   ⌐Ealles ðæs⌐ Iūdith   gave (to +d)   clever *dsf*
  sægde°   declared
wuldor weroda° Dryhtne   þe hyre weorðmynde°   of hosts   esteem *as*
  geaf°,   had given
mǣrðe° on moldan° rīce,   swylce ēac mēde on heofonum,   renown *as*   of earth
sigorlēan° in swegles wuldre,   ⌐þæs þe⌐ hēo āhte   victory-reward *as*
  sōðne gelēafan
345 ⌐ā⌐ tō° ðām ælmihtigan.   Hūru° æt þām ende ne   in   Certainly
  twēode°   doubted +*g*
þæs lēanes þe hēo lange gyrnde°.   Dæs° sȳ° ðām   desired   For that   be *sbj*
  lēofan Dryhtne
wuldor ⌐tō wīdan aldre⌐   þe gesceōp° wind ond lyfte°,   created   skies
roderas° ond rūme° grundas°,   swylce ēac   heavens   spacious   lands
  rēðe° strēamas°   fierce   seas
ond swegles drēamas°   ðurh his sylfes miltse.   joys

338–9 **eal ... sinces ...** gen. of specification: 'everything (by way) of treasure ...', etc.
341 **Ealles ðæs** gen. of respect: 'For all that'.
344 **þæs þe** 'because'.
345 **ā** 'ever'; absent from the manuscript but added for alliterative and metrical purposes.
347 **tō wīdan aldre** 'for eternity'.

IV

EXAMPLE AND EXHORTATION

The literature of Anglo-Saxon Christianity dominates the surviving Old English corpus in the sheer volume of texts – and all of them, whether targeted at monks and clergy or at the laity, have ultimately a single aim: to encourage the faithful. They do this through example and exhortation, and through the clear exposition of Christian doctrine and practice in relation to life here on earth. Implicitly, and often explicitly, the theme of 'end things' (a subject known as eschatology) is at the heart of such writings. At the end of human time, according to St Paul in his Epistle to the Romans (14.10), 'we shall all stand before the judgement seat of Christ', and there all shall be judged according to how they lived their earthly life. Christian writers thus urge the faithful to conduct that life in the clear knowledge of its transitoriness and in the expectation of better things to come. It is Paul also, in his Epistle to the Ephesians (6.10–17), who defines for us the ideal Christian hero – the *miles Christi* ('soldier of Christ'), whose weapons are spiritual and include the 'sword of truth' and the 'breastplate of righteousness'.

Prose is the medium most favoured by militant Anglo-Saxon Christian writers, and three modes of discourse feature prominently: homily, sermon and hagiography. 'Homily' and 'sermon' are useful ways to describe two different sorts of address, both designed to be read out at church services, though in practice the terms have always been used loosely and indiscriminately. A homily, properly speaking, is Bible-based; it takes a passage of scripture – usually one set to be read at mass on a particular day in the church year – and analyses it in detail, explaining both its literal significance and what it stands for figuratively as a lesson on right Christian behaviour. Ælfric's *Homily for Easter Sunday* (Text 22) is a classic example, which uses a passage from the gospel of Matthew to unravel the meaning of Christ's crucifixion and subsequent events. A sermon, on the other hand, is not tied to a Bible reading but addresses a specific topic related to church practice or doctrine and explores it in detail. It might be on the Trinity or baptism, or a more general theme, such as the problem of the worship of pagan deities which Archbishop Wulfstan faces in his *On False Gods* (Text 24); or it might be something more topical (and distinctly political), as in another of Wulfstan's works, *The Sermon of the Wolf* (Text 25), in which he interprets the pressing problem of Viking attack and English cowardice around the year 1014 as divine punishment for the people's sins. The third main type of Christian discourse is the saint's life. Though Protestant

Christians since the Reformation have played down the importance of saints, or even excluded them altogether, in the medieval church (as in the Roman Catholic Church today) they performed a major role in the doctrine, liturgy and daily practice of Christianity. The role of hagiography, i.e. the recording of saints' lives (the word is derived from *hagios*, Greek for 'holy'), was correspondingly crucial. Ælfric produced a volume of such lives in OE, including both saints who died peacefully and those who were martyred for their faith (see 21/headnote). Among Ælfric's lives is that of an English virgin saint of the seventh century, Æthelthryth, much admired by Bede (Text 21a). Briefer accounts of saints were catalogued in 'martyrologies'; in the *Old English Martyrology* is to be found the story of St Eugenia, an illustrious near-eastern predecessor of Æthelthryth, who was both a virgin and a martyr (Text 21b).

The role of OE poets in the promotion of Christian ideas was crucial too, however. Indeed, the brief *Death Song* attributed to Bede is a perfect evocation of that most basic imperative which Christians are urged to face – self-scrutiny in the face of certain judgement to come – and it stands as a fitting epigraph for this section as a whole (Text 20). The theme is shared by *The Dream of the Rood* (Text 23), in which the anxieties of an individual Christian (the 'dreamer' of the poem) provoke a compelling personal meditation on the significance of Christ's crucifixion; the cross itself speaks to the dreamer and, through him (so the poet hopes), to the reader or auditor. In *The Seafarer* (Text 26), too, the lyric voice of the storm-tossed speaker modulates, under the force of a startling paradox, into a didactic one, which again submits life on earth to a ruthless analysis by Christian logic and ends in the contemplation of the true 'home' in heaven.

Further reading

M. McC. Gatch, *Preaching and Theology in Anglo-Saxon England: Ælfric and Wulfstan* (Toronto and Buffalo, 1977)

D. G. Scragg, 'The Corpus of Vernacular Homilies and Prose Saints' Lives', *ASE* 8 (1979), 223–77

L. Carruthers, 'Apocalypse Now: Preaching and Prophecy in Anglo-Saxon England', *Études Anglaises* 51 (1998), 399–410

C. A. Lees, *Tradition and Belief: Religious Writing in Late Anglo-Saxon England* (Minneapolis, MN, 1999)

20
Bede's *Death Song*

Even as he lay dying at Jarrow in 735, the Venerable Bede (see p. 69) was working and teaching, according to an account of the great scholar's last days given in a letter written by a pupil of his, Cuthbert. During this time, Bede, who was 'well versed in our [i.e. English] poetry', recited a poem 'in our own language' about death, for he was 'skilled in the art of poetry in his own language'. Cuthbert gives us only a Latin paraphrase of the poem, but from at least the ninth century onwards copies of his letter were accompanied by an OE version too. More than thirty such copies survive, some made as late as the sixteenth century. A third of them (all apparently in manuscripts made on the Continent) have a text in the Northumbrian dialect; the rest are in a WS recension.

It is nice to think that Bede actually composed the song just before his death, but there can be no proof that he did not simply recite a poem already known to him. The theme is that favourite one of Christian writers, and one which Bede seems to have treated at length in a Latin poem, too – Judgement Day and the fate of the individual soul when it shall be called to account for its owner's conduct on earth. The *Death Song* implicitly avows a greater and simpler wisdom beyond that of even the wisest of earthly men (such as Bede himself). It consists of a single sentence, given in the style of an enigma but conveying a clear logic, structured as it is on the balance of the first and last lines: 'before . . .' and 'after . . .'. The metaphor of a 'compulsory (or inevitable) journey' in the opening line gives way to stark 'death' at the close, and the subjunctive mood of the final verb (*weorþe*, 5), contrasting with the earlier indicative (*wyrþeþ*, 1), leaves an ominous question mark over every individual's future.

Both Northumbrian and WS versions of the song are given below. In the former, taken from the earliest known copy in a ninth-century manuscript, now in the library of the monastery of Sankt Gallen in Switzerland, orthography and language suggest that it represents quite faithfully the version which Cuthbert says he heard at Bede's monastery in Northumbria in 735. The scribe – presumably working (perhaps at Sankt Gallen itself) from a much earlier English original – uses none of the characteristic Anglo-Saxon letters adopted during the eighth century (see p. xxix): ð and þ are written *th*, the digraph æ is written *ae*, and *w*, which had its own Anglo-Saxon character (the 'wynn'), is written *uu*. Our knowledge of the early OE dialects is limited (indeed, the *Death Song* is itself a significant piece of the evidence), but *aeththa*, *hiniongae*, and *neid-* seem to be Northumbrian, and *tharf*, which shows the older Germanic retention of the 'unbroken' vowel *a* before *r* + consonant (cf. later *ea*), is at least Anglian (i.e. shared by both Northumbrian and Mercian dialects). Features such as *t* for *th* at the end of *uuiurthit* and *e* for *ae* in *them*, both in line 1, may be due to scribal idiosyncrasy; *e* and *ae* in written Latin seem to have been interchangeable at this time. As for the WS version (b), taken here from a manuscript in the Bodleian Library, Oxford (Digby 211), it occurs in manuscripts not copied until the twelfth century, and all of them in England. Its orthography and language show characteristic late OE changes but the source of the original WS version, from which all the copies seem to derive, cannot be located precisely.

There are three differences in vocabulary between the Northumbrian and WS versions. The compound noun *thoncsnotturra* in line 2 of the former has become a two-word phrase in the latter, *þances snotera*, with the genitive termination added to *þanc* but the meaning hardly altered. In line 3, *gehicgenne* replaces the former *ymbhycggannae*, the loss of the prepositional prefix arguably weakening the force of the verb. In the case of *æfter dēaþe heonon* for the former *aefter deothdaege* in line 5, the adverb *heonon* is awkward and unnecessary and results almost certainly from a scribal error in the archetype of the WS versions (perhaps influenced by *heonen-* in line 3).

Further reading

E. V. K. Dobbie, *The Manuscripts of Cædmon's Hymn and Bede's Death Song* (New York, 1937)

A. H. Smith, ed., *Three Northumbrian Poems: Cædmon's Hymn, Bede's Death Song and the Leiden Riddle*, rev. edn. (Exeter, 1978)

B. Mitchell, 'Postscript on Bede's *Mihi cantare habes*', *NM* 70 (1969), 369–80

A. Crépin, 'Bede and the Vernacular', in *Famulus Christi: Essays in Commemoration of the Thirteenth Centenary of the Birth of the Venerable Bede*, ed. G. Bonner (London, 1976), pp. 170–92

G. H. Brown, *Bede the Venerable* (Boston, MA, 1987)

E. G. Stanley, 'The Oldest English Poetry Now Extant', *Poetica* (Tokyo) 2 (1974), 1–24; rep. in E. G. Stanley, *A Collection of Papers with Emphasis on Old English Literature* (Toronto, 1987), pp. 115–38.

20a
Northumbrian version

Fore° ⌐thēm neidfaerae⌐   nāēnig° uuiurthit°   Before   no one   becomes
⌐thoncsnotturra   than him tharf sīe
tō ymbhycggannae⌐,   āēr° his hiniongae°,   before   going hence
huaet° ⌐his gāstae   gōdaes aeththa yflaes   what
5   aefter dēothdaege°   dōēmid uueorthae⌐.   death-day

20b
West-Saxon version

For ⌐þām nēdfere⌐   nǣni wyrþeþ
⌐þances snotera⌐   ⌐þonne him þearf sȳ
tō gehicgenne⌐,   ǣr his heonengange,
hwæt ⌐his gāste   gōdes oþþe yfeles
5   æfter dēaþe heonon°   dēmed weorþe⌐.   henceforth

1 **thēm neidfaerae / þǣm nēdfere** 'the inevitable journey', i.e. death. The first element of the noun, late WS *nīed*, means 'need', 'necessity' or 'compulsion'; and Cuthbert's Latin paraphrase (see headnote) indicates that the second element should be interpreted as *fær* 'journey' or 'passage', rather than *fǣr* 'calamity' or 'sudden danger' – though the idea of 'the unavoidable calamity (of death)' might not be inappropriate in the context.

2 **thoncsnotturra** lit. 'thought-wiser'.   **þances snotera** lit. 'wiser of thought'.

2–3 **than him tharf sīe tō ymbhycggannae / þonne him þearf sȳ tō gehicgenne** 'than (that) it is necessary for him to consider' (*sīe/sȳ* is the sbj. of hypothesis, *gehicgenne* the infl. inf.: §G6d.ii.1). 1b–3a could be paraphrased: 'no one is so wise in thought that he does not need to consider . . .'.

4–5 **his gāstae . . . dōēmid uueorthae / his gāste . . . dēmed weorþe** sbj. of hypothesis: 'may be adjudged to his soul [*gāstae/gāste*, dat. sg.]'.   **gōdaes aeththa yflaes / gōdes oþþe yfeles** gen. of respect: 'by way of good or evil'. Cf. the words of St Paul cited in the section headnote, p. 165.

21

Two Holy Women

'To strengthen your faith' was how Ælfric described the purpose of his collection of *Lives of Saints* to the patron for whom they were written, in about 990. Such 'lives' constituted one of the most extensive genres of literature in the Christian world from the second century AD onwards. The earliest saints were the Christian martyrs of the Roman Empire who had died, often horrifically, for their faith, as the apostles had done before them; but sainthood could be achieved also by people who died naturally but had lived exemplary, holy, lives. The term 'confessor' was used for these, to distinguish them from the true 'martyr' (a Greek word meaning 'witness'). The recorded life of a confessor saint is called by the Latin word *uita* ('life'), that of a martyr a *passio* ('passion', in the sense of suffering). Saints are important for a unique double reason: their holiness brings them close to God, but their human nature makes them also accessible to ordinary people. Thus a saint may be persuaded by prayer to intercede with God on behalf of a Christian seeking forgiveness for sins or a cure for illness. Such, at least, was the hope which stimulated the veneration of saints in so-called 'cults' during the medieval period and in turn gave rise to a veritable industry of pilgrimage to saints' shrines and the collecting of (and trade in) 'relics' – for it was believed that contact with anything connected with a saint (a piece of clothing or a fragment of bone, for instance) might expedite one's petition.

Individual saints' lives in Latin had circulated widely in Anglo-Saxon England since the seventh century, but Ælfric was the first to put a substantial number of them into the vernacular. His collection of forty items complemented the two series of *Catholic Homilies* which he had already produced (see p. 181). Among Ælfric's saints were five Anglo-Saxons: two male confessors (Cuthbert and Swithun), two male martyrs (the kings Oswald and Edmund) – and a virgin saint, Æthelthryth. Her true witness as a Christian is demonstrated by her ascetic inclinations, her joyful acceptance of illness and, above all, her commitment (despite the active opposition of at least one of her two husbands) to lifelong virginity. Ælfric's account of Æthelthryth (a name, spelt with a final *d* in the manuscript, which would later develop into 'Audrey') is Text 21a, below.

Records of the martyr saint were kept in works known as 'martyrologies', too, where they were catalogued in chronological order of their feast-days (usually the day on which they died). In some such books, the entries may do no more than record the date and place of martyrdom, but in what are called 'historical' martyrologies, a somewhat longer narrative of each saint's life is given. The earliest surviving work of this kind in any vernacular language is the *Old English Martyrology*. This may have been modelled on a Latin *Martyrologium* by Bede, but the material is derived from an impressively wide range of other (Latin) sources, including Bede's *Historia ecclesiastica* (see p. 69), various Anglo-Saxon saints' lives, and works by Isidore of Seville and Gregory the Great. The two hundred-plus entries in the *Old English Martyrology* range in length from a short paragraph to a page or more. Five manuscripts of the work, in the dialect of Mercia, are preserved, but each is fragmentary and even between them they do not provide us with anything like a complete copy; entries for the months of February and December are mostly absent. As the earliest of the manuscripts dates from the late ninth century (i.e. the time of Alfred the Great), we know that the *Martyrology* was composed at least as early as this. One of the entries is for Saint Eugenia, whose story was treated also, at some length, by Ælfric in his *Lives of Saints* (item 2). Eugenia is a martyr, who suffers grievously for her steadfast faith and the preservation of her virginity; her entry is given as Text 21b.

Further reading

R. Woolf, 'Saints' Lives', in her *Art and Doctrine: Essays on Medieval Literature*, ed. H. Donoghue (London, 1986), pp. 219–44

M. Lapidge, 'The Saintly Life in Anglo-Saxon England', in *Cambridge Companion*, pp. 43–63

D. W. Rollason, *Saints and Relics in Anglo-Saxon England* (Oxford, 1989)

P. E. Szarmach, ed., *Holy Men and Holy Women: Old English Prose Saints' Lives and Their Contexts* (Albany, NY, 1996)

21a
Saint Æthelthryth
(from Ælfric's *Lives of Saints*)

Ælfric's main source for the story of Æthelthryth in his *Lives of Saints* (item 20) was the account by Bede in his *Historia ecclesiastica* (bk. 4, ch. 19). Æthelthryth was a royal princess of East Anglia, born about 630, who was married first, in about 652, to ealdorman Tondberht, and then, after the latter's early death, to the king of Northumbria, Ecgfrith. She was still probably only about fifteen years old and the king twice that age. In 671, Ecgfrith allowed Æthelthryth her long held desire to be a nun, and she entered the monastery at Coldingham (leaving Ecgfrith to take a new wife). A year later, she became founding abbess of a monastery at Ely, in East Anglia, and she died in 679, from an illness whose symptoms included a large swelling on her neck. Bede's claim that she remained a virgin through her two marriages cannot of course be verified; nor can the counter-claim by some historians that she was in fact sterile and that Ecgfrith alleged non-consummation as a pretext for divorce. Bede certainly believed in Æthelthryth's virginity, and he records that bishop Wilfrid (his informant) had been offered a reward by the king if he could persuade Æthelthryth to consummate the marriage (a point included by Ælfric in his version). Æthelthryth had been brought up surrounded by enthusiastic Christians, including her recently converted father, named Anna, and a sister and step-sister who both became nuns. Thus her own ambition to take the veil, and the vow of chastity that went with it, need not surprise us. Whatever the case, it has been noted that for Bede, and later for Ælfric, Æthelthryth was an ideal hagiographical model, the nearest England could come to the virgin martyrs of the early Christian church, such as Eugenia. Bede composed a fifty-four-line 'hymn' on virginity in Æthelthryth's honour (*Historia ecclesiastica*, bk. 4, ch. 20).

In the works written late in his career, including the *Lives of Saints*, Ælfric adopted a metrical style in his prose which bears at least a superficial resemblance to the metres of OE poetry (see p. xxii). It is a style characterised by an alliterating stress rhythm, which links pairs of (usually) two-stressed phrases. An example is *And Sexburh sēo abbudisse* / *hēt slēan ān geteld* // *bufan ðā byrgene* / *wolde þā bān gaderian* (59–60), where there is stress on the initial, alliterating, syllables of *Sexburh* and *slēan*, and of *bufan*, *byrgene* and *bān*. However, the habit adopted by earlier editors of Ælfric's works of setting out the lines as though they were poetry cannot be justified. An alliterative stress rhythm may be an important aspect of the prose but is not its essence; the unit of meaning remains the sentence, whose effect depends on the movement and shape of the whole.

Several manuscripts of *Lives of Saints* are preserved, the most complete being the one used here, London, British Library, Cotton Julius E. vii. It was copied early in the eleventh century, not long after composition of the work. The late WS language shows great inconsistency of spelling. These mainly involve the use of *i* and *y* (the latter characteristic of later WS): thus we find *swilce* (45) as well as *swylce* (65) and *micclum* (80) as well as *mycclum* (58). *Swustor* occurs twice (48 and 51), *swuster* once (66); intrusive *c* appears before *g* in *woruldþincg* (23) and *cynincg(e)* (5, 11, etc) but not in *cyning* (16).

Further reading

W. W. Skeat, ed. and trans., *Ælfric's Lives of Saints*, 2 vols. in 4, EETS 76/82 and 94/114 (London, 1881–1900, repr. 1966)

C. E. Fell, 'Saint Æðelþryð: a Historical-Hagiographical Dichotomy Revisited', *Nottingham Medieval Studies* 38 (1994), 18–34

P. A. Thompson, 'St Æthelthryth: the Making of History from Hagiography', in *Studies in English Language and Literature: 'Doubt Wisely': Papers in Honour of E. G. Stanley*, ed. M. J. Toswell and E. M. Tyler (London and New York, 1996), pp. 475–92

L. A. Donovan, *Women Saints' Lives in Old English Prose Translated from Old English with Introduction, Notes and Interpretive Essay* (Cambridge, 1999)

⌐VIIII *Kalendas Iulii natale sancte Æðelðrȳðe Virginis*⌐.

⌐WĒ WYLLAÐ⌐ NŪ ĀWRĪTAN, ⌐ÞĒAH ÐE⌐ HIT WUNDORLIC° SȲ°, be°
ðǣre hālgan° ⌐sancte⌐ Æðeldrȳðe þām Engliscan mǣdene°, ⌐þe wæs mid twām
werum⌐ and swāðēah° wunode° mǣden, ⌐swā swā⌐ þā wundra° geswuteliað° þe
5   hēo wyrcð° gelōme°. ⌐Anna hātta⌐ hyre fæder Ēastengla cynincg, swȳðe° crīsten
man, swā swā he cȳdde° mid weorcum°, and eall his tēam° wearð° gewurðod°
þurh God. Æðeldrȳð wearð þā forgifen° ānum ealdormenn° tō° wīfe, ac hit
nolde° se ælmihtiga God þæt hire mægðhād° wurde° mid hǣmede° ādȳlegod°
ac hēold° hī° on clǣnnysse°, ⌐forðan þe⌐ hē is ælmihtig God and mæg dōn eall
10   þæt hē wile and on manegum wīsum° his mihte° geswutelað. Se ealdorman
gewāt° ⌐þā ðā⌐ hit wolde God, and hēo wearð forgifen ⌐Ecfride⌐ cynincge and
twelf gēar wunode ungewemmed° mǣden ⌐on þæs cynincges synscype⌐, swā

2 miraculous may be *sbj* concerning   **3** holy maiden   **4** even so remained miracles show   **5** performs often deeply   **6** showed (his) deeds family was honoured   **7** given (to +*d*) ealdorman as   **8** did not wish virginity should be intercourse destroyed   **9** (he) kept her chastity   **10** ways power   **11** departed (*i.e.* died)   **12** unblemished

1 **VIIII... Virginis** Lat. title to the text: 'The ninth of the kalends of July on the birthday [*or* anniversary] of saint Æthelthryth, Virgin'. 'Kalends' was the first day of the month in the ancient Roman calendar and one of the reference points for a complex process of dating; here the date is in fact 3 June.

2 **Wē wyllað** Ælfric characteristically uses the 1st pers. pl.; see also 82 and 83.   **þēah ðe** conj. phr. 'though'.

3 **sancte** From Lat. *sanctus*, 'saint', here with dat. sg. OE inflection; see 7b/50n.

3–4 **þe wæs mid twām werum** 'who was [*i.e.* had lived] with two husbands'.

4 **swā swā** 'just as', or simply 'as'. See also 12–13, 21, etc.

5 **Anna** He ruled the kingdom of the East Angles, probably from the early 640s until his death in 654. Among his notable Christian deeds (see next line) was the conversion of the West-Saxon king, Cenwealh (*d.* 672).   **hātta** 'was called'; a passive vb., more usually *hātte*.

9 **forðan þe** conj. phr.: 'because'. See also 39 and 53.

11 **þā ðā** 'then when', i.e. 'when'.   **Ecfride** 'to Ecgfrith'. He was the Christian king of Northumbria (670–85) who had donated the land for Bede's monastery of Wearmouth-Jarrow.

12 **on þæs cynincges synscype** lit. 'in the king's cohabitation', i.e. 'in cohabitation (*or* marriage) with the king'. A similar construction is used in 17.

swā swutele° wundra hyre mǣrða° cȳðaþ° ⌐and hire mægðhād⌐ gelōme. Hēo
lufode° þone hǣlend° þe hī° hēold unwemme°, and Godes ðēowas° wurðode°.

15   Ān þǣra° wæs ⌐Wilfrid⌐ bisceop þe° hēo swȳðost° lufode, and hē sǣde ⌐Bēdan⌐
þæt se cyning Ecfrid him oft behēte° mycel° on° lande and on fēo° gif hē lǣran°
mihte Æðeldrȳðe his gebeddan° þæt hēo brūce° his synscipes. Nū cwæð se
hālga Bēda, þe þās bōc gesette°, þæt se ælmihtiga God mihte ēaðe° gedōn°, ⌐nū
on ūrum dagum⌐, þæt Æðeldrȳð þurhwunode° ungewemmed mǣden, þēah ðe

20   hēo wer hæfde, swā swā on ealdum dagum hwīlon° ǣr° getīmode° þurh þone
ylcan° God þe ǣfre° þurhwunað mid his gecorenum° hālgum°, swā swā hē sylf
behēt°.

      Æðeldrȳð wolde ðā ealle woruldþincg° forlǣtan° and bæd° georne° þone
cynincg þæt hēo Crīste mōste° þēowian° on mynsterlicre° drohtnunge° swā hire
25   mōd° ⌐hire tō spēon⌐. Þā lyfde° hire se cynincg, þēah þe hit embe° lang° wǣre
⌐þæs þe hēo gewilnode⌐, and Wilfrid bisceop þā hī gehādode° tō mynecene°
and hēo syððan° on mynstre° wunode sume° twelf monað swā°, and hēo syððan
wearð gehādod eft° tō abudissan° on ⌐Elig-Mynstre⌐ ofer manega mynecena,
and hēo hī mōdorlīce° hēold° ⌐mid gōdum gebysnungum tō þām gāstlican līfe⌐.

13 clear glorious deeds *ap* make known   **14** loved Saviour her unblemished servants
honoured   **15** of them whom most deeply   **16** promised *sbj* much in money persuade
+*d*   **17** spouse enjoy *sbj* +*g*   **18** composed easily bring about   **19** remained *sbj*   **20** at
times formerly occurred   **21** same ever chosen saints   **22** promised   **23** worldly
affairs abandon entreated eagerly   **24** might be allowed *sbj* to serve +*d* monastic way
of living   **25** heart permitted (it to +*d*) after (a) long (time)   **26** consecrated (a) nun
27 afterwards convent about thus   **28** next abbess   **29** as a mother ruled

13 **and hire mægðhād** This phr. joins with *mǣrða* to form the pl. subj. of *cȳðaþ*. Such
intervention of the vb. to break up 'heavy groups' of words is common in OE.
      15 **Wilfrid** Northumbrian bishop (*d.* 709), who founded the monastery at Hexham and
at one time wielded considerable ecclesiastical and political power.   **Bēdan** 'to Bede'. His
account of what Wilfrid said is in bk. 4, ch. 19 of the *Historia ecclesiastica* (see headnote).
      18–19 **nū on ūrum dagum** In stressing the continuity between God's present powers
and those of 'the old days' (20), Bede was explicitly associating the exemplary Æthelthryth
with the virgin saints of the early church, some of whom were martyred for their faith.
      25 **hire tō spēon** The prep. *tō* comes after its obj.: 'urged to her', i.e. 'urged her'. In 24,
the same pron. form *hire* is gen.
      26 **þæs þe hēo gewilnode** gen. of respect: 'for that which she desired', i.e. 'before she
had what she desired'. As we learned above (12), she was married to the king for twelve
years before he released her.
      28 **Elig-Mynstre** 'the monastery of Ely', in East Anglia, founded by Æthelthryth in
672.
      29 **mid gōdum ... līfe** lit. 'with good examples (pertaining) to the spiritual life'; perhaps,
'by her good example of the spiritual life'.

30   Be hire is āwrytan þæt hēo wel drohtnode°, ⌜tō ānum mæle fæstende⌝ būtan°
hit frēolsdæg° wǣre, and hēo syndrige° gebedu° swȳðe lufode and wyllen°
weorode°, and wolde seldhwænne° hire līc° baðian° būtan tō hēahtīdum°, and
ðonne hēo wolde ǣrest° ealle ðā° baðian þe on ðām mynstre wǣron, and
wolde him ðēnian° mid hire þīnenum°, and þonne hī sylfe baðian. Þā on þām

35   eahtēoðan° gēare siððan° hēo abbudisse wæs, hēo wearð geuntrumod°, ⌜swā
swā hēo ǣr wītegode°⌝, swā þæt ān geswel° wēox° on hire swūran° ⌜mycel⌝
under þām cynnbāne°, and hēo swīðe þancode° Gode þæt hēo on þām swūran
sum° geswinc° þolode°. Hēo cwæð, 'Ic wāt° geare° þæt ic wel wyrðe° eom
þæt min swūra bēo geswenct° mid swylcere° untrumnysse°, forðan þe ic on

40   iugoðe° frætwode° mīnne swūran mid mænigfealdum° swūrbēagum° and ⌜mē
is nū geþūht⌝ þæt Godes ārfæstnyss° þone gylt° āclǣnsige°, þonne° mē nū þis
geswel scȳnð° for golde° and þæs hāta° bryne° for hēlicum° gymstānum°.' Þā
wæs þǣr sum lǣce° on ðām gelēaffullum° hēape°, Cynefryð gehāten°, and ⌜hī
cwǣdon þā sume⌝ þæt se lǣce sceolde āscēotan° þæt geswell. Þā dyde hē sōna°

45   swā and þǣr sāh° ūt ⌜wyrms⌝. Wearð him þā geðūht swilce° hēo gewurpan°
mihte, ac hēo gewāt of worulde mid wuldre° tō Gode on þām ðriddan° dæge
syððan se dolh° wæs geopenod° and wearð bebyrged°, swā swā hēo bæd sylf
and hēt°, betwux° hire geswustrum° on trēowenre° cyste°. Þā wearð hire swustor

30 conducted herself unless **31** feast-day private prayers *ap* woollen clothes
32 wore seldom body bathe major holy days **33** first those **34** wait on female
servants **35** eighth after ill **36** (had) prophesied tumour grew neck **37** chin- (*or*
jaw-)bone thanked +*d* **38** a certain pain suffered know well deserving **39** afflicted
such illness **40** youth adorned numerous necklaces **41** grace sin may remove *sbj*
when **42** glistens gold hot inflammation glorious gem-stones **43** physician
faithful group named **44** lance immediately **45** fell as though recover **46** glory
third **47** wound opened buried **48** commanded among sisters wooden coffin

30 **tō ānum mǣle fǣstende** lit. 'fasting to one meal', i.e. 'fasting save for one meal (a
day)'. On feast-days, the rule was relaxed. Fasting is an aspect of Æthelthryth's asceticism,
along with (as we now learn) her wearing of wool (not linen) and her restricted bathing
habits.

35–6 **swā swā hēo ǣr wītegode** We are given no details about Æthelthryth's foretelling
of her illness; Bede reports it as hearsay.

36 **mycel** The adj. describes *geswel*.

40–1 **mē is nū geþūht** impers.: 'now it seems to me'. Similarly in 45, with *wearð* used
as auxil. vb.

43–4 **hī cwǣdon þā sume** The pers. pron. anticipates *sume*: 'then some of them
said'.

45 **wyrms** This has sometimes been taken to be a mistake for *wyrmas*, 'worms', but
the meaning is in fact rather less dramatic, namely 'corrupt matter' or 'pus'; cf. the OE vb.
wyrmsan, 'fester'.

⌐Sexburh⌐ gehādod tō abbudissan æfter hire geendunge°, sēo ðe ǣr wæs cwēn°

50 on Cantwarebyrig°.

Þā wolde sēo Sexburh æfter syxtȳne gēarum ⌐dōn° hire swustor bān° of ðǣre byrgene° ūp⌐ and beran° intō þǣre cyrcan°, and sende° ⌐þā gebrōðra⌐ tō sēcenne° sumne stān° tō° swilcere nēode°, forðan þe on þām fenlande ⌐synd fēawa weorcstāna⌐. Hī hrēowan° þā tō Grantanceastre° and God hī sōna gehradode°,

55 swā þæt hī þǣr gemetton° āne mǣre° þrūh° wið° þone weall standende, geworht of marmstāne° eall° ⌐hwītes blēos⌐ bufan° þǣre eorðan, and þæt hlyd° ðǣrtō° gelimplīce° gefēged° ēac° of hwītum marmstāne ⌐swā swā⌐ hit macode° God. Þā nāman° ðā gebrōðra blȳðelīce° þā ðrūh and gebrohton° tō mynstre, mycclum° ðancigende Gode. And Sexburh sēo abbudisse ⌐hēt slēan⌐ ān geteld° bufan ðā

60 byrgene, wolde þā bān gaderian°. Hī sungon ðā ealle° sealmas° and līcsang°, ⌐þā hwīle þe⌐ man° ðā brygene bufan geopenode. Þā læg° hēo on ðǣre cyste swilce hēo lǣge on slǣpe, hāl° ⌐eallum limum⌐, and se lǣce wæs ðǣr ðe þæt geswell geopenode, and hī° scēawode° georne. Þā wæs sēo wund gehǣled°, þe se lǣce worhte ǣr; ēac swilce° þā gewǣda°, ⌐þe hēo bewunden wæs mid⌐, wǣron swā

65 ansunde° swylce° hī eall nīwe wǣron.

⌐Sexburh þā hyre swuster⌐ swīðe þæs fægnode°, and hī þwōgon° ðā syððan þone sāwllēasan° līchaman° and mid nīwum gewǣdum bewundon ārwurðlīce°

---

49 death queen **50** Canterbury **51** take bones **52** burying place carry church sent seek **53** stone for (a) purpose **54** rowed Grantchester caused to succeed **55** found splendid coffin against **56** marble completely above +*d* lid to it **57** properly fitted also (had) made **58** took joyfully brought (it) greatly **59** tent **60** gather all *pron* psalms 'corpse-singing' (*i.e.* dirges) **61** someone lay **62** sound **63** her examined healed **64** likewise shrouds **65** intact as though **66** rejoiced washed **67** soulless (*i.e.* lifeless) body reverentially

---

49 **Sexburh** Another daughter of king Anna, and thus Æthelthryth's sister. She was married to a Kentish king, then widowed. It has been suggested that she is the same Seaxburh recorded later as the wife of the West-Saxon king, Cenwealh (see 5n).

51–2 **dōn ... ūp** 'take up' or 'exhume'. *Swustor* is here gen. [§B4c].

52 **þā gebrōðra** 'the brothers' or 'brethren', i.e. monks. Ely was a double house, catering for both women and men. In general, nuns and monks would be kept strictly apart in separate sections of the monastery.

53–4 **synd fēawa weorcstāna** 'there are few hewn stones'; *fēawa* is a noun/pron. made from *fēa* on the analogy of *fela* and governing likewise a gen. pl. noun. (lit. 'few of'). The fenland area of East Anglia was uniformly flat and marshy.

56 **hwītes blēos** descriptive gen.: 'of white hue', or 'white in colour'.

57 **swā swā** 'just as though'.

59 **hēt slēan** 'The infin. has a passive sense [§G6d.i.2]: 'commanded to be erected'.

60–1 **þā hwīle þe** conj. phr.: 'while'.

62 **eallum limum** dat. of specification: 'in all (her) limbs'.

64 **þe hēo bewunden wæs mid** 'with (*or* in) which she was wrapped'.

66 **Sexburh þā hyre swuster** i.e. *Þā Sexburh, hyre swuster, . . .*

and bǣron° intō ðǣre cyrcan, blyssigende° mid sangum°, and lēdon° hī on
ðǣre þrȳh, þǣr ðǣr° hēo līð° ᵓoð þis᷄ on mycelre ārwurðnysse°, mannum°
70 tō wundrunge°. Wæs ēac wundorlic þæt sēo ðrūh wæs geworht, þurh godes
foresċēawunge°, ᷄hire swā gemǣte swylce hēo° hyre sylfre᷄ swā gesċeapen°
wǣre, and æt hire hǣfde° wæs āhēawen° se stān, gemǣte þām hēafde þæs
hālgan mǣdenes. Hit is swutol þæt hēo wæs ungewemmed mǣden, þonne°
hire līchama ne mihte formolsnian° on eorðan. And Godes miht is geswutelod
75 sōðlīce° þurh hī, þæt hē mæg ārǣran° ðā formolsnodon līchaman, sē° ðe hire
līc hēold hāl on ðǣre byrgene gīt° oð þisne dæg. Sȳ° him ðæs° ā° wuldor.

Þǣr wǣron gehǣlede þurh ðā hālgan fēmnan ᷄fela᷄ ādlige° menn, swā swā
wē gefyrn° gehȳrdon°. And ēac ðā þe hrepodon° þæs rēafes° ǣnigne dǣl°, þe
hēo mid bewunden wæs, wurdon sōna hāle; and manegum ēac fremode° sēo
80 cyst micclum ᷄þe hēo ǣrest on᷄ læg, swā swā se lārēow° Bēda on ðǣre bēc°
sǣde þe hē gesette ᷄be ðysum᷄. Oft woruldmenn° ēac hēoldon, swā swā ūs ᷄bēc᷄
secgað, heora clǣnnysse on synscipe for Crīstes lufe°, swā swā wē mihton
reccan° gif gē rōhton° hit tō gehȳrenne. Wē secgað swāðēah be sumum ðegne°,
se wæs þryttig° gēara mid his wīfe on clǣnnysse. Þrȳ suna° hē gestrȳnde°, and hī
85 siððan būta° ðrittig gēara wǣron wunigende būtan hǣmede and fela ælmyssan°
worhton, oð þæt se wer fērde tō munuclicere° drohtnunge, and Drihtnes° englas°
cōmon eft on° his forðsīðe° and fēredon° his sāwle mid sange tō heofonum, swā
swā ūs secgað bēc. Manega bysna° synd on bōcum be swylcum°, hū oft weras
and wīf wundorlīce drohtnodon and on clǣnnysse wunodon, tō wuldre þām
90 hǣlende þe þā clǣnnysse āstealde°, Crīst ūre hǣlend, þām° is ā wurðmynt° and
wuldor on ēcnysse°. ĀMEN.

68 carried rejoicing songs laid   **69** where lies honour to people   **70** miraculous
sight   **71** foresight it shaped   **72** head cut away   **73** when (*or* since)᷄   **74** decay
75 truly raise up he (*i.e.* God)   **76** still (*or* even) Be for that eternally   **77** sick
78 of old (have) heard touched garment *gs* part   **79** helped +*d*   **80** teacher book *ds*
81 laypeople   **82** love *ds*   **83** relate cared thegn (*or* nobleman)   **84** thirty sons
fathered   **85** both almsgiving   **86** monastic the Lord's angels   **87** at passing carried
88 examples such (things)   **90** ordained to whom honour   **91** eternity

69 **oð þis** 'until this (time)', or 'until now'.

71 **hire swā gemǣte swylce** 'as suited to her (*or* fitting her) as if'.   **hyre sylfre** 'for
her herself'.

77 **fela** Here *fela*, usually treated in OE as a noun/pron. followed by the partitive
gen., is an adj., describing *ādlige menn* (nom. pl.). So also in 85 (where it is followed
by acc. sg.).

80 **þe ... on** 'in which'. The rel. clause modifies *cyst*, though the adv. *micclum* (modifying the vb. *fremode*) intervenes.

81 **be ðysum** The demons. pron. could be sg. or pl.: 'about this' or 'about these (things)'.
The book mentioned is of course Bede's *Historia ecclesiastica*.   **bēc** 'books' (nom. pl.).
These are volumes of saints' lives, homilies, etc, by church writers.

21b
Saint Eugenia
(from the *Old English Martyrology*)

Although Æthelthryth, as we have seen in Text 21a, had to fight opposition to her commitment to virginity, there is no record of persecution; nor is there any hint of disapproval directed by either Bede or Ælfric against her noble husband, King Ecgfrith. In the case of Eugenia, however, we meet an early Christian martyr whose story, even in its very condensed form in the *Old English Martyrology*, follows the more conventional, almost formulaic, pattern of the *passio*. This requires (1) a Christian devoted to Christ; (2) an evil persecutor demanding that the Christian renounce Christ and turn to devil-worship; (3) horrible tortures inflicted on the Christian because of a refusal to do this (though in fact she or he is left quite unscathed because of their faith); and (4) the eventual happy death of the Christian, usually by beheading. For a virgin martyr, an essential added element of tension is always the pressure to marry against her will. In the case of Eugenia, the strategy she uses to avoid such marriage is of particular interest: she dresses as a man and is so successful in her male role that she acts as the respected abbot of a monastery for some years, before reverting to life as a woman. The fuller story of Eugenia, transmitted by Ælfric in his *Lives of Saints* (item 2), reveals that her eventual unmasking as a cross-dresser happens after a noble lady has tried to seduce her (in her guise of abbot) and then reacted against rejection by accusing 'him' (Eugenia) of attempted rape.

Internal evidence seems to show that the *Old English Martyrology* was compiled in the mid-ninth century, and two of the preserved manuscript witnesses date from late in that century. The one used for the text below, however, Cambridge, Corpus Christi College 41 (the only copy to include the entry for Eugenia), was copied in the early or mid-eleventh century. There is an odd variety of spellings used by the scribe, but overall they suggest someone writing fairly late WS. Thus *dæig* is written for *dæg* (1), *dēoful-* for *dēofol* (12 and 17) and *mihtegu* for *mihtigu* (11), and the dative plural noun-inflection *-um* is reduced to *-on* in *dagon* (2), *æpelon* (6) and *cnihton* (8), although elsewhere *-um* is used. 'Smoothing' of the diphthong *īe* is seen in *hīrdon* (5) and *nīdde* (16). The change of *i/ī* to *y/ȳ*, characteristic of many eleventh-century texts, is not at all in evidence (hence *bið*, 1, *hire*, 7, *minster*, 8, and *swīðe*, 3). Only in *þēr* (8), rather than expected *þǣr*, and perhaps in *u* for *f* in *gerēua* (4 and 16), might we see relics of a Mercian dialect.

Further reading

G. Kotzor, ed., *Das altenglische Martyrologium*, Bayerische Akademie der Wissenschaften, phil.-hist. Klasse, Abhandlungen 88 (Munich, 1981)

G. Herzfeld, ed., *An Old English Martyrology*, EETS 116 (London, 1900)

G. Kotzor, 'The Latin Tradition of Martyrologies and the *Old English Martyrology*', in *Studies in Earlier Old English Prose: Sixteen Original Contributions*, ed. P. E. Szarmach (Albany, NY, 1986), pp. 301–33

P. E. Szarmach, 'Ælfric's Women Saints: Eugenia', in *New Readings on Women in Old English Literature*, ed. H. Damico and A. H. Olsen (Bloomington and Indianapolis, IN, 1990), pp. 146–57

G. Roy, 'A Virgin Acts Manfully: Ælfric's *Life of St Eugenia* and the Latin Versions', *LSE* n.s. 23 (1992), 2–27

⌐On þone forman° dæig¬ bið ⌐sancta Eugēnian¬ tīd°, þære æðelan° fǣmnan°.

⌐Sēo wæs on Commodes dagon þæs cāseres¬ ond hēo lufode° Crīst ǣr° hēo gefullod° wǣre. Hēo was swīðe° mǣres° weres° dohtur, se° wæs hāten° Philippus. Hē wæs þǣre mǣran burge° gerēua°, ⌐þe hātte° Alexsandria¬, ond

5   ealle Ēgipta° þēode° him hīrdon°. Þā þæt mæden wæs ⌐XV gēar¬, þā wolde se fæder hī sellan° sumum° æþelon men° tō° brȳde°. Þā on° niht bescear° hēo hire feax° swā° weras ond onfēng° weres gegyrlan° ond gewāt° of° hire fæder rīce° mid twām cnihton°. Þā ēode° hēo on wera minster°, þēr° nān wīfman° ǣr ne cōm°, ond hēo onfēng fulwihte° ond Gode þēnode° ond þēowode° ond mid þām°

10 wunode°, þæt° nān man ne mihte onfindan° þæt hēo wæs fǣmne. Ond binnan° III gēarum hēo wearð° þæs minstres abbud°. Ond hēo was swā mihtegu° wið

1 first feast-day noble maiden *gs* **2** loved before **3** baptised very famous man's who called **4** city *gs* prefect is called **5** of the Egyptians (*i.e.* Egypt) peoples obeyed +*d* **6** give +*d* a certain man *ds* as bride (*or* wife) at cut off **7** hair as (do) took clothing set out from **8** kingdom serving-boys went monastery where woman **9** (had) gone received baptism served +*d* followed +*d* them (*i.e.* the monks) **10** lived so that discover within +*d* **11** became abbot important

1 **On þone forman dæig** 'On the first day', i.e. the first day of the Yuletide festival, 25 Dec., Christmas Day itself. **sancta Eugēnian** 'saint Eugenia's'. *Sancta* has been left in its Latin nom. form (see 7b/50n), but *Eugenia* has been given an OE gen. *n*-inflection [§§B5c, 6a]. The phr. qualifying the name, *þǣre æðelan fǣmnan*, is also in the gen.

2 **Sēo wæs** i.e. 'she lived'. **on Commodes dagon þæs cāseres** 'in the days of the emperor Commodus', who ruled AD 182–92.

4 **þe hātte Alexsandria** The clause modifies *burge*.

5 **XV gēar** 'fifteen years (old)', with the numeral (*fīftȳne*) used as an adj. [§E3d], as also in 11 and 20.

God þæt hēo sealde° blindum men gesihðe° ond ⌐dēofulsēoce⌐ gehǣlde°. Ond
þā æfter manegum gēarum hēo wæs fram° hire fæder ongitenu° ⌐ond brōþrum⌐,
ond siððan° hēo wunode mid fǣmnum on hira hīwe°. Ond æfter hire fæder

15   dēaðe hēo gewāt mid hire mēder tō Rōme ond þær geþrōwode° martirdōm for
Crīste. Þǣr Necittius, Rōmeburge° gerēua, hī nīdde° þæt hēo Crīste wiðsōce°
ond dēofulgild° gelīfde°. Þā hēo þæt nolde, þā ⌐hēt hē bindan hire stān tō þām
swūran⌐ ond worpan° on Tifre° flōd°. Þā tōbǣrst° se stān ond hēo flēat° āweg
ofer þæt wæter tō lande. Ond þā hēt hē hī eft° sendan° on birnendne° ofon°,

20   ond sē° ācōlode° sōna°. Þā hēt hīe dōn° on carcern°, ond hēo wæs þær X niht
and dagas būtan° mete°. Þā ætēowde° hire Drihten silfa ⌐on þā ilcan° niht æt
his ācennisse°⌐ ond cwæð tō hire, 'Ic þē nime°, Eugēnie, ond ic eom sē° þe þū
lufodest. ⌐Þī illcan dæge⌐ ic tō heofnum° āstāh° ⌐þē þe⌐ ic tō eorþan cōm.' Ond
þī ilcan dæig hēo onsende° hire gāst° tō Gode, ond hire līchama° resteð wið°

25   Rōmebirig on þām wege° þe man nemneð° ⌐Latina⌐.

---

12 gave (to +*d*) (their) sight cured   **13** by recognised   **14** afterwards fashion
15 suffered   **16** of Rome   urged   might forsake *sbj*   **17** idolatry   might believe
18 throw   of the Tiber   river   shattered   floated   **19** then   be cast   burning furnace
20 it   cooled down   immediately   be put   prison   **21** without   food   appeared (to +*d*)
same   **22** nativity   (will) take   he   **23** the heavens (*or* heaven)   ascended   **24** yielded up
spirit   body   near   **25** street   calls

---

12 **dēofulsēoce** 'the devil-sick' (adj. used as noun), i.e. 'those possessed by the devil',
or simply 'the insane'.

13 **ond brōþrum** This combines with *hire fæder* to form the double obj. of *fram*: 'and
by (her) brothers'. OE commonly splits such 'heavy groups'.

17–18 **hēt hē ... swūran** 'he commanded (them) to tie a stone to her neck'; *hire* functions as the dat. of possession. The acc. and inf. construction [§G6d.i.3] is used also in 19
and 20.

21–2 **on ... æt his ācennisse** 'on the same night at his birth [i.e. "when he was born"]'.
Eugenia dies on the day of Christ's nativity; hence the date of her feast-day.

23 **Þī illcan dæge** instr. phr.: 'on the same day' (repeated, with different spellings, in
24). **þē þe** The best interpretation (assuming that the repetition of *þe* is not simply a copyist's
error) is to take the first word as the instr. pron. *þē*, correl. with (and a variant form of) *þȳ*;
the second *þe* is the rel. particle: lit. 'on that which', i.e. 'as that on which'.

25 **Latina** The *Via Latina* was one of the four major roads emanating from Rome; it
began at the *Porta Latina* ('Latin Gate').

22

A Homily for Easter Sunday
(from Ælfric's *Sermones catholicae*)

Between about 990 and 995, at Cerne Abbas (see p. 4), Ælfric wrote two series of *Sermones catholicae* (usually called his *Catholic Homilies* today) which, to judge from the many surviving copies, were immensely popular not only during his lifetime but well into the thirteenth century. Each volume contains forty items, including both homilies and sermons (see section headnote), and also a few saints' lives. Within each volume the various items are arranged chronologically, according to the use assigned to them at specific times during the church year, though there are a few sermons labelled to be read at any time. In the preface to the first volume, Ælfric explains that he has put the homilies into plain speech, both for reading and for hearing, in order to edify ordinary people and thus, he hopes, to effect the salvation of their souls. He claims that he has seen much error in English books, a reference probably to such compilations as the anonymous 'Blickling Homilies' and 'Vercelli Homilies', many of whose texts contain unorthodox material. For his own homilies, Ælfric drew on the work of the established fathers of the church, above all Jerome, Augustine, Gregory the Great and Bede, along with Smaragdus of Saint-Mihiel and Haymo of Auxerre. The two volumes were designed to form the basis of a comprehensive programme of orthodox teaching for Christians. Although the prefatory comments noted above suggest that Ælfric's primary audience was the laity, in which case the sermons and homilies would have been preached in parish churches, they nevertheless contain many passages which appear to be directed specifically at monks or at the secular clergy (see line 69 in the text below). There is evidence also that Ælfric expected private readers for his homilies, as well as auditors in monastic or church settings.

The fifteenth item in the first series of homilies, headed *Dominica Pascae* (Easter Sunday), has the typical homiletic structure of a gospel extract, specific to the day in question, followed by an interpretation. In a church setting, we may imagine that the gospel reading for Easter Day has already been read from the Latin Vulgate, relating the visit of 'the three Marys' to Christ's tomb following his crucifixion and the angel's report of his resurrection (Mk 16.1–7). After a brief introduction, Ælfric presents a much fuller version, in OE, of the biblical narrative (lines 5–61). It is a skilfully made conflation of parts of three different narratives of the Easter story, in the order Mt 27.62–6, Mk 15.47–16.4, Mt 28.8–13 and Lk 24.36–47. Then, after rounding off the gospel account with a look forward to the Ascension, Ælfric announces that he will expound the scripture according to the writings of Gregory (lines 62–8). This he proceeds to do, explaining for his audience the symbolic significance of every detail of the women's visit to the tomb (lines 69–104), and the Galilee episode and Resurrection (lines 105–29). Then he moves on to the mockery of Christ on the cross by the Jews, showing how this was foreshadowed in the OT account of Samson's humiliation by the Philistines; as Samson was able subsequently to tear down the gates of Gaza, so Christ broke the gates of hell (lines 130–66). Ælfric concludes with an account of the Trinity, and a reaffirmation of God's sacrifice of his son and the significance for Christians of the Resurrection (lines 167–77).

Ælfric's prose is celebrated for its clarity, which was an essential element in his mission to spread orthodox teaching. It is achieved largely by the syntactically balanced presentation of parallel and contrast. A good example occurs in lines 156–66, where the repetition of a formula – 'the heavens acknowledged Christ when they . . . , the sun acknowledged Christ when it . . .' – establishes what is for Ælfric the supreme logic, almost the inevitability, of faith, so that when the Jews are finally introduced *without* the formula, the point Ælfric wishes to make (that the Jews alone are without faith) has been demonstrated as well as stated. He thus persuades with the sort of argument that is both syntactical and intellectual, and such a quietly effective technique may be contrasted with that of his near-contemporary Wulfstan, whose dramatic repetitions are more like a succession of hammer-blows which bludgeon us into acceptance of his message (see especially Text 25).

The homily for Easter Day survives substantially in fourteen manuscripts, the youngest written in the second half of the twelfth century. The version edited here is that in London, British Library, Royal 7. C. xii, fols. 4–218, almost certainly written at Cerne Abbas during the first half of 990. There are many contemporary alterations, some of them apparently in Ælfric's own hand, but others have been made as late as the twelfth century. The late WS language shows, unusually, almost no sign of the levelling of inflections and is on the whole remarkable for its consistency. A notable exception to this, however, is the instability shown by the inflected forms of *burg* (14, 145, 146 and 150), *byrgen* (8, 21, 27, 31, etc) and *þrūh* (19, 78 and 81); and *bīo* (25) occurs as well as *bēo* (47, 92). In *āweig* (22) and *dæig* (8), the *i* is a characteristic late intrusion (which reflects the 'soft' pronunciation of *g*). Owing to an omission from the British Library manuscript, some text in lines 77–81 (*Se engel . . . of middangearde*) has had to be supplied from an almost contemporary manuscript, Cambridge, University Library, Gg. 3. 28 (also possibly copied at Cerne Abbas).

Further reading

N. Eliason and P. Clemoes, eds., *Ælfric's Catholic Homilies: British Museum Royal 7 C. xii, Fols. 4–218*, EEMF 13 (Copenhagen, 1965)

P. Clemoes, ed., *Ælfric's Catholic Homilies. The First Series. Text*, EETS s.s. 17 (Oxford, 1997) [see pp. 299–306 for our text]

M. Godden, ed., *Ælfric's Catholic Homilies. The Second Series. Text*, EETS s.s. 5 (London, 1979)

M. Godden, *Ælfric's Catholic Homilies. Introduction, Commentary and Glossary*, EETS s.s. 18 (Oxford, 2000)

B. Thorpe, ed. and trans., *The Homilies of the Anglo-Saxon Church*, 2 vols. (London, 1844–6) [see vol. I, pp. 220–9, for our text]

P. Clemoes, 'Ælfric', in *Continuations and Beginnings: Studies in Old English Literature*, ed. E. G. Stanley (London, 1966), pp. 176–209

M. Godden, 'Ælfric and the Vernacular Prose Tradition', in *The Old English Homily and its Backgrounds*, ed. P. E. Szarmach and B. F. Huppé (Albany, NY, 1978), pp. 99–117

A. P. Scheil, 'Anti-Judaism in Ælfric's *Lives of Saints*', *ASE* 28 (1999), 65–86

J. E. Cross, 'Vernacular Sermons in Old English', in *The Sermon*, ed. B. M. Kienzle, Typologie des Sources du Moyen Âge Occidental 81–3 (Turnhout, 2000), 561–96

⌐*Maria Magdalene et Maria Iacobi et reliqua*⌐.

Oft gē gehȳrdon° ymbe° ðæs hælendes° ǣrist°, hū hē on þisum dæge of° dēaðe ārās°, ⌐ac wē wyllað⌐ ēow° myningean°, þæt hit ne gange° ⌐ēow of gemynde⌐.

5 ⌐Đā ðā⌐ Crīst bebiriged° wæs, þā cwǣdon° ⌐þā Iūdēiscan tō heora ealdermen⌐ Pilāte, ⌐'Lā lēof⌐, se swīca° þe hēr ⌐ofslegen is⌐ cwæð gelōmlīce° þā ðā hē on līfe

2 (have) heard about Saviour's resurrection from 3 arose you remind goes *sbj*
5 buried said 6 deceiver frequently

1 *Maria Magdalene . . . reliqua* Lat.: 'Mary Magdalene and Mary [the mother of] James, and the rest'; the opening words of the gospel-reading set for Easter Day, from Mk 16.

3–4 **ac wē wyllað** Ælfric characteristically uses the first pers. pl. in his works. **ēow of gemynde** 'from your memory'; *ēow* is poss. dat. [§D4b].

5 **Đā ðā** double conj.: 'When' (lit. 'then when'); also in 6, 20, etc. **þā Iūdēiscan** 'the Jews'; i.e. the inhabitants of province of Judea. **tō heora ealdermen** 'to their governor (*or* ruler)'. Pilate is governor, under the Romans, of Judea, so the Anglo-Saxon term (here dat. sg.) is appropriate (see 8/4–5n).

6 **Lā lēof** 'Behold, lord', but the interj. *lā* may be om. in trans. **ofslegen is** perf. tense: 'has been executed'.

wæs þæt hē wolde ārīsan of° dēaðe on ðām þriddan° dæge. ⌈Bebēod nū for ðī
besittan⌉ his birigene° oð° ðone þriddan dæig, ⌈þē læs þe⌉ his leorningcnihtas°
cumon and forstēlan° his līc° and secgan° þām folce þæt hē of dēaðe ⌈ārīse⌉.

10 Þonne bið° þæt gedwyld° wyrse þonne° ⌈þæt ōðer⌉ wære'. Þā andwyrde° se
ealdorman Pilātus, 'Gē habbað° weardas°: farað° tō° and healdað°'. Hī ðā fērdon
tō and mearcodon° ðā þrūh° mid insegle° and besǣton þā birgine.

    Þā behēold Māria þæs hǣlendes mōder and þā wimmen þe hyre mid wǣron
hwǣr hē bebiriged wæs and ēodon° ðā ongēan° tō ðǣre birig°. And ⌈sēo Mag-
15 dalēnisce Māria⌉ and Māria Iācōbes° mōder bohton° dēorwyrðe° sealfe° ⌈þe bið
geworht° tō smyrigenne° dēadra manna līc° mid°, þæt hī scolon late° rotian°⌉.
And ēodon ðā° ðā wimmen on þisum dæge on ǣrnemerien° and woldon his līc
behwyrfan°, swā hit þǣr gewunlic° wæs on° ðǣre þēode°. Þā cwǣdon þā wīf
betwux° him, 'Hwā sceal° ūs° āwilian° þone stān° of ðǣre þyrih°? Se stān is
20 ormǣtlīce° micel'. Þā ðā hī þis sprǣcon, þā wearð° fǣrlīce° micel eorðstyrung°
and Godes engel flēah° of heofenum tō ðǣre birgene and āwylte þone stān
āweig and ⌈gesǣt him⌉ uppon þām stāne. Þā wæs þæs engles wlite° swilce°
līget° and his rēaf° swā hwīt° swā snāw°. Þā wurdon þā weardmen° āfyrhte°
and fēollon adūne° swilce° hī dēade wǣron. Þā cwǣð se engel tō þām wīfum,
25 'Ne bīo° gē ofdrǣdde°. Ic wāt° þæt gē sēcað° þone hǣlend þe wæs on rōde°

---

7 from third **8** tomb until 'learning-youths' (disciples) **9** steal away body say (to
+*d*) **10** will be heresy than answered **11** have guards go there(to) guard (it)
12 marked sepulchre seal **14** went back city **15** of James bought precious ointment
16 prepared anoint bodies with slowly decay **17** then early morning **18** prepare
customary among people **19** between is to (*or* shall) for us roll away stone tomb
20 extremely (there) was suddenly earthquake **21** flew **22** countenance like
23 lightning clothing white snow guards frightened **24** down as though **25** be
afraid know seek cross

7–8 **Bebēod . . . besittan** 'command to surround . . .', i.e. 'command that . . . be surrounded'.   **for ðī** instr. adv.: 'for that (reason)', i.e. 'therefore'.

8 **þē læs þe** conj. phr.: 'the less that' (instr. *þē*), i.e. 'in case'.

9 **ārīse** The form is pres. sbj., for hypothesis: 'may arise', or even 'has arisen'.

10 **þæt ōðer** The 'other' heresy referred to is the claim that Christ was the
Messiah.

14–15 **sēo Magdalēnisce Māria** 'the Mary of Magdala' (*Magdalēnisce* is an adj.); she
is usually known today as 'Mary Magdalene', to distinguish her from the other Marys
involved in Christ's life.

15–16 **þe bið geworht . . . rotian** Into his otherwise close trans. of the gospel text (here
Mk 15.47–16.4), Ælfric inserts his own explanatory note, as he does also in 18 (*swā hit . . .
þēode*); *scolon* is for *sculon*, 'ought', or (here) 'shall'.

22 **gesǣt him** 'sat', with the dat. rflx. pron. ('himself') om. in trans.

gefæstnod°. Nis° hē hēr; hē ārās of dēaðe, ⌜swā swā⌝ hē ēow ǣr° sǣde. Cumað and scēawiað° his birigene ⌜þǣr hē on læg⌝, þe nū is ǣmtig. Gāð° nū ongēan tō his leorningcnihtum and secgað him þæt Crīst ārās of dēaðe and hē cymð° tō him on ðām earde° þe is gehāten° Galilēa. Secgað þæt ⌜hī cumon him þǣr

30   tōgēanes⌝. Þǣr hī hine gesēoð°swā swā hē him behēt° ⌜ǣr ðām þe⌝ hē þrōwade°'. Þā lāgon° ðā scȳtan° innon þǣre byrgene þe hē mid° bewunden° wæs. And þā wīf gecyrdon° þā tō Crīstes leorningcnihtum mid miclum ege° and mid micelre blisse° and woldon him° cȳþan° Crīstes ǣrist.

⌜Þā mid ðām þā⌝ gemētton hī Crīst and hē hī gegrētte° and hī fēollon tō° his

35   fōtum. Ðā cwæð se hǣlend him tō, 'Farað and cȳþað mīnum gebrōðrum° þæt hī cumon tōgēanes mē on ðām lande Galilēa; þǣr hī gesēoð mē'. Þā mid þām þe ðā wīf ēodon°, þā cōmon þā weardmenn and cȳddon° þæt Crīst ārās of dēaðe. Þā nāmon° þā hēafodmen° þā weardas on sundersprǣce° and sealdon him micelne sceat° ⌜tō ðī þæt⌝ hī scoldon secgan þæt Crīstes līc him° wǣre° forstolen ⌜ðā

40   hwīle þe hī slēp fornam⌝, and þā wearð° þæt cūð° geond eall Iūdēa land þæt ðā weardas þone scet nāmon æt° ðām hēafodmannum and þæt Crīst ārās of dēaðe. Wē cweðað nū, gif hwā° his līc forstele°, nolde° hē hine unscrȳdan°, ⌜for ðan þe⌝ stale° ne lufað nāne° yldinge°.

Crīst wearð ætēowed° on ðām ylcan dæge Pētre° and ⌜ōðrum twām his⌝

45   leorningcnihtum, and hī° gefrēfrode°. Þā ⌜æt nēhstan⌝ cōm se hǣlend tō his leorningcnihtum þǣr hī gegaderode° wǣron and cwæð him tō: 'Sȳ° sib° betwux

---

26 fastened Is not [*ne is*] earlier **27** see Go **28** will come **29** place called **30** will see promised suffered **31** lay sheets with (*or* in) wrapped **32** returned fear **33** joy to them make known **34** greeted at **35** brethren **37** went made known **38** took captains private conversation **39** sum of money from them had been **40** became known **41** from **42** anyone were to steal would not want undress **43** theft any delay *as* **44** revealed to Peter **45** them comforted **46** gathered Be *sbj* peace

---

26 **swā swā** double conj.: 'just as'.

27 **þǣr hē on læg** 'wherein (*or* in which) he lay'.

29–30 **hī cumon him þǣr tōgēanes** 'they shall meet him there' (lit. 'come against him').

30 **ǣr ðām þe** conj. phr.: 'before'.

34 **Þā mid ðām þā** 'Then, with that'; the repeated adv. *þā* is redundant in trans.

39 **tō ðī þæt** conj. phr.: 'in order that' (instr. *ðī*).

39–40 **ðā hwīle þe** conj. phr.: 'while'. **hī slēp fornam** 'sleep had taken them', i.e. 'they had been asleep'.

42–3 **for ðan þe** conj. phr.: 'because'; also 76, etc, or simply *for ðan* (158) or *for ðon* (171–2).

44 **ōðrum twām his** 'to his other two . . .'.

45 **æt nēhstan** adv.: 'at last', or 'at length'.

ēow. ⌐Ic hit eom⌐: ne bēo gē ⌐nā⌐ āfyrhte°'. Ðā wurdon hī āfǣrede° and wēndon°
þæt hit sum gāst° wǣre. Þā cwæð hē him tō, 'Hwī° synd gē āfǣrede and mislīce°
þencað be° mē? Scēawiað mīne handa and mīne fēt þe wǣron mid næiglum
50   þurhdrifene°. Grāpiað° and scēawiað. Gif ic gāst wēre, þonne næfde° ic flǣsc
and bān swā swā gē gēseoð þæt ic hæbbe'. Þā ðā hē þis cwæð, þā ætēowde hē
him ⌐ǣgðer ge handa ge⌐ fēt ⌐ge sīdan þe hē on gewundod wæs⌐. Þā wæs heora
mōd° mid micelre wundrunga° and blisse ofernumen°. Þā cwæð se hǣlend
him eft° tō, 'Hæbbe gē hēr ǣnig þincg þe tō etenne° sī?' Þā brōhton hī him
55   gebrǣdne° fisc and sumne° dǣl° huniges and hē ǣt° þā beforan him and sealde
him ⌐his lāfe⌐, þus cweðende, 'Þis ic sǣde ēow ǣr mīnre þrōwunge°. Hit is nū
gefylled° be° mē, swā swā ⌐sēo ealde ǣ and wītegan⌐ be mē āwriton°'. And hē
ðā him forgeaf° andgit° þæt hī mihton þā gewritu° tōcnāwan° and cwæð þā gȳt°,
'Þūs wæs gewriten be mē, þæt ic þrōwian scolde and ārīsan of dēaðe on ðām
60   þriddan dæge, and sceal bēon gebodod° on mīnum naman dǣdbōt° and synna
forgifenyss on° eallum þēodum°'.

Se hǣlend wearð þā gelōmlīce ætēowod his leorningcnihtum and hī°
gewissode° tō ðǣre lāre° and tō þām gelēafan, hū hī eallum mancynne° tǣcan°
scoldon. And on ðām feowertigoðan° dæge his ǣristes hē āstāh° līchamlīce° tō
65   heofenum tō his fæder. Ac wē habbað nū ⌐micele māran endebyrdnysse þǣre
Crīstes bēc⌐ gesǣd° þonne ⌐ðis dægðerlice godspel⌐ behæfð°, for trymmynge°
ēowres gelēafan. Nū ⌐wille wē⌐ ēow gereccan° þæs dægðerlican godspelles
traht° æfter° þæs hālgan pāpan° Gregories trahtnunge°.

47 afraid frightened imagined **48** spirit Why erringly **49** about **50** pierced
Touch would not have [*ne hæfde*] **53** mind astonishment seized **54** further eat
55 baked a portion ate **56** passion **57** fulfilled concerning wrote **58** gave
knowledge scriptures understand further **60** preached penance **61** among peoples
62 them **63** guided learning humankind *ds* teach **64** fortieth ascended bodily
66 related contains strengthening **67** explain **68** exposition according to
pope *gs* commentary

47 **Ic hit eom** lit. 'I am it', i.e. 'It is I'. **nā** Emphatic neg. part., often rendered '(not)
at all', though it need not be trans. when *ne* is also present.
52 **ǣgðer ge ... ge** 'both ... and'. **ge sīdan þe hē on gewundod wæs** 'and (his) side,
in which he had been wounded'.
56 **his lāfe** 'its [i.e. the food's] remains', i.e. 'what was left of it'.
57 **sēo ealde ǣ and wītegan** 'the old law and the prophets'; i.e. the OT books
of Moses (the Pentateuch) and the books of the prophets, who foretold the coming of
Christ.
65–6 **micele māran ... bēc** *māran* is used as a noun with partitive gen.: 'much more of
the contents of Christ's book [i.e. the gospels]'.
66 **ðis dægðerlice godspel** 'this gospel-reading for today' (see 1n).
67 **wille wē** Reduced vb.-inflection when the pron. follows [§G6f]; also in 87. Cf. *wyllað*
in 3.

⌐Mīne gebrōðra þā lēofostan°⌐, gē gehȳrdon þæt ðā hālgan wīf þe Drihtne
70 on līfe filigdon° cōmon tō his birgene mid ðǣre dēorwyrðan sealfe, and þone°
þe hī lufedon on līfe, ⌐þām hī woldon dēadum mid menniscre° gecnyrdnysse°
þēnian⌐. Ac þēos dǣd° getācnað° ⌐sum ðing tō dōnne⌐ on Godes gelāðunge°. Wē
ðe ⌐gelȳfað Crīstes ǣriste⌐, wē cumað gewīslīce° tō his byrgene mid dēorwurðre
sealfe gif wē bēoð gefyllede° mid brǣðe° hāligra mihta° and gif wē mid hlīsan°
75 gōdra° weorca ūrne Drihten sēcað. Þā wīf þe ðā sealfa brōhton, hī gesāwon
englas, for ðan ðe ⌐ðā gesēoð þa heofenlican englas þā ðe⌐ mid brǣðum
gōdra weorca gewilniað° þæs ūplican° fǣreldes°. Se engel āwylte þæt hlid of
ðǣre ðrȳh. Nā þæt hē Crīste ūtganges° rȳmde° ac hē geswutelode° mannum
þæt hē ārisen wæs, sē° ðe cōm dēaðlic° tō ðisum middangearde°, ācenned°
80 ⌐þurh beclȳsedne innoð⌐ þæs mǣdenes°. Se ylca°, būtan twēon°, ðā ðā hē ārās
undēaðlic°, mihte° ⌐belocenre ðrīh⌐ faran of middangearde. Se engel sæt on ðā
swīðran° healfe° þǣre byrgene. Sēo swȳðre hand getācnað þæt ēce° līf and sēo
wynstre° ðis andwearde° līf. Rihtlīce° sæt se engel on ðā swȳðran hand, for ðan
þe hē cȳdde° þæt se hǣlend hæfde þā oferfarǣn° þā brosnunga° þises andwerdan
85 līfes and wæs þā wuniende° on° ēcum þingum undēadlic. Se bydel° wæs
ymbscrȳd° mid scīnendum rēafum° for ðan ðe hē bodade° þā blisse þisre
frēolstīde° and ūre mǣrða°. ⌐Hwæðer, cweðe wē, þe ūre þe ðǣra engla?⌐ Wē

69 dearest   70 followed him   71 human devotion   72 action signifies church
73 truly   74 filled odour power fame   75 good *gpn*   77 desire upward journey
78 departure opened the way for +*g* revealed (to +*d*)   79 he mortal world brought forth
80 virgin same (man) doubt   81 immortal was able   82 right side eternal   83 left
present Rightly   84 showed overcome corruptions   85 dwelling among herald
86 clothed garments proclaimed   87 festival (*i.e.* Easter) glories

69 **Mīne gebrōðra þā lēofostan** Ælfric seems to be addressing monks here.
71–2 **þām hī woldon dēadum...þēnian** The main vb. governs the dat., hence *þām*
(here a pron.) and *dēadum*: 'him, dead, they wanted to serve', i.e. 'they wanted to serve
him... when (he was) dead'.
72 **sum ðing tō dōnne** The infl. inf. is used passively: 'something to be done'.
73 **gelȳfað Crīstes ǣriste** Ælfric occasionally uses *geliefan* plus dat. obj. without a
prep.: 'believe in Christ's resurrection'.
76 **ðā gesēoð...þā ðe** In both cases, *þā* is the pl. pron.,'they', but it need be trans. only
once: 'they see..., who...'.
80 **þurh beclȳsedne innoð** 'by means of a closed womb'. Mary's womb was 'closed' in
that conception was believed to have occurred miraculously, not by normal physical means.
81 **belocenre ðrīh** 'from a closed tomb' (dat.). This miracle parallels that of the conception.
87 **Hwæðer... ðǣra engla?** ' "Ours or the angels?", we may say'; i.e. we may ask
ourselves whose glories are being referred to. When, as here, *hwæðer* functions as little
more than a sign of interrogation, it is best not trans.; similarly, the first of the pair *þe... þe*
('either... or ...?') may be om.

cweðað sōðlīce ǣigðer ge ūre ge heora°. Þæs hǣlendes ǣrist is ūre frēolstīd
and blis, for ðan ðe hē gelǣdde ūs mid his ǣriste tō ðǣre undēadlicnysse° þe
90   wē tō° gesceapene° wǣron. His ǣrist wæs ⸢þǣra engla blis⸣, for ðan þe God
gefylð° heora getæl° þonne hē ūs tō heofonan gebrincð°.

    Se engel gehyrte° þā wīf, þus cweðende, 'Ne bēo gē āfyrhte', swilce hē
swā cwǣde: ⸢Forhtian þā ðe⸣ ne lufiað engla tōcyme°; ⸢bēon ðā ofdrǣdde þā ðe⸣
synd ofsette° mid flǣsclicum lustum° and nabbað nǣnne hiht° tō° engla werede°.
95   Hwī forhtige gē, gē ðe gesēoð° ēowre° gefēran°? 'His wlite wæs swilce līget and
his rēaf swā hwīt swā snāw'. Sōðlīce on līgette is ōga°, and on snāwe līðnes°
þǣre beorhtnysse°. Rihtlīce wæs se bydel Crīstes ǣristes swā gehīwod°, ⸢for
ðī⸣ þonne° hē° cymð tō ðām miclan dōme° þonne° bið hē swīðe egefull° þām
synfullum and swȳðe līðe° þām rihtwīsan°. Hē cwæð, 'Gē sēcað þone hǣlend:
100 hē ārās, nis hē hēr'. Hē næs þā līchamlīce° on ðǣre birgene, sē° ðe ǣghwǣr° bið
þurh his godcundan° mihte. Þǣr læg þæt rēaf bæftan° þe hē mid bewunden wæs,
for ðan þe hē ne rōhte° þæs eorðlican rēafes syððan hē of dēaðe ārās. Ðēah°
man dēadne mannan mid rēafe bewinde°, ⸢ne ārīst þæt rēaf nā ðē raðor eft mid
þām men⸣ ac hē bið mid þām heofenlicum rēafe gescrȳd æfter his ǣriste.

105   Wel is gecweden° be ðām hǣlende þæt hē wolde cuman tōgēanes his gefērum
on Galilēa. Galilēa is gecweden° ⸢'oferfæreld'⸣. Se hǣlend ⸢wæs þā āfaren⸣
fram þrōwunge tō ǣriste, fram dēaðe tō līfe, fram wīte° tō wuldre°. And gif
wē farað fram leahtrum° tō hālgum mægnum°, þonne mōte° wē gesēon þone
hǣlend æfter ūrum færelde of þisum līfe. Twā līf sind° sōðlīce: þæt ān wē
110 cunnon°, þæt ōðer ūs wæs uncūð° ǣr Crīstes tōcyme. Þæt ān līf is dēaðlic, þæt
ōðer undēaðlic. Ac se hǣlend cōm and underfēng° þæt ān līf and geswutelode
þæt ōðer; þæt ān līf hē ætēowde mid his dēaðe and þæt ōðer mid his ǣriste. Gif hē

88 theirs 89 immortality 90 for created 91 completes number brings
92 encouraged 93 advent 94 beset desires trust in company 95 will see your
companions 96 terror mildness 97 brightness figured 98 when he (*i.e.* Christ)
judgement then awesome (to +*d*) 99 mild righteous 100 bodily he everywhere
101 divine afterwards 102 cared about +*g* Though 103 wraps 105 said
106 interpreted 107 torment glory 108 sins virtues may 109 (there) are
110 know unknown 111 assumed

    90 **þǣra engla blis** 'joy of the angels', i.e. 'a joy to the angels'.
    93 **Forhtian þā ðe** sbj. with optative sense: 'Let those fear who …' **bēon ðā
ofdrǣdde þā ðe** 'Let those be afraid who …' (with the first *ðā* om. in trans.).
    97–8 **for ðī** conj. phr.: 'because'.
    103–4 **ne ārīst … þām men** 'the clothing does not the sooner (*ðe raðor*) rise again (*eft*)
with the person'. None of our material possessions is held to go with us into the next life.
    106 **oferfæreld** 'passing over'. Ælfric took this etymology from Gregory. **wæs þā
āfaren** pluperf.: 'had then passed'.

ūs dēadlicum° mannum ǣrist and þæt ēce līf behēte° and þēahhwæðere° ⌐nolde
hit þurh hine sylfne geswutelian⌐, hwā wolde þonne his behātum° gelȳfan? Ac
115   þā ðā hē man bēon wolde, þā gemedemode° hē hine sylfne ēac° tō dēaðe, āgenes°
willan°. And hē ārās of dēaðe þurh his godcundan mihte and geswutelode þurh
hine sylfne þæt þæt hē ūs behēt.

Nū cwyð° sum man on his geþance°, 'Ēaðe° mihte hē ārīsan of dēaðe for ðan
þe hē is God. Ne mihte se dēað hine gehæftan°'. Gehȳre° se mann þe ðis smēað°
120   andsware° his smēagunge°: Crīst forðfērde° āna° ⌐on ðām tīman⌐ ac hē ne ārās
nā āna of dēaðe ac ārās mid miclum werode. Se godspellere° Mathēus āwrāt° on
Crīstes bēc þæt manega hālige men ⌐þe wǣron on ðǣre ealdan ǣ forðfarene þæt
hī⌐ ārison mid Crīste. And þæt sǣdon gehwilce° wīse lārēowas°, þæt hī habbað
gefremod° heora ǣrist tō ðām ēcan līfe, swā swā wē ealle dōn sceolon on°
125   ende þisre worulde. Þā lārēowas cwǣdon þæt ðā ārǣredan° men nǣron° sōðlice
gewitan° Crīstes ǣristes, gif hī nǣron ēcelīce° ārǣrde. Nū sind ādwǣscte° ealle
gelēaflǣstu° þæt nān man ne sceal° ortrūwian° be his āgenum ǣriste, þonne°
se godspellere āwrāt þæt fela ārison mid Crīste þe wǣron ānfealde° men, ⌐þēah
ðe Crīst God sȳ⌐.

130   Nū cwæð Gregorius se trahtnere° þæt⌐him cōme tō gemynde⌐hū ðā Iūdēiscan
clypodon° be Crīste þā ðā hē wæs on ðǣre rōde gefæstnod. Hī cwǣdon, 'Gif
hē sȳ Israhēla cyning, þonne āstīge° hē nū of ðǣre rōde and wē gelȳfað on
hine'. Gif hē þā of þǣre rōde ⌐āstīge⌐ and nolde heora hosp° forberan°, þonne

113 mortal (had) promised *sbj* (to +*d*) yet   **114** promises   **115** humbled even
of his own   **116** will *gs*   **118** will say mind Easily   **119** hold captive Let hear *sbj*
thinks   **120** the answer (to +*d*) (his) thought *ds* departed alone   **121** evangelist wrote
123 all teachers   **124** accomplished at   **125** raised were not   **126** witnesses (of +*g*)
eternally extinguished   **127** unbeliefs needs despair since   **128** simple
130 commentator   **131** cried out   **132** descend   **133** mockery tolerate

113–14 **nolde ... geswutelian** 'did not wish (*or* had not been willing) to make it [i.e.
resurrection and eternal life] manifest through himself'.

120 **on ðām tīman** i.e. the time of his crucifixion.

122–3 **þe wǣron ... forðfarene** 'who had died [lit. "were departed"] in the old law';
i.e. during the earliest OT period before the law of Moses was established.   **þæt hī** Both
the conj., correl. with *þæt* earlier in 122, and the pron. are redundant. The same construction
occurs in the next sentence.

128–9 **þēah ðe Crīst God sȳ** 'though Christ be God'. By emphasising the contrast
between simple men and exalted Christ, the homilist magnifies the value of Christ's gift of
salvation.

130 **him cōme tō gemynde** 'it had come into his mind'; *him* is poss. dat., *cōme* the sbj.
of indir. statement.

133 **āstīge** pres. sbj. (as in 132, 'let him descend'), but clearly the past conditional is
required in trans.: '(if he) had descended'.

būton twȳn° ⌜ne sealde⌝ hē ūs nāne bysne° his geþyldes°. Ac hē ābād° hwōn°
135 and forbær heora hosp and hæfde geðyld. Ac sē ðe nolde of þǣre rōde ābrecan°,
sē ārās of ðǣre byrgene. Māre° wundor wæs þæt hē of dēaðe ārās þonne° hē
cucu° of ðǣre rōde ābrǣce. Māre miht wæs þæt hē ðone dēað mid his āriste
tōbrǣc° þonne hē his līf gehēolde°, of ðǣre rōde āstīgende. Ac þā ðā hī gesāwon
þæt hē ne āstāh of ðǣre rōde for heora hospum ac þǣron° dēaðes gebād°,
140 þā gelȳfdon hī þæt hē oferswȳðed° wǣre and his nama ādwǣsced°. Ac ⌜hit
gelamp swā⌝ þæt of ðām dēaðe sprang° his nama geond° ealne middaneard. Ðā
wearð ⌜heora⌝ bliss āwend° tō ðām mǣstan° sāre°, for ðan þe heora sorh° bið°
endelēas°.

Þās þing° getācnode se stranga ⌜Samson⌝, se hæfde fǣhðe° tō ðām folce þe
145 is gehāten Philistēi°. Þā getīmode° hit þæt hē becōm° tō heora byri° þe wæs
Gaza gehāten. Þā wǣron þā Filistēi swīðe blīðe° and imbsǣton° þā buruh. Ac
se stranga Samson ārās on midre nihte and gelǣhte° þā burhgeatu° and ābǣr° hī
uppon ānre dūne° tō° bismre° his gefān°. Se stranga Samson getācnode Crīst. Sēo
burh Gaza getācnode helle and þā Philistēi hæfdon Iūdēisces folces getācnunge°
150 þe besǣton° Crīstes byrgene. Ac se Samson nolde gān ȳdel° of þǣre byrig ac hē
ābǣr þā gatu ūp tō ðǣre dūne, for ðan þe ūre hǣlend Crīst tōbrǣc hellegatu and
generode° Ādam and Ēuan and his gecorenan° of heora cynne° and frēolīce° of
dēaðe ārās, and hī samod°, and āstāh tō heofonum. Þā mānfullan° ⌜hē lēt bēon
bæftan⌝ tō þām ēcum wītum° and is nū hellegeat belocen° rihtwīsum mannum
155 and ǣfre° open unrihtwīsum.

134 doubt example patience remained a little while   **135** escape   **136** Greater than
137 alive   **138** destroyed should have saved *sbj*   **139** on it awaited +*g*   **140** vanquished
extinguished   **141** spread through   **142** changed greatest pain sorrow shall be
143 endless   **144** things *ap* enmity   **145** Philistines happened came city
146 joyful surrounded   **147** seized city gates bore   **148** hill in derision enemy *gs*
149 signification   **150** surrounded empty-handed   **152** saved chosen (ones) kin
jubilantly   **153** as well wicked (people)   **154** punishments locked (against +*d*)   **155** ever

134 **ne sealde** 'had not given', i.e. 'would not have given'.
140–1 **hit gelamp swā** 'it so turned out'.
142 **heora** i.e. Christ's mockers.
144 **Samson** An Israelite who suffered humiliation by the Philistines but then tore up
the gates of their city, Gaza; see Jdg 16.1–3. Samson is a 'type' of Christ, foreshadowing
both Christ's suffering and his subsequent 'harrowing of hell' – i.e. his breaking of hell's
gates and his rescue of the souls of the righteous, events specifically alluded to in 163–4.
See also 23/149n.
153–4 **hē lēt bēon bæftan** 'he let be behind', i.e. 'he left behind'.

Ungesǣlig° wæs þæt Iūdēisce folc þæt hī swā ungelēaffulle° wǣron. Ealle
gesceafta° oncnēowon° heora scyppend būton þām Iūdēiscan ānum°. Heofonas
oncnēowon Crīstes ācennednysse°, for ðan ðā hē ācenned wæs þā wearð
gesewen° nīwe steorra°. Sǣ oncnēow Crīst, þā ðā hē ēode mid drīgum fōtum
160   uppon hire ȳðum°. Eorðe oncnēow, þā ðā hēo eal bifode° on Crīstes ǣriste.
Sēo sunne oncnēow, þā ðā hēo wearð aþȳstrod° on Crīstes þrōwunge fram
middæge ⌐oð nōn⌐. Stānas oncnēowon, þā ðā hī tōburston° on heora scyppendes
forðsīðe°. Hel oncnēow Crīst, þā ðā hēo forlēt° hyre hæftlingas° ūt þurh ðæs
hǣlendes hergunge°. And þā heardheortan Iūdēi þēah°, þurh eallum þām
165   tācnum°, noldon gebūgan° mid gelēafan tō ðām mildheortan hǣlende, sē ðe
wile ⌐eallum mannum gehelpan on hyne gelȳfendum⌐.

Ac uton° wē gelȳfan þæt God fæder wæs ǣfre būton anginne° and ǣfre wæs
se sunu of ðām fæder ācenned, for ðan þe hē is se wīsdom and ⌐miht þe se
fæder ealle gesceafta þurh gescēop⌐. And hī ealle wurdon gelīffæste° þurh þone
170   hālgan gāst, sē ðe is willa and lufu þæs fæder and þæs suna. ⌐Hī þrȳ⌐, ān God
untōdǣledlic°, on ānre godcundnysse° wuniende, hī ealle gelīce° mihtige°, for
ðon ⌐swā hwæt swā⌐ læsse° bið and unmihtigre°, þæt ne bið nā God. Ac se fæder
sende þone sunu tō° ūre ālȳsednysse° and hē āna underfēng° þā menniscnysse°
and þrōwade dēað be his āgenum willan and ārās of dēaðe on þisum dæge and
175   āstāh tō heofonum on ðām fēowertigeðon dæge his ǣristes ætforan° manegra
manna gesihðe° and rīxað° mid ðām ælmihtigum fæder and þām hālgum gāste,
nū and ⌐ā on ēcnysse⌐. ĀMENN.

156 Unfortunate unbelieving **157** creatures acknowledged alone **158** birth **159** seen
star **160** waves trembled **161** darkened **162** shattered **163** departure released
captives **164** harrowing yet **165** signs bend **167** let us beginning **169** endowed
with life **171** indivisible Godhead (*i.e.* divine essence) equally powerful **172** lesser
weaker **173** for redemption assumed human form **175** before **176** sight rules

162 **oð nōn** 'until the ninth hour'; i.e. 3 p.m. (see 1/44n).
166 **eallum mannum ... on hyne gelȳfendum** 'all men believing [i.e. "who believe"]
in him'; dat. after *gehelpan*.
168–9 **miht þe ... þurh gescēop** The prep. belongs with the rel. pron.: 'the power
through which the father created all creatures'.
170 **Hī þrȳ** 'These three'; i.e. the Trinity of the Holy Spirit, the Father and the Son.
172 **swā hwæt swā** 'what(so)ever'.
177 **ā on ēcnysse** 'ever in eternity', i.e. 'for ever and ever'.

23

The Dream of the Rood

Since early in the fourth century, the cult of the cross has provided Christianity with its most powerful image – an enduring reminder of the sacrifice whereby Christ, through his crucifixion, offered redemption to fallen humankind. *The Dream of the Rood* presents an intense and original treatment of this theme. In its best-known, 156-line, version, the poem occurs only on fols. 104–6 of the 'Vercelli Book', a manuscript written in England in the later tenth century but now in the Biblioteca Capitolare at Vercelli in Italy. There are three other poems and eighteen prose homilies in the volume, which seems to have been compiled as a source of meditative and penitential reading for the faithful. However, a variant text of several lines of *The Dream of the Rood* appears also on a twenty-two-foot high Anglo-Saxon stone cross which was extensively damaged during the Reformation but is now restored and on display at Ruthwell in Dumfriesshire, Scotland. The lines are inscribed in runic characters, which were used regularly by the Anglo-Saxons before they learned the Roman alphabet from Christian monks and thereafter continued in use for decorative purposes. Traditionally, the inscription on the cross, which accompanies carved scenes of biblical and other events, has been dated to the eighth century, though this view has been challenged recently. In addition, two lines echoing the speech of the cross in the poem are engraved on a small silver reliquary cross, known as the Brussels Cross, dating from the end of the tenth century. These various occurrences are enough to suggest that our poem, in whole or in part, was known widely.

Meticulously structured, the poem is framed by the first-person testimony of the narrator (lines 1–27 and 122–56), to whom the vision of a speaking cross has been granted, apparently in a dream. Within this frame, the long central section is another first-person narrative, that of the cross itself on which Christ was crucified, which tells how it was torn from its roots and, initially against its will, became a participant in the events on Calvary. Re-enacting Christ's passion, burial and resurrection, the cross effects the transformation of the poet-dreamer from the anxious and confused sinner of the opening lines to the confident, evangelising Christian of the poem's conclusion, who now knows how and why to meditate on the cross in his personal devotions. The poet no doubt aims to stimulate the same sort of response in his audience.

Parallels for the personification of an inanimate object (a device known as 'prosopopoeia') are to be found in other OE verse, including the *Riddles* (see, for instance, Text 35d). The device in the present poem allows the poet to express the physical suffering of Christ through the parallel experience of the cross, thus avoiding a range of theological controversies concerning the balance between the human and divine aspects of Christ. Of special interest in this account is the character of Christ himself. In contrast to the suffering figure who has dominated the art and literature of Western Christianity since the later Middle Ages, the Christ of *The Dream of the Rood* is an heroic, warrior-like figure who actively embraces his fate and eagerly ascends the cross. In turn, the cross is required to show its loyalty by being complicit in Christ's death: it is a servant of its lord whose loyalty consists in not 'daring' to act in his defence, a point made three times in six lines (42–7). The texture of the poem is dense with verbal patterning, parallelism and repetition. To give just one example, the path to active and willing Christian devotion is mapped out by the threefold repetition of the phrase *elne mycle*, which may be translated 'with much courage' or 'with great zeal'. Used first of the heroic Christ (34), then of the obedient cross (60), and finally of the narrator himself (123), it becomes a paradigm for the evangelical dynamic of the poem and forces us to ask what 'heroic' action is in a Christian context.

A notable feature of the poem is its use of blocks of 'hypermetric' lines, which extend the normal metrical limits of the OE verse line (i.e. two main stresses in each half-line: see p. xxiv) with several extra stressed syllables. The main examples occur at lines 8–10, 20–3, 30–4, 39–43, 46–9 and 59–69. There has been no completely satisfactory explanation of them, but it will be seen that they tend to occur in passages of particular emotional intensity or portentousness, the effects of which are perhaps emphasised in the disruption of the reader's rhythmic expectations. The language of *The Dream of the Rood* in its manuscript version is characteristic of late WS usage, with the exception of a few apparently earlier forms (some of them possibly, but not convincingly, showing the influence of Anglian dialects), such as *meahte* (18, though *mihte* also occurs, 37), *gesīene* (46, not *gesȳne*), and forms in final -*g*, such as *hnāg* (59) and *āstāg* (103), but *fāh* (13) and *gestāh* (40) also occur. Levelling of unstressed vowels is apparent only in *þurhdrifan* (46; for -*on*). In line 28, *gȳta* (rather than *gȳt*) is a characteristic poetical form.

Further reading

M. J. Swanton, ed., *The Dream of the Rood* (Manchester, 1970)

R. Woolf, 'Doctrinal Influences on *The Dream of the Rood*', *MÆ* 27 (1958), 137–53

M. Schlauch, 'The *Dream of the Rood* as Prosopopoeia', in *Essential Articles for the Study of Old English Poetry*, ed. J. B. Bessinger and S. J. Kahrl (Hamden, CT, 1968), pp. 428–41

M. J. Swanton, 'Ambiguity and Anticipation in "The Dream of the Rood"', *NM* 70 (1969), 407–25

C. J. Wolf, 'Christ as Hero in *The Dream of the Rood*', *NM* 71 (1970), 202–10

P. R. Orton, 'The Technique of Object Personification in *The Dream of the Rood* and a Comparison with the Old English *Riddles*', *LSE* n.s. 11 (1980), 1–18

E. B. Irving, 'Crucifixion Witnessed, or Dramatic Interaction in *The Dream of the Rood*', in *Modes of Interpretation in Old English Literature: Essays in Honour of Stanley B. Greenfield*, ed. P. R. Brown, G. R. Crampton and F. C. Robinson (Toronto, 1986), pp. 101–13

S. McEntire, 'The Devotional Context of the Cross Before A.D. 1000', in *Sources of Anglo-Saxon Culture*, ed. P. E. Szarmach and V. D. Oggins (Kalamazoo, MI, 1986); repr. in *OE Literature*, ed. Liuzza, pp. 392–403

B. Cassidy, *The Ruthwell Cross: Papers from the Collegium sponsored by the Index of Christian Art, Princeton University, 8 December 1989* (Princeton, NJ, 1992)

⌐Hwæt⌐, ic ⌐swefna cyst⌐ secgan° wylle	tell
hwæt ⌐mē gemætte⌐ tō° midre° nihte	at mid
⌐syðþan reordberend reste wunedon⌐.	
Þūhte° mē° þæt ic gesāwe° ⌐syllicre trēow	(It) seemed to me saw
5 on lyft lædan⌐, ⌐lēohte⌐ bewunden°,	wrapped round
bēama° beorhtost°. ⌐Eall þæt bēacen wæs	of 'beams' brightest
begoten⌐ mid° golde. Gimmas° stōdon°	with Gems appeared

1 **Hwæt** lit. 'What!', an exclamation which often signals the start of OE poems (among them *Beowulf*) and harks back to the oral tradition. It is hard to trans., but 'Listen!' or the antique 'Lo!' are often used. Cf. *hwæt* as a conventional pron. ('what') at the start of 2. **swefna cyst** *cyst* is a noun from the vb. *cēosan* 'to choose'; hence: 'the choicest (*or* best) of dreams'.

2 **mē gemætte** impers. vb.: '(it) dreamed to me', i.e. 'I dreamed'.

3 **syðþan reordberend reste wunedon** Both *rest* and *wunian* have a range of meanings. The main possibilities here are 'when (the) voice-bearers remained (*or* dwelt *or* were) at rest' (dat. *reste*), or '... occupied their resting-place (*or* beds)' (acc. *reste*). The kenning *reordberend* (used again in 89) means of course human beings, with perhaps a hint of disapproval.

4–5 **syllicre** comp. adj. with intensive meaning: 'most wondrous'. **trēow on lyft lædan** acc. and inf. construction (G6d.i.3), with passive sense: 'a ... tree borne up into the sky'. See also the use of *þenian* in 52, and cf. 15n for active sense.

5 **lēohte** dat. of instrument: 'with light'; see also *synnum* (13), *wǣdum* (15), etc.

6–7 **Eall ... begoten** 'all (*or* altogether) drenched'. Adv. *eall* is used similarly in 20, 48 and 62. **bēacen** ModE 'beacon' retains the double sense of a flaming object and an abstract 'sign'.

⌐fægere æt foldan scēatum⌐:   swylce° þǣr fīfe wǣron   likewise
uppe° on þām ⌐eaxlegespanne⌐.   ⌐Behēoldon þǣr engel   above
   Dryhtnes ealle

10   fægere þurh forðgesceaft⌐.   Ne wæs ðǣr hūru° fracodes°   truly   a criminal's
   gealga°   gallows
ac° ⌐hine⌐ þǣr behēoldon   hālige° gāstas°,   but   holy   spirits np
⌐men ofer moldan°   ond eall þēos mǣre°   (the) earth   glorious
   gesceaft°⌐.   creation ns
Syllic wæs se sigebēam°   ond ic synnum° ⌐fāh⌐,   victory-tree   by sins
forwunded° mid wommum°.   Geseah° ic   badly wounded   faults   Saw
   wuldres° trēow,   of glory

15   ⌐wǣdum geweorðode,   wynnum scīnan⌐,   exalted
gegyred° mid golde.   Gimmas hæfdon°   adorned   had
bewrigene° weorðlice°   wealdendes⌐ trēow.   covered   splendidly
Hwæðre° ic þurh° þæt gold   ongytan° meahte°   Yet   beyond   perceive   could
⌐earmra ǣrgewin⌐   þæt° hit ǣrest° ongan°   in that   first   began

---

8 **fægere** Either an adj. describing *gimmas*: 'beautiful', or an adv.: 'beautifully'.   **æt foldan scēatum** An oft-favoured trans. is 'at the surface [lit. "surfaces"] of the earth' (see also 37 and 43), but 'at the corners of the earth' might better suit the idea of the cross spread out in different directions across the heavens (and thus the world). Cf. a similar expression, *ofer... eorþan sceatas*, in *The Seafarer* (26/60–1).

9 **eaxlegespanne** lit. 'shoulder-link'; presumably the transverse beam of the cross, 'the cross-beam', which passes behind the victim's shoulders. The five jewels may be thought of as arranged along this or (reflecting a pattern found on some contemporary sculptured stone crosses) in a 'quincunx' (like the five points on dice) at the point of intersection of cross-beam and upright.

9–10 **Behēoldon þǣr... forðgesceaft** The pron. *ealle* appears to be the subj. and *engel Dryhtnes* the obj., with the phr. *fægere þurh forðgesceaft* qualifying *ealle*: 'All (those) fair by eternal decree beheld there the angel of the Lord'. The 'angel' is presumably Christ (though the description is unusual) but might be the cross. Those 'fair by eternal decree' may be the saints and angels of 153–4, who are already established in heaven. Editors have made various attempts to emend this line-and-a-half (including the dropping of *ealle* from the metrically overloaded 9b), but none is satisfactory.

11 **hine** 'it' (acc.), with antec. *gealga* (masc.), obj. of *behēoldon*.

12 **men ofer moldan... gesceaft** The line is repeated in 82.

13 **fāh** An ambiguous adj.: both 'stained' and 'decorated'.

15 **wǣdum geweorðode** 'ennobled by (its) garments'; presumably, the jewels and ornamentation which adorn the cross.   **wynnum** 'with joys', or 'with joyful things', but the dat. pl. may be an adv.: 'joyously' or 'delightfully'.   **scīnan** part of an acc. and inf. construction with *trēow*.: 'shine' or 'shining'. See also *wendan* in 22 and *efstan* in 34.

17 **wealdendes** 'of the ruler'. The manuscript reading *wealdes*, 'of the forest', would also make sense, but parallel phrases in 25 and 53 support the emendation.

19 **earmra ǣrgewin** 'the former struggle of wretched ones'. The reference is presumably to the sufferings of Christ and the cross itself.

20	swǣtan° on þā swīðran healfe⌐. Ēall ic wæs mid sorgum°	to bleed sorrows
	gedrēfed°.	afflicted
	forht° ic wæs for° þǣre fægran gesyhðe⌐. Geseah ic	frightened before sight
	þæt fūse° bēacen	eager
	wendan° wǣdum ond blēom⌐; hwīlum° hit wæs mid	change at times
	⌐wǣtan⌐ bestēmed°,	drenched
	beswyled° mid swātes° gange°, hwīlum mid	soaked of blood flow
	since° gegyrwed.	treasure
	Hwæðre ic þǣr licgende° ⌐lange hwīle⌐	lying
25	behēold hrēowcearig° hǣlendes° trēow,	distressed *ns* Saviour's
	oððæt° ic gehŷrde° þæt hit hlēoðrode°,	until heard spoke
	ongan þā° word sprecan° wudu° sēlesta°:	these to speak tree best
	'Þæt wæs gēara iū°, ic þæt gŷta° geman°,	long ago once still remember
	þæt ic wæs āhēawen° ⌐holtes on ende⌐,	hewn down
30	āstyred° of° stefne° mīnum. Genāman° mē	removed from root Seized
	ðǣr strange° fēondas°,	strong enemies *np*
	⌐geworhton him þǣr tō wæfersŷne⌐, hēton° mē	ordered
	heora wergas° hebban°.	criminals to raise
	Bǣron° mē ðǣr beornas° on eaxlum° oððæt hīe	Carried men shoulders
	mē on beorg° āsetton°,	hill set up
	gefæstnodon° mē þǣr fēondas genōge°. Geseah ic	fixed enough
	þā frēan° mancynnes	lord
	efstan° elne mycle° þæt⌐ hē⌐ mē wolde on⌐ gestīgan°.	hurry climb
35	Þǣr ic þā ne dorste° ofer° Dryhtnes° word	dared against the Lord's
	būgan° oððe berstan°, þā° ic bifian° geseah	bend break when shake
	eorðan° scēatas. ⌐Ealle ic mihte⌐	earth's

20 **on þā swīðran healfe** 'on the right side'. Jn 19.34: 'But one of the soldiers with a spear opened his side, and immediately there came out blood and water'. According to an early church tradition, it was Christ's right side that was pierced. See also 49a.

22 **wǣdum ond blēom** dat. of respect: 'in respect of garments and colours'. **wǣtan** 'wetness' (dat. sg., weak noun); probably 'water', as the blood is referred to in the next line (see 20n).

24 **lange hwīle** acc. of duration of time: 'for a long time'; see also 64, 70 and 84.

29 **holtes on ende** 'from the end (*i.e.* border *or* edge) of the forest'.

31 **geworhton ... wæfersŷne** The obj. of the vb. is still 'me': 'they made me there into a spectacle for themselves (*him*)'.

34 **elne mycle** instr. of manner: 'with great fortitude (*or* zeal *or* courage)'. The phr. is repeated in 60 and 123 (see headnote). **þæt** Here, 'because' is an appropriate trans. **mē ... on** 'onto me'.

37 **Ealle** adj. qualifying *fēondas* in 38. **ic mihte** perf. conditional: 'I could have'.

feondas gefyllan°,   hwæðre ic fæste stod.   — *have knocked all my enemies down but I stood fast* — knock down

Ongyrede hine þa geong hæleð,   þæt wæs God ælmihtig,   — *Then the young man that was God almighty*

40 strang ond stiðmod.   Gestah° he on gealgan heanne°,   — *stood and stripped himself strong* — resolute Climbed high

modig° on manigra gesyhðe°,   þa he wolde°   — *brave in the thoughts of many that ... sights (many view)* — brave of many

mancyn lysan°.   — *he wanted to redeem mankind* — redeem

Bifode ic þa° me se beorn ymbclypte°.   Ne dorste ic hwæðre   — *I trembled when he embraced me. I dared not* — when

bugan to eorðan,   — *bend to earth*

feallan to foldan sceatum,   ac ic sceolde° fæste standan.   — *fell to the ground but I had to stand fast* — had to

Rod° wæs ic ared°,   ahof° ic ricne°   — *I was raised the cross was raised* — (A) cross raised lifted mighty

cyning,   — *lifted the mighty king*

45 heofona° hlaford°;   hyldan° me° ne dorste.   — *lord of the heavens I dared not bend myself* — of the heavens lord bend myself

Purhdrifan° hi me mid deorcan° næglum°;   on me   — *They pierced me with dark nails those scars* — Pierced dark nails

syndon þa dolg° gesiene°,   — *are visible on me* — scars visible

opene inwidhlemmas°;   ne dorste ic hira°   — *open malicious wounds I dared not* — malicious wounds of them

nænigum° sceððan°.   — *injure any of them* — none harm +d

Bysmeredon° hie unc° butu° ætgædere.   Eall ic wæs   — *they mocked both of us together I was* — Mocked us *dual* both

mid blode bestemed   — *all covered in blood*

begoten of þæs guman sidan°   siððan° he hæfde   — *from the man's side. when his* — when

his gast° onsended°.   — *spirit ascended* — spirit sent forth

50 Feala ic on þam beorge gebiden° hæbbe   — *I have suffered many* — suffered (*or* endured)

wraðra wyrda.   Geseah ic weruda° God   — *cruel events I saw God* — of hosts

pearle° þenian°.   Þystro° hæfdon   — *of hosts stretched out Darkness had hidden* — harshly Darkness *np*

bewrigen° mid wolcnum°   wealdendes hræw°,   — *with clouds the cross* — hidden clouds corpse

scirne sciman°;   sceadu° forð eode°,   — *shining splendour shadow went forth* — shadow went

wann° under wolcnum.   Weop° eal gesceaft,   — *dark under the clouds All of creation wept* — dark Wept

55 cwiðdon° cyninges fyll°.   Crist wæs on rode.   — *lamented the death of the king Crist was on the cross* — lamented death

---

39 **Ongyrede ... hæleð** 'Then the young hero (*or* man) stripped himself'. In the gospel version, the soldiers strip Christ (Mt 27.28: see 14/33–4); the details here (along with others in the poem) seem to derive from an account of the martyrdom of St Andrew. In 78, the cross calls the dreamer *hæleð*.

42 **ymbclypte** 'embraced'. This idea is alluded to in several Latin poems about the cross.

44 **Rod** This is the first time that the cross is actually named as such.

49 **begoten of þæs guman sīdan** The past part. is parallel with *bestemed*: '(drenched and) soaked (with blood) from that man's side'.

50–1 **Feala ... wrāðra wyrda** partitive gen. phr.: 'many cruel events'. See also 125 and 131.

52 **þenian** acc. and inf. construction (with acc. *God*): 'stretched out' or 'racked'.

54 **scīrne scīman** The phr. is a var. on *hrǣw* and thus a parallel obj. of *hæfdon bewrigen*: 'shining splendour (*or* light)' (contrasting dramatically with *sceadu* in the next half-line).
sceadu forð ēode Mt 27.45: 'Now from the sixth hour there was darkness over the whole earth' (see also 14/55).

Hwæðere þær ⌐fūse° feorran° cwōman°⌐	eager (people) from afar	came
tō þām æðelinge°. Ic þæt eall behēold.		prince
Sāre° ic wæs mid sorgum gedrēfed, hnāg° ic hwæðre	Grievously	bent
⌐þām secgum tō handa⌐		

60   ēaðmōd° elne mycle.   Genāmon° hīe þær ælmihtigne God,   humble Seized

āhōfon° hine of ðām hefian° wīte°.   Forlēton°   dire   torment   Left

   mē ⌐þā⌐ hilderincas°   warriors

standan stēame° bedrifenne°;   eall ic wæs ⌐mid   with moisture   spattered

   strǣlum°⌐ forwundod.   arrows

Ālēdon° hīe ðǣr limwērigne°,   ⌐gestōdon him   Laid down   'limb-weary (one)'

   æt his līces hēafdum⌐;

behēoldon hīe ðǣr heofenes Dryhten   ond hē hine° ðǣr   himself

   hwīle reste°,   rested

65   mēðe° æfter ðām miclan° gewinne°.   Ongunnon   worn out   great   struggle

   ⌐him⌐ þā moldern° wyrcan°   tomb *as*   make

beornas ⌐on banan gesyhðe⌐;   curfon° hīe ðæt of beorhtan   carved

   stāne°,   rock

gesetton° hīe ðǣron sigora° wealdend.   Ongunnon   placed   of victories

   him þā sorhlēoð° galan°   'sorrow-song'   sing

⌐earme⌐ on þā ǣfentīde°   þā hīe woldon eft° sīðian°   eveningtime   back   go

mēðe fram þām mǣran þēodne°.   Reste hē ðǣr ⌐mǣte weorode⌐.   prince

---

57 **fūse...cwōman** In Jn 19.38–9, Joseph of Arimathea and Nicodemus are named as coming to take down Christ's body. *Cwōman* is an older, uncontracted, form of *cōman* (or *cōmon*).

59 **þām secgum tō handa** 'to the men to hand', i.e. 'to the hands of the men' (*handa* appears to be dat. sg.).

61 **þā** adv. 'then', or perhaps the def. art. 'the' (nom. pl. masc.) with *hilderincas*.

62 **mid strǣlum** The arrows are a metaphor for the nails of 46.

63 **gestōdon him...hēafdum** *him* is a rflx. dat. pron. and *hēafdum* is pl. but with sg. meaning (known as a 'locative' dat. [§D4i]; cf. the use of *brēostum* in 118): 'they placed themselves at his body's head'.

65 **him** rflx. dat. pron. with *ongunnon* ('they began'), referring to *beornas*, or an indir. pron., 'for him'. The same applies to *him* in 67.

66 **on banan gesyhðe** 'in the sight of the slayer'. The cross refers to its own role in Christ's death.

68 **earme** 'wretched'. The adj. refers to men who are about to leave.

69 **mǣte weorode** instr. of accompaniment: 'with a small company'. This might be litotes, in that Christ is in fact alone in the tomb, or it could refer either to the 'three Marys' who attended the tomb or to the soldiers who guarded it: see Mt 27.61 and 65–6, and Texts 14 and 22. The phr. is repeated in 124, where the solitariness of the dreamer *does* seem to be implied. Interpretation as litotes to express the situation of the individual Christian alone 'except' for God, in the persons of the Trinity (see 22/170n), would cover both uses.

70	Hwæðere ⌈wē⌉ ðǣr grēotende° gōde hwīle	lamenting
	stōdon on staðole°, ⌈stefn ūp gewāt⌉	position
	hilderinca. Hrǣw cōlode°,	grew cold
	fæger feorgbold°. Þā ūs man fyllan° ongan	'soul-dwelling' (body) strike down
	ealle tō eorðan; þæt wæs egeslic° wyrd°!	dreadful fate
75	Bedealf° ūs man on dēopan sēaþe°. Hwæðre ⌈mē þǣr	Buried pit
	Dryhtnes þegnas
	frēondas gefrūnon⌉,
	gyredon° mē golde ond seolfre.	adorned (with +d)
	Nū ðū miht gehȳran, hæleð mīn se lēofa°,	beloved
	þæt ic ⌈bealuwara weorc gebiden hæbbe,
80	sārra sorga⌉. Is nū sǣl° cumen°	time come
	þæt mē weorðiað° wīde° ond sīde°	(shall) worship far wide
	menn° ofer moldan ond eall þēos mǣre gesceaft	people
	gebiddaþ° ⌈him⌉ tō þyssum bēacne. On mē bearn° Godes	(shall) pray son
	þrōwode° hwīle; forþan° ic þrymfæst° nū	suffered therefore glorious
85	hlīfige° under heofenum ond ic hǣlan° mæg	rise up save
	⌈ǣghwylcne ānra þāra þe him bið egesa tō mē⌉.
	Iū ic ⌈wæs geworden⌉ wīta° heardost	of punishments
	lēodum° lāðost° ⌈ǣr þan⌉ ic ⌈him līfes weg	to people most hateful
	rihtne⌉ gerȳmde°, reordberendum.	opened up
90	Hwæt, mē þā geweorðode° wuldres ealdor°	honoured prince ns

70 **wē** i.e. Christ's cross and its two companion crosses.

71 **stefn** The manuscript has *syððan*, but this cannot be right and *stefn* ('voice' or 'sound'), though only a guess, is appropriate (cf. 67); some editors keep *syððan* as well, but that is metrically awkward. **ūp gewāt** 'went upwards', i.e. 'passed away'.

75–6 **mē...gefrūnon** 'heard about me'; *þegnas* and *frēondas* are parallel subjs. These lines refer to the 'invention' (discovery) of the true cross by St Helena, the mother of the Roman emperor Constantine, a story told in another OE poem of the Vercelli Book, *Elene*. A half-line appears to be missing from 76, and the beginning of 77 probably lacks one or two words.

79–80 **bealuwara...sorga** The parallel gen. nouns are both dependent on *weorc*, the sense of which varies: 'the action of dwellers in iniquity, the affliction of painful sorrows'.

83 **him** The vb. *gebiddan* takes a dat. rflx. pron.; see also 122.

86 **ǣghwylcne ānra** 'each one'; lit. 'each of ones' (partitive gen., but cf. *ǣghwylc* used as simple adj. in 120); cf. 108–9. **þāra þe him bið egesa tō mē** lit. 'of those who in them is fear towards me', i.e. 'of those who have fear for me'.

87 **wæs geworden** 'was (*or* had) become', i.e. 'became'.

88 **ǣr þan** 'before' (lit. 'before that'), a conj. phr., with instr., used before a vb.-phr.

88–9 **him līfes weg rihtne** 'the right way of life for them'; *him* is parallel with dat. pl. *reordberendum*.

⌜ofer holmwudu⌝,   heofonrīces° weard°,   kingdom of heaven *gs*   guardian

⌜swylce swā hē⌝ his mōdor ēac°,   Mārian° sylfe,   also   Mary *as*

ælmihtig God   for° ealle menn   before

geweorðode   ⌜ofer eall wīfa cynn⌝.

95   Nū ic þē hāte°,   hæleð mīn se lēofa,   command

þæt ðū þās° gesyhðe   secge° mannum°,   this   tell   to people

onwrēoh° wordum°   þæt hit is wuldres bēam,   reveal   in words

⌜sē ðe ælmihtig God   on þrōwode⌝

for mancynnes   manegum synnum

100   ond Ādomes   ⌜ealdgewyrhtum°⌝.   deeds of old

Dēað hē þær byrigde°,   hwæðere eft° Dryhten ārās°   tasted   afterwards   arose

mid his miclan mihte°   mannum tō° helpe°.   power   as   a benefit

Hē ðā on° heofenas āstāg°.   Hider° eft fundaþ°   to   ascended   Here   (will) come

on þysne middangeard°   mancynn sēcan°   world   to seek

105   on dōmdæge°   Dryhten sylfa   judgement day

ælmihtig God   ond his englas mid°   as well

⌜þæt⌝ hē þonne wile dēman°,   se° āh° dōmes   judge +*d*   who   possesses

geweald°,   (the) power

⌜ānra gehwylcum   swā hē him ǣrur hēr

on þyssum lǣnum°   līfe geearnaþ⌝.   transitory

110   Ne mæg þǣr ǣnig   unforht° wesan°   unafraid   be

for° þām worde   þe se wealdend cwyð°.   because of   (will) say

Frīneð° hē for° þǣre mænige°   hwǣr se   (Will) ask   before   multitude

man sīe°,   is *sbj*

sē° ðe for Dryhtnes naman   dēaðes wolde   he

---

91 **ofer holmwudu** Often rendered 'above the trees of the forest' (i.e. the other trees), but the compound noun (occurring uniquely here) may mean 'tree(s) of the hill' and thus allude to Calvary, the site of the crucifixion.

92 **swylce swā hē** The pron. refers forward to the subj. of this clause, *ælmihtig God* (93): 'just as he, (almighty God . . .)'.

94 **ofer eall wīfa cynn** 'above all womankind [lit. "the race of women"]'. The Virgin Mary was picked out to be the mother of Christ; see Lk 1.28.

98 **sē ðe . . . on þrōwode** 'that on which almighty God suffered'.

100 **ealdgewyrhtum** The reference is to Adam's (and Eve's) disobedience in Eden.

107 **þæt** 'in as much as', or 'because'.

108–9 **ānra gehwylcum** 'each one' (*gehwylcum* dat. after *dēman*, plus partitive gen.); cf. 86. **swā hē him ǣrur . . . geearnaþ** The vb. is best understood as fut. perf.: 'even as he for himself earlier . . . will have earned (*or* deserved)'. All will be judged according to how they have lived on earth. **on þyssum lǣnum līfe** A familiar formula in OE Christian poetry; see 26/65–6 and 38/108–10.

⌐biteres⌐ onbyrigan°, swā hē ǣr° on ðām bēame dyde. taste +g formerly

115 Ac hīe þonne forhtiað° ond fēa° þencaþ° will be afraid scarcely imagine

hwæt hīe tō Crīste cweðan onginnen°. may begin

Ne þearf° ðǣr þonne ǣnig ⌐anforht°⌐ wesan, need terrified

þe ⌐him ǣr in brēostum⌐ bered° bēacna sēlest° carries the best (of +g)

ac ðurh ðā rōde sceal° rīce° gesēcan° shall kingdom *as* seek out

120 of° eorðwege° ǣghwylc° sāwl, away from the earthly path each

⌐sēo þe⌐ mid wealdende wunian° þenceð°.' to dwell desires

Gebǣd° ic mē þā tō þan bēame ⌐blīðe mōde⌐, Prayed

elne mycle, þǣr ic āna° wæs alone

mǣte werede. Wæs mōdsefa° (my) spirit

125 āfȳsed° on forðwege°, ⌐feala ealra gebād urged the journey ahead

langunghwīla⌐. Is mē nū līfes hyht° hope

þæt ic þone sigebēam sēcan mōte° may

āna oftor° þonne° ealle men, more often than

well° weorþian. ⌐Mē is willa tō ðām properly

130 mycel on mōde⌐ ond mīn ⌐mundbyrd°⌐ is hope of protection

geriht° tō þǣre rōde. Nāh° ic rīcra° feala directed Do not have powerful

frēonda on foldan ac hīe forð heonon° from here

gewiton° of worulde° drēamum°, ⌐sōhton him⌐ wuldres went world's joys

cyning,

lifiaþ nū on heofenum mid hēahfædere°, 'the high father' (*i.e.* God the father)

135 wuniaþ on wuldre, ond ⌐ic wēne mē⌐

daga gehwylce° hwænne° mē Dryhtnes rōd, each +gp when

114 **biteres** The adj., given special emphasis in this position, qualifies *dēaðes* in 113.

117 **anforht** This line closely parallels 110, but there is a crucial variation: while there is no one who can afford to be *un*afraid of God's word (for all must respect and fear it), no one who reveres the cross need be afraid of their future. The manuscript has *unforht* here as well as in 110 and it is conceivable that the poet deliberately planted more ambiguity, for the prefix *un-*, though it commonly has a neg. sense, is sometimes used in early Germanic languages to intensify the attached adj. But the emendation to *anforht* ensures the positive meaning, and *an-* still sounds enough like *un-* to suggest an instructive pun.

118 **him...in brēostum** poss. dat. pron. and 'locative' dat. noun: 'in his breast'.

121 **sēo þe** 'she who', i.e. 'which' (antecedent *sawl*).

122 **blīðe mōde** instr. of manner: 'with glad heart'.

125–6 **feala ealra gebād langunghwīla** 'experienced many of all periods of longing', i.e. 'very many periods of longing' (subj. *mōdsefa*).

129–30 **Mē is...mōde** lit. 'for me the desire for that is great in my heart'. **mundbyrd** A term with legal connotations: see 7/headnote.

133 **sōhton him** 'sought out for themselves', or (with rflx. *him* untrans.) 'approached'.

135 **ic wēne mē** 'I hope for' or 'look forward to', with rflx. pron. untrans.; the indir. obj. of the phr. is the clause beginning *hwænne*.

þe ic hēr on eorðan   ǣr scēawode°,   beheld
on° þysson lǣnan   līfe gefetige°   from   may fetch *sbj*
ond mē þonne gebringe   þǣr° is blis° mycel,   where   happiness
140   drēam on heofonum,   þǣr is Dryhtnes folc
geseted° tō° symle°   þǣr is singal° blis,   placed   at   the feast   continuous
ond mē þonne āsette°   þǣr ic syþþan° mōt   set down   then
wunian on wuldre,   well° mid þām hālgum°   fittingly   saints
drēames brūcan°.   Sī° mē Dryhten frēond,   enjoy +g   Be
145   sē ðe hēr on eorþan   ǣr þrōwode
on þām gealgtrēowe°   for guman° synnum.   gallows-tree   of man
Hē ūs onlȳsde°   ond ūs līf forgeaf°,   set free   gave
heofonlicne hām.   Hiht wæs genīwad°   renewed
mid blēdum° ond mid blisse   ⌜þām þe⌝ þǣr bryne°   splendours   burning
þolodan.
150   Se sunu wæs sigorfæst°   on þām sīðfate°   victorious   expedition
mihtig ond spēdig°   þā hē mid manigeo° cōm,   successful   the multitude
gāsta weorode°,   on Godes rīce,   (with a) host
anwealda° ælmihtig,   ⌜englum tō blisse⌝   ruler
ond eallum ðām hālgum   þām þe on heofonum ǣr
155   wunedon on wuldre,   þā heora wealdend cwōm,
ælmihtig God,   þǣr his ēðel° wæs.   homeland

149 **þām þe** 'for them who…'. These are the righteous people whom Christ rescued from the power of Satan during his 'harrowing' of hell (the *sīðfæt* of 150), to where he descended between his crucifixion and resurrection. In the following verses, allusion is made to his subsequent ascension to heaven, taking the rescued souls with him.

153 **englum tō blisse** 'as a joy to the angels'; the phr. *eallum ðām hālgum* in 154 is parallel with *englum*.

24

On False Gods
(Wulfstan's *De falsis deis*)

Little is known about Wulfstan before he was appointed bishop of London in 996, though he seems to have had family connections in the East Midlands, around Peterborough or Ely. Thereafter, however, he became a prominent and influential figure in church and state, being involved among other things in the drawing up of lawcodes for two kings, Æthelred and Cnut. In 1002, he was appointed bishop of Worcester and archbishop of York and held the two sees in plurality until 1016, after which he retained York until his death in 1023. Four sermons in Latin and twenty-two in OE have been identified as Wulfstan's, though the number of the latter should certainly be put higher, in view of several fragments which show his highly distinctive style (discussed below). Their subjects are often eschatological – dealing, that is, with 'end things': death, judgement, heaven and hell – or they offer guidance on specific aspects of faith, such as baptism. Among Wulfstan's other known works are the *Institutes of Polity*, which sets out the distribution of authority among members of church and state, and the *Canons of Edgar*, a handbook of instruction for the secular clergy.

The sermon *De falsis deis* is preserved in a single copy in Oxford, Bodleian Library, Hatton 113, a two-volume homiliary (a collection of homilies) compiled at Worcester between 1064 and 1083 for the presiding bishop (another Wulfstan); it contains several items by Ælfric, as well as most of Wulfstan's sermons. *De falsis deis* is in fact an expansion of part of one of Ælfric's homilies (not one of the main collection of *Sermones catholicae*), which in turn drew on the work of a sixth-century continental writer, Martin of Braga. Pagan practices had survived into Christian times in England and Wulfstan denounced them regularly in his works; each of the lawcodes with which he was involved includes injunctions against such practices. With his archiepiscopal see at York, in a strongly Scandinavian area, he may have been particularly aware of the problem. The equation of Germanic deities with classical counterparts was well established in the early medieval period, with consequences still visible today in the names of the days of the week in Germanic and Romance languages. Thus, for example, Woden is identified with Mercury, resulting in OE *wodnesdæg*, ModE 'Wednesday', but French *mercredi*, Italian *mercoledì*. It was also a commonplace of medieval thought, well exemplified in the works of Augustine, for instance, to explain away pagan gods as merely human beings well practised in deceits and vices of various kinds. This demythologising (known as euhemerism) is illustrated in the genealogies of Anglo-Saxon kings, all of whom have Woden as one of their remote ancestors. But with writers such as Ælfric and Wulfstan, euhemerism was developed further into a process of demonisation. In *De falsis deis*, the statement in line 1 that everything went awry ðurh dēofol, 'through the devil', becomes a theme which is reiterated with variations six times (in lines 9, 12, 14, 42, 56 and 64).

Wulfstan, the public orator and political manipulator, has one of the most distinctive of prose styles. Forthright, emotive and often bombastic, it makes a sharp contrast with the quietly persuasive style of Ælfric, scholarly monk and teacher (see 22/headnote). Wulfstan's style originated, as recent studies have demonstrated, in traditional OE poetical techniques – the 'oral-formulaic' or 'oral-traditional' practices of alliteration, variation and parallelism which we see most obviously in poems such as *Beowulf, Judith* and *The Battle of Maldon*. On these techniques, see the headnote to the most famous of Wulfstan's sermons, the *Sermo Lupi* (Text 25).

In its language, the sermon shows several non-standard late WS features typically found in manuscripts written at Worcester in the early years of the eleventh century (thus indicating an earlier Worcester exemplar for our surviving copy) and possibly classifiable as Mercian or Anglian, but they are not consistently used. Examples are *wurðedon* (13) and *wurðiaþ* (24 and 65, but cf. *weorðiaþ*, 46), *wyrðmente* (67, but cf. *weorðmynt* 77) and *strece* (28, not *stræce*). The form *embe* in 69 often occurs for *ymbe* in unstressed positions, as here; cf. *ymbe* in 40, where the word carries stress. In *lufiad* (24), *d* for *ð* is characteristic of late manuscripts. The interchange of *-a* and *-u*, as in *suna* (75, for nom. *sunu*), is frequent in some late manuscripts.

Further reading

D. Bethurum, ed., *The Homilies of Wulfstan* (Oxford, 1957)

D. Bethurum, 'Wulfstan', in *Continuations and Beginnings: Studies in Old English Literature*, ed. E. G. Stanley (London, 1966), pp. 210–46

E. G. Stanley, *The Search for Anglo-Saxon Paganism* (Cambridge, 1975)

J. Wilcox, 'The Dissemination of Wulfstan's Homilies: the Wulfstan Tradition in Eleventh-Century Vernacular Preaching', in *England in the Eleventh Century: Proceedings of the 1990 Harlaxton Symposium*, ed. C. Hicks (Stamford, 1992), pp. 199–217

D. Wilson, *Anglo-Saxon Paganism* (London, 1992)

T. Hofstra, L. A. J. R. Houwen and A. A. MacDonald, *Pagans and Christians: the Interplay between Christian Latin and Traditional Germanic Cultures in Early Medieval Europe*, Germania Latina 2 (Groningen, 1995)

R. North, *Heathen Gods in Old English Literature*, CSASE 22 (Cambridge, 1997)

Ēalā°, gefyrn° is þæt ðurh° dēofol fela þinga ⌐misfōr⌐ and þæt mancynn tō°
swȳðe° Gode mishȳrde° and þæt hǣðenscype° ⌐ealles tō wīde⌐ swȳðe gederede°
and gȳt° dereð wīde. Ne ⌐rǣde wē⌐ þēah° āhwǣr° on bōcum þæt man ārǣrde°
ǣnig hǣðengyld° āhwǣr on worulde on eallum þām fyrste° þe wæs ǣr° ⌐Nōes
5   flōde⌐. Ac syððan° þæt gewearð° þæt ⌐Nembrod and ðā entas⌐ worhton° þone
wundorlican° stȳpel° æfter Nōes flōde, and ⌐him ðā swā fela gereorda gelamp⌐,
⌐þæs þe bēc secgað, swā ðæra wyrhtena wæs⌐. Þā syððan° tōfērdon° hȳ wīde
⌐landes⌐ and mancyn þā sōna swȳðe wēox°. And ðā ⌐æt nȳhstan⌐ wurdon hī
bepǣhte° þurh ðone ealdan dēofol þe Ādam iū° ǣr beswāc°, swā þæt hī worhton
10   wōlīce° and gedwollīce° him° hǣþene godas and ðone sōðan° God and heora
āgenne° scyppend° forsāwon° þe hȳ tō° mannum gescōp° and geworhte.

Hī nāmon° ēac° him ðā þæt° tō° wisdōme, þurh dēofles lāre°, þæt hȳ
wurðedon° ⌐him⌐ for godas þā sunnan and ðone mōnan for heora scīnendan
beorhtnesse and him lāc° þā æt nȳhstan þurh dēofles lāre offrodon and forlēton°
15   heora Drihten þe hȳ gescōp and geworhte. Sume men ēac sǣdan be° ðām

1 Alas   long ago   because of   too   2 greatly   disobeyed +d   paganism   did harm   3 still
however   anywhere   established   4 idolatry   time   before   5 later   happened   built
6 wonderful   tower   7 afterwards   dispersed   8 increased   9 deceived   long ago   betrayed
10 perversely   heretically   for themselves   true   11 own   creator   scorned   as   created
12 took   also   it   as   teaching   13 worshipped   14 sacrifices *ap*   abandoned   15 about

1 **misfōr** 'went wrong'; sg. vb. because the subj. is *fela*, 'many', a sg. noun/pron.
(followed by a gen. pl. noun).
    2 **ealles tō wīde** 'altogether too widely'. A characteristic Wulfstanian phr.
    3 **rǣde wē** Reduced inflection (*rǣde*, not *rǣdaþ*) in pl. vb. preceding its pron. [§G6f];
cf. 61.
    4–5 **Nōes flōde** Noah's flood, described in Gen 7–8, marks the end of the first age of
the world (see 13/headnote).
    5 **Nembrod and ðā entas** 'Nimrod and the giants'. According to Gen 10.8–10, Nimrod,
a descendant of Noah, was 'mighty' and a 'stout hunter', but he is not associated (as implied
here) with the giants mentioned in Gen 6.4. Nor is he the leader of the presumptuous builders
of the tower of Babel (Gen 11.1–9), though this idea was popular in the medieval period,
being spread by Augustine among others.
    6 **him ðā swā . . . gelamp** impers. vb. with rflx. dat.: 'then as many languages came
about (*or* were created) for them'; *swā* is correl. with *swā* in 7 and *fela* is followed by the
partitive gen.
    7 **þæs þe bēc secgað** 'according to what books say'; i.e. scripture (see also 64).   **swā
ðæra wyrhtena wæs** 'as there were workmen'; *ðæra wyrhtena* is probably gen. because
notionally following *fela* in 6.
    8 **landes** descriptive gen.: 'by land' or, here, 'across the land'.   **æt nȳhstan** 'at last',
or 'in the end'; also 14 and 28.
    13 **him** rflx. pron. with *wurðedon* ('for themselves'), better left untranslated.

scīnendum steorrum þæt hī godas wǣron and āgunnan° hȳ weorðian georne°
and sume hȳ gelȳfdon° ēac on fȳr for his fǣrlicum° bryne°, sume ēac on wæter,
and sume hȳ gelȳfdon on ðā eorðan, ⌐forðan þe⌐ hēo ealle þing fēdeð°. Ac
hȳ mihton° georne° tōcnāwan°, gif hī ⌐cūdon þæt gescead⌐, þæt sē is sōð God
20   þe ealle þās ðing gescōp ūs mannum tō brīce° and tō note° for° his miclan
gōdnesse þe hē mancynne geūðe°. Ðās° gesceafta° ēac ealle dōð swā swā him
gedihte° heora āgen scyppend and ne magon nān þing dōn būtan° ūres Drihtnes
þafunge°, forðām þe nān ōðer scyppend nis° būton se āna° sōða God þe wē
on° gelȳfað° and wē hine ǣnne° ofer ealle ōðre þing lufiad and wurðiaþ mid
25   gewissum° gelēafan°, cweþende mid mūðe and mid mōdes° incundnesse° þæt
sē ān° is sōð God þe ealle ðing gescōp and geworhte.

        Gȳt ðā hǣþenan noldon° bēon gehealdene° on° swā fēawum° godum swā
hȳ ǣr hæfdan ac ⌐fēngon tō wurðienne⌐ æt nȳhstan mistlice° entas° and ⌐strece
woruldmen⌐ þe mihtige wurdan° on woruldafelum° and egesfulle° wǣran ⌐þā
30   hwȳle þe⌐ hȳ leofedon°, and heora āgenum lustum fūllīce° fullēodan°. Ān
man wæs on gēardagum° eardiende° on þām īglande þe Crēta hātte° ⌐se⌐ wæs
Saturnus gehāten, and sē wæs swā wælhrēow° þæt hē fordyde° his āgene bearn,
ealle būtan ānum, and unfǣderlīce° ⌐macode heora līf tō lyre⌐ sōna° on geogoðe°.
Hē lǣfde° swāþēah° unēaðe° ǣnne ⌐tō līfe⌐, þēah ðe hē fordyde þā brōðra
35   elles°, and sē wæs Iōuis gehāten and sē wearð° hetol° fēond. Hē āflȳmde° his
āgene fæder eft of ðām ylcan° foresǣdan īglande þe Crēta hātte and wolde hine

16 began keenly   17 believed sudden heat   18 nourishes   19 could readily
understand   20 enjoyment use because of   21 granted These created things
22 directed without   23 consent is not only   24 in believe alone   25 sure faith of
heart conviction   26 alone   27 would not restricted to few   28 various giants
29 became worldly powers awe-inspiring   30 lived foully followed   31 former days
living is called   32 savage did away with   33 unlike a father early youth   34 left
nevertheless reluctantly   35 otherwise became savage expelled   36 same

18 **forðan þe** conj.: 'because'; also 23 (*forðām þe*), 51 and 61.

19 **cūdon þæt gescead** 'knew reason', i.e. 'had the power of reason'.

28 **fēngon tō wurðienne** The infl. inf. completes the sense of the main vb.: 'took to worshipping'.

28–9 **strece woruldmen** 'violent men of the earth'; i.e. human beings. On the explaining away of pagan gods as mere humans, see headnote.

29–30 **þā hwȳle þe** conj. phr.: 'as long as'.

31 **se** In the following lines, *se* is used freely as either the rel. pron 'who', as assumed here, or the masc. pers. pron. 'he' (*sē*); the specific function is often ambiguous, and depends on the punctuation supplied.

33 **macode heora līf tō lyre** lit. 'made their lives to destruction', i.e. 'destroyed their lives'.

34 **tō līfe** 'alive'.

forfaran° georne gif hē mihte. And ⌜se Iōuis⌝ wearð swā swȳðe gāl° þæt hē ⌜on
his āgenre swyster gewīfode⌝; sēo wæs genamod Iūno and hēo wearð swȳðe
hēalic° gyden° æfter° hǣðenscype geteald°. Heora twā dohtra wǣron Minerua
40   and Uēnus. Þās mānfullan° men þe wē ymbe° specað wǣron getealde for ðā
mǣrostan° godas þā on ðām dagum and þā hǣðenan wurðodon hȳ swȳðe þurh
dēofles lāre°. Ac ⌜se sunu⌝ wæs swāþēah swȳðor° on hǣðenscype gewurðod
þonne° se fæder wǣre and hē is geteald ēac ārwurðost° ealra þǣra goda þe þā
hǣðenan on ðām dagum for godas hæfdon on heora gedwylde°. And hē hātte
45   Þor ⌜ōðrum naman⌝ betwux° sumum þēodum°, ðone° Denisca lēoda° lufiað
swȳðost and on heora gedwylde weorðiaþ geornost. His sunu hātte Mars, se
macode æfre gewinn° and wrōhte°, and saca° and wraca° hē styrede° gelōme°.
Ðysne yrming° æfter his forðsīðe° wurðodon þā hǣðenan ēac for hēalicne god
and swā oft swā hȳ fyrdedon° oððe ⌜tō gefeohte woldon⌝, þonne offrodon hȳ
50   heora lāc ⌜on ǣr⌝ tō weorðunge° þissum gedwolgode°. And hȳ gelȳfdon þæt hē
miclum° mihte heom fultumian° on gefeohte, forðan þe hē gefeoht and gewinn
lufude on līfe.

Sum man ēac wæs gehāten Mercurius on līfe, se wæs swȳðe facenfull°
and, ðēah full snotorwyrde°, swicol° on dǣdum and on lēasbregdum°. Ðone°
55   macedon þā hǣðenan be heora getæle° ēac heom° tō mǣran gode and ⌜æt wega
gelǣtum⌝ him lāc offrodon oft and gelōme þurh dēofles lāre and ⌜tō hēagum
beorgum⌝ him brōhton oft mistlice ⌜loflāc⌝. Ðes gedwolgod wæs ārwurðe ēac

---

37 destroy wanton   **39** exalted   goddess   according to   reckoned   **40** wicked   about
41 greatest   **42** teaching   more greatly   **43** than   most honourable   **44** error   **45** among
nations   whom   people *np*   **47** strife   contention   conflict   enmity   stirred up   often
48 wretch *as*   'journey forth' (death)   **49** went to war   **50** honour (to +*d*)   false god
51 greatly   assist   **53** crafty   **54** plausible in speech   deceitful   trickeries   Him
55 reckoning   for themselves

---

37 **se Iōuis** The def. art. is redundant but could be rendered as 'this'.
37–8 **on . . . gewīfode** 'took . . . as a wife'.
42 **se sunu** i.e. Jove.
45 **ōðrum naman** 'by another name'. Thor was identified with Jove (i.e. Jupiter), probably because he had been the principal god in the Germanic hierarchy; he was worshipped
as Thunor, the 'thunderer', in pre-Christian England.
49 **tō gefeohte woldon** A vb. of motion is needed [§G2d]: 'wanted (to go) into battle'.
50 **on ǣr** 'beforehand', or 'in advance'.
55–6 **æt wega gelǣtum** 'at the junctions of ways', i.e. 'at crossroads'. The ancient
practice of erecting images of Mercury (the god of travellers) at crossroads to avert evil
seems to have been taken over by Germanic peoples.
56–7 **tō hēagum beorgum** Rites at hill-top shrines are connected with the worship of
Woden (i.e. Óðinn, here *Ōðon*).
57 **loflāc** 'praise-offerings'; i.e. offerings in honour of the god.

betwux eallum hǣðenum on þām dagum and hē is Ōðon gehāten ōðrum naman
on Denisce wīsan°. Nū secgað ⸢sume þā Denisce men⸣ on heora gedwylde þæt se
60   Iōuis wǣre, þe hȳ Þor hātað, Mercuries sunu, ⸢þe hī Ōðon namiað⸣, ac hī nabbað
nā riht, forðan þe ⸢wē rǣdað on bōcum⸣, ge on° hǣþenum ge on Crīstenum, þæt
se hetula Iōuis tō° sōðan is Saturnes sunu. And sum wīf hātte Uēnus; sēo wæs
Iōues dohtor and sēo wæs swā fūl and swā fracod° on gālnysse° þæt hyre āgen
brōðor wið hȳ gehǣmde°, þæs þe man sǣde, þurh dēofles lāre, and ⸢ðā yfelan⸣
65   wurðiað þā hǣðenan ēac for° hēalice fǣmnan°.

Manege ēac ōðre hǣþene godas wǣron mistlīce° fundene° and ēac swylce°
hǣþene gydena ⸢on swȳðlicum wyrðmente⸣ geond middaneard, mancynne tō
forwyrde°, ac þās synd þā fyrmestan° ðēh° þurh° hǣðenscipe getealde, þēah ðe
hȳ fūlīce leofodon on worulde. And se syrwienda° dēofol þe ā° swīcað° embe°
70   mancyn gebrōhte þā hǣðenan men on þām hēalicon° gedwylde, þæt° hī swā
fūle° him tō godum gecuran° ⸢þe heora fūlan lust heom tō lage sylfum gesettan⸣
and on unclǣnnesse heora līf eal lyfedan þā hwīle ðe hī wǣran°. Ac sē bið
gesǣlig° þe eal swylc° oferhogað° and ðone sōðan Godd lufað and weorðað þe
ealle þing gescōp and geworhte. ⸢Ān is ælmihtig God on þrym hādum⸣, þæt is
75   fæder and suna and hālig gāst. Ealle þā ðrȳ naman befēhð° ān godcund° miht
and is° ān ēce° God, waldend° and wyrhta ealra gesceafta. Him symle° sȳ° lof
and weorðmynt ⸢in ealra worulda woruld ā būtan ende⸣. Āmen.

---

59 manner   **61** among   **62** in   **63** wicked lust   **64** copulated   **65** as   woman   **66** in
various ways   devised   likewise   **68** ruin   foremost   however [*ðēah*]   in   **69** scheming
ever   is treacherous   towards   **70** profound   so that   **71** vile (people) *ap*   chose
72 existed   **73** blessed   such   scorns   **75** encompass   divine   **76** (he) is   eternal   ruler
ever   be *sbj*

---

59   **sume þā Denisce men** *sume* is an adj.: lit. 'the some Danish men', i.e. 'some of the
Danish men'.
60   **þe hī Ōðon namiað** This clause modifies *Mercuries*, not *sunu*.
61   **wē rǣdað on bōcum** Wulfstan's sources are correct (i.e. that Jove was the son of
Saturn, not Mercury). Over-ambitious attempts to equate Germanic with classical gods led
to such confusion.
64   **ðā yfelan** adj. as noun (acc. sg. fem.), obj. of *wurðiað*: 'that evil (woman)'.
67   **on swȳðlicum wyrðmente** A vb. is needed: 'were held in great honour'.
71   **þe heora . . . sylfum gesettan** 'who (had) made their vile lust as a law for
themselves'.
74   **Ān . . . on þrym hādum** 'one in three persons'. A statement of the Trinity (see
16/48n).
77   **in ealra . . . ende** The modern formula is 'for ever and ever, world without end'; *in
ealra worulda woruld* is an amplified rendering of Lat. *in saecula saeculorum*.

25

The Sermon of the Wolf (Wulfstan's *Sermo Lupi*)

Wulfstan, bishop of Worcester and archbishop of York (see 24/headnote), appears to have been using the pen-name *Lupus* ('wolf') throughout his public life, but the name is memorialised most firmly in the Latin title given to a sermon in OE which we can pinpoint, in one of its versions at least, to the year 1014. This was only one bad year among many for the English during the last decade of the long reign of King Æthelred (978–1016; see p. 62). England had never been free from Danish attacks once they had restarted in earnest in about 980, despite the payment of ever increasing sums of money to the aggressors – £10,000 in 991, £24,000 in 1002 and £48,000 in 1012. Sporadic raids were replaced by major invasions, and that of 1013, led by the king of Denmark, Svein Forkbeard, threatened complete military defeat. After Christmas, Æthelred fled into exile in Normandy. The people of England acknowledged Svein as king and only the latter's fortuitous death in 1014 allowed Æthelred to return. He was to spend two years in hostilities against Svein's son Cnut until his own death in 1016, which brought Cnut to the throne. It is against this background of national humiliation, low morale and pusillanimous action by England's leaders that Wulfstan composed his *Sermo Lupi*.

The sermon is a direct warning to the English people to mend their ways and follow God's laws, or risk even worse disasters. It is meant to shock and is full of the emotive imagery of apocalypse, associating the nation's afflictions with the second coming of Christ and the end of the world. This was a sermon to be performed. The rhetoric is that of the pulpit preacher and so the themes are as much enacted in the style and syntax as developed by careful argument. Nevertheless, some thematic structuring may be discerned. A warning of approaching apocalypse is the point from which Wulfstan starts. The problems of England are going to be seen in terms of the simple polarisation of good and evil: 'we' have let the devil guide us too long and must pull our socks up before it is too late; while we despise God's laws, 'they' (the invaders), heathens though they may be, at least have the virtue that they are obedient to their deities. The sermon moves on to a sustained portrait of society, the world, in chaos. There is anarchy at all levels – hierarchies have collapsed, proprieties are ignored, and there are betrayals of all sorts. In the breakdown of order, kin are treated like strangers, thegns like servants – and all this because of our sins. From line 82, God's anger is a recurrent motif: that is why England has been without victory and the Vikings have been allowed to thrive. Then come the two main 'lists' of our sins (lines 109–21 and 134–9), packed with alliterating or assonating doublets, each ramming home the inescapable equation of sin with social and political decline. Wulfstan caps this with a sort of final proof, a reference to how the original Britons (according to the historian Gildas) similarly suffered invasion as a consequence of sin and God's anger. The sermon draws to an end with a succession of *utan* clauses ('let us . . .'), six in the last twenty-five lines, in which the preacher channels the momentum generated by the relentless series of images of chaos and horror towards what in the circumstances can only appear (or so he hopes) as logical steps: 'let us do what it is necessary for us to do' (144), etc.

All the features of Wulfstan's inimitable prose style – drawing heavily on the traditional techniques of oral poetry – are prominent in the sermon (see 24/head-note). Long balanced sentences are built up with a succession of two-stressed, often alliterating, phrases; there are rhetorical questions, frequent repetitions, and lists given in alliterating and tautological pairs of items. The dictional framework is provided by intensifying adverbs and adverbial phrases, often employing the formula *ealles tō* 'all too . . .' (see lines 11, 22, 53, etc), and the sense of social turmoil is emphasised by many nouns with the adversative prefix *un-* (*uncoþu*, 46, *uncræft*, 163, *undǣd*, 129, etc). Urgency is conveyed in the choice of verbs, too; there are sixteen with the intensifying prefix *for-* (*forbærnan*, 63, *forhealdan*, 21, *forlǣtan*, 158, *forlēogan*, 115, etc). Exclamations add drama to the oral delivery (*lā hwæt!*, 17, *and lā!*, 82, *ēalā!*, 141) and the didactic dimension, signalled by the imperative of the opening sentence, is consolidated by the frequent optative phrases (*gecnāwe se þe cunne*, 40, *understande sē þe wille*, 78). Irony abounds, mainly in expressions of understatement, such as *be ǣnigum dǣle* (126), 'to any extent' (i.e. not at all), and *be suman dǣle* (158), 'to some extent' (i.e. completely).

The language of the *Sermo Lupi* shows characteristic features of late WS, such as the levelling-off of vowels in weak verbs, as in *lehtreð* for *lehtrað* (124), and the use of *-an* for the dative plural, preterite and subjunctive endings (*wǣran*, 8, *spǣcan*, 8, *syndan*, 25, and *forwyrcan*, 130). *Þæne* for *þone* (85, 86, etc) is typical of late WS. Simplification of *synd(an)* to *syn* (57, 58, etc) is a characteristic of Wulfstan's works. Scandinavian influence on his vocabulary (the see of York was in an area of Danish settlement) may be seen in words such as *grið* (67), *griðian* (28), *lagu* (28) and *þrǣl* (85), and in what appear to be translations of Norse compounds, *nȳdgyld* (88) and *þegengylde* (87).

Further reading

D. Bethurum, ed., *The Homilies of Wulfstan* (Oxford, 1957)

D. Whitelock, ed., *Sermo Lupi ad Anglos*, 3rd edn. (London, 1963)

D. Whitelock, 'Archbishop Wulfstan, Homilist and Statesman', *Transactions of the Royal Historical Society* 24 (1942), 25–45

R. G. Fowler, 'Some Stylistic Features of the *Sermo Lupi*', *JEGP* 65 (1966), 1–18

S. Hollis, 'The Thematic Structure of the *Sermo Lupi*', *ASE* 6 (1977), 175–95; repr. in *OE Poetry*, ed. Liuzza, pp. 182–203

R. Jurovics, '*Sermo Lupi* and the Moral Purpose of Rhetoric', in *The Old English Homily and its Backgrounds*, ed. P. E. Szarmach and B. F. Huppé (Albany, NY, 1978), pp. 203–20

A. Orchard, 'Crying Wolf: Oral Style and the *Sermones Lupi*', *ASE* 21 (1992), 239–64

M. Godden, 'Apocalypse and Invasion in Late Anglo-Saxon England', in *From Anglo-Saxon to Early Middle English: Studies Presented to E. G. Stanley*, ed. M. Godden, D. Gray and T. Hoad (Oxford, 1994), pp. 130–62

J. Wilcox, 'The Wolf on Shepherds: Wulfstan, Bishops, and the Context of the *Sermo Lupi ad Anglos*', in *Old English Prose: Basic Readings*, ed. P. E. Szarmach with the assistance of D. A. Oosterhouse, Basic Readings in Anglo-Saxon England 5 (New York, 2000)

⌐*Sermo Lupi ad Anglos quando Dani maxime persecuti sunt eos, quod fuit anno millesimo XIIII ab incarnatione Domini nostri Iesu Cristi*⌐.

Lēofan° men, gecnāwað° ⌐þæt sōð is⌐: ðēos worold is on° ofste° and ⌐hit⌐ nēalǣcð° þām ende. And þȳ° ⌐hit is on worolde aa swā leng swā wyrse⌐ and swā
5 hit sceal° nȳde° for° folces synnan, ⌐ǣr Antecrīstes tōcyme⌐, yfelian° swȳþe and hūru° hit wyrð° þænne egeslic° and grimlic° wīde on worolde. Understandað ēac georne° þæt ⌐dēofol⌐ þās þēode° nū fela gēara dwelode° tō swȳþe° and þæt lȳtle° getrēowþa° wǣran mid° mannum, þēah° hȳ wel° spǣcan°, and unrihta° tō

3 Beloved know in haste **4** is nearing +*d* therefore **5** must necessarily on account of grow worse **6** indeed will become awful terrible **7** clearly people *as* led astray greatly **8** few +*g* loyalties *gp* among though fair spoke wrongs

1–2 **Sermo ... Cristi** A version of this Latin rubric is in three manuscripts (see headnote): 'The sermon of the Wolf to the English, when the Danes were most severely persecuting them, which was in the thousand and fourteenth year from the incarnation of our Lord Jesus Christ'.

3 **þæt sōð is** Probably *þæt* is a pron., with *sōþ* as either adj. or noun: 'what (*or* that which) is true', or 'what (the) truth is' (cf. 29, *Ac sōð is*); but it could be taken as a conj.: 'that the truth is (as follows)'. **hit** Probably a new impers. subj. (used again in the next line), rather than referring back (in false concord) to the fem. noun, *worold*.

4 **hit is ... aa swā leng swā wyrse** lit. 'it is ever so longer so worse', i.e. 'the longer it goes on (*or* things go on), the worse it will get' (*aa* for *ā*).

5 **ǣr Antecrīstes tōcyme** 'before the arrival of Antichrist'. He is the prince of Christ's enemies, referred to by name in 1Jn 2.18 and 22 and 4.3, and 2Jn 7. He is often associated with the strange beasts of Revelation or with 'the man of sin' in 2Thes 2.3–10, who will appear after a great apostasy (renunciation of faith) and claim to be God but will be slain by Christ at the second coming.

7 **dēofol** Om. of the def. art. before *dēofol* is a feature of Wulfstan's style.

fela ⌜rīcsode°⌝ on lande. And ⌜næs⌝ ā° fela manna þe smēade° ymbe° þā bōte°
10 swā georne° swā man scolde ac dæghwāmlīce° man īhte° yfel æfter ōðrum and
unriht rǣrde° and unlaga° manege ealles° tō wīde gynd° ealle þās þēode. And
wē ēac forþām° habbað fela byrsta° and bysmara° gebiden° and gif wē ǣnige
bōte gebīdan° scylan, þonne ⌜mōte wē þæs tō° Gode ernian⌝ bet° þonne wē
ǣr þysan dydan. Forþām mid miclan earnungan° wē geearnedan þā yrmða° þe
15 ūs onsittað° and mid swȳþe micelan earnungan wē þā bōte mōtan æt° Gode
gerǣcan° ⌜gif hit sceal heonanforð gōdiende weorðan⌝.

⌜Lā hwæt⌝, wē witan° ful georne þæt tō° miclan bryce° ⌜sceal micel bōt nȳde⌝
and tō miclan bryne° wæter unlȳtel°, gif man þæt fȳr sceal ⌜tō āhte⌝ ācwencan°.
And micel is nȳdþearf° ⌜manna gehwilcum⌝ þæt hē Godes lage° gȳme° heonan-
20 forð georne and Godes gerihta° ⌜mid rihte⌝ gelǣste°. On° hǣþenum þēodum
ne dear° man forhealdan° lȳtel ne° micel þæs° þe gelagod° is tō gedwolgoda°
weorðunge° and wē forhealdað ǣghwǣr° ⌜Godes gerihta⌝ ealles tō gelōme°. And
ne dear man gewanian° on hǣþenum þēodum ⌜inne ne ūte⌝ ǣnig þǣra þinga þe
gedwolgodan brōht ⌜bið⌝ and tō° lācum° betǣht° bið, and wē habbað Godes hūs
25 inne and ūte clǣne° berȳpte°. And Godes þēowas° syndan mǣþe° and munde°

9 prevailed ever thought about remedy **10** eagerly daily added **11** committed
unlawful acts altogether throughout **12** therefore injuries insults endured **13** expect
from better **14** deservings miseries **15** oppress from **16** obtain **17** know for
breach **18** burning no little quench **19** a necessity (for +d) law *gs* obey *sbj* +*g*
20 dues pay *sbj* Among **21** dare withhold nor of that appointed false gods *gp*
22 worship *ds* everywhere often **23** curtail **24** brought (to +*d*) as offerings
committed **25** utterly plundered servants (*i.e.* priests) respect *ds* protection *ds*

9 **rīcsode** Use of a sg. vb. with *fela* (see also *næs* and *smēade* in 9 and *gelimpð* in 89)
is common in poetry and in the writings of Alfred.   **næs** 'was not', because *fela* is treated
as sg., though followed by gen. pl.

13 **mōte wē** The pl. vb.-inflection is reduced to -*e* because it precedes its pron. [§G6f];
cf. pl. *mōtan* (for *mōton*) in 15.   **þæs... ernian** The vb. takes a gen. obj.: 'deserve it'.

16 **gif hit sceal... gōdiende weorðan** 'if it [i.e. the situation] is... to start [lit.
"become"] improving'.

17 **Lā hwæt** 'Behold!' or 'Listen!'.   **sceal micel bōt nȳde** 'be' must be supplied
[§G2d]: '(there) must (be) a great remedy of necessity', or 'a great remedy is required of
necessity'.

18 **tō āhte** adv.: 'at all'.

19 **manna gehwilcum** 'for each man' (lit. 'of men').

20 **mid rihte** adv. phr.: 'rightly' or 'properly'.

22 **Godes gerihta** 'God's dues (*or* rights)' would include monetary payments to the
church, such as tithes.

23 **inne ne ūte** 'inside or out'; little more than a rhetorical flourish, used again in 25,
etc.

24 **bið** The sg. vb. (as later in the line also) agrees with *ǣnig* rather than *þǣra þinga*,
but *lācum* is pl.

gewelhwǣr° bedǣlde°, and gedwolgoda þēnan° ne dear man misbēodan° on
ǣnige wīsan mid hǣþenum lēodum swā swā man Godes þēowum nū dēð tō
wīde þǣr Crīstene scoldan Godes lage healdan and Godes þēowas griðian°.

    Ac sōð is þæt ic secge: þearf° is þǣre bōte, forþām Godes gerihta wandean°
30   tō lange innan° þysse þēode° on ǣghwylcan° ænde° and folclaga° wyrsedan
ealles ⌐tō swȳþe⌐, and hālignessa° syndan tō° griðlēase° wīde, and Godes ⌐hūs⌐
syndan tō clǣne berȳpte ealdra gerihta and innan bestrȳpte ⌐ǣlcra gerisena⌐.
And wydewan syndan ⌐fornȳdde on unriht tō ceorle⌐ and tō mænege for-
yrmde° and gehȳnede° swȳþe, and earme men ⌐syndan⌐ sāre° beswicene° and
35   hrēowlīce° besyrwde° and ūt of þysan earde wīde gesealde°, swȳþe° unfor-
worhte°, ⌐fremdum tō gewealde⌐ and cradolcild gebēowede° þurh wælhrēowe
unlaga for lȳtelre° þȳfþe° wīde gynd þās þēode, and frēoriht° fornumene° and
⌐þrǣlriht°⌐ genyrwde° and ælmesriht° gewanode and, ⌐hrædest is tō cweþenne⌐,
Godes laga lāðe° and lāra° forsawene°. And þæs° wē habbað° ealle þurh Godes
40   yrre° bysmor° gelōme, ⌐gecnāwe sē þe⌐ cunne°. And se byrst° wyrð gemǣne°,
þēh° man swā ne wēne°, ⌐eallre þysse þēode⌐ būtan God beorge°.

26 nearly everywhere   deprived (of +*d*)   servants   ill-treat   **28** protect   **29** need
dwindled away   **30** within   nation   every   part   public law   **31** sanctuaries   too much
violated   **34** reduced to poverty   humiliated   grievously   deceived   **35** cruelly   ensnared
sold   completely   **36** 'uncondemned' (*i.e.* innocent)   enslaved   **37** petty   theft   rights of
free persons   taken away   **38** rights of slaves   restricted   right to alms   **39** hated   teachings
despised   (because) of that   experience   **40** anger   shame   can   injury   common
41 though   believe (it)   defend (us) *sbj*

    31 **tō swȳþe** One copy of the sermon adds here *syððan Ēadgār geendode*, 'since Edgar
died'. This was on 8 Jul., 975, and there are other references to how things deteriorated
thereafter.   **hūs** The ending of *berȳpte* shows the noun is pl. The allusion here may be
to the selling of church treasures and estates in order to meet payments of 'danegeld' –
protection money given to the Danes (probably the *ungylda* of 47).

    32 **ǣlcra gerisena** gen. of specification: 'of everything that is decent'.

    33 **fornȳdde ... tō ceorle** 'compelled to a husband'; i.e. forced to marry. Widows were
permitted by the church to remarry after one year but were encouraged instead to remain
chaste under the protection of church and king.

    34 **syndan** The one auxil. vb. controls eight past parts. and two adjs. in this breathless
sentence.

    36 **fremdum tō gewealde** 'to strangers into power' (poss. dat.), i.e. 'into the power of
strangers' (see also 74 and 77). The selling of Anglo-Saxons in foreign slave-markets may
have been especially common during the late tenth-century Viking attacks.

    38 **þrǣlriht** Slavery existed within Anglo-Saxon England, too; see 7/headnote.
hrædest is tō cweþenne 'quickest is to tell', i.e. 'to be brief'.

    40 **gecnāwe sē þe** sbj. with optative meaning: 'let (him) understand, he who ...'.

    41 **eallre þysse þēode** dat. of respect: 'for all this nation'.

Forþām hit is on ūs eallum swutol° and gesēne° þæt wē ǣr þysan oftor°
brǣcan° þonne wē bēttan° and þȳ° ⌐is þysse þēode fela onsǣge⌐. ⌐Ne dohte
hit⌐ nū lange inne ne ūte ac wæs here° and hunger, bryne and blōdgyte°, on
45   gewelhwylcan° ende° ⌐oft and gelōme⌐. And ūs stalu° and cwalu°, ⌐stric⌐ and
steorfa°, orfcwealm° and uncoþu°, hōl° and hete°, and rȳpera° rēaflāc° ⌐derede°⌐
swȳþe þearle; and ūs ungylda° swȳðe gedrehtan° and ūs unwedera° foroft°
wēoldan° unwæstma°. Forþām on þysan earde wæs, ⌐swā hit þincan mæg⌐, nū
fela gēara unrihta fela and tealte° getrȳwða° ǣghwǣr mid mannum. Ne bearh°
50   nū foroft gesib° gesibban ⌐þē mā þe⌐ fremdan, ne fæder his bearne, ne hwīlum°
bearn his āgenum fæder, ne brōþor ōþrum. Ne° ūre° ǣnig his līf fadode° swā swā
hē scolde, ⌐ne gehādode regollīce, ne⌐ lǣwede° lahlīce°, ac worhtan° lust ūs° tō
lage ealles tō gelōme and nāþor° ne hēoldan ne lāre ne lage Godes ne manna
swā swā wē scoldan. Ne ǣnig wið° ōþerne getrȳwlīce° þōhte° swā rihte swā hē
55   scolde ac mǣst° ǣlc° swicode° and ōþrum derede ⌐wordes and dǣde⌐, and hūru
unrihtlīce mǣst ǣlc ōþerne æftan° hēaweþ° mid sceandlican° onscytan°: ⌐dō
māre gif hē mæge⌐. Forþām hēr syn on lande ungetrȳwþa° micle for° Gode and
for worolde and ēac hēr syn on earde on mistlice° wīsan hlāfordswican° manege,

42 clear   evident   more often   **43** transgressed   amended   therefore   **44** devastation
bloodshed   **45** nearly every   region   theft   murder   **46** pestilence   cattle-plague   disease
malice   hatred   robbers *gp*   plundering   harmed   **47** excessive taxes   oppressed   bad weather
very often   **48** caused +*g*   crop failures   **49** wavering   loyalties   protects +*d*
50 kinsman   sometimes   **51** Nor   of us   regulated   **52** lay people   according to the law
(we) have made   for us   **53** neither   **54** towards   loyally   has intended   **55** almost
everyone   has betrayed   **56** in the back   stabs   shameful   attacks   **57** disloyalties   towards
58 various   traitors to their lords

43–4 **is þysse þēode fela onsǣge** 'much is assailing this nation'; the adj. *onsǣge* takes
the dat.   **Ne dohte hit** 'It has not availed', i.e. 'Things have not thrived (*or* prospered)'.

45 **oft and gelōme** 'often and frequently', or perhaps, 'over and over again'; a favourite
tautologous phr. of Wulfstan's (to be repeated four times).   **stric** This word occurs only in
Wulfstan's writings and presumably refers to some sort of 'sickness' or 'plague', but the
specific meaning scarcely matters here.

46 **derede** A sg. vb., perhaps because each individual item in the long list is sg.; it takes
a dat. obj. (*ūs*).

48 **swā hit þincan mæg** 'so it might be thought'.

50 **þē mā þe** instr. phr.: 'any more than'.

52 **ne gehādode regollīce, ne** 'neither those in holy orders [lit. "those consecrated",
past part. as noun] according to the rule [lit. "regularly"], nor . . .'. The 'rule' referred to is
the Rule of St Benedict, a form of which was followed by English monks in Wulfstan's
time.

55 **wordes and dǣde** gen. of respect: 'in word and deed'; see also 107.

56–7 **dō māre gif hē mæge** An ironical flourish: 'let him do more if he can [sbj.]'.
Similar phrs. occur in 69, 81, etc.

and ⌐ealra mǣst hlāfordswice se bið⌐ on worolde þæt° man his hlāfordes sāule°
60 beswīce. And ful micel hlāfordswice ēac bið on worolde þæt man his hlāford
⌐of līfe forrǣde⌐ oððon° of lande lifiendne° drīfe, and ǣgþer° is geworden° on
þysan earde. ⌐Ēadweard⌐ man forrǣdde and syððan ācwealde° and æfter þām
forbærnde° ⌐and Æþelrēd man drǣfde ūt of his earde⌐. And godsibbas° and
godbearn° tō fela man forspilde° wīde gynd þās þēode, ⌐tōēacan° ōðran ealles
65 tō manegan þe man unscyldgige° forfōr° ealles tō wīde⌐. And ealles tō manege
hālige stōwa° wīde forwurdan° ⌐þurh þæt þe man sume men ǣr þām gelōgode
swā man nā ne scolde⌐ gif man on° Godes griðe° mǣþe° witan° wolde. And
crīstenes folces tō fela man gesealde ūt of þysan earde nū ealle hwīle. And eal
þæt is Gode lāð°, gelȳfe° sē þe wille.
70   And scandlic° is tō specenne þæt° geworden is tō wīde and egeslic° is tō
witanne þæt° oft dōð tō manege, þe drēogað° þā yrmþe° þæt scēotað° tōgædere
and ⌐āne cwenan gemǣnum cēape bicgað gemǣne⌐ and wið þā āne° fȳlþe°
ādrēogað°, ān after ānum and ǣlc æfter ōðrum, hundum° geliccast° þe for fȳlþe
ne scrīfað°, and syððan wið° weorðe° syllað° of lande fēondum tō gewealde
75 ⌐Godes gesceafte⌐ and his āgenne cēap° þe hē dēore° gebohte°. Ēac wē witan
georne hwǣr sēo yrmð gewearð þæt fæder gesealde bearn wið weorþe and

59 (is) that soul **61** or living both happened **62** killed **63** burned godfathers *ap*
64 godchildren *ap* killed besides +*d* **65** guiltless destroyed **66** places *ap* fell to
ruin **67** to sanctuary respect show **69** hateful believe (it) **70** shameful what
dreadful **71** what commit atrocity (they) put in (*i.e.* club) **72** one foul sin *as*
73 practise dogs most like +*d* **74** care about for a price give up **75** purchase dearly
bought

59 **ealra mǣst hlāfordswice se bið** The adj. *mǣst* describes *hlāfordswice*; *ealra* is a
pron.: 'the greatest treachery of all that there is to a lord'.
   61 **of līfe forrǣde** 'betray from life', i.e. 'kill treacherously'.
   62 **Ēadweard** Edward the Martyr succeeded his father Edgar in 975 and was murdered
at Corfe Gap, Dorset, in 978; his half-brother Æthelred, who took the throne, was implicated.
   63 **and Æpelrēd … earde** Three copies of the sermon, including that in Hatton 113,
om. this sentence, perhaps for diplomatic reasons, because they were made during the reign
of Cnut (1016–35), whose father it was (Svein) who caused Æthelred to flee to Normandy
in 1013. See 8/headnote.
   64–5 **tōēacan … tō wīde** These words have been added in the margin of the manuscript
(i.e. Cotton Nero A. i) in a contemporary hand; they are in the other manuscripts.
   66 7 **þurh þæt þe** 'through this, that', i.e. 'for the reason that'.   **man sume men … ne
scolde** 'someone previously placed (*gelōgode*) certain men (there [i.e. in the *halige stōwa*,
"monasteries"]) as they should never have (done)'. The unsuitable men were probably
so-called 'secular' canons or other non-Benedictines.
   72 **āne cwenan … gemǣne** 'buy a woman in common (*gemǣne*) as a joint (*gemǣnum*)
purchase'.
   75 **Godes gesceafte** 'God's creature'; i.e. the woman, obj. of *syllað*. God sacrificed his
son to 'buy' redemption for humankind.

bearn his mōdor, and brōþor sealde ōþerne fremdum tō gewealde. And eal þæt
syndan micle and egeslice dǣda, understande sē þe wille. And gȳt hit is māre°
and ēac mænigfealdre° þæt dereð þysse þēode; mænige synd forsworene° and
80   swȳþe forlogene° and wed° synd tōbrocene oft and gelōme, and þæt is gesȳne
on þysse þēode þæt ūs Godes yrre hetelīce° onsit, gecnāwe sē þe cunne.

And lā, hū mæg māre scamu þurh Godes yrre mannum gelimpan° þonne ūs
dēð gelōme for āgenum° gewyrhtum°? Ðēh° þrǣla° wylc° hlāforde æthlēape°
and of crīstendōme ˥tō wīcinge weorþe˥ and hit æfter þām eft geweorþe þæt
85   wǣpngewrixl° weorðe ˥gemǣne˥ þegene and þrǣle, gif þrǣl þæne þegen fullīce°
āfylle°, ˥licge ǣgylde ealre his mǣgðe˥. And gif se þegen þæne þrǣl þe hē
ǣr āhte° fullīce āfylle, ˥gylde þegengylde˥. Ful earhlice° laga and scandlice
nȳdgyld° þurh Godes yrre ūs° syn gemǣne, understande sē þe cunne, and fela
ungelimpa° gelimpð þysse þēode oft and gelōme. Ne dohte hit nū lange inne ne
90   ūte ac wæs here and hete on gewelhwilcan ende oft and gelōme, and Engle nū
lange eal sigelēase° and tō swȳþe geyrigde° þurh Godes yrre, and flotmen° swā
strange þurh Godes þafunge° þæt oft on gefeohte° ān fēseð° tȳne° and hwīlum
lǣs hwīlum mā, eal for ūrum synnum. And oft tȳne oððe twelfe, ǣlc æfter
ōþrum, scendað° ˥tō bysmore˥ þæs þegenes cwenan and hwīlum his dohtor
95   oððe nȳdmāgan° þǣr° hē on lōcað þe° lǣt° hine sylfne rancne° and rīcne° and
genōh° gōdne° ǣr þæt gewurde°. And oft þrǣl þæne þegen þe ǣr wæs his hlāford
cnyt° swȳþe fæste and wyrcð° him tō þrǣle þurh Godes yrre.

Wālā° þǣre yrmðe° and wālā þǣre woroldscame° þe nū habbað Engle eal
þurh Godes yrre! Oft twēgen sǣmæn oððe þrȳ hwīlum drīfað þā drāfe° crīstenra
100   manna fram sǣ tō sǣ ūt þurh þās þēode, gewelede° tōgædere, ūs eallum tō

78 greater   **79** more diverse   forsworn   **80** perjured   pledges   **81** violently   **82** befall +d
83 (our) own   deeds   If slaves *gp* any +*gp* escape from   **85** armed encounter   outright
86 slay   **87** owned   cowardly   **88** exactions   among us   **89** misfortunes
91 'victory-less'   demoralised   seamen (*i.e.* Vikings)   **92** consent   battle   put to flight   ten
94 abuse   **95** near kinswoman   while   who   considered   proud   powerful   **96** enough
worthy   happened   **97** binds   makes   **98** Alas   for +d   misery   public disgrace   **99** herds
(*or* herd)   **100** huddled

84 **tō wīcinge weorþe** 'becomes a Viking'.
85 **gemǣne** 'in common to' (with dat.), i.e. 'between'.
86 **licge ǣgylde ealre his mǣgðe** 'he lies unpaid-for to all his family', i.e. 'he will
lie without payment to any of his family'. The penalty for the unlawful killing of a man
was payment to the man's relatives of an amount of *wergeld* (see 7/headnote) that varied
according to the status of the victim. The price for a thane was 1200 shillings.
87 **gylde þegengylde** 'They will pay the price of a thane'. It seems that the Danes were
exacting the thane-price, even if the victim were a runaway slave.
94 **tō bysmore** adv. phr. 'disgracefully'.

woroldscame, gif ⌜wē on eornost ænige⌝ cūþon° āriht° understandan. Ac ealne
þǣne bysmor þe wē oft þoliað° wē gyldað° mid weorðscipe° þām þe ūs scendað.
Wē him gyldað singallīce° and hȳ ūs hȳnað° dæghwāmlīce. Hȳ hergiað° and hȳ
bærnað, rȳpaþ° and rēafiað° and tō scipe lǣdað°. And lā, ⌜hwæt is ænig ōðer⌝ on
105   eallum þām gelimpum° būtan Godes yrre ofer° þās þēode, swutol and gesǣne?

Nis ēac nān wundor þēah° ⌜ūs mislimpe⌝, forþām wē witan ful georne þæt nū
fela gēara mænn nā ne rōhtan° foroft hwæt hȳ worhtan wordes oððe dǣde ac
wearð þes þēodscipe°, swā hit þincan mæg, swȳþe forsyngod° þurh mænigfealde
synna and þurh fela misdǣda: þurh morðdǣda° and þurh māndǣda°, þurh
110   ⌜gītsunga°⌝ and þurh gīfernessa°, þurh stala and þurh strūdunga°, þurh
mannsylena° and þurh ⌜hǣþene unsida⌝, þurh swicdōmas° and þurh seara-
cræftas°, þurh lahbrycas° and þurh ǣswicas°, þurh mǣgrǣsas° and þurh
manslyhtas°, þurh ⌜hādbrycas⌝ and þurh ǣwbrycas°, þurh ⌜siblegeru⌝ and þurh
mistlice forligru°. And ēac ⌜syndan⌝ wīde, swā wē ǣr cwǣdan, þurh āðbricas°
115   and þurh wedbrycas° and þurh mistlice lēasunga° forloren° and forlogen°
mā þonne scolde, and frēolsbricas° and fæstenbrycas° wīde geworhte oft and
gelōme. And ēac hēr syn on earde apostatan° ābroþene° and cyrichatan° hetole°
and lēodhatan° grimme ealles tō manege, and oferhogan° wīde godcundra°

101 could properly   **102** suffer repay (to +*d*) honour   **103** continually humiliate
ravage   **104** rob plunder take   **105** events towards   **106** even if   **107** cared about
108 nation ruined by sin   **109** deadly deeds evil deeds   **110** avarice greed robberies
111 sale of men deceptions   **112** frauds law-breaches transgressions attacks on
kinsmen   **113** manslaughters adulteries   **114** fornications oath-breakings
115 pledge-breakings falsehoods destroyed perjured   **116** failures to observe festivals
fast-breakings   **117** apostates degenerate opponents of the church fierce   **118** tyrants
despisers (of +*g*)   divine

101 **wē ... ænige** 'we any', i.e. 'any of us'.
104 **hwæt is ænig ōðer** 'what else is it'.
106 **ūs mislimpe** impers. vb.: '(it) goes wrong for us'.
110 **gītsunga** This, along with all the nouns in this long catalogue, is probably acc.
pl., though for nouns in -*ung* the ending -*a* may be used for acc. sg. too [§B3d] (see also
strudunga); a sg. noun is often appropriate in trans.
111 **hǣþene unsida** 'heathen abuses'. There were specific penalties in Anglo-Saxon
law for sacrifice, divination and any kind of idol-worship.
113 **hādbrycas** 'injuries to those in holy orders'. There were special penalties for such
acts also.   **siblegeru** 'acts of incest'; the term would apply to any breach of the church's
laws on who could marry whom, which were far stricter than those of most modern Western
countries.
114 **syndan** The auxil. controls two past parts. (*forloren* and *forlogen*) in 115 and its
subj. is the phr. *mā þonne scolde*, 'more (people) than should have been', in 116; it then
controls *geworhte*, also in 116.

rihtlaga° and crīstenra þēawa°, and ⌐hōcorwyrde dysige æghwǣr on þēode
120   oftost⌐ on° þā þing þe Godes bodan° bēodaþ° and swȳþost on þā þing þe æfre
tō Godes lage gebyriað° mid rihte.

And þȳ ⌐is nū geworden wīde and sīde tō ful yfelan gewunan⌐ þæt ⌐menn
swȳþor scamað⌐ nū for gōddǣdan þonne for misdǣdan, forþām tō oft man
mid hōcere° gōddǣda hyrweð° and godfyrhte° lehtreð° ealles tō swȳþe, and
125   swȳþost man tǣleð° and mid olle° gegrēteð° ealles tō gelōme þā° þe riht° lufiað
and Godes ege° habbað be° ǣnigum dǣle°. ⌐And þurh þæt þe⌐ man swā dēð, þæt
man eal hyrweð þæt man scolde heregian° and tō forð lāðet° þæt man scolde
lufian, þurh þæt man gebringeð ealles tō manege on yfelan geþance° and on
undǣde°, swā þæt hȳ ne scamað nā°, þēh hȳ syngian° swȳðe and wið God sylfne
130   forwyrcan° hȳ mid° ealle°. Ac for° īdelan° onscytan° hȳ scamað þæt hȳ bētan°
heora misdǣda, ⌐swā swā bēc tǣcan⌐, gelīce° þām dwǣsan° þe for heora prȳtan°
lēwe° nellað beorgan° ǣr° hȳ nā ne magan, þēh hȳ eal° willan.

Hēr syndan þurh synlēawa°, swā hit þincan mæg, sāre gelēwede° tō manege
on earde. Hēr syndan mannslagan and mǣgslagan and mæsserbanan° and
135   mynsterhatan°, and hēr syndan mānsworan° and morþorwyrhtan, and hēr
syndan myltestran° and bearnmyrðran° and fūle forlegene° hōringas° manege,
and hēr syndan ⌐wiccan and wælcyrian⌐, and hēr syndan rȳperas and rēaferas

---

119 just laws customs **120** about messengers command **121** pertain to **124** insult
derides God-fearing (people) reviles **125** slanders contempt attacks those justice *as*
126 fear to extent **127** praise hates [*lāðeð*] **128** thought **129** wicked deed not sin
sbj **130** do wrong *sbj* (along) with everything (else) because of empty calumnies atone
for **131** like (+*d*) fools pride **132** injury *ds* guard against +*d* until fully
133 injuries of sin hurt **134** priest-slayers **135** enemies of monasteries perjurers
136 whores child-killers adulterous fornicators

119–20 **hōcorwyrde dysige ... oftost** The second adj. (*dysige*) is used as a noun, the
first is modified by *oftost*: 'fools ... most often scornful'.

122 **is ... tō ful yfelan gewunan** 'it has become a very (*ful*) evil custom' (lit. 'as a very
evil custom').

122–3 **menn swȳþor scamað** impers. vb. with acc. (*menn* is acc. pl.): 'it shames people
more greatly', or 'people are more greatly ashamed'. See also 129, 130 and 139.

126 **And þurh þæt þe** The phr. is correl with *þurh þæt* in 128: 'And because ...
(therefore ...)'.

131 **swā swā bēc tǣcan** 'as (the) books teach (that we should)'. These are penitentials
(handbooks of penitence) which list sins and the penances that go with them, assigned by
a priest during confession. The sbj. mood of the vb. (*tǣcan* for *tǣcen*) is used presumably
because the whole tone is one of hypothesis; so also in 140.

137 **wiccan and wælcyrian** 'witches and sorcerers'. There are frequent references to
witchcraft in church laws and penitentials. *Wælcyrian* (lit. 'choosers of the slain') must refer
to some specific kind of witch or supernatural being; the word is cognate with 'valkyrie'.

and worolstrūderas° and, hrædest is tō cweþenne, ⌐māna and misdǣda ungerīm ealra⌐. And þæs° ūs ne scamað nā, ac ūs scamað swȳþe þæt wē bōte āginnan°,

140 swā swā bēc tæcan, and þæt is gesȳne on þysse earman forsyngodan þēode. Ēalā, ⌐micel magan manege gȳt hērtōēacan ēaþe beþencan, þæs þe⌐ ān man ne mehte on hrædinge° āsmēagan° hū° earmlīce° hit gefaren° is nū ealle hwīle wīde gynd þās þēode. And ⌐smēage hūru georne gehwā° hine sylfne and þæs° nā ne latige⌐ ealles tō lange. Ac lā, on Godes naman utan° dōn swā ūs nēod is, beorgan

145 ūs sylfum swā wē geornost magan þē lǣs wē ætgædere ealle forweorðan°.

Ān þēodwita° wæs on Brytta° tīdum ⌐Gildas⌐ hātte. Sē āwrāt° be heora misdǣdum hū hȳ mid heora synnum swā oferlīce° swȳþe God gegrǣmedan° þæt hē lēt æt nȳhstan° Engla here heora eard gewinnan° and Brytta dugeþe° fordōn° mid ealle. And þæt wæs geworden, þæs° þe hē sǣde, þurh rīcra° rēaflāc

150 and þurh gītsunge° wōhgestrēona°, ðurh lēode° unlaga and þurh wōhdōmas°, ðurh biscopa āsolcennesse° and þurh lȳðre° yrhðe° Godes bydela° þe sōþes geswugedan° ealles tō gelōme and clumedan° mid ceaflum° þǣr hȳ scoldan clypian°. Þurh ⌐fūlne⌐ ēac folces gǣlsan° and þurh oferfylla° and mænigfealde synna heora eard hȳ forworhtan and selfe hȳ forwurdan°. Ac wutan° dōn swā

155 ūs þearf is: warnian ūs be swilcan°. And sōþ is þæt ic secge: wyrsan dǣda wē witan mid° Englum þonne wē mid Bryttan āhwār° gehȳrdan. And þȳ ūs is þearf micel þæt wē ūs beþencan and wið God sylfne þingian° georne. And utan dōn swā ūs þearf is: gebūgan° tō rihte and be suman dǣle unriht forlǣtan° and bētan swȳþe georne þæt° wē ǣr brǣcan. And utan God lufian and Godes

138 pillagers **139** for that begin **142** hurry deal with (about) how wretched gone **143** everyone in respect of that **144** let us **145** perish **146** learned man of the Britons called wrote **147** excessively provoked **148** last conquer nobility **149** destroy according to of the powerful **150** coveting ill-gotten gains people's unjust judgements **151** laziness base cowardice messengers **152** kept silent about +g mumbled jaws **153** cry out wantonness gluttony **154** perished let us **155** such (things) **156** among anywhere **157** intercede **158** bow forsake **159** what

138–9 **māna and misdǣda ungerīm ealra** 'a countless number of all crimes and misdeeds'.

141 **micel ... beþencan** The subj. is *manege*, the obj. *micel*: 'many yet can easily bring to mind much in addition'. **þæs þe** 'to the extent that'.

143–4 **smēage ... latige** sbj. vbs. with optative meaning; the subj. of the sentence is *gehwā*: 'let everyone examine ... hesitate'.

146 **Gildas** Late fifth- or sixth-century British writer whose *De excidio Britanniae* ('On the ruin of Britain') lamented the sins of the Britons and saw invasion by what Wulfstan calls 'the army of the Angles' (*Engla here*, 148) as God's punishment. Wulfstan's source seems to be a letter written by Alcuin of York on hearing of the destruction of Lindisfarne by Vikings in 793. Like Gildas (and now Wulfstan), Alcuin attributed such calamities to the sins of the victim peoples. See also 9a/headnote and 10/65–73.

153 **fūlne** adj. describing *gǣlsan*: 'foul'.

160　lagum fylgean° and gelæstan° swȳþe georne þæt þæt wē behētan° þā wē fulluht°
　　　underfēngan° oððon þā þe æt fulluhte ūre forespecan° wǣran. And utan word
　　　and weorc rihtlīce fadian° and ūre ingeþanc° clǣnsian georne and āð and wed
　　　wærlīce° healdan and ⌜sume getrȳwða⌝ habban ūs betwēonan būtan uncræftan°.
　　　And utan gelōme understandan þone miclan dōm þe wē ealle tō sculon° and
165　beorgan ūs georne wið þone weallendan° bryne hellewītes° and geearnian ūs þā
　　　mǣrða° and þā myrhða° þe God hæfð gegearwod° þām þe his willan on worolde
　　　gewyrcað. ⌜GOD ŪRE HELPE⌝. ĀMEN.

160 follow fulfil promised baptism   **161** received sponsors   **162** order conscience
163 carefully deceit (*or* deceits)   **164** must (come)   **165** surging of hell-torment
166 glories joys prepared (for +*d*)

163 **sume getrȳwða** 'some loyalties' or 'a certain loyalty', depending on whether we
interpret *sume* as, respectively, an adj. in concord with *getrȳwða* (acc. pl. fem.), or as a pron.
(acc. sg. fem.) with *getrȳwða* in partitive gen. pl.

167 **GOD ŪRE HELPE** The pron. is the gen. obj. of *helpe* (sbj. with optative meaning):
'May God help us'.

26

The Seafarer

Interpretations of *The Seafarer* have suffered much from its being pigeon-holed almost invariably with *The Wanderer* (Text 38), a near-neighbour in the anthology of secular and religious poetry known as the Exeter Book (see below), as an 'elegy'. There is in fact little that is elegiac about it. Rather, it is an exhortatory and didactic poem, in which the miseries of winter seafaring are used as a metaphor for the challenge faced by the committed Christian, who perceives the spiritual emptiness of an easy life on 'dry land' and actively seeks to earn future heavenly bliss by embracing a rigorous exile from that life. This creates the crucial paradox of the poem, which is exposed in line 33: Seafaring is a wretched business – as the speaker has firmly persuaded us with his own 'true story' – and *therefore* (OE *forþon*) he must embrace it all the more. The more uncompromisingly realistic the opening account of seafaring, the more disturbing – and therefore effective – the paradox. This has been resisted by those readers of *The Seafarer* who have sought a smooth passage through the poem, yet the wilful desire of the seafarer to embrace the very hardship which he has just so graphically evoked is at its heart. At a literal level the message is harshly ascetic, but it is predicated unambiguously on hope and the (metaphorical) 'seafarer' will not therefore have regrets, though the allure of the life on land may still have its effects.

The theology underlying *The Seafarer* is unmistakably that of the most in-fluential of all Christian writers, St Augustine of Hippo (*d.* 430), reflecting his concept of two 'cities' – the earthly city of fallen mankind, who are preoc-cupied with ephemeral human concerns, and the heavenly city of God, where an eternity of bliss awaits those exiles who have waited patiently for salva-tion, distancing themselves from ungodly distractions as they live the life of *peregrini* ('pilgrims'), wanderers and exiles from the ancestral heavenly home (see Augustine's *De ciuitate Dei*, 'On the City of God', bk. 15, ch. 1). Anglo-Saxon Christians will have been familiar with the pilgrim-hermits who put into literal practice the idea of *peregrinatio pro amore Dei*, 'pilgrimage for the love of God'. The *Anglo-Saxon Chronicle* for 891 records the journey of three Irish monks who had cast off from Ireland in a boat without oars and with provisions for only a week, 'because for the love of God they wished to be on a pilgrimage, they cared not where'. The seafaring in *The Seafarer* is as real as we imagine it to be.

Thus in the first part of the poem the 'seafarer' sets up a contrast between himself, all too conscious of his spiritual needs, and complacent land-dwellers; even the delights of springtime in the earthly city only incite him to higher aspirations. A lyrical pivot between this and the second part of the poem is provided by lines 58–66, in which the mind escapes the confines of the body, has a glimpse of the future and returns greedy for it. With his oxymoron 'this dead life' in line 65, the poet encapsulates the hollowness of earthly existence and the second half of the poem becomes a homiletic development of the theme of the transitoriness of that existence. The conclusion is as logical as it is clear: Let us (good Christians, that is) remind ourselves where our true home lies and concentrate on getting there. If a comparison is to be made between *The Wanderer* and *The Seafarer*, it is better done in terms of contrast and complement, rather than congruence. In the course of the former poem, the poet steers his 'wanderer', who is in involuntary exile from human society, to a position of resigned acceptance of his earthly fate and preparedness to accept a new (Christian) perspective on life. The first-person poet of *The Seafarer*, on the other hand, has already accepted the consequences of the Christian position and goes further, voluntarily embracing hardship as a necessary step towards the promised salvation. Close parallels with the ideas of *The Seafarer* will be found in another OE poem, *Resignation*.

The Exeter Book (Exeter, Cathedral Library, 3501, fols. 8–130), in which *The Seafarer* is preserved, was compiled *c*. 975 somewhere in the south of England, and is one of the four major codices of OE poetry to have survived. It acquired its name because it has been in Exeter at least since it was donated to the cathedral library there by Bishop Leofric, some time before his death in 1072. The text of *The Seafarer* reached the Exeter Book in a defective state; there are apparent problems especially around lines 15–16, 23–6 and 112–15 (see notes below). Linguistic evidence for dating or place of composition is inconclusive. The consistent use of the prefix *bi-* rather than *be-* in *bigeat* (6), *bidroren* (16), etc, and *u* for *w* in *huilpan* (21), along with the 'unsyncopated' (i.e. uncontracted) verb-ending *-eð/-að* (as in *limpeð*, 13, and *gewītað*, 52: cf. *limpð*, 15a/7, and *gewīt*, 4/14), have been taken as 'early' features but in fact they occur also in poetical texts known to be of tenth- or eleventh-century composition. The lack of syncopation has been identified also as an Anglian feature, along with forms such as *calde* (8; not *cealde*), *ælda* (77; not *ealda*) and *meotudes* (103; not *metod*, but cf. *meotod*, 108), but as dialectal indications these are all very weak.

Further reading

I. L. Gordon, ed., *The Seafarer* (Manchester, 1979)

D. Whitelock, 'The Interpretation of *The Seafarer*', in *Essential Articles for the Study of Old English Poetry*, ed. J. B. Bessinger and S. J. Kahrl (Hamden, CT, 1968), pp. 442–57

P. A. M. Clemoes, '*Mens absentia cogitans* in the *Seafarer* and *The Wanderer*', in *Medieval Literature and Civilisation: Studies in Memory of G. N. Garmonsway*, ed. D. A. Pearsall and R. A. Waldron (London, 1969), pp. 62–77

R. Woolf, '*The Wanderer, The Seafarer* and the Genre of *planctus*', in *Anglo-Saxon Poetry: Essays in Appreciation for John C. McGalliard*, ed. L. E. Nicholson and D. W. Frese (Notre Dame, IN, 1975), pp. 192–207

R. F. Leslie, 'The Meaning and Structure of *The Seafarer*', in *The Old English Elegies: New Essays in Criticism and Research*, ed. M. Green (Rutherford, NJ, 1983), pp. 96–122

P. Orton, 'The Form and Structure of *The Seafarer*', *SN* 63 (1991), 37–55; repr. in *OE Poetry*, ed. Liuzza, pp. 353–80

MÆG° ic be° mē° sylfum° ⌐sōðgied⌐ wrecan°, Can about me myself relate

sīþas° secgan°, hū ic ⌐geswincdagum⌐ journeys (*or* experiences) tell

earfoðhwīle° oft þrōwade°, times of hardship *ap* suffered

bitre brēostceare° gebiden° hæbbe, 'heart-care' *as* endured

5 gecunnad° in cēole° ⌐cearselda⌐ fela, experienced 'keel' (*i.e.* ship)

⌐atol ȳþa gewealc⌐. Þǣr ⌐mec oft bigeat⌐

nearo° nihtwaco° æt nacan° stefnan° oppressive night-watch ship's prow

þonne° hē be° clifum ⌐cnossað⌐. ⌐Calde⌐ geþrungen° when along pinched

wǣron mīne fēt, forste° gebunden° by frost fettered

10 caldum clommum°, þǣr þā ceare° seofedun° chains *dp* anxieties sighed

⌐hāt⌐ ymb° heortan. Hungor innan° slāt° around within rent

merewērges° mōd°. Þæt se mon ne wāt° of the sea-weary one mind *as* knows

⌐þe him on foldan° fægrost limpeð⌐, land

1 **sōðgied** 'true story (*or* song)' (acc. sg.); cf. the start of *The Wife's Lament* (40/1).

2 **geswincdagum** dat. of time: 'in days of toil'.

5 **cearselda** 'dwellings of sorrow' (partitive gen. after *fela*, 'many'); an ironical metaphor, for *seld* is normally used of solid land-dwellings.

6 **atol ȳþa gewealc** Parallel with *cearselda fela* as a further obj. of *gecunnad*: 'the terrible surging of the waves'. The phr. is partly repeated in 46 and also occurs in the OE *Exodus* (18/10). **mec ... bigeat** 'seized (*or* came upon) me' (*mec* is an alternative form of acc. *mē*); the subj. is *nearo nihtwaco* in 7. Cf. a similar use of the vb. in 40/32.

8 **cnossað** 'beats' or 'dashes'. The switch to the pres. tense is presumably made because an habitual action is now being described; the vb. is intrans. (cf. the related trans. form used in 33). **Calde** dat. of instrument: 'by cold'; similarly *forste* (9) and *caldum clommum* (10).

11 **hāt** Either adj. 'hot' (nom. pl. fem.), describing *ceare*, or adv. 'hotly', modifying *seofedun*; in either case, the ending -e has been elided before the vowel of the following word. 'Hot', meaning here 'intense' or 'violent', makes a telling contrast with the external coldness of the seafarer's situation.

13 **þe him ... limpeð** impers. vb. with dat. rflx. pron.: 'whom [lit. "who, for him"] it suits (*or* happens) most agreeably', or 'for whom it goes most agreeably'.

	hū ic earmcearig°	īscealdne° sǣ	wretched ice-cold
15	ꜰwinterꜰ wunade°	ꜰwræccan lāstumꜰ,	inhabited
	winemǣgum° bidroren°,		kinsfolk bereft (of +d)
	bihongen° hrīmgicelum°; hægl scūrum°		hung about with icicles in showers
	flēag°.		flew
	Þǣr ꜰic ne gehȳrde būtan hlimman sǣꜰ,		
	īscaldne wǣg°. Hwīlum° ylfete° song		wave *as* At times swan's
20	dyde° ic ꜰmē tō gomeneꜰ, ganetes° hlēoþor°		took gannet's cry
	ond huilpan° swēg° fore ꜰhleahtor°ꜰ wera°,		curlew's sound laughter of men
	mǣw° singende° fore medodrince°.		seagull singing mead-drinking
	Stormas þǣr stānclifu° bēotan° ꜰþǣr him stearn		rocky cliff *as* pounded
	oncwæðꜰ		
	īsigfeþera°. Ful° oft ꜰþæt earn bigealꜰ		icy-feathered Very
25	ūrigfepra°. Nǣnig° hlēomǣga°		wet-feathered No protecting kinsman
	fēasceaftig° ferð° frefran° meahte°.		desolate spirit *as* comfort might *sbj*
	Forþon° ꜰhim gelȳfeð lȳtꜰ, sē° þe ꜰāh līfes wyn°		Therefore he pleasure
	gebidenꜰ in burgum° bealosīþa° hwōn°,		cities bitter experiences few +g
	ꜰwlonc ond wīngālꜰ, hū ic wērig oft.		
30	in brimlāde° bīdan° sceolde°.		ocean-path remain had to
	Nāp° nihtscūa°, norþan° snīwde°,		Darkened night-shadow from north snowed

15 **winter** acc. of time: 'in the winter'.   **wræccan lāstum** adv. clause: 'in the paths of exile' (*wræccan* is an *n*-noun, gen. sg.). It has been suggested that this formulaic half-line is a late accretion to the text and has pushed the succeeding phr. into a metrically incomplete line by itself (16).

18 **ic ne gehȳrde būtan** 'I did not hear (anything) except', or 'I heard nothing but'. **hlimman sǣ** acc. and infin. construction [§G6d.i.3] after *gehȳrde*: 'the sea resounding'.

20 **mē tō gomene** poss. dat. *mē*: 'for my entertainment'.

21 **hleahtor** The form is acc., whereas *medodrince* in 22 (also following *fore*, 'for') is dat. Such variation is not unusual in OE (and *for(e)* may take acc. or dat.), but possibly *hleahtor* is an error for *hleahtre*.

23 **þǣr him stearn oncwæð** 'where the tern answered them [i.e. the storms]'.

24 **þæt earn bigeal** *þæt* is puzzling. The simplest solution would be to take it as the demons. pron., but *earn* is usually masc., not neut. If *þæt* is obj. pron. 'it', *bigeal* could be interpreted transitively: 'screamed around it' – but what then is 'it'? Some critics have assumed that the vb. is intrans. and (less convincingly) that *ful oft þæt* is an elliptical way of saying 'it happens very often that'. Perhaps *þæt* is simply a scribal error for *þǣr*, which would offer a parallel with 23a; then again, *þæt* does *sound* better here than *se*.

27 **him gelȳfeð lȳt** impers. vb. with rflx. dat. pron.: 'he little believes'.

27–8 **āh...gebiden** The 3rd-pers. pres. of *āgan* is used instead of a part of *habban* as an auxil. vb. with past part.: 'has experienced'.

29 **wlonc ond wīngāl** 'proud and merry (*or* elated) with wine'. A stock poetic description of the good-living town-dweller, used also in *The Ruin* (37/34).

hrīm° hrūsan° bond°,   hægl fēol on eorþan,   — frost earth *as* bound
corna° caldast.   — of grains
        ⌐Forþon cnyssað nū
heortan geþōhtas⌐   þæt ic hēan° strēamas°,   — deep currents *ap*
35 sealtȳþa° gelāc°,   sylf cunnige°.   — salt-waves' tumult *as* experience
Monað° mōdes lust°   ⌐mæla gehwylce⌐   — Urges desire *ns*
ferð° tō fēran°   þæt ic feor heonan°   — spirit *as* set out from here
⌐elþēodigra   eard⌐ gesēce°.   — seek out *sbj*
Forþon° ⌐nis þæs mōdwlonc   mon ofer eorþan⌐   — Because
40 ne° his gifena° þæs gōd°   ne in geoguþe tō þæs   — nor of (*or* in) gifts generous
   hwæt°   — bold
ne in his dædum tō þæs dēor°   ⌐ne him his dryhten tō þæs hold⌐   — brave
þæt hē ⌐ā his sæfōre   sorge næbbe⌐,
⌐tō hwon hine Dryhten   gedōn wille⌐.
⌐Ne biþ him tō° hearpan hyge⌐   ne tō hringþege°,   — for ring-receiving
45 ⌐ne tō° wīfe° wyn⌐   ne ⌐tō worulde hyht⌐,   — in woman
ne ymbe° ōwiht° elles,   nefne° ymb ȳða gewealc.   — for anything except

---

33–4 Forþon This very common word, with the basic sense of 'for that (reason)' or 'for (the reason) that', may operate as an adv. ('therefore...'), as apparently in 27, or conj. ('... because'). This allows for a certain amount of creative ambiguity in OE. A contrastive meaning, 'yet', is less easy to demonstrate. In this line, *forþon* ('therefore') launches the key paradox of the poem: the seafarer embraces the very hardship he has so graphically evoked. (A case might be made for the trans. 'because', with the sentence beginning *monað* then consequential, but that reduces the dynamic of the poem to a mere list of loosely connected ideas.) **cnyssað nū heortan geþōhtas** The probable subj. of the vb. is the phr. *heortan geþōhtas*, with *heortan* as gen. sg. of an *n*-noun and the vb. intrans.: 'the thoughts of my heart press (*or* urge) now (that...)'. Alternatively, *heortan* could be the acc. sg. obj. of *cnyssað* taken as trans.: '(my) thoughts press (my) heart now (that...)'.

36 mæla gehwylce dat. of time: 'time and again' (lit. 'in each of times').

38 elþēodigra eard 'the land of foreigners (*or* strangers)'. This may be an unspecified place of further pilgrimage or exile, or perhaps heaven (see Heb 11.13–16 and Augustine, *De ciuitate Dei*, bk. 15, ch. 1).

39 nis þæs...ofer eorþan Here, and in 40–1, *þæs* is used as an adv. (with additional *tō* in three cases) and is best translated 'so': 'there is not anyone on earth so proud of heart'.

41 ne him...þæs hold 'nor (a man) whose lord is so gracious to him'.

42 ā his sæfōre sorge næbbe 'never has anxiety about his sea-voyage [gen. of respect]'.

43 tō hwon...gedōn wille '(as) to what the Lord will bring him to', or 'as to how the Lord will treat him'.

44 Ne biþ him...hyge poss. dat.: 'his thought is not'.

45 ne...wyn 'nor (is his) joy...'.   **tō worulde hyht** 'in hope of the world'; i.e. trust in worldly things.

Ac ā° hafað ⌈longunge⌉   sē þe on lagu° fundað°.   ever   sea   sets out
Bearwas° ⌈blōstmum nimað⌉,   byrig ⌈fægriað,   Groves
wongas wlitigað⌉,   woruld ōnetteð°.   hurries onward
50 Ealle þā° gemoniað°   ⌈mōdes fūsne   these (things)   urge
sefan⌉ tō sīþe°,   ⌈þām þe⌉ swā þenceð°,   journey   intends
on flōdwegas°   feor ⌈gewītað°⌉.   ocean-paths   sets out
Swylce° ⌈gēac°⌉ monað   ⌈gēomran reorde⌉,   Likewise   cuckoo
singeð sumeres weard°,   sorge bēodeð°   watchman   announces
55 ⌈bitter⌉ in brēosthord°.   Þæt se beorn° ne wāt,   heart   man
ēstēadig° secg°,   hwæt ⌈þā sume⌉ drēogað°   'favour-blessed'   man   suffer
þe þā ⌈wræclāstas⌉   wīdost° lecgað°.   most widely   follow
⌈Forþon⌉ nū mīn hyge hweorfeð°   ofer°   journeys   beyond
     hreþerlocan°,   breast
mīn mōdsefa°   mid° mereflōde°   mind *ns*   with   ocean tide
60 ofer hwæles° ēþel°   hweorfeð wīde,   whale's   home

47 **longunge** Probably the 'longing' or 'yearning' is for the onward journey and the half-line is a restatement of the seafarer's spiritual urge; but he might be making the point that, even though he turns his back on earthly pleasures, he is still human enough to have longings for them.

48–9 **blōstmum nimað** Apparently, 'take with blossoms', i.e. 'come into flower', although there are no other examples in OE of *niman* construed thus with the dat. (and *blōstman*, acc. pl., may have been intended).   **fægriað ... wlitigað** If these vbs. are trans., the subj. of both is still *bearwas*, and the (acc.) objs. are *byrig* and *wongas*, respectively: '(they) make the cities lovely, adorn the meadows'. Alternatively, the vbs. may be taken as intrans. and the nouns as their (nom.) subjs.: 'the cities become lovely, the meadows become beautiful'.

50–1 **mōdes fūsne sefan** Both *sefan* and *fusne* are best taken as objs. of *gemoniað*: 'the (one) eager of spirit, his heart'.   **þām þe** Here *þām* is a pron.: 'in the one who'.

52 **gewītað** The ending -*eð* would be more usual in the sg. Many editors emend to inf. *gewītan*, which is then the complement of *þenceð* in 51.

53 **gēac** The cuckoo as a bird of lament with a sad voice appears also in the OE poem *The Husband's Message* (23), and is a notable feature of early Celtic elegies.   **gēomran reorde** dat. of manner: 'with sad voice'.

55 **bitter** If the adj. describes *sorge*, 'sorrow', it is acc. sg. fem., with terminal *e* elided before the vowel of *in*. Alternatively, it may qualify *weard* (nom. sg. masc.), in which case its form is correct.

56 **þā sume** *þā* is probably the demons. pron. in apposition with pron. *sume*: 'those ones', i.e. 'certain people' or simply 'some'.

57 **wræclāstas** The 'paths of exile' (acc. pl.) are a recurring motif in OE poetry; see *The Wanderer* (38/5 and 32).

58 **Forþon** Again the paradoxical 'therefore'. The active mind of the seafarer anticipates the intended journey and returns with longing. The repetition of *forþon* in 64 may be best interpreted as correl., 'because', marking the start of the explanation of the paradox; but it might be argued to be a parallel 'therefore'.

⌜eorþan scēatas⌝,   cymeð eft° tō mē   again
gīfre° ond grǣdig;   gielleð° ⌜ānfloga⌝,   avid   cries
hweteð° on ⌜wælweg⌝   hreþer° unwearnum°   incites   heart *as*   irresistibly
ofer holma° gelagu°.   Forþon mē hātran° sind   seas'   expanses   more inspiring
65   Dryhtnes drēamas°   þonne þis dēade līf,   joys
lǣne° on londe.   Ic gelȳfe nō°   fleeting   not
þæt ⌜him° eorðwelan°   ēce° stondeð°;   earthly riches   eternally   remain
simle° ⌜þrēora sum   þinga gehwylce⌝   always
ǣr his tīdege°   ⌜tō twēon weorþeð⌝:   final day
70   ⌜ādl° oþþe yldo°   oþþe ecghete°⌝   sickness   old age   sword-violence
⌜fǣgum fromweardum⌝   feorh° oðþringeð°.   life *as*   wrests
⌜Forþon þæt bið eorla gehwām   æftercweþendra
lof lifgendra   lāstworda betst,
þæt hē gewyrce⌝,   ǣr hē on weg ⌜scyle⌝,
75   ⌜fremum⌝ on foldan°   wið° fēonda nīþ°,   earth   against   malice
dēorum° dǣdum   dēofle tōgēanes°,   brave   against +*d*
þæt hine ælda° bearn°   æfter hergen°   of men   children *np*   may praise *sbj*
ond his lof° siþþan°   lifge° mid englum   glory   then   may live *sbj*

61 **eorþan scēatas** A phr. parallel with *hwæles ēþel*: '(over) the regions (*or* surfaces) [acc. pl.] of the earth'.

62 **ānfloga** i.e. the cuckoo; almost certainly not the soul, as some critics have suggested.

63 **wælweg** Probably for *hwælweg*, 'whale's path', i.e. the sea (cf. 60); *w*- for *hw*- occurs elsewhere in the Exeter Book. But conceivably *wæl* is the word meaning 'slaughter' or 'the dead'.

67 **him** 'for him'. There is no obvious antec. for the pron. here, nor for *his* in 69, but both clearly refer to 'a man', the land-living man of 71 who is subject to the trials of mortal life and fated to die (*fǣge* and *fromweard*).

68 **þrēora sum** 'one of three (things)'. **þinga gehwylce** 'in each of circumstances', i.e. 'invariably'.

69 **tō twēon weorþeð** 'becomes (a matter) for doubt'.

70 **ādl ... yldo ... ecghete** These three earthly enemies are listed also by King Hrothgar in *Beowulf*, 1735–9, in a speech about kingship and destiny.

71 **fǣgum fromweardum** 'from (the man) fated to die (and) about to depart' (*fromweard*, lit. 'from-ward', on the pattern of 'to-ward').

72–4 **Forþon þæt bið ... hē gewyrce** The syntax is complex but the meaning is clear: 'Therefore for each man (*eorla gehwām*) the best of reputations to leave behind (*lāstworda* ['track-words']) is the praise (*lof*) of those who will speak after his death (*æftercweþendra*), the living (*lifgendra*), that he may bring about (*gewyrce*) ...'. The pron. *þæt* in 72 is correl. with conj. *þæt* in 74, and both are better left out of the trans. The obj. of *gewyrce* is the clause beginning *þæt hine* in 77.

74 **scyle** A vb. of motion is needed: 'must (go)' [§G2d].

75 **fremum** dat. of instrument: 'by good actions'; this is an emendation of the manuscript's *fremman*, which is impossible to construe plausibly. The phr. *dēorum dǣdum* in 76 is parallel.

⌐āwa tō ealdre⌐,   ēcan līfes ⌐blǣð⌐,   splendour

80   drēam⌐ mid dugeþum°. ⌐Dagas° sind gewitene°⌐,   hosts Days departed

ealle onmēdlan°   eorþan rīces;   pomps

⌐nearon⌐ nū cyninges   ne cāseras°   emperors

ne goldgiefan   swylce° iū° wǣron   such as once

þonne hī ⌐mǣst mid° him°   mǣrþa⌐ gefremedon°   among themselves performed

85   ond on dryhtlicestum°   dōme° lifdon.   most noble renown *ds*

Gedroren° is þēos duguð° eal,   drēamas sind gewitene,   Perished company

wuniað° þā wācran°   ond þās woruld healdaþ°,   remain weaker (people) inhabit

⌐brūcað þurh bisgo⌐.   Blǣd is gehnǣged°,   humbled

eorþan indryhto°   ealdað° ond sēarað°   nobility *ns* ages withers

90   ⌐swā nū monna gehwylc⌐   geond° middangeard°.   throughout world

⌐Yldo him on fareð⌐,   onsȳn° blācað°,   face grows pale

gomelfeax° gnornað°,   wāt his iūwine°,   grey-haired (man) mourns past friends

æþelinga bearn,   eorþan forgiefene°.   committed (to +*d*)

Ne mæg ⌐him þonne se flǣschoma⌐,   þonne ⌐him⌐

þæt feorg° losað°   life fails

95   ne swēte° forswelgan°   ne sār° gefēlan°,   sweetness swallow pain *as* feel

ne hond onhrēran°   ne mid hyge° þencan.   move mind

⌐Þēah þe græf wille   golde strēgan

brōþor his geborenum⌐,   ⌐byrgan be dēadum⌐

79–80 āwa tō ealdre 'always in eternity', i.e. 'for ever and ever'. **blǣð, drēam** These appear to be parallel with *lof* as subjs. of *lifige*, i.e. states which it is hoped will endure for ever. *blǣð* is for *blǣd*, showing a confusion of *ð* and *d* common in late manuscripts.

80 Dagas sind gewitene . . . For an expression of the transience of the world similar to that expressed here (80–102), particularised in terms of the passing of the heroic way of life, see *The Wanderer* (38/92–6, etc). In 82, cf. the rhetorical question from the author of the tenth Vercelli Homily: 'Where are the powerful emperors and kings that there once were?' There are also classical parallels.

82 nearon 'are not' (*ne + earon* [§G1a.ii]). The scribe wrote *nǣron* ('were not'), which seems illogical; hence the emendation.

84 mǣst . . . mǣrþa 'the greatest [acc.] of glorious deeds'.

88 brūcað þurh bisgo '(they) use (it) in toil', or 'occupy it with trouble'.

90 swā nū monna gehwylc 'just as now each man (does)'.

91 Yldo him on fareð Here *on* is an adv. (and takes the alliterating stress): 'For him old age marches onwards (*or* advances)'.

94 him . . . se flǣschoma poss. dat.: 'his body'; this is the subj. of the vbs. in 95–6. **him** poss. dat., referring either to the dying man or to his body.

97–8 Þēah þe . . . his geborenum The subj. is *brōþor* and the obj. *græf*: 'Though a brother may wish to strew the grave with gold for his brother' (*geborenum*: lit. 'one born [in the same family]'). These lines carry an implicit censure of heathen burial practices (cf. Text 24) and express the Christian warning that material wealth will count for nothing on Judgement Day.

māþmum mislicum   ⌜þæt hine mid wille⌝,

100 ⌜ne mæg þære sāwle   þe biþ synna ful

gold tō gēoce⌝   for° Godes egsan°,   in face of   awesomeness

þonne° ⌜hē⌝ hit ǣr hȳdeð°   þenden° hē hēr   (even) when   hides   while

leofað°.   lives

Micel biþ se meotudes° egsa   ⌜for þon hī sēo molde oncyrreð⌝.   creator's

Sē° gestaþelade°   stīþe° grundas°,   He   established   firm   foundations

105 eorþan scēatas   ond ūprodor°.   the heavens above

⌜Dol° biþ sē þe him his Dryhten ne ondrǣdeþ°⌝:   cymeð   Foolish   fears

him° se dēað unþinged°.   to him   unexpected

Ēadig° bið sē þe ēaþmōd° leofaþ: cymeð him   Blessed   humble

sēo ār° of heofonum.   grace

Meotod him° þæt mōd° gestaþelað°   forþon hē   in him   heart   makes firm

in his meahte° gelȳfeð.   might

Stīeran° mon sceal strongum° mōde   ond ⌜þæt on   Restrain +d   headstrong

staþelum healdan⌝;

110 ond, ⌜gewis wērum   wīsum⌝ clǣne°,   pure

scyle monna gehwylc   ⌜mid gemete°⌝ healdan   moderation

⌜wiþ° lēofne°   ond wið lāþne° bealo°⌝   against   friend   enemy   malice

---

98–9 **byrgan . . . mislicum** The infin. is still governed by *wille* and *deādum* (adj. as noun) may be sg. or pl.; either 'to bury (it [gold]) beside the dead (man), along with various treasures', or 'to bury him [the brother] among the dead, with various treasures'. **þæt hine mid wille** 'that he may wish (to go) with him' (*mid* may take acc. as well as dat.).

100–1 **ne mæg þære sāwle . . . tō gēoce** The vb. 'be' is required for the modal [§G2d]: 'cannot (be) of (any) help to the soul'.

102 **hē** i.e. the dead man.

103 **for þon hī . . . oncyrreð** Here *þon* is best taken as an instr. pron., with antec. *egsa*, and *hī* as a rflx. pron. (acc. sg. fem.) with antec. *sēo molde*: 'before which the earth turns itself away'. Cf. Rev 20.11.

106 **Dol . . . ondrǣdeþ** This line occurs in almost the same form in the OE poem *Maxims I*, 35. Rflx. *him* is best not trans.

109 **þæt on staþelum healdan** 'keep it on firm foundations'; i.e. under control.

110 **gewis wērum** 'true to (his) pledges'; but, conceivably, the noun here is *wer* 'man' and the meaning 'reliable among men'. **wīsum** dat. of respect: 'in (his) ways'.

111 **mid gemete** The wisdom of acting with moderation is emphasised also in *The Wanderer* (38/65–72).

112 **wiþ lēofne . . . bealo** This and the next three lines are clearly incomplete. As it stands, the meaning of this one seems to be '(govern with moderation) malice against friend and against foe'. One speculative restoration adds *lufan* at the beginning: 'love towards friend, malice (*bealo*) towards foe'.

⌐þēah þe hē hine wille fȳres   fulne

oþþe on bǣle   forbærnedne

115   his geworhtne wine⌐.   Wyrd° biþ swīþre°,   Fate   stronger

meotud meahtigra°   þonne ǣnges° monnes gehygd°.   mightier   any   conception

Uton° wē hycgan°   hwǣr wē hām āgen°   Let us   consider   may have *sbj*

ond þonne geþencan°   hū wē þider° cumen°   think   there   may come

ond wē þonne ēac tilien°   ⌐þæt wē tō mōten⌐   strive *sbj*

120   in þā ēcan   ēadignesse°,   blessedness

þǣr is līf gelong°   in° lufan Dryhtnes,   dependent   on

hyht° in heofonum.   Þæs° sȳ° þām halgan°   hope   For that   be   holy one

þonc°   thanks (to +*d*)

þæt hē ūsic° geweorþade°,   wuldres ealdor°,   us   (has) honoured   prince

ēce Dryhten,   in° ealle tīd°.   through   time

125   Āmen.

113–15 **þēah þe ... wine** If we assume that the antec. of *hine* is *lāþne* (112), a possible interpretation is: 'though he may wish him [his foe] full of fire and the friend he has made (*geworhtne*) consumed on the funeral-pyre (*bǣle*)'. A contrast is then being made between the fires of hell for the foe and a proper cremation for the friend.

119 **þæt wē tō mōten** adv. *tō* ('thither'), belonging to an unexpressed vb. of motion: 'that we may (arrive) there'.

V

TELLING TALES

The telling of tales is one of the world's oldest professions. In pre-literate societies it was the bard, minstrel, poet or (to use an OE term) *scop* on whom the roles not only of entertainer but also of historian fell. The oral poet was the keeper of the collective memory and transmitter of the narratives which recreated a nation's or tribe's past and the achievements of its heroes, and thereby forged its present sense of identity. The OE poem known as *Widsith*, which is a sort of catalogue of the professional poet's repertoire, shows this well, and so does *Deor*, given below in section VI (Text 36). The poet of *Beowulf*, too, never misses the chance to promote his own craft within his story. After Beowulf's defeat of Grendel, the monster's blood is hardly dry on the ground before a bard among the Danish king's thegns is produced to commemorate the hero's exploit in song. Then, that same evening, a minstrel performs at a celebratory feast, applying a timely check on the triumphalism of the occasion by telling the sad tale of the Danish princess Hildeburh's ill-fated marriage to Finn of the Frisians (Text 31a below). It is a reminder to the Danes of how sorrow invariably seems to follow joy, and the allusive way in which this tale is told shows that the *Beowulf*-poet's audience were thoroughly familiar with it. Indeed, they may have known it from a version of another OE poem which has come down to us, though only in a fragment – *The Fight at Finnsburh* (Text 32). The surviving lines present a blow-by-blow account of an encounter between Danes and Frisians which is only lightly sketched in the longer poem. The arrival of Grendel's mother to avenge her son after the Danish celebrations proves the minstrel's point about changing fortunes. The details of Beowulf's subsequent tracking down and killing of this she-monster suggest how close in character monsters and heroes may be (Text 29b). They illustrate, too, with the inclusion of an episode of divine intervention to enable the hero to complete his task, how Christianity can be used to colour a tale of the Germanic pagan world without diminishing it.

Whatever its origins in, and debts to, oral culture, *Beowulf* itself, in the form in which we have it, is a work of written literature. As the idea of written historical record took root and developed after the coming of Christianity to Anglo-Saxon England, the demand for the minstrel's creative talents did not lessen. The distinction between story and history is a modern one, and in any case all written history is to a greater or lesser extent creative in its selection and shaping of fact for a particular audience or for a particular polemical purpose. The *Anglo-Saxon Chronicle* illustrates this point well. Every now and then in the humdrum year-by-year record a space is cleared for something more substantial and artful. Thus an eighth-century dynastic squabble between King Cynewulf of Wessex and his brother Cyneheard is transformed into a carefully constructed exemplum about loyalty to a leader, the language of which may reflect its own origins in oral reportage (Text 29). A similar theme is celebrated in a poem (this one not in the *Chronicle*) about an encounter between the English and the Danes which took place right at the end of the tenth century. *The Battle of Maldon* (Text 30) was composed by a poet well versed in the old heroic narrative style. The circumstances of composition are elusive but the traditional craft by which military defeat is processed into moral victory is clear.

This section of tales begins, however, not with Germanic material at all but with two texts which reveal an Anglo-Saxon taste for the stories of the late antique Mediterranean world also. One is an OE translation of a hugely popular Latin work, known as the 'Letter of Alexander', in which the great king tells of his adventures in India. In the extract given here, he encounters magical trees which tell future events – including his own early death (Text 28). Latin was also the language in which the genre of what later would be termed 'romance' reached England, in the form of the story of *Apollonius of Tyre*, which enjoyed as much popularity as the Alexander legends in the medieval period. An OE translation, included curiously in a manuscript of the works of Wulfstan, is the earliest known example of the genre in England. In the extract with which this section begins (Text 27), we encounter something rare indeed in Anglo-Saxon literature – a love story.

Further reading

J. E. Cross, 'The Ethic of War in Old English', in *England before the Conquest: Studies in Primary Sources Presented to Dorothy Whitelock*, ed. P. Clemoes and K. Hughes (Cambridge, 1971), pp. 269–82

J. Opland, *Anglo-Saxon Oral Poetry: a Study of the Traditions* (New Haven, CT, and London, 1980)

T. A. Shippey, 'Boar and Badger: an Old English Heroic Antithesis?', *LSE* n.s. 16 (1985), 220–39

N. Howe, *Migration and Mythmaking in Anglo-Saxon England* (New Haven, CT, and London, 1989)

S. S. Evans, *Lords of Battle: Image and Reality of the Comitatus in Dark-Age Britain* (Woodbridge, 1997)

J. D. Niles, *Homo Narrans: the Poetics and Anthropology of Oral Literature* (Philadelphia, PA, 1999)

27

Falling in Love
(from *Apollonius of Tyre*)

The story of *Apollonius of Tyre* started life as a Greek popular narrative, probably in the second or third century BC. It was translated into Latin a number of times and subsequently found its way into most of the European vernaculars, but the OE version is the earliest of these known. The popularity of this somewhat gaudy and gory tale, with its successive themes of incest, deception, murder and enforced prostitution, was as long-lasting as it was widespread: in the late sixth century a celebrated poet and man of letters, the bishop Venantius Fortunatus, could allude almost casually to Apollonius as a celebrated figure of exile, and the fourteenth-century poet Gower devoted an entire book of his *Confessio Amantis* to retelling the tale. Chaucer, however, was less approving, characterising it in the introduction to his *Man of Law's Tale* (lines 81–5) as 'so horrible a tale for to rede'. Shakespeare used it for his *Pericles Prince of Tyre*.

The OE version is markedly less spectacular than some of the later retellings, thanks in part to its evidently pedestrian rendering of a now-lost Latin source, including what appear to be a number of simple blunders, but mostly because that part of the tale which contains the most salacious elements is absent from the extant text. This was probably a deliberate omission by the translator, but the loss of some pages from the (only) manuscript, Cambridge, Corpus Christi College 201 (B), makes it impossible to be certain. The manuscript was copied in the early or middle eleventh century and mainly consists of legal, juridical and homiletic texts associated with Archbishop Wulfstan of York (see Texts 24 and 25). The explanation for the tale's inclusion might be that Apollonius was seen as having saintly qualities, in view of his many stoically borne sufferings.

A nobleman from Tyre, Apollonius has been shipwrecked in Cyrenaica (part of present-day Libya) while on the run from the king of Antioch, after discovering the latter's incestuous relationship with his daughter. The Cyrenaican king, Arcestrates, has observed the ragged and destitute Apollonius taking part in a ball game and has been so impressed with his nobility that he has invited him to a feast. As the extract begins, the king's daughter is seeing the multi-talented Apollonius for the first time. Soon infatuated, she contrives to get closer by persuading her father that she could benefit from the stranger's pedagogical skills. This episode is remarkable for being one of only a handful in OE literature in which the emotional life of a female figure is explored.

Several obvious scribal errors have been corrected in the text below. Late WS spelling features include some levelling, as in *-an* for the subjunctive ending *-en* (*cuman*, 69, and *berēafian*, 69) and *namon* for *naman* (13, but cf. *naman* elsewhere), and the intrusion of *c* after *g* (*onfengc*, 84, but cf. *onfeng*, 71); *cyning* occurs both in full and contracted form, with or without intrusive *c* (1, 4, 17, 36, 39, etc). The form *lēofa* is used consistently before a feminine noun, where we might expect the strong adjectival form *lēofu* (6, 18, 25 and 77). The translator has mostly kept the Latin grammatical forms of the name of the hero, including not only the accusative (*Apollonium*, 66 and 80) and dative (*Apollonio*, 3, 10, etc), but also the 'vocative' case (used for direct address), which OE does not have (*Apolloni*, 22, 30, etc); but an anglicised form of the name with dative ending is used also (*Apollonige*, 36, 75 and 79).

Further reading

P. Goolden, ed., *The Old English 'Apollonius of Tyre'* (London, 1958)

E. Kobayashi, 'On the "Lost" Portions in the Old English *Apollonius of Tyre*', in *Explorations in Linguistics: Papers in Honor of Kazuko Inoue*, ed. G. Bedell *et al.* (Tokyo, 1979), pp. 244–50

J. McGowan, 'The Old English *Apollonius of Tyre* and the Latin Recensions', *Proceedings of the Patristic, Medieval, and Renaissance Conference* 12–13 (1989), 179–95

A. R. Riedinger, 'The Englishing of Arcestrate: Woman in Apollonius of Tyre', in *New Readings on Women in Old English Literature*, ed. H. Damico and A. H. Olsen (Indianapolis and Bloomington, IN, 1990), pp. 292–306

E. Archibald, *Historia Apollonii Regis Tyri. English and Latin 'Apollonius of Tyre': Themes and Variations* (Woodbridge, 1991)

⌈Mid þī ðe⌉ se cyning þās word gecwæð°, ðā° fǣringa° þār° ēode° in ðæs cynges iunge° dohtor and cyste° hyre fæder and ðā ymbsittendan°. ⌈Þā hēo becōm° tō Apollonio, þā⌉ gewænde° hēo ongēan° tō hire fæder and cwæð: 'Ðū° gōda° cyningc and ⌈mīn se lēofesta fæder⌉, ⌈hwæt⌉ is þes iunga man þe° ongēan°

1 (had) said   then   by chance   there went   **2** young   kissed   those sitting around   came
3 turned   back   You   good   **4** who   opposite

1 **Mid þī ðe** conj. phr. with instr. *þī*: 'When...'. It is used again in 17, 19 and 48 (with *þȳ*). 'These words' just spoken by the king were an injunction to Apollonius to 'be happy' and put his hope in God for better things.

2–3 **Þā..., þā...** A common OE construction, with correl. conj. and adv.: lit. 'When..., then...', but 'then' is best om. in trans.

4 **mīn se lēofesta fæder** The def. art. *se* is redundant in trans.: 'my dearest father'. **hwæt** 'what', in the sense 'what kind'; modern idiom would use 'who'.

5 ðē° on swā° wurðlicum° setle° sit mid° sārlicum° andwlitan°? Nāt° ic hwæt hē
besorgað°.' Ðā cwæð se cyningc: 'Lēofa dohtor, þes iunga man is forliden° and
hē gecwemde° mē ⌐manna betst on ðām plegan⌐; forðām° ic hine gelaðode° tō
ðysum ūrum° gebēorscipe°. Nāt ic hwæt hē is ne° hwanon° hē is, ac° gif ðū
wille° witan° hwæt hē sȳ°, axsa° hine, forðām° ⌐þē gedafenað⌐ þæt þū wite°.' Ðā
10 ēode þæt mæden tō Apollonio and mid forwandigendre° sprǣce° cwæð: '⌐Ðēah
ðū stille° sȳ and unrōt°, þēah⌐ ic þīne æðelborennesse° on ðē gesēo°. Nū þonne,
⌐gif ðē tō hefig ne þince⌐, sege° mē þīnne naman, and þīn gelymp° ārece° mē.'
Ðā cwæð Apollonius: 'Gif ðū for nēode° axsast æfter mīnum namon, ic secge
þē ic hine° forlēas° on° sǣ. Gif ðū wilt mīne æðelborennesse witan, wite ðū þæt
15 ic hig° forlēt° on° Tharsum°.' Ðæt mæden cwæð: 'Sege mē gewīslicor° þæt ic hit
mǣge° understandan.' Apollonius þā sōðlīce° hyre ārehte ealle his gelymp and
æt þāre sprǣcan° ende ⌐him fēollon tēaras of ðām ēagum⌐. Mid þȳ þe se cyngc
þæt geseah°, hē bewænde° hine° ðā⌐tō ðāre dohtor⌐ and cwæð: 'Lēofa dohtor, þū
gesingodest°; mid þȳ þe þū woldest° witan his naman and his gelimp, þū hafast°
20 nū geednīwod° his ealde sār°. Ac ic bidde° þē þæt þū gife him⌐swā hwæt swā⌐ðū
wille.' ⌐Ðā ðā⌐ þæt mæden gehīrde þæt ⌐hire wæs ālȳfed fram hire fæder þæt hēo
ǣr hyre silf gedōn wolde⌐, ðā cwæð hēo tō Apollonio: 'Apolloni, sōðlīce þū eart

---

5 you   so   honoured   (a)   seat   with   sorrowful   face   Do not know [*ne wāt*]   **6** is troubled
about   shipwrecked   **7** pleased   therefore   invited   **8** our   feast   nor   from where   but
9 wish *sbj* to know   is *sbj*   ask *imp*   because   know *sbj*   **10** respectful   speech   **11** silent
sad   nobility   see   **12** tell   circumstances   relate   **13** necessity   **14** it ('him')   lost   at
15 it ('her')   left   in   Tarsus   more precisely   **16** can *sbj*   truly   **17** speech's   **18** saw
turned   himself   **19** have done wrong   wished   have   **20** renewed   sorrow   ask

---

7 **manna betst on ðām plegan** gen. of comparison: 'the best of (*or* among) the
men in the game'; i.e. in the ball game at which the king had first encountered
Apollonius.

9 **þē gedafenað** impers. vb. with dat. pron.: 'it is proper for you'.

10–11 **Ðēah... þēah** correl. conj. and adv.: 'Though ..., nevertheless ...'.

12 **gif ðē tō hefig ne þince** impers. vb.: 'if it does not seem too oppressive to you
[*ðē*, dat.]'.

17 **him... of ðām ēagum** 'from him fell tears from the eyes' (poss. dat.), i.e. 'tears fell
from his eyes'.

18 **tō ðāre dohtor** 'to the [i.e. his] daughter'. Nouns of relationship may have the same
forms in all the sg. cases [§B4c]; here *dohtor* is dat., but gen. in 24. See also gen. *fæder*
in 76.

20 **swā hwæt swā** 'what(so)ever'; also in 51 and 52–3.

21–2 **Ðā ðā** double conj.: 'When' (lit. 'then when'); also in 84.   **hire wæs ālȳfed ...**
gedōn wolde 'she was allowed [lit. "to her it was allowed"] by [lit. "from"] her father to do
what (*þæt*) she already (*ǣr*) herself wanted to do'.

ūre°. Forlǣt þīne murcnunge°, and nū ic mīnes fæder lēafe° habbe, ic gedō° ðē
weligne°.' Apollonius hire ⌐þæs þancode⌐, and se cyngc blissode° on° his dohtor
25   welwillendnesse° and hyre tō cwæð: 'Lēofa dohtor, ⌐hāt feccan þīne hearpan⌐
and gecīg° ⌐ðē tō⌐ þīnum frȳnd and āfirsa° fram þām iungan° his sārnesse.'

Ðā ēode hēo ūt and hēt feccan hire hearpan and sōna° swā hēo hearpian°
ongān°, hēo mid° winsumum° sange° gemǣgnde° þāre hearpan swēg°. Ðā
ongunnon ealle þā men hī° herian° on° hyre swēgcræft° and Apollonius āna°
30   swīgode°. Ðā cwæð se cyningc: 'Apolloni, nū ðū dēst° yfele°, ⌐forðām þe⌐ ealle
men heriað mīne dohtor on hyre swēgcræfte and þū āna ⌐hī swīgende tǣlst⌐.'
Apollonius cwæð: 'Ēalā° ðū gōda cyngc, gif ðū mē gelīfst° ic secge° þæt ic
ongite° þæt sōðlīce þīn dohtor ⌐gefēol on swegcræft⌐ ac hēo næfð° hine° nā
wel geleornod°. Ac hāt mē nū sillan° þā hearpan; ⌐þonne wāst þū þæt þū nū
35   gīt nāst⌐.' Arcestrates se cyning cwæð: 'Apolloni, ic oncnāwe° sōðlīce þæt þū
eart on eallum þingum wel gelǣred°.' Ðā hēt se cyng sillan Apollonige þā
hearpan. Apollonius þā ūt ēode and hine° scrīdde° and sette ænne° cynehelm°
uppon his hēafod and nam° þā hearpan on his hand and in ēode and swā stōd
þæt se cyngc and ealle þā ymbsittendan wēndon° þæt hē nǣre° Apollonius
40   ac þæt hē wǣre Apollines° ðāra hǣðenra° god. Ðā ⌐wearð stilnes and swīge°
geworden⌐ innon° ðāre healle. And Apollonius his hearpenægl° genam° and hē
þā hearpestrengas mid cræfte āstirian° ongān and þāre hearpan swēg mid winsumum sange gemǣgnde. And se cyngc silf° and ealle þe þār andwearde° wǣron

---

23 (one) of us grief permission (will) make **24** wealthy rejoiced in **25** kindness
26 summon *imp* take away *imp* young (man) **27** (as) soon play the harp **28** began
with delightful song blended sound *as* **29** her *asf* praise for musical skill alone
30 was silent do wrong **32** Alas trust say **33** perceive has not [*ne hæfð*] it
34 learned to be given **35** recognise **36** taught **37** himself dressed a garland
38 took **39** imagined was not *sbj* [*ne wǣre*] **40** Apollo heathens *gp* silence
41 within 'harp-nail' (*i.e.* plectrum) took **42** to excite **43** himself present

---

24 **þæs þancode** The vb. takes an indir. obj. in the gen.: 'thanked for that'.
25 **hāt feccan þīne hearpan** 'command (them) to fetch your harp', or 'command your
harp to be fetched'. The same acc. and inf. construction [§G6d.i.3] is used in 27, 34, 36, 70
and 80.
26 **ðē tō** 'to you'.
30 **forðām þe** conj. phr.: 'because'.
31 **hī swīgende tǣlst** 'insult her (by) being silent'.
33 **gefēol on swegcræft** This is a lit. rendering of the Latin: 'has fallen into musical
craft (*or* skill)'. The sense is that she has made a start in the craft.
34–5 **þonne wāst ... nāst** 'then you (will) understand what (*þæt*) you do not now (as)
yet understand' (*nāst* for *ne wāst*).
40–1 **wearð ... geworden** The pres. of *weorðan* ('become' or 'happen') is used as an
auxil. with its own past. part.: 'was come about', i.e. 'there was'.

⌐micelre stæfne¬ cliopodon° and hine heredon°. Æfter þisum forlēt Apollonius
45   þā hearpan, and ⌐plegode and fela fægera þinga þār forð tēah¬, þe° þām folce
ungecnāwe° wæs and ungewunelic°, and ⌐heom eallum þearle° līcode¬ ǣlc° þāra
þinga ðe hē forð tēah.

Sōðlīce mid þȳ þe þæs cynges dohtor geseah þæt Apollonius on eallum
gōdum cræftum swā wel wæs getogen°, þā ⌐gefēol hyre mōd on his lufe¬. Ðā
50   æfter þæs bēorscipes geendunge° cwæð þæt mǣden tō ðām cynge: 'Lēofa fæder,
þū lȳfdest° mē ⌐lītle ǣr¬ þæt ic mōste° gifan Apollonio° swā hwæt swā ic wolde
of þīnum goldhorde.' Arcestrates se cyng cwæð tō hyre: 'Gif him swā hwæt
swā ðū wille.' Hēo ðā swīðe° blīðe° ūt ēode and cwæð: 'Lārēow° Apolloni, ic
gife þē be mīnes fæder° lēafe twā hund punda goldes and fēower hund punda
55   gewihte° seolfres and ⌐þone mǣstan dǣl¬ dēorwurðan° rēafes° and twēntig
⌐ðēowa manna¬.' And hēo þā þus cwæð tō ðām þēowum mannum: 'Berað° þās°
þingc mid ēow° þe ic behēt° Apollonio mīnum lārēowe and lecgað° innon būre°
⌐beforan mīnum frēondum¬.' Þis wearð° þā þus gedōn æfter° þāre cwēne° hǣse°
and ealle þā men hire gife° heredon ðe hig° gesāwon.
60   Ðā sōðlīce geendode ⌐þe¬ gebēorscipe and þā men ealle ārison° and grētton°
þone cyngc and ðā cwēne and ⌐bǣdon hig gesunde bēon¬ and hām gewǣndon.
Ēac° swilce° Apollonius cwæð: 'Ðū gōda cyngc and ⌐earmra gemiltsigend¬, and

44 cried out praised **45** that **46** unknown (to +*d*) unusual greatly each (of +*g*)
49 instructed **50** end **51** granted might to Apollonius **53** very happy Master
54 father's **55** by weight *ds* costly clothing **56** Carry these **57** you have promised
(to +*d*) lay (them) apartment **58** was according to princess's command **59** gifts *ap*
them **60** arose saluted **62** Also likewise

44 micelre stæfne dat. of manner: 'with great voice'.
45 plegode ... forð tēah 'entertained and performed [lit. "brought forth"] there many pleasing things' (*fela* with gen. pl.).
46 heom eallum ... līcode impers. vb.: 'to them all it pleased', i.e. 'it pleased them all'. The vb. is used again in 68. *Heom* is a frequent late WS form of *him*.
49 gefēol hyre mōd on his lufe 'her heart fell into his love', i.e. 'fell in love with him'.
51 lītle ǣr 'a little before', or 'a little while ago'; the adj. *lītle* may be construed as a noun in the acc. of time.
55 þone mǣstan dǣl 'the greatest portion', i.e. 'a great quantity' ('of', with gen.).
56 ðēowa manna 'serving men'; gen. pl., following the numeral [§E3d].
58 beforan mīnum frēondum 'in front of my friends'. In the Latin, the reference to friends belongs at the beginning of the sentence, where the gifts are to be conveyed in the view of '(my) friends (who are) present' – so that they can see how worthily Apollonius is being treated (as the next sentence shows).
60 þe A late form of the def. art. (for *se*), anticipating later developments in the language.
61 bǣdon hig gesunde bēon 'bade them be healthy', i.e. 'said farewell to them'.
62 earmra gemiltsigend The pres. part. ('pitying') functions as a noun: 'pitier of the poor'; similarly *lāre lufigend* in 63.

þū cwēn, lāre° lufigend°, bēon gē gesunde.' Hē besēah° ēac tō ðām þēowum
mannum þe þæt mǣden him forgifen hæfde and heom cwæð tō: 'Nimað° þās
65   þing mid ēow þe mē sēo cwēn forgēaf and gān° wē sēcan ūre gesthūs° þæt wē
magon° ūs° gerestan.' Ðā ādrēd° þæt mǣden þæt hēo nǣfre eft° Apollonium ne
gesāwe° swā° raðe° swā hēo wolde and ēode þā tō hire fæder and cwæð: 'Ðū
gōda cyningc, līcað° ðē wel þæt Apollonius, þe þurh ūs tōdæg gegōdod° is, þus
heonon° fare° and cuman yfele men and berēafian° hine?' Se cyngc cwæð: 'Wel
70   þū cwæde°. ⌐Hāt him findan hwār⌐ hē hine mǣge wurðlīcost° gerestan.' Ðā dide
þæt mǣden swā hyre beboden° wæs, and Apollonius onfēng° þāre wununge°
ðe hym getǣht° wæs and ðār in ēode, Gode þancigende° ðe him ne forwyrnde°
cynelices° wurðscipes° and frōfres°.

Ac þæt mǣden hæfde unstille° niht mid þāre lufe onǣled° þāra worda and
75   sanga þe hēo gehȳrde æt° Apollonige, and nā° leng° hēo ne gebād° ðonne° hit
dæg wæs ac ēode sōna swā hit lēoht° wæs and gesæt beforan hire fæder bedde.
Ðā cwæð se cyngc: 'Lēofa dohtor, ⌐for hwī⌐ eart ðū þus ǣrwacol°?' Ðæt mǣden
cwæð: 'Mē āwehton° þā gecnerdnessan° þe ic girstandæg° gehȳrde. Nū bidde ic
ðē forðām° þæt þū befæste° mē ūrum cuman° Apollonige tō° lāre.' Ðā wearð se
80   cyningc þearle geblissod° and hēt feccan Apollonium and him tō cwæð: 'Mīn
dohtor girnð° þæt hēo mōte° leornian æt ðē ðā gesǣligan° lāre ðe þū canst° and
gif ðū wilt þisum þingum gehȳrsum° bēon, ic swerige° ðē þurh mīnes rīces°
mægna° þæt swā hwæt swā ðū on sǣ forlure°, ic ðē þæt on lande gestaðelige°.'
Ðā ðā Apollonius þæt gehȳrde, hē onfengc þām mǣdenne tō lāre and hire tǣhte
85   swā wel swā hē silf geleornode.

63 of learning lover ('loving') looked **64** Take **65** go lodging **66** can ourselves *ap*
was afraid again **67** would see as quickly **68** (does it) please enriched **69** from here
should go rob **70** (have) said most honourably **71** commanded accepted +*g* dwelling
gs **72** assigned thanking +*d* denied +*g* **73** regal dignity comfort **74** restless
enflamed (by +*g*) **75** from no longer waited when **76** light **77** awake early
78 awakened accomplishments yesterday **79** therefore entrust (to +*d*) guest *ds* for
80 pleased **81** desires may beneficial know **82** amenable (to +*d*) swear (to +*d*)
kingdom's **83** powers lost restore

70 **Hāt him findan hwār** 'Command (them) to find for him (a place) where . . .'.
77 **for hwī** adv. phr. 'why' (lit. 'for why', instr. *hwī*).

28

The Trees of the Sun and the Moon (from the *Letter of Alexander*)

Alexander the Great (356–323 BC) was the renowned king of Macedonia, educated by Aristotle, who led the Greeks to victory over Darius of Persia and then extended his conquests to Egypt and India. He died of fever at the age of thirty-two and thereafter became the subject of many legends. One of the most popular vehicles for these in the medieval period was the Latin *Epistola Alexandri ad Aristotelem* – 'the Letter of Alexander to Aristotle' – supposedly an account, sent to his tutor, of Alexander's military campaigns in India and some of his adventures by the way. The letter circulated in England in both Latin and OE versions and Alexander is mentioned in two other Anglo-Saxon 'travel' texts, the OE *Orosius* (a much modified version of a world history by Paulus Orosius, made in the time of King Alfred) and *Marvels of the East* (see below). Alexander is also among the legendary characters listed by the narrator of the OE poem *Widsith*, who alludes to him positively as a fine prince, 'the most powerful among all of humankind'. This reflects an admiration for Alexander that was widespread in the Middle Ages, but there was another view, too, a less favourable one promoted especially by Christian writers. They tended to play down Alexander's positive characteristics and to emphasise instead his over-weening pride, and it is this line which the OE version of the *Letter* follows. There are considerable departures from the Latin original, apparently designed to produce an exemplum about the pride of earthly rulers, with the spotlight on Alexander's egotism and belligerence. This Alexander, it has been suggested, might be interpreted as a monster-killer who is himself monstrous in his pride and whose *Letter* is thus a most suitable companion piece for *Beowulf*, which follows it in the *Beowulf*-manuscript (London, British Library, Cotton Vitellius A. xv, fols. 126r–129v). Before it were copied two other prose texts which deal with forms of the monstrous: a version of a work known as *Marvels of the East*, deriving from a tradition of Latin texts describing bizarre men and animals purportedly seen in eastern parts of the world, and an account of the life of the dog-headed St Christopher.

In the OE *Letter*, Alexander relates how he reaches India, putting to flight King Porus of 'Fasiacen' (an unexplained name: Porus's kingdom was in northern India, south of the Indus) and moving through the interior of India in pursuit of him. On the way he endures various tribulations, after which he routinely, and with great cruelty, punishes his guides; there are encounters with fantastical beasts, too, such as three-headed fire-breathing serpents and mice the size of foxes. Having caught up with Porus and accepted his surrender and friendship, Alexander, in company with his huge army, continues his explorations. Eventually he meets two old men and asks them whether there is anything worth seeing in their country. When they tell him that ten days' march away are to be found 'the trees of the sun and the moon', which answer questions put to them about the future, Alexander determines to seek them out, taking a small part of his army with him. This is where the extract begins, towards the end of the *Letter*.

Although the OE translation from the Latin is mostly accurate, the style is often awkward. One particularly common syntactical trait is the use of both a personal pronoun and a demonstrative adjective before a noun; thus *hē se bisceop*, 'he the bishop', for simply 'the bishop' (14 and 18) and *þā mīne frȳnd*, 'those my friends', for 'my friends' (74). Inconsistency is the main characteristic of the late WS copyist (or his exemplar). Varying word-forms include *gegyrde* (7) and *gegerwed* (18), *sōcerd* (26) and *sācerd* (48), and *þrēo* (1) and *þrīo* (23). The preterite plural ending *-on* is often levelled to *-an*: *fōran* (2), *wǣran* (9) (but cf. *wǣron*, 4); conversely, the infinitive ending *-an* may appear as *-on*: *ābidon* (2), *unārefndon* (4). The short vowel *i* breaks to *io* in *siogorum* (53), *sioþþan* (52) and *siodðan* (46); in the latter, *d* is written for *ð*, as also in *cwæd* (55), but cf. *cwæð* (34). The forms of *trēow*, 'tree', are the most varied: *trīow* (nom. sg.), *trīo* (nom. sg. and acc. pl.), *trēow* (nom. pl.), *trēowu* (acc. pl.), *trēowa* (gen. pl.), and *trēowum* and *trīowum* (both dat. pl.). *K* is used for *kyninge* (2) and *kynnes* (8), but cf. *cyning* (56) and *gimcynne* (17). Finally, the accusative pronominal forms *mec* (1, 8, etc) and *ūsic* (3), usually associated with poetry, are used.

Further reading

S. Rypins, ed., *Three Old English Prose Texts in Ms. Cotton Vitellius A. xv*, EETS 161 (London, 1924)

G. Cary, *The Medieval Alexander*, ed. D. J. A. Ross (Cambridge, 1956)

H. L. C. Tristram, 'More Talk of Alexander', *Celtica* 21 (1990), 658–63

R. Stoneman, trans., *Legends of Alexander the Great* (London, 1994)

A. Orchard, *Pride and Prodigies: Studies in the Monsters of the 'Beowulf'-Manuscript* (Cambridge, 1995; rev. edn. Toronto, 2002)

B. McFadden, 'The Social Context of Narrative Disruption in *The Letter of Alexander to Aristotle*', *ASE* 30 (2001), 91–114

Genom° þā mid° mec° þrēo þūsendo° ond forlēt° ⌐mīne fyrd elcor⌐ in Fasiacen
under Pore° þǣm kyninge ond under mīnum gerēfum° ðǣr ābīdon°. Ðā fōran°
wē ond ūsic° þā lādtēowas° lǣddon þurh° ⌐þā wǣdlan stōwe wǣtres⌐ ond þurh
þā unārefndon° lond° wildēora° ond wyrma° þā° wǣron ⌐wunderlicum nomum⌐
5　on Indisc° geceged°. ⌐Mid þȳ⌐ wē þā nēalehtan° ðǣm þēodlonde°, þā gesāwon°
wē ⌐ǣgþer ge wīf° ge⌐ wǣpnedmen° mid palthera° fellum° ⌐ond tīgriscum þāra
dēora hȳdum⌐ gegyryde°, ond nānes° ōðres brūcon°. Mid þȳ ic þā frægn° hīe
ond āhsode° ⌐hwelcre ðēode kynnes⌐ hīe wǣron, ðā ondswarodon hīe mec ond
sǣgdon on hīora geþēode° þæt hīe wǣran Indos°. Wæs sēo stōw rūm° ond
10　wynsumo° ond ⌐balzamum ond rēcels ðǣr wæs genihtsumnis⌐ ond þæt ēac°
of° þǣra trēowa telgan° wēol° ond þā men þæs londes ⌐bī ðȳ⌐ lifdon ond þæt
ǣton. Mid þȳ, wē ðā geornlicor° þā stōwe scēawodon° ond betwih° þā bearwas°
ēodon° ond ic ðā wynsumnesse° ond fǣgernesse° þæs londes wundrade°.

　　Ðā cwōm° se bisceop þǣre stōwe ūs tōgēanes°. Wæs hē se bisceop X
15　fōta ūphēah° ond ⌐eall him wæs se līchoma⌐ sweart° būton° þǣm tōþum ðā
wǣron hwīte, ond þā ēaran him þurh° þyrelode° ond ēarhringas onhongedon°
of mǣnigfealdan° gimcynne° geworhte° ond hē wæs mid wildēora fellum
gegerwed. Þā hē se bisceop tō mē cwōm, ðā grētte° hē mē sōna° ond hālette°

1 (I) took with me thousand (men) *ap* let　**2** Porus officers remain *inf* set out
[*fōron*]　**3** us *ap* guides through　**4** inhospitable lands *ap* of wild animals of serpents
which　**5** (the) Indian (language) called approached country saw　**6** women men
panthers' skins　**7** dressed no 'used' (*i.e.* wore) +*g* questioned　**8** asked　**9** language
Indians spacious　**10** pleasant also　**11** from branches *dp* flowed　**12** more closely
inspected among groves　**13** went pleasantness marvelled at (+*a*)　**14** came towards
15 tall black except　**16** through (were) pierced hung down　**17** numerous kind(s) of
jewel *ds* made　**18** greeted at once saluted

　1 **mīne fyrd elcor** 'my army else', i.e. 'the rest of my army'.
　3 **þā wǣdlan stōwe wǣtres** The adj. describes *wǣtres*: 'the place devoid of water'.
　4 **wunderlīcum nomum** dat. of instrument: 'by marvellous names'.
　5 **Mid þȳ** conj. phr. (instr. *þȳ*): 'When ...'. So also in 7, 60, 63 and 69; in 12 and 50,
the adv. 'then' seems to be the appropriate trans.
　6 **ǣgþer ge ... ge** 'both ... and ...'.
　6–7 **ond tīgriscum þāra dēora hȳdum** 'and (in) the hides of the animals (called) tigers';
tīgrisc is an adj., 'tigerish', i.e. 'of tigers'.
　8 **hwelcre ðēode kynnes** 'of which people's kind' (all gen.), i.e. 'what kind of people'.
　10 **balzamum ond rēcels ðǣr wæs genihtsumnis** The syntax is not clear; *recels* might
pass for a gen. form but *balzamum* would not. Nevertheless, 'an abundance of balsam and
incense' is clearly what is meant, and, to judge from the Latin version, *þæt* in the same line
(the subj. of *wēol*) refers to both together, rather than simply the balsam.
　11 **bī ðȳ** instr. phr.: 'by (means of) that'.
　15 **eall him ... se līchoma** The adj. goes with *līchoma*, and *him* is poss. dat (as also in
16): 'his whole body'.

⌐his lēodþēawe⌐; frægn hē ēac mē ⌐tō hwon⌐ ic þider cwōme° ond hwæt ic
20 þǣr wolde°. Þā ondswarode ic him þæt ⌐mec lÿste gesēon⌐ þā hālgan° trīo°
sunnan ond mōnan. Đā ondswarode hē: 'Gif þīne gefēran° bēoð ⌐clǣne from
wīfgehrīne⌐, þonne mōton° hīe gongan° in þone godcundan° bearo.' Wæs ⌐mīnra
gefērana mid mē þrīo hund monna⌐. Þā hēt° se bisceop mīne gefēran þæt hīe
hīora gescīe° ond ealne heora gerelan° ⌐him of ādyden⌐, ond ⌐hēt ic ǣghwæt
25 swā dōn swā⌐ hē ūs bebēad°. Wæs hit þā sīo endlefte° tīd° dæges.
    Đā bād° se sōcerd° sunnan setlgonges°, forþon° sunnan trīo āgefēð° ondsware
æt þǣm ūpgonge° ond eft° æt setlgonge, ond þæt mōnan trīow gelīce° swā on
niht dyde. Đā ongon° ic geornlīcor° þā stōwe scēawigan ond geond° þā bearwas
ond trēowu gongan, þā gesēah ic þēr ⌐balzamum þæs betstan stences genōh⌐
30 of þǣm trēowum ūtweallan°. Þæt balzamum ǣgþer ge ic ge mīne gefēran þǣr
⌐betwih þǣm rindum nōman þǣra trīo⌐. Þonne° wǣron ðā hālgan trīo sunnan ond
mōnan on middum° þǣm ōðrum trēowum; meahton° hīe bēon huntēontiges° fōta
ūphēah ond ēac þǣr wǣron ōþre trēow ⌐wunderlicre hēanisse⌐ ðā hātað° Indeos
⌐bebronas⌐. Þāra trīowa hēannisse ic wundrade ond cwǣð þæt ic wēnde° þæt
35 hīe for° miclum wǣtan° ond regnum° swā hēage° wēoxon°. Đā sǣgde se bisceop
þæt þǣr nǣfre in þǣm londum regnes dropa ne cwōme, ⌐ne⌐ fugel° ne wildēor
ne nǣnig° ǣtern° wyrm þæt hēr dorste° gesēcean° ðā hālgan gemǣro° sunnan

19 (had) come *sbj* 20 wanted sacred trees 21 companions 22 may go divine
23 commanded 24 shoes clothes 25 ordered eleventh hour 26 waited for (+*g*)
priest setting because gives 27 (sun)rise again likewise 28 began more carefully
through 30 flow out 31 Now 32 middle might hundred 33 call 34 imagined
35 on account of wetness rains high grew 36 bird 37 not any poisonous dared
visit precincts

19 **his lēodþēawe** descriptive gen.: 'according to the custom of his people'.   **tō hwon**
'why' (lit. 'as to what', instr.).
    20 **mec lÿste gesēon** *lÿste* is impers.: 'it pleased me to see', or 'I desired to see'.
    21–2 **clǣne from wīfgehrīne** 'unblemished by sex with a woman [lit. "woman-
contact"]'.
    22–3 **mīnra gefērana ... þrīo hund monna** 'three hundred of my companions'.
    24 **him of ādyden** 'should take from themselves', i.e. 'should take off'.
    24–5 **hēt ic ǣghwæt swā dōn swā** 'I ordered everything to be so done as . . .'.
    29 **balzamum þæs betstan stences genōh** 'balsam enough of the best odour'; i.e. plenty
of it.
    31 **betwih ... þǣra trīo** 'gathered (from) between the bark [lit. "barks"] of the trees'
(*nōman* for *nāmon*).
    33 **wunderlicre hēanisse** descriptive gen.: 'of wondrous height'.
    34 **bebronas** The name (*hibrionas* in the Latin version) is otherwise unknown.
    36 **ne** 'nor (was there) . . .'.

ond mōnan. ⌐Ēac þonne hē sægde se bisceop þonne þæt eclypsis wǣre⌐, þæt is
þonne° ⌐ðæs sunnan āsprungnis oðþe þǣre mōnan⌐, þæt ðā hālgan trīow swīðe
40   wēpen° ond mid micle sāre° onstyred° wǣron, forþon hīe ondrēdon° þæt hīe
hīora godmægne° sceoldon bēon benumene°.

Ðā þōhte ic, sægde Alexander, þæt ic wolde onsægdnisse° þǣr onsecgan° ac
þā forbēad° mē se bisceop ond sægde þæt ðæt nǣre° ālȳfed° ænigum men þæt hē
þǣr ænig nȳten° cwealde° oþþe blōdgyte° worhte° ac mec hēt þæt ⌐ic mē tō° þāra
45   trīowa fōtum gebǣde⌐ þæt sunna ond mōne mē ⌐sōþre ondsware geondwyrdon
þāra þinga⌐ ðe ic frūne°. Sioððan° ⌐þās þing⌐ þūs gedōn wǣron, þā gesāwon
wē westan° þone lēoman° sunnan, ond se lēoma gehrān° þǣm trēowum ufon-
weardum°. Ðā cwæð se sācerd: 'Lōciað nū ealle ūp ond ⌐be swā hwylcum
þingum swā⌐ gē willon frīnan°, ⌐þence⌐ on his heortan dēagollīce° ond nǣnig
50   mon his geþōht ⌐openum wordum⌐ ūt° ne cȳðe°.' Mid þȳ wē þā wel° nēah° stōdan
þām bearwum ond þǣm godsprecum°. Þā ðōhte ic on mīnum mōde hwæþer
ic meahte ealne middangeard° ⌐mē on onweald⌐ geslēan° ond þonne sioþþan,
mid þǣm siogorum° geweorþad°, ic eft meahte becuman° in Macedōniam
tō Olimphiade mīnre mēder° ond mīnum geswustrum°. Ðā ondswarode mē

---

39 namely **40** would weep *sbj* sorrow moved dreaded **41** divine power *ds* deprived
(of +*d*) **42** sacrifice offer **43** forbade was not permitted (to +*d*) **44** animal should
kill *sbj* bloodshed should commit *sbj* at **46** might ask *sbj* After **47** from the west
light touched +*d* **48** at the top **49** ask secretly **50** publicly make known very near
to +*d* **51** oracles **52** world win **53** victories honoured come **54** mother *ds* sisters

---

38 Ēac þonne... eclypsis wǣre Repetitions make for awkward syntax: 'Then the
bishop said also that, when there was [*wǣre* sbj.] an eclipse...'.

39 ðæs sunnan... mōnan OE splits up 'heavy groups' (see 29/1n): 'the failing of the
sun or the moon'.

44–5 ic mē... gebǣde rflx. vb.: 'I should pray'; also in 64.

45–6 sōþre ondsware geondwyrdon 'answer with a truthful answer' (dat. of instrument). The manuscript has *ge ond wyrdum* and the assumption made here is that *-um* is likely
to be an error for the vb. ending *-on*, though sbj. *-en* would be more appropriate. **þāra
þinga** gen. of respect: 'about the things'.

46 þās þing There is no obvious pl. referent for 'these things', for the OE version oms.
a further exchange between Alexander and the priest given in the Latin; but the phr. could
be understood to refer to Alexander's actions in praying.

48–9 be swā hwylcum þingum swā 'about what(so)ever things'.

49 þence 'let him think'; sbj. with optative meaning. The subj. switches from 2nd-pers.
pl. (*gē*) to 3rd-pers. sg.

50 openum wordum dat. of instrument: 'with clear words'.

52 mē on onweald 'into my power' (poss. dat. *mē*).

55 þæt trīow ⌐Indiscum wordum⌐ ond þus cwæd: '⌐Đū unoferswȳðda° Alexander
in gefeohtum°⌐, þū weorðest° cyning ond hlāford ealles middangeardes ac
hwæþre° ne cymst þū on þīnne ēþel° ðonan° þū ferdest° ǣr, forþon ⌐ðīn wyrd
hit swā be þīnum hēafde ond fōre hafað ārǣded⌐.' ⌐Đā⌐ wæs ic unglēaw° þæs
geþēodes° þāra Indiscra worda þe þæt trīow mē tō sprǣc, ðā rehte° hit mē se
60 bisceop ond sægde°. Mid þȳ hit mīne gefēran gehȳrdon° þæt ic eft cwic° ne
mōste in mīnne ēþel becuman, ðā wǣron hīe swīðe unrōte° for þon°.
      Þā wolde ic eft on þā æfentīd mā° āhsian° ac þā næs° se mōna þā gȳt° uppe.
Mid þȳ wē þā eft ēodon in þone hālgan bearo ond wē þā eft be þǣm trēowum
stōdan, gebǣdon ūs þā sōna tō þǣm trēowum swā wē ǣr dydon. Ond ic ēac in
65 mid mec gelǣdde° mīne þrīe ðā getrēowestan frȳnd ðā° wǣron mīne syndrige°
trēowgeþoftan°, þæt wæs ǣrest° Perticam ond Clitomum ond Pilotan, forþon ic
⌐mē⌐ ne ondrēd þæt mē þǣra ǣnig beswīce°, forþon þǣr næs riht° on þǣre stōwe
ǣnigne tō ācwellanne° ⌐for þǣre stōwe weorþunge⌐. Đā þōhte ic on mīnum mōde
ond on mīnum geþōhte° on hwelcre stōwe ic sweltan° scolde. Mid þȳ ðā ǣrest
70 se mōna ūpēode°, þā gehrān hē mid his scīman° þǣm trīowum ufeweardum°
ond þæt trīow ondswarode þǣm mīnum geþōhte ond þus cwæd: 'Alexander,
fulne° ende° þines līfes þū hæfst gelifd°, ac ⌐þȳs æftran gēare⌐ þū swyltst° on
Babilōne on Maius° mōnðe: ⌐from þǣm⌐ þū lǣst° wēnst°, from þǣm þū bist°
beswicen.' Đā wæs ic swīðe ⌐sāriges mōdes⌐ ond ⌐þā mīne frȳnd swā ēac⌐, þā
75 mē þǣr mid wǣron. Ond hīe wēopon swīðe, for þon him wǣre mīn gesynto°
lēofre° þonne hīora seolfra hǣlo°.

55 invincible **56** battles shall become **57** however homeland from where journeyed
58 ignorant of **59** language interpreted **60** told (to me) heard alive **61** downhearted
that *is* **62** more ask was not yet **65** took who special **66** faithful comrades first (*or*
above all) **67** would betray *sbj* proper **68** kill **69** mind die **70** rose radiance
'upwards' (*i.e.* on the upper parts) **72** (the) full limit lived will die **73** of May (*Lat.*)
least expect will be **75** welfare **76** dearer health

      55–6 Indiscum wordum 'with Indian words'; i.e. in the Indian language. **Đū...**
gefeohtum i.e. *Đū Alexander, unoferswȳðda in gefeohtum, ...*
      57–8 ðīn wyrd...ārǣded Apparently, 'your fate has so decreed it on your head al-
ready', taking *fore* as an adv. and omitting *ond* in trans. *Wyrd* is an emendation, replacing
the manuscript's *eþel*, which appears on the previous line and was probably recopied in error.
      58 Đā The conj. is correl. with adv. *ðā* in 59, and the relationship between the two parts
of the sentence is consequential: 'Since ..., (therefore) ...'.
      67 mē rflx. pron., redundant in trans.
      68 for þǣre stōwe weorþunge 'on account of the veneration of [i.e. due to] that place'.
      72 þȳs æftran gēare instr. phr.: 'in this next year'.
      73 from þǣm Probably, 'from whom', with parallel 'from him' to follow, but 'from
what ... from that' is also possible (Lat. *a quo*).
      74 sāriges mōdes descriptive gen. 'sorrowful in (my) heart'.

29

Cynewulf and Cyneheard
(From the *Anglo-Saxon Chronicle*:
annal for 755)

The entry for 755 in the *Anglo-Saxon Chronicle* is remarkable for its length. Breaking from the pattern of terse entries restricted to the major events of successive years, it expands into an account of a power struggle lasting almost thirty years between two royal kinsmen for the kingdom of Wessex. The entry is a carefully crafted narrative with a purpose beyond mere record. It has been argued that the piece, the 'Cynewulf and Cyneheard' episode, must have derived from a pre-existing source outside the *Chronicle*, perhaps a poem or an oral tradition; it has been claimed also that the style has something in common with that of the Icelandic sagas, though there is little to support this. Lexical evidence in fact associates the writer of this annal with the one who put together the entries for the 870s. After the episode, the *Chronicle* returns to 756 and resumes with a more typical assortment of short annals.

The style of the episode, with its paratactic syntax (mostly short sentences joined by 'and'), is breathless. It can be confusing, too, as the result of the swift alternation of subjects, which often leaves the reader doubtful about the referents of 'he' and 'they'. The copyist of the 'Parker Chronicle' (Cambridge, Corpus Christi College, 173), the version used for the text below, seems to have become confused himself at one point, writing plural *cȳðdon* instead of the correct singular *cȳðde* (24). Below, the subjects of pronouns are indicated by glosses where confusion is likely. After allusion to the events which saw Cynewulf take the throne of Wessex from Sigebyrht, thus fomenting future trouble from the latter's brother, Cyneheard, the narrative is largely taken up with events towards the end of the thirty-year period covered. Two armed encounters are presented, with clearly parallel features. First, a small group of King Cynewulf's men, caught off-guard in an attack on their stronghold by Prince Cyneheard, are offered safety and reward if they will desert their king; they choose not to do so and die fighting. The victorious Cyneheard and his men are now besieged in the stronghold by a newly arrived group of Cynewulf's supporters, who make the same offer of safety and reward to those of Cyneheard's men who are their kin; but these too refuse, putting loyalty to their leader above ties of kinship, and they too, along with Cyneheard, die in the subsequent fighting. The symmetry is highlighted by the fact that each phase of fighting leaves all dead bar one man, who is badly wounded.

The problem of conflicting duties to lord and kin was an important one in Anglo-Saxon times, with implications for the stability of kingdoms. One of King Alfred's laws for Wessex would explicitly state that loyalty to one's lord must override kinship ties (7b/42–3). Matters are complicated in the episode of Cynewulf and Cyneheard, however, by the fact that the struggle between the main actors, king and prince, is itself a dynastic one. This becomes clear towards the end of the annal, when we read that Cynewulf and Cyneheard had a shared paternal ancestry. The theme of family ties is driven home by the genealogy of King Offa which closes the annal; like most such genealogies, it traces the royal line back to the pagan god Woden (or Óðinn). Chronological dislocation in the annals between 754 and 845 in the Parker manuscript has led to events being dated two or three years too early: Sigebyrht was in fact deposed in 757, and Cynewulf died in 786.

The Parker manuscript is the oldest surviving version of the *Chronicle*, begun in the closing years of the ninth century and continued at intervals, in Winchester, throughout the tenth. One scribe wrote in all the annals until 891. The episode shows that he used a variety of early WS spellings (of the sort we would expect up to about 900), but they are slightly outnumbered by later forms. Thus we find the preterites *wǣran* (17) and *wǣrun* (10, 13, etc) as well as later WS *wǣron* (25 and 31), and *wunade* (4) and *locude* (12), as well as *wunode* (3) and *gewundode* (13). Early *hiene* occurs twice (3 and 4) but thereafter only *hine* (9, 10, etc). Other early forms are *hwelc* (15) and *gehwelcum* (16), *was* (7, but cf. *wæs* in 20 and 33), *alle* (18) and *aldormon* (3, 5 and 20). In *tæt* (28), *t* is written for *þ*, and in *cuǣdon* (25, 28 and 29) and *uuiþ* (6), *u* or *uu* are written for *w* (represented elsewhere in the text by its own OE character: see p. xxix).

Further reading

J. Earle and C. Plummer, eds., *Two of the Saxon Chronicles Parallel with Supplementary Extracts from the Others*, 2 vols. (Oxford, 1892–9; repr. 1952)

J. Turville-Petre, 'The Narrative Style in Old English', in *Iceland and the Mediaeval World: Studies in Honour of Ian Maxwell*, ed. J. S. Martin and G. Turville-Petre (Melbourne, 1975), pp. 116–25

R. W. McTurk, ' "Cynewulf and Cyneheard" and the Icelandic Sagas', *LSE* n.s. 12 (1981), 81–127

T. A. Shippey, 'Bear and Badger', *LSE* n.s. 16 (1985), 220–39

K. Ferro, 'The King in the Doorway: the Anglo-Saxon Chronicle, A.D. 755', *Acta* 11 (1986), 17–30

S. D. White, 'Kinship and Lordship in Early Medieval England: the Story of Sigeberht, Cynewulf and Cyneheard', *Viator* 20 (1989), 1–18; repr. in *OE Literature*, ed. Liuzza, pp. 157–81

R. H. Bremmer, 'The Germanic Context of "Cynewulf and Cyneheard" Revisited', *Neophil.* 81 (1997), 445–65

D. G. Scragg, '*Wifcyþþe* and the Morality of the Cynewulf and Cyneheard Episode in the Anglo-Saxon Chronicle', in *Alfred the Wise: Studies in Honour of Janet Bately on the Occasion of her Sixty-Fifth Birthday*, ed. J. Roberts and J. Nelson with M. Godden (Cambridge, 1997), pp. 179–85
See also the works listed for Text 8, p. 63.

⌐Hēr Cynewulf benam° Sigebryht his rīces° ond Westseaxna wiotan⌐ for un-ryhtum° dǣdum būton° Hamtūnscīre, ond hē hæfde° ⌐þā⌐ oþ° hē ofslōg° þone aldormon° þe° him° lengest wunode°. Ond hiene° þā Cynewulf ⌐on Andred⌐ ādrǣfde° ond hē þǣr wunade oþþæt° hiene ān swān° ofstang° ⌐æt Pryfetes
5   flōdan⌐; ond hē wræc° þone aldormon ⌐Cumbran⌐. Ond ⌐se⌐ Cynewulf oft ⌐miclum gefeohtum⌐ feaht° uuiþ° ⌐Bretwālum⌐. Ond ⌐ymb XXXI wintra þæs þe⌐ hē rīce hæfde, hē wolde° ādrǣfan ānne æþeling° se° was Cyneheard hāten° ond se Cyneheard wæs ⌐þæs Sigebryhtes brōþur⌐. Ond þā geascode° hē þone

1 deprived (of +*g*) kingdom   **2** unlawful   except +*d*   held   until   killed   **3** ealdorman who   with him   (had) remained   him *as* [*hine*]   **4** drove out   until   swineherd *ns*   stabbed to death   **5** avenged   **6** fought   against [*wiþ*]   **7** wished   prince   who   called   **8** discovered

1 Hēr 'here'; i.e. at this point in the annals or 'in this year' (see 8/headnote). **Cynewulf... ond Westseaxna wiotan** OE compound subjects ('heavy groups') such as this are usually split in OE; the vb. agrees in number with the nearest part of the subj., here *Cynewulf*, hence *benam*: 'Cynewulf and the counsellors of the West-Saxons (deprived...)'. **Sigebryht** The 'Laud' Chronicle adds the detail that Sigebyrht and Cynewulf were related, underlining the theme of strife between kin that is central to this narrative. See also 8n.
2 **þā** 'that'; acc. sg. fem. pron., agreeing with *Hamtūnscīre* ('Hampshire').
3 **on Andred** 'into the Weald', then a large forest extending from Kent to Hampshire. Such forests were commonly used for pasturing swine.
4–5 **æt Pryfetes flōdan** 'at the stream at [lit. "of"] Privett', a village near Petersfield in Hampshire.
5 **Cumbran** 'Cumbra' is the loyal ealdorman slain by Sigebyrht (3). On ealdormen, see 8/4–5n. **se** 'that' or 'this', or om. in trans.
6 **miclum gefeohtum** dat. of definition: 'in great battles'.   **Bretwālum** 'the Britons', i.e. descendants of the tribes who inhabited Britain before the coming of the Anglo-Saxons; here they are probably Cornishmen.
6–7 **ymb XXXI wintra þæs þe** lit. 'after thirty-one of winters from that (in) which', i.e. 'thirty-one years after'. The Anglo-Saxons often reckoned years in terms of winters. Cynewulf's death is in fact recorded twenty-nine years on, in the annal for 784 (though properly this is 786: see headnote). The figure 'thirty-one' is repeated in 35.
8 **þæs Sigebryhtes brōþur** 'the brother of that Sigebyrht'. On the basis of twelfth-century evidence, it has been argued that, in addition, Cyneheard was Cynewulf's nephew. This would strengthen the theme of a family feud.

cyning ⌜lȳtle werode on wīfcȳþþe on Merantūne⌝ ond hine þǣr berād° ond þone
10 ⌜būr⌝ ūtan° beēode° ǣr° hine þā men onfunden° þe mid þām kyninge wǣrun.
Ond þā ongeat° se cyning þæt ond hē on° þā duru° ēode° ond þā unhēanlīce°
hine° werede° oþ hē ⌜on þone æþeling locude⌝ ond þā ūt rǣsde° on hine ond hine
miclum° gewundode°. Ond hīe alle on° þone cyning ⌜wǣrun feohtende⌝ oþþæt
hīe hine ofslægenne° hæfdon. Ond þā on° þæs wīfes gebǣrum° onfundon þæs
15 cyninges þegnas þā unstilnesse° ond ⌜þā þider urnon swā hwelc swā þonne gearo
wearþ ond radost⌝. Ond ⌜hiera se æþeling gehwelcum feoh ond feorh⌝ gebēad°
ond hiera nǣnig° hit geþicgean° nolde°, ac° hīe simle° feohtende wǣran oþ hīe
alle lǣgon° būtan ⌜ānum Bryttiscum gīsle⌝, ond sē° swīþe° gewundad wæs.
    Ðā on morgenne° gehīerdun° ⌜þæt þæs cyninges þegnas þe him beæftan
20 wǣrun þæt⌝ se cyning ofslægen wæs. Þā rīdon° hīe þider, ond his aldormon
Ōsrīc ond Wīferþ his þegn ond þā men þe hē beæftan him lǣfde° ǣr°, ond þone

---

9 overtook   **10** outside   surrounded   before   discovered   **11** realised   to   door (*or* doors)
went 'unbasely' (*i.e.* nobly)   **12** himself   defended   rushed   **13** greatly   wounded   against
14 slain   from   screams   **15** disturbance *as*   **16** offered   **17** none [*ne ǣnig*]   accept
would not [*ne woldon*] but   continuously   **18** lay (dead)   he   severely   **19** morning   heard
20 rode   **21** had left   previously

---

    9 **lȳtle werode** instr. of accompaniment [§D5d]: 'with a little troop'.   **on wīfcȳþþe**
lit. 'at woman-knowing', i.e. (apparently) 'meeting a woman'. The later Latin *Chronicle*
of Ealdorman Æthelweard represents the phr. by stating that Cynewulf passed the time
cum quadam meretrice morando, 'dallying with a certain prostitute', and this derogatory
interpretation has been adopted by most later commentators, but there is no conclusive
evidence for it.   **on Merantūne** 'at Merton', probably the place in Surrey.
    10 **būr** A chamber separate from the main hall; Cynewulf's men are in the latter. Both
buildings are part of a fortified compound (*burh*), protected by gates.
    12 **on ... locude** 'caught sight of' (lit. 'looked on').
    13 **wǣrun feohtende** past continuous: 'were fighting', i.e. 'continued to fight'.
    15–16 **þā þider urnon ... ond radost** lit. 'then ran there whosoever became
ready (*gearo*) and quickest'; i.e. each of his men ran to Cynewulf as quickly as he
could.
    16 **hiera ... gehwelcum** 'to each of them'; i.e. to each of Cynewulf's men, whom Cyne-
heard presumably knew individually.   **feoh ond feorh** 'money and life'; an alliterating
doublet, common as a formula in Germanic lawcodes, and here amounting to a formal
offer.
    18 **ānum Bryttiscum gīsle** 'a British hostage', no doubt acquired in one of the battles
against the British alluded to in 6. Cf. *The Battle of Maldon* (30/265–72).
    19–20 **þæt ... þæt** correl. conjs.; only the second need be trans.   **þe him beæftan
wǣrun** 'who were (left) behind him'; i.e. who had not come to Merton. Putting a prep.
after the pron. it governs is a stylistic trait of this chronicler; see also 22–3 (*him tō*) and 25
(*him mid* and *him from*), but cf. 21 (*beæftan him*).

æþeling on þǣre byrig° mētton þǣr° se cyning ofslægen læg, ond ⸢þā gatu him
tō belocen hæfdon⸣, ond ⸢þā þǣr tō ēodon⸣. Ond þā gebēad hē° him° ⸢hiera
āgenne dōm fēos ond londes⸣ gif hīe him° þæs rīces ūþon°, ond him° cȳðde°
þæt hiera mǣgas° him° mid wǣron, ⸢þā þe him from noldon⸣. Ond þā cuǣdon°
25   hīe° þæt him ⸢nǣnig mǣg lēofra° nǣre þonne hiera hlāford ond hīe nǣfre his
banan° folgian noldon⸣. Ond þā budon° hīe° hiera mǣgum þæt hīe gesunde°
from ēodon°, ond hīe° cuǣdon þæt tæt° ilce° ⸢hiera gefērum⸣ geboden wǣre, þe
ǣr mid þām cyninge wǣrun. Þā cuǣdon hīe° þæt ⸢hīe hīe⸣ þæs ne onmunden°
30   ⸢þon mā þe ēowre gefēran þe mid þām cyninge ofslægene wǣrun⸣. Ond
hīe° þā ymb þā gatu feohtende wǣron oþþæt hīe þǣrinne° fulgon° ond þone
æþeling ofslōgon ond þā men þe him mid wǣrun, alle būtan ānum, se wæs

22 fortification *ds*   where   **23** he [Cyneheard]   them [the king's men]   **24** to him   would
grant *sbj* +*g*   to them   made known   **25** kinsmen   him [Cyneheard]   said   **26** they [the
king's men]   dearer   **27** slayer   offered   they [the king's men]   unharmed   **28** might go *sbj*
[*ēoden*]   they [their kinsmen among Cyneheard's men]   the [*þæt*]   same   **29** they
[Cyneheard's men]   pay attention (to +*g*)   **31** they [the king's men]   within   penetrated

22–3 þā gatu him tō belocen hæfdon The referent of *him tō* ('against them') is not
clear. It could be that Cyneheard's men have locked themselves in, or that they had locked
the gates against Cynewulf's men, or even perhaps that Cynewulf's men locked the gates
to contain Cyneheard's men.
    23 þā þǣr tō ēodon 'then they [the king's men] went to there'; i.e. up to the gates.
    23–4 hiera āgenne dōm fēos ond londes 'their own choice (in respect) of money and
land'. This is settlement on their own terms, suggesting some deterioration in Cyneheard's
position, since he confidently offered the original king's men simply *feoh ond feorh* (16).
Offering enemies self-judgement in respect of compensation was common in Germanic
legal practice (see also 30/38). We learn from a later annal (784, a mistake for 786) that
Cyneheard had eighty-four men with him, but presumably the king's men outnumbered
them.
    25 þā þe 'who' (lit. 'those who'). **him from noldon** The vb. of motion is om. [§G2d]:
'were not willing (to go) from him'.
    26–7 nǣnig … nǣre … nǣfre … noldon The fourfold neg. stresses the utter rejection
of Cyneheard's offer by the king's men, who will now make an offer in return.
    28 hiera gefērum 'to their [the king's men's] companions'. So those kinsmen of the
king's men who are with Cyneheard cite the example of the original group of king's men,
who died the previous night after refusing an offer of terms from Cyneheard.
    29 hīe hīe subj. pron. 'they [Cyneheard's men]', plus rflx. pron. 'themselves' (better
not trans.), attached to *onmunden* (which takes a gen. obj., *þæs*).
    30 þon mā … wǣrun The use of *ēowre*, 'your', shows that there has been a sud-
den switch to direct speech (hence the editorial quotation marks): these are the words
actually used by Cyneheard's men, addressing the king's men outside the fortification.
This adds vividness to the narrative and is a feature common in Icelandic sagas, though
also found elsewhere in OE. *Þon mā þe* is an instr. phr.: 'the more than', or 'any more
than'.

⌐þæs aldormonnes godsunu¬, ond ⌐hē¬ his feorh generede° ond þēah° hē wæs°
oft gewundad.

35   Ond se Cynewulf rīcsode° XXXI wintra ond his līc° līþ° æt Wintanceastre°,
ond þæs æþelinges æt Ascanmynster°, ond hiera ryhtfæderencyn° gǣþ° tō
⌐Cerdīce¬. Ond ⌐þȳ ilcan gēare¬ mon ofslōg Æþelbald, Miercna° cyning, on
Seccandūne°, ond his līc līþ on Hreopadūne°. Ond Beornrǣd fēng° tō rīce ond
⌐lȳtle hwīle¬ hēold ond ungefēalīce°. Ond þȳ ilcan gēare Offa fēng tō rīce ond
40   hēold XXXVIIII wintra; ond his sunu Egferþ hēold XLI daga ond C daga. Se
Offa wæs ⌐Þincgferþing¬, Þincgferþ Eanwulfing, Eanwulf Ōsmoding, Ōsmod
Eawing, Eawa Pybing, Pybba Creoding, Creoda Cynewalding, Cynewald
Cnebing, Cnebba Iceling, Icel Eomǣring, Eomǣr Angelþowing, Angelþēow
Offing, Offa Wǣrmunding, Wǣrmund Wyhtlǣging, Wihtlǣg Wōdening.

33 saved nevertheless had been **35** reigned body lies Winchester **36** Axminster
direct paternal ancestry goes (back) **37** of the Mercians **38** Seckington Repton
succeeded **39** joylessly

33 **þæs aldormonnes godsunu** Osric's godson has been fighting on Cyneheard's side,
emphasising again the theme of kin against kin. **hē** Presumably the godson, who saved
himself, though possibly Osric, who did the saving.

37 **Cerdīce** Cerdic was the putative founder of the kingdom of Wessex and of the line
of WS kings. **þȳ ilcan gēare** instru. phr.: 'in the same year'.

39 **lȳtle hwīle** acc. of time: 'for a little while'.

41 **Þincgferþing** The ending *-ing*, attached to this and to other names below, is
patronymic, signalling 'son of'. The vb. 'was (the son of...)' must be understood in each
subsequent case. The ending *-a* on names is elided before the suffix is added (as in *Eawing*).

30
The Battle of Maldon

'In this year Ipswich was ravaged and quickly after that Ealdorman Byrhtnoth was slain at Maldon. And in this year tribute was first paid to the Danes because of the great terror they caused along the coast.' Thus reports one version of the *Anglo-Saxon Chronicle*'s annal for 991 (see 8/20–3 for the OE text). This incident at Maldon, in Essex on the east coast of England, might have gone unnoticed in the larger picture of defeat and capitulation which characterised England in the 990s; the Danes were stepping up their attacks, which would continue with little opposition from King Æthelred and his nobles until the Danish Cnut took the throne in 1016. But an anonymous poet ensured that posterity would know a little more about this particular defeat. Indeed, by invoking the old heroic ideals of his countrymen's Germanic past, and using the poetic style associated with the celebration of those ideals, he turned the dire events at Maldon into a sort of moral victory: English heroes died, but they died well.

How soon after August 991 the poem was written is not known, but nothing in its language or style precludes a more or less contemporary date. Yet its purpose in relation to events of the time is not clear. Stirring as the defiant speeches of loyal but doomed heroes may be, in practical terms they scarcely constitute an effective national rallying cry, and it may be that the poem had a more parochial aim, to commemorate the English leader Byrhtnoth. By all accounts the elderly ealdorman of Essex was a revered figure, and he seems to have been unusual in his willingness to stand up against the enemy. There is a strong possibility that the poem was written in one of the monasteries in eastern England which Byrhtnoth generously supported and where his memory would have been revered. In a Latin 'Life' of St Oswald, written a few years after 991 at Ramsey, also in East Anglia, Byrhtnoth figures prominently as a Christian martyr. In the *Liber Eliensis* ('the Book of Ely'), moreover, written about 1170 but based on earlier and in some cases oral sources, two battles against the Danes at Maldon are recorded; the first is a triumphant victory for Byrhtnoth and his forces, the second a long and fruitless struggle against overwhelming odds. Some linguistic evidence, such as the use of words of Norse origin (e.g. *drenga*, 149, and *grið*, 35), supports, but cannot confirm, an origin in eastern England.

A major problem in making assessments of the purpose of the poem is that our only version of it is incomplete, lacking beginning and end, so that the vital clues to purpose which introductory and concluding lines would have given are missing. We are lucky to have any of the poem at all. It was first catalogued in 1621, as a set of three folded leaves (and thus six pages) included in a composite volume owned by the collector Sir Robert Cotton. But in a fire in his library at Ashburnham House in 1731, the volume was severely damaged and all the *Maldon* leaves were destroyed. Fortunately, however, a careful transcription had been made a few years earlier by John Elphinston, under-keeper of the library, and the poem had been printed by the historian Thomas Hearne in 1726. The transcription is now in the Bodleian Library, Oxford (with the shelf-mark Rawlinson B. 203), and forms the basis of the text printed below. Given the coherence of the poem as it survives, it seems likely that comparatively little is missing at either end. We join the story as the English assemble beside the River Pante (now the Blackwater), a mile or two from the town of Maldon, and are being deployed by Byrhtnoth; and we leave it at a point when it would seem that just about all the heroes have had their say and died their exemplary deaths.

The poem is written entirely from an English viewpoint and is obviously not a factual account of the skirmish. The facts were presumably known to the poet, but he has manipulated them and recast them within the constraints of his chosen genre. Thus the relationships between the men on the English side reflect the traditional values of loyalty, familiar from the world evoked in *Beowulf* (Text 31a, b) and *The Fight at Finnsburh* (Text 32). There are two defining moments in the action. In the first, Byrhtnoth allows the Vikings, who are contained on a tidal island, to cross a causeway (which is exposed when the tide flows out) to the mainland and thus to engage the English troop, man to man; he does so because of his *ofermōd*, a word whose meaning and significance (a good thing, or bad?) are much debated (see 89n). In the second, some cowardly English participants escape (one of them on Byrhtnoth's horse), causing confusion and fatally weakening the English effort.

Other artfully contrived elements in the poem include the hawk, symbolic of aristocratic pleasures, which is dispatched by its owner to the safety of the woods, once he realises that duty calls; to those same woods the cowards later flee. In the latter part of the poem, after the death of Byrhtnoth, there is a distinctly hierarchical pattern in the presentation of the heroes: from the nobles of famed lineage to the simple freeman and even a hostage (see 265n), all show the loyalty till death required by the heroic ideal. A climactic speech of heroic futility is finally given by Byrhtwold, a veteran warrior. There is a Christian context to all this, at least to the extent that Byrhtnoth is shown to acknowledge, as a good Christian ought to, the hand of God in earthly events, and he properly commits his soul to God as he dies. The Viking invaders are given suitably short shrift; their heathenism is stressed and they are disparaged as 'slaughter-wolves' (*wælwulfas*, 96).

The style and diction of the poet of *Maldon* are fully characteristic of the old 'heroic' poetry and include variation, parallelism and formulaic expression: see the notes to lines 25, 26, 42 and 74. The poet's word-hoard is rich, bringing trouble for the would-be translator into ModE, who must scrape the current word-barrel to come up with synonyms for 'shield' (for which the OE poet has *scyld, bord, lind* and *rand*) and 'spear' (for which the poet has *æsc, daroð, franca, gār* and *spere*); there are eight OE words for a Viking or seaman, and fourteen for a warrior. Overall, the language of the poem shows great uniformity and is consistent with late WS usage. Specifically late forms include *swustersunu* (115, not *sweoster-*), *swurd* (15, 161, etc, not *sweord*) and *manega* (200; but cf. *manigne*, 243, *mænigne*, 188, and *mænig*, 282), as well as levelled inflections, with *-on* written both for *-um* (e.g. *handon*, 7, but cf. *handum*, 4 and 14) and for the subjunctive plural ending *-en* (e.g. *gangon*, 56, and *hēoldon*, 20). The interchange of *-a* and *-u*, as in *suna* (298; for nom. *sunu*), is frequent in some late manuscripts. The few earlier or non-WS spellings, such as *cald* (91), *bēron* (67), *waldend* (173) and *wēgon* (98), are characteristic of OE poetry generally and therefore not necessarily indicative of dialectal origin. On the writing of *d* for *ð*, see 113n.

Further reading

D. G. Scragg, ed., *The Battle of Maldon* (Manchester, 1981)

E. B. Irving, 'The Heroic Style in *The Battle of Maldon*', *SP* 58 (1961), 457–67

G. Clark, '*The Battle of Maldon*: a Heroic Poem', *Speculum* 43 (1968), 52–71

J. D. Niles, 'Maldon and Mythopoesis', *Mediaevalia* 17 (1974); repr. in *OE Poetry*, ed. Liuzza, pp. 445–74

H. Gneuss, '*The Battle of Maldon* 89: Byrhtnoð's *ofermod* Once Again', *SP* 73 (1976), 117–37

F. C. Robinson, 'God, Death, and Loyalty in *The Battle of Maldon*', in *J. R. R. Tolkien, Scholar and Storyteller: Essays in Memoriam*, ed. M. Salu and R. T. Farrell (Ithaca, NY, 1979), 76–98; repr. in *OE Poetry*, ed. Liuzza, pp. 425–44.

D. G. Scragg, ed., *The Battle of Maldon A.D. 991* (Oxford, 1991)

J. Cooper, ed., *The Battle of Maldon: Fiction and Fact* (London, 1993)

P. Cavill, 'Interpretation of *The Battle of Maldon*, Lines 84–90: a Review and Reassessment', *SN* 67 (1995), 149–64

no end / beginning . (handwritten)

had been broken (handwritten)
The... commanded to ⌐brocen wurde¬. *release his horse* (handwritten)

⌐Hēt þā° hyssa° hwæne°   hors forlǣtan | then of warriors each
feor° āfȳsan° and forð gangan°, | far drive off go
⌐hicgan tō handum¬ and tō hige° gōdum°. | courage noble

Offa's (handwritten)

5   Þā° ⌐þæt¬ Offan° mǣg° ǣrest° onfunde° | When Offa's kinsman first realised
þæt se eorl° nolde° yrhðo° geþolian°, | nobleman wouldn't cowardice tolerate
hē lēt° ⌐him þā of handon   lēofne° flēogan° | let beloved fly
hafoc°¬ wið° þæs holtes° and tō þǣre hilde° | hawk towards +g wood battle
stōp°. | advanced

know (handwritten)   *knight* (handwritten)

Be° þām° ⌐man mihte oncnāwan¬ þæt se cniht° nolde | By that young man
10 wācian° æt þām wīge° þā° hē ⌐tō wǣpnum fēng¬. | weaken battle now
Ēac° him wolde Ēadrīc his ealdre° | In addition to leader
gelǣstan°, | support +d
/⌐frēan°¬ tō° gefeohte°; ongan° þā forð beran° | lord in fight began carry
gār° tō gūþe°. / Hē hæfde gōd° geþanc° | spear battle firm purpose
⌐þā hwīle þe¬ hē mid° handum   healdan mihte | with
15 bord° and brād° swurd°; / bēot° hē gelǣste° | shield broad sword vow fulfilled
þā hē ætforan° his frēan   feohtan sceolde°. | in front of had to *sbj*
⌐Ðā þǣr Byrhtnōð¬ ongan   beornas° trymian°, | warriors to arrange
rād° and rǣdde°, rincum° tǣhte° | rode (about) instructed men showed +d

---

1 **brocen wurde** We can only guess what 'had been broken'. The opening of the poem must have told how Byrhtnoth gathered his army by the River Pante in response to the Viking threat.

2 **Hēt . . . forlǣtan** '(He, *i.e.* Byrhtnoth) commanded . . . to release'. The vb. controls three more infins. in 3–4 (*afȳsan, gangan* and *hicgan*). Variations on this infin. construction [§G5d.ii] are used in 30, 62, 74 and 101–2.   **hors** A poss. pron. is needed: 'his horse'.

4 **hicgan tō handum** 'to think about' or 'set (their) mind on (their) hands'; i.e. concentrate on the work that their hands must now do, wielding sword and spear in combat.

5 **þæt** 'it', the obj. of *onfunde*, but in trans. it is best to ignore it and simply to treat the *þæt* clause in 6 as the obj. ('that the nobleman . . .'). A similar construction occurs in 36–7.

7–8 **him . . . of handon** poss. dat. *him*: 'from his hands'.   **lēofne flēogan hafoc** The adj. (*lēofne*) is separated from its noun (*hafoc*, acc. sg.) for effect, and a better order for trans. is *hē lēt þā* ('then') *lēofne hafoc flēogan*. Cf. the similar separation of *ānne* and *flotan* in 226–7. On the hawk, see headnote.

9 **man mihte oncnāwan** 'one could understand', or 'it could be understood'.

10 **tō wǣpnum fēng** 'grasped at weapons', i.e. 'grabbed (*or* took up) (his) weapons'.

12 **frēan** Parallel with (and a variation on) *ealdre* as a dat. obj. of *wolde . . . gelǣstan*.

14 **þā hwīle þe** acc. of time: 'in the period that', i.e. 'while' or 'as long as'. See also 83.

17 **Ðā þǣr . . .** 'Then there . . .'. The need for such basic instructions here (17–22) suggests that this is an novice troop mustered for the occasion; but there is a poetic need also, to show Byrhtnoth in the role of experienced leader.

hū hī sceoldon standan and þone stede° healdan	position
20 and bæd° þæt hyra randas° rihte° hēoldon	ordered shields properly
fæste° mid folman° and ne forhtedon° nā°.	firmly hands be afraid not at all
Þā hē hæfde° þæt folc° fægere° getrymmed,	had troop carefully
hē lihte° þā ⌐mid lēodon þær him lēofost wæs⌐,	dismounted
þær hē his heorðwerod° holdost° wiste°.	'hearth-troop' loyalest knew (to be)
25 ⌐Þā stōd⌐ on stæðe° stīðlīce° clypode°	shore fiercely shouted
wīcinga° ār°, ⌐wordum mælde⌐;	the Vikings' messenger
⌐sē on bēot⌐ ābēad° brimlīðendra°	declared seafarers'
ǣrænde° tō þām eorle þær hē on ōfre° stōd:	message bank
'Mē sendon° tō þē° sǣmen snelle°,	have sent you ds bold
30 ⌐hēton ðē secgan⌐ þæt þū mōst° sendan raðe°	must quickly
bēagas° wið° gebeorge° and ēow°	treasures for protection for you
betere is	
þæt gē° þisne gārrǣs° mid gafole°	you 'spear-storm' tribute
forgyldon°	buy off
⌐þon wē swā hearde hilde dǣlon⌐.	
Ne ⌐þurfe° wē ūs⌐ spillan° ⌐gif gē spēdaþ tō þām⌐.	need kill
35 Wē willað wið þām golde grið° fæstnian°.	truce fix

23 **mid lēodon** 'among the people (*or* men)' (*lēodon* for dat. pl. *lēodum*; cf. 50).   **þær him lēofost wæs** 'where to him it was most pleasant (to be)'; i.e. among the household retainers of his own 'hearth-troop' or 'retinue' (*heorðwerod*, 24).

25 **Þā stōd . . .** In four lines, the poet describes the messenger's uttering of his message with threefold variation: *stīðlīce clypode . . . wordum mælde . . . ābēad brimlīðendra ǣrænde*. Such variation occurs also in 42–4, 168–70 and 209–11.

26 **wordum mælde** A formula much used in poetry: 'spoke out (*or* held forth) with (his) words'.

27 **sē** Probably the masc. pers. pron. 'he' (hence the vowel is marked long here: see p. xxxiii), but it could be interpreted as *se*, the rel. pron. 'who'; there is similar syntactical ambiguity in 75, 153 and 310.   **on bēot** The Vikings are in a typically aggressive mood: 'in boast' or 'in threat', i.e. 'cockily' or 'threateningly'.

30 **hēton ðē secgan** '(they) commanded (me) to say to you'. The context shows that *ðē* is the dat. form of the 2nd-pers. sg. pron., not the acc. (which would have made 'you' the obj. of 'commanded').

33 **þon** comp. conj. (more commonly *þonne*), following *betere* in 31: 'than (that)'.   **wē swā hearde hilde dǣlon** An ambiguous clause. If *hearde* is an adj. ('fierce' or 'cruel'), it may describe either *hilde* (acc. sg. fem.), with *dǣlon* interpreted as 'we should share (battle)', or the Vikings (nom. pl. masc.), with *dǣlon* interpreted as 'we should deal out (battle)'. If *hearde* is an adv. ('fiercely' or 'cruelly'), it may again refer either to the 'sharing' action of English and Vikings together or the 'dealing out' by the Vikings.

34 **þurfe wē** The ending of a pl. vb. (here *þurfaþ*) is commonly reduced to *-e* when its pron. follows [§G5f].   **ūs** 'us' (acc. pl.), i.e. 'each other'.   **gif gē spēdaþ tō þām** 'if you are prosperous (enough) for that'; i.e. if you have money enough to buy us off.

Gyf þū ꝼþatꝺ gerǣdest°   ꝼþe hēr rīcost eartꝺ,   decide
þæt þū þīne lēoda°   lȳsan° wille,   people   ransom
syllan° sǣmannum   ꝼon hyra sylfra dōmꝺ   give
feoh° wið frēode°   and niman° frið°   money   goodwill   accept   peace
    æt° ūs,   from
40   wē willaþ mid þām sceattum°   ꝼūs tō scype ganganꝺ,   money *dp*
    ꝼon flot fēranꝺ   and ēow° friþes healdan°.'   with you   keep *+g*
        ꝼByrhtnōð maþelode°,   bord hafenode°ꝺ,   spoke   lifted
    wand° wācne° æsc°,   wordum mǣlde,   brandished   slender   ash-spear
    yrre° and ānrǣd°   āgeaf° him andsware: angry   single-minded   gave back
45   'Gehȳrst° þū, sǣlida°,   hwæt þis folc segeð°?   Hear   seaman   says
    Hī willað ēow tō° gafole   gāras syllan,   as
    ꝼǣttrynneꝺ ord°   and ꝼealde swurdꝺ,   (spear-)point
    ꝼþā heregeatuꝺ   þe ēow° æt° hilde ne dēah°.   to you   in   be of use
    Brimmanna° boda°,   ābēod° eft°   Seamen's   messenger   report   again
        ongēan°,   back
50   sege þīnum lēodum   ꝼmiccle lāþre spellꝺ,
    þæt hēr stynt° unforcūð°   eorl mid his werode°   stands   undisgraced   troop
    þe wile° gealgean°   ēþel° þysne,   will   defend   homeland
    Æþelrēdes eard°,   ꝼealdres mīnesꝺ,   country

36 **þat** i.e. *þæt*, 'it'. **þe hēr rīcost eart** In trans., this phr. is best put immediately after *þū*: 'If you, who are the most powerful here'.

38 **on hyra sylfra dōm** 'at the judgement of them themselves', i.e. 'at their own judgement (*or* choice)'. The sum to be paid for peace is to be fixed by the Vikings. Cf. 29/23–4n.

40 **ūs tō scype gangan** A 'pleonastic' (superfluous) pron. is often used with vbs. of motion, but here it could be trans. as rflx.: 'take ourselves off to our ships'.

41 **on flot fēran** 'go (*or* put) to sea'.

42 **Byrhtnōð maþelode, bord hafenode** An heroic line echoed to great effect late in the poem (309). The end-rhyming of half-lines is uncommon in OE poetry, but see also 271 and 282.

47 **ǣttrynne** 'poisonous'. A metaphor, expressing the idea 'deadly' or 'fatal' (see also 146, with var. spelling).   **ealde swurd** The adj. ending (strong neut. pl., with late reduction of *-u* to *-e*) shows that *swurd* is pl. These 'ancient' or 'ancestral' swords are tried and trusted weapons with illustrious pedigrees.

48 **þā heregeatu** lit. 'war-gear', but Byrhtnoth, in the context of the exchange of tribute or tax, is using the term ironically by drawing on its technical sense as a sort of death-duty, payable to a lord when a retainer dies (and requiring the return of arms and armour given by the lord); in later English, the word became 'heriot'.

50 **miccle lāþre spell** 'a much more unpleasant tale'. More irony; the Vikings will be expecting news of an English capitulation.

53 **ealdres mīnes** modifies *Æþelrēdes*. Until now in this sentence, Byrhtnoth has talked about himself in the 3rd pers.

folc and foldan°. ⌐Feallan sceolon⌐   land
55 hæþene° æt hilde. Tō° hēanlic° mē þinceð°   heathens Too shameful (it) seems
þæt gē mid ūrum° sceattum   tō scype gangon°   our   should go *sbj*
unbefohtene°   nū gē þus feor hider°   unfought hither
on° ūrne eard   in becōmon°.   into   have come
Ne sceole gē swā sōfte°   sinc° gegangan°;   easily treasure gain
60 ūs sceal ord and ecg°   ⌐ǣr gesēman°,   (sword-)edge decide between
grim° gūðplega°,   ǣr⌐ wē gofol syllon°.'   fierce 'battle-game' give *sbj*
    Hēt þā bord beran,   beornas gangan
þæt° hī on þām ēasteðe°   ealle stōdon.   so that   river-bank
⌐Ne mihte þǣr for° wætere   werod⌐ tō þām ōðrum.   on account of
65 Þǣr cōm° flōwende   flōd° æfter ebban°,   came flood(-tide) ebb(-tide)
⌐lucon lagustrēamas⌐.   Tō lang hit him° þūhte°,   to them (it) seemed
⌐hwænne hī tōgædere   gāras bēron⌐.
Hī þǣr Pantan° strēam° ⌐mid prasse bestōdon⌐,   Pante *gs* river
Ēastseaxena° ord°   and se ⌐æschere⌐.   East Saxons' vanguard
70 Ne mihte hyra° ǣnig   ōþrum° derian°,   of them to the other do harm
būton° hwā° þurh flānes° flyht°   fyl°   unless someone arrow's flight death
genāme°.   took *sbj*
Se flōd ūt gewāt°;   þā flotan° stōdon gearowe°,   went seafarers ready
wīcinga fela°,   wīges georne°.   many +*gp* eager for +*g*
⌐Hēt þā hæleða° hlēo°⌐   healdan þā bricge°   of heroes protector *ns* causeway

54 **Feallan sceolon** The modal vb. seems to convey a sense of inevitability here; perhaps, 'are destined to fall'. The Vikings' paganism is stressed; see also 181.

60–1 **ǣr ... ǣr ...** OE often uses advs. and conjs. in correl. pairs which link two parts of a sentence. It is sometimes best to ignore one of them, but here both may be trans. effectively: 'first ... before ...'.

64 **Ne mihte ... werod** A vb. of motion is left unexpressed after the modal vb. [§G2d]: 'reach' or 'come'. Neither troop can get to the other because of the flood tide, which, following the ebb, has covered the causeway between island and mainland.

66 **lucon lagustrēamas** 'the sea-currents locked'; i.e. the incoming streams met round the island.

67 **hwænne hī ... bēron** The vb. is sbj. pret., with conditional meaning (*bēren* being the expected spelling; see also 229): 'when (*i.e.* until) they could bring spears together' or 'bring spears against each other'.

68 **mid prasse** Perhaps, 'in battle array', but *prass* is little used in OE and its origin is unknown. **bestōdon** 'stood around', or, as clearly the meaning is that the two groups stood either side of the water, 'stood alongside'.

69 **æschere** 'ship-army' (i.e. the Vikings). Ash-wood was used for spear shafts and for building boats, and *æsc* can be used as a metonym for either (see 43).

74 **Hēt** The dir. obj. of the vb. is *wigan*, which does not appear until the start of 75. **hæleða hlēo** An heroic epithet for Byrhtnoth, the subj. of the sentence (cf. *eorla hlēo* in *Deor*, 36/41).

75   wigan° wīgheardne°,   se° wæs hāten°   a warrior *as* 'war-hardened' who called
      Wulfstān,
      cāfne° ⌐mid⌐ his cynne°:   þæt wæs ⌐Cēolan° sunu⌐   bold kin Ceola's
      þe ðone forman° man   mid his francan° ofscēat°   first spear pierced
      þe þǣr baldlīcost°   on° þā bricge stōp.   most boldly onto
      Þǣr stōdon mid Wulfstāne   wigan unforhte°,   unafraid
80   Ælfere and Maccus,   mōdige° twēgen°;   heroic pair
      þā° noldon æt° þām forda°   flēam° gewyrcan°   they from ford flight take
      ac° hī fæstlīce°   wið° ðā fȳnd°   but resolutely against enemies
      weredon°   defended
      þā hwīle þe hī wǣpna   wealdan° mōston°.   to wield +*g* were able *sbj*
      Þā hī þæt ongēaton°   and georne° gesāwon°   realised clearly saw
85   þæt hī þǣr bricgweardas°   bitere° fundon°,   causeway-guardians fierce had met
      ongunnon° ⌐lytegian⌐ þā   lāðe° gystas°,   began hateful strangers
      bǣdon° þæt hī ūpgangan°   āgan° mōston,   implored passage (*or* access) have
      ofer þone ford faran°,   fēþan° lǣdan°.   go soldiers lead
      Đā se eorl ongan   for° his ⌐ofermōde⌐   because of
90   ālȳfan° ⌐landes tō fela⌐   lāþere° ðēode°.   yield to +*d* more hateful people *ds*
      Ongan ceallian° þā   ofer° cald wæter   call out across
      ⌐Byrhtelmes bearn°⌐;   beornas gehlyston°:   son *ns* listened
      'Nū ⌐ēow is gerȳmed⌐,   gāð° ricene° tō ūs,   come quickly
      guman° tō gūþe;   God āna° wāt°   men alone knows
95   hwā° þǣre wælstōwe°   wealdan° mōte°.'   who place of battle control may
      Wōdon° þā wælwulfas°   (for wætere ne   Advanced slaughter-wolves
      murnon°)   paid heed
      wīcinga werod,   west ofer Pantan:

76 **mid** Probably 'along with', or 'like'; i.e. he was as bold as all his kin were known
to be.   **Cēolan sunu** i.e. Wulfstan.
86 **lytegian** The word occurs uniquely here. It is usually taken to mean 'to act cunningly'
or 'deceitfully', but a less adversative meaning of 'to act pragmatically' has been suggested.
89 **ofermōde** Usually trans. as 'over-pride' or 'too much pride', but 'over-exuberance'
or 'excess of courage' may be more apt. Although Byrhtnoth's decision to allow the Vikings
across the causeway turns out to be a tactical error, the vaunting courage and belligerence
which he has already displayed, and of which this present behaviour is an extension, cannot
be faulted either within the conventions of heroic story or in the context of a dire period
in English history, when cowardice in the face of the enemy was the norm. In his general
demeanour, Byrhtnoth is proud but not arrogant.
90 **landes tō fela** 'too much land' (*fela* with partitive gen.). Perhaps, but not necessarily,
an ironic understatement.
92 **Byrhtelmes bearn** i.e. Byrhtnoth.
93 **ēow is gerȳmed** Perhaps, '(a space) has been cleared (*or* made) for you'; cf. 90.

ofer scīr° wæter   scyldas wēgon°,   gleaming carried

lidmen° tō lande   linde° bǣron.   seamen (linden-)shields

100 Þǣr ongēan° gramum°   gearowe stōdon   facing foes

Byrhtnōð mid beornum;   hē ⌐mid bordum hēt⌐   form

wyrcan° þone ⌐wīhagan⌐   and þæt werod healdan

fæste° wið fēondum.   Þā wæs feohte° nēh°,   firmly fighting near

tīr° æt getohte°.   Wæs sēo tīd° cumen°   glory battle time come

105 þæt þǣr fǣge° men   feallan sceoldon.   doomed

Þǣr wearð° hrēam° āhafen°,   ⌐hremmas°   was shouting raised ravens

    wundon°,   circled

earn° ǣses° georn⌐;   wæs on eorþan cyrm°.   eagle carrion uproar

Hī lēton þā of folman   ⌐fēolhearde⌐ speru°,   spears

⌐grimme°⌐ gegrundene°   gāras flēogan;   cruelly ground

110 bogan° wǣron bysige°,   bord ord onfēng°.   bows busy received

    Biter wæs se beadurǣs°,   beornas fēollon   onslaught

on gehwæðere° hand°,   hyssas lāgon°.   either side lay (dead)

Wund° ⌐weard⌐ Wulfmǣr,   ⌐wælræste⌐ gecēas°,   Wounded chose

Byrhtnōðes mǣg: hē mid billum° wearð,   swords

115 ⌐his swustersunu⌐,   swīðe° forhēawen°.   violently cut down

Þǣr wærd° wīcingum   weþerlēan° āgyfen°.   was requital given to +d

⌐Gehȳrde° ic⌐ þæt Ēadweard   ānne° slōge°   Heard one asm struck

swīðe mid his swurde,   swenges° ne wyrnde°,   blow gs withheld +g

---

101 **mid bordum** In trans., this belongs after *þone wīhagan* (102).   **hēt** The obj. of the vb., which governs both *wyrcan* and *healdan*, is *þæt werod*.

102 **wīhagan** 'battle hedge'; i.e. a defensive wall of interlocked shields held by the fighters.

106–7 **hremmas . . . georn** This is the 'beasts of battle' motif beloved of poets; here it is predatory birds only, but in other poems the wolf joins in as well (see 10/65 and 32/6).

108 **fēolhearde** 'file-hard'; probably 'hardened by files', a reference to the making of the spear-head.

109 **grimme** The transcription has only *gegrundene* for this half-line; *grimme* is a plausible addition.

113 **weard** i.e. *wearð* ('became' or 'was'). Confusion of *d* and *ð* is very common in late manuscripts (though the transcription could be at fault: see headnote); scc also 116 (*wærd.* again for *wearð*), 224 (*ǣgder*), 324 (*od-*) and 325 (*gūde*).   **wælrǣste** 'slaughter-bed'; i.e. a resting place among the slain.

115 **his swustersunu** 'his [Byrhtnoth's] sister's son'; i.e. Wulfmær. In describing this first casualty, the poet lays great stress on the bond of kinship, which seems to have been especially close between a man and his sister's son in Germanic societies.

117 **Gehȳrde ic** A dramatic 1st-pers. intervention by the poet, indicating that his authority stems from eye-witness accounts.

þæt ⌐him æt fōtum⌐   fēoll fǣge cempa°;   fighter
120 ⌐þæs him his ðēoden   þanc gesǣde
þām būrþēne⌐,   þā hē byre° hæfde.   opportunity
Swā° stemnetton°   stīðhicgende°   Thus stood firm resolute
hysas æt hilde,   hogodon° georne   set (their) minds on
hwā þǣr mid orde   ǣrost° mihte   first
125 on° fǣgean men°   feorh° gewinnan°,   from man *ds* life win
⌐wigan⌐ mid wǣpnum;   wæl° fēol on eorðan.   the slain
Stōdon stǣdefæste;   stihte° hī Byrhtnōð,   directed
bæd þæt hyssa gehwylc°   hogode tō wīge   each +*gp*
þe ⌐on Denon⌐ wolde   dōm° gefeohtan°.   glory   gain by fighting
130 Wōd þā ⌐wīges heard⌐,   wǣpen ūp āhōf°,   raised
bord tō gebeorge°   and wið° ⌐þæs beornes⌐ stōp.   protection towards +*g*
Ēode° swā° ānrǣd   eorl tō þām ⌐ceorle°⌐,   Went just as commoner
ægþer° hyra° ōðrum   yfeles hogode°.   both of them intended +*g*
Sende° ðā se sǣrinc°   ⌐sūþerne gār⌐   Sent sea-warrior
135 þæt gewundod° wearð   wigena° hlāford.   wounded of warriors
⌐Hē scēaf°⌐ þā mid ðām scylde   þæt° se sceaft°   thrust so that shaft
tōbærst°   broke
and þæt spere sprengde°   þæt hit sprang° ongēan°.   flexed sprang out again
Gegremod° wearð se gūðrinc°;   hē mid gāre stang°   Enraged warrior stuck

119 **him æt fōtum** poss. dat.: 'at his feet'.

120–1 **þæs him . . . þām būrþēne** *him* and *þām būrþēne* are parallel dat. objs. of the vb.: 'for that [*þanc* with gen.] his lord said to him, to the chamberlain, thanks'. The *būrþen* (lit. 'bower-thane'), i.e. Edward, is clearly an important member of his lord's household. Quite when Byrhtnoth, ever the gracious lord, has the opportunity to convey these thanks in the remaining minutes of his life is not clear.

126 **wigan** This *n*-noun [§B5a], used also in 75 and 79, is perhaps best taken as nom. pl., a variation on the *hysas* of 123, who compete to kill a Viking first: 'warriors (with their weapons)'; but it could be dat. sg., parallel with dat. sg. *men*: '(from) a warrior (with weapons)'.

129 **on Denon** 'from (*i.e.* at the expense of) the Danes'.

130 **wīges heard** '(one) hard of battle'; i.e. hardened in battle, or bold. He is a Viking who now challenges Byrhtnoth, and is the *ceorl* of 132 and the *sǣrinc* of 134.

131 **þæs beornes** 'the man' is of course Byrhtnoth.

132 **ceorle** On the meaning of this word (also in 256), see 7a/22n.

134 **sūþerne gār** 'a southern spear'; i.e. of southern make. Weapons made in France, south of the Vikings' homelands, were especially prized by them.

136 **Hē scēaf . . .** In this passage (136–42), Byrhtnoth (*Hē*) apparently uses his shield to knock the shaft of the spear which has penetrated him in such a way that it breaks, causing the part still in his body to vibrate or flex, so that it springs out again. Experienced as he is, he in turn sends a spear into his attacker, making it pierce the man's neck.

wlancne° wīcing   þe him þā wunde°   presumptuous   wound *as*
    forgeaf°.   had given
140 Frōd° wæs se fyrdrinc°;   hē lēt his francan wadan°   Experienced   soldier   travel
    þurh ðæs hysses hals°,   hand wīsode°   neck   guided (it)
    þæt hē on° þām færsceaðan°   feorh geræhte°.   from   sudden attacker   took
    Ðā hē ⌐ōþerne⌐   ofstlīce° scēat   speedily
    þæt sēo byrne° tōbærst;   hē wæs on ⌐brēostum⌐ wund   mail-coat
145 þurh ðā hringlocan°,   ⌐him æt heortan⌐ stōd   ring-links
    ætterne ord.   Se eorl wæs ⌐þē⌐ blīþra°;   happier
    hlōh° þā, mōdi° man,   sæde metode° þanc   laughed   spirited   creator *ds*
    ðæs dægweorces°   þe him Drihten forgeaf.   day's work
    Forlēt° þā drenga° sum°   daroð° of   Let go   (Viking) warriors   one of +*g*   spear
        handa,
150 ⌐flēogan⌐ of folman°   þæt sē° tō forð° gewāt   hands   it   far
    þurh° ðone æþelan°,   Æþelrēdes ⌐þegen⌐.   into   nobleman
    ⌐Him be healfe⌐ stōd   hyse° unweaxen°,   youth   'ungrown' (*i.e.* not fully grown)
    cniht° on gecampe°,   se° full° cāflīce°   boy   battle   who   very   boldly
    bræd° of þām beorne°   blōdigne gār.   pulled   man (*i.e.* Byrhtnoth)
155 Wulfstānes bearn,   Wulfmær se geonga°,   younger
    forlēt ⌐forheardne⌐   faran° eft ongēan;   go
    ord in gewōd°   þæt sē° on eorþan læg°   went   he   lay dead
    þe his þēoden ǣr   þearle° geræhte°.   grievously   (had) struck
    Ēode þā ⌐gesyrwed⌐   secg°⌐ tō þām eorle;   armed   warrior
160 hē wolde þæs beornes   bēagas° gefecgan°,   valuables   carry off
    rēaf° and hringas   and gerēnod° swurd.   armour   ornamented
    Þā Byrhtnōð bræd°   bill of scēðe°,   drew   sheath

---

143 **ōþerne** The pron. (acc. sing. masc.) presumably refers to 'another' Viking whom Byrhtnoth 'shot' or 'pierced' (*scēat*), with dramatic effect.

144 **brēostum** 'the breast'; the pl. form is usual in OE [§D4i].

145 **him æt heortan** poss. dat.: 'at his heart'.

146 **þē** intensive adv. 'the' (instr.), used with a comp. adj. See also 312–13.

150 **flēogan** The vb. from the previous line, *forlēt*, having governed its own dir. obj. there (*daroð*), is still needed to pair with *flēogan*: 'let fly'. See also 321–2.

151 **þegen** Byrhtnoth is a loyal 'thegn' or retainer of the king, just as his own men are loyal 'thegns' of his (see 205, etc). On the term, see 8/12n.

152 **Him be healfe** 'at his side', or 'alongside him'.

156 **forheardne** adj. used as noun: 'very hard object', or 'hardest of things' (acc. sg.); i.e. the spear that Wulfmær has just pulled from his lord.

159 **gesyrwed secg** Another Viking warrior, who hopes to strip Byrhtnoth of his valuable war-gear.

⌜brād and brūneccg°⌝,   and on þā byrnan° slōh°.   bright-bladed mailcoat struck

Tō raþe hine° gelette°   lidmanna sum,   him hindered

165 þā hē þæs eorles   earm° āmyrde°.   arm disabled

Fēoll þā tō foldan   fealohilte° swurd;   golden-hilted

ne mihte hē gehealdan   heardne mēce°,   blade

wæpnes wealdan.   Þā gȳt° þæt word° gecwæð°,   yet utterance spoke

hār° hilderinc°   hyssas bylde°;   grey-haired warrior encouraged

170 bæd° gangan forð°   gōde gefēran°.   urged onwards comrades

Ne mihte þā on fōtum leng°   fæste gestandan°.   (any) longer stand

⌜Hē tō heofenum wlāt°⌝:   looked

'Geþancie° þē,   ⌜ðēoda° waldend°⌝,   (I) thank (for +g) of nations ruler

ealra þæra wynna°   þe ic on worulde gebād°.   joys (have) experienced

175 Nū ic āh°, milde° metod,   mæste° þearfe°   have merciful greatest need

⌜þæt þū mīnum gāste   gōdes geunne⌝

þæt mīn sāwul° tō ðē   sīðian° mōte°   soul journey may

on° þīn geweald°,   þēoden engla°,   into keeping of angels

mid friþe ferian°.   ⌜Ic eom frymdi tō þē⌝   pass

180 þæt ⌜hī⌝ helsceaðan°   hȳnan° ne mōton.'   'hell-foes' harm

Ðā hine hēowon°   hæðene° scealcas°   hacked down heathen warriors *np*

⌜and bēgen° þā beornas⌝   þe him big° stōdon,   both by

Ælfnōð and Wulmǣr;   bēgen lāgon:

ðā° onemn° hyra frēan°   feorh gesealdon°.   they alongside lord gave

185 ⌜Hī būgon° þā⌝ fram beaduwe°   þe þær bēon noldon.   turned away battle

Þǣr wurdon° Oddan° bearn°   ǣrest on flēame°.   were Odda's sons flight

---

163 **brād and brūneccg** The same half-line is used in *Beowulf* (31b/55).

172 **Hē . . . wlāt** Probably a half-line has been lost here.

173 **ðēoda waldend** The first of three epithets for God which the good Christian uses (the others are *milde metod*, 175, and *þēoden engla*, 178).

176 **þæt þū . . . geunne** The vb. *geunnan* governs the dat. and gen.: 'grant (to) my spirit the favour (*gōdes*) . . .'. It was believed that the soul or spirit (*gāst* and *sāwul* seem to be interchangeable here) was in its greatest danger as it left the body and might be waylaid and carried off by 'hell-foes' (*helsceaðan*, 180), i.e. devils.

179 **Ic eom frymdi tō þē** 'I am suppliant to you', i.e. 'I beseech you'.

180 **hī** acc. sg. fem. pron., with antec. *mīn sāwul*: 'it'.

182 **and bēgen þā beornas** The punctuation in 182–4 has been imposed on the assumption that this phr. is a further obj. of *hēowon*, but it could be taken as the subj. of *lāgon*, with no essential change of meaning.

185 **Hī būgon þā . . .** The behaviour now described (185–97) is contrasted explicitly with that of the two loyal retainers who have just given their lives alongside their dead lord.

⌈Godrīc fram gūþe⌉ and þone gōdan° forlēt°   good (man) deserted
þe him ⌈mænigne oft   mearh⌉ gesealde°.   had given
Hē gehlēop° þone eoh°   þe āhte° his hlāford,   leaped onto +*a* horse owned
190 ⌈on þām gerǣdum   þe hit riht ne wæs⌉.
And ⌈his brōðru mid him   bēgen⌉ ærndon°,   ran away
Godwine and Godwīg,   gūþe ne gȳmdon°   cared for +*g*
ac wendon° fram þām wīge   and þone wudu sōhton°,   turned   made for
flugon on þæt fæsten°   and hyra fēore° burgon°,   place of safety life saved +*d*
195 and manna mā°   ⌈þonne hit ænig mǣð wǣre⌉,   more +*g*
gyf hī þā geearnunga°   ⌈ealle⌉ gemundon°   favours (had) remembered
þe hē him° tō° duguþe°   gedōn° hæfde.   to them as benefit done
Swā ⌈him⌉ Offa ⌈on dæg   ǣr⌉ āsǣde°   (had) said
on þām meþelstede°   þā hē gemōt° hæfde,   meeting-place assembly
200 þæt þǣr mōdelīce°   manega sprǣcon°   boldly spoke
þe eft° æt þearfe   þolian° noldon.   later suffer
        Þā wearð° āfeallen°   þæs folces ealdor,   had fallen
Æþelrēdes eorl;   ealle gesāwon
heorðgenēatas°   þæt hyra hēorra° læg.   hearth-companions *np* lord
205 Þā ðǣr wendon forð   wlance° þegenas,   proud
unearge° men   efston° georne: unflinching hurried
hī woldon þā ealle   ⌈ōðer twēga⌉:

---

187 **Godrīc fram gūþe** A vb. is needed in trans.: 'Godric (fled) from the battle'. He is the first of the sons of Odda noted in 186, as we see later.

188 **mænigne . . . mearh** 'many a horse' (acc. sg.).

190 **on þām gerǣdum** The noun designates the harness and trappings of Byrhtnoth's horse, from which he dismounted at the start of the encounter; they are obviously of the finest, fit for a nobleman of such status. Suggested trans.: 'into the trappings', or 'into the saddle'.   **þe hit riht ne wæs** *þe* may here be a rel. pron.: '*which* it was not right (to do)'; or a conj.: '*as* it was not right (to do)'; or even the reduced form of another conj., *þēh* (i.e. *þēah*): '*though* it was not right (*or* fitting)'.

191 **his brōðru . . . bēgen** Thus there are three cowardly (and conveniently alliterating) brothers.

195 **þonne hit ænig mǣð wǣre** lit. 'than it were any fitness (*or* respect)', i.e. 'than was in any way fitting'.

196 **ealle** The adj. qualifies *þā geearnunga*. Separation of *ealle* from the noun or pron. to which it relates is seen also in 203 and 207.

198 **him** Presumably 'to him', i.e. Byrhtnoth, who is the referent of *hē* in 199.   **on dæg ǣr** 'earlier in the day'. This gathering to discuss the Viking threat may have been mentioned in the lost opening part of the poem.

207 **ōðer twēga** As a pron., *ōþer* has a basic meaning of one of a pair of possibilities; thus: 'one of two (things)'.

līf forlǣtan   oððe° lēofne° gewrecan°.   or   beloved (man) *as*   avenge

Swā hī° bylde forð   bearn Ælfrīces,   them

210   wiga ⌈wintrum geong⌉,   wordum mǣlde,

Ælfwine þā cwæð,   hē on ellen° sprǣc: courage

'Gemunu° þā mǣla°   þe° wē oft æt meodo°   (I) remember   times   when   mead

sprǣcon

þonne wē on bence°   bēot° āhōfon°,   (the) bench   boast   put up

hæleð° on healle,   ymbe° heard gewinn°;   heroes   about   conflict

215   ⌈nū mæg cunnian⌉   hwā cēne° ⌈sȳ⌉.   brave

Ic wylle mīne æþelo°   eallum° gecȳþan°,   lineage   to all   make known

þæt ic wæs on° Myrcon°   ⌈miccles cynnes⌉;   among   Mercians

wæs mīn ⌈ealda fæder   Ealhelm⌉ hāten,

wīs ealdorman,   woruldgesælig°.   prosperous

220   Ne sceolon° mē on þære° þēode   þegenas ætwītan°   shall   that   reproach

þæt ic of° ðisse ⌈fyrde°⌉   fēran° wille,   from   army   run

eard° gesēcan°,   nū mīn ealdor ligeð°   homeland   make for   lies

forhēawen æt hilde.   Mē° is þæt hearma° mǣst: To me   of sorrows

hē wæs ǣgder° mīn mǣg   and mīn hlāford.'   both

225   Þā hē forð ēode,   fǣhðe° gemunde°,   revenge *as*   thought about

þæt hē mid orde   ⌈ānne gerǣhte°⌉   struck

flotan⌉ on þām ⌈folce⌉   þæt sē on foldan læg

forwegen° mid ⌈his⌉ wǣpne.   Ongan þā winas°   carried off   comrades *ap*

manian°,   to exhort

frȳnd° and gefēran,   þæt hī forð ⌈ēodon⌉.   friends

230   Offa gemǣlde°,   æscholt° āscēoc°:   spoke   ash-spear   shook

---

210 **wintrum geong** dat. of definition: 'young in winters'. The Anglo-Saxons often used 'winter' where ModE uses 'year'.

215 **nū mæg cunnian** impers. subj. unexpressed: 'now one (*or* we) can find out'.   **sȳ** sbj. to express hypothesis, but in ModE simple 'is' suffices.

217 **miccles cynnes** gen. of definition: 'of (*or* from) a great family'; see also *heardes cynnes*, 266. The use of pret. *wæs* in Ælfwine's statement seems a little premature, unless we think of it in the sense 'I was born into . . .'.

218 **ealda fæder** 'grandfather'.   **Ealhelm** He was ealdorman of central Mercia, 940–51.

221 **fyrde** See 8/28–9n.

226–7 **ānne . . . flotan** 'a seaman'.

227 **folce** Probably here 'host' or 'army', meaning the Vikings. In 22 and 241 *folc* is used of the English host, but there is more ambiguity in 259 (see note).

228 **his** i.e. Ælfwine's.

229 **ēodon** Despite the indic. form, the meaning is sbj. (i.e. *ēoden*): '(that) they should go (forward)'.

⌐Hwæt⌐, þū Ælfwine hafast°   ealle gemanode°   have exhorted
þegenas ⌐tō þearfe⌐,   nū ūre þēoden līð°,   lies (dead)
eorl on eorðan.   Ūs° is eallum þearf   To us
þæt ūre° æghwylc°   ōþerne bylde,   of us each

235 wigan tō wīge,   þā hwīle þe hē wǣpen mæge
habban° and healdan°,   heardne mēce,   hold keep
gār and gōd swurd.   Ūs Godrīc hæfð,
earh° Oddan bearn,   ealle beswicene°.   cowardly betrayed
Wēnde° ⌐þæs formoni man⌐,   þā hē on mēare° rād°   Believed steed rode (off)

240 ⌐on wlancan° þām wicge°⌐,   þæt wǣre hit ūre hlāford;   splendid horse
forþan° wearð hēr on felda°   folc° tōtwǣmed°,   therefore field army divided
scyldburh° tōbrocen°.   ⌐Ābrēoðe his angin⌐   shield-wall broken
þæt hē hēr swā° manigne°   man āflȳmde°!'   so many (a) put to flight
Lēofsunu gemǣlde   and his linde āhōf,

245 bord tō gebeorge;   hē þām beorne oncwæð°:   answered
'Ic þæt gehāte°   þæt ic heonon° nelle°   vow from here will not
flēon° ⌐fōtes trym⌐   ac wille furðor gān,   flee
wrecan° on gewinne   mīnne winedrihten°.   avenge beloved lord
Ne þurfon° mē embe° ⌐Stūrmere⌐ stedefæste hælæð   have occasion to around

250 wordum° ætwītan,   nū mīn wine° gecranc°,   with (their) words lord has fallen
þæt ic hlāfordlēas   hām ⌐sīðie⌐,
wende⌐ fram wīge,   ac mē sceal wǣpen niman°,   take
ord and īren°.'   Hē ful yrre wōd,   iron (sword)
feaht° fæstlīce,   flēam hē forhogode°.   fought scorned

255 Dunnere þā cwæð,   daroð ācwehte°,   brandished

231 **Hwæt** An exclamation: 'Indeed' or 'Truly', signalling Offa's approval of Ælfwine's exhortations.

232 **tō þearfe** lit. 'at need'. The idea is that Ælfwine has risen to the occasion, so 'in this time of need' or 'as is needed' are apt renderings.

239 **þæs** 'that', gen. obj. of *wēnan*. It anticipates the *þæt* clause, which starts on the next line, and so is not needed in trans. A similar construction is in 246.   **formoni man** The prefix *for-* is here an intensifier: 'very many men' or 'too many a man'.

240 **on wlancan þām wicge** The adj. precedes the def. art. for metrical reasons.

242 **Ābrēoðe his angin** The vb. is sbj., with optative meaning: 'May his action (*or* undertaking) fail!'.

247 **fōtes trym** adv. phr., with *trym* in the acc. of extent: 'the length of a foot', i.e. 'a single footstep'. Cf. *fōtmǣl*, 275.

249 **Stūrmere** Sturmer is a village in the north of Essex.

251–2 **sīðie, wende** pres. sbj. of hypothesis: '(that) I should travel..., turn...'; but in ModE we would adopt the point of view of a future speaker, so the pret. is better: '(that) I travelled..., turned...' (and in fact the form *wende* could be pres. or pret. sbj.).

⌐unorne° ceorl   ofer eall⌐ clypode,   simple
bæd þæt beorna gehwylc°   Byrhtnōð wrǣce°:   each +gp   (should) avenge
'Ne mæg nā° wandian°   sē þe wrecan þenceð   never   hesitate
frēan ⌐on folce⌐,   ne for fēore murnan.'
260 Þā hī forð ēodon,   fēores hī ne rōhton°;   cared about +g
ongunnon ⌐þā hīredmen⌐   heardlīce° feohtan,   fiercely
grame° gārberend°,   and God bǣdon°   hostile   spear-bearers   prayed
þæt hī mōston gewrecan   hyra winedrihten
and on hyra fēondum   fyl° gewyrcan°.   destruction   wreak
265 ⌐Him se gȳsel°⌐ ongan   geornlīce° fylstan°;   hostage   eagerly   support
hē wæs on° Norðhymbron°   ⌐heardes cynnes⌐,   from   Northumbria
Ecglāfes bearn,   him wæs Æscferð nama.
Hē ne wandode nā   æt° þām wīgplegan°   from   'battle-play'
ac hē fȳsde° forð   flān° genehe°.   shot   arrows   in abundance
270 Hwīlon° hē on° bord scēat,   hwīlon beorn tǣsde°;   Sometimes   into   lacerated
⌐æfre embe stunde⌐   hē sealde° sume° wunde   inflicted   some
þā hwīle ðe hē wǣpna   wealdan mōste°.   was able
        Þā gȳt on orde° stōd   ⌐Ēadweard se langa°⌐,   vanguard   tall
gearo° and geornful°,   gylpwordum° sprǣc   ready   eager   in vaunting words
275 þæt hē nolde flēogan   fōtmǣl° landes°,   a foot-space   of ground
⌐ofer bæc⌐ būgan°,   þā° his betera° leg°.   retreat   now   better   lay (dead)
Hē bræc° ⌐þone bordweall⌐   and wið° þā beornas feaht   broke   against

256 **unorne ceorl** A humble 'commoner' or 'yeoman' fights alongside great noblemen, and he has his say, too.   **ofer eall** 'over (it) all'; presumably, above the din of battle.

259 **on folce** Probably, 'upon (that) people', i.e. the Viking army, but it could simply mean 'among (their) people', i.e. the English army to which the would-be avengers belong.

261 **þā hīredmen** *þā* is either the adv. *then* or the nom. pl. def. art. with *hīredmen*, 'household men' (i.e. retainers).

265 **Him** Presumably, 'them' (the English warriors), dat. pl. obj. of *fylstan*.   **se gȳsel** It was not unusual for well-born hostages to be exchanged as pledges for peace-treaties between warring Anglo-Saxon kingdoms; they would live honourably among the nobles of the host kingdom and, as we now see, might display the same spirit of loyalty as they. Æscferth is from Northumbria, a troublesome region still not fully part of a united England at this time. A hostage behaves similarly in the 'Cynewulf and Cyneheard' episode (29/18).

266 **heardes cynnes** gen. of definition: 'from tough stock'.

271 **æfre embe stunde** 'time and again' (lit. 'ever at a time'). This awkward line has no alliterative pattern, but the two half-lines are linked by rhyme. See also 282 (*brōðor / ōþer*) and 42n.

273 **Ēadweard se langa** Presumably the same Edward whom we met in 117.

276 **ofer bæc** 'backwards'.

277 **þone bordweall** Presumably a defensive 'shield-wall' thrown up hastily by the Vikings (cf. 102).

oðþæt° hē his sincgyfan°   on° þām sǣmannum   until treasure-giver upon

wurðlīce° wrec°,   ǣr hē on° wæle° ⌐lǣge⌐.   worthily avenged among the slain

280   Swā dyde Æþerīc,   æþele° gefēra   noble

fūs° and forðgeorn°,   feaht eornoste,   willing eager to advance

Sībyrhtes brōðor,   and swīðe mænig ōþer

clufon° ⌐cellod⌐ bord: cēne hī° weredon.   split themselves

Bærst° bordes lǣrig°   and sēo byrne sang   Shattered rim

285   ⌐gryrelēoða sum⌐.   Þā æt gūðe slōh

Offa ⌐þone sǣlidan⌐   þæt hē on eorðan fēoll,

and ðǣr Gaddes mǣg   grund gesōhte.

Raðe wearð æt hilde   Offa forhēawen;

hē hæfde ðēah° geforþod°   þæt hē his frēan   nonetheless accomplished

gehēt°,   promised

290   swā° hē bēotode° ǣr wið° his bēahgifan°   inasmuch as (had) vowed to ring-giver

þæt hī sceoldon bēgen   on burh° rīdan   stronghold

hāle° tō hāme   oððe on here° crincgan°,   unharmed army perish

on wælstōwe°   wundum sweltan°.   slaughter-place die (from +d)

Hē læg ðegenlīce°   ðēodne gehende°.   like a thane close to +d

295   Ðā wearð° borda gebrǣc°.   Brimmen wōdon,   (there) was smashing

gūðe gegremode°;   gār oft þurhwōd°   enraged (with +d) passed through

fǣges° feorhhūs°.   Forð ðā ēode Wīstān,   (a) doomed one's 'life-house' (i.e. body)

Þurstānes suna,   wið þās secgas feaht;

hē wæs on geþrange°   ⌐hyra þrēora bana⌐   throng

---

279 **lǣge** A sbj. vb. is often preferred in OE in constructions with *ǣr* ('before' or 'until'), presumably because, in relation to the action of the main clause, the event alluded to is still in the future and thus hypothetical. See also 300.

283 **cellod** This unique word seems to be an adj. describing the shields (*bord*, acc. pl.), but its meaning is unknown; 'curved' has been suggested. Cf. *celæs bord* (similarly obscure) in 32/29.

285 **gryrelēoða sum** 'a certain terrible song' (*sum* with partitive gen.). The poet evokes the sound of sword on chain-mail; this and the shattering shield are not presented in relation to any specific combatant but are among the vivid general battle-images which become more frequent now: see esp. 295–7.

286 **þone sǣlidan** We are not told *which* Viking and perhaps the word is being used generically, i.e. the Vikings in general were being slain by Offa (just as in 284 a single shield shattering appears to signify a repeated happening); but some lines may have been lost here, which would explain the abruptness with which we are told next that *Gaddes mǣg* (i.e. Offa) fell.

299 **hyra þrēora bana** 'the slayer of three of them'.

300	ǣr ⸢him⸣ Wīgelines bearn on þām wæle læge.
	Þǣr wæs stīð° ⸢gemōt⸣. Stōdon fæste	tough
	wigan on gewinne; wīgend° cruncon,	warriors
	wundum wērige°; wæl fēol on eorþan.	exhausted (by +d)
	Ōswold and Ēadwold ealle hwīle,	
305	bēgen þā gebrōþru°, beornas trymedon,	brothers
	hyra winemāgas° wordon° bǣdon	dear kinsmen *ap* by (their) words
	þæt hī þǣr æt ðearfe þolian sceoldon,	
	unwāclīce° wǣpna nēotan°.	untiringly use +g
	⸢Byrhtwold maþelode, bord hafenode⸣,	
310	sē wæs eald genēat°, æsc ācwehte;	companion
	hē ful baldlīce beornas lǣrde°:	exhorted
	'Hige° sceal° þē heardra°, heorte þē cēnre°,	Intention must (be) firmer braver
	mōd° sceal þē māre°, þe° ūre ⸢mægen⸣ lȳtlað°.	courage greater as diminishes
	Hēr līð ūre ealdor eall forhēawen,	
315	gōd° on grēote°. ⸢Ā mæg gnornian⸣	good (man) dust
	sē ðe nū fram ⸢þīs⸣ wīgplegan wendan þenceð.	
	Ic eom frōd° fēores°; fram ⸢ic ne wille⸣	mature 'of life' away
	ac ic ⸢mē⸣ be healfe° ⸢mīnum hlāforde⸣,	side
	be swā lēofan men, licgan þence.'	
320	Swā° hī° Æþelgāres bearn ealle bylde,	Likewise them

300 **him** rflx. dat. pron., not translatable. Presumably it is Wistan who now lies among the slain, but it is odd that he is described as the son of both Thurstan (298) and Wigelin (300). Perhaps Wistan's father had two names (known to the original audience), or perhaps *bearn* (300) here means 'descendant' rather than specifically 'son'. Then again, a passage introducing yet another hero may have been lost between 298 and 299.

301 **gemōt** 'meeting' or 'encounter'; the same noun was used for the assembly of the English at which they boasted of their intentions, before the battle (199).

309 **Byrhtwold . . . hafenode** In presenting this last and most venerable of Byrhtnoth's retainers, the poet repeats precisely the introduction to Byrhtnoth's own earlier vaunting speech (42); it is a tribute to Byrhtwold's loyalty.

313 **mægen** Either bodily 'strength' or (the English) 'force' or 'troop'.

315 **Ā mæg gnornian** lit. 'ever will be able to regret', i.e. 'ever will have cause to regret'.

316 **þīs** Unusually, *fram* is followed by the instr. form of *þes* (masc. sg.).

317 **ic ne wille** A vb. of motion must be added: 'I will not go'.

318 **mē** rflx. pron. associated either with *licgan* (cf. *him* in 300) or with *þence*; either way, it need not be trans.   **mīnum hlāforde** poss. dat.: 'of my lord'.

Godrīc tō gūþe.   Oft hē gār ⌐forlēt,
wǣlspere° windan⌐   on þā wīcingas;   deadly spear
swā hē on þām folce   fyrmest° ēode,   foremost
hēow° and hȳnde°   odþæt hē on hilde gecranc.   hacked   felled
325   Næs þæt nā ⌐se Godrīc⌐   þe ðā gūde forbēah°.   fled from

321–2 **forlēt ... windan** 'let fly'; the vb. phr. governs both *gār* and *wǣlspere*.
325 **se Godrīc** For Godric the coward, see 187.

31
Beowulf

Although *Beowulf* is the earliest epic poem in English, it is not about England or England's heroes. Its setting is what we now call Scandinavia, particularly Denmark and southern Sweden (the latter area being referred to as Geatland in the poem), and its cast-list includes a selection of both historical and legendary figures from the period of the fourth to sixth centuries known as the 'age of migrations', when Germanic tribes spread across much of western Europe (some of them eventually reaching, and sacking, Rome). The settlement of Britain in the mid-fifth century by Angles, Saxons and other tribes – who would come to be known collectively as the 'English' – was itself part of this process. For them, therefore (and for the great number of later settlers, mainly Danes, who arrived during the ninth and tenth centuries), the world of *Beowulf* was, notionally at least, a familiar world, the world in which their ancestral identity had been created. It is within this world that the story of the young Geatish hero Beowulf unfolds: how he saved Denmark under King Hrothgar from the depredations of Grendel and his mother (in the first section of the poem), and how, in old age, he died defending his own kingdom from a dragon.

Our only copy of the 3182-line poem – known universally by the name of its principal character since it was first edited in 1815 – is on fols. 153r–155v of what today is known simply as 'the *Beowulf*-manuscript' (though its older name, the 'Nowell codex', referring to its sixteenth-century owner, may still be encountered); this constitutes the second half of a composite British Library volume, Cotton Vitellius A. xv. The manuscript was written out between about 1000 and 1010, by two scribes, but the poem's origins have long been a matter of great controversy. Historical references within it (such as the raid on the Swedes by Hygelac, lines 2922–98, which we know took place *c*. 510, and his death *c*. 520) show that it could not have been composed – in the form in which we know it – much before the middle of the sixth century; but the poet's knowledge of Christianity, and his obvious confidence that this is shared by his audience, pushes the earliest possible date further forward to the first half of the seventh century, after the conversion of the Anglo-Saxons. During two centuries of *Beowulf*-scholarship, various dates of composition covering the whole of the theoretically possible span (up to about 1000) have been championed. However, a recent analysis of the errors made by the scribe of the *Beowulf*-manuscript, which appear to include the repeated misreading of certain letters, has shown that he (or his predecessor) was probably copying from a version of the poem written in a particular Anglo-Saxon script (whose forms are likely to have given rise to specific copying errors) which was only in use until about 750. This would indicate that the poem in its literary form had indeed taken shape by then. Certainly, various linguistic, metrical and stylistic features of the poem add weight to a dating in the first half of the eighth century. However, the poem will not have reached its early eleventh-century form without modification and addition – and we can scarcely doubt, anyway, that the true origins of the poem lie in generations of oral tradition (probably commencing *c.* 520), of which the version we know represents merely a late stage.

The 'Christianity' of *Beowulf*, alluded to above, deserves a further note. Though set in a pagan world populated by pagan people, the poem as we know it is suffused by Christian reference (as the second of the extracts below shows particularly strongly). It should not, however, surprise us that a poet composing for a Christian audience, and himself a Christian, should use his religion's resources creatively, as in deriving Grendel's evil nature from that OT 'type' of wrongdoing, Cain. Poetic licence allows such anachronism, and the attempts of earlier scholars to interpret the poem as Christian allegory (with Beowulf as Christ) have rightly been dismissed as unworkable. Nevertheless, a good case can be made for the *Beowulf*-poet's deliberate highlighting of the flaws of pagan heroic society, even as he celebrates its glories. Implicit in such an approach would be affirmation of the superior claims of the Christian dispensation, with its promise of a bright heavenly future for the deserving, rather than shadowy remembrance in the mouth of a minstrel. The Hildeburh episode (extract 31a, below) well illustrates this unexpressed questioning of the values of a feud-dominated society.

The *Beowulf*-manuscript (which contains the poem *Judith* and several prose narratives also: see Texts 10 and 27) was one of the items damaged in a fire in Sir Robert Cotton's library in London in 1731. The bulk of the text remains intact but the edges of pages were charred, and then rather ineptly restored, and this has added to the number of problematical readings in the poem. Two transcripts made before the fire have as often as not compounded rather than solved the problems. Wherever possible, original manuscript readings are retained in the version below, but some emendations are made and the most important of these are discussed in the notes. For ease of reference, the lines in each extract are numbered from 1, but the line numbering in relation to the whole poem is indicated also in square brackets.

The issue of the linguistic character of the *Beowulf*-text as we know it is complex. Two scribes, with differing spelling habits, were responsible for our copy, and the one who wrote out lines 1–1939, thus including both of the extracts below, appears to have made a greater effort than the second to bring spellings into line with the conventions of written WS at the start of the eleventh century. Late use of *y* instead of *i* is seen, for example, in *scypon* (a/92 – where *-on* is a levelled spelling of *-um,*), *syn-* (a/73), *-wyrgenne* (b/27) and *fȳf-* (b/91), but is by no means universal. For the third-person plural pronoun, the late spelling *hig* is used (a/23), but also *hīe* (a/24, etc). There are many forms which might be thought to be of dialectal significance – often Anglian or sometimes, more specifically, Mercian; examples are *frioðu-* (a/34, not *friðu*) and *gescær* (b/35, not *gescear*). *Mehte* rather than *meahte* (a/20, b/5 and 24) could be an Anglian relic, yet the form occurs also in both Alfredian (i.e. early WS) and later WS texts. Such is the overall mix of forms in the poem that, on linguistic grounds alone, nothing can be reliably concluded about its origins.

Further reading

K. Malone, ed., *The Nowell Codex: British Museum Cotton Vitellius A. XV, Second MS.,* EEMF 12 (Copenhagen, 1963)

K. S. Kiernan, with A. Prescott *et al.,* eds., *Electronic 'Beowulf',* 2 CD-ROMS (London, 1999) [facsimile]

F. Klaeber, *'Beowulf' and the 'Fight at Finnsburg',* 3rd edn with suppls. (Boston, 1950)

G. Jack, *Beowulf: a Student Edition* (Oxford, 1994)

G. Turville-Petre, *The Heroic Age of Scandinavia* (London, 1951)

R. W. Chambers, *'Beowulf': an Introduction to the Study of the Poem,* with supplement by C. Wrenn (Cambridge, 1959)

G. N. Garmonsway and J. Simpson, *'Beowulf' and its Analogues* (London, 1968)

J. D. Niles, *'Beowulf'. The Poem and its Tradition* (Cambridge, MA, 1983)

P. S. Baker, ed., *'Beowulf': Basic Readings* (New York and London, 1995)

J. Hill, *The Cultural World in 'Beowulf'* (Toronto, 1995)

R. E. Bjork and J. D. Niles, *A 'Beowulf' Handbook* (Exeter, 1997)

M. Lapidge, 'The Archetype of *Beowulf'*, *ASE* 29 (2000), 5–41

A. Orchard, *A Critical Companion to 'Beowulf'* (Woodbridge, 2002)

31a
The Tragedy of Hildeburh (*Beowulf*, lines 1063–1159)

Much of the complexity of *Beowulf* results from the number of narrative levels on which the poem unfolds. Within and around the simple narrative past of the central story (the hero's fights against Grendel, Grendel's mother and the dragon) there operates a series of chronological dislocations (often described as 'digressions') which either take us back to a more remote past – historical, mythical, legendary or even biblical – or carry us forward to a future, known or unknown to the original audience. The tragedy of Hildeburh is one such dislocation. During the feast held in Heorot to celebrate Beowulf's mortal wounding of Grendel, the poet has King Hrothgar's scop perform a 'lay' whose theme of death and disaster is clearly meant to act as a sort of balance to the unbridled joy of the hall-people. It is set in the not too distant historical past of the Danes, and the abbreviated and allusive way in which it is told by the scop suggests that the poet knew his Anglo-Saxon audience (like the audience *within* the poem) to be already familiar with the details. The poetical fragment given later in this section (Text 32, 'The Fight at Finnsburh') seems to have come from just the sort of vehicle by which they could have come to know them. The OE poem *Widsith* corroborates several of the relationships mentioned in the *Beowulf*-account, such as those between Hoc and Hnæf and between Folcwalda and Finn.

The episode is told, not in the words of the minstrel himself, but in an allusive report of what he sang. It is hard to follow at a first reading and we have to supply the context ourselves and deduce many of the details.

1–17a. After setting the scene, the poet alludes to Hildeburh's tragedy. She was clearly a Danish (or at least 'half-Danish') princess, who had married Finn, prince of the Frisians, doubtless as a political move to secure peace between Danes and Frisians. Hildeburh had a brother, Hnæf, who apparently went to Finn with his Danish retinue in friendship. However, for an unexplained reason, they were attacked and Hnæf was killed. In an elliptical reference, the 'Jutes' (*Ēote*) are implicated. This, along with several later references, suggests that Jutes were allied with Finn (they were his geographical neighbours), or that at least a group of them was among his retinue (see also 10n). The unnamed son of Hildeburh (presumably fathered by Finn and, again presumably, fighting on Finn's side) was killed also. This is the phase – Frisians (and Jutes) attacking Danes – which seems to be the subject of Text 32.

17b–44. Despite these slayings, so many of Finn's thanes had been killed also that he was forced to call a truce with the Danes, leadership of whom had now been assumed by Hnæf's thane Hengest; he would set aside a hall for the Danes' use, to be shared with some Jutes. He would treat both groups equally; the Danes thus had to accept to serve the killer of their lord (Hnæf), and the Frisians were specifically forbidden to harbour thoughts of continuing the feud.

45–62. There was time now for the bodies of Hnæf and Hildeburh's son to be burned on a funeral pyre and for Hildeburh to mourn.

63–97. Winter set in, making it impossible for the Danes to go home. The Frisians dispersed but Hengest had to bide with Finn. Spring came, and in Hengest the desire for vengeance quickened, catalysed by the symbolic laying of a sword across his lap by a Danish warrior. And then it seems that two further Danes, Guthlaf and Oslaf (who had perhaps sailed back to Denmark for reinforcements), arrived to demand retribution. So the Danes attacked, killed Finn, looted his treasures and sailed home with the now triply bereaved Hildeburh.

In the lines that follow this extract, mirth is resumed in Heorot and the celebration concludes. Overnight, however, Grendel's mother wreaks *her* vengeance on the Danes; the sequel is described in Text 31b.

Further reading

L. E. Nicholson, 'Hunlafing and the Point of the Sword', in *Anglo-Saxon Poetry: Essays in Appreciation for John C. McGalliard*, ed. E. Nicholson and D. W. Frese (Notre Dame, IN, 1975), pp. 50–61

R. J. Schrader, *God's Handiwork: Images of Women in Early Germanic Literature* (Westport, CT, 1983)

J. Hill, ' "Þæt wæs geomuru ides!" A Female Stereotype Examined', in *New Readings on Women in Old English Literature*, ed. H. Damico and A. H. Olsen (Bloomington and Indianapolis, IN, 1990), pp. 235–47

See also 'Further Reading' for Text 32, p. 287.

Þǣr wæs sang° ond swēg° ⌈samod ætgædere⌉	singing music	
fore° ⌈Healfdenes hildewīsan⌉,	before +*d*	
gomenwudu° ⌈grēted, gid° oft wrecen⌉,	'mirth-wood' (*i.e.* lyre) song	
⌈ðonne healgamen Hrōþgāres scop		
5 æfter° medobence° mǣnan scolde⌉,	along mead-benches	
⌈be⌉ Finnes eaferum°, ðā hīe° se fǣr°	sons them sudden attack	
begeat°,	assailed	
⌈hæleð Healf-Dena, Hnæf Scyldinga⌉,		
[*1070*] in Frēswæle° feallan scolde°.	Frisian battlefield had to	

1 **samod ætgædere** 'at the same time together'; but 'both together' softens the tautology; see also 38/39.

2 **Healfdenes hildewīsan** 'Healfdene's battle-leader'; i.e. Hrothgar. This was perhaps the title given him while his father, Healfdene, still ruled.

3 **grēted ... wrecen** In the context, best trans. as '(had been) plucked [lit. "touched"] ... (had been) recited' (with *wæs* in 1 perhaps still in action, but now as the auxil. vb.). The next stage in the proceedings is anticipated.

4–5 **ðonne healgamen ... mǣnan scolde** lit. 'when ... was to relate (*mǣnan*) a hall-entertainment'; i.e. something to entertain the hall.

6 **be** 'about'. This is not in the manuscript but suits the sense; it is possible that a line is missing at this point.

7 **hæleð Healf-Dena, Hnæf Scyldinga** Hnæf, the subj. of this sentence (with vb. *sceolde*), is thus described as both 'hero of the Half-Danes' and 'of the Scyldings'; the latter (elaborated as 'Herescyldings' in 46) is the dynastic name of the Danes (see 28 and 96). Hnæf is Hildeburh's brother, and their father is Hoc (see 14).

⌐Ne hūru° Hildeburh   herian° þorfte°⌐   indeed to praise had occasion

10 ⌐Ēotena⌐ trēowe°: unsynnum° wearð°   good faith *as* guiltless (she) was

beloren° lēofum° æt   þām lindplegan°,   deprived of +*d* loved (ones) shield-play

⌐bearnum ond brōðrum⌐; hīe ⌐on gebyrd⌐ hruron°,   fell

gāre° wunde°. Þæt wæs gēomuru° ides°!   by spear wounded sad woman

Nalles° hōlinga°   Hōces dohtor   Not without cause

15 meotodsceaft° bemearn°   syþðan° morgen   decree of providence bewailed after
      cōm,

ðā hēo under swegle°   gesēon° meahte°   sky see could

morþorbealo° māga°. ⌐Þǣr hē ǣr mǣste hēold⌐   deadly slaughter of kinsmen

[*1080*] worolde wynne°, wīg° ⌐ealle⌐ fornam°   joy battle carried off

Finnes þegnas   nemne° fēaum° ānum°,   except for +*d* a few only

20 þæt° hē ne mehte   on þǣm ⌐meðelstede°⌐   so that 'meeting-place'

wīg Hengeste°   wiht° gefeohtan°,   against Hengest *ds* at all win

ne ⌐þā wēalāfe⌐   wīge forþringan°,   dislodge (from +*d*)

⌐þēodnes ðegne⌐; ac ⌐hig him⌐ geþingo° budon°   terms offered

þæt hīe him ōðer° flet° eal° gerȳmdon°,   another hall complete would clear

25 healle ond hēahsetl°,   þæt hīe ⌐healfre⌐ geweald°   'high seat' (*i.e.* throne) control

---

9 **Ne ... herian þorfte** A laconic understatement.

10 **Ēotena** 'of the Jutes'. The words *Ēote* 'Jutes' and *eoten* 'giant' have the same gen. pl. form but here it will be assumed that the tribal name is intended throughout the episode; see headnote [and §B6e]. The Jutes and Frisians were closely related and it seems that Finn (a prince of Frisia) has members of both tribes serving under him. There is ambiguity in relation to the Jutes later on (see 79 and 83). The Jutes and the Frisians were among the tribes who settled in Britain during the fifth century (see 9a/16–18).

12 **bearnum ond brōðrum** generic pl.; there is in fact only one of each: 'of son and brother'. **on gebyrd** Apparently, 'in accordance with destiny [lit. "birth"]'.

17 **Þǣr hē ǣr ... hēold** 'Where he [i.e. Finn] had previously possessed'. But many editors emend *hē* to *hēo* 'she', i.e. Hildeburh, with the clause then belonging to the previous sentence. **mǣste** adj. 'greatest', describing *wynne* (18; *worolde* is gen. sg.).

18 **ealle** describes *þegnas* in 19.

20 **meðelstede** A kenning for 'place of battle'.

22 **þā wēalāfe** 'the woe-remnant' (acc. sg.); perhaps, 'the survivors of the calamity' (also in 36).

23 **þēodnes ðegne** The phr., with dat. *ðegne*, must be parallel with *Hengeste* in 21: '... against Hengest, his prince's [i.e. Hnæf's] thane'. **hig him** After *ac*, 'but', and in the context of what follows, the most likely referent for *hig*, 'they', is Hnæf and his followers, in which case *him* is 'them', referring to the Frisians (or possibly 'him' for Finn); but *hig* might refer to the Frisians and *him* either to Hengest ('him') or to the survivors in general ('them'). The prons. in 24 must then be trans. as appropriate.

25 **healfre** 'of half (of it)'; gen. sg. fem., agreeing with *healle*.

⌐wið° Ēotena bearn⌐   āgan° mōston°;   with   possess   might

ond æt feohgyftum°   ⌐Folcwaldan sunu⌐   treasure-giving *dp*

[*1090*] ⌐dōgra gehwylce⌐   Dene° ⌐weorþode°⌐,   the Danes *ap*   would honour

Hengestes hēap°   hringum wenede°   company *as*   would favour (with +*d*)

30   ⌐efne swā swīðe⌐,   sincgestrēonum°   with treasures

fættan° goldes,   ⌐swā hē Frēsena° cyn   (of) ornamented   of the Frisians

on bēorsele°   byldan° wolde⌐.   drinking-hall   encourage

Ðā hīe getruwedon°   on twā° healfa°   trusted in +*a*   two (*i.e.* both)   sides

fæste° frioðuwǣre°.   Fin Hengeste   firm   peace-agreement *as*

35   ⌐elne unflitme⌐   āðum° benemde°   with oaths   declared (to +*d*)

þæt hē þā wēalāfe   ⌐weotena dōme⌐

ārum° hēolde°,   þæt ðǣr ǣnig mon   honourably   would treat

[*1100*] ⌐wordum ne worcum⌐   wǣre° ne brǣce°,   agreement   should break

nē þurh inwitsearo°   ǣfre ⌐gemǣnden°⌐   malicious intrigue   should complain

40   ðēah° hīe hira bēaggyfan°   bana° folgedon,   though   ring-giver's   slayer

ðēodenlēase°,   ⌐þā him swā geþearfod wæs⌐;   'prince-less'

gyf þonne Frȳsna hwylc°   ⌐frēcnen sprǣce⌐   any of +*g*

ðæs morþorhetes°   ⌐myndgiend wǣre⌐,   murderous hostility

26 **wið Ēotena bearn** As it is unlikely that the Danes would be asked to share a hall with their enemies, it is assumed that these 'men of the Jutes' are on the Danish side, in which case there are groups of Jutes serving both sides.

27 **Folcwaldan sunu** 'Folcwald's son' (nom.); i.e. Finn.

28 **dōgra gehwylce** 'every day' (lit. 'on each of days'). **weorþode** The mood of this and most of the vbs. in the following lines is the sbj. of hypothesis or command.

30 **efne swā swīðe** 'even as strongly', i.e. 'to the same extent'.

31–2 **swā... wolde** 'just as (*or* to the same extent that) he would wish...'. The agreement is that the Danes shall be treated just as well as the Frisians. **bēorsele** lit. 'beer-hall', but the drink alluded to was a sweet drink nothing like today's beer.

35 **elne unflitme** The noun *flit* means 'strife' or 'contention', and so *unflitme*, occurring here uniquely, might mean 'without contention', but its form is not clear. Both it and *elne* may be advs.: 'with courage and without argument'; or it may be an adj. qualifying *elne*: 'with undisputed courage'. Some editors emend *unflitme* to the adj. *unhlitme* (which occurs also, probably, in 67) and trans. as 'most unhappy' or 'ill-fated'.

36 **weotena dōme** This seems to refer to Finn's decision about how to treat the Danes; thus, 'in (accordance with) the judgement of (his) counsellors'.

38 **wordum ne worcum** 'in (neither) words nor deeds'.

39 **gemǣnden** The subj. *ǣnig mon*, treated as sg. with *brǣce*, is now given a pl. vb. (sbj.). The point of the hypothetical complaint, that one might be forced to follow the slayer of one's lord, is a crucial destabilising element in feud cultures.

41 **þā him swā geþearfod wæs** 'when [i.e. "since"] (it) had been thus forced on them'.

42 **frēcnen sprǣce** dat. of manner: 'with some daring remark'.

43 **myndgiend wǣre** lit. 'should be reminding of' (with gen.), i.e. 'should bring to mind'.

þonne ⌈hit sweordes ecg   syððan scolde⌉.

45 Ād° wæs geæfned° ond ⌈icge⌉ gold	Pyre made ready
āhæfen° of° horde. ⌈Here-Scyldinga⌉	brought up from
betst beadorinca° wæs on° bǣl° gearu°.	of warriors for fire ready
[*1110*] Æt þǣm āde wæs ēþgesȳne°	plain to see
swātfāh° syrce°, ⌈swȳn° ealgylden°⌉,	bloodstained mailcoat boar 'all-gilded'
50 eofer°⌉ īrenheard°, æþeling° manig	boar 'iron-hard' (a) nobleman
wundum āwyrded°; ⌈sume⌉ on wæle°.	maimed (by +*d*) carnage
crungon°	had fallen
Hēt ðā Hildeburh æt Hnæfes āde	
⌈hire selfre sunu⌉ sweoloðe° befæstan°,	flame *ds* be committed (to +*d*)
⌈bānfatu° bærnan°⌉, ond on bǣl dōn°	'bone-vessels' be burned be consigned
55 ⌈ēame on eaxle⌉. Ides gnornode°,	mourned
gēomrode° giddum°. Gūðrinc°	lamented with songs (The) warrior
āstāh°;	arose
wand° tō wolcnum° wælfȳra° mǣst°,	curled skies of 'slaughter-fires' greatest
[*1120*] hlynode° for° hlāwe°; hafelan° multon°,	roared before mound heads melted
bengeato° burston ðonne blōd ætspranc°,	'wound-gates' spurted out
60 lāðbite° līces°. Līg° ⌈ealle forswealg°⌉,	'hostile bites' body's Fire swallowed up
gǣsta gīfrost°, þāra⌉ ðe þǣr gūð fornam	greediest
bēga° folces; wæs hira blǣd° scacen°.	of both glory departed
Gewiton° ⌈him⌉ ðā wīgend wīca° nēosian°,	Went dwellings seek out +*g*
frēondum befeallen°, ⌈Frȳsland gesēon⌉,	bereft of +*d*

---

44 hit sweordes ecg syððan scolde 'it should thereafter (be) the sword's edge' (vb. 'to be' om. after the modal: §G2d), i.e. be a matter to be settled by the sword. Some editors emend *syððan* to a vb., such as *sēðan*, 'affirm' or 'settle', but this is unnecessary.

45 icge An unknown word; perhaps an adj., 'splendid' or 'rich'.

46 Here-Scyldinga 'of the army-Scyldings'; perhaps, 'warlike Scyldings'.

49–50 swȳn ... eofer The two nouns describe the same creature, the boar, whose image was used as a protective symbol on Anglo-Saxon weapons and items of armour, such as a famous helmet from the Sutton Hoo burial in Essex.

51 sume 'certain ones' or 'some'; the understated pron. is presumably emphatic: many notable ones had fallen.

53 hire selfre sunu 'the son of her herself', i.e. 'her own son'.

54 bānfatu bærnan The kenning is pl. (meaning 'bodies'), as though the poet's view is on the general picture, even as he tells specifically of Hildeburh's son.

55 ēame on eaxle 'to uncle at shoulder', i.e. 'at his uncle's side'.

60–1 ealle ... þāra 'all of those'.

63 him rflx. pron. with vb. of motion [§D4c].

64 Frȳsland gesēon Presumably Finn's citadel is outside the boundaries of Frisia, to which the Frisians are able to return for the winter, overland; Hengest and his men, however, cannot return by sea to their homeland in this season.

65 hāmas ond hēaburh°.   Hengest ðā gȳt°   *high stronghold still*
⌐wælfāgne winter⌐   wunode° mid ⌐Finne   *remained*
eal unhlitme⌐.   Eard° gemunde°   *Homeland as remembered*
[*1130*] þēah þe ne meahte   on mere° drīfan°   *sea drive*
hringedstefnan°;   holm° storme°   *ring-prowed (ship) ocean with storm*
wēol°,   *surged*
70 won° wið winde,   winter ȳþe° belēac°   *struggled waves ap locked*
īsgebinde°,   oþðæt ⌐ōþer cōm   *with icy bond*
gēar in geardas⌐   swā nū gȳt dēð°,   *does*
⌐þā ðe syngāles   sēle bewitiað°,   *observe*
wuldortorhtan weder⌐.
Đā wæs winter scacen,
75 ⌐fæger foldan bearm⌐.   Fundode° ⌐wrecca⌐,   *Was eager (to go)*
gist° of geardum;   hē tō° gyrnwræce°   *visitor about revenge for injury*
swīðor° þōhte   þonne° tō sǣlāde°,   *more intensely than sea-journey*
[*1140*] gif° hē torngemōt°   þurhtēon° mihte,   *whether hostile encounter bring about*
⌐þæt hē Ēotena bearn⌐   inne gemunde⌐.   *men*
80 Swā hē ne forwyrnde°   ⌐woroldrǣdenne⌐   *denied*
þonne ⌐him Hūnlāfing   hildelēoman°,   *gleaming sword as*
billa° sēlest°,   on bearm⌐ dyde°,   *of blades best put*
⌐þæs wǣron mid° Ēotenum   ecge⌐ cūðe°.   *among known*

66 **wælfāgne winter** acc. of duration of time: 'through (that) slaughter-stained winter'.

66–7 **Finne eal unhlitme** The manuscript has *Finnel un hlitme*. The conjectured *eal* is the adv. 'completely' or 'utterly'; suggested renderings of the otherwise unattested *unhlitme* (taking the root to be *hlytm*, 'the casting of lots') have included 'without lot', i.e. 'involuntarily' (with *un* as neg. prefix), or 'with misfortune', i.e. 'in a disastrous plight' (with *un* as adversative prefix).

71–2 **ōþer cōm gēar** i.e. *ōþer gēar cōm.*   **in geardas** 'to (the) dwellings (of men)'.

73–4 **þā ðe ... wuldortorhtan weder** This part of the sentence is a variation on 'another year' and what it brings: lit. 'those that always (*syngāles*) observe the seasons (*sēle*, acc. pl.), gloriously bright weathers'; perhaps, 'those times of gloriously bright weather that always observe their season'.

75 **fæger foldan bearm** An elliptical half-line; apparently, '(and) the lap of the earth (had grown) beautiful'.   **wrecca** 'the exile' (parallel with *gist* in 76); presumably Hengest.

79 **þæt ... inne gemunde** 'so that he might therein be mindful of ...'. An understated reference to his need for vengeance on the Jutes.

80 **woroldrǣdenne** 'the way (*or* condition) of the world'; i.e. the system of vengeance.

81–2 **him ... on bearm** 'into his lap'.   **Hūnlāfing** This is probably a Danish warrior, symbolically reminding Hengest of his duty; but some readers take the name to be that of the sword itself (a weapon well known, as we see in 83).

83 **þæs ... ecge** 'of which the edges', i.e. 'whose edges ...'.

Swylce° ferhðfrecan° Fin eft° begeat°	Thus bold-spirited *as* after assailed
85 sweordbealo° slīðen° æt his selfes hām,	sword-death *ns* cruel
˹siþðan° grimne° gripe° Gūðlāf ond Ōslāf	when savage attack *as*
æfter sǣsīðe°, sorge°, mǣndon°˺,	sea-journey grievance *as* bemoaned
[*1150*] ˹ætwiton˺ wēana° dǣl°; ne meahte ˹wǣfre mōd˺	sorrows *gp* (their) portion *as*
forhabban° in hreþre°. Ðā wæs heal ˹hroden˺	hold (itself) back breast
90 fēonda fēorum°, swilce Fin slægen°,	(with) lives (was) slain
cyning on° corþre°, ond sēo cwēn numen°.	in (his) troop taken
Scēotend° Scyldinga tō scypon feredon°	Warriors carried
eal ingesteald° eorðcyninges°,	household goods king of the land
swylce° hīe æt Finnes hām findan meahton	such as
95 ˹sigla, searogimma˺. Hīe on sǣlāde	
drihtlice° wīf tō Denum feredon,	noble
lǣddon tō lēodum°.	(her) people

86–7 **siþðan ... mǣndon** The objs. of *mǣndon* are *grimne gripe* and *sorge*. Presumably the two complainants, *Gūðlāf* and *Ōslāf*, clearly Danes, are new arrivals, having sailed to help their embattled comrades in the spring. The 'cruel attack' which they 'complained' of (an understatement) is that made by Finn's men on Hnæf and the Danes, which sparked this present problem; they want vengeance. In *The Fight at Finnsburh* (32/16), Hnæf's men include *Ordlāf* and *Gūþlāf*, names which correspond to those of the sons of a Danish king named in the saga literature; *Ōslāf* and *Ordlāf* are probably var. names for the same warrior.

88 **ætwiton** '(and) blamed (on him)'.   **wǣfre mōd** The 'enraged heart' is Hengest's.

89 **hroden** past. part. of *hrēodan*, 'adorn'. Many editors emend to *roden*, past. part. of *rēodan* 'redden', on the reasonable grounds that a fourth alliterating *h* in one line is unlikely; but the grim irony of the hall being 'adorned' with the lives (i.e. the life's blood) of enemies is quite acceptable.

95 **sigla, searogimma** gen. of respect: '(by way) of jewels (and) precious gems'.

31b
The Slaying of Grendel's Mother (*Beowulf*, lines 1492–1590)

As Danes and visitors alike sleep off the celebrations at Heorot following Beowulf's encounter with Grendel, the latter's mother comes to exact her revenge for the mortal wounding of her son. The poet has not mentioned this second monstrous creature before, but now we hear that she is in fact well known as one who stalks the fens 'in the likeness of a woman'. The warrior she devours turns out to be

King Hrothgar's favourite, Æschere, and the old king is distraught. But Beowulf calmly resolves to march off and challenge this second foe on her own territory – the bottom of the dark and dangerous pool (or mere) of Grendel and his kin. The poet has already given us a good sense of this place (1357–79 and 1408–17): it is so steeped in evil that even a hunted deer prefers to face death than to jump in. Not surprisingly, in view of the repeated association of Grendel and his mother with demons and devils, the mere is depicted as a sort of hell. Close similarities between the poet's description and a passage in one of the OE *Blickling Homilies* have been noted; both authors may be drawing on versions of a popular medieval text known as the *Visio Pauli* ('St Paul's Vision'). But nothing daunts Beowulf. Suitably kitted out and brandishing Hrunting, a renowned sword presented to him by Unferth (a thegn who had originally questioned his prowess), he concludes a valedictory speech and – as the extract opens – dives straight into the uninviting water and makes for the bottom. This is to be a far more dangerous fight than that with Grendel. Beowulf's chain-mail saves him initially but, once inside his antagonist's hall (as her 'guest'), his sword fails and he is in trouble. But in the nick of time he sees a great sword hanging on the wall; in calling this 'the work of giants', the poet alludes to the nature of evil and to an association between Cain and the giants of Genesis. With the sword, Beowulf decapitates Grendel's mother, and for good measure he seeks out the body of Grendel himself and removes his head as well.

Similarities in theme and incident between *Beowulf* and an Old Norse tale, *Grettis saga* (known to us only from the thirteenth century), have convinced many scholars of a relationship between the two, perhaps at the very least the influence of the same source-story on both. The *saga* includes, for instance, a struggle between the hero Grettir and a troll-wife in an underwater lair which boasts a mysterious light and a sword on the wall. But a recent study has made a good case for scepticism, arguing that coincidence of much-used themes is the most likely explanation.

Further reading

J. R. R. Tolkien, *The Monsters and the Critics and Other Essays*, ed. C. Tolkien (London, 1983)

E. B. Irving, 'The Nature of Christianity in *Beowulf*', *ASE* 13 (1984), 7–21

S. C. Hawkes, *Weapons and Warfare in Anglo-Saxon England* (Oxford, 1989)

A. Orchard, *Pride and Prodigies: Studies in the Monsters of the 'Beowulf'-Manuscript* (Cambridge, 1995; rev. edn Toronto, 2002)

M. Fjalldal, *The Long Arm of Coincidence: the Frustrated Connection between 'Beowulf' and 'Grettis saga'* (Toronto, 1998)

Æfter þǣm wordum ⌐Weder-Gēata⌐ lēod°   leader
efste° mid elne°, nalas° andsware°   hurried courage not answer *gs*
bīdan° wolde. Brimwylm° onfēng°   wait for +*g* 'Water-surging' received +*d*
hilderince°. Ðā wæs ⌐hwīl dæges⌐   battle-warrior
5 ǣr hē þone grundwong° ongytan° mehte°.   bottom make out could
Sōna° þæt onfunde°, ⌐sē ðe⌐ flōda°   At once discovered waters *gp*
begong°   region
heorogīfre° behēold° ⌐hund missēra⌐,   fiercely ravenous (had) guarded
grim° ond grǣdig, þæt þǣr gumena sum°   fierce a certain +*gp*
[*1500*] ælwihta° eard° ufan° cunnode°.   alien creatures' abode from above was probing
10 ⌐Grāp þā tōgēanes⌐, gūðrinc° gefēng°   battle-warrior *as* seized
⌐atolan clommum⌐. ⌐Nō þȳ ǣr in gescōd
hālan līce⌐: hring° ūtan° ymbbearh°,   ring-armour on the outside protected
þæt° hēo þone fyrdhom° ðurhfōn° ne mihte,   so that war-garment pierce
⌐locene leoðosyrcan⌐, ⌐lāþan fingrum⌐.
15 Bær° þā sēo brimwylf°, þā hēo tō botme° cōm,   Carried water-wolf bottom
⌐hringa þengel⌐ tō hofe° sīnum°   dwelling her
swā° hē ne mihte, ⌐nō hē þæs mōdig wæs⌐,   in such a way that
wǣpna gewealdan°, ac hine wundra° ⌐þæs fela⌐   wield +*g* weird creatures
[*1510*] swencte° on sunde°, sǣdēor° monig°   harassed swimming sea-beast many a
20 hildetūxum° heresyrcan° bræc°;   with battle-tusks battle-coat tore

1 **Weder-Gēata** 'of the Storm-Geats'. This is a variation on *Gēatas*, the name of Beowulf's tribe, which occupied part of what is now southern Sweden. They are called 'Battle-Geats' in 47.

4 **hwīl dæges** lit. 'a period of the day'; understatement for 'most (*or* a good part) of the day'.

6 **sē ðe** The pron. is masc. ('he who') but refers to Grendel's mother; fem. *hēo* is used in 13, etc.

7 **hund missēra** 'for a hundred half-years', i.e. 'fifty years'; probably simply a way of expressing a long time, for it is the same period for which Hrothgar is said to have ruled Denmark before Grendel's attacks and for which Beowulf will rule Geatland before his encounter with the dragon.

10 **Grāp þā tōgēanes** '(She) grabbed then towards (him)', i.e. 'made a grab for him'.

11 **atolan clommum** dat. of instrument: 'with (her) terrible clutches'.

11–12 **Nō þȳ ǣr in . . . līce** instr. phr., and *in* as an adv.: 'None the sooner did she hurt [*gescōd* with dat.] the healthy body within'.

14 **locene leoðosyrcan** 'locked limb-corselet' (acc. sg.), i.e. 'mail-coat of interlocked rings', a var. on *fyrdhom*. **lāþan fingrum** dat. of instrument: 'with (her) loathsome fingers'.

16 **hringa þengel** 'the prince of rings' (obj. of *Bær*); the reference is presumably again to Beowulf's mail-coat.

17 **nō hē þæs mōdig wæs** 'no matter how brave he was'; *þæs* (emended from manuscript *þæm*) functions as an adv. ('to the extent that' or 'so').

18 **þæs fela** 'so many' (with gen. pl.).

ēhton° ⌐āglǣcan⌐. Đā se eorl ongeat°   (they) pursued perceived

þæt hē in nīðsele° nāthwylcum° wæs   'strife-hall' some sort of

þǣr him nǣnig° wæter wihte° ne sceþede°,   no at all might injure

ne° him for° hrōfsele° hrīnan° ne   nor because of roofed hall touch +d

mehte

25 fǣrgripe° flōdes; fȳrlēoht° geseah°,   'sudden grip' *ns* 'fire-light' *as* (he) saw

blācne° lēoman° beorhte° scīnan.   glittering radiance brightly

Ongeat þā se gōda° grundwyrgenne°,   brave man cursed one of the deep

merewīf° mihtig: mægenrǣs° forgeaf°   'sea-woman' mighty assault gave

[*1520*] hildebille°, hond sweng° ne oftēah°,   with battle-sword stroke *as* held back

30 þæt ⌐hire on hafelan⌐ ⌐hringmǣl⌐ āgōl°   sang out

grǣdig gūðlēoð°. Đā se gist° onfand   battle-song *as* visitor

þæt ⌐se beadolēoma⌐ bītan° nolde°,   'bite' would not

aldre° sceþðan°, ac sēo ecg geswāc°   (her) life *as* damage failed +d

ðēodne° æt þearfe°. Đolode° ǣr fela   prince *ds* need (It had) endured

35 hondgemōta°, helm oft gescǣr°,   hand-encounters *gp* (had) cut through

fǣges° fyrdhrægl°; ðā wæs forma°   (a) doomed one's war-garment *as* first

sīð°   occasion

⌐dēorum māðme⌐ þæt his dōm° ālæg°.   renown failed

Eft° wæs ānrǣd°, nalas elnes læt°,   Again resolute slack (in +g)

[*1530*] mǣrða° gemyndig°, mǣg° Hȳlāces.   glorious deeds mindful of +g kinsman

40 Wearp° ðā ⌐wundenmǣl⌐ wrǣttum° gebunden° Threw with ornaments adorned

yrre° ōretta° þæt° hit on eorðan læg,   angry warrior *ns* so that

stīð° ond stȳlecg°. ⌐Strenge getruwode°,   sturdy steel-edged trusted in +d

mundgripe mægenes⌐. Swā sceal man dōn

þonne hē æt gūðe gegān° þenceð°   to gain intends

45 longsumne° lof°: nā ymb° his līf cearað°.   longlasting fame about cares

---

21 **āglǣcan** There is ambiguity here. The *n*-noun [§B5] might be nom. pl., a variation on the *monig sǣdēor* who pursued Beowulf; but it is more likely to be the acc. sg. obj. of *ēhton*, in which case it is the sea-beasts who pursued Beowulf. Often rendered as 'monster', the basic meaning of *āglǣca* seems to be 'awe-inspiring one' or 'formidable one' (apt here), and it is used elsewhere in the poem for Grendel, Grendel's mother, the dragon, the dragon and Beowulf together, and Sigemund the dragon-slayer.

30 **hire on hafelan** poss. dat.: 'on her head'. **hringmǣl** 'ring-sword' (also 73). The reference is probably to the patterns on the sword; thus perhaps, 'ring-marked sword'.

32 **se beadolēoma** 'the battle light' (a variation on the *hildebille* of 29). This is the 'gleaming sword', Hrunting, which has been lent to Beowulf by Unferth (1465–71).

37 **dēorum māðme** dat. of interest: 'for the precious treasure' (i.e. the sword).

40 **wundenmǣl** Probably, 'sword with twisted patterns' (acc. sg.).

42–3 **Strenge . . . mundgripe mægenes** 'in (his own) strength . . . in the hand-grip of his might'; i.e. the power of his hand-grip and his prowess in hand-to-hand combat.

Gefēng þā be eaxle°,   nalas for fǣhðe° mearn°   shoulder hostility felt sorrow

Gūð-Gēata° lēod,   Grendles mōdor.   'Battle-Geats' *gp*

Brægd° þā ⌐beadwe heard⌐,   þā° hē gebolgen° wæs,   Flung now that enraged

[1540]   feorhgenīðlan°,   þæt hēo on flet° gebēah°.   'life-enemy' *as* floor fell

50   Hēo him eft° hraþe°   andlēan° forgeald°   next quickly requital paid back

⌐grimman grāpum⌐   ond ⌐him tōgēanes fēng⌐.

Oferwearp° þā wērigmōd° wigena°   (She) overthrew dispirited *as* of warriors
      strengest,

fēþecempa°,   þæt hē ⌐on fylle wearð⌐.   'foot-soldier' *as*

Ofsæt° þā þone selegyst°   ond hyre seax°   (She) sat on +*a* hall-guest sword
      getēah°,   drew +*d*

55   ⌐brād ond brūnecg°⌐,   wolde hire bearn° wrecan°,   bright-edged son avenge

āngan° eaferan°.   ⌐Him⌐ on eaxle læg   only son *as*

brēostnet° brōden°:   þæt gebearh° fēore°,   corslet woven protected +*d* life

wið° ord ond wið ecge   ingang° forstōd°.   by entry prevented

[1550]   ⌐Hæfde ðā forsīðod⌐   sunu Ecgþēowes

60   under gynne° grund°,   Gēata cempa°,   broad earth warrior

⌐nemne⌐ him heaðobyrne°   helpe gefremede°,   battle-corselet afforded

herenet° hearde,   ond hālig God   'battle-mesh'

gewēold° wīgsigor°.   Wītig° Drihten,   controlled victory in war Wise

rodera° rǣdend°,   hit ⌐on ryht⌐ gescēd°   heavens' ruler decided

65   ȳðelīce°   syþðan° hē eft āstōd°.   easily when stood up

Geseah ðā ⌐on searwum⌐   sigeēadig° bil°,   'victory-blessed' sword *as*

ealdsweord ⌐eotenisc⌐,   ⌐ecgum þȳhtig⌐,

⌐wigena weorðmynd⌐:   þæt wæs wǣpna cyst°,   choicest

---

48 **beadwe heard** '(the man) hardy (*or* bold) in battle' (subj. of *brægd*).

51 **grimman grāpum** dat. of instrument: 'with her cruel clutches'.   **him tōgēanes fēng** 'grabbed towards him', i.e. 'made a grab for him'.

53 **on fylle wearð** 'was (brought) to a fall' or 'took a fall'.

55 **brād ond brūnecg** *ond* is not in the manuscript. The same half-line occurs in *The Battle of Maldon* (30/163).

56 **Him** poss. dat., and referring now to Beowulf.

59 **Hæfde ðā forsīðod** The auxil. vb. is sbj.: 'He would then have perished'.

61 **nemne** 'unless' or 'if ... not', controlling two vbs., *fremede* (subj. *heaðobyrne*) and *gewēold* (subj. *hālig God*).

64 **on ryht** 'according to right (*or* justice)'.

66 **on searwum** 'among (other) trappings (*or* arms)'. These are apparently hanging on the wall of the cave.

67 **eotenisc** 'gigantic', or 'forged by giants' (cf. 71); see also 31a/10n.   **ecgum þȳhtig** dat. of specification: 'firm in its edges'.

68 **wigena weorðmynd** 'a mark of distinction for [lit. "of"] warriors'.

[*1560*] būton° hit wæs māre° ðonne ǣnig mon ōðer	except that bigger	
70 tō beadulāce° ætberan° meahte°,	'battle-play' carry would be able	
gōd° ond geatolīc°, ⌐gīganta geweorc⌐.	noble splendid	
Hē gefēng þā ⌐fetelhilt⌐ freca° Scyldinga,	bold man	
hrēoh° ond heorogrim° hringmǣl gebrægd°,	fierce 'deadly grim' drew	
aldres° orwēna°, yrringa° slōh°	of life without hope angrily struck	
75 ⌐þæt hire wið hales heard grāpode⌐,		
bānhringas° bræc, bil eal° ðurhwōd°	'bone-rings' *ap* fully went through	
fǣgne° flǣschoman°. Hēo on flet gecrong°.	doomed body fell (dead)	
Sweord wæs swātig°, secg weorce gefeh°.	bloody rejoiced in +*d*	
[*1570*] Līxte° ⌐se lēoma⌐, lēoht ⌐inne⌐ stōd°,	Shone appeared	
80 efne° swā° of hefene hādre° scīneð	just as brightly	
rodores° candel. Hē æfter° recede° wlāt°,	sky's about hall gazed	
hwearf° þā be° wealle, wǣpen hafenade°	moved along raised	
⌐heard be hiltum⌐ Higelāces ðegn,		
yrre ond ānrǣd. ⌐Næs sēo ecg fracod°	useless (to +*d*)	
85 hilderince⌐ ac hē hraþe wolde		
Grendle forgyldan ⌐gūðrǣsa fela		
ðāra þe⌐ hē geworhte° tō° West-Denum	made on	
oftor° micle° ðonne on ǣnne sīð°,	more often much occasion	
[*1580*] þonne hē Hrōðgāres heorðgenēatas°	hearth-companions *ap*	
90 slōh on sweofote°, slǣpende fræt°	sleep ate	
folces Denigea fȳftȳne men		
ond ⌐ōðer swylc⌐ ūt offerede°,	carried	

71 **gīganta geweorc** 'the handiwork of giants'. A stock description of impressive artefacts belonging to older times; see 37/2n.

72 **fetelhilt** Probably, 'belted (*or* ringed) sword-hilt' (acc. sg.).

75 **þæt hire . . . heard grāpode** Theoretically the apparent adj. *heard* could describe
the *hringmǣl* of 73 (nom. sg. neut.), but it seems preferable to take it as an adv., though
normally the dat. sg. inflection -*e* would be expected: 'so that it caught her hard on her neck'
(poss. dat. *hire*).

79 **se lēoma** Presumably, this is the radiance in Grendel's mother's hall mentioned
in 26.   **inne** The sense seems to be that 'within' this radiance shines an even brighter light.

83 **heard** The adj. describes *wǣpen* in 82.   **be hiltum** pl. form of noun with sg. meaning: 'by the hilt'.

84–5 **Næs . . . hilderince** The blade is not *yet* useless, for it has a job still to do.

86–7 **gūðrǣsa fela ðāra þe** 'for the many assaults which . . .' (lit. 'those which'); *fela*
is the obj. of the vb.

92 **ōðer swylc** 'as many again' (lit. 'other such'); i.e. thirty altogether. Only during Beowulf's retelling of his adventures to his king in Geatland (2085) do we learn
that Grendel had a huge 'glove', made from dragons' skins, in which to carry off his
victims.

lāðlicu° lāc°. ⌐Hē⌐ him þæs° lēan°   loathsome booty for that reward *as*
    forgeald,

rēþe° cempa, ⌐tō ðæs þe⌐ hē on ræste° geseah   fierce resting-place

95 gūðwērigne° Grendel licgan   battle-weary

aldorlēasne°, swā° him ǣr gescōd°   lifeless so (much) had harmed +*d*

⌐hild æt Heorote⌐. Hrā° wīde sprong°   Corpse burst open

syþðan hē æfter dēaðe drepe° þrōwade°,   blow suffered

[*1590*] heorosweng° heardne, ond ⌐hine þā hēafde becearf⌐.   sword-stroke

93 **Hē** i.e. the *rēþe cempa* of 94, Beowulf.

94 **tō ðæs þe** 'to the extent that', or 'to such effect that'.

97 **hild æt Heorote** This was the battle in which Beowulf tore off Grendel's arm, leaving him mortally wounded as he escaped back to the mere.

99 **hine þā hēafde becearf** 'then deprived him of his head [dat.]', i.e. 'he (Beowulf) cut off his head'.

32

The Fight at Finnsburh

By a rare chance, one of the most prominent episodes in *Beowulf* – the tale of the tragedy at Finnsburh, in which a marriage alliance is shattered by fighting between ostensible allies (Text 31a) – has come down to us in a second version, albeit fragmentarily. A single sheet of parchment containing forty-seven lines from an apparent 'lay' about the incident (i.e. a simple narrative poem or ballad) survived at least until the early eighteenth century, when the antiquarian George Hickes found it in a manuscript codex in the library of Lambeth Palace, the London residence of the archbishops of Canterbury. The fragment has since disappeared and we must rely for the text on the version printed by Hickes, among other old items, in 1705.

Even from the few preserved lines, it is clear that the lay had a different purpose from the Finnsburh episode as told by the poet of *Beowulf*. For him it is an exemplum, reminding the revelling Danes (and us) that the cycle of victory and defeat is relentless in the feud-driven heroic world. His concern is with the social and ethical dimensions of the episode, and with the personal tragedy of the Danish princess Hildeburh, who loses brother, son and husband (Finn) in the feud. Furthermore, he is addressing an audience to whom the details are already well known, for he gives none of them. In the fragment, however, we have a detailed account of one part of the fighting between Frisians and Danes in Finnsburh, the citadel of the Frisian leader, Finn. It is a fast-moving narrative in which the focus is on the individual warriors, who are named. The poet marshals all the rhetorical devices of heroic war poetry, including vaunting speeches, the sounds of weapons clashing, and the gathering of the beasts of battle. A lay would have been comparatively short, perhaps two or three hundred lines. Among surviving OE poems, only *The Battle of Maldon* is comparable (Text 30); there also the fate of individual warriors is traced within a framework of a code of loyalty based on hall-companionship and the obligations due to a gift-giving lord.

Critics mostly agree that the 'Finnsburh fragment' (as it is often called) describes the first hostile encounter between Danes (or Scyldings) and Frisians during the visit of Hnæf and his troop to Frisia. The *Beowulf*-poet, viewing things retrospectively, remarks that Hildeburh has little reason to trust the Frisians, having lost her son (unnamed) and brother, Hnæf (see 31a/9–13). Presumably, then, the Frisians, for whatever reason, made an attack on Hnæf's troop during the Danes' ostensibly friendly visit, and it is that attack which is about to take place when the fragment opens. The action, which is confused by sudden changes of perspective, appears to go as follows.

1–13. A watching Dane has seen a strange light outside the hall where his comrades are sleeping. The young Danish 'king' (Hnæf) realises that it is the flashing of armour and weapons (a theme to which the poet returns in 35–6), borne by the attacking Frisians, and so he rouses his men for battle with heroic words.

14–17. Two pairs of Danish warriors go to the doors at either end of the hall (apparently – but the fragment tells us only about what happens at one end), and Hengest, next in status to Hnæf, follows.

18–27. The viewpoint shifts abruptly to the Frisians outside the hall as one warrior tries to restrain the impetuosity of another and calls to know who is holding the door from inside; a Dane, Sigeferth, answers in an appropriate manner.

28–48. The attack begins noisily and Frisians begin to fall (Garulf first), while the sixty Danes within defend magnificently and fight for five days without loss. But finally they, too, take casualties, and Hnæf is asking about the injuries as the fragment ends. Subsequently, as we know from *Beowulf*, Hnæf is killed and Hengest takes over as the Danish leader.

Hickes seems to have been a poor transcriber of Anglo-Saxon script, liable to confuse manuscript *a* with *u*, *c* with *g* or *t*, and so on, but probably he was not as slipshod as some editors have made him out to be, insisting as they do on a score of emendations to his printed text. It is likely that some of what to us are obscurities were already in the copy Hickes used, and certainly the writing of *d* for *ð* occurs regularly in manuscripts written late in the Anglo-Saxon period. In the edited version below, therefore, emendations have been kept to a minimum (see p. 352). The language of the copy would suggest a date for the lost manuscript in the early eleventh century; the forms are mainly typical of late WS: thus *y* for earlier *i* in *scȳneð* (7), intrusive *u* in *buruhðelu* (30) and *Finnsburuh* (36). But (as in *Beowulf*) there is a mix of other forms that could be earlier or dialectal: thus *wæg* (43; not *weg*) might be Anglian; *scefte* (7; not *sceafte*) could be Mercian or Kentish but it appears also in late WS, as does *sword* (15; not *sweord*), which otherwise might be Northumbrian; and *mænig* (13; not *manig* or another variant), though perhaps Anglian, occurs often enough in late WS texts to be unreliable as a dialectal marker. Clearly, the date of original composition of the poem is impossible to pin down with precision. It is likely, however, to have been contemporary with, or to have pre-dated, the received text of *Beowulf* itself, which may have been composed by about 750 (see pp. 270–1).

Further reading

D. K. Fry, ed., *Finnsburh Fragment and Episode* (London, 1974)
J. Hill, ed., *Old English Minor Heroic Poems* (Durham, 1983; rev. 1994)
R. Girvan, 'Finnsburh', *Proceedings of the British Academy* 26 (1940), 327–60

G. N. Garmonsway, 'Anglo-Saxon Heroic Attitudes', in *Franciplegius: Medieval and Linguistic Studies in Honour of Francis Peabody Magoun, Jr.*, ed. J. P. Bessinger and R. P. Creed (New York and London, 1965), pp. 139–46
J. R. R. Tolkien, *Finn and Hengest: the Fragment and the Episode* (London, 1982)
See also the bibliography for Text 31a, p. 274.

⌐... nas byrnað° næfre°⌐.	burn never
Hlēoþrode° ðā ⌐hearogeong° cyning⌐:	Proclaimed 'battle-young'
⌐'Ne ðis ne dagað⌐ ēastan°, ne hēr draca° ne	from the east dragon
flēogeð°,	flies
ne hēr ðisse healle° hornas° ne byrnað,	hall's gables
5 ⌐ac hēr forþ berað⌐, ⌐fugelas singað,	
gylleð° grǣghama⌐, ⌐gūðwudu⌐ hlynneð°,	howls resounds
scyld scefte° oncwyð°. Nū scȳneð þes mōna°	(spear-)shaft *as* answers moon
⌐waðol⌐ under wolcnum. Nū ārīsað° wēadǣda°	(will) occur 'woe-deeds'
ðe ⌐ðisne folces nīð⌐ fremman° willað.	carry out
10 Ac onwācnigeað° nū, wīgend° mīne;	awake *imp* warriors
habbað° ēowre linda°, hicgeaþ° on ellen°,	hold shields set minds glory
windað° on° orde°, wesað° onmōde°.'	turn to (the) front be resolute
Đā āras mænig goldhladen° ðegn, gyrde°	'gold-laden' girded (with +*d*)
hine° his swurde.	himself
Đā tō dura° ēodon° drihtlīce° cempan°	door went noble champions
15 Sigeferð and Ēaha, hyra sword getugon°,	drew

1 **...nas byrnað næfre** Several editors, taking their clue from 4, have completed the first word as *hornas* ('horns'). Less plausibly, citing metrical reasons, some have emended *næfre* to *Hnæf* and made it the first word of 2.

2 **hearogeong cyning** This is the youthful Danish leader, Hnæf, inexperienced in war.

3 **Ne ðis ne dagað** 'This does not dawn', i.e. 'this is not the dawn'.

5 **ac hēr forþ berað** An elliptical half-line, and it is possible that two further half-lines have been lost. The poet perhaps intended, 'But they (the Frisians) are carrying weapons towards us here', or simply, 'But they are attacking'.

5–6 **fugelas...grǣghama** The 'beasts of battle' motif (see also 10/60–5 and 30/106–7). The birds (*fugelas*) will include the raven (mentioned in 34) and the eagle; the 'grey-coated one' (*grǣghama*) is probably the wolf (though some translators take the compound to mean 'mail-coat').

6 **gūðwudu** 'battle-wood'; presumably a kenning for 'shield'.

8 **waðol** A word otherwise unknown, but presumably an adj. describing the moon. Analogies with words in other Germanic languages, and with the OE noun *wað* ('wandering' or 'roving'), suggest a meaning of 'wandering' or 'inconstant'.

9 **ðisne folces nīð** The demons. pron. *ðisne* is acc. sg. masc. and goes with *nīð*: 'the malice of this people' (i.e. the attacking Frisians).

and ⌜æt ōþrum durum⌝   Ordlāf and Gūþlāf,
and Hengest sylf   ⌜hwearf him on lāste⌝.
Ðā gȳt° Gārulf   Gūðere styrode°⌝   meanwhile   urged
ðæt hē swā° frēolic° feorh°   ⌜forman sīþe⌝   so   noble   life *as*
20 ⌜tō ðǣre healle durum,   hyrsta°, ne bǣre°⌝,   trappings *ap*   carry
nū ⌜hyt nīþa heard⌝   ānyman° wolde.   take away
Ac ⌜hē⌝ frægn° ⌜ofer eal⌝   undearninga°,   asked   openly
dēormōd° hæleþ°,   hwā° ðā duru hēolde.   brave-hearted   warrior   who
'Sigeferþ is mīn nama,' ⌜cweþ hē⌝,   'ic eom ⌜Secgena⌝ lēod°,   prince
25 wreccea° wīde cūð°;   fæla ic ⌜wēana gebād,   adventurer   known
heordra hilda⌝.   Ðē° is gȳt° hēr witod°   For you   even now   ordained
⌜swæþer ðū sylf tō mē   sēcean wylle⌝.'
Ðā wæs on healle   wælslihta° gehlyn°;   of 'slaughter-blows'   din

---

16 **æt ōþrum durum** A phr. such as 'so too' needs adding in the trans. There are presumably (double?) doors at each end of the hall; see also 20.

17 **hwearf him on lāste** 'went in their track' (poss. dat. *him*), i.e. 'followed in their footsteps'.

18 **Ðā gȳt...styrode** The viewpoint now switches to the Frisian side as they approach the door of the hall. Assuming that we interpret *styrode* as pret. of *styrian*, whose meanings include 'urge', the syntax is ambiguous: grammatically, either Garulf or Guthere could be the object of the urging by the other – an urging for restraint, we discover. The fact that it is Garulf who eventually falls (31) might suggest that it is he who is being warned by Guthere, yet there would be grim irony if the first Frisian to fall were in fact the urger himself. Some editors emend *styrode* to *stȳrde*, pret. of *stȳran* 'restrain', which takes a dat. obj.; the form *Gūðere* could be dat., but we would expect *Gārulf* to acquire an *e*.

19 **forman sīþe** dat. of definition: 'in the first foray', or 'on the first occasion'.

20 **tō...ne bǣre** *feorh* and *hyrsta* are parallel objs. of the vb.; Guthere is urged that he 'should not carry' so noble a life, and his fine armour (his 'trappings'), to the door; i.e. not to risk them.

21 **hyt** This, the obj. of *ānyman*, clearly refers back to *feorh*. **nīþa heard** adj. as noun (nom. sg.), with gen. of specification: 'one fierce in attack'. This is one of the Danes, presumably Sigeferth, who, as we shall see, claims to be the guardian of the door.

22 **hē** i.e. whichever of the two, Guthere or Garulf, was the obj. of (but is ignoring) the plea for restraint. **ofer eal** Either 'over (it) all', i.e. above all the commotion, or 'before everyone', which would reinforce *undearninga*; cf. 30/256n.

24 **cweþ hē** Metrically awkward and perhaps an interpolation; *cweþ* (for *cwæþ*) might be a dialectal form. 'He' is now Sigeferth, who, from inside the hall, answers Guthere's question. **Secgena** 'of the Secgens'. This unknown Germanic tribe is twice mentioned also in the OE poem *Widsith* (31 and 62), with the spelling *Sycgan*.

25–6 **wēana...heordra hilda** Parallel gen. pl. complements of *fæla*, 'many': 'woes ... fierce battles'.

27 **swæþer ðū sylf...wylle** 'whichever of two things (*swæþer*) you yourself will get [lit. "seek out"] from me'. The two things gnomically implied are death or victory, and Sigeferth's message to Guthere is that the outcome is already fated.

⌐sceolde celæs borð　cēnum on handa

30　bānhelm berstan⌐. Buruhðelu° dynede°,　Fortress-floor　resounded

oð æt ðǣre gūðe　Gārulf gecrang°,　fell dead

⌐ealra ǣrest°　eorðbūendra°⌐,　first　land-dwellers (*i.e.* Frisians) *gp*

⌐Gūðlāfes sunu⌐; ymbe° hyne ⌐gōdra fǣla　around

hwearflicra hrǣs⌐. ⌐Hræfen wandrode°⌐,　circled

35　sweart° and sealobrūn°.　dark　with dusky gleam

　　　　　　　　　Swurdlēoma° stōd°　'Sword-gleam'　appeared

swylce° eal Finnsburuh　fȳrenu° wǣre.　as though　on fire

Ne gefrægn° ic nǣfre ⌐wurþlīcor　æt wera hilde　heard

sixtig sigebeorna°　sēl⌐ gebǣran°,　'victory-warriors'　bear (themselves)

nē nēfre ⌐swanas° hwītne°⌐ medo　sēl forgyldan°　young men　bright　repay

40　ðonne° Hnæfe guldan°　his hægstealdas°.　than　paid to +*d*　young retainers *np*

Hig fuhton fīf dagas　swā° hyra nān° ne fēol　in such a way that　none

drihtgesīða°　ac hig ðā duru hēoldon.　of the noble-companions

Ðā ⌐gewāt him wund° hæleð　on wæg gangan⌐,　wounded

sǣde þæt his byrne°　ābrocen wǣre,　corselet

45　heresceorpum° hror°,　and ēac wæs his　in (his) battle-garments　brave

　　helm ðyrel°.　pierced

29–30 sceolde celæs bord ... berstan The meaning of *celæs* (whether an adj. defining *borð*, i.e. *bord*, 'shield', or a noun in gen. relationship with it) is unknown; cf. the similarly obscure *cellod* in *The Battle of Maldon* (30/283). Nor is the syntax clear. Either the *celæs bord*, 'in the hands of the bold ones' (*cēnum on handa*, poss. dat.), is to smash (*berstan*, trans.) the 'bone-protector' (*bānhelm*, probably 'helmet', as protector of the skull or perhaps partly made of bone plates), or the *celæs bord* and the *bānhelm* are both to 'shatter' (*berstan*, intrans.) in the conflict.

　32 ealra ... eorðbūendra 'of all the earth-dwellers [i.e. Frisians]'.

　33 Gūðlāfes sunu This is unlikely to be the same Guthlaf, one of the Danes, whom we met in 16.

　33–4 gōdra fǣla hwearflicra hrǣs An emendation of Hickes's *hrær* in 34 is necessary, and *hrǣs*, conjectured to be a form of the pret. of *hrēosan* 'fall', is one possibility. Its subj. is *fǣla* in 33, which is followed (in the gen. pl.) by both *gōdra* and *hwearflicra*; the latter is itself an emended form (from *hearflacra*), assumed to be, like *gōdra*, an adj. used as a noun: 'many good men, fleeting ones (*i.e.* mortals), fell'. **Hræfen wandrode** Cf. *hremmas wundon* in 30/106.

　37–8 wurþlīcor ... sēl The two comp. adjs. are in parallel: 'more worthily and better'. **æt wera hilde** 'in battle between [lit. "of"] men'.

　39 swanas hwītne Hickes's *swa noc hwitne* is clearly wrong and this emendation is preferable to others tried (such as the radically abbreviated *swētne*); *hwītne* (acc. sg. masc.) describes the mead for which the young men are now repaying their leader.

　43 gewāt him ... on wæg gangan 'went walking away' (with rflx. dat. pron. *him* untrans.). We are not given the name of this first warrior to retire – or his allegiance; see next note.

Ðā hine sōna° frægn° ⌜folces hyrde°⌝,   quickly asked protector
hū ðā wīgend hyra   wunda genǣson°,   were bearing
oððe hwæþer° ðǣra hyssa° . . .   which of (the) young warriors

46 **folces hyrde** Although the epithet has generally been assumed to denote Finn, thus meaning that the focus is still on the Frisian side, the referent could be Hnæf, enquiring of the wounded man (a Dane) how the others are faring.

VI

REFLECTION AND LAMENT

The making of wise observations on life, derived from experience and modified by reflection on that experience, and the formal (often formulaic) expression of these in song or poem, were part of the oral inheritance of the Anglo-Saxons and continued to have an essential place in their literature. Even the eponymous hero of *Beowulf* must find time for reflection before he performs his great deeds: 'fate proceeds always as it must', he announces before fighting Grendel, and 'it's better that a man avenge his friend than mourn much', before taking on Grendel's mother. Such sayings, whether we call them 'maxims' (the term usually applied to sayings with an ethical dimension) or 'gnomes' (more descriptive sayings) or 'aphorisms' (any wise or sententious sayings), pervade much of OE literature. There are two poems – known rather drearily as *Maxims I* and *Maxims II* – which are built entirely of such material; the second of the two begins this section (Text 33). Social regulation seems to be at least part of the purpose of such poems. They make sage and incisive comments on the world and its people, using the ordinary and the obvious to impart to their audience a sense of the necessary order of things. Closely related to maxims in their form are so-called 'proverbs', but they take a more robustly independent view of the world and express their truths through metaphor. As the OE collection known as the *Durham Proverbs* shows (Text 34), this is a more cunning and more subversive, and often humorous, method. Humour is a natural ingredient also, though not the only one, in many of the OE *Riddles*. Riddling is an active process of reflection, in which the mind is forced to participate in liberating dislocations of imagined experience; like maxims and proverbs, riddles direct us towards social and existential truths, but they do so with forensic intensity, erecting elaborate structures of double meaning and exploiting paradox as they scrutinise the things of the world and the creatures (including us) which inhabit it. A selection of five riddles is given below (Text 35).

There are other ways of transmitting worldly wisdom. Some poets use the language and landscape of lamentation to focus on the human experience of suffering and mutability, and in so doing they create a formal distance between the sufferer and the experience, allowing the latter to be set in its proper place in the universal scheme of things. The poet of *Deor*, for instance (Text 36), affects to draw comfort in his current predicament (unemployment) by recalling a succession of victims of misfortune from the legendary past, thereby reminding himself, and us, how time always heals. The poet of *The Ruin* (Text 37) also deals with change through time, but this is a resolutely impersonal poem, whose subject is the architectural wonders of a Roman city, which it seems to celebrate even as it chronicles their disintegration. Kingdoms rise and fall, the finest of buildings decay, and their heroes with them, in a perpetual cycle which is objectified as inexorable *wyrd* or 'fate' – 'what happened to happen', in Philip Larkin's memorable gloss.

For a Christian society, however, this worldly scheme of things, with all its oddities and circularities, is ultimately no more than a page of divine history, only a stage in the long and linear human progression from the error in Eden to the catharsis of Judgement Day, with its final reckoning – played out under the all-seeing eye of God. Most of the reflective and meditative literature in OE acknowledges this divine sanction: the dragon of *Maxims II* may be in his lair and the king in his hall, but just as surely, the poem reminds us, God is in his heaven. Some poets go a stage further, using secular lament to promote Christian hope. Wise reflection on one's own worldly problems under the rule of an apparently implacable fate then becomes a stepping-stone to a more confident focus on transcendent goals and the embracing of faith. Thus, in *The Wanderer* (Text 38), the long meditation of the 'wanderer' himself on the joys and sorrows of a past spent in the bosom of an heroic lord bring him to the point where, made wise through experience, he is ready for Christian consolation.

But literary reflection on suffering and the cruelty of fate is not always transmuted into wise resolution. *Wulf and Eadwacer* (Text 39) and *The Wife's Lament* (Text 40) are lyrics of loss and separation. Both are enigmatic (at least to the modern reader) and defy complete solution at a narrative level, but both give a voice to exiled women who are victims of the machinations of man or tribe, or of the destructive demands of society. As in *The Wanderer* and *Deor*, so in these two poems bitter lament is formalised in poetic meditation, but here we witness no enlightened leap forward, no hint of either temporal or spiritual healing. The raw edge of unhappy experience remains unsmoothed (and may even be inflamed) by the poems' gnomic conclusions, which seem to express the resignation of despair rather than of wisdom.

All the texts in this section, except *Maxims II* and the *Durham Proverbs*, are preserved in the Exeter Book (Exeter, Cathedral Library, 3501, fols. 8–130), which was compiled in the second half of the tenth century; see p. 222.

Further reading

A. L. Klinck, *The Old English Elegies: a Critical Edition and Genre Study*, 2nd edn (Montreal, 2001) [for Texts 36–40]

B. J. Muir, ed., *The Exeter Anthology of Old English Poetry: an Edition of Exeter Dean and Chapter Ms 3501*, 2 vols., 2nd edn (Exeter, 2000) [for Texts 35–40]

C. Fell, 'Perceptions of Transience', in *Cambridge Companion*, pp. 172–89

E. T. Hansen, *The Solomon Complex: Reading Wisdom in Old English Poetry* (Toronto, 1988)

33
Truth is Trickiest
(*Maxims II*)

The poem known as *Maxims II* is found in a mid-eleventh-century manuscript (London, British Library, Cotton Tiberius B. i, fol. 115r–v), where it is sandwiched between a metrical calendar, recording liturgical feasts and saints' days of the church year, and a copy of the *Anglo-Saxon Chronicle*. The OE maxims present an intimate view of the world in literal terms. Indeed, on the face of it, they may seem to state the obvious ('a king must rule his kingdom'), but that is the point. Their effect derives from their economy of expression, pared down to the simple unqualified statement of fact, which allows no escape into metaphorical interpretation, and so they demand a direct confrontation with meaning. There are numerous references in *Maxims II* to the Germanic 'heroic' culture out of which the Anglo-Saxons came: a king sharing out treasures, young men being exhorted to battle, the dragon guarding its hoard. The sense of order which the maxims cumulatively promote reflects and reinforces the divinely ordained laws of the natural world and the laws (by implication no less divinely inspired) of social hierarchy.

The essential simplicity of gnomic utterance in OE literature does not lead to ease of translation into ModE. Two main verbal formulae are used to present the maxims. The first one uses *byð* (or *bið*), 'is' (from *bēon*), known as the 'gnomic' present tense and in general expressing universal, unchanging truths, but used also to indicate future action ('will be'). Mostly, *byð* is used for the more abstract or unchanging truths ('winter is coldest'). The other formula uses *sceal* (present tense of *sculan*), which is more problematical. The essential meaning of OE *sculan* is 'must', but is it 'must be' in the sense of moral duty and obligation, or 'must needs be' in the sense of something customary or simply unavoidable? Perhaps, in a social context, there can be no essential difference, and the Anglo-Saxon poet and his audience were no doubt well aware of the ambiguities. Although translation of OE *sceal* as the future auxiliary 'shall' is usually to be avoided, in the case of maxims it may be a good choice, for even today the verb retains some of its sense of both obligation and necessity. A structural principle seems to be at work in the poem in its use of the two formulae. After an initial *sceal* statement, all ten *byð* (or plural *bēoð*) statements are concentrated in the first thirteen lines; then there are almost forty *sceal* statements, but from line 55 these give way to a more expansive closing section which exhibits increasing verbal certainty, mainly through the parallel statements that 'the Creator alone knows' and 'the Lord alone knows'. Linguistically, *Maxims II* exhibits expected late WS forms. There is some evidence of the levelling of inflections in verbs, for example in *syndan* (4; but. cf. *syndon*, 2) and *sceolan* (14, for *sceolon*). Loss of final *g* in *nǣni* (63) is characteristic of late texts; so too is the intrusion of *e* after palatalised ('soft') *c* in the infinitives *wyrcean* (21) and *hycgean* (54).

Further reading

T. A. Shippey, ed., *Poems of Wisdom and Learning in Old English* (Cambridge, 1976)

P. B. Taylor, 'Heroic Ritual in the Old English Maxims', *NM* 70 (1969), 387–407

J. K. Bollard, 'The Cotton Maxims', *Neophil.* 57 (1973), 179–87

S. B. Greenfield and R. Evert, '*Maxims II*: Gnome and Poem', in *Anglo-Saxon Poetry: Essays in Appreciation for John C. McGalliard*, ed. L. E. Nicholson and D. W. Frese (Notre Dame, IN, 1975), pp. 337–54

T. A. Shippey, 'Maxims in Old English Narrative: Literary Art or Traditional Wisdom?', in *Oral Tradition Literary Tradition: a Symposium*, ed. H. Bekker-Nielsen *et al.* (Odense, 1977), pp. 28–46

M. Nelson, ' "Is" and "Ought" in the Exeter Book Maxims', *Southern Folklore Quarterly* 45 (1981), 109–21

P. Cavill, *Maxims in Old English Poetry* (Cambridge, 1999)

Cyning ⌈sceal rīce° healdan⌉. ⌈Ceastra⌉ bēoð° feorran°	kingdom are from afar
gesȳne°,	visible
⌈orðanc enta geweorc⌉, ⌈þā þe⌉ on þysse eorðan syndon°,	are
wrǣtlic° weallstāna° geweorc. Wind byð°	wondrous of 'wall-stones' is
on° lyfte° swiftust,	in sky
þunar° byð ⌈þrāgum⌉ hlūdast°. ⌈Þrymmas syndan	thunder loudest
Crīstes⌉ myccle°,	great

1 **sceal... healdan** On *sceal*, see headnote; *healdan* means 'rule', but also 'keep' or 'watch over'.   **Ceastra** 'towns'. The Latin borrowing refers to the impressive stone-built towns which the Romans left behind them in Britain – such as the one described in *The Ruin* (Text 37), where the native noun *burgstede* is used for *ceaster*. With the exception of some churches, early Anglo-Saxon buildings were built mainly of wood.

2 **orðanc enta geweorc** 'the skilful handiwork (*or* structure) of giants'. Calling great Roman buildings, and other ancient artefacts, the work of giants is a poetic commonplace: see 37/2, 38/87 and 31b/71   **þā þe** 'those which'; *þā* is in concord with *ceastra* (nom. pl.), not *enta* (gen. pl.). See also 9.

4 **þrāgum** dat. of time: 'at times', or 'in (its) seasons'.   **Þrymmas syndan Crīstes** 'the powers of Christ are ...'.

5 ⌐wyrd⌐ byð swīðost°.   Winter byð cealdost,   mightiest
  lencten° hrīmigost°:   hē byð lengest° ceald,   spring   frostiest   longest
  sumor sunwlitegost°:   ⌐swegel⌐ byð hātost°,   'sun-fairest'   hottest
  hærfest° ⌐hrēðēadegost⌐:   hæleðum° bringeð   autumn   to men
  gēres° wæstmas°,   þā þe him° God sendeð.   year's   fruits   to them
10 Sōð° bið ⌐swicolost⌐,   sinc° byð ⌐dēorost⌐,   Truth   treasure
  gold, ⌐gumena gehwām⌐;   and gomol° snoterost°,   old man   wisest
  ⌐fyrngēarum frōd⌐,   sē° þe ær° feala° ⌐gebīdeð⌐.   he   previously   much
  ⌐Wēa° bið wundrum° clibbor°,   wolcnu°   Grief   wondrously   clinging   clouds
      scrīðað°⌐.   glide (by)
  ⌐Geongne° æþeling° sceolan   gōde gesīðas°⌐   Young   prince *as*   companions *np*
15 byldan° tō beaduwe°   and tō bēahgife°.   encourage   war-making   ring-giving
  Ellen° ⌐sceal on eorle⌐;   ecg° sceal wið°   Courage   blade   against
      hellme°   helmet

5 **wyrd** Juxtaposed with the reference to Christ, this should probably be understood as 'Providence', rather than simply 'fate'. Cf. its use in *The Wanderer* (38/5, 15, 100 and 107) and the explanation in King Alfred's version of *De consolatione Philosophiae* by Boethius (6/2–22).

7 **swegel** Usually meaning 'heavens' or 'sky', this word is also used for 'sun', which is apt here.

8 **hrēðēadegost** lit. 'most glory- (*or* victory-) blessed'; the abundance of harvest-time is being celebrated as though it were the finale of a campaign of a battle.

10 **swicolost** 'most deceitful', or 'trickiest'. Oddly, some editors emend to *swītolost* ('clearest'); would it were so! **dēorost** The ambiguities of ModE 'dear' ('beloved', 'costly', 'valuable', etc.) attach to OE *dēor* also.

11 **gumena gehwām** The pron. (dat. sg. masc. of *gehwā*) governs a gen. pl. noun: 'to each of men'.

12 **fyrngēarum frōd** dat. of instrument: 'experienced (*or* wise) through former [i.e. past] years'. **gebīdeð** The tense is pres. but the sense perf.: 'has experienced'.

13 **Wēa ... scrīðað** A surprising but effective contrast is set up between the properties of grief and of clouds.

14 **Geongne æþeling ... gōde gesīðas** Though placed first in the sentence, the *geongne æþeling* is the obj. of the vb. (as the acc. sg. masc. ending of the adj., *-ne*, shows) and the subj. is *gōde gesīðas*. For a similar reference to how a king's son should behave, see *Beowulf*, 20–5. *Æþeling* is also used generally for a nobleman of royal blood.

16 **sceal** The modal auxil. *sceal* is able to stand by itself, with the vb. 'be' understood [§G2d]; possible renderings include 'must be', 'must needs be' and 'belongs'. See also 22, 25, 26, etc. **on eorle** Late in the Anglo-Saxon period, *eorl* would come to replace *ealdorman* (see 8/4–5n) to describe noblemen of the highest rank; here it seems to convey the traditional sense of a noble 'warrior' (though often in poetry simply 'man' seems apt).

hilde° gebīdan°. ⌐Hafuc sceal on glōfe	battle *as* experience
wilde gewunian⌐. Wulf sceal on bearowe°,	forest
earm° ānhaga°. Eofor° sceal on holte°	wretched loner Boar wood
20 ⌐tōðmægenes trum⌐. Til° sceal on ēðle°	(The) good (man) (his) native land
dōmes° wyrcean°. Daroð° sceal on handa,	glory achieve *+g* Javelin
gār° golde fāh°. Gim° sceal on hringe	spear adorned with *+d* Gemstone
standan stēap° and gēap°. Strēam° sceal ⌐on ȳðum	high curved Current
mecgan, mereflōde⌐. Mæst° sceal on cēole°,	Mast 'keel' (*i.e.* ship)
25 ⌐segelgyrd seomian⌐. Sweord sceal on bearme°,	lap
drihtlic° īsern°. Draca° sceal on hlæwe°,	noble iron Dragon barrow
frōd, ⌐frætwum wlanc⌐. Fisc sceal on wætere	
cynren° cennan°. Cyning sceal on healle	(its) species *as* spawn
⌐bēagas⌐ dælan°. Bera° sceal on hæðe°,	distribute Bear heath
30 eald° and egesfull°. Ēa° of° dūne° sceal	old terrifying River from hill
flōdgræg° fēran°. Fyrd° sceal ætsomne°,	'water-grey' run Army together
tīrfæstra° getrum°. Trēow° sceal on eorle,	of 'glory-firm' (men) troop Loyalty
wīsdōm on were°. Wudu° sceal on foldan°	(a) man Tree earth
blædum° blōwan°. Beorh° sceal on eorþan	with leaves *dp* blossom Hill
35 grēne° standan. God sceal on° heofenum°,	green in (the) heavens
dæda° dēmend°. Duru° sceal on healle,	of deeds judge Door
rūm° recedes° mūð°. ⌐Rand⌐ sceal on scylde,	wide hall's mouth

17–18 **Hafuc … wilde gewunian** The adj. goes with *hafuc*, and a simple trans. would be, 'the wild hawk must become accustomed to (*or* simply remain on) the glove'; but the position of *wilde* (in a half-line which syntactically parallels, and partly rhymes with, the half-line above it) is emphatic, so that the meaning might be, 'the hawk, wild though it be, must get used to the glove'. Cf. 30/5–8.

20 **tōðmægenes trum** gen. of respect: 'secure in tusk-power', i.e. 'in the power of its tusks'.

23–4 **on ȳðum mecgan, mereflōde** Perhaps, 'mix (*or* mingle) in the waves with the sea-tide [dat.]'.

25 **segelgyrd seomian** An elliptical half-line: '(and) the sail-yard hang there' *or* 'from it [i.e. the mast]'.

27 **frætwum wlanc** 'proud (*or* magnificent) in (*or* with) its treasures'. The jealous guarding of the treasure deposited in burial mounds is one of a dragon's main duties; theft from such a hoard precipitates the disastrous conclusion to the poem *Beowulf*.

29 **bēagas** 'rings', referring to substantial gold arm-rings or neck-rings (torques), but also more generally to 'treasures', the distribution of which (to both reward and buy loyalty) is a classic feature of the heroic world.

37 **Rand** Probably either the 'rim' of a shield or its central 'boss'. The next clause could refer to this or to the shield as a whole.

fæst° ⌐fingra gebeorh⌐. Fugel° uppe° sceal   firm   Bird   above
lācan° on lyfte. Leax° sceal on wæle°   soar   Salmon   pool
40 mid° ⌐sceote⌐ scrīðan. Scūr° sceal on° heofenum   with   Storm   from
winde° geblanden° in þās° woruld cuman.   by wind *ds*   churned   this
Þēof° sceal gangan° ⌐þȳstrum wederum⌐. Þyrs°   A thief   go (out)   Monster
sceal on fenne° gewunian   fen
āna° innan° lande°. Ides° sceal ⌐dyrne   alone   within   (its) territory   Woman
cræfte⌐,
⌐fæmne hire frēond gesēcean⌐, gif hēo nelle° on°   does not wish   among
folce° geþēon°,   (her) people   to prosper
45 ⌐þæt hī man bēagum gebicge⌐. Brim° sceal sealte°   Ocean   with salt *ds*
weallan°,   seethe
lyfthelm° and laguflōd° ymb° ⌐ealra   'sky-cover' (cloud)   sea-tide   around
landa gehwylc⌐
flōwan, ⌐firgenstrēamas⌐. Feoh° sceal on eorðan   Cattle
tȳdran° and tȳman°. Tungol° sceal on heofenum   bring forth   propagate   Star
beorhte° scīnan°, swā° him bebēad°   brightly   shine   as   ordered +*d*
meotud°.   the ordainer
50 Gōd° ⌐sceal wið yfele,⌐ geogoð° sceal wið yldo°,   Good (man)   youth   old age
līf sceal wið dēaþe, lēoht° sceal wið þȳstrum°,   light   darkness *dp*
fyrd wið fyrde, fēond° wið ōðrum°,   (one) foe   another
lāð° wið lāþe ymb° land sacan°,   enemy   about   contend

38 **fingra gebeorh** 'protection for [lit. "of"] fingers'.

40 **sceote** Probably dat. sg. of *sceot*, meaning a 'shot' (from a weapon) and extended to denote a quick movement, such as the darting motion of a fish. This kind of detailed description of behaviour parallels that given of the salmon in the previous line, and in general of animals in the maxims. However, *sceote* could be dat. sg. of *scēota*, 'trout', a close relative of the salmon.

42 **þȳstrum wederum** dat. of definition: 'in gloomy weather [lit. "weathers"]'.

43 **dyrne cræfte** instr. phr.: 'with secret cunning'.

44 **fæmne** 'maiden'. A variation on the subj. *ides*; i.e. 'a woman, a maiden...'. **hire frēond gesēcean** 'seek out her friend (*i.e.* lover)'. This appears not to mean simply to contrive to visit him but to run away to him once and for all, in order to avoid being provided with a husband in the regular way, in return for a dowry of rings from his people (see 45).

45 **þæt hī man bēagum gebicge** 'in that someone might buy [sbj.] her with rings'.

46 **ealra landa gehwylc** lit. 'each of all lands', i.e. 'in each and every land'.

47 **firgenstrēamas** Probably 'mountainous streams', but it is not clear whether these are an addition to the flowing streams of cloud and sea or simply a variation which includes both of them.

50 **sceal wið yfele** i.e. 'must *contend* against evil'; the same vb. is understood in the next five half-lines and is finally given in 53 (*sacan*).

⌐synne stælan⌐.   Ā° sceal snotor° hycgean°   Ever prudent (man) think
55 ymb þysse worulde° gewinn°,   wearh° hangian,   world's conflict *as* criminal
    fægere° ongildan°   þæt° hē ǣr fācen° dyde   fairly atone because crime
    ⌐manna cynne⌐.   Meotod āna wāt°   knows
    hwyder° sēo sāwul° sceal   syððan° hweorfan°,   to where soul afterwards go
    and ealle þā gāstas°   þe ⌐for⌐ Gode hweorfað   spirits
60 æfter dēaðdæge,   dōmes° bīdað°   judgement await +*g*
    on fæder° fæðme°.   Is sēo forðgesceaft°   father's embrace shape of the future
    dīgol° and dyrne°;   Drihten° āna wāt,   obscure hidden the Lord
    nergende° fæder.   Nǣni° eft° cymeð   saving None again
    hider° under° hrōfas°   ⌐þe þæt hēr for sōð   here below 'roofs' (*i.e.* heavens)
65 mannum secge   hwylc sȳ meotodes gesceaft⌐,
    sigefolca° gesetu°   þǣr° hē sylfa°   of 'victory-people' seats where himself
    wunað°.   dwells

54 **synne stælan** The vb. may mean 'found', 'institute' or 'impute'. The sense here could be that, by entering into conflict, both sides will 'institute sin' (i.e. become sinful), with acc. *synne*; but 'impute (*or* charge) with sin', with dat. *synne*, is another possibility: i.e. both sides, in order to justify their action, will perhaps accuse the other of breaking some law or agreement.

57 **manna cynne** indir. dat. obj. of *dyde*: '(committed) against the race of men'.

59 **for** 'before', or 'into the presence of'.

64–5 **þe þæt hēr for sōð mannum secge** 'who may tell [sbj.] it (*þæt*) for sure [lit. "for truth"] here to people'; *þæt* is correl. with *hwylc* and could be left out in trans. **hwylc sȳ meotodes gesceaft** 'what the Creator's establishment may be [sbj. pres.]', i.e. what sort of place it may be; *gesetu* in 66 is parallel with *gesceaft*.

34

The *Durham Proverbs*

The *Durham Proverbs* are so called because they are found in a manuscript now in the library of Durham Cathedral. In one of the curious juxtapositions which characterise the preservation of OE literature, they were copied, by a none too skilful scribe, onto five blank pages between a collection of hymns and a series of liturgical canticles. These hymns and canticles are in Latin, but with an OE gloss, and they seem to have been copied out in the second quarter of the eleventh century, with the proverbs being added a little later. The manuscript was made at Canterbury, and a second part contains a copy of Ælfric's grammatical work, his *Excerptiones* (see p. 22). Two of the proverbs (nos. 37 and 39) appear also as additions to a mid-eleventh-century Latin psalter (London, British Library, Royal 2. B. v) and two (nos. 14 and 42) are included in the thirteenth-century Middle English collection of the *Proverbs of Hendyng*. There is one other major set of proverbs in OE (surviving in three manuscripts), a version of the *Disticha Catonis* (the 'Dicts of Cato'), a third-century collection of wise sayings in Latin which enjoyed great popularity throughout the Middle Ages; it was widely used as a class-text in the monastic schools of Anglo-Saxon England. The only connection between these and the *Durham Proverbs* is the occurrence of the first of the latter as part of dict no. 23 (see 1n, below).

The forty-six OE proverbs in the Durham collection are all accompanied by Latin versions, but these derive from no known source. It is indeed not certain that the Latin versions came first and scholars have been tempted to see the collection as an original vernacular work, a native English collection of proverbs which someone then tried to put into Latin. The uneven and in places incomprehensible nature of the latter might suggest that it was supplied by a novice monk attempting the translation as a learning exercise. However, comprehension problems occur in the OE versions of the *Durham Proverbs*, too, and there are several cases (such as no. 16) where we have to turn to the Latin to make sense of the OE. The relationship between the English and Latin versions thus remains unclear. (The Latin versions given for the two proverbs occurring in Royal 2. B. v are identical with those in the Durham manuscript.)

A 'proverb' – at least as represented in the Durham collection – has a special quality of transferability which a 'maxim' in general does not. Thus the statement that 'a man can't have a mouthful of meal and also blow the fire' (see no. 43) certainly has a simple practical truth in it, but the man's dilemma is also paradigmatic: it stands for any situation where it is impossible to do two things at once. The *Durham Proverbs* offer a compelling mixture of the familiar and the bizarre. The cheerful observation of everyday affairs allows, and probably demands, the incursion of humour, something which the more serious and cerebral maxims have little scope for, and one example borders on the surreal (no. 11). Some of the proverbs are hoary old favourites from antiquity, but others are unknown in Latin or any other literatures. Several are echoed in the proverbial statements made in many OE poems, and a few have fairly close Old Norse parallels, though this need not suggest any direct connection. Some of the proverbs in the Durham collection remain tantalisingly obscure, perhaps through textual corruption, though only one all but defies rational interpretation (no. 15).

No overall structural coherence is apparent in the collection, but there is a cluster of four proverbs on the theme of 'a friend', nos. 2–5 (with another at no. 26), and in a few cases, pairs of proverbs seem to be deliberately juxtaposed, such as nos. 8 and 9, and 24 and 25. Several distinct styles may be seen. The plain aphoristic statement with *sceal* ('must', with all its ambiguities: see p. 296) occurs in five proverbs. The gnomic *biþ* is used in eleven, and the formula *sē þe*, 'he who', occurs twelve times, along with two similar cases where the relative pronoun is omitted. Of especial note are five *cwæþ* proverbs (nos. 10, 11, 15, 44 and 45), which we are surely entitled to call jokes. Their structure is bipartite, with a comparatively unremarkable initial statement rendered ludicrous by a second, which reveals the unexpected identity of the first speaker. Half of the proverbs use alliteration for effect and in some cases this results in complete metrical lines (see especially nos. 17, 19, 27, 35, 40 and 42). The language of the proverbs is late WS with a few non-WS spellings, such as *fele* (no. 26), *gehere* (no. 39) and *gelpeð* (no. 46); these cannot be shown to be local to Kent, despite the apparent origin of the Durham manuscript in Canterbury (as noted above). Eight emendations have been made below (see p. 353), the most important being signalled in the notes. In the glosses and in the main Glossary, reference is made to proverb-number, not line-number; there is, however, no numbering in the manuscript.

Further reading

O. Arngart, *The Durham Proverbs*, Lunds Universitets Årsskrift 1.52.2 (Lund, 1956)
   'The Durham Proverbs', *Speculum* 56 (1981), 288–300
R. S. Cox, 'The Old English Dicts of Cato', *Anglia* 90 (1972), 1–42
N. F. Barley, 'A Structural Approach to the Proverb and Maxim with Special Reference to the Anglo-Saxon Corpus', *Proverbium* 20 (1972), 737–50
G. Schleich, 'Die Sprichwörter Hendings und die Prouerbs of Wysdom', *Anglia* 51 (1927), 220–77

B. J. Whiting, ed., in collaboration with H. W. Whiting, *Proverbs, Sentences and Proverbial phrases from English Writings mainly before 1500* (London, 1968)

T. A. Shippey, 'Miscomprehension and Re-Interpretation in Old and Early Middle English Proverb Collections', in *Text und Zeittiefe*, ed. H. L. C. Tristram, ScriptOralia 58 (Tübingen, 1994), pp. 293–311

[1]   Geþyld° byð ⌐middes ēades⌐.

[2]   Frēond dēah° feor° ge° nēah: byð nēar° nyttra°.

[3]   Æt þearfe° man ⌐sceal freonda cunnian⌐.

[4]   Nafað° ǣnig mann frēonda tō feala°.

[5]   Beforan his frēonde ⌐biddeþ⌐, sē° þe his wǣdle° mǣneþ°.

[6]   ⌐Gōd gēr° byþ⌐ þonne se hund þām hrefne° gyfeð°.

[7]   Oft on sōtigum° bylige° ⌐searowa⌐ licgað°.

[8]   Hwīlum° æfter medo° ⌐menn mǣst geþyrsteð⌐.

1 Patience **2** is useful far and nearer more useful **3** (time of) need **4** Does not have [*ne hafað*] many +*g* **5** he poverty laments **6** year raven gives **7** dirty bag lie **8** Sometimes mead *as*

1 **middes ēades** gen. of definition: 'of half of happiness', i.e. 'halfway to happiness'. This proverb forms the second half of an item in the OE *Disticha Catonis*, no. 23 (see headnote), and this has prompted emendation of the Durham manuscript's *ēa* to *ēades*. The first part of the dict is *Forbǣr oft ðæt þū ēaðe wrecan mæge*, 'suffer often what you might readily avenge'.

3 **sceal freonda cunnian** Either 'must needs put (his) friends to the test', or, taking *sceal* as the fut. auxil., 'shall find out (his) friends'. *Cunnian* takes a noun in the gen.

5 **biddeþ** 'entreats' or 'will entreat'. The Latin version has the sbj. vb. *postulet*, and OE sbj. *bidde* ('let him beg . . .') would better suit the context.

6 **Gōd gēr . . . gyfeð** Cf. 'Pigs might fly'.

7 **searowa** The noun *searo* has primary meanings of 'art', 'cunning' or 'craft', extended to that which is made skilfully or cunningly (including 'war-gear'), so a general sense of 'things of value' or 'treasure' may be intended; this would correlate with the Latin version's *aurum*, 'gold'. However, this meaning of the noun is not attested elsewhere and the more abstract treasure of 'cunning', issuing from an otherwise unprepossessing person, is a perfectly viable idea. The form *searowa* is unusual for nom. pl. [§B2g]. An Old Norse analogue has wisdom coming from a shrivelled leather bag, i.e. an old man. Whatever the case, the message is simple: Don't judge by appearances.

8 **menn . . . geþyrsteð** The construction is impers.: lit. 'it thirsts most to a person [dat. sg.]', i.e. 'a person thirsts most'. 'Man' might have been chosen as the more specific trans. here, for mead-drinking (with its ironical consequences) does seem to have been a male occupation in Anglo-Saxon England.

[9]   ⌐Æfter leofan menn langað swīðost⌐.

[10]   Nū hit ys ⌐on swīnes dōme⌐, cwæð ⌐se ceorl sæt⌐ on eoferes° hricge°.

[11]   ⌐Ne swā þēah trēowde þēah þū teala ēode⌐, cwæþ sē þe geseah° hægtessan° ⌐æfter hēafde geongan⌐.

[12]   ⌐Eall on mūðe þæt on mōde⌐.

[13]   ⌐Gemǣne sceal⌐ māga° feoh°.

[14]   Man dēþ° swā hē byþ ⌐þonne hē mōt swā hē wile⌐.

10 boar's back   **11** saw   witch   **13** of kinspeople   wealth   **14** will do

9 **Æfter... swīðost** The syntactical parallels between this and no. 8 suggest that the two were deliberately juxtaposed, but there are differences. The impers. vb. *langian* usually takes its obj. in the acc. (though dat. is also possible, as with *geþyrsteð*), in which case *menn* may be acc. pl.: 'people long most strongly'; then *leofan* is a noun: 'for the beloved'. But the first three words may be taken together as a prep. phr., 'for the beloved person' (*æfter* plus dat. sg. *menn*, with the apparently weak inflection of the adj., -*an*, standing for strong -*um*); the two-word shorter phr. at the end then means simply, 'one longs most strongly' – a sentiment which has a strong echo in *Beowulf*, 1879–80. The Latin version supports the second interpretation of the first three words (using *hominem*, 'man'), but the vb. used is *tedet* with the meaning 'it becomes most tedious (*or* wearying)'. That is a possible meaning for the OE vb. *langað*, but the whole proverb then becomes less clear. The Latin could in fact be seen as a bungled attempt to render the OE; *post* does not accurately reflect OE *æfter* when it has objective sense, rather than temporal or local.

10 **on swīnes dōme** 'in the judgement of the pig'; perhaps, 'up to the pig'.   **se ceorl sæt** 'the man who sat'. This proverb is as enigmatic as it is memorable. The *ceorl* astride the boar's back might simply be a 'peasant' or 'yeoman' but is more likely a 'husband' (as in the Latin: *maritus*). Presumably the *swīn* (often a domesticated pig) and the *eofor* (usually a wild boar) are the same creature; see the analogy in *Beowulf* (31a/49–50). Some joke about the perils of marriage is probably intended. Among the many grotesque little thirteenth-century stone carvings which are to be seen high up in the nave and in the chapter house of York Minster in England are two which depict a man precariously astride a pig.

11 **Ne... ēode** If, like *ēode*, *trēowde* be taken as sbj., the interpretation seems to be: 'I would not trust (you) anyway (*swā þēah*), even though you walked properly'.   **æfter hēafde geongan** Presumably the prep. has the sense 'by means of'; thus, 'go (*or* pass by) on (her) head'; *geongan* is emended from *geo...*

12 **Eall... mōde** 'Everything is in the mouth that is in the mind (*or* heart)', i.e. 'What the heart thinks, the mouth speaks'. There is a ME version: 'That the hert thynkyt the mowte spekyt', and Lk 6.45 provides a biblical analogue: '... for out of the abundance of the heart the mouth speaketh'.

13 **Gemǣne sceal** 'must (be) shared [lit. "in common"]'. Families ought to look after their own.

14 **þonne hē mōt swā hē wile** 'when he may (do) as he wishes'. A man will reveal his true character when free from constraints. Cf. *Proverbs of Hendyng*: 'Wan man mai done als [= as] he wille, þan doth he also [= as] he is'.

[15]   ⌐Ne saga sagan, cwæð sē gesēah hwer fulne hēalena sēoþan¬.

[16]   Eaðe° ⌐wīs¬ man mæg witan° spell° and ēac secgan.

[17]   Blind byþ ⌐bām ēagum, sē þe brēostum ne starat¬.

[18]   ⌐Ðā° ne sacað°¬ þe ætsamne° ne bēoð.

[19]   ⌐Ne dēah eall sōþ āsǣd ne eall sār ætwiten¬.

[20]   ⌐Gyf þū well¬ sprece°, wyrc° æfter° swā°.

[21]   ⌐Sōþ°¬ hit sylf ācȳþeð°.

[22]   Earh° ⌐mæg þæt ān¬ þæt hē ⌐him¬ ondrǣde°.

[23]   ⌐Ne sceal man¬ tō ǣr° forht° ne tō ǣr fǣgen°.

16 Easily understand narrative 18 Those quarrel together 20 speak do afterwards so 21 Truth reveals 22 Coward is afraid 23 soon fearful joyful

15 **Ne saga... sēoþan** This is the most obscure of the proverbs, no doubt owing to transmission error. The best that we can do with the OE as it stands is to accept *saga* as imper. of *secgan*, and *sagan* as acc. pl. of masc. *n*-noun *saga*, 'narrative' or 'tale'. In the second part of the proverb, *hēala* (here gen. pl.) is a 'hydrocele', a tumour filled with fluid – or so the Latin equivalent (*ponderosum*) seems to tell us. Thus we have: 'Tell no tales, said he who saw the pot full of hydroceles boil'. But what might it mean? One critic suggests, 'What you attempt to persuade us to is not good for us', but that seems a bit far-fetched. The Latin version has a vb. in the opening part with no equivalent in the OE and appears to say, 'He doesn't make good flesh with flesh (*caro carnem*), said he who boiled a pot full of hydroceles'. So far, we must accept defeat on this one.

16 **wīs** Although *wīs* is not in the manuscript, the Latin version indicates that it ought to be, and certainly it gives purpose to an otherwise rather empty idea: a wise man may easily understand a discourse or story and also explain it or pronounce on it.

17 **bām ēagum** 'in both eyes'. **sē þe brēostum ne starat** (with *starat* for *starað*, and *brēostum* used with sg. meaning [§D4i]). Perhaps 'he who does not see with (his own) heart', but 'into his own heart' has also been suggested. In either case, we are near to a sense of 'he who does not *understand* his own heart or mind'. Cf. 'There are none so blind as those who will not see', though this rather implies a conscious refusal to see truth.

18 **Ðā ne sacað... bēoð** Cf. 'It takes two to make a quarrel'.

19 **Ne dēah eall sōþ āsǣd** 'It does no good (for) all truth (to be) told'. **ne eall sār ætwiten** 'nor all wrong imputed', i.e. blamed on someone. Cf. 'You can tell too much of the truth'.

20 **Gyf þū... swā** Cf. 'Practice what you preach'.

21 **Sōþ... ācȳþeð** Cf. 'Truth will out', or the biblical 'Great is truth, and it prevails' (3 Esd 4.41).

22 **mæg þæt ān** 'can (do only) the one (thing)'. **him** The refl. dat. pron. can be ignored in trans.

23 **Ne sceal... fǣgen** The vb. 'be' must be supplied [§G2d]. There is striking correspondence with *The Wanderer* (38/65–8): *Wita... ne sceal nō tō hātheort... ne tō forht ne tō fǣgen*, but calls for moderation are a commonplace of wisdom literature; the OE *Disticha Catonis* include several.

[24] ⌐Forworht mann⌐ friþes° behōfað°.

[25] ⌐Sēlre° byþ þæt man hund heona gesēce þonne man hund hȳnþa° geþolie°⌐.

[26] Ne byð þæt fele° frēond, sē þe ⌐ōþrum facn hēleð⌐.

[27] ⌐Swā cystigran hīwan°, swā cynnigran⌐ gystas°.

[28] Gyfena° gehwilc° ⌐underbæc besihþ⌐.

[29] ⌐Ne wāt°⌐ swētes° ðanc°, sē þe biteres ne onbyrgeð°.

[30] ⌐Tō nāwihte ne hopað⌐, se° tō hāme ne ⌐higeð⌐.

[31] ⌐Eall here° byþ hwæt° þonne se lātēow° byþ hwæt⌐.

[32] ⌐Wīde timbreð, sē þe wegferendum hȳreð⌐.

[33] ⌐Tiligera hūs⌐ lencgest° standaþ.

24 refuge has need of +*g*   **25** Better oppressions endure   **26** faithful   **27** household guests **28** Gift(s) each +*gp*   **29** knows of sweetness pleasure *as* tastes +*g*   **30** who **31** army bold general   **33** longest

24 **Forworht mann** 'A condemned person' or 'outlaw'. In the Anglo-Saxon lawcodes, *friþ*, 'refuge' or 'sanctuary', may also indicate the restoration of rights to an outlaw.

25 **Sēlre ... geþolie** If *heona* is the gen. of the pl. noun *hiwan*, and if this is given its common meaning 'members of a religious household', then the proverb may allude to the refuge afforded by monasteries (but perhaps with an ironical suggestion that in normal circumstances monks are the last people one would wish to be with?): 'It is better to seek out a hundred (*hund*) monks than to endure a hundred oppressions'. The juxtaposition with no. 24 seems deliberate. See also no. 27, where *hiwan* is again used, though not in an alliterating environment.

26 **ōþrum facn hēleð** 'hides (*or* harbours) treachery against another'.

27 **Swā cystigran ... swā cynnigran** Here *swā* is used as an adv. with the comp. adj.: 'The better ... the nobler'.

28 **underbæc besihþ** 'looks back'. Gifts are always given in the expectation of a return. Cf. the Old Norse proverb, *Ey sér til gildis giof*, 'a gift always looks for a return' (*Hávamál*, 1145).

29 **Ne wāt ... onbyrgeð** Cf. Alfred's version of Boethius's *De consolatione Philosophiae* (ch. 23; see p. 38 for edition): *ælcum men þincð huniges biobrēad þȳ weorodra gif hē hwæne ǣr biteres onbirigð*, 'to every man the honeycomb seems the sweeter if he previously tastes something bitter'.

30 **Tō nāwihte ne hopað** 'he hopes for nothing', i.e. 'he has no hope'. **higeð** 'sets his mind on', 'hopes for' and 'remembers' are all possibilities here. Cf. 'There's no place like home'. It seems unnecessary to identify, as one editor has, a Christian dimension.

31 **Eall here ... hwæt** Cf. the similar sentiment about leadership expressed proverbially in the *Anglo-Saxon Chronicle* for 1003 (8/79–80).

32 **Wīde timbreð ... hȳreð** It is not clear whether the second vb. is from *hȳran*, 'obey' or 'serve' (with dat.), or *hȳrian*, 'hire'. The meaning seems to be, 'He builds widely (*or* spaciously?) who serves (*or* hires out to) wayfarers (*or* travellers)'. Perhaps some comment on the unpredictability and/or unreliability of travellers is intended. For *wīde*, the Latin version has *crebro*, 'repeatedly' or 'often', but the rest is senseless.

33 **Tiligera hūs** The noun *tiligea* (gen. pl.), from the vb. *tilian*, 'labour' or 'exert oneself', should perhaps be interpreted here as 'those who labour', rather than simply 'labourers'; *hūs* is pl.: 'the houses of those who labour'. Cf. 'Hard work brings prosperity'.

[34] ⌜Mete gæþ on banan hand⌝.
[35] Lēana° forlēosaþ°, sē ⌜þe hit lȳþran dēð⌝.
[36] ⌜Sēo nȳdþearf° feala° lǣreð°⌝.
[37] ⌜Betere byþ⌝ oft feðre° þonne° oferfeðre°.
[38] ⌜Cræfta gehwilc⌝ byþ ⌜cealde⌝ forgolden°.
[39] ⌜Ciggendra gehwilc⌝ wile° þæt hine man gehēre°.
[40] ⌜Weard seteð, sē þe wæccendum wereð⌝.
[41] ⌜Ne sceall sē for horse murnan°, sē þe wile heort° ofærnan°⌝.
[42] ⌜Swā fulre fæt swā⌝ hit mann sceal fægror° beran°.
[43] ⌜Ne mæg man mūþ fulne° melewes° habban and ēac fȳr blāwan°⌝.

35 Gifts *ap*   loses   **36** necessity   much   teaches   **37** loaded   than   overloaded   **38** repaid   **39** wants   listens to +*a*   **41** be anxious   stag   overtake   **42** more gently   carry   **43** full of meal   blow

34 **Mete ... hand** Apparently a statement about the positive consequences of (perhaps the justification for?) killing: 'Food comes to the slayer's hand'. Whether the killing referred to is of enemies or simply food-animals is not clear. It has been suggested that *banan* ought to be emended to *benan* 'supplicant', producing a proverb with the sense of 'ask and ye shall receive'. The Latin version uses a noun meaning 'dispenser', which has led to the further suggestion that OE *brytta* was meant.

35 **þe hit lȳþran dēð** The sg. pron. has the pl. antec. *leana*; the adj. *lȳþran* is used as a noun: 'who bestows them on a base [i.e. unworthy] person'.

36 **Sēo nȳdþearf ... lǣreð** Cf. 'Necessity is the mother of invention'.

37 **Betere byþ** 'It is better to be . . .'. This proverb occurs also in a later manuscript (see headnote), with the first word replaced by *sēlre* (with the same meaning). Cf. 'little by little'.

38 **Cræfta gehwilc** Here *cræft*, often meaning 'skill' or 'strength', must have a more negative sense: 'Every deceit (*or* trick)'. **cealde** lit. 'coldly' or 'with coldness'; the Latin has *acerbior*, 'more bitterly' or 'more harshly'.

39 **Ciggendra gehwilc** The noun is formed from the pres. part. of *ciegan*, 'call out' or 'shout': 'Everyone who shouts'. The version in a later manuscript (see headnote) has a rather different emphasis: *clipiendra gehwylc wolde þæt him man oncwæde*, 'everyone who calls out would like someone to answer him'.

40 **Weard ... wereð** In the manuscript, the OE version begins *eard seeð* and the emendation to *weard seteð* is made on the strength of Latin *custodem ponit*, but thereafter the Latin is not much help (*qui uigilans minat*). The (emended) OE version could mean, 'He sets a watchman, who guards against (*or* defends, *wereð*) the watchers'. This brings to mind (and perhaps answers) the question famously asked by Juvenal in the context of setting guards to keep a wife from lovers: *sed quis custodiet ipsos custodes?*, 'but who is to guard the guards themselves?'.

41 **Ne sceall ... ofærnan** Cf. 'Needs must'.

42 **Swā fulre fæt swā** 'The fuller the cup, the . . .'. Cf. *Proverbs of Hendyng*: 'When þe coppe is follest, þenne ber hire feyrest'.

43 **Ne mæg ... blāwan** Cf. 'No man can both sup and blow at once' and 'A man cannot whistle and drink at the same time'. There are close parallels in other Germanic languages, including one in Old High German more or less contemporary with the OE.

[44] ⌜Wīde⌝ ne biþ wel, cwæþ sē þe ⌜gehȳrde on helle hrīman⌝.

[45] ⌜Āge þē, sē þe æfter cīge⌝, cwæþ sē þe gesēah hungor of tūne faran°.

[46] ⌜Hwon° gelpeð°⌝, sē þe wīde sīþað°.

45 go   **46** Little   boasts   travels

44 **wīde** adv. 'widely', 'far and wide' or 'afar'; perhaps an understatement for 'every-where'.   **gehȳrde ... hrīman** A var. on the acc. and infin. construction [§G6d.i.3], with no obj. expressed: 'heard (people) wailing', or, treating the pres. part. as a noun: 'heard the wailing'. The whole proverb might be rendered: 'Far and wide things aren't well [or, with more irony, "Things are far from well"], said he who heard the wailing in hell'. In the OE poem *Christ and Satan*, hell is described as 'that miserable hall, where wailing and weeping are heard afar (*wīde*)' (331–2), in contrast with heaven, where 'holy rejoicing' is to be heard (327), and a few lines later we read: 'Therefore he who was twelve miles away from hell could hear that there was a loud and sad gnashing of teeth'.

45 **Āge þē** sbj. vb.: 'he may have you', or 'let him have you'.   **sē þe æfter cīge** 'he who calls (you) back'.

46 **Hwon ... sīþað** The taciturnity of the experienced wayfarer (who has seen much to talk about) is implicitly praised here; cf. the promotion of the same virtue in *The Wanderer* (38/11–14 and 111). There are several medieval analogues in other languages.

35

Five Anglo-Saxon Riddles

Riddling quickens the mind and lifts the spirit. It is an ancient and universal art which uses devices such as pun, *double-entendre* and metaphor to engage with the world in a sort of intellectual game-playing. Some ninety-five riddles in OE, all of them poems, are preserved in the Exeter Book, the exact number varying according to how editors divide them. They are copied in three groups, with other poems intervening, and some of the latter (such as *Wulf and Eadwacer*, Text 39) are themselves so enigmatic that critics have been tempted to include them in the riddling genre as well. It is likely that the OE riddles had a variety of different authors. They drew on a strong Latin tradition associated especially with Symphosius, whose collection of three-line *ænigmata*, compiled in the fourth century or the fifth, was enormously popular. In England, the early eighth-century bishop of Sherborne, Aldhelm, composed one hundred *ænigmata* in order to illustrate his study of Latin metre. (He composed OE verse as well, but none, as far as we can tell, survives.) In the eighth century, a collection of one hundred Latin riddles was put together by Tatwine, archbishop of Canterbury, and a writer calling himself 'Eusebius', who was possibly Bede's friend Hwætberht, abbot of Jarrow.

Though strongly influenced by such Latin precedents, the OE riddles, with a few exceptions, are not simply translations. In general they are longer than the Latin riddles and contain more detail, and they are far more playful in style. Their subjects are a heterogeneous mixture of the secular and the religious, the cosmological and the mundane: shield, sword, cross, chalice; beaker, onion, dough; sun, storm, wind, iceberg; badger, hen, fish. Some reflect a knowledge of Graeco-Roman learning, others are overtly popular, with sexual double-meanings, and many offer us a window on to aspects of Anglo-Saxon life which we rarely see in the other literature. Several riddles incorporate the challenge, 'say what I am' or 'ask what I am called'; this may take a lot of ingenuity (and a few riddles have never been satisfactorily solved), but in other cases the 'solution' is in fact obvious long before the end, and such riddles seem to be purely celebrations of the things they describe. Of the five OE riddles given here, (b), (c) and (d) use one of the most frequent devices of the Anglo-Saxon riddler, the personification of an object (a device known as prosopopoeia), which then describes itself in the first person. One of these is the 'Bible' riddle, which gives us a meticulous description of the process of making a biblical manuscript (perhaps a gospel-book rather than a complete Bible), from the procurement and preparation of the animal skin to the binding and decorating of the magnificent finished volume. In 'Bookworm', the viewpoint of the detached, quizzical, observer is used. This riddle is based on a Latin *ænigma* by Symphosius and playfully asks provoking questions about the ultimate value of our devouring of written knowledge. The world conjured up by the 'Onion' riddle, which is placed in the manuscript immediately before the 'Bible' riddle, is rather less elevated in its theme; it is one of half a dozen items in the collection which playfully describe, on one level, sexual arousal. If we are surprised to find such material in a manuscript produced in monastic scriptorium and owned by a bishop, it may be because we have too one-sided a view of the life of even the ostensibly devout Anglo-Saxon. The phrase with which this riddle starts (*Ic eom wunderlicu wiht*) is used to introduce other riddles, too (those usually numbered 18, 20 and 24), but none has a salacious theme.

The five riddles are presented here in the order in which they occur in the Exeter Book and are numbered according to the most widely used system. Linguistically, the texts of the OE riddles match those of the Exeter Book as a whole in their 'standard' late WS forms. There is very little sign in those below of the levelling of inflections, though *fēoldan* for *fēoldon* (d/7) is an exception. Confusion of *d* and *ð*, a characteristic feature of late manuscripts, is seen in a/6 (*forwurde* for *forwurðe*), and in d/12, *þ* is written for *d* in *hȳþe*.

Further reading

C. Williamson, ed., *The Old English Riddles of the Exeter Book* (Chapel Hill, NC, 1977)

N. F. Barley, 'Structural Aspects of the Anglo-Saxon Riddle', *Semiotica* 10 (1974), 143–75

M. Nelson, 'The Rhetoric of the Exeter Book Riddles', *Speculum* 49 (1974), 421–40

K. Crossley-Holland, trans., *The Exeter Book Riddles* (Harmondsworth, 1979)

C. Williamson, *A Feast of Creatures: Anglo-Saxon Riddle-Songs* (Philadelphia, PA, 1982)

J. Scattergood, 'Eating the Book: *Riddle* 47 and Memory', in *Text and Gloss: Studies in Insular Learning and Literature Presented to Joseph Donovan Pheifer*, ed. H. Conrad-O Briain, A. M. D'Arcy and V. J. Scattergood (Dublin, 1999), pp. 119–27

R. DiNapoli, 'In the Kingdom of the Blind, the One-Eyed Man is a Seller of Garlic: Depth-Perception and the Poet's Perspective in the Exeter Book Riddles', *ES* 81 (2000), 422–55

D. K. Smith, 'Humor in Hiding: Laughter between the Sheets in the Exeter Book Riddles', in *Humour in Anglo-Saxon Literature*, ed. J. Wilcox (Cambridge, 2000), pp. 79–98

35a

Riddle 5: 'Shield'

Ic eom ⌜ānhaga, ⌝īserne⌝ wund°,	wounded
bille° gebennad°, beadoweorca° sæd°,	by sword hurt war-deeds sated with
ecgum° wērig°. Oft ic wīg° sēo°,	by (sword-)edges exhausted battle *as* see
⌜frēcne feohtan⌝, frōfre° ne wēne°,	consolation *as* expect
5 þæt mē° ⌜gēoc cyme° gūðgewinnes⌝	to me (will) come *sbj*
ǣr° ic mid° ældum° eal° forwurde°,	before among men wholly perish *sbj*
ac° mec° hnossiað° ⌜homera lāfe⌝,	but me batter
heardecg° heoroscearp° hondweorc smiþa°	hard-edged deadly sharp of smiths
bītað° in burgum°. Ic ābīdan° sceal°	bite (me) strongholds await +*g* must
10 lāþran° gemōtes°. Næfre° lǣcecynn°	more hostile meeting Never physician
on folcstede° findan meahte°	town could (I)
⌜þāra þe mid wyrtum° wunde° gehǣlde⌝	herbs wounds *ap*
ac ⌜mē ecga° dolg° ēacen weorðað⌝	of swords wounds *np*
Þurh dēaðslege° ⌜dagum ond nihtum⌝.	death-stroke

1 **ānhaga** 'solitary one', 'loner'. The word is used also of the solitary exile in *The Wanderer* (38/1). **īserne** dat. of instrument: 'by iron', i.e. iron weapon(s); see also 2 (*bille*) and 3 (*ecgum*).

4 **frēcne feohtan** A second obj. of *seo*, in an acc. and inf. construction [§G6d.i.3]: 'bold ones fighting'.

5 **gēoc ... gūðgewinnes** 'relief from [lit. "of"] battle-strife'.

7 **homera lāfe** 'the legacy of hammers'; i.e. the sword (the 'handiwork' of 8) that the smith's hammer prepares. The same kenning is used in *The Battle of Brunanburh* (10/6).

12 **þāra þe ... gehǣlde** 'of those who might heal [sbj. pret.]', i.e. 'of the sort who might heal'.

13 **mē ... ēacen weorðað** 'become augmented on me', i.e. 'grow bigger on me'.

14 **dagum ond nihtum** dat. of time: 'by days and nights', or simply, 'day and night'.

35b

Riddle 7: 'Swan'

⌐Hrægl˥ mīn swīgað°   þonne° ic hrūsan° trede°   is silent   when   ground   tread
oþþe þā wīc° būge°   oþþe wado° drēfe°.   village   occupy   waters   stir up
Hwīlum° mec āhebbað°   ofer hæleþa°   Sometimes   raise up   men's
    byht°   habitation
⌐hyrste° mīne   ond þēos hēa° lyft°˥,   trappings *np*   lofty   air *ns*
5 ond mec þonne wīde°   ⌐wolcna strengu˥   widely
ofer folc byreð°.   Frætwe° mīne   carries   Ornaments
swōgað° hlūde°   ond swinsiað°,   resound   loudly   make melody
torhte° singað   þonne ic getenge° ne bēom°   brightly   near to (+*d*)   am
flōde° ond foldan°,   fērende° gæst°.   water *ds*   earth *ds*   travelling   spirit *ns*

---

1 **Hrægl** 'dress'. The poet uses this and two other metaphors, *hyrste* and *frætwe*, for the swan's plumage. There is a punning contrast made between *swīgað* here and *swōgað* in 7.

    4 **hyrste...lyft** double subj. of *āhebbað*, whose obj. is *mec*.

    5 **wolcna strengu** 'the power [nom. sg.] of the skies (*or* clouds)'; a kenning for the wind.

35c

Riddle 25: 'Onion'

Ic eom wunderlicu° wiht°   ⌐wīfum on hyhte˥,   wondrous   creature
nēahbūendum° nyt°.   ⌐Nǣngum sceþþe   neighbours   a service (to +*d*)
burgsittendra˥   nymþe° bonan° ānum°.   except   (my) slayer   alone
Staþol° mīn is stēaphēah°,   stonde° ic on° bedde,   Stem   erect   stand up   in
5 ⌐ncoþan rūh nāthwǣr˥.   Nēþeð° hwīlum°   Dares   sometimes

---

1 **wīfum on hyhte** lit. 'to women in expectation'; perhaps, 'in women's expectation'.

    2–3 **Nǣngum sceþþe burgsittendra** '(I) harm none of the citizens'; *sceþþan* governs the dat.: hence also *bonan ānum*.

    5 **neoþan rūh nāthwǣr** 'hairy somewhere down below' (*nāt* + *hwǣr*, lit. 'I don't know where').

ful° cyrtenu°   ceorles° dohtor,   very   comely   yeoman's
mōdwlonc° mēowle°,   ⌜þæt hēo on mē grīpeð⌝,   proud   maiden
⌜ræseð mec on rēodne⌝   rēafað° mīn hēafod,   plunders
⌜fēgeð mec on fæsten⌝.   Fēleþ° sōna°   Feels (+g)   directly
10   ⌜mīnes gemōtes⌝,   sēo° þe° mec nearwað°,   she   who   confines
wīf ⌜wundenlocc⌝.   Wæt° bið þæt ēage°.   Wet   eye

7 **þæt hēo on mē grīpeð** 'that she grasps at (*or* takes hold of) me'; in ModE we would say '(dares) to grasp . . .'.

8 **ræseð mec on rēodne** 'attacks me in (my) redness'; perhaps, 'attacks my red self'.

9 **fēgeð mec on fæsten** 'fixes (*or* confines) me in a stronghold'; perhaps, ' . . . in a firm grip'.

10 **mīnes gemōtes** 'my encounter' (gen. after *fēleþ*), i.e. 'her encounter with me'.

11 **wundenlocc** 'with braided hair' (see 19/77).

35d
Riddle 26: 'Bible'

⌜Mec fēonda sum   fēore besnyþede⌝,
⌜woruldstrenga binōm⌝,   wætte° siþþan°,   wetted   next
dȳfde° on wætre,   dyde° eft° þonan°,   dipped   took   again   out
sette on° sunnan°   þǣr° ⌜ic swīþe belēas   in   sun   where
5   hērum þām þe ic hæfde⌝.   ⌜Heard°⌝ mec siþþan   Hard
snāð° seaxses° ecg,   ⌜sindrum begrunden⌝   cut   knife's

1 **Mec . . . fēore besnyþede** 'robbed me of [lit. "from"] life'. The obj. pron. *mec* is repeated notionally after the other trans. vbs. in the succeeding lines (*wætte mec, dȳfde mec*, etc). Cf. the opening of the cross's story in *The Dream of the Rood* (23/28–33a). **fēonda sum** 'a certain one of enemies', i.e. 'a certain enemy'.

2 **woruldstrenga binōm** 'deprived (me) of worldly strengths [i.e. physical powers]'.

4–5 **ic swīþe belēas hērum þām þe ic hæfde** 'I was violently deprived of [lit. "from"] the hairs that [lit. "those that"] I had'. After the animal's skin has had several soakings in water and been stretched over a frame in the sun, the hairs come away very easily.

5 **Heard** The adj. describes *ecg* (the subj. of *snāð*) in 6.

6 **sindrum begrunden** '(once I had been) ground (*or* scraped) clean from impurities'. Using a curved knife, the parchment-maker has already scraped the surface of the hairless skin clean of any remaining bits of flesh or other impurities, before cutting it to shape.

	Fingras fēoldan° ond ⌐mec fugles° wyn°	folded (me) bird's delight
	geond spēddropum spyrede⌐ geneahhe°,	repeatedly
	⌐ofer brūnne brerd bēamtelge°⌐ swealg°,	tree-ink *as* swallowed
10	strēames° dǣle°, stōp° eft on mec,	of liquid portion *as* stepped
	sīþade° ⌐sweartlāst⌐. Mec siþþan wrāh°	travelled clad
	hæleð° hlēobordum°, hȳþe°	a man *ns* with protective boards with hide
	beþenede°,	covered
	gierede° mec mid golde. Forþon° mē glīwedon°	adorned Forthwith adorned
	wrǣtlic° ⌐weorc⌐ smiþa°, wīre°	ornamental of smiths with wire
	bifongen°.	encased
15	Nū þā gerēno° ond se rēada° telg°	trappings red dye
	ond þā wuldorgesteald° wīde° ⌐mǣre⌐	wondrous setting widely
	⌐dryhtfolca helm, nales dol wīte⌐.	
	Gif ⌐mīn⌐ bearn° wera° brūcan° willað,	children *np* of men use
	hȳ° bēoð° ⌐þȳ gesundran ond þȳ sigefæstran⌐,	they will be
20	⌐heortum⌐ þȳ hwætran° ond ⌐þȳ hyge° blīþran°⌐,	bolder in mind happier

7–8 **mec ... geond spēddropum spyrede** 'made tracks across me (*geond mec*) with its useful drops' (or 'with lucky droppings', as S. A. J. Bradley nicely puts it). Ink from the quill-pen (*fūgles wyn*) leaves a trail of the words of scripture. The prep. *geond* is metrically awkward and some editors add a conjectured missing vb. after it.

9 **ofer brūnne brerd** Perhaps, 'over the dusky margin (of the manuscript)'; another suggestion is 'across the burnished rim (of the ink-pot)'. Either way, we see the pen going back and forth between ink-pot and writing area. **bēamtelge** Tree products, including especially oak-galls, were used in the making of ink.

11 **sweartlāst** Apparently an adv.: 'with black track (*or* trail)'.

14 **weorc** 'objects' or 'artefacts', the pl. subj. of *glīwedon*. These lines suggest a binding embellished with filigree, a delicate tracery formed of fine gold wire.

16 **mǣre** sg. form for pl. sbj. vb., with optative meaning: 'let (the ornaments, etc) proclaim...', with obj. *dryhtfolca helm* in 17. Some editors take *mǣre* to be an adj., 'famous', describing the ornaments, etc, but that leaves us without a vb.

17 **dryhtfolca helm** 'the peoples' protector'; i.e. scripture itself, or perhaps Christ. **nales dol wīte** A problematical half-line, probably corrupt. The emphatic neg. adv. *nales* ('not' or 'not at all') suggests that a firm contrast is being made with what has gone before. If we take *wīte* to be a sbj. vb., from *wītan* ('guard' or 'keep', but also 'impute to' or 'blame'), parallel with *mǣre* in 16, we might understand: 'let (them) not in any way guard (*or* encourage?) folly', though the necessity for such a declaration is not apparent. Perhaps a little more satisfactory is to take *wīte* as the noun 'punishment' or 'misery'. *Dol* is an adj. meaning 'foolish' (or a noun, 'folly'). If the words (separated in the manuscript) are taken as a compound, the meaning might be '(not) punishment of the foolish' (interpreted by some as 'the pains of hell'); or perhaps '(not) the misery of the foolish' (i.e. of sinful people?).

18 **mīn** 'me', gen. obj. of *brūcan*.

19 **þȳ ... sigefæstran** instr. *þȳ* is the intensive adv. before a comp. adj.: 'the safer and the more sure of victory' (in a spiritual sense; cf. 23/13, 33/66, etc).

20 **heortum** dat. of respect: 'in (their) hearts'; similarly *hyge*, and *ferþe* in 21. **þȳ hyge blīþran** i.e. *hyge þȳ blīþran*.

ferþe° þȳ frōdran°.   Habbaþ° frēonda   **in spirit wiser (They will) have**
  þȳ mā°,   **more**
⌜swæsra° ond gesibbra°,   sōþra ond gōdra°,   **dearer closer more virtuous**
tilra° ond getrēowra°⌝,   ⌜þā⌝ hyra tȳr°   **more good more loyal glory**
  ond ēad°   **happiness**
ēstum° ȳcað°   ond hȳ° ⌜ārstafum   **gladly (will) increase them**
25 lissum⌝ bilecgað°   ond hī lufun° fæþmum°   **(will) cover of love with embraces**
fæste clyppað°.   Frige° hwæt ic hātte°,   **(will) clasp Ask am called** *pass*
niþum° tō° nytte°.   Nama mīn is mære°,   **to people as service renowned**
hæleþum° gifre°   ⌜ond hālig sylf⌝.   **to men bountiful**

22–3 swæsra . . . getrēowra All the compound adjs. in these lines complement *frēonda* ('of friends', gen. pl. after *mā*); a substitute pron. may be introduced in trans.: '(more) dear ones, more close ones, . . .'.

23 þā rel. pron., 'who', with antec. *frēonda*.

24–5 ārstafum lissum dat. of agency: 'with benefits (and) with kindnesses'; similarly *fæþmum*.

28 ond hālig sylf 'and (I) myself holy'.

35e

Riddle 47: 'Bookworm'

[handwritten: alliterative metre]

[handwritten: 2/3. 4 stresses]

Moððe° 'word' fræt°.   Mē° þæt þūhte°   **ate To me seemed**
wrætlicu° wyrd°,   þā ic þæt wundor°   **curious happening marvel**
gefrægn°,   **heard about**
þæt se° wyrm° forswealg°   'wera gied sumes',   **swallowed down**
þēof° in þȳstro°,   þrymfæstne° cwide°   **thief** *ns* **the dark glorious discourse**
5 ond þæs strangan staþol.⌉   Stælgiest° ne wæs   **Thieving visitor**
wihte° þȳ° gleawra°   þe° hē þām wordum   **at all the wiser when**
swealg°.   **swallowed** *+d*

[handwritten annotations interspersed: "The moth ate words", "eat - etam - scoff", "To me a curious", "that seemed to me a strange event", "wonder", "when I heard about that marvel", "prefix", "that the way he swallowed down some man's words", "the thieving", "the visitor was not at all the wiser when he swallowed the words", "prefix"]

1 **word** 'words'. The context suggests the pl., and this is confirmed in 6 (*wordum*, dat. pl.).

3 **wyrm** The 'worm' is the larval stage of the *moððe* of 1. Worm-holes in the leaves of manuscripts are very familiar to scholars. **wera gied sumes** 'the speech of a certain one of men', i.e. 'some man's speech (*or* words)'.

5 **þæs strangan staþol** 'the foundation of that mighty (thing)'; presumably an ironical reference to the man's utterance, whose very foundation (i.e. the parchment on which it is written) is being eaten away.

[handwritten: Moth / worm. they - human doesn't become wiser.]

36
Deor

'He who knows many songs sorrows the less', claims the poet of the OE *Maxims I* – and *Deor* seems to confirm this sentiment. It is a poem of consolation which draws on stock characters of Germanic legend to sketch a series of episodes of misfortune. Each episode is followed by a refrain which may be translated loosely as 'That passed away, so may this', and thus the philosophical detachment from the original misfortune allowed by the passage of time is transferred to a present calamity – 'this'. We do not learn what 'this' is until the last section of the poem, where the speaker identifies himself as a *scop* (professional poet) called Deor, who has been expelled from his position with a great lord in favour of a rival called Heorrenda. The diction of *Deor* (with nouns such as *earfoþ*, *sorg* and *wræc*, compound adjectives such as *winterceald* and *sorgcearig*, and verbs such as *drēosan* and *bidǣlan*) links it very obviously with the other lyrical or elegiac OE poems given in this section – *The Wanderer*, *The Wife's Lament* and *Wulf and Eadwacer*. Like the poet of *The Wanderer* (in line 30), the *Deor*-poet uses the image of sorrow as a companion (line 3).

As a poem in strophic form, with a refrain, *Deor* is a rarity in OE literature, and the scribe of the Exeter Book has taken note of this, providing a large capital at the start of each section following the refrain. The form is not regular, however. The first five 'stanzas' have, respectively, seven, six, four, three and seven lines, including in each case the one-line refrain. Then follow fifteen lines which, though often printed as a complete sixth stanza, are set out below as two stanzas, of seven and eight lines. These two parts seem to be self-contained, though complementary – the first a philosophical summing up what has gone before, which prepares us for the revelation of the second, namely the misfortune of Deor himself in his loss of his patron. Only the second, therefore, has the refrain. It is appropriate that a poet should draw his comfort from the very material by which he makes his living, when he can get a job, but we should perhaps ask whether irony is not intended in the elevation of his own mundane concerns into a subject worthy of a place in the hall of fame of Germanic history and legend.

Deor – a name which could be interpreted as 'bold' or 'dear', or even 'animal' – seems to be an invented figure, but the other names mentioned in the poem will no doubt have been well known to its Anglo-Saxon audience. The identities of some of the individuals named are now irrecoverable, however, and even when we can identify them, the specific details of the legends as they were known to the poet and his audience may be different from those that we know today. Indeed, the poet's allusions may serve as an 'advertisement' for his repertoire. The most readily identifiable reference is the first one, to Weland the Smith. His story features on one of the carved panels of the 'Franks Casket', a remarkable eighth-century Anglo-Saxon whalebone box (now in the British Museum) with a programme of Christian and secular legends depicted on it. So well known was Weland that King Alfred, when he translated Boethius's *De consolatione philosophiae* into OE (see Text 6) and wanted a memorable exemplar of mutability, used Weland in place of Fabricius, a renowned Roman consul and general who will have been familiar to Boethius's original audience but not to the Anglo-Saxons.

Little can be established about the date and origin of *Deor*. Some editors have reasonably argued for a comparatively early date of composition, in view of the richness of reference to common Germanic characters, though there is no need to suppose that knowledge of these was not still intact, and still a productive source for minstrels or poets, during the later years of Anglo-Saxon England. The language of the poem, though in general showing the comparatively late WS characteristics of most of the poems in the Exeter Book (copied in the second half of the tenth century), includes some apparently earlier forms – such as *nēde* (5, not *niede*), the double consonant in *gesīþþe* (3), regular *o* for *a* before nasal consonants (e.g. *monn*, 6, and *monegum*, 33), and uncontracted verb endings (e.g. *þinceð*, 29); but these are not in themselves reliable evidence for early composition. In *earfoda* (30), there has been graphic confusion between *d* and *ð*, a frequent occurrence in late copying, or perhaps aural confusion between *d* and *þ* (cf. *earfoþa*, 2).

Further reading

K. Malone, ed., *Deor*, rev. edn (Exeter, 1977)

J. Hill, ed., *The Old English Minor Heroic Poems*, rev. edn (Durham, 1994)

F. Norman, '*Deor*: a Criticism and an Interpretation', *Modern Language Review* 32 (1937), 374–81

P. J. Frankis, '*Deor* and *Wulf and Eadwacer*: Some Conjectures', *MÆ* 31 (1962), 161–75

F. Norman, 'Problems in the Dating of *Deor* and its Allusions', in *Medieval and Linguistic Studies in Honor of Francis Peabody Magoun, Jr.*, ed. J. P. Bessinger and R. P. Creed (London, 1965), pp. 205–13

⌐Wēlund him be wurman   wræces¬ cunnade°,   experienced +g

ānhȳdig° eorl°   earfoþa° drēag°,   single-minded man miseries suffered

hæfde him tō° gesīþþe°   sorge° ond longaþ°,   as companion sorrow longing

wintercealde wræce°.   Wēan° oft onfond°   suffering Misfortunes experienced

5   siþþan° ⌐hine Nīðhād on   nēde¬ legde°,   after   laid

swoncre° ⌐seonobende¬   on sȳllan° monn°.   supple good man

⌐Þæs oferēode,   þisses swā mæg¬.

Beadohilde° ne wæs   hyre brōþra dēaþ   To Beadohild

on sefan° swā° sār°   swā ⌐hyre sylfre¬ þing°,   (her) heart as grievous situation

10   þæt° hēo gearolīce°   ongieten° hæfde   in that (or when) clearly realised

þæt hēo ēacen° wæs.   ⌐Ǣfre ne meahte¬   pregnant

þrīste° geþencan°   ⌐hū ymb þæt sceolde¬.   confidently think

Þæs oferēode,   þisses swā mæg.

1 **Wēlund** In Germanic legend, Weland the Smith (Vǫlundr in the Old Norse *Edda*), renowned for his skill in metalworking, was forced to work for king Nithhad, who hamstrung him to stop him escaping; but Weland avenged himself on the king by killing the latter's two sons, raping his daughter Beaduhild (with a result we learn about in 11), and escaping by means of wings he had made. **him** Perhaps simply 'for him', but this depends on our interpretation of the next phr. **be wurman** It is generally assumed that *wurman* is a form of dat. pl. *wyrmum*, 'through serpents'. If this is right, 'serpents' must be a metaphor, perhaps for swords (with serpent-patterns on them), or for the bonds restraining Weland (*him*, 'on him'). Other interpretations have been suggested (including taking *Wurmas* to be the name of Nithhad's tribe), but none is convincing. **wræces** This noun (with the related *wræce* in 4, acc. sg. of *wracu*) encompasses the ideas of 'exile', 'persecution' and 'misery', but no single ModE word has the same range.

5 **hine ... on** 'on him', a reading confirmed by the parallel phr. *on syllan monn* in 6. **nēde** Probably acc. pl., 'constraints' or 'fetters', but possibly acc. sg.

6 **seonobende** 'sinew-bonds' (acc. pl., parallel with *nēde*). In theory, these could be either fetters made *from* sinew or fetters of rope applied *to* the sinews. If the allusion is to Nithhad's action in hamstringing Weland, as in the Norse version of the story, then the latter interpretation is appropriate; but as Nithhad is also said there to have bound the smith, 'supple sinew-bonds' could be a poetic reference to this and a variation on the *nēde* of the previous line.

7 **Þæs oferēode, þisses swā mæg** Syntactical analyses of the refrain have varied. The most plausible take *oferēode* to be impers., with *þæs* and *þisses* either in the gen. of respect: 'As regards that [the case of hardship just mentioned], it passed away; as regards this [my present predicament] it can likewise (pass away)', or the gen. of point of time: 'It passed over from that; it can likewise pass from this'.

9 **hyre sylfre** 'of her herself', i.e. 'her own ...'.

11 **Ǣfre ne meahte** 'Never could (she) ...'.

12 **hū ymb þæt sceolde** An extra vb. is needed [§G2d]: 'how in respect of that it must (be)', or 'what must needs become of that'.

Wē þæt ⌐Mǣðhilde   monge⌐ gefrugnon°   heard
15 wurdon° grundlēase°   ⌐Gēates frīge⌐,   became   boundless
⌐þæt hī sēo sorglufu   slǣp ealle binōm⌐.
Þæs oferēode,   þisses swā mæg.

⌐Ðēodrīc āhte⌐   þrītig° wintra   thirty +*gp*
⌐Mǣringa burg⌐; þæt wæs monegum cūþ°.   known (to +*d*)
20 Þæs oferēode,   þisses swā mæg.

Wē geāscodan°   ⌐Eormanrīces⌐   (have) learned of

14 **Mǣðhilde** Apparently a gen. form: 'of (*or* about) Mæthhild'. The two elements
of the compound are separated in the manuscript but attempts to establish that it is not a
name have largely failed. A comparatively modern Scandinavian ballad has a Magnhild
(or Magnild, depending on the version) and a Gauti (or Gaute) as a pair of tragic lovers,
but no connection can be established and we have to accept that the poet's allusion is lost
to us.   **monge** The word is unknown. On the assumption that it must be a noun-obj. of
gefrugnon, 'affair' has been offered as a meaning; emendation to *mōne* 'moans' has also
been suggested. Perhaps the least unsatisfactory solution is to assume that *monge* stands for
the pron. *monige*, 'many', in apposition with *wē*; the word-order is unusual but possible:
'we . . . many', i.e. 'many of us'. The complement of *gefrugnon*, 'have heard', is then the
clause (*þæt*) *wurdon . . . frīge*, with a notional second *þæt*, correl. with that in 14, inserted.

15 **Gēates frīge** *Gēates* (gen. sg.) presumably identifies either Mæthhild's lover or his
tribe. The name appears frequently in the mythical parts of Anglo-Saxon genealogies and is
associated with the Scandinavian Gautr (one of the names for Óðinn). From the evidence of
its use in other OE poems, *frīge* (here pl., as *wurdon* shows) is generally read as 'embraces'
or 'affections'. Attempts to take it as nom. pl. of *freo*, 'free man', do not help. Suggested
trans.: 'the affections of the Geat'.

16 **þæt hī . . . binōm** The pron. *hī* could be an acc. pl., 'them', or acc. sg. fem., 'her', but
the latter seems more likely, referring to Mæthhild. The vb. *biniman* can take an acc. and
dat. construction and *slǣp* may be dat., with final -*e* elided before the adv. *ealle*. A likely
trans. of the whole clause is: 'in that that unhappy love deprived her of sleep completely'.

18 **Ðēodrīc** Theodoric, Ostrogothic emperor, ruled in Italy 493–526. The Anglo-Saxons
certainly knew of him as a tyrant, through Boethius's *De consolatione Philosophiae* (see
p. 37) and Gregory's *Dialogi*, so that the approximately thirty years of his rule would make
a suitable example of an affliction (on his subjects) which eventually passed.   **āhte** 'ruled',
as in 22, following a common meaning of *āgan*. However, one of the legends surrounding
the king depicts him as a victim, suffering thirty years of exile at the court of Attila the Hun.
In this case *Mǣringa burg* in 19 must be the town in Hunnish territory where Theodoric and
his people dwelled during the exile (see 19n); *āhte* is a rather odd vb. to use in this case: it
could be ironical (or, in the view of some readers, it might simply mean 'inhabited').

19 **Mǣringa burg** Probably 'stronghold of the Mærings', who are linked with the Os-
trogoths in several medieval sources; the stronghold might be modern Ravenna, Theodoric's
capital, or possibly Verona.

21 **Eormanrīces** Eormanric was a Gothic king (*d.* 375) who became renowned as a
tyrant (see *Beowulf*, 1200–1, and *Widsith*, 7).

wylfenne° geþōht°.   Āhte wīde° folc   savage mind *as* widely
Gotena° rīces.   Þæt wæs grim° cyning.   of the Goths   cruel
Sæt secg° monig   sorgum gebunden°,   (a) man   fettered (by +*d*)
25   ⌐wēan on wēnan⌐,   wȳscte° geneahhe°   wished   often
þæt ⌐þæs cynerīces   ofercumen wǣre⌐.
Þæs oferēode,   þisses swā mæg.

Siteð sorgcearig°   sǣlum° bidǣled°,   sorrowing (man) from joys cut off
on sefan sweorceð°,   sylfum° þinceð°   grows dark to himself (it) seems
30   þæt sȳ° endelēas   earfoda dǣl°.   is *sbj* (his) share (of +*g*)
Mæg° þonne geþencan   þæt geond° þās woruld   (I) can   throughout
wītig° Dryhten   ⌐wendeþ⌐ geneahhe: wise
⌐eorle monegum   āre° gescēawað°,   mercy   shows
wīslicne° blǣd°,   sumum⌐ wēana dǣl.   certain   success

35   Þæt ⌐ic bī mē sylfum   secgan wille⌐,
þæt ic hwīle° wæs   ⌐Heodeninga⌐ scop°,   for a time   poet
dryhtne dȳre°.   ⌐Mē wæs Dēor noma⌐.   dear (to +*d*)
Āhte° ic fela wintra   folgað° tilne°,   Possessed position *as* good
holdne° hlāford,   oþþæt ⌐Heorrenda⌐ nū,   loyal
40   lēoðcræftig° monn,   londryht° geþāh°   'song-skilled' land-entitlement received
þæt mē eorla hlēo°   ǣr° gesealde°.   protector previously granted
Þæs oferēode,   þisses swā mæg.

25 **wēan on wēnan** 'in expectation [lit. "expectations"] of sorrow'.

26 **þæs cynerīces ofercumen wǣre** gen. of respect plus impers. vb.: lit. 'as regards the kingdom, it might be defeated'.

32 **wendeþ** vb. used without an obj.: 'changes (things)', or 'causes change'.

33–4 **eorle monegum . . . sumum** 'to many a man . . . , to some . . .'.

35 **ic bī mē . . . wille** Cf. the very similar opening of *The Seafarer* (26/1).

36 **Heodeninga** 'of the Heodenings', the tribe, or descendants, of King Heoden (Norse Heðinn).

37 **Mē . . . noma** poss. dat.: 'My name'.

39 **Heorrenda** This may be the famous singer Hôrant who features in the Middle High German epic *Kudrun*. In the Norse literature, Hjarrandi is the father of Heðinn (see 36n).

37
The Ruin

There is a nice irony in the fact that the poem we know as *The Ruin* is itself in such a state of disrepair. It comes near the end of the Exeter Book, where fire damage has left two sections of it, including the final lines, largely irrecoverable. The poem is a meditation on the remains of a Roman city and is decidedly elegiac in tone, though lacking the first-person viewpoint adopted in other OE elegiac verse. The voice is not apparently that of an actual victim of decay but a detached observer of it. The poem echoes a classical Latin tradition of lament on the fall of great cities and the celebration of their splendours, but there are many precedents for the theme among church writings also. Indeed, although the text (as we have it) is purely descriptive, and specific to a single place, we are bound to see it in the context of overtly didactic poems such as *The Wanderer* where the ruin of great buildings is symbolic of the disintegration of the human world in general (see 38/73–9; also 26/80–90). The first twenty lines of *The Ruin* describe in remarkable detail the decayed state of wondrously made structures which have long outlasted the lives of their boldly creative builders, and we are left with a sense of admiration for the achievements of the past. The theme is then given a distinctly Germanic gloss with an evocation of the revelry of the splendid warriors who once occupied the stronghold, but soon the focus turns again to the buildings and to a detailed description of the baths within them, including the very plumbing of the hot-water system. But at this point fate intervenes and the text itself finally disintegrates. It is possible that the closing lines of the poem established a clear moral, and probably Christian, viewpoint for the poem.

The city itself has been identified convincingly as Bath in Somerset, the Roman city of Aquae Sulis, celebrated for its temple and the hot springs around which elaborate bathing facilities were built. The earliest recorded use of the name Bath is in 796, in the dative plural form *Bathum*, '(place) at the (Roman) baths' (see 11/13n). From 675 onwards the town was an important monastic centre, first for nuns but later for monks, and it played a frequent role in Anglo-Saxon history. King Edgar was crowned there in 973 as 'emperor of Britain', recalling the imperial connotations of the place.

The poem naturally displays a large range of the vocabulary of decline and fall, collapse and decay, much of it common to other OE elegiac poems, such as *The Wanderer* and *The Wife's Lament*. Notable too is the use of internal rhyme

(5, 7, 11 and 31), uncommon in OE poetry. Despite its largely late WS vocabulary and linguistic forms, the poem has a number of features which suggest an origin outside Wessex, possibly in Mercia. Examples are the 'back mutation' of *e* to *eo* in *meodoheall* (23) and *undereotone* (6), *ē* for *ǣ* in *hwǣtrēd* (19; a unique word) and *fēlon* (13), and the gen. pl. form *cnēa* (8), where *cnēowa* would have been expected in late WS. Past participles ending in *-on*, as in *undereotone* (6) and *forweorone* (7), are rare and may be a scribal idiosyncrasy. Confusion of *ð* and *d* is seen in *gefrætweð* (33). In the text below, letters between square brackets are reconstructions of damaged letters still present in the manuscript.

Further reading

R. F. Leslie, ed., *Three Old English Elegies: The Wife's Lament, The Husband's Message, The Ruin* (Manchester, 1961)
J. F. Doubleday, 'The Ruin: Structure and Theme', *JEGP* 71 (1972), 369–81
K. Hume, 'The "Ruin Motif" in Old English Poetry', *Anglia* 94 (1976), 339–60
C. Abram, 'In Search of Lost Time: Aldhelm and *The Ruin*', *Quaestio* (Cambridge) 1 (2000), 23–44

⌐Wrǣtlic° is þes wealstān°¬; ⌐wyrde gebrǣcon		Wondrous 'wall-stone'
burgstede burston¬, brosnað° ⌐enta° geweorc°¬.		decays of giants construction
Hrōfas° ⌐sind¬ gehrorene°, hrēorge° torras°,		Roofs collapsed in ruins towers
⌐hringeat¬ berofen°, hrīm° on līme°,		destroyed rime mortar

1 **Wrǣtlic ... wealstān** Cf. the striking similarities in *Maxims II* (33/3).

1–2 **wyrde ... burston** It is tempting to take *wyrde* as dat. and *gebrǣcon* as a past part. ('shattered by fate'), but it is unlikely that the form *gebrǣcon* (pret. pl. of *gebrecan*) is a mistake for, or a var. of, *gebrocen* (which is in fact used in 32). So *wyrde* must be the nom. pl. subj. of the active vb., with obj. understood: 'the fates shattered it (i.e. the *wealstān*)'; then, in 2, *burgstede* is a new nom. pl. subj., with *burston* as its intrans. vb.: 'cities have crumbled'. Alternatively, *burgstede* could be taken as the acc. sg. obj. of *gebrǣcon*, with *burston* in parallel: 'the fates shattered the city, destroyed (it)', but there is effective consistency if all the main nouns in 1–5 are subjs. in the nom., presenting a succession of elliptically expressed images of decay. **enta geweorc** A poetic commonplace to describe the buildings left by the Romans; see 33/2n.

3 **sind** 'are', i.e. 'have'. The vb. controls all the past parts. in 3–5.

4 **hringeat** This is one of the simplest of the various emendations which have been suggested for the obviously defective manuscript reading *hrim geat* (followed by a superfluously repeated *torras*). It could be taken as a reduction of *hring-geat*, 'ring-gate', and might refer to an arched gate or doorway.

5 scearde° ⌜scūrbeorge⌝ scorene°, gedrorene°,	gaping stripped perished
ældo° undereotone°. Eorðgrāp°	age *ds* eaten away (by +*d*) 'Earth-grip'
hafað°	holds
⌜waldendwyrhtan⌝, forweorone° gelēorene°,	perished passed away
⌜heard gripe° hrūsan°⌝, oþ° hund cnēa°	grip of ground until generations
werþēoda° ⌜gewitan⌝. ⌜Oft⌝ þæs° wāg° gebād°,	of peoples this wall survived
10 ræghār° ond rēadfāh°, ⌜rīce⌝ æfter ōþrum°,	lichen-grey red-stained another
ofstonden° under stormum. ⌜Stēap gēap⌝ gedrēas°	left standing (it) decayed
⌜Wunað° gīet° se . . . . num	Remains still
gehēapen°,	heaped up
fēlon° i	was joined to
grimme° gegrunden°	harshly ground
15 . . . . re scān° heo	shone
. . . . g orþonc° ǣrsceaft°	skill ancient building
. . . . g . . . . . . lāmrindum° bēag°⌝	with a clay coating ring
⌜mōd mo . . . . yne swiftne gebrægd°	drew forth
hwætrēd° in hringas, hygerōf° gebond°	determined stout-hearted bound
20 weallwalan° wīrum° wundrum° tōgædre⌝.	walls with wires wonderfully
Beorht° wǣron burgrǣced°, ⌜burnsele⌝ monige,	Bright city-dwellings

5 **scūrbeorge** 'storm-protection'; presumably 'roof' (over the arched gate?).

7 **waldendwyrhtan** lit. 'ruling maker(s)' or 'ruling builder(s)' (the *n*-noun *wyrhta* could be acc. sg. or pl.). Probably the 'lordly builders' who had the buildings built, rather than the 'master builders' who actually did the building, for the image of even the most powerful of rulers ending up in the grave aptly parallels the inevitable decay of even the most wondrous of buildings. It is they whom the adjs. in 7b describe.

8 **heard gripe hrūsan** A variation on *eorðgrāp* in 6.

9 **gewitan** The sense is forward-looking: 'have passed away'.   **Oft** 'often' in the sense of 'again and again'.

10 **rīce** obj. of *gebād*: '(one) kingdom'.

11 **Stēap gēap** 'steep (*or* high) (and) curved'. Presumably the subj. is still *wāg*, to which the two adjs. refer, in which case we are to understand that, though often it had survived onslaught, it did eventually decay. Cf. the same phr. (but different context) in 33/23.

12–17 **Wunað . . . bēag** Little can be made of these damaged lines. With reference to 14, it may be noted that in *The Battle of Maldon* spears are described as *grimme gegrundene* (30/109).

18–20 **mōd . . . tōgædre** These lines appear to be part of a single sentence describing in detail the construction of a building. Perhaps one determined and renowned (assuming *hwætrēd* and *hygerōf* to be adjs., used as nouns, describing the builder) joined something together (*gebrægd*, assuming it is a vb.) in rings (or arches?), and wondrously bound the wall together with wire ties.

21 **burnsele** A *burn* is a 'stream' or 'spring', so the compound suggests 'halls with running water', i.e. bath-houses.

hēah ⌐horngestrēon⌐,   heresweg° micel,   martial sound

meodoheall° monig°   ⌐mondrēama⌐ full,   mead-hall   many a

oþþæt þæt° onwende°   ⌐wyrd sēo swīþe°⌐. that *as*   changed   mighty

25 Crungon° walo° wīde,   cwōman°   Fell   the slain   came

   wōldagas°,   days of pestilence

swylt° ⌐eall fornōm°   secgrōfra° wera⌐; death   carried off   'sword-renowned'

wurdon° hyra ⌐wīgsteal⌐   wēstenstaþolas°. became   desolate places

Brosnade° burgsteall°,   ⌐bētend⌐ crungon, Crumbled   city

⌐hergas⌐ tō hrūsan.   Forþon° þās hofu° drēorgiað° Therefore   courts   collapse

30 ond ⌐þæs tēaforgēapa   tigelum sceādeð⌐,

⌐hrōstbēages hrōf⌐.   Hryre° wong° gecrong° (To) ruin   place   has fallen

gebrocen° tō beorgum°   þær iū° ⌐beorn monig⌐, shattered   heaps   once

glædmōd° ond goldbeorht°   ⌐gleoma⌐ cheerful   'gold-bright'

   gefrætwed°   adorned

⌐wlonc ond wīngāl⌐, wīghyrstum° scān°, in war-trappings   gleamed

---

22 **horngestrēon** 'horn-treasure', usually interpreted as 'an abundance of arches (*or* curved gables)'.

23 **mondrēama** In the manuscript, the first element is represented by a rune which could be M or D, but M (for *mon*) makes good sense: '(full) of human revelries'.

24 **wyrd sēo swīþe** Cf. 26/115, 33/5 and 38/100.

26 **eall . . . wera** *eall* is a pron., followed by the partitive gen.: 'all of . . . men'.

27 **wīgsteal** 'fortresses' (lit. 'battle-places'). Some editors, identifying the element *wīg* as 'idol', rather than 'battle' or 'war(fare)', trans. as 'place of idols' or 'sanctuary', but this seems unnecessary.

28 **bētend** pres. part. of *bētan*, 'restore' or 'make good', used as a noun, suggesting those who might have repaired the damage to the buildings; hence 'rebuilders'.

29 **hergas** parallel subj., with *bētend*, of *crungon*: 'troops' or 'multitudes'. The word has also been interpreted as pl. of *hearh*, 'idol' (see 27n).

30 **þæs tēaforgēapa** The compound seems to consist of two adjs., *tēafor*, probably 'red', and *gēap*, among whose meanings are 'lofty', 'steep' and 'bent'; the result is an adj, used as a noun, which may depict a lofty, steep or curved red-tiled roof; *þæs* is for *þes*, 'this'. **tigelum sceādeð** 'separates (*or* splits) from its tiles', i.e. sheds its tiles.

31 **hrōstbēages hrōf** The phr. appears to be a var. on *þæs tēaforgēapa*. The rare word *hrōst* may refer to the framework of a roof, and so the compound might suggest a circular framework, perhaps of vaulting (although *bēag* is not, as *hring* is, found otherwise in an architectural setting): thus, perhaps, 'roof of vaulting', i.e. 'vaulted roof'. The manuscript has simply *rōf*, which would mean 'renowned', but it is difficult to accept in the context; hence the emendation to *hrōf*.

32 **beorn monig** 'many a man'. This is the subj. of a long clause whose vb. is first *scān* (34) and then *seah* (35).

33 **gleoma** Either a rare 'instrumental' gen. pl. of *gleomu*, and thus 'with brightness (*or* splendour)', or a dat. sg. form, with much the same result.

34 **wlonc ond wīngāl** 'proud and merry with wine'. The same formula is used in *The Seafarer* (26/29), with a tone of disapproval, but there is no evidence of this in *The Ruin*.

35 seah° on sinc°, on sylfor, on searogimmas°,	gazed treasure curious gems
on ēad,° on ǣht°, on eorcanstān°,	wealth property precious stone
on þās beorhtan burg° ⌐brādan° rīces⌐.	stronghold broad
Stānhofu° stōdan, strēam ⌐hāte wearp⌐	Stone courts
⌐wīdan wylme⌐, ⌐weal⌐ eall° befēng°	everything enclosed
40 ⌐beorhtan bōsme⌐ þǣr þa baþu° wǣron,	baths
⌐hāt on hreþre⌐. Þæt wæs hȳðelic°.	convenient
⌐Lēton° þonne gēotan°	(They) let pour
ofer hārne° stān hāte strēamas⌐	grey
un	
45 ..þþæt hringmere° hāte st	round pool
. . . . þǣr þā baþu wǣron	
Þonne is	
. . . . .re þæt is cynelic° þing,	royal
hū se . . . . .burg	

37 **brādan rīces** This is the gen. complement of *burg*.

38 **hāte wearp** Most likely *hāte* is an adv. (dat. sg. of *hāt*, 'heat'), 'hotly', modifying *wearp*, lit. 'hotly threw (up *or* out)', or here perhaps 'spouted' or 'gushed'. Alternatively, *hāte* may be trans. as the noun, so that the stream 'spouted with heat'. The result is the same.

39 **wīdan wylme** dat. of manner: 'in a broad surge'.   **weal** This is presumably the wall which encloses the bath ('everything').

40 **beorhtan bōsme** dat. of containment: 'in (its) bright bosom'.

41 **hāt on hreþre** Probably, 'hot at their heart', i.e. 'hot to the core' (which would explain the convenience alluded to in the next half-line). The same phr. occurs in the poems *Beowulf* (3148) and *Christ and Satan* (98).

42–3 **Lēton . . . strēamas** A description of how the hot water is used in the baths begins but then fragments.

38
The Wanderer

The Wanderer is a memorable example of meditation in a lyrical vein, in which universal rules are generated from intense personal experience. Though the context is unequivocally Christian, the poem is striking for the intimate allusions it makes to the conduct and ethos of the secular 'heroic' world. These occur notably in the retrospective brooding of the persona of the 'wanderer' himself (that being the widely accepted rendering of the word *eardstapa* in line 6 – literally 'earth-stepper' or 'earth-hopper'), as he mourns separation from his treasure-giving lord, on whose knees he once ceremoniously laid hands and head, and from his boon companions of the mead-hall. It is (or was) a world of ritual, good companionship and human warmth, the memory of which is all the more compelling in contrast with a forlorn present of coldness and isolation.

The Wanderer is a frame poem, which begins and ends with lines of explicit Christian statement – first about the availability of God's mercy, even to the abject exile (1–5), and last about the rewards of faith (112–15). Within this outer frame is another one (6–7 and 111), in which brief 'stage directions' are given, introduced by the formula *swā cwæþ*, 'thus spoke' – in the first place, 'thus spoke the wanderer', and in the second, 'thus spoke the wise man' (*snottor*). Enclosed by this double frame is the long central section of the poem (8–110), which, in the simplest interpretation, may be seen as the monologue of the wanderer, in whose reflective voice the poet develops his theme. The monologue itself is structured, moving from personal despair to detached observation, and its integrity need not be affected by its closing lines (92–110), in which the wanderer rounds off his own ruminations by invoking the voice of a world-weary 'everyman', who has perceived the transience of all people and all things and asks where they have all gone, using a literary topos known by the Latin words for 'where are they?', *ubi sunt*, frequently exploited in homiletic literature.

The main structural problem in the poem involves the question of whether those stage directions of the inner frame (6–7 and 111), which are clearly in the voice of the scene-setting poet, refer backwards or forwards – i.e. to the voice which speaks the Christian frame or to the voice of the central monologue. An attractive interpretation has the poet's first *swā cwæþ* referring forwards to the monologue that is about to start and the second referring back to it once it has ended; then the outer, Christian, frame may be attributed to the poet also, who enunciates the Christian precepts which the poem is designed to promote. Alternative interpretations (and there are several variations) would have the opening and closing lines (the outer frame) given to the wanderer himself. Whatever the case (and the creative possibilities of deliberate ambiguity are worth considering), if we accept that the same subject speaks both of the *swā cwæþ* passages, we accept that the *eardstapa* and the *snottor* are one and the same. The anguished wanderer, suffering the calamity of exile from an heroic community, has turned into a calmly philosophic man; he has thought his way through, and out of, suffering to reach a patient acceptance of the cruel fact that all worldly well-being is mutable. If we accept that the Christian frame is in the voice of the poet also, then the message of the poem is arguably the more powerful. The wanderer himself has not yet found the Christian answer to his predicament, but, as he sits apart in contemplation, he is on the brink of a revelation which we, of course (thanks to the poet), can see clearly.

The diction of *The Wanderer* links it closely with the other OE elegiac lyrics of exile and loss. The poet has a notable fondness for compound adjectives of suffering or longing, such as *seledrēorig* ('hall-sad', i.e. sad at the loss of a hall, 25) and *drēorighleor* ('sad-faced', 83), and three adjectives formed with *cearig* ('sorrowful' or 'anxious'): *mōdcearig* (2), *earmcearig* (20) and *wintercearig* (24). Like the other poems of the Exeter Book, *The Wanderer* shows predominantly WS features in its language, but non-WS influences are apparent in the 'back-mutated' *e* in *sweotule* (11) and *meoduhealle* (27), *ea* for *eo* in *wearþan* (64) and the prefix *bi* for *be* in *bidǣled* (20), *bihrorene* (77), etc.

Further reading

T. P. Dunning and A. J. Bliss, eds., *The Wanderer* (London, 1969)

R. F. Leslie, ed., *The Wanderer*, rev. edn (Exeter, 1985)

S. B. Greenfield, '*The Wanderer*: a Reconsideration of Theme and Structure', *JEGP* 50 (1951), 451–65

T. C. Rumble, 'From *eardstapa* to *snottor on mode*: the Structural Principle of *The Wanderer*', *MLQ* 19 (1958), 225–30

G. Richman, 'Speaker and Speech Boundaries in *The Wanderer*', *JEGP* 81 (1982), 469–79

R. E. Bjork, '*Sundor æt Rune*: the Voluntary Exile of The Wanderer', *Neophil.* 73 (1989), 119–29; repr. in *OE Poetry*, ed. Liuzza, pp. 315–27

C. B. Pasternack, 'Anonymous Polyphony and *The Wanderer*'s Textuality', *ASE* 20 (1991), 99–122

R. North, 'Boethius and the Mercenary in *The Wanderer*', in *Pagans and Christians: the Interplay between Christian Latin and Traditional Germanic Cultures in Early Medieval Europe*, ed. T. Hofstra *et al.* (Groningen, 1995), pp. 71–98

⌜OFT him⌝ ānhaga°   ⌜āre gebīdeð⌝,   solitary one
metudes° miltse°,   ⌜þēah þe⌝ hē mōdcearig°   ordainer's   mercy   anxious of mind
geond° lagulāde°   longe° sceolde°   across   sea-way   far   must
⌜hrēran mid hondum⌝   hrīmcealde° sæ,   ice-cold
5   wadan° ⌜wræclāstas⌝.   ⌜Wyrd⌝ bið ful° ārǣd°.   travel   fully   determined

Swā cwæþ eardstapa°,   earfeþa° gemyndig°,   wanderer   miseries   recalling +g
wrāþra° wælsleahta°,   winemǣga° ⌜hryre⌝.   of enemies   slaughters   dear kinsmen

Oft ic sceolde° āna°   ⌜ūhtna gehwylce⌝   have had to   alone
mīne ceare° cwīþan°.   Nis° nū ⌜cwicra nān⌝   sorrow   lament   (There) is not
10   ⌜þe ic him⌝ mōdsefan°   mīnne durre°   heart   dare
sweotule° āsecgan°.   Ic tō° sōþe° wāt°   plainly   express   as   (a) truth   know
þæt biþ° in eorle°   indryhten° þēaw°   (it) is   (a) man   excellent   virtue
þæt hē his ferðlocan°   fæste binde°,   heart   bind
healde° ⌜his hordcofan⌝,   hycge° swā° hē wille.   keep close   think   as
15   Ne mæg wērig mōd°   wyrde wiðstondan°,   heart   resist +d
ne se hrēo° hyge°   helpe gefremman°.   troubled   mind   provide

1 **OFT** In poetry, frequently an understatement for 'always'.   **him** dat. of interest: 'for himself'.   **āre gebīdeð** Possible meanings of the vb. (which usually governs a noun in the gen.; the fem. nouns *āre* and *miltse* in 2 may be acc. or gen.) include 'wait for', 'endure', 'experience' and 'obtain'. The ambiguity may be deliberate, but the most likely central meaning, in view of the preceding adv. (*oft*), is that the solitary one, even though he endures the hardship of exile, will obtain or experience the 'grace' (*āre*) and 'mercy' of the Ordainer (*metud*, i.e. God). *Ār* itself (repeated in 114) has a wide semantic range but in the context 'grace', 'favour' or 'pity' seem apt.

2 **þēah þe** conj. phr.: 'though'.

4 **hrēran mid hondum** 'stir with (his) hands'. Presumably a figure for rowing or paddling with an oar.

5 **wræclāstas** 'paths of exile'. For other examples of the exile topos expressed thus, see *The Seafarer* (26/57) and *Beowulf* (1352).   **Wyrd** Presumably 'fate' as divine Providence is implied here (see 33/5n); cf. 100 and 107.

7 **hryre** 'fall' or 'death'. We would expect a gen. here, parallel with *earfeþa* and *wælsleahta*, and so *hryre* (masc.) may be an error for gen. pl. *hryra* or gen. sg. *hryres*.

8 **ūhtna gehwylce** dat. of time: 'at each dawn [lit. "of dawns"]'. More precisely, *ūhte* is the pre-dawn period, when the night and the wanderer's spirits are still dark.

9 **cwicra nān** 'none of living-ones', i.e. 'not one living'.

10 **þe...him** 'who   to him', i.e. 'to whom'.

14 **his hordcofan** 'his treasure-chamber'; clearly the 'treasury of his thoughts (*or* heart)'. Cf. the similar *ferðloca* in 13 and 33, and *brēostcofa* in 18.

	Forðon° ⌐dōmgeorne drēorigne˥ oft	Therefore
	in hyra brēostcofan° bindað fæste.	'breast-chamber' (*i.e.* heart)
	Swā ic ⌐mōdsefan mīnne˥ sceolde°,	(have) had to
20	oft earmcearig° ēðle° bidæled°	care-worn homeland *ds* deprived of +*d*
	frēomægum° feor°, feterum° sælan°,	from noble kin far with fetters bind
	siþþan° gēara° iū° goldwine° mīne	since once long ago 'gold-friend' *as*
	⌐hrūsan heolstre biwrāh˥ ond ic ⌐hēan° þonan°	dejected from there
	wōd° wintercearig° ofer waþema°	went 'winter-sad' of waves
	gebind°,	mingling
25	sōhte° seledrēorig°˥ sinces° bryttan°	sought 'hall-sad' of treasure a giver
	hwǣr ic feor oþþe° nēah findan meahte°	or might
	þone° þe in meoduhealle ⌐mīne wisse˥	him
	oþþe mec° frēondlēasne° frēfran° wolde,	me friendless comfort
	wēman° mid wynnum°. Wāt° sē° þe	entice (me) pleasures Knows he
	cunnað°	tries (it)
30	hū slīþen° bið sorg° tō° gefēran°	cruel grief as companion
	þām° þe ⌐him lȳt° hafað˥ lēofra° geholena°.	for him few +*gp* dear comrades
	Warað° hine wræclāst, nales° wunden° gold,	Preoccupies not coiled
	ferðloca frēorig°, nalæs foldan° blǣd°.	frozen earth's splendour
	Gemon° hē selesecgas° ond	Remembers 'hall-men'
	sincþege°,	treasure-receiving
35	hū ⌐hine˥ on geoguðe° his goldwine	(his) youth
	wenede° tō wiste°. Wyn eal gedrēas°.	entertained feast perished

17 **dōmgeorne** adj. as noun (nom. pl.): 'those eager for glory (*or* renown)'. A recurrent theme of heroic literature is the eagerness of men to leave behind them a good reputation; see 26/72–80.   **drēorigne** Possibly another adj. as noun (acc. sg.): 'a sorrowful thing'. Many editors take it as an adj. qualifying *hyge* in the previous line, so it is 'the sad heart' which is to be hidden, but this is not very convincing. It is likely that another noun after *drēorigne* has been lost in transmission or even that *drēorigne* was originally *drēorignes(se)*, 'sadness'.

19 **mōdsefan mīnne** 'my heart', obj. of *sceolde... sælan*. Acc. sg. masc. *mīnne* has its 'correct' form here; cf. 22 and 27.

23 **hrūsan heolstre biwrāh** The subj. of the vb. is *ic* in 19 (repeated in 23b); *heolstre* is dat. of instrument and *hrūsan* (an *n*-noun) is gen.: '(since) I covered... with the darkness of the earth'.

23–5 **hēan... wintercearig... seledrēorig** Each adj. describes the state of mind of the wanderer; *seledrēorig* could be paraphrased 'sad for the want of a hall'.

27 **mīne wisse** This abrupt half-line has been emended in various (unsatisfactory) ways, but as it stands it can be interpreted 'might know (sbj. *wisse*) mine' or 'my own', i.e. be acquainted with his people and origins.

31 **him** rflx. dat., better not trans.   **lȳt hafað** A sort of litotes: the wanderer does not have *any* dear comrades.

35 **hine** obj. of *wenede* in 36.

Forþon ⌜wāt⌝ sē þe sceal°   his winedryhtnes°   must   friendly lord's
lēofes° lārcwidum°   longe forþolian°,   dear   precepts   do without +d
ðonne sorg ond slǣp   somod° ætgǣdre°   at the same time   together
40   earmne° ānhogan   oft gebindað°.   wretched   hold fast
Þinceð° him on mōde   þæt hē his mondryhten°   It seems   lord
clyppe° ond cysse°   ond on cnēo° lecge°   embraces   kisses   (his) knee   lays
honda ond hēafod,   swā° hē hwīlum° ǣr   just as   at times
in gēardagum°   ⌜giefstōlas⌝ brēac°.   days of old   enjoyed
45   Ðonne onwæcneð° eft°   winelēas° guma°,   awakes   again   friendless   man
gesihð° him biforan°   fealwe° wēgas°,   sees   before +d   grey   waves
⌜baþian brimfuglas⌝,   brǣdan° feþra°,   spread(ing)   feathers ap (i.e. wings)
hrēosan° hrīm° ond snāw,   hagle° gemenged°.   fall(ing)   frost   with hail   mingled
Þonne bēoð þȳ° hefigran°   heortan° benne°,   the   more grievous   heart's   wounds
50   ⌜sāre æfter swǣsne⌝.   Sorg bið genīwad°   renewed
þonne māga° gemynd°   mōd geondhweorfeð°.   of kin   memory   goes through
Grēteð glīwstafum°   georne° geondscēawað°   joyfully   eagerly   regards
secga° geseldan°.   ⌜Swimmað oft on weg⌝.   of men   companions
⌜Flēotendra ferð   nō þǣr fela bringeð
55   cūðra cwidegiedda⌝.   Cearo° bið genīwad   Care
þām° þe sendan sceal   swīþe geneahhe°   in him   often
ofer waþema gebind   wērigne sefan°.   spirit
Forþon ic geþencan° ne mæg   geond° þās woruld   think   in
⌜for hwan⌝ mōdsefa   mīn ne gesweorce°   grows dark sbj
60   þonne ic eorla līf   eal geondþence°,   contemplate
hū hī fǣrlīce°   ⌜flet ofgēafon⌝,   quickly
mōdge° maguþegnas°.   Swā þes middangeard°   brave   young retainers   world

37 **wāt** Here (cf. 29), the vb. ('knows' or 'understands') is used absolutely, though a notional obj., 'these things', could be assumed.

44 **giefstōlas** Apparently a late (or erroneous) spelling of gen. sg. *giefstōles*: 'the gift-throne'; *brūcan* usually takes a gen. (but occasionally dat.) obj.

47 **baþian brimfuglas** acc. and inf. construction [§G6d.i.3]: '(sees) seabirds bathing'; similarly *brǣdan* and, in 48, *hrēosan*.

50 **sāre æfter swǣsne** 'painful [i.e. the wounds] in pursuit of (*or* in longing for) the beloved (one)'.

53 **Swimmað oft on weg** 'Often they float away'. On *oft*, see 1n.

54–5 **Flēotendra ferð... cūðra cwidegiedda** The 'floating ones' or 'swimmers' are the speechless sea-birds who, in the return to reality, replace the dreamed-of loved ones: 'The spirit of the floating ones does not bring there many familiar utterances' (in fact, none at all).

59 **for hwan** 'for what [instr.]', i.e. 'why'.

61 **flet ofgēafon** 'gave up the floor [of the mead-hall]'; i.e. died.

⌐ealra dōgra gehwām⌐   drēoseð° ond fealleþ.   declines

Forþon ne mæg wearþan° wīs   wer° ǣr hē āge°   become   a man *ns*   has

65   ⌐wintra dǣl in woruldrīce⌐.   Wita° ⌐sceal⌐ geþyldig°,   A wise man   patient

ne sceal ⌐nō tō⌐ hātheort°   ne° tō hrædwyrde°,   fiery   nor   hasty of speech

ne tō wāc° wiga°   ne tō wanhȳdig°,   weak   warrior   reckless

ne tō forht° ne tō fægen°   ne tō feohgīfre°   fearful   joyful   'wealth-greedy'

ne nǣfre gielpes° tō georn°   ⌐ǣr hē geare cunne⌐.   boasting   eager for +*g*

70   Beorn° sceal gebīdan°,   þonne hē bēot° spriceð°,   Warrior   wait   boast   utters

oþþæt° collenferð°   cunne gearwe°   until   stout-hearted   fully

hwider° ⌐hreþra⌐ gehygd°   hweorfan° wille.   where   thought   to turn

Ongietan° sceal glēaw° hæle°   hū gæstlic° bið   Realise   prudent   man   awful

þonne ealre þisse worulde wela°   wēste° stondeð,   riches *ns*   desolate

75   swā nū missenlīce°   geond þisne middangeard   in various places

winde biwāune°   weallas stondaþ   blown (by +*d*)

hrīme bihrorene°.   Hrȳðge° þā ederas°,   covered (by +*d*)   Storm-beaten   buildings

wōriað° þā wīnsalo°, waldend° licgað°   crumble   wine-halls   rulers   lie (dead)

drēame° bidrorene°.   Duguþ° eal   joy   deprived (of +*d*)   Noble company

gecrong°   fell

80   wlonc° bī° wealle;   sume° wīg° fornōm°,   proud   near   some *ap*   war   destroyed

ferede° ⌐in forðwege⌐, sumne° fugel oþbær°   carried   one *as*   bird   bore away

ofer hēanne° holm°,   sumne se hāra° wulf   deep   ocean   grey

⌐dēaðe gedǣlde⌐,   sumne ⌐drēorighlēor°⌐   sad-faced

in eorðscræfe°   eorl gehȳdde°.   earth-grave   buried

85   Ȳþde° swā þisne eardgeard°   ælda°   Laid waste   habitation *as*   men's

scyppend°   creator

oþþæt burgwara°   breahtma° lēase°   of citizens   of the revelries   deprived

---

63 **ealra dōgra gehwām** 'on each of all days', i.e. 'each and every day'.

65 **wintra dǣl in woruldrīce** lit. 'a deal of winters in the kingdom of the world'; i.e. in *this* world.   **sceal** The vb. 'be' must be supplied [§G2d].

66 **nō tō** The use of the formula 'not too…' is rhetorical; warriors should not be passionate, etc, *at all*. Catalogues of 'dos and don'ts' are characteristic of wisdom literature; a biblical warning against consorting with bold, passionate or foolish people, and against speaking openly, is to be found in Ecclus 8.18–22; cf. also 34/23.

69 **ǣr hē geare cunne** 'before he clearly knows [sbj.]', i.e. before he is fully aware of what his boast may entail. The theme is continued in the next three lines.

72 **hreþra** 'of (his) heart (*or* mind)'. The OE idiom uses a pl. where ModE prefers sg.

81 **in forðwege** 'on the onward path (*or* way ahead)'; i.e. to death and whatever follows.

83 **dēaðe gedǣlde** The detail of this image is unclear. The vb. has a range of meanings, allowing 'received a share of in death' or 'shared with death', or even 'dismembered in death'.   **drēorighlēor** Describes *eorl* in 84.

⌐eald enta° geweorc°⌐   īdlu° stōdon.   giants *gp*   constructions *np*   empty
Sē° þonne þisne wealsteal°   wīse   He who   'wall-place'
  geþōhte°   (has) considered
ond þis deorce° līf   dēope geondþenceð,   gloomy
90 frōd° in ferðe°,   feor° oft gemon°   wise   heart   far back   recalls
wælsleahta worn°   ond þās word ācwið°:   a multitude (of +*gp*)   utters
⌐Hwǣr cwōm mearg?⌐   Hwǣr cwōm mago°? Hwǣr cwōm   kinsman
  māþþumgyfa°?   treasure-giver
Hwǣr ⌐cwōm⌐ symbla° gesetu°?   Hwǣr sindon   of banquets   places
  seledrēamas°?   hall-pleasures
⌐Ēalā beorht būne!⌐   Ēalā byrnwiga°!   mailed warrior
95 Ēalā þeodnes° þrym°!   Hū sēo þrāg° gewāt°,   prince's   majesty   time   went
genāp° under nihthelm°   ⌐swā hēo nō wǣre⌐.   grew dark   cover of night
Stondeð nū ⌐on lāste   lēofre duguþe⌐
weal wundrum° hēah,   wyrmlicum°   wondrously   with snake patterns
  fāh°.   decorated
Eorlas° fornōman°   asca° þrȳþe°,   The men *ap*   took off   of ash(-spears)   hosts
100 wæpen° wælgīfru°,   wyrd sēo mǣre°,   weapons   'slaughter-greedy'   renowned
ond þās stānhleoþu°   stormas cnyssað°,   rocky slopes *ap*   batter
hrīð° hrēosende° hrūsan bindeð,   snowstorm *ns*   falling
wintres wōma°. ⌐Þonne won⌐ cymeð,   howling *ns*
nīpeð° nihtscūa°,   norþan° ⌐onsendeð⌐   darkens   'night-shadow'   from north
105 hrēo° hæglfare°   hæleþum° on° andan°.   fierce   hailstorm   to men   as   terror

87 **eald enta geweorc** See 33/2n. A nom. pl. neut. inflection on *eald* has presumably been elided before the vowel of *enta*.

92 **Hwǣr cwōm mearg?** 'Where did the horse go?' On this rhetorical device, see the headnote; *cwōm* preserves an earlier form of the vb. before contraction.

93 **cwōm** A sg. form for a vb. whose pl. subj. (here *gesetu*) follows it is usual [§G6f] (but this does not apply to the vb. 'be').

94 **Ēalā beorht bune!** Either 'Alas (*or* O), the bright goblet!' or 'Alas for ...'.

96 **swā hēo nō wǣre** The pluperf. is appropriate in trans.: 'as though it had not [i.e. had never] been'.

97 **on lāste lēofre duguþe** 'in the track of the dear company'; i.e. after their departure.

103 **Þonne** Here interpreted as an adv.: 'Then'; but it could be (with adjustment of punctuation) the conj. 'when...'.   **won** This is probably the adj. meaning 'dark', in which case it must go, however awkwardly, with *nihtscūa* in 104, which is therefore complemented by both *cymeð* and *nīpeð*. Some editors argue that *won* is being used as a noun, the subj. of *cymeð*.

104 **onsendeð** 'sends'. The subj. is *nihtscūa*. Cf. 30/31.

⌐Eall⌐ is earfoðlic°   eorþan rīce;   full of hardship

onwendeð° ⌐wyrda gesceaft⌐   weoruld under heofonum.   changes

Hēr bið feoh° ⌐lǣne⌐,   hēr bið frēond lǣne,   wealth

hēr bið mon lǣne,   hēr bið mǣg° lǣne,   kinsman

110   eal þis eorþan gesteal°   īdel weorþeð°!'   foundation   will become

Swā cwæð snottor° on mōde,   gesæt° ⌐him⌐ sundor°   wise man   sat   apart
    ⌐æt rūne⌐.

Til° biþ sē þe his trēowe° gehealdeþ°; ⌐ne sceal nǣfre   Worthy   faith   keeps
    his torn tō rycene

beorn of his brēostum ācȳþan⌐   nemþe° ⌐hē⌐ ǣr°   unless   beforehand
    ⌐þā bōte⌐ cunne,

eorl mid elne° gefremman°.   ⌐Wel bið þām þe him⌐ āre   courage   to effect
    sēceð,

115   frōfre° tō° fæder on heofonum   þǣr ūs° eal sēo   comfort *as*   from   for us
    fæstnung° stondeð.   permanence

106   **Eall** This may be the subj. pron. 'all', in which case *eorþan rīce* is an adv. phr.: 'All
in the kingdom of earth . . .'. But *rīce* may itself be the subj., in which case *eall* is either an
adv., 'entirely', as in 36, 60 and 79, or an adj., describing *rīce*: 'The whole kingdom . . .'.

107   **wyrda gesceaft** 'the disposition of the fates'; i.e. the ordained course of events.
This is the subj. of *onwendeð*, with *weoruld* the obj.

108   **lǣne** lit. 'loaned' (cf. *lǣnan* 'to lend'), but 'temporary', 'transitory', 'passing' or
'ephemeral' are among the available renderings.

111   **him** rflx. dat., best not trans.   **æt rūne** Meanings of the noun (which is also used
for the letters of the runic alphabet) include 'consultation' or '(secret) counsel'. Here it is
clearly one man consulting with himself, so a suitable trans. is 'in contemplation' or 'in
thought'.

112–13   **ne sceal . . . ācȳþan** The subj. of this sentence is *beorn*, the obj. *torn* ('anger'):
'a man must never too hastily (*rycene*) reveal his anger from his breast'; pl. *brēostum* usually
has sg. meaning [§D4i].

113   **hē** Parallel with *eorl* in 114 and probably better not trans.   **þā bōte** 'the remedy',
obj. of *cunne gefremman*.

114   **Wel bið þām þe him** 'It will be well for the one (*þām*) who for himself . . .'.

39

Wulf and Eadwacer

Along with *The Wife's Lament* (Text 40), *Wulf and Eadwacer* is a rarity in the OE poetic corpus: a secular lyric in a female voice. It is also one of the most enigmatic of poems and has generated intense but largely unresolved argument about its interpretation, for at the simple narrative level it is full of undeveloped allusions and unexplained ambiguities – not least the question of who 'Wulf' is and what his relationship with the speaker is, and who 'Eadwacer' is and whether he is a separate person at all. In the Exeter Book, the poem immediately precedes a long section of riddles, and some readers have found it useful to see it in the same light, as a deliberate enigma. Only at the more abstract level of theme and tone does the poem become more or less coherent, as a bitter personal reflection on separation and longing, an expression of intense feeling, apparently addressed by the female speaker (her gender confirmed by the feminine form of the adjective *reotugu* in line 10) to an absent 'Wulf'. This has led to a plausible, but not particularly helpful, association of *Wulf and Eadwacer* with the genre of poems in Germanic literature known as *Frauenlieder* ('women's songs').

In the structure of the poem, there is a sense of both economy and completeness. What is striking, especially in view of the complexity (to us) of its literal meaning, is the comparative simplicity of its syntax. The obscurities do not arise from muddy grammatical relationships, syntactical dislocations or, as far as we can tell, from bad copying; they are in the semantics and the allusive terms of reference. Thus it is likely that the enigmas of the poem are deliberate. Simplicity is especially evident in the first eight lines, with the stark clarity of the discrete half-lines in 4 and 5 formally underlining the theme of separation. This section is given shape by the exact repetition of line 2 in line 7, followed in both cases by the cryptic statement, *ungelīc(e) is ūs*, meaning (apparently) either 'it is different for us' or 'there is a difference between us' (see 3n). The section containing lines 9 to 19, though lacking any repetition, is carefully crafted; four 'standard'-length lines of exposition are followed by an explanation of the speaker's pain, given in three much terser lines, with threefold variation, and then the poem ends with two longer lines whose sense is drawn out in each case by an additional half-line. The second of these units has the distinctive tone of aphorism or proverb, though the reference remains personal. That indeed is one of the unusual and compelling characteristics of the poem: there is no formal frame to contain the monologue, no introductory or concluding statement which might put some distance between the speaker and her experience, or between her and the auditor or reader. The intensity of personal feeling in the poem is shown by the number of first-person pronouns, which give way sometimes to the first-person plural or the dual (*uncerne*, 16, and *uncer*, 19: 'of the two of us'); it is in that interplay between singular and plural, or dual, that the hidden drama of the poem is surely enacted.

Such is the enigmatic nature of the poem's narrative detail that the sense of an individual word is often impossible to pin down, dependent as it is on other words equally hard to assess. Several such cases are dealt with in the notes below, where alternative interpretations are rehearsed, but no claim is made for their authority or completeness. Linguistically, the text shows consistency in its late WS forms.

Further reading

P. J. Frankis, '*Deor* and *Wulf and Eadwacer*: some Conjectures', *MÆ* 31 (1962), 161–75

P. Baker, 'The Ambiguity of *Wulf and Eadwacer*', *SP* 78 (1981), 39–51

S. B. Greenfield, '*Wulf and Eadwacer*: All Passion Pent', *ASE* 15 (1986), 5–14

L. Bragg, '*Wulf and Eadwacer*, *The Wife's Lament*, and Women's Love Lyrics in the Middle Ages', *Germanisch-romanische Monatsschrift* n.s. 39 (1989), 257–68

P. A. Belanoff, 'Women's Songs, Women's Language: *Wulf and Eadwacer* and *The Wife's Lament*', in *New Readings on Women in Old English Literature*, ed. H. Damico and A. H. Olsen (Bloomington and Indianapolis, IN, 1990), pp. 193–203

M. Desmond, 'The Voice of Exile: Feminist Literary History and the Anonymous Anglo-Saxon Elegy', *Critical Enquiry* 16 (1990), 572–90

P. Pulsiano and K. Wolf, 'The *hwelp* in *Wulf and Eadwacer*', *ELN* 28.3 (1991), 1–9

S. E. Deskis, 'The Gnomic Woman in Old English Poetry', *Philological Quarterly* 73 (1994), 133–49

⌐Lēodum is mīnum⌐   swylce° him mon ⌐lāc⌐ gife°;   as though   gives *sbj*

⌐willað hȳ° hine āþecgan   gif hē on þrēat cymeð⌐.   they

1 **Lēodum is mīnum** 'It is to (*or* for) my people'.   **lāc** The core meaning is 'offering' or 'gift', sometimes in the sense of 'sacrifice' to a deity; occasionally 'message' or even 'medical potion' are indicated.

2 **willað hȳ ... cymeð** This line, repeated exactly in 7, seems to be a statement, though some interpreters have taken it as a question.   **āþecgan** A rare vb., related to *þicgan* ('take', often in reference to food), whose central meaning appears to be 'receive' and can include the idea of 'take as food' or 'consume'. Ambiguity may be intended: 'receive'/'welcome' and 'consume'/'destroy' are simultaneously implicit.   **on þrēat** The usual sense of the noun is 'host' or 'troop', and, in the absence of a dat. ending (-*e*), we must assume that it is in the acc., making it probable that *on þrēat* means 'into (this? their?) troop', rather than 'in (*or* with) a troop'.

⌐Ungelīc is ūs⌐.

⌐Wulf⌐ is on īege°,   ic on ōþerre°.   island   another

5   ⌐Fæst⌐ is þæt ēglond,   fenne° biworpen°.   by marsh surrounded

Sindon wælrēowe°   weras° þǣr on īge°;   cruel   men   island

willað hȳ hine āþecgan   gif hē on þrēat cymeð.

Ungelīce is ūs.

⌐Wulfes ic mīnes wīdlāstum   wēnum dogode⌐.

10 Þonne° hit wæs rēnig weder   ond ic rēotugu° sæt,   When   mournful nsf

þonne° mec ⌐se beaducāfa°   bōgum bilegde⌐;   then   'battle-bold one'

wæs mē wyn° ⌐tō þon⌐,   wæs mē hwæþre° ēac°   pleasure yet   also

lāð°.   loathsome

Wulf, mīn Wulf,   ⌐wēna mē þīne⌐

sēoce° gedydon°,   þīne seldcymas°,   sick   made   'seldom-comings'

15 murnende° mōd°,   nales° metelīste°.   grieving heart not lack of food

---

3 **Ungelīc is ūs** The variation in 8, where the adj. has the form *ungelīce* (which could be an adv. form), may be a scribal whim; if deliberate, it is hard to see how it works. The phr. is impers., but what is the significance of *ūs*? Relating the line (here and in 8) to the preceding one, the difference alluded to must be that between the woman and her people: 'there is a difference between us'. She could be including her lover also, she and he as a unit, in which case we might interpret: 'it is different for us', but there is no sign of this, as there is later, with dual pronouns. If, however, we see *ungelīc is ūs* as prefacing the following line, which is about Wulf (here and again in 9), then 'the difference between us' is more likely to be between him and her.

4 **Wulf** This is usually assumed to be the name of the narrator's lover, as distinct from her husband Eadwacer (16), but it is by no means certain.

5 **Fæst** The narrator's island (if that is the one being referred to) is presumably 'secure' because inaccessible.

9 **Wulfes ... dogode** It would seem that *dogode* is the pret. sg. (here 1st-pers.) of a vb. *dogian*, governing the dat. (*wīdlāstum*), but the vb. is unknown elsewhere and its meaning is obscure; suggestions have included 'suffered', 'followed' and 'dogged' (i.e. 'trailed', 'hounded' or perhaps 'hunted'). The sense of this line seems to be that the woman has 'followed in the wide tracks (*wīdlāstum*)' of her lover 'in hope' or 'in expectation' (*wēnum*, dat. pl.), or possibly 'in her imagination'.

11 **se beaducāfa** Some have taken this to be Wulf, others the woman's husband. **bōgum bilegde** 'wrapped in (his?) arms'; assumed to be a euphemism for sexual intercourse. Other meanings of *bilecgan* include 'afflict' and 'accuse'.

12 **tō þon** Perhaps 'in that' (*þon* is instr.), rather than, as frequently trans., 'to an extent' (after which meaning a rel. conj. and clause would be expected to follow).

13 **wēna ... þīne** 'thy expectations'; presumably, 'expectations of you'. These, along with Wulf's rare appearances and her own grieving heart, have made the woman ill.

Gehȳrest° þū, ⌐Ēadwacer⌐? Uncerne° earmne°   Hear Our *dual* wretched
hwelp
bireð ⌐wulf⌐ tō wuda.
Þæt mon ēaþe° ⌐tōslīteð°⌐ þætte næfre gesomnad°   easily tears apart joined
wæs,
uncer giedd° geador°.   tale together

16 **Ēadwacer** Most critics take this to be the same man as the *beaducāfa* of 11, and
therefore the woman's husband, partly because the name suggests a socially acceptable
authority figure in contrast to Wulf, a name with connotations of outlawry. *Ēadwacer* is
usually interpreted as a name meaning 'property-watcher', though the element *ēad* can
equally well mean 'good fortune' or 'happiness'. This raises the possibility that we are
dealing with an epithet, not a proper noun at all; one imaginative suggestion is that the
woman is here addressing Wulf, her lover and thus the 'guardian' of her happiness, and that
there is no second man in her life.   **Uncerne earmne hwelp** A 'whelp' is the young of a
wolf or dog and so, if the reference in 'us two' is to the woman and Eadwacer (whoever he
is), it may be an ironic and dismissive reference to an unwanted child; but it could be the
(wanted?) child of the woman and her lover. Manuscript *earne* makes little sense; *earmne*,
confirming *hwelp* as the obj. of *bireð*, is the most satisfactory emendation.

17 **wulf** This is usually presented by editors as the animal (with lower-case *w*, as here)
rather than the man, but even if this is correct, we can scarcely avoid taking it *also* as the
man. It is not clear whether the sense of *bireð* (for *bereð*, 'bears') is pres. or fut., nor what
is to happen to the 'whelp': is it to be devoured in the wood or kept in safety?

18 **tōslīteð** Although the final observation seems to cover the woman's relationship
with Wulf in general, the savage action described by the vb. may be a clue to the fate of the
hwelp.

40

The Wife's Lament

Like *Wulf and Eadwacer* (Text 39), *The Wife's Lament* is a lyric of lament sung by a female voice; and it, too, has an enigmatic and allusive narrative which defies complete elucidation. Nevertheless, in many ways *The Wife's Lament* fits into a pattern familiar from other OE lyrical poems. The opening declaration by the first-person speaker of her ability to tell the true story of herself is remarkably like the opening of *The Seafarer*, and an inventory of key words reveals the unmistakable kinship of the poem with the OE lyrics of lament, especially *The Wanderer*. There is the diction of sadness and mental anguish (*geōmorre*, 1, *geōmormōd*, 42, *ūhtceare*, 7, *mōdceare*, 40 and 51, *brēostceare*, 44), of physical hardship (*yrmþa*, 3, *earfoþa*, 39), and of exile and the landscape of exile (*wræcsīþa*, 5 and 38, *winelēas wræcca*, 10, *eorðsele*, 29, *storme behrīmed*, 48). We may deduce that the narrator is a woman exiled from her husband's tribe (which is presumably not her own), probably during his absence, though he seems to have been instrumental in forcing her to live as she does. Some sort of feud is perhaps operating and there appear to be references to hidden enmities or betrayals. The woman's lament is that of a rejected or separated lover, and perhaps another man is involved as well; that could explain the 'very suitable man' referred to in line 18. The density of personal reference in the poem is remarkable. There are thirty-five first-person pronouns in all (fifteen of them the nominative *ic*) and five dual pronouns, which of course include the speaker in their reference (*unc*, 'us two', *wit*, 'we two', etc). Although the poem's concluding lines are ostensibly more objective, including a final aphorism, their subject is still '*my* lover'. There is no resolution, no release from sorrow.

Supplying modern punctuation for a poem whose narrative detail is so elusive presents great problems. At the end of line 10, for instance, a full stop dictates the translation 'then' for *Ðā* in line 9, but if a comma were used, *Ðā* would be the conjunction 'when'. Again, in lines 20–1, several sequences of punctuation are syntactically possible, and they may give radically different results. The punctuation provided below is only tentative. Extensive notes on the possible interpretations of individual lines are given, but they are not exhaustive.

Such are the difficulties in interpreting *The Wife's Lament* on a literal level that some critics have wondered whether this apparently secular poem is in fact quite the opposite, and that it should be read as a Christian allegory. They invoke the biblical tradition epitomised in the Song of Songs in the Old Testament, where the expression of intense erotic love between a groom and his bride is interpreted, according to commentators, as the relationship between Christ and his church. Following this lead, the female persona of the OE poem could be interpreted as Jerusalem (i.e. the Hebrew people) and also as the church, and all the topics of her lamentation – exile, suffering, betrayal, retribution – could be seen as aspects of the history of God's people, as told in the Old Testament, and then, by typological extension, of Christians in the present world. These ideas could be taken further, some critics think, to link this poem with another somewhat enigmatic lyric which occurs later in the Exeter Book and is known as *The Husband's Message*. This is a poem apparently anticipating imminent reunion and might be seen as a hopeful sequel to the despair of *The Wife's Lament*. However, nothing compels us to interpret either poem thus, and *The Wife's Lament*, whatever its obscurities, remains an evocative lyric in its own, ostensibly secular, right.

Several features of the vocabulary and phonology of the poem show a departure from general late WS usage and might suggest an Anglian, possibly Mercian, origin. Examples are *brērum* for *brǣrum* (31), *longade* for *longode* (14), *nemne* for *nefne* (22), the use of *wrecan* (1) in the sense of 'utter', and the use of the adverb *ūp* with the verb *wēox* (3; more usually *āwēox*).

Further reading

R. F. Leslie, ed., *Three Old English Elegies: The Wife's Lament, The Husband's Message, The Ruin* (Manchester, 1961)

S. B. Greenfield, 'The *Wife's Lament* Reconsidered', *PMLA* 68 (1953), 907–12

M. J. Swanton, '*The Wife's Lament* and *The Husband's Message*', *Anglia* 82 (1964), 269–90

A. M. Lucas, 'The Narrator of *The Wife's Lament* Reconsidered', *NM* 70 (1969), 282–97

M. Rissanen, 'The Theme of "Exile" in *The Wife's Lament*', *NM* 70 (1969), 90–104

B. Mitchell, 'The Narrator of *The Wife's Lament*: Some Syntactical Problems Reconsidered', *NM* 73 (1972), 222–34

A. Renoir, 'A Reading Context for *The Wife's Lament*', in *Anglo-Saxon Poetry: Essays in Appreciation for John C. McGalliard*, ed. L. E. Nicholson and D. W. Frese (Notre Dame, IN, 1975), pp. 224–41

K. P. Wentersdorf, 'The Situation of the Narrator in the Old English *Wife's Lament*', *Speculum* 56 (1981), 492–516

F. Walker-Pelkey, '"*Frige hwæt ic hatte*": *The Wife's Lament* as Riddle', *Papers on Language and Literature* 28 (1992), 242–66

S. Horner, 'En/closed Subjects: The *Wife's Lament* and the Culture of Early Medieval Female Monasticism', *Æstel* 2 (1994); repr. in *OE Poetry*, ed. Liuzza, pp. 381–91

K. A. Lowe, 'A Fine and Private Place': *The Wife's Lament*, ll. 33–34, the Translators and the Critics', in *'Lastworda Betst': Essays in Memory of Christine E. Fell with her Unpublished Writings*, ed. C. Hough and K. A. Lowe (Donington, 2002), pp. 122–43

(For studies treating *The Wife's Lament* together with *Wulf and Eadwacer*, see the headnote to the latter poem, p. 336.)

IC þis giedd° wrece° ⌐bī mē ful geōmorre⌐,   tale   tell
⌐mīnre sylfre sīð⌐. Ic ⌐þæt⌐ secgan mæg
hwæt ic ⌐yrmþa⌐ gebād° siþþan° ic ūp wēox°,   endured   after   grew
⌐nīwes oþþe ealdes⌐, nō° mā° þonne nū.   never   more
5 Ā° ic wīte° wonn° ⌐mīnra wræcsīþa⌐.   Always torment *as* suffered
Ǣrest° mīn hlāford gewāt° heonan° of   First   went   hence
   lēodum°   (his) people
ofer ⌐ȳþa gelāc⌐; hæfde ic ⌐ūhtceare°⌐   anxiety before dawn
⌐hwǣr mīn lēodfruma° londes⌐ wǣre.   'people-leader' (*i.e.* lord)
Đā ⌐ic mē fēran gewāt folgað sēcan⌐,
10 winelēas° wrǣcca°, for° mīnre   friendless exile *ns* because of
   wēaþearfe°.   woeful need
Ongunnon° ⌐þæt⌐ þæs monnes° māgas°   Began   man's   kinsmen
   hycgan°   to plot
þurh dyrne° geþōht° þæt hȳ tōdǣlden°   secret design might separate *sbj*
   unc°,   us two
þæt wit° ⌐gewīdost⌐ in woruldrīce°   we two 'world-kingdom' (*i.e.* this world)

1 **bī mē ful geōmorre** 'about me very melancholy', i.e. 'about my very melancholy self'. The fem. adj. (dat. sg., in concord with *mē*) confirms the speaker's gender.

2 **mīnre sylfre sīð** *sīð* is another acc. obj. of *wrece*, in parallel with *giedd*: 'the experience of my self', i.e. 'my own experience'.   **þæt** correl. with *hwæt* in 3 and better not trans.

3 **yrmþa** gen. of respect: '(by way) of troubles'.

4 **nīwes oþþe ealdes** gen. of respect: 'of new or of old', i.e. 'recently or of old'.

5 **mīnra wræcsīþa** '(the torment) of my miserable journeys (*or* exile's paths)'.

7 **ȳþa gelāc** 'the play (*or* rolling) of the waves'. The same phrase is used twice in *The Seafarer* (26/6 and 46).   **ūhtceare** See 38/8n; *ūhta* is used also in 35.

8 **hwǣr ... londes** gen. of place: '(as to) where in the land ...'.

9 **ic mē fēran gewāt** 'I went travelling'; rflx. pron. with vb. of motion [§D4c].   **folgað sēcan** It is not clear whether the *folgað* that the woman seeks is that of her exiled lord, and thus 'retinue' or 'following', or a new lord, and thus perhaps 'service'.

11 **þæt** pron. obj. of *hycgan*, correl. with conj. *þæt* in 12, and better not trans.

13 **gewīdost** 'most widely'; presumably as far apart as could be contrived.

⌐lifdon⌐ lāðlīcost°,   ond ⌐mec longade⌐.   most wretchedly

15 Hēt° mec hlāford mīn   ⌐hēr heard niman⌐;   Commanded

āhte° ic ⌐lēofra lȳt⌐   on þissum londstede°,   possessed   region

holdra° frēonda.   Forþon° is mīn hyge° geōmor.   loyal   Therefore   spirit

Ðā ic mē ful gemæcne°   monnan funde°,   suitable   found

heardsǣligne°,   hygegeōmorne°,   ill-fortuned   sad-spirited

20 mōd° mīþendne°,   morþor°   heart *as*   concealing   murder *as*

hycgendne°.   plotting

Blīþe gebǣro⌐,   ful oft wit bēotedan°   vowed

þæt ⌐unc ne gedǣlde   nemne° dēað āna°,   except   only

ōwiht elles⌐.   Eft° is þæt onhworfen°;   Now   reversed

⌐is nū   swā° hit ño wǣre⌐   as if

---

14 **lifdon** Presumably, 'have lived', with the situation continuing.   **mec longade** impers. vb. with acc. pron.: 'I pined'.

15 **hēr heard niman** There are four possibilities here. (1) In the manuscript, the first two words are written as one (an otherwise unknown compound); if the first element, *herh*, be taken as *hearh*, 'grove' or '(pagan) sanctuary', and the second *eard*, then the whole line might be read, 'My lord commanded me to take up this residence in a grove (*or* sanctuary)'. (2) If we separate the compound into *hēr* and *heard* (as here), then *heard* seems to be an adj. modifying *hlāford*: 'my cruel lord commanded me to be seized (*or* brought) here'. (3) Emendation of *heard* to the adv. *hearde*, 'cruelly', would overcome the awkward separation of adj. from noun: '...cruelly commanded me...'. (4) We could posit a redundant *h* and read as *hēr eard niman*, 'to take up residence here'.

16 **lēofra lȳt** partitive gen.: 'few loved ones'. There are in fact none at all; cf. the similar use of understatement in 38/31. In 17, *frēonda* is parallel with *lēofra*.

18–21 **Ðā ic ... bēotedan** The most obscure passage in the poem. Can the man be 'suitable' *because* he is unfortunate, sad at heart, etc, or is a deeper irony intended – i.e. he is clearly not suitable at all?   **Blīþe gebǣro** This seems to be a dat. phr.: 'with a happy demeanour' (with *gebǣro* uninflected [§B3h]); the punctuation given here has the phr. relate to the double subj. of the following sentence ('we two'), but it could equally well be part of the previous description of the man only. In 20, the manuscript has *hycgende*; most editors emend, as here, to the acc. sg. masc. form, which is in concord with the previous four adjs. and adds the anticipation of killing to the other aspects of the man's character. If the manuscript reading be retained, then we need a full-stop after *mōd mīþende*, for the adj. must, along with *blīþe gebǣro*, describe both the man and the woman, who were contemplating deadly deeds as they exchanged their love-vows.

22–3 **unc ne gedǣlde ... ōwiht elles** 'nothing else would separate us (except ...)'.

24 **is nū ... wǣre** A very short line, but the abruptness could be for effect. Some editors conjecture an added past part. (such as *geworden*, 'come about') after *nū* and put the caesura after it. For the second part, cf. the similar half-line in 38/96.

25	⌜frēondscipe⌝ uncer°. Sceal° ic feor ge° nēah	our Must and
	mīnes felalēofan° ⌜fǣhðu⌝ drēogan°.	'much-loved one' gs endure
	Heht° mec ⌜mon⌝ wunian° on wuda°	Commanded to dwell of trees
	bearwe°,	grove ds
	⌜under āctrēo⌝ in þām ⌜eorðscræfe⌝.	
	Eald is þes eorðsele°, eal ic eom oflongad°;	earth-dwelling seized with longing
30	sindon dena° dimme°, dūna° ūphēa°,	dales dark hills high
	bitre° ⌜burgtūnas⌝, brērum° beweaxne°,	'biting' with briars overgrown
	wīc° wynna lēas°. Ful oft mec hēr wrāþe°	habitation without +g cruelly
	begeat°	assailed
	fromsīþ° frēan°. ⌜Frȳnd sind on eorþan,	departure ns of (my) lord
	lēofe lifgende, leger° weardiað°⌝	beds ap occupy
35	þonne ic on ūhtan° āna gonge°	dawn walk
	under āctrēo geond° þās eorðscrafu.	around
	Þǣr ic sittan mōt° ⌜sumorlangne dæg⌝,	must
	þǣr ic wēpan° mæg mīne wræcsīþas,	bewail
	earfoþa° fela. Forþon ic ǣfre° ne mæg	hardships gp ever
40	þǣre mōdceare° mīnre gerestan°,	heart-sorrow gs find rest from +g
	ne ealles þæs longaþes° þe mec on þissum līfe begeat.	longing gs

25 frēondscipe Presumably 'love'; cf. *frēond* in the apparent sense of 'lover' in 33/44; see also 33, below. *Frēondscipe* is the subj. of *is* in 24 and is predicted by neut. *hit*, though the noun is masc.

26 fǣhðu Perhaps 'enmity', giving further definition to the end of the 'friendship'; but otherwise 'feud', involving the speaker's lover, in which she too is caught up.

27 mon Perhaps '*the* man', i.e. the woman's husband, otherwise '*a* man' or the indef. 'they' or 'someone'.

28 under āctrēo There is a similarly enigmatic allusion to a woman being made to live 'beneath an oak-tree' in an Old Norse poem (*Helreið Brynhildar*, stanza 6). **eorðscræfe** The 'earth-cave' under an oak-tree has been seen as a place associated with pagan worship (especially by those who read *he(a)rh* in 15); in *The Wanderer*, however, the word signifies 'earth-grave' (38/84).

31 burgtūnas 'fortified enclosures'. Perhaps an abandoned settlement or ancient earthworks; *bitre* may refer literally to the lacerating effect of the briars.

33–4 Frȳnd ... leger weardiað The last two words – 'occupy (their) beds' – may be a metaphor for the death of 'friends' who were 'beloved while living' (in which case *on eorþan* means 'in the earth'); or perhaps a literal reference to 'lovers' (which could be the meaning of *frȳnd*: see 25n) whose happy plight 'on earth' – they are 'beloved (and) living' – contrasts with the loneliness of the speaker.

37 sumorlangne dæg acc. of duration of time: 'the summer-long day'.

⌐Ā scyle geong mon   wesan° gēomormōd°,   be   sad-hearted
heard heortan geþōht;   swylce habban sceal
blīþe gebǣro,   ēac þon brēostceare°,   'heart-care'
45 sinsorgna° gedreag°⌐.   ⌐Sȳ æt him sylfum gelong   of constant sorrows   (a) host *as*
eal his worulde wyn,   sȳ⌐ ful wīde ⌐fāh⌐
⌐feorres folclondes⌐,   þæt mīn frēond siteð
under stānhliþe°   storme° behrīmed°,   stony slope   by (the) storm   frost-coated
wine° wērigmōd°,   wætre beflōwen°   friend *ns*   sad-spirited   surrounded (by +*d*)
50 on drēorsele°.   Drēogeð° ⌐se mīn wine⌐   sad abode   (Will) endure
micle° mōdceare;   hē gemon° tō oft   great   (will) think about
wynlicran° wīc.   ⌐Wā° bið þām þe sceal   more pleasant   Woe
of langoþe   lēofes ābīdan°⌐.   wait for +*g*

42–45a **Ā scyle . . . gedreag** Although these lines begin gnomically, the situation to which they refer is specific, not universal; *geong mon* is thus presumably the husband, '*the* young man', rather than '*a* (hypothetical) young man'. **scyle . . . sceal** Presumably a distinction is intended between the sbj. *scyle* (hypothetical: 'may have to') and the indic. *sceal* (certain: 'must'). **heard heortan geþōht** This is another predicate of *scyle wesan*: perhaps, '(and) his heart's thought (may have to be) painful'. **swylce . . . ēac þon** The syntax suggests 'just as he must have . . . , so also (he must have) . . .' (*ēac þon*, instr. phr., 'in addition to that' or 'besides'). **blīþe gebǣro** The phr. is acc. sg. (cf. 21), parallel with *brēostceare* and *gedreag*.

45b–47 **Sȳ . . . sȳ** Two interpretations seem possible. (1) The sense of the two sbj. vbs. may be optative: 'Let all his joy in the world be dependent (*gelong*) on himself, let him be . . .'. (2) The sbj. vb. may express alternative hypotheses: 'Whether all his joy in the world be . . . , (or) whether he be . . .' **fāh** This suggests a state of guilt and/or hostility, and 'outlawed' may be an apt trans. The following subord. clause (*þæt . . .*, 'so that . . .') expands on the predicament expressed in the second *sȳ* clause. If the first interpretation be accepted, then the following lines become a sort of curse by the woman on the husband; if the latter, they are merely a comment on his condition, which is to be an unhappy one, whether he be comfortably situated or in exile. **feorres folclondes** gen. of place: 'in a far country'.

50 **se mīn wine** 'that (*or* this) friend of mine'.

52–3 **Wā bið . . . ābīdan** A statement about forlorn lovers, using a common gnomic formula (*wā bið*, 'woe be (to) . . .'). The converse formula, *wel bið . . .* , is also much used by poets; see 38/114. **of langoþe** '(to come) from longing', or perhaps the idea is simply that a lover will await 'in longing'.

Manuscripts and textual emendations

1. In the Schoolroom

British Library, Cotton Tiberius A. iii (mid-11th cent.), fols. 60v–61r and 63v–64r

4 behese > behefe; **6** ge beon *supplied*, bewugen > beswungen; **8** swincgla us > us swincgla; **12** and *omitted*; **18** weorc þin > þin weorc; **22** æþer > æcer; **28** binnan oxan > oxena binnan, hig > hige; **29** sceasn heora > heora scearn; **31** ge > gea; **33** sceap mine > mine sceap; **35** and > on, treowa > tweowa; **36** on þærto 7 cyse 7 buteran ic do > and cyse and buteran ic do þærto; **40** cycean > cyrcean; **41** þa > þam; **43** mæssa > mæssan, sungan > sungon; **44** drucon > druncon; **51** deor > dear; **58** paxgeorn > waxgeorn, synd *supplied*; **59** ne eom > neom; **62** hwilon *supplied*; **65** hæbbe > næbbe, eala > ealu; **66** drncst > drincst; **67** ne eom > neom; **69** þu *supplied*; **72** crise > arise.

2. A Personal Miscellany

London, British Library, Cotton Titus D. xxvi–xxvii (1023–35), fols. 55v–56v.

(a) A Divinatory Alphabet

20 blis seo > blisse; **22** bycna > bycnaþ; **24** soldan > foldan.

(b) The Moon and Tide, (c) The Age of the Virgin

No emendations.

3. Medicinal Remedies

London, British Library, Royal 12 D. xvii (mid-10th cent.), fols. 9v–10r, 70v–71r and 106r–v.

(a) For Dimness of the Eyes

No emendations.

(b) For Vomiting

1 viþ > wiþ.

(c) For Dysentery

No emendations.

4.   Learning Latin

Oxford, St John's College 154, fols. 1–160 (early 11th cent.).

47 of > on; **51** of > on; **57** se *supplied before* u; **59** þam *supplied*; **65** þr-winne > þrowigenne; **69** coniunctio > coniugatio; **85** ne > nu; **90** on *supplied*; **94** mann mm > nan mann.

5.   A New Beginning

Oxford, Bodleian Library, Hatton 20 (807–7), fols. 1–2.

11 don *supplied.*

6.   The Wagonwheel of Fate

London, British Library, Cotton Otho A. vi (mid-10th cent.), fols. 110v–113v. Emendations and restorations are mostly from Oxford, Bodleian Library, Bodley 180 (first half of the 12th cent.) and a transcription of the Cotton version, made before it was damaged by fire. Restorations of text originally in the Cotton manuscript but now illegible or missing, owing to damage, are given here between square brackets.

4 þæ > þæm (*before* anfealdan), God[e]; **5** an[dwlitan], [Ond forþæm hit swa gescea]pen; **7** syle > symle; **13** hit > hi; **17** ðe *supplied*; **18–19** ealle [gesceafta þæt hi ne moton toslupan of]; **22** þonne *supplied*; **30** e[ng]las; **43** ond (*before* welt) *supplied*, hw[eo]l; **44** nex[t þæ]re, fæ[stlicor]; **45** fe[lgan don]; **45–6** g[od þe we] nemnað [God ond þa selestan men fa]ren; **47** ælces span > ælces spacan; **49** lif *supplied*; **56** [fe]lga [þ]eah; **57** þær[e e]orðan, [men o]n; **58** mid[mestan], [on God]e; **59** hio[ra luf]e, [hi ne magon] þæron; **65** ond swiðor þas eorðlicon þing forsioð *supplied*; **68** f[rom]; **70** andweadan > andweardan; **71** tow[ear]dan; **74** Swylc [is þæt þæt we] wyrd [hatað]; **75** sio *supplied after* ond.

7.   Laws of the Anglo-Saxon Kings

(a) Æthelberht

Rochester, Cathedral Library, A. 3. 5 (*Textus Roffensis*; early 12th cent.), fols. 1r–2v.

No emendations.

(b) Alfred

Cambridge, Corpus Christi College 173 (mid-10th cent.), fols. 39v–41v, 43r, 45r–v.

15–16 Gif he þonne ðæs weddie þe hym riht sy to gelæstanne *supplied from Textus Roffensis* (*see above and p. 47)*; **48** XXXVIII > XXXVIIII.

(c) Æthelred

Cambridge, Corpus Christi College 201 (mid-11th cent.), pp. 93–6.
No emendations.

8. England Under Attack

Oxford, Bodleian Library, Laud misc. 636 (first half of 12th cent.).

1 scipum > scipu; **12** dænisca > dæfenisca; **20** G .... wic > Gypeswic; **25** his > þis; **32** fram hþære > fram þære; **56** æt ætefingstoce > æt Tefingstoce.

9. Bede's *Ecclesiastical History of the English People*

(a) The Founding of England

Cambridge, University Library, Kk. 3. 18 (second half of 11th cent.) as far as 46, *sticode* (with emendations from Cambridge, Corpus Christi College 41, first half of 11th cent.), and Oxford, Bodleian Library, Tanner 10 (first half of 10th cent.) from 46, *sume*, to the end.

13 he > hi; **24–5** þæs fæder wæs Witta haten *supplied*; **40** wæs forhergiende > forheregeode wæron, hrusan o > hruran ond; **41** ond (*before* mæssepreostas) *supplied*.

(b) The Miracle of Cædmon

Oxford, Bodleian Library, Tanner 10 (first half of 10th cent.).

30 endebyrdnesse > endebyrdnes; **41–2** godes wordes > gode wyrðes; **59** in *supplied*; **85** ne *supplied*; **102** ohhylde > onhylde.

10. *The Battle of Brunanburh*

Cambridge, Corpus Christi College 173 (*c.* 900–late 11th cent.), fols. 26r–27r

13 secgas hwate > secga swate; **25** he eardes > heardes; **26** þæ > þæra þe; **29** cyninges > cyningas; **35** cnearen > cnear on; **39** hildering > hilderinc; **43** fer grunden > forgrunden; **49** cum bodgehnastes > cumbolgehnastes; **56** hira land > Iraland; **66** æfer > æfre; **72** weealles > Wealas.

11.   The Will of Ælfgifu

London, British Library, Additional 15350 (first half of 12th cent.), fol. 96.
No emendations.

12.   *The Fonthill Letter*

Canterbury, Dean and Chapter, Chart. Ant. C. 1282 (Red Book, no. 12) (*c.* 920).

17 æst > ærest; **31** ... n ond *supplied*; **32** ðæt land me se ... *supplied.*

13.   After the Flood

London, British Library, Cotton Claudius B. iv (mid-11th cent.); corrections from
Oxford, Bodleian Library, Laud Misc. 509 (late 11th cent.).

20 flæsc *supplied.*

14.   The Crucifixion

Cambridge, Corpus Christi College 140 (first half of 11th cent.), fols. 42r–45r.

45 tewgen > twegen.

15.   King Alfred's Psalms

Paris, Bibliothèque Nationale, lat. 8824 (mid-11th cent.), fols. 1r, 11r–v, 23r–v.

(a) Psalm 1, (c) Psalm 22
No emendations.

(b) Psalm 12
11 y > þy; **12** strenga > strengra.

16.   A Translator's Problems

Oxford, Bodleian Library, Laud misc. 509 (second half of 11th cent.), fols. 1r–3r.
Shown here, in addition to several emendations, are restorations of letters lost from
the edges of the first folio; they are in square brackets.

2 eadmo[d]lice; **3** [L]ydene; **6** þ[a]; **8** g[e]hyrþ; **9** niw[an]; **21** furþo[n]; **27** [w]æs; **29** [w]if; **30** [n]e, [þ]æt; **31** 7 (= and) *after* com *omitted*, [t]o (*after* began); **32** [h]im; **62** na *supplied*; **63** andfealdlice > anfealdlice; **90** fandunge > fadunge; **94** ealdan *supplied after* habban þa.

17.   Satan's Challenge

Oxford, Bodleian Library, Junius 11 (10/11th cent.), pp. 19–22.

9 widman > winnan; **21** on *supplied*; **55** . . . htes > leohtes; **88** on mode. minum > on minum mode.

18.   The Drowning of Pharaoh's Army

Oxford, Bodleian Library, Junius 11 (10/11th cent.), pp. 166–70.

25 barenodon > basnodon; **41** wer beamas > werbeamas; **48** flod wearde sloh > flodweard gesloh; **53** on bogum > onbugon; **54** mode wæga > modewæga; **56** on feond > onfond; **57** grund *supplied*; **59** huru fæðum > heorufæðum; **64** heoro > heora; **68** eac *supplied*; **71** moyse > moyses; **73** nemnað > ne mað; **92** gehylces > gehwylces; **100** is *supplied*; **110** ufon > us on.

19.   *Judith*

London, British Library, Cotton Vitellius A. xv (early 11th cent.), fols. 202r–209v.

85 þearffendre > þearfendre; **87** heorte ys onhæted > heorte onhæted; **134** hie hie > hie; **144** iudithe > Iudith; **179** stariað > starian; **201** þufas > sigeþufas; **207** westan > wistan; **234** rice > ricne; **249** weras ferhðe > weras werigferhðe; **251** hyldo > hilde; **297** lind(w?). . > lindwig; **347** gesceow > gesceop.

20.   Bede's *Death Song*

(a) St Gallen, Stiftsbibliothek 254 (9th cent.), p. 253.
        No emendations.
(b) Oxford, Bodleian Library, Digby 211 (12th cent.), fol. 108r.
        No emendations.

21.   Two Holy Women

(a) Saint Æthelthryth

British Library, Cotton Julius E. vii (early 11th cent.), fols. 94v–96v.
        No emendations.

(b) Saint Eugenia

Cambridge, Corpus Christi College 41 (early or mid-11th cent.), pp. 125–8.

15 deaðe *supplied*; **18** tobærs > tobærst.

22.   A Homily for Easter Sunday

London, British Library, Royal 7 C. xii (*c*. 1000), fols. 76v–80v.

77–81 Se engel awylte . . . faran of middangearde *supplied from Cambridge, University Library, Gg. 3. 28 (c. 1000).*

23.   *The Dream of the Rood*

Vercelli, Cathedral Library, CXVII (second half of 10th cent.), fols. 104–6.

2 hæt > hwæt; **17** wealdes > wealdendes; **20** surgum > sorgum; **59** sorgum *supplied from Ruthwell Cross text*; **70** reotende > greotende; **71** syððan > stefn; **117** unforht > anforht; **142** he > me.

24.   *On False Gods*

Oxford, Bodleian Library, Hatton 113 (*c*. 1070), fols. 58v–61.

13 godes > godas; **25** incunnesse > incundnesse; **28** fenge > fengon.

25.   *The Sermon of the Wolf*

London, British Library, Cotton Nero A. i (early 11th cent., with additions possibly by Wulfstan himself), fols. 110–15. Emendations mostly from Oxford, Bodleian Library, Hatton 113 (third quarter of 11th cent.).

8 swæcan > spæcan; **19** mana > manna; **47** us (*before* ungylda) *supplied*; **49** getryða > getrywða; **63** and Æþelred man dræfde ut of his earde *supplied*; **81** gecnewe > gecnawe; **101** wolodscame > woroldscame; **114** þur > þurh; **119** of > on; **124** godfyhte > godfyrhte; **129** hyne > hy ne; **149** fordom > fordon; **164** miclam > miclan.

26. *The Seafarer*

Exeter, Cathedral 3501 (second half of 10th cent.), fols. 81v–83r.

26 feran > frefran; **56** eft eadig > esteadig; **72** bið *supplied*; **75** fremman > fremum; **82** næron > nearon; **109** mod > mon; **115** swire > swiþre; **117b** se > we.

27. Falling in Love

Cambridge, Corpus Christi College 201 (B) (11th cent.), pp. 138–40.

11 stilli > stille; **27** heapian > hearpian; **34** nu þæt þu > þæt pu nu; **45** plegod > plegode; **53** sweoðe > swiðe.

28. The Trees of the Sun and the Moon

London, British Library, Cotton Vitellius A. xv (early 11th cent.), fols. 126r–129v.

18 alette > halette; **20** hin > him; **24** gesci > gescie; **26** setlgongen > setlgonges; **40** instyred > onstyred; **45** ge ond wyrdum > geondwyrdon; **57** eþel > wyrd.

29. Cynewulf and Cyneheard

Cambridge, Corpus Christi College 173 (9th/10th cent.), fol. 10r–v.

24 cyðdon > cyðde.

30. *The Battle of Maldon*

Oxford, Bodleian Library, Rawlinson B. 203 (an early 18th-cent. transcription of lost late 10th/early 11th-cent. manuscript; see headnote).

4 t hige > to hige; **5** þ > þa; **10** w . . . . ge > wige; **20** randan > randas; **33** ulde > hilde; **61** þe > we; **86** luðe > laðe; **103** fohte > feohte; **109** grimme *supplied*; **171** ge stundan > gestandan; **173** ge þance > geþancie; **188** mear > mearh; **191** ær don > ærndon; **192** godrine > Godwine; **201** þære > þearfe; **208** for lætun > forlætan; **274** gearc > gearo; **292** crintgan > crincgan; **297** forða > forð ða; **299** geþrang > geþrange.

31. *Beowulf*

London, British Library, Cotton Vitellius A. xv (early 11th cent.), fols. 153r–155v and 163r–164v.

(a) The Tragedy of Hildeburh

6 be *supplied*; **11** hild plegan > lindplegan; **45** að > ad; **55** earme > eame; **66–7** finnel un hlitme > Finne eal unhlitme; **68** he > ne.

(b) The Slaying of Grendel's Mother

15 brimwyl > brimwylf; **17** þæm > þæs; **19** swecte > swencte; **22** in *supplied*; **29** hord swenge > hond sweng; **40** wundel mæl > wundenmæl; **50** handlean > andlean; **54** seaxe > seax; **55** ond *supplied*; **68** wæs *supplied*.

32. *The Fight at Finnsburh*

Text printed by George Hickes in his *Linguarum Veterum Septentrionalium Thesaurus* [Collection of Ancient Languages of the North], vol. 1, pp. 192–3, from a single leaf, since lost, which he claimed to have found in a manuscript in Lambeth Palace Library, London. This may have been MS 487, a 13th-cent. collection of homilies. The emendations are to Hickes's printed text (see headnote, p. 287).

3 Eastun > eastan; **11** landa > linda, Hie geaþ > hicgeaþ; **20** bæran > bære; **25** Wrecten > wreccea, weuna > weana; **29** Genumon > cenum on; **34** Hwearflacra hrær > hwearflicra hræs; **38** gebærann > gebæran; **39** swa noc > swanas; **45** ðyrl > ðyrel.

33. Truth is Trickiest

London, British Library, Cotton Tiberius B. i (mid-11th cent.), fol. 115r–v.

19 earn > earm.

34. The *Durham Proverbs*

Durham, Cathedral Library, B. III. 32 (mid-11th cent.), fols. 43v–45v.

1 ea > eades; **11** geo.. > geongan; **16** wis *supplied*; **28** undebæc > underbæc; **40** eard > weard, seeð > seteð, weeð > wereð; **46** hwn > hwon.

35.   Five Anglo-Saxon Riddles

Exeter, Cathedral 3501 (second half of 10th cent.), fols. 102v, 103r, 106v–107v, 112v–113r.

(a) 'Shield'

8 7[*i.e.* ond] weorc > hondweorc.

(b) 'Swan'

No emendations.

(c) 'Onion'

10 se > seo.

(d) 'Bible'

6 ecge > ecg.

(e) 'Bookworm'

No emendations.

36.   *Deor*

Exeter, Cathedral 3501 (second half of 10th cent.), fol. 100r–v.
  No emendations.

37.   *The Ruin*

Exeter, Cathedral 3501 (second half of 10th cent.), fols. 123v–124v.

3–4 torras hrim geat torras > torras hringeat; **12** wo-að > wunað; **23** *the rune for 'man'* + dreama > mondreama; **26** secg rof > secgrofra; **31** rof > hrof.

38.   *The Wanderer*

Exeter, Cathedral 3501 (second half of 10th cent.), fols. 76v–78r.

14 healdne > healde; **24** waþena > waþema; **28** freond lease > freondleasne; **59** mod sefan > modsefa; **74** ealle > ealre; **89** deornce > deorce; **102** hruse > hrusan.

39.   *Wulf and Eadwacer*

Exeter, Cathedral 3501 (second half of 10th cent.), fols. 110v–111r.

16 earne > earmne.

40.   *The Wife's Lament*

Exeter, Cathedral 3501 (second half of 10th cent.), fol. 115r–v.

20 hycgende > hycgendne; **25** seal > sceal; **31** beweax. ne > beweaxne; **37** sittam > sittan.

Reference Grammar of Old English

For readers unfamiliar with grammatical terminology, a Guide to Terms is given on pp. 504–12. The 'cases' (nominative, accusative, genitive, dative and instrumental) relevant to pronouns, nouns and adjectives are explained in §D. Where appropriate, specific grammatical usage is illustrated by quotation from, or reference to, the texts of the main Reader, cited by text-number and line-number (e.g. 12/33). Where alternative inflections are given in the paradigms, the first form will usually be the one occurring more commonly. Paradigms are for reference, but beginners in Old English are heartily encouraged to learn at least the first one (§A1a) by heart. This gives the forms of the word for 'the' (or 'that/those'), some of which will not be immediately recognisable but which are often the key to the understanding of a sentence. For nouns, familiarity with the general paradigms given for each gender [§§B1a, B2a/b and B3a/b] is recommended; the minor variations [§§B1b–h, B2c–i and B3c–h] can be noted as and when necessary.

§A PRONOUNS

§A1 **Demonstrative Pronouns**

(a) **se, þæt, sēo**   'the', 'that', 'those'

	Sg.			Pl.
	Masc.	*Neut.*	*Fem.*	*All genders*
Nom.	se	þæt	sēo	þā
Acc.	þone	þæt	þā	þā
Gen.	þæs	þæs	þǣre	þāra, þǣra
Dat.	þǣm, þām	þǣm, þām	þǣre	þǣm, þām
Instr.	þȳ, þī, þon	þȳ, þī, þon		

Variations. 1. *sēo* frequently occurs as *sīo* in early texts (6/14, 19, etc).

2. *se* and *sēo* occasionally appear as *þe* and *þēo*, respectively, in late manuscripts: *þe gebēorscipe* (27/60).

3. *þām* replaces *þǣm* in later WS texts, and *þæne* replaces *þone*.

Uses

(i) As the DEFINITE ARTICLE 'the': e.g. *se mōna* '*the* moon'.

(ii) As the DEMONSTRATIVE ADJECTIVE 'that', 'those', e.g. *þæne ræd ġerædde Siric* 'Siric gave *that* advice' (8/24; *þæne* for *þone*). There is in effect little distinction between 'the' and 'that'/'those'; context will usually suggest the appropriate rendering.

(iii) As PRONOUNS, often in place of the personal pronouns listed in §A2; thus *sē* for *hē* 'he', *sēo* for *hēo* 'she', *þā* for *hī* 'they', and so on, e.g. *ðā ne sacað* '*they* do not quarrel' (35/18), *þone þe hī lufedon on līfe* '*him* who they loved in life' (22/70–1), *æfter þām* 'after *that*' (1/41). See also §A6. When *se* is used as a pronoun, it inevitably takes more stress than in its other uses and may be expected to be pronounced with a longer vowel; hence in this book it will be printed *sē* when so used (see p. xxxiii).

(iv) The above forms are also sometimes used as RELATIVE PRONOUNS, with meanings 'who', 'which', 'that', 'whose', etc, e.g. *se tōþ se bīstandeþ* 'the tooth *which* stands next' (7a/26–7). But this function is more commonly performed by the indeclinable relative particle, *þe* [§A7].

(v) The INSTRUMENTAL forms are used often in adverbial and conjunctive phrases, e.g. *æfter þon* 'after that' (3a/14), *æfter þon þe* 'when' (9a/50), *tō ðī þæt* 'in order that' (22/39). See also §D5.

(vi) *þæt* occurs often before a plural verb, e.g. *þæt synd dǣdliċe word* '*those* are [*or* that is] active verbs' (4/73).

(b) **þes, þis, þēos** 'this', 'these'

	Sg.			Pl.
	Masc.	*Neut.*	*Fem.*	*All genders*
Nom.	þes	þis	þēos	þās
Acc.	þisne	þis	þās	þās
Gen.	þis(s)es	þis(s)es	þisse, þisre	þissa, þisra
Dat.	þis(s)um	þis(s)um	þisse	þis(s)um
Instr.	þ̄ys, þ̄is	þ̄ys, þ̄is		

Variations. 1. Medial *i* is often replaced by *y*, especially in late WS: *þyssum, þysra,* etc.

2. In early WS, *io* is frequent for *i* and *ēo*: *þios, þīos.* Alternative forms with *eo* for *i* occur: *þeosse, þeossa, þeossum.*

3. *-um* may be levelled to *-an* or *-on*, especially in later texts.

Uses

(i) As the DEMONSTRATIVE ADJECTIVE, 'this', 'these', e.g. *ðās fīf stafas* 'these five letters' (4/38), *on ðissum ġēare* 'in this year' (8/39).

(ii) As PRONOUNS, e.g. *Godes sunu wæs þes* 'this (i.e. man) was God's son' (14/70–1), *hwæt cunnon þās þīne ġeferan?* 'what can these, your companions, do?' (1/14), *æfter þysum* 'after this' (1/41–2).

§A2 Personal Pronouns

(a) *1st Pers.* **ic, wit, wē**

'I', 'we two', 'we', 'me', 'us', 'my', 'our', etc

	Sg.	Dual	Pl.
Nom.	iċ	wit	wē
Acc.	mē, meċ	unc	ūs, ūsiċ
Gen.	mīn	uncer	ūre, ūser
Dat.	mē	unc	ūs

(b) *2nd Pers.* **þū, git, gē**

'you', 'you two', 'yours', etc

	Sg.	Dual	Pl.
Nom.	þū	ġit	ġē
Acc.	þē, þeċ	inċ	ēow
Gen.	þīn	inċer	ēower
Dat.	þē	inċ	ēow

Uses

(i) The separate DUAL pronouns are used mostly in poetry, e.g. *ful oft wit bēotedan* 'very often we two vowed' (40/21), *frēondscipe uncer* 'the friendship of us two' (40/25). The alternative dat. forms *uncit* and *incit* occur occasionally.

(ii) The 2ND-PERS. SG. forms (*þū, þē, þīn, þē*, early ModE 'thou', 'thee', 'thine', 'to thee') are always used when only one person is involved; there is no separation of 'polite' and 'intimate' forms, as there was in the English of later periods and as there is in many modern languages.

(iii) The alternative ACCUSATIVE forms *meċ, ūsiċ* and *þeċ* are found in older poetry; see 26/123, 35a/7.

(c) *3rd Pers.* **hē, hit, hēo, hī**

'he', 'it', 'she', 'they', 'him', 'her', 'them', 'his', etc

	Sg.			Pl.
	Masc.	*Neut.*	*Fem.*	*All genders*
Nom.	hē	hit	hēo	hī, hīe, hēo
Acc.	hine	hit	hīe, hī	hī, hīe, hēo
Gen.	his	his	hire	hira, hiera, heora, hiora
Dat.	him	him	hire	him, heom

Variations. 1. The forms with medial *i* are regularly found with *y* in later WS texts (*hyne, hyt, hym, hȳ, hyra,* etc); *hine* may occur as *hiene, hire* as *hiere.*

2. *hīo* may occur for *hēo* in early texts.

3. The varied forms of the fem. sg. and the pl. pronouns should be noted especially, including the congruence of certain of the nom./acc. pl. forms with those of the acc. sg. fem.

§A3 Reflexive Pronouns

The acc. and dat. forms of the personal pronouns are frequently used as REFLEXIVE PRONOUNS, in constructions where the action of a verb relates back to its subject, in order to establish personal relation or interest, e.g. *sōhton him wuldres cyning* lit. '(they) sought out for themselves [dat. *him*] the king of glory' (23/133). Often such pronouns are better left untranslated, e.g. *ne ondrǣde ic mē* 'I shall not fear' (15c/11); cf. early ModE 'I fear me'. The verb *ġebiddan* 'pray' is almost always used with a reflexive dat. pronoun; *verbs of motion* often attract one also. For examples, see §D4c.

§A4 Possessive Pronouns (Possessive Adjectives)

The *genitive* or possessive personal pronouns listed in §§A2a, 2b and 2c are used as ADJECTIVES before nouns ('*my* book', '*your* mother'). Those in §A2c (*his, hire, hira,* etc) do not alter their forms when so used: *on eallum his mihtum* 'with all his powers' (2a/14). But those in §§2a and 2b (*mīn, uncer, ūre* and *þīn, incer, ēower*) alter *to agree grammatically* with the nouns they qualify; their declension follows the pattern of 'strong' adjectives [§C2], except that *-e*, not *-u*, is invariably used in the neut. pl., e.g. *on mīnum naman* 'in my name' (22/60), *oþ ende ūres līfes* 'until the end of our life' (16/83). As an example, here is the full declension of **mīn** 'my', 'mine':

	Sg.			Pl.		
	Masc.	*Neut.*	*Fem.*	*Masc.*	*Neut.*	*Fem.*
Nom.	mīn	mīn	mīn	mīne	mīn	mīne
Acc.	mīnne	mīn	mīne	mīne	mīn	mīne
Gen.	mīnes	mīnes	mīnre	mīnra	mīnra	mīnra
Dat.	mīnum	mīnum	mīnre	mīnum	mīnum	mīnum

Variation. Medial *n* is sometimes doubled: *mīnnum.*

(i) An additional possessive pronoun **sīn** ('his', 'hers', 'its', 'their'), originally a general reflexive form, is found in verse (and some prose) texts; it is declined like *mīn.* For examples, see 7a/51, 17/63, 19/29.

§A5 Indefinite and Interrogative Pronouns

There is a number of other useful words serving in effect as pronouns, though often fulfilling an adjectival role also.

(a) **hwā, hwæt**. This serves as both INDEFINITE PRONOUN ('someone', 'anyone', 'whoever', 'someone's', 'to someone', etc) and INTERROGATIVE PRONOUN ('who?', 'what?', 'whose?', 'to whom?'). The instr. form *hwī* (or *hwȳ*), 'by what', is used as the INTERROGATIVE ADVERB 'why?'

	Masc./Fem.	*Neut.*
Nom.	hwā	hwæt
Acc.	hwone, hwæne	hwæt
Gen.	hwæs	hwæs
Dat.	hwǣm, hwām	hwǣm, hwām
Instr.	hwī, hwon	hwī, hwon, hwan

(b) **hwylċ** (or *hwilċ, hwelċ*) 'which'; **hwæþer** 'which of two'; **swylċ** (or *swilċ, swelċ*) 'such'; **ǣlċ** 'each', 'every'; and **þylliċ** 'such', 'such-like'. All these are declined like 'strong' adjectives [§C2]. See also §A6.

(c) Further indefinite pronouns, and pronominal phrases built from the above pronouns, include: **ġehwā, ġehwylċ** 'each', 'every'; **āhwæþer, āhwylċ** 'anyone'; **ǣġhwā, ǣġhwylċ** 'each one'; **swā hwā swā** 'who(so)ever'; **swā hwæt swā** 'what(so)ever'; and **nāthwā, nāthwylċ** 'someone', 'something'.

(d) The following are indeclinable: **wiht** (or **wuht**) 'anything', **āwiht** (or **āwuht**) 'anything', and **hwætwugu** 'something'.

§A6 Pronoun-Adjectives

There are some more very common words which function both as indefinite pronouns and as adjectives: **ǣniġ** 'any', **maniġ** 'many', **eall** 'all', **nān** 'none' and **ōþer** 'second' or 'other'. They are declined like adjectives, with 'strong' or 'weak' endings, as explained in §C1, with the exception of *ōþer*, which is always declined 'strong'. The basic functions of these words are straightforward – as PRONOUN, e.g. *ealle friðsumaþ God* 'God reconciles all' (2a/14), where *ealle* is independent and stands for 'all people' or 'all things'; as ADJECTIVE, e.g. *eall here byþ hwæt* 'every army is bold' (34/31), where *eall* describes the noun. But many cases are syntactically ambiguous: *ðe wē ealle ġecnāwan mæġen* 'which we all may know' (5/50). Here it can be argued that *ealle* is not so much an adjective describing *wē* as another pronoun, in apposition to it (i.e. standing grammatically parallel with it), as though it were 'we, all of us, . . .'. In the Glossary, an attempt has been made to give representative examples of these words distinguished according to apparent pronominal or adjectival use; but we interpret these constructions in exactly the same way, however we choose to analyse them.

§A7 Relative Pronouns

(i) The most common relative pronoun is the indeclinable RELATIVE PARTICLE *þe*; it serves for all genders and numbers and may be translated 'who', 'which' or 'that', as appropriate, e.g. *his ēahðyrl ðe hē on ðām arce gemacode* 'his window which he had made in the ark' (13/1), *wē þe gelyfað Crīstes ǣriste* 'we who believe in Christ's resurrection' (22/72–3).

(ii) As noted in §A1a.v, the DEMONSTRATIVE pronoun may be used as a relative pronoun, e.g. *þurh þone gelīffæste se Fæder ealle þā gesceafta* 'through whom the Father brought to life all created things' (16/54). Very often, a demonstrative is paired with *þe*, e.g. *þā þe on synnum lyfiað* 'those who live in sin' (2a/19). Often in translation a single relative pronoun is sufficient, e.g. *sum mæsseprēost, sē þe mīn magister wæs* 'a certain mass-priest, who was my master [lit. "he who"]' (16/12). Whether or not a pronoun is being used relatively is sometimes a moot point, depending on how we notionally punctuate a sentence (see, for instance, 24/31n).

§B NOUNS

Overview

Every OE noun belongs to one of the three GENDERS – masculine, neuter or feminine (though a few behave inconsistently, wavering between two or even all three of them). Gender does not necessarily correspond with sex; for example, *wīf* 'woman' is neuter (*þæt wīf* 'the woman'), not feminine, and a pronoun referring to *wīf* ought therefore to be neuter (so that 'she' would be *hit*, literally 'it'). In fact, OE was already tending to ignore this tradition and to move towards 'natural' gender; for examples, see 1/7, 5/23 and 9a/35. Usually, the gender of a noun has to be learned, but in a few cases it can be identified from the noun's form [§§B1 and 3].

The nouns of OE and their systems of declension have traditionally been classified on historical principles, taking account of the forms which they had long before the founding of Anglo-Saxon England, in the ancestral Germanic language from which OE derived. Very many masc. and neut. nouns, for example, belong to the '*a*-**declension**', so called because historically their case-endings in the singular incorporated an *a*: for example, the nom. form of OE *stān*, 'stone', is assumed to have been originally *stānaz*. The other two main declensions are the '*o*-**declension**', restricted to fem. nouns, and the '*i*-**declension**', to which belonged nouns from all three genders; as with *a*-nouns, the identifying vowels *o* and *i* no longer appear in the OE forms. Many nouns left their traditional declensions and took on the characteristics of others (especially the *a*-declension), and many anomalies arose due to sound-change through time. The *a*-, *o*- and *i*-declensions, with their various subdivisions ('*wa*-' and '*ia*-nouns', for instance), plus some so-called 'minor' declensions, are often described (not very helpfully) as the 'strong' declensions [§§B1–4]; they contrast with a so-called 'weak' declension (containing nouns of each gender), which is, however, more usefully known as the '*n*-**declension**', since -*n* is the dominant inflection [§B5]. The simplified system of classification used below is based primarily on gender, rather than on historical principles, and is designed to describe how nouns actually behave in the texts included in this Reader. The complexity of noun declension is far less than may at first appear, for many inflections are shared (as they are in adjectives and pronouns also). The following patterns may be observed:

  (i)   Nom. and acc. forms are the same in all *neut.* nouns in the sg., and for nouns of *all* genders in the pl.
 (ii)   Gen. and dat. endings are shared by masc. and neut. nouns.
(iii)   Fem. gen. and dat. forms are the same in the singular.
 (iv)   The ending -*(e)s* signals the gen. case in masc. and neut. nouns in the sg. (but the fem. ending is -*e*).
  (v)   The ending -*m* marks the dat. case; in the pl., *all* nouns and adjectives end in -*um* (though this may be spelled -*an* or -*on* in late writings).
 (vi)   The ending -*a* (sometimes -*ena*) is characteristic of (though not exclusive to) the genitive plural case in *all* nouns.

Some essential terminology

A SHORT SYLLABLE is one with a short vowel, e.g. the single syllable of *scip* or the first syllable of *metod* (*met*-). A LONG SYLLABLE is one in which either there is a long vowel, e.g. *stān*, or a short vowel followed by two consonants, e.g. *word* and the first syllable of *engel* (*eng*-). The STEM of a word is the most basic form, without the addition of suffixes or inflections; *eng* is the stem of *engel* – and is LONG because formed of a long syllable, and *met* is the stem of *metod* – and is SHORT. The prefix *ġe* is ignored when assessing syllable-structure; thus *ġebed* is treated as a short-stemmed monosyllable.

On the use of the CASES – nom(inative), acc(usative), gen(itive) and dat(ive) – see §D. Separate *instrumental* forms [§D5] are not shown in the noun-paradigms, for when this case occurs, its form is invariably the same as the dative. It is, however, identified where appropriate in the Glossary.

§B1 Masculine Nouns

Almost half of OE nouns are masc. Always masc. are nouns in *-dom, -els, -hād* and *-scipe,* 'agent' nouns in *-end* and *-ere,* and abstract nouns in *-ing* and *-ling.*

The General Masculine Declension [the 'a-Declension']

§B1a The pattern of **stān**, 'stone', is followed by most monosyllabic nouns and by disyllabic nouns with long second syllable, plus a few with two short syllables.

	Sg.	*Pl.*
Nom.	stān	stānas
Acc.	stān	stānas
Gen.	stānes	stāna
Dat.	stāne	stānum

So also *hlāf* 'bread', *mūþ* 'mouth', *prēost* 'priest', *biscop* 'bishop', *cyning* 'king', *hlāford* 'lord', *wīsdōm* 'wisdom', and many others. *Hām* 'home' often occurs without inflection in the dat. when location is expressed (examples: 1/21, 7a/7). Monosyllables ending in a doubled consonant may simplify in the uninflected form: e.g. *weal(l)* 'wall'.

Variations in the Masculine Declension

§B1b DISYLLABLES with long first and short second syllable, and a few with a short first syllable, usually show *syncopation* (i.e. contraction) of the second syllable when the inflections are added; thus **engel** 'angel':

	Sg.	*Pl.*
Nom.	engel	englas
Acc.	engel	englas
Gen.	engles	engla
Dat.	engle	englum

Similar are *dēofol* 'devil', *dryhten* 'lord', *ealdor* 'leader', *ellen* 'courage', *finger* 'finger', *heofon* 'heaven', *mōnaþ* 'month', and others.

(i) In nouns ending in *l, r, m* and *n,* the vowel of the second syllable (which was in any case an historical accretion) sometimes does not show up in the uninflected forms either: *fugl* 'bird' (also *fugol*), *nægl* 'nail' (also *nægel*), *þegn* 'thegn' (also *þegen*). But conversely, the 'floating' vowel may after all show up in *inflected* forms: thus *fugelas* (as well as *fuglas*).

§B1c In monosyllables with *æ*, this becomes *a* in the plural; thus **dæġ** 'day':

	Sg.	Pl.
Nom.	dæġ	dagas
Acc.	dæġ	dagas
Gen.	dæġes	daga
Dat.	dæġe	dagum

So *hwæl* 'whale', *pæþ* 'path', *stæf* 'letter', and others. The same pattern may be followed by long-stemmed *mǣġ* 'kinsman' in late WS, giving nom./acc. pl. *māgas*, but *mǣgas* also occurs. In *dæġ* itself, an uninflected dat. sg. form may occur (for examples, see 1/22, 27, 6/17).

§B1d In stems ending in *-lh* and *-rh*, the *h* is dropped in declined forms and the stem vowel lengthens; thus **wealh** 'foreigner':

	Sg.	Pl.
Nom.	wealh	wēalas
Acc.	wealh	wēalas
Gen.	wēales	wēala
Dat.	wēale	wēalum

Similarly *mearh* 'horse' gives *mēares*, *mēare*, etc. In such nouns, *g* often replaces *h* (thus *mearg*).

§B1e In stems ending in a VOWEL/DIPHTHONG + *h*, the endings are those of *stān* but the *h* and the unstressed vowel of the inflections *-es* and *-as* are absorbed: *sceōh* 'shoe' (*sceōs*, *sceō*, *sceōna*, *sceō(u)m* or *sceō*), *eoh* 'horse' (*eōs*, etc) and *hōh* 'heel' (*hōs*, etc).

§B1f *w*-NOUNS. In **bearo** 'grove' (deriving from the '*wa*-declension', in which *w* was part of the stem), *w* is present before inflections: *bearwes*, *bearwe*, *bearwas*, *bearwa*, *bearwum*; the *o* may be retained also: *bearowe*. Other nouns, ostensibly of this type, have (usually) retained the *w* and behave as 1a nouns (e.g. *þēow* 'servant', *þēaw* 'custom').

§B1g NOUNS IN *-e* (associated with the '*i*-declension') are declined like *stān* with the *-e* dropped in the pl. Thus **ende** 'end':

	Sg.	Pl.
Nom.	ende	endas
Acc.	ende	endas
Gen.	endes	enda
Dat.	ende	endum

So also *ege* 'fear', *fiscere* 'fisherman' (and other agent nouns in *-ere*), *hyrde* 'shepherd', *hyġe* 'thought', *mēċe* 'sword', *siġe* 'victory', and others; and nouns in *-scipe* (e.g. *ġebeorscipe* 'feast', *wurþscipe* 'honour'). There were many more of this type, but most lost the *e* and now behave as 1a nouns.

(i) A few nouns in -*e* have an alternative nom./acc. pl. in -*e* also, instead of the expected -*as*: *cwide* 'saying', *stede* 'place', *wine* 'friend' (with an alternative gen. pl. *winiġ(e)a*).

(ii) ***here*** 'army' often has *g(e)* or *iġ(e)* before case-endings: *her(i)ġes*, *her(i)ġe*, *her(i)ġ(e)as*, *her(i)ġ(e)a*, *her(i)gum*.

(iii) A few nouns double the medial consonant in the pl.: *hyse* 'warrior' (*hyssas*), *mete* 'food' (*mettas*).

(iv) *sǣ* 'sea' belongs here but is reduced to nom./acc./dat. sg. *sǣ*, gen. sg. and nom./acc. pl. *sǣs*, and dat. pl. *sǣm*. It may also be treated as a fem. noun, with *sǣ* throughout the sg. and in the nom./acc. pl.

§B1h PLURAL-ONLY NOUNS IN -*e*. A few nouns occurring only in the pl. have nom./acc. -*e*. They include *ælde* (also *ielde* or *ylde*) 'men', along with the names of tribes or peoples: see §B6.

§B2 Neuter Nouns

The General Neuter Declension [the 'a-Declension']

§B2a SHORT-STEMMED NOUNS, as **scip** 'ship':

	Sg.	Pl.
Nom.	scip	scipu
Acc.	scip	scipu
Gen.	scipes	scipa
Dat.	scipe	scipum

So also *ġebed* 'prayer', *hliþ* 'slope', *hof* 'dwelling', *lim* 'limb' (with pl. *limu* or *leomu*), *ġewrit* 'letter', and many others. In later WS, -*a* often occurs for -*u* in the plural.

§B2b LONG-STEMMED NOUNS, as **word** 'word':

	Sg.	Pl.
Nom.	word	word
Acc.	word	word
Gen.	wordes	worda
Dat.	worde	wordum

So also *bān* 'bone', *bearn* 'son', *brēost* 'breast', *hūs* 'house', *land* 'country', *mōd* 'mind', *ġeþanc* 'thought', *þing* 'thing', and many others. *Brēost* is used mostly in the pl. (examples: 23/118, 34/17).

(i) In nouns ending with a DOUBLED CONSONANT (and thus long-stemmed, like *word*), this is very often simplified when there is no inflection: *bil(l)* 'sword' (dat. sg. *bille*, gen. pl. *billa*, etc), *hlot(t)* 'lot', *geswel(l)* 'swelling', *wed(d)* 'pledge', and others.

(ii) Like *word* are DISYLLABLES with long second syllable, e.g. *īsern* 'iron' (whose late form is *īren(n)*); or with two short syllables but stress on the first, e.g. *reced* 'hall', *werod* 'troop' (but nom./acc. pl. *weredu* also occurs).

(iii) **cild** 'child' may follow *word* but has the alternative pl. endings of *scip*, with added *-r-*: *cildru, cildra, cildrum* (cf. ModE 'children' and dialect 'childer'). Similarly **ǣġ** 'egg': *ǣġru, ǣġra, ǣġrum*. Linguists sometimes classify these and similar nouns (including *lomb* 'lamb' and *cealf* 'calf') as members of an '*er*-declension'.

Variations in the Neuter Declension

§B2c In DISYLLABLES with short second syllable, there is often *syncopation* (see §B1b), and the endings are those of *scip*. Thus **wuldor** 'glory':

	Sg.	Pl.
Nom.	wuldor	wuldru
Acc.	wuldor	wuldru
Gen.	wuldres	wuldra
Dat.	wuldre	wuldrum

So also *morþor* 'murder', *tungol* 'star', *wæter* 'water', *wundor* 'marvel', and others. In the case of **hēafod** 'head', the nom./acc. pl. form *hēafod* occurs, as well as *hēafdu*; a 'locative' dat. sg. form *heafdum* occurs too (for an example, see 23/63). **Mynster** 'church' has an endingless locative form, especially in names (examples: 11/8, 12/63).

(i) The medial vowel is often, or in some cases nearly always, absent from the nom. sg. form also: *beac(e)n* 'beacon', *fāc(e)n* 'sin', *hrægl* 'garment', *husl* 'housel', *setl* 'seat', *tāc(e)n* 'sign', *wǣp(e)n* 'weapon', *wolc(e)n* 'cloud'.

(ii) Nouns with the diminutive suffix *-en* do not usually show syncopation but still add *-u* in the pl.; there is often doubling of *-n* before the dat. sg. *-e* inflection: *mǣden* 'maiden' (dat. sg. *mǣdenne*), *nȳten* 'animal' (nom. pl. *nȳtenu*).

(iii) Several nouns originally ending in *-enn* or *-ett* tend to simplify the double consonant in their uninflected forms but usually retain it elsewhere; there is no syncopation: *ǣfen* 'evening' (dat. sg. *ǣfenne*), *fæsten* 'fastness' (*fæstenne*), *liġet* 'flame' (*liġette*), *bærnet* 'burning' (*bærnette*).

§B2d In monosyllables with **æ**, this becomes *a* in the plural: so *fæt* 'vessel' (*fatu*, *fata*, *fatum*), *bæc* 'back', *bæþ* 'bath', and *dæl* 'valley'. Note also **ġeat** 'gate', with nom./acc. pl. *gatu* (though *ġeatu* also occurs).

§B2e In stems in **-rh**, *h* is lost in inflection and the stem vowel then lengthens. So **feorh** 'life':

	Sg.	Pl.
Nom.	feorh	feorh
Acc.	feorh	feorh
Gen.	fēores	fēora
Dat.	fēore	fēorum

Interchange of *h* and *g* is frequent in *rh*-stems: *feorg*.

§B2f In stems ending in a VOWEL/DIPHTHONG + **h**, the *h* is dropped and the unstressed vowel of the inflection is absorbed: *feoh* 'money' has gen. sg. *fēos*, dat. sg. *fēo* (there is no pl.); *wōh* 'error' has dat. sg. *wō* or *wōge*, nom./acc. pl. *wōh*; and *blēo* 'colour' may have *h* in nom./acc. pl. only.

§B2g **w-NOUNS.** In a few nouns ending in *-u* or *-o* (originating in the '*wa*-declension'; cf. §§B1f and B3f), a *w* is present before inflection and the *-o/u* is usually, but not always, dropped. Thus **searu** (or *searo*) 'device':

	Sg.	Pl.
Nom.	searu	searu
Acc.	searu	searu
Gen.	searwes	searwa
Dat.	searwe	searwum

So also *bealu* 'harm', *lysu* 'evil', and *melu* 'meal'. When the vowel is retained, its form may vary: *bealowes, bealuwes, melewes, searowa*, etc. Nom./acc. pl. often appear with *-a*.

(i) In nouns with stem in **-eow**, the *w* may appear in the uninflected forms also: *cnēo(w)* 'knee', *hlēo(w)* 'protector' and *trēo(w)* 'tree'.

§B2h **NOUNS IN -e** (originating in the '*i*-declension') are declined like *scip* with the *-e* dropped in the pl. Thus **spere** 'spear':

	Sg.	Pl.
Nom.	spere	speru
Acc.	spere	speru
Gen.	speres	spera
Dat.	spere	sperum

So also *ǣrende* 'message', *ierfe* 'inheritance', *ġemǣre* 'boundary', *rīċe* 'kingdom' (with alternative nom./acc. pl. *rīċiu*), *ġeþēode* 'language', *wīte* 'punishment', and others. There were many more of this type but most lost the -*e* and behave as type 2b or 2b.i nouns. In later WS, -*a* often occurs for -*u* in the pl.

§B2i NEUT./FEM. NOUNS. There is a group of long-syllable nouns which fluctuate between neut. and fem. (type 3g); their pl. is the neut. -*u*: *wiht* 'creature', *fulwiht* 'baptism', *ġecynd* 'race', *ġehyġd* 'thought', *ġemynd* 'memory', *ġesceaft* 'creation', *ġeþeaht* 'counsel', *ġeþyld* 'patience', and others. In ABSTRACT nouns of this type, the pl. forms in -*u* are often treated as indeclinable fem. sg., and thus become type 3h nouns (see below).

§B3 Feminine Nouns

Always fem. are nouns in -*nes* (or -*nis*/*nys*), -*ung*, -*rǣden* and -*þu* (or *þo*), and abstract nouns in -*ing*.

The General Feminine Declension [the 'o-Declension']

§B3a SHORT STEMMED NOUNS, as **ġiefu** (or *ġifu*) 'gift':

	Sg.	Pl.
Nom.	ġiefu	ġiefa, -e
Acc.	ġiefe	ġiefa, -e
Gen.	ġiefe	ġiefa, -ena
Dat.	ġiefe	ġiefum

So also *andswaru* 'answer', *cwalu* 'death', *frymþu* 'beginning' (which often loses its -*u*), *scamu* 'shame', and others; *lufu* 'love' often adopts these forms but is primarily an *n*-noun [§B5c].

(i) Rarely, stems with ***a*** change this to *æ* in inflected forms: thus *wracu* 'vengeance', acc. sg. *wræce* (as well as *wrace*).

§B3b LONG-STEMMED NOUNS, as **lār** 'teaching':

	Sg.	Pl.
Nom.	lār	lāra, -e
Acc.	lāre	lāra, -e
Gen.	lāre	lāra
Dat.	lāre	lārum

So also *ār* 'grace', *bricg* 'bridge', *healf* 'half', *rest* 'rest', *rōd* 'cross', *sorg* 'sorrow', *stōw* 'place', *þēod* 'people', and others.

Variations in the Feminine Declension

§B3c DISYLLABIC NOUNS with a short second syllable do not take -*u* in the nom. sg. and usually *syncopate* their medial vowel in inflected forms: *ċeaster* 'town' (*ċeastre, ċeastra, ċeastrum*); *feþer* 'feather' (*feþre*, etc), *frōfor* 'comfort' (*frōfre*, etc), *sāwol* 'soul' (*sāwle*, etc).

(i) Some of these nouns rarely show the medial vowel even in their uninflected forms: *ādl* 'illness', *eaxl* 'shoulder', *nǣdl* 'needle', *stefn* 'voice'.

§B3d ABSTRACT NOUNS in -*ung* and -*ing* may decline like *lār*; but in early and later WS -*a* is often used for acc./dat. sg., as well as for nom./acc. pl. (e.g. acc./dat. sg. *liornunga*, 5/10, 53; dat. sg. *geþafunga*, 11/6).

§B3e In nouns (usually monosyllables) ending in a DOUBLED CONSONANT (and hence long-stemmed) there is often *simplification* in the nom. sg. form, and sometimes in inflected forms also, but there is much inconsistency: *ben(n)* 'wound', *heal(l)* 'hall', *hel(l)* 'hell', *sib(b)* 'peace', *syn(n)* 'sin'.

(i) Doubling occurs also in nouns in -*en(n)*, including abstract nouns such as *woroldrǣden* 'worldly rule' (acc. sg. *woroldrǣdenne*), and those derived from masc. nouns, such as *þīnen* 'handmaiden' (dat. sg. *þīnenne*). However, *þēowen* 'servant' more often than not behaves as a 3c noun, with syncopation.

(ii) Similar are nouns in -*is(s)*, such as *blis* 'happiness' (dat. sg. *blisse*), *cnēoris* 'tribe', and the many nouns in -*nes*/-*nis*/-*nys*, such as *fæġernes* 'beauty' (acc. pl. *fæġernissa*), *stilnes* 'peace'. Sometimes the doubled *s* is found in the uninflected form also.

§B3f *w*-NOUNS. A few nouns (deriving from the '*wo*-declension'; cf. §B1f and §B2g) have *w* before inflections: *beadu* 'battle' (in which -*u* is often retained: *bead(u)we, beadwa, beadwum*), *lǣs* 'pasture' (*lǣswe*, but note dat. pl. *lǣsum*). *Þrēa* 'pain' belongs here but has lost the *w* throughout and now has the nom. sg. form in all cases, sg. and pl., except dat. pl.

§B3g INFLECTIONLESS ACCUSATIVE NOUNS. An important group of nouns, with long stem-syllable, may have acc. sg. the same as nom. sg. They derive from the '*i*-declension'. Thus **cwēn** 'woman':

	Sg.	*Pl.*
Nom.	cwēn	cwēna, -e
Acc.	cwēn, -e	cwēna, -e
Gen.	cwēne	cwēna
Dat.	cwēne	cwēnum

So also *ǣht* 'property', *dǣd* 'deed', *fyrd* 'army', *hyht* 'hope', *miht* (or *meaht*) 'power', *nīed* 'necessity', *tīd* 'time', *wynn* 'joy', *wyrd* 'fate', and others. There were many more nouns of this type, but most adopted the endings of the '*o*-declension' [§B3a].

(i) Three other nouns belong here: *ǣ* 'law' is often unchanged in all sg. cases and in nom./acc. pl. (but may have *ǣwe* in the gen./dat. sg.); **woruld** 'world' usually behaves as a type 3g noun; *ǣrist* 'resurrection' does also (acc. sg. *ǣriste*: 22/2, 33), but sometimes shows the endings of a masc. 1b noun (gen. sg. *ǣristes*: 22/64, 97).

§B3h A number of ABSTRACT NOUNS in -*þu* or -*u* (or -*þo* or -*o*), mostly formed from adjectives, may stay unchanged in all sg. cases and in nom./acc. pl.; alternatively, -*e* may occur in these cases (or -*a* in nom./acc. pl.). The -*u* (or -*o*) of the nom. sg. is often dropped. Gen. and dat. pl. are regular (-*a* and -*um*). Thus *bisgo* 'trouble' (dat. sg. *bisgo*, dat. pl. *bisgum*) and *yrhþo* 'cowardice' (acc. sg. *yrhþo* and *yrhþe*). Other common examples are *fyrhtu* 'fear', *yrmþ(u)* 'misery', *mǣrþu* 'glory', *yldo* 'age', *menigeo* 'multitude', *ġesynto* 'welfare' and *þȳstro* 'darkness'. Apparently *ġebǣro* 'demeanour' belongs here, though its form has also been interpreted as a neut. pl.

§B4 Minor Declensions

§B4a THE '*u*-DECLENSION'

A few masc. and fem. nouns belong here, their most notable feature being gen./dat. sg. in -*a*. There are two variations, represented by masc. **sunu** 'son' (short stem) and fem. **hand** 'hand' (long stem).

	Sg.	*Pl.*	*Sg.*	*Pl.*
Nom.	sunu	suna	hand	handa
Acc.	sunu	suna	hand	handa
Gen.	suna	suna	handa	handa
Dat.	suna	sunum	handa	handum

Like *sunu* are masc. *lagu* 'lake', *magu* 'youth', *medu* 'mede', *wudu* 'wood', and fem. *duru* 'door'. Like *hand* are masc. *æppel* 'apple', *feld* 'field' and *ford* 'ford'.

§B4b STEMS WITH '*i*-MUTATION'

Early in the history of the Germanic languages, there was a widespread process of MUTATION (i.e. modification) in the pronunciation of the stem-vowels of nouns when the next syllable (usually an inflection) contained an -*i*. In anticipation of producing this *i*, the shape of the mouth modified while the stem-vowel was still being articulated, and so the latter's quality mutated towards that of *i*. One effect of this was that *a* and *o* began to sound more and more like *e*. As the language developed, the change-inducing *i* disappeared from the words in question, but its effect remained in the dat. sg. and nom./acc. pl., and sometimes in the gen. sg. also. Two prominent OE examples of nouns affected by this '*i*-mutation' are masc.

mann 'man' (originally *maniz*) and fem. **bōc** 'book' (originally *bōkiz*); nom. and acc. sg. are not distinguished in either gender.

	Sg.	Pl.	Sg.	Pl.
Nom.	mann	menn	bōc	bēċ
Acc.	mann	menn	bōc	bēċ
Gen.	mannes	manna	bēċ, bōce	bōca
Dat.	menn	mannum	bēċ	bōcum

Other examples are masc. *fōt* 'foot'(dat. sg. and nom./acc. pl. *fēt*) and *tōþ* 'tooth' (*tēþ*); and fem. *burg* (or *burh*) 'fortification' (*byriġ*), *gōs* 'goose' (*gēs*), *lūs* 'louse' (*lȳs*) and *mūs* 'mouse' (*mȳs*). Most of these anomalies survived into ModE. So also fem. *sulh* 'plough' (*syl*) and *þrūh* 'tomb' (*þrȳh*), in both of which there may be loss of the *-h*.

(i) **niht** 'night': Mutated forms predominate (*niht* itself is one) but others occur also, resulting in a range of forms that include acc. sg. *neaht* (as well as *niht*) and dat. sg. *neahte*; pl. forms are nom./acc. *niht*, gen. *nihta*, dat. *nihtum*.

(ii) **ēa** 'river': The one form can be used for all cases, except dat. pl. (which is *ēaum*, *ēam* or *ēan*).

(iii) **meol(u)c** 'milk': Mutated forms, such as dat. pl. *milcum*, seem to appear in Anglian but not in WS, which has *meolcum*. The latter may be used as a 'locative' dat. sg. form; see 3c/4.

§B4c NOUNS OF RELATIONSHIP IN *-r*

Although always regular in the gen. and dat. pl., these nouns may remain uninflected in all the other cases, but commonly there is an '*i*-mutated' stem in the dat. sg. Collectively, they are sometimes ascribed to an '*r*-declension'. Thus masc. **brōþor** 'brother' (also *brōþer*, *brōþur*):

	Sg.	Pl.
Nom.	brōþor	brōþor
Acc.	brōþor	brōþor
Gen.	brōþor	brōþra
Dat.	brēþer	brōþrum

So also fem. *mōdor* 'mother' (with alternative dat. sg. *mēder*) and *dohtor* 'daughter' (*dehter*), where the mutated dat. sg. forms may also occur for the gen. sg. The alternative nom./acc. pl. forms *dohtru*/*dohtra* and *mōdra*/*mōdru* occur. Similar is fem. *sweostor* 'sister', but this is unchanged in the dat. sg.; there is great variety in the vowels of both the stem and the second syllable: *swustor*, *swuster*, *swostor*, etc.

(i) **fæder** 'father': This noun belongs to §B1a (with nom./acc. pl. *fæderas*), but it retains the form *fæder* in the dat. sg. and sometimes in the gen. sg.

§B4d NOUNS IN -*end*

These are AGENT NOUNS (all masc.), derived from the present participles of verbs (and sometimes collectively ascribed to an '*nd*-declension'). They have alternative inflections, or no inflection, in the nom./acc. pl. and insert an *r* before the gen. pl. ending. So **wīġend** 'warrior':

	Sg.	Pl.
Nom.	wīġend	wīġend, -as, -e
Acc.	wīġend	wīġend, -as, -e
Gen.	wīġendes	wīġendra
Dat.	wīġende	wīġendum

So also *āġend* 'owner', *dēmand* 'judge', *hǣlend* 'saviour', *wealdend* 'ruler', and many others.

(i) **frēond** 'friend' and **fēond** 'enemy' belong here but also show *i*-mutation [§B4b]; thus dat. sg. and nom./acc. pl. *frȳnd* and *fȳnd*. But 'regular' dat. sg. *frēonde* and *fēonde* occur, and also nom./acc. pl. *frēondas* and *fēondas*.

§B4e NOUNS WITH A *þ*-STEM

A few nouns of all genders in -*þ* have an alternative uninflected pl., in addition to that expected for nouns of their gender. Thus masc. **hæleþ** 'man':

	Sg.	Pl.
Nom.	hæleþ	hæleþ, -as
Acc.	hæleþ	hæleþ, -as
Gen.	hæleþes	hæleþa
Dat.	hæleþe	hæleþum

So also masc. *mōnaþ* 'month', in which the medial vowel is usually elided before inflection (*mōnþe*, *mōnþas*, etc). For *hæleþ*, the older form *hæle* occurs in poetry for nom./acc. sg. (example: 32/73).

(i) Fem. **mæġ(e)þ** 'maiden' has nom./acc/ pl. *mæġ(e)þ* or *mæġ(e)þe*; the uninflected form may also appear in gen./dat. sg. Also in this sub-group is neut. **ealu** 'ale', which appears as *ealoþ* in gen. and dat. sg.

§B5 The *n*-Declension

This is also known as the WEAK DECLENSION. The majority of OE nouns in -*a* (nearly all masc.) are '*n*-nouns', along with many in -*e* (most fem., with a few neut.).

§B5a MASC. **nama** 'name':

	Sg.	Pl.
Nom.	nama	naman
Acc.	naman	naman
Gen.	naman	namena
Dat.	naman	namum

§B5b NEUT. **ēage** 'eye':

	Sg.	Pl.
Nom.	ēage	ēagan
Acc.	ēage	ēagan
Gen.	ēagan	ēag(e)na
Dat.	ēagan	ēagum

§B5c FEM. NOUNS in *-e*, follow the pattern of *nama*, except for nom. sg. Thus *sunne* 'sun': acc. sg. *sunnan*, etc. Short-stemmed fem. nouns often adopt the nom. sg. form of fem. 3a-type nouns in *-u* (such as *giefu*) but usually still decline 'weak'; they include *wicu* 'week' (acc. sg. *wican*, etc). An oddity is **lufu** 'love', which is often declined 'strong', as a 3a-type noun (acc. sg. *lufe*: 6/59), as well as 'weak' (acc. sg. *lufan*: 26/112).

§B5d Nouns with a LONG VOWEL or DIPHTHONG in the nom. sg. have *-na* in the gen. pl. and *-m* in the dat. pl., with all other cases in *-n*: masc. *ġefēa* 'joy' (*ġefēan*; gen. pl. *ġefēana*; dat. pl. *ġefēam*); masc. *ġefā* 'enemy' (*ġefān*, *ġefāna*); fem. *sēo* 'pupil (of the eye)' (acc. sg. *sēon*, etc).

§B6 Proper Names

There is much variation and inconsistency in the inflection of proper names, but some observations may be made.

§B6a NATIVE NAMES OF PERSONS characteristically consist of two elements, the second of which will usually be an OE noun whose regular declension is followed: *Æþelrēd* (< *rǣd* m:B1a): gen. *Æþelrēdes*, dat. *Æþelrēde*; *Ælfġyfu* (< *ġyfu* f:B3a): acc./gen./dat. *Ælfġyfe*. Some have the form of '*n*-nouns' and are declined accordingly: *Ċeola* (m:B5a): acc./gen./dat. *Ċeolan*.

§B6b FOREIGN NAMES OF PERSONS may follow the pattern of native names, e.g. *Abraham* (m:B1a): gen. *Abrahames*, dat. *Abrahame*. But Latin names are sometimes declined as in Latin, or with a mixture of native and Latin endings, e.g.

Lat. nom. *Petrus* ('Peter'), Lat. acc. *Petrum*, OE dat. *Petre*; Lat. nom. *Agustinus* ('Augustine'), OE 'gen.' *Augustinus*; *Agustus* ('Augustus'), Lat. dat. *Augusto*.

§B6c NATIVE PLACE-NAMES and the names of COUNTRIES are often compounds, their second elements being a topographical or administrative designation; the latter determine the gender of the name and decline regularly, e.g. *Lēġċeaster* 'Chester' (f:B3c *ċeaster*): acc./dat. *Lēġċeastre*; *Mǣldūn* 'Maldon' (f:3b *dūn*): dat. *Mǣldūne*; *Defnanscīr* 'Devonshire' (f:B3b *scīr*): acc./dat. *Defnanscīre*; *Cumerland* 'Cumberland' (n:B2b *land*): dat. *Cumerlande*.

However, names in *-hām*, *-mynster* and *-wīc* often have an endingless 'locative' dat., e.g. *Hæfæreshām* (11/14), *Worġemynster* (12/63), *Ascanmynster* (29/36), *Gyssīċ* (last element originally *wīċ*; 11/15).

§B6d NAMES OF TRIBES and PEOPLES are usually in the pl., with one of two endings in the nom.:

(i) *-as* [m:B1a]: So *Bryttas* 'Britons' (gen. pl. *Brytta*), *Cornwēalas* 'the Cornish' or 'Cornwall' (dat. pl. *Cornwēalum*).

(ii) *-e* [m:B1h]: So *Dene* 'Danes' (gen. pl. *Dena* or *Deniġ(e)a*), *Engle* 'English', *Ēote* 'Jutes' (gen. pl. *Ēotena*; *Ēotan* and *Ēotenas* have also been conjectured as the nom. pl. forms), *Mierċe* 'Mercians' (gen. pl. *Mierċna*), *Norþymbre* 'Northumbrians', *Seaxe* 'Saxons' (but nom./acc. pl. *Seaxan* also occurs; gen. pl. *Seaxna*, dat. pl. *Seaxum*), and names in *-ware* and *-sǣte*, such as *Cantware* 'people of Kent' and *Sumorsǣte* 'people of Somerset'.

§C ADJECTIVES

Overview

Adjectives describe nouns and must be in grammatical concord with them, but most of them may take two different sets of endings, known as 'weak' and 'strong', which are used in specific circumstances, as described in §C1. The terms 'strong' or 'weak' are also sometimes used to describe noun declensions [§B/overview], but the concept of strong and weak adjectives is unconnected with this. The inflections which an adjective adopts are determined purely by the circumstances of its use, not the sort of noun to which it is attached.

§C1 The Use of Weak and Strong Adjectives

The inflections described below in §§C2–6 are used as follows:

(a) If the noun described already has the support of a definite article, the WEAK endings are used: *þā gōdan menn* 'those good men'.

(b) If the noun stands alone, the STRONG endings must be used: *gōde menn*, 'good men'.

(c) A few adjectives decline only weak *or* only strong:

Always WEAK: *ilca* 'same'; comparatives (e.g. *lengra* 'longer'); ordinal numerals [§E2] (e.g. *þridda* 'third'), except *ōþer* 'second'.

Always STRONG: *eall* 'all'; *fēa* 'few'; *ġenōg* 'enough'; *maniġ* 'many'; *ōþer* 'other' or 'second'; and possessive pronoun/adjectives (*mīn* 'my', *þīn* 'your', etc) [§A4].

(d) When an adjective is used predicatively, i.e. when it follows its noun after an intervening form of 'to be', it may be inflected, using the STRONG endings, but as often as not will carry no inflection, especially in later OE; e.g. *sēo bōc is gōdu* or *sēo bōc is gōd*, 'the book is good'.

§C2 Weak Forms

The weak endings of adjectives show little variation and closely resemble those of *n*-nouns [§B5]. Thus **dol** 'foolish':

	Sg.			Pl.
	Masc.	Neut.	Fem.	All genders
Nom.	dola	dole	dole	dolan
Acc.	dolan	dole	dolan	dolan
Gen.	dolan	dolan	dolan	dolra, dolena
Dat./Instr.	dolan	dolan	dolan	dolum

1 The gen. pl. form with *r* may cause confusion with the comparative form of adjectives [§C6].

§C3 Strong Forms

Strong adjectival endings closely resemble those of most nouns and pronouns. It should be noted that strong adjectives have a distinct inflection for the *instrumental case* [§D5] in masc. and neut. sing.

(a) SHORT-STEMMED MONOSYLLABLES. So **dol** 'foolish':

	Sg.			Pl.		
	Masc.	Neut.	Fem.	Masc.	Neut.	Fem.
Nom.	dol	dol	dolu	dole	dolu, -e	dola, -e
Acc.	dolne	dol	dole	dole	dolu, -e	dola, -e
Gen.	doles	doles	dolre	dolra	dolra	dolra
Dat.	dolum	dolum	dolre	dolum	dolum	dolum
Instr.	dole	dole				

1 Like *dol* are compound adjectives in *-lić* (*heofonlić* 'heavenly') and *-sum* (*wynsum* 'pleasant').

2 Possible confusion between the parallel nom. sg. fem and nom./acc. pl. neut. forms should be noted.

3 Nom./acc. pl. neut. *-u* is found in poetry and older prose texts, but in later WS, *-e* is commonly used; similarly, nom./acc. pl. fem. *-a* is usually replaced by *-e* in later texts. Thus the nom./acc. pl. forms in the masc., neut. and fem. may be the same.

4 Occasionally, *-o* occurs for *-u* in nom. sg. fem. and nom./acc. pl. neut.

(b) LONG-STEMMED MONOSYLLABLES: These differ from the forms in (a) only in that there is *no inflection* in the *nom. sg. fem.* and *nom./acc. pl. neut.* forms where *dol* has *-u*. Thus, *gōd* 'good' appears simply as unchanged *gōd* in these instances; see the paradigm of *mīn* in §A4.

(c) DISYLLABIC AND OTHER ADJECTIVES:

(i) Where the stressed syllable is SHORT, the pattern of *gōd* (b) is normally followed: e.g. acc. pl. neut. *maniġ* 'many', nom. sg. fem. *ġemyndiġ* 'mindful'.

(ii) Where the stressed syllable is LONG, the pattern of *dol* (a) is usually followed: e.g. nom. sg. fem. *rēotugu* 'mournful', nom. pl. neut. *unstillu* 'moving'.

§C4 Modifications in Disyllables (weak and strong forms)

(a) CONTRACTION: In disyllabic adjectives there may be syncopation before an inflection beginning with a vowel, e.g. strong masc./neut. gen. sg. *hālġes* 'holy', not *hāliġes*; *yfles* 'evil', not *yfeles*; and weak masc. acc. sg. (etc) *miclan* 'great', not *miċelan*. Examples such as the last two, where the stems are short, are very frequent. In syncopated forms of *miċel*, doubled *c* is very common (*micclan*, etc).

(b) ADJECTIVES IN *-e*: These drop the *e* before all inflections, e.g. *blīþe* 'happy' gives masc. acc. sg. *blīþne*, fem. nom. sg. *blīþu*, gen. pl. *blīþra*, etc.

(c) ADJECTIVES IN *-u*: These change *u* to *w* before vowels and to *o* before consonants, e.g. *ġearo* (or *ġearu*) 'ready' gives strong masc. gen. sg. *ġearwes*, acc. sg. *ġearone*.

§C5 Stem-Changes (Weak and Strong Forms)

(a) SHORT-STEMMED MONOSYLLABLES WITH *æ*: There is fluctuation between *æ* and *a*; usually *æ* becomes *a* when the following inflection begins with a vowel. So, from *glæd* 'glad', masc. gen. sg. *glades* and dat. pl. *gladum*, but masc. acc. sg. *glædne* and fem. gen./dat. sg. *glædre*.

(b) ADJECTIVES IN **-h**: The *h* may be dropped or 'voiced' to a *g*. So *hēah* 'high' becomes masc./neut. gen. sg. *hēas*, dat. pl. *hēam* or *hēagum*, fem. gen./dat. sg. *hēare*, nom. pl. *hēa* or *hēage*, etc.

§C6 Comparison of adjectives

(a) Most adjectives form the COMPARATIVE ('more . . .') with **-ra** and the SUPERLATIVE ('most . . .') with **-ost** (or *-ast*, *-ust*):

beorht 'bright'   beorhtra 'brighter'   beorhtost 'brightest'
blīþ 'happy'   blīþra 'happier'   blīþost 'happiest'

> 1 The possible confusion between comparative forms in *-ra* and the similar strong gen. pl. form of the basic adjective [§C2a] should be noted.
> 2 Sometimes the comparative conveys an intensive sense that is best translated with 'very' or 'most', e.g. *syllicre trēow* 'a very (*or* most) wondrous tree' (23/4).

(b) A few adjectives form the comparative regularly with *-ra* but the superlative with **-est**.

eald 'old'   ieldra   ieldest
hēah 'high'   hīehra, hīerra   hīeh(e)st, hēhst
long 'long'   lengra   lengest

(c) IRREGULAR comparison occurs in four very common OE adjectives (and is preserved in ModE):

gōd 'good'   bet(e)ra, sēlra 'better'   betst, sēlest 'best'
yfel 'bad'   wyrsa 'worse'   wyrrest, wyrst 'worst'
miċel 'big'   māra, mǣra 'bigger'   mǣst 'biggest'
lȳtel, lȳt 'little'   lǣssa 'littler', 'less'   lǣs(e)st, lǣrest 'littlest', 'least'

> 1 *wyrsa*, *wyrrest*, *wyrst* appear also as *wiersa*, *wierrest*, *wierst*; *miċel* as *myċel*; and *lȳtel*, *lȳt* as *lītel*, *līt*.

(d) DECLENSION. Comparative and superlative adjectives are declined in the same way as simple adjectives, taking weak or strong endings as appropriate, e.g. *betran*: weak, nom. pl. masc. (6/54); *lēofre*: strong, nom. sg. neut. (1/7); *lēofostan*: weak, nom. pl. masc. (22/69); *ryhtoste*: strong, nom. pl. masc. (7b/8).

§D THE USE OF THE CASES

The 'cases' of nouns (and of the pronouns and adjectives which are dependent on them) are used in a variety of ways to define the noun's function in a phrase or sentence.

§D1 Nominative

(a) For the subject of the verb, e.g. *se hrem flēah . . . ūt* 'the raven flew out' (13/2)

(b) For direct address, e.g. *ēalā lārēow!* 'O teacher!' (1/1).

§D2 Accusative

(a) For the direct object, e.g. *Hē āsende . . . ūt āne culfran* 'He sent out a dove' (13/3–4).

(b) For a reflexive object, e.g. *se rīca hyne reste* 'the ruler rested himself' (19/44). See also §A3.

(c) In adverbial expressions, especially of spatial extent and the duration of time, e.g. *fōtes trym* 'the length of a foot' (30/247), *lītle hwīle* 'for a short time' (8/15).

(d) After certain prepositions, such as *on* 'onto' or 'into' (with motion usually implied), *geond* 'throughout', *ofer* 'over' or 'along', *þurh* 'through', etc; e.g. *on Angelcyn* 'into England' (8/10), *ofer þā wegas* 'along the paths' (15c/10).

(e) In the 'accusative and infinitive' construction: see §G6d.i.3.

§D3 Genitive

(a) For possession, e.g. *ðæs cynges iunge dohtor* 'the king's young daughter' (27/1–2); *ðæra eorðan brādnis* 'the breadth of the earth' (13/13).

(b) Partitive genitive, e.g. *fela manna* 'many men [lit. "of men"]' (25/9), *fēawa hiora* 'few of them' (5/16), *L scillinga* '50 shillings' (7a/6); see also §E3d.

(c) In adverbial expressions of definition, description, time and place, e.g. *ealles* 'altogether' (24/2); *heardes cynnes* 'from tough stock' (30/266); *dæġes ond nihtes* 'day and night' (15a/3); *ūtanbordes* 'abroad' (5/11).

(d) In expressions of respect and comparison, e.g. *Hwæt hæfst þū weorkes?* 'what do you have by way of work?' (1/10); *beaduweorca beteran* 'superior in battle-deeds' (10/48); *þæs* 'in respect of that' or 'to that degree' (21a/76).

(e) For the object of certain verbs, including *brūcan* 'enjoy' (21a/17), *ehtan* 'persecute' (7c/6), *ġefēon* 'rejoice in' (19/205), *forġietan* 'forget' (15b/6), *ġīeman* 'care for' (17/9), *nēotan* 'use' (30/308), *þancian* 'thank for' (27/24) and *wēnan* 'expect' (19/20).

(f) Occasionally after prepositions, such as *wiþ* in the sense of 'towards' (19/248).

§D4 Dative

(a) For the indirect object, e.g. *þæt hē ðone dō nytne ōðrum mannum* 'that he make it useful to other people' (4/6).

(b) For possession: e.g. *healfne . . . þone swēoran him* 'half his neck [lit. "the neck to him"]' (19/105–6).

(c) For reflexive pronouns [§A3], often with verbs of motion and with *ġebiddan* 'pray'; they are usually untranslatable, e.g. *ēodon him þā ūp* 'then they went up' (8/52); *ġebiddaþ him tō þyssum bēacne* 'they will pray to this beacon' (23/83).

(d) With some impersonal verbs [§G5], such as *līcian* 'please', e.g. *heom eallum þearle līcode* '(it) pleased them all greatly' (27/46); and *þynċan* 'seem', e.g. *þūhte mē þæt ic ġesāwe* 'it seemed to me that I saw' (23/4).

(e) After many verbs which today are transitive (i.e. take a direct object) but in OE were considered intransitive, e.g. *iċ . . . mē selfum andwyrde* 'I answered myself [lit. "to myself"]' (5/39). Among others are *ætwindan* 'escape', *beorgan* 'save', *limpan* 'happen', *ġelȳfan* 'believe' and *sceþþan* 'injure'.

(f) In adverbial expressions of time, manner, agency, definition, respect, place and containment, e.g. *hwīlum* 'at times' (5/61); *listum* 'cunningly' (19/101); *sumre tīde* 'at a certain time' (9b/20); *ecgum ġecoste* 'tried in respect of (*or* as to) its edges' (19/231); *ferþe* 'in spirit' (35d/21).

(g) To express instrument, e.g. *atolan clommum* 'with (her) terrible clutches' (31b/11).

(h) After a majority of prepositions: always after *of*; nearly always after *fram*; usually after *be, mid, for, tō*, etc; often after *ǣr, æt, wiþ*, etc.

(i) There is a special usage of the dat. pl., known as the 'locative' dat., to express place or position in a sg. sense, e.g. *æt his līces hēafdum* 'at the head of his body' (23/63); *him . . . in brēostum* 'in his breast' (23/118).

§D5 Instrumental

Originally a separate case expressing manner or instrument, whose function became absorbed into the dat. The case survives mainly in the demonstrative pronouns *þȳ* (or *þī, þē*), *þon* (or *þan*) and *þȳs* (or *þīs*) [§§A1a–b]. Remnants of an instrumental inflection on nouns may survive: see 7a/44.

(a) In expressions of comparison, e.g. *habbaþ frēonda þȳ mā* 'they will have friends the more' (35d/21); *þē nēar* 'the nearer' (19/53).

(b) In expressions of measure and time, e.g. *tō þon þæt* 'to the extent that' or 'until' (9a/27); *tō þan swīðe* 'to such an extent that' (9a/29); *ēac þon* 'in addition to that' or 'besides' (18/100); *þȳs æftran ġēare* 'during this next year' (28/72).

(c) After prepositions of instrument (where dat. is more commonly used), e.g. *mid þȳs sweorde* 'with this sword' (19/89).

(d) In adverbial phrases of manner or accompaniment, e.g. *elne mycle* 'with great courage' (23/34), *lȳtle werode* 'with a little company' (29/9). (The inflection on the adjectives *mycle* and *lȳtle* would be -*um* if they were dative, but for the accompanying nouns, -*e* is the sg. inflection in both dat. and instr.)

§E NUMERALS

§E1 Cardinal numerals

1	ān	20	twēntiġ
2	twēġen	21	ān ond twēntiġ
3	þrī, þrȳ		*etc*
4	fēower	30	þrītiġ, þrittiġ
5	fīf	40	fēowertiġ
6	syx, siex	50	fīftiġ
7	seofon	60	syxtiġ
8	eahta	70	hundseofontiġ
9	nigon	80	hundeahtatiġ
10	tȳn, tīen	90	hundnigontiġ
11	endleofan	100	hundtēontiġ, hund(red)
12	twelf	101	ān ond hundtēontiġ
13	þrēotȳne		*etc*
14	fēowertȳne	110	hundendleofantiġ
15	fīftȳne	120	hundtwelftiġ
16	syxtȳne	200	twā hund
17	seofontȳne	300	þrēo hund
18	eahtatȳne		*etc*
19	nigontȳne	1000	þūsend

1 Considerable variation occurs in the spelling of the cardinal numerals, especially in the ending *-tȳne* (*-tīene, -tēne*).

2 The OE equivalents for 70–100 should be noted. Historically, **hund** was a word indicating 'ten' of something and so *hundseofontiġ* is in effect 'seven tens', i.e. 70, *not* 170, and *hundtēontig* is 'ten tens', i.e. 100; already the Anglo-Saxons had begun to abbreviate the latter to *hund*, and also used the form *hundred*. Similarly, 110 and 120 are *hundendleofantiġ* ('ten elevens') and *hundtwelftiġ* ('ten twelves'), respectively.

§E2 Ordinal numerals

1st	forma, fyrst, fyrmest	9th	nigoþa
2nd	ōþer	10th	tēoþa, tēogoþa
3rd	þridda	11th	endleofta
4th	fēorþa	12th	twelfta
5th	fīfta	13th	þrēotēoþa
6th	syxta	14th	fēowertēoþa
7th	seofoþa		*etc*
8th	eahtoþa	20th	twēntigoþa

21st	ān ond twēntigoþa	30th	þrītigoþa
	etc	40th	fēowertigoþa
			etc

1 Considerable variation occurs in the spelling of the ordinals, especially in the ending *-tigoþa* (*-tēogoþa*, *-tigþa*, etc).

§E3 Declension and use of the cardinals

(a) Only the first three regularly decline.

    (i) *ān* 'one' declines like a strong or weak adjective, as appropriate [§§C1–2]; *ǣnne* is a frequent alternative for acc. sg. masc. *ānne*.

    (ii) *twēġen* 'two':

       Nom./Acc. Masc. twēġen, *Neut.* twā, tū, *Fem.* twā

       Gen. (all genders) twēġra, twēġ(e)a; *Dat. (all genders)* twǣm, twām

    (iii) *bēġen* 'both' or 'a pair' declines like *twēġen*: bā, bū, bēġra, bēġ(e)a, bǣm, bām. There is a further form *būtū* used for nom./acc. in all genders.

    (iv) *þrīe* 'three':

       Nom./Acc. Masc. þrīe, *Neut.* þrēo, *Fem.* þrēo

       Gen. (all genders) þrēora; *Dat. (all genders)* þrim, þrym

(b) The numerals 4–19 are not normally declined when used ATTRIBUTIVELY (i.e. before a noun) but sometimes they are given endings when they stand alone. Numerals in *-tiġ* may be declined like neut. nouns but more often are not.

(c) *hund(red)* and *þūsend* are treated as neut. nouns, often uninflected: *twā hund, þrēo þūsend*, etc.

(d) Most numerals are followed by the PARTITIVE GENITIVE, e.g. *fēower hund wintra*, lit. 'four hundred of winters'. But the declinable numerals (1–3) are usually used as ADJECTIVES: *twēġen sceaþan*, 'two criminals' (14/45), the numeral agreeing here with the noun in the nom. pl.; other examples: 4/2, 8/1, 9a/5. But the other numerals are sometimes also used as adjectives: *XV gēar* '15 years' (21b/5).

(e) In place of the sometimes cumbersome OE words, Roman numerals were usually employed in the manuscripts (signalled by full-stops at each end). The scribes, however, often got them wrong; see 8/17n.

§E4 Declension and use of the ordinals

(a) The ordinal numerals are also known as NUMERICAL ADJECTIVES and are de-clined, and used, like weak adjectives, except for *ōþer* 'second', which is always strong: *oþ þā nigoþan tīd* 'until the ninth hour' (14/56); *ōðres mannes dǣd* 'the action of the second (*or* other) man' (4/79).

(b) No ordinal forms are recorded for *twā hund*, etc, or *þūsend*.

§F ADVERBS

§F1 Adverbs define – in terms of place, manner or time – the action of a specific verb, or give context to a whole sentence. They are formed freely in OE, often by the addition of *-e* or *-līċe* to an adjective, e.g. *beorht* 'bright' > *beorhte* 'brightly', *sōþ* 'true' > *sōþlīċe* 'truthfully'. Other characteristic endings are *-a* (*āninga* 'at once') and *-an* (*feorran* 'from afar'). Adverbs are frequently made from nouns, especially by putting them in the dat. pl. with *-um*, e.g. *ār* > *ārum* 'honourably', *wundor* > *wundrum* 'wondrously'; see also §D4f. The acc., gen. and instr. cases are much used for forming adverbs and adverbial phrases [§§D2c, 3c and 5b].

§F2 The COMPARATIVE and SUPERLATIVE of adverbs are formed, as in adjectives, by adding *-or* (or *-ur*, *-ar*) and *-ost* (or *-ust*, *-ast*), respectively, e.g. *fæġere* 'fairly' > *fæġror* 'more fairly', *fæġrost* 'most fairly'.

§G VERBS

Overview

Verbs in OE may be categorised in four main types: 1. BASIC; 2. so-called PRETERITE-PRESENT, including MODAL VERBS; 3. STRONG; and 4. WEAK. The OE verb has only a PRESENT tense (which may serve for the future also) and a PRETERITE (or past) tense [§§G6a–b]; each tense may modify into the 'subjunctive mood' [§G6e]. There is no independent 'passive' mood (to express action done *to* the subject, rather than *by* it), except as represented by a single historical relic, *hātte*, from *hātan* 'call', and in itself meaning 'is called'. The INFINITIVE form of the verb (defined in ModE by the preposition 'to': 'to sing') is the one used in glossaries and usually ends in *-an* (*singan*). Verbs CONJUGATE by adopting various forms, derived by inflection and/or stem-modification from the infinitive, to indicate one of the three *persons* (1st, 2nd or 3rd) in the *sg.* or *pl.* ('I' or 'we', 'you', 'he/she/it' or 'they'). A few general points about conjugation are worth noting.

(i) For all verbs, in whatever tense, there is only ever *a single pl. form* to include 'we' (1st pers.), 'you' (2nd pers.) and 'they' (3rd pers.).

(ii) The endings *-(e)þ* and *-aþ* signal the *present tense* of any verb; *-(e)þ* is usually 3rd-pers. sg. (cf. early ModE 'she cometh'), *aþ* very often the pl. form.

(iii) The ending *-on* is always the sign of a *pl.* verb in the *preterite* (i.e. past) tense (*-don* if it is a weak verb); *-(e)de* always signals a *sg.* weak verb in the *preterite* tense.

(iv) In the *subjunctive* mood, for both tenses, verbs invariably end in *-e* for all sg. persons and *-en* for the pl.

(v) In the *imperative* (for commands), there is a special form only in the sing.; for the imperative pl., the present pl. is used.

Note. In all the verb-paradigms given below, pronouns are notionally present: *Sg. 1*: ic 'I', *Sg. 2*: þū 'you', *Sg. 3*: hē, sēo, hit 'he/she/it'; *Pl.*: wē, gē, hī 'we/you/they'; thus *ic eom, þu eart, hē/sēo/hit is, wē sind*, and so on. Sample translations will be indicated in the paradigms of the basic verbs, but not thereafter.

§G1 Basic Verbs

The essential Basic Verbs are known as ANOMALOUS, because they show great anomalies (i.e. irregularities) when compared with the other more regularly conjugated verbs dealt with in §§G3–4. They might profitably be committed to memory by beginning students.

(a) bēon-wesan 'to be'

Historically, parts of three quite separate verbs came together to provide a range of ways of expressing 'to be' in OE. *Bēon* and *wesan* are the two surviving infinitives, from which derive the present-tense *b-* forms and the preterite *w-* forms, respectively. There are two forms of the present tense, for the use of which see (iv), below.

		Pres.		*Pret.*
		('I am', 'you are', etc)		('I was', 'you were', etc)
Sg.	1	eom	bēo	wæs
	2	eart	bist	wēre
	3	is	biþ	wæs
Pl.		sind(on), sint	bēoþ	wēron

	Sbj. ('I may be', etc)		('I may have been', etc)
Sg.	sīe	bēo	wēre
Pl.	sīen	bēon	wēren

	Imp. ('be!')		*Pres. part.* ('being')
Sg.	wes	bēo	wesende
Pl.	wesaþ	bēoþ	

(i) Spelling variations include *ys*, *synd(on)*, *synt*, *sī*, *sȳ*, and *byþ*.

(ii) A present pl. form *earan*, *earon* or *earun* (or *aron*, *arun*), 'are', occurs in early Mercian and Northumbrian documents. Thus, in 26/82, the negative *nearon* (*ne + earon*) is conjectured, though the scribe actually wrote *nǣron*.

(iii) The NEGATIVE is formed by the contraction of *ne* + verb: thus *neom*, *neart*, *nis* and *nǣs*, *nǣre*, *nǣron*, *nǣre*, *nǣren* ('I am not', 'you are not', etc, and 'I/he/she/it was not', etc).

(iv) USE OF *bēon-wesan*. 1. The present forms *eom*, *is*, etc are used to express the continuous and passing present tense: *iċ eom ġeanwyrde munuc* 'I am a professed monk' (1/11), *ðēos worold is on ofste* 'this world is in haste' (25/3). 2. The forms *bēo*, *biþ*, etc, are used to express the future: *þū bið wel* 'you will be well' (2a/2), and also the so-called 'gnomic' present, used to express eternal truths: *winter byð cealdost* 'winter is coldest' (33/5).

(b) **dōn** 'do'		(c) **gān** 'go'		(d) **willan** 'wish, will'	
Pres.		*Pres.*		*Pres.*	
('I do', etc)		('I go', etc)		('I wish', etc)	
Sg. 1	dō	Sg. 1	gā	Sg. 1	wille
2	dēst	2	gǣst	2	wilt
3	dēþ	3	gǣþ	3	wil(l)e
Pl.	dōþ	Pl.	gāþ	Pl.	willaþ
Pres. sbj.		*Pres. sbj*		*Pres. sbj.*	
('I may do', etc)		('I may go', etc)`		('I may wish', etc)	
Sg.	dō	Sg.	gā	Sg.	wil(l)e
Pl.	dōn	Pl.	gān	Pl.	willen
Imp. ('do!')		*Imp.* ('go!')			
Sg.	dō	Sg.	gā		
Pl.	dōþ	Pl.	gāþ		

Pres. part. ('doing') dōnde

Pres. part. ('going') gangende

Pres. part. ('wishing') willende

Pret.		*Pret.*		*Pret.*	
('I did', etc)		('I went', etc)		('I wished', etc)	
Sg. 1	dyde	ēode	Sg. 1	wolde	
2	dydest	ēodest	2	woldest	
3	dyde	ēode	3	wolde	
Pl.	dydon	ēodon	Pl.	woldon	
Pret. sbj.		*Pret. sbj.*		*Pret. sbj*	
('I might do', etc)		('I might go', etc)		('I might wish', etc)	
Sg.	dyde	ēode	Sg.	wolde	
Pl.	dyden	ēoden	Pl.	wolden	

Past part. ('done') (ġe)dōn

Past part. ('gone') (ġe)gān, (ġe)gangen

(i) In *gān*, the present participle *gangende* and the alternative past participle *ġegangen* are provided by the strong verb *(ġe)gongan* (VII).

(ii) In *willan*, the variant spellings *wylle, wylt, wyle,* etc will be found.

(iii) The NEGATIVE form of *willan* is the contracted verb *nellan* (*ne* + *willan*, 'to not wish'); it conjugates similarly to *willan*: *nelle, nelt, nele, nellaþ, nolde, noldest, noldon*. Variant spellings are many, including in the present tense *nylle, nile, nyle,* etc. Unlike *willan*, *nellan* has an imperative (in the pl.): *nellaþ* or *nyllaþ*.

(iv) USE OF *willan*. The original meaning was 'wish' or 'want', or 'will' (in the sense of intending something), e.g. *hē wolde ārīsan of dēaðe* 'he wanted (*or* intended) to arise from death' (22/7). However, present-tense examples such as *wē willaþ...ūs tō scype gangan*, 'we will go to our ship' (30/40), indicate how *willan* in OE was already coming to function as an important marker of the future tense.

§G2 Preterite-Present Verbs, including Modal Verbs

These important verbs are known as PRETERITE-PRESENT verbs because what were once their 'strong' preterite forms [§G3] were shifted historically to present-tense use; new preterite tenses were then needed and these were made on a 'weak' pattern (i.e. ending in a suffix with *d* [§G4]). They include four very important MODAL verbs, so called because they express a 'mood' – usually of necessity, possibility or desire: *cunnan* 'know (how to)', *magan* 'be able', *mōtan* 'may' and *sculan* 'must'. A fifth modal verb is *willan*, dealt with under 'basic verbs', in §G1. The OE modal verbs have a very wide semantic range, as do their ModE equivalents.

In (a), *sculan* is given as an example of a preterite-present modal verb; in (b) *witan* illustrates a non-modal preterite-present verb.

(a) **sculan** 'must'

		Pres.	*Pret.*
Sg.	1	sceal	sc(e)olde
	2	scealt	sc(e)oldest
	3	sceal	sc(e)olde
Pl.		sculon	sc(e)oldon

	Sbj.		
Sg.		scyle	sc(e)olde
Pl.		scylen	sc(e)olden

(i) USE OF *sculan*. The basic function is to express obligation: *hē sceal Crīstes ābilġðe wrecan* 'he must avenge offences against Christ' (7c/12–13); and some-times it seems to express what is customary: *fisc sceal on wætere* 'a fish must be (*i.e.* always is) in the water' (33/27; and see 33/headnote). But there are many cases where it seems to become a simple marker of the future: *hwā sceal ūs āwilian þone stān?* 'who is to (*or simply* will) roll away the stone for us?' (22/19).

(b) **witan** 'know'

	Pres.	*Pret.*
Sg. 1	wāt	wisse, wiste
2	wāst	wistest
3	wāt	wisse, wiste
Pl.	witon	wisson, wiston

Sbj.		
Sg.	wite	wisse, wiste
Pl.	witen	wissen, wisten

Imp.			
Sg.	wite	*Pres. part.*	witende
Pl.	witaþ	*Past part.*	(ġe)witen

(i) There is a contracted NEGATIVE form (*ne* + *witan*, 'to not know'): *nāt, nāst, nyton, nyte, nysse, nyste.*

(c) The following table summarises the behaviour of the preterite-present verbs; the numerals refer to the classes of 'strong' verbs [§G3] from which they derive. In the case of *dūgan* and *unnan*, no 2nd-pers. sg. forms have been recorded.

	Pres. Sg.		*Pres. Pl.*	*Pret. Sg.*
	1, 3	2		
(I) **witan** 'know'	wāt	wāst	witon	wiste, wisse
āgan 'possess'	āh	āhst, āht	āgon	āhte
(II) **dūgan** 'avail'	dēag, dēah		dugon	dohte
(III) **cunnan** 'know'	cann, conn	canst	cunnon	cūþe
durran 'dare'	dearr	dearst	durron	dorste
þurfan 'need'	þearf	þearft	þurfon	þorfte
unnan 'grant'	ann, onn		unnon	ūþe
(IV) **munan** 'remember'	ġeman, ġemon	ġemanst	ġemunon	ġemunde
sculan 'must'	sceal	scealt	sculon	sceolde
(V) **magan** 'be able'	mæġ	meaht	magon	mihte, meahte
(VI) **mōtan** 'be permitted'	mot	mōst	mōton	mōste

(d) AUXILIARY VERBS. One of the most important uses of the modal verbs is as auxiliaries with the *infinitive* of another verb, e.g. *ic sceal erian fulne æcer* 'I must plough a full acre' (1/22); *hēo . . . ne mihte findan* 'she could not find' (13/5); *ic þæt secgan mæġ* 'I can tell that' (40/2). But frequently the infinitive is *omitted* when it is the verb 'to be' or a *verb of motion*, e.g. *ellen sceal on eorle* 'courage must (be) in a warrior' (33/16); *þæt wē tō mōten* 'that we may (arrive) there' (26/119). Further examples: 17/44, 36/12.

§G3 Strong Verbs

Strong verbs form their preterite tense by means of *a change in the stem-vowel*, just as the equivalent verbs in ModE do. Thus OE *scīnan* corresponds to ModE 'to shine' (the infinitive form) and has the preterite form *scān* (3rd-pers. sg.), corresponding to 'shone'; the stem-vowel of the verb (in both OE and ModE) has been changed. The term 'strong' (cf. 'weak' in §G4) has no significance in itself, though it may be helpful to remember that only 'strong' verbs have the resources to make radical alterations to their structure. The complete 'strong' verb conjugation is illustrated here by two examples.

(a) **scīnan** 'to shine'		(b) **singan** 'to sing'	
Pres.		*Pres.*	
Sg.	*Pl.*	*Sg.*	*Pl.*
1 scīne	scīnaþ	singe	singaþ
2 scīn(e)st	scīnaþ	sing(e)st	singaþ
3 scīn(e)þ	scīnaþ	sing(e)þ	singaþ
Pres. sbj.		*Pres. sbj.*	
Sg. scīne	*Pl.* scīnen	*Sg.* singe	*Pl.* singen
Imp.		*Imp.*	
Sg. scīn	*Pl.* scīnaþ	*Sg.* sing	*Pl.* singaþ
Pres. part.		*Pres. part.*	
scīnende		singende	
Pret.		*Pret.*	
Sg.	*Pl.*	*Sg.*	*Pl.*
1 scān	scinon	sang	sungon
2 scine	scinon	sunge	sungon
3 scān	scinon	sang	sungon
Pret. sbj.		*Pret. sbj.*	
Sg. scine	*Pl.* scinen	*Sg.* sunge	*Pl.* sungen
Past part.		*Past part.*	
ġescinen		ġesungen	

(i) The stem-vowel of the infinitive is used for all present forms (*scīnan* > *scīne, scīnaþ; singan* > *singe, singeþ, sing!, singend*, etc.).

(ii) One mutated stem-vowel is used for the 1st- and 3rd-pers. pret. sg. (*scān*; *song*); a second is used for the 2nd-pers. sg. and for all the pl. forms (*scine, scinon*; *sunge, sungon*). These are known as the 1ST and 2ND PRETERITES. In some verbs (those in classes VI and VII, as given below) the same vowel is in fact used for both.

(iii) CONTRACTION. In the present tense, the 2nd- and 3rd-pers. forms are often (but *not* always) contracted, or 'syncopated', i.e. the *-e-* of the inflection is dropped (*scīnest > scīnst, singeþ > singþ*). Such contraction may have secondary effects, especially in the 3rd pers., leading to forms which are not easily recognisable for what they are. Thus *bītþ* is a contraction of *bīteþ* (from *bītan* 'to bite') but is very awkward to pronounce, so it is taken a stage further with the 'assimilation' of the two consonants, resulting in *bītt*. In the table of stem modifications given below, 3rd-pers. sg. forms in the present tense are included.

(iv) VOWEL MUTATION. When contraction takes place, as described in (iii), the verb-stem's vowel (if *a, ā, o, ō, æ, ǣ* or *e*) or diphthong (if *ea, ēa, eo* or *ēo*) 'mutates', e.g. *cuman* 'come' > *cymst*; *cweþan* 'speak' > *cwiþ(þ)*; *wealdan* 'control' > *wylst*.

(c) **The Seven Classes**

Strong verbs have been divided into seven main series, or CLASSES, according to the pattern of change of their stem-vowels. In this book they are designated by the Roman numerals I–VII (though some editors use Arabic 1–7, reserving Roman numerals for the three classes of weak verbs). The classes are summarised in the following table, with examples. A synopsis of the probable original 'proto-Germanic' vowel series for each class is given first, but certain regular but complex sound-changes have resulted in the stem-vowels in some parts of some verbs being not those apparently required of their class. This is especially the case in class III, where the 'nasal' and 'liquid' consonants (*n, m* and *h, l, r*) caused modification of the vowels which preceded them. All the standard grammars of OE give details. It should be noted that the 3rd-pers. present sg. form given in the second column is *not* part of the graded vowel series.

	Pres. 3 sg.	*1st pret.*	*2nd pret.*	*Past part.*
I ī ā i i				
scīnan 'shine'	scīneþ/scīnþ	scān	scinon	(ġe)scinen
þēon 'prosper'	þīehþ	þāh	þigon	(ġe)þigen
II ēo ēa u o				
cēosan 'choose'	cīest	cēas	curon	(ġe)coren
flēon 'flee'	flīehþ	flēah	flugon	(ġe)flogen
brūcan 'enjoy'	brȳcþ	brēac	brucon	(ġe)brocen

III

(a) **i a u u** (*inf. with* i + m/n + *cons.*)

| bindan 'bind' | bindeþ/bint | band | bundon | (ġe)bunden |

(b) **e/eo ea u o** (*inf. with* e/eo + h/l/r + *cons.*)

| helpan 'help' | hilfþ | healp | hulpon | (ġe)holpen |
| weorþan 'become' | wierhþ | wearþ | wurdon | (ġe)worden |

(c) **e æ u o** (*'irregular' verbs*)

| berstan 'burst' | bi(e)rst | bærst | burston | (ġe)borsten |
| breġdan 'weave' | – | bræġd | bruġdon | (ġe)broġden |

IV **e æ ǣ o**

| beran 'bear' | bi(e)rþ | bær | bǣron | (ġe)boren |
| cuman 'come' | cymþ | cōm | cōmon | (ġe)cumen |

V **e æ ǣ e**

cweþan 'say'	cwiþþ	cwæþ	cwǣdon	(ġe)cweden
ġiefan 'give'	ġiefþ	ġeaf	ġēafon	(ġe)ġiefen
þicgan 'receive'	þiġ(e)þ	þeah	þǣgon	(ġe)þeġen
sēon 'see'	si(e)hþ	seah	sāwon	(ġe)sewen
sittan 'sit'	sitt	sæt	sǣton	(ġe)seten

VI **a ō ō a**

| standan 'stand' | standeþ/stent | stōd | stōdon | (ġe)standen |
| scieppan 'create' | sciepþ | scōp | scōpon | (ġe)scapen |

VII **ea ēo ēo ea**

healdan 'hold'	hielt	hēold	hēoldon	(ġe)healden
hātan 'call'	hǣtt	hēt	hēton	(ġe)hāten
slǣpan 'sleep'	slǣpþ	slēp	slēpon	(ġe)slǣpen
fōn 'seize'	fēhþ	fēng	fēngon	(ġe)fangen

(i) CONTRACTED VERBS. The verbs *þēon*, *flēon*, *sēon* and *fōn* in the above list, and others like them, are known as 'contracted' or 'contract' verbs. Originally they had an 'intervocalic' *h* (i.e. between vowels), which was lost, with consequent absorption of the following vowel into the preceding vowel or diphthong, which then lengthened in compensation, if it was not already long. Thus, a form *seohan* is conjectured to have preceded *sēon*. A series of regular but complex sound-changes affect in particular the present-tense forms of these verbs; thus for *sēon* they are *sēo*, *si(e)hst*, *si(e)hþ*, *sēoþ*.

§G4 Weak Verbs

'Weak' verbs form their preterite tense by adding the suffix *-de* (sg.) or *-don* (pl.) to their *unaltered* stem. Thus OE *fæstnian* 'fasten' has the preterite form *fæstnode* (3rd-pers. sg.), corresponding to ModE 'fastened'. There are three classes of weak verbs: CLASS 1: with infinitive in *-an* or *-rian*; CLASS 2: with infinitive in *-ian* (except *-rian*); and CLASS 3: the quartet **habban**, **libban**, **secgan** and **hycgan**, which combine characteristics of both the other classes and in which there is much variation.

(a) CLASSES 1 AND 2

The most important differences between Class 1 and Class 2 verbs are in the vowels of the present 3rd-pers. sg. ending and the preterite 3rd-pers. sg. and pl. endings and the past participle. Within Class 1, three types may be distinguished: the *fremman* type (with a short vowel and double consonant before *-an*), the *herian* type (those in *-rian*), and the *dēman* type (most of which have a long vowel or diphthong and single consonant in their stem); the first types retain an *-e-* in the preterite ending.

	CLASS 1			CLASS 2
	fremman 'do'	**herian** 'praise'	**dēman** 'judge'	**lufian** 'love'
Pres.				
Sg. 1	fremme	heri(ġ)e	dēme	lufi(ġ)e
2	fremest	herest	dēm(e)st	lufast
3	fremeþ	hereþ	dēm(e)þ	lufaþ
Pl.	fremmaþ	heriaþ	dēmaþ	lufiaþ
Pres. sbj.				
Sg.	fremme	herie	dēme	lufi(ġ)e
Pl.	fremmen	herien	dēmen	lufien
Imp.				
Sg.	freme	here	dēm	lufa
Pl.	fremmaþ	heriaþ	dēmaþ	lufiaþ
Pres. part.	fremmende	heriende	dēmende	lufiende
Pret.				
Sg. 1	fremede	herede	dēmde	lufode
2	fremedest	heredest	dēmdest	lufodest
3	fremede	herede	dēmde	lufode
Pl.	fremedon	heredon	dēmdon	lufodon
Pret. sbj.				
Sg.	fremede	herede	dēmde	lufode
Pl.	fremeden	hereden	dēmden	lufoden
Past part.	(ġe)fremed	(ġe)hered	(ġe)dēmed	(ġe)lufod

1 In the 2nd- and 3rd-pers. present, weak verbs are subject to the same possible processes of CONTRACTION and vowel MUTATION as strong verbs: thus the 3rd-pers. pres. of *sendan* 'send' is *sint*; see above, §G3a/b.iii and iv.

2 In -*(r)ian* verbs, *g* may come between *i* and *e* or may replace *i*: *heriġe, herġende, lufiġe, lufiġende, lufġende.*

3 Some SIMPLIFICATIONS occur in the preterite and past participle, including *ht* for hypothetical *cd* or *ccd* (thus *tǣcan > tǣhte, tǣhton, ġetǣht, reċċan* 'relate' > *rehte*) and *t* for *þ* after certain 'voiceless' consonants (thus *mētan* 'meet' > *mētte, berȳpan* 'plunder' > *berȳpte*); there may be further simplification, too, as in *restan* 'rest' > *reste.*

4 Examples of Class 1 verbs: *settan* 'set' (pres. 3 *sett*, pret. 3 *sette*, past. part. *ġesett*), *lecgan* (pres. 3 *leġþ*, pret. 3 *leġde*, past. part. *ġeleġd*), etc; *derian* 'injure' (*dereþ, derede, ġedered*), *ġyrwan* 'prepare' (*ġyreþ, ġyrede, ġeġyrwed*), *ġelīefan* 'believe' (*ġelīefþ, ġelīefde, ġelīefed*), *sendan* 'send' (*sent, sende, ġesend*), *āweċċan* 'awake' (*āwehte*).

5 Examples of Class 2 verbs: *andswarian* 'answer', *bodian* 'announce', *folgian* 'follow', *leornian* 'obey', *maþelian* 'speak', *weorþian* 'honour'.

(b) CLASS 1 VERBS WITH STEM-VOWEL CHANGE

Contrary to the usual practice in weak verbs, some verbs in Class 1 change their stem-vowel in the preterite, as well as adding inflections. Most will be recognisable from their ModE equivalents:

	Pres. 3s	*Pret. 3s*	*Past part.*
cwellan 'kill'	cwel(e)þ	cwealde	ġecweald
þenċan 'think'	þenc(e)þ	þōhte	ġeþōht
bringan 'bring'	bring(e)þ	brōhte	ġebrōht
bicgan 'buy'	big(e)þ	bohte	ġeboht
sellan 'give'	syl(e)þ	sealde	ġeseald
wyrċan 'make'	wyrċ(e)þ	worhte	ġeworht
sēċan 'seek'	sēċ(e)þ	sōhte	ġesōht

(c) CLASS 3

	habban 'have'	**libban** 'live'	**secgan** 'say'	**hycgan** 'think'
Pres.				
Sg. 1	hæbbe	libbe	secge	hycge
2	hæfst	leofast, lifast	sæġst, se(ġe)st	hogast
3	hæfþ, hafaþ	leofaþ, lifaþ	sæġþ, se(ġe)þ	hogaþ
Pl.	habbaþ	libbaþ, leofaþ	secgaþ	hycgaþ
Pres. sbj.				
Sg.	hæbbe	libbe	secge	hycge
Pl.	hæbben	libben	secgen	hycgen
Imp.				
Sg.	hafa	leofa	saga, seġe	hyge, hoga
Pl.	habbaþ	libbaþ, leofaþ	secgaþ	hcygaþ
Pres. part.	hæbbende	libbende, lifiende	secgende	hycgende

Pret.

Sg. 1	hæfde	lifde, leofode	sæġde, sæde	hog(o)de
2	hæfdest	lifdest	sæġdest, sædest	hog(o)dest
3	hæfde	lifde, leofode	sæġde, sæde	hog(o)de
Pl.	hᴗᶠdon	lifdon, leofodon	sæġdon, sædon	hog(o)don

Pret. sbj.

Sg.	hæfde	lifde, leofode	sæġde, sæde	hog(o)de
Pl.	hæfden	lifden, leofoden	sæġden, sæden	hog(o)den

Past part.	(ġe)hæfd	(ġe)lifd, (ġe)leofod	(ġe)sæġd	(ġe)hogod

(i) There is a contracted NEGATIVE form of *habban* (*ne* + *habban* 'not to have'): *næbbe, nafaþ, nabbaþ*, etc.

§G5 Impersonal Verbs

These are verbs whose subject is a neutral 'it', usually not expressed: *snīwde* '(it) snowed' (26/31). Often they are used with a REFLEXIVE PRONOUN in the dat. to reflect the action back on to the subject [§§A3 and D4c]: *him þūhte* 'it seemed to them' (9b/85), *ðā ðe mē līcodon* 'those that I liked' (7b/2; lit. 'those which liked me': cf. early ModE 'it likes me not' for 'I don't like').

§G6 The Use of Verbs

(a) PRESENT TENSE

(i) Used for the *simple* present and for the *continuous* present, e.g. *wē ċildra biddaþ ġē* 'we children ask you' (7/1).

(ii) Used for the *future*, with only the context making this clear, e.g. *cymeð him sēo ār of heofenum* 'grace will come to him from heaven' (26/107). Present forms of *bēon* 'be' (mainly *biþ*) often have a future sense [§G1a.ii]. The Germanic languages did not possess a 'dedicated' future tense.

(b) PRETERITE TENSE

Used for the simple past, e.g. *hēr forðfērde Ælfere* 'here Ælfhere died' (8/4); but often best translated with the perfect, e.g. *ðæt mē cōm swīðe oft on ġemynd* 'it has come to me very often in my mind' (5/3). But see also §G6c.i.

(c) COMPOUND TENSES

The verbs *bēon-wesan* 'be' and *habban* 'have', and to a lesser extent *weorþan* 'become', are used with the present or past participles of other verbs to form the so-called 'compound' (or 'resolved') tenses. The participles originally functioned as adjectives, and some accordingly carry inflections. Compound verbs were used far less in OE than they are in ModE.

(i) ***habban*** With past participles forms perfect and pluperfect tenses, e.g. *bitre brēostceare ġebiden hæbbe* '(I) have experienced bitter heart-care' (26/4); *hēo hæfdon ūtamǣrede þā bīgengan* 'they had driven out the population' (9a/50–1). In OE, *habban* is more often used in its basic sense of 'possess' or 'hold', e.g. *wē . . . habba∂ lārēowa* 'we have teachers' (5/18–19).

(ii) ***bēon-wesan*** With present participles forms 'continuous' tenses, e.g. *hē of worulde gongende wæs* 'he was going from the world' (9b/83); with the past participles of intransitive verbs forms perfect and pluperfect tenses, e.g. *ofsleġen is* 'has been executed' (22/6); *∂ā wætera wǣron ādrūwode* 'the waters had dried up' (13/10).

(iii) ***weorþan*** With past participles forms perfect and pluperfect tenses, e.g. *þǣr wear∂ hrēam āhafen* 'a din was raised there' (30/106).

(d) INFINITIVES

(i) **Simple infinitive** (formed with *-an*):

1. Used (as in ModE) in conjunction with other verbs, including the 'modal' auxiliaries [§G2d], to express intention, obligation, feeling, causation or inception, e.g. *ongan ċeallian* '(he) began to call out' (30/91), *iċ wolde . . . leornian sprecan* 'I would like to learn to speak' (1/12–13).

2. Commonly used with verbs of COMMAND, e.g. *hēt þā hyssa hwæne hors forlǣtan* '(he) commanded each warrior to let go (his) horse' (30/2). The direct object of the verb may be unexpressed, e.g. *hēo . . . hēt feċċan hire hearpan* 'she commanded (someone) to fetch her harp', or, translating with a passive construction, 'she commanded her harp to be fetched' (27/27).

3. Used with verbs of *motion, rest* or *observation*, usually plus an *accusative* object (hence this is known as the ACCUSATIVE AND INFINITIVE construction), to express duration; the sense may be active, rendered with a present participle or with a subordinate clause with 'that', e.g. *ġesih∂ . . . baþian brimfuglas* '(he) sees seabirds bathing [lit. "to bathe"]' (38/46–7), *ġefræġen iċ ∂ā Hōlofernus wīnhātan wyrċean* 'I heard that Holofernes then issued invitations' (19/7–8); or it may be translated with a past participle, e.g. *ġeseah iċ weruda God þearle þenian* 'I saw the lord of hosts sorely racked' (23/51–2).

(ii) **Inflected infinitive** (formed with *-anne* or *-enne* and preceded by *tō*):

1. To express purpose, necessity or fitness, and usually translated with the passive, e.g. *sind tō flēoganne* 'are to be avoided' (3a/10). Other examples: 4/17, 16/92, 25/70–1.

2. To complete the sense of other verbs, e.g. *fēngon tō wurðienne... entas* '(they) began to worship giants' (24/28). Other examples: 7b/17, 8/28, 78, 14/26.

3. To complete the sense of a noun or adjective, e.g. *hæbbe ġē hēr ǣniġ þincg þe tō etenne sī?* 'have you here anything that may be eaten?' (22/54), *wynsumu tō ġehȳranne* 'pleasing to hear' (9b/61). Other examples: 7b/15, 55, 16/39–40, 92.

4. To complement adverbially a main sentence, e.g. *tō metanne wið ðā ēċan* 'when measured against the eternal' (6/76).

(e) SUBJUNCTIVE MOOD

(i) The mood of most verbs is 'indicative': they state something as a fact. When in the subjunctive mood (shown by sg. *-e* or pl. *-en* on the present or preterite root of a verb), they express something less certain, usually involving a wish, condition, hypothesis, claim, concession or doubt, e.g. *ġif frīġman cyninge stele* 'if a free man steal from the king' (7a/9), *þæt ic hit mæġe understandan* 'so that I may understand' (27/15–16), *oþþæt hit ġesoden sīe* 'until it be cooked' (3a/3), *ġif iċ onstyred bēo* 'if I should be roused up' (15b/12–13), *cweð þet hē ġesiclod wǣre* '(he) said that he was sick' (8/78). The subjunctive is much used in OE; it hardly survives in ModE but still appears in commonly used expressions such as 'if I *were* you'.

(ii) The meaning is often OPTATIVE, i.e. expressing an admonition or command, e.g. *L scillinga ġebēte* 'let (him) make good with (a payment of) 50 shillings' (7a/10), *wuldor sȳ ðē* 'be glory to you' (2a/23).

(f) REDUCED PLURAL FORMS

When a pl. pronoun subject immediately follows its verb, very often a sg. form of the verb is used; if the pl. inflection is *-on*, *-en* or *-aþ*, it is replaced by simple *-e*, e.g. *hwǣr cwōm symbla ġesetu?* 'where went the places of banquets?' (38/93), *nū wille wē ēow ġereċċan* 'now we will relate to you' (22/67; cf. *wē wyllað ēow myningean* 'we will remind you', 22/3).

§H USEFUL OLD ENGLISH

The following frequently used words often cause confusion because of their variety of function in OE or their misleading association with ModE words. Specific examples of their use may be found by reference to the Glossary.

(a)

hī, hīe, hȳ	*pron.* 'they' (3rd pers., nom. pl.)
	pron. 'them' (3rd pers., acc. pl.)
	pron. 'she' (3rd pers., nom. sg. fem., for *hēo*)
	pron. 'her' (3rd pers., acc. sg. fem.)
him	*pron.* 'to/for/from him/it' (3rd pers., dat. sg. masc./neut.)
	pron. 'to/for/from them' (3rd pers., dat. pl. *all* genders)
se	*def. art.* or *demons. pron.* 'the' or 'that' (nom. sg. masc.)
	rel. pron. 'which', 'that' or 'who' (an alternative to *þe*)
sē	*pers. pron.* 'he' (nom. sg. masc., for *hē*)
þā	*adv.* 'then'
	conj. 'when'
	def. art. or *demons. pron.* 'the' or 'that' (acc. sg. fem.)
	def. art. or *demons. pron.* 'the' or 'those' (nom./acc. pl. *all* genders)
	pers. pron. 'they' or 'them' (3rd pers., nom./acc. pl.)
	rel. pron. 'who'
þæt	*def. art.* 'the' (nom./acc. sg. neut.)
	demons. pron. 'that', sometimes with pl. sense (nom./acc. sg. neut.)
	pers. pron. 'it', 'that', 'what' (3rd pers., nom./acc. sg. neut.)
	conj. 'that', 'so that', 'on condition that'
þæs	*def. art.* or *demons. pron.* 'of the' or 'of that' (gen. sg. masc./neut.)
	adv. 'afterwards', 'therefore', 'on that account'
	conj. 'as', 'according to'
þe	*rel. part.* 'who', 'which', 'that' or 'what'
	def. art. 'the' (for *se*, nom. sg. masc.)
	conj. part. 'either/or'
þē	*pers. pron.* (2nd pers., acc./dat. sg.) 'you' or 'to you'
	comp. adv. 'the (more of something)' (form of instr. *þȳ*)
þonne	*adv.* 'then' (also 'now', 'therefore', etc)
	conj. 'when' (also 'since', 'while', etc)
	comp. adv. 'than'

(b)

mæġ	*verb* (1st- or 3rd-pers. sg. of *magan*): 'can'
mǣġ	*noun* (masc.): 'kinsman' (pl. *mǣgas* or *māgas*); note long vowel

mæġen	*verb* (pres. sbj. pl. of *magan*): 'can' or 'may be able'
mæġen	*noun* (neut.): 'force' or 'power'
mæġþ	*noun* (fem.): 'maiden' or 'woman'
mǣġþ	*noun* (fem.): 'nation' or 'tribe'; note long vowel
miht, mihte	*verb* (2nd- and 3rd-pers. sg. pret. of *magan*): 'could'
miht, mihte	*noun* (fem.): 'might' or 'power' (nom. sg. *miht*, acc./gen./dat. *mihte*)
maga	*noun* (masc.): 'stomach'
māga	*noun* (masc.): 'relative' or 'kin'
māġe	*noun* (fem.): 'relative' or 'kin'
mago	*noun* (masc.): 'male kinsman' or 'young man'

Glossary

ORGANISATION

The scope of the Glossary is discussed on p. xvii. Citation is by text number and line number, e.g. 22/30 indicates that the word cited will be found on line 30 of Text 22. Occurrences of the headword itself, if there are any, are cited first; then follow variant or derivative forms, given in strict alphabetical order for ease of finding. All the OE words are in bold type. In the alphabetising, the letter *æ* follows *a*. The letters *þ* and *ð* are treated as one and follow *t*; headwords are standardised with initial *þ*, and this is the letter privileged in subsequent listings within an entry, in cases where a word occurs in the texts both with initial *þ* and with *ð*. The prefix *ġe* is ignored in alphabetical ordering; e.g. *ġehelpan* will be found under *h*. [*Note.* In many dictionaries and glossaries, especially older ones, *æ* is treated as though it were *ae*: i.e. it is alphabetised between *ad* and *af*; *þ/ð* may be treated as though they were *th*, thus appearing immediately before words in *ti*; and all *ġe*-words may be arranged under *g*.] The wide variation in the spelling of OE means that some forms of a word may not be found where expected. Names of people and places have been designated primarily as 'proper nouns' (pr n) without regard to gender, though this is sometimes indicated, along with type of declension followed (see below).

ABBREVIATIONS

(For explanation of grammatical terms, see Guide to Terms, pp. 504–12, and relevant sections of the Reference Grammar, pp. 355–95.)

The main abbreviations are those used throughout the Reader, with a few additions:

adj *adjective*
adv *adverb*
anom *anomalous* (verb)
comp *comparative* (adjective or adverb)
conj *conjunction*
impers *impersonal* (verb)
indecl *indeclinable*
inf *infinitive*
infl inf *inflected infinitive*
interj *interjection*
neg *negative*

num *numeral*
num adj *numerical adjective*
prep *preposition*
pret pres *preterite present* (verb)
pron *pronoun*
pr n *proper noun*
rel part *relative particle*
rflx *reflexive* (verb or pronoun)
sbj *subjunctive*
sup *superlative* (adjective or adverb)
< *is a part of* or *derived from*

396

In the analysis of NOUNS, PRONOUNS and ADJECTIVES, the following more contracted abbreviations are used, as appropriate:

For case: **n** *nominative*, **a** *accusative*, **g** *genitive*, **d** *dative* or **i** *instrumental*
For number: **s** *singular* or **p** *plural*
For gender: **m** *masculine*, **n** *neuter* or **f** *feminine*.

The order in which the information is provided is always case–number–gender. Thus **gp** indicates a noun being used in the *genitive plural*, **nsn** indicates an adjective (or verb participle) in the *nominative singular neuter*. The double role of *n* (for nominative and neuter) will not cause confusion if it is remembered that case is *always* given first. The gender of all nouns is given (*m, n* or *f*), followed after a colon by an identification of the category of declension to which the noun belongs, made by reference to the appropriate paragraph in section B of the Reference Grammar (e.g. **B1b, B2a, B4e.i**).

VERBS are listed in their infinitive form and are identified by their class and class-number: Classes **1–3** of *weak* verbs [§G4] are indicated by Arabic numerals, Classes **I–VII** of *strong* verbs [§G3] by Roman numerals. Derived forms are then analysed according to tense (**p** *present* or **pt** *preterite*), person (**1** *1st*, **2** *2nd* or **3** *3rd*) and number (**s** *singular* or **p** *plural*); if the mood of the verb is **sbj** *subjunctive* or **imp** *imperative*, this is indicated; otherwise, all verbs are indicative. Examples: **p3s** *present tense, third-person singular*; **sbj pt1p** *subjunctive preterite first-person plural*; **imp s** *imperative singular*. The form may alternatively be an **infl inf** *inflected infinitive*, or a **prp** *present participle* or **pp** *past participle*; if a participle carries an inflection, this is analysed as for adjectives (see above).

The case of noun required by PREPOSITIONS (and a few verbs) is shown as follows: **+a** *with accusative*, **+g** *with genitive*, **+d** *with dative*, **+i** *with instrumental*, **+a/d** *with accusative or dative*, etc. **=noun** signals that a noun is functioning as an adjective, **=adv** as an adverb.

ABBREVIATIONS OF ENGLISH COUNTY NAMES

Berks.	Berkshire	Lincs.	Lincolnshire
Bucks.	Buckinghamshire	Northants.	Northamptonshire
Cambs.	Cambridgeshire	Northum.	Northumberland
Corn.	Cornwall	Oxon.	Oxfordshire
Derbys.	Derbyshire	Som.	Somerset
Dev.	Devon	Suf.	Suffolk
Dor.	Dorset	Sur.	Surrey
Ess.	Essex	Warks.	Warwickshire
Hants.	Hampshire	Wilts.	Wiltshire
Herts.	Hertfordshire		

A

ā adv *always, continuously, eternally, for ever* 7c/28, 16/106, 17/38, 19/7, 345, 21a/90, 22/177, 26/42, 47, 30/315, 33/54, 40/5, 42 **aa** 25/4

ābād < **ābīdan**

Abbandūn pr n *Abingdon* (Berks.) **Abbandūnæ** ds 11/12 **Abbandūne** ds 8/7

abbod m:B1a *abbot* ns 8/17, 37 ds 8/7 **abbodæ** ds 11/28, 30 **abbud** 21b/11

abbotrīċe n:B2h *abbey, abbacy* ds 8/38

abbudisse f:B5c *abbess* ns 9b/54, 21a/35, 59 **abbudissan** gs 9b/1 ds 9b/44, 21a/49 **abudissan** ds 21a/28

Abēl pr n *Abel* **Abēles** gs 16/64

ābelġan III *enrage* **ābolġen** pp 17/93

ābēodan II *declare, report* **ābēad** pt3s 30/27 **ābēod** imp 2s 30/49

āberan IV *bear, carry* **ābær** pt3s 22/147, 151

ābīdan I (+g) *await, remain, suffer* inf 35a/9, 40/53 **ābād** pt3s 13/8, 11, 22/134 **ābīdon** pt3p 28/2

ābilġðu f:B3h *anger, offence* **ābilġðe** ap 7c/13

ābītan I *bite* **ābīte** sbj pr3s 7b/32

āblendan 1 *blind* inf 8/44

Abrahām pr n *Abraham* **Abrahāmes** gs 16/5 **Abrahāme** ds 16/63

ābrǣce < **ābrecan**

ābrecan IV *break, destroy, sack, violate, escape* inf 22/135 **ābrǣce** sbj pr3s 22/137 **ābrece** sbj pr3s 7c/5 **ābrocen** pp 7c/18, 8/71, 32/44

ābreġdan III *draw* **ābrǣd** pt3s 19/79

ābrēoþan II *fail, degenerate, fall away* **ābrēoðe** sbj pr3s 30/242 **ābroþene** pp npm 25/117

ābrocen < **ābrecan**

abudissan < **abbudisse**

ābūtan prep +a *around, about* 8/50, 54

ac conj *but, nevertheless, however, and yet, moreover, because* 1/61, 3a/9, 4/22, 50, 6/9, 11, 7b/6, 8/75, 9b/9, 14/22, 27/20, 34, 40, etc

ācennan 1 *conceive, bring forth, give birth to* **āccenned** pp 16/51 **ācende** pt3s 2c/2 **ācenned** pp 22/79, 158, 168

ācennednys f:B3e.ii *birth, nativity* **ācennednysse** as 22/158

ācennesse f:Be.ii *birth, nativity* **ācennisse** ds 21b/22

āclǣnsian 2 *cleanse, remove* **āclǣnsige** sbj pr3s 21a/41

ācōlian 2 *cool, wane* **ācōlað** pr3s 4/13 **ācōlige** sbj pr3s 4/18 **ācōlode** pt3s 21b/20

āctrēo n:B2g.i *oak tree* ds 40/28, 36

ācwǣð < **ācweðan**

ācweċċan 2 *shake, brandish* **ācwehte** pt3s 30/255, 310

ācwellan 1 *kill* **ācwealde** pt3s 25/62 pp npm 9a/44 **ācwellanne** infl inf 28/68

ācwenċan 1 *quench, extinguish* inf 25/18

ācweðan V *speak, utter, declare* **ācwǣð** pt3s 19/82, 151, 283 **ācwið** pr3s 38/91

ācȳþan 1 *make known, reveal* 38/113 **ācȳþeð** pr3s 34/21

ād m:B1a *funeral pyre, fire* ns 31a/45 **āde** ds 31a/48, 52

Ādam pr n *Adam* ns 17/28, 82 as 22/152, 24/9 **Ādame** ds 17/50, 61 **Ādomes** gs 23/100

ādīlegian 2 *destroy* **ādȳlegod** pp 21a/8

ādl f:B3c.i *sickness, disease* 26/70 **ādle** as 3a/6

ādlig adj *ill, sick* **ādlige** npm 21a/77

ādōn anom *take off* **ādyden** sbj pt3p 28/24

ādrǣdan VII *dread* **ādrēd** pt3s 27/66

ādrǣfan 1 *drive out, exile* inf 29/7 **ādrǣfde** pt3s 29/4 **ādrǣfed** pp 8/8

ādrenċan 1 *submerge, drown* **ādrenċed** pp 18/13

ādrēogan II *practise, commit* **ādrēogað** pr3p 25/73

ādrīfan I *drive away* **ādrifan** pt3p 9a/32

ādrūwian 2 *dry up* **ādrūwod** pp 13/13 **ādrūwode** pp npn 13/10 **ādrūwodon** pt3p 13/3

ādūne adv *down* 22/24

ādwǣscan 2 *wash away, extinguish, destroy* **ādwǣsced** pp 22/140 **ādwǣscte** pp npf 22/126

ādȳdan 1 *destroy* **ādȳdon** inf 13/20

aēththa see **oþþe**

afaran < **eafera**

āfaran VI *travel, pass* **āfaren** pp 22/106

āfǣran 1 *frighten* **āfǣred** pp 18/1 **āfǣrede** pp npm 22/47, 48

āfeallan VII *fall away, decay* **āfeallen**
pp 5/57, 30/202

āfer adj *bitter, sour* npn 3a/10

āfirsian *take away* **āfirsa** imp sg 27/26

āflȳman 1 *put to flight, drive out* **āflȳmde**
pt3s 24/35, 30/243

āfor adj *fierce, ferocious* nsm 19/257

āfrēfran 2 *comfort, console* **āfrēfredon** pt3p
15c/12

after see **æfter**

āfyllan 1 *strike down, slay* **āfylle** sbj pr3s
25/86, 87

āfyrhtan 1 *frighten, terrify* **āfyrhte** pp npm
22/23, 47, 92

āfyrran 1 *remove* **āfyrred** pp 17/42

āfȳsan 1 *drive, impel* inf 30/3 **āfȳsed**
pp 23/125

āgalan VI *sing* **āgōl** pt3s 31b/30

āgan pt-pr *have, possess, own, rule, control*
inf 7a/48, 17/22, 85 sbj pr3p 7a/49 pt3p
17/90 **āge** sbj pr3s 7a/15, 46, 47, 7b/22, 24,
28, 34/45, 38/64 **āgen** sbj pr1p 26/117
āgon pt2p 19/196 **āh** pr1s 26/27 pr3s
23/107 **āhte** pt1s 17/31, 51 pt3s 12/16, 50
18/68; with neg **nāge** sbj pr3s 7b/29 **nāh**
pr1s 4/25, 16/107, 23/131 **nāhte** pt1s
19/91

āġeaf, **āġēafon**, **āġefēð** < **āġiefan**

āġēat < **āġēotan**

āgen adj *own* nsm 24/22, 63 dsn 5/30, 38, 44,
46, 47 **āgene** asm 24/36 asf 16/91 apm
24/32 **āgenes** gsm 22/115 **āgenne** asm
7c/10, 24/11, 29/24 **āgenre** dsf 15c/4,
16/18, 24/38 **āgenum** dsm 22/127, 174 dsn
14/29, 34 dpm 24/30

āgend m:B4d *owner* ds **āgende** 7a/50, 51

āġēnlǣdan 1 *lead back* **āġēnlǣde** pr1s 1/35

āġēotan II *drain, empty, void, destroy* **āġēat**
pt3s 18/69 **āġēted** pp 10/18 **āgotene** pp
npm 19/32

āġiefan V *give, give back* **āġeaf** pt1s 12/55
pt3s 9b/52, 12/37, 41 **āġēafon** pt3p 19/341
āġefeð pr3s 28/26 **āġīfan** inf 12/29 **āġife**
sbj pr3s 7b/31 **āġifen** pp 12/42 **āġyfe** sbj
pr1s 14/11 **āġyfen** pp 30/116

āġinnan III *begin, proceed* sbj pr1p 25/139
āgunnan pt3p 24/16

āglǣca m:B5a *awe-inspiring one* **āglǣcan** np
31b/21 (see note)

ġeāgniġean 2 rflx +d *prove one's right to* inf
12/14

āgol < **āgalan**

āgunnan < **āġinnan**

āġyf- < **āġiefan**

Agustinus pr n *Augustine* gs 7a/1

Agustus pr n *Augustus* **Agusto** ds 9a/3

āh < **āgan**

āhafen < **āhebban**

āhangian 2 *hang* **āhangen** pp 14/20, 21, 45
āhangene pp npm 14/53

āhæfen < **āhebban**

āhēawan VII *cut away, hew* **āhēawen**
pp 21a/72, 23/29

āhebban VI *raise, lift up, exalt, lift down,*
remove **āhafen** pp 15b/9, 30/106 **āhæfen**
pp 31a/46 **āhebbað** pr3p 35b/3 **āhōf** pt1s
23/44, pt3s 30/130, 244 **āhōfon** pt3p 23/61,
30/213

āhengon < **āhōn**

āhōf, **āhōfon** < **āhebban**

āhōn VII *hang, crucify* **āhengon** pt3p 14/40
āhongen pp 19/48 **āhōnne** infl inf 14/26,
35

āhreddan 1 *rescue, save* **āhredde** pt3s 12/47,
16/68, 70

(ġe)**āhs**- see (ġe)**āscian**

āhte < **āgan**

āhte, **āhtes** < **āwiht**

āhwār adv *anywhere* 24/3, 4, 25/156

āhwyrfan III *turn* inf 15b/7

āhwettan 1 *cast away, reject* **āhwet** pr3s
17/69

al < **eall**

ālǣdan 1 *bring, lead, carry off* **ālǣd** pp 15c/2
ālǣde sbj pr3s 7b/26

ālǣġ < **ālicgan**

ālǣnan 1 *blend* **ālǣneð** pp 11/28 **ālēnǣð**
pp 11/27

alde < **eald**

aldor n:B2c *life, age, eternity* **aldre** ds 31b/33
aldres gs 31b/74 **ealdor** ns 19/185 **caldre**
ds 19/76, 26/79; in phrs **āwa tō aldre** *for*
ever and ever 19/120 **on aldre** *ever, forever*
17/65 **tō aldre** *to eternity, ever* 17/90, 99 **tō**
wīdan aldre *for ever* 19/347

aldorlēas adj *lifeless* **aldorlēasne** asm
31b/96

aldormon see **ealdorman**

ālecgan 1 *lay down, put down* **ālēde** pt3s
19/101 **ālēdon** pt3p 23/63
ālēd, ālēdon < ālecgan
ālēnæð < ālǣnan
ālēogan II *leave unfulfilled* **ālēoganne** infl
inf 7b/15 **ālēoge** sbj pr3s 7b/16
Alexander pr n *Alexander* ns 28/42, 55,
71
Alexsandria pr n *Alexandria* ns 21b/4
ālicgan V *fail, cease, lie down* **ālæ̆ġ** pt3s
31b/37
alle < eall
alwalda m:B5a *'all-wielder', the Almighty*
alwaldan gs 19/84 ds 17/22
ālȳfan 1 *grant, allow* inf 30/90 **ālȳfed** pp
18/87, 27/21, 28/43
ālȳsan 1 *release, deliver* inf 14/62 **ālȳse** sbj
pr3s 14/52
ālȳsednys f:B3e.ii *redemption* **ālȳsednysse**
ds 22/173 **ālȳsnesse** gs 15c/5, 7
ambihtsmið m:B1a *court smith* or *carpenter*
as 7a/12
Ambrosius pr n *Ambrosius* ns 9a/55
āmen interj *amen* (Lat < Hebrew *certainly*)
2a/26, 24/77, 26/125 **āmenn** 22/177
āmyrran 1 +g *disable, hinder, obstruct*
āmyrde pt3s 30/165 **āmyrred** pp 17/41
ān adj/indef art *one, a single, alone, only* nsm
5/66, 7b/55, 22/170 nsn 7a/48, 21a/36 asn
5/15, 8/33, 13/9, 21a/59 **āna** nsm 4/48,
22/120, 121, 23/123, 27/29, 33/43, 57
ānæs gsm 11/18, 19, 34 **āne** asf 3b/7, 13/4,
14/60, 17/32, 21a/55 **ānnæ** adj asm 11/10
ānne asm 4/20, 7b/53 **ānræ** adj gsf 11/16,
33 **ānre** gsf 11/20 dsf 1/59, 7b/45, 22/148
ānum dsm 13/9, 21a/7, 35c/3 dsn 21a/30
dpm 22/157, 29/18, 31a/19 **ǣnne** asm 3b/4,
4/77, 5/24, 13/2, 14/8, 27/37 [etc]
ān pron/num *one, the one, a, an* nsm 14/45,
60, 21a/15, 24/26, 25/73 nsf 7c/2, 12/59
asn 6/32, 34/22 **āne** asf 5/66 **ānne** asm
5/17, 30/117 **ānra** gpm 1/51, 23/86, 108
(see also **ǣġhwylċ, ġehwylċ**) **ānum** dsm
16/64, 25/73, 29/32 dsn 16/89 [etc]
an, ann < unnan
anbid n:B2b *period of waiting, expectation*
ns 18/88
anbyhtscealc m:B1a *retainer, servant*
anbyhtscealcas np 19/38

and conj *and* 1/43, 64, 8/4, 7, 13/2, 5, etc
ond 3a/4, 7, 5/2, 3, 7a/2, 5, 7b/1, 2, 9a/1, 2,
etc
anda m:B5a *malice, envy, grudge, terror*
andan as 17/62, 38/105 ds 14/12
āndaga m:B5a *appointed day* **āndagan** ds
12/31, 36
āndagian 2 *fix a day for appearance, adjourn*
āndagade sbj pt3s 12/30
andġit n:B2a *meaning, understanding, sense,
knowledge, perception* ns 16/41 as 4/4,
5/61, 16/25, 22/58 **andġiete** ds 5/61
andġite ds 16/47, 67, 86 **andġyt** ns 4/13
andġyte ds 4/5
andġitfullīċe adv *intelligibly, clearly*
andġitfullīcost sup 5/65
andġyt, andġyte see andġit
andlēan n:B2b *reward, requital* as 31b/50
andleofen f:B3c *money, food* **andlifne** as
9a/47 **andlyfne** as 9a/14, 34
Andred pr n *the Weald* (Kent) ds 29/3
andsaca m:B5a *adversary* ns 18/57
andswarian 2 *answer, respond* **andswarode**
pt3s 14/4, 24 **ondswarade** pt3s 9b/95
ondswarede pt3s 9b/24 **ondswaredon**
pt3p 9b/93, 100 **ondswarode** pt1s 28/20
pt3s 28/21, 54, 71 **ondswarodon** pt3p
9b/89, 28/8
andswaru f:B3a *answer, reply* **andsware** as
9b/28, 22/120, 30/44 gs 31b/2 **ondsware** as
28/26, 45
andweard adj *present, actual* **andweardan**
gsn 6/70 **andwearde** asn 22/83 npm 27/43
andwerdan gsn 22/84
andwerd, andwerdan see andweard
andwerde < andwyrdan
andwlita m:B5a *form, face* **andwlitan** as 6/5,
15b/7 ds 27/5 **anwlitan** as 6/19
(ġe)andwyrdan 1 *answer* (+d) **andwerde**
pt3s 14/5 **andwyrde** pt1s 5/39 pt3s 14/16,
22/10 **ġeondwyrdon** pt3p 28/45
ānfaldnes f:B3e.ii *unity, oneness*
ānfaldnesse gs 6/7
ānfeald adj *undivided, uniform, simple* nsf
6/33 nsn 6/27 **ānfealdan** dsm 6/4, 40 dsf
16/41 **ānfealde** npm 22/128
ānfealdlīċe adv *in the singular* 16/63
anfēng < onfōn
ānfloga m:B5a *lone flier* ns 26/62

anforht adj *very afraid, terrified* nsm 23/117
ānforlǣtan VII *abandon* **ānforlēte** sbj pr3s
9b/55
ānga adj *sole* **āngan** asm 31b/56
Angel pr n *Angeln* (Denmark), *the land of the
Angles* **Angle** ds 9a/17 **Engle** ds 9a/20
Angelcynn pr n (n:B2b.i) *the English people,
England* **Angelcyn** as 8/10 **Angelcynn** as
5/4, 5, 27, 37, 58 **Angelcynne** ds 5/13, 52,
7b/8, 8/67 **Ongolcynne** ds 9a/61
Ongolcynnes gs 9a/61
Angelþēod pr n (f:B3b) *the people of the
Angles; the English language* ns 9a/4
Ongelþēode ds 9b/9
Angelþēow pr n *Angeltheow* ns 29/43
Angelþowing adj *son of Angeltheow* nsm
29/43
anġinn n:B2b.i *beginning, introduction,
undertaking* ns 16/48 **andġinne** ds 16/45
anġin ns 16/48, 30/242 as 16/49 **anġinne**
ds 16/16, 47, 22/167 **anġyn** ns 4/23
Angle < **Angel**
Angulus pr n (Lat) *Angeln, the land of the
Angles* ns 9a/21
anġyn see **anġinn**
ānhaga m:B5a *solitary one, loner* ns 33/19,
35a/1, 38/1 **ānhogan** asm 38/40
ānhȳdiġ adj *strong-minded, resolute* nsm
36/2
āninga adv *at once* 19/250
Anlāf pr n *Olaf* ns 10/46 **Anlāfe** ds 10/26
Anlāfes gs 10/31
ānlēpe adj *single, solitary, private* **ānlēpne**
asm 5/17 **ānlīpie** npn 9a/41
ānlīcnis f:B3e.ii *likeness, image* **ānlīcnisse** ds
16/60, 61, 63 **ānlīcnissum** dp 16/62
onlīcnesse ds 17/59
ānlīpie see **ānlēpe**
ānmōd adj *wholehearted, unanimous,
resolute* **ānmōdre** dsf 9a/53 **onmōde** npm
32/12
Anna pr n *Anna* ns 21a/5
ānnæ, ānne < **ān**
ānnis f:B3e.ii *oneness, unity* ns 16/62
ānrǣd adj *single-minded, resolute, agreed*
nsm 30/44, 132, 31b/38, 84 **ānrǣde** npm
8/81
ānrǣdliċ adj *one-minded, firmly resolved*
ānrǣdliċe npf 8/74

ānre < **ān**
ansīn f:B3g *face, countenance, form* **onsȳn**
ns 26/91
ansunde adj *sound, intact* npf 21a/65
Antecrīst pr n (m:B1a) *Antichrist*
Antecrīstes gs 25/5
ānwealda m:B5a *ruler, lord* ns 23/153
anwlitan < **andwlita**
ġeanwyrde adj *professed, known* nsm 1/11
ānyman IV *take away, deprive of* inf 32/21
āparian 2 *discover, apprehend* **āparade** pt3s
12/47
āplantian 2 *plant* **āplantod** pp 15a/4
Apollines pr n *Apollo* ns 27/40
Apollonius pr n *Apollonius* ns 27/13, 32, 37,
etc **Apolloni** (Lat vocative) 27/22, 30, 35,
53 **Apollonium** as 27/66, 80 **Apolloniġe** ds
27/36, 75, 79 **Apollonio** ds 27/3, 10, 22,
etc
apostata m:B5a *apostate* **apostatan** np
25/117
apostol m:B1a *apostle* ns 16/29 **apostola** gp
9b/68 **apostolas** np 15c/6, 16/33, 37, 95 ap
16/73
ār m:B1a *messenger* ns 30/26
ār f:B3b *grace, mercy, favour, benefit, pity,
respect; estate* ns 26/107 **āra** gp 15c/3 **āre**
as 9a/14, 12/56, 36/33 as/gs 38/1, 114 gs
9a/43 **ārum** dp 31a/37 (=adv *honourably*)
ārās < **ārīsan**
ārǣdan 1 *appoint, decree, determine; read*
inf 5/55, 58 **ārǣd** pp 38/5 **ārǣded** pp 28/58
ārǣran 1 *raise up, erect, establish* inf 21a/75
ārǣrde pt3s 16/34, 24/3 pp npm 22/126
ārǣrdon pt3p 4/21 **ārǣred** pp 23/44
ārǣredan pp npm 22/125
arc m:B1a *ark* **arce** ds 13/1, 7, 14, 17, 20
arces gs 13/12
arċebiscop m:B1a *archbishop* ns 8/13, 47, 66
arċebisceop ns 4/21 **arċebiscope** ds 8/18,
48 **arċebiscopes** gs 8/36 **ærċebiscepe** ds
5/62
arċebiscopstōl m:B1a *archiepiscopal see*
arċebiscopstōle ds 8/14
Arcestrates pr n *Arcestrates* ns 27/35, 52
āreċċan 1 *relate, tell, render, translate*
āreċċean inf 5/15, 65 **āreċe** imp s 27/12
ārehte pt3s 27/16
ārētan 1 *gladden, delight* **ārēted** pp 19/167

ārfæst adj *compassionate, gracious, virtuous, pious* nsm 19/190

ārfæstnis f:B3e.ii *piety, virtue, grace* **ārfæstnisse** ds 9b/3 **ārfæstnyss** ns 21a/41

ārhwæt adj *eager for glory* **ārhwate** npm 10/73

āriht adv *rightly, properly* 25/101

ārīsan I *arise, spring up, originate, come to pass* inf 9b/99, 22/7, 59, 118 **ārās** pt1s 1/39 pt3s 9b/19, 40, 22/3, 26, 23/101, etc **ārīsað** pr3p 15a/8, 32/8 **ārīse** pr1s 1/72 pr3s 22/9 **ārisen** pp 22/79 **ārison** pt1p 1/44 pt3p 22/123, 128, 27/60 **ārīst** pr3s 22/103 **āryson** pt3p 14/66

āriste < **ǣrist**

ārlēas adj *impious, wicked* **ārlēasan** dsf 9a/39

arn < **irnan**

arod adj *ready, bold* nsm 19/275

ārstæf m:B1a *benefit, grace* **ārstafum** dp 35d/24

ārwurðe adj *honourable* nsm 24/57 **ārwurðost** sup nsm 24/43

ārwurðnysse f:B3e.ii *reverence, honour* ds 21a/69

āryson < **ārīsan**

āsǣd, āsǣde < **āsecgan**

asca < **æsc**

Ascanmynster pr n *Axminster* (Dev.) ds 29/36

āsceacan VI *shake* **āscēoc** pt3s 30/230

āscēotan II *lance* inf 21a/44

āscian 2 *ask, inquire* **āhsast** pr2s 1/51 **āhsian** inf 28/62 **āhsode** pt1s 28/8 **āscade** pt3s 12/51 **āxie** pr1s 1/10 **āxode** pt3s 14/1 **āxsa** imp s 27/9 **āxsast** pr2s 27/13

ġeāscian 2 *learn (by asking), discover* **ġeāscodan** pt1p 36/21 **ġeāscode** pt3s 29/8

āsecgan 3 *say, tell, express* inf 19/330, 38/11 **āsǣd** pp 34/19 **āsǣde** pt3s 30/198

āsendan 1 *send forth* **āsende** pt3s 13/2, 3, 8, 11, 14/63

āsēon I *strain* **āsēownes** pp gsn 3a/5

āsettan 1 *set down, place, put* **āsette** pt3s 7a/1, 14/60 sbj pr3s 13/6, 23/142 **āsetton** pt3p 14/30, 43, 23/32

āsingan III *sing* **āsong** pt3s 9b/52

āsmēaġan 1 *consider, deal with, explicate* inf 25/142 **āsmēaġean** inf 4/20

āsolcennes f:B3e.ii *laziness* **āsolcennesse** as 25/151

āsong < **āsingan**

āsprungnis f:B3e.ii *failing, eclipse* ns 28/39

Asser pr n *Asser* **Assere** ds 5/62

Assȳria pr n *Assyria* **Assīriam** ds 15b/4

Assȳrias pr n *the Assyrians* **Assīria** gp 19/232, 309 **Assȳria** gp 19/265 **Assȳrium** dp 19/218

āstāg, āstāh < **āstīgan**

āstandan VI *stand up* **āstōd** pt3s 31b/65

āstellan 1 *establish, ordain* **āstealde** pt3s 16/72, 21a/90

āstīgan I *ascend, mount, descend* **āstāg** pt3s 23/103 **āstāh** pt1s 21b/23 pt3s 18/5, 22, 22/64, 139, 153, 175 **āstīge** sbj pr3s 22/132, 133 **āstīgende** prp nsm 22/138

āstirian 1 *stir, excite, move, remove* inf 27/42 **āstyred** pp 23/30

āstōd < **āstandan**

āstyred < **āstirian**

āswāmian 2 *die away, cease* **āswāmað** pr3s 17/39

āswǣscan VI *wash away, extinguish* **āswǣscte** pp npf 22/126

āswebban 1 *put to sleep, put to death* **āswefede** pp npm 10/30 apm 19/321

āswefede < **āswebban**

āsyndran 1 *separate* **āsyndrede** pp npm 6/71

ātēon II *draw off, remove* **ātēah** pt3s 18/45 **ātuge** sbj pr3s 9b/72

ātēorian 2 *fall away, fail* **ātēoriað** pr3p 4/16 **ātēorige** sbj pr3s 4/18

atol adj *terrible, dire, monstrous* nsn 18/10 asn 26/6 **atolan** asm 19/75 (=noun) dpm 31b/11 **atolne** asm 19/246

ātuge < **ātēon**

āð m:B1a *oath* ns 12/33, 42 as 7b/12, 12/29, 31, 37, 25/162 **aða** ds 12/39 **aðe** ds 12/23 is 12/18

āðbriċe m:B1g *oath-breaking* **āðbricas** ap 25/114

āþecgan 1 *take food, consume* 39/2, 7

Aþelwold pr n *Athelwold* ns 4/21, 8/6 **Aþelwoldæ** ds 11/20

āþenċan *plan, contrive* inf 17/63

āþȳstrian 2 *darken, be eclipsed* **āþȳstrod** pp 22/161

āðswaru f:B3a *swearing of an oath* **āðsware** ds 18/113

Aðulf pr n *Æthelwulf* **Aðulfe** ds 12/17

Aurelianus pr n *Aurelianus* ns 9a/55

āwa adv *ever, always* 26/79; in phr **āwa tō aldre** *for ever and ever* 19/120

āwearp < **āweorpan**

āweċċan 1 *awake, awaken* inf 19/258, 273 **āwecþ** pr3s 1/71, 72 **āwehte** pt3s 9b/73 **āwehton** pt3p 27/78

āweiġ adv *away, out* 22/22

āwendan 1 *change, vary, translate* inf 4/1, 16/2, 5, 88, 101, 104 **āwend** pp 16/6, 22/142 **āwende** pt1s 4/2, 5/65 pp npm 4/54 **āwent** pr3s 16/90

āweorpan III *throw (away), cast down, reject* **āwearp** pt3s 7b/3 **āweorpe** imp s 3a/14 **āworpene** pp npm 17/83 **āwurpan** inf 16/94 (twice)

āwierġan 1 *curse, damn* **āwyrġed** pp 18/87

āwiht indef pron *aught, anything, nothing* **āhtes** gs 8/27 **āwuht** as 7b/4 (=adv *at all*) **ōwiht** ns 40/23 as 7b/29, 26/46; in phr **tō āhte** *at all, in any way* 25/18

āwilian 2 *roll* inf 22/19

āworpene < **āweorpan**

āwrītan 1 *write, write down, copy* inf 4/24, 7b/1, 16/88, 106, 21a/2 **āwrāt** pt3s 22/121, 128, 25/146 **āwriten** pp 4/39, 16/67 **āwritene** pp npf 5/30 **āwritenne** pp asm 14/44 **āwriton** pt3p 22/57 **āwrytan** pp 21a/30

āwðer adv *either* **āwðer oððe ... oððe** *either ... or* 7b/6–7

āwuht see **āwiht**

āwurpan < **āweorpan**

āwyltan 1 *roll, roll away* **āwylte** pt3s 22/21, 77

āwyrdan 1 *maim, destroy, damage, impair* **āwyrded** pp 31a/51

āwyrġed < **āwierġan**

āx-, āxs- see **āscian**

Æ

æ f:B3g.i *law, scripture* ns 5/43, 16/10, 25, 22/57 as 15a/3, 16/30, 94 ds 15a/3, 16/9, 11, 20, 21, 22/122

æcer m:B1a *acre, field* as 1/22

ǣdre adv *swiftly, at once* 19/64, 95, 246

Ǣdwine r n *Edwin* ns 8/17

ǣfen n:B2c.iii *evening, vespers* as 1/46 (see note) **ǣfenne** ds 9b/82

ǣfenġeweorc n:B2b *evening work* **ǣfenġeweorce** ds 3b/3

ǣfentīd f:B3g *evening, evening-time* as 28/62 **ǣfentīde** as 23/68

ǣfest adj *pious, religious* nsm 9b/73 **ǣfeste** apn 9b/9 **ǣfestan** asf 9b/14

ǣfestnes f:B3e.ii *religion, piety* **ǣfestnesse** ds 9b/14 **ǣfestnisse** ds 9b/3

Ǣfiċ pr n *Æfic* as 8/64

æflāst m:B1a *deviant course* **æflāstum** dp 18/28

æfnan 1 *make ready* **ġeæfned** pp 31a/45

ǣfnung f:B3d *evening* **ǣfnunge** ds 13/9

ǣfre adv *always, ever* 2a/4, 4/78, 5/40, 7c/5, 20, 10/66, 15b/11, 16/50, 17/61, 21a/21, 22/155, 40/39, etc

æftan adv *from behind, in the back* 10/63, 25/56

æfter adv *after, afterwards, then, back* 9b/38, 17/99, 26/77, 34/20, 45

æfter prep +a/d/i *after, following, according to, by means of, about, along* 1/41, 2c/3, 3a/14, 3b/2, 4/48, 52, 5/33, 6/21, 25, 7b/6, 7c/28, 8/14, 15, 9a/31, 9b/4, 13/1, 14/67, 15c/7, 16/20, 17/59, 18/65 (*through*), 22/68, 109, 23/65, 27/44, 50, 31a/5, 31b/81, etc **aefter** 20a/5; in phrs **æfter þām þe** *after, according as* 14/33, 40 **æfter þon þe** *after, when* 9a/50

æftera comp adj *next, second, subsequent* **æfteran** dsm 7b/33 **æftran** isn 28/72

æftercweþende mp:B4d *those speaking afterwards* **æftercweþendra** gp 26/72

æftran < **æftera**

æfðonca m:B5a *grudge* **æfðoncan** ap 19/265

ǣġ n:B2b.iii *egg* **ǣiġra** np 1/56

ǣġhwā pron *every one, everything, anything* **ǣġhwæt** asn 7b/55, 28/24

ǣġhwǣr adv *everywhere, completely* 9a/54, 22/100, 25/22, 49, 119

ǣġhwylċ adj *each, every* nsf 23/120 **ǣġhwelċ** nsm 7b/12 **ǣġhwylċan** dsm 25/30

ǣġhwylċ pron *each, each one* nsm 30/234 **ǣġhwylċne** asm 23/86 (**ǣġhwylċne ānra** *each one*), 19/50 **ǣġhwylċum** dsm 19/166

ǣġþer adj *either, each* ǣġðrum dsm 6/52
    dsn 4/23
ǣġþer conj *both* 16/96 ǣġder 30/224 ǣġþer
    ġe...ġe *both...and* 5/4, 9, 6/13, 17, 8/41,
    51, 15b/2, etc ǣiġðer...ġe 22/88
ǣġþer pron *each, either, both* nsm 8/77,
    12/13, 30/133 ǣiġþær nsm 11/15
ǣġylde adj *unpaid, receiving no
    compensation* nsm 25/86
ǣht f:B3g *property, possessions, ownership*
    as 12/15, 37/36 ǣhta as 7b/17 ap 16/33
    ǣhtan ap 7a/16
ǣiġra < ǣġ
ǣlċ adj *each, every, any* nsm 4/12, 32, 6/13,
    23 asn 8/55 ǣlċæ dsn 11/25 ǣlċe asm 6/17
    dsm 1/22, 3a/12, 15, 15b/9 ǣlċes gsm 6/47,
    16/65 gsn 6/33 ǣlchum dsm 11/28 ǣlċne
    asm 12/40 ǣlċra gpn 25/32 ǣlċum dsm
    4/5, 5/66, 11/7 dsn 16/43 [etc]
ǣlċ pron *each, everyone* nsm 7c/7, 15b/3,
    15c/4, 25/55, 56 nsn 27/46 ǣlċes gsm
    12/20 ǣlċre asf 5/66
ælde mp:B1h *men, human beings* ælda gp
    26/77, 38/85 æ ldum dp 35a/6
ældo see yldo
Ælfere pr n *Ælfhere* ns 8/4, 30/80
Ælfgār pr n *Ælfgar* as 8/44
Ælfġyfu pr n *Ælfgifu* Ælfġyfæ gs 11/1
Ælfnōð pr n *Ælfnoth* ns 30/183
Ælfred pr n *Alfred* ns 5/2, 7b/1, 9, 12/18, 40
    Ælfrede ds 12/7
Ælfrīċ pr n *Ælfric* ns 4/1, 8/4, 8, 31, 48, 75,
    12/10, 16/2 Ælfrīċes gs 8/44, 30/209
    Ealfrīċe ds 8/28
ælfscīne adj *of elfin beauty* ælfscīnu nsf
    19/14
Ælfstān pr n *Ælfstan* Ælfstāne ds 8/29
    Ælfstānes gs 12/65
Ælfwar pr n *Ælfwar* Ælfwaræ ds 11/23
    Ælfwæræ ds 11/26
Ælfwerd pr n *Ælfweard* Ælfwerdæ ds 11/23,
    33
Ælfwine pr n *Ælfwin* ns 30/211, 231
ælmesriht n:B2a *right to alms* np 25/38
ælmesse f:B5c *almsgiving, charity* ælmessan
    ds 12/62 ælmyssan as 21a/85
ælmihtiġ adj *almighty* nsm 9b/39, 16/46,
    19/300, 23/39, 93, 98, 153, 156
    ælmehtigan gsm 6/21 ælmihtiga nsm

21a/8, 18 ælmihtigan dsm (=noun) 19/7,
    345 ælmihtiġne asm 23/60 ælmihtigum
    dsm 5/18, 22/176
ælne < eall
ælwiht f:B3g *alien creature* ælwihta gp
    31b/9
ġeǣmetiġan 2 *empty* ġeǣmetiġe sbj pr2s
    5/20
ǣmtiġ adj *empty* nsf 22/27
ænde see ende
ænge *narrow, constricted* nsm ænga
    17/19
æniġ adj *any* nsm 7b/55, 7c/5, 16/22, 19/329,
    31b/69, 34/4 asn 9b/88, 22/54 æneġum
    dsm 17/72 dpn 7b/56 ænġes gsm 26/116
    ænġum dsm 7b/14 æniġ asn 1/32 æniġe
    asf 17/54 æniġne asm 1/24, 4/6, 5/18,
    21a/78 æniġre dsf 9a/43 æniġum dsm
    16/7, 25/126 enġu nsf 12/39 [etc]
æniġ pron *any, anyone* nsm 9a/44, 17/90,
    18/10, 63, 23/110, 117, 25/51, 54, etc
ǣnne < ān
æppel m:B4a *apple* æppla np 3b/8
ǣr adv *before, previously, formerly, already,
    early, soon* 6/28, 7a/46, 9a/8, 9b/78, 87,
    12/6, 24, 14/66, 21a/20, 36, 23/137, 34/23,
    etc; in phrs nō þȳ ǣr *none the sooner*
    31b/11 on ǣr *beforehand* 24/50; see also
    ǣrest, ǣrur
ǣr conj *before, until* (usually +sbj) 3c/5,
    6/15, 23, 12/6, 24, 26/74, 27/51, 29/10, etc;
    in conj phrs *before* ǣr ðām þe 22/30 ǣr
    ðǣm ðe 5/26, 6/11 ǣr þan 23/88 ǣr þan
    þe 13/3, 16/10 ǣrðon þe 19/252
ǣr prep +d *before, until* 7b/52, 16/20, 22/56,
    110, 26/69
ǣr (for ēar) m:B1a *sea, wave* ǣra gp 10/26
ǣrǣnde see ǣrende
ærċebiscepe < arċebiscop
ǣrdēað m:B1a *premature death* ns 18/94
ǣrende n:B2h *message* as 18/73 ǣrænde as
    30/28
ǣrendgewrit n:B2a *letter* as 5/15
ǣrendraca m:B5a *messenger, minister*
    ǣrenddracan ap 9a/9 ǣrendwrecum
    dp 5/6
ǣrenfæt n:B2d *brass vessel* asn 3a/2
ǣrest adj *first* ǣreste nsf 9b/64; in phr æt
    ǣrestan dsn *first of all* 7b/12

ǣrest adv (sup of **ǣr**) *first, at first, before all*
7b/7, 7c/4, 10, 8/1, 10, 9a/23, 9b/35, 12/17,
21a/33, 80, etc **ǣræst** 11/4 **ǣrost** 30/124

ǣrġewin n:B2b *former struggle* as 23/19

ǣrist m:B1a/f:3g.i *resurrection* ns 22/88, 90
as 22/2, 33, 113, 124 **āriste** ds 22/137
ǣriste gs 15c/6 ds 22/73, 89, 104, etc
ǣristes gs 22/64, 97, 126, etc **ǣryste** ds
14/67

ǣrndon < **irnan**

ǣrnemerġen m:B1a *early morning,*
day-break **ǣrnemerien** ds 22/17

ǣrost < **ǣrest**

ǣrsceaft f:B3g *ancient building* ns 37/16

ǣrðon < **ǣr**

ǣrur adv (comp of **ǣr**) *earlier* 23/108

ǣrwacol adj *awake early* 27/77

ǣryste < **ǣrist**

ǣs n:B2b *carrion, food* **ǣses** gs 10/63,
30/107

ǣsǣlan 1 *ensnare, encumber* **ǣsǣled**
pp 18/25

æsc m:B1a *ash(-spear)* as 30/43, 310 **asca** gp
38/99

Æscferð pr n *Ashferth* ns 30/267

æschere m:B1g *army in ships* ns 30/69

æscholt n:B2b *spear made of ash* as 30/230

æscplega m:B5a *spear-play, battle*
æscplegan ds 19/217

æscrōf adj *spear-renowned, brave with spear*
æscrōfe npm 19/336

Æscwīġ pr n *Æscwig* **Æscwīġe** ds 8/29

æstel m:B1b *book-marker, pointer* ns 5/67 as
5/68

æswic m:B1a *offence, transgression* **æswicas**
ap 25/112

æt prep +d *at, in, from, to, next to, with, by*
1/21, 5/62, 63, 70, 7a/7, 7b/32, 44, 45,
7c/24, 8/9, 56, 69, 15b/8, 16/19, 21a/72,
27/17, etc

ǣt n:B2b *food, prey* **ǣtes** gs 19/210

ǣt < **etan**

ætbærst < **ætberstan**

ætberan IV *bear away* inf 31b/70

ætberstan III *escape* **ætbærst** pt3s 8/33
ætberste sbj pr3s 7c/7

ætbrǣd < **ætbreġdan**

ætēowan 1 *appear, show, reveal* **ætēowde**
pt3s 8/46, 21b/21 **ætēowdon** pt3p 14/67

ætēowed pp 22/44 **ætēowiað** pr3p 4/38

ætēowod pp 22/62 **ætȳwan** inf 19/174

ǣtern < **ǣtterne**

ætforan prep +d *before, in front of* 1/45,
22/175, 30/16

ætgædere adv *together, at the same time,*
united 9a/43, 9b/87, 23/48, 25/145, 31a/1
ætgædre 38/39

ætġebycgan 1 *buy* **ætġebicge** sbj pr3s 7a/51

æthlēapan VII *escape from* **æthlēape** sbj
pr3s 25/83

ætlicgan V *lie idle* **ætlicge** sbj pr3s 4/8

ǣton < **etan**

ætsacan VI *deny* inf 12/49

ætsomne adv *together, united, at the same*
time 9b/82, 33/31 **ætsamne** 10/57, 34/18

ætspringan III *spurt out* **ætspranc** pt3s
31a/59

ǣtterne adj *poisonous, deadly* nsm 30/146
ǣtern nsm 28/37 **ǣttrynne** asm 30/47

ætwītan 1 *censure, reproach, blame, impute*
inf 30/220, 250 **ætwiten** pp 34/19 **ætwiton**
pt3p 31a/88

ætȳwan see **ætēowan**

Æþælfledæ pr n *Æthelflæd* ds 11/27

Æþelbald pr n *Æthelbald* as 29/37

æðelborennes f:B3e.ii *nobility*
æðelborennesse as 27/11, 14

Æþelbryht pr n *Ethelbert* **Æðelbirht** ns 7a/1
Æþelbryhtes gs 7b/7

Æðeldrȳð pr n *Æthelthryth, Audrey* ns 12/15,
21a/19, 23 **Æðeldrȳðe** ds 12/19, 21a/3, 17
Æðelðrȳðe gs 21a/1

æþele adj *noble* nsm 30/280 nsf 10/16,
19/256 nsf 19/176 (=noun) **æþelan** asm
30/151 gsf 21b/1 **æþelon** dsm 21b/6

ġeæþele adj *inborn, natural* nsn 10/7

Æðelgār pr n *Æthelgar* ns 8/14 **Æþelgāres**
gs 30/320

æþeling m:B1a *atheling, prince, nobleman,*
lord (see 33/14n) ns 10/3, 58, 29/22, 31a/50
as 29/7, 12, 16, 32 **æþelinga** gp 26/93
æþelingæ ds 11/17 **æþelinge** ds 23/58
æþelinges gs 29/36

Æðelm pr n *Æthelhelm* ns 12/2, 24, 27, 63 as
12/9, 25 **Æðelme** ds 12/36

Æðelnōð pr n *Æthelnoth* **Æðelnāð** ns 12/20
Æðelnōðes gs 12/65

æþelo np:B2a *noble lineage* ap 30/216

Æþelrēd pr n *Æthelred* as 25/63 **Æþelrēdes**
gs 30/53, 151, 203

Æþelstān pr n *Athelstan* ns 10/1

Æðelward pr n *Ætheweard* **Æðelwærd** as
16/2 **Æþelwærdæ** ds 11/23 **Æþelwerdæ**
ds 11/34

Æðelwine pr n *Æthelwine* ns 8/26

Æðelwold pr n *Athelwold* ns 8/6 **Æþelwoldæ**
ds 11/20

Æðerēd pr n *Æthered* **Æðerēdes** gs 12/3

Æþerīċ pr n *Ætheric* ns 30/280

ǣwbryċe m:B1g *adultery* **ǣwbrycas** ap
25/113

ǣwe adj *lawful, legitimate* **ǣwum** dsn 7b/44,
46

ǣwerdlan < æfwerdla

ǣwiscmōd adj *ashamed, humiliated*
ǣwiscmōde npm 10/56

ǣwum adv *lawfully, legitimately* 7b/45, 46

ǣwum < ǣwe

Ǣypta < Ēgypte

B

bā < bēġen

Babilōnia pr n *Babylon* gs 15c/2 **Babilōne** ds
28/73

(ġe)bād < (ġe)bīdan

baldlīċe adv *boldly, rashly* 30/311 **baldlīcost**
sup 30/78

baldor m:B1a *prince, lord* ns 19/9, 32, 49,
338

balzamum n:B2a *balsam* as 28/29, 30 ?gs
28/10

bām < bēġen

bān n:B2b *bone* as 22/51 ap 21a/51, 60

bana m:B5a *slayer, murderer* ns 30/299
banan gs 23/66, 34/34 ds 29/27 **bonan** ds
35c/3

bānfæt n:B2d '*bone-vessel*', *body* **bānfatu**
ap 31a/54

bānhelm m:B1a '*bone-protector*', *?helmet*,
?shield ns 32/30

bānhring m:B1a '*bone-ring*', *vertebra*
bānhringas ap 31b/76

bānhūs n:B2b '*bone-house*', *body* **bānhūses**
gs 18/78

Barrabbas pr n *Barabbas* ns 14/10
Barrabban as 14/11, 16 etc

bāsnian 2 +d *await, expect* **bāsnodon** pt3p
18/25

baþian 2 *bathe* inf 21a/32, 33, 34, 38/47

baþu < bæþ

Baþum pr n *Bath* (Som.) dp 11/13 (see note)

bæ see be

bǣagas < bēag

Bæbbanburh pr n *Bamborough* (Northum.)
ns 8/39

bæc n:B2a *back* as 30/276 (**ofer bæc**
backwards)

bæcere m:B1g *baker* **bæceras** np 1/17

(ġe)bæd, (ġe)bǣd- see (ġe)biddan

bæftan adv *afterwards, behind* 22/101, 154

bǣl n:B2b *fire, flame, funeral-pyre* as 31a/47,
54 **bǣle** ds 26/114

bælc m:B1a *pride* ns 19/267

bænd m:B1a *headband, chaplet* **bændes**
gs 11/28

bær, bǣr- see beran

ġebǣran 1 *bear oneself, enjoy oneself* inf
32/38 **ġebǣrdon** pt3p 19/27

bærnan 1 *burn* inf 31a/54 **bærnað** pr3p
25/104 **bærndon** pt3p 8/55, 9a/35, 37

bærnett n:B2c.iii *burning, arson* **bærnette**
ds 8/53

ġebǣro f:B3h *demeanour, behaviour,
gesture, outcry* as 40/44 ds 40/21
ġebǣrum dp 29/14

bǣron < beran

bærst < berstan

bætǣcen < betǣcan

bæþ n:B2a *bath* **baþu** np 37/40, 46

be prep +d/i *about, according to, by,
concerning, with, along, near, beside, by,
by means of, through* 1/41, 51, 2a/7, 4/58,
6/13, 36, 7a/54, 7b/25, 8/23, 9b/18, 14/19,
15c/1, 3, 9, 16/13, 18, 21a/2, 22/49, 57, etc
bæ 11/3, 6, 22 **bī** 5/72, 9b/63, 64, 28/11,
40/1, etc; in phr **be ... twēonum** *between*
18/117 (see note); see also **full, hwȳ**

bēacen n:B2c.i *beacon, sign, portent* ns 23/6,
as 23/21 **bēacna** gp 23/118 **bēacne** ds
23/83

ġebēad < (ġe)bēodan

Beadohild pr n (f:B3b) *Beadohild*
Beadohilde ds 36/8

beadolēoma m:B5a '*battle light*', *gleaming
sword* ns 31b/32

Beadonesc adj *of Badon* **Beadonescan** gsf
9a/60
beadorinc m:B1a *warrior* **beadorinca** gp
19/276, 31a/47
beadoweorc n:B2b *warlike deed*
beadoweorca gp 35a/2
beadu f:B3f *battle, conflict, fighting*
beadowe ds 19/213 **beaduwe** ds 19/175,
30/185, 33/15 **beadwe** gs 31b/48
beaducāfa m:B5a *one bold in battle* ns 39/11
beadulāc n:B2b *battle-play, battle* **beadulāce**
ds 31b/70
beadurǣs m:B1a *rush of battle, onslaught* ns
30/111
beaduweorc n:B2b *work of battle,*
battle-deed **beaduweorca** gp 10/48
bēag m:B1a *ring, bracelet, treasure,*
valuables ?ns 37/17 **bǣagas** ap 11/15,
18/111, 30/31, 160, 33/29 **bēages** gs 11/18,
19 **bēagum** dp 19/36, 33/45
bēagġyfan < **bēahġifa**
ġebēah < (**ġe**)**būgan**
bēahġifa m:B5a *ring-giver, lord* ns 10/2
bēaġġyfan gs 31a/40 **bēahġifan** 30/290
bēahġifu f:B3a *ring-giving* **bēahġife** ds
33/15
bēahhroden adj *ring-adorned* **bēahhrodene**
npf 19/138
beald adj *bold* **bealde** npm 19/17
bealo n:B2g *harm, malice* as 26/112
bealofull adj *wicked, evil* nsm 19/63
bealofulla nsm 19/48 **bealofullan** asm
19/100 gsm 19/248
bealosīþ m:B1a *bitter journey, painful*
experience **bealosīþa** gp 26/28
bealospell n:B2b.i *baleful message*
bealospella gp 18/65
bealuware mp:B1h *dwellers in iniquity, evil*
men **bealuwara** gp 23/79
bēam m:B1a *tree, cross* ns 23/97 **bēama** gp
23/6 **bēame** ds 23/114 is 23/122
bēamtelg m:B1a *ink* or *dye from a tree*
bēamtelge ds 35d/9
bēan f:B3b *bean* **bēana** ap 1/56
(**ġe**)**bearh** < (**ġe**)**beorgan**
bearhtm m:B1a *brightness, flash* **bearhtme**
ds 19/39 (=adv *in an instant*)
bearm m:B1a *lap, bosom, breast* ns 31a/75,
82 **bearme** ds 33/25

bearn n:B2b *child, son, descendant* ns 7a/48,
23/83, 25/51, 77, 30/92, 155, etc as 7a/46,
49, 7b/29, 30, 19/84, 25/76, 31b/55 np
19/24, 26/77, 30/186, 35d/18 ap 14/25,
17/71, 26/93 **bearna** gp 19/51 **bearne** ds
25/50 **bearnum** dp 7a/47, 9b/35, 17/66,
19/33
bearnmyrðra m:B5a *child-murderer*
bearnmyrðran np 25/136
bearo m:B1f *grove, wood* as 28/22, 63
bearowe ds 33/18 **bearwas** np 26/48 ap
28/12, 28 **bearwe** ds 40/27 **bearwum** dp
28/51
bēatan VII *beat, pound* **bēotan** pt3p 26/23
bēotun pt3p 14/33
beæftan adv *behind* 19/112
beæftan prep +d *behind* 29/19, 21
bebēodan I *command, bid, enjoin, commend,*
assign (+d) **bebēad** pt3s 7b/4, 16/75,
17/68, 18/75, 19/38, 144, 33/49 **bebēod**
imp s 22/7 **bebēodende** prp nsm 9b/108
bebīode pr1s 5/19, 67 **beboden** pp 9b/21,
53, 16/81, 27/71 **bebudon** pt3p 9b/49
bibēad pt3s 9b/86
bebiriġed < **bebyrġian**
bebod n:B2a *command, decree* as 9a/6
beboden, bebudon < **bebēodan**
bebyrġan 1 *bury* **bebyrġed** pp 21a/47
bebyrġian 2 *bury, inter* **bebiriġed** pp 22/5,
14
bebyriġnys f:B3e.ii *burial, burying*
bebyriġnysse as 9a/44
bēċ < **bōc**
beċeorfan III *deprive by cutting off* **beċearf**
pt3s 31b/99
beclȳsan 1 *close, enclose* **beclȳsedne**
pp 22/80
becōm, becōm- < **becuman**
becuman IV *come, arrive, reach, meet with,*
happen, overcome inf 28/53, 61 **becōm**
pt3s 22/145, 27/2 **becōman** pt3p 10/70
becōmon pt3p 5/22 **becume** sbj pr3s 2a/5
becumon pt3p 4/5 **becwōm** pt3s 9b/106,
18/1, 10
bed < **bedd**
ġebed n:B2a *prayer* **ġebedu** ap 21a/31
Bēda pr n (m:B5a) *Bede* 21a/18, 80 **Bēdan** as
21a/15
bēdan 1 *compel, constrain* **ġebēded** pp 10/33

bedǣlan 1 *deprive* (+d *of*) **bedǣlde** pp npm 25/26 **bidǣled** pp 38/20

bedd n:B2b.i *bed, resting-place* **bed** as 19/48 **bedde** ds 1/40, 3a/11, 19/72, 278, 27/76, 35c/4 **beddes** gs 19/63

ġe**bedda** m/f:B5a/c *bedfellow, spouse* ġe**beddan** as 21a/17

ġe**bēded** < **bēdan**

bedelfan III *bury* **bedealf** pt3s 23/75

bedrest f:B3b *bed* **bedreste** ds 19/36

bedrīfan I *drive, spatter* **bedrifenne** pp asm 23/62

beēode < **begān**

befangen < **befōn**

befaran VI *surround* **befarene** pp npm 18/52

befǣllan *strike down* **befǣlled** pp 17/24

befǣstan 1 *entrust, commit, apply oneself* (+d *to*) inf 5/21, 31a/53 **befǣste** sbj pr2s 5/22, 27/79 sbj pr3s 4/7

befeallan VII *befall, happen to, bereave* (+d *of*) **befeallen** pp 31a/64 **befylð** pr3s 4/79, 82, 91

befēhð, befēng < **befōn**

befēolan III +d *apply oneself to* inf 5/53

beflōwan VII *flow round, surround* **beflōwen** pp 40/49

befōn II *clasp, encompass, enclose, include* **befangen** pp 17/37 **befēhð** pr3s 24/75 **befēng** pt3s 12/18, 37/39

beforan prep +d *before, in front of, in the presence of* 10/67, 14/1, 23, 31, 15c/13, 22/55, 27/58, 76, 34/5 **biforan** 38/46

befylð < **befeallan**

bēga < **bēġen**

began < **beġinnan**

begān anom *practise, carry out, surround* **beēode** pt3s 29/10 **begǣst** pr2s 1/18

beġēat, beġēat- see **beġietan**

bēġen dual pron/adj *both* npm 3c/1, 10/57, 19/207, 30/183, 191, 291, 305 apm 30/182 **bā** npf 19/133 **bām** dpn 34/17 **bēġa** gsn 31a/62 **bēġea** gpf 19/128

beġēotan II *pour over, soak* **begoten** pp 23/7, 49

beġietan V *come upon, acquire, get, seize, assail* inf 5/12 **beġeat** pt3s 31a/6, 84, 40/32, 41 **beġēatan** pt3p 10/73 **beġēaton** pt3p 5/32 **beġite** sbj pr3s 7c/16 **biġeat** pt3s 26/6

beġinnan III *begin* **began** pt3s 16/31

beġiondan prep +d *beyond* 5/16

begong m:B1a *expanse, region* as 31b/6

begrindan II *grind, scrape clean* **begrunden** pp 35d/6

behabban 3 *include, contain* **behæfð** pr3s 22/66

behāt n:B2b *promise* **behātum** dp 22/114

behātan VII *promise, vow* **behēt** pt3s 21a/22, 22/30, 117, 27/57 **behētan** pt1p 25/160 **behēte** sbj pt3s 21a/16, 22/113

behæfð < **behabban**

behēafdian 2 *behead, decapitate* **behēafdod** pp 19/289

behealdan VII *behold, gaze on, watch over, guard, occupy* inf 17/29 **behēold** pt1s 23/25, 58 pt3s 13/12, 22/13, 31b/7 **behēoldon** pt3p 14/43

behēfe adj *proper, necessary* nsf 1/4

behēt, behēt- see **behātan**

behindan adv *behind* 18/11

behindan prep +d *behind* 10/60

behionan prep +d *on this side of* 5/14

behōfian 2 +g *have need of, require* **behōfað** pr3s 34/24

behrēowsian 2 *repent* **behrēowsiað** pr3p 16/80

behrīman 1 *encrust with rime* or *frost* **behrīmed** pp 40/48

bēhð f:B3b *sign, proof* **bēhðe** ds 19/174

behwyrfan 1 *prepare* inf 22/18

behȳdan 1 *hide, conceal* **behȳdde** pp npm 9a/53

belēac < **belūcan**

belēosan II +d *be deprived of, lose* **belēas** pt1s 35d/4 **beloren** pp 31a/11

ġe**belgan** III *be* or *become enraged* ġe**bolgen** pp 31b/48

belimpan III *pertain, concern, conduce to* **belumpen** sbj pt3p 9b/3 **belumpon** pt3p 9b/14

belīðan I +g *deprive of* **belidenne** pp 19/280

belocen, belocenre < **belūcan**

beloren < **belēosan**

belt m:B1a *belt* as 12/3

belūcan II *lock, close, surround, shut in, contain* **belēac** pt3s 18/11, 31a/70 **belocen** pp 16/41, 22/154, 29/23 **belocenre** pp dsf 22/81

belump-, belympð see **belimpan**

bemurnan III *mourn over, bewail* **bemearn** pt3s 31a/15

benam < **beniman**

benǣman 1 +d *take away, deprive of* inf 19/76

benċ f:B3g *bench* **benċe** ds 30/213 **benċum** dp 19/18

benċsittend m:B4d '*bench-sitter*', *guest* **benċsittende** ap 19/27

benemman 1 *name, declare* **benemde** pt3s 31a/35

benġeat n:B2d '*wound-gate*', *gash* **benġeato** np 31a/59

beniman IV *take away from, deprive (of* +d) **benam** pt3s 29/1 **benumen** pp 17/25 **benumene** pp npn 28/41 **binōm** pt3s 35d/2, 36/16

benn f:B3e *wound* **benne** np 38/49

bennian 2 *wound, injure* ġe**bennad** pp 35a/2

benumen, benumene < **beniman**

bēo < **bēon-wesan**

bēod m:B1a *table* as 15c/14

(ġe)**bēodan** II *offer, give, announce, proclaim* ġe**bēad** pt3s 29/16, 23 **bēodaþ** pr3p 25/120 **bēodeð** pr3s 26/54 ġe**boden** pp 29/28 **budon** pt3p 29/27, 31a/23

bēom < **bēon-wesan**

bēon-wesan anom *be, exist, become* (often as auxil + infin) **bēo** sbj pr1s 15b/13, 16/105 sbj pr3s 4/8, 7b/17, 7c/18, 14/13, 16/41, 21a/39 imp p 22/47, 92 **bēom** pr1s 35b/8 **bēon** inf 1/6, 4/16, 39, 7c/4 sbj pr3p 22/93, 27/63 **bēoþ** pr1p 22/74 pr3p 4/31, 6/60, 17/92, 28/21, 33/1, 34/18 imp p 13/16 **bī** sbj pr3s 1/8 **bīo** sbj pr3s 6/52 imp p 22/25 **bīon** inf 6/61 **bīoð** pr3p 6/38, 61 **bist** pr2s 2a/5, 28/73 **biþ** pr3s 2a/1, 3a/3, 5/66, 8/80, 13/21, 23/86 **byst** pr2s 15c/12 **byþ** pr3s 1/47, 4/12, 13/24, 15a/1; **eart** pr2s 1/58, 14/2, 27/22 **eom** pr1s 1/11, 14/23, 21a/38, 21b/22 **is** pr3s 2a/16, 7a/44, 7b/12, 8/79; **sī** sbj pr3s 11/32, 22/54, 23/144 **sīe** sbj pr3s 3a/3, 7b/13, 23/112 **sīen** sbj pr3p 3c/1, 7b/48, 54 **siendon** pr3p 5/70 **sig** sbj pr3s 16/67, 105 **sind** pr3p 22/109, 26/64 **sindon** pr3p 16/35 **sint** pr3p 6/13 **sīo** sbj pr3s 7a/18 **sȳ** sbj pr2s 14/48, 27/11 sbj pr3s 2a/23, 7a/40, 7b/16, 7c/6, 14/19, 22/46 **syn** pr3p 25/57, 58 **sȳn** sbj pr3p 7c/22, 18/83 **synd** pr1p 1/45 pr2p 22/48 pr3p 4/36, 37, 21a/53, 22/94 **syndan** pr3p 25/25, 31, 33/4 **syndon** pr1p 1/2 pr3p 4/37, 7a/1, 33/2 **synt** pr3p 1/15; **was** pt3s 12/42, 16/50, 21b/3, 11 **wǣran** pt3p 12/10, 28/9, 29/17 **wǣre** pt 2s 1/48 sbj pt1s 12/5 sbj pt3s 7b/46, 8/78, 12/23, 21a/25 **wǣren** sbj pt3p 7b/6 **wǣron** pt3p 8/28, 13/6, 10, 14/44, 16/93 **wǣrun** pt3p 29/13, 20 **wæs** pt1s 12/9, 55 pt3s 2c/1, 2, 8/7, 13/13, 22/5 **wēre** sbj pt1s 22/50 **wes** pt3s 8/11 imp s 14/32 **wesan** inf 1/8, 2a/15, 17/30, 23/110 **ys** pr3s 1/26, 30, 16/16, 34/10 [etc]; with neg **nǣre** pt3s 27/39 sbj pt3s 29/26 **nǣren** sbj pt3p 5/16 **nǣron** pt3p 5/30, 8/81, 22/125 **næs** pt1s 1/49 pt3s 12/24, 22/100 **nearon** pr3p 26/82 **neom** pr1s 1/31, 59, 67 **nis** pr3s 2a/3, 6/6, 9b/100, 22/26, 26/39 **nys** pr3s 1/20, 67 [etc]

beorg m:B1a *hill, heap, barrow* as 23/32 **beorge** ds 23/50 **beorgum** dp 24/57, 37/32 **beorh** ns 33/34

ġe**beorg** n:B2b *defence, protection* ġe**beorge** ds 30/31, 131, 245 ġe**beorh** ns 33/38

(ġe)**beorgan** III +d *protect, save, seek a cure for* inf 25/132, 144, 165 **bearh** pr3s 25/49 ġe**bearh** pt3s 31b/57 **beorge** sbj pr3s 25/41 **beorh** imp s 2a/10 (rflx *beware*) **burgon** pt3p 30/194

ġe**beorh** see ġe**beorg**

beorhhlið n:B2a *hillside, steep slope* **beorhhliðu** np 18/3

beorht adj *bright, gleaming, illustrious, radiant, beautiful* nsm 18/78, nsf 10/15, 38/94 npn 37/21 **beorhtan** asf 19/58, 37/37 dsm 23/66, 37/40 dsf 19/326, 340 **beorhte** nsf 19/254 **beorhtost** asm 23/6 **beorhtra** gpm 19/340

beorhte adv *brightly* 31b/26, 33/49

beorhtnes f:B3e.ii *brightness, clearness, splendour* **beorhtnesse** ds 24/14 **beorhtnysse** gs 22/97

Beorhþanstæðæ pr n *Berkhampstead* (Herts.) ds 11/23

beorn m:B1a *man, warrior* ns 10/45, 23/42, 26/55, 37/32, as 30/270 **beorna** gp 10/2, 18/118, 19/254, 30/257 **beornas** np 19/213, 267, 23/32, 66, 30/92, 111 ap 30/17, 62 etc

beorne ds 30/154, 245 **beornes** gs 30/131, 160 **beornum** dp 30/101

Beornrǽd pr n *Beornræd* ns 29/38

(ġe)**bēorscipe** m:B1g *feast, revels* ns 27/60 ds 9b/16, 25, 27/8 **bēorscipes** gs 27/50 ġe**bēorscipes** gs 9b/20

bēorsele m:B1g *'beer-hall', drinking-hall, banquet hall* **bēorselas** ap 18/118 **bēorsele** ds 31a/32

bēot n:B2b *boast, boastful speech, vow, threat* as 30/15, 27, 213, 38/70

bēotan, bēotun < **bēatan**

bēotian 2 *vow* **bēotedan** pt1p 40/21 **bēotode** pt3s 30/290

bēotung f:B3d *threat* **bēotunge** as 9a/35

bēoð < **bēon-wesan**

bepǽċan 1 *deceive, seduce* **bepǽhte** pp npm 24/9

bera m:B5a *bear* ns 33/29

berād < **berīdan**

(ġe)**beran** IV *bear, carry, bring, give birth to* inf 1/29, 21a/52, 30/12, 62, 34/42 **bær** pt3s 12/21, 31b/15 **bǽre** sbj pt3s 14/37 **bǽron** pt3p 19/201, 21a/68, 23/32, 30/99 **berað** imp p 9b/91, 19/191, 27/56 **berenne** infl inf 19/131 **bereþ** pr3s 23/118 **bēron** sbj 3p 30/67 **bireð** pr3s 39/17 **boren** pp 19/18 ġe**borene** pp dsm 7b/42 **borenre** pp dsf 7b/45, 46 ġe**borenum** pp dpm 26/98 (=noun *one born in same family, brother*) **byreð** pr3s 35b/6 ġe**byreþ** pr3s 7a/46, 49 **byrð** pr3s 6/42

berēafian 2 *rob, plunder* sbj pr3p 27/69

berēofan II *bereave, destroy* **berofen** pp 37/4

berīdan I *overtake* **berād** pt3s 29/9

berstan III *burst, break, shatter* inf 23/36 **bærst** pt3s 30/284 **berstende** prp nsn 18/32 **burston** pt3p 18/38, 31a/59, 37/2

berȳpan 1 *plunder, rob* **berȳpte** pp npm 25/25 npn 25/32

besǽton < **besittan**

bescyrian 1 +a +g *cut off (from), deprive of* **bescear** pt3s 21b/6 **bescyrede** pp 17/55, 57

besēon V *look, have regard, look to, attend to* **besēah** pt3s 27/63 **besēoh** imp s 15b/10 **besihþ** pr3s 34/28

besihþ < **besēon**

besittan V *surround, occupy* inf 22/8 **besǽton** pt3p 22/12, 150

beslaġen < **beslēan**

beslēan VI *strike, take away by violence* **beslaġen** pp 10/42

besmītan 1 *besmirch, defile* inf 19/59

besnyþian 2 +d *rob, deprive of* **besnyþede** pt3s 35d/1

besorgian *be troubled about* **besorgaþ** pr3s 27/6

bestandan VI *stand about, stand next, surround* **bestōdon** pt3p 30/68 **bīstandeþ** pr3s 7a/27

bestēman 1 *bedew, make wet, drench* **bestēmed** pp 18/3, 23/22, 48

bestrȳpan 1 *strip, plunder* **bestrȳpte** pp npn 25/32

beswāc < **beswīcan**

beswīcan I *deceive, betray* **beswāc** pt3s 8/79, 24/9 **beswīce** sbj pr3s 25/60, 28/67 **beswicen** pp 28/74 **beswīcen** sbj pr2p 17/96 **beswicene** pp npm 25/34 apm 30/238

beswillan 1 *soak, drench* **beswyled** pp 23/23

beswincan III *toil, wear out* **beswuncen** pp 4/97

beswingan III *flog, beat* **beswuncgen** pp 1/48, 52 **beswungen** pp 1/6, 7

besyrewian 2 *entrap, deceive* inf 8/69

besyrwan 1 *ensnare, deceive* **besyrwde** pp npm 25/35

bet comp adv (< **gōd**) *better* 25/13

(ġe)**bētan** 1 *amend, atone for, compensate, pay compensation, make good, restore, satisfy* **bēt** pr3s 3b/5 **bētan** inf 7c/18, 25/159 sbj pr3p 25/130 ġe**bētan** sbj pr1p 17/62 **bēte** sbj pr3s 7b/35, 39, 7c/14, 20, 24 ġe**bēte** sbj pr3s 7a/8, 10, 15 etc, 7b/38 **bēttan** pt1p 25/43

betǽċan 1 *entrust, commit, hand over, commend, offer* **betǽċe** pr1s 1/40 **bætǽċen** inf 11/29 **betǽht** pp 25/24 **betǽhte** pt3s 8/28

betǽhte < **betǽċan**

bētend m:B4d *restorer, rebuilder* np 37/28

betera comp adj (< **gōd**) *better, superior* nsm 30/276 (=noun) **beteran** npm 10/48 apf 18/85 **betere** nsn 30/31, 34/37 **betran** npm 6/54 **betre** nsn 5/48

Bēthūlia pr n *Bethulia* **Bēthūliam** as 19/138, 326

betran < **betera**

betræppan 1 *entrap, catch* **betræppen** inf 8/30

betre < **betera**

betst sup adj (< **gōd**) (often =noun +g) *best* nsm 27/7, 31a/47 nsn 26/73 **betstan** gsm 28/29 gsf 7a/41 isn 9b/52 npm 6/58 dpm 6/58

betst sup adv *best* 27/7

betwēnan adv *between, in the meantime* 1/13

betweohx see **betwux**

betweonan prep +d *between* 25/163

betwih see **betwux**

betwux prep +d/a *among, between, during* 4/35, 13/22, 24, 21a/48, 22/19, 46, 24/45, 58 **betweohx** 16/16 **betwih** 9a/13, 42, 28/12, 31 **betwyh** 9a/21

betȳnan 1 *close, conclude* **betȳnde** pt3s 9b/76, 108 **betȳnedum** pp dpf 7b/45

beðeċċan 1 *cover, protect* **beðeahte** pp 19/213

beþenċan 1 *bring to mind, reflect on* inf 25/141, 157

beþenian 2 *cover, stretch over* **beþenede** pt3s 35d/12

bewǣnde < **bewendan**

beweaxan VII *overgrow* **beweaxne** pp npm 40/31

beweddian 2 *betroth, marry* **bewyddod** pp 7a/52

bewendan 1 *turn* **bewǣnde** pt3s 27/18

beweorpan II *cast out, cast down; surround* **beworpen** pp 17/56 **biworpen** pp 39/5

bewindan III *wrap, surround, envelop, coil about* **bewinde** sbj pr3s 22/103 **bewunden** pp 17/83, 19/115, 21a/64, 79, 22/31, 101, 23/5 **bewundon** pt3p 21a/67

bewitian 2 *watch, observe* **bewitiað** pr3p 31a/73

beworpen < **beweorpan**

bewrēon I *cover (over), hide* **bewriġen** pp 23/54 **bewriġene** 23/17 **biwrāh** pt3s 38/23

bewunden < **bewindan**

bewyddod < **beweddian**

bī < **be**, **bēon-wesan**

bibēad < **bebēodan**

(ġe)**bicgan** 1 *buy, purchase* ġe**bicge** sbj pr3s 33/45 **bicgean** inf 1/66 **bicgað** pr3p 25/72 ġe**biġeð** pr3s 7a/44 **bohte** pt3s 12/19 ġe**bohte** pt3s 25/75 **bohton** pt3p 22/15

ġe**bīcnian** 2 *signify, indicate* ġe**bīcnod** pp 16/61

bīdan I (+g) *remain, wait for, expect* inf 9b/101, 26/30, 31b/3 **bād** pt3s 18/105 **bīdað** pr3p 33/60 **bīde** imp s 2a/6

ġe**bīdan** I (+g) *wait, remain, experience, endure, attain, reach* inf 25/13, 33/17, 38/70 ġe**bād** pt1s 23/125 pt3s 22/139, 27/75 ġe**biden** pp 23/50, 79, 25/12, 26/4, 28 ġe**bidenne** pp 19/64 ġe**bīdeð** pr3s 33/12, 38/1 ġe**bīdon** pt3p 9a/48

bidǣlan 1 +d *deprive of, cut off from* **bidǣled** pp 36/28

biddan V *ask, ask for, demand, entreat, pray, beg (for* +g) **bæd** pt1s 12/30 pt3s 9b/82, 12/5, 31, 21a/23, 47 **bǣde** pt2s 16/2 sbj pt3s 9b/84 **bǣdon** pt3p 9b/94, 14/16, 27/61 **biddaþ** pr1p 1/1 **biddæ** pr1s 11/32 **bidde** pr1s 4/23, 11/21, 16/104, 106, 27/20, 78 sbj pr2s 16/105 **biddende** prp npm 9a/54 **biddeþ** pr3s 34/5 **bitt** pr3s 11/1

ġe**biddan** V *pray* +rflx d ġe**bæd** pt1s 23/122 pt3s 9b/101 ġe**bǣde** sbj pt1s 28/45 ġe**bǣdon** pt1p 28/64 ġe**biddaþ** pr3p 23/83

bidrēosan II *deprive* **bidroren** pp 26/16 **bidrorene** pp npm 38/81

bifian 2 *shake, tremble* inf 23/36 **bifode** pt1s 23/42 pt3s 14/65, 22/160

bifōn VII *surround, encase* **bifongen** pp 35d/14

biforan see **beforan**

big see **be**

(ġe)**bīgan** 1 *bend, turn, convert* **bīgdon** pt3p 14/31 ġe**bīgean** inf 16/102

biġeal < **biġiellan**

biġeat < **beġietan**

bīġenġa m:B5a *inhabitant* **bīġenġan** ap 9a/51

ġe**biġeð** < ġe**bicgan**

biġiellan III *scream around, screech* **biġeal** pt3s 26/24

bihōn VII *hang round (with* +i) **bihongen** pp 26/17

bihrēosan II *cover* **bihrorene** pp npm 38/77

bil see **bill**

bilecgan 1 *cover, wrap* **bileġde** pt3s 39/11

bilewit adj *innocent, gentle, kind, sincere* **bilewitne** asm 1/8 **bilwitre** isn 9b/104

bilewitnes f:B3e.ii *mildness, mercy*
bilewitnesse gs 6/8
bilġesliht n:B2b *sword-clash, battle*
billġeslehtes gs 10/45
bilicgan V *surround, encompass* **bilecgað**
pr3p 35d/25
bill n:B2b.i *sword, blade* as 30/162 **bil** as
31b/66 **billa** gp 31a/82 **bille** ds 35a/2
billum dp 30/114
bilwitre < **bilewit**
ġebind n:B2b *binding, mingling* as 38/24,
57
(ġe)**bindan** III *bind, fetter, hold fast,
constrain, fasten, join* inf 21b/17 **bindað**
pr3p 38/18 ġe**bindað** pr3p 38/40 **binde** sbj
pr3s 38/13 **bindeð** pr3s 38/102 **bond** pt3s
26/32 ġe**bond** pt3s 37/19 ġe**bunden** pp 4/8,
19/115, 26/9, 31b/40, 36/24 ġe**bundene**
pp npm 17/42
binnan prep +d *within, in* 16/80, 21b/10
binnon 7c/6
binne f:B5c *bin, manger* **binnan** ap 1/28
binōm < **beniman**
bīo, **bīoð** < **bēon-wesan**
birele f:B3c/5c *cup-bearer, serving-woman*
as 7a/21 **birelan** as 7a/22
birġine, **biriġene** < **byrġen**
biriġ < **burg**
ġe**biriġe** < ġe**byrian**
birnendne < **byrnan**
bisceop, **biscep**, **biscep-** see **biscop**
biscepstōl m:B1a *episcopal see* **biscepstōle**
ds 5/66
biscop m:B1a *bishop* ns 8/6, 14, 29 (twice),
12/59 **bisceop** ns 4/21, 21a/15, 26, 28/14,
18, 23, etc **bisceopæ** ds 11/20 **bisceope** ds
11/30 **biscep** ns 5/71, 7b/18 as 5/2 **biscepas**
np 5/69 **biscepe** ds 5/63, 7b/27 **biscepes** gs
7b/27 **biscopa** gp 25/151 **biscopas** np 9a/42
biscope ds 12/57 **biscopes** gs 7a/2, 12/6
biscoprīċe n:B2g *bishopric, diocese* as 8/9
bisgo f:B3h *toil, care, occupation* as 26/88
bisgum dp 5/59
bismore, **bismre** < **bysmor**
bīsnian 2 *set an example, instruct by example*
inf 16/38
bīspell n:B2b.i *example, parable* as 6/37
bist < **bēon-wesan**
bīstandeþ < **bestandan**

bītan I *bite, wound, cut, tear* inf 31b/32 **bītað**
pr3p 35a/9
biter adj *biting, sharp, bitter, fierce, grim,
cruel* nsm 30/111 **bitere** apm 30/85 **biteres**
gsm 23/114 gsn 34/29 (=noun) **bitre** asf
26/4 npm 40/31 **bitter** asf 26/55
biþ < **bēon-wesan**
biwāwan VII *blow upon* **biwāune** pp npm
38/76
biworpen < **beweorpan**
biwrāh < **bewrēon**
blāc adj *shining, bright, pale, black* **blāca**
nsm 12/11 **blācne** asm 19/278, 31b/26
blāchlēor adj *pale-cheeked* nsf 19/128
blācian 2 *grow pale* **blācað** pr3s 26/91
gebland n:B2b *commotion, turmoil* as
10/26
blandan VII *blend, mingle, churn, infect*
ġe**blanden** pp 18/31, 33/41 ġe**blonden**
pp 19/34
blandenfeax adj *grey-haired* nsm 10/45
blāwan VII *blow* inf 34/43
blǣd m:B1g *breath, spirit, life; blessings,
riches, success, glory, splendour* ns 18/100,
118, 88, 38/33 as 19/63, 122, 36/34 **blǣð**
ns 26/79 **blēdum** dp 23/149
blǣd f:B3b *shoot, leaf, fruit, flower* **blǣda** np
15a/5 **blǣdum** dp 33/34
Bleddanhlǣw pr n *Bledlow* (Bucks.)
Bleddanhlǣwe ds 11/10
bledu f:B3a *dish, bowl* **blede** as 3c/5
blēdum < **blǣd**
blēo n:B2f *colour, hue* **blēom** dp 23/22 **blēos**
gs 21a/56
bleriġ adj *bald* **blerian** gsm 12/66
blīcan I *shine, gleam* inf 19/137
blind adj *blind* nsm 34/17 **blindum** dpm
21b/12 (=noun)
bliss f:B3e.ii *bliss, happiness, gladness, joy*
ns 22/142 **blis** ns 22/89, 90, 23/139, 141
blisse as 2a/16, 22/86 gs 9b/17 ds 22/33,
53, 23/149, 153 np 2a/5, 20, 21
blissian 2 *be glad, make happy, please,
rejoice* **blissað** pr3s 15b/13 ġe**blissod**
pp 27/80 **blissode** pt3s 27/24 **blyssiġende**
prp 21a/68
blīþe adj *glad, cheerful, joyful, pleased,
gracious* nsm 19/58, 154 nsf 27/53 asn
9b/92, 40/44 dsn 23/122 isn 40/20 npm

9b/95, 19/159, 22/146 **blīþra** comp nsm
30/146 **blīþran** comp npm 35d/20
blīþelīċe adj *joyfully* **blȳðelīċe** 21a/58
blīðemōd adj *friendly, kindly disposed* nsm
9b/96 **blīðemōde** npm 9b/94
blīðnys f:B3e.ii *joy, pleasure* **blīðnysse** as
2a/3
blōd n:B2b *blood* ns 14/25, 16/64, 18/17
blōde ds 14/24, 15/48, 18/3
blōdeġesa m:B5a *blood-terror* **blōdeġesan** ds
18/32
blōdġyte m:B1g *bloodshed* ns 25/44 as
28/44
blōdiġ adj *bloody, gory* asn 19/126, 174
blōdiġne asm 30/154
ġeblonden < **blandan**
blōstma m:B5a *blossom* **blōstman** as 3a/1
blōstmum dp 26/48
blōwan VII *flourish, blossom* inf 33/34
blyssiġende < **blissian**
blȳðelīċe see **blīþelīċe**
bōc f:B4b *book, deed, charter* ns 4/4, 22,
16/39, 42, etc as 4/1, 24, 30, 5/60, 68,
12/21, 41, 16/3, 8, etc **bēċ** gs 16/5, 22/66 ds
5/68, 16/52, 59, 21a/80, 22/122 np 10/68,
21a/81, 89, 24/7 ap 4/2, 5/37, 45, 49 **bōca**
gp 4/3, 5/28, 29, 9b/66, 16/43 **bōcon** dp
12/14 **bōcum** dp 4/29, 21a/88, 24/3, 61
booc ns 9b/64
bōcere m:B1g *scholar, writer, scribe* **bōceras**
np 18/85 ap 9b/4 **bōcerum** dp 14/49
boda m:B5a *messenger* ns 30/49 **bodan** np
25/120
bodade < **bodian**
ġeboden < **(ġe)bēodan**
bodian 2 *proclaim, announce, preach* inf
19/251 **bodade** pt3s 22/86 **bodedon** pt3p
19/244 **bodienne** infl inf 16/31 **bodiġean**
inf 18/65 **ġebodod** pp 22/60
bodiġean see **bodian**
ġebodod < **bodian**
bōg n:B2b *arm, shoulder, branch* **bōgum** dp
39/11
boga m:B5a *bow* **bogan** np 30/110
ġebogen < **būgan**
(ġe)bohte, bohton < **(ġe)bicgan**
ġebolgen < **ġebelgan**
bolla m:B5a *bowl, cup* **bollan** as 3b/2 np
19/17

bolster n:B2c *pillow* **bolstre** ds 9b/102
bonan < **bana**
bond < **bindan**
bonena < **bana**
booc < **bōc**
bord n:B2b *shield* ns 30/110, as 30/15, 42,
131, etc ap 19/192, 317, 30/62, 283 **borda**
gp 30/295 **bordes** gs 30/284 **bordum** dp
19/213, 30/101 **borð** ns 32/29
bordweal m:B1a *shield-wall* as 10/5
bordweall as 30/277
boren, (ġe)boren- see **beran**
bōsm m:B1a *bosom, breast* **bōsme** ds 10/27,
37/40
bōt f:B3b *remedy, relief, compensation,
atonement* ns 7b/34, 25/17 **bōtæ** ds 11/30
bōte as 25/9, 13, 139 gs 25/29 ds 7c/9, 11,
11/29
bōtlēas adj *without compensation* nsn 7c/6
botm m:B1a *bottom* **botme** ds 17/24, 31b/15
bōtwurðe adj *that can be atoned for*
bōtwurðan dpn 7c/24
brād adj *broad, wide, spacious, widespread*
asn 30/15, 163, 31b/55 apn 10/71, 19/317
brādan gsn 37/37 **brāde** asn 18/111
brādne asm 15c/14
brādnis f:B3e.ii *breadth, surface* ns 13/13
brādnysse as 13/5
bræc < **brecan**
ġebræc n:B2a *breaking, smashing* ns 30/295
bræcan, bræce < **brecan**
bræd < **bregdan**
ġebræd < **ġebrēdan**
brædan 1 *spread* inf 38/47
ġebrædan 1 *bake, cook* **ġebrædne** pp asm
22/55
brægd < **breġdan**
ġebrægd < **ġebreġdan**
brǣð m:B1a *breath, odour, scent* **brǣðe** ds
22/74 **brǣðum** dp 22/76
brēac < **brūcan**
breahtm m:B1a *sound of merriment, revelry*
breahtma gp 38/86
brēber see **brēmbel**
brecan IV *break, tear, force, transgress,
breach, violate* inf 8/78 **bræc** pt3s 30/277,
31b/20, 76 **bræcan** pt3p 25/43, 159 **bræce**
sbj pr3s 31a/38 **brecað** pr3s 17/93
ġebroced pp 7a/30 **brocen** pp 30/1

(ġe)**breġdan** III *draw, pull out, fling, weave,*
  feign **bræd** pt3s 30/154 ġe**bræd** pt3s 8/77
  (*feigned*) **bræġd** pt3s 31b/48 ġe**bræġd**
  pt3s 31b/73, 37/18 **brōden** pp 31b/57
  (*woven*) **bruġdon** pt3p 19/229
brego m:B4a *prince, chief, leader* ns 19/39,
  254 **bregu** ns 10/33
brēmbel m:B1b *briar, bramble* ns 3c/1
  brēber ns 12/48
brēme adj *famous, noble* **brēma** nsm 19/57
(ġe)**brengan** 1 *bring* **brenge** sbj pr3s 6/66
  ġe**brenge** sbj pr3s 7a/45 **brengð** pr3s 6/27
brēost n:B2b (used in pl) *breast, heart, mind*
  brēostum dp 18/78, 19/192, 23/118,
  30/144, 34/17, 38/113
brēostcearu f:B3a *heart-care, sorrow,*
  anxiety **brēostceare** as 26/4, 40/44
brēostcofa m:B5a '*breast-enclosure*', *heart*
  brēostcofan ds 38/18
brēosthord n:B2b *inmost feelings, heart* as
  26/55
brēostnet n:B2a *corselet* ns 31b/57
Breotone < **Bryten**
brēr m:B1a *briar, bramble* **brērum** dp 40/31
brerd m:B1a *brim, margin* as 35d/9
Brettas see **Bryttas**
Bretwālas pr n (mp:B1a) *the Britons*
  Bretwālum dp 29/6
brīce n:B2h *use, enjoyment, profit* ds 24/20
bricg f:B3b *bridge, causeway* **bricge** as
  30/74, 78
bricgweard m:B1a *guardian of the causeway*
  bricgweardas ap 30/85
Bricius pr n (*St*) *Brice* gs 8/68
Brihtnōð see **Byrhtnōð**
brim n:B2a *sea, water* ns 18/32, 33/45 **brimu**
  ap 10/71
brimfugol m:B1bi *seabird* **brimfuglas** ap
  38/47
brimlād f:B3b *sea-way, ocean path*
  brimlāde ds 26/30
brimlīþend m:B4d *seafarer, Viking*
  brimlīþendra gp 30/27
brimman m:B4b *seafarer, Viking*
  brimmanna gp 30/49 **brimmen** np 30/295
brimwylf f:B3b *she-wolf of the sea* or *lake* ns
  31b/15
brimwylm m:B1a *water-surging, turbulent*
  water ns 31b/3

ġe**brincð** < ġe**bringan**
(ġe)**bringan** 1 *bring, lead, carry, present,*
  produce, offer ġe**brincð** pr3s 22/91 **bringe**
  sbj pr3s 16/108 ġe**bringe** sbj pr3s 4/25,
  23/139 ġe**bringeð** pr3s 25/128 **brōht**
  pp 25/24 **brōhtan** pt3p 8/57 **brōhte** pt3s
  12/54, 13/9, 16/74 **brōhton** pt3p 16/75,
  22/54, 75, 24/57 ġe**brōhton** pt3p 21a/58
brocen < **brecan**
brōden < **bregdan**
brōga m:B5a *terror, danger* **brōgan** gs 19/4
  ds 8/23
(ġe)**brōht**, (ġe)**brōht-** see (ġe)**bringan**
brosnian 2 *decay, crumble* **brosnade** pt3s
  37/28 **brosnað** pr3s 37/2
brosnung f:B3d *decay, corruption*
  brosnunga ap 22/84
brōþor m:B4c *brother* ns 9b/1, 10/2, 24/64,
  26/98 np 9b/95, 99 **brōþer** 16/17 **brōðra**
  ap 24/34 **brōðru** np 30/191 **brōþrum** dp
  21b/13 **brōþur** ns 29/8
ġe**brōþor** m:B4c *brother, fellow-man,*
  fellow-monk ġe**brōþer** np 10/57 ġe**brōðra**
  np 9a/24, 21a/58, 22/69 ap 21a/52
  ġe**brōþru** np 30/305 ġe**brōþrum** dp 1/12,
  40, 70, 22/35
brūcan II +g(/d) *use, make use of, benefit*
  from, enjoy, partake of, possess inf 10/63,
  12/43, 23/144, 35d/18, **brēac** pt3s 38/44
  brūcað pr3p 26/88 **brūcæn** sbj pr3p 11/26
  brūce sbj pr3s 21a/17 **brūcon** pt3p 28/7
bruġdon < **breġdan**
brūn adj *gleaming, polished, dark, brown* dsf
  18/53 **brūne** apm 19/317 **brūnne** asm
  35d/9
Brūnanburh pr n (f:B4b) *Brunanburh* as
  10/5
brūnecg adj *with bright edge, bright-bladed*
  asn 31b/55 **brūneccg** asn 30/163
bryċe m:B1g *breach, violation* ds 25/17
brycge < **bricg**
brȳd f:B3g *bride, wife* **brȳde** ds 21b/6
bryne m:B1g *burning, fire, flame, heat* ns
  21a/42, 25/44 as 23/165, 25/165 ds 24/17,
  25/18
Bryten pr n (f:B3a) *Britain* **Breotone** as 9a/5,
  62 **Brytene** as 10/71
brytta m:B5a *giver, dispenser* ns 19/30, 93
  bryttan as 19/90, 38/25

Bryttas pr n (mp:B1a) *the Britons* np 9a/12
  ap 9a/33 **Brettas** np 9a/57, 59 **Brytta** gp
  9a/10, 25/146, 148 **Bryttan** dp 25/156
bryttian 2 *divide out, distribute* inf 10/60
Bryttisc adj *British* **Bryttiscum** dsm 29/18
būan 1 *inhabit, occupy* **būge** pr1s 35b/2
budon < (ġe)**bēodan**
bufan adv *from above* 21a/61
bufan prep +d *above* 7b/79, 21a/56, 59
(ġe)**būgan** II *bend, bow down, turn (away),*
  withdraw, depart, sink, fall inf 7a/47,
  22/165, 23/36, 42, 25/158, 30/276 ġe**bēah**
  pt3s 31b/49 ġe**bogen** pp 12/56 **bugon** pt3p
  30/185
būge < **būan**
ġe**bund-** see (ġè)**bindan**
būne f:B5c *goblet, drinking cup* ns 38/94
  būnan np 19/18
būr m:B2b *chamber, apartment* as 29/10
  būre ds 27/57 is 12/26
Burch pr n *Peterborough* (Cambs.) ds 8/37,
  38
burg f:B4b *stronghold, fort, dwelling place,*
  town, city **biriġ** ds 22/14 **burge** gs 21b/4
  burgum dp 18/65, 26/28, 35a/9 **burh** ns
  22/149 as 8/72, 82, 18/111, 30/291 **buruh**
  as 22/146 **byri** ds 22/145 **byriġ** ds 15b/5,
  22/150, 29/22 ap 26/48
būrġeteld n:B2b *pavilion, tent* as 19/276
  būrġetelde ds 19/57 **būrġeteldes** gs 19/248
burglēode fp:B3g *citizens, town-dwellers*
  burglēoda gp 19/187 **burhlēodum**
  dp 19/175
burgon < **beorgan**
burgrǣċed n:B2a *city-dwelling, fortress* np
  37/21
burgsittende mp:B4d *town-dwellers*
  burgsittendra gp 35c/3 **burhsittende**
  np 19/159
burgsteall n:B2b.i *city* ns 37/28
burgstede m:B1g.i *city, fortress* np 37/2
burgtūn m:B1a *fortified enclosure,*
  habitation **burgtunas** np 40/31
burgwaru f:B3a *population, inhabitants*
  burgwara gp 38/86
burh see **burg**
burhġeat n:B2d *town gate* **burhġeatu** ap
  22/147
burhsittende see **burgsittende**

burnsele m:B1g *bath-house* np 37/21
burston < **berstan**
būrþēn m:B1b *chamberlain, household*
  officer **būrþēne** ds 30/121
buruh < **burg**
buruhðelu f:B3a *floor of the fortress* ns 32/30
būta see **būtū**
būtan conj *except, except that, except for,*
  unless, but, only, as long as 9a/33, 16/65,
  etc **būton** 1/4, 4/15, 91, 5/70, 7b/43, 7c/7,
  16/5, 19, 31b/69, etc
būtan prep +d (/a) *without, except* 4/39, 64,
  7b/26, 48, 8/15, 12/43, 21b/21, 22/80,
  29/18, 32 **būton** 8/33, 9a/42, 9b/92,
  22/134, 157, 29/2
butere f:B5c *butter* **buteran** as 1/36
būton see **būtan**
būtū m/n/f dual *both* n 7c/33 a 23/48 **būta** n
  21a/85
bȳcnian 2 *make sign, signify* **bȳcnaþ** pr3s
  2a/22
bydel m:B1a *herald, messenger, preacher* ns
  22/85, 97 **bydela** gp 25/151
byht m:B1g *dwelling, habitation* ap 35b/3
byldan 1 *encourage, cheer, exhort,*
  embolden, excite, agitate inf 31a/32, 33/15
  bylde pt3s 30/169, 209, 320 sbj pt3s
  30/234 ġe**bylde** pp npm 19/268
byliġ m:B1b *bag, pouch* **byliġe** ds 34/7
ġe**byrd** n/f:B2i *destiny* as 31a/12
byre m:B1g *time, opportunity* as 30/121
(ġe)**byreþ** < (ġe)**beran**
byrġan 1 *bury* inf 26/98
byrġen f:B3e.i *burying place, grave,*
  sepulchre **birġene** ds 22/21, 70, 100
  birġine as 22/12 **biriġene** as 22/8, 27
  byrġena np 14/65 **byrġene** as 21a/60, 61,
  22/150 gs 22/82 ds 21a/52, 76, 22/31, 73,
  136 **byrġenum** dp 14/66
Byrhthelm pr n *Brihthelm* ns 12/11, 36
  Byrhtelmes gs 30/92
Byrhtnōð pr n *Byrhtnoth* ns 30/17, 42, 101
  etc as 30/257 **Brihtnōð** ns 8/21
  Byrhtnōðes 30/154
Byrhtwold pr n *Byrhtwold* ns 30/309
byri, byriġ see **burg**
ġe**byrian** 2 impers *be fitting, be appropriate,*
  pertain to ġe**biriġe** sbj pr3s 7c/16 ġe**byrað**
  pr3s 4/6 ġe**byriað** pr3p 25/121

byriġan 1 *taste* byriġde pt3s 23/101

byrnan III *burn* birnendne prp asm 21b/19
   byrnað pr3p 32/1, 4

byrne f:B5c *coat of mail, corselet* ns 30/144,
   284, 32/44 byrnan as 19/337, 30/163 ap
   19/327

byrnhom m:B1a *coat of mail, corselet*
   byrnhomas ap 19/192

byrnwiġa m:B5a *mailed warrior* ns 38/94
   byrnwiġena gp 19/39

byrnwiġġend m:B4d *mailed warrior*
   byrnwiġġende np 19/17

byrst m:B1g *loss, injury* ns 25/40 byrsta gp
   25/12

byrð < beran

bysen f:B3c *example, exemplar, model* bysna
   np 21a/88 bysne as 22/134 ds 4/25, 16/107

ġebysenung f:B3d *example, model*
   ġebysnungum dp 21a/29

bysġian 2 *occupy, employ* bysgod pp 1/12

bysiġ adj *busy* bysiġe npm 30/110

bysmerian 2 *mock, revile* bysmeredon pt3p
   14/33, 46, 49, 23/48 bysmorudun pt3p
   14/31

bysmerlīċe adv *shamefully, ignominiously*
   19/100

bysmor m:B1b *disgrace, shame, insult,*
   derision as 25/40, 102 bismore ds 8/33
   bismre ds 22/148 bysmara gp 25/12
   bysmore ds 12/44, 25/94

bysmorudun < bysmerian

bysna, bysne < bysen

ġebysnungum < ġebysenung

byst, byþ < bēon-wesan

C

cāf adj *bold, active* cāfne asm 30/76

cāflīċe adv *boldly, bravely* 30/153

cald adj *cold* caldast sup nsn 26/33
   caldum dpm 26/10 ċeald asn 3a/7 ċealdost
   sup nsm 33/5

cald n:B2b *cold* calde is 26/8

(ġe)camp m:B1a *battle, combat* campe ds
   10/8, 19/200 ġecampe ds 30/153

campian 2 *strive, fight* campodon pt3s 9a/13
   compedon pt3p 9a/8 compian inf 9a/7

campstede m:B1g *battle-field* ds 10/29, 49

can < cunnan

Cananēas pr n *Canaanites* Cananēa gp
   18/110

candel f:B3c *candle, light* ns 31b/81 condel
   ns 10/15

cann, canst < cunnan

canōn m:B1a *canon* canōnes gs 9b/66

Cantware pr n (mp:B1h) *inhabitants of Kent*
   np 9a/17

Cantwareburg pr n (f:B4b) *Canterbury*
   Cantwarebyriġ ds 21a/50

capitolmæsse f:B5c *first mass*
   capitolmæssan as 1/42

carcern n:B2c *prison* as 21b/20 carcerne ds
   7b/17

cāsere m:B1g *emperor* ns 9a/2 ds 9a/3
   cāseras np 26/82 cāseres gs 21b/2

cāsus m:B1a (Lat) *case* cāse ds 4/64

cawel m:B1b *kale, cabbage* ns 3a/10

cǣġ f:B3b *key* ns 4/3 cǣġon dp 18/79

Cæstæleshamm pr n *Chesham* (Bucks.)
   Cæstæleshammæ ds 11/12

ċeafl m:B1a *jaw* ċeaflum dp 25/152

ċeald, ċealdost < cald

ċealde adv *coldly, bitterly* 34/39

ċeallian 2 *call, shout* inf 30/91

ċēap m:B1a *purchase, bargain, price* as 25/75
   ċēape ds 25/72 ċēapi ds/is 7a/44 (see note)

ċēapian 2 *buy* ġeċēapod pp 7a/44

ceare < cearu

cearian 2 *care, be anxious* cearað pr3s
   31b/45

cearseld n:B2b *'care-seat', dwelling of*
   sorrow cearselda gp 26/5

cearu f:B3a *care, sorrow* ceare np 26/10 as
   38/9 cearo ns 38/55

ġeċēas < ġeċēosan

ċeaster f:B3c *town, city, stronghold* ċeastra
   ds 6/6 np 5/1 ċeastre as 14/67

Cedmon pr n *Cædmon* ns 9b/24

celæs adj nsn 32/29 (see note)

cellod adj apn 30/283 (see note)

celþenie f:B5c *celandine* celþenian gs 3a/1

cempa m:B5a *champion, soldier, warrior* ns
   30/119, 31b/60, 94 cempan np 14/27,
   32/14

cēne adj *brave, keen, bold* nsm 30/215 npm
   19/332 npm 30/283 (=noun) cēnra gp
   19/200 cēnre comp nsf 30/312 cēnum dpm
   32/29 (=noun)

cennan I *beget, produce* inf 33/28

ċēol m:B1a *keel, ship* ċēole ds 26/5, 33/24

Ċēola pr n (m:B5a) *Ceole* Ċēolan gs 30/76

ċeorfan III *carve, hew out* curfon pt3p 23/66

ċeorl m:B1a *man, peasant, commoner, freeman of lowest class, husband* (see 7a/22n) ns 7a/46, 48, 34/10 as 8/71 ċeorle ds 7a/54, 7b/23, 38, 25/33, 30/132 ċeorles gs 7a/22 (twice), 7b/37, 35c/6

ġeċēosan II *choose, decide* ġeċēas pt3s 16/32, 30/113 ġecoren pp 9b/46 ġecorenan pp apm 22/152 (=noun *chosen ones, disciples*) ġecorenum pp dpm 16/28 (=noun), 21a/21 ġecuran pt3p 24/71

Cerdiċ pr n *Cerdic* Cerdīċe ds 29/37

ċerr m:B1a *occasion, time* ċerre ds 7b/33

Chaldēas pr n *the Chaldeans* np 9a/37

Chrīste < Crīst

(ġe)ċīeġan I *call out, shout, summon, name* ġeċeġed pp 28/5 ġeċīġ imp s 27/26 ċīġe sbj pr3s 34/45 ċiġġendra prp gpm 34/39 (=noun) ċȳġdon pt3p 9a/30

ċiġġendra < ċīeġan

ċild n:B2b.iii *child* ns 1/54 ċilda gp 1/68 ċildra np 1/1 ċildum dp 4/4

ċinbān n:B2b *chin-bone, jaw-bone* as 7a/25 ċynnbāne ds 21a/37

cincges < cyning

ġecind n:B2i *species, kind* ġecinde ds 16/43

cinehlāford m:B1a *royal lord* cinæhlāfordæ 11/13 cinehlāfordæ ds 11/1 cinelāford as 11/32 cynehlāforð ds 11/24

cing, cing- see cyning

cinna < cynn

Ċippanhom pr n *Chippenham* (Wilts.) Ċippanhomme ds 12/55

ċiriċe f:B5c *church* ns 7b/30 ċirċan np 7c/4 gs 7c/21 ds 7c/21 ċiriċan gs 7b/28 ċiriċean gs 7a/2 ds 11/4 np 5/27 ċyrċan ds 21a/52, 68 np 7c/22 ċyrċean ds 1/40, 8/49

ċiriċfriþ m:B1a *right of church sanctuary, penalty for breach* ns 7a/3

ċiriċgrið n:B2a *church-peace, right of sanctuary* ns 7c/18 as 7c/5, 15

ċiriċwāg m:B1a *church wall* ċiriċwāgum dp 7c/6

ċirman see ċyrman

ċirran I *turn, return* ċirdon pt3p 19/311

clǣne adj *clean, pure* nsm 26/110 nsn 9b/60 npm 28/21 apn 1/56

clǣne adv *utterly, completely* 5/13, 25/25, 32

clǣnnis f:B3e.ii *purity* clǣnnisse ds 16/34 clǣnnysse as 21a/82, 90 ds 21a/9, 84, 89

clǣnsian 2 *purify* inf 25/162

clēofan II *split, cleave* clufan pt3p 10/5 clufon pt3p 30/283

cleofum < clif

cleroc m:B1a *clerk in holy orders* cleroces gs 7a/3

clibbor adj *clinging* nsm 33/13

clif n:B2a *cliff, rock, crag* cleofum dp 9a/49 clifum dp 26/8

cliopodon, clipode < clypian

Clitomum pr n *Clitomus* ns 28/66

clomm m:B1a *fetter, chain, grip, clutch* clommas np 17/36 clomme ds 17/71 clommum dp 26/10, 31b/11

clufan < clēofan

clumian 2 *mumble* clumedan pt3p 25/152

clūstor n:B2c *bar, barrier* clūstro ap 17/79

clypian 2 *call, cry out, summon* inf 25/153 cliopodon pt3p 27/44 clipode pt3s 16/64 clypað pr3s 14/59 clypode pt3s 14/56, 62, 30/25, 256 clypodon pt3p 14/21, 22/131

clypiendliċ adj *vocalic, vocative* (=noun *vowel*) clypiendliċe npm 4/37 clypiendlicum dpm 4/43, 51

clyppan I *embrace, clasp, cherish* inf 9b/54 clyppað pr3p 35d/26 clyppe sbj pr3s 38/42

clypung f:B3d *sounding, sound* clypunge as 4/46, 50

cnapa m:B5a *boy* ns 1/38 cnapan as 1/25

ġecnāwan VII *know, perceive, understand* inf 5/50 ġecnāwað imp p 25/3 ġecnāwe sbj pr3s 25/40, 81

cnēa < cnēow

cnear m:B1a *small ship, galley* ns 10/35

Cnebba pr n *Cnebba* ns 29/43

Cnebing adj *son of Cnebba* nsm 29/43

cnēo < cnēow

cnēomǣġ m:B1c *kinsman, ancestor* cnēomǣġum dp 10/8

cnēoris f:3e.ii *tribe, nation* ns 19/323

cnēow n:B2g.i *knee; generation* as 14/31 cnēa gp 37/8 cnēo as 38/42

ġecnerdnes f:B3e.ii *accomplishment* ġecnerdnessan np 27/78

cniht m:B1a *youth, boy, servant* ns 30/9, 153
  cnihton dp 21b/8
cnossian 2 *dash, beat, drive* cnossað pr3s
  26/8
cnyll m:B1a *knell, sound of bell* as 1/39, 72
ġecnyrdnys f:B3e.ii *zeal, devotion*
  ġecnyrdnysse ds 22/71
cnyssan 1 *batter, press, urge* cnyssað pr3p
  26/33, 38/101
cnyttan 1 *bind, knot* cnyt pt3s 25/97
cohhetan 1 *clear throat* inf 19/270
cōlian 2 *cool, grow cold* cōlode pt3s 23/72
collenferhð adj *bold-spirited, elated*
  collenferhðe npf 19/134 collenferð
  nsm 38/71
cōm, cōm- see cuman
cometa m:B5a *comet* ns 8/46
Commodus pr n *Commodus* Commodes gs
  21b/2
compedon, compian < campian
compwīġ n:B2b *battle, fray* compwīġe ds
  19/332
con < cunnan
condel see candel
ġecoren, ġecoren- see ġeċēosan
corn n:B2b *corn, grain* corna gp 26/33
Cornwēalas r n (mp:B1a) *the Cornish
  people, Cornwall* Cornwēalum dpm
  8/51
corþor n:B2c *troop, retinue, pomp* corþre ds
  18/20, 31a/91
ġecost adj *tried, proven* ġecoste npn 19/231
Costontīnus pr n *Constantine* ns 10/38
cradolċild n:B2b.iii *child in the cradle, infant*
  np 25/36
ġecranc < ġecrincgan
cræft m:B1a *craft, trade, study, skill,
  cunning, power, strength* as 4/6, 17/79
  cræfta gp 34/38 cræfte ds 16/71, 17/65,
  27/42 is 33/43 cræftes gs 4/5 cræftum dp
  27/49
cræftega m:B5a *craftsman* ns 6/23
Crēacas see Grēcas
crēad < crūdan
Creoda pr n *Creoda* ns 29/42
Creoding adj *son of Creoda* nsm 29/42
Crēta pr n *Crete* ns 24/31, 36
(ġe)crincgan III *fall, fall dead, die in battle,
  perish* inf 30/292 ġecranc pt3s 30/250, 324

ġecrong pt3s 31b/77, 37/31, 38/79
cruncon pt3p 30/302 crungon pt3p 18/36,
  31a/51, 37/25, 28 crungun pt3p 10/10
Crīst pr n *Christ* ns 7b/50, 14/11, 15b/3, 22/5,
  28, 37, 23/56, etc as 2c/2, 22/34, 148, etc
  Chrīste ds 7c/11 Crīste ds 16/28, 21a/24,
  22/78, 123, 23/116, etc Crīstes gs 7c/12,
  13, 8/49, 9b/66, 16/20, 22/32, 33, etc
  Xrīste ds 11/11
crīsten adj *Christian* nsm 7c/12, 16/21, 22,
  21a/5 crīstene nsn 15c/6 npm 15c/6
  crīstenes gsn 25/68 crīstenra gpm 25/99
  gpn 25/119 crīstenre dsf 7c/12 crīstnæ npf
  5/47 crīstne npm 5/24
Crīsten m:B1b *a Christian* Crīstene np
  25/28 Crīstenum dp 24/61
crīstendom m:B1a *Christendom,
  Christianity, the Church* crīstendōme ds
  25/84
crocca m:B5a *pot, vessel* croccan as 3a/13
ġecrong < ġecrincgan
crūdan II *hasten, press on* crēad pt3s 10/35
cruma m:B5a *crumb* cruman ap 3b/11
cruncon, crung- see crincgan
cuǣdon < cweðan
cuclermǣl n:B2b *spoonful* as 3b/5
cucu adj *living, alive* nsm 22/137
culfre f:B5c *dove* culfran as 13/4, 8, 11
culter m:B1b *coulter, knife* cultre ds 1/22
cuma m:B5a *guest* cuman ds 27/79
cuman IV *come, go* inf 4/14, 17/79, 22/105
  sbj pr3s 27/69 cōm pt3s 5/3, 8/10, 9a/5, 28,
  9b/42, 10/37, 13/8, 16/31 cōman pt3p
  9a/19, 20, 27 cōme subj pt3s 18/29, 22/130
  cōmon pt3p 8/1, 55, 9a/16, 14/37, 16/63
  cōmun pt3p 14/67 cumað pr1p 22/73 pr3p
  15a/10 imp p 22/26 cume sbj pr3s 14/62
  cumen sbj pr1p 26/118 pp 9b/47, 19/146,
  168, 23/80 cumende prp asm 14/36 cumon
  inf 8/32 sbj pr3p 22/9, 29, 36 cwōm pt3s
  9b/51, 23/155 cwōman 3p 23/57, 37/25
  cwōme sbj pt1s 28/19 sbj pt3s 28/36 cyme
  sbj pr3s 35a/5 cymeð pr3s 17/101, 26/61
  cymst pr2s 28/57 cymð pr3s 6/20, 15a/6,
  18/94, 22/28, 98 [etc]
cumbol n:B2c *standard, banner* cumblum
  dp 19/332
cumbolġehnāst n:B2b *clash of standards*
  cumbolġehnāstes gs 10/49

cumbolwiġa m:B5a *warrior* cumbolwiġan
as 19/259 ap 19/243

Cumbra pr n *Cumbra* Cumbran as 29/5

ġecunnad < cunnian

cunnan pt-pr *know, know how to, be able,
have the power to* inf 1/7 can pr3s 16/93
cann pr1s 1/45 canst pr2s 1/44, 27/81 con
pr1s 9b/25 cunne sbj pr3s 25/40, 81, 88
cunnen sbj pr3p 5/54 cunnon pr1p 5/33,
22/110 pr3p 1/14, 16/25 cūþe pt1s 9b/26
pt3s 4/20, 16/13, 17/48 cūðen sbj pt3p 5/14
cūþon pt1p 5/42, 58, 17/20 pt3p 16/36,
24/19 [etc]

cunnian 2 (+g) *try, put to the test, explore,
find out, experience* inf 8/30, 34/3, 30/215
ġecunnad pp 26/5 cunnade pt3s 36/1
cunnað pr3s 38/29 cunniġan inf 12/29
cunniġe 26/35 cunnode pt3s 31b/9

ġecunnian 2 *seek to know* inf 19/259

ġecuran < ġeċēosan

curfon < ċeorfan

cūð adj *known, familiar* nsn 6/32, 22/40,
36/19 cūðe npf 31a/83 cūðra gpn 38/55

cūþe, cūðen, cūþon < cunnan

cwalu f:B3a *death, murder* ns 25/45 cwale ds
16/69

cwæd, cwæd-, cwæþ < cweþan

cwealm m:B1a *death* cwealme ds 18/23

cweċċan 1 *shake* cwehton pt3p 14/46

ġecwed- see (ġe)cweþan

cwehton < cweċċan

cwellan 1 *kill* cwealde sbj pt3s 28/44

ġecwēman 1 *please* ġecwēmde pt3s 27/7

cwēn f:B3g *woman, wife, queen, royal
princess* ns 21a/49, 27/63, 65 cwēne as
27/61 gs 27/58 cwēnum dp 18/66

cwene f:B5c *woman, wife* cwenan as 25/72,
94 cwynan ds 7a/54

(ġe)cweþan V *say, speak, utter, declare,
proclaim, call, propose, consider, regard*
inf 4/82, 16/100, 23/116 cuǣdon pt3p
29/25, 28, 29 cwæd pt3s 28/55 cwǣdan
pt1p 12/37 cwǣde pt2s 16/4 cwǣde pt2s
27/70 sbj pt3s 22/93 cwǣden sbj pt3p 5/31
cwǣdon pt3p 7b/10, 9b/89, 14/18, 22/5,
18, etc cwǣdun pt3p 14/50 cwæþ pt1s
5/39, 12/29, 33 pt3s 6/2, 9b/26 etc, 13/18,
14/2, 16/14, etc ġecwæð pt3s 27/1, 30/168
ġecweden 4/94, 14/41, 22/105, 106

ġecwedene pp npm 4/49 cwest pr2s 4/56
cweþ pr3s 4/92, 8/78, 32/24 cweþaþ pr1p
7b/40, 22/42, 88 pr3p 16/28 cweþe pr1s
4/22, 80, 81, 16/103 sbj pr1s 15b/11 sbj
pr1p 22/87 ġecweðen pp 8/79 cweþende
prp nsm 13/14 npm 14/2, 21, 32, 22/56, 92,
24/25 cweþenne infl inf 25/38, 138 cwyst
pr2s 4/55, 81, 83 cwyþ pr 3s 4/91, 22/118,
23/111 [etc]

cwic adj *living, alive* (often =noun) asn 7a/46
cwicera gpm 19/235, 311 gpn 19/323
cwicra gpm 38/9 cwicum dsm 7a/54 dpm
7c/18

cwide see cwyde

cwideġiedd n:B2b.i *spoken utterance, speech*
cwideġiedda gp 38/55

cwīþan 1 *mourn, lament* inf 38/9 cwīðdon
pt3p 14/56

cwōm, cwōman < cuman

cwyde m:B1g *saying, speech, discourse, will,
sentence, phrase* cwide as 35e/4 cwydas ap
4/30 cwydes gs 11/2 cwydum dp 4/30

cwylmian 2 *kill, murder* cwylmde pp npm
9a/42

cwynan < cwene

ġecȳdd, cȳdd- see (ġe)cȳþan

ċȳġdon < ċīeġan

cyldu f:B3a *cold* cylde ds 1/26

cyle m:B1g *coolness, cold* ns 3a/11 ds
1/34

cyme m:B1g *coming, arrival* ds 9b/67 cymes
gs 9a/62

cymen m:B1a *cumin* cymenes gs 3b/7

cyme, cym(e)þ, cymst < cuman

cyn see cynn

ġecyndbōc f:B4b *book of origins, Genesis* ns
16/43

Cynefryð pr n *Cynefrith* ns 21a/43

Cyneheard pr n *Cyneheard* ns 29/7, 8

cynehelm m:B1a *royal crown, diadem,
garland* as 14/30, 27/37

cynehlāforð see cinehlāford

cyneliċ adj *kingly, royal, noble, public
(building)* nsn 37/48 cyneliċan apn 9a/38
cyneliċes gsm 27/73 cynelico npn 9a/41

cynerīċe n:B2b *kingdom, rule, sovereignty*
cynerīċes gs 36/26 kynerīċes gs 5/59

cynerōf adj *renowned, noble* cynerōfe npm
19/200, 311

cynescype m:B1g *royal power, majesty*
  cynescypæ ds 11/2
Cynewald pr n *Cynewald* ns 29/42
Cynewalding adj *son of Cynewald* nsm 29/42
Cynewulf pr n *Cynewulf* ns 29/1, 3, 5, 35
cyning m:B1a *king, ruler* ns 7a/1, 5, 7b/1, 9,
  8/9, 10/1, 14/2, 22/132, etc as 23/44, 133
  cincges gs 1/49 **cing** ns 12/18 etc as 12/30
  cinge ds 12/7, 24, 52 **cinges** gs 12/52 **cyng**
  ns 8/27, 28 etc, 15b/4, 27/36 **cyngc** ns
  7c/14, 27/17, 24, etc **cynge** ds 8/68 **cynges**
  gs 8/61, 64, 27/1 **cynincge** ds 21a/11
  cynincges gs 21a/12 **cyningas** np 10/29,
  18/20 **cyningc** ns 7c/2, 8, 27/4, 6, etc
  cyninge ds 7a/6, 53, 7b/27, 31, 9a/4, etc
  cyninges gs 7a/10, 7b/7, 7c/15, 9a/6,
  23/56, etc **kyning** ns 5/2 **kyningas** np 5/6
  kyninge ds 28/2, 29/10 **kyninges** 7b/26
cyningcynn n:B2b.i *royal line* ns 9a/26
cynn n:B2b.i *kin, race, stock, tribe, people,
  kind, gender* ns 9a/21 as 23/94 ap 1/59
  cinna gp 16/80 **cyn** as 18/110, 31a/31
  cynna gp 19/323 **cynne** ds 17/88, 19/226,
  22/152, 30/76, 33/57 **cynnes** gs 4/89, 9a/56,
  19/52, 310, 30/217, 266 **kynnes** ds 28/8
ċynnbāne < **ċinbān**
cynniġ adj *noble, of good family* **cynniġran**
  comp npm 34/27
cynren n:B2a *kind, species, progeny* as
  33/28
cȳpmann m:B4b *merchant* **cȳpmenn** np
  1/16
ċyrċan, ċyrċean < **ċiriċe**
cyre m:B1g *choice* ns 18/20
Cyrēnisc adj *of Cyrene* **Cyrēniscne** asm
  14/36
ċyriċhata m:B5a *opponent of the church*
  ċyriċhatan np 25/117
ċyrm m:B1a *cry, shout, uproar* ns 30/107
ċyrman 1 *cry out, shout, shriek, wail* pt3p
  ċirman inf 19/270 **ċyrmdon** 18/16
(ġe)ċyrran 1 *return, proceed* inf 13/3
  ġeċyrde pt3s 13/6, 12 **ġeċyrdon** pt3p 22/32
cyrten adj *fair, comely* **cyrtenu** nsf 35c/6
ċȳse m:B1g *cheese* as 1/56
cyssan 1 *kiss* **cysse** sbj pr3s 38/42 **cyste** pt3s
  27/2
cyst f:B3g *choice, the choicest, the best* ns
  31b/68 as 23/1

ċyst f:B3b *chest, coffin* **ċyst** ns 21a/80 **ċyste**
  ds 21a/48, 61
cystiġ adj *good, of good quality* **cystiġran**
  comp npm 34/27
Ċytlid pr n *Chicklade* (Wilts.) ds 12/47
(ġe)cȳþan 1 *announce, reveal, make known,
  proclaim, inform* inf 5/3, 19/56, 243, 22/33,
  30/216 **ġecȳdd** pp 8/68 **cȳdde** pt3s 22/84
  cȳddon pt3p 22/37 **cȳð** pr3s 11/3 **cȳþað**
  pr3p 21a/13 imp p 22/35 **cȳðe** pt3s 9b/44,
  29/24 **cȳðdon** pt3p 9a/33 **cȳðe** pr1s 12/1
  sbj pr3s 28/50 **ġecȳðed** pp 19/155
ġecȳþnis f:B3e ii *testament* ns 16/26, 27
  ġecȳþnissa ap 16/98 **ġecȳþnisse** ds 16/37
cȳþþu f:B3h *kinsfolk, home, native land*
  cȳþþe as 10/38, 58 ds 19/311

D

(ġe)dafenian 2 impers +d *befit, be proper*
  ġedafenað pr3s 4/10 (twice), 27/9 **dafnað**
  pr3s 1/63 **ġedafnode** sbj pt3s 16/35
  ġedeofanode pt3s 9b/14
ġedafenliċ adj *suitable* nsn 4/59
Dāfid pr n *David* ns 15b/1 **Dāuid** ns 15c/1
dag- see **dæg**
dagian 2 *dawn* **dagað** pr3s 32/3
ġedāl n:B2b *separation, break* **ġedāles** gs
  9a/33
dalo < **dæl**
daroð m:B1a *dart, spear* ns 33/21 as 30/149,
  255 **daraða** gp 10/54
Dāuid see **Dāfid**
dǣd f:B3g *deed, act, action* ns 4/79, 7c/19,
  21, 22/72 **dǣda** np 25/78 ap 4/77, 25/155
  gp 9b/73 **dǣde** as 4/67 gs 25/55, 107 ds
  7c/28 **dǣdum** dp 2a/13, 9a/35, 24/54,
  26/41, 29/2, etc
dǣdbōt f:B3b *atonement, penance* ns 22/60
  dǣdbōte as 16/79 **dǣtbōte** as 16/57
dǣdliċ adj *active* **dǣdliċe** npn 4/73, 77, 85
Dæfenisca adj *from Devon* nsm 8/12
dæġ m:B1c *day; lifetime* ns 18/96, 27/76 as
  7b/49, 51, 10/21, 15a/9, etc ds 1/22, 27, 36,
  6/17, etc **daga** gp 23/136, 29/40 **dagas** np
  7b/48, 26/80 ap 7b/49, 51, 13/8, 11, 15c/16,
  21b/21 **dagon** dp 21b/16 **dagum** dp 4/18,
  9b/78, 13/1, 14/47, 21a/19, 20, etc **dæġe** ds
  1/43, 3a/12, 15, 7a/1, 7b/6, 9b/68, etc is

21b/23 **dæġes** gs 3a/11, 15a/3, 31b/4 **dǽi**
as 8/32 **dæiġ** as 22/8 is 21b/24

dæġfeorm f:B3b *day's provisions*
dæġfæorman ap 11/25

dæġhwāmlīċe adv *daily* 25/10, 103

dæġrǣd n:B2b *dawn, dawning* as 1/19
dæġrēd as 19/204

dæġrēdliċ adj *dawn, morning* **dæġrēdliċe**
apm 1/41

dæġðerliċ adj *of the day* **dæġðerliċe** nsn
22/66 **dæġðerliċan** gsn 22/67

dæġweorc n:B2b *day's work* ns 18/73
dæġeweorce ds 19/266 **dæġweorces** gs
18/61, 30/148

dæi, dæiġ see **dæġ**

dæl n:B2d *valley* **dalo** ap 17/84

dǽl m:B1a *part, share, measure, extent,
quantity, unit, word* ns 4/29, 36/30 as
7b/31, 21a/78, 22/55, 27/55, 31a/88, 36/34,
38/65 **dǽlas** np 4/30 as 14/64 ap 3b/3 **dǽle**
ds 6/60, 16/13, 25/126, 158, 35d/10 **dǽlum**
dp 4/30

(ġe)**dǽlan** 1 *share, deal out, distribute* inf
33/29 **dǽlað** pr3p 18/93 **dǽlænne** infl inf
11/30 ġe**dǽlde** pt3s 38/83 **dǽlon** sbj pt3p
30/33 **dǽlð** pr3s 6/8, 19

dænnede < **dennian**

dǣtbōte < **dǣdbōt**

dēad adj *dead* nsm 19/107 **dēade** nsn 26/65
npm 22/24 **dēadne** asm 22/103 **dēadra**
gpm 22/16 **dēadum** dsm 22/71, 26/98
(=noun)

dēadliċ adj *subject to death, mortal*
dēadliċum dpm 22/113

dēag- see **dīgol, dīgollīċe**

dēah < **dugan**

dear, dearr < **durran**

dēaþ m:B1a *death* ns 22/119, 26/106, 36/8 as
2a/6, 22/137, 174, 23/101 **dēaþe** ds 2a/6,
9b/105, 15b/11, 18/2, 20b/5, 22/3, 7, 9,
31b/98, etc **dēaþes** gs 15c/11, 22/139,
23/113

dēaðdæġ m:B1c *day of death* **dēaðdæġe** ds
33/60 **dēothdaeġe** ds 20a/5

dēaðdrepe m:B1g *death-blow* is 18/50

dēaðliċ adj *subject to death, mortal* nsm
22/79 nsn 22/110

dēaðsleġe m:B1g *death-blow, deadly stroke*
ds 35a/14

ġe**dēaw** adj *dewy, moist* ġe**dēawre** gsf 3a/4

Defenas pr n (mp:B1a) *people of Devon,
Devon* **Defenan** dp 8/52

Defnanscīr pr n (f:B3b) *Devon* **Defnanscīre**
as 8/50

dehter < **dohtor**

delfan III *dig* **delf** imp s 3c/2

dēma m:B5a *judge, governor, ruler* ns 14/1,
6, 7, 16, 20, 19/59, 94 **dēman** gs 14/27,
19/4 ds 14/1

dēman 1 +d *judge, adjudge, decide, ordain,
decree* inf 23/107 **dēmed** pp 20b/5
ġe**dēmed** pp 9b/17, 19/196 **dēmeð** pr3p
18/97 **dōēmid** pp 20b/5

dēmend m:B4d *judge* ns 33/36

Dene pr n (mp:B1h) *Danes* ap 31a/28
Deniġea gp 31b/91 **Denon** dp 30/129
Denum dp 31a/96

Denisc adj *Danish* **Denisca** npf 24/45
Deniscan apm 8/67 dpm 8/22 **Denisce** dsf
24/59 npm 24/59

dennian 2 ?*stream* **dænnede** pt3s 10/12 (see
note)

denu f:B3a *valley, dale* **dena** np 40/30

ġe**deofanode** < ġe**dafenian**

dēofol m:B1b *devil, the devil* ns 24/69, 25/7
as 7b/50 **dēofle** ds 26/76 **dēofles** gs 24/42,
56 **dēoflum** dp 15b/3

dēofolcund adj *devilish, diabolical*
dēofulcunda nsm 19/61 (=noun)

dēofulgild n:B2b *devil-worship, idolatry* as
21b/17

dēofulsēoc adj *possessed by the devil, insane*
dēofulsēoce dsm 21b/12 (=noun)

dēop adj *deep, profound, solemn, great* nsf
16/39, 66 nsn 18/61 asn 10/55, 18/73
dēopan dsm 23/75 apn 17/84 **dēope** asf
7c/8

dēope adv *deeply, profoundly* 38/89

dēoplīċe adv *deeply* 16/86

dēor adj *bold, brave* nsm 26/41 **dēorum** ipf
26/76

dēor n:B2b *wild beast, animal* as 10/64
dēora gp 28/7

Dēor pr n *Deor* ns 36/37

deorc adj *dark, gloomy* **deorcan** dpm 23/46
dēorce asn 38/89

dēore adj *dear, precious, beloved, costly,
valuable* **dēorost** sup nsn 33/10 **dēorum**

dsm 31b/37 **dȳre** nsm 17/3, 36/37 apm 19/318

dēore adv *dearly, at great cost* 25/75

ġe**deorf** n:B2b *labour, toil* ns 1/30, 31 as 1/32

deorfan III *labour* **deorfe** pr1s 1/19

dēormōd adj *fierce-minded, brave* nsm 32/23

Dēormōd pr n *Deormod* ns 12/20

dēorwurðe adj *valuable, precious, costly* **dēorwirþe** apm 16/74 **dēorwurðan** gsm 27/55 **dēorwurðre** dsf 22/73 **dēorwyrðan** dsf 22/70 **dēorwyrðe** asf 22/15

dēothdaeġe < **dēaðdæġ**

(ġe)**derian** 2 +d *injure, harm, do harm to* inf 30/70 **derede** pt3s 25/46, 55 ġe**derede** pt3s 24/2 **dereð** pr3s 24/3, 25/79

dēst, (ġe)**dēþ** < (ġe)**dōn**

dīacon m:B1a *deacon, minister* **dīacones** gs 7a/3

dide < **dōn**

dīgol adj *obscure, hidden* nsf 33/62 **dēaglum** dpf 9a/52

dīgol n:B2c *secret* **dīgla** ap 1/51

dīgollīċe adv *secretly* **dēagollīċe** 28/49

(ġe)**dihtan** 1 *direct, compose, write* inf 4/20 ġe**dihte** pt3s 7c/2, 16/72, 87, 24/22

dil m:B1a *dill* **diles** gs 3b/6

dim adj *dark, gloomy* **dimme** npf 40/30

dimnes f:B3e.ii *dimness* **dimnesse** ds 3a/4

Dinges-Mere pr n *Dingesmere* as 10/54

dō < **dōn**

dōēmid < **dēman**

dogian 2 ?*endure,* ?*dog* **dogode** pt3s 39/9 (see note)

dōgor n:B2c *day* **dōgore** is 19/12 **dōgra** gp 3b/28, 31a/28, 38/63

dohte < **dugan**

dohtor f:B4c *daughter* ns 8/65, 24/63, 27/2, 6, 18, 25, 31a/14, 35c/6, etc as 25/94, 27/31 gs 27/24 ds 27/18 **dehter** ds 7b/45, 16/18 **dohtra** np 24/39 **dohtur** ns 21b/7

dol adj *foolish* nsm 26/106

dol n:B2a *folly* **dole** ds 17/3

dolg n:B2b/m:B1a *wound, scar* np 23/46, 35a/13 **dolh** ns 21a/47

dolgbōt f:B3b *compensation for wounding* **dolgbōte** as 7b/36

dolhwund adj *wounded* nsm 19/107

dolwīte n:B2h *pain of punishment* as 35d/17

dōm m:B1a *decree, judgement, choice, glory, renown* ns 7c/28, 12/38, 31b/37 as 12/40, 25/164, 29/24 **dōma** gp 18/75 **dōmas** np 7a/1 **dōme** ds 9a/39, 9b/46, 22/98, 26/85, 34/10 **dōmes** gs 9b/68, 15a/9, 23/107 **dōmum** dp 9b/71

dōmærn n:B2b *judgement-hall, tribunal* **dōmerne** ds 14/27

dōmdæġ m:B1c *day of judgement* **domdæġe** ds 23/105

dōmġeorn adj *eager for glory* **dōmġeorne** npm 38/17 (=noun)

dōmlīċe adv *gloriously* 19/318

dōmsetl n:B2c.i *judgement-seat, tribunal* **dōmsetle** ds 14/13

(ġe)**dōn** anom *do, act, perform, make, cause, treat, take, gain, put, bestow, consign* **dōn** inf 2a/12, 9b/10, 16/83, 21a/9, 52, 21b/20, 22/124, 31b/43 sbj pr3p 6/45 ġe**dōn** inf 5/50, 17/67, 21a/18, 26/43, 27/22 pp 4/19, 12/27, 60, 16/46, 17/23 **dēst** pr2s 1/27, 16/101, 27/30 **dēþ** pr3s 4/26, 6/27, 78, 15a/7, 16/99, 34/15 ġe**dēþ** pr3s 7a/39 **dide** pt3s 27/70 **dō** pr1s 1/28, 36, 13/22, 14/18, 16/105 sbj pr3s 4/6, 5/68, 7b/22 imp s 3b/7, 3c/6, 7, 4/77 ġe**dō** pr1s 27/23 sbj pr3s 7a/5, 7 imp s 3a/2, 13 **dōnne** infl inf 2a/13, 4/65 **dōð** pr3s 25/71 pr3p 4/74, 6/57, 16/95 **dydan** pt1p 25/14 **dyde** pt1s 1/39, 26/20 pt3s 9b/20, 12/30, 14/20, 15b/3, 23/114 ġe**dyde** pt3s 12/3, 6 **dydest** pt2s 1/38 **dydon** pt1p 1/43 pt3p 9a/49, 15c/5 [etc]

dora m:B5a *humble-* (or *bumble-*)*bee* **dorena** gp 3a/2

dorste < **durran**

dōð < **dōn**

draca m:B5a *dragon, serpent* ns 32/3, 33/26

drāf f:B3b *drove, herd* **drāfe** as/ap 25/99

drǣfan *drive, drive out* **drǣfde** pt3s 25/63

ġe**dreag** n:B2b *multitude, host* as 40/45

drēam m:B1a *joy, bliss, delight, happiness* ns 18/86, 23/140, 26/80 **drēamas** np 26/65, 86 ap 19/349 **drēame** ds 18/101, 38/79 **drēames** gs 23/144 **drēamum** dp 23/133

ġe**drēas** < ġe**drēosan**

ġe**dreċċan** 1 *afflict, oppress* ġe**drehte** pt3p 18/55 ġe**drehtan** pt3p 25/47

drēfan 1 *trouble, stir up, disturb, afflict* **drēfe**
pr1s 35b/2 ġe**drēfde** pp npm 6/72 ġe**drēfed**
pp 19/88, 23/20, 59

ġe**drehtan** < ġe**dreċċan**

drenċ m:B1g *drink* ns 1/67

drenċan 1 *drench, ply with drink* **drenċte**
pt3s 19/29

dreng m:B1a *man, warrior* **drenga** gp 30/149

drēogan II *suffer, undergo, endure* inf 40/26
drēag pt3s 36/2 **drēogað** pr3p 25/71, 26/56
drēogeð pr3s 40/50 **drugon** pt2p 19/158

drēorgian 2 *be sad, grow desolate* **drēorgiað**
pr3p 37/29

drēoriġ adj *sad, dejected* nsf 10/54
drēoriġne asm 38/17

drēoriġhlēor adj *sad-faced* nsm 38/83

drēorsele m:B1g *dreary abode, hall of
sorrow* ds 40/50

(ġe)**drēosan** II *decline, fail, fall, collapse,
perish* ġe**drēas** pt3s 18/54, 37/11, 38/36
drēoseð pr3s 38/63 ġe**droren** pp 26/86
ġe**drorene** pp npf 37/5

drepe m:B1g *blow* as 31b/98

drīfan I *drive, expel* inf 31a/68 **drāf** pt3s
12/47 **drīfað** pr3p 25/99 **drīfe** pr1s 1/33 sbj
pr3s 25/61

drīġe adj *dry* **drīġum** dpm 22/159

driht f:B3g *multitude, troop* **drihte** np 18/50

drihten m:B1b *lord, the Lord, prince* ns
2a/23, 9b/34, 38, 10/1, 15b/6, 15c/8, 17/49,
etc as 18/101, 22/75 **drihtne** ds 9b/48, 104,
17/3, 22/69 **drihtnes** gs 9a/2, 10/16, 17/15,
21a/86 **dryhten** ns 10/1, 19/21, 23/101,
26/41, etc as 23/64, 26/106 **dryhtne** ds
19/342, 346 **dryhtnes** gs 23/9, 35, 26/65,
121, etc

drihtġesiд̄ m:B1a *noble companion, fellow
warrior* **drihtġesiд̄a** gp 32/42

drihtinbēag m:B1a *payment (to a lord) for
killing a freeman* **drihtinbēage** ds 7a/11

drihtliċ(e) < **dryhtliċ**

drinca m:B5a *drink* **drincan** np 3a/8

(ġe)**drincan** III *drink* inf 3b/10, 14/38, 39, 61
ġe**drincanne** infl 3b/2 (*swallow*)
drinċþ pr3s 7a/7 **drince** pr1s 4/95 **drincst**
pr2s 1/64, 66 ġe**druncen** pp 4/96 **druncon**
pt1p 1/44

drincehorn m:B1a *drinking-horn*
drinċhornæs gs 11/34

drohtnian 2 *conduct oneself, live*
drohtniende prp nsm 1/54 **drohtnode** pt3s
21a/30 **drohtnodon** pt3p 21a/90

drohtnung f:B3d *way of living* **drohtnunge**
ds 21a/24, 86

dropa m:B5a *drop* ns 28/36

ġe**droren**, ġe**drorene** < (ġe)**drēosan**

drugon < **drēogan**

druncen adj *drunk* nsm 19/67, 107

ġe**druncen**, **druncon** < **drincan**

dryhten, **dryhtnes** see **drihten**

dryhtfolc n:B2b *people, troop* gp 35d/17

dryhtguma m:B5a *retainer, warrior*
dryhtguman ap 19/29

dryhtliċ adj *lordly, noble, magnificent*
drihtliċ nsn 33/26 **drihtliċe** asn 31a/96
npm 32/14 **dryhtliċestum** sup dsm 26/85

dugan pt-pr *be of use, avail, thrive, be good*
dēah pr3s 30/48, 34/2, 19 **dohte** pt3s
25/43, 89

duguþ f:B3b *noble band (of warriors), troop,
company, host; prosperity, benefit* ns 18/55,
101, 26/86, 38/79 **dugeða** gp 19/61 **dugeþe**
as 25/148 gs 19/31, 38/97 ds 30/197
dugeþum dp 26/80

dumb adj *dumb, mute* **dumbe** npm 4/45, 49

dūn f:B3b *hill, mountain, height* **dūna** np
40/30 **dūne** gs 9a/60 ds 22/148, 151, 33/30

Dunnere pr n *Dunnere* ns 30/255

Dūnstān pr n *Dunstan* ns 4/20, 8/13

dura < **duru**

durran pt-pr *dare* dear pr1s 1/51 pr3s 25/21,
23, 26 **dearr** pr1s 16/103 **dorste** pt1s 7b/4,
23/35, 42, 45, 47 pt3s 19/258 **durre** sbj
pr1s 1/20 **durron** pr1p 16/87

duru f:B4a *door* ns 33/36 as 29/11, 32/23 ap
32/42 **dura** ds 32/14 ap 7b/30 **durum** dp
7b/45, 32/16, 20

dūst n:B2b *dust* ns 3a/12 **dūste** ds 15a/8

dwǣs adj *dull, foolish* **dwǣsan** dp 25/131
(=noun)

dwelian 2 *lead astray, deceive* **dwelode** pt3s
25/7

ġe**dwolgod** m:B1a *false god* ns 24/57
ġe**dwolgoda** gp 25/21, 26 ġe**dwolgodan** dp
25/24 ġe**dwolgode** ds 24/50

ġe**dwollīċe** adv *foolishly, heretically* 24/10

ġe**dwolmann** m:B4b *heretic* ġe**dwolmen** np
16/93

ġe**dwolsum** adj *misleading, confusing* nsn
16/92

ġe**dwyld** n:B2b *error, heresy* ns 22/10
ġe**dwylde** ds 24/44, 46, 59, 70

(ġe)**dyd**- see (ġe)**dōn**

dȳfan 1 *dip, immerse* **dȳfde** pt3s 35d/3

Dyflin pr n *Dublin* as 10/55

dynian 2 *make a din, clamour* **dynedan** pt3p
19/204 **dynede** pt3s 19/23, 32/30

dȳres see **dēore**

dyrne adj *secret, hidden* nsf 33/62 asm 40/12
ism 33/43

dysiġ adj *ignorant, foolish* nsm 16/8 **dysġra**
gpm 1/68 (=noun) **dysiġe** npm 25/119
(=noun)

E

ēa f:B4b.ii *river, stream* ns 33/30

ēac adv *also, likewise, besides, moreover,
even* (often in adv phrs **ēac swilċe**, **swelċe
ēac**, etc *likewise, in the same way*) 1/15, 25,
4/53, 7b/23, 9a/58, 9b/8, 70, 10/2, 19,
14/49, 15a/7, 15c/4, 16/17, 23/92, 27/62,
63, etc

ēac prep +d/i *in addition to, plus* 9a/3,
18/100, 40/44

ēaca m:B5a *increase* **ēacan** ds 16/18

ēacen adj *increased, augmented, pregnant*
npn nsf 35a/13, 36/11

ēad n:B2b *happiness, good fortune,
prosperity, riches* as 35d/23, 37/36 **ēades**
gs 17/65, 19/273, 34/1

ēadhrēðiġ adj *triumphant* **ēadhrēðiġe** npf
19/135

ēadiġ adj *blessed, happy, prosperous* nsm
15a/1, 26/107 **ēadiga** nsm 8/25, 16/30
ēadigan asf 19/35 **ēadiġe** apm 18/99

ēadiġnes f:B3e.ii *blessedness* **ēadiġnesse** as
26/120

ēadmōdlīċe adv *humbly* 16/2

Ēadmund pr n *Edmund* ns 10/3

Ēadrīċ pr n *Eadric* ns 30/11

Ēadwaċer pr n *Eadwacer* ns 39/16

Ēadweard pr n *Edward* ns 12/20, 30/117,
273 as 25/62 **Ēadweardes** gs 10/7,
52

Ēadwine pr n *Eadwine* ns 8/7

Ēadwold pr n *Eadwold* ns 30/304

eafera m:B5a *son, heir, offspring, descendant*
afaran np 10/7 ap 10/52 **eaferan** as 31b/56
eafrum dp 17/62 **eaferum** dp 31a/6

ēage n:B5b *eye* ns 35c/11 **ēagan** ds 6/50 np
3a/6 ap 3a/5, 16, 15b/10, 16/97 **ēagna** gp
3a/1, 3, etc **ēagum** dp 3a/13, 27/17, 34/17

Ēaha pr n *Eaha* ns 32/15

eahtatēoða num adj *eighteenth* **eahtēoðan** ds
21a/35

ēahðyrl n:B2c *'eye-hole', window, hatch* as
13/1

eal see **eall**

ēalā interj *oh!, ho!, alas!* 1/1, 19, 24/1,
25/141, 27/32

eald adj *old, ancient, senior* nsm 2b/2, 6,
10/46, 30/310, 33/30, 40/90 nsf 2c/2 npn
38/87 **alde** ism 18/49 **ealda** nsm 30/218
ealdan asf 16/36, 94 (twice), 96, 99 dsn
11/5, 24 dsf 16/16, 22/122 npm 16/10 apm
8/76 **ealde** nsf 16/10, 25, 27, 22/57 asn
27/20 npm 10/69, 19/166 apm 19/265
ealdne asm 2b/1 **ealdra** gpm 1/68 (=noun)
gpn 25/32 **ealdum** dpm 2b/3, 4 etc, 4/10
yldestan sup apm 19/10 dpm 19/242

ealdfēond m:B4d.i *ancient enemy*
ealdfēondum dp 19/315

ealdġenīðla m:B5a *ancient enemy*
ealdġenīðlan ap 19/228

ealdġewyrht f:B3g *deed of old, former
action* **ealdġewyrhtum** dp 23/100

ealdhettend m:B4d *ancient enemy*
ealdhettende ap 19/320

ealdian 2 *grow old, age* **ealdað** pr3s 26/89

ealdor m:B1b *leader, elder, prince, lord,
master, chief, God* ns 14/68, 19/38, 58 etc,
23/90, 26/123, 30/202, 222, 314 **aldor**
19/32 **ealdras** np 14/3, 15, 49 **ealdre** ds
30/11 **ealdres** gs 30/53 **ealdrum** dp 14/50

ealdor see also **aldor**

ealdordōm m:B1a *eladormanry, office of
ealdorman* **ealdordōme** ds 8/5

ealdorduguð f:B3b *chief nobility*
ealdorduguðe gs 19/304

ealdorlang adj *lifelong* **ealdorlangne** asm
10/3

ealdorman m:B4b *ealdorman, nobleman,
ruler* (see 8/4–5n) ns 8/4, 8, 21 etc, 16/104,
22/11, 30/219 as 8/64 **aldormon** ns 29/20
as 29/3, 5 **aldormonnes** gs 29/33

ealdermen ds 22/5 **ealdormann** as 16/2
ealdormannes gs 8/45 **ealdormenn** ds
21a/7 **ealdormon** ns 9b/43
ealdorþeġn m:B1b *chief thegn, retainer*
ealdorþeġnum dp 19/242
ealdr- < ealdor
ealdra < eald
ealdre < aldor
Ealdseaxan pr n (mp) *the Old Saxons, Old
Saxony* np 9a/19
ealdsweord n:B2b *ancient sword* asn
31b/67
Ealdulf pr n *Ealdulf* ns 8/37, 66
Ealfrīċ < Ælfrīċ
(ġe)**ealgian** 2 *defend* **ealgodon** pt3p 10/9
ġealgean inf 30/52
ealgylden see **eallgylden**
Ealhelm pr n *Ealhelm* ns 30/218
eall adj *all, every, each, the whole of* nsm
8/80, 21a/6, 34/31 nsn 9a/21, 14/24 nsf
5/51, 23/12 asn 5/27, 15b/14, 23/94 npn
6/35 apn 6/32 **al** asf 2a/17 **ælne** asm 11/7
eal nsf 23/55 npm 12/59 asn 13/20 **ealla**
npf 6/2 **ealle** asf 2a/11, 9b/79, 13/6 npm
4/41, 8/27, 23/128 npf 7c/4, 21b/5 apm
5/10, 8/67, 23/37 apn 1/56, 21a/23 apf 5/45
ealles gsm 6/77 gsn 6/43 **eallra** gpm 7b/53
gpf 6/41 **eallre** dsf 25/41 **eallum** dsm
9b/92 dsn 22/63 dpm 1/41 dpn 13/19, 22,
27/36 dpf 6/8, 22/61 **ealne** asm 6/43,
14/28, 22/141 **ealra** gpm 32/32 gpn 23/125
[etc]
eall pron *all, each, everything* nsn 5/27,
15a/6, 34/12, 38/106 asm 37/26 asn 5/26,
6/6, 23/58 **alle** npm 29/13, 18 apm 29/32
eal nsn 19/331, 25/68 asn 12/17, 13/15 npn
3a/10 **eallan** dpm 12/13, 22 **eallæ** apf 5/37
eallæs asn 11/27 **ealle** asf 5/44 npm 5/50,
8/81, 13/17, 14/19, 23/9 npn 26/50 apm
21a/33 apn 2a/14 **ealles** gsn 7b/21, 24
eallon dpm 16/64 **eallra** gpn 6/9, 70,
30/174 **eallum** dpm 7b/10, 9b/47, 27/46,
30/216 dpn 2a/14 **ealra** gpm 9a/53, 9b/46
gpn 17/14; in phr **mid ealle** *altogether,
fully, completely* 4/50, 8/73, 12/46, 25/130,
149 [etc]
eall adv *all, fully, utterly, altogether* 5/27,
6/24, 8/35, 12/24, 21a/56, 65, 23/6, 35a/6,
etc **eal** 12/22, 22/160, 25/91, 31b/76, etc

eallan < ġealla
ealles adv *fully, completely, quite* 19/108,
24/2, 25/11, 22, 31, 53, etc
eallgylden adj *all-golden* nsn 19/46
ealgylden nsn 31a/49
eallswā conj/adv *just as, even as, likewise*
11/6 **ealswā** 4/75
eallunga adv *altogether, entirely* 6/56
ealneġ adv *always* 5/70
ēalond n:B2b *island* as 9a/18 **ēalondes**
gs 9a/6, 51
ealra < eall
ealu n:B4ei *ale* as 1/65 (twice)
ēam m:B1a *(maternal) uncle* **ēame** ds 31a/55
ealswā see **eallswā**
Eanwulf pr n *Eanwulf* ns 29/41 **Eanulf**
ns 12/49
Eanwulfing adj *son of Eanwulf* nsm 29/41
ēaran < ēare
eard m:B1a *country, homeland, region, land,
dwelling-place* as 10/73, 12/56, 25/148,
154, 26/38, 31a/67, 31b/9 **earde** ds 8/65,
22/29, 25/35, 48, 58, etc
eardġeard m:B1a *habitation, world* as 38/85
eardian 2 *live, dwell* **eardiende** prp nsm
24/31
eardungstōw f:B3b *place of settlement,
habitation* **eardungstōwe** as 9a/12 gs 9a/6
ēare n:B5b *ear* **ēaran** np 28/16 ap 16/97
earfoþe n:B2a *hardship, suffering,
tribulation, misery* **earfeþa** gp 38/6
earfoda ap 36/30 **earfoþa** ap 36/2 gp 6/70,
40/39 **earfoðum** dp 15c/5
earfoðhwīl f:B3b *hard time* **earfoðhwīle** as
26/3
earfoðliċ adj *full of hardship, laborious* nsn
38/106
earh adj *cowardly* nsm 34/22 (=noun) nsn
30/238
earhliċ adj *shameful, cowardly* **earhliċe** npf
25/87
ēarhring m:B1a *ear-ring* **ēarhringas** np
28/16
earm adj *poor, wretched, miserable* (often
=noun) **earman** gsf 9a/45 dsf 25/140
earme npm 23/68, 25/34 **earmra** gpm
18/88, 27/62 gpn 23/19 **earmum** dpm
11/30
earm m:B1a *arm* ns 7b/80 as 30/165

earmceariġ adj *wretchedly anxious,*
care-worn nsm 26/14, 38/20
earmlīċe adv *miserably, wretchedly* 25/142
earmscanca m:B5a *arm-bone* **earmscancan**
np 7b/81
earn m:B1a *eagle* ns 19/210, 26/24, 30/107
as 10/63
(ġe)**earnian** 2 *earn, deserve, gain* inf 7b/56,
25/165 ġe**earnaþ** pr3s 23/109 ġe**earnedan**
pt1p 25/14 ġe**earnedon** pt3p 15a/10 **ernian**
inf 25/13
(ġe)**earnung** f:B3d *deserving, deserts, merit,*
favour ġe**earnunga** ap 30/196 **earnungan**
dp 25/14, 15
eart < **bēon-wesan**
ēastan adv *from the east* 10/69, 19/190, 32/3
ēastdǣl m:B1g *eastern part, the East*
ēastdǣle ds 9a/5
Ēastengle pr n (mp:B1h) *the East Anglians,*
East Anglia np 9a/20 **Ēastengla** gp 21a/5
Ēastenglum dp 8/34
ēasteð n:B2a *river-bank* **ēasteðe** ds 30/63
Ēastre f:B5e *Easter* **Ēastron** dp 7b/51
ēastsǣ m:B1g *eastern sea* ds 9a/36
Ēastseaxe pr n (mp:B1h) *the East Saxons,*
Essex **Ēastseaxan** np 9a/19 **Ēastseaxena**
gp 30/69
ēaþe adv *easily, readily* 5/51, 21a/18, 22/118,
25/141, 34/16, 39/18
ēaðmēdu f:B3a *humility, reverence*
ēaðmēdum dp 7b/16
ēaþmōd adj *humble, obedient, gentle* nsm
23/60, 26/107
ēaðmōdlīċe adv *humbly* 9b/74
ēaðost sup adv *most easily* 19/75, 102
Ēawa pr n *Eawa* ns 29/42
Ēawing adj *son of Eawa* nsm 29/42
eax f:B3b *axle* ns 6/42, 45 **eaxe** as 6/77 ds
6/42, 44, 46, 55, etc
Eaxeċeaster pr n *Exeter* ns 8/71
eaxl f:B3c.i *shoulder* **eaxle** ds 7b/78, 31a/55,
31b/46 **eaxlum** dp 23/32
eaxleġespann n:B2b *cross-beam, junction*
eaxleġespanne ds 23/9
ebba m:B5a *ebb-tide* **ebban** ds 30/65
Ebrēas pr n (mp:B1a) *the Hebrews* np 19/218
Ebrēa gp 19/253, 262, 298
Ebreiscġeðīode n:B2h *Hebrew language* ds
5/43

Ebrisc adj *Hebrew* **Ebrisce** npm 19/241, 305
ēċe adj *eternal, endless, everlasting,*
perpetual nsm 9b/34, 38, 24/76, 26/124 nsn
2a/21, 18/92 asn 22/82, 113 apm 18/28, 70
ēċan asf 26/120 gsn 26/79 dsm 16/70 dsn
22/124 apn 6/76 **ēċes** gsm 10/16 **ēċne** asm
9a/47 **ēċum** dpm 13/23 dpn 22/85, 154
[etc]
ēċe adv *eternally* 26/67
eċed m:B1a *acid, vinegar* **eċede** ds 14/60
ēċelīċe adv *eternally* 22/126
ecg f:B3b *edge, sword* ns 30/60, 31a/44,
31b/33, 84, 35d/6 **ecga** gp 35a/13 **ecge** as
31b/58 np 31a/83 **ecgum** dp 10/4, 68,
31b/67, 35a/3
Ecgfrid pr n *Ecgfrith* **Ecfrid** ns 21a/16
Ecfride ds 21a/11
ecghete m:B1g *sword-hate, violence of the*
sword ns 26/70
Ecglāf pr n *Ecglaf* **Ecglāfes** gs 30/267
ecgplega m:B5a *sword-play, battle*
ecgplegan as 19/246
Ecgþēow pr n *Ecgtheow* **Ecgþēowes** gs
31b/59
eclypsis n:B3e.ii *eclipse* ns 28/38
ēċne < **ēċe**
ēċnys f:B3e.ii *eternity* **ēċnisse** ds 16/106
ēċnysse ds 16/58, 21a/91, 22/177
ġe**ednīwian** 2 *renew, restore* ġe**ednīwod**
pp 27/20
edor m:B1a *building, dwelling* **ederas** np
38/77
edwīt n:B2b *insolence, abuse* as 19/215
efelāste f:B5c *everlasting* (a plant) **efelāstan**
as 3c/4
efne adv *even, just, thus, now, only* 9b/13,
13/18, 31a/30, 31b/80
efstan 1 *hurry* inf 23/34 **efste** pt3s 31b/2
efston pt3p 30/206
eft adv *again, then again, back, after,*
afterwards, next, now 1/44, 2b/5, 3a/4,
3c/6, 4/21, 7a/45, 8/54, 9a/59, 9b/26,
10/56, 13/2, 4, 8, 9, 14/48, 15c/13, 23/68,
27/66, 28/27, 33/63, 35d/3, etc
eftwyrd f:B3g *after-event, judgement day* ns
18/94
eġe m:B1g *fear, dread, terror* as 25/126 ds
1/21, 9a/29, 22/32
eġefull see **eġesful**

eġesa m:B5a *awe, fear, terror, awesomeness,*
monstrous thing ns 19/252, 23/86 **eġesan**
np 18/46 **eġsa** ns 26/103 **eġsan** ds 26/101
eġesful adj *awful, awesome, dreadful,*
terrifying nsm 19/21 **eġefull** nsm 22/98
eġesfull nsm 18/60, 19/257, 33/30
eġesfulle npm 24/29
eġesliċ adj *fearful, dreadful* nsf 23/74 nsn
25/6, 70 **eġesliċe** nsf 25/78
Eġferþ pr n *Ecgferth* ns 29/35
Ēgipta < Ēgypte
eġlan 1 +d *plague, trouble* inf 19/185
ēġlond see īġland
eġsa, eġsan see eġesa
Ēgypte pr n (m:B1g) *Egyptians* np 18/6
Ǣgypta gp 9b/64 Ēgipta gp 16/68, 21b/5
Ēgypta gp 18/55 Ēgyptum dp 18/60
ēhtan 1 +g *pursue, assail, persecute* ēhte sbj
pr3s 7c/6 **ēhton** pt3p 19/237, 31b/21
eiġlande < īġland
elcor adv *else, otherwise* 28/1
ele m:B1g *oil* ds 15c/15
elebēam m:B1a *olive-tree* **elebēame** ds
13/9
Eliġ-Mynster pr n (n:B2c) *monastery at Ely*
Eliġ-Mynstre ds 21a/28
ellen n:B2c *strength, courage, fortitude, zeal*
as 30/211 **elne** ds 19/95, 23/34, 60, 123,
31a/35, 31b/2, 38/114 **elnes** gs 31b/38
ellendǣd f:B3g *brave deeds* **ellendǣda** gp
19/273
ellenrōf adj *daring, courageous* nsf 19/109,
146
ellenþrīste adj *boldly daring, audacious* npf
19/133
ellenwōdnis f:B3e.ii *zeal, fervour*
ellenwōdnisse gs 9b/75
elles adv *else, otherwise* 16/92, 24/35, 26/46
elleshwæt adv *otherwise* 12/61
ellor adv *elsewhere* 19/112
elmboga m:B5a *elbow* **elmbogan** ds 7b/80
elne < ellen
elðēod f:B3b *foreign people* **elðēoda** gp
19/237
elþēodiġ adj *foreign, hostile* **elþēodiġra** gpm
(=noun) 26/38, 19/215
em (for efen) adv *equally, evenly* 3a/5
embe see ymbe
emnēah adv *equally near* 6/53

ende m:B1g *end, conclusion, boundary, limit,*
district, region ns 6/48, 52 as 6/51, 15b/6,
16/6, 83, 19/64 ds 6/27, 18/21, 19/120,
22/125, 23/29, 25/4, 45, 90, 27/17 **ænde** ds
25/30 is 9b/76 **endas** np 3c/1
endeberd-, endebird- see endebyrdnes
endebyrdan 1 *arrange, dispose* ġeendebyrd
pp 16/86
endebyrdlīċe adv *in an orderly way, in*
succession 4/70
endebyrdnes f:B3e.ii *order, arrangement,*
sequence, contents ns 2b/1, 9b/30
endeberdnesse as 6/4 **endebirdnisse** as
16/88 **endebyrdnesse** as 9b/17 ds 6/19
endebyrdnysse gs 22/65
endelēas adj *endless* nsm 36/30 nsf 22/143
ġeendian 2 *end, finish, complete* ġeendade
pt3s 9b/76, 103 ġeendað pr3s 4/52, 53
ġeendedu pp nsf 12/39 ġeendiað pr3p
4/47, 51, 52, 73, etc ġeendigan inf 12/36
ġeendod pp 2a/9 ġeendode pt3s 27/60
ġeendodu pp nsf 12/38
endlefta num adj *eleventh* **endlefte** nsf 28/25
endlyfenġylde adv *elevenfold* 7a/2
ġeendung f:B3d *end, death* ġeendunge as
21a/49, 27/50
engel m:B1b *angel* ns 17/12, 22/21, 24, 76,
etc as 23/9 **engla** gp 16/44, 17/1, 65,
18/113, 22/87, 90, etc **englas** np 16/63,
21a/86, 23/106 ap 6/30, 22/76 **engles** gs
22/22 **englum** dp 23/153, 26/78
Engle pr n (mp:B1h) *Angles, the English,*
England np 10/70, 25/90, 98 Engla gp
7c/2, 25 Englum dp 25/156
Engle < Angel
Englisc adj *English* nsm 4/19 asn 5/54, 58 dsf
9b/6 Engliscan dsn 21a/3 Engliscum
dsn 4/1, 41
Englisc n:B2b *English (the language)* ns
16/89, 91 as 4/29, 59, 5/15, 58, 60, 61,
14/57, 16/3, 45, 53, 88, 91
enġu < ǣniġ
ent m:B1a *giant* enta gp 33/2, 37/2, 38/87
entas np 24/5 ap 24/28
(ġe)ēod- see (ġe)gān
eodorcan 1 *chew the cud* **eodorcende** prp nsn
9b/60
eofer m:B1a *boar, figure of boar on helmet* ns
31a/50, 33/19 **eoferes** gs 34/10

Eoferwīċstōl m:B1a *the (episcopal) see of
York* **Eoferwīċstōle** ds 8/37
eoh m:B1e *horse* as 30/189
eom < **bēon-wesan**
Ēomǣr pr n *Eomǣr* ns 29/43
Ēomǣring adj *son of Eomǣr* nsm 29/43
eorcanstān m:B1a *precious stone* as 37/36
eorl m:B1a *nobleman, warrior, hero, man*
(see 33/16n) ns 8/29, 30/6, 51, 89, 132,
31b/21, 36/2, 38/114, etc as 38/84 **eorla** gp
10/1, 19/21, 257, 26/72, 36/41 **eorlas** np
10/31, 19/273, 336 ap 38/99 **eorle** ds
7b/23, 30/28, 159, 33/16, 32, 36/33, 38/12
eorles gs 7a/20, 30/165
eorlcund adj *noble* **eorlcundre** gsf/dsf 7a/41
Eormanrīċ pr n *Eormanric* **Eormanrīċes** gs
36/21
eornost f:B3b *earnestness* as 25/101 (**on
eornost** *in earnest, seriously*)
eornoste adv *resolutely, in earnest* 19/108,
231, 30/281
ēorodċist f:B3g *troop, contingent*
ēorodċistum dp 10/21
eorðbifung f:B3d *earthquake* **eorðbifunge**
as 14/69
eorðbūend m:B4d *earth-dweller, inhabitant*
eorðbūendra gp 32/32
eorðcyning m:B1a *king of the land*
eorðcyninges gs 31a/93
eorþe f:B5a *earth, world, ground, clay* ns
14/65, 22/160 **eorþan** as 3c/1, 13/3, 6, 11,
16, 14/55, 16/46, 49, 17/28, etc gs 9b/35,
13/5, 13, 23/37, 26/61, 38/104, 110 ds
6/51, 57, 13/24, 23/42, 74, 30/157, 33/2,
34, etc
eorðgrāp f:B3b *grip of earth* ns 37/6
eorðliċ adj *earthly, worldly* **eorðliċan** gsn
22/102 **eorðliċe** asn 6/49 **eorðlicon** apn
6/65
eorðrīċe n:B2h *kingdom of the earth* ds 17/82
eorðscræf n:B2d *earth-cave, grave*
eorðscræfe ds 38/84, 40/28 **eorðscrafu**
ap 40/36
eorðsele m:B1g *earth-hall, barrow* ns 40/29
eorðstyrung f:B3d *earthquake* ns 22/20
eorðweġ m:B1a *earthly way* **eorðweġe**
ds 23/120
eorðwela m:B5a *earthly wealth* **eorðwelan**
np 26/67

Ēote pr n (m:B1h) *the Jutes* **Ēotena** gp 31a/10
(see note), 26, 89 **Ēotenum** dp 31a/83
eotenisc adj *made by giants* asn 31b/67
ēoton < **etan**
ēow < **ġē**
ēowan 1 *show, display* **ēowdon** pt3p 19/240
eowend m:B1a *genitals* **eowende** ds 7b/39
ēower poss pron *your* nsm 18/118 **ēowere**
npm 19/195 **ēowre** npm 19/195, 29/30 apm
22/95 apf 32/11 **ēowres** gsm 22/67
ēowrum dsm 13/19; see also **ġē**
ġeēowian 2 *show* **ġeēowde** pt1s 7b/10
erian 2 *plough* inf 1/22 **erad** pr3s 4/93 **erast**
pr2s 4/93 **erige** pr1s 4/93 **ġeerod** pp 4/94,
95
ernian see (ġe)**earnian**
erðan < **eorþe**
esne m:B1g *servant* **esnes** gs 7a/54
esnewyrhta m:B5a *hireling, unfree labourer*
esnewyrhtan dp 7b/49
ēstēadiġ adj *'favour-blessed', fortunate* nsm
26/56
ēstum adv *freely, gladly* 35d/24
etan V *eat, feed, provision oneself* inf 1/60 **ǣt**
pt3s 22/55 **ǣton** pt1p 1/44 pt3p 28/12 **ete**
pr1s 1/57, 4/96 sbj pr3s 16/22 **ġeeten**
pp 4/96 **etenne** infl inf 22/54 **etst** pr2s 1/58
ytst pr2s 1/53, 55
eþel m:B1b *native land, home, country,
territory* ns 23/156 as 5/8, 26/60, 28/61
ēðle ds 9a/9, 47, 19/169 **ēðles** gs 9a/13
ēðellēas adj *homeless, outcast* **ēðellēase** npm
18/88
ēðelweard m:B1a *defender of the homeland*
ēðelweardas np 19/320
ēþgesȳne adj *easily visible, plain to see* nsf
31a/48
ēðle, ēðles < **eþel**
Ēua pr n *Eve* **Ēuan** as 22/152 **Ēue** ns 17/82
Eugēnie pr n *Eugenia* ns 21b/22 **Eugēnian**
gs 21b/1
Ezēchias pr n *Ezechias* or *Hezekiah* ns 15b/3

F

ġefā m:B5d *foe, enemy* **ġefān** gs 22/148
fācen n:B2c.i *treachery, evil, wickedness,
crime* as 33/56 **fācn** as 34/26
fācenfull adj *deceitful, crafty* nsm 24/53

fācne adj *deceitful, treacherous* **fācne** nsn 7a/45

(ġe)**fadian** 2 *arrange, order, phrase* inf 16/91, 25/162 **fadode** pt3s 25/51

fadung f:B3d *arrangement, order of words, syntax* **fadunge** ds 16/90

fāgum < **fāh**

fāh adj *hostile, guilty; decorated, gleaming, stained* nsm 18/30, 96, 23/13, 33/22, 40/46 nsn 38/98 **fāgum** dsm 19/104 dp 19/194, 264, 301

fāhmon m:B4b *man who is object of a blood-feud* ns 7b/24

fala see **fela**

fāmgian 2 *foam, seethe* **fāmgode** pt3s 18/36

fāmiġbōsma adj *foamy-bosomed* nsn 18/48

fanggene < **fōn**

(ġe)**faran** VI *set out, go, travel, advance, die* inf 22/81, 30/88, 156, 34/45 **faraþ** pr1p 22/108 pr3p 6/63 imp p 22/11, 35 **fare** sbj pr3s 27/69 **faren** sbj pr3p 6/46 ġe**faren** pp 25/142 **fareð** pr3s 26/91 **færþ** pr3s 6/25, 44, 46, 63, 64, 16/55 ġe**fōr** pt3s 8/26 **fōran** pt1p 28/2 **fōron** pt3p 19/202

Faraon pr n *Pharaoh* ns 18/56

faru f:B3a *journey* **fare** as 18/109

Fasiacen pr n *Fasiacen* ds 28/1 (see 28/headnote)

fæc n:B2d *interval, time* as 9b/102 **fæce** ds 9b/5

fædde < **fēdan**

fæder m:B1a/4ci *father, patriarch* ns 2a/24, 8/7, 9a/25, 16/17, 22/167, 169, 172, 27/4, 51, 30/218, 33/63 as 24/36, 27/2 gs 12/54, 22/170, 27/23, 54, 76, 33/61 ds 7b/47, 16/51, 22/65, 168, 176, 27/3, 21, 67 **fæderas** np 16/10

fæderyncynn n:B2b.ii *our fathers' race, forefathers* **fæderyncynne** ds 18/114

fædrenmǣġ m:B1c *paternal kinsman* **fædrenmǣġum** dp 7b/31 **fæderingmāgas** ap 7a/49

fǣġe adj *fated, doomed to die* (often =noun) nsm 30/119 npm 10/12, 28, 18/36, 19/19 apm 19/195 **fǣġean** dsm 30/125 **fǣġes** gsm 31b/36 gsm 30/297 **fǣġne** asm 31b/77 **fǣġum** dpm 19/209, 26/71 dpf 18/17

fæġen adj *glad, joyful* nsm 34/23, 38/68

fæġer adj *fair, beautiful, fine, pleasant, pleasing* nsm 31a/75 nsn 19/47, 23/73 **fæġera** gpm 27/45 **fæġere** nsn 2a/24 npm 23/8, 10 **fæġerum** dpm 16/73 **fæġran** dsf 23/21 **fæġre** ism 9b/76

fæġere adv *fairly, agreeably, splendidly, carefully, gently* 30/22, 33/56 **fæġre** 19/300 **fæġror** comp 34/42 **fæġrost** sup 26/13

fæġernes f:B3e.ii *beauty, excellent feature* **fæġernesse** as 28/13 **fæġernissa** ap 16/78

fæġnian 2 *rejoice* **fæġniað** pr3p 15b/12 **fæġnode** pt3s 21a/66

fæġrian 2 *make beautiful, adorn* **fæġriað** pr3s 26/48

fǣhðu f:B3h *feud, hostility, violence, revenge* as 40/26 **fǣhðe** as 22/144, 30/225 ds 31b/46

fǣla see **fela**

fǣmne f:B5c *maid, wife, woman* ns 21b/10, 33/44 **fǣmnan** ds 24/65 **fǣmnum** dp 21b/14 **fēmnan** as 21a/77 gs 21b/10

fǣr m:B1a *calamity, sudden danger, attack* ns 31a/6 as 18/7

fǣreld n:B2b/m1a *journey, way, passage, movement* **fǣrelde** ds 22/109 **fǣreldes** gs 22/77 **fǣrelte** ds 6/61 **fǣreltes** gs 6/43

fǣrgripe m:B1g *sudden attack, peril* ns 31b/25

fǣringa adv *suddenly, by chance* 27/1

fǣrliċ adj *sudden* **fǣrlīcum** dsm 24/17

fǣrlīċe adv *suddenly, quickly* 22/20, 38/61

fǣrsceaða m:B5a *sudden attacker* **fǣrsceaðan** ds 30/142

fǣrspel n:B2b.i *dreadful news* as 19/244

fǣrþ < **faran**

fæst adj *firm, fixed, constant, motionless, secure* nsm 6/48, 52 nsf 6/15 asn 18/91 **fæste** npm 6/55, 62, 71 asf 31a/34 **fæstum** dsm 17/72

fæstan 2 *fast* **fæstende** prp 21a/30

fæste adv *fast, firmly, securely, closely, completely* 9b/40, 17/37, 23/38, 43, 25/97, 30/21, 103, 35d/26, etc

fæsten n:B2c.iii *fastness, place of safety, enclosed place, stronghold* as 30/194, 35c/9 **fæstenne** ds 19/143

fæstenbryċe m:B1g *non-observance of fasts* **fæstenbrycas** np 25/116

fæstende < **fæstan**

fæstenġeat n:B2d *gate of stronghold*
fæstenġeates gs 19/162
fæstlīċe adv *resolutely, constantly,*
unremittingly 30/82, 254 **fæstlīcor** comp
6/44
(ġe)**fæstnian** 2 *establish, fasten, fix* inf 30/35
ġe**fæstnod** pp 22/26, 131 ġe**fæstnode**
pp npm 6/60 ġe**fæstnodon** pt3p 23/33
pp dpm 1/21
fæstnung f:B3d *stability, permanence* ns
38/115
fæt n:B2d *vessel, cup* ns 34/42
fǣtan 1 *adorn* **fǣttan** pp gsn 31a/31
(*ornamented, plated*)
fǣtels m:B1a *bag, pouch* **fǣtelse** ds 19/127
fæþm m:B1a *embrace, grasp, protection,*
keeping **fæðme** ds 18/81, 33/61 **fæþmum**
dp 35d/25
fēa adj *few, a few* **fēaum** dpm 31a/19 **fēawe**
apm 5/25 (see note) **fēawum** dpm 4/19,
24/27; see also **fēawa**
fēa adv *little, scarcely* 23/115
ġe**fēa** m:B5d *joy* ġe**fēan** ds 15c/10
ġe**feah** < ġe**fēon**
feaht < **feohtan**
feala see **fela**
fealdan VII *fold, wrap* **fēoldan** pt3p 35d/7
fealene < **fealu**
(ġe)**feallan** VII *fall, fall in battle, die, fall to*
ruin inf 23/143, 30/54, 105, 31a/8 **fealleþ**
pr3s 38/63 **fēol** pt3s 26/32, 30/126, 303,
32/41 ġe**fēol** pt3s 18/37 (*fall on* +a), 46,
19/67, 27/33, 49 **fēoll** pt3s 30/119, 166,
286 ġe**fēoll** pt3s 19/280, 307 **fēollan** pt3p
9a/40, 10/12 **fēollon** pt3p 22/24, 34, 27/17,
30/111
fealohilte adj *golden-hilted* nsn 30/166
fealu adj *yellow, dusky, grey* **fealene** asm
10/36 **fealwe** apm 38/46
fealwian 1 *fade, wither* **fealwiað** pr3p 15a/5
fēasċeaftig adj *wretched, desolate* asn 26/26
fēaum < **fēa**
fēawa indecl noun/pron *few* (+gp) 5/14, 16,
21a/53
fēawe, fēawum < **fēa**
feax n:B2b *hair* as 19/281, 21b/7 **feaxe** ds
19/99
(ġe)**feċċan** 2 *fetch, bring, carry off* inf 27/25,
27, 80 ġe**fecgan** inf 30/160

fēdan 1 *feed, provision, nourish* **fǣdde** pt3s
10/63 **fēdde** pt3s 11c/9, 15c/9 **fēden** sbj
pr3p 7b/19 **fēdeð** pr3s 24/18
fēdesl m:B1a ?*nobleman*, ?*boarder* ns 7a/19
(see note)
fēfer m:B1b *fever* **fēfre** ds 3b/9
fēġan 1 *fix, confine, fit* ġe**fēġed** pp 21a/57
fēġeð pr3s 35c/9
ġe**fēġednyss** f:B3e.ii *derivation, form* ns 4/69
ġe**feh** < ġe**fēon**
ġe**fehð** < ġe**fōn**
fela adv *much* **feala** 34/36
fela indecl noun/pron (usually +gp); also adj
many, much, many things 7b/5, 14/4, 14,
16/80, 21a/77, 85, 22/128, 25/7, 9 etc,
25/64, 27/45, etc **fæla** 32/25, 33 **feala**
23/50, 125, 131, 33/12, 34/4; in adv phrs
swā fala *as many* 11/16 **þæs fela** *so many*
31b/18
felalēof adj *much loved, very dear* **felalēofan**
gsm 40/26 (=noun)
(ġe)**fēlan** 1 *feel* inf 26/95 **fēleþ** pr3s 35c/9
(+g)
feld m:B4a *field, battlefield* ns 10/12 **felda** ds
1/20, 30/241
feldċiriċe f:B5c '*field-church*', *country*
church **feldċirċan** ds 7c/27
fēle adj *faithful, true* nsm 34/26
fēleþ < (ġe)**fēlan**
felġ/felġe f:B3b/5c *felloe, (segment of) rim*
felġa np 6/56, 61, 67 **felġan** np 6/45 **felġe**
ds 6/48, 51, 53 **felġea** np 6/62 **felġum** ds
6/54
fell n:B2b.i *skin, hide* **fellum** dp 28/6, 17
fēlon < **fēolan**
fēmnan < **fǣmne**
(ġe)**fēng, fēngon** < (ġe)**fōn**
fenland n:B2b *fenland, marsh* **fenlande** ds
21a/53
fenn n/m:B2b/1a *fen, marsh, moor* **fenne** ds
33/42, 39/5
feoh n:B2f *money, price, wealth, goods,*
property, cattle ns 4/8, 7a/2, 3, 33/47,
34/13, 38/108 as 29/16, 30/39 **fēo** ds 12/15,
39, 21a/16 **fēos** gs 29/24 **fioh** as 7a/49
feohġifre adj *greedy for wealth, avaricious*
nsm 38/68
feohġyft f:B3g *giving of treasure, valuable*
gift **feohġyftum** dp 31a/27

feohland n:B2b *pasture* as 15c/9

ġe**feoht** n:B2b *battle, fight, fighting, war* as
9a/32, 24/51 ġe**feohte** ds 9a/57, 58, 10/28,
19/189, 24/49, 25/92, 30/12, etc
ġe**feohtum** dp 28/56, 29/6

feohtan III *fight, attack* inf 7b/40, 42 (twice),
44, 9a/7, 30/261, 35a/4 **feaht** pt3s 19/291,
29/6, 30/254, 277, 281, 298 **feohtende** prp
npm 29/13, 17, 31 **fiohte** sbj pr3s 7b/41
fuhton pt3p 19/262, 32/41

ġe**feohtan** III *achieve (by fighting), win* inf
30/129, 31a/21

feohte f:B5c *fighting, battle* ns 30/103

feohtlāc n:B2b *fighting* as 7c/19

(ġe)**fēol** < (ġe)**feallan**

fēolan III *penetrate* **fulgon** pt3p 29/31

fēolan IV *be joined to, persist* **fēlon** pt3p
37/13

fēolheard adj *hard as a file* **fēolhearde** apn
30/108

(ġe)**fēoll, fēoll-** see (ġe)**feallan**

ġe**fēon** V +g/i *rejoice, exult* ġe**feah** pt3s
19/205 ġe**feh** pt3s 31b/78 ġe**fēonde** prp isn
9b/86

fēond m:B4d.i *enemy, foe, devil* ns 15b/9, 11,
24/35 **fēonda** gp 18/116, 26/75, 35d/1
fēondas np 23/30, 33 ap 23/38 **fēondum**
dp 9a/14, 46, 15b/2, 18/30, 25/74, 30/264
fȳnd np 19/195 ap 19/319, 30/82

fēondsceaða m:B5a *fiendish enemy* or
criminal **fēondsceaðan** as 19/104

feor adj *far, far away* (*from* +d) nsn 9b/100,
16/42 nsm 38/21 **feorres** gsn 40/47

feor adv *far, far back, from long ago* 9a/32,
26/37, 52, 34/2, 38/26, 90, 40/25 **fyr** comp
3a/7 (*further*) **fyrrest** sup (*farthest*) 6/62

fēore, fēores, feorg < **feorh**

feorgbold n:B2b *soul's dwelling, body* ns
23/73

feorh n:B2e *life, soul* as 7b/20, 10/36, 26/71,
29/16, 33, 30/142, 184 **fēore** ds 18/102,
30/194, 259, 31b/57, 35d/1 **fēores** gs
7b/21, 24, 7c/8, 30/260, 317 **feorg** ns 26/94
fēorum dp 31a/90 **fiorh** as 7b/24

feorhġenīðla m:B5a *life-enemy, mortal foe*
feorhġenīðlan as 31b/49

feorhhūs n:B2b *'life-house', body* as 30/297

feormung f:B3d *harbouring* **feormunge** as
7b/21

feorr < **feor**

feorran adv *from afar* 6/1, 19/24, 23/57, 33/1

fēorða num adj *fourth* **fēorðan** gsf 7a/42 isn
19/12

fēos < **feoh**

fēower num *four* 3b/7, 7a/26, 9a/1, 61, 12/59,
16/14, 27/54

fēowertiġ num *forty* 7b/17, 9a/1, 61
fēowertigum dsm 9a/3, 13/1

fēowertigoþa num adj *fortieth*
fēowertigeðon dsm 22/175 **fēowertigoðan**
dsm 22/64

fēowertȳne num *fourteen* **fēowertȳnum** dpm
9b/78 **fēowortȳne** 2c/2

ġe**fēra** m:B5a *companion, comrade* ns 30/280
ġe**fēran** as 1/24 ds 16/32 np 1/14, 50,
28/21, 30, 60, 29/30 ap 22/95, 28/23,
30/170, 229 ġe**fērana** gp 28/23 ġe**fērum**
dp 1/42, 22/105, 29/28

fēran 1 *go, journey, set out, depart, proceed,
run* inf 19/12, 26/37, 30/221, 33/31, 40/9
fērde pt3s 2c/2, 8/50, 83, 21a/86 **fērdest**
pt2s 28/57 **fērdon** pt3p 14/79, 91, 22/11
fērende prp nsm 35b/9

ġe**fēran** 1 *reach, attain* ġe**fērde** pt3s 8/14, 25

(ġe)**fērde** < (ġe)**fēran**

ferhðfreċ adj *bold in spirit* **ferhðfrecan** asm
31a/84

ferhðglēaw adj *wise, prudent* **ferhðglēawe**
asf 19/41

(ġe)**ferian** 2 *carry, take, convey* inf 30/179
ferede pt3s 38/81 **feredon** pt3p 21a/87,
31a/92, 96 ġe**ferod** pp 16/53

fers n:B2b *verse* ap 9b/29 **ferse** ds 16/52

ferþ n:B2b *heart, spirit, mind* ns 38/54 as
26/26, 37 **ferþe** ds 35d/21, 38/90

ferðloca m:B5a *breast, heart* ns 38/33
ferðlocan as 38/13

ġe**fērum** < ġe**fēra**

fēsan 1 *drive away, put to flight* **fēseð** pr3s
25/92

festlīċe see **fæstlīċe**

fēt < **fōt**

fetelhilt n:B2b *belted sword-hilt* as 31b/72

feter f:B3c *fetter* **feterum** dp 38/21

ġe**feterian** 2 *fetter, bind* ġe**feterod** pp 18/24

(ġe)**fetian** 2 *fetch* sbj pr3s ġe**fetiġe** 23/138
fetiġan inf 19/35

fēþa m:B5a *foot-troop, soldier* **fēþan** as 30/88

fēðe n:B2h *motion, power of movement* as 17/42

fēþecempa m:B5a *foot-warrior* ns 31b/53

fēðegāst m:B1a *roving spirit* ns 18/30

fēðelāst m:B1a *'walking-track'*, *way* **fēðelāste** ds 19/139

feþer f:B3c *feather* **feþra** as 38/47

feðerhama m:B5a *feather-cloak, wings* **feðerhoman** ds 17/80

feðre adj *loaded* nsn 34/37

fierste < **first**

fif num *five* 4/37, 38, 43, 11/28, 12/1, 58, 32/41 **fife** npm 10/28, 23/8

fifteġ num *fifty* **fifteġum** dpm 5/67

filiġian 2 *follow* +d **filiġdon** pt3p 22/70

Filistēi see **Philistēi**

ġefillednys f:B3e.ii *fulfilment* ns 16/27

Fin see **Finn**

findan III *find, meet, devise, recover* inf 9a/35, 13/5, 18/8, 35a/11 **findað** pr3p 18/74 **fintst** pr2s 2a/2, 4 **funde** pt3s 19/2, 278 **funden** pp 5/43 **fundene** pp npm 24/66 **fundon** pt3p 19/41, 30/85

finger m:B1b *finger* ns 7b/86, 90 as 7a/38 **fingra** gp 33/38 **fingras** np 35d/7 **fingrum** dp 31b/14

Finn pr n *Finn* **Fin** ns 31a/34, 90 as 31a/84 **Finne** ds 31a/66 **Finnes** gs 31a/6, 19, 94

Finnsburuh pr n *Finnsburh* ns 32/36

finul m:B1a *fennel* as 3a/13, 15 **finoles** gs 3b/3

fioh see **feoh**

fiohte < **feohtan**

fiorh see **feorh**

fiorm f:B3b *use, benefit* **fiorme** as 5/29

fiorran adv *from afar, far-off* 6/1

fīras mp:B1a *men, people* **fīra** gp 17/71, 19/24, 33 **fīrum** dp 9b/39

firġenstrēam m:B1a *mountain stream* **firġenstrēamas** np 33/47

firmest see **fyrmest**

first m:B1a *(space of) time, duration, period* as 5/54 **fierste** ds 7b/31 **fyrst** as 19/324 **fyrste** ds 24/4

fisc m:B1a *fish* as 1/56, 22/55, 33/27

fiscere m:B1g *fisherman* **fisceras** np 1/16

flān m:B1a *arrow, barb* as 30/269 **flāna** gp 19/221 **flānes** gs 30/71

flǣsc n:B2b *flesh* as 13/20, 22/50

flǣschoma m:B1a *covering of flesh, body* ns 26/94 **flǣschoman** as 31b/77

flǣscliċ adj *corporeal, carnal* **flǣsclicum** dpm 22/94

flǣscmete m:B1g.ii *meat* **flǣscmettum** dp 1/54

flēag, flēah < **flēogan, flēon**

flēam m:B1a *flight, retreat* as 8/43, 19/291, 30/81, 254 **flēame** ds 10/37, 30/186

ġeflēmed < **ġeflȳman**

flēogan II *fly* inf 17/80, 19/221, 30/7, 109 etc **flēag** pt3s 26/17 **flēah** pt3s 13/2, 5, 19/209, 22/21 **flēoganne** infl inf 3a/10 **flēogeð** pr3s 32/3 **flugon** pt3p 18/7

flēohnet n:B2a *fly-net, mosquito curtain* ns 19/47

flēon III *flee, run, avoid* inf 30/247 **flēah** pt3s 12/48 **flugon** pt3p 19/296, 30/194

flēotan II *float, swim* **flēat** pt3s 21b/18 **flēotendra** prp gpm 38/54 (=noun)

flet n:B2a *floor, dwelling, hall* as 31a/24, 31b/49, 77, 38/61

fletsittend m:B4d *'hall-sitter'*, *guest* **fletsittendum** dp 19/19, 33

ġeflit n:B2a *dispute, suit* **ġeflite** ds 12/63

flōd m:B1a *flowing water, sea, stream, flood-tide, tide* ns 13/21, 18/36, 30/65, 72 as 10/36, 18/17, 21b/18 **flōda** gp 31b/6 **flōde** ds 24/5, 6, 35b/9 **flōdes** gs 13/20, 31b/25

flōde f:B5c *stream* **flōdan** ds 29/52

flōdblāc adj *flood-pale* nsm 18/52

flōdeġsa m:B5a *terror of the flood* or *sea* ns 18/1

flōdgrǣġ adj *'water-grey'*, *grey like water* nsf 33/31

flōdweard m:B1a *guardian of the flood* ns 18/48

flōdweġ m:B1a *ocean path* **flōdwegas** ap 26/52

flōr f:B3b *floor* **flōre** as 19/111

flot n:B2a *sea* as 10/35, 30/41

flota m:B5a *ship, fleet, seaman, Viking* **flotan** as 30/227 ds 8/59, 60 np 30/72 gp 10/32

flotman m:B4b *seaman, Viking* **flotmen** np 25/91

flōwan VII *flow* inf 33/47 **flōwende** prp nsm 30/65

flugon < **flēogan, flēon**

flyht m:B1a *flight* as 30/71

flȳma m:B5a *fugitive, exile* **flȳman** as 12/54
ġeflȳman 1 *put to flight* **ġeflēmed** pp 10/32
ġefō < **ġefōn**
ġefohten < **ġefeohtan**
folc n:B2b *people, tribe, nation, troop, army,
  crowd* ns 9a/28, 14/10, 24, 15c/6, 16/74,
  23/140, 14, 30/45, etc as 8/78, 14/14,
  16/68, 30/22, 54, 241, 35b/6, 36/22 **folce** ds
  4/15, 14/8, 23, 16/35, 37, 22/9, 27/45,
  30/227, 259, 323, 33/44, etc **folces** gs
  9a/38, 9b/64, 10/67, 15c/2, 16/18, 22/149,
  30/202, etc **folcum** dp 9a/16, 42, 18/56
folclagu f:B3a *public law* **folclaga** np 25/30
folclond n:B2b *country* **folclondes** gs 40/47
folcstede m:B1g *dwelling-place, place of
  assembly, battlefield* ds 10/41, 19/319,
  35a/11
folctoga m:B5a *leader of the people, general*
  folctogan gs 19/47 ap 19/194
Folcwalda pr n *Folcwalda* **Folcwaldan** gs
  31a/27
folde f:B5c *earth, ground, soil, land* **foldan**
  as 9b/39, 30/54 gs 23/8, 43, 31a/75 ds
  2a/24, 18/91, 23/132, 30/166, 227, etc
folgað m:B1a *following, retinue, service,
  position* as 36/38, 40/9
folgian 2 +d *follow* inf 29/27 **folgie** sbj pr3s
  15c/16 **folgedon** pt3p 31a/40 **folgodon**
  pt3p 16/34
folm/folme f:B3b/5c *hand* **folman** ds 30/150
  dp 30/21, 108 **folme** ds 19/80 **folmum** dp
  19/99
(ġe)**fōn** VII *catch, seize, clutch, grasp, take,
  encounter* (**fōn tō** +d *succeed to, receive*)
  fanggene pp npm 9a/45 **fēng** pt1s 12/57
  pt3s 5/18, 8/4, 14, 12/52, 19/299, 29/38,
  39, 31b/51, etc **ġefēng** pt3s 31b/10, 46, 72
  fēngon pt3p 8/62, 24/28
for prep +d/a/i *for, because of, before, in, in
  the face of, in the presence of, as, through*
  1/7, 2a/16, 4/19, 7b/55, 8/22, 9a/7, 13,
  9b/7, 14/12, 15c/10, 20b/1, 22/66, 23/21,
  33/64, etc; **for ðī** see **furðȳ**; **for
  þǣm/þan/þon** see **forþǣm**
(ġe)**fōr** < (ġe)**faran**
forad adj *broken, useless* nsm 7b/80 **forade**
  npm 7b/81
foran adv *beforehand* 16/39
fōran < **faran**

forbær < **forberan**
forbærnan 1 *burn down, consume by fire*
  forbærnde pt3s 25/63 **forbærndon** pt3p
  8/56, 82 **forbærned** pp 5/27 **forbærnedne**
  pp asm 26/114
forbēah < **forbūgan**
forberan IV *forbear, bear, tolerate* inf
  22/133 **forbær** pt3s 22/135
forberstan III *break, fail* **forburste** sbj pt3s
  12/33
forbīgan 1 *bring low, humble* **forbīged**
  pp 19/267
forbrecan IV *break* **forbrocen** pp 7a/31
forbūgan II *flee from* **forbēah** pt3s 30/325
forburste < **forberstan**
forċeorfan III *cut through* **forċearf** pt3s
  19/105
ford m:B4a *ford* as 30/88 **forda** ds 30/81
fordīlġian 2 *blot out, destroy* **fordīlgode**
  pp npm 9a/54
fordōn anom *do away with, destroy* inf
  25/149 **fordyde** pt3s 8/9, 73, 24/32, 34
  fordydon pt3p 14/16
fordrīfan I *drive, compel* **fordrāf** pt3s 19/277
fore adv *beforehand, already* 6/15, 28/58
fore prep +d/a *for, on behalf of, before, in the
  presence of, because of* 12/7, 46, 20a/1,
  26/21, 22, 31a/2
foregenga m:B5a *predecessor, attendant* ns
  19/127 **foregengan** np 7b/2
foremǣre adj *very illustrious, outstanding*
  foremǣrne asm 19/122
foresǣd adj *aforesaid* **foresǣdan** dsn 24/36
  foresǣde nsf 16/85
foresċēawung f:B3d *foresight* as 6/10
  foresċēawunge as 21a/71
forespǣċ (for **foresprǣċ**) f:B3b *advocacy,
  defence* **forspǣċe** ds 12/8
forespeca (for **forespreca**) m:B5a
  intercessor, advocate, sponsor ns 12/5
  forespecan np 25/161
foresprecen adj *above-mentioned*
  foresprecenan dsm 9a/4
foretiohhung f:B3d *preordaining* ns 6/29, 33
foreþonc m:B1a *providence, forethought* ns
  6/14 (twice), 18, 78 as 6/10 **foreþanc** ns
  6/29 **foreþonce** ds 6/21, 22, 36, 74
  forþonce ds 6/25
forewerd adj *early* **forewerdne** asm 1/32

forfaran VI *ruin, destroy, cause to perish* inf 24/37 **forfōr** pt3s 25/65

forfōr < **forfaran**

forġēaf, forġēaf- see **forġīefan**

forġeald, forġelde < **forġieldan**

forġīefan V *give, grant, release* **forġeaf** pt3s 14/25, 22/58, 23/147, 27/65, 30/148, 31b/28 **forġēafan** pt3p 12/59 **forġēafe** pt2s 12/56 sbj pt1s 17/73 **forġēafen** pt3p 9a/14 **forġefe** sbj pt3s 9a/47 **forġiefene** pp nsm 26/93 **forġifen** pp 7b/47, 54, 9b/48, 21a/7, 11, 27/64 **forġifene** pp npm 7b/48 **forġȳfan** inf 14/8 **forġȳfe** sbj pr1s 14/17

forġieldan III *repay, requite, indemnify, reward* **forġeald** pt3s 31b/50, 93 **forġelde** sbj pr3s 7a/17, 19, 25, 12/7 **forgolden** pp 19/217, 34/38 **forġyldan** inf 31b/86, 32/39 **forġylde** sbj pr3s 7a/9 **forġyldon** sbj pt3p 30/32

forġietan V +g *forget* **forġitan** inf 15b/6

forġif- see **forġīefan**

forġifenyss f:B3e.ii *forgiveness, remission* ns 22/61 **forġifenisse** as 16/57 **forġifnisse** as 16/56

forġitan < **forġietan**

forgolden < **forġieldan**

forgrindan III *grind to pieces, destroy* **forgrunden** pp 10/43

forġȳf- see **forġīefan**

forġyld- see **forġieldan**

forhabban 3 *hold back, hinder* inf 18/42, 31a/89

forhealdan VII *withhold* inf 25/21 **forhealdað** pr1p 25/22

forheard adj *exceedingly hard* **forheardne** asm 30/156 (=noun)

forhēawan VII *cut down, hack down* **forhēawen** pp 30/115, 223, 288, 314

forherġian 2 *plunder, ravage, devastate* **forherġeode** pp npf 9a/40 **forherġod** pp 5/27

forhogdnis f:B3e.ii *contempt* **forhogdnisse** ds 9b/7

forhogode < **forhycgan**

forht adj *afraid, fearful* nsm 23/21, 34/23, 38/68

forhtian 2 *fear, be afraid, dread* sbj pr3p 22/93 **forhtedon** sbj pt3p 30/21 **forhtiaþ** pr3p 23/115 **forhtiende** prp npm 9a/48

forhtiġe pr2p 22/95 **forhtiġende** prp npm 18/7

forhtlīċe adv *fearfully, in alarm* 19/244

forhycgan 2 *despise, scorn* **forhogode** pt3s 30/254

forlǣtan VII *let go, loose, abandon, neglect, leave, forsake* inf 21a/23, 25/158, 30/2, 20 **forlǣt** imp s 2a/17, 27/23 **forlǣte** sbj pr3s 11/32 **forlǣten** pr3p 17/67, 92 pp 5/34 **forlǣtende** prp nsm 9b/105 **forlǣton** inf 19/150 **forlēt** pt1s 7b/9, 27/15, 28/1 pt3s 8/13, 25, 9b/20, 10/42, 16/32, 22/163, 27/44, 30/149, etc **forlēte** pt2s 14/58 **forlēton** pt3p 5/41, 16/33, 19/170, 23/61

forleġene < **forlicgan**

forlēogan II *lie, perjure oneself* **forlogen** pp 25/115 **forlogene** pp npm 25/80

forlēosan II *lose* inf 19/63 **forlēas** pt1s 27/14 **forlēosaþ** pr3s 34/35 **forloren** pp npm 25/115 **forlure** pt2s 27/83

forlēt, forlēt- see **forlǣtan**

forlicgan V *fornicate, commit adultery* **forleġene** pp npm 25/136 (=noun *adulterer*)

forliden adj *shipwrecked* 27/6

forliġer n:B2c *fornication* **forliġru** ap 25/114

forlogen, forlogene < **forlēogan**

forloren, forlure < **forlēosan**

forma sup adj *foremost, first* nsm 31b/36 **forman** asm 21b/1, 30/77 dsm 32/19 dsn 16/52 dsf 7b/32

formolsnian 2 *decay* inf 21a/74 **formolsnodon** pp apm 21a/75

formoni adj *very many* nsm 30/239

forniman IV *take away, carry off, overcome, plunder, destroy* **fornam** pt3s 22/40, 31a/18, 61 **fornāmen** pt3p 9a/38 **fornōm** pt3s 37/26, 38/80 **fornōman** pt3p 38/99 **fornumene** pp npm 9a/43 npn 25/37

fornȳdan 1 *force, compel* **fornȳdde** pp npf 25/33

foroft adv *very often* 25/47, 50, 107

forrǣdan 1 *betray* **forrǣdde** pt3s 25/62 **forrǣde** sbj pr3s 25/61

forsawene < **forsēon**

forsēon V *despise, scorn, reject, renounce* **forsawene** pp npf 25/39 **forsāwon** pt3p 24/11 **forsihð** pr3s 16/57 **forsīoð** pr3p 6/65 forsīðian 2 *journey disastrously, perish* forsīðod pp 31b/59

forslēan VI *cut through, break* forslǣhð pr3s 7a/25

forspanan I *entice, seduce* forspēon pt3s 17/13

forspǣċe < forespǣċ

forspēon < forspanan

forspillan I *destroy, kill* forspilde pt3s 25/64

forst m:B1a *frost* forste ds 26/9

forstandan VII *hinder, prevent; understand* forstōd pt1s 5/64 pt3s 31b/58

forstelan IV *steal away, rob, deprive* forstæl pt3s 12/3, 46 forstēlan sbj pr3p 22/9 forstele sbj pr3s 22/42 forstolen pp 22/39

forswāpan VII *sweep away* forswāpen pp 17/54

forswelgan III *swallow up, swallow down, devour* inf 26/95 forswealg pt3s 31a/60, 35e/3 forswelgen sbj pr3p 1/35

forswerian VI *forswear, swear falsely* forsworene pp npm 25/79

forsyngian 2 *sin greatly* forsyngod pp (*ruined by sin, corrupt*) 25/108 forsyngodan pp dsf 25/140

forþ adv *forth, forward, onwards, away, henceforth, still* 2a/12, 7b/35, 7c/5, 8/76, 10/20, 12/14, 21, 17/11, 100, 18/80, 116, 23/54, 132, 25/127, 27/45, 47, 30/3, 12, 32/5, etc

forþām, forþan see forþǣm

forþǣm adv (often written as two words) *therefore, for that reason, assuredly, forthwith* 5/33, 6/5, 63 forþām 2a/16, 7b/4, 7c/12, 27/7 forþan 23/84 forþon 5/20, 9b/13, 16, 26/27, 33, 58, 35d/13, 37/29, 38/17, 37, etc for þon 28/61

forþǣm conj (often written as two words) *because, for, seeing that, inasmuch as* 6/5, 27, 77 forþām 1/1, 30, 7b/5, 18/62, etc for ðan 22/158 forþon 8/68, 9b/2, 10, 12/5, 16, 26/39, 64 for þon 22/171; in phrs for þām þe *because* 16/5, 43 forþan þe 4/3, 11 for ðan þe 13/6, 16/8, 50, 22/42 for þǣm þe 5/29, 30 [etc]

forþbringan I *bring forth, produce* forþbrōhte pt3s 9b/6

forðēodon < forðgān

forðfaran VI *depart, die* forðfarene pp npm 22/122

forðfēran 1 *go forth, die* forðfērde pt3s 8/4, 6, 17, 47, 66, 22/120

forðfōr f:B3b *faring forth, death* ns 9b/85 forðfōre gs 9b/77, 109 ds 9b/81, 90

forðgān anom *go forth, leave* forðēodon pt3p 9a/52

forðgang m:B1a *advance, escape* forðganges gs 18/24

forðgangan VII *go forth, advance* forðgenġe pp nsm 4/16

forðġeċīgan 1 *call forth* forðġeċeġde pt3s 9a/57

forðġeorn adj *eager to advance* nsm 30/281

forðġesceaft f:B3g *preordination, eternal decree, future* ns 33/61 as 23/10

forþian 2 *carry out, accomplish* ġeforþod pp 30/289

forþolian 2 *do without, lack* inf 38/38

forþon see forþǣm

forþonce < foreþanc

forþringan II *dislodge* inf 31a/22

forðsīð m:B1a *going forth, departure, passing, death* forðsīðe ds 8/37, 21a/87, 22/163, 24/48

forðweġ m:B1a *the onward path, the journey ahead* forðweġe ds 23/125, 38/81

forðȳ adv/conj *therefore, because* 5/48, 70, 6/63 for ðī 4/17, 22, 39, 22/7, 97

forðylman 1 *enwrap, envelop* forðylmed pp 19/118

forwandian 2 *respect* forwandiġendre prp dsf 27/10 (*respectful*)

forwearð < forweorðan

forwegan V *carry off, destroy* forwegen pp 30/228

forweorðan III *fall to ruin, become ruined, deteriorate, perish* inf 19/288 sbj pr1p 25/145 forwearð pt3s 12/46 forwurdan pt3p 25/66, 154 forwurde pr1s 35a/6

forweosan I *perish, decay* forweorone pp apm 31/7

forworht, forworht- < forwyrcan

forwundian 2 *wound badly* forwunded pp 23/14 forwundod pp 23/62

forwurdan, forwurðe < forweorðan

forwyrċan 1 (+g) *forfeit, destroy, obstruct, do wrong, condemn* inf 12/53 sbj pr3s

25/130 **forworht** pp 34/24 **forworhtan**
pt3p 25/154 **forworhte** pp npm 17/44
forwyrhtne pp asm 14/8
forwyrd n/f:B2i *destruction, ruin,*
annihilation ns 19/285 as 9a/54 **forwyrde**
ds 24/68
forwyrnan 1 *deny, refuse* **forwyrnde** pt3s
27/72, 31a/80
foryrman 1 *reduce to poverty* **foryrmde**
pp npf 25/33
fōt m:B4b *foot* as 13/6 **fēt** np 17/42, 26/9 ap
16/98, 22/49, 52 **fōta** gp 28/32 **fōtes** gs
30/247 **fōtum** dp 22/35, 159, 30/119, 171
fōtmǣl n:B2b *the space of a foot* as 30/275
fracod adj *base, wicked, useless* nsf 1/5,
24/63, 31b/84 **fracodes** gsm 23/10 (=noun
criminal)
fram adv *away* 30/317 **from** 29/28
fram prep +d/i *from, of, since, concerning,*
on account of, by 2a/6, 2b/3, 4/13, 8/32,
9a/1, 14/23, 15b/2, 16/6, 22/107, 23/69,
27/21, 30/316, etc **from** 9b/10, 19, 10/8,
17/69
franca m:B5a *spear, lance* **francan** as
30/140 ds 30/77
ġefrǣġen, (ġe)**frǣġn** < (ġe)**friġnan**
Frǣna pr n *Frǣna* ns 8/43
frǣt < **fretan**
frǣtwe fp:B3f *treasures, adornments,*
trappings np 35b/6 **frǣtewum** dp 16/73
frǣtwum dp 33/27
(ġe)**frǣtwian** 2 *adorn, ornament, dress,*
equip ġe**frǣtewod** pp 19/171, 328
ġe**frǣtweð** pp 37/33 **frǣtwode** pt3s 21a/40
frēa m:B5a *lord, master, the Lord* ns 9b/39,
19/300 **frēan** as 23/33, 30/184, 259 gs
40/33 ds 30/12, 16, 289
freca m:B5a *bold man, warrior* ns 31b/72
frēcne adj *dangerous, savage, bold* apm
35a/4 (=noun *savage ones, enemies*)
frēcnen ds 31a/42
frēcnys f:B3e.ii *harm, danger* **frēcnysse**
as/ds 2a/10
frēfran 1 *comfort, console* inf 26/26, 38/28
ġe**frēfrian** 2 *comfort, cheer* ġe**frēfrode** pt3s
22/45
frēfrung f:B3d *consolation, comfort* ns
15c/13

fremde adj *foreign, strange* (=noun
foreigner, stranger) **fremdan** ds 25/50
fremdum dp 25/36, 77
fremena < **fremu**
(ġe)**fremian** 2 (+d) *help, avail, do good,*
effect, accomplish inf 4/4, 22 ġe**fremod**
pp 22/124 **fremode** pt3s 14/22, 21a/79
(ġe)**fremman** 1 *do, perform, commit,*
perpetrate, accomplish, provide inf 17/56,
38/16, 114 ġe**fremed** pp 6/11 ġe**fremede**
pt3s 19/6, 181, 31b/61 **fremedon** pt3p
19/37 ġe**fremedon** pt3p 17/55, 26/84
fremsumnes f:B3e.ii *benefit, blessing*
fremsumnessum dp 9b/70
fremu f:B3a *benefit, good action* **fremena** gp
17/101 **fremum** dp 26/75
Frencisc adj *French* **Frenciscan** asm 8/71
frēo adj *free* **frēoh** nsm 1/30 **frēum** dsm
7a/15 **frīġes** gsm 7a/40 **frīġne** asm 7a/11
frīora gpm 5/52 **frīoum** dpm 7b/48
frēod f:B3b *friendship, peace* **frēode** as 30/19
frēodōm m:B1a *freedom* **frēodōme** ds 15c/2
frēoġan 2 *free* **frēoġe** sbj pr3s 11/7
frēoliċ adj *glorious, noble* 32/19
frēolīċe adv *with festivity, jubilantly* 22/152
frēolsbriċe m:B1g *non-observance of*
festivals **frēolsbricas** np 25/116
frēolsdæġ m:B1c *feast-day* ns 21a/31
frēolstīd f:B3g *festival, feast-day* ns 22/88
frēolstīde gs 22/87
frēomǣġ m:B1c *noble kinsman* **frēomǣġum**
dp 38/21
frēond m:B4d.i *friend, relative, lover* ns 7c/7,
23/144, 34/2, 26, 38/108, 40/47 **frēonda** gp
10/41, 23/132, 34/3, 4, 35d/21, 40/17
frēondas np 23/76 **frēonde** ds 34/5
frēondum dp 7b/17, 27/58, 31a/64 **frȳnd**
np 40/33 ap 27/26, 30/229
frēondlēas adj *friendless* **frēondlēasne** asm
7c/24, 38/28
frēondlīċe adv *in a friendly manner,*
affectionately 5/3
frēondscipe m:B1g *friendship, love* ns 40/25
frēoriġ adj *frozen, chilled* nsm 19/281, 38/33
frēoriht n:B2b *rights of freemen* np 25/37
frēowīf n:B2b *free woman, freeborn woman*
frīwīf ns 7a/39
Frēsena < **Frȳsen**

Frēswæl n:B2a *Frisian battle-field* Frēswæle
ds 31a/8
fretan V *eat up, devour* fræt pt3s 31b/90,
35e/1
frēum < frēo
frīġ f:B3b *affection, embrace, love* ns 36/15
(see note)
frīġes < frēo
frīġman m:B4b *free-man, freeborn man* ns
7a/9, 15
friġnan III *ask, question, inquire* fræġn pt1s
28/7 pt3s 9b/88, 91, 98, 28/19, 32/22, 46
friġe imp s 35d/26 frīnan inf 28/49 frīneþ
pr3s 23/112 frūne sbj pt1s 28/46
ġefriġnan III *hear of, find out, learn (by
asking)* ġefræġen pt1s 19/7, 35e/2
ġefræġn pt1s 19/246, 32/37 ġefruġnon
pt1p 36/14 ġefrūnon pt3p 23/76
frīġne < frēo
frīora, frīoum < frēo
frioðuwǣr f:B3b *peace-agreement*
frioðuwǣre as 31a/34
friþ m:B1a *peace, refuge, (right of)
sanctuary, protection* as 7b/24, 8/59, 30/39
friþe ds 30/179 friþes gs 7b/27, 30/41,
34/24
Friðegist pr n *Frithegist* ns 8/44
ġefriðian 2 *protect, defend* ġefriðoðe sbj pt3s
19/5
friðsōcn f:B3b *sanctuary, asylum* friðsōcne
as 7c/8
friðsumian 2 *make peaceful, reconcile*
friðsumaþ pr3s 2a/14
frīwīf see frēowīf
frōd adj *old, mature, wise, experienced* nsm
30/140, 317, 33/12, 27, 38/90 frōda nsm
10/37 (=noun) frōdran comp npm 35d/21
frōfor f:B3c *consolation, joy, comfort, refuge*
frōfre as 35a/4, 38/115 gs 19/83 ds 19/296
frōfres gs 27/73
from see fram
fromlīċe adv *boldly, promptly* 19/41, 220, 301
fromsīþ m:B1a *journey away, departure* ns
40/33
fromweard adj *about to depart*
fromweardum dp 26/71 (=noun)
fruma m:B5a *origin, beginning* fruman as
9a/26 ds 6/41, 9a/17, 9b/63, 16/19

frumgār m:B1a *leader, chief* frumgāras ap
19/195
frumsceaft f:B3g *first creation, the beginning
of creation* as 9b/28
frūne, ġefrūnon < (ġe)friġnan
frymdi adj *suppliant, entreating* nsm 30/179
frymð(u) f:B3a *beginning, origin, creation*
frymða gp 19/5, 83, 189
frȳnd < frēond
Frȳsen pr n (mp:B1b) *(West) Frisians*
Frēsena gp 31a/31 Frȳsna gp 31a/42
Frȳsland pr n (n:B2b) *Friesland* as 31a/64
fugel m:B1bi *bird, fowl* ns 19/207, 28/36,
33/38, 38/81 fugelas np 32/5 fugles gs
35d/7 fuglum dp 19/296
fugelere m:B1g *fowler, bird-catcher*
fugeleras np 1/16
fuhton < feohtan
ful, fulan < full
fūl adj *foul, disgusting* nsf 24/63 fūla nsm
19/111 fūlan asm 24/71 fūle asm 24/71
(=noun *vile people*) npm 25/136 fūlne asm
25/153
fulfremed < fullfremman
fulgon < fēolan
fūlīċe adv *foully, shamefully* 24/69 fūllīċe
24/30
full adj *full, filled (with), entire, completed,
utter* nsf 26/100, 37/23 asn 3b/5 ful nsn
18/5 asn 16/15 fullan asf 7b/52 dsm 7b/36,
7c/15 fulle asf 3c/5, 4/46 npm 19/19 fulles
gsn 7c/4 fulne asm 1/22, 3b/2, 26/113,
34/15, 43 fulre comp nsn 34/43 dsf 7c/9; in
phr be fulan *fully, in full* 12/37 be fullan
5/37, 12/31
full adv *fully, completely, very* 24/54, 30/153
ful 25/17, 60, 87, 106, 122, 26/24, 30/253,
311, 33/127, 35c/6, 40/32, 46
fullēst m:B1a *help, support* fullēsta gp
18/109
fullfremman 2 *accomplish, complete*
fulfremed nsn 4/72 (*completed*)
fullfremed pp 6/10
fullgān anom *perform, follow* fullēodan pt3p
24/30
fullīċe adv *fully, completely, outright* 12/24,
25/85, 87
ġefullod < fulwian

fulluht n/f:B2i *baptism* as 25/160 **fulluhte**
ds 7b/8, 15c/7, 16/56, 25/161 **fulwihte** as
21b/9

fulne, fulre < **full**

fultum m:B1a *help, support* as 19/186, 300
fultom as 9a/58 **fultomes** gs 9a/53 **fultume**
ds 5/51, 7b/14

fultumian 2 *help, support* inf 24/51
fultemade sbj pt1s 12/32 ġe**fultumed**
pp 9b/12

fulwian 2 *baptise* ġe**fullod** pp 21b/3

fulwihte < **fulluht**

funde, fund- see **findan**

fundian 2 *be eager for, set out, come* **fundaþ**
pr3s 23/103, 26/47 **fundode** pt3s 31a/75

Funtial pr n *Fonthill* (Wilts.) ds 12/1, 46

furþon see **furðum**

furðor adv *further, any more* 5/55, 17/64
furður 5/55

furðum adv *furthermore, moreover, even*
5/15, 17 **furþon** 16/21

fūs adj +g *eager, ready, hastening* asm
30/281 **fūse** asn 23/21 npm 23/57 (=noun)
fūsne asm 26/50

fȳftȳne num *fifteen* 31b/91

fyl see **fyll**

fylde < **fyllan**

fylġan 1 *follow, observe, attend to* +d inf
19/33 **fylġean** inf 25/160

fyll m:B1a *fall, death, destruction* as 23/56
fyl as 30/264 **fylle** ds 31b/53

fyllo f:B3h *fill, feast* **fylle** gs 19/209

(ġe)**fyllan** 1 *fill, fulfil, complete* **fyllan** inf
1/28 ġe**fyldæ** pp npf 5/28 **fylde** pt3s 14/60
ġe**fyldon** pt3p 9a/35 ġe**fylle** imp s 3a/14
ġe**fylled** pp 12/38, 14/41, 22/57 ġe**fyllede**
pp npm 22/74 ġe**fylð** pr3s 22/91

(ġe)**fyllan** 1 *fell, strike down, kill* inf 19/194,
23/38, 73 ġe**fylled** pp 10/41, 67

fylstan 1 +d *help, support* inf 12/34, 30/265

fȳlþ f:B3b *foul sin* **fȳlþe** ds 25/72 ds 25/73

ġe**fylð** < (ġe)**fyllan**

fȳnd see **fēond**

fyr < **feor**

fȳr n:B3b *fire, hell-fire* ns 17/37, 18/91 as
24/17, 25/18, 34/43 **fȳre** ds 9a/38, 17/24,
100 **fȳres** gs 26/113

fyrd f:B3g *campaign, expedition, army, levy*
(see 8/28–9n) ns 33/31, 52 as 28/1 **fyrde** as

8/28, 42, 74, 75, 17/72 gs 18/26 ds 8/32,
30/221, 33/52

fyrdhom m:B1a *war-garment, mailcoat* as
31b/13

fyrdhræġl n:B2b *war-garment, mailcoat* as
31b/36

fyrdian 2 *go to war* **fyrdedon** pt3p 24/49

fyrdrinc m:B1a *warrior* ns 30/140

fyrdwīc n:B2b *army camp* **fyrdwīcum** dp
19/220

fȳren adj *fiery, afire* **fȳrenu** nsf 32/36

fyrestum < **fyrst**

fyrhtan 1 *fear* **fyrhteð** pr3s 2a/19

fyrhtu f:B3h *fear, terror* ds 9b/68

fȳrlēoht n:B2b *firelight* as 31b/25

fyrmest sup adj (< **forma**) *foremost, first,
chief* nsm 30/323 **firmest** nsf 16/43
fyrmestan npm 24/68

ġe**fyrn** adv *formerly, long ago* 12/61, 21a/78,
24/1

fyrndagas mp:1c *days of old* **fyrndagum** dp
18/114

fyrnġēar m:B1a *far-off year, bygone year*
fyrnġēarum dp 33/12

fyrnġeflit n:B2a *ancient strife, former
quarrel* **fyrnġeflitu** ap 19/264

fyrrest < **feor**

fyrst adj *first, foremost, front* **fyrestum** dpm
7a/26

fyrst, fyrste see **first**

fȳsan 1 *send forth, hasten, prepare oneself*
sbj pr2p 19/189 **fȳsde** pt3s 30/269

G

gā < **gān**

Gadd pr n *Gadd* **Gaddes** gs 30/287

(ġe)**gaderian** 2 *collect, gather* inf 21a/60
ġe**gaderode** pt1s 7b/1, 9 pt3s 8/42, 73 sbj
pt3s 8/27 pp npm 22/46 ġe**gaderodon** pt3p
14/28

gādīsen n:B2b '*goad-iron*', *cattle-prod*
gādīsene ds 1/25

gafol n:B2c *tribute* as 8/22, 59 **gafle** ds 8/62
gafole ds 30/32, 46 **gofol** as 30/61

gāl adj *wanton, wicked* nsm 24/37

galan VI *sing* inf 23/67

gālferhð adj *lustful, lascivious* nsm
19/62

Galilēa pr n *Galilee* ns 22/29, 106 ds 22/36, 106

gālmōd adj *wanton, licentious* **gālmōda** nsm 19/256

gālnys f:B3e.ii *wantonness, lust* **gālnysse** ds 24/63

gālscipe m:B1g *wantonness, pride* ds 17/4

gān anom *go, advance, proceed* inf 3b/10, 8/42, 12/14, 19/149, 22/150 sbj pr1p 27/65 **ēodan** pt1p 12/24 **ēode** pt1s 1/40, 9b/25 pt3s 9b/19, 12/63, 13/17, 23/54, 27/1, 10, 29/11 sbj pt2s 34/11 **ēodon** pt3p 8/52, 55, 9a/46, 13/20, 14/66, 19/15, 22/14, 17, 37, 29/23, 28, 32/14 **gā** pr1s 1/19 sbj pr3s 7b/34, 14/51 imp s 14/48 **gāþ** imp p 22/27 **gǣþ** pr3s 4/32, 15a/1, 18/80, 29/36, 34/33 [etc]

ġegān anom *arrive at, reach, come to, gain, win* inf 31b/44 pp 19/140, 219 **ġeēodon** pt3p 19/331 **ġegā** sbj pr3s 7c/14

ganet m:B1a *gannet* **ganetes** gs 26/20

gang m:B1a *going, progress, motion, flow* **gange** ds 23/23 **gonges** gs 2b/1

gang, (ġe)gang- see **(ġe)gongan**

gār m:B1a *spear, javelin* ns 30/296 as 30/13, 134, 154, etc **gāras** ap 19/224, 30/46, 67, 109 **gāre** ds 30/138 **gārum** dp 10/18

gārberend m:B4d *spear-bearer, warrior* np 30/262

gārġewinn n:B2b *spear-conflict, battle with spears* **gārġewinnes** gs 19/307

gārmitting f:B3d *spear-encounter* **gārmittinge** gs 10/50

gārrǣs m:B1a *spear-storm, battle* as 30/32

gārsecg m:B1a *sea* ns 18/44

Gārulf pr n *Garulf* ns 32/18, 31

gāst m:B1a *ghost, spirit, soul, demon* ns 16/53, 54, 55, 57, 22/48, 50, 24/75 as 9b/108, 14/63, 21b/24, 22/170, 23/49 **gāsta** gp 23/152 **gāstae** ds 20a/4 **gāstas** np 23/11 ap 18/2, 99 **gāste** ds 2a/25, 20b/4, 22/176, 30/176 **gāstes** gs 9b/67, 18/79 **gǣst** ns 19/83, 112, 35b/9 **gǣsta** gp 31a/61 **gǣstes** gs 19/279

gāstliċ adj *spiritual, ghostly, ghastly, awful, terrifying* **gāstlican** dsn 21a/29 **gāstliċe** asn 16/25 **gāstlicum** dsn 16/47, 67, 86 dpm 15b/2 **gǣstliċ** nsn 38/73

gāstlīċe adv *spiritually* 16/36, 39, 96

gātehǣr n:B2b *goat-hair* ns 16/79 as 16/75

gatu < **ġeat**

gāþ < **gān**

Gaza pr n *Gaza* ns 22/146, 149

gǣlsa m:B5a *pride, wantonness, luxury* **gǣlsan** as 25/153

gǣngang m:B1a ?*return* ns 7a/53 (see note)

gǣst see **gāst**

gǣstliċ see **gāstliċ**

gǣþ < **gān**

ġe conj *and* 19/176, 34/2, 40/25 **ġe ... ġe** *both ... and* 6/70, 72, 7b/23, 7c/9, 9b/79, etc; see also **ǣgþer**

ġē pers pron *ye, you* np 1/3, 13/16, 14/17, 17/97, 18/115, 22/25, etc **ēow** ap 22/3 dp 13/19, 22, 14/11, 17 **ēower** gp 17/91 (*of you*) **īow** dp 5/48; see also poss pron **ēower**

ġēa interj *yes* 1/31, 33

ġēac m:B1a *cuckoo* ns 26/53

geador adv *together* 39/19

ġeaf, ġeafan < **giefan**

ġeald < **ġieldan**

ġealga m:B5a *gallows, cross* ns 23/10

ġealgan as 23/40

ġealgean see **(ġe)ealgian**

ġealgtrēow n:B2g.i *gallows-tree* **ġealgtrēowe** ds 23/146

ġealla m:B5a *gall, bile* **eallan** ds 14/39

ġēap adj *curved, arched, broad* nsm 33/23, 37/11

ġear n:B2b *year* ns 31a/72 as 8/15, 12/45 ap 2c/3, 9a/2, 21a/12, 21b/5 **ġēara** gp 2c/2, 3, 21a/84, 85 **ġēare** ds 2a/6, 8/26, 39, 44 etc, 11/25, 21a/35 is 28/72, 29/37, 39 **ġēarum** dp 4/19, 21a/51, 21b/11, 13 **ġēr** ns 34/6 as 9a/60 **ġēres** gs 33/9

ġēara adv *'of yore', once, long ago* 17/74, 38/22 **ġēara iū** *once long ago, years ago* 23/28

ġeard m:B1a *enclosure, dwelling* **ġeardas** ap 31a/72 **ġeardum** dp 31a/76

ġēardagas mp:B1c *days of yore, former days* **ġēardagum** dp 24/31, 38/44

ġeare see **ġearwe**

ġearo adj *ready, prepared* nsm 29/15 nsn 17/99 **ġearuwe** npm 1/45

ġearolīċe adv *clearly* 36/10

ġearoþoncol adj *ready-witted, clever* **ġearoþoncolre** dsf 19/341

ġearowita m:B5a *intellect, understanding*
  ġearowitan as 6/75

ġearuwe < ġearo

ġearwe adv *readily, well* 19/2 ġeare 21a/38

ġeġearwian 2 *prepare* ġeġearwod pp 19/199
  ġeġearwod pp 25/166 ġeġearwode pt3s
  9b/83, 98 ġeġearwodest pr2s 15c/13

ġeat n:B2d *gate, door* as 19/151 gatu ap
  22/151, 29/22, 31

Ġēat pr n *a Geat* Ġēates gs 36/15

Ġēatas pr n (mp:B1a) *Geats, Jutes* Ġēata gp
  9a/17, 31b/60 Ġēatum dp 9a/17, 21

Ġeatolic adj *well-equipped, noble* nsm 31b/71

Ġeġnum adv *straight, directly* 19/132

Ġēhhol pr n *Yule(tide), Christmas* ds 7b/49

ġelpan III *boast, exult* inf 10/44 ġelpeð pr3s
  34/46

ġēmde < ġīeman

Genesis pr n *(the book of) Genesis* ns 16/42
  as 16/3, 13 gs 9b/63

ġēoc f:B3b *help, rescue, relief* ns 35a/5 ġēoce
  ds 26/101

ġeofon n:B2a *sea, ocean* ns 18/2

ġeoguþ f:B3b *youth, youthfulness* ġeogoð ns
  33/50 ġeogoðe ds 24/33 ġeoguþe ds 26/40,
  38/35 ġioguð ns 5/52 iugoþe ds 4/15,
  21a/40

ġēomor adj *troubled, sorrowful, sad, gloomy,
  mournful* nsm 19/87, 40/17 ġēomorre dsf
  40/1 ġēomran dsf 26/53 ġēomre apm 18/2
  ġēomuru nsf 31a/13

ġēomormōd adj *sad-hearted, despondent*
  nsm 40/42 ġēomormōdum dsn 19/144

ġēomrian 2 *mourn, lament* ġēomrode pt3s
  31a/56

ġeond prep +a *through, throughout, over,
  across* 22/40, 141, 24/67, 26/90, 35d/8
  ġiond 5/4, 5, 27 etc ġynd 25/11, 37, 64,
  143

ġeondhweorfan III *pass through, pervade*
  ġeondhweorfeð pr3s 38/51

ġeondscēawian 2 *survey, regard*
  ġeondscēawað pr3s 38/52

ġeondþenċean 1 *contemplate, meditate on*
  ġeondþenċe pr1s 38/60 ġeondþenċeð pr3s
  38/89

ġeong adj *young* nsm 23/39 ġeonge npm
  19/166 ġeongne asm 33/14 ġiunge npm
  10/29 ġiungne asm 10/44 iunga nsm 27/4,

6 iungan dsm 27/26 (=noun) iunge nsf
  27/2 iungum dpm 4/9 dpn 4/4

ġeongan see gongan

ġeongra m:B5a *subordinate, servant*
  ġiongrum dp 17/71

ġeorn adj *eager, zealous* nsm 19/210 ġiorne
  npm 5/10

ġeorne adv *eagerly, readily, well, carefully,
  clearly, earnestly, keenly* 4/17, 7c/13, 17,
  18, 17/60, 21a/23, 63, 24/16, 19, 25/7, 10,
  17, etc ġeornost* sup 24/46, 25/145 ġiorne
  5/10

ġeornful adj *eager* nsm 30/274

ġeornfulnes f:B3e.ii *yearning, desire*
  ġeornfulnesse ds 9b/72

ġeornlīċe adv *eagerly, earnestly, carefully,
  closely* 9b/71, 30/265 ġeornlīcor comp
  28/12, 28

ġēotan II *pour, gush* inf 37/42

ġēr, ġēres see ġēar

ġerela m:B5a *apparel, clothes* ġerelan as
  28/24

Germānie pr n (mp:B1h) *the Germans,
  Germany* gp 9a/16

ġeġerwed < ġeġyrwan

ġēsne adj (+g) *empty, bereft of, deprived of,
  lacking* nsm 19/210 asm 19/279 npm 18/83

ġesthūs n:B2b *guesthouse, lodging* 27/65

ġēt see ġīet

ġiedd n:B2b.i *song, poem, story, narrative,
  word, speech* ns 39/19 as 40/1 ġid ns 31a/3
  ġiddum dp 31a/56 ġied as 35e/3

ġiefan V *give, grant, bestow, devote* ġeaf pt3s
  19/342 ġeafan pt3p 9a/12 ġif imp s 27/52
  ġifan inf 27/51 ġife pr1s 27/54 sbj pr2s
  27/20 ġyfeð pr3s 34/6

ġiefstōl m:B1a *gift-throne* ġiefstōlas gs
  38/64

ġieldan III *pay, repay, requite, render* ġeald
  pt3s 8/63 sbj pt3s 8/22 ġielde sbj pr3s
  7b/37 guldan pt3p 32/40 ġyldan inf 17/77
  ġyldað pr1p 25/102, 103 ġylde sbj pr3s
  25/87 ġyldon inf 8/59

ġiellan III *yell, cry* ġielleð pr3s 26/62

ġielpes < ġylp

ġīeman 1 (+g) *care for, take heed, take
  charge of, control* inf 17/12 ġēmde pt3s
  9b/71 ġȳman inf 17/9 ġȳmdon pt3p
  30/192 ġȳme sbj pr3s 25/19

ġīen adv *still, yet, now* 17/77

ġierede < ġyrwan

ġīet, ġīeta see ġȳt

ġif conj *if, whether, lest* 1/52, 3b/9, 3c/6, 4/23, 7a/5, 7b/13, 7c/5, 8/30, 9b/50, 12/39, 15b/12, etc ġyf 2a/15, 4/24, 13/4, 14/48, 51, 16/19, etc

ġif, ġifan see ġiefan

ġifena < ġifu

ġīfernes f:B3e.ii *greed, gluttony* ġīfernessa ap 25/110

ġifeðe adj *granted* nsm 19/157

ġifre adj *useful, bountiful* 35d/28

ġīfre adj *eager, avid, greedy* nsm 26/62 ġīfrost sup nsm 31a/61

ġifu f:B3a *gift, favour, grace* ns 9b/48 ġife as 9b/12, 43, 54, 17/77 ds 9b/2 ap 27/59 ġifena gp 19/2, 26/40 ġyfena gp 34/28

ġīgant m:B1a *giant* ġīganta gp 31b/71

ġihðu f:B3h *anxiety, sorrow* ġihðum dp 18/89

Gildas pr n *Gildas* ns 25/146

ġim m:B1a *gem, jewel* ns 33/22 ġimmas np 23/7, 16

ġimcynn n:B2b.i *precious stone, gem* ġimcynne ds 28/17

ġimstān m:B1a *jewel* ġimstānas np 16/78 ap 16/74 ġymstānum 21a/42

ġinfæst adj *ample* ġinfæsten apn 18/79

ġingre f:B5c *handmaid, female servant* ġingran dsf 19/132

ġinn adj *spacious, wide* ġinnan ism 19/2 dsf 19/149 ġynne asm 31b/60

gio- see ġeo-

ġirnan 1 *yearn for, desire* ġirnþ pr3s 27/81 ġyrnde pt3s 19/346

ġirstandæġ adv *yesterday* 27/78

ġīsle < ġȳsel

ġist see ġyst

ġīt see ġȳt

ġītsung f:B3d *avarice, greediness* (+g *for*) ġītsunga ap 25/110 ġītsunge as 25/150

ġiū adv *formerly* 5/37

ġiunge, ġiungne < ġeong

glād < glīdan

glædlīċe adv *joyfully* 9b/90

glædmōd adj *glad at heart, cheerful* nsm 37/33 glædmōde npf 19/140

glēaw adj *wise, prudent, clear-sighted* nsm 38/73 nsf 19/13 glēawe asf 19/333 nsf 19/171 (=noun) glēawra comp nsm 35e/6

glēawhȳdiġ adj *thoughtful, prudent* nsn 19/148

glēd f:B3b *glowing coal, ember* glēdum dp 3a/3

glenġan 1 *adorn* ġeglænġde pp asn 9b/6 ġeglenġed pp 9b/52

gleomu f:B3a *splendour, brightness* gleoma gp 37/33 (see note)

glēowian 2 *make merry* glēowiende prp nsm 9b/87 glīwedon pt3p 35d/13

glīdan I *glide* glād pt3s 10/15

glīwedon < glēowian

glīwstæf m:B1a *melody, joy* glīwstafum dp 38/52 (=adv *joyfully*)

glōf f:B3b *glove* glōfe ds 33/17

gluto Lat *glutton* ns 1/63 (see note)

ġegnīdan I *rub, grind, crumble* ġegnīd imp s 3b/2, 7

gnorn adj *sad, troubled* gnornra comp nsm 18/9

gnornian 2 *mourn, lament, regret* inf 30/315 gnornað pr3s 26/92 gnornode pt3s 31a/55

god n:B1a *a god* ns 27/40 as 24/48 goda gp 24/43 godas np 24/16, 66 ap 24/10, 13, 41, 44 gode ds 24/55 godum dp 24/27, 71

God m:B1a *God* ns 2a/14, 12/7, 13/14, 18, 14/52, 15a/10, 22/90, etc as 2a/11, 21a/7, 21, 21b/12, 24/10 Godæs ds 11/31 Godæs gs 11/2, 4, 32 Godd as 24/73 Gode ds 2a/18, 9b/41, 15b/14, 15c/3, 21b/9, 24, 24/2, 33/59, etc Godes gs 2a/6, 7a/2, 7b/55, 9a/38, 14/47, 23/83, etc

gōd adj *good, excellent, favourable, worthy, virtuous, noble, generous* nsm 3a/3, 9a/56, 26/40 nsn 31b/71, 34/6 gōda nsm 27/32, 62, 31b/27 (=noun) gōdan isn 17/73 gōde asf 3c/5, 16/76, 23/70 apm 30/170, 33/14 gōdena gpm 5/36 gōdne asm 4/6 gōdra gpn 22/15, 77 gpf 9b/73 comp gpm 35d/22 gōdum dsm 6/27 dpm 27/49 dpn 16/38 dpf 21a/29 good nsn 6/27 asn 15c/9 goodan apm 6/30

gōd n:B2b *good, goodness, benefit, possession, goods, virtue, mental faculty* ns 6/45 as 2a/2, 6, 15b/14 ap 18/79 gōda gp

19/32 **gōde** ds 15a/5, 15b/12, 19/271 **gōdes**
gs 15c/8, 20b/4, 30/176 **gōdum** dp 9b/57
good ns 6/26, **goode** ds 6/27

Goda pr n *Goda* ns 8/12

godbearn n:B2b *godchild* ap 25/64

godcund adj *divine, religious, spiritual* asf
24/75 **godcunda** nsm 6/18, 78 **godcundan**
asm 28/22 asf 22/101, 116 dsm 6/36, 74
npm 5/9 dpf 9b/70 **godcunde** nsf 6/14
godcundra gpm 5/4 gpf 25/118 **godcundre**
gsf 9b/49 dsf 9b/1 **godcundum** dpm 9b/4

godcundliċ adj *divine, spiritual* **godcundliċe**
asn 6/50

godcundlīċe adv *divinely, in divine matters*
7c/22, 9b/11

godcundnys f:B3e.ii *divine nature, godhead*
godcundnysse ds 22/171

gōddǣd f:B3g *good deed* **gōddǣda** ap
25/124 **gōddǣdan** dp 25/123

godfyrht adj *godfearing* **godfyrhte** ap
25/124 (=noun)

gōdian 2 *improve, enrich* **gōdiende** prp nsn
25/16 ġe**gōdod** pp 27/68

godmæġen n:B2c *divine power* **godmæġne**
ds 28/41

gōdne < **gōd**

gōdnes f:B3e.ii *goodness, virtue* **gōdnesse** ds
24/21

gōdra < **gōd**

Godrīċ pr n *Godric* ns 30/187, 237, 321, 325

godsibb m:B1a *sponsor, godfather*
godsibbas ap 25/63

godspel n:B2b.i *gospel, gospel-reading* ns
4/9, 22/66 as 16/31 **godspelles** gs 22/67

godspellere m:B1g *evangelist* ns 22/121, 128

godsprǣce n:B2h *oracle* **godsprecum** dp
28/51

godsunu m:B4a *godson* ns 29/33

Godwīġ pr n *Godwig* ns 30/192

Godwine pr n *Godwin* ns 8/43, 30/192

gofol see **gafol**

gold n:B2b *gold* ns 26/101, 31a/45, 38/32 as
16/74, 76, 23/18 **goldæs** gs 11/8, 10 **golde**
ds 19/171 etc, 23/7, 16, 77, 35d/13 is 26/97
goldes gs 27/54, 31a/31

goldbeorht adj *bright with gold* nsm 37/33

goldfinger m:B1b *ring-finger* as 7a/37

goldġiefa m:B5a *gold-giver, lord* **goldġiefan**
np 26/83 **goldġifan** as 19/279

goldhladen adj *gold-adorned* nsm 32/13

goldhord n:B2b *gold-hoard, treasure*
goldhorde ds 27/52

goldwine m:B1g *'gold-friend', lord,*
generous lord ns 19/22, 38/35 as 38/22

Golgotha pr n *Golgotha* ns 14/38

gomelfeax adj *grey-haired* nsm 26/92
(=noun)

gomen n:B2a *entertainment* **gomene** ds
26/20

gomenwudu m:B4a *'mirth-wood', lyre, harp*
ns 31a/3

gomol adj *old* ns 33/11 (=noun)

(ġe)**gongan** VII *go, advance, proceed, walk*
inf 9b/80, 28/22, 29, 32/43 **gang** imp s
13/14 **gangan** inf 30/3, 40, 62, 170, 33/42
ġe**gangan** inf 19/54, 30/59 (*gain*) **gange**
pr1s 4/89 sbj pr1s 15c/11 sbj pr2s 2a/10 sbj
pr3s 22/3 **gangeð** pr3s 2a/1 **gangon** sbj
pr3p 30/56 **geongan** inf 34/11 **gonge** pr1s
40/35 **gongende** pp nsm 9b/21, 83

gonges < **gang**

good, good- see **gōd**

Gotan pr n (mp) *the Goths* **Gotena** gp 36/23

gram adj *angry, fierce, hostile* **grame** npm
19/224, 238, 30/262 **gramum** dpm 30/100
(=noun *enemy*)

Grantanceaster pr n (f:B3c) *Grantchester*
(Cambs.) **Grantanceastre** ds 21a/54

grāp f:B3b *grasp, claw* **grāpum** dp 31b/51

grāp < **grīpan**

grāpian 2 *grab, grasp, take hold of, touch*
grāpiað imp p 22/50 **grāpode** pt3s 31b/75

grǣdiġ adj *greedy, fierce* nsm 26/62 nsf
31b/8 asn 31b/31 **grǣdiġne** asm 10/64

græf n:B2c *grave* as 26/97

grǣġ adj *grey* **grǣġe** asn 10/64

grǣġhama adj *grey-coated* nsm 32/6
(=noun)

ġe**grǣmedan** < ġe**gremian**

grēat adj *great, huge* **grēate** npm 17/47

Grēcas pr n (mp:B1a) *the Greeks* **Crēacas** np
5/44 **Grēcum** dp 4/53

grēcisc adj *Greek* **grēcisca** nsm 4/40, 53
grēciscra gpm 4/40 **grēciscum** dpn 4/54

Gregorius pr n *Gregory* ns 22/130 gs 7b/50
Gregories gs 22/68

ġe**gremian** 2 *enrage, incense, provoke*
ġe**grǣmedan** pt3p 25/147 ġe**gremede**

pp npm 19/305 ġegremod pp 30/138
ġegremode pp npm 30/296
grēne adj *green* nsm 33/35 **grēnne** asm 3a/13
  grēnum dpn 13/9
Grendel pr n (m:B1b) *Grendel* **Grendle** ds
  31b/86 **Grendles** gs 31b/47
grēot n:B2b *'grit', earth, dust* as 19/307
  grēote ds 30/315
grēotan II *weep, lament* **grēotende** prp npm
  23/70
(ġe)**grētan** 1 *greet, address, approach,*
  accost, touch inf 5/2 **grēt** pr3s 16/2 **grēted**
  pp 31a/3 **grēteð** pr3s 38/52 ġe**grēteð** pr3s
  25/125 **grētte** pt3s 9b/23, 28/18 ġe**grētte**
  pt3s 22/34 **grētton** pt3p 27/60
grim adj *fierce, severe, cruel, angry* nsm
  30/61, 36/23 nsf 31b/8 **grimman** apm
  17/70 dpf 31b/51 **grimme** npm 25/118 apf
  17/53
Grimbold pr n *Grimbold* **Grimbolde** ds 5/63
grimliċ adj *cruel, terrible* nsn 25/6
grimme adv *fiercely, harshly* 37/14
grindan III *grind, sharpen* **grindende** pp nsf
  7a/18 ġe**grunden** 37/14 ġe**grundene**
  pp apm 30/109
grindel m:B1b *bolt, bar* **grindlas** np 17/47
grīpan I *seize, grab, take hold* **grāp** pt3s
  31b/10 **grīpeð** pr3s 35c/7
gripe m:B1g *grip* ns 37/8
grīstbitian 2 *gnash the teeth, cough* inf
  19/271
grið n:B2a *truce, peace, sanctuary* as 8/61,
  30/35 **griðe** ds 25/67 **griðes** gs 7c/4
griðbryċe m:B1g *breach of sanctuary* as
  7c/20, 24
griðian 2 *protect* inf 25/28
griðlēas adj *unprotected, violated* **griðlēase**
  npf 25/31
grund m:B1a *ground, land, earth, region,*
  bottom, abyss, depth as 18/57, 30/287,
  31b/60 **grundas** ap 10/15, 19/348, 17/70
  grunde is 19/2 **grundes** gs 17/9, 12
ġe**grund** see **grindan**
grundlēas adj *fathomless, boundless*
  grundlēase apf 17/53, 36/15
grundwong m:B1a *bottom, ground* as 31b/5
grundwyrġen f:B3e.i *accursed one of the*
  deep **grundwyrġenne** as 31b/27
gryre m:B1g *horror, terror* is 18/44

gryrelēoð n:B2b *terrible song* **gryrelēoða**
  gp 30/285
guld- see **ġieldan**
guma m:B5a *man* ns 10/18, 38/45 **guman** gs
  23/49 np 19/305 gp 23/146 **gumena** gp
  10/50, 19/9, 22, 32, 31b/8, etc
ġe**gurning** f:B3d *desire, request* ns 11/1
gūþ f:B3b *battle, combat* **gūde** as 30/325
  gūþe gs 30/192 ds 10/44, 19/123, 305,
  30/13, 94, 187 etc, 31b/44
Gūðere pr n *Guthere* ns 32/18
gūðfana m:B5a *battle-standard, banner*
  gūðfanum dp 19/219
gūðfreca m:B5a *fighting-man, warrior*
  gūðfrecan np 19/224
Gūð-Ġeatas pr n *'battle-Geats'* **Gūð-Ġeata**
  gp 31b/47
gūðġewinn n:B2b *battle, the strife of battle*
  gūðġewinnes gs 35a/5
gūðhafoc m:B1a *war-hawk* as 10/64
Gūðlāf pr n *Guthlaf* ns 31a/86, 32/16
  Gūðlāfes gs 32/33
gūðlēoð n:B2b *war-song* as 31b/31
gūðplega m:B5a *the game of battle, conflict*
  ns 30/61
gūðræs m:B1a *battle-storm, assault*
  gūðræsa gp 31b/86
gūðrinc m:B1a *warrior* ns 30/138, 31a/56 as
  31b/10
gūðsceorp n:B2b *war-apparel, armour* as
  19/328
gūðweriġ adj *battle-weary* **gūðweriġne** asm
  31b/95
gūðwudu m:B4a *'battle-wood', ?spear,*
  ?shield ns 32/6
gyden f:B3e.i *goddess* ns 24/39 **gydena** np
  24/67
ġyf see **ġif**
ġyfena < **ġifu**
ġyfeð < **ġiefan**
ġyld- see **ġieldan**
ġylian 1 *yell, shout* **ġylede** pt3s 19/25
ġyllan III *yell, shriek, howl* **ġyllende** prp ism
  18/44 **ġylleð** pr3s 32/6
ġylp m:B1a *boast, boasting, vaunting* ns 18/9
  as 18/69 **ġielpes** gs 38/69
ġylpword n:B2b *vaunting word, boast*
  ġylpwordum dp 30/274
gylt m:B1a *crime, sin* as 14/44, 21a/41

ġȳm- see ġīeman

ġynne < ġinn

ġynd see ġeond

Ġypeswīċ pr n *Ipswich* (Suf.) ns 8/20

ġyrd f:B3b *rod, staff* ns 15c/12 ġyrda ds 1/54 ġyrde ds 1/73

gyrdan 1 *gird, encircle* gyrde pt3s 32/13

ġeġyrla m:B5a *clothing, attire* ġeġyrlan as 21b/7

ġyrnde < ġirnan

ġyrnwræcu f:B3a *revenge for injury* ġyrnwræce ds 31a/76

ġyrwan 1 *prepare, adorn, dress* ġeġerwed pp 28/18 gierede pt3s 35d/13 ġeġyred pp 23/16 ġyredon pt3p 23/77 ġeġyrwed pp 23/23 ġeġyryde pp apm 28/7

ġȳsel m:B1bi *hostage* ns 30/265 ġīsle ds 29/18

Gyssīċ pr n *Gussage* (Dor.) ds 11/15

ġyst m:B1a *guest, visitor, stranger* ġist ns 31a/76, 31b/31 ġystas np 30/86, 34/27

ġystern n:B2b *guest-house* ġysterne ds 19/40

ġystsele m:B1g *hall of visitors, lodging house* as 18/89

ġȳt adv *yet, further, still, even, up to now* 1/54, 4/43, 9b/98, 18/74, 25/78, 31a/72, etc ġēt 6/41 ġīet 5/33 ġīeta 10/66 ġīt 7c/26, 16/16, 27/35 ġȳta 23/28; in adv phr þā ġȳt *yet, still, further* 19/107, 22/58, 30/168, 273, 31a/65, etc ðāġȳt 13/4, 8

ġytesǣl f:B3g *merriness at wine-pouring* ġytesālum dp 19/22

H

habban 3 *have, possess, hold, keep, watch over, be subject to* inf 5/13, 8/69, 12/20, 14/8, 16/29, 30/236, 34/43 sbj pr3p 7c/23 habbaþ pr1p 5/19, 22/65 pr2p 22/11 pr3p 4/50, 58, 17/36, 40, 22/123, 35d/21 habbe pr1s 27/23 sbj pr1p 12/41 hafast pr2s 27/19 hafaþ pr3s 17/26 etc, 18/81, 110, 19/197, 26/47 hæbbe pr1s 1/25, 65, 14/14, 22/51, 23/50, 79, 26/4 pr1s 1/33 pr2p 22/54 sbj pr3s 3b/4, 7b/35, 16/91 hæbben sbj pr3p 5/52 hæfdan pt3p 12/28, 24/28 hæfdæ pt1s 11/27, 28 hæfde pt1s 5/64, 12/6, 27 pt3s 9a/3, 9b/41, 12/15, 14/9, 16/6,

23/49 sbj pt3s 31b/59 hæfdon pt3p 5/6, 9a/50, 9b/89, 14/7, 15b/4, 16/18, 23/16 hæfst pr2s 1/10 etc, 28/72 hæfþ pr3s 4/6, 6/41, 12/56, 16/88, 17/24 heafde pt3s 8/72; with neg nabbaþ pr3p 4/46, 16/89, 22/94, 24/60 nafaþ pr3s 34/4 næbbe pr1s 1/65 sbj pr3s 7b/19, 26/42 næfde sbj pt1s 22/50 næfþ pr3s 16/100, 17/23, 27/33 [etc]

ġehabban 3 *hold, retain* inf 3b/6

hād m:B1a *order, office, rank; person, gender* ns 4/69 hāda gp 5/4 hādas np 5/9, hāde ds 4/64, 92, 94 hādum dp 7b/23

hādbryċe m:B1g *violation of holy orders* hādbrycas ap 25/113

ġehādian 2 *consecrate, ordain* ġehādod pp 8/18, 21a/28, 49 ġehādode pt3s 21a/26 pp npm 25/52 (=noun *those in holy orders*)

hādre adv *clearly, brightly* 31b/80

hafaþ < habban

hafela m:B5a *head* hafelan np 31a/58 ds 31b/30

hafenian 2 *raise, lift up* hafenade pt3s 31b/82 hafenode pt3s 30/42, 309

hafoc m:B1a *hawk, falcon* as 30/8 hafuc ns 33/17

hāl adj *whole, sound, safe, uninjured* nsm 2a/18 (twice), 14/32 nsf 21a/62 asn 21a/76 hālan dsn 31b/12 hāle npm 21a/79, 30/292

ġehāl adj *whole* ns 16/82

hālettan 1 *greet, salute* hālette pt3s 9b/23, 28/18

hālga m:B5a *holy person, saint* hālgan ds 26/122 hālgum dp 1/41, 21a/21, 23/143, 154 hāliġra gpm 7b/53 gpf 22/74 hāliġre dsf 19/98; see also adj hāliġ

ġehālgian 2 *hallow, consecrate* ġehālgod pp 8/7, 48

hālgung f:B3d *consecration* hālgunge as 7c/23

hāliġ adj *holy, divine, saintly* nsm 9b/36, 31b/62, 35d/28 asn 9b/49 hālga nsm 8/6, 13, 16/54, 21a/18, etc hālgan asm 22/170, 28/63 asf 16/77, 19/260, 21a/77 gsm 9b/65, 67, 22/68 gsn 9b/58, 21a/73 dsf 4/13, 21a/3 npn 22/69, 28/31 apn 28/20 hālgum dpm 22/176 dpn 22/108 hāligan asf 14/67 dsf 19/203 hāliġe nsn 4/9 nsf 4/18, 16/58, 19/56 asn 16/31 asf 18/40, etc npm 14/66, 22/122, 23/11; see also noun hālga

hāliġdōm m:B1a *sanctuary, relics*
  hāliġdōmæ ds 11/9
hāliġnes f:B3e.ii *sanctuary* **hāliġnessa** np
  25/31
hals m:B1a *neck* as 30/141 **halse** ds 31b/75
  healse ds 17/48
hālwende adj *salutary* apn 9b/106
hām adv *home, homewards* 9a/9, 50, 9b/19,
  51, 18/62, 19/131, 27/61, 30/251
hām m:B1a *home, dwelling, abode* as 23/148
  as 26/117 ds 1/21, 7a/7, 45, 31a/85, 94
  hāmas ap 10/10, 18/8, 31a/65 **hāme** ds
  18/11, 30/292, 34/30
hamor m:B1a *hammer* **hamora** gp 10/6
  homera gp 35a/7
Hamtūn pr n (m:B1a) *Southampton* (Hants.)
  as 8/2
Hamtūnscīr pr n (f:B3b) *Hampshire*
  Hamtūnscīre ds 8/74, 29/2
hāmweardes adv *on the way home* 15c/3
hand f:B4a *hand* ns 22/82, 30/141 as 3c/2,
  9a/46, 18/34, 40, 27/38, 30/112, 34/34
  handa ds 23/59, 30/149 np 17/43 ap 14/23,
  16/98, 22/49, 52, 38/43 gp 17/31, 51
  handon dp 30/7 **handum** dp 30/4, 14 **hond**
  ns 31b/29 as 19/130, 26/96 **honda** ds 9b/91,
  108 ds 12/6 ap 12/26, 38/43 **hondum** 38/4
handweorc n:B2b *handiwork* ns 18/47
hangian 2 *hang, depend on, be joined to* inf
  33/55 **hongiað** pr3p 6/56
hār adj *hoary, old and grey* nsm 10/39,
  30/169 **hāra** nsm 38/82 **hāre** apf 19/327
  hārne asm 37/43
hās adj *hoarse* nsm 1/26
hasewanpād adj *dusky-coated*
  hasewanpādan asm 10/62 (=noun)
hāt adj *hot, fervent, intense, inspiring* nsm
  17/17 nsn 17/40 npf 26/11 **hāta** nsm
  21a/42 **hātan** asf 17/102 dsf 17/25 **hātost**
  sup nsn 33/7 **hātran** comp npm 26/64
hāt n:B2b *heat* **hāte** ds 37/38 (see note)
(ġe)hātan II (1) *order, command, summon*
  (often +inf) **hāt** imp s 27/25, 34, 70 **hāte**
  pr1s 23/95 **hāteþ** pr3s 5/2 **ġehāteþ** pr3s
  7a/5 **heht** 9b/44, 58 **hēt** pt3s 7b/1, 8/31, 44,
  67, 12/9, 17/8, 27/27, 36, etc **hēte** sbj pt3s
  19/53 **hēton** pt3p 9a/9, 23/31, 30/30; (2)
  call, be named **hātan** inf 17/7 **hātaþ** pr1p
  6/9, 12, 16, 24, 28, 74 pr3p 24/60 **hāten**

pp 9a/25 (twice), 55, 21b/3, 30/75, 218
  ġehāten pp 4/2, 34, 14/11, 16/42, 22/29,
  24/32, etc **ġehātene** pp npm 4/40, 42 npn
  4/76, 85, 88 **hāteþ** pr3s 9a/19 **hātta** passive
  pt3s 21a/5 **hātte** passive pr1s 35d/26 pr3s
  21b/4, 24/31, 44, 46 **hēte** pt2s 12/54
ġehātan VII *promise, vow* **ġeheht** pt3s 9a/58
  ġehēt pt1s 12/42 pt3s 18/112 **ġehēton** pt3p
  9a/47
hāte adv *hotly, searingly* 17/46, 19/94
hatedon < **hatian**
hātheort adj *passionate, impulsive* nsm 38/66
hatian 2 *hate, treat as an enemy* **hatedon**
  pt3p 15c/14
ġehātland n:B2b *promised land* **ġehātlandes**
  gs 9b/65
hātta, hātte < (ġe)**hātan** (2)
hāwian 2 *look, gaze* **hāwede** pt3s 8/77
hǣ see **hē**
hæbb- see **habban**
hæfd-, hæfst see **habban**
Hæfæreshām pr n *Haversham* (Bucks.) ds
  11/14
hæft n:B2a *handle, sword-hilt* **hæfte** ds
  19/263
ġehæftan 1 *catch, shackle, fetter, hold
  captive* inf 22/119 **ġehæfte** pp 17/43
  ġehæfted pp 17/48, 19/116 **ġehæftne**
  pp asm 14/9
hæftling m:B1a *prisoner, captive* **hæftlingas**
  ap 22/163
hæfþ < **habban**
hæġl m:B1bi *hail* ns 26/17, 32 **haġle** ds 38/48
hæġlfaru f:B3a *hailstorm* **hæġlfare** as
  38/105
hæġsteald adj *unmarried, young*
  hæġstealdas npm 32/40
hæġtesse f:B5c *witch* **hæġtessan** as 34/11
(ġe)hǣlan 1 *heal, cure, save* inf 14/50, 23/85
  ġehǣl imp s 14/48 **ġehǣlde** pt3s 14/50,
  21b/12 sbj pt3s 35a/12 **ġehǣled** pp 21a/63
  gehǣlede pp npm 21a/77 **hǣlþ** pr3s 3b/5
hǣle m:B1g *man, warrior* ns 38/73
hǣlend m:B4d *saviour* ns 14/1, 2, 21a/90,
  22/35, 45, 53, etc as 21a/14, 22/25, 99
  hǣlende ds 14/19, 21a/90, 22/105, 165
  hǣlendes gs 22/2, 13, 88, 23/25 **hǣlyn** as
  14/16 **hǣlynd** ns 14/44, 62 as 14/11, 26,
  27, 69

hæleþ m:B4e *man, hero, warrior* ns 23/39, 78, 95, 32/23, 35d/12 np 19/56, 177, etc ap 19/247 **hæleþa** gp 10/25, 18/66, 19/51, 35b/3 **hæleþum** dp 18/22, 35d/28, 38/105

hǣlo f:B3h *safety, security, salvation* ns 28/76 ds 9a/13, 15b/14

ġehǣman 1 *have intercourse with, copulate* **ġehǣmde** pt3s 24/64

hǣmed n:B2c *cohabitation, sexual intercourse* as 7c/20 **hǣmede** ds 21a/8, 85

hærfest m:B1a *harvest time, autumn, fall* ns 33/8 **hærfeste** ds 7b/52

hǣs f:B3g *bidding, command* **hǣse** ds 27/58

hǣto f:B3h *heat* ns 17/52 **hǣte** ds 1/33

hǣþ m:B1a *heath* **hǣðe** ds 33/29

hǣþen adj *heathen* (often =noun) **hǣþenan** npm 24/27, 41, etc asm 19/98, 110 **hǣþene** npm 24/66, 30/55, 181 npf 24/67 apm 24/10, 25/111 **hǣþenes** gsm 19/179 **hǣþenra** gpm 27/40 gp 19/216 **hǣþenum** dpm 24/58, 61 dpf 25/20, 23, 27

hǣþenġild n:B2b *idolatry, heathen sacrifice* **hǣþenġyld** as 24/4

hǣþenscype m:B1g *heathenism, paganism, idolatry* ns 24/2 ds 24/42 **hǣðenscipe** as 24/68

Hæþfeld pr n *Hatfield* (Herts.) **Hæþfælda** ds 11/14

hǣwen adj *blue* **hǣwene** nsf 18/31

hē pers pron *he, him, his* ns 1/52, 2a/1, 7b/15, 13/1 **hæ** ns 11/20 **hiene** as 5/21, 29/3, 4 **him** ds 2c/3, 7a/5, 8/13, 13/12 **hinæ** as 11/21 **hine** as 7b/20, 22, 8/64 **his** gs 2a/14, 7a/5, 8/27, 13/1 **hym** ds 14/13, 15 **hyne** as 11/1, 14/1, 19/44 **hys** gs 14/23, 24 [etc]; see also **sē**

hēa see **hēah**

hēaburh f:B4b *high stronghold* as 31a/65

heafde < **habban**

hēafod n:B2c *head* ns 19/110 as 9b/102, 14/30, 33, 44, 15c/15, 19/126, 173, 179, 27/38, 35c/8, 38/43 ap 14/47 **hæfde** ds 21a/72 **hēafde** ds 21a/72, 28/58, 31b/99, 34/11 **hēafdum** dp 23/63

hēafodġerīm n:B2b *head-count, muster* **hēafodġerīmes** gs 19/308

hēafodmann m:B4b *head man, captain* **hēafodmen** np 22/38 **hēafodmannum** dp 22/41

hēafodmynster n:B2c *chief minister* **hēafodmynstres** gs 7c/24

hēafodpanne f:B5c *skull* **hēafodpannan** gs 14/38

hēafodweard m:B1a *chief guard, sentinel* **hēafodweardas** np 19/239

hēage, hēagum < **hēah**

hēah adj *high, lofty, tall, deep, sublime, illustrious, proud* nsm 38/98 nsn 37/22 **hēa** nsf 35b/4 **hēage** npn 28/36 **hēagum** dpm 24/56 **hēan** asm 17/21 dsm 10/14 dsn 19/43 dsf 6/7 apm 26/34 dpn 9a/49 **hēanne** asm 19/161, 23/40, 38/82 **hēhsta** sup nsm 15b/15, 17/7, 19/94 **hēhstan** gsm 19/4 **hēhste** nsn 6/45 **hīeran** comp dsm 5/56 **hȳhsta** sup nsm 19/308

hēah adv *high, aloft* 18/15, 22, 47

hēahfæder m:B1a/4c *patriarch, God the father* **hēahfædere** ds 16/14, 23/134

hēahġerēfa m:B5a *high sheriff, chief officer* **hēahġerēfan** as 8/64

hēahsetl n:B2c.i *high seat, throne* as 31a/25

hēahtīd f:B3g *high festival, major holy day* **hēahtīdum** dp 21a/32

hēahþungen adj *of high rank, illustrious* nsm 18/72

heal see **heall**

hēala m:B5a *rupture, hydrocele* **hēalena** gp 34/15

(ġe)healdan VII *hold, possess, keep, maintain, preserve, observe, guard, keep close, watch over, control, rule, treat, occupy* inf 4/12, 12/44, 17/11, 26/109, 111, 30/14, 19, etc **healdanne** infl inf 7b/4, 11 **ġehealdanne** infl inf 7b/17 **healdaþ** pr3s 22/11, 26/87 **ġehealdað** pr3p 18/115 **healde** sbj pr3s 7b/13, 38/14 **ġehealden** pp 4/12, 12/61 **ġehealdene** pp npm 24/27 (*restricted*) **healdende** prp npm 14/69 **healdenne** infl inf 16/96 **healdeþ** pr3p 18/89 **ġehealdeþ** pr3s 38/112 **hēold** pt1s 1/49 pt3s 21a/9, 14, 29/30, 40, 31a/17, etc **hēoldan** pt1p 25/53 **hēolde** pt3s 32/23 sbj pt3s 31a/37 **ġehēolde** sbj pt3s 22/138 **hēoldon** pt3p 7b/2, 19/142, 21a/81, 30/20, 32/42 **hīoldon** pt3p 5/31 **ġehīoldon** pt3p 5/8 **hylt** imp s 2a/13

healdend m:B4d *guardian, lord* ns 19/289

healf adj *half* **healfne** asm 7a/46, 47, 19/105
ōþer healf *one-and-a-half* asn 12/45
healf f:B3b *half, side* as 7b/27 (twice) **healfe**
as 14/45, 22/82, 23/20 **healfre** gsf 31a/25
healfa ap 31a/33
healfclypiende adj *semi-vowel* npm 4/44,
46
Healf-Dene pr n (mp:B1h) *Half-Danes*
Healf-Dena gp 31a/7
Healfdene pr n *Healfdene* **Healfdenes** gs
31a/2
healgamen n:B2c *hall entertainment* as 31a/4
hēaliċ adj *high, exalted, illustrious, glorious*
nsf 24/39 **hēaliċe** asf 24/65 **hēaliċne** asm
24/48 **hēalicon** dsn 24/70 **hēlicum** dpm
21a/42
heall f:B3e *hall, palace* **heal** ns 31a/89 **healle**
as 31a/2 gs 32/4, 20 ds 27/41, 30/214,
32/28, 33/28, 36
ġehealp < **ġehelpan**
healse < **hals**
hēan adj *lowly, dejected, despised* nsm 38/23
hēanne asm 19/234
hēan, hēanne < **hēah**
hēanis f:B3e.ii *height* **hēanisse** gs 28/33
hēannisse as 28/34
hēanliċ adj *humiliating, shameful* nsn 30/55
hēap m:B1a *crowd, troop, company* as 31a/29
hēape ds 21a/43 **hēapum** dp 19/163
hēapian 2 *heap up, pile high* **ġehēapen**
pp 37/12
hēapmǣlum adv *in troops, in droves* 9a/227,
46
heard adj *hard, strong, brave, fierce, stern,
cruel, bitter* nsm 31b/48 (=noun +g),
32/21 nsf 17/95, 35d/5 asn 31b/83 **hearde**
nsn 31b/62 npm 17/36 **heardes** gsm 10/25
gsn 17/46 **heardne** asm 19/79, 31b/99
heardost sup nsn 23/87 **heardra** comp
gpm 19/225 (=noun) **heardum** dpn 19/263
heordra gpf 32/26
hearde adv *painfully, harshly, firmly* 19/116,
216 **heard** 31b/75
heardecg adj *hard-edged* nsn 35a/8
heardheort adj *hard-hearted* **heardheortan**
npm 22/164
heardlīce adv *resolutely, bravely* 30/261
heardsēliġ adj *ill-fortuned* **heardsēliġne** asm
40/19

hearm m:B1a *harm, affliction, sorrow* as
17/31 **hearma** gp 30/223
hearmscearu f:B3a *affliction, punishment*
17/95
hearoġeong adj *young in war, inexperienced*
nsm 32/2
hearpe f:B5c *harp* **hearpan** as 9b/18, 27/25,
27, 34, etc gs 27/28, 42 ds 9b/18, 26/44
hearpenæġl m:B1bi *plectrum* as 27/41
hearpestreng m:B1a *harp-string*
hearpestrengas as 27/42
hearpian 2 *play the harp* 27/27
hearra m:B5a *lord* ns 17/21 **hearran** ds 17/2,
19/56 **heorra** ns 30/204
heaþobyrne f:B5c *war-corselet* ns 31b/61
heaþolind f:B3b *battle-shield* (of linden
wood) **heaþolinde** ap 10/6
heaþorian 2 *restrain, control* **heaþeraþ** pr3s
6/18
heaðorinc m:B1a *warrior* **heaðorincas** np
19/212 **heaðorinces** gs 19/179
(ġe)hēawan VII *hew, cut down, hack, slay* inf
19/90 **ġehēawen** pp 19/288, 294 **hēaweþ**
pr3s 25/56 **hēow** pt3s 30/324 **hēowan** pt3p
10/6, 23 **hēowon** pt3p 19/303, 30/181
hebban VI *lift up, bear aloft* inf 23/31
hefene < **heofon**
hefiġ adj *heavy, dire, grievous* nsn 27/12
hefian dsn 23/61 **hefiġran** comp npf
38/49
hefiġan 2 *weigh down, burden* **hefgad**
pp 9b/79
hefiġtīme adv *burdensome, troublesome* 16/4
hēhst- see **hēah**
(ġe)heht < **(ġe)hātan**
hēlan IV *conceal, harbour* **hēleþ** pr3s 34/26
heldor n:B2a *door of Hell* **heldora** gp 17/43
Helias pr n *Elias* ns 14/62 **Heliam** as 14/59
hēlicum < **hēaliċ**
hell f:B3e *hell* **hel** ns 22/163 **helle** as 17/11,
40, 69, 102, 22/149 gs 16/70, 17/8, 36 ds
17/25, 31, 52, 34/44
hellebryne m:B1g *hell-fire* ds 19/116
helleġeat n:B2d *gate of hell* ns 22/154
hellegatu ap 22/151
hellewīte n:B2h *hell-torment* **hellewītes** gs
25/165
helm m:B1a *helmet, protection, protector* ns
32/45 as 19/337, 31b/35, 35d/17 **hellme** ds

33/16 **helmas** ap 19/193, 317, 327 **helmum**
19/203
Helmstān pr n *Helmstan* ns 12/3, 13, 17, 23
help f:B3b *help* **helpe** as 31b/61, 38/16 ds
19/96, 23/102
(ġe)**helpan** II +g/d *help* inf 22/166 **helpe** sbj
pr3s 25/167
helpend m:B4d *helper, support* **helpendra**
gp 18/42
helsceaþa m:B5a *fiend from hell, devil*
helsceaþan np 30/180
ġe**hende** adv *near, at hand* 8/76
ġe**hende** prep +d *near, near to* 30/294
Henġest pr n *Hengest* ns 9a/24, 31a/65, 32/17
Henġeste ds 31a/21, 34 **Henġestes** gs
31a/29
hēo pers pron *she, her, hers* ns 11/1, 2, 13/4,
5, 16/67, 21a/5, 11, 27/2 as 21a/15 **hī** as
13/7, 21a/14, 26, 26/103, 30/180, 33/45 **hīe**
as 5/11, 44, 7b/29 **hig** as 16/107, 27/15 **hīo**
ns 2c/1, 2 etc, 5/13, 6/64, 7a/17, 46 **hīræ** ds
11/1, 7 **hire** gs 7b/30, 13/5, 21a/8, 27/3, 21
ds 8/72, 27/21 **hyre** gs 13/10, 21a/5, 27/2,
22 ds 19/123, 124, 22/13 [etc]; see also **sēo**
hēo < **hī**
Heodeningas pr n (mp:B1a) *the Heodenings*
Heodeninga gp 36/36
heofon m:B1b *heaven* as 9b/36 **hefene** ds
31b/80 **heofenan** as 16/46, 49 **heofenas** ap
23/103 **heofenes** gs 23/64 **heofenum** dp
22/21, 65, 23/85, 134 **heofne** ds 17/2, 13
heofnum dp 21b/23 **heofona** gp 17/60,
23/45 **heofonan** dp 22/91 **heofonas** np
22/157 ap 9b/67 **heofones** gs 6/31
heofonum dp 6/50, 22/153, 175, 23/140,
26/107, etc
heofoncyning m:B1a *king of heaven*
heofoncyninges gs 17/3
heofonlic adj *heavenly* nsf 9b/48 **heofenlican**
apm 22/76 **heofenlicum** dsn 22/104
heofonlecan gsn 9b/69 isn 9b/97
heofonlican gsn 9b/8 **heofonliċe** asn 8/14,
26 **heofonliċne** asm 23/148
heofonrīċe n:B2h *heavenly kingdom, heaven*
as 17/51, 67, 89, etc ds 17/21, 25, 86
heofonrīċes gs 9a/53, 9b/31, 18/40, 23/91
(ġe)**hēold-** see (ġe)**healdan**
heolfor n:B2c *blood, gore* **heolfre** ds 18/4, 31
heolfriġ adj *bloody, bloodied* asn 19/130, 316

heolstor adj *dark, shadowy* **heolstran** dsm
19/121
heolstor n:B2c *darkness* **heolstre** ds 38/23
heom (**him**) < **hī**
heona < **hīwan**
heonan see **heonon**
heonengang m:B1a *going hence, departure*
heonengange ds 20b/3 **hiniongae** 20a/3
heonon adv *hence, from here, henceforth*
17/78, 20b/5, 23/132, 27/69, 30/246
heonan 7c/5, 26/37, 40/6
heononforð adv *henceforth, from here* 13/20,
21 **heonanforþ** 25/19
heora < **hī**
heord f:B3b *herd, flock, care* ns 9b/21
heordra < **heard**
heoroġīfre adj *fiercely ravenous, greedy for*
slaughter nsf 31b/7
heorogrim adj *deadly grim, ferocious* nsm
31b/73
heoroscearp adj *deadly sharp* nsn 35a/8
heorosweng m:B1a *sword-stroke* as 31b/99
Heorot pr n *Heorot* **Heorote** ds 31b/97
hēorra see **hēarra**
Heorrenda pr n *Heorrenda* ns 36/39
heort m:B1a *hart, stag* as 34/41
heorte f:B5c *heart, will, courage* ns 15b/13,
19/87, 30/312 **heortan** as 17/17, 26/11 gs
26/34, 38/49, 40/43 ds 15b/8, 28/49,
30/145 ap 16/55 **heortum** dp 35d/20
heorþġenēat m:B1a *hearth-companion,*
retainer **heorþġenēatas** as 31b/89
np 30/204
heorþwerod n:B2b.ii *hearth-troop, body of*
household retainers as 30/24
heorufæþm m:B1a *deadly embrace*
heorufæþmum dp 18/59
heoruwǣpen n:B2c *bloody weapon, sword*
heoruwǣpnum dp 19/263
hēow, hēow- see **hēawan**
hēr adv *here, in this place, at this time* 1/45,
4/57, 58, 8/1, 4, 9a/39, 10/1, 22/26, 100,
23/108, 137, 26/102, etc
hēr n:B2b *hair* **hērum** dp 35d/5
hērbūend m:B4d *dweller here (on earth)*
hērbūendra gp 19/96
here m:B1g.ii *army, (invading) host; war,*
devastation ns 8/33, 34, 40, 9a/50, 18/52,
105, 19/161, 25/44, 90, 34/31, etc as 8/30,

31, 81 ds 30/292 **heres** gs 8/75 **herġas** np
37/29 **herġes** gs 18/11 **heriġe** ds 19/135
heriġes gs 10/31, 18/62, 19/293
ġehēre < **ġehȳran**
hereblēaþ adj *battle-shy, cowardly*
   hereblēaþe npm 18/8
heredon < **herian**
hereflȳma m:B5a *fugitive from an army*
   hereflȳman ap 10/23
herefolc n:B2b *army* **herefolces** gs 19/234,
   239
hereġeatu f:B3a *war-equipment, heriot* ap
   30/48
hereġian see **herian**
herehuð f:B3g *booty* **herehuðe** ns 8/40 as
   8/57, 73
herelāf f:B3b *army remnant, survivors*
   herelāfum dp 10/47
herenes f:B3e.ii *praise* **herenesse** ds 9b/29
   herenisse ds 9b/107
herenet n:B2a '*war-mesh*', *corselet* ns
   31b/62
hererēaf n:B2b *war booty, plunder* as 19/316
heresceorp n:B2b *war-garment, armour*
   heresceorpum dp 32/45
Here-Scyldinga see **Scyldingas**
hereswēġ m:B1a *martial sound* ns 37/22
heresyrċe f:B5c *war corselet, mailcoat*
   heresyrċan as 31b/20
heretoga m:B5a *leader of army, commander*
   ns 8/79, 9a/55 **heretogan** np 8/43, 9a/23
herewǣþa m:B5a '*war-hunter*', *warrior*
   herewǣþan gs 19/126, 173
herewōp m:B1a *shrieking of army,*
   lamentation **herewōpa** gp 18/15
herġas, herġes < **here**
herġen < **herian**
herġian 2 *plunder, lay waste, seize* inf 9a/34
   herġedon pt3p 9a/36 **herġiað** pr3p 25/103
ġeherġian 2 *harry, lay waste* **ġeherġodon**
   pt3p 8/51, 82 **ġeherġoden** pt3p 8/1
   ġeherġod pp 8/11, 20
herġung f:B3d *harrowing* **herġunge** ds
   22/164
herian 1 *praise, glorify, extol* inf 27/29 **hera**
   imp s 2a/11 **heredon** pt3p 27/44, 59
   hereġian inf 25/127 **herġen** sbj pr3p 26/77
   heriaþ pr3p 27/31 **heriġaþ** pr3p 18/101
   heriġean inf 9b/31

heriġe, heriġes < **here**
heriġean see **herian**
hērinne adv *herein* 17/99
hēron adv *herein* 7b/8
herpaþ m:B1a *war-path, passage for army* as
   19/302
hērtōēacan adv *besides* 25/141
(ġe)**hēt**, (ġe)**hēt**- see (ġe)**hātan**
hete m:B1g *hatred, malice* ns 25/46, 90
hetelīċe adv *terribly, violently* 25/81
heteþoncol adj *hostile-minded, savage*
   heteþoncolne asm 19/105
hetol adj *hating, evil, hostile, savage* nsm
   24/35 **hetole** npm 25/117 **hetula** nsm 24/62
hettend m:B4d *persecutor, enemy* np 10/10
hī pers pron *they, them, their* **hēo** np 9a/50
   heom dp 7a/5, 14/7, 17, 27/46 **heora** gp
   1/29, 8/60, 77, 13/15, 14/7 **hī** np 8/23, 30,
   13/17 ap 8/59, 61, 21a/29, 22/45, 62 **hīe** np
   7b/10, 56 ap 5/45, 12/9 **hiġ** np 14/5, 7,
   16/36, 37 ap 1/20, 28, 14/68 **him** dp 7b/10,
   8/33, 52, 57 **hiera** gp 29/23, 25 **hiora** gp
   5/7, 7b/31, 56 **hira** gp 23/47 **hȳ** np 33/19
   hym dp 14/25 **hyra** gp 19/128 [etc]
hī < **hēo**
(ġe)**hicg**- see (ġe)**hycgan**
hīd f:B3g *hide (of land)* **hīda** ap 12/1, 58
   hīdan dp 12/58
hider adv *hither, here* 8/66, 9a/6, 10 etc,
   9b/26, 10/69, 17/83, 23/103, 33/64 **hieder**
   5/12
hīe < **hī**, **hēo**
hiene < **hē**
hiera < **hī**
hīeran < **hēah**
ġehīer- see **ġehȳran**
hierdebōc f:B4b *shepherd-book* ns 5/61
hīersumian 2 +d *obey* **hīersumedon** pt3p 5/7
Hierusalēm pr n (f:B3b) *Jerusalem*
   Hierusalēme gs 9a/37
hig interj *o!, ho!* 1/30
hiġ < **hēo**, **hī**
hīġ n:B2b *hay* **hīġe** ds 1/28
Higa pr n *Higa* ns 12/2, 4, 63
hiġe see **hyġe**
Hiġelāc see **Hyġelāc**
hiġerōf adj *brave-hearted* **hiġerōfe** npm
   19/302
hiġeþ < **hycgan**

hiġeþoncol adj *thoughtful, discreet*
   hiġeþoncolre dsf 19/131

hiht see **hyht**

hild f:B3b *battle, war* ns 31b/97 **hilda** gp
   32/26 **hilde** as 18/59, 19/251, 30/33, 33/17
   ds 19/293, 30/8, etc

hildebil n:B2b.i *battle-sword* **hildebille** ds
   31b/29

Hildeburh pr n *Hildeburh* ns 31a/9, 52

hildelēoma m:B5a *battle light, sword*
   hildelēoman as 31a/81

hildelēoþ n:B2b *war-song* as 19/211

hildenǣdre f:B5c '*battle-adder*', *arrow*
   hildenǣdran ap 19/222

hilderinc m:B1a *warrior, hero* ns 10/39,
   30/169 **hilderinca** gp 23/72 **hilderincas** np
   23/61 **hilderince** ds 31b/4, 85

hildetūx m:B1a *battle-tusk* **hildetūxum** dp
   31b/20

hildewīsa m:B5a *leader in battle* **hildewīsan**
   ds 31a/2

hilt n:B2b *hilt* **hiltum** dp 31b/83

him < **hē, hit, hī**

hinæ (hine) < **hē**

hindan adv *from behind* 10/23

hindrian 2 *hinder, impede* ġe**hindred**
   pp 8/80

hiniongae < **heonengang**

hinsīþ m:B1a *journey hence, death* **hinsīþe**
   ds 19/117

hīo see **hēo**

(ġe)hīoldon < **(ġe)healdan**

hiora, hira < **hī**

(ġe)hīr- see **(ġe)hȳran**

hiræ, hire < **hēo**

hīredman m:B4b *household man, warrior*
   hīredmen np 30/268

hirre see **irre**

hirsode < **irsian**

his < **hē, hit**

hit pers pron *it, its* ns 1/4, 20, 2a/3, 3a/3,
   4/18, 26, 7a/44, 8/79, 9a/22 as 1/7, 2a/2, 4,
   5/23, 6/2, 24, 12/16 **his** gs 12/6, 17/75 **hyt**
   ns 1/30, 47, 14/22 as 19/174, 32/21 [etc]

hīw n:B2b *form, fashion, appearance* ns 4/33,
   34, 69 **hīwe** ds 21b/14

hīwan mp:B5a *household, community,*
   religious house np 12/59, 34/27 **heona** gp
   34/25

ġehīwian 2 *give shape to, figure* ġe**hīwað**
   pr3s 6/34 ġe**hīwod** pp 22/97

hlāf m:B1a *bread* **hlāfes** gs 3b/11

hlāford m:B1a *lord, master, ruler* ns 1/19,
   7b/41 as 7b/41, 23/45, 25/60, etc **hlāfordas**
   np 14/3, 15 **hlāfordæs** gs 11/22 **hlāforde**
   ds 1/37, 7b/28, 19/251, etc **hlāfordes** gs
   1/21, 7b/23, 25, etc

hlāfordlēas adj *without a lord* nsm 30/251

hlāfordsearu n:B2g *treachery against one's*
   lord **hlāfordsearwe** ds 7b/14

hlāfordswica m:B5a *traitor against a lord*
   hlāfordswican np 25/58

hlāfordswice m:B1g *treachery against a lord*
   ns 25/59, 60

hlanc adj *lean, gaunt* **hlanca** nsm 19/205

hlāw m:B1a *mound, barrow* **hlāwe** ds 31a/58
   hlǣwe ds 33/26

hlǣfdiġe f:B5c *lady* ns 8/65 **hlǣfdiġan** ds
   11/18

ġehlǣstan 1 *load, deck* ġe**hlǣste** pp asf
   19/36

hlǣwe < **hlāw**

hleahtor m:B1b *laughter* as 26/21

ġehlēapan VII *leap onto, mount* ġe**hlēop** pt3s
   30/189

hlehhan VI *laugh, rejoice* inf 10/47 **hlōh** pt3s
   19/23, 30/147

hlēo n:B2g.i *protector, lord* ns 30/74, 36/41

hlēobord n:B2b *protecting board*
   hlēobordum dp 35d/12

hlēomǣġ m:B1c *protecting kinsman*
   hlēomǣga gp 26/25

hlēoþor n:B2c *sound, cry* as 26/20

hlēoþrian 2 *sound, speak, proclaim*
   hlēoþrode pt3s 23/26, 32/2

hlid n:B2a *lid, cover, door* as 22/77 **hlyd** ns
   21a/56

Hlidaford pr n *Lydford* (Dev.) **Hlidaforda** ds
   8/55

hlifian 2 *rise up, tower* **hlifiġe** pr1s 23/85

hlimman III *roar, resound* inf 26/18
   hlummon pt3p 19/205

Hlincgeladæ pr n *Linslade* (Bucks.) ds 11/14

hlīsa m:B5a *fame, glory* **hlīsan** ds 22/74

hlōh < **hlihhan**

hlot n:B2b.i *lot, share* ap 14/41, 43

hlūd adj *loud* **hlūdan** dsf 18/105 **hlūdast** sup
   nsm 33/4

hlūde adv *loudly, aloud* 19/205, 223, 270, 35b/7

hlummon < hlimman

hlūttor adj *pure* hlūttre isn 9b/104 hlūttrum dsf 17/60

hlyd see hlid

ġehlȳd n:B2b *uproar, disturbance* ns 14/22

hlȳdan 1 *roar, shout* hlȳdde pt3s 19/23

ġehlyn n:B2a *sound, din* ns 32/28

hlynian 2 *roar, resound* hlynode pt3s 31a/58

hlynnan 1 *resound, roar, clamour* hlynede pt3s 19/23 hlynneþ pr3s 32/6

ġehlystan 1 *listen* ġehlyston pt3p 30/92

hnāg < hnīgan

Hnæf pr n *Hnæf* ns 31a/7 Hnæfe ds 32/40 Hnæfes gs 31a/52

hnǣġan 1 *humble, bring low* ġehnǣġed pp 26/88

hnæppan 1 *strike* hnæppen sbj pr3p 6/67 (twice)

hnīgan 1 *bend down, bow* hnāg pt1s 23/59

hnossian 2 *strike, batter* hnossiaþ pr3p 35a/7

Hōc pr n *Hoc* Hōces gs 31a/14

hōcor n:B2b.ii *insult, derision* hōcere ds 25/124

hōcorwyrde adj *derisive, scornful* npm 25/119

hof n:B2a *dwelling, court* hofe ds 31b/16 hofu np 37/29

hogian 2 *set one's mind on, consider, intend* (+g) hogedon pt3p 19/250, 273 hogode pt3s 30/133 sbj pt3s 30/128 hogodon pt3p 30/123

hōl n:B2b *slander, malice* ns 25/46

ġehola m:B5a *companion, comrade* ġeholena gp 38/31

hold adj *friendly, loyal, gracious* nsm 26/41 holdne asm 36/39 holdost sup asn 30/24 holdra gpm 40/17

hōlinga adv *in vain, without cause* 31a/14

holm m:B1a *ocean, sea, water* ns 18/4, 31a/69 as 38/82 holma gp 26/64

holmweall m:B1a *wall of seawater* ns 18/22

holmwudu m:B4a *tree on the hill* as 23/91 (see note)

Hōlofernus pr n *Holofernes* ns 19/21, 46 as 19/7 gs 19/180, 250 Hōlofernes gs 19/336

holt n:B2b *wood, forest, copse* holte ds 33/19 holtes gs 23/29, 30/8

homer see hamor

hond, honda see hand

hondġemōt n:B2b *hand-encounter, battle* hondġemōta gp 31b/35

hondplega m:B5a *hand-to-hand combat* hondplegan gs 10/25

hondseten f:B3e *signature, ratification* ns 12/22 hondsetene as 12/18

hondweorc n:B2b *handiwork* ns 35a/8

hongiað < hangian

hopian 2 *hope* inf 19/117 hopaþ pr3s 34/30

hord n:B2b *hoard, treasure* as/ap 10/10 horde ds 31a/46

hordcofa m:B5a *treasure chamber, heart* hordcofan as 38/14

hordweard m:B1a *guardian of treasure, lord* hordwearda gp 18/66

hōring m:B1a *fornicator* hōringas np 25/136

horn m:B1a *horn, gable* hornas ap 32/4

hornboga m:B5a *horn(-tipped) bow* or *bow curved like horn* hornbogan dp 19/222

hornġestrēon n:B2b *wealth of arched structures* ns 37/22

hors n:B2b *horse* as 30/2 horsa 11/16 horse ds 34/41

Horsa pr n *Horsa* ns 9a/24

hosp m:B1a *scorn, insult, mockery* as 19/216, 22/133, 135 hospum dp 22/139

hrā < hrǣw

ġehradian 2 *hasten along, cause to succeed* ġehradode pt3s 21a/54

ġehrān < ġehrīnan

hraþe adj *quick* sup npm radost 29/16

hraþe adv *quickly, soon, at once* 18/56, 19/37, 31b/50, 85 raþe 8/20, 27/67, 30/30, 164, 288 raþor comp 22/103

hræd adj *quick, alert* hrædest sup nsn 25/38, 138

hræding f:B3d *haste* hrædinge ds 25/142

hrædlīce adv *forthwith, quickly* 14/59

hrædwyrde adj *hasty of speech* nsm 38/66

hræf(e)n see hrefn

hræġl n:B2c.i *dress, garment, clothing* ns 4/97, 35b/1 as 19/282

hrælþēn m:B1bi *master of wardrobe* ns 12/11

hrǣw n:B2b *corpse, body* ns 23/72 as 23/53 np 32/34 ap 19/313 hrā ns 31b/97 hrǣ ap 10/60

hrēam m:B1a *outcry, shouting, uproar* ns
18/4, 30/106 **hrēame** ds 1/26
hrefn m:B1a *raven* ns 19/206 **hræfen** ns
32/34 **hræfn** as 10/61 **hrefne** ds 34/6 **hrem**
ns 13/2 **hremmas** np 30/106 **hremn** as
13/2
hrēman 1 +d *exult about* inf 10/39
hrēmiġ adj +g *exulting, boasting* **hrēmiġe**
npm 10/59
hremmas, hremn < **hrefn**
hrēo see **hrēoh**
hrēod n:B2b *reed, rush* as 14/30, 33, 61
hrēodan II *adorn* **hroden** pp 31a/89
ġe**hrodene** pp asf 19/37
hrēoh adj *fierce, savage, distraught, troubled*
nsm 19/282, 31b/73 **hrēo** nsm 38/16 asf
38/105
Hreopadūn pr n (f:B3b) *Repton* (Derbys.)
Hreopadūne ds 29/38
hrēoriġ adj *collapsing, in ruins* **hrēorġe** npm
37/3
hrēosan II *fall, collapse, crumble* inf 38/48
hrēosende prp nsf 38/102 ġe**hrorene**
pp npm 37/3 **hruran** pt3p 9a/40 **hruron**
pt3p 31a/12
hrēowan I impers *grieve* **hrēoweð** pr3s 17/89
hrēowan < **rōwan**
hrēowceariġ adj *sorrowful, distressed* nsm
23/25
hrēowiġmōd adj *grieving at heart, dejected*
hrēowiġmōde npm 19/289
hrēowlīċe adv *cruelly, wretchedly* 9a/44,
25/35
hrepian 2 *touch* **hrepodon** pt3p 21a/78
hrēran 1 *move, stir* inf 38/4
hrēþēadeġ adj *glorious, victorious*
hrēþēadeġost sup nsn 33/8
hreþer n:B2c *breast, heart, spirit* **hreþra** gp
38/72 **hreþre** as 26/63 ds 19/94, 37/41,
31a/89
hreþerloca m:B5a *heart-enclosure, breast*
hreþerlocan as 26/58
hricg m:B1a *back, ridge* **hricge** ds 34/10
hrīm m:B1a *rime, frost* ns 26/32, 37/4 as
38/48 **hrīme** is 38/77
hrīman 1 *cry out, wail* inf 34/44
hrīmċealde adj *ice-cold* asf 38/4
hrīmġiċel m:B1a *icicle* **hrīmġiċelum** dp
26/17

hrīmiġ adj *rimy, frosty* **hrīmiġost** sup nsn
33/6
(ġe)**hrīnan** I +d *touch, reach* inf 31b/24
ġe**hrān** pt3s 28/47, 70
hring m:B1a *ring, link, ringed mail-coat;
circle, circular structure* ns 31b/12 **hringa**
gp 17/40, 31b/16 **hringas** ap 37/19
hringum dp 19/37, 31a/29
hrinġeat n:B2d *arched gate* ns 37/4
hringedstefna m:B5a *ring-prowed ship*
hringedstefnan as 31a/69
hringloca m:B5a *ring-link* (in mail-coat)
hringlocan ap 30/145
hringmǣl n:B2b *ring-marked sword* ns
31b/30 as 31b/73
hringmere m:B1g *round pool* as 37/45
hringþegu f:B3a *receiving of rings*
hringþege ds 26/44
Hrisanbeorgan pr n *Princes Risborough*
(Bucks.) dp 11/6
hrīþ f:B3b *snowstorm* as 38/102
hroden < **hrēodan**
hrōf m:B1a *roof, sky, heavens* ns 37/31 as
13/12 **hrōfas** np 37/3 ap 33/64 **hrōfe** ds
9b/36, 19/67
Hrōfeċeaster pr n (f:B3c) *Rochester* (Kent)
Hrōfeċeastre ds 8/9
hrōfsele m:B1g *roofed hall* ds 31b/24
hror adj *active, brave* nsm 32/45
ġe**hrorene** < **hrēosan**
hrōstbēag m:B1a ?*vaulted roof* **hrōstbēages**
gs 37/31 (see note)
Hroþgār pr n *Hrothgar* **Hroþgāres** gs 31a/3,
31b/89
hruran < **hrēosan**
hrūse f:B5c *earth* **hrūsan** as 26/32, 35b/1,
37/29, 38/102 gs 37/8, 38/23
hryre m:B1g *ruin, fall, destruction, decay* as
18/66 gs 38/7 ds 37/31
hrȳþiġ adj *storm-beaten* **hrȳþġe** npm
38/77
hū adv *how* 1/18, 50, 61, 15b/6, etc
hū conj *how* 5/68, 9b/98, 12/1, 25, 14/4,
17/96, 19/25, 26/2, 14, 38/30, 35, etc
huaet see **hwæt**
Hugon pr n *Hugh* as 8/72
huilpe f:B5c *curlew* **huilpan** gs 26/21
Humbre pr n (f:B5c/indecl) *(River) Humber*
ds 5/14, 16 **Humbran** gs 8/40

hund m:B1a *dog, hound* ns 7b/32, 34, 35, 34/6 as 19/110 **hundum** dp 1/34, 25/73
hund num *hundred* 9a/1, 11/8, 10, 27/54 (twice), 28/23, 31b/7, 34/25, 37/8 (twice)
hundeahtatiġ num *eighty* **hundeahtatiġum** dpn 4/3
hundred num *hundred* **hundredes** gsn 14/68
hundtwelftiġ num *one hundred and twenty* 7b/27 **hundtwælftiġum** dpm 11/15 **hundtwelftiġan** dpm 7c/26 **hundtweltifġum** dpm 11/19
hungor m:B1b *hunger, famine* ns 26/11 as 34/45 **hunger** ns 25/44 as 16/69 **hungre** ds 9a/46, 16/70
huniġ n:B2a *honey* as 3a/2 **huniġes** gs 3a/5, 3b/3, 22/55
Hūnlāfing pr n *Hunlafing* ns 31a/81
hunta m:B5a *huntsman* **huntan** np 1/16
huntēontiġ num *hundred* **huntēontiġes** gsn 28/32
hupseax n:B2b *short sword* (worn at hip) ap 19/327
hūru adv *certainly, indeed, truly, especially* 7c/16, 19/345, 23/10, 25/6, 55, 143, 31a/9
hūs n:B2b *house, family* ns 9b/80 as 9b/20 np 25/24, 31, 34/33 **hūse** ds 9b/19, 51, 83, 15c/17
hūsl n:B2c.i *eucharist, host* as 9b/88 (see note), 91 **hūsles** gs 9b/89
hwā, hwæt indef/interrog pron *who, what, one, whoever, anyone, someone, something* **huaet** nsn 20a/4 **hwā** nsm 1/71, 4/24, 25, 5/71, 7b/13, 16/19, 57, 22/19, 42 **hwām** dsm 4/23 **hwæne** asm 4/81, 19/52 **hwæt** nsn 7b/5, 9b/27 asn 1/3, 4 etc, 7a/7, 39, 16/23, 23/2, 116, 27/5 **hwī** isn (see separate entry) **hwȳ** isn (see **hwī**); in adv/conj phrs (isn) **for hwan** *why* 38/59 **for hwon** *why* 9b/84, 26/43 **tō hwon** *as to what, why* 28/19; see also **swā swā** [etc]
ġehwā pron (+g) *each, every, everyone* nsm 25/143 **ġehwām** dsm 26/72 **ġehwæne** asm 10/9, 19/186 **ġehwæs** gsn 9b/33 **ġehwone** asm 18/116
hwanon adv *whence, from where* 4/14, 27/8 **hwonon** 9b/47
hwār see **hwǣr**
hwæl m:B1c *whale* **hwæles** gs 26/60
(ġe)**hwæne** < (ġe)**hwā**

hwænne adv *when, then* 1/46 (interrog) **hwonne** 12/38, 41
hwænne conj (*the time*) *when, until* (*the time when*) 23/136, 30/67 **hwonne** 18/26
hwǣr adv *where, somewhere* 1/69, 5/71, 26/117, 38/92, 93
hwǣr conj *where* 13/5, 22/14, 23/112, 38/26, 40/8 **hwār** 27/70
ġehwǣr adv *everywhere* 9a/41
(ġe)**hwæs** < (ġe)**hwā**
hwæt adj *bold, brave, brisk, active* nsm 34/31 (twice) nsm 26/40 **hwætran** comp npm 35d/19
hwæt interj and adv *behold!, listen!, now, indeed* 6/56, 23/1, 90, 30/231
hwæt < **hwā**
Hwætædūn pr n (f:B3b) *Whaddon* (Bucks.) **Hwætædūnæ** ds 11/11
hwæthwugu adv *somewhat* 6/68
hwæthwugu pron *something* as 9b/24
hwætran < **hwæt** adj
hwætrēd adj *determined, quick in thought* nsm 37/19
hwæþer interrog adv *whether, which of two* 15b/6, 9 (see note), 22/87
hwæþer conj *whether* 9b/88, 92, 14/62 **hweðer ðe** *or* 12/45
hwæþer pron *either, which* (*of two*) asm 14/10 **hwæþerne** asm 14/17 **hwæþrum** dsn 7b/13
ġehwæþer adj *either, each* **ġehwæþere** asf 30/112
hwæþere adv *nevertheless, yet, still, but, and indeed* 9a/39, 23/57, 70, 101 **hwæþre** 7b/35, 9b/10, 27, 79, 85, 23/18, 24 etc, 28/57, 39/12
hwealf adj *hollow, curved* **hwealfum** dpf 19/214
hwearf m:B1a *crowd* **hwearfum** dp 19/249
hwearfian 2 *turn, change, revolve* **hwearfað** pr3s 6/39 **hwearfiað** pr3p 6/42 **hwearfiende** prp nsf 6/39 **hwerfð** pr3s 6/13
hwearfliċ adj *changing, fleeting* **hwearflicra** gp 32/34 (=noun)
hwelċ, hwelċ- see **hwilċ**
hwelp m:B1a *whelp, the young of an animal* as 39/16
hwēol n:B2b *wheel* ns 6/43, 76 np 6/42 **hwēoles** gs 6/61

hwēop < **hwōpan**

hweorfan III *turn, depart, journey, come, go, roam, move* inf 33/58, 38/72 **hwearf** pt3s 31b/82, 32/17 **hweorfaþ** pr3p 33/59 **hweorfende** prp 9a/50 **hweorfeþ** pr3s 26/58, 60

hwer m:B1a *pot, bowl* 34/15

ġehwerfde < **ġehwierfan**

hwettan 1 '*hwet*', *incite, urge* **hweteþ** pr3s 26/63

hweþer see **hwæþer**

hwī interrog adv/conj (isn of **hwæt**) *why* 16/29, 101, 22/48, 95 **hwȳ** 12/27, 51; in adv/conj phrs (*why*) **for hwī** 27/77 **tō hwī** 14/58 **be hwȳ** 12/25; see also **swā**

hwider adv *whither, in which direction* 38/72

ġehwierfan 1 *turn, change* **ġehwerfde** pt3s 9b/60 **ġehwyrfde** pt3s 9b/50, 15c/9 **ġehwyrfst** pr2s 2a/18

hwīl f:B3b *time, while, period* ns 31b/4 **hwīle** as 3c/5, 8/15, 19/214, 23/24, 64 etc, 25/68, 142, 29/39 ds 6/49; in conj phr **þā hwīle þe** as *while, as long as* 6/10, 11, 12/43, 21a/60, 22/39, 24/72 **þā hwȳle þe** 24/29 **þā wīlæ þæ** 11/26; see also **hwīlum**, **lȳtel**

hwilċ adj *which, what kind of* **hwelċre** gsf 28/8 dsf 28/69 **hwilċe** npm 6/38 **hwylċ** nsf 9b/89 **hwylċe** asm 15a/10 asf 9b/43 npm 6/38 **hwylċum** dpn 28/48

hwilċ pron (+g) *which, any* nsm 17/77 **hwelċere** dsf 7b/34 **hwylċ** nsm 31a/42 nsn 33/65 **wylċ** nsm 25/83

ġehwilċ adj *each, every, all* **ġehwilċe** npm 22/123 **ġehwilċne** asm 18/75 **ġehwylċ** nsm 7a/28 **ġehwylċum** dpm 7a/26

ġehwilċ pron (+g) *each, any, some, whoever, whatever* nsm 34/38, 39 nsf 34/28 **ġehwelċum** dpm 29/16 **ġehwilċum** dsm 25/19 **ġehwylċ** nsm 26/90, 111, 30/128, 257 asn 33/46 **ġehwylċe** nsf 9a/40 dsm 30/8 dsn 30/28 ism 23/136 isn 26/36, 68 **ġehwylċes** gsn 18/92, 19/32; + **ānra** (gp) *each one, every one:* **ġehwylċ** nsm 1/52 **ġehwylċum** dsm 23/108 **ġehwylċne** asm 19/95

hwīlon see **hwīlum**

hwīlstiċċe n:B2h *interval of time, spare moment* **hwīlstiċċum** dp 7b/56

hwīlum adv *at times, sometimes* 5/61, 6/29, 9a/59 (twice), 23/22, 23, 26/19, 34/8, 35b/3, 35c/5, etc **hwīlon** 1/72 (twice), 16/12, 17, 21a/20

hwīt adj *bright, radiant, white* nsm 17/13 nsn 22/23, 96 asm 10/63 **hwīte** npm 28/16 **hwītes** gsn 21a/56 **hwītne** asm 32/39 **hwītost** sup nsn 17/2 **hwītum** dpm 21a/57

hwon < **hwā**

hwōn adv *little, for a little while* 22/134, 34/46

hwōn indecl noun/pron +g *little, few* 26/28

ġehwone < **ġehwā**

hwonne see **hwænne**

hwonon see **hwanon**

hwōpan VII *threaten* **hwēop** pt3s 18/2

hwȳ see **hwī**

(ġe)**hwylċ**, (ġe)**hwylċ-** see (ġe)**hwilċ**

ġehwyrf- see **ġehwierfan**

ġehwyrftnes f:B3e.ii *return* **ġehwyrftnesse** ds 15c/4

(ġe)**hycgan** 3 *think, consider, plot, determine, set one's mind (on), be mindful of, hope (for)* inf 17/60, 26/117, 40/11 **hicgan** inf 30/4 **hicgeaþ** imp p 32/11 **ġehicgenne** infl inf 20b/3 **hiġeþ** pr3s 34/30 **hycgaþ** imp p 17/95 **hycge** sbj pr3s 38/14 **hycgean** inf 33/54 **hycgendne** prp asm 40/20

hȳd f:B3g *hide, skin* **hȳdum** dp 28/7 **hȳþe** ds 35d/12

hȳdan 1 *hide, hoard* **hȳdeþ** pr3s 26/102

ġehȳdan 1 *hide, bury* **ġehȳdde** pt3s 38/84

ġehȳġd f:B3g *thought, intention, conception* ns 26/116, 38/72

hyġe m:B1g *spirit, mind, heart, intention, reason, thought, courage, ambition, pride* ns 17/13, 17, 26/44, 58, 38/16 ds 17/89, 26/96, 35d/20 **hiġe** ns 19/87, 30/312 as 17/48 ds 30/4

hyġeġeōmor adj *sad-spirited* **hyġeġeōmorne** asm 40/19

Hyġelāc pr n *Hygelac* **Hȳlāces** gs 31b/39 **Hiġelāces** gs 31b/83

hyġerōf adj *stout-hearted, resolute* nsm 37/19

hȳhsta < **hēah**

hyht f:B3g *hope, trust, joy, expectation, desire* ns 19/98, 23/126, 26/45, 122 **hiht** ns 23/148 as 22/94 **hyhte** ds 35c/1

hyhtwynn f:B3g *joy of hope* **hyhtwynna** gp 19/121

hyldan 1 *bend, bow down* inf 23/45

hyldo f:B3h *favour, grace* as 17/67, 19/4 ds 17/69

hylt < **healdan**

hȳnan 1 *lay low, harm, fell, humiliate* inf 30/180 **hȳnaþ** pr3p 25/103 **hȳnde** pt3s 30/324 ġe**hȳnede** pp npf 25/34

hȳnþo f:B3h *humiliation, affliction* **hȳnþa** gp 34/25

(ġe)**hȳran** 1 *hear, hear of, understand, serve, obey* (+d) inf 1/45, 19/24, 23/78 ġe**hēre** sbj pr3s 34/39 ġe**hīerdun** pt3p 29/19 ġe**hīran** inf 16/30 ġe**hīrde** pt3s 27/21 **hīrdon** pt3p 21b/5 ġe**hȳr** imp s 15b/10 ġe**hȳranne** infl inf 9b/61 ġe**hȳrdan** pt3p 12/37, 25/156 ġe**hȳrde** pt1s 1/39, 23/26, 26/18, 27/78, 30/117 pt3s 9b/30, 27/75, 84, 34/44, etc **hȳrdon** pt1p 9b/110 ġe**hȳrdon** pt3p 14/59, 19/160, 21a/78, 22/2, 69 ġe**hȳre** pr1s 1/72, 4/75 sbj pr3s 22/119 ġe**hȳrenne** infl inf 21a/83 ġe**hȳrest** pr2s 39/16 **hȳreþ** pr3s 34/32 ġe**hyrst** pt2s 14/4, 30/45 ġe**hȳrþ** pr3s 16/8

hyrde m:B1g *herdsman, shepherd, guardian, keeper* ns 19/60

hyre < **hēo**

hyrnednebba m:B5a *horny-beaked one* ns 19/212 **hyrnednebban** as 10/62

ġe**hȳrnes** f:B3e.ii *hearing, listening* ġe**hȳrnesse** ds 9b/59

hyrst f:B3b *ornament, trapping, armour* **hyrsta** ap 19/316, 32/20 **hyrste** np 35b/4

ġe**hȳrsum** adj *obedient, amenable* nsm 27/82

ġe**hyrtan** 1 *cheer, encourage* ġe**hyrte** pt3s 22/92

hyrwan 1 *abuse, deride* **hyrweþ** pr3s 25/124, 127

hys (**his**) < **hē, hit**

hyse m:B1g.iii *warrior, youth* ns 30/152 **hysas** np 30/123 **hyssa** gp 30/2, 128, 32/48 **hyssas** np 30/112 ap 30/169 **hysses** gs 30/141

hyspan 1 *mock, scorn* **hyspdun** pt3p 14/54

hyt see **hit**

hȳþe < **hȳd**

hȳþeliċ adj *convenient, advantageous* nsn 37/41

I

Iācōb pr n *Jacob* **Iācōbe** ds 16/14 **Iācōbes** gs 22/15

iċ pers pron *I, me, my* ns 1/10, 4/1, 2, 5/16, 18, 7b/1, 3, 9b/25, 13/18, 20 **ig** 11/26 **mǣ** ds 11/25, 31 **mē** as (often rflx) 1/49, 51, 14/58, 15b/10, 22/36 ds (often rflx) 1/67, 4/79, 5/3, 7b/2, 13/22, 24, 21a/40, 23/4 **meċ** as 26/6, 28/1, 8, 35a/7, 35b/3, 5, 35c/8, 35d/1, 40/14 **mīn** gs 15b/6, 35d/18 (*me*) [etc]; see also poss pron **mīn**

īhte < **ȳcan**

Iċel pr n *Icel* ns 29/43

Iċeling adj *son of Icel* nsm 29/43

icge adj ?*rich*, ?*splendid* nsn 31a/45 (see note)

īdel adj *idle, vain, worthless, empty, desolate* nsm 38/110 nsf 1/5 **īdelan** dpm 25/130 **īdles** gsn 9b/13 **īdlu** npn 38/87

ides f:B3b *woman, wife, lady* ns 19/14, 109 etc, 31a/13, 55, 33/43 **idesa** np 19/133 **idese** as 19/55, 58 ds 19/340

īeġ f:B3b *island* **īeġe** ds 39/3 **īġe** ds 39/6

ieldran mp (comp of **eald**) *elders, ancestors* np 5/31

ierfe n:B2h *possessions, property, inheritance* **ierfes** gs 7b/29, 30

ig see **iċ**

īġe < **īeġ**

īġland n:B2b *island* **ēġlond** ns 39/5 **eiġlande** is 10/66 **īġlande** ds 24/31, 36

ilca adj *same, like, very* **ilcan** asf 21b/21 dsm 8/5, 65, 66 dsn 8/26, 44 dsf 7b/42 ism 21b/24 isn 29/37, 39 **ilce** asn 9b/41 **illcan** ism 21b/23 **ylcan** asm 21a/21 gsm 9a/6 dsm 22/44 dsn 24/36 [etc]

ilca pron *same, the same* **ilcan** ism 3a/4 isn 3b/3 **ilċe** nsn 29/28 **ylca** nsm 4/41, 22/80

imbsǣton < **ymbsittan**

in adv *in, inwards, inside, within* 27/1, 38, 72, 28/64, 30/58, 157, 31b/11

in prep +a/d/i *in, into, on, within, at, among, during, through* 7a/10, 52, 8/54, 9a/48, 9b/1, 5, 18/78, 19/2, 116, 23/118, 28/22, 33/41, etc

inbryrdnes f:B3e.ii *inspiration* **inbryrdnisse** as 9b/5

inca m:B5a *grievance, rancour* **incan** as 9b/93 ds 9b/92

incundnes f:B3e.ii *inward conviction,
sincerity* **incundnesse** ds 24/25
Indeos pr n *Indians* np 28/33 **Indos** np 28/9
Indisc adj *Indian* as 28/5 (=noun *the Indian
language*) **Indiscra** gpn 28/59 **Indiscum**
dpn 28/55
indryhten adj *noble, excellent* nsm 38/12
indryhto f:B3h *nobility* ns 26/89
Ine pr n *Ine* **Ines** gs 7b/6
ingang m:B1a *entrance, entry, penetration* as
31b/58 **ingong** as 9b/98 **ingonge** ds 9b/65
inġehīd f:B3g *intention, conscience* as
16/76
inġesteald n:B2b *household possessions* as
31a/93
inġeþanc m:B1a *inner thought, conscience* as
25/162
ingong, ingonge < **ingang**
inlagian 2 *reverse a legal sentence* **inlagiġe**
sbj pr3s 7c/11
inlǣdan 1 *bring in* **inlǣdon** inf 9b/81
inn n:B2b *chamber, room* **inne** ds 19/70
innan adv *within, from within, inside* 17/5,
25/32, 26/11
innan prep +d/a/i *in, within* 12/26, 25/30,
33/43 **innon** 22/31, 27/41, 57
innanbordes adv *within the country, at home*
5/8
inne adv *inside, within, retained* 9b/87, 88,
13/15, 25/23, 25, 44, 89, 31b/79
innon see **innan**
innoð m:B1a *womb* as 22/80
inntō see **intō**
inseġl n:B2c.i *seal* **inseġle** ds 22/12 **insiġle** as
12/54, 55
instyred < **onstyrian**
intinga m:B5a *matter, cause, occasion* ns
9b/17 **intingan** as 9a/32 ds 4/40
intō prep +d/a *into, to, against, in, for* 4/9,
7c/15, 21, 8/51, 81, 11/4, 10, 13/7, etc
inntō 11/9
inwidda m:B5a *malicious foe, villain, enemy*
ns 10/46, 19/28
inwidhlemm m:B1a *malicious wound*
inwidhlemmas np 23/47
inwitsearo n:B2g *malicious cunning, intrigue*
as 31a/39
Iōhannes pr n *John* **Iōhanne** ds 5/63
Iōsēp pr n *Joseph* ns 16/68

Iōuis pr n *Jove* ns 24/35, 37, 60, 62 **Iōues** gs
24/63
īow (ēow) < **ġē**
Īraland pr n (n:B2b) *Ireland* as 10/56
īren, īrenes see **īsern**
īrenbend f:B3b *iron bands* **īrenbenda** np
17/34
īrenheard adj *iron-hard* nsm 31a/50
irnan III *run, hurry* **arn** pt3s 14/59 **ærndon**
pt3p 30/191 **urnon** pt3p 19/164, 29/15
is < **bēon-wesan**
Īsaac pr n *Isaac* **Īsaace** ds 16/5, 6
īsceald adj *ice-cold* **īscealdne** asm 26/14
īscaldne 26/19
īsern n:B2b.ii *iron, iron weapon, sword* ns
33/26 **īren** ns 30/253 **īrenes** gs 17/9 **īserne**
ds 9a/43, 35a/1
īsġebind n:B2b *icy bond* **īsġebinde** ds 31a/71
īsiġfeþera adj *icy-feathered, icy-winged* nsm
26/24
Israhēlas pr n (mp:B1a) *Israelites, Israel*
Israēla gp 15c/1 **Israhēla** gp 9b/64, 14/51,
22/132 **Israhēlum** dp 18/70
iū adv *formerly, of old, long ago* 5/4, 9a/37,
23/28, 87, 24/9, 26/83, 37/32
Iūdēi pr n *the Jews* np 22/164 **Iūdēa** gp 14/2,
22, 44, 22/40 **Iūdēum** dp 15b/3
Iūdēisce adj *Jewish*, noun *the Jews* nsn
22/156 **Iūdēiscan** np 16/95, 22/5, 130 dp
22/157 **Iūdēisces** gsn 22/149 **Iūdēiscum**
dp 16/48
Iūdith pr n (f:B3b) *Judith* ns 19/13, 123 etc
Iūdithe gs 19/333 **Iūdithðe** as 19/40
iugoþe < **geoguþ**
iukian 2 *yoke* **iugie** pr1s 1/20 ġe**iukodan**
pp dpm 1/21
iung see **ġeong**
iungling m:B1a *youth, young man*
iunglingum dp 4/11
Iūno pr n *Juno* ns 24/38
iūwine m:B1g.i *friend of former days* ap
26/92

K

Kenulf pr n *Kenulf* ns 8/38
kynerīċes < **cynerīċe**
kyning, kyning- see **cyning**
kynnes < **cynn**

L

lā interj *lo!*, *behold!*, *o!* 22/6, 25/17, 82, 104, 144

laadrincmanna m:B5a *conductor, escort* **laadrincmannan** as 7a/12

lāc n:B2b *offering, sacrifice, booty* as 10/14, 39/1 ap 24/50, 56, 31b/93 **lāce** ds 16/80 **lācum** dp 25/24

ġelāc n:B2b *play, rolling, tumult* 26/35 as 40/7

lācan VII *move up and down, soar* inf 33/39

lādtēowas < **lāttēow**

lāf f:B3b *what is left, remnant, legacy* ns 10/54 **lāfan** dp 10/6 **lāfe** as 22/56 gs 9a/45, 18/63 np 35a/7

laga, lage < **lagu**

lāgen, lāgon < **licgan**

ġelagian 2 *appoint by law, ordain* **ġelagod** pp nsn 25/21

lagu m:B4a *sea, water* ns 18/37 as 26/47

lagu f:B3a *law* **laga** np 25/39, 87 **lage** as 25/28, 53 gs 25/19 ds 7c/25, 24/71, 25/53, 121 **lagum** dp 25/160

ġelagu np:B2a *expanses, stretches* ap 26/64

laguflōd m:B1a *sea-tide, ocean* ns 33/46

lagulād f:B3b *sea-way, sea* **lagulāde** ap 38/3

lagustrēam m:B1a *water, river* **lagustrēamas** np 30/66

lāgon < **licgan**

lahbryċe m:B1g *breach of law* **lahbrycas** ap 25/112

lahlīce adv *lawfully* 25/52

ġelamp < **ġelimpan**

lāmrind f:B3b *clay coating, tile* **lāmrindum** dp 37/17

land n:B2b *land, country, earth, region, realm* ns 4/95, 9a/21, 40 as 10/9, 27, 59, 12/32, 18/37, 33/53, etc **landæs** gs 11/5 etc **lande** ds 8/66, 9a/19, 16/68, 17/55, 30/45, 47, etc **landes** gs 9a/10, 24/8, 30/90, 275 **lond** as 5/12, 12/1, 5, etc **londe** ds 9b/64, 12/53, 57, 26/66 is 12/58 **londes** gs 12/43, 29/24

landbīgenga m:B5a *peasant, native* **landbīgengan** dp 9a/30

landbūend m:B4d *land-dweller, native* **landbūende** np 19/226 **londbūendum** dp 19/314

landscipe m:B1g *region* as 17/39

lang adj *long, tall, long-lasting, long-coming* nsn 21a/25, 30/66 **langa** nsm 30/273 **lange** asf 15c/17 (twice), 23/24 **lengran** comp gsn 19/184 apf 18/86

lange adv *long, for a long time, far* 15b/6, 7, 9, 17/64, 19/158, 25/30, etc **lencgest** sup 34/33 **leng** comp 7b/28, 6/69, 16/104, 19/153, 25/4, 27/75, etc **lengest** sup 29/3, 33/6 **longe** 5/69, 38/3, 38

langian 2 impers +a *long, pine* **langaþ** pr3s 34/9 **longade** pt3s 40/14

langoþ m:B1a *longing, discontent* **langoþe** ds 40/53 **longaþ** as 36/3 **longaþes** gs 40/41

langunghwīl f:B3b *period of longing* **langunghwīla** gp 23/126

lār f:B3b *learning, teaching, instruction, doctrine, precept, advice, knowledge* ns 4/16, 18, 5/40, 57 **lāra** np 25/39 ap 16/77 **lāre** as 4/11, 5/10, 16/34, 17/104, 18/115, 27/63, 79, etc gs 9b/49 ds 1/7, 4/13, 9b/68, 22/63, etc

lārcwide m:B1g *precept, counsel* **lārcwidum** dp 38/38

lārēow m:B1a *teacher, master* ns 1/1, 72, 21a/80, 27/53 **lārēowa** gp 5/19 **lārēowas** np 9b/62, 4/15, 16, 16/24, 22/123, 125 **lārēowe** ds 27/57 **lārēowum** dp 16/35

lāst m:B1a *track, step* as 10/22, 19/209, 291 **lāste** ds 19/297, 32/17, 38/97 **lāstum** dp 26/15

lāstword n:B2b *word left behind, reputation* **lāstworda** gp 26/73

late adv *late, slowly* 22/16; in phr **sīð ond late** *at last* 19/275

lātēow see **lāttēow**

latian 2 *delay, hesitate* **latiġe** sbj pr3s 25/144

lāttēow m:B1a *leader, general, guide* ns 9a/55 **lādtēowas** np 28/3 **lātēow** ns 34/31 **lāttēowas** np 9a/23

lāþ adj *hostile, hateful, loathsome, harmful, evil* (very often =noun *hostile one, enemy,* etc) nsn 25/69, 39/12 asm 19/45 **laþan** gsn 19/310 dpm 31b/14 **laðe** npm 18/16 **lāðestan** sup gsm 19/178 dpm 19/314 **lāþne** asm 19/72, 101, 26/112 **laðost** sup nsm 23/88 npm 19/322 **lāþra** gpm 10/9, 19/297, 303 **lāðran** comp asm 17/39 gsn

35a/10 npm 17/92 **lāþre** comp asn 30/50
lāþum dsn 19/226 dp 10/22
lāð n:B2b *harm, injury* as 17/55 **lāðes** gs
17/57
lāðbite m:B1g *hostile bite, wound* np 31a/60
lāðettan 1 *loathe, hate* **lāðet** pr3s 25/127
(ġe)**laðian** 2 *invite, summon* **laðedon** pt3p
9a/30 ġe**laðod** pp 9a/4 ġe**laðode** pt3s 9a/7,
27/7
lāðliċ adj *horrible, repulsive* **laðlicu** apn
31b/93
lāðlīċe adv *horribly, wretchedly* **lāðlīcost** sup
40/14
ġe**laþung** f:B3d *church, congregation*
ġe**laþunge** gs 16/72 ds 22/72
lǣċe m:B1g *physician* ns 21a/43, 44, 62,
63
ġe**lǣċċan** 1 *seize, take* ġe**lǣhte** pt3s 22/147
lǣċecynn n:B2b.i *race of physicians, kind of
physician* as 35a/10
lǣċedōm m:B1a *remedy, medicine* ns 3a/3
lǣċedōmas np 3a/1
(ġe)**lǣdan** 1 *lead, bring, take, derive* inf 8/75,
79, 19/42, 23/5 **lǣd** imp s 13/15 **lǣdað**
pr3p 25/104 **lǣdde** pt3s 8/81, 9a/26,
19/129 ġe**lǣdde** pt3s 9b/44, 12/31, 15c/10,
22/89 **lǣddon** pt3p 14/35, 19/72, 325 **lǣde**
pr1s 1/39 **lǣdene** infl inf 8/28 **lǣdeð** pr3s
18/98, 109
Lǣden, Lǣdene see **Lēden**
lǣdene < **lǣdan**
Lǣdenġeðīode n:B2h *Latin language* ds 5/55
Lǣdenġeðīodes gs 5/57
Lǣdenware mp:B1h *the Romans* np 5/45
lǣfan 1 *leave, bequeath* **lǣfde** pt3s 24/34,
29/21 **lǣfdon** pt3p 5/32 **lēfdon** pt1p 5/23
lǣġ, lǣgun < **licgan**
ġe**lǣhte** < ġe**lǣċċan**
lǣn n/f:B2b/3g *loan* as 12/53 **lǣne** ds 5/71
lǣne adj *transitory, fleeting, passing,
temporary, temporal* nsm 18/86, 38/108
(twice), 109 (twice) nsn 26/66, 38/108
lǣnan dsn 23/138 apn 6/76 **lǣnum**
dsn 23/109
(ġe)**lǣran** 1 *teach, exhort, persuade* (+d),
instruct, guide, advise inf 5/55, 9b/58,
21a/16 **lǣrað** pr1p 7b/12 **lǣrde** pt3s 9b/55,
30/311 **lǣrdon** pt3p 14/15 **lǣre** sbj pr3s
5/55 ġe**lǣred** pp 4/83, 9b/11, 27/36

ġe**lǣrede** pp npm 5/69 (*learned*)
ġe**lǣredestan** pp sup apm 9b/45 (*most
learned*) **lǣreð** pr3s 34/36
læriġ m:B1a *rim of shield* ns 30/284
lǣs adv (comp of **lȳt**) *less* 6/65
lǣs indecl noun/pron *less, fewer* as 25/93; in
conj phr **þȳ/þē lǣs(þe)** (+sbj) *lest, in case*
1/34, 3a/6, 6/69, 15b/11, 16/105, 22/8,
25/145
lǣs f:B3f *pasture* **lǣse** ds 1/34
lǣssa adj (comp of **lȳtel**) *less* **lǣssan** gsn
7c/26 **lǣsse** nsn 22/172
lǣst adj (sup of **lȳtel**) *least, smallest* **lǣsta**
nsm 4/29
lǣst adv *least* 28/73
ġe**lǣstan** 1 *perform, fulfil, achieve, support*
inf 18/112, 30/11 ġe**lǣstanne** infl inf 7b/15,
16 ġe**lǣste** pt3s 30/15 ġe**lǣsteð** pr3s 17/98
lǣt adj *slow, slack* nsm 31b/38
lǣtan VII *let, allow, cause to do, set, leave
behind* **lǣt** pt3s 25/95 imp s 14/61 **lǣtað**
pr3p 6/65 **lǣte** pr1s 17/101 **lēt** pt3s 14/26,
22/153, 25/148, 30/7, 140 **lētan** pt3p 10/60
lēton pt3p 19/221, 30/108, 37/42
ġe**lǣte** n:B2h *junction (of roads)* ġe**lǣtum** dp
24/56
lǣðð f:B3b *affliction, injury* **lǣðða** gp 19/158
lǣðð um dp 19/184
lǣwed adj *unlearned, lay* **lǣwede** npm 25/52
(noun *lay people*) **lǣwedum** dp 16/35
le < **lecgan**
lēaf n:B2b *leaf* np 15a/5 **lēafum** dp 13/10
lēaf f:B3b *leave, permission* **lēafe** as 27/23,
54
ġe**lēafa** m:B5a *belief, faith* ns 4/11, 16
ġe**lēafan** as 16/76, 19/6, etc gs 22/67
ds 16/38, 19/97, 22/63, 165, 24/25
ġe**lēaffull** adj *believing, faithful* ġe**lēaffullum**
dsm 21a/43
ġe**lēaflēast** f:B3h *unbelief, infidelity*
ġe**lēaflǣstu** np 22/127
leahtor m:B1b *vice, sin* **leahtrum** dp 22/108
lēan n:B2b *reward, payment, requital* ns
17/98, 18/61 as 31b/93 **lēana** ap 34/35
lēanes gs 19/346 **lēanum** dp 17/75
ġe**lēanian** 2 *reward* inf 17/57
lēap m:B1a *container, carcass* ns 19/111
lēas adj +g *lacking, without, deprived of* nsm
17/35, 19/121 nsn 40/32 **lēase** npn 38/86

lēas adj *false, lax, unreliable* nsm 16/105
   lēase apm 4/26, 16/108
lēasbreġd n:B2b *cheating, trickery*
   lēasbreġdum dp 24/54
lēasung f:B3d *lying, falsehood, frivolity*
   leasunga ap 25/115 lēasunge gs 9b/13
leax m:B1a *salmon* ns 33/39
lecgan 1 *lay, set, place, apply, go* le imp s
   3b/10 lecgað pr3p 26/57 imp p 27/57 lecge
   sbj pr3s 38/42 lēdon pt3p 21a/68 leġde
   pt3s 36/5 leġdun pt3p 10/22 (see note)
   licge sbj pr3s 3a/11
lēddon < lǣdan
lēden adj *Latin* dsf 1/13
Lēden n:B2c *Latin (language)* ns 16/89 as
   4/20 Lǣden as 5/60 Lǣdene ds 5/15
   Lēdene ds 16/90, 103 Lēdenes gs 16/92
   Līden ns 16/88 Lӯden as 16/13 Lӯdene ds
   16/3
Lēdensprǣċ f:B3b *Latin language*
   Lēdensprǣċe gs 4/64 ds 4/36, 54, 80
lēdon < lecgan
lēfdon < lǣfan
lēfnes f:B3e.ii *leave, permission* lēfnesse
   ds 7b/26
leġ < licgan
leġdun < lecgan
leġer n:B2c *couch, grave* ap 40/34
lehtrian 2 *blame, revile* lehtreð pr3s
   25/124
lencgest < lange
lenċten m:B1a *Lent, spring* ns 33/6 lenġtene
   ds 8/65
leng, lengest < lange
lengran < lang
lēod m:B1a *man, chief, leader* ns 31b/1, 47,
   32/24
lēode fp:B3g *people, nation* ap 7a/5 gp
   25/150 lēoda np 10/11, 24/45 ap 30/37
   gp 19/178 lēodum dp 19/147, 23/88,
   25/27, 30/50
lēodfruma m:B5a *leader of people, lord* ns
   40/8
lēodġeld n:B2b *fine for manslaughter*
   lēodġelde ds 7a/13
lēodhata m:B5a *persecutor, tyrant*
   lēodhatan as 19/72 np 25/118
lēodþēaw m:B1a *popular usage, customary
   way* lēodþēawe ds 28/19

lēof adj *dear, beloved, agreeable, pleasing*
   nsm 1/19, 16/104, 17/2 nsf 19/147 (=noun)
   lēofa nsm 23/78, 95, 27/50 nsf 27/6, 18, 25
   lēofan npm 9b/96 dsm 34/9 dsm 19/346
   lēofesta sup nsm 27/4 lēofne asm 26/112
   (=noun) lēofost sup npm 7b/54 lēofostan
   sup npm 22/69 lēofra nsm 29/26 lēofran
   comp asf 17/75 lēofre comp nsn 1/7, 12/32;
   lēof in addressing persons, *sir, sire* ns 1/31,
   11/3, 29, 12/1, 38, 60, 16/3, 6, 22/6
leofaþ < libban
leofede, leofode, leofodon < libban
Lēofsiġ pr n *Leofsige* as 8/60, 64
Lēofsunu pr n *Leofsunu* ns 30/244
lēoht adj *bright, radiant* lēohtne asm 19/191
lēoht n:B2b *light, daylight, the world* ns
   18/100, 27/76, 31b/79, 33/51 lēohte ds
   2a/3, 23/5 lēohtes gs 17/55, 57, 64
lēohtliċ adj *lucid, straightforward* lēohtlicum
   dpn 16/67
lēoma m:B5a *ray of light, gleam, radiance* ns
   28/47, 31b/79 leoman as 19/191, 28/47,
   31b/26
leomu < lim
lēoran 1 *pass away, depart* ġelēorene
   pp npm 37/7
leornere m:B1g *scholar* leorneras ap 9b/45
(ġe)leornian 2 *learn, study* inf 1/13, 4/13,
   9b/59, 27/81 leornade pt3s 9b/11
   ġeleornade pt3s 9b/16 leornion sbj pr3p
   4/10, 15 ġeleornod pp 27/34 ġeleornode
   pt3s 9b/4, 27/85 leornodon pt3p 9b/62
   ġeliornod pp 5/38, 64 ġeliornode pt1p
   5/62 ġeliornodon pt3p 5/44, 46
leorningcniht m:B1a *disciple*
   leorningcnihtas np 22/8 leorningcnihtum
   dp 22/28, 32, 45, 46, 62
leornung f:B3d *learning, study* leornunge ds
   1/6 liornunga as 5/10 ds 5/53
lēoð n:B2b *song, poem, poetry* as 9b/16, 46,
   60 np 9b/62 ap 9b/2, 9, 69 leoðe is 9b/52
   lēoþes gs 9b/13
lēoðcræft m:B1a *art of song, poetry* as 9b/11
lēoðcræftiġ adj *skilled in song* nsm 36/40
leoðosyrċe f:B5c *corselet, mail-coat*
   leoðosyrċan as 31b/14
lēoþsong m:B1a *song, poem, poetry*
   lēoþsonges gs 9b/50 lēoþsongum dp 9b/7
lēswǣs < lysu

lēt, lētan, lēton < lǣtan

letanīa m:B5a *litany* letanīan as 1/42

ġelettan 1 *hinder, prevent* ġelette pt3s 30/164

lēw f:B3b *blemish, injury* lēwe ds 25/132

ġelēwian 2 *blemish, hurt* ġelēwede pp npm 25/133

libban 3 *live, exist* leofaþ pr3s 26/102, 107 leofede pt3s 16/30 leofedon pt3p 24/30 leofode pt3s 8/15 leofodon pt3p 16/10, 11 etc, 24/69 libbe sbj pr3s 7b/28 libbendum prp dpn 13/19, 22 ġelifd pp 28/72 lifde pt3s 12/43 lifdon pt3p 26/85, 28/11 lifġe sbj pr3s 26/78 lifġendra prp gpm 26/73 (=noun) lifiaþ pr3p 23/134 lifiendne prp asm 25/61 lybban inf 16/9, 20 lybbe pr1s 4/89 lyfdon pt3p 19/296 lyfedan pt3p 24/72 lyfiað pr3p 2a/19

līċ n:B2b *body, corpse* ns 22/39, 29/35, 38 as 12/54, 21a/32, 76, 22/9, 42, etc ap 22/16 līċe ds 31b/12 līċes gs 23/63, 31a/60

ġelīċ adj +d *like, similar to* nsn 3a/12 ġeliċċast sup npm 25/73 ġelīċe asf 7c/23 npm 25/131 ġelīċran comp npm 15a/78 ġelīċre comp gsf 7c/22

ġelīċe adv *equally, likewise, similarly* 9b/10, 14/53, 22/171, 28/27

licgan V *lie, lie down, lie dead, remain* inf 19/278, 30/319, 31b/95 lāgon pt3p 18/12, 19/30, 22/31, 30/183 læġ pt3s 10/17, 19/106, 22/27, 101, 29/22, 30/157, 204, 227, 31b/41, 56, etc lǣġe sbj pt3s 21a/62, 30/279, 300 lǣgon pt3p 29/18 lǣgun pt3p 10/28 leġ pt3s 30/276 liċeð pr3s 30/222 licgað pr3p 17/34, 45, 34/7, 38/78 licge sbj pr3s 25/86 licgende prp 23/24 līð pr3s 19/288, 21a/69, 29/35, 38, 30/232, 314

ġelicgan V *lie, sleep (with)* ġeliġeþ pr3s 7a/17, 21, 22, 54

līċhama m:B5a *body* ns 21a/74, 21b/24 līċaman as 11/5 līċhaman np 14/66 as 21a/67 ap 21a/75 līċhoma ns 28/15 līċhoman ds 6/73

līċhamliċ adj *bodily, in the body, physical* līċhamlicum dpm 15b/2 līċhomlicre dsf 9b/78

līċhamlīċe adv *bodily, in the flesh* 22/64, 100

līcian 2 impers/+d *please, be pleasing* inf 7b/5 līcað pr3s 27/68 līcode pt3s 7b/10, 27/46 līcodon pt3p 7b/2, 3

ġelīċran < ġelīċ

līċsang m:B1a *'corpse-singing', funeral hymn* as 21a/60

lid n:B2a *ship* lides gs 10/27, 34

Līden see Lēden

Lidġeard pr n *Lydiard* (Wilts.) ds 12/58

lidmann m:B4b *seaman, Viking* lidmanna gp 30/164 lidmen np 30/99

(ġe)līef-, ġelīfst see (ġe)lȳfan

līf n:B2b *life* ns 2a/21, 18/100, 22/110, 111, 26/65, etc as 6/49, 8/13, 25, 9a/48, 9b/76, 22/82, 112, 113, 23/147, 31b/45, etc np 22/109 līfe ds 8/69, 21a/29, 22/107, 23/109, etc līfes gs 2a/11, 6/70, 9b/8, 15c/16, 22/85, 23/88, etc; in phrs **on līfe** *in life, when alive* 22/6, 70, 24/52 **tō līfe** *alive* 24/34

ġelifd, lifd- see libban

ġelīfde < ġelȳfan

lifer f:B3c *liver* lifre as 3b/5

ġelīffæstan 1 *quicken, bring to life* ġelīffæste pt3s 16/54 pp npm 22/169

lifġ-, lifi- see libban

līġ m:B1g *flame, fire* ns 17/39, 31a/60 līġe ds 9a/43

līġet n:B2c.iii *lightning, flash of lightning* ns 22/23, 95 līġette ds 22/96

līhtan 1 *alight, dismount* līhte pt3s 30/23

lim n:B2a *limb* leomu ap 9b/22 limum dp 21a/62

līm m:B1a *lime, mortar* līme ds 37/4

ġelimp n:B2b *occurrence, event, fortune, circumstances* as 27/19 ġelimpum dp 25/105 ġelymp as 27/12, 16

(ġe)limpan III impers +d *happen, be, befall, suit, turn out, belong (to)* inf 25/82 ġelamp pt3s 22/141, 24/6 limpeþ pr3s 26/13 limpþ pr3s 15a/7 ġelimpþ pr3s 4/67, 25/89

ġelimpliċ adj *belonging, relevant, fitting* ġelimpliċe dsf 9b/22 apn 4/67

ġelimplīċe adv *properly, suitably* 21a/57

limwēriġ adj *weary in limb* limwēriġne asm 23/63

lind f:B3b *shield (of linden-wood)* linda ap 32/11 linde as 30/244 ap 19/191, 303, 30/99 lindum dp 19/214

Lindesīġ pr n *Lindsey* (Lincs.) Lindesīġe ds 8/41

lindplega m:B5a *shield-play, battle* lindplegan ds 31a/11

lindwīġ n:B2b *shield-army* as 19/297
lindwiġġend m:B4d *shield-warrior*
   lindwiġġende np 19/42
linnan III +d *lose, yield up* **lunnon** pt3p
   18/51
ġeliorn- see ġeleornian
liornung see leornung
lioþobend f:B3b *limb-bond, fetter*
   lioþobendum dp 17/45
liss f:B3b *love, kindness, joy* **lissa** gp 18/100
   lissum dp 35d/25
listum adv *skilfully, cunningly, carefully*
   3a/2, 19/101
lītl- see **lȳtel**
līð < **licgan**
līðe adj *gentle, mild* nsm 22/99
līðnes f:B3e.ii *mildness, softness* ns 22/96
līxan 1 *shine, gleam* **līxte** pt3s 31b/79
loc n:B2a *enclosure, fold* **loca** ap 1/35, 136
locbore f:B5c ?*one in position of*
   responsibility ns 7a/39 (see note)
locene < **lūcan**
lōcian 2 *see, look, gaze* **lōcaþ** pr3s 25/95
   lōciaþ pr3p 3a/6 imp p 28/48 **lōcie** sbj pr3s
   6/50 **lōcude** pt3s 29/12
lof n:B2a *praise, fame, glory* ns 24/76, 26/73,
   78 as 9b/99, 107, 31b/45
lofian 2 *praise* **lofie** pr1s 15b/14
loflāc n:B2b *offering of praise, sacrifice* ap
   24/57
lofsang m:B1a *song of praise, hymn*
   lofsanges ap 1/41
ġelōgian 2 *place, fill* **ġelōgode** pt3s 25/66
ġelōme adj *frequent* npn 25/40
ġelōme adv *often, constantly* 19/18, 21a/5,
   13, 24/47, 25/22, 53, 80, etc
ġelōmlīċe adv *repeatedly, frequently* 22/6,
   62
lond, lond- see **land**
londbūendum < **landbūend**
londryht n:B2b *land-entitlement* as 36/40
londstede m:B1g *region, country* ds 40/16
ġelong adj *dependent on, belonging to* nsf
   40/45 nsn 26/121
longade < **langian**
longaþ, longaþes < **langoþ**
longe see **lange**
longsum adj *long-lasting, enduring*
   longsumne asm 31b/45

longung f:B3d *longing, anxiety* **longunge** as
   26/47
losian 2 *be lost, fail, perish, escape* inf
   19/287 **losaþ** pr3s 17/97, 26/94 **losiġe** sbj
   pr3s 7b/34
lotwrenc m:B1a *deceit, trick* **lotwrencas** ap
   6/31
lūcan II *lock, join, link* **locene** pp asf 31b/14
   lucon pt3p 30/66
lufan < **lufu**
lufian 2 *love, cherish, delight in* inf 25/128
   lufast pr2s 4/81 **lufaþ** pr3s 4/12 pr3p
   22/43, 24/73 **lufedon** pt3p 22/71 **lufiad**
   pr1p 24/24 **lufiaþ** pr3p 22/93, 24/45,
   25/125 **lufiġe** pr1s 4/74, 80, 81 **lufiġean** inf
   9b/54 **lufiġend** prp 27/63 (=noun *lover*)
ġelufod pp 4/83 **lufode** pt3s 21a/14, 15, 31
   lufodon pt1p 5/23, 24, 31 **lufude** pt3s
   24/52
lufflīċe adv *lovingly, warmly* 5/2
lufu f:B3a/5c *love, affection* ns 4/82, 22/170
   lufan as 26/121 gs 35d/25 ds 9b/72 (twice)
   lufe as 6/59, 64 ds 21a/82, 27/74 11/32
   lufun ds 11/2
Lunden pr n *London* ds 8/34
Lundenburg pr n (Bf:4b) *London*
   Lundenbyriġ ds 8/28
lungen f:B3d *lung* **lungenne** ap 3b/5
lungre adv *at once, quickly* 19/147, 280
lunnon < **linnan**
lust m:B1a *joy, ecstasy, desire, pleasure* ns
   26/36 as 24/71, 25/52 **lustum** dp 16/102,
   19/161, 22/94, 24/30
lūtian 2 *hide* inf 1/21
lybb- see **libban**
Lȳden, Lȳdene see **Lēden**
Lȳdenbōc f:B4b *Latin book* **Lȳdenbōcum**
   dp 16/24
lȳfan 1 *allow, grant* **līefað** pr1p 7b/43 **lȳfde**
   pt3s 12/8, 21a/25 **lȳfdest** pt2s 27/51
ġelȳfan 1 *believe, trust in, hope for, grant,*
   concede inf 22/114, 167 ġelīefe pr1s 5/19
   ġelīfde sbj pt3s 21b/17 ġelīfst pr2s 27/32
   ġelȳfaþ pr1p 14/51, 22/73, 132, 24/24
   ġelȳfdon pt3p 22/140, 24/17, 18, 50 ġelȳfe
   pr1s 15b/13, 17/64, 26/66 sbj pr3s 25/69
   ġelȳfed pp 18/110 ġelȳfendum prp dpm
   22/166 ġelȳfeþ pr3s 26/27, 108 ġelȳfþ pr3s
   14/52

lyfdon, lyfedan < **libban**
ġelȳfed adj *weakened, advanced* (*in age*)
   ġelȳfdre gsf 9b/15
lyft f:B3g *air, mist, cloud* ns 18/16, 31, 37,
   35b/4 **lyfte** ds 33/3, 39 ap 19/347; in phr **on
   lyft** as *aloft, on high* 23/5
lyfthelm m:B1a *air, cloud* ns 33/46
lyftwynn f:B3g *joy in heaven* **lyftwynna** ap
   18/86
lyre m:B1g *loss, destruction* ds 24/33
lȳsan 1 *release, redeem, ransom* inf 23/41,
   30/37
lystan 1 impers +a/inf *please, desire* **lyste**
   pt3s 28/20
ġe**lystan** 1 impers +g *desire* ġe**lyste** pt3s
   19/306
lysu n:B2g *evil* **lēswæs** gs 7a/39 **lyswæs** gs
   7a/7
lȳt adv *little* 26/27
lȳt indecl noun +g *little, few* 38/31, 40/16
lytegian 2 *use guile, deceive* inf 30/86
lȳtel adj *little, small, petty* (often =noun) asn
   25/21 **lītle** isn 10/34 **lītles** gsn 16/23 **lītlum**
   dsn 16/66 **lȳtelre** dsf 25/37 **lȳtlan** asm
   7a/38 asf 4/1 **lȳtle** asf 4/50, 5/29, 25/8 isn
   29/9 **lȳtlum** dsn 4/14; in adv phrs **lītle ǣr**
   asn *a little while ago* 27/51 **lītle hwīle** as
   (*for*) *a little while* 8/15, 29/39
lȳthwōn pron +g *few* ns 19/310
lȳtlian 2 *diminish* **lȳtlaþ** pr3s 30/313
lȳþre adj *wicked, base* asm 4/8 asf 25/151
   lȳþran ds 34/35 (=noun *unworthy person*)

M

mā indecl noun/comp adj (usually +g) *more*
   ns 3c/6 as 5/42, 7b/35, 12/12, 16/18, 18/84,
   25/93, 116, 28/62; in adv/conj phrs **þȳ mā**
   more, the more 10/46, 35d/21 **þē mā þe** *any
   more than* 25/50 **þon mā þe** 6/61, 29/30
mā adv *more* 40/4
Maccus pr n *Maccus* ns 30/80
Macedōnia pr n *Macedonia* **Macedōniam**
   as 28/53
(ġe)**macian** 2 *make, form, do, cause* **macedon**
   pt3p 24/55 **maciað** pr3p 4/86, 92 **macode**
   pt3s 21a/57, 24/33, 47 ġe**macode** pt3s 13/2
mādm- see **māþm**
maga m:B5a *stomach* **magan** as 3b/10

māga, māgas < **mǣg**
magan pt-pr *be able, can, be competent, have
   power to, avail* **magan** pr1p 25/145 pr3p
   25/132 sbj pr3p 25/141 **magon** pr1p
   16/102, 17/56, 27/66 pr2p 19/177 pr3p
   3a/7, 9, 6/59, 61, 16/24 **mæġ** pr1s 17/44,
   23/85, 26/1 pr3s 12/39, 14/51, 21a/9, 75,
   23/110 sbj pr3s 36/7 **mæġe** sbj pr1s 1/60,
   67, 12/12, 27/16 sbj pr2s 5/21 sbj pr3s
   3b/6, 17/90, 27/70 **mæġen** sbj pr1p 17/61
   sbj pr3p 5/54, 7b/56 **meaht** sbj pr2s 6/37,
   68, 9b/27 **meahte** pt1s 5/65, 23/18, 35a/11
   sbj pt1s 28/52, 53, 38/26 pt3s 9b/10, 12/53,
   31a/68, 36/11 sbj pt3s 9b/50, 12/28, 17/75,
   26/26 **meahton** pt3p 5/30 sbj pt3p 28/32
   mehte pt3s 31b/5 sbj pt3s 25/142, 31a/20,
   31b/24 **miht** pr2s 4/82, 23/78 **mihte** pt1s
   23/37 pt3s 13/5, 16/19, 21a/18, 46, 22/81
   sbj pt3s 17/78, 21a/17 **mihten** pt3p 19/24
   mihton pt1p 4/58, 21a/82 pt3p 9a/35,
   16/37, 22/58 **muhton** sbj pt3p 8/30 [etc]
Magdalēnisc adj *of Magdala, Magdalene*
   Magdalēnisce nsf 22/14
magister m (Lat) *teacher* ns 16/12
mago m:B4a *male kinsman, young man* ns
   38/92
magon < **magan**
magoþeġn m:B1bi *young retainer*
   magoþeġnas np 19/236 **maguþeġnas** np
   38/62
man impers pron *one, a person, someone,
   anyone, they* 7a/7, 10, 8/21, 22, 16/19,
   22/118, 23/73, 31b/43, etc **mann** 34/42
   mon 3a/11, 7a/5, 7b/12, 30, 9a/19, 47,
   12/20, 19/291, etc
man see **mann**
mān n:B2b *evil deed, crime* **māna** gp 25/138
ġe**man** < ġe**munan**
ġe**mana** m:B5a *community, common property*
   ġe**mānan** ds 11/23
mancus m:B1a *mancus* (see 5/67n) **mancessa**
   gp 5/67 **mancussa** gp 11/10 **mancussum**
   dp 11/16, 18, 19 **mandcussa** gp 11/8
mancynn n:B2b.i *humankind, mankind,
   people* ns 24/1 as 23/104 **mancyn** 23/41 ns
   24/8 as 24/70 **mancynne** ds 22/63, 24/21,
   67 **mancynnes** gs 23/33, 99 **moncynne** ds
   17/26 **moncynnes** gs 9b/63 **monncynnes**
   gs 9b/37

māndǣd f:B3g *evil deed* māndǣda ap
25/109 gp 9b/72
mandcussa < mancus
maneġ- see maniġ
mānful adj *full of evil, wicked* mānfullan
npm 24/40 apm 22/153 (=noun)
ġemang n:B2a *throng, crowd* as 19/225
ġemong as 19/193, 303
ġemang prep +d *among* on ġemang 8/63
mānhūs n:B2b *house of wickedness, hell* as
18/90
manian 2 *urge, exhort, admonish* manode
pt3s 19/26 ġemanode pp apm 30/231
monade pt3s 9b/55
maniġ adj *many, many a* nsm 31a/50 manega
npm 22/122 npf 21a/88 apn 1/39 apf 6/8,
21a/28 maneġe npm 24/66, 25/58, 118,
141 npf 25/65 apf 25/11 maneġra gpm
22/175 manegum dpf 16/85, 21a/10,
21b/13, 23/99 maniġe npm 14/66 mæniġ
nsm 10/17, 32/13 mæniġne asm 30/188
monegum dsm 36/33 dpn 9b/65 moniġ
nsm 36/24 nsn 31b/19 nsf 37/23 etc
moniġe npm 3a/6, 37/21 moniġra gpm
9b/7 gpf 9a/26 [etc]
maniġ pron *many, a multitude* manega npm
16/18, 30/200 manegan dpm 25/65
maneġe npm 25/71, 133, 136 npf 25/33
apm 25/128 apf 7b/2 manegum dpm
14/68, 18/43, 97 etc maniġra gpm 23/41
mæneġe npf 25/33 mænegum dpm 18/107
mæniġ nsm 30/282 mæniġe npm 25/79
moneġe apf 7b/1 monegum dpm 36/19
moniġ apn 9b/41, 69 etc moniġe npm 5/16,
58, 9a/45, 9b/9 [etc]
maniġeo < meniġu
maniġfaldliċ adj *manifold, complex* nsf
6/26
maniġfeald adj *manifold, numerous,*
abundant, various, diverse, complex
maniġfealdum dpf 5/59 mæniġfealdan
dsn 28/17 mæniġfealde apf 25/108, 153
mæniġfealdre comp nsn 25/79
mæniġfealdum dpm 21a/40 meniġfælde
apf 16/75 meniġfældum dpf 16/73
meniġfeald nsf 16/81
maniġfealdlīċe adv *in various ways, in the*
plural meniġfealdlīċe 4/59 menifealdlīċe
16/56

mann m:B4b *person, man* ns 4/94, 22/119,
34/4 as 14/8, 36 man ns 4/12, 7c/5, 16/6,
22/115, 23/112 manna gp 7b/21, 16/55,
18/104 mannes gs 4/79, 7a/7, 52, 16/65
mannum dp 4/93, 7c/18, 8/22, 16/31,
23/96 mæn ds 7a/52 mænn np 25/107 ap
11/33 men ds 4/5, 7c/9, 9b/55, 15a/6, 16/7
is 7b/41 np 4/74, 15b/6, 16/11, 23/12 ap
8/67, 9b/45, 71, 31b/91 menn ds 4/91,
34/8, 9 np 5/40, 21a/77, 23/82 ap 23/93
mon ns 3b/9, 7a/5, 7b/12, 9a/56, 9b/15,
12/47, 19/329 as 7b/32, 9b/11, 17/58 monn
as 36/6 monna gp 9b/7, 12/10, 17/66,
26/90 monnes gs 9a/56, 26/116 monnum
dp 6/48, 7b/48, 49, 54, 9b/10 [etc]
manna m:B5a *man* mannan as 7a/10, 11, 20,
16/60, 22/103
mannslaga m:B5a *manslayer* mannslagan
np 25/134 manslēaga ns 7c/6
mannsylen f:B3b *selling of people*
mannsylena ap 25/111
mansliht m:B1g *manslaughter, murder*
manslihtum dp 8/53 manslyhtas ap
25/113
mānswora m:B5a *perjurer* mānsworan np
25/135
māra adj (comp of miċel; often =noun +g)
more, greater, larger nsn 5/41 māran asm
8/53, 9a/10 asf 7b/29, 9a/34, 22/65 asf
19/92 dsn 4/5 npn 9a/27 apf 4/58 māre
nsm 14/22 nsn 10/65, 22/136, 25/78,
30/313, 31b/69 nsf 22/137, 25/82 asm 1/23
asn 1/27, 28, 55, 16/5, 25/57, etc isn 7b/30
Māria pr n (f:B5c) *Mary* ns 2c/1, 22/13, 15
Mārian as 23/92 gs 7b/52 ds 11/12
marmstān m:B1a *marble* marmstāne ds
21a/56, 57
Mars pr n *Mars* ns 24/46
Martianus pr n *Martian* ns 9a/2
martirdōm m:B1a *martyrdom* martirdōm
as 21b/15
Mathēus pr n *Matthew* ns 22/121
māð < mīðan
maþelian 2 *speak, speak out, declare*
maþelode pt3s 17/10, 30/42, 309
māþm m:B1a *treasure, precious thing*
mādma gp 19/329 mādmas ap 19/318
mādme ds 31b/37 māðma gp 5/28, 19/340
māþmum dp 26/99

māþþumġyfa m:B5a *treasure-giver* ns 38/92

mǣ (me) < **iċ**

ġemæc adj *suitable, well suited* **ġemæcne**
asm 40/18

mǣċan < **mēċe**

mǣden n:B2c.ii *maiden, virgin* ns 21a/4, 12,
19, 73, 21b/5, 27/10 **mǣdene** ds 21a/3
mǣdenes gs 21a/73, 22/80 **mǣdenne** ds
27/84

mǣġ m:B1c *kinsman, kin, parent* ns 29/26,
30/5, 114, 224, 287, 31b/39, 38/109 **māga**
gp 34/13, 38/51 **mǣga** gp 10/40 **mǣgas** np
7b/18, 29/25 **mǣġe** ds 7b/42 **mǣgum** dp
29/27

mǣġ, mæġ- see **magan**

mæġdenman m:B4b *maid, virgin* as 7a/17

mæġen n:B2c *force, strength, power, army* ns
18/13 etc, 19/253, 261, 30/313 as 9a/52, 57
mæġenes gs 31b/43 **mæġna** ap 27/83
mæġnum dp 22/108

mæġenēacen adj *increased in strength,
mighty* nsn 19/292

mæġenrǣs m:B1a *mighty assault* as 31b/28

mæġenþrēat m:B1a *mighty host*
mæġenþrēatas ap 18/67

mæġenþrymm m:B1g *power, glory*
mæġenþrymma gp 18/95

mæġenwīsa m:B5a *leader* ns 18/108

mæġnum < **mæġen**

mǣġrǣs m:B1a *attack on kinsmen*
mǣġrǣsas ap 25/112

mǣġslaga m:B5a *slayer of a kinsman*
mǣġslagan np 25/134

mǣġþ f:B4ei *maiden, virgin, (unmarried)
woman* ns 19/78, 125 etc as 7a/44, 19/35,
43 etc gs 19/334 np 19/135

mǣġþ f:B3b *tribe, nation, race, generation,
kin* **mǣġða** gp 9a/26, 19/324 **mǣġþe** ds
25/86 **mǣġðum** dp 13/23

mǣġþbōt f:B3b *compensation payable to* (or
by) *an unmarried woman* ns 7a/40

mæġðhād m:B1a *virginity* ns 21a/8 as 21a/13

mæġþmann m:B4b *unmarried woman*
mæġþmon as 7a/50

mǣl n:B2b *time, occasion, meal* **mǣla** ap
30/212 gp 26/36 **mǣle** ds 21a/30

(ġe)mǣlan 1 *speak* **mǣlde** pt3s 30/26, 43,
210 **ġemǣlde** pt3s 30/230, 244

Mǣldūn pr n *Maldon* (Ess.) **Mǣldūne** ds
8/21

mæn < **mann**

(ġe)mǣnan 1 *complain of, lament, mention,
relate, mean* inf 31a/5 **mǣnde** pt3s 6/2
ġemǣnden sbj pt3p 31a/39 **mǣndon** pt3p
31a/87 **mǣneþ** pr3s 34/5

ġemǣne adj *common (to +d), shared (with
+d), in common, mutual, joint* nsm 25/40
nsn 14/14, 25/85, 34/13 npm 25/72 npn
25/88 **ġemānan** dpm 10/40 **ġemǣnum**
dsm 25/72

ġemǣne n:B2h *sharing, fellowship* ns 2a/24

mæneġe, mæniġ, mæniġe < **maniġ**

mæniġe < **meniġeo**

mæniġfeald, mæniġfeald- see **maniġfeald**

ġemǣnifyldan 1 *multiply, increase*
ġemǣnifylde pp npm 13/16

mænn < **mann**

mǣran 1 *celebrate, make known, glorify*
mǣre sbj pr3p 35d/16 **ġemǣred** pp 9b/2

mǣre adj *famous, renowned, great,
illustrious, splendid* nsm 35d/27 nsn 10/14,
15c/15 nsf 23/12, 82, 38/99 asf 21a/55 npm
16/24 **mǣran** gsf 21b/4 dsm 19/3, 23/69
dpm 24/55 **mǣres** gsm 21b/3 **mǣrost** sup
nsf 19/324 **mǣrostan** sup apm 24/41
mǣrra comp gpm 19/329

mǣre < **māra, mǣran**

ġemǣre n:B2h *boundary, precinct* **ġemǣro**
ap 28/37

Mǣringas pr n (mp:B1a) *the Mærings*
Mǣringa gp 36/19

mǣrþu f:B3h *fame, renown, glory, glorious
deed* **mǣrþa** ap 16/75, 21a/13, 22/87,
25/166 gp 26/84, 31b/39 **mǣrðe** as 19/343

Mæssanwyrð pr n *Masworth* (Bucks.)
Mæssanwyrðæ ds 11/14

mæsse f:B5c *mass, feast-day* **mæssan** as 1/43
ds 7b/52

mæsseprēost m:B5a *(mass-)priest,
clergyman* ns 16/12 **mæsseprēostas** np
9a/41 **mæsseprēoste** ds 5/64
mæsseprīoste ds 5/63

mæsserbana m:B5a *slayer of a priest*
mæsserbanan np 25/134

mæst m:B1a *mast* ns 33/24

mǣst adj (sup of **micel**) *most, greatest* nsm
25/59 **mǣstan** asm 27/55 asf 9b/5 dsn
22/142 **mǣste** asn 17/39 asf 30/175

mǣst adv *most, almost, mostly* 7b/12, 25/55,
56, 34/8

mǣst indecl noun +g *the most, the greatest, the greatest number* ns 17/27, 18/15, 54, etc as 18/65, 19/181, 26/84

ġemǣtan 1 impers +d *dream* **ġemǣtte** pt3s 23/2

mǣte adj *small, inferior, base* dsn 23/69, 124 **mǣtestan** sup npm 6/57, 58 **mǣtran** comp npm 6/54

ġemǣte adj *suitable for, fitted to* +d nsm 21a/72 nsf 21a/71

mæþlfriþ m:B1a *security at a public assembly* ns 7a/4

ġemǣtte < **ġemētan**

mǣð f:B3g *respect, honour, status, fitness* ns 7c/21, 30/195 **mǣðe** as 25/67 gs 7c/22 ds 7c/28, 25/25

Mǣðhild pr n (f:B3b) *Mæthhild* **Mǣðhilde** gs 36/14

mǣw m:B1a *seagull* as 26/22

mē < **iċ**

meagollīċe adv *earnestly* 18/82

meaht, meaht- see **magan**

meahte < **miht**

meahtiġra < **mihtiġ**

(ġe)mearcian 2 *mark, mark out, designate, appoint* **mearcað** pr3s 6/23 **ġemearcod** pp 17/26, 58 **mearcodon** pt3p 22/12

mearh m:B1d *horse, steed* as 30/188 **mēare** ds 30/239 **mearg** ns 38/92

mearn < **murnan**

mearu adj *tender, soft* **merwe** npn 3b/9

meċ < **iċ**

mēċe m:B1g *sword, blade* as 19/78, 30/167, 236 ds 19/104 is 18/49 **mǣċan** dp 10/40 **mēċum** dp 10/24

mecgan 1 *mingle, mix* inf 33/24

mēd f:B3b *reward* **mēde** as 19/343 ds 19/334

mēdder < **mōdor**

ġemēde adj *agreeable, suitable* **ġemēdan** dsn 12/15

medeme adj *middling, ordinary* **medemran** comp gsn 7c/25 **meduman** dsn 7a/12

ġemedemian 2 *humble* **ġemedemode** pt3s 22/115

mēder < **mōdor**

medmiċel adj *moderate, short* asn 9b/102 **medmiclum** ds 9b/5

medmung f:B3d *measure, amount* ns 7c/28

medo m:B4a *mead* as 32/39, 34/8 **meodo** ds 30/212

medobenċ f:B3g *mead-bench* **medobenċe** ds 31a/5

medoburh f:B4b *city with a mead-hall* **medobyriġ** ds 19/167

medodrinc m:B1a *mead-drinking* **medodrince** ds 26/22

medowēriġ adj *'mead-weary', stupefied with mead* **medowēriġe** apm 19/229 **medowērigum** dpm 19/245

mēdrenmǣg m:B1c *maternal kinsman* **mēdrenmǣga** gp 7b/31

medugāl adj *'mead-merry', drunk* nsm 19/26

mehte < **magan**

melkan III *milk* **melke** pr1s 1/35

meltan III *melt, dissolve, digest* inf 3a/9 **multon** pt3p 18/39, 31a/58

melu n:B2g *meal, flour* **melewes** gs 34/43

men < **mann**

ġemengan 1 *mix, mingle, blend* **ġemǣgnde** pt3s 27/28, 43 **ġemeng** imp s 3a/2, 4 **ġemenged** pp 14/39, 38/48

meniġeo f:B3h *multitude, company* ns 18/108 **mæniġe** ds 23/112 **menġeo** ns 5/28

meniġfeald- see **maniġfeald-**

menn < **mann**

mennen n:B2b *handmaiden, slave* as 7b/37

mennisc adj *human, natural* **menniscre** dsf 22/71

menniscnes f:B3e.ii *incarnation, humanness, human form* **menniscnesse** ds 9b/66 **menniscnisse** ds 16/26 **menniscnysse** as 22/173 ds 9a/2

meodo see **medo**

meodoheall f:B3b *mead-hall* ns 37/23 **meoduhealle** ds 38/27

meolc f:B4b.iii *milk* **meolcum** dp 3c/4

meotod, meotud, meotudes < **metod**

meotodsceaft f:B3g *decree of fate, death* as 31a/15

mēowle f:B5c *woman, maiden* ns 19/56, 35c/7 **mēowlan** as 19/261

Mcrantūn pr n *Merton* (Surr.) **Merantūne** ds 29/9

Merċna < **Myrċe**

Mercurius pr n *Mercury* ns 24/53 **Mercuries** gs 24/60

mere m:B1g *mere, lake, pool, sea* ns 18/13 as 10/54, 31a/68

mereðēað m:B1a *death in the sea* ns 18/67 **mereðēaða** gp 18/19

mereflōd m:B1a *sea-flood, ocean tide, ocean*
mereflōde ds 26/59, 33/24 **mereflōdes** gs
18/58

merehwearf m:B1a *sea-shore* **merehwearfe**
ds 18/71

merestrēam m:B1a *sea-current, flood* ns
18/23 **merestrēames** gs 18/43

meretorr m:B1a *tower of sea-water*
meretorras np 18/39

merewēriġ adj *sea-weary* or *sad* **merewērġes**
gs 26/12 (=noun)

merewīf n:B2b *woman of the water* as 31b/28

merwe < **mearu**

messedæġ m:B1c *mass-day, festival* as 8/68

ġemet n:B2a *measure, moderation, manner,
mood* ns 4/68 as 9b/41 **ġemete** ds 26/111

metan V *measure, compare* **metanne** infl inf
6/75, 76

(ġe)**mētan** 1 *meet, encounter, come upon, find*
ġemǣtte pt3s 8/34 **ġemēteð** pr3s 7b/44
ġemētte pt1s 7b/56 **mētton** pt3p 29/22
ġemētton pt3p 8/56, 14/35, 21a/55, 22/34

mete m:B1g.iii *food* ns 3b/1, 34/34 as 3b/6,
3c/5, 7b/19, 33 ds 21b/21 **metta** gp 1/59
mettas np 3a/8 **mettum** dp 1/62

metelīst f:B3g *lack of food* **metelīste** np 39/15

ġemetfæst adj *moderate, modest* nsm 9a/56

ġemetgung f:B3d *measure, proportion,
ordinance* **ġemetgunga** ap 6/8, 20
ġemetgunge as 6/5

ġemetlīce adv *moderately* 9b/79

metod m:B1a *creator, ordaining lord, God* ns
19/154, 30/175 **meotod** ns 26/108, 33/57
meotodes gs 9b/32, 33/65 **meotud** ns
26/116, 33/49 **meotudes** gs 26/103 **metod**
ns 18/33 **metode** ds 30/147 **metodes** gs
18/84, 19/261 **metudes** gs 38/2

metsung f:B3d *provisioning, provisions*
metsunge ds 8/62

ġemētte, ġemētton < **ġemētan**

mēðe adj *worn out, dejected* nsm 23/65 npm
23/69

meþelstede m:B1g *meeting-place, place of
assembly* ds 18/97, 30/199, 31a/20

miċel adj *big, great, much, intense* nsm 1/59,
2a/16, 16/16, 17/37, 22/19, etc nsn 1/30 nsf
5/28, 12/60, 22/20, etc asn 3a/5, 4/26,
9a/60, 25/141 (=noun *much*) **micclum**
dpm 4/22 (=noun *many*) **miċelan** dpf

25/15 **miċele** nsn 16/70 asf 22/65 **miċelne**
asm 22/38 **miċelre** gsf 9b/75 dsf 1/57,
22/32, 53, 27/44 **miclan** asm 16/69 dsm
3b/6, 22/98 dsn 23/65 dsf 23/102 **miclum**
dsm 22/32 dsn 22/121 dpn 29/6 **myccla**
nsm 8/10 **mycclan** dsm 8/22 **mycclum** dsn
8/33 dpf 19/10, 70 **myċel** nsm 23/130 nsn
8/13, 21a/36 nsf 8/40, 23/139 asn 8/35, 41,
53, 16/109, 21a/16 (=noun) **myċele** asf
8/42, 74 **myċelre** dsf 14/56, 21a/69 **mycle**
asf 8/73 dsn 23/34, 60, 123 **myclum** dsm
9a/29 dpm 9a/5 [etc]; see also **māra** comp,
mǣst sup, **micle** adv, **miclum** adv

micle adv *much, greatly* 6/44, 69, 17/85,
31b/88 **miccle** 30/50

miclum adv *much, greatly* 24/51, 29/13
micclum 21a/80 **mycclum** 21a/58

ġemiclian 2 *make great, strengthen* **ġemiclað**
pr3s 2a/12

mid adv *likewise, as well* 12/26

mid prep +d/a/i *with, together with, amid,
among, by, by means of, through* 1/40, 42,
2a/25, 2c/3, 3a/5, 14, 7a/25, 47, 7b/3, 7c/2,
8/13, 9a/38, 13/9, 15, 20, 14/5, 29, 16/22,
21a/3, 8, 22/12, etc **mit** 1/22, 12/55; in phrs
mid þām þā adv *with that, thereupon*
22/34 **mid þām þe** conj *when* 16/60, 61,
22/36 **mid þȳ** adv *when* 9b/86, 28/5, 7, 12,
etc **mid þī ðe** conj *when* 27/1 **mid þȳ ðe**
14/3, 27/17, 19, 48

midd adj *middle, mid* **middan** ds 19/68
(=noun) **midde** asf 15c/11 **middum** dsn
28/32 **midre** dsf 22/147, 23/2

middanġeard m:B1a *middle-earth, earth,
world* ns 38/62 as 9b/37, 105, 17/58, 18/95,
23/104, 28/52, 38/75 **middaneard** as
22/141, 24/67 **middanearde** ds 2c/1, 3
middanġearde ds 22/79, 81
middanġeardes gs 9b/62, 28/56

middæġ m:B1c *midday, sext* as 1/43
middæġe ds 22/162

Middelengle pr n (mp:B1h) *Middle Angles*
np 9a/20

middelfinger m:B1b *middle finger* as 7a/36

middeneaht f:B4b.i *midnight* as 9b/88

middes prep +g *halfway (to)* 34/1

middeweard adv *in the middle* 6/52

midlest adj (sup of **middel**) *middlemost*
midlestan dpm 6/48

midmest adj *midmost, the middle sort of*
midmestan npm 6/47, 53, 58 **midmestum**
dpm 6/57
Mierċna < **Myrċe**
miht f:B3g *might, power, strength, virtue,*
ability, authority, function ns 4/34, 21a/74,
22/137, 168 as 24/75 **meahte** as 9b/32,
26/108 **mihta** gp 22/74 **mihte** as 22/101,
118 ap 4/58, 21a/10 ds 23/102, 24/51
mihtum dp 2a/14, 18/104
mihte < **miht, magan**
mihtiġ adj *mighty, strong, powerful,*
important nsm 2a/18, 17/5, 19/92, 198,
23/151 asn 31b/28 **mihteġu** nsf 21b/11
mihtiga nsm 18/39 (=noun) **mihtiġe** npm
22/171, 24/29 **mihtiġes** gsm 17/66
mihtiġra comp nsm 18/58, 26/116
mihton < **magan**
milde adj *mild, merciful, kind* nsm 16/105,
30/175 **mildost** sup nsm 18/104
mildheort adj *merciful, compassionate*
mildheortan dsm 22/165
mildheortnes f:B3e *loving-kindness, mercy*
ns 15c/16 **mildheortnesse** ds 15b/13
milts f:B3b *mercy, favour* **miltsa** gp 18/84
miltse as 19/349, 38/2 gs 19/85, 92
ġemiltsian 2 *pity* **ġemiltsiġend** prp 27/62
mīn poss pron *my, mine* nsm 1/72, 21a/39,
23/78, 27/4 nsn 35b/1 nsf 23/130 asn
13/18, 33/8 npm 15b/9 **mīnan** dsn 12/57
mīnæ apm 11/32 dsf 11/21 **mīnæn** dsm
11/13 **mīnæs** gsm 11/22, 27 **mīne** asf
15b/8, 17/76, 28/1 npm 22/69, 26/9 npf
35b/4 apm 22/49 apn 1/33, 14/42 (twice),
15b/10 apf 22/48 **mīnes** gsm 1/21, 7b/6 gsn
13/22 **mīnnæ** dsm 11/32 **mīnne** asm 13/23,
15b/6, 17/29, 21a/40 **mīnnum** dpm 7b/9
mīnon dsm 1/37, 40 **mīnra** gpm 7b/3, 4,
17/77 gpf 17/31 **mīnre** dsf 22/56 **mīnum**
dsm 22/60, 23/30 dsn 17/88 dpm 22/35
mīræ dsf 11/26 **mīre** dsf 12/8 [etc]; see
also pers pron **iċ**
Minerua pr n *Minerua* ns 24/39
mīnn- < **mīn**
minster, minstres see **mynster**
minte f:B5c *mint* as 3b/8
misbēodan II +d *ill-treat, injure* inf 25/26
misdǣd f:B3g *misdeed* **misdǣda** np 16/65 ap
25/131 gp 7b/34, 35, 25/109, 138

misdǣdan dp 25/123 **misdǣde** ds 7b/32
misdǣdum dp 25/147
misfaran VI *go wrong, err* **misfōr** pt3s 24/1
mishȳran 1 +d *not to listen to, disobey*
mishȳrde pt3s 24/2
misliċ adj *various, diverse, manifold* **misleca**
apf 6/8 **misliċe** apm 6/31 apf 16/78
mislicum dpm 26/99 dpf 5/59 **mistliċe**
apm 24/28, 57 apn 25/114 apf 25/58, 115
mislīċe adv *variously, in various way,*
erringly 22/48 **mistlīċe** 24/66
mislimpan III impers +d *go wrong* **mislimpe**
sbj pr3s 25/106
missenlīċe adv *variously, in various places*
38/75
missēre n:B2h *half-year* **missēra** gp 31b/7
mist m:B1a *mist, cloud, dimness* **mistas** ap
17/54 **miste** ds 3a/1, 5, 13
mistliċe see **misliċ, mislīċe**
mit see **mid**
mīþan I *hide, conceal, keep to oneself* **māð**
pt3s 18/73 **mīþendne** prp asm 40/20
mōd n:B2b *heart, mind, spirit, will, courage,*
resolution ns 19/167, 22/53, 27/49, 30/313,
38/15, etc as 9a/51, 57, 9b/7, 92, 15c/9,
17/66, 18/34, 26/12, etc **mōde** ds 5/35,
6/11, 9a/49, 19/57, 23/122, 26/109, etc is
9b/86 **mōdes** gs 26/36, 50, etc **mōdum** dp
18/82
mōdceariġ adj *sad at heart, anxious of mind*
nsm 38/2
mōdcearu f:B3a *grief of heart, sorrow*
mōdceare gs 40/40 ds 40/51
mōdelīċe adv *boldly, heroically* 30/200
mōder see **mōdor**
mōdewǣġ m:B1a *violent wave* **mōdewǣġa**
gp 18/54
mōdgeþanc m:B1a *purpose of mind* as 9b/32
mōdġian 2 *exult, rage* **mōdgode** pt3s 18/13
mōdiġ adj *spirited, brave, proud, heroic,*
arrogant, impetuous nsm 18/23, 19/26,
23/41, 31b/17 **mōdġe** npm 38/62 **mōdi**
nsm 30/147 **mōdiga** nsm 19/52 (=noun)
mōdiġe npm 18/19, 30/80 **mōdiġes** gs
18/107 (=noun) **mōdiġre** gsf 19/334
mōdor f:B4c *mother* ns 7b/30 as 23/92,
25/77, 31b/47 **mēdder** ds 7b/46 **mēder**
ds 28/54 **mōder** ns 22/13, 15 **mōdor** ds
11/21

mōdorlīce adv *maternally, as a mother* 21a/29

mōdsefa m:B5a *mind, spirit, heart* ns 23/124, 26/59, 38/59 **mōdsefan** as 38/10, 19

mōdwlonc adj *proud of spirit, confident* nsm 26/39 nsf 35c/7

Moises pr n *Moses* ns 16/71 gs 16/20, 21, 30 **Moise** ds 16/87 **Moyses** ns 18/71 gs 9b/64, 16/11, 18/34

molde f:B5c *earth* ns 26/103 **moldan** as 23/12, 82 gs 19/343

moldern n:B2b *earth-house, tomb* as 23/65

mon see **man, mann**

mōna m:B5a *moon* ns 2b/2, 5, 28/62, 70, 32/7 **mōnan** as 2b/2, 24/13 gs 2b/1, 28/21, 27, 32, etc ds 2b/3 (twice), 4 (twice), 5 **mōne** ns 28/45

monade < **manian**

mōnað m:B4e *month* ap 21a/27 **mōnðas** ap 8/16 **mōnðe** ds 28/73 **mōnðes** gs 19/324

moncynn, moncynnes < **mancynn**

mondryhten m:B1b *lord, master* as 38/41

moneġ- see **maniġ**

ġemong see **ġemang**

(ġe)monian 2 *remind, urge, admonish* inf 9a/52 (*recover*; see note) **monað** pr3s 26/36, 53 **ġemoniað** pr3p 26/50

moniġ, moniġ- see **maniġ**

monn, monn- see **mann**

mōnð- see **mōnað**

monuc see **munuc**

morgen m:B1a *morning* ns 31a/15 as 1/33 **morgenne** ds 9b/42, 52, 29/19

morgencolla m:B5a *morning slaughter* **morgencollan** as 19/245

morgenġifu f:B3a *morning-gift* ns 12/17 **morgenġyfe** as 7a/49

morgentīd f:B3g *morning-tide, morning* as 10/14, 19/236

morðdǣd f:B3g *deadly deed, murder* **morðdǣda** ap 25/109

morðor n:B2c *violent crime, deadly evil, murder* as 40/20 **morðer** as 17/5 **morðra** gp 19/181 **morðres** gs 19/90

morþorbealo n:B2g *deadly slaughter* as 31a/17

morþorhete m:B1g *murderous hate* or *hostility* **morþorhetes** gs 31a/43

morþorwyrhta m:B5a *murderer* **morþorwyrhtan** np 25/135

mōst, mōst- see **mōtan**

ġemōt n:B2b *assembly, meeting, encounter* ns 30/301 as 30/199 **ġemōtes** gs 10/50, 35a/10, 35c/10

ġemōtad < **mōtian**

mōtan pt-pr *be able, may, be allowed to, must* **mōst** pr2s 30/30 **mōste** pt3s 18/64, 19/185, 30/272 sbj pt1s 17/32, 27/51, 28/61 sbj pt3s 12/8, 21a/24 **mōston** pt1p 17/22 sbj pt3p 30/83, 87, 263 **mōt** pr1s 23/142 pr3s 7b/41, 34/14 **mōtæ** sbj pr1s 11/29 **mōte** sbj pr1s 19/89, 23/127 sbj pr3s 7b/40, 12/60, 16/9, 19/118, 27/81, 30/95, 177 sbj pr1p 22/108 **mōten** sbj pr3p 26/119 **mōton** pr1p 17/67 pr3p 6/18, 16/29, 28/22, 30/180 [etc]

mōtian 2 *plead, dispute* **ġemōtad** pp 12/41

mōton < **mōtan**

moððe f:B5c *moth* ns 35e/1

Moyses see **Moises**

mucgwyrt f:B3g *mugwort* as 3c/4

muhton < **magan**

multon < **meltan**

ġemunan pt-pr *think about, be mindful of, remember, consider* (+g) **ġeman** pr1s 23/28 **ġemon** pr3s 38/34, 90, 40/51 **ġemunde** pt1s 5/26 (twice), 36, 43, 57 pt3s 31a/67 sbj pt3s 30/79 **ġemunu** pr1s 30/212

mund f:B3b *hand; security, trust, protection* ns 7a/41, 43 **munde** ds 7c/25, 25/25 **mundum** dp 19/229

mundbryċe m:B1g *breach of protection laws* ds 7c/15

mundbyrd f:B3g *protection, hope of protection* ns 7a/14 (see note), 22, 23/130 as 19/3

mundgripe m:B1g *hand-grip* ds 31b/43

Mundingwill pr n *Mongewell* (Oxon.) **Mundingwillæ** ds 11/22

munuc m:B1a *monk, nun* ns 16/2 as 7b/28 **monuc** ns 1/11 **muneca** gp 8/6 **munece** ds 1/63

munuchād m:B1a *monastic orders, monastic life* as 9b/56

munucliċ adj *monastic* **munucliċere** dsf 21a/86

munuclīf n:B2b *monastic life, monastery* **munuclīfum** dp 4/21 murcnung f:B3d *complaint, grief* murcnunge as 27/23

murnan III *care for, be anxious about, feel sorrow, mourn* inf 19/154, 30/259, 34/41 **mearn** pt3s 31b/46 **murnað** pr3p 18/90 **murnende** prp nsn 39/15 **murnon** pt3p 30/96

mūþ m:B1a *mouth* ns 33/37 as 34/43 **mūðe** ds 8/40, 9b/62, 13/10, 24/25, 34/12

mūða m:B5a *mouth* (of river) **mūðan** ds 8/54 **mūðon** ds 8/51

mūðhǣl f:B3g *wholesome speech, speech of salvation* as 18/107

myccl-, myċel, mycl- see miċel

mycclum see miclum

myclian 2 *increase* inf 9a/29

mylenscearp adj *sharp from grinding* **mylenscearpan** dpm 10/24

myltestre f:B5c *whore* **myltestran** np 25/136

ġemynd n/f:B2i *mind, memory, remembrance, commemoration* as 5/3, 38/51 **ġemynde** ds 9b/40, 22/4, 130

ġemynddæġ m:B1c *anniversary* as 7b/50

myndgian 2 *remind* **myndgiend** prp 31a/43

ġemyndgian 2 *remember* **ġemyndgade** pt3s 9b/59

ġemyndiġ adj (+g) *mindful (of), preoccupied, recollecting, intent on* nsm 18/103, 31b/39, 38/6 nsf 19/74

mynecen f:B3a *nun* **mynecena** ap 21a/28 **mynecene** ds 21a/26

ġemynegian 2 *remember, mention* **ġemynegodon** pt1p 9a/28

myningean 2 *remind* inf 22/3

mynster n:B2c *church, monastery, minster, cathedral, nunnery* as 8/56, 9b/56 **minster** as 21b/8 **minstres** gs 21b/11 **mynstær** ds 11/5, 8, 9, 11, 24 **mynstere** ds 7b/26 **mynstre** ds 5/68, 9b/1, 21a/27, 33, 58 **mynstres** gs 7c/25, 11/29 **mynstrum** dp 11/26

mynsterclǣnsung f:B3d *purification of a minster* **mynsterclǣnsunge** as 7c/16

mynsterhata m:B5a *persecutor of monasteries* **mynsterhatan** np 25/135

mynsterliċ adj *monastic* **mynsterlicre** dsf 21a/24

mynstermann m:B4b *monk* **mynstermannum** dp 4/17

myntan 1 *intend, think, suppose* **mynton** pt3p 19/253

Myrċe pr n (mp:B1h) *the Mercians* np 9a/20, 10/24 **Merċna** gp 7b/7 **Mierċna** gp 29/37 **Myrċon** dp 30/217

myrhð f:B3h *joy, mirth* **myrhða** ap 25/166

N

nā adv *no, not, not at all, never, by no means* 1/52, 4/26, 6/1, 7c/22, 12/24, 15a/7, 16/5, 17/75, 22/47, 78, 24/61, 27/33, 75, etc **nō** 19/117, 26/66, 31b/11, 17

nabbað < habban

naca m:B5a *boat, ship* **nacan** gs 26/7

nacod adj *naked, bare* nsm 18/29 **nacedan** asf 16/40

nafa m:B5a *nave* (of wheel) ns 6/55

nafað < habban

nafola m:B5a *navel* **nafolan** ds 3b/3

nafu f:B3a *nave* (of wheel) ns 6/44, 46, 63, etc **nafe** ds 6/48, 51, 53, 54, 55

nāge (ne āge), nāh (ne āh) < āgan

nāht indef pron (+g) *nothing* ns 4/32 as 9b/26, 14/22 **nāuhte** ds 6/60 **nōht** as 9b/13, 25

nāhte (ne āhte) < āgan

nalas, nales, nalles see nealles

(ġe)nam < (ġe)niman

nama m:B5a *name, noun* ns 4/33, 14/36, 22/140, 141, 30/267, 32, 35d/27 **naman** as 5/24, 15b/14, 17/6, 27/12, 19 ds 4/24, 5/67, 15c/11, 22/60, 23/113, 24/45, 58 np 6/13, 24/75 ap 4/38 **namena** gp 4/41 **namon** ds 27/13 **noma** ns 36/37 **noman** ds 7b/55, 9a/55, 9b/24 **nomum** dp 28/4

(ġe)nāman, ġenāmen < (ġe)niman

(ġe)namian 2 *name, call, invoke* **namiað** pr3p 24/60 **ġenamod** pp 24/38 **nāmon** pt3p 24/12

(ġe)namon < (ġe)niman

nān (ne ān) adj *none, not one, not any, no* nsm 1/63, 4/19, 32, 94, 5/67, 16/100, 22/127, 24/23 nsn 4/39, 90, 14/13 asn 14/3, 15c/11 apn 24/22 **nānan** dsn 12/34 **nāne** asf 16/103, 22/43, 134 **nānes** gsn 15c/8, 28/7 **nānne** asm 3b/6 **nānre** dsf 5/54 **nānum** dsm 4/91, 6/60 dsn 14/5 **nǣnne** asm 5/38, 16/100, 22/94

nān pron *none, not one, nothing* nsm 19/257
asn 12/28 **nānne** asm 19/68, 233 **nānum**
dpm 10/25

nānwiht adv *not at all, not* **nānwuht**
6/35

nānwiht indef pron (+g) *nothing* ns 6/6
nāwihte ds 34/30

(ġe)**nāp** < (ġe)**nīpan**

nāt < **witan**

nāteshwōn adv *not at all, in no way* 13/20

nāthwǣr adv *somewhere (or other)* 35c/5

nāthwylċ adj *some, some sort of*
nāthwylċum dsm 31b/22

nāþor adj/pron *neither* nsn 4/65 nsf 4/68
nāðres gsn 4/88

nāþor conj *neither* **nāþor ne ... ne**
neither ... nor 4/12, 25/53

nāuhte < **nāht**

næ see **ne**

næbbe (ne hæbbe), **næbben** (ne hæbben) <
habban

næfde (ne hæfde) < **habban**

næfre adv *never* 9b/13, 16, 30, 12/34, 15b/11,
27/66, 35a/10, 38/112, etc **nēfre** 32/39

næfþ (ne hæfþ) < **habban**

næġl m:B1b.i *nail* ns 7a/33 **næġlum** dp 23/46
næiġlum dp 22/49

næġledcnearr m:B1a *nailed ship*
næġledcnearrum dp 10/46

nænig adj *no* nsn 31b/23 nsm 28/37, 49,
29/26 asn 9b/16 **nænigne** asm 9b/93

nænig pron *none, no one* nsm 9a/36, 9b/10,
19/51, 20a/1, 26/25, 29/17 **næni** nsm
20b/1, 33/63 **nængum** dsm 35c/2
nænigum dsm 23/47

nænne < **nān**

nære (ne wǣre), **næron** (ne wǣron) <
bēon-wesan

nærolīċe adv *narrowly, concisely* 16/85

næs adv *not, not at all* 1/5, 63

næs m:B1a *earth, ground* as 19/113

næs (ne wæs) < **bēon-wesan**

ne neg part before vb *not* 1/7, 51, 2a/4, 4/18,
5/17, 7a/49, 7b/3, 7c/22, 9a/26, 9b/25,
13/21, 15a/1, 16/4, etc **næ** 11/32

ne conj *nor* 1/68, 2a/4, 5/23, 9b/11, 13, 13/21,
15a/1, 2, 18/10, etc **ne ... ne** *neither ... nor*
4/13, 25/53

nēde < **nīed**

nēah adj *near, close (to* +d) nsf 9b/85, 90, 98
nsn 15a/4; see also **nēahst**

nēah adv *near, nearly* 19/287, 28/50, 34/2;
see also **nēar**

nēahbūend m:B4d *neighbour*
nēahbūendum dp 35c/2

ġe**neahhe** adv *in abundance, very often,
constantly* 19/26, 35d/8, 36/25, 32, 38/56
ġe**nehe** 30/269

nēahst sup adj (< **nēah**) *nearest, last*
nēhstan dsm 19/73; in adv phr **æt nēhstan**
at length, in the end, finally, next 22/45 **æt
nȳhstan** 24/8, 14, 28, 25/148

nēahst sup adv (< **nēah**) +d *nearest, next to*
6/46 **nēaxst** 6/63 **nēhste** 6/46 **nēxt** 6/44

neaht, neahte < **niht**

neahtnestigum adv *having fasted for a night*
3b/4

nēalēċan 1 *draw near, approach* inf 9b/18
nēalǣcte pt3s 9b/77 **nēalǣcð** pr3s 25/4
nēalǣhte pt3s 19/34, 261 **nēalehtan** pt3p
28/5

nealles adv *not, not at all, in no way* **nalas**
31b/2, 38 **nalæs** 38/33 **nales** 9b/10, 35d/17,
38/32 **nalles** 17/9

nēar comp adv (< **nēah**) +d *nearer* 6/54, 64,
12/23, 19/53, 34/2

nearo adj *narrow, oppressive* nsf 26/7

nearon (ne + earon) < **bēon-wesan**

nearwian 2 *force in, confine* **nearwað** pr3s
35c/10

nēat n:B2b *beast, ox, cattle* **nēata** gp 9b/21

ġe**nēat** m:B1a *companion, follower* ns 30/310

nēawest f:B3b *neighbourhood* **nēaweste** ds
9b/80

nēaxst see **nēahst**

nebb n:B2b.i *nose, face* as 12/48

Necittius pr n *Necitius* ns 21b/16

nēde < **nīed**

ġe**nēde** < ġe**nīedan**

nēdfær n:B2a *compulsory* or *inevitable
journey* **nēdfere** ds 20b/1 **nēidfaerae** ds
20a/1

nēdhǣmed n:B2c *rape* **nēdhǣmde** ds 7b/37,
39

nefne see **nemne**

nēfre see **næfre**

nēhċeaster f:B3c *neighbouring town*
nēhċeastra gp 9a/40

ġenehe see ġeneahhe

nēhstan, nēhste < nēahst

nellan (ne willan) anom *not to wish* inf 1/8
nele pr3s 4/12, 27, 16/109 nellað pr3p
16/29, 25/132 nelle pr1s 13/20, 16/103,
30/24 sbj pr3s 33/44 nelt pr2s 2a/15
noldan pt3p 9a/31 nolde pt3s 13/2, 14/39,
22/42, 29/17, 30/9, 31b/32, etc noldon
pt1p 5/35, 38 pt3p 22/165, 29/25, 27, 30/81
[etc]

Nembroð pr n *Nimrod* ns 24/5

(ġe)nemnan 1 *call, name, appoint* inf 12/12,
19/81 nemnað pr1p 6/45 nemneð pr3s
21b/25 nemnde pt3s 9b/24 nemned
pp 9a/21, 26 ġenemned pp 5/60, 12/10,
14/8, 19, 37

nemne conj *unless, except, if not* 31b/61,
40/22 nefne 26/46

nēod, nēode see nīed

nēodðearf see nӯdþearf

neom (ne eom) < bēon-wesan

ġenēop < ġenēpan

nēosan II +g *seek out, go to* inf 18/29,
19/63

nēosian 2 +g *seek out, go to* inf 31a/63

nēotan II +g *use, make use of* inf 30/308

neoþan adv *below* 35c/5 neoðone 17/38

neowel adj *steep, deep* neowelne asm 19/113

nep adj *enfeebled, powerless* nsn 18/24

ġenēpan VII +d *engulf, overwhelm* ġenēop
pt3s 18/30

nerġend m:B4d *saviour* as 19/81 nerġende
ds 19/45 nerġendes gs 19/73

nerġendliċ adj *saving* nsm 2a/16

(ġe)nerian 2 *save, rescue* ġenerede pt3s
10/36, 29/33 nerġende prp nsm 33/63
ġenerode pt3s 22/152

ġenesan V *survive, bear* ġenǣson pt3p
32/47

nest n:B2b *food, provisions* as 19/128

nestiġ adj *fasting* 3c/5

neten see nyten

nēþan 1 *venture, dare* nēðde pt3s 19/277
nēþeð pr3s 35c/5

nēxt see nēahst

nīdde, ġenīed < (ġe)nӯdan

nīedbeðearf adj *necessary, essential*
nīedbeðearfosta sup npf 5/49

nīġean < nīwe

nigon num *nine* 3c/2, 3, 4/49, 9a/1

nigonġylde adv *ninefold* 7a/9

nigoþa num adj *ninth* nigoþan asf 14/56
nygoðan asf 14/56

niht f:B4b.i *night* ns 19/34 as 1/39, 8/32,
21b/6, 21, 27/74 ap 21b/20 neaht as 3c/5
neahte ds 9b/21, 82 nihta gp 2b/1, 2 etc,
3a/13, 7b/17 nihte ds 8/31, 19/64, 22/147,
23/2, etc nihtes gs 15a/3, 19/45 (=adv *at
night*) nihtum dp 35a/14

nihthelm m:B1a *cover of night* as 38/96

nihtsangc m:B1a *Compline* as 1/46

nihtscūa m:B5a *shadow of night* ns 26/31,
38/104

ġenihtsumnis f:B3e.ii *abundance, plenty* ns
28/10

nihtwaco f:B3a *night-watch* ns 26/7

(ġe)niman IV *take, take away, grip, seize,
bring, add* inf 8/59 nam pt3s 16/17, 27/38
ġenam pt3s 13/7, 14/22, 60, 19/77, 98,
27/41 nāman pt3p 21a/58 ġenāman pt3p
23/30 ġenāmen pt3p 8/73 nāmon pt3p
14/32, 22/38, 41 ġenāmon pt3p 23/60
ġenim imp s 3a/1, 13, 3b/1, 3 etc, 3c/1, 3
nimað pr3p 26/48 imp p 27/64 nime pr1s
21b/22 ġenimeþ pr3s 7a/43, 50 nimst pr2s
2a/15 (*accept*) ġenom pt3s 12/50, 28/1
nōman pt1p 28/31 ġenumen pp 4/40, 53,
87, 8/40

nīobedd n:B2b.i *corpse-bed, hell* as 17/6

nīotan II +g *enjoy, use* inf 17/64

(ġe)nīpan I *grow dark, darken* nāp pt3s
26/31 ġenāp pt3s 38/96 nīþeð pr3s 38/104

nis (ne is) < bēon-wesan

nīþ m:B1a *evil, malice, violence, strife, attack*
as 26/75, 32/9 nīða gp 19/34, 32/21 nīðe ds
19/53 nīðum dp 19/287

niðer see nyþer

Nīðhād pr n *Nithhad* ns 36/5

nīðheard adj *brave in battle, daring* nsm
19/277

nīðhycgend m:B4d *evil schemer, one intent
on battle* nīðhycgende ap or np 19/233

nīðsele m:B1g *hostile hall* ds 31b/22

niþþas mp:B1a *men* niþum dp 35d/27

ġeniwad < nīwian

Nīwanhām pr n *Newnham Murren* (Oxon.)
ds 11/17

nīwe adj *new* nsf 16/26 nsm 22/159 npf
21a/65 nēowran comp asm 3c/1 nīgean
dsn 11/9 nīwan asf 16/95, 96, 99 dsf 16/9,
16, 34, 37 nīwes gsn 40/4 (=adv *recently*)
nīwum dpf 21a/67

ġenīwian 2 *renew, restore* ġenīwad
pp 23/148, 38/50, 55 ġenīwod pp 19/98

nō see nā

Nōe pr n *Noah* ns 13/1, 10, 12, 16 ds 13/7, 9,
14, 18 Nōes gs 24/4, 6

ġenōg adj *enough, plenty of* ġenōge npm
23/33

ġenōh adv *enough, abundantly* 25/96, 28/29

nōht adv *not at all, not* 5/16

nōhwæðer conj *neither* 5/23 nōwðer
12/39

nold- see nellan

ġenom, nōman < (ġe)niman

noma, noman < nama

nōn n:B2b as *the ninth hour* (3 p.m.), *nones*
as 1/44, 22/162

norð adv *north* 10/38

norþan adv *from the north* 9a/8, 26/31,
38/104

norþerne adj *northern, Norse* norþerna nsm
10/18

Norðhymbre pr n (mp:B1h) *the
Northumbrians, Northumbria*
Norðhembra gp 9a/21 Norðhymbran dp
8/41 Norðhymbron dp 30/266

norþmann m:B4b *norseman* norðmanna gp
10/33 norþmen np 10/53

Norðwālas pr n (mp:B1a) *the Welsh, Wales*
Norðwālum dp 8/52

nosþirl n:B2c.i *nostril* nosþirlu ap 16/97

notu f:B3a *employment, use, advantage* note
ds 5/54, 24/20

nōwiht see nānwuht

nōwðer see nōhwæðer

nū adv *now, just now, presently* 1/25, 45,
4/17, 19, 5/12, 18, 9b/31, 13/18, 14/48,
16/6, 17/52, 21a/2, 17, 23/78, 27/11, 20,
30/93, etc

nū conj *now that, in as much as, since* 9b/90,
18/85, 27/23, 30/57, 232, 250

ġenumen < (ġe)niman

nunne f:B5c *nun* nunna gp 11/10 nunnan as
7b/26

nȳd f:B3g *need, constraint, necessity,
purpose* ns 19/277 nēde as/ap 36/5 ds

7a/50, 10/33 nēod ns 25/144 nēode ds
21a/53, 27/13

(ġe)nȳdan 1 *compel, force, urge* ġenēde sbj
pr3s 7b/39 nīdde pt3s 21b/16 ġenīed
pp 7b/13 nȳddon pt3p 14/37

nȳdboda m:B5a *herald of disaster* ns 18/29

nȳddon < nȳdan

nȳde adv *of necessity, necessarily* 25/5, 17

nȳdgyld n:B2b *forced tribute, exaction, tax*
np 25/88

nȳdmāge f:B5c *near kinswoman* nȳdmāgan
as 25/95

nȳdþearf f:B3b *need, necessity* ns 25/19,
34/36 nēodðearf ns 12/60

nygoðan < nigoþa

nȳhstan < nēahst

nymþe conj *unless, except* 19/52, 35c/3
nemþe 38/13

nyrwan 1 *narrow, restrict* ġenyrwde pp npn
25/38

nys (ne ys) < bēon-wesan

nyste (ne wyste) < witan

nyt see nytt

nyte (ne wite) < witan

nȳten n:B2c.ii *beast, animal, ox, cattle* as
28/44 nēten ns 9b/60 nȳtene ds 16/82
nȳtenum dp 13/19, 22

nytt adj *useful, helpful* nytne asm 4/6 nyttra
comp nsm 34/2

nytt f:B3b *use, benefit, service* nyt ns 35c/2
nytte ds 35d/27

nyþer adv *down, downwards* 14/48, 51 niðer
17/6

ġenyðerian 2 *bring low, abase* ġenyðerad
pp 19/113

nyþeweard adj *low, lowermost part of* as
14/64 (=noun)

O

Odda pr n (m:B5a) *Odda* Oddan gs 12/64,
30/186, 238

odþæt see oþ

of adv *off* 3a/15

of prep +d *from, out of, away from; about,
concerning* 2b/2, 4, 2c/1, 4/1, 37, 5/15, 61,
6/19, 7b/26, 8/34, 37, 9a/16, 13/9, 14, 17,
17/28, 18/47, 21a/46, 51, 22/3, 33/30, etc

ofāslēan VI *cut off, strike off* ofāslǣhð pr3s
7a/33, 35, 36, 37, 38

ofǽr see **ofer**
ofǽrnan III *overtake, ride down* inf 34/41
ofdrǽdan VII *fear, be afraid* **ofdrǽdde**
 pp npm 22/93 npf 22/25
ofdūne adv *down* 19/290
ofen m:B1b *oven, furnace* **ofon** as 21b/19
ofer adv *over, after* 7b/51
ofer prep +a *over, across, beyond, along,*
 above, upon, through(out), after, against,
 towards 1/34, 7b/51, 9a/47, 9b/88, 10/15,
 19, 12/48, 13/3, 4, 6, 16, 14/25, 15b/9,
 15c/10, 16/53, 17/40, 18/22, 95, 23/12,
 26/39, 30/88, 91, 35b/3, etc **ofǽr** 11/24
ōfer m:B1b *edge, river-bank* **ōfre** ds 30/28
ofercuman IV *overcome* inf 19/235
 ofercōman pt3p 10/72 **ofercumen**
 pp 36/26
oferdrencan 1 *drench, make drunk*
 oferdrencte pp npm 19/31
oferēaca m:B5a *surplus, remainder*
 ofǽrēacan as 11/30
oferfaran VI *pass over, overcome* **oferfarǽn**
 pp 22/84
oferfǽreld n:B2b/m:B1a *journey across,*
 passage ns 22/106
oferfeðre adj *overloaded* nsn 34/37
oferfyllu f:B3h *gluttony* **oferfylla** ap 25/153
ofergān anom *go over, pass away* **oferēode**
 pt3s 36/7, 13, 17, 20, 27, 42
ofergangan VII *overcome* **ofergangað** pr2p
 18/116
oferhoga m:B5a *despiser* **oferhogan** np
 25/118
oferhogian 2 *despise* **oferhogað** pr3s 24/73
oferhrops f:B3b *voracity* **oferhropse** ds 1/63
oferlīce adv *excessively* 25/147
ofermētto f:B3h *pride, presumption* as 17/14
ofermōd adj *proud, overbearing* **ofermōda**
 nsm 17/1
ofermōd n:B2b *over-exuberance, excess of*
 courage **ofermōde** ds 30/89
oferniman IV *seize, carry off* **ofernumen**
 pp 22/53
oferswȳðan 1 *overpower, conquer*
 oferswīðde pt3s 7b/50 **oferswȳðed**
 pp 22/140
oferweorpan III *throw over, throw down*
 oferwearp pt3s 31b/52
oferwinnan III *defeat, conquer* **oferwunnen**
 pp 19/319

Offa pr n *Offa* ns 29/39, 41, 44, 30/198, 230,
 286, 288 **Offan** gs 7b/7, 30/5
offerian 2 *carry off* **offerede** pt3s 31b/92
Offing adj *son of Offa* nsm 29/44
offrian 2 *offer, sacrifice* inf 16/76 ġe**offrod**
 pp 16/84 **offrode** pt3s 16/80 **offrodon** pt3p
 24/14, 49, 56
offringdisc m:B1a *offering-dish, paten* as
 11/10
offrung f:B3d *offering, sacrifice* **offrunge** ds
 16/82
ofġiefan V *abandon, give up* **ofġēafon** pt3p
 38/61
oflongian 2 *seize with longing* **oflongad**
 pp 40/29
ofon see **ofen**
ofost f:B3c *haste, speed* **ofste** ds 25/3 **ofstum**
 dp 19/10, 35, 70
ofostlīce adv *speedily* 19/150, 169
ofscēotan II *shoot, pierce to death* **ofscēat**
 pt3s 30/77
ofsettan 1 *beset, oppress* **ofsette** pp npm
 22/94
ofsittan V *sit on* **ofsæt** pt3s 31b/54
ofslaġen, ofslæġen < **ofslēan**
ofslēan VI *strike off, kill, slay, destroy* inf
 8/67 **ofslagen** pp 8/12 **ofslæġen** pp 8/21,
 29/20, 22 **ofslæġene** pp npm 29/30
 ofslæhþ pr3s 7a/20 **ofslēa** sbj pr3s 7a/10,
 7b/30 **ofslēahþ** pr3s 7a/11 **ofsleġen** pp 22/6
 ofslēhð pr3s 7a/12 **ofslōg** pt3s 29/2, 37
 ofslōgon pt3p 8/35, 29/32 **ofslōh** pt3s 8/34,
 63
ofslōg, ofslōgon, ofslōh < **ofslēan**
ofspring m:B1a *offspring, descendant(s)*
 ofspringe ds 13/19
ofstang < **ofstingan**
ofste, ofstum < **ofost**
ofstingan III *stab to death* **ofstang** 29/4
ofstlīce adv *quickly, speedily* 30/143
ofstondan VI *remain standing, endure*
 ofstonden pp 37/11
oft adv *often, frequently* 5/3, 9a/8, 9b/7, 10/8,
 16/28, 22/2, 26/3, 31b/35, 34/7, 37, 35a/3,
 37/9, 38/1, etc **oftor** comp 3c/7, 23/128,
 25/42, 31b/88 **oftost** sup adv *most often*
 5/20, 25/120
oftēon II *withhold, hold back* **oftēah** pt3s
 31b/29
oftor, oftost < **oft**

ōga m:B5a *fear, terror* ns 22/96
Olimphiad pr n *Olimphias* Olimphiade ds
    28/54
oll n:B2b *contempt, scorn* olle ds 37/126
on adv *on, in, into, within, down* 18/45,
    22/27, 52, 26/91
on prep +d/a/i *on, onto, in, into, to, at,*
    against, during, among, amid, for, as, with,
    according to 1/6, 12, 2a/6, 2c/1, 3a/2, 6,
    3b/2, 8, 3c/2, 4, 6/13, 7a/1, 8/10, 9a/4, 13/1,
    9, 10, 23, 15a/1, 15b/8, 22/2, 23/138,
    33/16, etc
onǣlan 1 *kindle, enflame* onǣled pp 27/74
onbærnan 1 *fire, inspire* onbærnde pt3s 9b/8
    onbærned pp 9b/75
onbelǣdan 1 *inflict upon* onbelǣden inf 1/8
onbryrdan 2 *excite, inspire* onbryrde pt3s
    19/95
onbūgan II +d *bow to, submit to* onbugon
    pt3p 18/53
onbyriġan 1 +g *taste* inf 23/114 onbyrġeð
    pr3s 34/29 onbyriġde pt3s 14/39
oncnāwan VII *recognise, know,*
    acknowledge, understand inf 30/9
    oncnāwe pr1s 27/35 oncnēow pt3s 22/159,
    160, 161, 163 oncnēowon pt3p 22/157,
    158, 162
oncweðan V +d *answer, respond* oncwæð
    pt3s 26/23, 30/245 oncwyð pt3s 32/7
onċyrran 1 *turn away, change* onċyrde
    pp 18/6 onċyrreð pr3s 26/103
ond see and
ondlong adj *entire, whole* ondlongne asm
    10/21
ondrǣdan VII *be afraid, dread* (often rflx)
    ondrǣde pr1s 15c/11, 16/8 pr3s 34/22
    ondrǣdeþ pr3s 26/106 ondrēd pt1s 28/67
    ondrēdon pt3p 14/70, 28/40
ondswar- see andswar-
ondweard adj *present* ondweardum dpm
    9b/45
ġeondwyrdon < (ġe)andwyrdan
ondwyrdum < andwyrde
oneardian 2 *inhabit* oneardað pr3s 9a/18
onemn prep +a/d *alongside* 30/184
ōnettan 1 *hurry onward, be busy* pt3p 19/139
    ōnette pt3s 19/162 ōnetteð pr3s 26/49
onfand < onfindan
onfēng, onfēng- < onfōn

onfeohtan III *attack, fight with* onfeohteð
    pr3s 7b/43
onfindan III *find out, discover, realise,*
    perceive, experience inf 21b/10 onfand
    pt3s 31b/31 onfond pt3s 18/56, 36/4
    onfunde pt3s 31b/6 sbj pt3s 30/5 onfunden
    sbj pt3p 29/10 onfundon pt3p 29/14
onfōn VII (+d/a) *receive, accept, take,*
    undertake, undergo, sponsor onfēng pt3s
    7b/8, 9a/2, 6, 9b/12, 28, 43, 57, 21b/7, 9,
    27/71, 31b/3 onfēngc pt3s 27/84 onfēnge
    sbj pt3s 9b/56 onfēngon pt3 9a/57, 59
    onfongen pp 12/6 onfongne pp asf 9b/51
    onfōð pr3p 6/3
onfond < onfindan
onfong-, onfōð see onfōn
onfund- see onfindan
ongan < onginnan
onġēan adv *again, back* 22/14, 27, 27/3,
    30/49, 137, 156
onġēan prep +d/a *against, opposite, facing,*
    contrary to, towards, to meet 13/3, 7, 12,
    18/9, 19/165, 27/4, 30/100 onġēn 14/5, 14
onġeat, onġēaton < onġietan
Ongelþēode < Angelþēod
onġemang prep +d *among, amidst* 5/59
onġēn see onġēan
onġēton < onġietan
onġietan V *know, perceive, understand,*
    recognise, witness, experience inf 38/73
    onġeat pt3s 29/11, 31b/21, 27 onġēaton
    pt3p 19/168, 238 onġēton pt3p 18/7, 106
    onġieten pp 36/10 onġiotan inf 5/30
    onġitan inf 6/37, 68 onġite pr1s 27/33
    onġitenu pp asf 21b/13 onġytan inf 23/18,
    31b/5
onġildan III *pay, atone for* inf 33/56
onġinnan III *begin, precede, attempt,*
    undertake ongan pt1s 5/58 pt3s 6/1, 8/77,
    9a/28, 9b/54, 19/80, 281, 23/19, 27/28, 42
    onġin imp s 2a/9 onġinnað imp p 17/71
    onġinnen sbj pr3p 23/116 onġinst pr2s
    2a/2 onġinð pr3s 16/44 ongon pt1s 28/28
    pt3s 9b/29, 12/3 ongunnon pt3p 9a/51,
    9b/9, 19/42, 270, 23/65, 67, 27/29
    onġynnað pr3p 4/47, 51 onġynð pr3s 4/48
onġitan see onġietan
Ongolcynn- see Angelcynn
ongon, ongunnon, onġyn- see onġinnan

onġyrwan 1 *unclothe, strip* onġyrede pt3s
23/39

onġytan see onġietan

onhangian 2 *hang* onhongedon pt3p 28/16

onhǣtan 1 *heat, inflame* onhǣted pp
19/87

onherġian 2 *harass* onherġedon pt3p 9a/8

onhongedon < onhangian

onhrēran 1 *stir up, disturb, move* inf 26/96
onhrēred pp 18/37

onhwerfan III *turn, change, reverse*
onhworfen pp 40/23

onhyldan 1 *bend, incline* onhylde pt3s
9b/102

oninnan prep +d/a *within, amidst* 17/16,
19/312

onlāg < onlēon

onleġen f:B3b *application, poultice* onleġena
ap 3b/11

onlēon I +d *grant, bestow, allot* onlāg pt3s
17/21 onlēah pt3s 19/124 onlȳhð pr3s
18/84

onlīcnesse < ānlīcnis

onlīhtan 1 *illuminate, give light to* onlīht imp
s 15b/10

onlūcan II *unlock* inf 18/77

onlūtan II *bend, bow* inf 5/35

onlȳhð < onlēon

onlȳsan 1 *free, redeem* onlȳsde pt3s 23/147

onmēdla m:B5a *pomp, magnificence*
onmēdlan np 26/81

onmiddan prep +d *in the middle of* 6/53

onmōd, onmōde see ānmōd

onmunan pt-pr +g *pay attention to, care for*
onmunden sbj pt3p 29/29

onsæġdnis f:B3e.ii *sacrifice, offering*
onsæġdnisse as 28/42

onsǣġe adj (+d) *attacking, assailing* nsn
25/43

onscyte m:B1g *attack, calumny* onscytan dp
25/56, 130

onsecgan 3 *offer, sacrifice* inf 28/42

onsendan 1 *send forth, yield up* inf 5/66
onsende pt3s 21b/24 onsended pp 23/49
onsendeð pr3s 38/104

onsittan V *assail, oppress* onsit pr3s 25/81
onsittað pr3p 25/15

onslēpan 1 *fall asleep* onslēpte pt3s 9b/22,
102

onspecend m:B4d *accuser, claimant*
onspecendan dp 12/4

onstal m:B1a *supply* as 5/18

onstellan 1 *establish, institute, set the
example of* onstealde pt3s 9b/34
onstealdon pt3p 8/43

onstyrian 1 *stir up, move, rouse* onstyred
pp 15b/12, 28/40

onsȳn see ansīn

ontȳnan 1 *open* ontȳne imp s 3a/15

onufan prep +a *above, upon, on top of* 12/45,
19/252

onwacnian 2 *wake up, arise* onwacniġeað
imp p 32/10

onwǣcan 1 *weaken, soften* onwǣcen sbj
pr1p 17/66

onwæcnan VI *awake* onwæcneð pr3s 38/45
onwōce sbj pt3s 19/77

onweald m:B2b *control, authority, power*
(+g *over*) as 5/7, 28/52 onwald as 5/6

onwendan 1 *change, overturn, upset, reverse,
pervert, transgress against* inf 12/40 sbj
pr1p 17/63 onwende pt3s 37/24 onwended
pp 17/94 onwendeð pr3s 38/107
onwendon sbj pr3p 17/68

onwrēon I *disclose, reveal* onwrēoh imp s
23/97

onwrīðan I *unwrap* inf 19/173

open adj *open, clear* nsn 18/92, 22/155 opene
npm 23/47 openum dpn 28/50

(ġe)openian 2 *open* ġeopenod pp 21a/47
ġeopenode pt3s 13/12, 21a/61, 63
pp npf 14/65

openlīċe adv *openly, plainly* 6/32, 9a/33

ōr n:B2b *beginning, origin* as 9b/34

orc m:B1a *pitcher, cup* orcas np 19/18

ord m:B1a *point, spear, vanguard* ns 30/60,
69, 146, 157, 253 as 30/47, 110, 31b/58
orde ds 30/124, 226, 273, 32/12

Ordlāf pr n *Ordlaf* ns 12/52, 32/16 Ordlāfes
gs 12/64

Ordulf pr n *Ordwulf* Ordulfes gs 8/56

ōretmæcg m:B1c *warrior* ōretmæcgas ap
19/232

ōretta m:B5a *warrior* ns 31b/41

orf n:B2b *cattle, livestock* as 16/80

orfcwealm m:B1a *cattle-plague* ns 25/46

orfeorme adj +d *destitute of, alienated from*
npm 19/271

ormǣtlīċe adv *excessively, extremely* 22/20
orsāwle adj *lifeless* nsm 19/108
orsorg adj *without anxiety, secure*
  orsorgestǣ sup npm 6/70 orsorgran comp
  npm 6/65
orsorglīċe adv *securely* orsorglīcor comp
  6/44
ortrūwian 2 *despair, doubt* inf 22/127
orðanc adj *cunning, skilful* nsn 33/2
orðian 2 *breathe* orðiġe pr1s 4/89
orþonc m:B1a *ingenuity, skill* ?ns 37/16
orwena adj *without hope of, despairing* nsm
  31b/74
orwīġe adj *not liable to a charge of homicide*
  nsm 7b/41, 44
Ōsferð pr n *Osferth* Ōsferðes gs 12/65
Ōslāf pr n *Oslaf* ns 31a/86
Ōsmōd pr n *Osmod* 29/41
Ōsmōding adj *son of Osmod* nsm 29/41
Ōsrīċ pr n *Osric* ns 29/21
Ōsulf pr n *Oswulf* Ōsulfe ds 12/15, 16
Ōswald pr n *Oswald* ns 8/25 Ōswaldes gs
  8/36 Ōswold ns 30/304
oþ conj *until* 10/16, 17/3, 13, 29/12, 17,
  31b/31, 37/8, etc oþ þæt *until* 8/55,
  16/30, etc oþþæt 2b/2, 5, 3a/3, 3b/4,
  3c/4, 4/5, 18/33, 23/26, etc odþæt
  30/324
oþ prep +a *until, to, as far as, for* 2b/3, 4,
  5/54, 9a/22, 9b/15, 14/56, 64, 15b/5,
  15c/16, 16/6, 83, 21a/69, 76, 22/8, etc
oþberan IV *bear away, carry off* oþbær pt3s
  38/81
ōþer adj *other, another, second, next, one of
  two* nsm 6/47, 16/6, 31b/69 nsn 31a/71
  ōþere dsf 7a/23 ōþerne asm 3c/5 ōðerra
  gpf 6/30 oðerre dsf 5/54 ōðran dpm 12/4
  ōþre asm 19/109 gsf 7a/41 dsf 7b/3, 9b/74
  ism 9a/55 npm 3a/8, 4/41, 48 apm 13/8 apf
  5/45 ōþres gsn 4/79, 9b/97 ōðron dsm 4/91
  ōþrum dsm 7a/52, 17/20 dpm 1/62, 4/6,
  5/24, 22/44 dpn 4/93, 9b/65 dpf 5/59; see
  also healf [etc]
ōþer pron *one, other, another* nsm 14/45,
  30/282 nsn 22/10, 111, 112, 25/104 asm
  8/77 asn 2a/8, 22/112 apn 9b/70 ōþere apm
  14/50 oþerne asm 7b/44, 25/54, 56, 77,
  30/234 ōðran dpm 25/64 ōþre asf 5/71
  npm 9b/9, 14/61 apf 7b/9 ōþres gsn 28/7
  ōþrum dsm 25/73, 94, 33/52, 34/26 dpm

25/55; in correl use ōðer ... ōðer *the
  one ... the other* nsm 6/47, 51 ōðre ... ōðre
  dsn 6/49 [etc]
oðfæstan 1 *set* oðfæste pp npm 5/53
oðfeallan VII *fall away, decay* inf 5/41
  oðfeallenu pp nsf 5/13
oðflītan 1 *obtain by legal process* inf 12/4
Ōðon pr n *Óðinn* or *Odin* ns 24/58, 60
ōþr- see ōþer
oþþæt see oþ
oþþe conj *or, or else, and* 1/5, 46, 2b/2, 3a/1,
  3b/8, 4/18, 7a/12, 7b/7, 20, 9b/47, 12/33,
  16/7, 23/36, 30/208, etc aēththa 20a/4
  oððon 25/61, 161 oþþe ... oþþe
  either ... or 4/64, 6/29, 7b/14, etc; see also
  āwðer
oðþringan III (+d) *wrest from, force*
  oðþringeð pr3s 26/71 oðþrong pt1s
  19/185
oðwendan I *take away from* inf 17/66
ōwiht see āwiht
oxa m:B5a *ox* oxan ap 1/25, 12/46 dp 1/21
  oxena gp 1/28 oxon ap 1/20
oxanhyrde m:B1g *oxherd* oxanhyrdas np
  1/15
oxon < oxa

P

palþer m:B1b *panther* palthera gp 28/6
Pante pr n *River Pant* (Ess.) Pantan as 30/68,
  97
pāpa m:B5a *pope* pāpan gs 22/68
pað m:B1c *course, path* as 18/42
Paulus pr n *Paul* Paules gs 7b/52
pæning m:B1a *penny* pæniga gp 11/28
Pehtas pr n (mp:B1a) *the Picts* Pehtum dp
  9a/31
Penearding pr n *Penearding* ns 12/49
Penwihtsteort pr n *Land's End* (Corn.) as
  8/54
Perticas pr n *Perticas* Perticam ns 28/66
Pētrus pr n *Peter* ns 16/29, 30, 32 Pētre ds
  16/28, 22/44 Pētres gs 7b/51 Pētrum as
  16/32
Philippus pr n *Philippus* ns 21b/4
Philistēi pr n *the Philistines* np 22/145, 149
  Filistēi np 22/146
ġepīcian 2 *cover with pitch* ġepīcod pp
  3a/14

Pilātus pr n *Pilate* ns 14/4, 10, 18, 21, 22/11
 Pilāte ds 22/6
Pilotas pr n *Pilotas* **Pilotan** ns 28/66
pīnung f:B3d *torment, punishment* **pīnunge**
 as 4/78
pipor m:B1a *pepper* **pipores** gs 3b/7
pistol m:B1a *epistle, letter* as 4/20
plega m:B5a *sport, entertainment* **plegan** ds
 27/7
plegian 2 *entertain, play, contend* **plegodan**
 pt3p 10/52 **plegode** pt3s 27/45
Plegmund pr n *Plegmund* **Plegmunde** ds
 5/62
plēoh n:B2c *danger, risk, responsibility* ns
 4/26, 16/108
plēolić adj *dangerous* nsn 16/7
por n:B2a *leek* ns 3a/10
Porus pr n *Porus* **Pore** ns 28/2
prass m:B1a *battle array* **prasse** ds 30/68
prēost m:B1a *priest* ns 4/20 **prēostas** np
 16/23, 35 **prēostes** gs 7a/2
prīm n:B2b *prime* as 1/42
Pryfet pr n *Privett* (Hants.) **Pryfetes** gs 29/4
prȳte f:B5c *pride* **prȳtan** ds 25/131
pund n:B2b *pound* as 4/7, 11/28 **punda** gp
 8/23, 63, 27/54 (twice) **pundum** dp 7c/25
Pybba pr n *Pybba* ns 29/42
Pybing adj *son of Pybba* nsm 29/42

R

racente f:B5c *chain, fetter* **racentan** gs 17/35
 racentum dp 17/97
rād < **rīdan**
ġe**rād** n:B2b *consideration, understanding,*
 condition as 4/11 ġe**rāda** as 12/34 (see
 note)
radost < **hraðe**
ranc adj *proud, brave* **rancne** asm 25/95
rand m:B1a *boss* or *rim of shield, shield* ns
 33/37 **randas** ap 30/20
randburh f:B4b *rampart* **randbyriġ** np 18/18
randwiġġend m:B4d *shield-warrior*
 randwiġġendra gp 19/188 **rondwiġġende**
 np 19/11, 20
raþe, raðor < **hraþe**
ġe**rǣcan** 1 *reach, attain, obtain, strike* inf
 25/16 ġe**rǣhte** pt3s 30/142, 158, 226
rǣd m:B1a *advice, benefit, precept, wisdom,*
 reason ns 17/87, 18/80 as 8/24 **rǣda** gp

 18/103, 19/68 **rǣdas** ap 18/70 **rǣde** ds
 19/97
rǣdan 1 *read* inf 16/8 **rǣda**ð pr1p 24/61
 rǣdde pt3s 12/22 **rǣde** pr1s 4/75
 pt1s 24/3 **rǣdenne** infl inf 16/92 **rǣt** pr3s
 16/8
(ġe)**rǣdan** 1 *advise, guide, decree, determine*
 ġe**rǣdde** pt3s 8/22, 24, 27, 58 ġe**rǣdest**
 pt2s 30/36 **rǣt** pr3s 15c/8
rǣdbora m:B5a *adviser* **rǣdboran** as 16/100
(ġe)**rǣdde** < (ġe)**rǣdan**
rǣdend m:B4d *ruler* ns 31b/64
ġe**rǣdnes** f:B3e.ii *decree, ordinance*
 ġe**rǣdnessa** gp 7c/2
ġe**rǣdu** np:B2g *harness, trappings* ġe**rǣdum**
 dp 30/190
ræfnan 1 *do, perform* **ræfndon** pt3p 19/11
ræghār adj *grey with lichen* nsm 37/10
ġe**rǣnod** adj *ornamented* ġe**rǣnodæs** gsm
 11/34
rǣran 1 *lift up, promote, commit* inf 9b/99
 rǣrde pt3s 25/11
rǣsan 1 *rush (upon), attack* **rǣsde** pt3s 29/12
 rǣseð pr3s 35c/8
rǣste < *rest*
rǣswa m:B5a *leader, chief* **rǣswan** ds 19/12
 np 19/178
rǣt < **rǣdan**
rēad adj *red* **rēada** nsm 35d/15 **rēadum** dsn
 19/338
rēadfāh adj *red-stained* nsm 37/10
rēadian 2 *redden* sbj pr3p 3c/4
rēaf n:B2b *garment, clothing, armour* ns
 22/23, 96, 101 as 30/161 ap 14/40, 42
 (twice) **reafe** ds 14/29, 34, 22/103, 104
 rēafes gs 21a/78, 22/102, 27/55 **rēafum** dp
 22/86
rēafere m:B1g *robber, plunderer* **rēaferas** np
 25/137
rēafian 2 *rob, plunder* **rēafað** pr3s 35c/8
 rēafiað pr3p 25/104
rēaflāc n:B2h *robbery, plunder* ns 25/46 as
 7c/19 as/ap 25/149
ġe**reaht, reaht-** see (ġe)**recċan**
rēc m:B1a *smoke* ns 3a/11
recċan 1 (+g) *care about, care for, be*
 interested in inf 21a/83 **recċað** pr3p 6/66
 rēċe pr1p 1/4 **rōhtan** pt3p 25/107 **rōhte**
 pt3s 22/102 **rōhton** pt2p 21a/83 pt3p
 30/260

(ġe)reċċan 1 *relate, explain, interpret, decide*
inf 22/67 ġereaht pp 12/28 **reahte** pt3s
12/13 **reahtan** pt1p 12/25 (twice) **rehte**
pt3s 28/59 ġerehte pt3s 12/52 (*adjudge to*)
rehton pt3p 9b/48

reċċelēas adj *negligent, careless* reċċelēase
npm 5/40

reċed n:B2b.ii *building, hall* reċede ds
31b/81 **reċedes** gs 33/37

ġereċednis f:B3e.ii *narrative* ġereċednisse as
16/40 ds 16/42

rēċels n:B2b *incense, frankincense* ?gs 28/10

recene adv *instantly, hastily, quickly* 19/188
ricene 30/93 **rycene** 38/112

ġereċenian 2 *explain* ġereċenod pp 18/80

ġerēfa m:B5a *reeve, steward, officer, prefect*
ns 12/50 ġerēfan ds 8/72 ġerēfum dp 28/2
ġerēua ns 21b/4, 16

reġn m:B1a *rain* reġnes gs 28/36 **reġnum**
dp 28/35

reġnþēof m:B1a *arch-thief* reġnþēofas np
18/93

regolliċ adj *regular, according to monastic
rule* regollecum dpm 9b/73

regollīċe adv *according to rule* 25/52

(ġe)rehte, rehton < (ġe)reċċan

rēnboga m:B5a *rainbow* as rēnbogan 13/23

ġerēne n:B2h *ornament* ġerēno np 35d/15

ġerēnian 2 *adorn, ornament* ġerēnode
pp 19/338

rēniġ adj *rainy* nsn 39/10

ġerēnod adj *ornamented, decorated* asn
30/161

rēnwæter n:B2c *rainwater* rēnwætere ds
3a/14

rēocan 2 *reek, smoke* rēoċende prp apn
19/313

rēod n:B2b *red colour, redness* rēodne as
35c/8

rēofan II *rend, break* rofene pp npf 18/18

rēon < rēowe

reord f:B3b *speech, voice* reorde ds 26/53

ġereord f:3b *speech, voice, language*
ġereorda np 24/6 ġereorde ds 1/13, 4/1,
23, 41, 9b/6

reordberend m:B4d *speech-bearer, person*
np 23/3 reordberendum dp 23/89

reordiġean 2 *speak* reordode pt3s 18/103

ġereording f:B3d *meal* ġereordinge ds 1/59

rēotiġ adj *mournful, tearful* rēotugu nsf
39/10

rēowe f:B5d *blanket* rēon ds 7b/45

rest f:B3b *rest, resting place, bed* ræste ds
31b/94 reste ds 3b/10, 9b/22, 86, 23/3

(ġe)restan 1 *rest* inf 9b/84, 17/97, 27/66, 70,
40/40 (*find rest from* +g) **ræstan** inf 11/5
reste pt3s 19/44, 23/64, 69 sbj pr3s 3c/6
resteð pr3s 21b/24 **reston** pt3p 19/321

rēþe adj *cruel, raging* nsm 31b/94

ġerēua see ġerēfa

rīca m:B5a *ruler* ns 19/44

Ricard pr n *Richard* Ricardes gs 8/65

rīċe adj (often =noun) *powerful, mighty,
great, noble* rīca nsm 19/20, 24, 68 **rīcan**
dsm 19/11 **rīċne** asm 19/234, 23/44, 25/95
rīcost sup nsm 30/36 **rīcra** gpm 23/131,
25/149

rīċe n:B2h *kingdom, realm, authority, rule,
power* ns 17/97 as 8/70, 17/60, 18/93,
23/119, 152, 33/1, etc ds 5/18, 66, 9a/2,
19/343, 21b/8, 29/38, 39, 38/106 (see note)
is 17/73 **rīċes** gs 9b/69, 17/23, 26/81,
27/82, 29/1, etc

ricene see recene

rīċne < rīċe adj

rīcsian 2 *reign, rule, prevail* rīcsode pt3s
25/9, 29/35 **rīxað** pr3s 22/176

rīdan I *ride, swing* inf 30/291 pt1p 12/35 **rād**
pt3s 12/36 (twice), 30/18, 239 **rīdeð** pr3s
17/35 **rīdon** pt3p 29/20

riht adj *just, true, fitting, right, due* nsn 7b/16
nsf 1/4 **rihte** dsm 9a/39, 19/97 **rihtne** asm
23/89 **rihtre** dsf 15a/5 **ryht** nsn 12/27, 62
ryhtoste sup npm 7b/8 **ryhtre** comp nsn
7b/15 asn 12/28

riht n:B2b *justice, right, what is right* as
2a/15, 17/23, 24/61, 25/125 **rihte** ds 4/52,
7c/28, 17/87, 25/20, etc **ryht** as 31b/64
ryhte ds 12/34 **ryhtes** gs 12/8; see also
rihte adv

ġeriht n:B2b *what is right* or *direct, right,
privilege* ġerihta np 25/29 ap 25/20, 22 gp
25/32; in phr on ġerihte ds *directly* 19/202

ġerihtan 1 *correct, direct* inf 4/27, 16/109
ġeriht pp 23/131 ġerihte sbj pr3s 4/24,
16/107

rihte adv *rightly, justly* 25/54, 30/20

rihtlagu f:B3a *just law* rihtlaga gp 25/119

rihtlīċe adv *justly, properly* 22/83, 97, 25/162
rihtne, rihtre < **riht**
rihtwīs adj *just, righteous, upright* **rihtwīsan**
  npm 15a/10 dpm 22/99 **rihtwīsena** gpm
  15a/9 **rihtwīsum** dpm 22/154
rihtwīsa m:B5a *righteous man* **rihtwīsan** as
  14/14 gs 14/24
rihtwīsnes f:B3e *righteousness* **rihtwīsnesse**
  gs 15c/10
rinc m:B1a *man, warrior* **rinca** gp 19/54, 338
  rincum dp 30/18
rinde f:B5c *bark* **rindum** dp 28/31
ġerisene n:B2b *what is seemly* or *decent*
  ġerisena gp 25/32
ġerisenliċ adj *fitting, proper* **ġerisenliċe** apn
  9b/2
rīxaðð, rīxode < **rīcsian**
rōd f:B3b *cross* ns 23/44, 136 **rōde** as 14/37,
  23/119 ds 14/19, 40, 49, 51, 22/25, 131,
  132, etc, 23/56, 131
roder- see **rodor**
rōdetācen n:B2c *sign of the cross* **rōdetācne**
  ds 9b/101
rodor m:B1a *sky, heaven, the heavens*
  as 18/18 **rodera** gp 31b/64 **roderas** ap
  19/348 **roderum** dp 19/5 **rodores** gs
  31b/81
rōf adj *renowned, brave* **rōfe** npm 19/20
  rōfra gp 19/53
rofene < **rēofan**
rōht- see **reċċan**
Rōm pr n *Rome* **Rōme** ds 21b/15
Rōmanisc adj *Roman* **Rōmanisces** gsn
  9a/56
Rōmeburg pr n *Rome* **Rōmebiriġ** as 21b/25
  Rōmeburge gs 21b/16
rōmigan 2 +g *extend* inf 17/23
rondwiġġende < **randwiġġend**
rotian 2 *rot, decay* inf 22/16
rotlīċe adv *gladly, cheerfully* 9b/90
rōwan VII *row* **hrēowan** pt3p 21a/54
rūde f:B5c *rue* **rūdan** gs 3a/4
rūh adj *coarse, hairy* nsm 35c/5
rūm adj *broad, spacious, open* nsm 33/37 nsf
  28/9 **rūme** apm 19/348
rūm m:B1a *space, opportunity* ns 19/313
rūme adv *spaciously, abundantly* 19/97
Rummæsiġ pr n *Romsey* (Hants.)
  Rummæsiġæ ds 11/11

rūn f:B3b *consultation, secret council,
  mystery* ns 18/80 **rūne** ds 19/54, 38/111
rycene see **recene**
ryht see **riht**
ryhtfæderencyn n:B2b.i *direct paternal
  ancestry* ns 29/36
ryhtracu f:B3a *true account* **ryhtrace** ds
  12/9
ryhtre < **riht**
(ġe)rȳman 1 *clear, open, open a way for,
  make space for, extend* **rȳmde** pt3s 22/78
  ġerȳmde pt1s 23/89 pt3s 18/34 **ġerȳmdon**
  pt3p 5/8 sbj pt3p 31a/24 **ġerȳmed**
  pp 30/93
ryne m:B1g *course, running* **rynum**
  dp 15a/4
rȳpan 1 *plunder, rob* **rȳpaþ** pr3p 25/104
rȳpere m:B1g *robber, plunderer* **rȳpera** gp
  25/46 **rȳperas** np 25/137

S

sacan VI *fight, quarrel, contend* inf 33/53
  sacað pr3p 34/18
sācerd m:B1a *priest* ns 28/48 **sācerda** gp
  14/3, 15, 49 **sācerdas** np 9a/41 **sōcerd** ns
  28/26
sacu f:B3a *conflict, strife* **saca** as 24/47
saga m:B5a *story, narrative* **sagan** ap 34/15
saga < **secgan**
sagu f:B3a *report, testimony* **sagena** gp 14/5
sāh < **sīgan**
sāl m:B1a *cord, halter, loop* ns 17/35, 41
salowiġpād adj *dark-coated* **salowiġpāda**
  nsm 19/211 **saluwiġpādan** apm 10/61
  (=noun)
same see **some**
ġesamnod < **ġesomnian**
samod see **somod**
Samson pr n *Samson* ns 22/144, 147, 148,
  150
sanct m/f *saint* (see 7b/50n) **sancta** gs 7b/52,
  21b/1 **sanctan** ds 11/12 **sancte** gs 7b/51,
  52 ds 21a/3
sand n:B2b *sand* np 18/25
sang < **singan, song**
sanga, sange < **song**
sār adj *sore, painful, grievous* nsn 17/88
  sārra gpf 19/182, 23/80**

sār n:B2b *pain, wound, suffering, sorrow* as 15b/8, 26/95, 27/20 **sāre** ds 22/142, 28/40

sāre adv *sorely, grievously* 23/59, 25/34, 133

sāriġ adj *sorrowful* **sāriġes** gsn 28/74

sārian 1 *grieve, be sad* **sāriġende** prp npm 9a/48

sārliċ adj *sorrowful, grievous* **sārlicum** ds 27/5

sārnes f:B3e.ii *grief, sorrow* **sārnesse** as 27/26

sārra < **sār**

Sātan pr n *Satan* 17/8, 10

Saturnus pr n *Saturn* ns 24/32 **Saturnes** gs 24/62

sāule, sāulum < **sāwol**

ġesāwe, ġesāwon < **ġesēon**

sāwol f:B3c *soul, spirit, mind* **sāule** as 25/59 ds 12/8 **sāulum** dp 17/60 **sāwl** ns 23/120 **sāwla** ap 6/30, 18/98 **sāwlæ** ds 11/4 **sāwle** as 15b/8, 21a/87 ds 26/100 **sāwlum** dp 18/51 **sāwul** ns 30/177, 33/58

sāwollēas adj *soulless* **sāwllēasan** asm 21a/67

sǣ m:B1g.iv *sea* ns 18/27, 22/159 as 9a/48, 26/14, 18, 38/4 ds 8/83, 25/100 (twice), 27/14, 83 **sǣm** dp 18/117 **sǣs** gs 18/21

sǣċċ f:B3e *strife, battle* **sǣċċe** ds 10/4, 42, 19/288

sǣd adj +g *sated with, weary of* nsm 10/20, 35a/2

sǣd n:B2b *seed* **sǣdes** gs 3b/7

(ġe)sǣd- see **(ġe)secgan**

sǣdēor n:B2b *sea-beast* ns 31b/19

sǣdon < **(ġe)secgan**

Sǣfern pr n *(River) Severn* gs 8/51

sǣflōd m:B1a *sea-tide* ns 2b/2, 3 etc **sǣflōdes** gs 2b/1

sǣfōr f:B3b *sea-voyage* **sǣfōre** ds 26/42

ġesǣgan 1 *lay low, destroy* **ġesǣged** pp 19/293

sǣġde, sǣġdon, sǣġest < **secgan**

sǣl m:B1a/f:B3g *time, occasion, season; prosperity, joy* ns 23/80 **sǣlum** dp 36/28 **sēle** ap 31a/73

sǣlād f:B3b *sea-journey, voyage* **sǣlāde** ds 31a/77, 95

sǣlan 1 *bind, fetter, secure* inf 38/21 **ġesǣled** pp 19/114

sǣlida m:B5a *sailor, Viking* ns 30/45 **sǣlidan** as 30/286

ġesǣliġ adj *happy, blessed, favoured, beneficial* nsm 4/12, 24/73 **ġesǣligan** asf 27/81 **ġesǣliġe** npm 17/74

ġesǣliġliċ adj *blessed, happy* **ġesǣliġlica** npf 5/5

sǣm < **sǣ**

sǣmann m:B4b *sailor, Viking* **sǣmanna** gp 18/33 **sǣmannum** dp 30/38, 278 **sǣmæn** np 25/99 **sǣmen** np 30/29

ġesǣne < **ġesȳne**

sǣrima m:B5a *sea-shore, coast* **sǣriman** ds 8/23

sǣrinc m:B1a *sea-warrior, Viking* ns 30/134

sǣs < **sǣ**

sǣsīð m:B1a *sea-journey, voyage* **sǣsīðe** ds 31a/87

(ġe)sǣt, sǣt- see **(ġe)sittan**

scacen < **sceacan**

scamian 2 impers +a (+g) *shame, be ashamed* **scamað** pr3s 25/123, 129, 130, 139 (twice)

scamu f:B3a *shame, dishonour* ns 25/82 **scome** ds 9b/19

scandliċ adj *shameful* nsn 25/70 **scandliċe** npn 25/87 **sceandlican** dpm 25/56

scæcð < **sceacan**

ġescær, scæron < **(ġe)scieran**

scæt, scætta < **sceatt**

sceacan VI *hasten, hurry away, depart* inf 19/291 **scacen** pp 31a/62, 74 **scēoc** pt3s 8/32

ġescead n:B2a *distinction, reason* as 24/19

sceādan VII *part, come away from* **sceādeð** pr3s 37/30

ġescēadan VII *decide* inf 18/59 **ġescēd** pt3s 31b/64

sceadu f:B3f *shadow, darkness* ns 23/54 **sceade** as 15c/11

ġesceadwīsnes f:B3e.ii *discrimination, reason* ns 6/14, 75

scēaf < **scūfan**

sceaft m:B1a *shaft, arrow, spear* ns 30/136 **scefte** ds 32/7

ġesceaft n/f:B2i *creation, created thing, creature, establishment, disposition, destiny* ns 6/39, 10/16, 23/12, 55, 82,

38/107 ġescēafta np 6/2, 22/157, 24/21 ap
6/18, 16/47, 50, 54, 22/169 gp 6/30, 41,
24/76 ġescēafte as 25/75 ġescēaftum dp
6/9, 19

sceal, sceall, scealt < sculan

scealc m:B1a *retainer, warrior, man*
scealcas np 19/230, 30/181

sceandlican < scandliċ

scēap n:B2b *sheep* ap 1/33

ġescēap n:B2b *creation* ġescēape ds
9b/63

ġescēapen, ġescēapene < (ġe)scieppan

ġescēapenis f:B3e.ii *creation* ġescēapenisse
ds 16/44

scear m:B1a *ploughshare* sceare ds 1/22

sceard adj *cut, bereft, gaping* nsm 10/40
scearde npf 37/5

scearn n:B2b *dung, muck* as 1/29

scearp adj *sharp, acid* asn 3b/2 scearpne
asm 19/78

sceat see sceatt

scēat m:B1a *corner, region, surface (of the
earth)* scēatas ap 23/37, 26/61, 105
scēatum dp 23/8, 43

sceatt m:B1a *(sum of) money, property,
tribute, sceat (a coin; see 7a/23n)* scæt ns
7a/45 as 7a/46, 47 scætta gp 7a/23, 24
sceat as 22/39 sceattum dp 30/40, 56 scet
as 22/41

scēat < scēotan

scēað f:3b *sheath, scabbard* scēaðe ds 19/79
scēaðena gp 19/193 scēaðum dp 19/230
scēðe ds 30/162

sceaþa m:B5a *ravager, criminal* sceaþan np
14/45, 53

scēawian 2 *see, behold, look at, inspect*
scēawiað imp p 22/27, 49, 50 scēawigan
inf 28/28 scēawode pt1s 23/137 pt3s
21a/63 sbj pt3s 13/4 scēawodon pt1p
28/12

ġescēawian 2 *show* ġescēawað pr3s 36/33

scēawung f:B3d *show, regard* scēawunge
ds 9a/43

ġescēd < ġescēadan

scefte < sceaft

scendan 1 *shame, insult* scendað pr3p 25/94,
102

scēoc < sceacan

ġescēod < ġescēon, ġesceþþan

sceold- see sculan

ġescēon 1 +d *befall* ġescēod pp 18/61

(ġe)scēop < (ġe)scieppan

sceot n:B2b *darting motion, rapid movement*
sceote ds 33/40

scēotan II *shoot, throw, hit, put in* scēat pt3s
30/143, 270 scēotað pr3p 25/71 scoten
pp 10/19

scēotend m:B4d '*shooter*', *spear-thrower,
warrior* np 19/304, 31a/92

Scottas pr n (mp:B1a) *the Scots* Scotta gp
10/11, 32

scēphyrde m:B1g *shepherd* scēphyrdas np
1/15

sceppende < scyppend

scet < sceat

scēðe < scēað

(ġe)sceþþan VI +d *injure, harm, destroy* inf
23/47, 31b/33 ġescēod pt3s 18/43 sceþede
sbj pt3s 31b/23 sceþþað pr3p 3a/12 sceþþe
pr1s 35c/2 ġescōd pt3s 31b/96

scēwyrhta m:B5a *shoemaker* scēwyrhtan np
1/17

ġescīe < ġescȳ

(ġe)scieppan VI *create, shape, destine,
assign* ġescēapen pp 4/34, 6/5, 21a/71
ġescēapene pp npm 22/90 scēop pt3s
9b/35, 17/6 ġescēop pt3s 6/6, 16/45, 50,
97, 19/347, 22/169 ġescōp pt3s 24/11, 15,
20, etc

(ġe)scieran IV *shear, split, cut through, strip*
ġescær pt3s 31b/35 scǣron pt3p 19/304
scorene pp npf 37/5

scild m:B1a *shield* as 10/19 scildas np 19/204
scyld ns 32/7 scylda gp 11/16 scyldas
ap 30/98 scylde ds 33/37, 30/136

scildburh f:B4b *shield-wall* as 19/304
scyldburh ns 30/242

scilling m:B1a *shilling* ns 7a/28 scillinga
gp 7a/6, 10, 7b/27, 33, etc scillingas
np 7a/18, 22 etc scillingum dp 7a/23, 25,
31, 7b/37, 7c/26, 27

scīma m:B5a *light, radiance, splendour*
scīman as 23/54 ds 28/70

scīnan I *shine, flash, gleam* inf 23/15, 31b/26
scān pt3s 37/15, 34 scīnendan prp dsf
24/13 scīnendum dpm 24/16 dpn 22/86
scīnon pt3p 18/21 scȳneð pr3s 32/7 scȳnð
pr3s 21a/42

scip n:B2a *ship* as 8/33, 35 **scipa** ds 8/57
  scipe ds 25/104 **scipu** np 8/1 ap 8/27, 34
  scype ds 30/40, 56 **scypon** dp 31a/92
  scypum dp 9a/5
scipen f:B3a *stall, cattle-shed* **scipene** ds
  9b/21
scipflota m:B5a *seaman, Viking* **scipflotan** np
  10/11
sciphere m:B1g *ship-army, fleet* as 9a/11
scīr adj *clear, bright, gleaming* asn 30/98
  scīre apm 19/193 **scīrne** asm 23/54
scīrmæled adj *brightly decorated* apn
  19/230
Scittisc adj *Scottish* nsm 10/19
ġescōd < ġesceþþan
scoldan, scolde < sculan
scome < scamu
scop m:B1a *poet, singer* ns 31a/4, 36/36
ġescōp < (ġe)scieppan
scopġereord n:B2b *poetical language*
  scopġereorde ds 9b/5
scoten < scēotan
scræf n:B2d *pit* ns 18/92
scridde < scrȳdan
scrīfan I *prescribe, ordain, care about*
  scrīfað pr3p 25/74 **scrīfe** sbj pr3s
  7b/18
scrīn n:B2b *chest, shrine* as 11/9
scrīðan I *move, glide* inf 33/40 **scrīðað** pr3p
  33/13
scrȳdan I *dress, clothe* **scrīdde** pt3s 27/37
  ġescrȳd pp 22/104 **scrȳddon** pt3p 14/29,
  34
scucca m:B5a *sprite, evil spirit* **scuccena** gp
  6/31
scūfan II *shove, thrust* **scēaf** pt3s 30/136
sculan pr-pt *have to, ought to, must, must
  needs, shall* **sceal** pr1s 9b/27, 12/61, 15b/7,
  35a/9 pr3s 5/1, 7c/12, 16/91, 17/28, 22/19,
  23/119 **sceall** pr3s 6/15, 34/41 **scealt** pr2s
  2a/7 **sceolan** pr3p 33/14 **sceoldan** pt3p
  8/30, 42, 9a/7 sbj pt3p 8/60 **sceolde** pt1s
  23/43, 26/30 sbj pt1s 16/3 pt3s 14/7, 16/82,
  17/11 sbj pt3s 8/59, 79, 17/7 **sceolden** sbj
  pt3p 5/40 **sceoldon** pt1p 17/86 pt3p 8/32,
  9b/81, 28/41 sbj pt3p 5/12, 13, 15c/2
  sceolon pr1p 16/76, 22/124 pr3p 4/14
  scoldan pt1p 25/54 pt3p 25/28 **scolde** pt1s
  22/59 pt3s 25/10, 52, 28/69 sbj pt3s 25/67

scolden sbj pt3p 9b/17, 99 **scoldon** pt3p
  5/11, 22/64 sbj pt3p 22/39 **scolon** sbj pr3p
  22/16 **sculon** pr1p 17/60, 19/287, 25/164
  pr3p 9b/31, 17/69 **scylan** sbj pr1p 25/13
  scyle sbj pr1s 15b/9 sbj pr3s 26/74, 111,
  40/42 [etc]
scūr m:B1a *a shower, storm, tempest* ns
  33/40 **scūras** ap 19/221 **scūrum** dp 19/79,
  26/17
scūrbeorg f:B3b *storm-protection*
  scūrbeorge np 37/5
ġescȳ n:B2h *shoe, pair of shoes* ġ**escīe** ap
  28/24
scyċċels m:B1a *cloak, mantle* **scyċċelse** ds
  14/29, 34
scylan < sculan
scyld f:B3g *sin, fault* **scyldum** dp 15c/7
scyld < scild
scyldburh < scildburh
scyldiġ adj +g *guilty, liable (for)* nsm 7b/21,
  24
Scyldingas pr n (mp:B1a) *Scyldings, Danes*
  Scyldinga gp 31a/7, 92, 31b/72
  Here-Scyldinga gp '*army-Scyldings*' gp
  31a/46
scyle < sculan
scȳne adj *bright, radiant, beautiful* apf
  19/316 **scȳnost** sup nsm 17/1
scȳneð, scȳnð < scīnan
scype, scypon < scip
scyppend m:B4d *creator* ns 9b/36, 24/22, 23,
  38/85 as 22/157, 24/11 **sceppende** ds 6/15
  scyppendes gs 9b/29, 107, 19/78, 22/162
scypum < scip
ġescyrian I *ordain, allot* ġ**escyred**
  pp 17/87
scȳte f:B5c *linen cloth, sheet* **scȳtan**
  np 22/31
scytefinger m:B1b *forefinger* ns 7a/35
se, sēo, þæt def art *the*; demons pron/adj *that,
  those*; pers pron *he, it, that, she, they*, etc;
  rel pron *who, which, that, what* [§A1a]:
  se nsm 2b/2, 8/6, 9, 13/2 **sē** nsm (*he*) 2a/18,
  7a/25, 17/11, 30/27, 33/12 **sēo** nsf 2b/1,
  7a/43, 7b/30, 16/10 **sīo** nsf 6/14 **tæt** asn
  29/28 **thaem** dsf 20a/1 **thēm** dsn 20a/1 **þā**
  asf 2a/17, 8/28, 16/3, 23/119 npm 2a/19,
  6/70, 7a/1, 14/15 apm 9a/31 apn 8/27,
  23/27 apf 7a/16 **þām** dsm 7a/27, 8/5, 13/1

dsn 1/41, 51, 8/15 dpm 9a/30, 14/49 **þan**
ism 23/122 isn 17/73, 23/88 dpm 4/37 **þāra**
gpm 7b/31, 23/86 **þāre** gsf 7a/41, 42 dsf
7a/23 **þat** asn 30/36 **þǣm** dsm 6/3, 21 dsn
5/53 **þæne** asm 8/24, 25/85, 86 **þǣra** gpn
16/27 gpf 4/3 **þǣre** gsf 7b/28, 13/5 dsf
1/22, 8/32, 13/5 **þæs** gsm 8/61, 9b/20,
13/12 gsn 7b/30, 9b/8 (see also **þæs** adv)
þæt nsn 7b/10, 8/23, 13/21 asn 7a/15, 8/14,
23/58 **þe** nsm 27/60 **þēre** dsf 8/31 **þet** asn
8/9, 62 **þī** ism 21b/23, 24 **þon** ism 3a/4,
12/17, 26 isn 3a/14, 3b/3, 9b/100, 12/42,
62, 28/61, 39/12 **þonæ** asm 11/30 **þone**
asm 3a/15, 5/6, 7b/28, 8/30, 14/36, 38/27
þȳ ism 7b/41 isn 3a/15, 9b/97 (see also **þȳ**
adv) **þys** gsm 12/65; for phrs with instr
þī/þy, **þan/þon** see **for**, **mā**, **mid**, **tō**, **wiþ**
[etc]
(ġe)**seah** < (ġe)**sēon**
(ġe)**seald**, (ġe)**seald-** see (ġe)**sellan**
sealf f:B3b *ointment* **sealfa** ap 22/75 **sealfe** as
22/15 ds 22/70, 74
sealm m:B1a *psalm* as 15b/1, 15c/1 **sealmas**
ap 21a/60 **sealme** ds 15b/2, 15c/7 **seolmas**
ap 1/42
sealobrūn adj *dusky*, *dark brown* nsm 32/35
sealt adj *salt* **sealtum** dpf 18/27
sealt n:B2b *salt* **sealte** ds 33/45
sealtere m:B1g *salter* **sealteras** np 1/17
sealtȳþ f:B3b *salt-wave* **sealtȳþa** gp 26/35
searacræft m:B1a *fraud* **searacræftas** ap
25/111
searað < **searian**
Searburg pr n *Salisbury* (Wilts.) **Searbyriġ**
ds 8/82
sēarian 2 *wither*, *dry up* **sēarað** pr3s 26/89
sēariað pr3s 15a/5
searo n:B2g *war-gear*, *arms*, *things of value*
searowa np 34/7 **searwum** dp 18/25,
31b/66
searoġim m:B1a *curious gem*, *precious stone*
searoġimma gp 31a/95 **searoġimmas** ap
37/35
searoþoncol adj *discerning*, *shrewd* nsf
19/145 **searoþoncelra** gp 19/330 (=noun)
sēaþ m:B1a *pit* **sēaþe** ds 23/75
sēaw n:B2b *juice* as 3a/1, 5 **sēawes** gs 3b/3
seax n:B2b *knife*, *short sword* as 31b/54
seaxses gs 35d/6

Seaxe pr n (mp:B5a) *the Saxons*, *Saxony* np
10/70 **Seaxan** np 9a/8, 32, 59 **Seaxna** gp
9a/4 **Seaxum** dp 9a/16, 18, 22
sēċan 1 *seek*, *seek out*, *approach*, *make for*,
visit, *reach by seeking* inf 10/55, 17/69,
23/104, 119, 127 pr1p 27/65 ġe**sāhte** pt3s
12/54 ġe**sǣċen** sbj pr3p 11/33 **sēċað** pr1p
22/75 pr2p 22/25, 99 ġe**sēċe** sbj pr1s 26/38
sbj pr3s 7c/8, 34/25 **sēċean** inf 32/27
ġe**sēċean** inf 28/37, 33/44 **sēċende** prp npm
9a/32 **sēċenne** infl inf 21a/52 **sēċeð** pr3s
19/96, 38/114 **sōhtan** pt3p 10/71 **sōhte**
pt1s 38/25 pt3s 5/12, 12/5 ġe**sōhte** pt3s
19/14 **sōhton** pt3p 10/58, 23/133 ġe**sōhtun**
pt3p 10/27 (*invaded*)
Seccandūn pr n *Seckington* (Warks.)
Seccandūne ds 29/38
secg m:B1a *man*, *retainer*, *warrior* ns 10/17,
26/56, 30/159, 31b/78, 36/24 **secga** gp
10/13, 38/53 **secgas** np 19/201 ap 30/258
secgum dp 23/59
(ġe)**secgan** 3 *say*, *tell*, *declare*, *report*,
explain, *ascribe* inf 4/58, 70, 6/37, 9a/9,
9b/45, 110, 17/101, 18/64, 23/1, etc sbj
pr3p 22/9 **saga** imp s 34/15 **sǣd** pp 9a/22
ġe**sǣd** pp 22/66 **sǣdan** pt1p 12/24 pt3p
24/15 **sǣde** pt3s 12/49, 14/17, 52, 16/15,
21a/15, etc ġe**sǣde** pt3s 30/120 **sǣdon**
pt1p 4/87 pt3p 9a/33, 22/123 **sæ̇gde** pt3s
9b/43, 44, 18/71, 28/60 **sæ̇gdon** pt3p 9b/49
sæ̇gest pr2s 1/18, 32 **secgað** pr1p 21a/83
pr3p 10/68, 16/39, 18/85, 21a/82, 88, etc
imp p 22/28, 29 **secge** pr1s 27/13, 32 sbj
pr2s 1/45, 23/96 sbj pr3s 33/65 **secgeað**
pr3p 14/5 **seġe** imp s 27/12, 15, 30/50 **seġeð**
pr3s 30/45 **seġst** pr2s 14/2 **seġð** pr3s 4/9
Secgen pr n *Secgen* (unknown Germanic
tribe) **Secgena** gp 32/24
secgrōf adj *renowned with the sword*
secgrōfra gpm 37/26
sefa m:B5a *spirit*, *mind*, *heart* **sefan** as 26/51,
38/57 ds 36/9, 29
sēfte < **sōfte**
seġe < **secgan**
seġelġyrd f:B3b *sail-yard* ns 33/25
ġe**seġen** < ġe**sēon**
(ġe)**seġnian** 2 *cross oneself*, *bless* **seġniende**
prp nsm 9b/108 ġe**seġnode** pt3s 9b/101
seġst, **seġð** < **secgan**

sēl adj *good, noble* **sēlest** sup (*best*) asm
23/118 asn 31a/82 **sēlesta** nsm 23/27
sēlestan npm 6/46, 64 **sēlre** comp (*better*)
nsn 34/25 **sӯllan** asm 36/6

sēl comp adv *better* 32/38, 39

ġeselda m:B5a *companion* **ġeseldan** ap 38/53

seldcyme m:B1g *infrequent coming*
seldcymas np 39/14

seldhwænne adv *seldom* 21a/32

sele m:B1g *hall* as 38/25

sēle < **sǣl**

seledrēam m:B1a *hall-joy* **seledrēamas** np
38/93

seledrēoriġ adj *sad for want of a hall* nsm
38/25

seleġyst m:B1a *hall-guest, visitor* as 31b/54

selesecg m:B1a *hall-man, retainer* **selesecgas**
ap 38/34

self, self- see **sylf**

(ġe)sellan 1 *give, give up, surrender, supply,*
sell, restore inf 21b/6 **ġesæld** pp 16/68
seald pp 2a/13 **ġeseald** pp 2a/8, 20, 12/42,
16/69 **sealdan** pt3p 9a/12 **sealde** pt1s
12/57 pt3s 5/21, 9a/44, 12/18, 14/26, 61,
21b/12, etc sbj pt3s 12/32 **ġesealde** pt3s
12/15, 25/68, 76, 30/188 pp npm 25/35
sealdon pt3p 9a/34, 14/12, 38, 22/38
ġesealdon pt3p 30/184 **sele** imp s 3b/2, 4, 9
sellanne infl inf 7b/55 **selle** sbj pr3s 7b/16,
33 **ġeselle** sbj pr3s 7b/27, 32 **sillan** inf
27/34, 36 **ġesille** sbj pr3s 7c/10 **silþ** pr3s
16/55 **syleð** pr3s 15b/14 **syllan** inf 30/38,
46 sbj pr3p 11/25 **syllanne** infl inf 12/16
syllað pr3p 25/74 **syllon** sbj pr3p 30/61
sylþ pr3s 15a/4, 16/57

(ġe)sēman 1 *reconcile, bring to an*
agreement, arbitrate between **sēman** inf
12/9 **ġesēman** inf 30/60 **sēmdan** pt3p
12/21

sendan 1 *send, cast* inf 21b/19 pt3p 9a/9
sende pt3s 8/31, 60, 14/13, 21a/52, 22/173
sbj pr3s 19/190 **sendon** pt3p 9a/10, 19/224,
30/29

ġesēne < **ġesӯne**

sēo f:B5d *pupil (of eye)* **sēon** as 3a/7

sēo < **se** (pron), **sēon** (vb)

sēoc adj *sick, weak* **sēoce** nsf 39/14 **sēocne**
asm 8/77

seofan num *seven* 4/45, 13/8, 11 **seofene** npm
10/30 **seofon** 1/11, 1/42

seofian 2 *lament, sigh* **seofedun** pt3p 26/10
seofode pt3s 15b/1

seolf- see **sylf**

seolfor n:B2c *silver* ns 16/77 as 16/74 **seolfre**
ds 23/77 **seolfres** gs 27/55 **sylfor** as
37/35

seolmas < **sealm**

seomian 2 *hang, sway* inf 33/25

sēon < **sēo**

(ġe)sēon V *look, see, observe, perceive* inf
3a/7, 14/62, 22/108, 31a/16, 64 **ġesāwe** sbj
pt1s 23/4 sbj pt3s 27/67 **ġesāwon** pt3p
14/69, 22/75, 138, 27/59 **seah** pt3s 37/35
ġeseah pt1s 5/26, 17/38, 23/14, 21, etc pt3s
8/80, 9b/18, 13/13, 14/21, 27/18, 48, 34/11,
etc **ġeseġen** pp 9b/47, 109 **sēo** pr1s 35a/3
ġesēo pr1s 27/11 **ġesēoð** pr2p 14/24, 22/51,
95 pr3p 22/30 **ġesewen** pp 22/159 **ġesīon**
inf 5/33 **ġesīoð** pr1p 6/17

seonobend f:B3b *sinew-bond, fetter*
seonobende ap 36/6

sēoþan II *boil, seeth, cook* inf 34/15 **sēoþ** imp
s 3b/4 **ġesoden** pp 3a/3, 3b/8 **ġesodene**
pp apm 3b/10

ġeset n:B2a *seat, habitation* **ġesetu** np 33/66,
38/93

ġeset < **settan**

setl n:B2c.i *seat, throne, resting place* **setla**
gp 17/74 **setle** ds 10/17, 15a/2, 27/5

setlgong m:B1a *setting, sinking* **setlgonge** ds
28/27 **setlgonges** gs 28/26

ġesetnis f:B3e.ii *law, decree* **ġesetnissa** ap
16/102 **ġesetnissum** dp 16/101

(ġe)settan 1 *set, set up, set out, set down, put,*
place, settle, arrange, establish, make,
compose inf 7b/5, 15b/8, 17/59 pt3p 24/71
ġesætte pt3s 8/61 **ġeset** pt3s 15c/8 pp 16/99
ġeseted pp 9b/15, 23/141 **seteð** pr3s 34/40
ġesett pp 8/72 (*appointed*), 16/10, 85
ġesettanne infl inf 17/27 **settað** pr1p 7b/23
sette pr1s 13/18, 23 pt3s 27/37, 35d/4
ġesette pt3s 9b/22, 107, 12/40, 21a/18, 81
pp 4/55, 16/35 **ġesetton** pt3p 23/67

ġesewen < **(ġe)sēon**

ġesewenliċ adj *visible* **ġesewenlica** npf 6/3

Sexburh pr n *Sexburh* ns 21a/49, 51, 59,
66

sī, sīe < **bēon-wesan**

sibb f:B3e *peace, concord* **sib** ns 22/46 **sibbe**
as 2a/22, 5/7 ds 9a/13

ġesibb adj *related, close* ġesib ns 25/50
(=noun) ġesibban ds 25/50 (=noun)
ġesibbra comp gpm 35d/22
sibleġer n:B2c *incest* sibleġeru ap 25/113
sibling m:B1a *sibling, kinsman* siblingum
ds 16/19
Sībyrht pr n *Sibyrht* Sībyrhtes gs 30/282
sīclian 2 *sicken, become ill* ġesīclod pp 8/78
sīd adj *ample, wide* sīde asf 19/337
sīde adv *widely*; in phr wīde ond sīde *far and
wide* 23/81, 25/122
sīde f:B5c *side* sīdan as 22/52 ds 23/49
sīe, sīen, sīendon < bēon-wesan
ġesīene see ġesȳne
sierwan 1 *plot* sierwe sbj pr3s 7b/20, 24
siġ < bēon-wesan
sīgan I *sink, fall* sāh pt3s 10/17, 21a/45
siġe m:B1g *victory* as 9a/9, 58, 59
siġebēam m:B1a *tree of victory* ns 23/13
as 23/127
siġebeorn m:B1a *victory-warrior, hero*
siġebeorna gp 32/38
Siġebryht pr n *Sigebryht* 29/1 Siġebryhtes
gs 29/8
siġeēadiġ adj *blessed with victory* asn 31b/64
siġefæst adj *sure of victory, triumphant*
siġefæstran comp npm 35d/19
Siġeferþ pr n *Sigeferth* ns 32/15, 24
siġefolc n:B2b *victorious people* siġefolca
gp 33/66 siġefolce ds 19/152
siġelēase adj *without victory, defeated* npm
25/91
siġerīċe n:B2h *victorious kingdom* as 18/117
siġerōf adj *triumphant, victorious* siġerōfe np
19/177
siġeþūf m:B1a *victory banner* siġeþūfas ap
19/201
siġewong m:B1a *field of victory* siġewonge
ds 19/294
siġle n:B2c.i *jewel, brooch, neckless* siġla gp
31a/95
sigor m:B1a *victory, triumph* as 19/89 sigora
gp 23/67 sigore ds 19/298 sigores gs
19/124 siogorum dp 28/53
sigorfæst adj *victorious, triumphant* nsm
23/150
sigorlēan n:B2b *reward of victory* as 19/344
ġesihð f:B3b *sight, vision, presence* ġesihðe
as 21b/12 ds 9b/106, 22/176 ġesyhðe as
14/15, 23/96 ds 23/21, 41, 66

silf, silfa, silfne < sylf
sillan, ġesille, silþ < (ġe)sellan
simle see symble
sīn poss pron *his, its, her* sīne apm 19/29
sīnes gsm 17/63 sīnne asm 7a/51 sīnre dsf
19/132 sīnum dsn 19/99, 31b/16
sinc n:B2b *treasure* ns 33/10 as 30/59, 37/35
since ds 23/23 sinces gs 19/30, 339, 38/25
sincald adj *ever cold* sincalda nsm 18/27
sincġestrēon n:B2b *treasure* sincġestrēonum
dp 31a/30
sincġyfa m:B5a *giver of treasure, lord*
sincġyfan as 30/278
sincþegu f:B3a *receiving of treasure*
sincþege as 38/34
sind, sindon < bēon-wesan
sinder n:B2c *dross, impurity* sindrum dp
35d/6
sinfulle f:B5c *house-leek* sinfullan as 3b/1
singal adj *continuous, everlasting* nsf 23/141
singallīċe adv *continually, incessantly* 25/103
singan III *sing, recite, chant, cry* inf 9b/14,
18 etc sang pt1s 1/40 pt3s 15b/1, 15c/1,
19/211 sincge pr1s 1/11 sing imp s 3c/3,
9b/24, 28 singað pr3p 35b/8 singe pr1s
15b/14 singende prp asm 26/22 singeð
pr3s 26/54 singð pr3s 15b/3, 15c/5 song
pt3s 9b/40, 62 sungon pt1p 1/41, 43, 44
pt3p 21a/60 syngan inf 1/46
ġesingian 2 *sin, do wrong* ġesingodest pr2s
27/19
sīnne see sīne
sinsorg f:B3b *constant sorrow* sinsorgna gp
40/45
sint < bēon-wesan
sīo < bēon-wesan
siodo m:B4a *custom, morality* as 5/7
siodðan see siþþan
ġesīoð < ġesēon
sioþþan see siþþan
Sirīċ pr n *Sigeric* ns 8/18, 24, 47
(ġe)sittan V *sit, dwell, remain, occupy* inf
17/101, 19/15 sæt pt3s 12/53, 14/12, 34/10,
etc ġesæt pt3s 22/22, 27/76, 38/111 sǣte
sbj pt3s 19/252 sǣton pt1p 17/74 pt3p
19/141 sit pr3s 2a/18, 27/5 sitt pr3s 15a/2,
ġesittað pr3p 18/117 sitte pr1s 4/90
sittende prp npm 14/43
sīþ adv *late, tardily*; in phr sīð ond late *at last*
19/275

sīþ m:B1a *journey, venture, experience, fate, time, occasion, movement* ns 31b/36 as 18/33, 64, 19/145, 31b/88 **sīþas** ap 26/2 **sīþe** ds 3c/7, 19/73, 109, 26/51, 32/19 **sīðes** gs 17/41 **sīþun** dp 3c/3

ġesīþ m:B1a *companion, retainer, comrade* **ġesīðas** np 19/201, 33/14 **ġesīþþe** ds 36/3

sīþfæt m:B2d *journey, expedition, venture* ns 2a/1 **sīðfate** ds 18/76, 19/335, 23/150

sīþian 2 *travel, go* inf 23/68, 30/177 **sīþade** pt3s 35d/11 **sīþað** pr3s 34/46 **sīðie** sbj pr1s 30/251

siþþan adv *afterwards, after, later, then, next, after that* 5/55, 6/24, 7a/28, 17/6, 8, 26/78, 35d/2, 5, etc **siodðan** 28/46 **sioþþan** 28/52 **syþþan** 1/42, 4/30, 31, 8/69, 16/56, 21a/27, 66, 23/142, etc

siþþan conj *after, since, when, once* 5/45, 64, 6/12, 28, 10/13, 69, 18/53, 57, etc **syþþan** 4/2, 19/189, 218, 21a/47, 22/102, 23/3, 49, 71, 31b/65, 98, etc

sixġylde adv *sixfold* 7a/3

sixtan < **syxta**

sixtiġ, sixtigan < **syxtiġ**

slāpan see **slǣpan**

slāt < **slītan**

(ġe)slæġene < **(ġe)slēan**

slǣp m:B1a *sleep* ns 38/39 ds 36/16 (see note) **slǣpe** ds 9b/40, 19/247, 21a/62 **slēp** as 22/40

slǣpan VII *sleep, fall asleep* **slāpan** inf 15b/11 **slǣpende** prp nsm 9b/40, 31b/90 **slǣpst** pr2s 1/69 **slēpon** pt1p 1/44 pt3p 14/66

slǣpern n:B2b *dormitory* as 1/70

slēan VI *strike, strike down, slay, slaughter, erect* inf 21a/59 **slæġene** pp npm 9a/42 **slogan** pt3p 9a/36 **sloge** sbj pt3s 30/117 **slōgon** pt3p 8/56, 19/231 **slōh** pt3s 18/39, 30/163, 285, 31b/74, 90

ġeslēan VI *strike, win (by fighting), conquer, inflict* inf 28/52 **ġeslæġene** pp npn 17/46 (*forged*) **ġesleġene** pp npm 19/31 **ġeslōgan** pt3p 9a/9 **ġeslōgon** pt3p 9a/60, 61, 10/4 **ġeslōh** pt3s 18/48

slēap < **slūpan**

sleġefǣġe adj *death-doomed* apm 19/247

slēp see **slǣp**

slēpon < **slǣpan**

slītan I *tear, rend* **slāt** pt3s 26/11

slīþen adj *cruel, terrible, dire* nsf 38/30 nsn 31a/85

slīðheard adj *cruel-hard, savage* **slīðhearda** nsm 17/41

(ġe)slōg-, (ġe)slōh see **(ġe)slēan**

slūpan II *slide* **slēap** pt3s 18/45

smale adv *finely* 3b/7

smēaġan 1 *ponder, think, meditate on, examine* **smēade** pt3s 25/9 **smēaġe** sbj pr3s 25/143 **smēaġende** prp nsm 15a/3 **smēað** pr3s 6/49, 22/119

smēagung f:B3d *thought, reflection* **smēagunge** ds 22/120 **smēaung** ns 6/75

smið m:B1a *smith, craftsman* **smiþa** gp 35a/8, 35d/14

smolt adj *peaceful, still* asn 9b/92

smylte adj *calm, serene* ism 9b/105 **smyltre** dsf 9b/104

smyrian 2 *smear, anoint* **smyriġenne** infl inf 22/16

(ġe)smyrwan 1 *smear, anoint* **smyre** imp s 3a/5 **ġesmyredest** pt2s 15c/14

snāð < **snīðan**

snāw m:B1a *snow* ns 22/23, 96 as 38/48 **snāwe** ds 22/96

snel adj *bold, keen* **snelle** npm 30/29 **snelra** gpm 19/199 (=noun)

snīðan I *cut, mow* **snāð** pt3s 35d/6

snīwan 1 *snow* **snīwde** pt3s 26/31

snotor adj *wise, clever, prudent, discerning* ns 33/54 (=noun) **snotera** comp nsm 20b/2 **snoteran** asf 19/55 **snotere** nsf 19/125 **snoterost** sup nsm 33/11 **snottor** nsm 38/111 (=noun)

snotorwyrde adj *wise of speech, plausible* nsm 24/54

snūde adv *quickly, at once* 19/55, 125, 199

sōcerd see **sācerd**

ġesoden, ġesodene < **sēoþan**

sōfte adv *softly, easily, quietly* 3c/6, 30/59 **sēfte** comp 17/96

(ġe)sōht- see **(ġe)sēċan**

sōm f:B3b *arbitration, agreement* **sōme** ds 12/23

some adv; in phr **swā some** *in the same way, likewise* 17/62 **swǣ same** 5/45

ġesomnian 2 *assemble, join* inf 9b/44 **ġesamnod** pp 14/10 **ġesomnad** pp 39/18

ġesomnung f:B3d *community, assembly*
  ġesomnunge ds 9b/57
somod adv *together (with), at the same time,*
  as well 19/163, 269, 282, 288, 38/39
  samod 4/42, 43, 22/153, 31a/1
sōna adv *at once, directly, soon* 5/39, 9a/7,
  10, 35, 9b/29, 41, 12/4, 16/24, 17/92,
  21a/44, 54, etc; in phr sōna swā *as soon as*
  8/76, 12/42, 27/27, 76, etc
song m:B1a *song, singing* ns 9b/61 as 26/19
  sang ns 31a/1 sanga gp 27/75 sange ds
  1/12, 21a/87, 27/28, 43 sangum 21a/68
  songes gs 9b/42
song < singan
songcræft m:B1a *art of singing, composing*
  poetry as 9b/12
sopcuppe f:B5c *sop-cup, drinking cup*
  sopcuppan gs 11/16, 20, 34
sorg f:B3b *sorrow, grief, trouble, care,*
  grievance ns 38/30, 39, 50 sorga gp 17/27,
  19/182, 23/80 sorge as 26/42, 54, 31a/87
  sorgum dp 19/88, 23/20, 59 sorh ns 22/142
sorgceariġ adj *anxious, sorrowing* nsm 36/28
  (=noun)
sorgian 2 *sorrow, grieve* sorgiende prp dsn
  9a/49 npm 17/10
sorglufu f:B3a *sad love* ns 36/16
sorh see sorg
sorhful adj *sad, anxious* sorhfulle asn 15b/8
sorhlēoð n:B2b *song of sorrow, lament* as
  23/67
sōtiġ adj *sooty, dirty* sōtigum dsm 34/7
sōþ adj *true, just, righteous* nsm 18/34 sōða
  adj nsm 24/23 sōðan asm 24/10, 73 sōðe
  nsf 16/61 sōðne asm 19/89, 344 sōþra
  comp gpm 35d/22 sōþre dsf 28/45 sōðum
  dsm 2a/25 dpn 18/76
sōþ n:B2b *truth* ns 34/19, 21 as 16/15, 25/29,
  155, 33/64 sōðan ds 24/62 sōþes gs 25/151;
  in phr tō sōþe ds *as a truth, in truth* 38/11
sōðfæst adj *steadfast in truth, righteous*
  sōðfæstra gpm 18/98 (=noun)
soðgied n:B2b.ı *true tale* as 26/1
sōþlīce adv *truly, indeed, certainly, really*
  14/9 (see note), 14, 40, 16/46, 96, 21a/75,
  22/88, 96, 109, 125, 27/16, 22, etc
spāca m:B5a *spoke* ns 6/52 spācan np 6/47,
  51, 62 gs 6/47 ds 6/53, 56 spācum dp 6/62
spanan VII *urge, allure* spēon pt3s 21a/25

sparian 2 *spare* sparedon pt3p 19/233
spāw < spīwan
spæc < sprecan
spǣċ < sprǣċ
spæcan < sprecan
spæra < spere
spætton < spittan
specan see sprecan
spēd f:B3g *success, means, power,*
  opportunity as 18/68 spēda ap 5/52
spēdan 1 *be prosperous, be wealthy* spēdaþ
  pr3p 30/34
spēddropa m:B5a *useful drops* spēddropum
  dp 35d/8
spēdiġ adj *successful, wealthy* nsm 1/67,
  23/151
spelboda m:B5a *messenger* spelbodan ap
  18/68
ġespelia m:B5a *vicar, deputy* ns 7c/12
spell n:B2b.i *narrative, tale, message,*
  statement, homily as 9b/49, 12/13, 30/50,
  34/16 spelles gs 9b/58 spellum dp 4/3,
  9b/65
spēon < spanan
spēow < spōwan
spere n:B2h *spear* ns 30/137 spæra gp 11/17
  speru ap 30/108
speremon m:B4b *track-man, tracker* ns 12/47
spillan 1 *destroy, kill* inf 30/34
spittan V *spit* spætton pt3p 14/32
spīwan 1 +d *spew, vomit* spāw pt3s 18/4
  spīwenne infl inf 8/78
spiwþa m:B5a *vomiting* spiweþan ds 3b/6
  spiwþan ds 3b/1
spōn m:B1a *sliver, shaving* spōnas ap 3c/2
ġespong n:B2a *fastening, clasp* np 17/40
sponge f:B5c *sponge* spongean as 14/60
spor n:B2a *track, trail* spore ds 5/35
sporwreċel m:B1b *what is tracked after*
  being driven off sporwreclas ap 12/48
(ġe)spōwan VII impers +d *avail, prosper,*
  succeed spēow pt3s 5/9, 19/274 ġespēow
  pt3s 19/175 ġespēwð pr3s 2a/12
sprǣc < sprecan
sprǣċ f:B3b *utterance, speech, language,*
  point, suit, charge ns 1/4, 7a/29 spǣċ ns
  12/38, 39 sprǣca ap 16/77 sprǣcan gs
  27/17 sprǣċe as 6/1, 18/72 gs 16/90 ds
  27/10, 31a/42

sprecan V *speak, say, utter* inf 1/1, 3, 4/59, 6/1, 9b/79, 23/27 **spæc** pt1s 12/7 **spǣcan** pt3p 25/8 **specan** inf 12/4 **specað** pr1p 24/40 **specenne** infl inf 25/70 **spræc** pt3s 13/14, 16/64, 17/1, 10, 18/107, 30/211 **sprǣcon** pt3p 22/20, 30/200, 212 **sprecaþ** pr1p 1/2 **sprece** pr1s 16/49 sbj pr2s 34/20 **sprecende** prp nsm 9b/27, 87, 90 **spriceð** pr3s 38/70 **spricþ** pr3s 16/43, 44 **sprycst** pr2s 1/10 **spycð** pr3s 12/2

sprengan 1 *spring, flex, split* **sprengde** pt3s 30/137

springan III *jump, spring out, burst open, spread* **sprang** pt3s 22/141, 30/137 **sprong** pt3s 31b/97

spycð < **sprecan**

spyrian 2 *make a track, track, travel* **spyrede** pt3s 35d/8 **spyriġean** inf 5/33

staf- see **stæf**

ġestāh < **ġestīgan**

stalu f:B3a *theft, stealing* ns 25/45 **stala** ap 25/110 **stale** np 22/43

stān m:B1a *stone, rock* ns 21a/72, 21b/18, 22/19 as 21a/53, 21b/17, 22/19, 21 **stānas** np 14/65, 22/162 **stāne** ds 22/22, 23/66

stānclif n:B2a *rocky cliff* **stānclifu** ap 26/23

(ġe)**standan** VI *stand, be positioned, sit, stand up, arise, remain, last, occupy, be, exist* inf 23/43, 62, 30/19, 171 **standaþ** pr3p 34/33 **stande** pr1s 1/34, 4/89 **standende** pp asf 21a/55 **stænt** pr3s 11/6 **stent** pr3s 15a/1 **stint** pr3s 6/42 **stōd** pt1s 23/38 pt3s 9b/23, 12/22, 25, 26, 14/1, 27/38, 31b/79, etc **stōdan** pt1p 28/50, 64 pt3p 37/38 **stōdon** pt1p 23/71 pt3p 5/28, 14/58, 19/267, 23/7, etc **ġestōdon** pt3p 23/63 **stondan** inf 12/19, 60 **stondað** pr3p 17/81, 26/67, 38/76 **stonde** pr1s 35c/4 **stondeð** pr3s 38/74, 115 **stynt** pr3s 16/52, 30/51

stang < **stingan**

stānhliþ n:B2a *rocky slope, cliff* **stānhleoþu** ap 38/101 **stānhliþe** ds 40/48

stānhof n:B2a *stone building* **stānhofu** np 37/38

starian 2 *stare, see (into), gaze (at)* inf 19/179 **starat** pr3s 34/17

ġestaþelian 2 *establish, restore, make steadfast* **ġestaþelade** pt3s 26/104

ġestaþelað pr3s 26/108 **ġestaðeliġe** pr1s 27/83

staþol m:B1a *fixed position, foundation, base, stem* ns 35c/4 as 35e/5 **staþelum** dp 26/109 **staþole** ds 23/71 **staðulas** ap 18/28

staðum < **stæð**

stædefæste < **stedefæst**

stæf m:B1a *letter, writing* (p) ns 4/29, 32, 53 **stafa** gp 4/36 **stafas** np 4/31, 38, 42, 57 **stafum** dp 4/31, 35, 39, 51, 59, 9b/4 **stæfe** ds 4/47

stæf m:B1c *staff, rod* ns 15c/12

stæfcræft m:B1a *grammar* ns 4/3 **stæfcræfte** ds 4/2

stæfġefēġ n:B2h *syllable* **stæfġefēgu** np 4/31 **stæfġefēgum** dp 4/31

stæfne, stæfnum < **stefn**

stǣlan 1 +d *accuse of, charge with* inf 33/23

ġestǣlan 1 *attribute, accuse* inf 17/54

stælġiest m:B1a *thieving visitor* ns 35e/5

stǣr n:B2b *history, narrative* as 9b/63 **stǣres** gs 9b/58

stæð n:B2a *shore, river-bank* **stæðe** ds 30/25 **staðum** dp 15c/9

ġestæððiġ adj *firm, unchanging* **ġestæððegan** dsm 6/4, 40

ġesteal n:B2b.i *structure, foundation* ns 38/110

stēam m:B1a *moisture* **stēame** ds 23/62

stēap adj *steep, deep, high, prominent* nsm 33/23, 37/11 **stēape** npm 19/17

stēaphēah adj 'steep-high', *erect* nsm 35c/4

stearc adj *severe* nsm 1/20

stearn m:B1a *tern* ns 26/23

stede m:B1g *place, position* as 30/19 **styde** 17/19

stedefæst adj *steadfast, unyielding* **stædefæste** npm 30/127 (=noun) **stedefæste** npm 30/249

stedeheard adj *firmly fixed* **stedehearde** apm 19/223 (see note)

stefn m:B1a *stem, root* **stefne** ds 10/34, 23/30

stefn f:B3c.i *voice, sound* ns 23/71 **stæfne** ds 27/44 **stæfnum** dp 18/17 **stefne** ds 14/57, 63, 18/105

stefna m:B5a *prow, stern of ship* **stefnan** ds 26/7

stelan IV *steal, rob* stele sbj pr3s 7a/9 stelþ
pr3s 7a/15

stemn see stefn

stemnettan 1 *stand firm* stemnetton pt3p
30/122

stenċ m:B1a *odour* stenċes gs 28/29

stent < standan

steorfa m:B5a *pestilence* ns 25/46

steorra m:B5a *star* ns 8/46, 22/159 steorrum
dp 24/16

steppan VI *step, go, march, advance* stōp
pt3s 30/8, 78, 131, 35d/10 stōpon pt3p
19/39, 69, 200, 212, 227

sterċedferhð adj *stout-hearted, determined*
sterċedferhðe npm 19/55, 227

stiċċemǣlum adv *little by little* 9a/51

stician 2 *stick, fix, stab, butcher* sticiað pr3p
6/50 sticode pp npm 9a/46

(ġe)stīeran 1 +d (person) +g (thing) *control,
restrain, prevent* inf 26/109 ġestīreð pr3s
3b/5 ġestȳrde pt3s 19/60

ġestīgan I *ascend, mount, descend, reach* inf
23/34 ġestāh pt3s 18/57, 23/40

stihtan 1 *direct, exhort* stihte pt3s 30/127

stillan < stille

stille adj *silent, unmoving, fixed* nsm 27/11
stillan dsm 6/3, 40 stillu npn 6/3

stille adv *still, quietly* 6/42, 18/105

stilnes f:B3e.ii *peace, silence* 27/40 stilnesse
as 5/51 ds 9b/103

stingan III *stab, pierce* stang pt3s 30/138

stint < standan

ġestireð < ġestīeran

stīþ adj *hard, severe, strong, resolute* nsn
30/301, 31b/42 stīþan asf 16/79 stīþe apm
26/104

stīðhicgende adj *firm of purpose, resolute*
30/122

stīþlīċe adv *fiercely, loudly* 1/72, 30/25

stīðmōd adj *resolute, stern-hearted* nsm
23/40 stīðmōda nsm 19/25

stōd, stōdon < standan

stōl m:B1a *chair, throne* as 17/29

stond- see standan

stōp, stōpon < steppan

storm m:B1a *storm, tumult, turbulence*
ns 18/14 stormas np 26/23, 38/101
storme ds 31a/69, 40/48 stormum dp
37/11

stōw f:B3b *place, religious foundation* ns
14/38, 28/9 stōwa as 5/31 np 25/66 ap 6/20
stōwe as 9b/83, 14/37, 28/12, 28 gs 28/14,
68 ds 5/70, 28/67, 69 stōwum dp 9a/52,
16/85

strang adj *strong, mighty, firm, bold, wilful,
resolute* nsm 23/40 stranga nsm 22/144,
147, 148 strangan gsm 35e/5 (=noun)
strange npm 23/30 strangestan sup dpn
9a/16 strangne asm 14/9 strengest sup
nsm 31b/52 strengra comp nsm 15b/12
strengran comp gpm 9a/11 strongum dsm
26/109

strǣl m:B1a *arrow* strǣlas ap 19/223
strǣlum dp 23/62

strēam m:B1a *current, stream, water, sea,
liquid* ns 33/23, 37/38 as 30/68 strēamas
np 18/14 ap 19/348, 26/34, 37/43 strēames
gs 35d/10

streċe adj *severe, violent* apm 24/28

strēgan 1 *strew, spread* inf 26/97

streng- see strang

strenġu f:B3h *strength, power* ns 35b/5
strenġe ds 31b/42

stric n:B2a *?sickness, ?contagion* ns 25/45

Strica pr n *Strica* ns 12/11

ġestrīenan 1 *beget, father* ġestrīene sbj pr3s
7b/29 ġestrȳnde pt3s 21a/84

strong see strang

stronglìċ adj *strong, firm, mighty* stronglican
asm 17/29

strūdung f:B3d *spoilation, robbery*
strūdunga ap 25/110

strȳnd f:B3g *race, stock* strȳnde ds 9a/26

ġestrȳnde < ġestrīenan

stund f:B3b *time, short while* stunde as
30/271

Stūrmere pr n *Sturmer* (Ess.) as 30/249

styde see stede

stȳlecg adj *steel-edged* nsn 31b/42

stynt < standan

stȳpel m:B1b *steeple, tower* as 24/6

ġestȳrde < ġestīeran

styrian 2 *stir up, urge* styrede pt3s 24/47
styrode pt3s 32/18

styrman 1 *storm, rage, bellow* styrmde pt3s
19/25 styrmdon pt3p 19/223

styrnmōd adj *stern-minded* styrnmōde npm
19/227

sulh f:B4b *plough* **syl** ds 1/20
sum adj *a certain, a, an, some, about* nsm
9b/1, 23, 16/6, 8, 12, 21a/43, 22/48, 118
nsn 4/23 nsf 17/95 asn 4/11, 64, 65, 6/37,
9b/49, 21a/38, 22/72 **suman** dsm 25/158
sumæ apf 5/48 **sume** asf 30/271 npm 16/93
apm 21a/27 **sumne** asm 4/10, 5/47, 21a/53,
22/55 **sumre** dsf 9a/31, 9b/20 **sumu** npn
6/34 apn 9b/87 **sumum** dsm 4/7, 21a/83,
21b/6 [etc]
sum pron *one, a certain one, some one* nsm
12/10, 35d/1 nsn 6/26 (twice), 26/68 **sume**
npm 9a/46, 47, 14/58, 16/75, 19/148,
21a/44 npn 4/92, 6/35 [etc]
sumor m:B4a *summer* ns 33/7 **sumera** ds
8/66 **sumeres** gs 26/54
sumorlang adj *long as in summer*
sumorlangne asm 40/38
Sumortūn pr n *Somerton* (Wilts.)
Sumortūne ds 12/11
suna < **sunu**
sund n:B2b *sea, water, swimming* **sunde** ds
31b/19
ġesund adj *sound, safe, well, unharmed*
nsm 2a/1, 5, 6/69 nsf 6/67 **ġesunde** npm
27/61, 63, 29/27 **ġesundran** comp npm
35d/19
sundersprǣċ f:B3b *private conversation*
sundersprǣċe ds 22/38
ġesundlīċe adv *safely, soundly* **ġesundlīcost**
sup 6/64
sundor adv *apart* 38/111
sundoryrfe n:B2h *private inheritance,
personal wealth* **sundoryrfes** gs 19/339
sune, sunena < **sunu**
sunna m:B5a *sun* ns 28/45 **sunnan** gs 28/21,
26 (twice), 31, 37, 39, 47
sunne f:B5c *sun* ns 10/13, 22/161 **sunnan** as
24/13, 35d/4
sunu m:B4a *son* ns 14/48, 53, 70, 22/168,
23/150, 24/42, 29/40, 30/76, 31a/27,
31b/59, 32/33 as 8/44, 16/50, 22/173,
31a/53 ds 2a/25 ap 10/42 **suna** ns 24/75,
30/298 gs 22/170 ds 16/5 np 9a/24, 13/15
ap 21a/84 **sunum** dp 13/18
sunwliteġ adj *beautiful with sunshine*
sunwlitegost sup nsn 33/7
sūpan II *sip, swallow* **sūpe** sbj pr3s 3c/5
sūr adj *sour* **sūre** npm 3b/8

sūsl f:B3ci *torment, misery* **sūsle** gs 16/70 ds
19/114
sūðan adv *from the south* **be sūðan** *south of*
5/17
sūþerne adj *southern* asm 30/134
sūðhealf f:B3b *south side* **sūðhealfe** as
8/54
Sūðseaxan pr n (mp:B5a) *the South Saxons,
Sussex* np 9a/19
swā adv *so, such a, as, thus, likewise, in this
fashion, in this respect, very* 1/20, 59, 67,
3a/10, 3c/7, 4/14, 7b/22, 41, 7c/8, 9a/39,
44, 9b/61, 15a/5, 7, 15b/2, 3, 15c/5, 16/20,
46, 21a/27, 22/93, 27/5, 30/33, etc **swǣ**
5/13, 16 etc; see also **þēah**
swā conj *as, just as, so, equivalent to, such
that, when, although* 7a/40, 48, 7b/18, 8/76,
9b/3, 33, 10/7, 13/11, 14/5, 15a/3, 17/44,
22/18, 23/92, 27/71, etc **swǣ** 5/19, 20 etc;
see also **sōna**
swā swā adv/conj (joined or separated) *as,
just as, just like, such as, just as though*
1/62, 4/9, 6/22, 9b/47, 60, 16/9, 21a/4, 6,
etc **swǣ swǣ** 5/69 **swā...swā** *such...as*
7b/36 *as* (or *so*)*...as* 22/23, 96, 27/67,
36/9 *the...the* 34/42; **swā hwā swā**
who(so)ever 17/101 **swā hwæt swā**
what(so)ever 6/20, 9b/3, 22/172, 27/20, 52,
etc **swā hwelċ swā** *who(so)ever* 29/15
swāf < **swīfan**
swān m:B1a *swineherd* ns 29/4
swāpan VII *sweep, rush* **swēop** pt3s 18/35
swāt m:B1a *blood* **swāte** ds 10/13 **swātes** gs
23/23
swātfāh adj *blood-stained* nsf 31a/49
swātiġ adj *bloody* nsn 31b/78 **swātiġne** asm
19/337
swāþēah see **þēah**
swaðu f:B3a *track, trail* **swaðe** ds
19/321
swǣs adj *beloved, dear* **swǣsne** asm 38/50
swǣsra comp gpm 35d/22
swǣsendo np:B2c *food, banquet* ap 19/9
swǣtan 1 *bleed* inf 23/20
swæð n:B2a *track, trail* as 5/33
swæþer (**swā + hwæþer**) pron *whichsoever,
whichever of two* asn 32/27
swealg, ġeswealh < (**ġe)swelgan**
ġeswearc < **sweorcan**

sweart adj *dark, black* sweartan nsm 28/15,
32/35 asm 10/61 gsf 17/8 apm 17/54
sweartlāst adv *with black trail* 35d/11
swefan V *sleep, die* swǣfon pt3p 18/50
swefn n:B2c.i *dream* as 9b/23, 46 swefna gp
23/1
swēġ m:B1a *sound, voice, noise, music* ns
31a/1 as 26/21, 27/28, 42
swēġan 1 *make a noise, sound* swēġaþ pr3p
4/43 swēġende prp npm 4/42 swēġendum
dpm 4/44 (=noun *vowel*)
swēġcræft m:B1a *musical skill* as 27/29, 33
swēġcræfte ds 27/31
sweġel n:B2c *heaven, sky* ns 33/7 sweġle ds
31a/16 sweġles gs 19/80, 88, 124, etc
Sweġen pr n *Svein* ns 8/80
swēġendlic adj *vocal* swēġendlicum dpm
4/55 (=noun *vowel*)
swelċ- see swilċ-
(ġe)swelgan III +d *swallow, imbibe* swealg
pt3s 35d/9, 35e/6 ġeswealh pt3s 18/67
swelgere m:B1g *swallower, glutton* ns 1/59
ġeswell n:B2b.i *swelling, tumour* as 21a/44,
62 ġeswel ns 21a/36, 42
sweltan III *die, perish* inf 28/69, 30/293
swulton pt3p 18/19 swylteþ pr3s 7a/46
swyltst pr2s 28/72
swenċan 1 *harass, afflict, oppress* swenċað
pr3p 15b/12 ġeswenct pp 21a/39 swencte
pt3s 31b/19 ġeswencte pp apm 6/72
sweng m:B1g *blow, stroke* as 31b/29
swenges gs 30/118
sweofot m/n:B1a/2c *sleep* sweofote ds
31b/90
sweoloð m/n:B1a/2c *burning heat, flame*
sweoloðe ds 31a/53
swēop < swāpan
swēora m:B5a *neck* swēoran as 19/106
swūra ns 21a/39 swūran as 21a/40 ds
21a/36, 37, 21b/18
swēorbēag m:B1a *necklace, torque*
swūrbēagum dp 21a/40 swȳrbēages as
11/18
(ġe)sweorcan III *grow dark, despair*
ġeswearc pt3s 18/16 ġesweorce sbj pr3s
38/59 sweorceð pr3s 36/29
sweorcendferhð adj *with darkening thought,
gloomy-hearted* sweorcendferhðe npm
19/269

sweord n:B2b *sword* ns 31b/78, 33/25 as
19/337 sweorda gp 10/4 sweorde ds
19/288 is 19/89 sweordes gs 10/68, 31a/44
sweordum dp 10/30, 19/194, 294 sword
ap 32/15 swurd ns 30/188 as 30/15, 47,
161, 237 ap 30/47 swurde ds 30/118, 32/13
swyrd ap 19/230, 317 swyrdum dp 19/264
sweordbealo n:B2g *sword-evil, death by
sword* ns 31a/85
sweoster f:B4c *sister* swistær ds 7b/46
swuster ns 21a/66 as 16/17 swustor ns
21a/48 gs 21a/51 ġeswustra ap 16/15
ġeswustrum dp 21a/48, 28/54 swystær ds
11/26 swyster ds 24/38
swēot n:B2b *army, company* ns 19/298 np
18/51
sweotole adv *clearly, openly* 19/177
sweotolor comp 6/37 sweotule 38/11
sweotollīċe adv *clearly, plainly* 19/136
sweotule see sweotole
swerian 2 *swear* sweriġe pr1s 27/82
swēte adj *sweet, pleasant* asn 26/95 (=noun
sweetness, what is sweet) swētes gsn 34/29
(=noun) swēteste sup asn 9b/60
swētnis f:B3e.ii *sweetness* swētnesse
ds 9b/69 swētnisse as 9b/5
ġeswētte adj *sweetened* npm 3a/8
swica m:B5a *deceiver, traitor* ns 22/6
swīcan I *deceive, be treacherous* swīcað
pr3s 24/69
ġeswīcan I *cease (from +g), abandon, fail*
(+d) inf 8/60 ġeswāc pt3s 31b/33
ġeswicon pt3p 13/4
swicdōm m:B1a *deception, fraud, treachery*
swicdōmas ap 25/111
swician 2 *deceive, betray, fail* swicode pt3s
25/55
swicol adj *false, deceitful, tricky* ns 24/54
swicolost sup nsn 33/10
swīfan 1 *intervene* swāf pt3s 12/49
swift adj *swift, fast* swiftne asm 37/18
swiftust sup nsn 33/3
swīge f:B5c *silence, quiet* ns 27/40
swīgian 2 *to be silent, become quiet* swīgað
pr3s 35b/1 swīġende prp nsm 27/31
swīgode pt3s 27/30
swilċ adj *such, similar* apf 3b/11 swilċere dsf
21a/53 swylċere dsf 21a/39 swylċum dsm
15b/11

swilċ pron/rel pron *such, whichever, such as, like* **swilċan** dpn 25/155 **swilċe** nsm 22/22 **swylċ** nsn 6/74 asn 24/73, 31b/92 **swylċe** npm 26/83 **swylċne** asm 14/8, 19/65 **swylċum** dpn 21a/88 [etc]

swilċe adv *likewise, also, thus, again, in addition to* (often in adv phrs **ēac swilċe**, **swelċe ēac**, etc *likewise, in the same way*) 10/19, 27/62 **swelċe** 6/45, 9b/8, 70, 107, 109 **swylċe** 9b/105, 15a/7, 19/18, 26/53, 31a/84, etc

swilċe conj *as if, as though, just as, such that, such a* 6/50, 21a/45, 61, etc **swelċe** 5/31, 6/1 **swylċe** 4/78, 6/74, 19/31, 23/8, 31a/94, 32/36, 40/1, etc; in phr **swylċe swā** *just as* 23/92

swīma m:B5a *stupor, swoon* **swīman** ds 19/30, 106

swimman III *swim* **swimmað** pr3p 38/53

swīn n:B2b *pig, boar, boar-image* **swīnes** gs 34/10 **swȳn** ns 31a/49

ġeswinċ n:B2b *affliction, pain* as 21a/38

swincan III *labour* **swinċe** pr1s 4/97

ġeswincdæġ m:B1c *day of toil* **ġeswincdagum** dp 26/2

swingan III *beat, scourge* inf 14/26

swingell f:B3c *stroke, blow* **swincgla** ap 1/8

swinsian 2 *sound melodiously, make melody* **swinsiað** pr3p 35b/7

swinsung f:B3d *sound, melody* **swinsunge** ds 9b/50

swistær see **sweoster**

swipian 2 *lash, scourge* **swipode** pt3s 18/18

swīþ adj *mighty, strong, great* **swīðran** comp *right* asf 14/45, 22/82, 23/20 dsf 14/31 (=noun *right hand*), 19/80 **swīþe** asf 37/24 **swīþre** comp nsf 26/115 **swȳðran** comp asf 22/83 **swȳðre** comp nsf 22/82

swīðan 1 *strengthen, fortify* **swīðed** pp 18/104

swīþe adv *very, greatly, deeply, strongly, firmly, violently* 2a/16, 3b/7, 7c/13, 8/42, 73, 9a/29, 9b/73, 94, 15c/14, 16/7, 27/53, 30/115, etc **swīðe swīðe** *very greatly* 5/36 **swīþor** comp *more, more firmly* 6/65, 14/21 **swīþost** sup *most of all, especially* 3a/8, 17/14, 34/9 **swīður** comp 6/71, 72 **swȳþe** 1/58, 8/20, 15c/8, 19/88, 22/99 **swȳþor** comp 19/182 **swȳðost** 21a/15; in instr phr **tō þan swīðe** *to such an extent that* 9a/29

swīðliċ adj *violent, great, excessive* asn 19/240 **swȳðlicum** dsf 24/67

swīþlīċe adv *greatly* 14/6

swīðmōd adj *arrogant, insolent* nsm 19/30, 339

swīþor < **swīþe**

swīðran < **swīþ**

swiðrian 2 *diminish, abate* **ġeswiðrod** pp 19/266 **swiðrode** pt3s 18/20 (see note)

swōgan VII *sound, resound* **swōgað** pr3p 35b/7

swoncor adj *slender, supple* **swoncre** apf 36/6

sword see **sweord**

ġeswugian 2 *keep silent* (+g *about*) **ġeswugedan** pt3p 25/152

swulton < **sweltan**

swūra, swūran < **swēora**

swūrbēagum < **swēorbēag**

swurd, swurde see **sweord**

swurdlēoma m:B5a *sword-light, flashing of swords* ns 32/35

swuster, swustor see **sweoster**

swustersunu m:B4a *sister's son* ns 30/115

ġeswustr- see **sweoster**

ġeswutelian 2 *reveal, show, make clear, make manifest* inf 22/114 **ġeswutelað** pr3s 4/74, 21a/10 **ġeswuteliað** pr3p 4/74, 77, 21a/4 **ġeswutelod** pp 4/76, 16/59, 62, 19/285, 21a/74 **ġeswutelode** pt3s 22/78, 111, 116

swutol adj *clear, evident* nsn 21a/73, 25/42, 105 **swutele** npn 21a/13

swylċ, swylċ- see **swilċ, swilċe**

swylt m:B1a *death* ns 37/26

swylteþ, swyltst < **sweltan**

swȳn see **swīn**

swȳrbēages < **swēorbēag**

swyrd, swyrdum see **sweord**

swyrdgeswing n:B2b *sword-stroke* as 19/240

swyster see **sweoster**

swȳþ- see **swīþ-**

sȳ < **bēon-wesan**

sȳfernyss f:B3e.ii *moderation* **sȳfernysse** ds 1/62

ġesyhðe < **ġesihð**

syl < **sulh**

syleð < (**ġe**)**sellan**

sylf adj *self, same* **seolfan** npm 9b/61 **sylfan** dsm 2a/25 dpm 9a/29

sylf pron *self, himself, herself, themselves*, etc
  self nsm 7b/19 **selfe** npm 5/23 **selfes** gsm
  31a/85 **selfne** asm 7b/22 **selfre** gsf 31a/53
  selfum dsm 5/39 **seolfes** gsm 9b/109
  seolfne asm 9b/108 **seolfra** gpm 28/76 **silf**
  nsm 16/34, 36, 87, 27/43 nsf 27/22 **silfa**
  nsm 21b/21 **silfne** asm 7c/11, 16/99 **sylf**
  nsm 12/25, 16/48, 26/35, 35d/28 asn 34/21
  sylfa nsm 17/4, 53, 18/96, 23/105 **sylfe** asf
  21a/34, 23/92 npm 9a/34 apm 4/38 **sylfne**
  asm 14/48, 50, 17/101, 22/114 **sylfra** gpm
  30/38 **sylfre** gsf 36/9, 40/2 dsf 19/335,
  21a/71 **sylfum** dsm 8/33, 9b/48, 26/1 dpm
  4/48, 51 dpn 4/86 [etc]
sylfor, sylfore < seolfor
syll- see (ġe)**sellan**
sȳllan < sēl
sylliċ adj *wonderful, marvellous* nsm 23/13
  syllicre comp asn 23/4
sylð < (ġe)**sellan**
symbel adj *continuous*; in phr **on symbel**
  always 19/44 (=noun asn)
symbel n:B2c *banquet, feast* **symbla** gp 38/93
  symble ds 9b/19 **symle** ds 19/15, 23/141
symbeldæġ m:B1c *feast-day, festival*
  symbeldæġe ds 14/7
symblan 1 *feast, banquet* **symblað** pr3p
  15c/15
symble adv *always, ever, continuously* 2a/5
  simle 16/83, 26/68, 29/17 **symle** 6/7, 67,
  9a/49, 24/76 **symlie** 11/21
symble, symle < symbel
Symon pr n *Simon* ns 14/36
syn see **synn**
sȳn, synd, synd- < bēon-wesan
syndriġ adj *special, private* **syndriġe** npm
  28/65 apn 21a/31
syndriġlīċe adv *specially, separately* 9b/1
ġesȳne adj *visible, seen, evident, conspicuous*
  nsn 25/80, 140 npf 33/1 **ġesǣne** nsn 25/105
  ġesīene nsn 25/42 **ġesīene** npm 23/46
synful adj *sinful, guilty* (usually =noun)
  synfullan npm 15a/9 **synfullra** gp 18/51
  synfullum dpm 22/99 **synfulra** gpm 15a/2
syngāla adv *continually, always* **syngāles**
  31a/73
syngian 2 *sin* sbj pr3p 25/129
synlēaw f:B3b *injury caused by sin* **synlēawa**
  ap 25/133

synn f:B3e *sin* ns 16/58 **sinna** ap 16/80 **syn**
  as 2a/17 **synna** gp 9b/72, 16/56, 22/60,
  25/109, 26/100 **synnan** dp 25/5 **synne** as
  17/54 a/ds 33/23 (see note) **synnum** dp
  2a/19, 9a/38, 23/13 etc
synscipe m:B1g *cohabitation, marriage* ds
  21a/82 **synscipes** gs 21a/17 **synscype** ds
  21a/12
synt < bēon-wesan
ġesynto f:B3h *success, deliverance,*
  salvation, welfare ns 28/75 **ġesynta** as
  2a/22 gp 19/90
syrċe f:B5c *mailshirt* ns 31a/49
ġesyrwed adj *armoured, armed* nsm 30/159
syrwian 2 *be deceitful, scheme* **syrwienda**
  prp nsm 24/69
sȳð see **sīþ**
syþþan see **siþþan**
syx num *six* 4/47, 11/16
syxta num adj *sixth* nsm 9a/3 **sixtan** dsf 14/55
syxtiġ num *sixty* **sixtiġ** 32/38 **sixtigan** dpm
  7c/27 **syxti** 2c/1
syxtȳne num *sixteen* 2c/3, 21a/51

T

tācen n:B2c.i *sign, portent, token, evidence*
  tācn ns 13/21, 24 **tācne** ds 12/49 **tācnum**
  dp 22/165
(ġe)tācnian 2 *show, signal, prefigure,*
  betoken, signify, mean, denote **tācnað** pr3s
  2a/6 **ġetācnað** pr3s 2a/3, 22/72, 82
  ġetācniende prp nsm 4/64 **ġetācniġe** sbj
  pr3s 4/67, 72 **ġetācnion** sbj pr3p 4/79
  ġetācnod pp 19/197, 286 **ġetācnode** pt3s
  16/27, 76, 77, etc, 22/144, 148, 149
  ġetācnodon pt3p 16/78
ġetācnung f:B3d *token, prefiguring,*
  signification, meaning ns 4/67, 72, 91,
  16/26, 81 **ġetācnunge** as 16/69, 72, 22/149
  ds 16/83
Tamer pr n *(River) Tamar* (Corn./Dev.) gs
  8/54
Tæafersceat pr n *Tæafersceat* (unidentified
  place) ds 11/20
tǣċan 1 *teach, instruct, show, interpret,*
  direct inf 4/13, 18/82, 22/63 sbj pr3p
  25/131, 140 **tǣċe** pr1s 4/75, 83 sbj pr2s 1/1
  tǣċon sbj pr3p 4/11 **tǣċþ** pr3s 16/90

ġetæ̆ht pp 27/72 tæ̆hte pt3s 16/37, 27/84
tæ̆hton pt3p 16/95
tæ̆ċing f:B3d *teaching* tæ̆ċinge ds 4/48
tæġel m:B1b *tail* ns 16/82, 84
tæ̆hte, tæ̆hton < tæ̆ċan
ġetæl n:B2a *number, sequence, reckoning* as
9b/58, 22/91 ġetæle ds 24/55 ġetel ns 4/70
tælan 1 *slander, wrong* tæleð pr3s 25/125
tælst pr2s 27/31
tæsan 1 *lacerate, tear* tæsde pt3s 30/270
tæt (þæt) < se
tē (ðē) < þū
tēaforġēap adj '*red-wide*' tēaforġēapa nsm
37/30 (=noun ?*wide red roof*)
tēah < tēon
teala adv *well, properly* 9b/100 (interj *good!*),
34/11
ġeteald, ġetealde < ġetellan
tealt adj *unstable, wavering* tealte npf 25/49
tēam m:B1a *family, progeny* ns 21a/6
tēar m:B1a *tear* tēaras np 27/17
Tefingstoc pr n *Tavistock* (Dev.) Tefingstoce
ds 8/56
ġetel see ġetæl
ġeteld n:B2b *tabernacle, tent* ns 16/70 as
21a/59 ġetelde ds 16/81
telġ m:B1a *dye, colour* ns 35d/15
telga m:B5a *twig, branch* telgan dp 28/11
ġetellan 1 *reckon, consider* ġeteald pp 24/39,
43 ġetealde pp npm 24/40, 68
Temese pr n *(River) Thames* ds 5/17
templ n:B2c.i *temple* as 14/47 temples gs
14/63
ġetenġe adj +d *near to, resting on* 35b/8
ġetēode < ġetēogan
teohhian 2 *intend, direct* tiohhað pr3s 6/25
ġetiohhod pp 6/41
tēon 1 *prepare, create, adorn* tēode pt3s
9b/38
(ġe)tēon II *drag, draw, bring* tēah pt3s 8/76,
19/99, 27/45, 47 ġetēah pt3s 31b/54
ġetogen pp 27/49 ġetugon pt3p 32/15
tēoðinglond n:B2b *land subject to tithe* ns
12/59
teran IV *tear* inf 19/281
than see þonne
tharf see þearf
Tharsus pr n *Tharsus* Tharsum as 27/15
thēm (þǣm) < se

thoncsnottur adj *discerning of thought,
prudent* thoncsnotturra nsm 20a/2
tīd f:B3g *time, season, occasion, feast-day,
hour, tense* ns 4/68, 21b/1 as 2a/11, 9a/55,
57, 9b/79, 14/56, 17/22, 75, 19/306,
26/124, etc tīda np 5/5 ap 6/20 gp 1/11 tīde
as 9b/77 ds 4/64, 7b/51, 9a/22, 31, 59,
9b/15, 14/55, 16/10, etc tīdum dp 25/146
tiid as 15c/17; in phrs sumre tīde *on a
certain occasion* 9b/20 tō sumre tīde *at a
certain time* 9a/31
tīddæġ m:B1c *final day, final hour* tīdeġe ds
26/69
Tifer pr n (f:B3c) *Tiber* Tifre gs 21b/18
tiġel f:B3c *tile* tiġelum dp 37/30
tīgrisc adj *of a tiger* tīgriscum dpf 28/6
tiid see tīd
til adj *good, brave, praiseworthy, useful* nsm
33/20 (=noun *good man*), 38/112 tilne asm
36/38 tilra comp gpm 35d/23
tilian II +g *provide for, support*
tilian 2 *strive, labour, provide for* (+d)
inf 19/208 (+ g of thing) tilien sbj pr1p
26/119
tiliġea m:B5a *labourer, toiler* tiliġera gp
34/33
tīma m:B5a *time* ns 1/47 tīman ds 16/13, 31,
22/120
ġetimbre n:B2h *building, structure* ġetimbro
np 9a/41 ap 9a/38
timbrian 2 *build* timbreð pr3s 34/32
ġetimbrian 2 *build* ġetimbrað pr3s 14/48
ġetīmian 2 *happen, fall out* ġetīmode pt3s
21a/102, 22/145
tintreġliċ adj *tormenting, infernal*
tintreġlican gsn 9b/69
tiohhað, ġetiohhod < teohhian
tīr m:B1a *fame, glory, honour* ns 19/157,
30/104 as 10/3, 19/197 tīres gs 19/93, 272
tȳr as 35d/23
tīrfæst adj *sure of glory* tīrfæstra gpm 33/32
(=noun)
tīð f:B3b *assent, favour* tīðe as 19/6
tīþian 2 *grant* tīþienne infl inf 16/4
tō adv *thereto, there* 8/17, 22/11, 12, 26/119
tō adv *too, too much* 25/11, 27, 30, 30/55, 66,
34/4, 23, 38/66, 67, 40/51, etc
tō prep +d/i/(g) *to, into, for, as, as to, in, of,
with* 1/20, 33, 2a/18, 4/53, 7a/5, 11, 7b/13,

8/4, 10/17, 12/7, 13/7, 9, 22/5, 33/15, etc;
with infl inf *to* (do something), *for* (doing
something) 5/49, 7b/4, 10, 15, 8/28, 78,
9b/61, 12/16, 22/16, etc; in instr phrs **tō ðī
þæt** *in order that* 22/39 **tō þon þæt** *to the
extent that, until* 9a/27; see also **swīðe, þæs**
(conj)

tōberstan III *burst open, break, shatter*
tōbærst pt3s 21b/18, 30/136, 144
tōburston pt3p 14/65, 22/162

tōblāwan V *blast, scatter* **tōblǣwð** pr3s
15a/8

tōbrecan IV *break to pieces, destroy, violate,
break open* **tōbræc** pt3s 22/138, 151
tōbrocen pp 30/242 **tōbrocene** pp npn
25/80 **tōbrocon** pp 8/39

tōbrēdan III +d *shake off, start awake from*
tōbrēdon inf 19/247

tōburston < **tōberstan**

tōcnāwan VII *understand, acknowledge,
recognise* inf 22/58, 24/19

tōcyme m:B1g *coming, arrival, advent* as
22/110 ds 16/20, 22/93, 25/5

tōdāl n:B2b *distinction, difference* ns 16/16

tōdæġ adv *today* 1/38, 48, 14/14, 27/68
tōdæġe 9a/22

tōdǣlan 1 *part, separate, share out* **tōdǣlað**
pr1p 4/30 **tōdǣlden** sbj pt3p 40/12
tōdǣldon pt3p 14/40, 42 **tōdǣled** pp 6/68,
69

tōēacan prep +d *in addition to, besides* 25/64

tōfēran 1 *be scattered, disperse* **tōfērdon**
pt3p 24/7

tōforan prep +d *before, in front of* 1/58

tōgædere adv *together* 4/55, 7b/1, 8/32, 42,
9a/12, 25/71, 100 **tōgædre** 37/20

tōġēanes adv *against, opposite* 31b/10

tōġēanes prep +d *against, towards, at* 22/30,
36, 105, 26/76, 31b/51 **tōġēnes** 14/36

ġetogen < **tēon**

tōġenȳdan 1 *compel* **tōġenȳdd** pp 1/9

tōġeþēodan 1 *add* **tōġeþēodde** pt3s 9b/42

ġetoht n:B2b *battle, conflict* **ġetohte** ds
30/104

tohte f:B5c *battle* **tohtan** ds 19/197

tōhweorfan III *go apart, disperse* **tōhwurfon**
pt3p 8/81

torht adj *radiant, beautiful* **torhtan** asf
19/43

torhte adv *brightly, splendidly* 35b/8

torhtliċ adj *splendid* nsm 19/157

torhtmōd adj *illustrious, glorious* nsm 19/6,
93

torn n:B2b *anger, misery, affliction* as
19/272, 38/112

torne adv *bitterly* 19/93

tornġemōt n:B2b *hostile meeting* as 31a/78

torr m:B1a *tower* **torras** np 37/3

tōrȳpan 1 *scratch* **tōrȳpte** pt3s 12/48

tōsenċan 1 *submerge, drown* **tōsenċende** prp
nsm 13/21

tōslītan I *tear apart, rend, separate, destroy*
tōslīte sbj pr3s 7b/32 **tōsliten** pp 14/64
tōslīteð pr3s 39/18

tōslūpan II *slip away, fall apart* inf 6/18

tōtwǣman 1 *divide, break up* **tōtwǣmed**
pp 30/241

tōþ m:B4b *tooth* ns 7a/26 **tōðon** dp 19/272
tōþum dp 7a/26, 28/15

tōðmæġen n:B2c *strength of tusks*
tōðmæġenes gs 33/20

tōweard adj *coming, imminent, future* nsm
19/157 nsf 19/286 **tōweardan** gsm 9b/68
gsn 6/71 **tōweardra** gpn 16/26

tōwearde adv *beforehand* 16/28

tōweorpan III *cast down, destroy* **tōwyrpð**
pr3s 14/47

tōwyrd f:B3g *opportunity* **tōwyrde** as 9a/32

traht m:B1a *text, exposition* as 22/68

trahtnere m:B1g *expounder, commentator* ns
22/130

trahtnung f:B3d *exposition, commentary*
trahtnunge ds 22/68

træf n:B2a *tent* as 19/268 **træfe** ds 19/43,
255

tredan V *step on, trample* **trede** pr1s 35b/1

trēow n:B2g.i *tree* as 23/4 etc np 28/33
trēowa gp 28/11 **trēowe** ds 15a/4 **trēowu**
ap 28/29 **trēowum** dp 28/30, 32 etc **trīo** ns
28/26 np 28/31 ap 28/20 gp 28/31 **trīow** ns
28/27, 55, 59 **trīowa** gp 28/45 **trīowum** dp
28/70

trēow f:B3f *truth, faith, good faith* ns 33/32
trēowe as 31a/10, 38/112

(ġe)**trēowan** 1 *believe in, trust; exculpate
oneself, clear oneself* **trēowde** sbj pt1s
34/11 **trīowan** inf 7b/22 **ġetrīowe** sbj pr3s
7b/25

ġetrēowe adj *faithful, loyal, trustworthy*
ġetrēowestan sup apm 28/65 ġetrēowra
comp npm 35d/23 ġetrȳwe nsm 1/37
trēowen adj *wooden* trēowenre dsf 21a/48
trēowġeþofta m:B5a *faithful comrade*
trēowġeþoftan np 28/66
ġetrēowþ f:B3h *truth, loyalty* ġetrēowþa gp
25/8 ġetrȳwða np 25/49 ap 25/163
ġetrifullan 1 *bruise, crush* ġetrifuladre
pp gsf 3a/4
trīo, trīo- see trēow
trīowan, ġetrīowe < (ġe)trēowan
trum adj *strong, firm, secure, vigorous* nsm
18/108, 33/20 trumne asm 19/6
ġetrum n:B2a *army, troop, company*
ns 33/32
ġetruwian 2 *trust, put trust in, confirm*
ġetruwedon pt3p 31a/33 ġetruwode pt3s
31b/42
trym n:B2a *piece, short length* as 30/247
trymian 1 *arrange, draw up, exhort* inf 30/17
trymedon pt3p 30/305 ġetrymmed
pp 30/22
ġetrymman 1 *strengthen, comfort*
ġetrymmende prp nsm 9b/97
trymmyng f:B3d *strengthening, encouraging*
trymmynge ds 22/66
ġetrȳwe see ġetrēowe
ġetrȳwlīċe adv *truly, loyally* 25/54
ġetrȳwða < ġetrēowþ
tū see þū
tūa < twēġen
tūn m:B1a *enclosure, estate, manor,*
homestead, village tūnæ ds 11/7 tūne ds
7a/10, 20, 7b/18, 34/45
tunge f:B5c *tongue* ns 9b/106 tungan as
9b/14
tūnġerēfa m:B5a *estate steward* tūnġerēfan
ds 9b/42
tungol n:B2c *star, planet, constellation* ns
10/14, 33/48 tungl ap 6/31
twā, twām < twēġen
twēġen num *two, a pair* npm 4/57, 6/13,
9a/23, 30/80 apm 3b/3, 14/45, 64, 16/97,
98 tūa apn 12/45 twā npn 6/13, 11/8,
22/109 apm 4/32, 15c/1 apn 16/97 (thrice),
27/54 apf 4/2, 16/14, 15, 98 (twice) twām
dpm 14/17, 21a/3, 21b/8, 22/44 dpn 11/25
twēġa gpn 30/207 twēġea gsm 11/15

twelf num *twelve* 16/33, 21a/12, 27 twelfe
npm 25/93
twelfġylde adv *twelvefold* 7a/2
twelfta num adj *twelfth* twelftan asm 15b/1
twēnteogeþa num adj *twentieth*
twēnteogeþan asm 15c/1
twēntiġ num *twenty* 4/36, 27/55
twēo m:B5a *doubt, hesitation, uncertainty*
twēon ds 22/80, 26/69 twȳn ds 22/134
twēon II +g *doubt, hesitate* (+g) twēode
pt3s 19/1, 345
twēonum see be
tweowa adv *twice* 1/35
twibōte adv/adj *with* (or *subject to*) *double*
compensation 7a/8
twig n:B2a *twig, shoot* as 13/9 twigu np 3b/9
twiġylde adv *twofold* 7a/4
twȳn < twēo
tȳde < tīd
tȳdran 1 *beget offspring, propagate* inf
33/48
tȳma see tīma
tȳman 1 *bring forth, beget offspring* inf 33/48
tȳmde pt3s 16/18
tȳn num *ten* tȳne npm 25/93 apm 25/92
tȳr see tīr
Tysseburg pr n (f:B4b) *Tisbury* (Wilts.)
Tyssebyriġ ds 12/50

þ

þā adv *then, at that time, after that time,*
thereupon, there 7b/1, 10, 8/1, 28, 9a/1, 9,
9b/22, 24, 13/1, 2, 3, 14/1, 2, 21a/25,
22/10, 23/27, 33, 27/1, 3, 35e/2, etc; see
also ġȳt
þā conj *when, seeing that, now that, if, as,*
since, because, where 2c/2, 3, 8/42, 9a/11,
9b/22, 28, 14/10, 23/36, 41, 27/2, etc þā þā
(often joined) *when* 1/39, 21a/11, 22/5,
27/21, etc
þā (dem adj, pron) < se
ġeþafa adj indecl +g *consenting* (to), *in*
agreement (with) 12/24, 17/77
(ġe)þafian 2 *allow, assent to, consent to* (+a)
ġeþafian inf 19/60 ġeþafiġe sbj pr3s 7c/14
þafode pt3s 9b/56
(ġe)þafung f:B3d *consent, permission,*
accord ġeþafunga ds 11/3, 29 ġeþafiungæ

ds 11/22 ġeþafunga ds 11/6 þafunge as 25/92 ds 24/23 ġeþafunge ds 9a/53

þāġȳt see ġȳt

ġeþāh < ġeþicgan

þām < se

þan (þām, þon) < se

þanc m:B1a *thought, reflection, pleasure*; *thanks* (for +g) as 30/120, 147, 34/29 þances gs 20b/2 þonc ns 5/18, 69, 26/122

ġeþanc m:B1a/n:B2b *thought, mind, purpose* as 30/13 ġeþance ds 22/118, 25/128 ġeðonce ds 19/13

(ġe)þancian 2 +d (person) +g (for a thing) *thank, give thanks to* inf 15c/3 þancað pr3s 15c/5 ġeþance pr1s 30/173 þanciað pr3p 15c/6 þanciġende prp nsm 21a/59, 27/72 þancode pt3s 21a/37, 27/24

þancolmōd adj *thoughtful, attentive* þancolmōde asf 19/172

þancung f:B3d *thanksgiving, thankfulness* þancunge ds 1/57

þanon adv *thereupon, after that; thence, from there, out* 7c/7, 8/82, 9a/22, 18/70 þanonne 19/132 þonan 6/8, 9, 19/118, 35d/3, 38/23

þār, þārtō see þǣr, þǣrtō

þāre < se

þæ, þǣ see þe, þē

þæġn, þæġne < þeġn

þǣm < se

þæne (þone) < se

þænne see þonne

þǣr adv *there, then, in that respect* 3a/9, 6/10, 7a/5, 7, 45, 7b/18, 8/35, 40, 9b/17, 22, 14/58, 69, 17/63, 22/29, 30, 36, 23/8, 9, etc þār 27/1, 43

þǣr conj *where, when, while* 9a/34, 17/51 (see note), 58, 18/91, 100, 22/27, 23/123, 139, 26/6, 10, 35d/4, etc þēr 21b/8; often in conj phr þǣr þǣr *there where, where, wherever* 5/21, 21a/69, etc

þǣræt adv *thereat, there* 12/47

þǣre < se

þǣrinne adv *therein* 12/25, 13/15, 19/50, 29/31

þǣrofer adv *thereover* 14/41

þǣron adv *thereon, therein* 6/59, 12/22, 14/61, 22/139, 23/67

þǣrrihte adv *immediately* 14/63, 16/32

þǣrtō adv *thereto, pertaining to (it), as well,*

for that (purpose) 1/36, 4/87, 12/10, 16/25, 21a/56 þārtō 7c/16

þæs adv (gs of þæt) *afterwards, in respect of that, to that degree, so, therefore* 12/23, 21a/76, 25/39, 139, 143, 26/39, 40, 31a/17, 18; in phr tō þæs *so* 26/40, 41

þæs conj (gs of þæt) *as, because, after* 10/51; in phrs þæs þe *according to what, as, to the extent that* 6/6, 17, 10/68, 24/7, 64, 25/141, 149 tō ðæs þe 31b/94

þæs (demons adj/pron) < sē, þes

þæt conj *that, so that, on condition that, because* 1/1, 20, 2a/10, 12, 3a/11, 4/6, 7, 5/17, 19, 20, 7b/10, 12, 40, 8/22, 27, 13/4, 10, 13, etc þet 8/62, 78; see also oð

þæt (def art, demons pron) < se

þætte (þæt þe) conj *that, which, so that* 5/16, 18, 6/9, 9b/3, 61, 18/64, etc

þe indecl rel part/conj *who, which, that, when, as, because* 1/25, 58, 2a/19, 3a/8, 10, 11, 4/2, 7a/1, 27, 8/23, 27, 9b/3, 13/1, 14/11, 19, 27/4, 33/2, 9, etc þæ 11/26 þe ... þe *either ... or* 14/11, 22/87 þe *than*; see mā

þē (instr of se, þæt) see þȳ

þē (pron) < þū

þēah adv *nevertheless, even so, yet, still, however* 5/58, 6/2, 26, 42, 15b/13, 16/86, 17/23, 55, 22/164, 27/11, 29/33, 30/289, etc swā þēah 4/23, 92, 13/11, 16/25, 47, 34/11, etc swāþēah 21a/4, 83, 4/34, 42

þēah conj *though, although, even if* 4/25, 6/26, 52, 7c/22, 15c/11, 17/22, 25/106, 26/97, 113, 27/10, 34/11, etc þēah þe 16/67, 107, 21a/2, 19, 25, 22/128 þēh 24/68, 25/41, 129, 132

þēahhwæþere adv *yet, moreover* 1/12, 22/113

ġeþeaht n/f:B2i *advice, counsel, purpose* as 15a/1, 15b/8 ġeþeahte ds 6/25, 7b/3, 7c/3, 15a/9

þearf f:B3b *need, hardship, distress* ns 3c/6, 7b/12, 9b/89, 20b/2, 25/29, 155, 157, 158 tharf ns 20a/2 þearfe as 19/3, 92, 30/175 ds 30/201, 31b/34, 34/3

þearf, þearft < þurfan

þearfende adj (prp of þurfan) *in want, needy, wretched* asn 9a/48 þearfendre dsf 19/85

ġeþearfian 2 *necessitate, force* ġeþearfod pp 31a/41

þearfliċ adj *advantageous* þearflucustþ sup
nsn 11/31

þearle adv *very hard, harshly, violently,
sorely, keenly* 1/19, 10/23, 14/70, 19/74,
86, 262, 23/52, 25/47, 27/46, 80, etc

þearlmōd adj *stern-hearted, severe* nsm
19/66, 91

þēaw m:B1a *custom, practice, disposition,
virtue* ns 9b/80, 38/12 þēawa gp 25/119
ðēawas ap 5/25 ðēawum dp 16/73, 19/129

þeġenġylde n:B2h *payment for a thegn* as
25/87

þeġenlīċe adv *like a thegn, loyally* 30/294

þeġn m:B1b.i *thegn, nobleman, retainer,
warrior, follower* (see 8/12n) ns 9b/84,
31b/63, 32/13 as 9b/82 þæġn ns 8/12 þeġen
ns 25/86 as 25/85, 96, 30/151 þeġenas np
30/205, 220 ap 30/232 þeġene ds 25/85
þeġenes gs 25/94 þeġna gp 17/77 þeġnas
np 19/306, 23/75, 29/15, 19 ap 19/10
þeġne ds 17/72, 21a/83 þēnan dp 25/26

þeġnian 2 *serve, minister to* +d inf 9b/82
þēnian inf 21a/34, 22/72 þēnode pt3s
21b/9

þēgon < þicgan

þēh see þēah

þēnan < þeġn

(ġe)þenċan 1 *think, think of, consider, reflect,
remember, intend, desire* inf 12/28, 26/96,
118, 36/12, 31, 38/58 þæncþ pr3s 11/5
þenċ imp s 2a/8 ġeðenċ imp s 5/22 þenċaþ
pr2p 22/49 pr3p 2a/19, 23/115 þenċe sbj
pr3s 28/49 þenċean inf 17/71 ġeðenċean
inf 5/17 þenċeð pr3s 17/64, 23/121, 26/51,
31b/44 ðencð pr3s 6/23 ġeþōht pp 6/11
þōhte pt1s 4/4 pt3s 19/58 ġeþōhte pt3s
38/88 þōhton pt3p 19/208

þenden conj *so long as, while* 17/73, 19/66,
26/102

þengel m:B1b *prince* as 31b/16

þenian 2 *stretch out, rack* inf 23/52

þēnian see þeġnian

þēning f:B3d *divine service* ðēninga ap 5/14

þēo see sēo

þēod f:B3b *nation, people, tribe* ns 9a/18
þēode as 22/18, 25/7, 11, 64, 100, etc gs
28/8 ds 7c/12, 9a/39, 25/30, 41, 43, 79, etc
np 18/41, 21b/5 þēodum dp 9a/28, 10/22,
22/61, 24/45, 25/20 ðīoda np 5/47

ġeþēodan 1 *join* ġeþēodde pp npm 9b/57

þēode < þēod, þēowan

ġeþēode n:B2h *speech, language* ġeðēoda gp
5/42 ġeþēode ds 28/9 ġeþēodes gs 28/59
ġeðīode as 5/50 ds 5/30, 38, 44, 46, 47

þēoden m:B1b *lord, prince, ruler, the Lord* ns
19/66, 91, 30/120, 178, 232 as 30/158
þēodne ds 19/11, 23/69, 30/294, 31b/34
þēodnes gs 19/268, 38/95 þēoðnes gs
19/165

þēodenlēas adj *lordless* ðēodenlēase npm
31a/41

þēodenmāðm m:B1a *princely treasures*
þēodenmāðmas ap 17/72

þēodguma m:B5a *man, people* np 19/208
þēodguman np 19/331

þēodlond n:B2b *country* þēodlonde ds 28/5

þēodne, þēodnes < þēoden

ġeþēodnis f:B3e.ii *joining, conjugation*
ġeþēodnisse ds 9b/8 ġeþēodnyss ns 4/69

þēodrīċ pr n *Theodric* ns 36/18

þēodscipe m:B1g *nation; discipline, law* ns
25/108 þēodscipes gs 18/83 þēodscipum
dp 9b/74

þēodwita m:B5a *learned man* ns 25/146

þēof m:B1a *criminal, thief* ns 12/51, 33/42,
35e/4

þēofmann m:B4b *thief* as 14/9

ġeþēon I/II *thrive, prosper* inf 2a/7, 33/44

þēos, þeoss- see þes

þēostrum < þȳstro

þēow adj *serving, enslaved* þēowa gpm 27/56
þēowum dpm 7b/49, 54, 27/56, 63

þēow m:B1fi *slave, servant* þēowa as 4/8 gp
9b/57 þēowas np 25/25 ap 21a/14, 25/28
þēowum dp 4/17, 25/27 ðīowa gp 5/28

þēowa f:B5c *slave-woman* ns 7a/18 ðēowan
ds 7a/23

þēowan 1 *serve* þēode pt3s 9b/104

þēowdōm m:B1a *slavery, servitude* as 9a/47
þēowdōme ds 15c/2

þēowen f:B3c *handmaiden, female slave* ns
19/74 þēowne as 7b/38

þēowian 2 *be subject to, enslave, serve,
follow* (+d) inf 21a/24 ġeþēowede pp npn
25/36 þēowode pt3s 21b/9 ġeþēowuð
pp 11/8

þēowmon m:B4b *slave* ns 7b/38

þēr see þǣr

þes, þis, þēos demons pron/adj *this, these*
[§A1b]:
þās asf 4/1, 16/8, 23/12 npm 1/14, 4/38,
7b/1 npn 22/144 apn 17/84 þæs nsm 17/19,
37/9 þēos nsf 4/4, 22/72, 23/12 þeosse gsf
9b/1 þeossum dsm 9b/25 þes nsm 14/20,
71, 27/6 þios nsn 6/39 þīos nsf 6/24 þis
nsm 14/44 nsn 13/21 nsf 7c/2 asn 8/13,
14/59 þīs ism 30/316 þises gsn 22/84 þisne
asm 14/14, 38/88 þisre gsf 22/86, 125
þissa gpn 7b/13 gpf 7b/34 þisse dsf 1/39,
2a/7, 6/34 þissere dsf 16/98, 103 þisses gsn
9a/51 þissum dsm 8/39 dsn 2a/3, 9a/31,
10/68 þisum dsn 1/43, 4/40 dpm 14/17 þȳs
ism 19/2 isn 19/89, 28/72 þysan dsm 25/35,
48 dsn 25/14 þyses gsm 14/23 þysne asm
15b/1 þyson dsm 15c/7 þyssa gpm 19/187
þysse dsf 19/66, 25/41, 43 þysses gsn 9a/9
þysson dsn 23/138 þyssum dsn 2a/6,
17/100, 23/83 þysum dsn 1/42 [etc]
þet (þæt) < se, sēo, þæt
þī < se, sēo, þæt, þȳ
þiċċe adj *thick, viscous* apm 3a/10
(ġe)þicgan V *receive, accept, take, consume*
ġeþāh pt3s 36/40 ġeþicgean inf 29/17
þēgon pt3p 19/19 þicge sbj pr3s 3c/6
þicnes f:B3e.ii *thickness* þicnesse as 3b/4
þider adv *thither, there, to that place* 12/36,
26/118, 28/19, 29/15, 20
þiderweardes adv *thither* 6/2
þīn poss pron *thy, thine, your, yours* þīn nsm
15c/12 nsf 27/33 nsn 13/14, 15c/15 þīne
npm 1/14, 13/15 asf 15b/13 þīnes gsn
2a/11 þīnne asm 15b/14 asf 27/11 þīnre
gsf 19/85 dsf 11/3, 15b/13 þīnum dpf
2a/13 þȳræ dsf 11/4 [etc]
þinc- see þynċan
þincg see þing
Þincgferþ pr n *Thingferth* ns 29/41
Þincgferþing adj *son of Thingferth* nsm
29/41
þīnen f:B3e.i *handmaiden, female servant*
þīnena ap 16/15 ðīnenne as 19/172
þīnenum ds 21a/34
þing n:B2b *thing, matter, event, case,
circumstance, cause, act, property* ns 14/13
as 4/64, 65, 8/55, 14/3, 22/72, etc np 3a/12,
6/34, 36, 76 ap 1/39, 4/33, 66, 6/34, 65,
9b/87, 14/69, 22/144, 27/65 þincg as 22/54

np 6/14 þinga gp 16/26, 27, 26/68, 27/45,
47 þingan dp 7c/24 þingc ap 1/56, 58
þinges gs 6/33, 19/60 þingum dp 4/93,
22/85, 27/36, 82, 28/49
ġeþing n:B2a *agreement, terms* ġeþingo ap
31a/23
þingian 2 *pray, intercede (for +d), supplicate*
inf 7c/16 sbj pr1p 25/157 ðingade pt1s
12/7 þingiæ sbj pr3s 11/21
þingð < þynċan
ġeþīode < ġeðēode
þios, þīos < þes
þīowa < þēow
þīowotdōm m:B1a *service* ðīowotdōmas
ap 5/11
þis, þis-, þiss- see þes
ġeþōht m:B1a *thought, mind, purpose* as
36/22 ġeþōhtas np 26/34 ġeþōhte ds
28/69, 71
ġeþōht < ġeþenċan
þōhte, þōhton < þenċan
ġeþōhtung f:B3d *idea, counsel* ġeþōhtnunge
ds 2a/7
(ġe)þolian 2 *suffer, endure* inf 30/6, 201, 307
þoledon pt3p 19/215 þoliað pr1p 17/52,
25/102 ġeþolie sbj pr3s 34/25 þolien sbj
pr1p 17/30 þoliġende prp npm 19/272
ġeþolod pp 14/14 þolodan pt3p 23/149
þolode pt3s 21a/38, 31b/34
þon < se; see also æfter, ēac, tō, wið
þon see þonne
þonan conj *whence, from where* 28/57
þonan see þanon
þonæ (þone) < se
þonc see þanc
ġeðonce < ġeþanc
þoncwyrðe adj *'thankworthy', gratifying* asn
19/153
þone < se
þonne adv *then, now, therefore, henceforth,
rather, however, besides* 3b/4, 8, 4/13, 26,
6/12, 19, 7a/27, 7b/14, 7c/6, 10, 8/80,
9a/39, 12/41, 16/24, 40, 21a/33, 22/10, 50,
23/107, 115, 26/94, 118, 27/11, 28/39,
35b/5, etc þanne 7a/27 þænne 1/28 þonnæ
11/3
þonne conj *when, while, since, namely, yet*
1/58, 3b/10, 8/79, 15a/8, 21a/41, 73, 22/91,
98, 26/8, 65, 34/6, 14, 35b/1, 8, etc

þonne conj + comp *than* 4/58, 7b/15, 12/12, 28, 33, 15b/12, 22/10, 66, 23/128, 26/65, 34/25, 37 **than** 20a/2 **þænne** 1/7 **þon** 30/33

Þor pr n *Thor* ns 24/45, 60

þorfte, þorftun < þurfan

þorn m:B1a *thorn* þornum dp 14/30

Þorod pr n *Thorod* Þorode ds 8/29

þrāg f:B3b *time period, season* ns 38/95 þrāgum dp 33/4 (=adv *at times*); in phr **ealle þrāge** as *continuously* 19/237

ġeþrang n:B2b *throng, crowd* ġeþrange ds 30/299

þrǣl m:B1a *slave* ns 25/85, 96 as 25/86 þrǣla gp 25/83 þrǣle ds 25/85, 97

þrǣlriht n:B2b *rights of a slave* np 25/38

þrēa f:B3f *pain, punishment* ap 17/52

þrēat m:B1a *troop, host, oppression* as 14/28, 39/2, 7 ðrēate ds 19/62 ðrēatum dp 19/164

ġeþrēatian 2 *force, attack* ġeðrēatað pr3s 7b/37

þrēaung f:B3d *reproof, correction* ns 15c/13

þrēo, þrēora < þrīe

þridda num adj *third* þriddan asm 22/8 gsf 7a/42 dsm 3c/7, 4/92, 94, 7b/33, 21a/46, 22/7, 60 dsf 7a/23 þridde nsf 7a/18

þrīe num *three* asm 28/65 þrēo nsn 28/1 npm 4/36 apn 3b/7, 3c/4, 4/33 þrēora gp 2b/1, 5, 26/68 gpm 30/299 þrī npm 16/63 þrīm dpm 14/47, 16/64 dpn 9a/5, 16 þrīo nsn 28/23 þrȳ npm 22/170, 24/75 apm 21a/84 þrȳm dpm 24/74

þrih < þrūh

þrīm < þrīe

þringan III *throng, press, constrict, pinch* inf 19/249 ġeþrungen pp 19/287, 26/8 þrungon pt3p 19/164

þrīnnys f:B3e.ii *trinity* ns 16/58 þrīnnis ns 16/61 ðrȳnesse gs 19/86

þrīste adv *boldly, confidently* 36/12

ġeþrīstlǣċan 1 *presume, dare* inf 7b/4

þrītiġ num *thirty* 36/18 þrītæġum dpn 11/18 þrīteġum dpn 11/19 ðrittiġ 21a/85 þryttiġ 21a/84

þriwa adv *three times* 3c/3

(ġe)þrōwian 2 *suffer, endure* inf 3a/6, 22/59 þrōwade pt1s 26/3 pt3s 22/30, 174, 31b/98 þrōwiġe sbj pr3s 7b/18 þrōwiġenne infl inf 4/65 þrōwode pt3s 23/84, 98, 145 ġeþrōwode pt3s 21b/15

þrōwiendliċ adj *suffering, passive* ðrōwiendliċe npn 4/78, 86

þrōwung f:B3d *passion, suffering* þrōwunge as 4/68 ds 9b/66, 22/56, 107, 161

þrūh f:B4b *tomb, coffin* ns 21a/70 as 21a/55, 58, 22/12 þȳrih ds 22/19 þrȳh ds 21a/69, 22/78 ðrīh ds 22/81

ġeþrungen < þringan

þrȳ < þrīe

þryċċan 1 *oppress, crush* þryċċed pp 9b/78

þrȳh < þrūh

þrym m:B1a *might, glory, majesty* ns 19/86, 38/95 þrymmas np 33/4 þrymme ds 19/331 þrymmes gs 19/60 ðrymmum dp 19/164

þrȳm < þrīe

þrymfæst adj *illustrious, mighty* nsm 23/84 þrymfæstne asm 35e/4

þrymful adj *magnificent, glorious* nsf 19/74

þrymliċ adj *glorious* apn 19/8

þrȳnesse < þrīnnys

þrȳþ f:B3h *might, host* þrȳþe np 38/99

þū pers pron *thou, thee, you* ns 1/1, 10, 2a/2, 4, 3b/7, 4/81, 82, 13/14, 16/2, etc tē ds 12/55 tū ns 12/54 þē ds 11/3 þē as 1/10, 71, 2a/10, 12, 4/81, 83, 16/105, etc ds 1/1, 58, 2a/2, 8, 12, 4/82, 83, 12/1, 13/15, 16, 27/12 [etc]; see also p ġē, dual ġit, poss pron þīn

ġeþūht, þūht- see þynċan

þuma m:B5a *thumb* þuman as 7a/33 gs 7a/33

þunar m:B1b *thunder* ns 19/4

ġeþungen adj (pp of þēon) *excellent, distinguished* nsf 19/129

þurfan pt-pr *need, have occasion to, must* þearf pr3s 16/100, 19/117, 23/117 þearft pr2s 3c/7 þorfte pt3s 10/39, 44, 16/4 þorftun pt3p 10/47 þurfe pr1p 30/34 sbj pr2s 3c/7 þurfon pr3p 30/249 þyrfen sbj pr2p 19/153

þurh adv *through* 19/49, 28/16

þurh prep +a/d *through, by, by means of, because of, on account of, in, into, beyond* 4/11, 26, 5/32, 46, 6/29, 7b/20, 7c/8, 19, 8/71, 9a/6, 31, 9b/4, 11, 14/14, 41, 16/49, 17/79, 18/34, 21a/7, 20, 22/80, 23/10, 27/68, 82, 30/71, etc

þurhdrīfan I *drive through, pierce* pt3p
23/46 þurhdrifene pp npm 22/50

þurhfōn VI *penetrate* inf 31b/13

þurhstingan III *pierce, puncture* þurhstinð
pr3s 7a/31

þurhtēon II *bring about, effect* inf 31a/78

þurhwadan VI *pass through* þurhwōd pt3s
30/296, 31b/76

þurhwunian 2 *remain, abide continuously*
þurhwunað pr3s 21a/21 þurhwunode sbj
pt3s 21a/19

Þurstān pr n *Thurston* Þurstānes gs 30/298

þus adv *thus, in this way, so* 9b/90, 13/14,
14/1, 33, 16/44, 22/56, 27/56, 58, 28/55,
71, 30/57, etc þuss 14/32, 44, etc

þūsend num *thousand* ns 8/23 as 8/63
þūsendo ap 28/1

þūsendmǣlum adv *in thousands* 19/165

þuss see þus

þwēan VI *wash, anoint* þwēah imp s 3a/15
þwōgon pt3p 21a/66 þwōh pt3s 12/26,
14/23

þwītan I *cut off, whittle* þwīt imp s 3c/2

þwōgon, þwōh < þwēan

þȳ (demons pron isn) < se

þȳ adv *therefore, for this reason* 15a/7, 25/4,
122; see also for, tō

þȳ adv + comp *the, by that* 10/46, 35d/19,
20, 21 þē 12/23, 30/312, 313; see also
lǣs

þyder see þider

þȳfþ f:B3b *theft* þȳfþe ds 25/37

þȳhtiġ adj *firm, powerful* asn 31b/67

ġeþyld n/f:B2i *patience* ns 34/1 as 22/135
ġeþyldes gs 22/134

ġeþyldiġ adj *patient* nsm 38/65

þyllic pron *such, such-like* ðyllice npn 4/76

þynċan 1 impers +d *seem, appear, think*
þinċan inf 25/48, 108, 133 þinċæ sbj pr3s
11/31 þinċe pr3s 6/26, 27/12 þincð pr2s
12/62 pr3s 16/6, 41 þingð 16/24 ġeþūht
pp 21a/41, 45 þūhte pt3s 9b/85, 12/13, 22,
27, 16/4, 23/4, 35e/1 ðūhton pt3p 7b/8
ðyncð pr3s 5/48

þyrel adj *pierced, perforated* nsm 32/45

þyrelian 2 *pierce* þyrelode pp npn 28/16

þyrfen < þurfan

þȳrih see þrūh

þyrs m:B1g *monster, demon* ns 33/42

ġeþyrstan 1 impers +d *thirst* ġeþyrsteð pr3s
34/8

þȳs, þys-, þyss- see þes

þȳstre adj *dark, gloomy* nsf 19/34 þȳstrum
dpn 33/42

þȳstro f:B3h *darkness* ns 17/52 ds 35e/4 np
23/52 ðēostrum dp 4/9 þȳstru np 14/55
þȳstrum dp 19/118, 33/51

þȳwan 1 *urge, drive* þȳwende prp nsm 1/19

U

Ubba pr n *Ubba* ns 12/12

Uēnus pr n *Venus* ns 24/40, 62

ufan adv *above, from above* 17/38, 31b/9

uferra comp adj *upper, higher* uferan dsf
3a/8

ufeweard adj *upper, topmost part of* (usually
=noun) npn 3b/9 ufeweardon dsn 14/64
ufeweardum dpm 28/70 ufonweardum
dpn 28/48

ūhta m:B5a *period before dawn, early
morning* ūhtan ds 40/35 ūhtna gp 38/8

ūhtcearu f:B3a *anxiety before dawn*
ūhtceare as 40/7

ūhtsong m:B1a *morning song, Matins* as
9b/99

unāgen adj *not one's own* unāgne asf 7a/43

unandwendliċ adj *unchanging* nsf 6/33

unārefned adj *unendurable, inhospitable*
unārefndon asn 28/4

unāsecgendliċ adj *indescribable, ineffable*
unāsecgendliċe asf 8/57 unāsecgendlicum
dsm 6/21

unbefohten adj *without a fight* unbefohtene
npm 30/57

unc, uncer < wit

uncer poss pron dual *our, of the two of us* nsn
39/19 uncerne asm 39/16

unclǣnnes f:B3e.ii *uncleanness, impurity*
unclǣnnesse ds 24/72

uncoþu f:B3a *disease* ns 25/46

uncræft m:B1a *evil practice, deceit*
uncræftan dp 25/163

uncūð adj *unknown* nsn 5/68, 7b/5, 22/110

undǣd f:B3g *wicked deed, crime* undǣde as
12/3, 6 ds 25/129

undær see under

undēadliċ adj *immortal* nsm 22/85

undēadlicnys f:B3e.ii *immortality*
  undēadlicnysse ds 22/89
undearninga adv *without concealment,*
  openly 32/22
undēaðliċ adj *immortal* nsm 22/81
under adv *under, down* 3b/1
under prep +d/a *under, beneath, covered by*
  or in 1/54, 7b/45, 16/11, 21, 18/91, 19/67,
  113, 203, 219, 332, 23/55, 85, 31b/60,
  38/96, 107 **undær** 11/7
underbæc adv *backwards, behind* 34/28
underbeġinnan III *undertake*
  underbeġinnenne infl inf 16/7
underetan V *eat away, undermine*
  undereotone pp npf 37/6
underfēng < **underfōn**
underfōn VII *receive, accept, assume,*
  conduct **underfēng** pt3s 22/111, 173
  underfēngan pt1p 25/161 **underfēngon**
  pt3p 8/62, 14/27
underġietan V *perceive, understand*
  underġeat pt3s 13/10
understandan VI *understand, comprehend*
  inf 16/13, 36, 66, 25/101, 164, 27/16
  understandað pr3p 16/23 imp p 25/6
  understande sbj pr3s 25/78, 88
  understandenne infl inf 16/39
  understondan inf 5/14
undertīd f:B3g *terce, the third hour*
  undertīde as 1/43
underþēodan 1 *subject, devote*
  underþēoded pp 9b/74
underðīed adj *subject, subjected* npn 6/35,
  36 (twice) npm 6/38
undōn anom *undo, open* **undyde** pt3s
  13/1
unearh adj *not cowardly, unflinching*
  unearge npm 30/206
unēaðe adv *not easily, unwillingly* 24/34
unfācne adj *without deceit* nsn 7a/44
unfæderlīċe adv *in an unfatherly way*
  24/33
unflitme adj ?*undisputed* 31a/35 (see note)
unforcūð adj *undisgraced, honourable* nsm
  30/51
unforht adj *unafraid, fearless* nsm 23/110
  unforhte npm 30/79
unforworht adj *uncondemned, innocent*
  unforworhte npm 25/35

unġecnāwe adj *unknown* npn 27/46
unġefēalīċe adv *miserably, joylessly* 29/39
unġehīrsum adj *disobedient* nsm 16/105
unġelǣred adj *uneducated, ignorant*
  unġelǣredan npm 16/23 **unġelǣrede** npm
  1/2 **unġelǣredum** dp 16/41
unġelēafful adj *unbelieving* **unġelēaffulle**
  npm 22/156
unġelīċ adj (+d) *unlike, unalike, different*
  nsm 17/19 nsn 9a/37, 39/3 **ungelīċe** 39/8
unġelimp n:B2b *misfortune* **unġelimpa**
  gp 25/89
unġerēdelīċe adv *roughly, violently*
  unġerēdelīcost sup 6/63
unġerīm n:B2b *countless number* ns 25/138
unġesǣliġ adj *unfortunate* nsn 22/156
unġesewenlīċ adj *invisible* nsn 6/17
  unġesewenlica npf 6/3
unġetrȳwþ f:B3h *disloyalty, treachery*
  unġetrȳwþa np 25/57
unġewemmed adj *unblemished, pure* nsn
  21a/12, 19, 73
unġewunelīċ adj *unusual, unfamiliar* 27/46
unglēaw adj *ignorant* nsm 28/58
ungrund adj *fathomless, vast* **ungrundes**
  gsm 18/63
unġylde n:B2h *excessive tax* **unġylda** np
  25/47
unhēanlīċe adv *not basely, nobly* 29/11
unhlēow adj *unprotective* **unhlēowan** asm
  18/49
unhlitme adv ?*involuntarily,* ?*disastrously*
  31a/67 (see note)
unlagu f:B3a *violation of law, unlawful act,*
  injustice **unlaga** ap 25/11, 37, 150
unlǣd adj *wretched, wicked, untended*
  unlǣdan gsm 19/102 apm 12/46
unlīcð < **unlūcan**
unlūcan II *unlock* **unlīcð** pr3s 4/4
unlyfiġend adj *lifeless, dead* **unlyfiġendes**
  gsm 19/180 **unlyfiġendum** dpm 19/315
unlȳtel adj *not a little, much, great* nsn 25/18
unmihtiġ adj *powerless, weak* **unmihtiġre**
  comp nsn 22/172
unmyltsiendlīċ adj *unforgivable* nsf 16/58
(ġe)**unnan** pt-pr +d (person) +g (thing)
  grant, bestow, intercede **an** pr3s 11/9, 21
  ann pr1s 11/13, 20, 22, 33 pr3s 11/4
  ġeunne sbj pr3s 7c/8, 30/176 imp s 19/90

ūðe pt3s 19/123, 183 sbj pt3s 12/35 ġeūðe
pt3s 24/21 ūþon subj pt3p 29/24
unnyt adj *useless, unprofitable* nsn 6/6
unoferswīðendliċ adj *unconquerable,
invincible* nsn 9a/11
unoferswȳðed adj *unconquerable, invincible*
unoferswȳðda nsm 28/55
unorne adj *simple, humble* nsm 30/256
unriht adj *unlawful, wrong* asn 7c/20
unryhtum dsm 7b/14 dpf 29/1
unriht n:B2b *injustice, wrong* as 25/11, 33,
158 unrihta gp 25/8, 49
unrihtlīċe adv *unjustly, wrongly* 25/56
unrihtwīs adj *unrighteous* (often used as
noun) unrihtwīsan npm 15a/7, 8, 10
unrihtwīsra gpm 15a/1 unrihtwīsum dpm
22/155
unrīm n:B2b +g *a countless number* (*of*) ns
10/31
unrōt adj *unhappy, dejected* nsm 27/11
unrōte npm 19/284, 28/61
unrōtnes f:B3e.ii *sadness, dejection*
unrōtnesse ds 15c/10
unryhtum < unriht
unscrȳdan 1 *undress, strip* inf 22/42
unscrȳddon pt3p 14/28, 34
unscyldiġ adj *guiltless* nsm 14/23
unscyldgiġe apm 25/65
unsidu m:B4a *abuse, vice* unsida ap 25/111
unsōfte adv *ungently, roughly* 19/228
unstille adj *moving, changeable* 27/74 nsf
6/39 unstillu npn 6/3
unstilnes f:B3e.ii *disturbance* unstilnesse as
29/15
unswǣsliċ adj *unpleasant, cruel*
unswǣsliċne asm 19/65
unsȳfre adj *unclean, filthy* unsȳfra
nsm 19/76
unsynnum adv *without sins, guiltlessly*
31a/10
untōdǣledliċ adj *inseparable, indivisible*
nsm 4/29, 22/171 untōdǣledliċe
npm 4/32
untrum adj *infirm, sick* untrumra gpm 9b/80
untrumran comp apm 9b/81 (=noun)
untrumian 2 *fall ill* ġeuntrumod pp 21a/35
untrymnes f:B3e.ii *infirmity, illness*
untrymnesse ds 9b/78 untrumnysse ds
21a/39

unþinged adj *unexpected, sudden* nsm
26/106
unwāclīċe adv *untiringly, without weakening*
30/308
unwæstm m:B1a *crop failure* unwæstma gp
25/48
unwearnum adv *irresistibly* 26/63
unweaxen adj *not fully grown* nsm 30/152
unweder n:B2c *bad weather, storm*
unwedera np 25/47
unwemme adj *unblemished, pure* 21a/14
unwrītere m:B1g *bad scribe, inaccurate
copyist* ns 4/27, 16/109
unwurðlīċe adv *dishonourably* 17/103
ūp adv *up, above, upwards, upstream, ashore,
inland* 3c/2, 8/52, 55, 10/13, 70, 17/78,
18/16, 45, 19/9, 21a/52, 23/71, 30/130,
40/3 ūpp 15b/9
ūpāstīġnes f:B3e.ii *ascension* ūpāstīġnesse
ds 9b/67
ūpēode < ūpgān
ūpgān anom *go up, rise* ūpēode pt3s
28/70
ūpgang m:B1a *rising, sunrise* ūpgonge ds
28/27
ūpganga m:B5a *passage to land, access*
ūpgangan as 30/87
ūphēah adj *high, lofty, tall* nsm 28/15 npn
28/33 ūphēa npf 40/30
ūpliċ adj *upward* ūplican gsn 22/77
ūpp see ūp
uppe adv *above, aloft* 23/9, 28/62, 33/38
uppon prep +d *on, upon, up to* 22/22, 148,
160, 27/38
ūprodor m:B1b *heaven, the heavens above*
as 18/99, 26/105
ūpweard adv *upwards, recumbent* 3a/11
ūre poss adj *our* nsm 21a/90 nsf 22/88 asn
27/65 dsf 16/61 dsn 5/35 npm 5/31, 7b/2
apn 1/51, 14/25 apf 22/87 ūres gsm 9a/1
gsn 16/83, 17/23 ūrne asm 16/76, 22/75,
30/58 ūrum dsn 22/109 dpm 21a/19, 27/8
[etc]; see also pers pron wē
ūriġfeðera adj *dewy-feathered,
?speckled-winged* nsm 19/210 (=noun)
ūriġfeþra nsm 26/25
ġeurnen < ġeiernan
urnon < irnan
ūs, ūsiċ < wē

ūt adv *out, outside, abroad, publicly, forth, away* 1/19, 29, 5/8, 7b/26, 8/8, 9b/20, 10/35, 13/2, 4, 8, 14/66, 21a/45, 22/163, 27/27, 37, 53, 28/50, 31b/92, etc

ūtamǣran 1 *drive out, depopulate* **ūtamǣrede** pp npm 9a/51

ūtan adv *outside, from outside, from abroad* 3a/14, 3b/10, 17/17, 29/10, 31b/12

ūtanbordes adv *outside the country, from abroad* 5/11

ūte adv *out, outside, abroad* 5/12, 17/32, 78, 19/284, 25/23, 25, 90

ūtene adv *from the outside, outside* 8/30

ūtfēran 1 *go out* **ūtfērdon** pt3p 14/35

ūtgang m:B1a *exit, exodus* **ūtganges** gs 22/78 **ūtgonge** ds 9b/64

ġe**ūtian** 2 *banish, expel* ġe**ūtode** pt3s 8/64

ūtlǣdan 1 *bring out* **ūtlǣdde** pt3s 7b/29

uton anom (pr1p of **wītan** *depart*) +inf *let us* 16/59, 17/66, 22/167, 26/117 **utan** 25/144, 158, 159, 161, 164 **utun** 14/61 **wutan** 25/154 **wuton** 9b/100

ūtwærċ m:B1a *dysentery* **ūtwærċe** ds 3c/1

ūtweallan VII *well out, flow* inf 28/30

ūðe, ūþon < **unnan**

ūðwita m:B5a *scholar, sage, authority* **ūðwitan** np 10/69 **ūðwitena** gp 4/48

uu- see **w-**

W

wā interj *alas!, so!* 14/47; see also **wālā**

wā see **wēa**

wāc adj *weak, slender, inferior* nsm 38/67 **wācne** asm 30/43 **wācran** comp npm 26/87 (=noun)

wācian 2 *weaken, be weak* inf 30/10 **wācað** pr3s 8/80

wācran < **wāc**

wadan VI *go, advance, travel, traverse* inf 30/140, 38/5 **wōd** pt1s 38/24 pt3s 30/130, 253 **wōdon** pt3p 30/96, 295

ġe**wadan** VI *pervade, pass* ġe**wōd** pt3s 18/17, 30/157

wado < **wæd**

wāg m:B1a *wall* ns 37/9

wāhryft n:B3a *veil, curtain* ns 14/63

wālā interj (**wā** + **lā**) *woe!, alas!* (+d *for*) 17/31, 25/98 (twice)

walde < **weald**

waldend see **wealdend**

waldendwyrhta m:B5a *ruler's builder, master builder* **waldendwyrhtan** ap 37/7

wamb f:B3b *stomach* **wambe** ds 3a/9

wan indecl adj +g *wanting, lacking* 15c/8

wand < **windan**

wandean < **wanian**

wandian 2 *hesitate, flinch* inf 30/258 **wandode** pt3s 30/268

wandrian 2 *wander, circle, change* **wandriende** prp nsf 6/24 **wandriġe** sbj pr3s 6/66 **wandrode** pt3s 32/34

wanhȳdiġ adj *foolhardy, rash* nsm 38/67

(ġe)**wanian** 2 *lessen, dwindle away, wane, curtail* **wanaþ** pr3s 2b/2, 4 **wandean** pt3p 25/29 ġe**wanode** pp npn 25/38

wann adj *dark, black* nsf 23/55 **wanna** nsm 19/206 **won** nsn 38/103

warian 2 *hold, preoccupy* **warað** pr3s 38/32

warnian 2 *warn, caution* inf 8/31, 25/155 **warniġenne** infl inf 4/17

was < **bēon-wesan**

wāst, wāt < **witan**

ġe**wāt** < ġe**wītan**

waterian 2 *water* inf 1/29

waðol adj *?wandering* nsm 32/8

waþum m:B1a *wave* **waþema** gp 18/26, 38/24, 57

waxġeorn adj *greedy* nsm 1/58

wæċċan 2 *be awake, watch* **wæċċende** prp npm 19/142 (=adj *watchful, vigilant*) **wæċċendum** prp dpm 34/40 (=noun *watchers*)

wæd n:B2d *water, sea* **wado** ap 35b/2

wǣd f:B3b *clothing, covering* **wǣdum** dp 23/15, 22

ġe**wǣde** n:B2h *covering, shroud* ġe**wǣda** np 21a/64 ġe**wǣdum** dp 21a/67

ġe**wǣdian** 2 *dress, equip* ġe**wǣdod** pp 8/36

wǣdl f:B3b *poverty* **wǣdle** as 34/5

wǣdla adj *poor, barren, devoid of* **wǣdlan** asf 28/3

wǣfersȳn f:B3b *show, spectacle* **wǣfersȳne** ds 23/31

wǣfre adj *restless, wandering* nsn 31a/88

wæġ see **weġ**

wǣġ m:B1a *water, wave, sea* as 18/49, 26/19
  wǣgas np 18/38 **wǣġe** ds 18/12 **wēgas** ap
  38/46
wægon < **wegan**
wæl n:B2a *slaughter, carnage, the slain,*
  battlefield ns 8/13, 10/65, 30/126, 303 as
  8/35, 9a/60 **walo** np 37/25 **wæle** ds 30/279,
  300, 31a/51
wæl m:B1a *pool, river* **wǣle** ds 33/39
wælbenn f:B3e *mortal wound* **wælbenna** np
  18/46
wælcyrie f:B5c *sorceress* **wælcyrian** np
  25/137
wælfāg adj *slaughter-stained* **wælfāgne** asm
  31a/66
wælfæðm m:B1a *deadly embrace*
  wælfæðmum dp 18/35
wælfȳr n:B2b *slaughter-fire, funeral pyre*
  wælfȳra gp 31a/57
wælfeld m:B4a *battlefield* **wælfelda** ds 10/51
wælġīfre adj *greedy for carrion* or *slaughter*
  bloodthirsty nsm 19/207 **wælġīfru** npn
  38/100 **wælġīfrum** dp 19/295
wælhrēow adj *cruel, savage, bloodthirsty*
  nsm 24/32 **wælhrēowe** apf 25/36
  wælrēowe npm 39/6
wælmist m:B1a *mist* or *pall of death* ns 18/5
wælræst f:B3b *bed of slaughter, death in*
  battle **wælræste** as 30/113
wælrēowe < **wælhrēow**
wælscel n:B2a *?carnage* as 19/312 (see note)
wælsleaht m:B1g *slaughter-stroke, slaughter*
  wælsleahta gp 38/7, 91 **wælslihta** gp 32/28
wælspere n:B2h *deadly spear* as 30/322
wælstōw f:B3b *place of slaughter, battlefield*
  wælstōwe gs 30/95 ds 10/43, 30/293
wælweġ m:B1a *whale-path, sea* as 26/63 (see
  note)
wælwulf m:B1a *wolf of slaughter, (Viking)*
  warrior **wælwulfas** np 30/96
ġewæmmodlīċe adv *corruptly, badly* 1/2
wæn m:B1a *wagon, cart* ns 6/69 as 6/43
  wǣnes gs 6/42, 77
ġewǣnd- see ġe**wendan**
wǣpen n:B2c.i *weapon* ns 30/252 as 30/130,
  235, 31b/82 np 38/100 ap 19/290 **wǣpn** as
  7b/16 **wǣpna** gp 18/5, 30/83, 272, 308,
  31b/18, 68 **wǣpne** ds 30/228 **wǣpnes** gs
  30/168 **wǣpnum** dp 30/10, 126

wǣpenġewrixl n:B2b *exchange of weapons,*
  armed encounter **wǣpnġewrixl** ns 25/85
  wǣpenġewrixles gs 10/51
wǣpnedmann m:B4b *male person, man*
  wǣpnedmen ap 28/6
ġewǣpnian 2 *arm, furnish with weapons*
  ġe**wǣpnod** pp 8/35
wǣre < **wēr**
wǣran, wǣre, wǣren < **bēon-wesan**
Wǣrferð pr n *Wærferth* as 5/2
wǣrlīċe adv *warily, carefully* 1/49, 7b/13,
  25/163
wǣrloga m:B5a *troth-breaker, liar*
  wǣrlogan as 19/71
Wǣrmund pr n *Wærmund* ns 29/44
Wǣrmunding adj *son of Wærmund* nsm
  29/44
wærod see **werod**
wǣron, wǣrun, wǣs < **bēon-wesan**
wǣstenum < **wēsten**
wæstm m:B1a *fruit* **wæstmas** ap 15a/4 ap
  33/9
wæstmbærnys f:B3e.ii *fertility*
  wæstmbærnysse as 9a/10
wǣt adj *wet, moist* nsn 35c/11
wǣta m:B5a *wetness, blood, fluid, humours*
  wǣtan ds 23/22, 28/35 ap 3a/9
wǣtan 1 *wet, moisten* **wǣtte** pt3s 35d/2
wæter n:B2c *water, sea, river* ns 18/5,
  31b/23 as 1/65, 3a/7, 3b/8, 10/55, 14/22,
  16/56, 21b/19, 24/17, 30/91, 98 **wætera** np
  13/4, 6, 10 gp 15a/4, 15c/9 **wætere** ds
  30/64, 96, 33/27 is 3a/15 **wæteru** np 13/3
  ap 16/53 **wæterum** dp 13/21 **wætre** ds
  40/49 **wætres** gs 28/3
ġewæterode < **waterian**
wǣtte < **wǣtan**
wǣðan 1 *wander, hunt* **wǣðde** pt3s 18/35
wē pers pron *we, us, ours* np 1/1, 2, 18/83 **ūs**
  ap 1/1, 8, 14/25, 21a/81, 88 dp 1/7, 9, 45,
  7b/6, 10/68, 18/84 **ūre** gp 22/87, 25/51,
  167, 27/23, 30/234 **ūsiċ** ap 26/123, 28/3
  [etc]; see also poss pron **ūre**, dual **wit**
wēa m:B5a *woe, misfortune, evil, harm, grief,*
  misery, sin ns 33/13 **wā** ns 40/52 **wēan** gs
  36/25 ap 36/4 **wēana** gp 31a/88, 32/25,
  36/34; see also **wā, wālā**
wēadǣd f:B3g *deed of woe, evil deed*
  wēadǣda np 32/8

wēaġesīð m:B1a *companion in evil* or *misery* wēaġesīðas np 19/16

weal see weall

wēalāf f:B3b *survivor(s) of calamity* wēalāfe as 31a/22, 36

Wealas < Wealh

ġewealc n:b2b *rolling, surging* ns 18/10 as 26/6, 46

weald m:B1a *forest, wood* walde ds 19/206 wealde ds 10/65

ġeweald n:B2b *control, use, power, dominion* as 2a/20, 4/25, 16/107, 17/31, 23/107, 30/178 ġewealde ds 25/36, 74, 77

(ġe)wealdan VII +g *wield, control, manage, possess, cause* inf 19/103, 30/95, 31b/18 ġewealdest pr2s 2a/4 welt pr3s 6/9, 33, 40, 43, 77 ġewēold pt3s 31b/63 wēoldan pt3p 25/48

wealdend m:B4d '*wielder*', *ruler, the Lord* ns 23/111, 155 as 23/67 waldend ns 19/5, 61, 24/76, 38/78 wealdende ds 23/121 wealdendes gs 23/53

wealġeat n:B2d *wall-gate, city-gate* wealgate ds 19/141

Wēalh m:B1d *foreigner, Welshman* Wēalas ap 10/72

wealhstod m:B1a *interpreter, translator* ns 18/77 wealhstodas ap 5/46

weall m:B1a *wall, rampart* as 19/161, 21a/55 weal ns 37/39, 38/98 weallas np 38/76 ap 9a/37, 19/137 wealle ds 31b/82, 38/80 wealles gs 19/151

weallan VII *well up, seethe, surge, boil, flow* weallendan prp asm 25/165 wēol pt3s 28/11, 31a/69 wēoll pt3s 17/16 wēollon pt3p 18/46

weallfæsten n:B2c *rampart* np 18/38

weallstān m:B1a *wall-stone, masonry, construction made of stone* wealstān ns 37/1 weallstāna gp 33/3

weallwala m:B5a *wall, foundation* weallwalan ap 37/20

wealowian 2 *roll* wealowiġen sbj pr3p 6/57

wealsteal m:B1a *place of walls, ruined site* as 38/88

wēana < wēa

weard adv *towards* 8/75

weard m:B1a *guard, watchman, guardian, protector, possessor* ns 9b/37, 18/40, 78

as 9b/31, 19/80, 23/91, 26/54, 34/40 weardas np 22/41 ap 22/11, 38

weard f:B3b *watch, guard* wearde as 19/142

weardian 2 *possess, occupy, guard* weardiað pr3p 40/34

weardmann m:B4b *watchman, guard* weardmen np 22/23 weardmenn 22/37

Weardora pr n *Wardour* (Wilts.) Weardoran ds 12/21, 26

wearh m:B1a *criminal* ns 33/55 wergas ap 23/31

wearm adj *warm* wearmum dpf 3a/2

wearme adv *warmly* 3c/6

wearp < weorpan

(ġe)wearþ, wearþan < (ġe)weorþan

wēaþearf f:B3b *woeful need* wēaþearfe ds 40/10

weaxan VII *grow, increase, wax, be fruitful* inf 9a/28 weaxe imp p 13/16 weaxeð pr3s 2b/3, 5 wēox pt1s 40/3 pt3s 21a/36, 24/8 wēoxon pt3p 28/35

Weċedport pr n *Watchet* (Som.) ns 8/11 ds 8/52

wēdan 1 *become mad, rage* wēdde pt3s 18/44

wedbryċe m:B1g *pledge-breaking* wedbrycas ap 25/115

wedd n:B2b.i *pledge, oath* wed as 7b/13, 13/18, 25/162 np 25/80 wedde ds 12/35 is 12/42 weddes gs 13/22, 24

weddian 2 +g *pledge, promise* weddie sbj pr3s 7b/15

weder n:B2c *weather, storm* ns 39/10 np 31a/74 wederum dp 33/42

Weder-Ġēatas pr n (mp:B1a) *the Geats* Weder-Ġēata gp 31b/1

weġ m:B1a *path, road, way, direction, course* ns 2a/20, 21 as 15a/10, 23/88 wega gp 24/55 wegas np 17/44, 18/12 ap 15c/10 weġe ds 15a/1, 15c/3, 21b/25; in phr on weġ *away* 26/74, 38/53 on wæġ 32/43

wegan V *carry, bear* wǣgon pt3p 19/325 wēgon pt3p 30/98

wēgas < wǣġ

weġfērend m:B4d *wayfarer, traveller* weġfērendan np 14/46 weġfērendum dp 34/32

weġnest n:B2b *provisions for a journey, eucharist* weġneste isn 9b/97

wel adv *well, fully, properly, effectively,*
 quite, readily, indeed 2a/2, 4/24, 5/8, 9b/6,
 56, 100, 12/16, 16/37, 19/27, 103, 21a/30,
 38, 22/105, 27/34, 36, 34/44, etc **well**
 23/129, 143, 34/20
wela m:B5a *prosperity, riches, happiness* ns
 17/94 **welan** as 5/32, 34, 17/85 ds 17/83
ġewelede < welwan
welega < weliġ
weler m:B1a *lip* **weleras** ap 16/97
(ġe)welhwǣr adv *nearly everywhere* 5/69,
 25/26
ġewelhwilċ adj *nearly every* ġe**welhwilċan**
 dsm 25/90 ġe**welhwylċan** dsm 25/45
weliġ adj *prosperous, well-to-do* **weliġne** asm
 27/24
well see wel
welm m:B1a *fervour, zeal* **welme** ds 9b/75
welt < wealdan
Wēlund pr n *Weland* ns 36/1
welwan 1 *roll, huddle* ġe**welede** pp apm
 25/100
welwillendnes f:B3e.ii *goodwill, kindness*
 welwillendnesse ds 27/25
wēman 1 *win over, entice* inf 38/29
wēn f:B3g *hope, expectation, belief* **wēna** np
 39/13 **wēnan** dp 36/25 **wēnum** dp 39/9
wēnan 1 *think, believe, imagine, expect,*
 suspect, hope inf 16/9 **wēnde** pt1s 28/34
 pt3s 19/20, 30/239 **wēndon** pt3p 5/40,
 22/47, 27/39 **wēne** pr1s 5/16, 23/135, 35a/4
 sbj pr3s 25/41 **wēnst** pr2s 28/73
wendan 1 *turn, turn away, go, change,*
 translate inf 5/39, 60, 23/22, 30/316 **wende**
 sbj pr1s 30/252 **wenden** sbj pr1p 5/50 sbj
 pr3p 6/59 **wendeþ** pr3s 36/32 **wendon** pt3p
 5/44, 46, 48, 8/53, 54, 30/193, 205
ġewendan 1 *go, return, bring about* inf 17/91
 ġe**wǣnde** pt3s 27/3 ġe**wǣndon** pt3p
 27/61
wēnde, wēndon < wēnan
wenian 2 *accustom, entertain* **wenede** pt3s
 38/36 sbj pt3s 31a/29
wēol < weallan
weolcenrēad adj *scarlet, purple*
 weolcenrēadum dsm 14/29
ġewēold, wēoldan < (ġe)wealdan
wēoll, wēollon < weallan
wēop, wēopon < wēpan

weorc n:B2b *work, action, deed, task,*
 achievement; affliction, pain ns 4/76, 6/16,
 16/7 as 1/18, 4/74, 6/23, 9b/33, 23/79 np
 35d/14 **weorca** gp 22/75, 77 **weorce** ds
 31b/78 **weorcum** dp 16/38, 78, 84, 96,
 21a/6 **weorkes** gs 1/10
ġeweorc n:B2b *work, labour, handiwork,*
 construction ns 31b/71, 33/2, 3, 37/2 np
 38/87 ġe**weorce** ds 16/67
weorcstān m:B1a *hewn stone* **weorcstāna** gp
 21a/54
weorod, weorode < werod
weorpan III *throw, fling, cast down, gush*
 wearp pt3s 17/5, 31b/40, 37/38 **worpan** inf
 21b/18 ġe**worpen** pp 4/9 **wurpon** pt3p
 14/41, 43, 19/290
weorþ n:B2b *price* **weorðe** ds 25/74, 76
weorþ- see also wurþ-
weorþan III *become, be, come to, happen;*
 often = auxil vb (*is, will be, was,* etc) inf
 5/40 **uueorthae** sbj pr3s 20a/5 **uuiurthit**
 pr3s 20a/1 **wǣrd** pt3s 30/116 **weard** pt3s
 30/113 **wearþ** pt3s 10/32, 14/64, 18/9,
 19/21, 21a/6, 28, 27/40, etc **wearþan** inf
 38/64 **weorþ** pr3s 7a/29, 31, 17/68
 weorðað pr3p 6/60, 35a/13 **weorþe** sbj
 pr3s 6/11, 20b/5 **weorðest** pr2s 28/56
 weorþeð pr3s 7a/30, 33, 26/69 ġe**worden**
 pp 9b/103, 23/87, 25/61, 70, 122, 149,
 27/41 **wurdan** pt3p 24/29 **wurde** pt3s 30/1
 sbj pt3s 21a/8 **wurdon** pt3p 17/3 (*turned*),
 19/159, 21a/79, 22/23, etc **wurdun** pt3p
 10/48, 14/65 **wurðan** sbj pr3p 17/77
 wurðe sbj pr3s 7c/6 **wurðeþ** pr3s 17/93
 wyrð pr3s 17/94 **wyrþeþ** pr3s 20b/1
ġeweorþan III *happen, come about, turn out;*
 impers *please* inf 6/15 ġe**wearð** pt3s 24/5
 ġe**weorðe** sbj pr3s 6/16 ġe**weorðeþ** pr3s
 7a/53 ġe**worden** pp 19/260 ġe**wurde** pt3s
 14/22 ġe**wurden** pp 14/55 ġe**wurdon** pt3p
 14/70 ġe**wurðan** inf 17/50 ġe**wurðe** sbj
 pr3s 7c/7 ġe**wyrð** pr3s 16/100
(ġe)weorþian 2 *honour, worship, exalt,*
 enrich, reward, respect, obey inf 23/129,
 24/16 ġe**weorðad** pp 9b/2, 28/53
 ġe**weorþade** pt3s 26/123 **weorðað** pr3s
 24/73 **weorðiað** pr3p 23/81, 24/46
 ġe**weorðod** pp 19/298 **weorþode** sbj pt3s
 31a/28 ġe**weorþode** pt3s 23/90, 94 pp asn

23/15 **wurðedon** pt3p 24/13 **wurðian**
17/16 **wurðiaþ** pr1p 24/24 pr3p 24/65
wurðienne infl inf 24/28 ġe**wurðod**
pp 21a/6, 24/42 **wurðode** pt3s 21a/14
wurðodon pt3p 24/41, 48
weorðlīċe see **wurðlīċe**
weorðmynt f:B3b *esteem, honour, mark of*
honour ns 24/77 **weorðmynd** as 31b/68
weorðmynde as 19/342 **wurðmynt** ns
2a/23, 21a/90 **wyrðmente** ds 24/67
weorðscipe m:B1g *honour, dignity* ds 25/102
wurðscipes gs 27/73
weorþung f:B3d *honour, veneration,*
worship, celebration **weorþunge** ds 7b/53,
24/50, 25/22, 28/68
weorud, weoruda see **werod**
weoruld, weorulde see **woruld**
weoruldhād see **woruldhād**
weotena < **wita**
Weowungum pr n *Wing* (Bucks.) dp 11/13
(see 11/headnote)
wēox, wēoxon < **wēaxan**
wēpan VII *weep, bewail, mourn over* inf
40/38 **wēop** pt3s 23/55 **wēopon** pt3p 28/75
wēpen sbj pr3p 28/40
wer m:B1a *man, husband, 'man-price'* ns
15a/1, 18/72, 21a/86 as 7c/10, 21a/20 **wera**
gp 18/69, 21b/8, 26/21, 35d/18, 35e/3,
37/26 **weras** np 19/71, 142, etc **were** ds
7b/25, 36 **weres** gs 21b/3, 7 **werum** dp
21a/4
wēr f:B3b *covenant, pledge, treaty,*
agreement **wǣre** as 31a/38 **wērum** dp
26/110
wērbeam m:B1a *protecting barrier*
wērbeamas ap 18/41
wēre < **bēon-wesan**
wereda, werede < **werod**
wergas < **wearh**
werġeld n:B2b *'man-price'*, *wergeld*
werġelde ds 7b/22
werian 1 *put on, wear* **weorode** pt3s 21a/32
werian 1 *protect, defend* **werede** pt3s 29/12
wereð pr3s 34/40 **weredon** pt3p 30/82, 283
ġe**werian** 1 *make a (defensive) alliance*
ġe**weredon** pt3p 9a/31
wēriġ adj *weary, exhausted, wretched, sad*
nsm 10/20, 26/2, 35a/39 nsn 38/15 **weriġe**
npm 30/303 **wēriġne** asm 38/57

wēriġferhð adj *weary-hearted, demoralised*
wēriġferhðe npm 19/290 apm 19/249
wēriġmōd adj *weary, disheartened* nsm
31b/52, 40/49
werod n:B2b.ii *company, band, host, army,*
multitude ns 30/64 as 30/102 **weorod** np
9a/27 **weorode** ds 10/34, 23/69, 152
weorud ns 9a/11 **wereda** gp 2a/23, 17/15
werede ds 22/94, 23/124 **weroda** gp 17/49,
18/102 **werode** ds 22/121, 30/51 is 17/33,
29/9 **weruda** gp 23/51
werþēod f:B3b *people, nation* **werþēoda** gp
37/9 **werðēode** np 18/74
wes, wes- see **bēon-wesan**
Wesseaxe, Wesseaxena see **Westseaxe**
west adv *west* 30/97
westan adv *from the west* 28/47
West-Dene pr n (mp:B1h) *Danes*
West-Denum dp 31b/87
wēste adj *deserted, desolate, empty* nsm
38/74 nsn 9a/23
wēsten n:B2c.iii *desert place, wasteland*
wēstene ds 16/71 **wēstenum** dp 9a/45, 49
wēstenstaþol m:B1a *desolate place*
wēstenstaþolas ap 37/27
westsǣ f:B3g *western sea* ds 9a/36
Westseaxe, -seaxan pr n (mp:B1h/5a) *West*
Saxons **Wesseaxe** np 10/20 **Wesseaxena** gp
10/59 **Westseaxan** np 9a/20 **Westseaxna**
gp 7b/9, 29/1
wībed n:B2c *altar* **wībedum** dp 9a/42
wīċ n:B2b *dwelling-place, habitation, village*
ns 40/31 as 35b/2 ap 40/52 **wīca** gp 31a/63
wican I *yield, give way* **wicon** pt3p 18/38
wican < **wicu**
wiċċa m:B5a *wizard* / **wiċċe** f:B5c *witch*
wiċċan np 25/137
wicg n:B2b *horse* **wicge** ds 30/240
Wichām pr n *Wickham* (Hants.) ds 11/12
wīcing m:B1a *Viking* as 30/139 **wīcinga** gp
30/26, 73, 97 **wīcingas** ap 30/322 **wīcinge**
ds 25/84 **wīcingum** dp 30/116
wicu f:B5c *week* **wican** as 7b/52
wīd adj *wide, broad, long* **wīdan** dsm 37/39
dsn 18/102 (*everlasting*); in phr **tō wīdan**
aldre *for ever* 19/347
wīde adv *widely, spaciously, far afield, far*
and wide 18/35, 19/156, 25/6, 11, 28,
31b/97, 34/32, 44, 46, 35b/5, 35d/16, etc

wīdost sup 26/57 **wīde ond sīde** *far and wide* 23/81

ġewīde adv *far apart* ġewīdost sup *as far apart as possible* 40/13

wīdl m:B1a *defilement, filth* **wīdle** ds 19/59

wīdlāst m:B1a *'wide track', far wandering* **wīdlāstum** dp 39/9

widobān n:B2b *collar-bone* **widobāne** ns 7a/30

widuwe f:B5c *widow* **widuwan** as 7a/43 gs/ds 7a/41 **wydewan** np 25/33

wīf n:B2b *woman* ns 13/15, 14/13, 24/62, 35c/11 np 13/15, 21a/89, 22/18, 32, etc ap 16/14, 29, 22/92 **wīfa** gp 16/18, 23/94 **wīfæ** ds 11/27 **wīfe** ds 7b/44, 46, 16/17, 21a/7, 84, 26/45 **wīfes** gs 2a/15, 29/14 **wīfum** dp 22/24, 35c/1

wīfcȳþþu f:B3a *meeting a woman* **wīfcȳþþe** ds 29/9

Wīferþ pr n *Wiferth* ns 29/21

wīfġehrine m:B1g *'woman-touch', sexual intercourse* ds 28/22

(ġe)wīfian 2 *take to wife, marry* inf 16/19 ġewīfode pt3s 24/38

wīfmann m:B4b *woman* **wīfman** ns 21b/8 **wimmen** np 22/13, 17

wīġ n:B2b *war, warfare, battle, fighting, strife, struggle* ns 38/80 as 35a/3 **wīġe** ds 5/9, 30/10, 128, 193, 235, 252 **wīġes** gs 10/20, 59, 30/73, 130

wiġa m:B5a *warrior, fighter* ns 30/210, 38/67 **wiġan** as 30/75, 235 np 30/79, 126, 302 **wiġena** gp 19/49, 30/135, 31b/52, 68 **wiġhena** gp 9a/11

wīġbord n:B2b *shield* np 18/21

Wīġelin pr n *Wigelin* **Wīġelines** gs 30/300

wiġena < wiġa

wīġend m:B4d *warrior* np 30/302, 31a/63, 32/10, 47 **wiġġend** as 19/258 np 19/69, 141, 312 **wiġġendum** dp 19/283

Wigeraċeastre < Wigoraċeastor

wiġġend see wīġend

wīġheard adj *hard in war, fierce* **wīġheardne** asm 30/75

wīġhyrst f:B3g *war-trappings* **wīġhyrstum** dp 37/34

Wigoraċeastor pr n (f:B3c) *Worcester* **Wigeraċeastre** ds 8/37 **Wiogoraċeastre** ds 5/1

wīġplega m:B5a *battle-play, fighting* **wīġplegan** ds 30/268 is 30/316

wīġsigor m:B1a *victory in war* as 31b/63

wīġsmiþ m:B1a *war-smith, warrior* **wīġsmiþas** np 10/72

wīġsteal n:B2b.i *place for warfare, fortress* np 37/27

wīhaga m:B5a *battle-wall* (of shields) **wīhagan** as 30/102

wiht adv *at all* 19/274, 31a/21

wiht n/f:B2i *creature, being, something, anything* ns 35c/1 **wihte** ds 17/57; in phr **mid wihte** *at all, somehow* 17/44, 91; see also **wihte** (adv)

Wiht pr n *Isle of Wight* ns 9a/18

Wihta pr n *Wecta* ns 9a/25 gs 9a/25

Wihtbord pr n *Wihtbord* ns 12/10, 36 **Wihtbordes** gs 12/64

wihte adv *in any way, at all* 17/63, 31b/23, 35e/6

ġewihte n:B2h *weight* as 27/55

Wihtgyls pr n *Wihtgisl* **Wihtgylses** gs 9a/24

Wihtlæġ pr n *Wihtlæg* ns 29/44

Wihtsǣtan pr n *inhabitants of the Isle of Wight* np 9a/18

wiites < wīte

wilde adj *wild* nsm 33/18 **wildre** asf 3a/4

wildēor n:B2b *wild animal* ns 28/36 **wildēora** gp 28/4, 17

wile < willan

Wilfrid pr n *Wilfrid* ns 21a/15, 26

willa m:B5a *desire, purpose, determination, consent, pleasure* ns 15a/2, 22/170, 23/129 **willan** as 15c/13, 17/63 gs 17/63, 18/106, 22/116 ds 7a/51, 19/295, 22/174

willan anom *want, wish, will, intend, desire; also auxil vb will, shall* inf 16/101 **wile** pr3s 7c/4, 12/40, 16/83, 22/166, 23/107, 30/52 sbj pr3s 6/22, 7c/4 **willað** pr1p 30/35, 40 pr3p 30/46, 35d/18 **wille** pr1s 5/66 pr3s 3b/10, 26/43 pr1p 22/67 pr2p 1/3, 6 sbj pr2s 2a/9, 5/20, 27/9 sbj pr3s 3b/10, 7a/47, 7b/22, 16/9, 26/13 **willon** sbj pr2p 28/49 **wilt** pr2s 2a/4, 12, 15b/6, 7, 27/14, 82 **wolde** pt1s 4/1, 5/70, 12/34 pt3s 1/12, 12/4, 22/105, 23/34, 30/11 sbj pt1s 28/20 sbj pt3s 7b/6, 12/43, 22/7, 23/113 **woldest** pt2s 27/19 **woldon** pt3p 5/41, 8/68, 9b/75, 14/8, 22/17, 23/68 **wylæ** sbj pr3s 11/4, 6

wyle pr3s 16/20 **wyllað** pr1p 4/58, 70,
21a/2, 22/3 **wylle** pr1s 12/61, 23/1, 30/216
sbj pr2s 15b/6 sbj pr3s 4/24, 14/52, 62,
16/106 sbj pr2p 1/46, 14/10 [etc]; for
negative forms, see **nellan**
ġe**wilnian** 2 *desire, yearn, entreat* ġe**wilniað**
pr3p 22/77 ġe**wilnode** pt3s 21a/26
wilnung f:B3d *desire* **wilnunga** ds 5/41
wilsumnes f:B3e *willingness, devotion*
wilsumnesse ds 9b/104
wilt < **willan**
Wiltūn pr n *Wilton* (Wilts.) **Wiltūne** ds 8/81
Wiltūnscīr pr n *Wiltshire* **Wiltūnscīre** ds 8/74
wimmen < **wīfmann**
wīn n:B2b *wine* ns 1/67, 4/95 as 1/66, 67,
3b/2, 14/38 **wīne** ds 3b/9, 19/29, 67
winas < **wine**
wind m:B1a *wind* ns 3a/12, 15a/8, 33/3 as
19/347 **winde** ds 33/41, 38/76
windan III *wind, circle, fly, roll, curl, weave,*
brandish inf 17/81, 30/322 **wand** pt3s
19/110, 30/43, 31a/57 **wundon** pt3p 14/30,
30/106
wine m:B1g *friend, lord* ns 30/250, 40/49, 50
as 26/115 **winas** ap 30/228
winedrihten m:B1b *beloved lord, lord and*
friend as 19/274, 30/248, 263
   winedryhtnes gs 38/37
winelēas adj *friendless, lordless* nsm 38/45,
40/10
winemǣġ m:B1c *beloved kinsman, near*
kinsman **winemāgas** ap 30/306 **winemǣga**
gp 38/7 **winemǣgum** dp 26/16
wīngāl adj *merry with wine* nsm 26/29, 37/34
wīnġeard m:B1a *vineyard, vine* **wīnġeardes**
gs 3b/8
wīngedrinc n:B2b *wine-drinking* ns 3a/8
   wīngedrince ds 19/16
wīnhāte f:B5c *invitation to wine* **wīnhātan** as
19/8
ġe**winn** n:B2b *conflict, war, struggle, labour,*
hardship as 24/47, 51, 30/214, 33/55
ġe**winne** ds 9a/15, 23/65, 30/248, 302
ġe**winna** m:B5a *adversary* ġe**winnan** ds 9a/8
winnan III *struggle, suffer, contend, vie* inf
17/9 **won** pt3s 31a/70 **wonn** pt1s 40/5
   wunnon pt3p 9a/14, 18/69
ġe**winnan** III *bring about, win, conquer* inf
17/65, 100, 25/148, 30/125

wīnsæd adj *sated with wine* **wīnsade** npm
19/71
wīnsæl n:B2d *wine-hall* **wīnsalo** np 38/78
winsumum < **wynsum**
Wintanċeaster pr n (f:B3c) *Winchester*
   Wintanċeastre ds 29/35
winter m:B1b *winter* ns 1/20, 31a/70, 74,
33/5 as 26/15, 31a/66 **wintra** gp 2c/1, 9a/1,
61, 29/6, 35, 40, 38/65 **wintres** gp 38/103
wintrum dp 30/210
winterċeald adj *wintry-cold* **winterċealde**
asf 36/4
winterceariġ adj *winter-sad* nsm 38/24
winterstund f:B3b *winter-hour, short time*
   winterstunde as 17/33
Wiogoraċeastre < **Wigoraċeastor**
wiotan, wiotona < **wita**
wiotonne < **witan**
wīr m:B1a *wire, metal thread, filigree* **wīre** ds
35d/14 **wīrum** dp 37/20
wirċean see **wyrċan**
wirðe < **wurþ**
wīs adj *wise, learned* nsm 34/16, 38/64 **wīsan**
dsm 16/51 **wīse** npm 4/15, 22/123 apm
5/46 **wīsra** comp gpm 1/68 (=noun)
ġe**wis** adj *aware, sure, certain, true* nsm
9b/109, 26/110 ġe**wissum** dsm 24/25
wīsan < **wīse**
wīsdōm m:B1a *wisdom, knowledge, learning*
ns 5/42, 16/51, 22/168 as 4/10, 12, 5/11,
21, 32, 34 **wīsdōme** ds 5/9
wīse adv *wisely* 38/88
wīse f:B5c *way, manner, idiom, fashion,*
matter **wīsan** as 9b/51, 16/89, 92 ds 7b/3,
42, 9b/74, 24/59, 25/27 ap 25/58 **wīsum** dp
21a/10, 26/110
wīsian 2 *guide, instruct* **wīsode** pt3s
30/141
wīsliċ adj *wise, certain* **wīsliċne** asm 36/34
wīslicu apn 18/81
ġe**wīslīċe** adv *truly, carefully, precisely* 4/70,
22/73 ġe**wīslīcor** comp 27/15
wissian 2 +d *guide, instruct* inf 16/38
ġe**wissian** 2 *direct, guide* ġe**wissode** pt3s
22/63
ġe**wissum** < ġe**wis**
wist f:B3g *feast, feasting* **wiste** ds 38/36
Wīstān pr n *Wistan* ns 30/297
wist- see **witan**

wit pron dual *we two* n 40/13, 21 **unc** a 23/48, 40/12, 22 d 17/50 **uncer** g 40/25

wita m:B5a *wise man, counsellor, adviser, philosopher* **weotena** gp 12/58, 31a/36 **wiotan** np 5/4, 29/1 **wiotona** gp 5/37 **witan** np 8/27, 58 ap 8/69 **witena** gp 7b/3, 7c/2, 8/61 **witum** dp 7b/10

ġewita m:B5a *witness* ġe**witan** np 22/126

witan pt-pr *know, understand, be aware of, be conscious of, feel, show* inf 6/13, 16/30, 25/67, 27/9, 19, 34/16 pr1p 25/156 **wāst** pr2s 27/34 **wāt** pr1s 6/6, 15, 17/48, 22/25 pr3s 1/52, 15a/10, 26/12, 55, 92, 33/62, 34/29, etc **wiotonne** infl inf 5/49 **wistan** pt3p 19/207 **wiste** pt1s 16/12 pt3s 8/83, 14/12, 17/49 **wiston** pt3p 5/29, 9b/93 **witanne** infl inf 16/93, 25/71 **wite** sbj pr2s 27/9, 15 **witon** pr3p 18/90 **witun** pr1p 1/8; with neg **nāst** pr2s 27/35 **nāt** pr1s 12/45, 27/8 **nyste** pt3s 16/15, 19/68

ġewītan I *set out, depart, go, pass away* ġe**wāt** pt3s 9b/26, 19/61, 145, 21a/11, 46, 21b/7, 15, 30/72, 150, 38/95 ġe**wīt** pr3s 4/14 ġe**witan** pt3p 10/53, 19/290, 37/9 ġe**wītaŏ** pr3s 26/52 ġe**witon** pt3p 9a/48, 31a/63

wīte n:B2h *punishment, torment, penalty, fine* ns 17/18, 94 as 7a/15, 17/30, 35d/17 ds 7b/38, 7c/26, 23/61 **wiites** gs 9b/69 **wīta** gp 17/56, 23/87 **wītu** np 5/22 **wītum** dp 15a/11, 19/115, 22/154

wītega m:B5a *wise man, prophet* **wītegan** np 22/57 as 14/42

wītegian 2 *prophesy, predict* **wītegode** pt3s 15c/1, 21a/36

witena < wita

ġewitenes f:B3e.ii *departure, death* ġe**witenesse** gs 9b/77

witenne < witan

wīteþēow adj *reduced to slavery by law* **wītæþǣownæ** asm 11/7

wītgode < wītegian

wītiġ adj *wise* nsm 31b/63

ġewitloca m:B5a *mind* ġe**witlocan** ds 19/69

ġewitnes f:B3e *witness* ġe**witnesse** as 12/57 ds 12/64

witod adj *appointed, ordained, fated* nsn 32/26 **witodes** gsm 18/106 (=noun) **witodre** ?dsf 18/26 (see note)

witodlīċe adv *certainly, verily, truly, therefore, but* 14/18, 20, 46, 52, 55, 61, 68

witon < wita, witan

wītrod n:B2a *route of battle* as 18/46

ġewitt n:B2b *mind, understanding* ġe**witte** ds 6/20

Witta pr n *Witta* ns 9a/25

wītu, wītum < wīte

wiþ prep +a/d/g/i *to, towards, with, against, from, by, in return for* 3a/1, 2, 3b/1, 3, 3c/1, 7a/20, 22, 7b/24, 43, 7c/9, 8/59, 74, 9a/8, 14, 9b/26, 10/9, 52, 12/9, 14/38, 15c/14, 16/68, 21a/55, 26/75, 33/16, etc **uuiþ** 29/6; in instr phr **wiþ þon þe** *in the case that, on condition that* 3b/1, 8/59, 9a/47

wiþerlēan n:B2b *requital* ns 30/116

wiðertrod n:B2a *retreat, way back* as 19/312

wiðsacan VI *forsake* **wiðsoce** sbj pt3s 21b/16

wiðstandan VI (+d) *withstand, resist* **wiðstōd** pt3s 9a/36 **wiðstondan** inf 38/15

wīves < wīf

wlanc adj *proud, noble, bold, boastful, exulting in, presumptuous* nsm 33/27 nsf 19/325 **wlancan** dsn 30/240 **wlance** npm 10/72, 19/16, 30/205 npf 18/41 **wlancne** asm 30/139 **wlonc** nsm 26/29 nsf 38/80

wlāt < wlītan

wlætta m:B5a *nausea* **wlættan** ds 3b/5

wleċċan I *make tepid, warm* **wleċe** imp 2s 3a/2

wlītan I *look, gaze, see* inf 19/49 **wlāt** pt3s 30/172, 31b/81

wlite m:B1g *face, appearance, countenance* ns 22/22, 95

wlitiġ adj *splendid, beautiful* **wlitegan** gsf 19/137 dsn 19/255

wlitiġian 2 *make beautiful, adorn* **wlitigaŏ** pr3p 26/49

wlonc see wlanc

wō see wōh

(ġe)wōd, wōdon < (ġe)wadan

Wōden pr n *Woden* ns 9a/25

Wōdening adj *son of Woden* nsm 29/44

Wōdnesdæġ m:B1c *Wednesday* **Wōdnesdagas** np 7b/53

wōg, wōge < wōh

wōh n:B2f *crookedness, error, wrong* as 4/27 ap 16/109 **wō** ds 12/34 **wōge** ds 4/25,

16/108; in adv phr **on wōh** as *wrongfully*
7b/13, 43

wōhdōm m:B1a *unjust judgement*
wōhdōmas ap 25/150

wōhġestrēon n:B2b *ill-gotten gains*
wōhġestrēona gp 25/150

wōlberend adj *bearing pestilence,
pestilential* **wōlbærendum** dsn 15a/2

wolcen n:B2c.i *cloud(s), sky* **wolcna** gp
19/67, 35b/5 **wolcne** ds 17/81 **wolcnu** np
33/13 **wolcnum** dp 13/24, 23/53, 55, 32/8

wōldæġ m:B1c *day of pestilence* **wōldagas**
np 37/25

wolde, woldon < **willan**

wōlīċe adv *perversely, wrongly* 24/10

wōma m:B5a *howling, terror* ns 38/103

womfull adj *foul, evil, sinful* nsm 19/77

womm m:B1a *stain, sin* **womme** ds 19/59
wommum dp 18/87, 23/14

won see **wann**

wong m:B1a *ground, plain, place* ns 37/31
wongas np 26/49 (see note)

wonn < **winnan**

word n:B2b *word, command, speech, saying,
utterance, verb* ns 4/39, 63, 66, etc as 5/61,
17/16, 91, 23/35, 30/168 np 4/73, 86, 87 ap
9b/29 etc, 18/81, 23/27, 27/1 **worda** gp
27/74 **worde** ds 5/61, 8/61, 14/5, 16/59,
17/18, 68, 23/111 **wordes** gs 25/55
wordon dp 30/306 **wordum** dp 4/54, 76,
77, 90, 5/2, 9b/41, 16/66, 67, 17/103,
18/76, 23/97, 30/26, 43, 31b/1, etc

ġe**worden**, ġe**wordene** < **weorðan**

Worġemynster pr n (n:B2c) *Warminster*
(Wilts.) ds 12/63

(ġe)**worht**, (ġe)**worht-** see (ġe)**wyrċan**

wōrian 2 *crumble to pieces, decay* **wōriað**
pr3p 38/78

worldlīċe adv *temporally, in secular matters*
7c/22

worn m:B1a *crowd, swarm, multitude* as
38/91 **wornum** dp 19/163

worold, worolde see **woruld**

woroldrǣden f:B3e.i *worldly rule, way of
the world* **woroldrǣdenne** as 31a/80

woroldscamu f:B3a *public disgrace*
woroldscame ds 25/98, 101

worolstrūdere m:B1g *spoliator, pillager*
worolstrūderas np 25/138

worpan, ġe**worpen** see **weorpan**

woruld f:B3g.i *world, age, eternity* ns 26/49
as 26/87, 38/58 **weoruld** as 38/107
weorulde ds 6/34, 59 **worold** ns 25/3
worolde gs 31a/18 ds 25/4, 6, 58, etc
woruld as 19/156, 24/77 **worulda** gp 24/77
worulde gs 16/17, 22/125, 23/133, 38/74
ds 2c/4, 5/22, 9b/7, 83, 16/99, 19/66,
21a/46, 24/4, 69, 26/45

woruldafel n:B2a *worldly strength, secular
power* **woruldafelum** dp 24/29

woruldbūend m:B4d *dweller on the earth*
woruldbūendra gp 19/82

woruldcund adj *secular, worldly*
woruldcundra gpm 5/5

woruldġesǣliġ adj *blessed with worldly
wealth, prosperous* nsm 30/219

woruldhād m:B1a *secular life* as 9b/55
weoruldhāde ds 9b/15

woruldman m:B4b *man of the world, human
being, layperson* **woruldmen** ap 24/29
woruldmenn np 21a/81

woruldrīċe n:B2h *kingdom of the world, this
world* ds 38/65, 40/13

woruldstrenġu f:B3a *worldly strength,
physical power* **woruldstrenga** gp
35d/2

woruldþing n:B2b *worldly affair*
woruldþincg ap 21a/23 **woruldðinga** gp
5/20

wōum < **wōh**

wracu f:B3a *suffering, pain, enmity,
vengeance* **wraca** as 24/47 **wrace** as 17/56
wrǣce as 36/4

wrāh < **wrēon**

wrāð adj *wrathful, angry, hostile, cruel* nsm
17/68 **wraðra** gp 23/51, 38/7 (=noun
enemies)

wrāðlīċ adj *cruel, hard* nsn 17/18

wræc n:B2a *misery, persecution, exile* **wræcc**
ns 9a/37 **wræces** gs 36/1

wræc, wrǣce < (ġe)**wrecan**

wræcca see **wrecca**

wrǣce < **wracu**

wræclāst m:B1a *path of exile* ns 38/32
wræclāstas ap 26/57, 38/5

wræcsīþ m:B1a *journey of misery, path of
exile* **wræcsīþa** gp 40/5 **wræcsīþas** ap
40/38 **wræcsīðe** ds 15c/4

wrǣtliċ adj *artfully made, wondrous, curious* nsm 37/1 nsn 33/3 npn 35d/14 **wrǣtlicu** nsf 35e/2

wrǣtt f:B3b *work of art, ornament* **wrǣttum** dp 31b/40

wrecan V *recite, tell* **wrece** pr1s 40/1 **wrecen** pp 31a/3

(ġe)wrecan V *avenge* **wrecan** inf 7c/13, 30/248, 258, 31b/55 ġe**wrecan** inf 30/208, 263 **wræc** pt3s 29/5 **wrǣce** sbj pt3s 30/257 **wrec** pt3s 30/279 ġe**wrec** imp s 19/92

wreċċa m:B5a *fugitive, exile, adventurer, outcast* ns 31a/75 **wræċċa** ns 40/10 **wreċċea** ns 32/25 **wreċċena** gp 7b/20 **wreccum** dp 18/87

wreċċan 1 *awake, arouse* **wrehton** pt3p 19/228, 243

wrēgan 1 *accuse* **wrēgaƌ** pr3p 16/65 **wrēgdon** pt3p 14/3

wrenċ m:B1a *trick, wile* **wrenċeas** ap 8/76

wrēon 1 *cover, clad, wrap up* **wrāh** pt3s 35d/11 **wrēo** imp s 3c/6

wreoton < **wrītan**

ġewrit n:B2a *writing, document, book, scripture* as 5/54, 58, 7b/5 ġe**writes** gs 9b/66 ġe**writu** ap 22/58 ġe**writum** dp 18/74

wrītan 1 *write* **wreoton** pt3p 9b/62 **wrītaþ** pr1p 16/40 **wrīte** sbj pr3s 5/72 ġe**writen** pp 22/59

wrītere m:B1g *writer, scribe* ds 16/87 **wrīteras** ap 4/26, 16/108

ġewritu < ġe**writ**

wrixendlīċe adv *in turn* 9b/94

wrōht f:B3b *enmity, contention* **wrōhte** as 24/47

(ġe)wroht- see (ġe)**wyrċan**

wudu m:B4a *forest, wood, tree* ns 23/27, 33/33 as 30/193 **wuda** ds 9a/49, 39/17

wuduæppel m:B1b *wild apple, crab* **wuduæpla** ap 3b/11

wuldor n:B2c *wonder, glory, splendour, heaven* ns 2a/23, 19/155, 347, 21a/76, 91 as 19/342 **wuldre** ds 19/344, 21a/46, 89, 22/107, 23/135, 143, 155 **wuldres** gs 19/59, 23/14, 90, 97, 133

wuldorblǣd m:B1g *glorious success* ns 19/156

wuldorcyning m:B1a *glorious king* as 18/102

wuldorfæder m:B1a/4c *father of glory* gs 9b/33

wuldorġesteald n:B2b *wondrous setting* np 35d/16

wuldortorht adj *gloriously bright* **wuldortorhtan** npn 31a/74

wuldre, wuldres < **wuldor**

wulf m:B1a *wolf* ns 19/206, 33/18, 38/82, 39/16 as 10/65 **wulfas** np 1/34 **wulfum** dp 19/295

Wulf pr n *Wulf* ns 39/13 (twice) **Wulfes** gs 39/9

Wulfgār pr n *Wulfgar* ns 8/17

Wulfhun pr n *Wulfhun* ns 12/11

Wulfmǣr pr n *Wulfmær* ns 30/113, 155 as 30/183

Wulfstān pr n *Wulfstan* ns 30/75 **Wulfstāne** ds 30/79 **Wulfstānes** gs 30/155

ġewuna indecl adj +d *accustomed to* 18/28

ġewuna m:B5a *custom, practice, rite* ġe**wunan** ds 14/7, 25/122

wunade, wunaƌ < **wunian**

wund adj *wounded, sore* nsm 30/113, 144, 32/43, 35a/1 **wunde** npm 31a/13

wund f:B3b *wound, wounding* ns 21a/63 **wunda** ap 32/47 **wunde** as 30/139, 271 ap 35a/12 **wundum** dp 30/293, 303, 31a/51 **wundun** dp 10/43

wunden adj *twisted, coiled* nsn 38/32

wundenlocc adj *curly-haired, with braided locks* nsf 19/77, 103, 325 nsn 35c/11

wundenmǣl n:B2b *sword with curved markings* as 31b/40

wunder- see **wundor-**

ġewundian 2 *wound* ġe**wundad** pp 29/18, 34 ġe**wundod** pp 22/52, 30/135 ġe**wundode** pt3s 29/13

wundon < **windan**

wundor n:B2c *marvel, miracle, wondrous thing, strange creature* ns 22/136, 25/106 as 18/106, 35e/2 **wundra** np 21a/4, 13 gp 9b/33, 31b/18 **wundrum** dp 19/8; see also adv **wundrum**

wundorliċ adj *wonderful, remarkable* nsn 21a/2, 70 **wunderlicre** gsf 28/33 **wunderlicu** nsf 35c/1 **wunderlicum** dsn 16/71 dpm 28/4 **wundorlican** asm 24/6

wundorlīċe adv *wondrously, remarkably* 21a/89

wundrian 2 *wonder, be astonished at*
wundrade pt1s 5/36, 28/13, 34 **wundrode**
pt3s 9b/84, 14/6
wundrum adv *wondrously* 33/13, 37/20,
38/98
wundrung f:B3d *wonder, astonishment*
wundrunga ds 22/53 **wundrunge** ds
21a/70
ġe**wuneliċ** adj *common, customary* nsm 4/41
ġe**wunliċ** nsn 22/18
(ġe)**wunian** 2 *dwell, live, inhabit, remain,
exist* inf 15c/16, 19/119, 23/121, 143, 40/27
wunade pt1s 26/15 ġe**wunade** pt3s 9b/2
(*was accustomed to*) **wunaо** pr3s 6/7,
33/66 **wunedon** pt3p 23/3, 155 **wuniaþ**
pr3p 23/135, 26/87 ġe**wuniaо** pr3p 3a/9
wuniende prp nsm 22/85 npm 22/171
wuniġan inf 6/59 **wuniġe** sbj pr3s 9a/23
ġe**wuniġe** sbj pr3s 3b/1 **wuniġende** prp
npm 21a/85 **wunode** pt3s 19/67, 21a/4, 12,
27, 21b/10, 14, 29/3, 31a/66 **wunodon** pt3p
21a/89
ġe**wunliċ** see ġe**wuneliċ**
wunnon < **winnan**
wunung f:B3d *dwelling, abode* **wununge**
gs 27/71
(ġe)**wurd-** < (ġe)**weorþan**
wurman < **wyrm**
ġe**wurpan** see ġe**wyrpan**
wurpon < **weorpan**
wurð adj *valued, dear, worth, worthy,
deserving, entitled* (*to* +g) **wirðe** npf
7c/22 **wurðe** npf 7c/4 **wurðran** comp npm
17/85 **wyrðæ** nsf 11/2 npm 11/33 **wyrðe**
nsm 12/8, 16/21 nsf 21a/38 **wyrðes** gsn
9b/42
(ġe)**wurþ-** see (ġe)**weorþ-**
wurðliċ adj *honoured, splendid* **wurðlicum**
dsm 27/5
wurðliċe adv *worthily, honourably,
splendidly* 30/279 **weorðliċe** 23/17
wurþlicor comp 32/37 **wurðlicost** sup
27/70
wurðmynt see **weorðmynd**
wurðran < **wurð**
wurðscipes < **weorðscipe**
wūtan, wūton see **ūton**
wycg see **wicg**
wydewan < **widuwe**

Wyhtlæging adj *son of Wihtlæg* nsm 29/44
wylæ, wyle < **willan**
wylfen adj *wolfish, savage* **wylfenne** asm
36/22
wyllan 1 *boil* **wyl** imp s 3c/4
wyllað, wylle < **willan**
wyllen adj *woollen* asn 21a/31 (=noun
woollen material)
wylm m:B1a *surge, surging* **wylme** ds 37/39
wylst < **wealdan**
wylt < **willan**
wynliċ adj *pleasant* **wynlicran** comp apn
40/52
wynn f:B3g *joy, delight, pleasure, bliss* ns
35d/7 **wyn** ns 26/45, 38/36 as 26/27 **wynne**
ds 17/30 **wynnum** dp 23/15 (=adv
delightfully)
wynstre adj *left* nsf 22/83 **wynstran** asf 3c/2,
14/46
wynsum adj *pleasant, delightful* **winsumum**
ds 27/28, 43 **wynsumo** nsf 28/10
wynsumu npm 9b/61
wynsumnes f:B3e.ii *pleasantness*
wynsumnesse as 28/13
(ġe)**wyrċan** 1 *do, make, prepare, perform,
carry out, cause, wreak, bring about,
achieve* inf 9b/3 etc 23/65, 30/81, 102, 264
wirċean inf 16/60 (twice) ġe**worht**
pp 6/28, 9b/6, 17/28, 81, 21a/55, 70, 22/16
worhtan pt3p 8/23 **worhte** pt3s 16/49, 71,
19/65, 21a/64, etc ġe**worhte** pt3s 9b/70,
71, 16/46, 31b/87, etc pp npm 25/116
ġe**worhtne** pp nsm 17/58 asm 26/115
worhton pt3p 19/302, 21a/86 ġe**worhton**
pt3p 23/31 **wrohtan** pt3p 8/53 ġe**wrohtan**
pt3p 8/41 **wyrċ** imp s 34/20 ġe**wyrċað**
pr3p 25/167 **wyrċe** sbj pr3s 6/24, 7b/36
(*inflict*) ġe**wyrċe** sbj pr3s 7b/35, 26/74
wyrċean inf 19/8 (*issue*), 33/21 **wyrċeað**
pr3p 3a/9 **wyrċð** pr3s 6/17, 21 [etc]
wyrd f:B3g *happening, event, fate, chance,
destiny, Providence* ns 6/14, 19, 20, 18/12,
23/74, 26/115, 33/5, 35e/2, 37/24, 38/5,
100, etc as 6/12, 16, 24, 28/57, etc **wyrda**
gp 23/51, 38/107 **wyrde** ds 6/32, 35, 38/15
np 37/1
wyrdan 1 *injure, spoil* **wyrt** pr3s 3a/7
ġe**wyrht** n/f:B2i *deed, merit* ġe**wyrhtum**
dp 25/83

wyrhta m:B5a *maker* ns 24/76 **wyrhtena** gp
24/7

wyrm m:B1a *worm, serpent, snake* ns 18/91,
28/37, 35c/3 **wurman** ds 36/1 **wyrma** gp
28/4 **wyrmum** dp 19/115

wyrmlīċ n:B2b *form of a serpent, snake
pattern* **wyrmlīcum** dp 38/98

wyrms m:B1a *corrupt matter, pus* ns 21a/45

wyrmsele m:B1g *hall of serpents* ds 19/119

wyrnan 1 +g *withhold, be sparing of*
wyrnde pt3s 30/118 **wyrndon** pt3p 10/24

ġewyrpan 1 *get well, recover* **ġewurpan** inf
21a/45

wyrsa adj (comp of **yfel**) *worse* **wyrsan** apf
25/155 **wyrse** nsn 22/10, 25/4

wyrsian 2 *grow worse, deteriorate* **wyrsedan**
pt3p 25/30

wyrt f:B3g *herb, plant, vegetable* **wyrta** np
1/56 **wyrtum** dp 35a/12

wyrt < **wyrdan**

wyrttruma m:B5a *root* **wyrttruman** as 3c/2

(ġe)**wyrð** < (ġe)**weorþan**

wyrð- see **wurð**

wyrðmente < **weorðmynd**

wyrðode < **weorþian**

wȳscan 1 *wish* **wȳscte** pt3s 36/25

ġewyslīċe adv *certainly, truly* 1/28

X

Xrīste < **Crīst**

Y

ȳcan 1 *increase, add to* inf 19/183 **īhte** pt3s
25/10 **ȳcað** pr3p 35d/24 **ȳce** imp s 3b/9

ȳdel adv *empty-handed* 22/150

yfel adj *bad, evil, wicked* nsn 6/26 **yfelan** asf
24/64 (=noun *evil creature*) dsn 25/128
npm 25/122 **yfele** npm 27/69 apm 3a/9,
35e/9

yfel n:B2c *evil, harm, wickedness* as 2a/19,
4/26, 8/41, 53, 15c/12, 16/109, 25/10 **yfela**
gp 18/92 **yfeles** gs 8/60, 14/20, 20b/4,
30/133 **yflaes** gs 20a/4

yfele adv *badly, evilly* 17/50, 27/30

yfelian 2 *become bad, grow worse* inf 25/5

ylca, ylcan see **ilca**

ylde < **yldu**

yldestan < **eald**

ylding f:B3d *delay, tarrying* ns 9a/27 **yldinge**
as 22/43

yldran, yldrena < **eald**

yldo f:B3h *age, old age* ns 18/94, 26/70, 91
ds 33/50 **ældo** ds 37/6 **ylde** as 15c/17 gs
9b/16

ylfetu f:B3a *swan* **ylfete** gs 26/19

ymb prep +a/d *about, concerning, in respect
of, after, around, near, at, over, towards,
against* 5/10, 6/49, 7b/20, 23, 9a/1, 61,
12/1, 2, 15a/3, 17/17, 51, 71, 26/11, 29/6,
31, 31b/45, 33/46, 53, 55, 36/12, etc **embe**
21a/25, 24/69, 30/249, 271 **ymban** 12/45
ymbe 10/5, 14/56, 17/34, 45, 19/47, 268,
22/2, 24/40, 26/46, 30/214, 32/33

ymbbeorgan III *protect round about*
ymbbearh pt3s 31b/12

ymbclyppan 1 *embrace* **ymbclypte** pt3s
23/42

ymbe see **ymb**

ymbhycgan 3 *think about, meditate*
ymbhycgannae infl inf 20a/3

Ymbrenwicu f:B5c *Ember-week*
Ymbrenwicum dp 7b/54

ymbscrȳdan 1 *clothe* **ymbscrȳd** pp 22/86

ymbset n:B2a *siege* **ymbsetes** gs 9a/60

ymbsittan V *sit around, sit at table,
surround, besiege* **imbsǣton** pt3p 22/146
ymbseten pp 15b/4 **ymbsittendan** prp
npm 27/39 apm 27/2

ymbsprecan V *speak about* **ymbsprǣcon**
pt1p 15a/6

ymbūtan adv *round, around* 6/1, 43

yntse f:B5c *ounce* **yntsan** as 3b/7

yppan 1 *reveal, betray* inf 1/51

ypping f:B3d *manifestation, mass* **yppinge** ds
18/53

yrfcwalm m:B1a *cattle-plague* ns 8/10

yrfe n:B5b *property, bequest* as 12/50, 52

yrgan 1 *dishearten, demoralise* **ġeyriġde**
pp npm 25/91

yrhþo f:B3h *cowardice* **yrġþo** as 9a/10, 30/6
yrhðe as 25/151

yrming m:B1a *wretched creature, wretch* as
24/48

yrmþ f:B3h *misery, hardship, crime* ns 25/76
yrmþa ap 25/14 gp 40/3 **yrmþe** as 25/71
ds 25/98

yrre adj *angry, enraged, fierce* nsm 17/5,
  18/60, 30/44, 253, 31b/41, 84 npm
  19/225
yrre n:B2h *anger* ns 25/81, 105 as 25/40, 82,
  88, 91, 97, 99
yrringa adv *angrily* 31b/74
yrþlincg m:B1a *ploughman* ns 1/18
  yrþlincgas np 1/15

ys < **bēon-wesan**
ȳtmæst adj *last* **ȳtmæstan** apn 9b/107
ȳþ f:B3b *wave* **ȳþa** gp 26/6, 46, 40/7 **ȳþe**
  ap 31a/70 **yðum** dp 18/4, 27, 22/160, 33/23
ȳþan 1 *lay waste* **ȳþde** pt3s 38/85
ȳðelīċe adv *easily* 31b/65
ȳðhenġest m:B1a *wave-horse, ship*
  ȳðhenġestas np 8/83

Guide to terms

This guide defines the grammatical and other descriptive terminology used in this book. The illustrative examples are all from modern English. Cross-reference is made in square brackets to sections of the Reference Grammar on pp. 355–95. Italicised words direct the user to other entries in the Guide.

Ablative A *case* used in Latin but not in OE, although it is sometimes mimicked in OE translations from Latin. In OE, the sense of 'by', 'with' or 'from' (something), conveyed by the ablative, is more commonly expressed by the *dative*.

Accusative The *case* of the *direct object*.

Active The most common function or '*voice*' of verbs, in which the *subject* performs the action; if there is an *object*, the action directly affects it: 'the dog barks', 'the dog chased the cat'. Cf. *passive*.

Adjective A word that describes a *noun* or *pronoun*. It may be attributive ('The *big* dog') or predicative ('It is *lazy*'). (Derived adjective: adjectival.) See also *comparative* and *superlative*.

Adverb A word that modifies a *verb* or *adjective* to define manner, location, time, etc ('He spoke *loudly*'; 'She arrived *yesterday*'. '*Then* he spoke'), or carries an argument forward ('Therefore . . .', 'However . . .'), or intensifies ('very'). (Derived adjective: adverbial.) See also *comparative*, *superlative*.

Affix A general term which may denote either a *prefix* or a *suffix*.

Agreement The process by which different words in a sentence are brought into grammatical *concord* (i.e. they 'agree') with each other: 'the *dog barks* often', 'the *dogs bark* often', 'the *woman* brings *her* dog'. The necessity for agreement affects OE far more than ModE.

Anomalous 'Irregular', describing an important category of basic OE verb [§G1].

Article A word specifying whether a noun is 'definite': '*the* dog' (i.e. a particular one) or 'indefinite': '*a* dog' (i.e. no particular one). 'The' is thus the definite article, 'a' or 'an' the indefinite article. Pronouns such as 'some' and 'many' also may be described as indefinite.

Auxiliary verb A 'helping' verb (usually 'have', 'will' or 'shall' in ModE) which is used with various forms of another verb to specify meaning: 'I *have* arrived', 'She *is* eating'. See also *participle*.

Case The form of a *noun*, *pronoun* or *adjective* defining its relationship with other words in a sentence, usually marked by *inflection*. OE had four main cases (*nominative*, *accusative*, *genitive* and *dative*) and the remnants of a fifth (*instrumental*); for details of their use, see §D. In ModE the concept of case is redundant, except in the *genitive*: 'the dog*'s* bone' (where *'s* marks the genitive or possessive case).

Clause Within a sentence, a grammatically complete unit larger than a *phrase*, with a *subject* and *verb*. If it is a *main* clause, it will be a sentence in itself: '*The man shouted loudly*, when he saw the dog'; if a *subordinate* clause, it will not really make sense if separated from the main clause which it modifies: 'The man shouted loudly, *when he saw the dog*'. Here 'when' is a *subordinating conjunction*. Two clauses of equal status, joined by a *coordinating conjunction* such as *and* or *but*, are called *coordinate sentences*: 'The man shouted loudly and the dog barked'.

Comparative Denotes the forms of *adjectives* and *adverbs* which express increase in extent relative to a standard quality or quantity: 'a bigg*er* bone', 'he moved fast*er*'. Cf. *superlative*.

Complement A word or phrase which completes the sense of a grammatical unit: in 'he killed the prisoners', 'prisoners' is the complement of the verb 'killed'; in 'the army of the king', the phrase 'of the king' complements the noun 'army'.

Compound noun A composite form of noun, such as 'wordhoard'.

Compound tense See *tense*.

Concord See *agreement*.

Conditional Used of verbal phrases or clauses (and the verbs themselves) that express a condition or hypothesis: '*if it stopped raining*, I would go out'.

Conjugation (1) The schematic representation of the *inflections* of verbs. (2) A class of such verbs sharing the same inflections. Verbs are said to 'conjugate' according to particular patterns.

Conjunction A word which joins sentences, clauses, phrases or words: 'Man *and* boy'; 'The dog barked *but* the cat was silent'; 'She laughed *when* she saw it'. See also *clause*. (Derived adjective: conjunctive.)

Contraction The shortened form of a word or pair of words combined: *can't* for *cannot*; *it's* for *it is*.

Coordination See *clause*.

Correlative Used of words or phrases which are grammatically related in a sentence and often give structure to the whole: '*neither* the dog *nor* the cat was here'; '*as* you sow, *so* shall you reap'. OE makes much use of this sort of structure.

Dative The *case* associated with the *indirect object* and also used to express the sense of 'to', 'for', 'by', 'with' and 'from' [§D4].

Declension (1) The schematic representation of the inflections of *nouns, pronouns* or *adjectives*. (2) A class of such words sharing the same inflections. Nouns, etc, are said to 'decline' according to particular patterns.

Definite See *article*.

Diphthong A vowel which starts with one quality but moves towards another (as in 'boy' or 'sigh'), within a single syllable. In OE, always written as a sequence of two vowels, but they represent a single sound.

Direct object See *object*.

Disyllable, disyllabic See *syllable*.

Dual See *number*.

Ending On a word. See *inflection*; *suffix*.

Formulaic See *variation*.

Future See *tense*.

Gender The grammatical classification of words into the notional categories, *masculine, neuter* or *feminine*. ModE employs a system of 'natural' gender, so that we refer to a woman as 'she', a book as 'it', and so on, but in OE this was not usually the case [§B/overview].

Genitive The possessive *case*: 'the dog*'s* bone' [§D3].

Grammar The study of the forms, functions and interrelationships of words in *sentences*.

Guttural See *velar*.

Imperative See *mood*.

Impersonal Used of verbs which express an action with no definite subject and no direct object: 'It rained'. Such verbs were far more common in earlier periods of English (cf. 'methought', meaning literally 'it thought to me').

Indefinite See *article*.

Indicative See *mood*.

Indirect object See *object*.

Infinitive The base form of a verb, preceded by 'to' in ModE ('to bark'). For the OE infinitive, including a special form called the *inflected infinitive*, see §G6d.

Inflection (or **Inflexion**). The change in the form of a noun, verb or other word to show *number, case, mood, person*, etc, usually made by the addition of *suffixes* (endings) to the basic word. In ModE, *-s* and *-es* are the *plural* inflections: 'dogs', 'lenses'. The adjectives *inflected* and *uninflected* describe words that carry or do not carry such endings. See also *infinitive*.

Instrumental A *case* expressing means or agency [§D5].

Interjection An exclamatory word: 'Hail!', 'Alas!'

Interrogative Describes a word or phrase which asks a question: 'Why?' 'Is she here?'

Intransitive See *verb*.

Kenning A metaphorical *compound noun* or *phrase*: 'whale's road' (i.e. the ocean).

Levelling A tendency in pronunciation (which is then reflected in writing) for various word-endings to sound the same when unstressed. For example, most speakers of ModE do not distinguish between *-el*, *-al* and *-ol* in the words *kennel*, *cymbal* and *symbol*, respectively.

Litotes Understatement, in which something is affirmed by the negation of its opposite: 'he was less than helpful' (i.e. not helpful at all).

Locative Used to describe a specific form of the *dative* in phrases defining location [§D4i].

Medial Adjective used to specify a vowel or consonant occurring at, or towards, the middle of a word.

Modal Used to describe verbs such as *shall, may, must, will*, and *can* (mostly used as *auxiliary* verbs) which express a 'mood' of necessity, possibility, striving or desire: 'we *may* overcome'.

Modify Any word, but especially an adjective or adverb, which defines or expands the meaning of another word may be said to 'modify' that word.

Monosyllable, monosyllabic See *syllable*.

Mood The form of a verb which puts it into one of three categories: (1) *indicative*, denoting the action of, or state described by, the verb to be objective fact; (2) *subjunctive*, denoting the action or state to be a possibility or wish; or (3) *imperative*, conveying a command. ModE retains the subjunctive only vestigially; its most familiar use will be in such phrases as 'if I *were* you ...', as an alternative to the indicative form 'if I *was* you'. OE used the subjunctive more frequently but the majority of forms met are indicative. The subjunctive is sometimes used to denote the *optative* mood, which expresses more forcibly a wish or desire: 'May he be successful!', 'Let him do it at once!'

Morphology The structure of individual words, especially in relation to the addition of *inflections*.

Negative Used of a verb or verbal phrase which expresses denial or contradiction of the 'positive' sense of the verb. The sense is usually conveyed by means of a negative *particle*: 'She has *not* arrived'.

Nominal See *noun*.

Nominative The *case* of the *subject* [§D1].

Noun A word denoting a thing, person, animal, state or abstract concept. (Derived adjective: nominal.)

Number There are two categories of number in ModE: words are *singular* when denoting one person, thing or instance; and *plural* when denoting more than one of these. The distinction is made by *inflection*: 'dog', 'dogs'. Some OE pronouns have a third set of forms, the *dual* forms, used in reference to two persons or things.

Object The element in a clause which, in ModE, usually follows the verb. When it expresses the direct result of the action of the verb, it is called a *direct object*: 'The dog bit *the man*'; when the action is indirect (which in ModE usually involves the intervention of a preposition), it is an *indirect object*: 'The man took the bone from *the dog*' (where the *direct* object is of course the bone).

Optative See *mood*.

Orthography The use of letters in the spelling system of a language or a specific text.

Pal(a)eography The study of old forms of writing.

Palatalisation The process by which consonants are made *palatal*, i.e. sounded by placing the tongue at the back of the hard palate and restricting the flow of air (as *y* in 'yes' and *c* in 'church').

Paradigm A table illustrating all the possible forms of a noun, pronoun, adjective, verb or another *part of speech*.

Part of speech A class of words distinguished by idea or function, such as *noun*, *adjective*, *verb* or *preposition*; every word may be assigned to at least one such class.

Participle A form of the *verb* that functions as an *adjective* and can be used to form *compound* tenses. The *present participle* suggests continuing action: 'the *barking* dog'; 'the dog was *barking*'. The *past participle* signals completed action: 'a *defeated* man'; 'the man has been *defeated*'.

Particle A small uninflected unit of speech. See *negative*; *relative*.

Passive The relationship between the *subject* and *object* of a sentence in which the action affects the subject: 'the cat *was chased* by the dog'; the verb is said to be in the 'passive voice'. Cf. *active*.

Past See *participle*; *tense*.

Perfect See *tense*.

Person The aspect of a *verb* or *pronoun* (usually conveyed by a specific form) which refers to a speaker (*1st person*), a thing or person addressed (*2nd person*), or some other thing or person involved (*3rd person*). Each 'person' will also be *singular* or *plural* (or possibly, in OE, *dual*) and, in the case of pronouns, may vary with *gender*. Thus, 'we sing' (1st-person plural pronoun and verb), 'she sings' (3rd-person singular feminine pronoun and verb).

Phrase Within a sentence, a small unit of two or more words ('in a loud voice'; 'until now'). It is often convenient to think of such units as functioning in effect like single nouns, verbs, adjectives, etc. Such phrases may be described as 'noun-phrases', 'verb-phrases', etc; 'in a loud voice' may be described as an adverbial phrase.

Pluperfect See *tense*.

Plural See *number*.

Possessive Describes a word or *inflection* which indicates possession. See *genitive*, *pronoun*.

Predicate The part of a sentence which contains the verb and describes the *subject*: 'The dog *bit the man*'.

Prefix An addition to the beginning of a word, usually modifying its meaning or grammatical function: '*un*friendly', '*be*devil'.

Preposition A linking word usually denoting position, direction, time or manner: 'the dog is *in* the kennel'; 'she runs *to* the house'; 'he was bitten *by* the dog'.

Present See *participle*; *tense*.

Preterite See *tense*.

Preterite-present A special type of verb in OE [§G2].

Pronoun A word used as a substitute for a noun or a noun-phrase: '*he* [e.g. 'the man'] is here'; '*it* [e.g. 'eating'] is fun'; 'I saw *them* [e.g. 'the women']'. *Possessive pronouns* function as *adjectives*, describing nouns: '*my* dog', '*their* house'. *Relative pronouns* relate a noun or noun-phrase to a verb or verbal clause: 'the man *who* arrived'. (Derived adjective: pronominal.)

Proper noun The name of a person, place, etc.

Referent Used to describe a noun (or noun-phrase) occurring previously, to which a pronoun or a descriptive phrase refers.

Reflexive Describes pronouns which reflect back to the subject of the verb: 'he bit *himself*'; or to the verbs themselves with which such pronouns are commonly used.

Relative Describes a relative *pronoun* (or *particle*) which relates a clause to a previous clause or noun: 'the dog *who* (or *which* or *that*) came home'.

Sentence A segment of speech making sense in itself. Normally a sentence will be grammatically complete, containing at least a *subject* (or *object*) and a *verb*. It may be *simple*, with a single statement: 'the dog was hungry'; or *complex*, consisting of a *main clause* and one or more *subordinate* clauses: 'the dog was hungry, because the food was late'.

Singular See *number*.

Stem The basic part of a word, to which inflectional *endings*, other *suffixes*, or *prefixes* may be attached: *fold* is the stem of *fold*ed, *fold*ing, *fold*er, un*fold*s, etc.

Stress The emphasis or accent given to one part of a word in pronunciation: *bark*ing, un*do*ing.

Strong Used of verbs, nouns and adjectives when they are categorised according to certain patterns of inflection: see *weak*.

Subject The element of a *clause* which performs the action of the *verb*: '*the dog bit the man*'.

Subjunctive See *mood*.

Subordination See *clause*.

Suffix An addition to the end of a word, usually modifying its meaning or use: 'shout*ing*', 'loud*ly*'.

Superlative Used to denote the forms of *adjectives* and *adverbs* which express the extreme degree of comparison: 'the bigg*est* bone', 'he barked loud*est*'. Cf. *comparative*.

Syllable The smallest unit of pronunciation; 'undo' has two syllables: 'un' + 'do'. Such words are called *disyllables* (they are *disyllabic*); those with only one syllable are *monosyllables* (and are *monosyllabic*); and those with more than two are *polysyllabic*.

Syncopation The contraction of a word through the loss of a vowel from one of its syllables: 'can't' is a syncopated form of 'cannot'.

Syntax The way in which words are arranged to form sentences or parts of sentences. (Derived adjectives: syntactic, syntactical.)

Tense The aspect of a *verb* (shown by *inflection* or by the use of additional *auxiliary* verbs) which defines when its action takes place. Thus *present* tense: 'I sing'; *past* tense (also known as *preterite*): 'I sang'; *future* tense: 'I shall sing'; *perfect* tense: 'I have sung'; *pluperfect* tense: 'I had sung'; *future perfect* tense: 'I shall have sung'; etc. Tenses formed with other verbs are known as *compound* tenses (also called periphrastic). OE had only simple present and past tenses, with present doubling for future, but compound tenses were emerging [§§G6a–c].

Transitive See *verb*.

Variant Any of two or more different spellings or grammatical forms of the same word.

Variation Repetition of the meaning or essence of a word or descriptive phrase in a subsequent word or phrase, which gives a different emphasis or describes a different aspect of the subject referred to by the original word or phrase. So-called 'formulaic' variation is much used by OE poets. See p. xxiv–xxv.

Velar Describes a sound produced when the back of the tongue is in contact with the soft palate (the velum), as *g* in 'got' and *k* in 'kick'; such sounds are also described as *guttural*.

Verb Word expressing an act, occurrence or state, such as 'go' (which cannot be followed by a *direct object*, and is therefore called an 'intransitive' verb) and 'make' (which takes a *direct object* and is therefore called 'transitive'). See also *auxiliary, conjugation, infinitive, impersonal, mood, tense.* (Derived adjective: verbal.)

Voice (1) See *active, passive.* (2) Describes the breathing out of air with the vocal cords closed, so that they vibrate: *z* is a 'voiced' sound, *s* is not.

Weak Used to describe: (1) OE verbs whose stem stays unchanged in the past tense, as distinct from *strong* verbs, in which it changes [§§G3–4]; (2) OE nouns with a simple range of inflections mostly ending in -*n*, as distinct from *strong* nouns (the majority), which have more complex inflectional patterns [§§B1–5]; and (3) the forms of an OE adjective used when it is supported by a definite article, as distinct from *strong* forms, which are used when the adjective is not so supported [§§C1–2].

Index

The index covers the Introduction, section-notes, headnotes and text-notes; only the names of the more important people and places are included. An *n* after a page-number indicates that the reference will be found in a text-note on that page.